The Cambridge History of
Latin American Literature

VOLUME 3

The Cambridge History of Latin American Literature
Edited by
Roberto González Echevarría and Enrique Pupo-Walker

The Cambridge History of Latin American Literature is by far the most comprehensive and authoritative work of its kind ever written. Its three volumes cover the whole sweep of Latin American literature (including Brazilian) from pre-Columbian times to the present, and contain chapters on Latin American writing in the US. Over forty specialists in North America, Latin America, and Britain have contributed to what is not only the most reliable, up-to-date, and convenient reference work on its subject, but also a set of books containing innovative approaches and fresh research that will expand and animate the field for years to come. The *History* is unique in its thorough coverage of previously neglected areas, in its detailed discussion of countless writers in various genres, and in its inclusion of extensive annotated bibliographies.

Volume 1 begins with pre-Columbian traditions and their first contact with European culture, continuing through to the end of the nineteenth century. New World historiography, epic poetry, theatre, the novel, and the essay form are among the areas covered in this comprehensive and authoritative treatment.

Volume 2 provides coverage of all genres from the end of the nineteenth century up to García Márquez's *One Hundred Years of Solitude* and beyond to 1990, thus including discussion of Spanish American literature's best-known works. The novel, poetry, autobiographical narrative, the short story, Afro-Hispanic American literature, theatre, and Chicano literature are among the areas treated in this wide-ranging volume.

Volume 3 is devoted partly to the history of Brazilian literature, from the earliest writing through the colonial period and the Portuguese-language traditions of the nineteenth and twentieth centuries; and partly also to an extensive bibliographical section in which annotated reading lists relating to the chapters in all three volumes of *The Cambridge History of Latin American Literature* are presented. These bibliographies are a unique feature of the *History*, further enhancing its immense value as a reference work.

Contents of the other two volumes

The Cambridge History of Latin American Literature

VOLUME 3

Brazilian literature; bibliographies

Edited by

Roberto González Echevarría
Yale University

and

Enrique Pupo-Walker
Vanderbilt University

CAMBRIDGE
UNIVERSITY PRESS

PUBLISHED BY THE PRESS SYNDICATE OF THE UNIVERSITY OF CAMBRIDGE
The Pitt Building, Trumpington Street, Cambridge, United Kingdom

CAMBRIDGE UNIVERSITY PRESS
The Edinburgh Building, Cambridge CB2 2RU, UK
40 West 20th Street, New York, NY 10011–4211, USA
10 Stamford Road, Oakleigh, VIC 3166, Australia
Ruiz de Alarcón 13, 28014 Madrid, Spain
Dock House, The Waterfront, Cape Town 8001, South Africa

http://www.cambridge.org

© Cambridge University Press 1996

First published 1996
Reprinted 2001

Printed in Great Britain at the University Press, Cambridge

Library of Congress Cataloguing in Publication Data
The Cambridge history of Latin American literature / edited by Roberto
González Echevarría and Enrique Pupo-Walker.
p. cm.
Contents: v. 1. Discovery to Modernism – v. 2. The twentieth
century – v. 3. Brazilian literature; bibliographies.
ISBN 0 521 34069 1 (v. 1). – ISBN 0 521 34070 5 (v. 2). – ISBN
0 521 41035 5 (v. 3)
1. Latin American literature – History and criticism. I. González
Echevarría, Roberto. II. Pupo-Walker, Enrique.
PQ7081.A1C35 1995
860.9′8 – dc20   93-37750 CIP

ISBN 0 521 41035 5 hardback

SE

Contents

Bibliographies

Volume 1

List of contents

Contributors

Severino João Albuquerque, University of Wisconsin-Madison
Mary L. Daniel, University of Wisconsin-Madison
John Gledson, University of Liverpool
David T. Haberly, University of Virginia
K. David Jackson, Yale University
Fábio Lucas, University of Brasília
J. G. Merquior (deceased)
Massaud Moisés, University of São Paulo
Benedito Nunes, Federal University of Pará
Marta Peixoto, New York University
Giovanni Pontiero, University of Manchester
Thomas E. Skidmore, Brown University
Candace Slater, University of California, Berkeley

General preface

In 1893, the renowned Spanish critic and historian Marcelino Menéndez y Pelayo published his vastly influential *Antología de la poesía hispano-americana*: not only the first history of Spanish American poetry, but truly the first history of Spanish American literature. The *Antología* appeared just as *Modernismo* [Modernism], the first poetic movement developed in Spanish America, was achieving its greatest acclaim throughout the Hispanic world. With *Modernismo* Spanish American literature came of age, while the *Antología*, compiled and prefaced by the most authoritative critic of the language, gave it institutional substance and academic respectability. The present *History* appears in the wake of the most remarkable period of expansion and international recognition ever enjoyed by Latin American literature. The consolidation of Latin American literature as an academic discipline and a recognized category in the world book market was made possible by the achievements of writers as diverse as Jorge Luis Borges, Alejo Carpentier, Julio Cortázar, João Guimarães Rosa, José Lezama Lima, Gabriel García Márquez, Octavio Paz, Mario Vargas Llosa, and many others. García Márquez and Paz attained the ultimate recognition, the Nobel Prize. Without the distinction and accomplishments of these writers, the public at large, not to mention publishing houses and universities throughout the world, would have continued to treat Latin American literary production as an appendix to Spanish literature, dependent on someone like Menéndez y Pelayo for legitimation. It is to them too that this *History* owes its existence. *Modernismo* gave Latin America a place in the Spanish-language literary world; writers like the ones mentioned above placed it at the center of world literature.

Latin American literature today enjoys a truly international currency. Latin American novelists in particular are read and imitated not only in the west but throughout the world. For instance, Leo Ou-fan-Lee, a professor of Chinese literature at the University of Chicago, has written recently that Latin American writers "now exert a powerful impact on many young Chinese writers." As recently as thirty years ago such a statement would have been unthinkable. Given its universal reach and appeal, it is perhaps appropriate that this *History* should be the effort of a group of scholars working in the United States, England, and continental Europe, as well as in Latin America. Latin American literature is today at the pinnacle of the international literary movements that began with the Avant-Garde in the 1920s. Those movements as well as their aftermath are cosmopolitan in essence.

The *History* attempts to take full advantage of its collective and international cast, while at the same time aiming to be a coherent statement, conceived within a common set of scholarly guidelines and academic values. As an academic history, ours is concerned with historical fact and accuracy, with sources and influences, and with the relationship of literature to history in general. Our work, in other words, takes full account of the past, not only in the object of our study, but in the previous studies of that object. We build on what has been done before, and if and when we do not, we give our reasons. We aim not just to tell a story, but also to tell how that story has been told before. Aside from those givens, issuing no doubt from large ideological investments, ours is a work that is not dominated by narrow philosophical or methodological constraints. In contrast to most others, the *History* is not limited by the ideological or aesthetic values of a single author. In the invitations to participate in the project, the editors asked each contributor to be innovative in his or her approach to the field. Each was consulted about the limits of his or her area of study and about the very assumptions that make it a coherent subset within Latin American literary history. Everyone was asked, in short, to be self-conscious in her or his choices, not merely to review a field and to furnish an *état présent*. In this sense the *History* is not only a history of Latin American literature, but equally a statement on the current status of Latin American historiography. While the latitude given to each contributor has resulted in some unevenness, the editors believe that eclecticism enhances the value of the *History*, both as a reference tool and as an intellectual venture. Some literary works that previously had not been given much attention (in some cases none at all) have been examined by our contributors, thus effectively incorporating them into the canon. For instance, this is the first history of Latin American literature to provide detailed coverage of the colonial period, the works of women writers, and the literature written in Spanish by Chicano and other Hispanic authors in various regions of North America. Similarly, this is the first history of Latin American literature to link meaningfully the works of Afro-Hispanic and Afro-American authors. The *History* also brings together Brazilian and Spanish American literatures, giving the former the full individual attention it naturally deserves, but also underscoring their contiguities, continuities, and discontinuities. In short, the editors feel that our *History* is a reassessment and expansion of the canon of Latin American literature, seen in a broad, new-world context.

We are fully aware, of course, that large ideological presuppositions underlie our enterprise. The first concerns the very existence of Latin American literature as such. Since its deliberate creation as a concept and field of endeavor in the 1830s, Latin American literature has debated whether it is a literature at all or in fact a series of national literatures that share a common language. The most prominent writers, from Andrés Bello to Paz, have argued in favor of the existence of a Latin American literature that transcends national boundaries; and if one thinks of tradition as being made up by the major works, as we do here, then one can assume the existence of a Latin American literature. But not everyone has always been convinced, and we do not question that there are peculiarities that distinguish some national literatures within Latin America. The case of Brazil is a special one, of course: there is no doubt that Brazilian literature is a national literature as original and self-contained as French, Italian, or Spanish literature; its ties to a broader Latin American literature, however, are strong, if fluid and ever-changing over time. But Cuban, Mexican, Argentinian, Chilean, and Colombian literatures are also marked by national characteristics that are undeniable. These national inflections are for the most part thematic. For instance, the lives of Blacks and their African retentions play a very significant role in Caribbean literature, whereas in the Southern cone it is the *gaucho* and his mores that provide a strong thematic strain. There is, however, a certain homology in the way these figures appear in their respective national or regional literatures, one that extends to how the Indian is portrayed in areas such as Peru and Mexico. National traditions stress the differences and remain local. But the stronger authors and works cross frontiers or dwell in the homology. They constitute a kind of overarching literature to which all aspire. Our assumption here has been that the most significant and influential part of Latin American literature is the one engaged in a transnational intertextual exchange. The recuperation of the colonial period, when Spanish America was one, is part of this struggle to constitute a continental literature with a common origin and discourse. This is one of the strongest forces behind the recent increase in scholarship on the colonial period.

The breadth of this undertaking is particularly evident in the chapters on colonial literature, both Brazilian and Spanish American. Until a few years ago, colonial literature was chiefly the object of antiquarian interest, but in recent years this has changed drastically in fundamental and irreversible ways. The editors and contributors have sought to reflect that change. Before the 1960s, few universities (in Latin America or elsewhere) offered courses on Latin American writers of the colonial period, but now many include in their programs of study Sor Juana Inés de la Cruz, Bernal Díaz del Castillo, Garcilaso de la Vega, El Inca, and many others. At the post-graduate level there are now monographic courses dealing with those figures, as well as with Columbus, Gonzalo Fernández de Oviedo, and many other historians of the discovery and conquest of America. Scholarship on these authors has increased significantly in scope and sophistication. There are now international symposia devoted solely to colonial literature, as well as sessions within established, periodical meetings, such as the yearly conventions of the Modern Language Association of America.

Appropriately, given the nature of the chronicles, this *History* incorporates scholarly materials and methodological tools that are not common to literary scholarship. The interdisciplinary bent of this part of our venture is enhanced by the contributions of Asunción Lavrín (in Volume 1) and Thomas Skidmore (in Volume 3), well-known historians of Spanish and Portuguese America respectively. This productive linkage of disciplines is the natural byproduct of recent scholarship. In the past two decades, the study of colonial Spanish American literature has been enriched by its broad interdisciplinary scope. The reassessment of early historiography of the Americas combines quite freely the findings of rhetorical analyses, historical scholarship, anthropology and archaeology. This unprecedented and expanding convergence of disciplines has made possible forms of scholarly cooperation that are exceptional in Hispanic studies, and that certainly point to the research agendas of the future.

The incorporation of the colonial period into the study of Latin American literature has improved the overall quality of the criticism devoted to this literature by showing the inadequacy of journalistic approaches that are based exclusively on the most recent literary production. This development is intimately tied to the legitimation of Latin American literature as an academic discipline, a fairly recent phenomenon. Curiously, this movement also brings out the strong ties Latin American literature still has with Spanish and Portuguese literatures, both in the colonial period and in the present. If the Iberian Middle Ages, Renaissance, and Baroque are such a powerful presence in Latin American literature, then this literature shares a living past with its metropolitan counterparts. From a scholarly perspective what this means is that scholars of colonial literature (and one hopes, also of modern literature) must now have a strong background in Medieval, Renaissance, and Golden Age literatures. A full sixth of the *History* is devoted to the

General preface

colonial period, and the chapters devoted to the modern periods reflect the
weight of that living past.

One reason for this increase in colonial studies is that modern Latin
American authors have discovered in the works of the colonial Baroque,
or in the chronicles of the Discovery and Conquest, the starting point of
the literary tradition to which they belong. Octavio Paz's voluminous
study of Sor Juana is but the latest evidence of this phenomenon.
Carpentier, García Márquez, Neruda, and many other contemporary
writers have either written about colonial figures or declared their debt to
them in interviews and other pronouncements. Haroldo de Campos has
developed theories of Brazilian literature based on the continued presence
of the Colonial Baroque, or the self-conscious return to it. Many
contemporary works, both in Spanish and Portuguese, include topics,
characters, and stories drawn from colonial texts. This return to the
colonial past, highlighting its pertinence in the present, rounds out the
Latin American literary tradition and endows it for the first time with a
density of five centuries. It does not matter that, if examined closely, this is
nothing more than an enabling pretext, or a fable about origins. Literature
creates its own historical fictions, its own history being one of them. Our
History, while being as concrete and factual as possible, reflects the
fullness and influence of that fiction. In this sense, too, ours is a history of
the history of Latin American literature.

The editors feel that the History is the first to recognize the richness and
diversity of Latin American literature in the nineteenth century (preceding
Modernismo). This field, which has yet to acquire the institutional
recognition accorded to the colonial period, has of late begun to draw
attention from scholars as well as writers. The chapters devoted to both
Spanish American and Brazilian literature of the nineteenth century are
among the most innovative, and constitute the area where the freshest
research is offered by our contributors. More than a history bringing to
closure the study of this promising field, work on the nineteenth century in
the History may very well constitute the founding of a new area of
specialization.

The richness and depth of Latin American literature in the colonial
period and during the past century is one of the features, perhaps the
strongest, that distinguishes it from other literatures of the so-called Third
World. In the 1960s, in the wake of the Cuban Revolution and other
political movements aimed at breaking the grip of colonialism, many
Latin American authors allied themselves with authors whose plight
seemed similar to theirs. Regardless of the outcome of those political
alliances the fact is that if by Third World one refers to countries that
emerged from the debacle of nineteenth-century colonialism, then Latin
America, being the product of a much older and different colonialism, had

to have a very different literary tradition. The literatures of the Third World emerged, for the most part, in our own century, whereas those of Latin America reach back really to, at least, the sixteenth. The burden of Latin American culture is a Western culture that reaches back to the Middle Ages, when the foundations of the Spanish Empire in the New World were set. Latin American culture, particularly Spanish, was from the beginning one of ostentatious viceregal capitals, surpassing in splendor cities of the Old World, often because they had to compete with magnificent urban centers constructed by the Aztecs, Mayas, or Incas. This urban quality of Latin American culture also obeyed Spanish Neo-Scholasticism, grounded on the Aristotelian notion that civilization was, as the etymology indicates, something proper to cities. Latin American colonial culture, in many ways medieval, is so distant from that of North America, or countries of the Third World, that gross distortions and misreadings are bound to occur in comparing them. Desire for solidarity with the Third World is a significant element of recent Latin American literature perhaps even as a movement, but it does not make of Latin American literature a Third-World literature. Latin American literature is not a new literature, even if one of its enabling pretexts or founding fables is its newness. Our *History*, we hope, makes this very clear, with abundant supporting evidence.

The question of the new is so poignant in Latin American literature precisely because it is such an old culture, both back through our European roots, and through those of the native and African cultures. The entire history of Macondo, the fictional town in García Márquez's *One Hundred Years of Solitude* that is a microcosmic representation of Latin America, has been written in advance, in Sanskrit, by a wizard; it is a story that emerges from the very origins of history and writing. In those origins writing precedes history. The literatures of the Third World are recent; some came into being in the twentieth century. Latin American writers find predecessors, within what they consider as their own literature, in the sixteenth and seventeenth centuries. Octavio Paz's passionate and polemical literary biography of Sor Juana Inés de la Cruz is a case in point. There were Renaissance-style literary academies in Lima at the turn of the sixteenth to the seventeenth century, and hundreds of Petrarchan poets in seventeenth-century Mexico. If anyone should doubt this he or she ought to read Alicia de Colombí-Monguió's superb *Petrarquismo peruano*, and Irving A. Leonard's classic *Books of the Brave* and *Baroque Times in Old Mexico*.

The editors and contributors have spared no effort in making the *History* a reliable, informative, and useful reference work and research tool. Hence, we have been careful to be thorough in providing dates and bibliographic information in general. In fact, we feel that the selective, annotated bibliographies relating to each chapter (and reproduced in Volume 3) constitute in and of themselves a significant contribution to the field, as does the general bibliography at the end, which was compiled by a professional bibliographer. In some instances (Carlos Alonso's comprehensive list of regionalist novels is a good example) the bibliographies are the result of ground-breaking research. All secondary bibliographies are selective and the annotations are meant to guide future scholars to the latest, the newest, and the most promising work. Read in conjunction with their respective chapters, these bibliographies should bring a critic to the point where he or she can begin to make the next original contribution. The editors sincerely hope that this will very often be the case and that the *History* will help to provide an auspicious opening to the second one hundred years of Latin American literary historiography.

The *Cambridge history of Latin American literature* draws upon a long tradition of collaborative scholarship that began with the *Cambridge modern history* (1902–1912), and includes the eight-volume *Cambridge history of Latin America*. In its format, general guidelines and scholarly values, the *Cambridge history of Latin American literature* aspires to the rigor and accessibility for which these predecessors are known.

RGE and EPW

Acknowledgments

A collaborative work such as this is by its very nature the product of many people, some whose names appear as contributors or editors, and others whose contributions are not so obvious. We should like to thank here as many of those as possible, painfully aware that we are bound to make errors of omission. We apologize for them in advance.

First of all, we must thank those contributors who have also helped us in many ways other than writing their chapters. First and foremost we thank Professor David Haberly, who was our consultant for the volume on Brazilian literature. Professor Haberly discussed possible contributors with us, read the chapters for volume 3, and offered many valuable suggestions about how to shape the material. He also completed the chapter written by José Guilherme Merquior, whose premature death occurred in February 1991. In editing that volume, we were also aided by Professor K. David Jackson, whose expertise in all matters Brazilian and his abilities as a translator were both crucial. Other contributors also assisted us in similar ways in editing volumes 1 and 2. Professor Cathy L. Jrade read several manuscripts, offered detailed suggestions about various matters, helped us with the prologues, and participated with the two editors in meetings at which critical decisions were made. We acknowledge our great debt to Professor Jrade, who also served as a sounding board for ideas, several of which she helped sharpen or discard. Professor Sylvia Molloy gave us important advice concerning the selection of contributors, and also on how best to incorporate the work of women writers into the *History*. Professors Aníbal González Pérez, Gustavo Pérez Firmat and Kathleen Ross also aided us with their counsel, friendship, and erudition. We are especially grateful to Andrew Bush and José Quiroga. We asked them for important contributions which they had to write in a very limited period of time.

The library staffs at both Yale and Vanderbilt helped with bibliographical matters, and the respective staffs at the offices of grants and contracts were our link to the foundations that made the *History* possible. We should like to single out here Steven H. Smartt at Vanderbilt, and Alice Oliver at Yale. We have, of course, an enormous debt of gratitude to the National Endowment for the Humanities, which provided a three-year grant that allowed us to continue work during the summers, and to the Rockefeller Foundation for a grant to round out the sum provided by the Endowment. At the Endowment we were graciously assisted by David Wise, who was always patient with our queries and requests. Completion of a project as complex and time-consuming as this would have been impossible without the financial backing of these institutions, and we wish to make public our heartfelt appreciation.

During the five-year period that we have spent in this project, the office for the *Cambridge history of Latin American literature* has been the Center for Latin American and Iberian Studies at Vanderbilt. We have profited from all the facilities available at the Center, and want to thank Vanderbilt for its generosity in putting them at our disposal. The most invaluable resource at the Center, and the person to whom we owe the greatest debt of gratitude, is Mrs. Norma Antillón, Secretary Technical to the Director. Given the demands of our many other academic responsibilities, which often took us from the *History*, Mrs. Antillón was the one continuous presence; at times she seemed to *be* the *History*, as the many contributors who dealt with her in our absence know well. It would be impossible even to attempt to enumerate her many contributions and we would rather simply express to her our profound gratitude for her loyalty, devotion, attentiveness, and unswerving commitment to the successful completion of this work. We also wish to convey our appreciation to Mrs. Sandra Guardo, secretary to the Department of Spanish and Portuguese at Yale University. She was a valuable resource on many occasions. In addition, Mrs. Suzan McIntire, secretary to the Center for International Programs at Vanderbilt, was helpful to us in administrative aspects of this project.

We would also like to recognize as well Mr. Kevin Taylor at Cambridge University Press (England) for his exemplary attention to all matters pertaining to this *History*. We are also grateful to Mrs. Jay Williams, who provided valuable advice about contractual matters and helped improve the style of several chapters. We also wish to thank the translators, who labored hard to transform Spanish and Portuguese prose into academic English; they are Susan Griswold, Georgina Dopico Black, K. David Jackson and Cindy Najmulski.

Finally, we gratefully thank our wives Betty and Isabel for their patience and encouragement, and for making our meetings not only possible, but enjoyable.

ROBERTO GONZÁLEZ ECHEVARRÍA   ENRIQUE PUPO-WALKER

Introduction to Volume 3

Brazil's is the most independent, and perhaps most original, national literature in the New World. Whereas the United States' powerful literary tradition is, nevertheless, in some synchrony with that of England, its former metropolis, as is the case with the Spanish American literary tradition with regards to that of Spain, Portugal ceased long ago to be a significant literary presence in Brazil. This is ironic because, of all the American nations, with the exception of Canada, Brazil is the one whose break from the mother country was least painful and radical. Instead of becoming independent from the metropolitan government, the metropolitan government actually moved to Brazil. Brazil absorbed its origins, like some mythological figure who swallows its parents. The emergence of Brazilian literature is, thus, the product of this assimilation.

The foregoing does not mean that modern Portugal is devoid of influential literary figures. Eça de Queiroz, Fernando Pessoa, and currently José Saramago are authors of well deserved world-wide acclaim, who are much respected in Brazil. Yet Brazil itself was able to boast, as early as the nineteenth century, of a writer second to none in the Hispanic world (Spain included, of course); Joaquim Maria Machado de Assis. Machado was the first world-class Latin American writer; he enjoyed a reputation whose only worthy predecessor may have been Sor Juana Inés de la Cruz in colonial Mexico. In the twentieth century, Brazil has generated its own artistic movements, and produced a number of writers of indisputable quality, from Euclides da Cunha, whose *Os sertões* (1902) [*Rebellion in the Backlands*] is an influential masterpiece in all of Latin America, to João Guimarães Rosa, whose *Grande sertão, veredas* is considered by some (for instance, the late Uruguayan critic, Emir Rodríguez Monegal) the greatest Latin American novel ever. The Brazilian novelistic tradition, which includes the regionalist movement of the Northeast, with Graciliano Ramos, and has continued more recently with Jorge Amado, Clarice Lispector, and Nélida Piñón, rivals in richness that

1

of all of Spanish America, as well as that in the United States. In poetry, Brazil's Concrete poets founded a movement without parallel in the rest of the world, and the *Modernista* (that is to say, avant-garde) movement, which began with the Week of Modern Art in São Paulo in 1922, was the most original in Latin America, and one of the most original in the entire world.

At first glance the literary history of Brazil resembles that of Spanish America, but those similarities can often be deceiving, and in most instances have to be restricted to broad analyses or to the mechanics of periodization. To be sure, the distinctiveness of Brazilian letters can be perceived without resorting to contrastive views of the literatures of the Americas. Yet, in the context of this *History*, it seeems desirable to underscore, at the outset, some of the affinities and divergent qualities that stand out when one compares the literary output of Brazil and Spanish America. Differences between both literary traditions are due to their dissimilar origins, and are informed by contrasting historical processes.

In the colonization of Brazil, Portuguese settlers remained mostly in the coastal areas and were not confronted by populous and complex indigenous cultures. When compared to the Spanish viceroyalties, Brazilian colonial society seems less developed institutionally. The economic growth of the colony was sustained mainly by a feudal agricultural economy which depended largely on slave labor imported from Africa. Centers of higher learning were not established in Brazil until 1827, and the first university was authorized only in 1920. In Spanish America, on the other hand, the Dominican college of Santo Domingo was elevated to the rank of a university (called St Thomas) in 1538, and Mexico City and Lima had printing presses by 1535. Much to its advantage, colonial Brazil was a society receptive to the foreign intellectual currents that often came with trade. French, British, and US ships frequently anchored in Brazilian ports. Though the Portuguese crown sought a strict administrative control of its vast American colony, it never developed the paranoid fear of foreigners displayed by Spanish authorities. This is all the more remarkable when one realizes that portions of Brazil were contested by Spain, Holland, and other European powers. In fact, due to dynastic mishaps, the Spanish crown ruled Portugal and its Empire from 1580 to 1640. Moreover, from 1630 to 1654 the Dutch occupied most of the Brazilian northeast, from São Francisco river to Maranhão. These adverse developments, however, did not lead to the kind of political fragmentation that eventually took place in Spanish America after Independence. In part, the cohesion of Brazilian society was enhanced when, in 1808, this colony became the center of the Portuguese Empire. After fleeing Napoleonic troops with a British naval escort, the Prince Regent (later King João VI) settled his court in Rio de Janeiro, and remained there until 1821.

2

On December 16, 1815, Brazil became a kingdom and as such an equal of Portugal. Obviously, such an extraordinary turn of events has no equivalent in the history of Spanish America.

By the middle of the eighteenth century, Brazilian society was an intense amalgamation of Indians, Africans, and Europeans. The large African slave labor employed in agriculture and mining rapidly became an important sector of the total population. Yet, contrary to the expectations of some conservative sectors, this growing pattern of ethnic diversity did not prove to be a destabilizing factor. On the whole, the political history of Brazil has not included the extended periods of violence withstood by most Spanish American nations. Tolerance and a penchant for compromise have held sway, even when the colony was seeking its independence. Nevertheless, political tolerance and the stability enjoyed by the ruling elite did not improve the ruthless treatment endured, for centuries, by Indians, slaves, and immigrant labor.

In Brazil, as elsewhere in Latin America, proclamations of a national literature derived mostly from political discourses which sought to abolish colonial rule and to strengthen national identity. In that context, literature became an important contributor to an emerging rhetoric of nationhood. As Professor Benedito Nunes makes clear in the introductory chapter to this volume of this *History*, arguments for and against the existence of a Brazilian literary history lasted well into the twentieth century. Conflicting statements focused on a varied assortment of manifestos, learned documents, and detailed commentaries of certain key texts. Yet, it is clear that those controversial initiatives stemmed mainly from a nationalistic historiography which coveted a *sui generis* representation of the cultural legacies of Brazil.

Romantic historians depicted the indigenous populations, exotic flora, mythic wealth, and artistic achievements as interrelated components. Indeed, this kind of iconographic scheme was already present in *Tropical Harvest* (1640–1643), by the Dutch painter Albert Eckhourt, and also in *Virgin Forest* (1834–1839), by the French artist Jean-Baptiste Debret. Not surprisingly, a similar perspective is evident in Domingos José Gonçalves de Magalhães's "Ensaio sobre a história da literatura do Brasil" (1836), and also in Francisco Adolfo de Varnhagen's *História geral do Brasil* (1854). No less can be said of earlier works by the Frenchman Ferdinand Denis. Particularly relevant is his *Résumé de l'histoire littéraire du Portugal, suivi du résumé de l'histoire littéraire du Brésil* (1826), as well as other treatises produced by historians such as João Manuel Pereira da Silva and Joaquim Norberto de Sousa e Silva. The central goal of these writers was to establish the documentary basis for a national history of Brazil, one that would be articulated in a singular manner and that would vindicate an earlier corpus of texts such as Sebastião da Rocha Pita's

3

História da América portuguesa 1500–1724 (1730). These attempts amounted to the collective origination of a master narrative meant to encompass factual data of almost any kind, as well as the creative achievements of *belles lettres* and the popular arts. Preliminary notions of historical periodization surfaced from these efforts and eventually they were duplicated by a less than assured literary historiography which began to emerge in the second half of the nineteenth century.

Evidently, the formulation of a national Brazilian history stands as an enterprise carried out by political leaders, historians, literary scholars, and creative writers among others. Their task is clearly akin to the Hegelian conception of universal history; that is, a narrative of considerable poetic breadth that takes as its subject all that is known about the past. As such, romantic historical writing fashioned its content in response to idealized notions that are largely depicted by means of metaphorical representations. As might be expected, the historical accounts of Denis, Magalhães, Varnhagen, and their followers, are the sort of narrative representation in which verbal sophistication seems to matter as much as documentary evidence. Thus, in the guise of fictional narratives, romantic historians often blurred relationships between general and particular data, or between individuals and society. In many, such imaginative discourse is clearly linked to literary texts, such as the *Diálogos das grandezas do Brasil* (1618), by Ambrósio Fernandes Brandão, or to the *Cultura e opulência do Brasil* (1711), by the Italian Jesuit André João Antonil.

If nothing else, the contrastive appraisal of historical accounts and literary texts delineated above shows that both kinds of writing contributed generously to the formation of a codified discourse of praise which, through the centuries, has depicted Brazil as a land of splendid beauty and immense richness. Literature and history articulated an elaborate rhetoric of abundance and promise which was meant to feed national pride and that is clearly evident in F. Denis's *Scènes de la nature sur les tropiques et de leur influence sur la poésie* (1824). David Haberly documents perceptively this recurring convergence of literary and historical discourses generated by the liberal ideology of Romanticism. By the end of the eighteenth century literary creation in Brazil had surpassed Portuguese letters in quality and output. With a renewed sense of assurance, Brazilian authors looked to French, English, and German models as incentives for renovation. Yet, the idealized cultural motifs and Indianist themes that surfaced in Gonçalves de Magalhães's *Suspiros poéticos e saudades* (1836) remained visible through most of the nineteenth century. Inevitably, the sentimental excesses of romantic verse faded as French Parnassian and symbolist poets became better known in Brazil. The poetry of Charles Baudelaire, Leconte de Lisle, and Théophile Gautier, among others, changed in many ways the tone and general orientation of Brazilian poetry. Through parodies and ingenious adaptations the theatre also entered a period of renovation toward the end of the century. It did so as it enlarged its repertoire, while linking its modes of representation to those prevalent in advanced nations. Severino João Albuquerque documents this process thoroughly and shows as well the surprising development achieved by this genre in the nineteenth century. Fiction, on the other hand, did not fare as well in most of Latin America during the first half of the nineteenth century. Mary L. Daniel describes the growing interaction that existed between fictive prose and journalism, as Brazil moved toward political independence. The growing impact of the *folhetins* (serials), literary supplements, and similar tracts of fictional narratives, becomes particularly visible in the second half of the nineteenth century. As in the rest of Latin America, the absence of native novels of merit was partially compensated for by frequent translations of European authors. Perhaps the most notable exception among the works of that period was *Memórias de um sargento de milícias* (1855), a novel written by Manuel Antônio de Almeida (1831–1861), which was first published in a series of *folhetins*. Recognition, however, came to it quite belatedly.

David Haberly also depicts the remarkable development of the Brazilian novel in the second half of the nineteenth century. José de Alencar's *Iracema* (1865), *O gaúcho* (1870), and *O sertanejo* (1875), among other novels, enriched considerably the telluric narratives that emerged in the latter part of the century. In his fiction the social and economic roles of women and other marginal sectors of Brazilian society came into sharper focus. However, it is in *O mulato* (1881), *O cortiço* (1890), and *Demônios*, by Aluísio Azevedo (1857–1913) that the oppressing effects of rural and urban deprivation are depicted in ways that often evoke the harsh fictions of Charles Dickens and Emile Zola. Those and other disheartening features of Latin American society at the turn of the century are just as evident in the works of Machado de Assis, yet his novels do not resort to the bulky proto-scientific data and crude episodes cherished by the Naturalists. In *Memórias póstumas de Brás Cubas* (1881), *Dom Casmurro* (1900), and *Quincas Borba* (1891) Machado displays the artistry of a master storyteller. The sophistication achieved in *Memórias* and *Dom Casmurro* reminds one of Flaubert and Eça de Queiroz. By 1900 Machado was already the finest Latin American novelist, though few knew his work outside Brazil. His subtle fictions reflected the increasing complexities of Brazilian society as it entered the twentieth century. Yet, regrettably, as in earlier times, literary and cultural activities still remained the prerogatives of small elites. As the new century approached, Brazil expanded its many links with the industrialized nations. Like other Latin American republics it did so with the hope of sharing in the promising achievements of modern science and technology. Not unexpectedly, Brazilian literature of that period, and the novel in particular, reveal the paradoxical fate of Latin American nations that seemed unable to reconcile the rhetoric of modernity with protracted states of social and economic stagnation. Yet, ironically, those persisting contradictions invigorated much of the Brazilian prose produced in the first decade of the twentieth century.

This is particularly so in *Os sertões*, a text that gains strength from the contradictions between its scientific approach and the elusiveness of Brazilian reality. As in the Spanish American work that is its closest counterpart, Sarmiento's *Facundo* (1845), the central dynamic of Euclides da Cunha's book is the tension between the Eurocentrism inherent in the science or pseudo-science he attempts to apply to his subject and the visceral nationalism that compels him to identify with landscapes, societies, and individuals defined by Eurocentrism as negative factors in Brazil's development as a modern nation. *Os sertões* is the foundational text of a powerful modern tradition of sometimes anguished elitist introspection in Brazil. This tradition, as represented by da Cunha, Oliveira Vianna, Paulo Prado, and Gilberto Freyre, is described and analyzed here by Thomas Skidmore; the enormous literary and historiographical consequences of the tradition, which seeks nothing less than a totalizing definition of Brazil's past and future, are studied in Mary Daniel's account of prose fiction in the first half of the twentieth century, and by Benedito Nunes.

Another fundamental Brazilian text, as pessimistic as *Os sertões* and almost as influential, also appeared in 1902: Graça Aranha's novel *Canaã*. The contrast between these two works and José Enrique Rodó's *Ariel* (1900) could not be sharper, and serves to illustrate both the gap between Brazilian and Spanish American self-definitions at the turn of the century and the important differences between Brazilian literature during this period and Spanish American *Modernismo* as defined by its most influential prose text.

For much of the nineteenth century, Brazil's romantic poetry, studied here by Fábio Lucas, was not fundamentally different in form and function from that produced in Spanish America. This is not to say that the two traditions did not occasionally diverge in important ways: the poetic Indianism exemplified in the works of Gonçalves Dias did not appear with similar force in Spanish America until the publication of Juan Zorrilla de San Martíns's *Tabaré* in 1888; the idealized and distant Indian was far more appealing to the Brazilian elite than the mixed-race inhabitants of the nation's interior, and nothing approaching *poesía gauchesca* ever developed in Brazil; the campaign against African slavery was largely waged through prose fiction in the Spanish-speaking Caribbean, but its most influential Brazilian champion was a poet, Antônio de

Castro Alves. In formal and technical terms, however, the two poetic traditions were more similar than distinct.

That similarity ended quite abruptly toward the close of the nineteenth century. While Spanish American *Modernismo* managed, more-or-less successfully, to assimilate and integrate the theories and techniques of Hugoan Romanticism and French Parnassianism and Symbolism, no such integration occurred in Brazilian poetry in the period from about 1880 to 1922. Romanticism, *parnasianismo*, and *simbolismo* are three distinct movements there, and are analyzed in the essays by Massaud Moisés and Marta Peixoto. While the differences between these movements are perhaps more sharply defined in Brazilian literary historiography than in the reality of texts from this period, and while the formation of the *parnasianista* and *simbolista* movements was influenced by personal relationships and geography as well as by French poetic theory, the fact remains that Brazilian poetry of this period was both less innovative and more closely tied to European models than that of Spanish America. Brazil produced no single figure comparable in talent and influence to the Nicaraguan Rubén Darío, although two *simbolista* poets, Augusto dos Anjos and João da Cruz e Sousa, are among the most powerful and unique New World voices; in particular, Cruz e Sousa is perhaps the greatest black poet of Latin America.

After the turn of the century, the self-contented Formalism of the *parnasianistas* triumphed decisively in Brazilian poetry, and remained the dominant poetic force until the modernist explosion of 1922. Prose fiction often appeared equally stale and repetitious, and both genres seemed intent upon validating the famous dictum of Afrânio Peixoto that literature should be no more than "the smile on society's face." The one interesting fictionist of the period, Afonso Henriques de Lima Barreto (like Machado de Assis, a mulatto), did not achieve the reputation he deserved until well after his death in 1922.

Nothing comparable to the 1922 Week of Modern Art, as a defining intellectual and artistic event, can be found in North American or Spanish American literary history. Organized by a handful of young writers and artists in São Paulo, the Week decisively influenced Brazilian literature, painting, sculpture, and architecture for decades. Giovanni Pontiero's article describes and analyzes the overwhelming impact of the Week on verse; that impact can also be seen in the studies by Mary Daniel (on prose fiction), by K. David Jackson (on the short story), and by Severino João Albuquerque (on the twentieth-century theatre). A number of the fundamental texts of modern Brazilian literature – the poetry of Manuel Bandeira and Carlos Drummond de Andrade, the verse and fiction of Mário de Andrade and Oswald de Andrade – derive directly from Modernism, and the enduring influence of the movement can be seen in the Concrete poets (the spiritual, intellectual, and technical heirs of Oswald de Andrade) and in the linguistic experimentation of Guimarães Rosa.

Brazilian Modernism, in its essence, was an attempt to utilize the forms of the contemporary European Avant-Garde to disrupt the ideological and linguistic code implicit in the introspective tradition begun by Euclides da Cunha, a tradition which appeared ever more pessimistic in its assessment of Brazil's character and potential. This effort was not always consistent, nor was it ultimately successful; what is perhaps the most pessimistic Brazilian introspective essay, Paulo Prado's *Retrato do Brasil* (1928), was written by a friend and ally of the São Paulo Modernists, and the most complex and innovative text the movement produced, Mário de Andrade's *Macunaíma* (1928), is in large measure a myth of national destruction rather than creation.

The Modernists, despite their good intentions and their enthusiasm for the artifacts of modernity and technology found in the city of São Paulo, in fact tended to reinforce the code. Ironically, it was a sociologist from the plantations of the Northeast, Gilberto Freyre, who effected the disruption the Modernists envisioned; his influence, beginning with the publication of *Casa grande e senzala* [*The Masters and the Slaves*] in 1933, is studied in the article by Thomas Skidmore. Freyre buttressed his radically positive view of the nation's heritage and its potential with careful analyses of colonial and nineteenth-century society and with references to contemporary European and North American social theorists, theorists whose view of racial and ethnic diversity was very different indeed from that of the nineteenth-century French and German theorists on race and determinists whose ideas had long served as the basis for the introspective tradition.

Freyre's ideas and the force of his personality helped to create what is often called the "New Novel" of the Northeast. The works this movement produced from about 1930 to 1945, surveyed by Mary L. Daniel, are a very mixed bag, combining Freyrean optimism and naturalistic pessimism, late nineteenth-century Regionalism and Socialist Realism. Nonetheless, the "New Novelists" include several major figures, notably José Lins do Rego, Graciliano Ramos, and Jorge Amado. Nevertheless, despite the literary and commercial success of these Northeastern novelists, the great fictionist of Brazil in the twentieth century is João Guimarães Rosa. His novels are discussed here by John Gledson, his short fiction by K. David Jackson. Fusing extraordinary linguistic and philosophical complexity with the authenticity of regional landscapes and characters, Guimarães Rosa's works finally completed the program envisioned by the most serious and sophisticated of the Modernists, Mário de Andrade.

While the poetry of Carlos Drummond de Andrade and the prose fiction of Guimarães Rosa are the high points of the Brazilian twentieth century, that is not to say that the nation has been a literary wasteland since 1950; the diverse accomplishments of recent fictionists are here described by Jackson and Gledson. Nonetheless, as the late J. G. Merquior points out in his comparative essay on Brazilian and Spanish American letters, those writers have been considerably overshadowed, on the international literary scene, by the major figures of the *Boom* – Borges, Cortázar, García Márquez, and others. As Merquior notes, at least some Brazilian intellectuals have attempted to explain this phenomenon as the result of a conspiracy of French Structuralist critics, Spanish publishing houses, and North American readers of Hispanic ancestry. The theory, of course, is ludicrous, but there is a kernel of truth to it. By about 1960, the Spanish-speaking world contained enough educated and sophisticated readers to support the authors of the *Boom* and to project those authors onto the international scene; Brazil, despite its vast area and large population, has not yet developed that kind of market for serious fiction, and even the best modern novelists – Clarice Lispector or Nélida Piñón, for example – have only recently begun to attract foreign attention.

The development of Brazilian literature since 1960 was also hampered by the military dictatorship that lasted from 1964 to 1984 – the first extended period of repression and relatively rigid censorship in the nation's history. It can be argued that while Spanish American writers, through historical experience stretching back to the early nineteenth century, had long since developed strategies for coping with censorship and repression, Brazilians were largely unprepared, and therefore spent much of those two decades exploring their limited options. One option was hermetic experimentalism, creating works impenetrable to the government's censors; such works, however, were sometimes equally impenetrable to readers. Another option, explicit or implicit in some of the most interesting texts of the period, was to seek to move beyond the limited market for serious literature by borrowing and reformulating the discourse of popular culture in Brazil. The unique richness and importance of that culture, in one of its most remarkable manifestations, are explored by Candace Slater in her essay on the *literatura de cordel*. All in all, however, theatre – a relatively weak genre in the colonial period and the nineteenth century – was most successful in adapting to the realities of the dictatorship, as Severino Albuquerque's article makes clear.

This volume, the work of distinguished contributors from Europe, North America, and Brazil, is the fullest and most detailed account of the whole development of Brazilian literature available in English. While its chief purpose is to assist both scholars and general readers, it also possesses, for both Brazilians and Brazilianists, a symbolic value that transcends its utility. It may not be entirely true that, as the Parnassian poet Olavo Bilac asserted, the Portuguese language is "the cemetery of literature," but the language has undeniably served as a barrier, limiting international recognition of the richness and originality of Brazilian literature and of its great writers. The publication of this collection of essays is an important step in achieving that recognition.

Roberto González Echevarría
Enrique Pupo-Walker
David Haberly

The literary historiography of Brazil

Benedito Nunes

Literature in Brazil began to exist from the moment of the discovery of the country by the Portuguese in 1500, commemorated by a literary event in the broadest sense of the word: the *Carta* by Pero Vaz de Caminha, scribe of Pedro Álvares Cabral's fleet, reporting the finding of new land and its inhabitants to King Manuel. However, the first title that legitimized the identity of literature as Brazilian appeared after three centuries of colonization, at the time when political subordination to Portugal had been severed. For only after Independence was proclaimed on September 7, 1822 would literary historiography begin to appear in Brazil, concomitant with the implantation of Romanticism, to which it owes its legitimacy, and in direct relation to the appearance of a national historiography. Amounting to a second beginning, that legitimacy conferred a lawful existence on literature as opposed to its earlier *de facto* existence during the colonial period. Historiography as the writing of history thereby carried out the singular recuperation of the past of which it is capable in accord with its founding function – a function more pronounced in the countries to which European colonialism gave rise, as in those of the Portuguese and Spanish Americas.

A consequence of political separation, the ambiguous relationship between the Americas and Europe, at times antagonistic and at other times identifying with the earlier state of dependence on the external capitals, disposed the countries of the Americas to the writing of their own history, capable of recuperating the past as a long and continuous phase of preparation for nationhood, highlighting the struggles or the yearning for emancipation during the colonial period of subjugation. Part of a broader process of cultural legitimation as a result of a strong ideological motivation brought about by newly established political power, this effort engendered in Brazil the founding function of historiography, whether national or literary, both treated by Romantic thought according to the same common principles.

One can thus affirm that the Romantics created literary historiography in Brazil, at the same time that literary historiography, impregnated by the very ideology with which national historiography supported the nascent monarchy, created literature, giving birth to the Brazilian identity that legitimized it. Through the retrospective view of the historian – who always arrives at the past through a perspective conditioned by the present – the state of literature before Independence was seen as a reflection of an original and fitting character as defined after Independence. At the beginning of the nineteenth century, literature was configured as the first draft of a unique literary realm on the road to complete autonomy.

In the Spanish American countries an analogous process occurred, defining the identity of their respective literatures: a conceptual identity, theoretically constituted and ideologically based. Thus, the dubious reality that literature manifests is underwritten by its founding philosophy – a dubious and paradoxical reality, which always existed, but only began to have effective existence at the moment that the Romantics conceived of it. "There is a Latin American literature even before the romantics, but this is only so because it was conceived retrospectively by romantic thought."[1]

That paradox may also be applied to Latin America itself, since its literature does not stand alone as a consequence of modern thought. Conceived as a political and cultural entity, Latin America embodies equally the dubious existence of what came before, and what comes after, the concepts that make it thinkable as a reality. The same paradox connects the entity to its literature by a relationship of mutual genesis, given that literature expresses something unique and original that the entity holds in its very reality. Both would constitute a "metaphoric field" (González Echevarría, *The Voice of the Masters*, 4), as a single form of new cultural expression that has its nucleus in the conversion of Nature into landscape. In Brazilian literature, also implicated in the stated paradox, we can discover similar relationships. The question of its identity extends to that of the country itself. And the idea of Nature as landscape enters into the conception of both the country and its literature.

Keeping these crossed relationships in mind, the first part of this exposition will follow the concomitant processes of the genesis of historiography and of literature that was produced following the curve of ascension and decline of Romanticism, from the first moments of Independence to the beginning of the social and political crisis of the Second Empire (1870). The second part will focus on the systematization of historiography as the product of anti-Romantic thought rooted in Naturalism (1888–1919), and, immediately following, the revision of

[1] Roberto González Echevarría, *The Voice of the Masters* (Austin: University of Texas Press, 1985) 4.

historiography that came to be felt in the 1950s in the aftermath of the modernist upheaval (1922), above all as a function of the spreading of the social sciences in Brazil, beginning about 1930.

The conclusion will set forth the problematics and the perspectives of contemporary literary historiography, as a synthesis of the questions formulated in earlier sections.

With the weakening of Portugal's political domination and the end of its cultural hegemony in the early years of the nineteenth century, the preliminary signs of Romanticism reached Brazil by the same transatlantic routes that brought foreign scholars, writers, and artists, after the arrival of Doña Maria I and her court, who were fleeing the invasion of Napoleonic troops during the regency of D. João. In 1808 a new period for the reception of European ideas, particularly French, was then inaugurated due to the influence of this singular episode in the annals of the colonization of American lands.

One should remember that on arrival in Bahia, the first stop of this untimely move, the Prince Regent, who would be proclaimed King João VI in 1818, decreed the opening of the colony's ports to all nations friendly with Portugal, particularly England, and declared the colony to be part of a single realm with Portugal and the Algarve. Docking in Rio de Janeiro in 1808, D. João VI created a royal press, alongside scientific establishments and facilities for higher education, and opened to public consultation the 60,000 volumes of the library of the Palácio da Ajuda, brought by the royal family, out of which the holdings of the National Library were born.[2] After the return of King João VI to Portugal in 1821, D. Pedro I, while still Regent, lifted the censorship of imported books (Azevedo, *A cultura brasileira*, 382). The heights of liberalization introduced by these measures in a country deprived of printing presses and public libraries for three centuries by strict prohibition of the Portuguese Crown, prepared a favorable climate for the regular arrival of foreign figures in greater number than before, through their own initiative, alone, or in groups carrying out official duties.

Thus there arrived in Brazil, in addition to the French writer Ferdinand Denis (1798–1890), who remained there from 1817 to 1821, painters such as Nicolas Antoine Taunay (1755–1830) and Jean-Baptiste Debret (1768–1848) (members, among others, of the French Artistic Mission, contracted in 1816 by the government to found an Academy of Fine Arts), and Johann Morits Rugendas (1802–1858), Aimé-Adrien Taunay (1803–1828), and Hercules Florence (1804–1879), part of the Langsdorf Mission (1824–1829), under the sponsorship of Russia. Even Naturalists arrived, such as

---

[2] Fernando de Azevedo, *A cultura brasileira*, 5th. edn. (São Paulo: Edições Melhoramentos, 1971) 382.

the Prince of Wied-Neuwied (1782–1867), from 1815 to 1817, August de Saint-Hilaire (1799–1853), from 1816 to 1822, Karl Friedrich Philip von Martius (1794–1868), and Johan Baptist von Spix (1781–1826) – the latter two members of the Austrian Scientific Mission (1817).

These scholars, artists, and writers, above all voyagers and explorers, traveled throughout Brazil cataloguing zoological and botanical species, drawing or painting indigenous peoples, describing majestic natural panoramas. The enraptured vision of these pre-romantic voyagers in search of the exotic in Brazilian Nature was manifested in the *Scènes de la nature sur les tropiques et de leur influence sur la poésie* (1824), by Ferdinand Denis. The foreign writer's distanced gaze, the result of a sentimental infusion similar to Chateaubriand's of the forests of Canada and Florida, revealed Nature to be an entrancing and enveloping landscape, identified with the country and embodied in its people. In a later work, Denis would try to demonstrate that the landscape was not merely the setting for native life but something that literature could make profound. Authentic source of a new tradition, that profoundly changed landscape should supply literature with the elements of its marvelous but previously unexplored reality.

This was the central idea of his *Résumé de l'histoire littéraire du Portugal, suivi du résumé de l'histoire littéraire du Brésil* (Paris, 1826) which, while not the first appreciation of Brazilian literature by an educated European, was the one that brought immediate and profound repercussions. In fact, two other publications by foreigners who did not come to Brazil preceded that of Denis in this regard.

In his *Geschichte der Portuguesischen Poesie und Beredsamkeit* (1805), volume IV of a collective panoramic work about modern literatures in 12 volumes – *Geschichte der Poesie und Beredsamkeit seit dem Ende des 13.Jahrhunderts*, published from 1801 to 1819 – Friedrich Bouterwek of Göttingen (1765–1828) included two authors born in Brazil: the author of comedies António José da Silva, "The Jew" (1705–1739), and the poet Cláudio Manuel da Costa (1729–1789). Also, the Genevan Jean Charles Leonard Simonde de Sismondi, of the circle of the Schlegel brothers and Mme. de Stäel, in his *De la Littérature du Midi de l'Europe* (1813), besides the two Brazilians cited by the German professor, includes the eighteenth-century poet Manuel Inácio da Silva Alvarenga (1749–1814), studying them within the "overseas projection" of a meridional literature such as the Portuguese, rich in imagination and sensibility.

Unlike these other foreigners, Denis separates Brazilian literature from Portuguese, whose history, by the way, he was the first to study. He also separates them materially; to each one he dedicates a distinct part of the same volume – "O resumo da história literária do Brasil," which came after the one relating to the "História literária de Portugal" – perhaps already wishing to figure into this internal schism between subjects the autonomy that Brazilian literature should assume after the colony's political break with its external metropolis. However, before taking up history, in the introductory part of the study, a mixture of romantic interpretation of the geography and the psychology of the country and its people and a program to put into place the development of letters, he enumerates the features that enabled Brazil to have its own literature, the autonomous expression of its originality as a people and as a nation.

It becomes very clear, therefore, that for Denis that autonomous expression was not yet a fact, but something that the country's situation allowed to be foreseen according to the potentialities inherent in those features. That was the source of the book's enormous repercussions, a sort of prelude to the articulating concepts of Brazilian literary historiography.

The first of these concepts, after political liberty, is certainly that of Nature – in the sense of physical ambience and also climate – with which we begin, because without the magical romantic vision that originates in its contemplation there would be no essence of local color to guarantee the independence of expression of what is particular to the land and to the people who live there. "In these beautiful lands, so favored by nature, one's thought should spread wings to match the spectacle offered to it; majestic, thanks to the classics of the past, such thought must remain independent, having no guide but observation. In sum, America must be free as much in her poetry as in her government."[3]

The connection between the motif of liberty and that of youth is highlighted, above all, thus associating recent independence with the future proclivities of the new nation. Along with the other countries of Latin America, Brazil would be considered, as part of the mythical prestige that it was already acquiring, a young country of which one could expect "new and energetic thoughts . . ." (Denis, *Resumo* [1968] 30). Yet Denis also pointed to the archaic side of this young nation where, as Montaigne would say, one could witness humanity in its infancy: the indigenous peoples who with their ancient customs represented the wellspring of the magical new reality proportioned by Nature, and from whom all that is genuinely Brazilian would flow. Denis knew them firsthand: he traveled among the Botocudos of the Rio Doce Valley and among the Machakalis, the theme of his novella of the same title included in *Scènes de la nature*, considered a precursor of Romantic Indianism.[4] Like Nature that is in harmony with the "savage" peoples, this third motif

---

[3] Ferdinand Denis, *O resumo da história literária do Brasil* (Porto Alegre, Editora Lima, 1968) 30–1.
[4] Guilhermino César, *Historiadores e críticos do romantismo*, vol. I (EDUSP, 1978) xxv.

distanced Brazilian literature from the imitative classical tradition that Denis summarizes as the predominance of Greco-Roman mythology.

"Greek mythology, based in large part on the phenomena of Nature, would play a sad role under the tropical sky," wrote C. Schlichthorst, who was known only as a German mercenary in the service of D. Pedro I from 1824 to 1826, in his *Rio de Janeiro wie es ist – Beiträge zur Tages und Sittengeschichten der Hauptstadt von Bresilien* (1829) [*O Rio de Janeiro como é – 1824–1826*] (1943). These words of the lieutenant-grenadier echo the question of the French writer: "Will the dawn of Greece with its rosy fingers open that splendorous sky, whose brilliance would make Apollo himself turn pale?" (*Resumo*, 32). Instead of relying on these comparisons inherited from the European world, Brazilian poets should look for inspiration to the sumptuous landscapes and to the "free nations" of the Indians, repositories of poetry and courage that protect the reserves of a heroism similar to that found in the Middle Ages, with its "ardent and adventurous spirit of the age of chivalry."

Finally, the natural disposition of the people – which corresponds to the Romantic notion of genius formed by the diverse races that constituted it – predisposes them "to receive profound impressions; and to abandon themselves to poetry for which a city education is not necessary; it is assumed that the peculiar genius of so many diverse races is patent in it" (*Resumo*, 33–4). The Brazilian, therefore, would synthesize different levels of sensibility: the chivalry of the Portuguese, the boldness and fantasy of the Indian – who for Denis is simply the American – and the credulity of the black slave. What the writer last affirms as the ethnic germ of an autonomous Brazilian literature is the motif of miscegenation, destined to play a role as a vehicle of sensibility and even of character in the long course of literary historiography.

In the historical part *per se*, merely a weak recapitulation of what had been produced in prose and verse up to the period of Independence, among lists of poems by Cláudio Manuel da Costa, Tomás Antônio Gonzaga (1744–1809 or 1812), and Antônio Pereira de Sousa Caldas (1762–1814), Denis highlights in a long exposition the two eighteenth-century epics, *O Caramuru* (1781) by Frei José de Santa Rita Durão (1722–1784) and *O Uraguai* (1769) by José Basílio da Gama (1741–1795), from which he transcribes stanzas that show the incorporation of the natural environment into the scenario in which indigenous characters play a role. Either aspect, the scenic or the ethnic, would attest to the national character of both poems. In this way, without stretching his conclusion, the French Indianist accepts that in the colonial period both epics anticipated the literary autonomy later demanded by political independence.

Thus Denis opened the retrospective trail on which Brazilian literary identity would be formed, bringing together in its past, just as it should in its present, the autonomous expression of national originality and local reality.

Coinciding with the nationalistic tone of the *Résumé*, but not with its historical survey, is the assessment made of Brazilian poetry in the eighteenth century, published in the same year under the title *História abreviada da língua e da poesia portuguesa* (1826) by a young Portuguese romantic poet then exiled in France, João Batista da Silva Leitão de Almeida Garrett. Garrett highlighted the sonnets of Cláudio Manuel da Costa and the collection of lyric poetry by Tomás Antônio Gonzaga, *Marília de Dirceu* (1792).

According to Garrett, Portuguese literature, in decline since the seventeenth century, its "Iron Age" after the Renaissance "Golden Age," had been rescued in the eighteenth century with the "production of Brazilian plantations." Inseparable, therefore, from Portuguese poetry into which they breathed a new life, these authors' works, for the Portuguese Romantic, would be of still larger merit if they had taken advantage of "the majestic and new scenes of nature in that vast region." It seemed to him that "they hesitate to show themselves as American; and from that comes the affection and impropriety that represents a flaw in their best qualities" (César, *Historiadores*, 90).

Almeida Garrett, however, who valued the national as an expression of local color – and particularly in relation to da Gama's *Uraguai* – did not consider it, as had Denis, to be a distinctive sign of the literature of a free country, one by that time already politically independent.

Romanticism was not the cause of Brazil's political independence, but as a factor in the "encounter of two movements – the political and the literary,"[5] it opened to Brazil's literature the desire to become independent.

After the return of King João VI to Portugal, Independence resulted from the joining of the elites of Rio de Janeiro and São Paulo around the Prince Regent, who remained in Brazil and who would reign as Pedro I against the recolonizing measures of the Portuguese constitutional government. The immediate hope was to neutralize the wave of antilusitanism and cut off the political radicalism then diffused throughout the country by means of a "great and strong monarchy."[6] A cruel conquest, the separation from Portugal was imposed through the armed struggles that repressed the Portuguese reaction in the provinces, such as Bahia and Pará. Later, with the abdication of King Pedro I, who had been the

---

[5] Dante Moreira Leite, *O caráter nacional brasileiro – história de uma ideologia* (São Paulo: Livraria Pioneira Editora, 1969) 171.

[6] Hamilton de Mattos Monteiro, "Da Independência à vitória da ordem," *História geral do Brasil*, ed. Maria Yedda Linhares *et al.* (Rio de Janeiro: Editora Campus, 1990) 116.

sponsor of the former alliance between Brazilians and Portuguese, the painful consolidation of the new monarchy endured a regency that ended in 1840 with the declaration of the majority of the heir to the throne, Pedro II. During the Regency, nationalism was exacerbated, impassioned and moderate liberals confronted each other, and the radical foci of the insurrections spread from north to south reignited, some being truly revolutionary explosions of a popular nature, for example the *Cabanagem* (Pará and Amazonas, 1833–1836), the *Sabinada* (Bahia, 1837–1838), and the *Balaiada* (Maranhão, 1839–1841), as well as others of a separatist and republican nature such as the *Guerra dos Farrapos* (Rio Grande do Sul, 1835–1845).

With D. Pedro's majority, imperial peace was established. The military suppression of the uprisings – also called Pacification – reinforced the political centralization that would go along with the practice of alternating the conservative and liberal parties in power. This mechanism would last until the end of the Second Reign, whose structure of slavery and latifundia began to crumble in 1888, when the monarchy itself signed the *Lei áurea* (the Golden Law) abolishing slavery.

Between the Regency and the Majority, before the stable period around 1850 to which the new coffee-producing and commercial elite contributed (Monteiro, "Da Independência," 124), Romanticism took root, establishing the "conscious desire to define an independent literature in Brazil"[7] that reinitiated Denis's program, and further disposing itself to renew the potentialities for autonomous literary expression perceived by the French writer.

The author of the *Résumé* proposed that this replica of the political act of 1822 intended to separate the new poetry to be written in Brazil from the aesthetic standards adopted by Portugal. Its patriotic intention to construct a national literature, defending, restoring, perfecting, and highlighting its Brazilian particularities, led toward the development of a literary history that would conjoin two main lines of romantic thought – historicism and nationalism.

Neither the union of the political and the literary nor the proximity to history are strangers to the essence of the contradictory Romantic movement, begun in Germany in the late eighteenth century and disseminated in the early 1800s. With a reactive nature that opposed it to the French Revolution and to the incipient industrial society, causing a return to the past that crystallized in the value attributed to the Middle Ages and to Christian antiquity, the Romantic movement also had a liberal and progressive side of confidence in the future. These two temporally opposing directions, a return to the past and confidence in the future,

---

[7] Antônio Cândido, *Formação da literatura brasileira: momentos decisivos*, vol. I: *1750–1836*; vol. II: *1836–1880* (São Paulo: Livraria Martins Editora, 1959) I, 300.

produced historical consciousness in modern thought. From that consciousness comes the penchant for connecting the romantic movement to history as science and to historicism. Without the Romantics' historical consciousness, nineteenth-century historicism would be inconceivable.[8] Yet without historicism – the idea that reality is historical and as such explainable by causes outside of the individual will – the idea of "nation" as conceived by the Romantics, as the ultimate cohesive force, essence of the collective soul or the spirit of a people that gave rise to nationalism, would be inconceivable also.

Thus, whoever tells the history of history that began to form during this period cannot lose sight of these two directions, nationalism and historicism, particularizing the union of the literary and political aspects of the same romantic movement that guided the formation of Brazilian historiography in general, the motivating goal of a considerable portion of the intellectual endeavor in this period. "During the years of Romanticism, historical activity is placed in the foreground of the intellectual concerns alongside novel and poetry."[9] Thus even less can the historian of history disregard the institutional apparatus controlling this activity; the historian is obliged to examine its effects in order finally to appreciate the interpenetration of historical writing with the literary production of the period.

The institutional frame was provided by the *Instituto Histórico e Geográfico Brasileiro*, founded in 1838 to "collect, organize, publish, or archive the documents necessary for the history and geography of the Empire of Brazil,"[10] according to the methods of the German school that linked history as science to historicism.[11] The function that the Institute attempted to fulfill, in accord with what was stated in its charter, was the formation of a documentary base, upon which to construct the history of the country, stimulating regional monographs and the writing of history of an openly nationalistic nature, since the only history existing at that time was the *History of Brazil* (1810) by the English poet Robert Southey (1774–1843).

The concern with the way to elicit this writing is reflected in the proposal by Januário da Cunha Barbosa (1780–1846) in 1840 "to offer one hundred *mil = réis* as a prize to whoever presented to the Institute a plan to write the ancient and modern history of Brazil, organized in such a way as to encompass the political, civil, ecclesiastical, and literary parts"

---

[8] Arnold Hauser, *The Social History of Art*, vol. III (London: Routledge & Kegan Paul, 1962) 157–8.
[9] Antônio Soares Amora, *História da literatura brasileira – Séculos XVI–XX* (São Paulo: Edição Saraiva, 1960) 74.
[10] José Honório Rodrigues, *Vida e história* (Rio de Janeiro: Civilização Brasileira, 1966) 37.
[11] Salgado Guimarães, Manoel Luiz Lima, Arno Wehling, *et al. Origens do Instituto Histórico e Geográfico Brasileiro* (Rio de Janeiro: Instituto Histórico e Geográfico Brasileiro, 1989) 50–1.

(Honório Rodrigues, *Vida e história*, 157). A practical–political purpose, however, would end up making this history of nationality compatible with the ideological orientation of historical studies, considered useful in the exercise of the functions of government, according to Joaquim Manuel de Macedo's insinuation when as Secretary of the Institute he recommended that ministers, legislators, and diplomats read its *Revista*.[12]

The service that these studies could render to the strengthening of nationality would not cease to be useful, by extension, to the imperial government in which the nation was embodied, safe from the conflicts that had threatened it during the turbulent period of the Regency. There were no radicals among the members of the Institute because the intelligentsia of the period was as small as it was moderate, confident in the centralized state, in the justice of the Emperor, and in the civilizing course of the Nation. This latter aspect of the nationalist ideology of Brazilian history made itself apparent principally in the debate in the *Revista* concerning one of the topics most discussed by scholars: the possible use of indigenous peoples as workers, given the end of the African slave trade in 1850 and the convenience of their integration into civilization, guided by the state "that held the key role as promoter of the national project" (Salgado Guimarães, "Idéias filosóficas," 32–3).

Given that the discussion took this route, the problem would not have held the same meaning for all the members of the most influential cultural institution of the period. The composition of the *Instituto Histórico* was heterogeneous; it counted on the patronage of the Emperor himself, who frequently attended its sessions. If historians such as Cunha Barbosa, Joaquim Norberto de Sousa e Silva (1820–1891), Francisco Adolfo de Varnhagen (1816–1878), and João Manuel Pereira da Silva (1817–1897) belonged to it, working with literary history, many other members were writers, including the previously mentioned Joaquim Manuel de Macedo (1820–1882), one of Brazil's first novelists, and poets Domingos José Gonçalves de Magalhães (1811–1882) and Gonçalves Dias (1823–1864), who was also an ethnographer. That heterogeneous membership, bringing together men of letters who were not specialists, facilitated the confluence of literary history and general history, which began to be written based on the collection of firsthand documents.

It is not by chance, therefore, that the matrix of Brazilian literary history resulted from the conjunction of the efforts of these men of letters, principally from the work of two of them: Magalhães – at once "pioneer of literary nationalism," and "herald of Brazilian Romanticism" [and]

[12] Manoel Luiz Lima, Salgado Guimarães, "Idéias filosóficas e sociais e estruturas de poder no Segundo Reinado," *Origens do Instituto Histórico e Geográfico Brasileiro*, ed. Arno Wehling (Rio de Janeiro: Instituto Histórico e Geográfico Brasileiro, 1989) 27.

"of the French orientation of our spiritual life,"[13] and Varnhagen, who would author the awaited nationalistic *History of Brazil*. In Magalhães, who had a degree in medicine, the "French orientation" extended from his book of verses, *Suspiros poéticos e saudades* (1836), to philosophy, disciple that he was of the eclecticism of Victor Cousin (1792–1867). In 1858 he would publish *Os fatos do espírito humano*, derived from an idealist line of Hegelian thought. Varnhagen, who was an engineer, dedicated himself to the social sciences, having studied paleography before pursuing historical investigation and entering the Brazilian diplomatic corps in 1841. Magalhães's book-length *Ensaio sobre a história da literatura do Brasil* (1836) and Varnhagen's *Ensaio histórico sobre as letras no Brasil* (1847) appeared within the cycle of research on the documentary sources of the country's literature and historical past.

Between 1829 and 1830, Cunha Barbosa edited in eight fascicles the *Parnaso brasileiro ou coleção das melhores poesias dos poetas do Brasil, tanto inéditos como já impressos* (Rio de Janeiro) that harks back to the poetic production of the seventeenth century. The same anthological criterion guided Pereira da Silva's *Parnaso brasileiro ou seleção dos melhores poetas brasileiros desde o descobrimento do Brasil* (1843), preceded by an introductory study. These publications that already dealt with and inventoried works of the past as historical material did not reach the threshold of literary historiography, which could only be achieved "by making canons that are in some sense transhistorical, and by inventing historical periods."[14]

The cited works of Magalhães and Varnhagen stand out within the cycle of which they are a part precisely for having crossed that threshold: they delineated the chronological outlines that served in the construction of periodicity and linked the supporting criteria to the establishment of a canonical romantic tradition, extending to the seventeenth and eighteenth centuries. Yet, although both supplied the seminal outline of literary history that acquired its definitive shape in the second half of the nineteenth century, their studies are distinguished by the differing concepts that tie them to the history of the country in the framework of the same conservative ideology.

Published in Paris in the first volume of *Niterói: Revista Brasiliense* that he edited in 1836 in collaboration with the poet Manuel José de Araújo Porto Alegre (1806–1879), Magalhães's work is superior not only for its chronological precedence in relation to Varnhagen's work (1847) but also

---

[13] Sérgio Buarque de Holanda, "Prefácio," to Domingos J. Gonçalves de Magalhães, *Suspiros poéticos e saudades*, 5th. edn. (Editora Universidade de Brasília, 1986) 15.
[14] Frank Kermode, "Canon and Period," in his *History and Value* (Oxford: Clarendon Press, 1989) 108–9.

for the scope of the problems it raises. Although it may be only the model for a historiography, a probing of the origin and progress of literature not including those who cultivated it, Magalhães's work is based on the relationship established by the Romantics between each people and its history. With the end of Portuguese rule, the free progress of nations in the nineteenth century had brought the idea of fatherland to Brazil, "child of French civilization" and its great Revolution. Yet the literature that the colonizer bequeathed the nation as an inheritance had lost nothing of its classical form when transplanted to the American milieu. So that literary development could accompany the progress of history, it was then necessary to recover through letters the presence of the fatherland and of Christian religious sentiment, which had been extinguished by the European classical tradition.

Thus the preeminent issue of independence or of literary autonomy presented itself to Magalhães when he questions whether "Brazil can inspire the imagination of its poets" and, again, whether "its indigenous people perchance cultivated poetry."[15] As placed in these twin concerns, the question could only be resolved through sources of autochthonous inspiration: Nature on one side and indigenous peoples on the other. Fundamentally, they are the same themes of Denis that return in Magalhães with the same affirmation that the Frenchman lent to them: the exuberance of natural scenery, already described in the "sublime pages of Langsdorf, Neuwied, Spix and Martius, Saint-Hilaire, and a multitude of other travellers . . ." (Magalhães, "Ensaio," 154), and the "free nations of indigenous peoples," according to him a primitive wellspring still capable of stimulating the imagination of poets just as the "fortunate proclivities of Nature" inspired the first inhabitants of the land, whom he does not hesitate to call Brazilian after Denis called them American. Who would the Brazilians born as musicians and poets be if not the Tamoios, who were musicians and poets drawn to church psalms translated by the Jesuits into *língua geral* or Tupi? From all evidence, the autochthony of the sources, for an autonomous literature, extends from the native land to the Indian as a congenital protobrazilian. Magalhães's romantic expectation is that the indigenous chants, when translated into Portuguese, could enrich Brazilian poetry just as the Scottish bards had influenced northern European poetry.

At the same time, through the effect of an "occult instinct," an independent, truly Brazilian literature, nurtured by patriotic sources guaranteeing its progress, would have already sprung up here and there during the colonial period. A literary history of Brazil forming part of its

[15] Domingos José Gonçalves de Magalhães, "Ensaio sobre a história da literatura do Brasil," *Niterói: Revista Brasiliense* (1836), vol. 1, Biblioteca Nacional (Rio de Janeiro).

history as a nation also could be written thanks to its connection with the colonial past.

Magalhães would not write that history. He delineated for it, however, the first chronological order, the outline of a periodicity following the division of the history of Brazil into two moments: from the discovery of the country to 1808, and from 1808 onward. Since he said "that all history, as all drama, presupposes a setting, actors, passions, a progressive plot that unfolds, that has its justification, just as it has an origin and an end" ("Ensaio," 142), it can be said that his "Ensaio" sketched, at least for Brazilian historiography, Nature as setting (including in it the forest dweller), religious and patriotic sentiment as passions, and, as a progressive trait in consonance with the local color valued by Denis, the expression of national character.

The value of Varnhagen's *Ensaio histórico*, the introduction to his *Florilégio da poesia brasileira*, resides in the global vision of authors and works of the seventeenth and eighteenth centuries as elements of a unified literary activity that illustrate the development of Brazilian intellectual life, dated by the military, political, and economic events to which it is related. With these characteristics in mind, the introduction may be better understood if read in tandem with his pioneering work, the *História geral do Brasil* (1854, I; 1857, II), which the introduction in a certain way anticipates, and which goes from the Discovery to the eve of Independence.

Varnhagen attributes the delay in this literary activity – which did not begin with the occupation of the land, contrasting with the colonial literature of Spanish America – to the predatory and exploratory objectives of the initial colonial undertaking. Those "ambitious for glory" took part in the conquests of Asia and Africa, while "no poets travelled" to Brazil.[16] Poets did travel to Spanish America, a source of glory for the Spaniards who there found their Indies. Camões's great epic *Os Lusíadas* appeared in 1572, three years after the first part of the *Araucana* by the soldier–poet Ercilla had been published, so Varnhagen affirms at the beginning of this comparison, possibly the first in Brazil between the letters of Portuguese America and those of Spanish America (Varnhagen, "Ensaio histórico," 71).

Besides printing sixteenth-century accounts such as the *Tratado descritivo do Brasil* (1587) by Gabriel Soares de Sousa, the *Diário de navegação* (1530–1532) by Pero Lopes de Sousa, and the *Narrativa epistolar* (1583–1590) by Fernão Cardim, among the innumerable sources which gave to

---

[16] Francisco Adolfo de Varnhagen, "Ensaio histórico sobre as letras no Brasil," *Textos que interessam à história do romantismo*, ed. José Aderaldo Castelo (São Paulo: CEC, 1960) 71.

his *História geral* the most abundant documentary support yet found in works of this type, Varnhagen would publish in 1876 the *Arte, vocabulario y tesoro de la lengua guarani* by Montoya, revealing his interest in the study of the languages of primitive populations. Nevertheless, he did not subscribe to Magalhães's version of a rich precolonial poetry. Poets had not traveled to Brazilian lands, and neither were there native poets before the land was civilized. Varnhagen recognized, as did Magalhães, the same poetic and musical talents of the indigenous peoples, who were capable of improvising chants and orations that the Jesuits used in the work of catechism, writing sacramental plays for the entertainment and Christian edification of their "little native converts" (Varnhagen, "Ensaio histórico," 71). The beginnings of poetry and theatre in Brazil descended from those plays and not from chants similar to those of the bards (p. 71).

When refined by the religious and humanistic education taught in the colleges founded by the Jesuits, these beginnings gave birth to the first poets, such as the Bahian Bento Teixeira, whose epic poem *Prosopopéia*, printed in 1601, Varnhagen had discovered in Lisbon. However, the literary activity that he presented as a more or less continuous flow of works written by Brazilians in seventeenth-century Bahia and Pernambuco began only after the wars against the Dutch, during the period of Restoration of the Portuguese throne (1640). These works contributed to the solidarity of the native-born with the Portuguese colonizer, since Varnhagen asserts that "the conquest of glory is as necessary to a people-nation as is the increase in its income" (p. 74). That same activity became institutionalized in the eighteenth century with the Academia dos Esquecidos (Bahia, 1724) and the Academia dos Seletos (Rio, 1752), favored by the Illuminist administration of José de Carvalho e Melo, Marquis of Pombal (1750–1777), and found new support in the gold-producing region of Minas Gerais, the land of the *Mineiro* poets – of Basílio da Gama, Santa Rita Durão, Silva Alvarenga, who lived in Rio, and also of Cláudio Manuel da Costa, Inácio José de Alvarenga Peixoto (1744–1793), and Tomás Antônio Gonzaga. The latter three, who graduated from the University of Coimbra after having studied with the Jesuits, participated in the conspiracy of 1789 in Vila Rica – the *Inconfidência Mineira* against the Portuguese Crown, underrated by Varnhagen in his *História geral* as a movement with no political consistency.

The movement's separatist insurrections did not earn a favorable review from him. A member of the titled nobility of the Empire as Viscount of Porto Seguro, Varnhagen had written his history using documentary research favored by the historical method of the German school, with a view to facts "more in relation to the true development and civilization of the country"[17] – which reached fulfillment through the

---

[17] Francisco Adolfo de Varnhagen, *História geral do Brasil: antes de sua separação e Independência de Portugal*, 3rd. edn. (5 vols., São Paulo: Companhia Melhoramentos, 1926) 10, XI.

benefits of colonization, with the sacrifice of many generations and due to the discernment of the Crown, and culminated immediately following Independence in the monarchist state, which was equated with the Nation.

The interference of utilitarian morals implicated in that conservative ideology, apparent in Varnhagen's literary appraisals, nevertheless does not compromise the compilation he made of seventeenth-century poets: a certain Gregório de Matos e Guerra (1623?–1696) – not mentioned by Denis – "the first poet who became notable in Brazil" (Varnhagen, "Ensaio histórico," 77) – whose reputation as a satirist began at that point, and one Manuel Botelho de Oliveira (1636–1711), "the first Brazilian who published a volume of verse," entirely too cultured or "contorted," but the author of a *silva* describing the picturesque Ilha da Maré off the Bahian coast (p. 79). Following the example of this *silva* and of Silva Alvarenga's rondos – "erotic essays of American color" referred to by Varnhagen – other seventeenth- and eighteenth-century works constituted the romantic canon, given their local flavor and description of the land. Also in the romantic period, the *Uraguai* and the *Caramuru* came to be considered precursors of Indianism.

A comparison of the essays by Varnhagen and Magalhães shows that they share a romantic valuing of local color and a search for the specific signs of the native land and nature. In both, the landscape is now taken to be a homeland that furnishes literary works with an identity. However, they differ on the representativeness of the Indian in relation to that same homeland. Under this perspective one can focus on the relationship between nascent historiography and the literary production of the period that was so marked by Indianism.

To comprehend this point fully, one needs to keep in mind that the discussion concerning integration of the Indians raised by the Historical Institute's *Revista* was closely linked to questions about the origin and culture of these peoples. When it was accepted that they were not remnants of an advanced civilization, it was also admitted that it would be difficult, if not impossible, to enlist them to serve the nation that was being civilized. The "irremediable antagonism" between barbarism and civilization will continue to be the principal cause of the extermination of indigenous groups, concluded João Francisco Lisboa (1812–1863), in his *Jornal de Timon* (1864–1865), citing as evidence long passages of *Democracy in America* by Alexis de Tocqueville on the fate of North American tribes. One understands, therefore, that on concluding the description of the traditions of Brazil's indigenous peoples in the initial sections of his *História do Brasil*, Varnhagen may have considered "not at all flattering" the portrayal of these peoples "who more or less by default, without benefit of spiritual peace or culture, enjoyed the fertile and beautiful land of Brazil . . ." (Varnhagen, *História geral*, I: 54). In that work, in which the efforts of the colonizer to adapt to the harsh elements and to conquer the hostility of the first inhabitants are elevated to heroism, its ethnocentrism, rooted in the utilitarian morals of the conservative ideology, deprived the Indians of nationality by classifying them as barbarians. A literary Jacobin, Magalhães, Viscount of Araguaia, in his opposing defense of the Indian, merely bypasses ethnocentrism without being free of it; his epic, A confederação dos tamoios (1856), revives the savage as providential agent of a future Brazilian civilization.

Actually, the historian's attitude of rejection and the poet's of commitment, anchored in one and the same ideology, simply reveal the contradictory sociocultural and political background of the Second Reign, which brought about the literary ascension of the Indian who was at the time the object of ethnographic interest. The Indian was idealized in poetry and in the new genre that then appeared, the novel, while existing outside society, neither slave laborer nor free citizen, orphan of the state since the Regency and soon to be under its protection–tutelage. Whether indomitable warrior battling for the national cause, tragic hero of declining traditions, or ally of the Portuguese, with pagan strength and Christian soul, the Indian was consecrated in the most popular novel of the period, O guaraní (1857) by José de Alencar (1829–1877), and incorporated into the thematics of romantic poetry, from A confederação dos tamoios by Magalhães to the Primeiros cantos (1846) by Gonçalves Dias (1823–1864), from the Cantos meridionais (1869) by Fagundes Varela (1841–1875) to the Americanas (1875) by Machado de Assis (1839–1908).

Given the extensive penetration of the Indianist theme – a true source for the whole imagination of the period, integrating images of Nature into the "metaphoric field" of the similarity between the country's reality and its literature – there can be no doubt about the ideological role played by Indianism that would subsist, metamorphosized, until the twentieth century. However the Indian's role is viewed, whether it was to channel the antilusitanian reaction or the spirit of national conciliation with the colonizer, whether to justify the slavery of the submissive African by the fierce freedom of the Tupi, or whether to project a Middle Ages in the soul of the forests to compensate for colonization, it is no less certain that the Indianist current created an image of national origin. It is a mythified image of collective beginnings, beyond history, appearing at the moment when incipient historiography, by the force of the will to independence previously mentioned, appropriated the past and reshaped colonial literature into the nativist mold it then coined. "It was required [that nativism], to be legitimized, connect the present to prehistoric times, to the period that had preceded the Conquest and Colonization," writes Ferdinand Wolf (1796–1866) in Le Brésil littéraire-histoire de la littérature Brésilienne (1863) [O Brasil literário-história da literatura Brasileira] indicating the most extreme point of the conquest of identity in Brazil's literature, *pari passu* with the delineation of literary historiography.

The sense of identity joining the recent state of that literature to its colonial past is missing in the historical sketch traced a year earlier by Padre Joaquim Caetano Fernandes Pinheiro (1825–1876). In his *Curso elementar de literatura nacional* (1862), the sense of identity is only treated separately from Portuguese literature as the Brazilian romantic school, after independence. Francisco Sotero dos Reis (1800–1877) follows a similar orientation, connecting the two, so alike "as if they could be two twin sisters,"[18] in his *Curso de literatura portuguesa e brasileira* (1866–1873). The poets of each literature are distinguished by the "certain air of individuality of each people, each nation" (Sotero, *Curso*, I: 82). "But ours is a graft of the Portuguese," Pinheiro would observe in a later *Resumo de história literária*, where he divides the literature into three periods: formation (sixteenth and seventeenth centuries), development (eighteenth century), and reform (nineteenth century) (Pinheiro, *Resumo de história*, II: 294).

Written in Vienna, published in French, and dedicated to the Emperor Pedro II, the O *Brasil literário* by Wolf – an Austrian scholar of Hispanic culture, personally connected to Magalhães – presents us with the periodicity adopted by Joaquim Norberto de Sousa e Silva (1820–1891) in *Bosquejo da história da poesia brasileira* (*Modulações poéticas*, 1841), which broadens the chronological markers of the literary activity established by Varnhagen into five phases, corresponding to those of the history of Brazil: (1) from the Discovery until the end of the seventeenth century (Jesuit production and imitation of Portuguese and Spanish models); (2) the first half of the eighteenth century (expansion of literary activity); (3) the second half of the eighteenth century (the *Mineira* school); (4) from the beginning of the nineteenth century until 1822 (advance in the expression of national character); (5) from 1840 on (national literature with the rise of the romantic school).

However, Wolf conceived the succession of these phases in terms of a uniform development, from the imitation of Portuguese and Spanish models to national originality, without preparing himself, as is shown by one aspect of the militant criticism of the period – outside of historiography but compromised by historicism – either for conflicting elements in the definition of identity in Brazilian literature or for what in it was most vacillating and ambiguous.

Around 1840, at the height of romantic nationalism, the possible separation of Brazilian literature from Portuguese literature as an independent whole was defended by the critic of Chilean origin Santiago

---

[18] Francisco Sotero dos Reis, *Curso de literatura portugueza e brasileira*, (5 vols., Maranhão, 1866–1873; I–IV: Typografia de B. de Mattos; V: Typografia de Paiss) I, 77.

Nunes Ribeiro (d. 1847) in the pages of the journal *Minerva Brasiliense* (1843–1845). The Portuguese journalist José da Gama e Castro presented opposing arguments in an article from 1842 in the *Jornal do Comércio do Rio de Janeiro*, where he lived from 1837 to 1842, according to which this independence was found lacking in view of the linguistic base common to both literatures. Santiago's counterargument transferred the characterization of literature from the realm of language to two separate nonliterary factors: that of beliefs and customs, which today we call culture, and that of climate conditions as related to environment.

Peoples who are differentiated by culture and climate will have different literatures even when written in the same language. Not only had Portuguese literature modified itself in passing to the New World – which contradicts the thesis of the unaltered acclimation of its classical forms propounded by Magalhães – but also, due to this change – as Santiago admitted – literature in Brazil could not have resulted from any other than spiritual inclinations made possible in accordance with historical moments and the authors' lives. The exception to the requirement of local color as an indicator of the originality of Brazil's poetry during the colonial period, as implied by this last criticism, would not be pursued even in the anti-romantic period of historiography.

Meanwhile, literature's vacillating identity was also ambiguous: its independence could not be allowed to suffocate the Portuguese heritage or the principle of environmental determinism – which was reputed to have guaranteed its autonomy – in order to neutralize the repercussion of European ideas on Brazil's writers.

In the prologue to his *História da literatura brasileira*, released five days after the abolition of slavery on May 13, 1888, Sílvio Vasconcelos da Silveira Ramos Romero (1851–1914) discusses political and social problems of the period: the Republic, the "utilization of the productive energy of the proletariat, labor organization in general, the fair distribution of territorial property" and "foreign colonization" that substituted the "obstacle of the servile question" recently removed by the Golden Law.[19] Beyond the polemical temperament of the author and the political tempering of his varied work as an essayist, embodied in the *História da literatura brasileira*, these topics of analysis, presented in the combative tone of a critical manifesto, allow one to see the extent of the crisis felt by the monarchy, which fell in a little more than a year, with the proclamation of the Republic on November 15, 1889.

Between 1870 and 1880, after the Paraguayan War (1864–1870), premonitory signs of crisis appeared, despite the decade's prolongation of

19 Sílvio Romero, *História da literatura brasileira*, 5th. edn. (5 vols., Rio de Janeiro: Livraria José Olympio Editora, 1953) I, 47.

the period of prosperity initiated in 1850 with the extinction of the slave trade. The challenge to the personal power of Pedro II – who should reign but not govern – placed the Empire's political centralism in check; the status of free labor – stimulated by foreign immigrants utilized in the coffee plantations to replace slave labor – which had contributed to that prosperity, conflicted with the state's archaic structure of latifundia; finally, the appearance of the Republican party (1870) came to question the legitimacy of the monarchist government.

This "rise in the democratic tide in Brazil"[20] rocked the institutional stability of the Second Reign at the same moment that the ideology that had legitimized it began to crumble under the impact of "new ideas" on the rise: the Neo-Kantism of Frederico Alberto Lange (1828–1875), the evolutionist Monism of Ernest Haeckel (1834–1919), and the synthetic-evolutionist philosophy of Herbert Spencer (1820–1903), disseminated in the academic circles of the Recife Law School under the intellectual leadership of the Germanist Tobias Barreto de Meneses (1839–1889) and of Romero, after 1866. The Positivism of Auguste Comte (1798–1857) "found a reception in Brazil that it did not have in its country of origin,"[21] disseminated initially by the Positivist Society installed in Rio de Janeiro in 1876 under the initiative of Benjamin Constant (1833–1891), a member of the Republic's provisional government (1889–1891).

These doctrines made possible an articulation of the "earlier isolated manifestations of inconformity with the eclectic doctrine" adapted by Magalhães[22] and were unanimous in their rejection of metaphysics, to be replaced by scientific investigation of reality. Not only were the new concepts opposed to Romantic religiosity and to the exalted patriotism with which it joined forces, but they marked the continuing substratum of nationalism with the stamp of a critical platform concerning the solution of Brazilian social, political, and economic problems. Yet, whether because of the biological matrix of the Darwinian concept of evolution which came to the fore in Spencerian evolutionism (*First Principles*, 1862), or because of the generally accepted presuppositions of the export of models of physics and biology to sociology and anthropology practiced by Positivism, such philosophies shared in common a Naturalistic vision of the world, according to which even social and historical phenomena, a category including art and literature, could be explained by the action of constant natural factors, physical or organic.

Thus one can understand why Sílvio Romero, one of the eminent

[20] João Cruz Costa, *Contribuição à história das idéias no Brasil* (Rio de Janeiro: Livraria José Olympio Editora, 1956) 183.
[21] Caio Prado, Jr., *Evolução política do Brasil* (São Paulo: Editora Brasiliense, 1932) 207.
[22] Antônio Paim, *História das idéias filosóficas no Brasil*, 2nd. edn. (São Paulo: EDUSP/Editorial Grijalbo Ltda., 1974) 255.

spokesmen of that naturalistic vision of the world, particularly tied to Spencerian philosophy, after a prologue to his work of 1888 on the country's political situation, under the critical perspective of a nationalism opposed to the romantic idealism and the conservative ideology of the Romantics, used milieu and race as explicatory factors, primary and secondary respectively, for the evolution of national literature, which also passed into the orbit of the naturalistic aesthetic. However, milieu, which was nurtured in the *History of Civilization in England* (1857–1861) by Henry Thomas Buckle (1821–1862), and race, which Romero found in the *Histoire de la littérature Anglaise* (1865) by Hippolyte Taine (1829–1893), were not sufficient to explain the spiritual life of the Brazilian people, of which literature would be the most complete expression. Political and economic facts, together with the influence of foreign currents, were third within this fluctuating hierarchy of causes. They were as influential as, if not more than, ecological or ethnic concerns, in the configuration of literature and its tendencies.

If the milieu, including the not always healthy tropical climate and the scarce and inadequate alimentation, generated "a morbid population, with short lives, bothersome and remorseful in its majority" (Romero, *História da literatura* [1953] I: 100–1), for whom intellectual production became a martyrdom, predisposed to the quick exhaustion of generally precocious talents and more inclined to lyricism than to painstaking works of science and philosophy, this same natural milieu, earlier described as landscape within the admiring register of the Romantics, also produced, as the denominator of geographic diversity, "worthy men" and jovial and humorous aspects in Brazilian literature (I: 103). However, the "sentimental effusion of our lyricism, sweeter, softer, and more ardent than the lyricism inherited from the Portuguese" (I: 104), promoted by the effects of climate, is a definitive product of the second factor, race.

The determinism in vogue in the nineteenth century receives another setback in the fact that the Brazilian people are anything but a homogeneous ethnic group, having received their identity from the three races that engendered them – the Portuguese, the Indian, and the African. Corresponding here with Denis's intuition, Romero carries miscegenation, rich from a physical point of view, to the moral and spiritual plane of the mixture of the races. Here, miscegenation becomes a causal factor in Brazilian literature, benefited by the crossing of sentiments and ideas from each of the formative races that brought into being, as the author describes, "the rich and ardent colors of our lyricism, of our painting, of our music, of our art in general" (I: 336).

Flexibility in the use of natural factors makes Romero's *História da literatura* compatible with the application of a historical and comparative method that allowed him to relate literary development to the effect of political causes – the war against the Dutch, Independence, the installation of the Empire – and economic causes – sugar in the seventeenth century, gold in the eighteenth, and coffee at the advent of Romanticism. Evaluating that development, however, Romero emphasizes in a pessimistic tone the scanty, poor, and inefficient results that, as a consequence, illustrated the precarious condition of intellectual production. Lacking originality and imitative of foreign models, literature paralleled the apathy and disinterest of the Brazilian and what is palliative in the nation itself, which lacks "its own form or characteristic individuality" (1: 166).

Both the flexibility of Naturalism and the evolutionist aspect of the *História da literatura brasileira* lead to two affirmations: the first, consonant with the broad notion it contains of literature, including not only the *belles lettres* but "all manifestations of intelligence of a people: – politics, economics, art, popular creations, science . . ." (1: 60), is the extraliterary nature of this work, extrapolating to the field of history of ideas or to the history of culture; the second is the peculiarity of its writing, which instead of the mechanicist paradigm that might be expected, given the extrahistorical factors invoked by its Naturalism,[23] follows an organicist paradigm, lending marks of dramatic development to its evolution.

One may say, therefore, according to Magalhães's image referred to in the first part, that Romero's historiography is written as a drama, but with noticeable differences in relation to the Brazilian romantic poet's project. Besides Nature as landscape, the setting of this drama also encompasses culture and history. Among the actors, one no longer finds the forest dweller, who is substituted by miscegenation; once religiosity is excluded, patriotic feeling gives way, in the roll of passions, to interest in the discovery of the country's reality itself – or of the "Brazilian reality" as it will soon be called. Meanwhile, the progressive issue that conveys the reasoning behind Sílvio Romero's periodicity, from which subsequent chronological demarcations of Brazilian literary history are derived, remains that of national character.

After a long formative period that extends from 1592 – the then supposed publication date of the *Prosopopéia* – to 1768, publication date of the poetic works of Cláudio Manuel in Lisbon, there follow the periods of autonomous development (1768–1836), of romantic reaction until 1875, and, finally, of critical and naturalist reaction, then Parnassian and symbolist. Since the author is situated in the period of critical and naturalist reaction, one concludes that his *História da literatura* will reevaluate romantic canons in the light of Naturalism, according to the

---

[23] Hayden White, *Metahistory: The Historical Imagination in Nineteenth Century Europe* (Baltimore: Johns Hopkins University Press, 1973) 16.

theory of miscegenation and the directive of philosophical evolutionism.

Within that perspective, the colonial literary past is united with the present time of the naturalist period by means of a succession of schools (the *Bahian*, with the name of Gregório de Matos, the *Mineira* of the eighteenth century, the *Fluminense*, with the first Romantics), of trends (principally the classical and the romantic, Sílvio Romero not having used the term Gongorism except in a deprecating sense for the bulk of seventeenth-century poetic production), and also of genres (epic, lyric, dramatic, oratorical, novelesque), which he treated in *Quadro sintético da evolução dos gêneros na literatura brasileira* (1909). These schools, trends, and genres succeed each other as phases of a single open evolutionary course, under the gradual collective effect of intrinsic causes (primary and secondary factors) and of extrinsic causes (foreign influence), at times relating to the particularities of the country and at others to universal themes. Thanks to such a particular conjunction of factors projected in an evolutionary scale, Romero constructed the first organic system of literary historiography, more as a lineage of authors, considering the works almost only for the content of their ideas in a predominantly historical, documentary dimension.

Meanwhile, the naturalist reevaluation of romantic canons, establishing the ranking of authors, upheld the primacy of national characteristics in the works. In this way, for Romero, Brazilian literature's function is to reproduce and express through sentiment the nation's original reality of which literature is the image.

Polemical, militant, the nationalism of this ideologically liberal and progressive historiographer is the corollary of a concept of the history of Brazil as a "product of our efforts, suffered with our tears and our blood" (II: 459). Such a position distances Romero from Varnhagen while drawing him nearer to a historian of his generation, Capistrano de Abreu (1853–1927), who is responsible for a revision of Romero's work in the *Capítulos de história colonial* (1907).

Uniting the country's identity with its literary expression, the national characteristic that reached its decisive moment in the pre-Romanticism of the *Mineiro* poets, becomes the touchstone of the Romerian system. Yet while authenticating the work of romantic poets such as Gonçalves Dias, Casimiro de Abreu (1839–1860), Fagundes Varela (1841–1875), and Castro Alves (1847–1871), that touchstone – to a certain point applicable to the Parnassians, above all to Olavo Bilac (1865–1918), to the romantic novels of Manuel de Macedo, such as *A moreninha* (1845), to *O guaraní*, *Iracema* (1865), *Ubirajara* (1874), *Minas de prata* (1865), *O gaúcho* (1870), and *O sertanejo* (1876) by José de Alencar, to the realist and naturalist novels such as *Inocência* (1872) by Alfredo Taunay, *O cabeleira* (1876) by Franklin Távora, *O missionário* (1888) by Inglês de Sousa, *O cortiço*

(1890) by Aluísio de Azevedo, and further to the *costumbrista* theatre of Martins Pena, such as *O juiz de paz na roça* (1838) – fails however in relation to the short stories and novels of Machado de Assis (*Iaiá Garcia* [1878], *Memórias póstumas de Brás Cubas* [1881], *Papéis avulsos* [1882], etc.) and to the symbolist poetry of Cruz e Sousa (*Missal e broquéis* [1893]).

At this point the signs of nationality are fluid, including features of Brazilian sensibility possessed by the animistic reserves of its ethnic patrimony. It is to that sensibility that one appeals, as a last resort, to guarantee the right of entry into national literature of the Jesuit priest José de Anchieta (1534–1597), considered its progenitor, because although born in Tenerife he later became Brazilianized; of the Portuguese Gonzaga, who lived for many years in Brazil; and even of Antônio José da Silva, "The Jew," who acquired the Brazilian tone of his lyricism from his Bahian cradle, despite having lived in Portugal since boyhood. However, what certifies and reinforces Brazilian literary identity, even for those born in Brazil, is the expression of "original emotion" (Romero, I: 169), guaranteed by the miscegenation of a Silva Alvarenga or a Gonçalves Dias. In summary, the animistic reserves of the ethnic patrimony preserving that sensibility are found in the poetry and popular dramaturgy of the oral tradition. Sílvio Romero, one of the first students of national folklore, included them to strengthen his ethnographic thesis in the pages of the *História da literatura*.

As an equivalent to miscegenation, perhaps this melting pot of ethnic patrimony, inclusive of the mentality of the three races, could transform itself with the continuation of racial mixing by new European contributors. Italian and German migration had mixed with the Portuguese. National psychology, determined by the initial melting pot, would not become definitive, however. Sílvio Romero rushes to clarify that he is far from admitting that Brazil is "a nation of mulattoes." After all, his praise of miscegenation, fueled by the belief that the "white form is prevailing and will prevail" (Romero, I: 132), introduced into Brazilian historiography, with the ambiguity of its Naturalism, the racist preference for whitening.

For Romero the historiographer, folklore, as a popular substrate of the identity of Brazilian literature separating it from the Portuguese, was more important than linguistic differentiation, even though at the time the novels of Alencar, especially the Indianist ones such as *O guaraní*, *Iracema*, and *Ubirajara*, were carrying indigenous language into literary language, artistically elaborated in Brazilian vocabulary and syntax.

Accompanying Santiago in the idea that the autonomy of Brazilian literature is ecological and cultural, Romero does not forget the circumstance that intellectual culture, like that of America in general, is a transplanted culture, passing through a "process of acclimation and, inevitably, of transformation."[24] The germs of the literature came from abroad, selectively provoking change by the action of endogenous elements. Thus, as in political history, literary history will translate the result of an arduous victory over the enduring Lusitanian heritage, modified by national sentiment and by the repercussion of foreign trends, mainly the French, beginning with Romanticism.

The Romerian system endured in its broad lines until Modernism suffered its first blow before the end of the nineteenth century, when José Veríssimo Dias de Matos (1857–1916), of the same generation receptive to the "new ideas," brought into question in a study published in 1894 the validity of the nationalist criteria, "for being too narrow for us to form an exclusive critical principle from it . . . We would narrow the field of activity of our writers too much if we did not want to recognize in the talent with which a work is conceived and executed a criterion of its value, independently of an inspiration more attached to national life."[25] The search for this other value criterion led Veríssimo to a more narrow conceptualization of literature and its historical development in the *História da literatura brasileira – de Bento Teixeira (1601) a Machado de Assis (1908)* (1916).

Observing that it is the read books, enduring and living, that give existence to modern literature, Veríssimo thinks that literary history is the history of the works, "of the movements, serious literary manifestations and their derivations" that give us intellectual pleasure and contribute to "interior culture" (*Literatura brasileira*, 11–18). With the idea of survival of the works as "the Nation's collective memory," he discerned a historical continuity not coincident with chronology or with political and social history. In addition, in a way that anticipated what later would be characterized as tradition, he intuited the specifically literary criterion that would superimpose itself on that of nationality: "Literature is literary art" (p. 13).

The works capable of outliving their authors will belong therefore to the realm of Fine Arts, according to "the vernacular classical notion." Although unpolished, that intuition of the artistic nature of literature according to the classical notion, or rather, according to the rhetorical concept of an art of the word, became a theoretical question for criticism and not history to resolve. Faced with the naturalist orthodoxy dominant at the time, however, it was a heresy, as Veríssimo realized. Criticism affiliated with the naturalist current identified the nature of literature

---

[24] Sílvio Romero and João Ribeiro, *Compêndio de história da literatura brasileira*, 2nd. edn. revised. (Rio de Janeiro: Livraria Francisco Alves, 1909) liv.

[25] José Veríssimo, *Estudos brasileiros*, 2nd. series (1889–1893) (São Paulo: Laemmert & Co. Editores, 1894) 198–9.

through the idea of the work of art taken from Emile Zola – "un coin de la création vu à travers un tempérament"[26] – and that favored the rise of Regionalism (for example *Pelo sertão* [1898], stories by Afonso Arinos; *Os caboclos* [1922], stories by Valdomiro Silveira; *D. Guidinha do Poço* [posthumous, 1952], novel by Manuel de Oliveira Paiva). In any case, the ironic skepticism apparent in Veríssimo's heresy[27] was a personal way of externalizing the political disillusionment of his generation in relation to the Republic that had inscribed the supreme positivist dictate, "Order and Progress," on the Brazilian flag.

When Pedro II was deposed by a *coup d'état* led by a military group under the influence of Positivism, the astonished population witnessed the movement of troops at the moment the Republic was proclaimed by Marshal Deodoro da Fonseca. Many believed "sincerely that they were seeing a parade" (Barbosa, *A tradição do impasse*, 131). Once the federation was established, the diverse local oligarchies, the soul of *coronelismo*[28] rose to power. The agrarian structure consolidated during the Empire did not change; control of the coffee economy reinforced the political supremacy of the former presidents of the provinces of São Paulo and Minas Gerais, now state governors, who began to generate the succession to power in the presidential elections.[29]

The "mantle of royalty" that had hidden many things had barely fallen. "The republic showed Brazil as it is," ironized Romero (*A América Latina*, 9). The Canudos War (Bahia, 1897), about which the historiographer may have been thinking when he said this, revealed behind the illusion of unity and of the "people's internal organization" the existence in the interior of Brazil of indigent populations outside the regime's representative institutions and the coast's urban civilization. The indomitable *sertanejos* besieged in the tiny village of Canudos, bombarded by the government troops' cannons as if it were a new Vendée, were not agents of a monarchist conspiracy but rather millenary believers awaiting final defeat of the Anti-Christ, as promised them by Antônio Conselheiro, the rustic prophet around whom they gathered.

The massacre's impact, representing military violence of the Republican order, and the shock of discovering this anachronic religious belief that went against the law of progress established by Positivism, joined together in the revealing book, *Os sertões* (1902) [*Rebellion in the Backlands*] by Euclides da Cunha (1866–1909). This mixture of essay and

---

[26] René Wellek, *História da crítica moderna* (3 vols., São Paulo: Editora Herder, 1967–1971) 15.
[27] João Alexandre Barbosa, *A tradição do impasse: linguagem da crítica e crítica da linguagem em José Veríssimo* (São Paulo: Editora Atica, 1974) 129.
[28] Monteiro, "Da Independência," 211.
[29] Sônia Regina de Mendonça, "As bases do desenvolvimento capitalista dependente: da industrialização restringida à internacionalização," in Yedda Linhares *et al. História geral do Brasil*, 230.

narrative brought to Brazilian literature the image of the desperate penury of the resistant *sertanejo*, "a strong type above all" (Euclides, *Os sertões*, 179), and of the messianic and lawless *sertão*, to a point unattained by the regionalist novel. In the wake of Abolition and an increase in foreign immigration this novelistic modality gave shape to "the writers' desire to record in all of its aspects the lives of our people, of the part of the population free of outside influences and contacts."[30]

Translating the author's lacerated theoretical conscience, *Os sertões*, redirecting the novel toward Brazil's hinterland, also was invigorated by a nationalism now vexed by its consciousness of an excessive imported intellectual culture used to defend the most genuinely Brazilian elements, and by the pessimistic tone of Romero's thought. Instead of exalting the land's potential, praising the youth of Brazil, its riches and natural wonders, as in the pages of *Por que me ufano do meu país* (1900) by Count Afonso Celso (1860–1938), a work that established *ufanismo* as a pattern of naive national conscience, Euclides da Cunha's pessimism highlighted the "instability of an unsuspected and long ethnological formation," and "our vacillating political structure and our incomplete historical background,"[31] that made him fear for the misrepresentation of the "originality of our tendencies," against which he reacted.

In the midst of the growing urbanization of Rio de Janeiro in the first decade of the twentieth century, a climate of routine literary activity was polarized by the Brazilian Academy of Letters, an institution intended to consecrate the man of letters, dominated by the formal and descriptive pattern of Parnassianism, transposed into oratory by the legal consultant and liberal political thinker Rui Barbosa (1849–1923) for an intellectual class, sensitive to European styles, that prided itself on imitating Wilde and Nietzsche.[32] There was an emphasized opposition between "industrious city – indolent countryside"[33] as two antagonistic portions of Brazilian society. In fiction, alongside the *caboclo* and the *sertanejo*, the *caipira* Jeca Tatu was profiled in *Urupês* (1918) by Monteiro Lobato (1882–1948), a caricature of a sad race "vegetating on its haunches, incapable of evolution, impenetrable by progress,"[34] who became the mobilizing image for the nationalism of political and social regeneration accompanying the country's modernization at the time of the First World

[30] Lúcia Miguel-Pereira, *Prosa de ficção – de 1870 a 1920* (*História da literatura brasileira*, vol. XII) 3rd. edn. (Rio de Janeiro: Livraria José Olympio Editora, 1973) 181.

[31] Euclides da Cunha, "Nativismo provisório," *Contrastes e confrontos* (Porto: Empresa Litterária e Typographica, 1907) 292–3.

[32] Brito Broca, *A vida literária no Brasil: 1900* (Rio de Janeiro: Ministério da Educação e Cultura, 1956) 109–17.

[33] Nicolau Sevcenko, *Literatura como missão – tensões sociais e criação cultural na Primeira República* (São Paulo: Editora Brasiliense, 1983) 32.

[34] Monteiro Lobato, *Urupês*, 26th. edn. (São Paulo: Editora Brasiliense, 1982) 147.

War. The racial side of that resurging ideology was manifested in the platform in defense of an autonomous American culture, with which Ronald de Carvalho (1893–1935), a participant in the modernist movement, concluded his *Pequena história da literatura brasileira* (1919).

A derivation of Romero's history, even in the dramatic outline enhanced by the eloquent style then in vogue, bringing no essential modification to periodicity nor altering the canon, this book subjects the former theme of literary independence to the obligation of acquiring its own American culture, capable of destroying "European prejudice" and affirming Brazil's barbarism.[35] Carvalho's Americanism, however, reflected the thought of Graça Aranha (1868–1931), belated descendant of the Recife Law School who detached himself from the Academy of Letters in 1924 in an act of fidelity to the "modern spirit." That spirit represented for him the overcoming of the African's fetishism and of the Indian's religious fear, enabling Brazilians to dominate the Nature that dominated them. Such a work of subjugation would be possible only, as he said in his *Estética da vida* (1921), if the "barbarous metaphysics," ancestral heritage of those ethnicities, were extirpated from the Brazilian psychology.

Thus, for Carvalho, American, as a substitute for European, culture would serve as a vehicle of modernization. Conceding that it teaches us to conquer the conservatism of a society with archaic habits and a frightening Nature "by the discipline of intelligence,"[36] he also concedes, contradictorily, the need to reject the ancestral basis of the historical Brazilian man. According to him, the change shown by industrialization was also the threshold of a "new nationality, of more temperate blood . . ." (Carvalho, *Pequena história*, [1944]) which was therefore whitened by contact with the ethnic contingents that "brought the machine to our economy" (*Pequena história*). It is not difficult to recognize in this a broadening of Romero's theory of miscegenation that mixes the ethnic and the cultural, hesitating between one and the other as the defining principle. Racial prejudice, still discreet in that conception, loomed as declared racism in the *Evolução do povo brasileiro* (1923) by Oliveira Vianna (1883–1951), who was nevertheless a renewer of Brazilian studies through the sociological focus that he gave to historical facts.

In February of 1922 the modernist movement exploded with the Modern Art Week that took place in São Paulo as a commemoration of the centenary of political independence in the city, which had industrialized after the First World War. Initially with no other theoretically defined position beyond freedom of expression by means of free verse in

---

[35] Ronald de Carvalho, *Estudos brasileiros* (Rio de Janeiro: Edição do Anuário do Brasil, 1924) 62.
[36] Ronald de Carvalho, *Pequena história da literatura brasileira*, 7th. edn. (Rio de Janeiro: F. Briguiet & Cia., Editores, 1944) 367.

poetry, and the rejection of both Parnassian academic Formalism and realist representation in prose and the plastic arts, Modernism appeared out of the convergence between socio-economic modernization and the renewal of philosophical, aesthetic, and political thought. Naturalist conceptions of the past century receded due to the spiritualist reaction against Positivism of the thinker Raimundo de Farias Brito (1862–1917), augmented by the mobilization of Catholic intellectuals headed by Jackson de Figueiredo (1891–1928), preacher of a rightist nationalism. In 1922, the Communist Party was founded. The doctrines of Henri Bergson, Sigmund Freud, Benedetto Croce, and Karl Marx spread. Add to this the interchange of European and American artistic ideas, particularly with the cubist-futurist tradition and with the French poetry to which it was related, and one will have outlined the context of the movement.

Essentially "destructive" as far as its "revolt against what was called national intelligence,"[37] Modernism created a spirit favorable to the Revolution of 1930, which was in a certain sense a victory of regenerating nationalism that levelled the Old Republic (1899–1929) and that seven years later, when Brazilian Fascism had already developed (Brazilian Integralist Party) on the eve of the Second World War, supported the paternalist and authoritarian *Estado Novo* of Getúlio Vargas (1937–1945). Meanwhile, it was during the 1930s that the hesitation between ethnic determinism and historical or cultural causality disappeared in the renewed field of social sciences. Three books published at the time, relevant to the comprehension of the whole of Brazilian society, *Casa grande e senzala* (1933) by Gilberto Freyre (1900–1987), *Raízes do Brasil* (1935) by Sérgio Buarque de Holanda (1902–1982), and *Evolução política do Brasil* (1932) by Caio Prado Júnior (1907–1990), draw on cultural anthropology, cultural sociology, and on Marxist sociology. Others, including *Negros bantus* (1937) by Edison Carneiro (1912–1972), *Costumes africanos no Brasil* (1938) by Manuel Quirino (1851–1923), and *Aculturação negra no Brasil* (1942) by Artur Ramos (1903–1949), set a new course of study in an area up until then preterated on indigenous ethnography.

Besides representing a fortunate detour from the generalizing tendencies of the mentality of the law school graduate, which were depicted by Holanda in a profile of Ibero-Brazilian roots in his 1935 book and against which the Modernists reacted, these works signal the spread of social sciences that began to underpin historiography in general, counterbalancing the long reign of historicism. Together with such support, new aesthetic ideas prepare the way for a theoretical revision of literary historiography.

---

[37] Mário de Andrade, "O movimento modernista," (1942) *Aspectos da literatura brasileira* (São Paulo: Livraria Martins Editora, 1974) 235.

Successively rewritten by the author from 1938 to 1960, but in no way altering the theoretical foundation of traditional historiography, the *História da literatura brasileira – seus fundamentos econômicos* (1938, 1942, 1960) by Nelson Werneck Sodré (b. 1911), takes up Romero's idea of cultural transplanting, adding to it the onus of colonization: the shared mechanisms of economic exploitation and political domination.

The colonialist structure with its ideology, rooted in the transplanted culture transformed in Brazil, impeded the possession of real literary autonomy, which only came about when, with the growth of the middle class and the appearance of the working class, motives Sodré places among the causes of the Revolution of 1930, conditions for normal economic development of the country were in place. The industrial spurt that preceded 1930 made the modernist movement possible, emphasizing literature "from then on autonomous, defined, and characterized."[38] José Osório de Oliveira (1900–1964) will say it in other words in his *História breve da literatura brasileira*, according to which the movement, above all in the novel cycle of the Northeast from 1930 on, with José Américo de Almeida (1887–1980), Raquel de Queiroz (b. 1910), José Lins do Rego (1901–1957), Graciliano Ramos (1892–1953), and Jorge Amado (b. 1912) – which was in a certain way, a ramification of Regionalism – marked the fixation of national physiognomy in a literature attuned from the beginning to the stylistic expression of patriarchal life, under the direct influence of the sugar economy as described by Freyre in *Casa grande e senzala*.

An essential reference mark of literary history since then, the modernist movement that loomed as an aesthetic revolution, and that was the conductor of a new circuit of nationalism as much artistic as political, influencing the evaluation of Brazilian culture in both critical and traditionalist ways, also changed the historical appreciation of the past. That interference may already be seen in the Brazilian part of *Noções de história das literaturas*, authored by Manuel Bandeira (1886–1968).

Participant as poet in the aesthetic revolution of 1922, in which he consolidated the Brazilianizing of literary language, even asserting the existence of a Brazilian language for polemical purposes, as did Mário de Andrade (1893–1945), Manuel Bandeira as historiographer was able to accentuate the linguistic aspect of cultural differentiation as a principle of literary autonomy in his panoramic work of a didactic nature. On the other hand, in a pioneering work, *Tendências e repercussões literárias do Modernismo* (1953), Lúcia Miguel-Pereira (1903–1959) showed that Modernism, through the impetus of its rebellion in the overturning of Parnassian canons, when it was not due to the thematic broadening of

---

[38] Nelson Werneck Sodré, *História da literatura brasileira – seus fundamentos econômicos*, 4th. edn. (Rio de Janeiro: Civilização Brasileira, 1964) 526.

poetry and prose that broke the classical decorum of language, also presented similarities and affinities with Romanticism through its "raving nationalism," even as an aesthetic revolution that allied itself with the ascendant European vanguards of the first quarter of the century, from Futurism to Surrealism. As did Romanticism, Modernism valued the popular and the folkloric but, contrary to the romantics who overpraised the Indian while only dwelling on the African to denounce his slave status, as in the abolitionist poetry of Castro Alves (*Espumas flutuantes* [1870]), the modernist poets utilized African rhythms and traditions.

The regressive effect in the elucidation of the past, brought about by the promotion of modernity's new canons in poetry and in prose, also made possible the correction of established periods. Modernist critic Tristão de Athayde, pseudonym of Alceu de Amoroso Lima (1893–1983), began to do this by rethinking the nexus of subordination of literary history to general history in *Quadro sintético da literatura brasileira* (1956) and *Introdução à literatura brasileira* (1956).

Amoroso Lima interwove in the modern phase, after the colonial and the imperial, a pre-modernist subperiod between Symbolism and Modernism. He even tried to lift the yoke of the historical or social over the literary. "Literary history does not necessarily accompany social history. Nor does it ever dissociate from it."[39] The unexpected reigns over this domain, although according to geographic conditions of the various regions the authors within this tendency bring to it the supposed unifying factors of literature, such as race, already known, for a portrait of the psychology of the Brazilian people. On the positive side of these works one may register the relevant confrontation between national elements and foreign influence, generalized in the internal phenomenon of repercussion. In a literature of colonial origin, born of direct transmission from the Lusitanian trunk, the conflict between its inherent characteristics and its acquired characteristics is constant. That debate took on its broadest dimensions in Modernism, as the internal dialectic in national culture in which the Brazilian endogenous is opposed to the foreign heterogeneous and, as exemplified by Regionalism, localist tendencies conflict with universalist.

One must consider, however, that the complete revision of the nineteenth-century theoretical apparatus of literary history resulted, above all, from the contribution of two other critics, Afrânio Coutinho (b. 1911) and Antônio Cândido (b. 1918). The first allied to New Criticism and the second to a sociological orientation, both were able from different perspectives – Coutinho in the directives of the collective text he

---

[39] Alceu Amoroso Lima, "Introdução à literatura brasileira," *Tristão de Athayde: Teoria, crítica e história literária*, ed. Gilberto Mendonça Teles (Rio de Janeiro: Livros Técnicos e Científicos Ltda., 1980) 462.

organized, planned, and directed, *A literatura no Brasil* (1955–1959; 1968–1971, 1986), and Cândido in his own text, *Formação da literatura Brasileira – momentos decisivos –* to relate criticism to history with the introduction of the aesthetic point of view in the appraisal of the works, both succeeding in what Veríssimo had only been able to glimpse.

Coutinho's text grafts the aesthetic point of view onto the nationalist tradition of criticism that originated in Romanticism, reformulating the old periodicity as a history of styles; Cândido's grafts it onto the great trunk of Romerian history, redirecting the idea of transplanting and literary development through the double consideration of the existence of literature as a social fact and of its link with the country's society and culture.

For Coutinho, there is no problem of origin: the literature was born with the country, developed in the course of colonization with the new man who appeared after the European set foot on tropical soil, and was completed with miscegenation in a process of adaptation to the physical environment and to different historical circumstances. Thus, too, he attempts to resolve the problem of literary identity as an effect of the very environmental and cultural differentiations that were consolidated by the transformation of the same Portuguese language: linguistic miscegenation accompanied ethnic. If the literature identifies itself as Brazilian, it is because since the beginning it has expressed the new experience of a new man. The European in the tropics will have begun to change according to the process, referred to by the critic Araripe Júnior (1848–1911) as the principle of "obnubilation": obscured by light, surrounded by Nature, dizzied by the climate, the European forgets his past situation. Coutinho does not criticize the Romantic's nationalist criticism; he accepts the search for national identity that they undertook as a vector of literary development that resulted in the "fortunate tradition," initiated again by seventeenth-century Nativism. But if Romanticism guaranteed the autonomy of Brazilian literature, its first aesthetic was not romantic. "Literature was born in Brazil under the sign of the Baroque, by the baroque hand of the Jesuits."[40] Thus, as Baroque, it was born in the writings of the founding patriarch Anchieta.

Thus two distinct criteria preside over Coutinho's historiography: one strictly historical that gives rise to investigation of nativist elements; the other stylistic, that shapes the literary periods aesthetically. To the long duration of the Baroque, extending to the eighteenth century, there succeeded the neoclassical form of Arcadism practiced among the *Mineiro* poets in the second half of that same century, the start of "personal Brazilian lyricism" with the fusion of individualism, the sense

---

[40] Afrânio Coutinho, *Introdução à literatura no Brasil* (Rio de Janeiro: Livraria São José, 1964) 113.

of Nature, and the classical ideal.[41] To that variant of Rococo at the end of the 1700s there follow Romanticism and Realism, respectively in the first and second half of the nineteenth century and, preceding Modernism, Impressionism with the novels *O Ateneu* (1888) by Raul Pompéia, *Canaã* (1902) by Graça Aranha, and the fiction of Adelino Magalhães (*Casos e impressões* [1916]).

Cândido places the questions of origin and differentiation in the context of one and the same problem: that of the literature's development, concomitant with the constitution of the social nexus of production, reception, and transmission of works that fulfill the minimal existing conditions of literary phenomena. The union of these questions modifies the chronological extension of the formative period in Romerian historiography, now converted into the process of the literary phenomenon's continuity, that will define itself only from the middle of the eighteenth century. At that time, the tie between producers and readers forms a tradition, or rather, a symbolic system, in a line that extends from the *Mineiro* poets to the pre-Romantics at the start of the nineteenth century, consolidating itself through Romanticism.

The initial segment of this line, as a decisive moment of development, articulates three distinct currents: the Neoclassical, a reaction to cultism; the ideology of Enlightenment; and the poetics of the Arcadists – compatible among themselves, in the same period. Each one of the currents contributes its part to constitute the system, made up of four themes: "familiarity with local reality; valuing of native populations; desire to contribute to the country's progress; incorporation of European standards."[42]

Thus, the aesthetic and ideological components of the system, being at the same time elements of the period's style – such as the exaltation of Nature carried to local color, the Arcadian pastoral idyll of the Indian as a natural man, the Enlightenment's reason aimed at a free and independent society and, finally, classical equilibrium in the Western literary tradition – were condensed in different ways by Brazilian writers who between 1750 and 1856 "created the bases of an organic Brazilian literature as a coherent system and not isolated manifestations" (Cândido, *Formação*, 64).

That focusing as a literature indebted to, and interwoven with, the country's destiny from the beginning, attests to the degree of historical consciousness in the process of Brazil's formation. A certain "infused nationalism" as the "fruit of historical conditions" (pp. 19–20) appears to gain strength from the fact of its transplanted origin: "Our literature is a branch of the Portuguese; it may be considered independent since Gregório de Matos or only after Gonçalves Dias and José de Alencar,

---

[41] Afrânio Coutinho, *A literatura no Brasil*, 3rd. edn. (6 vols, Rio de Janeiro: José Olympio Editora, 1986) 134.   [42] Cândido, *Formação*, 64.

according to the perspective adopted" (p. 22). As a result, one sees that Cândido resolves the problem of autonomy, which in Coutinho is still attached to independence in relation to Portuguese literature, through the historical and cultural genesis of a different literary system.

Formação da literatura brasileira, Cândido's historiographical text *par excellence*, limited chronologically to the two "decisive moments" – 1750–1786 and 1836–1880 – is complemented in later essays. Some that treat the earlier colonial period specify the stylistic function situated outside of the devised system: the Baroque, against which, under the name of cultism, the Neoclassicists reacted. Characterized as a style of trans-figuration in the religious spirit of the Counter-Reformation and, conse-quently, of Jesuit catechism in Brazil, the Baroque, whose symbolic religious space embraces the sacred oratory "of the century's greatest Luso-Brazilian, the Jesuit Antônio Vieira" (1608–1697) and the poetry of Gregório de Matos, represents an embellished, contrasting, and hyperbo-lic form of expression, within which chroniclers like Gabriel Soares de Sousa and historiographers such as Sebastião da Rocha Pita (1660–1738) – in his *História da América portuguesa 1500–1724* (1730) – descanted the marvels of Brazil's prodigal Nature.[43] The transfiguration of the land, so achieved, has the double effect of confirming on one hand the ideology of colonial domination while serving on the other as a link with the nativist sentiment that in the Arcadian period took on the dimension of a national political aspiration.

Other essays by the same author, dedicated to the modern period, highlight the matrixes of modernist nationalism, inseparable from the dialectic between the national and the foreign that marked the limits of the aesthetic revolution led by the movement of 1922.

The critical matrix of the nationalist wave that then appeared would revoke the Romerian pessimism persistent in Euclides da Cunha. "Our deficiencies, supposed or real, are reinterpreted as superiorities" (Cân-dido, *Literatura e sociedade*, 143). Whether it be miscegenation or the search for Native American and African heritage – Graça Aranha's "barbarous metaphysics" – both play a role in the recurrence of "native originality" that now was unleashed violently by means of the expressive freedoms of the European artistic vanguards, synchronous with the prelogical and prehistorical content of primitive cultures.

One of the high points of this tendency toward the primitive that imprinted an anarchist direction on nationalism, converted into an American current, was the "Manifesto Antropófago" (1928) of Oswald de Andrade. Turning Indianism inside out, it exalts the anthropophagist, the Tupi cannibal, taken as a symbol of opposition to the traditionalist

---

[43] Antônio Cândido, *Literatura e sociedade: estudos de teoria e história literária* (São Paulo: Companhia Editora Nacional, 1965) 110, 112.

nationalism (Grupo Verde-Amarelo, 1926) that revived *ufanismo*,[44] and further as a flag of the transgressions against patriarchal society and as the cultural devouring of the European element. The type "of expression, at once local and universal, reencountering European influence through immersion in Brazilian detail" (Cândido, *Literatura e sociedade*, 145) that the Modernists achieved, exemplifies the regime of devouring assimilation of European culture by the "native originality" that, from then on in Brazilian literature, normalized the dialectic of the particular and of the universal.

Perhaps owing to the affinities of the modern with earlier historical styles, the clarifying regressive effect of Modernism instilled a reaccommodation with the literary past, placing the literature of the seventeenth century in a new focus, still criticized in the nineteenth century on the basis of the Camonian epic and of the classical prose writers. Modernism thus made possible the critical rediscovery of authors and works that occupied secondary or inferior places in the canonical hierarchy of the Romanticism and Naturalism of the early twentieth century.

In the same way that the "baroque gentleman," to use Lezama Lima's expression, became a new center of historiographical interest, Joaquim de Sousa Andrade (Sousândrade; 1833–1902), esteemed by poetic Concretism beginning in 1964 – date of the *Re-visão de Sousândrade* by Augusto de Campos (b. 1931) and Haroldo de Campos (b. 1929) – comes to the foreground in the literary setting of Romanticism. In large part, Brazilian literary historiography from 1960 to 1990, by force of the historicizing of past canons, is motivated by the dynamic of rediscoveries and reevaluations: social originality is rediscovered in *Memórias de um sargento de milícias* (1855) by Manuel Antônio de Almeida (1831–1861) – a novel of customs misunderstood by Romantics and Naturalists – as well as in the poetry of dense pessimism, expressed in scientific terms, neither Parnassian nor symbolist, of *Eu* (1912) by Augusto dos Anjos (1884–1914); the urban novels of Lima Barreto (1881–1922), principally the satirical mural of naive nationalism, *O triste fim de Policarpo Quaresma* (1915), are brought out of obscurity, while Machado de Assis, already consecrated as a distinguished classic with a work considered uncompromised by politics, is revealed to be a novelist out of his time, at once modern in form and critical of his time and of his society.

Parallel to this, the mythical rhapsody of the national anti-hero "without any character," *Macunaíma* (1928) by Mário de Andrade (1893–1945), and the parodic and anthropophagous novels of José Oswald de Sousa Andrade (1890–1954), *Memórias sentimentais de João Miramar* (1924) and *Serafim Ponte Grande* (1933), become classics of

[44] Antônio Cândido, "Una palabra inestable," *Escritura, teoría y crítica literaria*, Caracas, 14:27 (1989), 35.

modern prose, attaining a position equal to the great modernist poetry of Manuel Bandeira (1886–1968), Cecília Meireles (1901–1964), Carlos Drummond de Andrade (1902–1987), Murilo Mendes (1901–1975), Jorge de Lima (1895–1953), and Cassiano Ricardo (1895–1974). Through the epic and dramatic accents of expression reworked by intelligence these authors rectify what would be seen as the inevitability of Brazil's exclusively lyrical vocation, according to the literary historiography of the past century.

Between 1960 and 1990, historiography abounds in the sectors of different authors and genres, to which are added panoramas, anthologies, and syntheses of essayistic nature that broaden and refine the critical, aesthetic, and ideological judgments of literary history. Nevertheless, that plethora of production accompanies a theoretical crisis in literary historiography, argued in terms of the permanent link that has joined it to general history, perhaps prejudicing the definition of its specific object, possibly the study of changes in forms of discourse by means of distinct families and genres of works.[45] What is argued, furthermore, are the presuppositions – also historical – of its writing, guided by organic metaphors tending to order the sequence of works in an evolving scale, even when not expressly evolutionist, and to utilize periodicity as a chronological scale of literary perfection.[46]

It is, after all, the temporal chain model of writing, based on the principle of uniform succession, that seems to have entered into crisis after Walter Benjamin's fragmentary conception of history and the deconstruction of Jacques Derrida. Proposing in that sense a literary historiography as "transformation," from a vertiginous origin and with ulterior points of rupture with tradition, Haroldo de Campos questions Cândido's system, that would correspond to the idea of a "rectilinear history," according to Campos responsible for the reduced importance of the Baroque in the *Formação da literatura brasileira*.[47]

Yet, outdated as are the questions of the independence and autonomy of Brazilian literature that resulted from its polemical origin, and no matter what may be the path of historiography in the future, there will remain the genealogical function that it played in the formulation of that literature's identity and, concomitantly, of the very identity of the country, interconnected by a single "metaphoric field," seen through the nationalist propensity to be both so fluid and so structured.

That "metaphoric field," spread throughout Indianism, Regionalism,

---

[45] Gilberto Mendonça Teles, "Introdução a uma filosofia da história literária," *Revista Letras de Hoje*, Rio Grande do Sul-PUC, 33 (Sept. 1978), 21.

[46] Fábio Lucas, "Literatura e história: história da literatura," *Revista de Letras*, São Paulo, 22 (1982), 83–98.

[47] Haroldo de Campos, *O sequestro do barroco na formação da literatura brasileira: o caso Gregório de Mattos* (Salvador: Fundação Casa de Jorge Amado, 1989).

and in other variants, local and particular, of things Brazilian, belongs to the symbolic and critical whole, with its political and ideological scope, that is called Brazilian culture, which limits literary historiography but which literary historiography itself contributed to develop. However, after the Brazilian writer learned with Machado de Assis to give as proof of his national identity "a certain intimate emotion that makes him a man of his time and of his country even when he treats subjects remote in space and time,"[48] it also became the responsibility of historiography to take into consideration the transnational.

[48] J. M. Machado de Assis, "Instinto de nacionalidade," *Obra completa*, vol. III. (Rio de Janeiro: Nova Aguilar, 1985) 804.

Colonial Brazilian literature
David T. Haberly

Brazil entered the consciousness of the European world late in April of 1500. Beginning with its conquest of Ceuta in 1415, Portugal had moved beyond the narrow confines of the western shore of the Iberian peninsula, eager to discover a sea route to the rich spice lands of India and the East. The Portuguese sailed down the African coast, reaching the Cape of Good Hope in 1488; Vasco da Gama's small fleet entered the Indian harbor of Calicut only ten years later. The Portuguese regarded da Gama's voyage as one of the greatest accomplishments of human history, but the rulers of Calicut were clearly less than impressed. When da Gama returned to Lisbon, it was decided to mount a much more considerable show of force. A new fleet, 13 ships and about 1,100 men under the command of Pedro Álvares Cabral, set sail in early 1500. This fleet – perhaps accidentally carried off-course, perhaps keeping to a pre-arranged plan to follow up on secret reports of a land mass in the South Atlantic – landed on the Brazilian coast on April 22, 1500.

Cabral's scribe, one Pero Vaz de Caminha, was greatly moved by the beauty of all that he saw during the ten days he spent in this new land, setting down a poetic and profoundly mythic vision of fertility and innocence. Caminha was struck, almost at first glance, by the apparently inexhaustible abundance and goodness of the land – and by the fact that all this visible and latent fertility served no useful purpose. He wrote:

> All the land along the coast, from one end to the other, is . . . very level and beautiful . . . So far we have been unable to discover whether there is any gold or silver or any other metal or iron there; we have not seen any . . . There is a great abundance, an infinite abundance of water. The country is so beautiful that, if one wished to make use of it, it would produce everything because of its wealth of water.
> (Cortesão, *A Carta de Pêro Vaz de Caminha*, 256)

Caminha viewed the native inhabitants of this land in the same terms – inherently good, but desperately in need of development. The Indian men, he noted twice, were uncircumcised, and he took this as the most basic proof possible that Brazil's inhabitants had not been corrupted by contact with the circumcised enemies of Catholic Portugal, Moslems and Jews.

> It seemed to me and to us all that this people needs only to understand us to become completely Christian; for they accepted, just as we do, all that they saw us do [during the celebration of the Mass], which led us to believe that they are without idolatry or worship. I truly believe that if your Majesty could send someone to stay among them a while, they would all be converted as Your Majesty wishes. (pp. 254–5)

The clearest indication of the natural goodness and innocence of this new world, however, was the nakedness of its inhabitants: "the innocence of these people with respect to shame about their bodies is such that that of Adam himself could not be greater" (p. 255).

In Caminha's several detailed discussions of the Indian women, his attention was clearly focused on their genitals; the Portuguese word he used, *vergonhas* – literally, "shames" – sums up the conflict of cultural patterns that both perturbed and excited him: "One of the [Indian] girls was all colored from head to toe with that paint they use, and surely she was so rounded and well-formed, and her shameful parts (about which she felt no shame) were so attractive that many women of our own land, seeing such perfection, would be ashamed that their parts were not as perfect" (p. 232).

The subtext of Caminha's letter, then, is his conviction that he and his companions have somehow returned to Eden before the Fall – a fair and fertile garden whose inhabitants do not know shame. Moreover, within this garden even European sailors can regain the lost innocence of Adam, looking upon the *vergonhas* of Indian girls: "we felt no shame at all" (p. 231).

Caminha's implicit vision of an American Eden echoed a similar but much more explicit claim by Christopher Columbus. In his third letter (1498), Columbus used the image of Eden as a justification for Spain's investment in his search for the Indies. He claimed to have found something even more valuable than Eastern riches: Venezuela was the nipple-shaped protuberance that crowned a pear-shaped globe, its geography symbolic of its original function as the site of Eden and of Man's betrayal by Satan and by Woman.

Within two generations of Columbus and Caminha writing, however, the almost incomprehensible wealth of Mexico and Peru had provided a non-theological justification for Columbus's enthusiasm about his New World. From Cape Horn to Colorado, Spaniards were busily engaged in exploring and conquering. The essential cultural institutions of Renaissance Europe arrived almost on the heels of the *conquistadores*: universities were founded in Santo Domingo, in Mexico, in Peru; printing presses were actively functioning throughout much of Spanish America within a few decades. These institutions helped form what we now call Spanish American literature, and provided that literature with a unifying continuity capable of spanning geography and chronology.

The history and culture of Portuguese America are very different indeed, and these differences had a fundamental impact upon the development and character of literature in colonial Brazil. When Cabral's fleet left Brazil in 1500, it went on to the real Indies – lands whose wealth was concrete and readily exploited rather than potential and metaphorical. Caminha's letter, written directly to the King, appears to have awakened no interest whatsoever in the Court; it disappeared into the files, and was not rediscovered until 1817. Intent upon its trading empire in India and Asia, Portugal largely ignored Brazil for decades, taking an interest in the territory only when other European nations appeared to covet it.

This disinterest was eventually replaced by an iron determination to maintain absolute control over every aspect of Brazilian life, but both approaches severely limited the development of colonial culture. No printing presses existed in Brazil until 1808, almost three hundred years after they began functioning in Spanish America. Only a few of the works written in Brazil during this period were published in Portugal; others circulated in manuscript form among colonial readers. Those readers, moreover, were very few and far between, for education was virtually non-existent in Brazil. There were a few elementary schools and even fewer secondary schools, but the first institutions of higher education – scattered independent faculties of law or medicine – were not established until after 1827; the first Brazilian university opened in 1920.

As a result of Brazil's cultural underdevelopment during the period before 1808, far fewer works of literature were produced there than in Spanish America, and fewer yet were published before the nineteenth century. There is, however, an even more striking difference between the colonial literature of Brazil and that of Spanish America: the lack of a clear consensus among Portuguese and Brazilian intellectuals on the canon which comprises colonial Brazilian literature – or, in fact, on whether such a literature exists at all.

The post-Independence creation of national literatures which included works produced before Independence was, of course, a problematical enterprise in many areas of the world, including the United States and Spanish America. Nonetheless, it is clear that consensus was reached, at some point in the first half of the nineteenth century, on the authors and works included under the rubric of colonial literature of the United States; precisely the same sort of consensus can be seen in the case of Spain and Spanish America after about 1870.

No such consensus exists, even today, in the case of Brazil. Portuguese literary historians have insisted that geopolitics has no real impact on the essential character of literature; the key factor, rather, is the language used to produce a given work. Language, they argue, molds and controls form and content alike, and the literatures of Portugal and Brazil, written in Portuguese, must therefore be regarded as a single entity. This approach led Portugal, during much of the nineteenth century, to deny the existence of a separate Brazilian literature even after political independence. That separateness has now been accepted, but major histories and anthologies of Portuguese literature produced in Portugal continue to include the major works of what Brazilians simultaneously define as their own colonial literature.

The reason behind Portugal's insistence that colonial Brazilian literature does not exist is the severe decline of Portuguese literature after about 1580, a decline that continued until the first half of the nineteenth century. The Spain of Cervantes, Quevedo, Góngora, and Calderón has felt no need to claim Bernal Díaz, the Inca Garcilaso, nor even Sor Juana Inés de la Cruz; the literary glory of England most assuredly does not depend upon Cotton Mather. However, Portuguese literature of the seventeenth and eighteenth centuries would be almost a wasteland without Brazilians like Father Antônio Vieira or the Arcadian poets of Minas Gerais.

The lack of a trans-Atlantic consensus has sometimes forced Brazilian literary historians to be tentative and defensive, compelled to prove that there is something inherently Brazilian about each author they seek to include in the canon. For the purposes of this account of the period from 1500 to 1822, however, I am defining Brazilian colonial literature as simply, logically, and inclusively as possible: works whose primary purpose is the description of Brazil; works by authors born or educated in Brazil; and works by authors whose lives are inextricably bound up with events in Brazil.

The essence of Brazil's early history and of its first literature, as Caminha's letter suggests, is that the territory served as a kind of vast green *tabula rasa*, upon which national or individual fantasies could easily be projected. When Portugal stopped completely ignoring its new territory, in 1532, its administrative model was entirely feudal. The Crown divided the land into twelve strips running west from the Atlantic to the boundary line established by the 1496 Treaty of Tordesillas; that line extended, in rough terms, from the mouth of the river Amazon to what is now the state of São Paulo. These strips were awarded to hereditary Captains-General, but few of these worthies even visited their Brazilian fiefdoms. As a result, much of what we know about Brazil during this period comes from the representatives of other European nations, all far more interested in the possibilities of this new land than its largely absentee owners. Italians, Dutch, Germans, and French were active all along the coast, both as pirates and as traders; they, along with a handful of energetic and ambitious Portuguese settlers, rapidly exploited and destroyed the land's first commodity of value, the brazilwood tree, which produced a valuable dye and gave the territory its name. Foreigners also played a role in the gradual development of sugar plantations along the northeastern coast.

By the middle of the sixteenth century, it seemed evident that the system of Captains-General had failed. A single royal governor, Tomé de Sousa, was appointed in 1549, and the city of Bahia became his headquarters. This centralization of Portuguese authority was accelerated by a short-lived French invasion of Rio de Janeiro between 1555 and 1567. Accounts of the conquest and settlement of what was fantasized as "la France Antartique," written by André Thévet (1502–1590) and Jean de Léry (1534–1611), presented a highly colored and sympathetic vision of Brazil and its native inhabitants – a vision that was to influence Sir Thomas More's *Utopia* and, in a more distant future, late eighteenth-century French speculations about natural law and the inherent goodness of humanity. A very different view of the Indians of Brazil appeared, almost simultaneously, in Germany: the *Warhaftige Historia . . . [True History of His Captivity]* of Hans Staden, a young sailor from Hesse. Staden's account of his experiences in Brazil focuses on hair-raising descriptions of fantastic and utterly demonic cannibals; he escaped only because a providential toothache made him thin and unappetizing.

Brazilian literature in Portuguese, in the fifty years or so that followed Tomé de Sousa's arrival, can be divided into two general categories: examples of what Brazilians call *ufanismo* – the glorification of the land and all it contains; and the writings of members of the Jesuit Order. The *ufanistas* include: Pero de Magalhães Gândavo, a Portuguese of Flemish descent who was in Brazil around 1570 and who wrote the *História da província de Santa Cruz a que vulgarmente chamamos Brasil [The Histories of Brazil]* and the *Tratado da terra do Brasil*; Gabriel Soares de Sousa (1540?–1591), a Portuguese plantation-owner in Bahia, whose *Tratado descritivo do Brasil em 1587* was published in Rio in 1851; and Ambrósio Fernandes Brandão, a Portuguese New-Christian and the author of the *Diálogos das grandezas do Brasil [Dialogues of the Great Things of Brazil]*, written in 1618 but first published in full in Rio de Janeiro, 1930.

All of these triumphant catalogues of the wonders of Brazil list its natural resources, praise its climate and its social life, and endeavor to elucidate its curiosities. They were written, in short, to attract immigrants. There is doubtless a good bit of exaggeration in these paeans, and their tone is sometimes a bit forced, as if the authors were attempting to convince not only their readers but themselves. Moreover, they stress that even greater riches – comparable to those of India, Mexico, or Peru – are just waiting to be discovered: there are precious gems and metals somewhere in the interior, and El Dorado lies at the headwaters of the São Francisco river.

These three writers provide enormously useful ethnographic and historical information. Above all, however, they allow us a glimpse of the fantasies upon which the development of the Northeast and its plantations – and of Brazil itself – was constructed. The surface texture of these writings is that of the Renaissance: clarity of organization and presentation, allusions to classical models, Brandão's adaptation of the didactic dialogue. The *ufanistas'* attitude toward their material, however, is essentially Medieval; observation and legend are given equal weight as they seek to describe phenomena so fantastic that they can best be understood in terms of novels of chivalry – texts to which Brandão explicitly refers.

The essence of their message about Brazil, moreover, is the fantasy that Medieval feudalism can be recovered and democratized within a society built upon slavery – first of Indians, then of Africans. That society, according to the *ufanistas*, enabled any Portuguese immigrant, no matter how poor, to live the kind of life once reserved for Europe's nobility. Magalhães Gândavo declared that "if someone manages to acquire four or six slaves here, even if he owns nothing else, he will instantly have the means to support his family in an honorable fashion, because one slave fishes for him, another hunts for him, the rest cultivate and till his lands" (*The Histories of Brazil*, fo. 15 of facsimile). Equally powerful, if less visible in these works, was the fantasy of the dark-skinned harem – the powerless and dependent Indian and African women of this slave-owning patriarchy. The concrete result of this fantasy in action was the rapid growth of a large mixed-race population in the colony.

The transmutation of Portuguese peasants into Brazilian lords was not the only Medieval fantasy that flowered in the colony. The first Jesuit missionaries in Brazil, commanded by Father Manuel da Nóbrega (1517–1570), arrived in 1549, only nine years after the founding of their order. Moved by the destruction of the Indian in the Spanish Caribbean, the Jesuits were determined to try a new approach to the salvation and preservation of the natives. The basis of that approach was a return to feudalism – theocratic, monastic feudalism, but feudalism nonetheless.

The Jesuits in Brazil gathered groups of Indians into protected villages, called *aldeias*, built around primitive churches and schools and defended against the incursions of white slave-hunters. The Indians were to learn to read and write Portuguese as an aid to their conversion, but the language of daily life would remain their native Tupi; furthermore, only native customs in direct conflict with Catholic doctrine – cannibalism and polygamy, for example – were to be abolished. It was anticipated that the fundamentally innocent inhabitants of the *aldeias*, instructed in the catechism and in the rudiments of agriculture and the arts, protected and guided by the Jesuits, would quickly become the perfect Christians Caminha had envisioned.

The enterprise turned out, however, to be considerably more difficult than expected. The area the Jesuits chose as their center of operations, the southern coast from about Rio de Janeiro to what is now São Paulo, had relatively few European settlers, but those settlers were often hostile; throughout Brazil, the colonial administration was rarely as supportive as the Jesuits had hoped. The fundamental problem, however, was that the Indians were not at all eager to be saved: they resisted resettlement and conversion, sometimes violently, and even those who appeared devout slipped easily into their old ways. There is no question that, while the idea behind the *aldeias* remains an appealing fantasy of the perfectibility of human society, in practice the system was often very close to slavery, or at least to serfdom. On the other hand, life in these villages, however constrained and regimented, was generally still better than the fate which awaited Indians enslaved by white settlers.

The prose texts of three major Jesuit missionaries in Brazil chronicle both the successes and the failures of this enterprise. Nóbrega wrote a very large number of letters to colleagues in Europe and the East; most of these were not printed until the twentieth century. José de Anchieta (1534–1597), a Spanish Jesuit born in the Canaries, arrived in Brazil at the age of nineteen and remained there until his death. He also wrote a number of epistolary accounts of his activities, as well as the one Jesuit prose text published in the sixteenth century – his *Arte de gramática da língua mais usada na costa do Brasil*, a grammar of the Tupi language spoken in the *aldeias*. A younger Jesuit, the Portuguese Fernão Cardim (1548?–1625), produced a long epistolary narrative and several extremely useful treatises on Brazilian ecology and ethnography, first published in book form in Rio de Janeiro, 1925.

Manuel da Nóbrega began the *aldeia* system; he also began the vitally important Jesuit tradition within Brazilian literature. While few of these works appeared in print, they were transmitted in manuscript form within the Jesuit community in Brazil and elsewhere, and passed from one generation of missionaries to the next – from Nóbrega's time until at least the end of the seventeenth century. This kind of continuity, facilitated in the rest of the hemisphere by superior educational systems and by the ready availability of locally printed texts, existed in Brazil only for the Jesuits.

Nóbrega's letters about events in Brazil swing back and forth between extreme optimism and profound depression, between gentle affection for the natives and violent authoritarianism. His most consciously literary text, and his most coherent discussion of the Jesuit enterprise in Brazil, is his *Diálogo sobre a conversão do gentio*, written around 1556. The two interlocutors, Mateus Nogueira and Gonçalo Álvares, are real people, relatively uneducated participants in Nóbrega's mission. As structured by its author, the *Diálogo* presents arguments both for and against the conversion of the Indians. Nogueira and Álvares debate the issue with humor, common sense, and references to Scripture and to their own mundane occupations. While the inevitable conclusion of the discussion is that the effort to save the natives can and must succeed, there are no more illusions about their inherent innocence; they are, rather, no better and no worse than any other peoples – Jews, Greeks, Romans, contemporary white Portuguese, and Brazilians. The salvation of the Indian will not be accomplished miraculously, but will require generations of sacrifice and struggle.

At the heart of the *Diálogo* is Nóbrega's remarkable vision of human history as a seamless whole, stretching back to the days of Abraham and independent of chronology, geography, and race. This vision is perhaps the central element in the Jesuit intellectual tradition in Brazil, and is omnipresent in Cardim's prose texts and in the poems and plays of the most famous of the early Jesuits, José de Anchieta. For Anchieta, the sense of seamless continuity is formal and literary as well as ideological, and serves both his purposes and those of his audiences in Brazil. In many of his verses, as in the accounts of Nóbrega and Cardim, we can sense the importance to the psychological survival of the first Jesuits of precisely this continuity: they saw both their victories and their defeats as part of a continuum, defining themselves as the direct successors of those first Christians who sought to convert Romans and barbarians alike. The Jesuits in Brazil buttressed this sense of continuity with sacred relics of early Christians, carefully chosen with an eye to the specific dangers they faced in Brazil: a leg of Saint Sebastian provided protection against the natives' arrows; a relic of Saint Lawrence (believed martyred on a red-hot grill) would preserve the missionaries from being roasted and eaten; the sexual immorality of Indians and settlers alike would be conquered by the power of the preserved heads of three of Saint Ursula's 11,000 virgins.

For Anchieta, traditional literary forms provided the same assurance of continuity as holy relics. His moving elegies for fallen comrades derive from martyrological poetry of the Middle Ages; his two epic poems in Latin, the *De Beata Virgine Dei Matre Maria* and *De gestis Mendi de Saa* (on Mem de Sá, the second Portuguese governor of Brazil), formally link Anchieta and his Jesuit audience to Medieval Marist epics and to the tradition of Virgil. The self-affirming and consoling function of literary texts in an alien environment is particularly evident in the *De Beata*

Virgine, written during long months spent as the captive of hostile Indians. Anchieta is said to have scratched each of its 5,786 lines into beach sand, correcting, memorizing, and then erasing it; he reconstructed the whole epic after his release. The most striking examples of the coexistence of past and present in Anchieta's poetry are his lyrics; their themes and metrics derive from Medieval Iberian *cancioneiros*, but they are written not only in Spanish and Portuguese, but in Tupi.

Anchieta's simple verse plays, primarily designed for presentation in the *aldeias*, were written both to enlighten and entertain, allowing his Indian audiences to sing and dance, to create rudimentary sound-effects, to rush back and forth across a primitive stage as angelic armies or diabolical hordes. Their style derives from Medieval mystery plays and from the *autos* of Gil Vicente, as does their vision of history as an endless struggle between Good and Evil, between God and Satan. Anchieta's characters, drawn from the Bible, from Medieval hagiography, and from his experiences in Brazil, speak Portuguese, Spanish, and Tupi. The fact that Satan and his devils almost invariably speak Tupi may well be a reflection of Anchieta's underlying cultural biases – but it also reflects the missionaries' belief that their problems in converting the natives were of demonic origin.

Quite another view of the Indian appeared in the first Brazilian poem to be published, the *Prosopopéia* of Bento Teixeira Pinto (1564?–?), which appeared in Lisbon in 1601. Teixeira was a Portuguese Jew who emigrated to Brazil, was accused by the Inquisition, and was sent back to Portugal to face trial. His truncated and pedestrian epic of 752 lines was apparently written to please members of the powerful Coelho and Albuquerque families, influential both in Pernambuco and in Portugal, in the hope that they would save him from the Holy Office. Teixeira was certainly not much of a poet, but the *Prosopopéia* is the first Brazilian text that is a product of the Renaissance rather than a late throw-back to the Middle Ages. Through his imitation of the *Lusiads* of Luís de Camões, Teixeira attempts to equate his various topics – the family history of his patrons, brief descriptions of Pernambuco, and a 1565 shipwreck involving Jorge de Albuquerque Coelho – with the glories of Portuguese history and the voyage of Vasco da Gama. He also uses one of the central conventions of the *Lusiads*, the superimposed apparatus of contentious classical deities, as a way to finesse a question which perplexed both the Jesuits and the *ufanistas* – the origin of the Indian; in the *Prosopopéia*, the natives are Vulcan's assistants in his subterranean workshops, burned red-brown by the fires of his forges.

Near the end of Teixeira's poem, Jorge de Albuquerque Coelho and his brother participate in the ill-fated Portuguese invasion of North Africa of 1578. That campaign, based upon King Sebastião's belief that God had chosen him to retake Jerusalem, fundamentally altered the history of the Portuguese-speaking world. The King and most of his court were killed, leading to a crisis of succession; Spain took advantage of this catastrophe and Portugal and all of its territories became part of the Spanish Empire from 1580 until the restoration of independence in 1640.

During those sixty years, Portugal lost almost all of its trading empire in Africa and the East. These events – in combination with a dramatic fall in the world price of sugar and a Dutch Protestant invasion of the major sugar-producing areas of the northeastern coast – challenged all of the optimistic assumptions of Jesuits and *ufanistas* alike. The *História do Brasil* of a Brazilian-born Franciscan, Frei Vicente do Salvador (1564–1636?), finished in 1627 but first published in Rio de Janeiro in 1889, details the political and military history of this crisis. Its enduring psychological and cultural consequences, however, are far more visible in the works of the two greatest Brazilian writers of the seventeenth century, Gregório de Matos and Father Antônio Vieira.

Gregório de Matos e Guerra (1623–1696?) was born into a wealthy and influential Bahian family; his Portuguese grandfather and father owned sugar plantations in the area around Salvador. Educated at the University of Coimbra in Portugal from 1652 to 1661, Gregório became a successful and respected judge in Portugal. He returned to Bahia in 1682, anticipating even more rapid advancement in the colonial bureaucracy there, but he was removed from office in 1683. He stayed in Bahia, working as a lawyer and holding various minor administrative and ecclesiastical posts, but his satirical verses – the fruit of his failure and disappointment – antagonized everyone of importance in the city; he also developed a reputation as a wastrel. He was briefly exiled to Angola in 1694, but returned to die in Recife. His poems were published only long after his death, but many of them appear to have circulated widely in manuscript.

The hundreds of poems attributed to Gregório de Matos include a number of deeply religious pleas for divine forgiveness; he held minor orders and appears, at times, to have sincerely repented the excesses so graphically catalogued in some of his other works. He also wrote refined, philosophical love poetry, dedicated to white women of the Bahian upper class, which stressed the mutability of emotions and the impermanence of physical beauty. There is something forced and artificial about these verses, many of which borrow heavily from Camões, Calderón, Quevedo, and Góngora. Gregório's debt to Góngora, for example, can be seen in the first stanza of one of his best-known love poems, a sonnet dedicated to his second wife:

Gregório
Discreta, e formosíssima Maria
Enquanto estamos vendo a qualquer hora

Em tuas faces a rosada Aurora,
Em teus olhos, e bôca o Sol, e o dia: . . .

(*Obras completas*, III: 659)

Góngora
Ilustre y hermosísima María
mientras se dejan ver a cualquier hora
en tus mejillas la rosada aurora,
Febo en tus ojos, y en tu frente el día, . . .
(Luis de Góngora, *Sonetos completos* [Madrid: Castalia, 1976] 231)

Gregório
[Mary, most beautiful and wise, we see,
Regardless of the hour, the rosy Dawn
Gleam in your cheeks, and in your eyes
The Sun, and in your mouth the dawning day: . . .]

Góngora
[Mary, most beautiful and famed, we see,
Regardless of the hour, the rosy dawn
Gleam in your cheeks, and in your eyes
Phoebus, and on your brow the dawning day, . . .]

Gregório's complete works also include detailed descriptions of another Bahia – not the world of the bureaucracy, the church, and the upper class, but the underworld of slums and slave quarters, bars and brothels. Gregório moved freely between these two worlds, and portrayed both in his poetry; he very occasionally allowed the two to meet – no doubt relishing the shock such juxtaposition caused. One of his sonnets, for example, explores the conflict between idealism and reality, between metaphysics and physiology, between the conceits of Baroque poetics and the earthy language of everyday life:

Rubi, concha de perlas peregrina,
Animado Cristal, viva escarlata,
Duas Safiras sobre lisa prata,
Ouro encrespado sobre prata fina.

Este o rostinho é de Caterina; . . .
Viu Fábio uma tarde transportado . . .
Disse igualmente amante e magoado:
Ah muchacha gentil, que tal serias,
Se sendo tão formosa não cagaras!

[Ruby, shell of rarest pearls,
Living Crystal, scarlet red,

57

Sapphires rest on silver smooth,
Chased gold enlaid on a silver bed.

This is Catherine's lovely face; ...
Fábio saw her, and lost his wits ...
And said – in love and sorrow too –
"Oh fairest maid, how fair you'd be
If you looked like this, but didn't shit!"]
(*Obras completas*, V: 1174)

The focus of Gregório's numerous pornographic poems, most of which were not published until 1969, is the utterly immoral woman of color who gladly and cheerfully bestows her abundant favors upon white males in general, and upon Gregório in particular. These works are extremely graphic, as well as very funny, but they also clearly reflect an attitude toward non-white women – as sexual objects, as nameless and almost faceless orifices – which has remained a constant in much of Brazilian culture.

His satires on Brazilian colonial life, closer to his pornographic poems than to his religious and sentimental verses, are the most interesting of Gregório's works. At the heart of his complaints is a profound crisis of faith shared by many other Brazilians in the last years of the seventeenth century: life in the colony simply had not worked out as promised in the *ufanistas'* fantasies of tropical feudalism. Like other Brazilian-born whites, Gregório felt trapped between the arrogance of powerful and well-connected immigrants from Portugal and the aggressive drive for success of those farther down the social scale. Brazil, he complained, had become a cruel stepmother to her native sons, who were surrounded and oppressed by uneducated Portuguese:

A cada canto um grande conselheiro,
Que nos quer governar cabana, e vinha,
Não sabem governar sua cozinha,
E podem governar o mundo inteiro.
(*Obras completas*, I: 3)

[A councilor waits at every corner,
Ready to govern our huts and our lands;
They can't even keep a kitchen in order,
Yet hold our whole world in their hands.]

At the same time, Gregório and his audience of native-born whites greatly feared the talents and potential for success of black freedmen and of the increasing numbers of mulattoes, both of whom he believed were given too much liberty and too many opportunities by the Portuguese colonial administration. Convinced that he and others of his race and class had become exiles in their own land, Gregório summed up his complaints about Bahia in echoed tercets:

> Quais são seus doces objetos? . . . Pretos
> Tem outros bens mais maciços? . . . Mestiços
> Quais destes lhe são mais gratos? . . . Mulatos.
>
> (I: 32)

> [What are her favorite geegaws? . . . Nigras.
> And what other goods suit her needs? . . . Half-breeds.
> But which are her best-loved beaus? . . . Mulattoes.]

The crisis of faith and sense of betrayal in the works of Father Antônio Vieira (1608–1697) went far deeper than Gregório's complaints about the loss of privilege and status. Vieira was born in Lisbon, probably of African descent. His family moved to Bahia, where he was educated and joined the Jesuit Order. He witnessed the Dutch invasion of Pernambuco, and his early sermons deal with what he viewed as Portugal's fall from divine grace; in his famous "Sermão pelo bom sucesso das armas de Portugal contra as de Holanda" of 1640, Vieira pugnaciously took God to task for deserting his chosen people in favor of Protestant Dutchmen:

> Consider, my God – and forgive me if I speak thoughtlessly – consider from whom You are taking these lands of Brazil, and to whom You are giving them. You are taking these lands from the Portuguese, to whom You first gave them; and simply to state to whom You have given them imperils Your credibility, since gifts given and then taken back are no signs of generosity . . . If You were determined to give these lands to the pirates of Holland, why didn't You do so when the lands were wild and barren, rather than now? Has that perverted and apostate nation served You so well that You sent us here first to clear the way for the Dutch, to till the soil for them, to build cities for them, planning only then – only after these lands were civilized and enriched – to turn these lands over to them? Can it be that heretics and enemies of the faith will so profit from Portuguese toil and Catholic sweat? . . . But since, Lord, You will and order that it be so, do as You please. Hand over Brazil to the Dutch, give them India, give them Iberia, . . . give them everything we have and hold (You have already given them so much); place the world in their hands; and as for us, Portuguese and Spaniards, desert us, repudiate us, tear us apart, have done with us. But I would say, I would remind Your Majesty, Lord, that the day may come when You will again need those whom You now turn against and cast away from You – and You will not have them. (*Sermões*, XIV: 308–11)

Vieira was sent to Lisbon, in 1641, as part of a delegation of Brazilians to the court of King João IV, the ruler of a newly independent Portugal. He very quickly became João's advisor and one of the most powerful men in

Portugal. Vieira gave all this up, in 1652, to live and work among the Indians in the northern Brazilian province of Maranhão. Vieira used his many talents to defend the natives from exploitation, but he and the other members of his order were expelled from Maranhão in 1661. Father Vieira returned to Lisbon, but his protector, João IV, had died in 1656; he was forbidden to preach, and pursued by the Inquisition. He returned to Bahia in 1681, remaining there until his death in 1697.

Many of Vieira's sermons are remarkable, even today, for their verbal brilliance and their openly subversive disregard for religious and social orthodoxy in defense of groups who possessed no other champion – the Indians of Brazil, the Jews of Iberia and the rest of Europe, the poor of Portugal. His central preoccupation, however, remained the problem he had raised in his early diatribes against the Dutch invaders of Brazil: why had God deserted the Portuguese, His chosen people who had explored and christianized the globe for Him, and what did Portugal have to do to regain His favor? At the end of his life, in the bitter resignation of his "Sermão vigésimo-segundo, da série 'Maria, rosa mística'", Vieira concluded that the Portuguese Empire – and, by extension, the promise of its Brazilian colony – had been forever betrayed by its own unworthiness. All of Portugal's many military and political misfortunes throughout the world, during more than a century of captivity and defeat and failure, were necessary and well-deserved penalties imposed by God for the nation's monstrous sins of racial prejudice and exploitation, sins made manifest in Indian and African slavery in Brazil.

Almost as Vieira delivered this sermon to his congregation in Bahia, Brazil's fortunes changed dramatically. Whites in the south of the colony, centered in the city of São Paulo, had long been organizing expeditions, called *bandeiras* and *entradas*, to explore the unmapped interior in search of new sources of Indian slaves; along the way, they looked for the rich deposits of precious metals and gems the *ufanista* tradition insisted could be found somewhere in Brazil. First gold and then diamonds were discovered, at the very end of the seventeenth century, in the province of Minas Gerais.

The discoveries helped Brazilians to recover their lost faith in the promise of the land. This restored faith is evident in the panegyric to the area around Bahia found in the "Ilha da Maré," the best-known poem in the first book by a Brazilian to be printed in the eighteenth century, the *Música do Parnaso* of Manuel Botelho de Oliveira (1636–1711); this is also the first volume of poetry published by any native-born Brazilian. Botelho de Oliveira's praises for the beauties – and, in particular, the foods – of Bahia are, nonetheless, almost the only local references in this collection of mediocre and imitative verse.

Two central problems confronted Brazil's writers in the eighteenth century: how to find stylistic and thematic approaches to local reality, for despite the rebirth of faith in the land and its potential, it was clearly impossible to return to the essentially Medieval traditions of both the Jesuits and the *ufanistas*; and how to construct a literary society and achieve personal success in a colony still crippled by an inferior educational system, by limited intellectual opportunities, and by Portugal's refusal to allow printing presses to operate in Brazil.

One solution to this second problem was simply to leave the colony to live and work in Portugal. The most tragic Brazilian intellectual in early eighteenth-century Portugal was Antônio José da Silva, known as "The Jew." Da Silva was born in Rio de Janeiro in 1705; he died in Lisbon in 1739, strangled and then burned by the Inquisition. He wrote a number of comic plays and operas during his brief career, and was the most important dramatist writing in Portuguese during this period. Other Brazilians flourished in Portugal, despite the continued power of the Inquisition, rigid censorship, and Byzantine politics. Matias Aires Ramos da Silva de Eça (1705–1768?) and his sister, Teresa Margarida da Silva e Orta (1711?–1787?), spent most of their lives in Portugal. Matias Aires's *Reflexões sobre a vaidade dos homens*, first published in Lisbon in 1752, went through four editions in the eighteenth century; it is, as its title suggests, a pessimistic and moralizing disquisition on the essentially evil nature of humanity – a far cry from the ideas propounded by his contemporary Rousseau. His sister's *Aventuras de Diófanes*, a moralizing novel modeled on Greek narrative and on Fenelón's *Adventures of Telemachus*, is the first work known to have been written by a Brazilian woman; it was published in Lisbon in 1752, under an anagramatic pseudonym, and went through three additional Portuguese editions before 1818.

Other colonial emigrants to eighteenth-century Portugal were eager to write about Brazil, but were constrained both by the stylistic preferences of their European readers and by Portuguese politics of the period. Nuno Marques Pereira (1652?–1728?), was probably born in Bahia and spent considerable time in the mining areas before going to Lisbon. His one work is the *Compêndio narrativo do peregrino da América*, the first part of which was published in Lisbon in 1728; four other editions appeared by 1765, but the second part was not published until 1939, in Rio de Janeiro. Pereira's text is an allegorical dialogue in which two characters, The Old Man and The Pilgrim, moralize about the generally sorry state of morals in Brazil. It includes a number of interesting notes on colonial society, but it was not meant to be realistic; Pereira designed it, rather, as the response of the Iberian Counter-Reformation to John Bunyan's *Pilgrim's Progress*.

Two Brazilians in eighteenth-century Portugal endeavored to revitalize the epic as a vehicle for descriptions of the colony and its history – and for wholesale revisions of that history in order to follow the changing winds of Portuguese politics. José Basílio da Gama (1741–1795) was born in Minas Gerais and was studying to be a Jesuit when the powerful Prime Minister of Portugal, the Marquis de Pombal, expelled that order from all Portuguese territories in 1759. He continued his studies in Rome, but by 1768 was in Portugal, where he was arrested on suspicion of Jesuitism and exiled to Angola. Da Gama saved himself with a laudatory poem to Pombal's daughter, and structured his O Uraguai [The Uruguay] to conform to the Marquis's policies. He changed tack again when Pombal fell, and remained an honored and respected member of Portuguese society until his death.

Da Gama's Uraguai, set in southern Brazil in the 1750s, mixes fact and fiction in its account of warfare between Spaniards and Portuguese on one side and some 30,000 Indians commanded by Jesuits on the other. Its five cantos of blank verse are very often pure propaganda – but nonetheless are wonderfully resonant, filled with sublime Portuguese heroes, noble Indian allies, and villainous and lascivious Jesuits. The nobility of some of da Gama's Indian characters, in fact, makes him seem a liberal Romantic born before his time, a great precursor of nineteenth-century Brazilian Indianism. However, his treatment of the natives was largely determined by his motives: in order to establish the valor of the Portuguese and Spanish, he had to extol the bravery and warlike virtue of the natives – a beautiful people, like the Indians who came out to meet Caminha in 1500, if only they could be freed from Jesuit domination.

The other epic of the eighteenth century, the Caramuru of José de Santa Rita Durão, published in Lisbon in 1779, is considerably less successful. Durão was born in Minas Gerais in 1722, and educated in Portugal. He entered the Augustinian order, but ran afoul of ecclesiastical politics and was forced to spend a number of years in exile in Italy; he was back in Portugal in 1777, and died there in 1784. His wordy and pedestrian epic, which follows the model of Camões far more closely than does the Uraguai, deals with the early history of Bahia. Durão had never visited that province, but he chose his topic for two very simple reasons: he wanted to glorify the conversion of Brazil's Indians, but was afraid to use the much more suitable theme of Anchieta and the Jesuits; and he remembered very little of his youth in the colony, and found that the best sources for the flora and fauna of his native land were histories and descriptions of the area around Bahia.

The hero of Durão's epic is Diogo Álvares, the central character in a legend which quite closely parallels the North American story of John Smith and Pocahontas. As Durão structures the narrative, Álvares is shipwrecked off Bahia and captured by Indians, who threaten to eat him. He saves himself by firing his gun; this astonishes the natives, who christen him Caramuru, "Son of Thunder," and make him their chief. Álvares falls in love with the beautiful and entirely un-Indian Paraguassu, the native princess, whom Durão describes as:

> De cor tão alva como a branca neve,
> E donde não é neve, era de rosa.
> (*Caramuru* [1961] canto II, v. 78, l. 55)

> [White in color, white as drifted snow,
> And where not snowy, colored like a rose.]

Álvares and Paraguassu are taken to Europe by French traders, and are married before the King and Queen in Paris. The French try to get Álvares's help in conquering Brazil, but he patriotically refuses and he and his bride sail back to Brazil. During a fierce storm at sea, the newly converted Paraguassu has a vision in which a statue of the Virgin shows her the entire history of Brazil into the eighteenth century. That history begins to become reality, at the end of the poem, as Diogo Álvares becomes the first governor of the province of Bahia.

Durão's quite incredible plot is padded with vast chunks of rhymed and metered data on Brazil's geography, plants, animals, birds, and native life. The riches of the land are catalogued at immense length, following the poet's *ufanista* sources, but he is generally unsympathetic toward the Indian inhabitants of this Eden. There are a very few Good Indians like Paraguassu, described as white, well-spoken, aristocratic, and naturally Christian. Against these paragons of virtue and their Portuguese allies stand diabolical Protestants and the masses of animalistic natives, described with curious juxtapositions of intolerant hostility and ethnological erudition:

> Na boca, em carne humana ensangüentada,
> Anda o beiço inferior todo caído,
> Porque a têm toda em roda esburacada,
> E o lábio de vis pedras embutido.
> (canto I, v. 20, l. 24)

> [Blood from human flesh drips down
> From a gaping mouth; the lip hangs low,
> For they have hollowed it all round
> And filled the hole with vile stones.]

Within Brazil, meanwhile, two imported cultural institutions made life at least a little more bearable for those colonial intellectuals unable or unwilling to emigrate: the academy and the Arcady. The tradition of the literary and scientific academy, begun in Italy and transmitted to Brazil through Portugal, was both healthy and utilitarian in the European context. Out of these baroque societies came both a serious interest in the study of history, economics, and science, and the first tentative experiments with self-governance.

However, the academies were marginal institutions in Brazil. The first of these gatherings of isolated intellectuals, founded in Bahia in 1724, admitted its marginality in the name it chose – the Brazilian Academy of the Neglected. The Neglected, the Happy Men, the Reborn Academics all met sporadically, composed their statutes, and laid great plans for the study of literature, history, botany, and zoology. Largely cut off from contemporary developments in Europe and equally alienated from the land they sought to investigate, the academics of Brazil saw most of their projects come to naught – leaving posterity with little more than a handful of bad verse.

Arcadianism appeared in Europe well after the formation of the first academies, but the two movements arrived almost simultaneously in Brazil. As understood in Europe, Arcadianism preached a return to the peaceful joys of Nature and to the purity and simplicity of both thought and diction associated with Greek and Roman verse. In Brazil – and most specifically and importantly in the province of Minas Gerais – neoclassic Arcadianism became both an emotional escape from reality and a catalyst for violence.

Minas, the site of the first great gold rush of modern history, was at least as wild and woolly as early California or the Klondike. The seemingly infinite flow of precious metal and diamonds had slowed to a trickle by the last quarter of the eighteenth century, but economic decline scarcely altered the character of the population – adventurers and prostitutes, criminals and renegade priests. Yet the attractions of great wealth and the complexities of managing that wealth within the colonial system had also brought in some very different settlers – highly educated lawyers and administrators. This group included a few very remarkable poets, as talented as any of their European contemporaries: Tomás Antônio Gonzaga (1744–1810?), Cláudio Manuel da Costa (1729–1789), and Inácio José de Alvarenga Peixoto (1744?–1793).

It is hard, as we read historical accounts of life in Minas Gerais, of whores and fugitive slaves, bar-room brawls and shoot-outs, to imagine these refined and sensitive intellectuals within that context. We can sense the appeal of the isolated and imaginary world these lawyers and bureaucrats created in the verse they wrote above all for themselves, a world that combined the intellectual elitism of the academies with the consoling fantasy of Arcady: a land of peace and well-clipped grass; of lovely nymphs; of the handsome, freedom-loving, and deeply poetic shepherds found in this self-portrait by Gonzaga:

> Eu, Marília, não sou algum vaqueiro,
> Que viva de guardar alheio gado;

De tosco trato, de expressões grosseiro,
Dos frios gelos e dos sóis queimado.
Tenho próprio casal e nele assisto;
Dá-me vinho, legume, fruta, azeite;
Das brancas ovelhinhas tiro o leite,
E mais as finas lãs, de que me visto.

(Marília de Dirceu [1972] 3)

[Marília, I am not some cowherd,
Living to tend another's kine,
Hard-bitten, coarse-mouthed features burned
By endless suns and winter's rime.
I have my own farm; there I dwell;
It gives the wine, the fruit I use.
I drink the milk of snow-white ewes
And weave their wool to dress so well.]

These poets and their friends met in the provincial capital, Vila Rica do Ouro Preto, to talk of literature, to discuss political events in Europe and North America, to read their verses – the sonnets of da Costa (in *Orbas*, 1768), the finest written in Portuguese after Camões; the love poems Gonzaga wrote to the teenaged girl he called Marília, first published as *Marília de Dirceu* in Lisbon in 1792 and still immensely popular; Alvarenga Peixoto's charming verses to his wife, Bárbara Heliodora (in his *Obras poéticas*, 1865). Yet though they called themselves by fanciful names they liked to think had once belonged to shepherds in the Greek pastures of Theocritus, all had been irrevocably marked by the society in which they lived and worked. Alvarenga Peixoto seduced Bárbara Heliodora, the daughter of a close friend, and their daughter was born two years before they married. Marília appears to have given birth to an illegitimate child, paternity unknown, in 1794; Gonzaga, exiled to Mozambique in 1792, prospered in the slave trade there and very probably never wrote another line of verse.

Reality intruded on Arcady in 1789, when the Portuguese authorities in Minas Gerais rounded up a motley group of dissidents, intellectuals, soldiers, and clerics; they were charged with conspiring to utilize the very real local discontent with heavy taxes and autocratic administration as the fulcrum for active revolt against Portugal and in favor of Brazilian independence. Gonzaga and Alvarenga Peixoto were convicted of participation in this abortive uprising, which Brazilians call the *Inconfidência Mineira*, and both were exiled to Africa; Cláudio Manuel da Costa, awaiting trial on similar charges, was found hanged in his cell.

In a more perfect universe, the *Inconfidência* would have triumphed and colonial Brazilian literature would end at the high point of the Arcadian poets of Minas Gerais. In reality, however, Brazil's political and cultural independence owed very little to Arcady, and a great deal to Napoleon. When the French invaded Portugal in 1807, the Portuguese royal family abandoned Lisbon and led a mass exodus – some 15,000 refugees in all – to the security of Brazil. João VI of Portugal ruled from Rio de Janeiro until he returned to Lisbon in 1821, and his presence dramatically transformed the colony: ports were opened to trade with friendly nations, libraries and schools were founded, and the first printing press was established at long last. Within a few months of João's departure, events slowly, peacefully, and inexorably moved toward full political independence under the leadership of his eldest son, who became Pedro I, Emperor of Brazil.

Brazilian literature, during this period from the *Inconfidência Mineira* to Independence, is generally inferior, in both form and content, to the works produced by the Arcadians; it rarely reflects the enormous social, cultural, and political changes taking place in Portugal and Brazil. Gaspar da Madre de Deus (1715–1800), a Benedictine friar, published a massive history of the colonization of São Paulo in Lisbon in 1797. José Elói Otôni (1764–1851) produced verse paraphrases of the Bible; his *Paráfrase dos Provérbios de Salomão em verso português* appeared in Bahia in 1815. Antônio Pereira de Sousa Caldas (1762–1814) managed to combine success in the church with considerable enthusiasm for the theories of Rousseau. Born in Brazil and educated in Portugal, he returned to Brazil with the royal family in 1807, and enjoyed a remarkable contemporary reputation as a preacher and as the author of religious verse; his translation of the Psalms was published in Paris in 1820.

The most interesting of the religious poets who flourished at the very end of the eighteenth century is Francisco de São Carlos (1768–1829). A Franciscan who spent his life in Brazil, São Carlos became a leading preacher in the court chapel after 1807. A few of his sermons have survived, but his reputation depends upon his massive epic, *A Assunção da Santíssima Virgem* – eight cantos of rhymed couplets dedicated to the Virgin and published in Rio de Janeiro in 1819. Many critics today consider it simply unreadable, but readers in the early nineteenth century compared it favorably to the *Divine Comedy* and *Paradise Lost*. I would not dispute José Veríssimo's judgment that it is "one of the most worthless and boring works in our poetry" (*História da literatura brasileira* 115), at least in terms of its monotonous and pedestrian versification, but ideologically it represents a remarkable attempt, at the very end of the colonial period, to return to and revitalize the fantasies of the past. In São Carlos's epic, the Virgin rises into Heaven, witnesses Saint Michael's defeat of Satan, and then describes the Paradise she has entered – in reality the New World Eden of Caminha, its plants and animals clearly Brazilian. She then narrates the tribulations of the first missionaries in Brazil, forging a link with Anchieta and Nóbrega, but moves forward to a description of Rio de Janeiro at the turn of the century and a vision of that city as the future center of the Portuguese-speaking world.

The last three writers who can be classified as part of the colonial period look not toward the past but to the literature of a politically and culturally independent Brazil that was to arise about two decades after 1822 – a literature in which writers of color were to play central roles. Manuel Inácio da Silva Alvarenga (1749–1814) was a mulatto, raised in Minas Geras and educated in Portugal. He returned to his native province, where he participated in the Ouro Preto Arcady, but he moved to Rio de Janeiro in 1782 and thereby escaped the consequences of the *Inconfidência Mineira* seven years later. He taught rhetoric and poetics in the capital, and was imprisoned from 1794 to 1797 for membership of a literary society suspected of subversive discussions. His *Glaura: poemas eróticos* was published in Lisbon in 1799 and re-issued in 1801; after the arrival of the Portuguese court in Rio de Janeiro, he edited one of Brazil's first newspapers, *O Patriota*.

Glaura's rondeaus and madrigals are, at least superficially, very much part of Arcady. Beneath the surface of classical allusions and pastoral fantasies, however, lie elements which foreshadow Brazilian Romanticism: an effort to be simple, even ingenuous rather than clever and erudite; stronger, more openly personal emotionalism; and the use of the native landscape not as an externally observed source of wonder and beauty – in the tradition that stretches from Caminha and the early *ufanistas* to da Gama and Durão – but as a mirror whose primary purpose is to reflect the poet's emotions.

Another mulatto, José da Natividade Saldanha (1796–1830) published his *Poesias oferecidas aos amantes do Brasil* (1822) in Portugal, where he was studying at the University of Coimbra. He returned to Brazil, to Pernambuco, where he practiced law and became one of the leaders of the "Confederation of the Equator," a failed attempt to secede from Pedro I's Empire and form a republic; Natividade Saldanha died in exile in Colombia. His early poems move beyond the limited emotionalism of Silva Alvarenga; they are filled with melancholy complaints of personal distress and with somewhat bombastic exclamations of patriotic fervor focused not upon Brazil but upon Pernambuco. In both his verses and his life, in short, we can see Natividade Saldanha attempting to define himself as the new romantic hero – an icon of emotional alienation and heroic nationalism.

Curiously enough, the most authentically Brazilian voice of the poets of the late eighteenth century spent most of his mature life in Portugal. Domingos Caldas Barbosa (1739?–1800), the very dark son of a Portuguese father and an African mother, was born in Brazil but lived in Lisbon after about 1775. He found powerful patrons there, and his performances of simple songs using poetic and musical forms of African origin made him famous. He was also very much an eighteenth-century intellectual, however, and was one of the founders of the Lisbon New Arcady, where he took "Lereno Selinuntino" as his pastoral name. He wrote neoclassical poems for notable occasions, but his reputation in his own time and today rests entirely upon the lyrics in his *Viola de Lereno*, published in Lisbon in 1798 and reprinted in Bahia in 1813. Several of those lyrics, folkloric in inspiration, eventually reversed the cycle and became folksongs in Brazil.

Caldas Barbosa is constantly aware of his color and his race – and his rivals in Portugal would not have allowed him, in any case, to forget his origins; the poet Bocage called him an "orangutang" (cited in Caldas Barbosa, *Viola* [1980] 22). However, race was not the only factor that made him an anomaly in Arcady. His lyrics openly deny the whole apparatus of Arcadian Neoclassicism – not merely because he is non-white, but because he is a Brazilian, the product of a new world and a new culture. He is not a swan, he tells us, but a parrot; not a shepherd, but

> O teu moleque sou eu,
> Chegadinho do Brasil
> (p. 267)

> [Just your little black boy
> Off the boat from Brazil.]

His use of Indianisms and Africanisms and his gentle melancholy and nostalgia for a world left far behind – like Natividade Saldanha's attempt to cast himself as a romantic hero, like Silva Alvarenga's poet-centered landscapes, like Francisco de São Carlos's effort to recover the vision of Brazil as Eden – are emblems of the independent literature which Brazilian poets and novelists would create in the nineteenth century.

Brazilian poetry from the 1830s to the 1880s
Fábio Lucas

Brazilian poetry of the nineteenth century was strongly influenced by political tensions. From this period forward, the relationship between literature and social values in Brazil would become very intimate. The first political event of consequence to provoke a reaction in the literary arena was the transference of the Portuguese court to Brazil in the years between 1808 and 1820. This resulted in the development of a metropolis–colony and colony–metropolis relationship that was subject to waves of internationalism and to a strong patriotic reaction on the part of the Brazilians.

In 1822, Brazil gained its political independence. This event fed the nativist tendencies of the poets, who took advantage of the circulation of romantic ideas in order to expand their discourse.

The Portuguese upper class, with opportunistic motives in mind, allied itself politically with the aristocratic nobility, the clergy, and the bourgeoisie exporting goods from Brazil. These groups shared a conservative view of the world and showed themselves to be directly or indirectly linked to the latifundia system of exploitation.

However, the lower-middle and middle classes, in alliance with bureaucratic groups, were receptive to the ideas of liberalism, where aspirations of liberty and equality favored the strengthening of the individual's conscience. Nevertheless, this attitude soon experienced moments of disenchantment that would be expressed in the phase of the romantic "spleen." The lack of initiative on the part of the bourgeoisie initially lent itself to a diffuse sense of religion, in which devout Catholicism and a belief in Divine Providence prevailed. All of this combined with a certain sentimental Humanism.

Thus, the inception of Romanticism occurred under the influence of several European and Brazilian tendencies. These tendencies developed as a series of metamorphoses, each characterized by the predominance of thematic and stylistic features drawn from a given period. For example, the first phase of Brazilian Romanticism was marked by the popularity of the indigenous element. The Indian and his civilization were idealized and exalted, resulting in the cultivation of an enchanted vision of nature and the subsequent desire to protect it. This also contributed to a robust and xenophobic patriotism. One of the first things that the Romantics sought to do was to create an epic poem that would narrate, in elevated terms, the deeds of native heroes.

Because of the growing importance of popular forms of writing, the poetic tradition, which had previously been marked by its archaic, rococo and neoclassical roots, yielded to literary modernization. A clear schism was provoked between Portuguese literary expression and a type of composition markedly Brazilian. The ideological forces of the era thus favored the formation of a national consciousness.

Romantic literature's reading public was composed primarily of adolescents and well-to-do women. Because this public was not very demanding, it allowed artists to seek out sources for their work in folk literature, in sentimental fiction, and in melancholy and subjective poetry. These superficial works were open to every sort of concession, since they aimed to please an immature public eager for cheap emotions. This explains the popularity of the romantic writers and their identification with the bourgeois ideals of the prosperous urban classes, with the students, and the slave-mistresses who were kept in an ambiguous relationship with a patriarchal, slave-owning society.

The strength of Romanticism resides in its multifaceted nature. In the case of Brazil, the most important facet was characterized by intense feelings of nationality and the desire to create regional identities. Certain myths and heroes of the past were resuscitated in order to emphasize the romantic ideals of nation, liberty, family, and Nature.

Concentrating on the individual rather than the collective, the theme of love, almost always idealized, became extremely popular, primarily in the expression of young writers. Under the influence of writers such as Byron and De Musset, a generation of precocious and sickly lyric poets emerged. They dealt with pessimism and the *mal du siècle*, imagining declarations of love under a veil of fear. "Fear and love" came to be one of the dialectics most touched upon by the youthful ardor of the second generation of Romantics.

The third generation of poets allowed themselves to be influenced by political themes, especially by the eloquent style of Victor Hugo. The social poetry of the Brazilian Romantics became linked to suggestions of Abolitionism and republican propaganda, in opposition to the imperial–slavocrat model. They cultivated a style that was boldly Brazilian. After the reign of Romanticism, the neo-lusitanian tendency of Parnassianism did not succeed in halting the process of differentiation between the two forms of the language, the Portuguese and the Brazilian.

The patriotic Romanticism of 1836

Two events signal the entry of Romanticism into Brazil: the first was the publication of *Niterói – Revista Brasiliense* (1836) which brought together three friends living in France: Domingos José Gonçalves de Magalhães (1811–1882), Francisco Sales Torres-Homem, and Manuel de Araújo Porto Alegre. The journal was short-lived but called attention to the patriotic side of the generation with its motto, "Everything because of Brazil and for [the good of] Brazil." In the first edition, an article by Gonçalves de Magalhães appeared, inspired by nativist ardor, entitled "Ensaio sobre a história da literatura do Brasil." This essay was originally presented at the Institut Historique de France in 1834, when Gonçalves de Magalhães was admitted as a corresponding member.

The second event that marked the entry of Romanticism into Brazil was the publication of a collection of poetry, *Suspiros poéticos e saudades* (1836) by Gonçalves de Magalhães. This collection is generally recognized in Brazilian literary historiography as having officially introduced Romanticism to Brazil.

The first generation of Romantic poets did not succeed in breaking completely with the preceding Arcadian spirit, characterized by Greco-Roman mythology, pastoral writing, and the rigid composition of strophes and lines, but they had in Gonçalves de Magalhães their first shining star.

Gonçalves de Magalhães

Gonçalves de Magalhães was born in Rio de Janeiro on August 13, 1811, and died in Rome on July 10, 1882. His collection, *Suspiros poéticos e saudades*, revealed his commitment to the poetic renovation that was sweeping Europe. The title itself gave an indication of the subjective sentimentality that lay within. Religious fervor and patriotism dominated Magalhães's thematic production. Myths of liberty and heroism permeated his poems. A good example of this, in spite of its imperfect form, is "Napoleão em Waterloo," which is full of oratorial hyperbole. Magalhães recognized and exalted the messianic or visionary mission of poetry. In his poems, he evoked friends and close relatives and pointed out the value of history and historical figures. He showed, even at this early date, his sympathy for slaves, and called attention to the injustice they suffered. His homeland was of great importance to him and he used his longing for his distant country in poems such as "O dia de ano bom de 1835" and "Suspiros à pátria." This sort of homesick nostalgia became common in Brazilian Romanticism.

Besides being the initiator of Brazilian Romanticism, Gonçalves de Magalhães was highly respected in his time, as a writer – his poetry appeared in three editions between 1836 and 1865, an extraordinary occurrence at that time – and as a public figure. Besides poetry, he also involved himself in theatre and in the writing of philosophical, historical, and literary essays. He even attempted an epic poem, A confederação dos tamoios, centered on the idea of liberty. According to Hélio Lopes (A divisão das águas, p. 215), the hero of this epic poem does not serve any king, does not obey the whims of the gods, and does not descend from divine lineage. He succeeds through his own valor, and submits only to the voice of the land. Gonçalves de Magalhães's epic was received with reservations by José de Alencar, the most popular novelist of the romantic era, resulting in a polemic about the poem. His great admirer, Araújo Porto Alegre, who matured alongside him, wrote an Americanist epic poem, Colombo, extolling the facts of European expansion through the voice of the navigator after whom the poem was named.

Gonçalves Dias

If Gonçalves de Magalhães was considered the initiator of Brazilian Romanticism, then Antônio Gonçalves Dias was consecrated as the greatest poet of this new school. He not only made Romanticism popular, but also gave Indianism its finest expression.

Gonçalves Dias was born on August 10, 1823, in Caxias, Maranhão, the illegitimate son of a Portuguese merchant and his mestizo wife, probably a "cafusa" (a mixture of Indian and African ancestry). He was killed in a shipwreck near Guimarães, Maranhão, on November 3, 1864.

While studying in Portugal, he wrote one of the most famous of Brazilian poems, the "Canção do exílio," the masterpiece of the nostalgic tradition.

In his first book, Primeiros cantos (1846), the best section is the "Poesias Americanas," where we find not only the famous "Canção do exílio," but also songs based on Brazilian Indian life. Americanism and Indianismo [Indianism] thus came to be an integral part of his work.

Indianism has a curious history within Romanticism, one that illustrates the nature of colonial relationships. French Indianism was directly inspired by Brazil. However, Brazilian writers imitated the French, in spite of the existence of their own tradition of popular stories of "caboclo" heroes who use their cunning to outwit Europeans.

Beyond its nativist affirmation, Indianism was utilized by the Brazilian

Romantics as a substitute for the Medieval themes much in fashion in European literature. Nevertheless, in the case of Gonçalves Dias, Indianism has clear political overtones that transcend identification with the remote Indian past.

Primeiros cantos was a great success, and it was followed by *Segundos cantos e sextilhas de Frei Antão* (1848), and by *Ultimos cantos* (1851). In 1857, while in Germany, Gonçalves Dias published his greatest Indianist poem, *Os timbiras*. With this, he brought to Brazilian lyric verse the newness of a poetry that was much more free in its use of versification, strophes, and rhyme.

The great popularity of Gonçalves Dias is due to the fact that he was the first poet to express the themes that most mattered to a people intent upon establishing a national identity. At that time, in Brazil, the word "nation" was laden with emotion. It represented an emotional as well as a physical space.

Given that the romantic spirit fed on escape or flight, whether through time (for example, the return to the Middle Ages) or through space (diaries of travel to exotic regions), the theme of the "pátria ausente" ["distant homeland"] was a focus of poetic inspiration, and was particularly meaningful to the sons of the rural aristocracy and the urban bourgeoisie, who went to Europe in search of education. The "pátria ausente" theme created a climate of remoteness and estrangement mixed with feelings of pain, sadness, and homesickness. All this was perfectly suited to the themes preferred by romantic writers.

Gonçalves Dias's "Canção do exílio," composed during his first trip to Europe, thus enjoyed a degree of fame rare in Brazil's literary history. It is a brief piece made up of lines of seven syllables, with a regular and melodic rhythm that is highly evocative. This poem, free of descriptive adjectives, is based on substantive values evoking, with simplicity, the contrast between life in the homeland and existence in exile.

The lyrical and *indianista* [Indianist] tendencies in Gonçalves Dias's work have received most critical attention. Cassiano Ricardo identifies three poetic genres in Dias's Indianist works: the lyric, in "Leito de folhas verdes"; the dramatic, in "I-Juca-Pirama"; and the epic, in "Os timbiras."

Gonçalves Dias was the first great poet of Brazilian Romanticism who did not pay tribute to the reigning sentimentality. He rejuvenated the language of poetry, although his Portuguese education gave him a strongly neoclassical vision which is particularly evident in the *Sextilhas de Frei Antão*. As Cassiano Ricardo noted, Dias broke with classical circumspection and brought great rhythmic freedom to Brazilian poetry; he also endorsed metrical irregularities and asymmetries that would later be widely accepted.

73

Alvares de Azevedo and the second generation of Romantics

On the heels of the nationalist generation came the introspective poets who were affected overwhelmingly by a bohemian lifestyle and a fantastic pessimism. Byron was in fashion, and his influence, along with that of Alfred de Musset and of Portuguese poets like Soares dos Passos, João de Lemos, and Mendes Leal, can be found everywhere in the large body of poetry produced by young writers during the fourth decade of the nineteenth century. The "mal du siècle" took possession of many poets who, full of inspiration, nonetheless ended up dying very young. Ultra-Romanticism dominated the literary scene during this second poetic generation.

The first great star of the generation was Manuel Antônio Alvares de Azevedo, who was born in São Paulo on September 12, 1831, and died in Rio de Janeiro on April 25, 1852. He lived but twenty-one years. He left a great number of works, all published posthumously: a very popular collection of poems, entitled *Lira dos vinte anos*, which appeared in his *Poesias*; some long dramatic poems, including *Macário* (1855), and *Conde Lopo*; and the fantastic tales of *A noite na taverna* (published in his *Obras*, vol. II). Alvares de Azevedo enrolled in the São Paulo Law School and became involved in a group called the "Sociedade Epicuréia" ["Epicurean Society"], founded in 1845 by students steeped in Byronic delirium. A certain mental instability and derangement filled the minds of these young poets who were unfamiliar with the limits between the real and the imaginary. There are depositions recording incidents of dissipation and even perversion on the part of the Epicureans. Even so, it is not certain whether Alvares de Azevedo was involved in these incidents. Important poets like Bernardo Guimarães, Aureliano Lessa, and Francisco Otaviano also took part in these sessions.

Azevedo's work is dominated by the presence of Satanism, Don Juanism, Epicureanism, and black magic in the style of Byron. These characteristics are not sufficient to guarantee the quality of his verses, but it is important to point out Alvares de Azevedo's contribution to the spirit of the era and how his poetry was filled with the morbid sentiments common to his generation. Brazilian literary history and criticism have duly recorded his contributions to Romanticism. For example, Alvares de Azevedo was the most perfect sonnet writer of Brazilian Romanticism, even though that movement, unlike neoclassical Arcadianism, generally avoided this form. At the same time, he was ahead of his contemporaries in the inclusion of prosaic themes of daily life in his poetic expression.

In his verses, Byronic deliriums found their most elevated and perfect expression. He was able to define the two opposite poles of his spirit:

ironic and amusing play on one hand, and, on the other, a bitter and sad rendition of life. "Spleen e charutos" illustrates the first attitude; "Idéias íntimas" exemplifies the second (both poems from *Lira dos vinte anos*, second part).

A master of escapism, praising the abuse of alcohol and tobacco, Alvares de Azevedo became, as well, one of the greatest singers of the dream-like state. The entire first part of *Lira dos vinte anos* is permeated with the idea of the dream.

Another dominant theme in Alvares de Azevedo's work is death. The poem "Se eu morresse amanhã" is one of the most popular in Brazilian literature. It combines the emotions linked to death with his homesickness for his mother and sister, both the true Muses of his adolescence and important components of his lyricism. In the poem "Vida," he identifies the images of his mother and sister with the beloved. His strong lyricism was also evident in his treatment of the theme of "love and fear," brilliantly analyzed by Mário de Andrade in his *Aspectos da literatura brasileira* as a central *topos* of Brazilian Romanticism, one especially vivid in Alvares de Azevedo and Casimiro de Abreu. The love poetry which predominates in the first part of *Lira dos vinte anos* is matched by his licentious Byronic lyrics, frequently mediated by Musset.

Luís José Junqueira Freire was born in Salvador, Bahia, on December 31, 1832, and died there on June 24, 1855, less than twenty-three years old. He is the author of *Inspirações do claustro* and *Contradições poéticas* (posthumously published in his *Obras poéticas*). In the first work, he sings of the traumas that led him to a cloistered and religious life. In the second work, he attempts, with the same confessional exaggeration, to express the contradictions of lost faith and a tormented life. He also wrote erotic poetry.

Laurindo José da Silva Rabelo was born in Rio de Janeiro on July 3, 1826, and died there on September 28, 1864. He received minor orders in the church and went on to graduate with a degree in medicine. His life was tormented by the successive deaths of his sister, his mother, and his brother, who was murdered.

Laurindo Rabelo was called the "lizard poet." He enjoyed great prestige during this era. His works reveal run-of-the-mill emotions of nostalgia, sadness, love for his mother and sister, all explored in mediocre verses. His poems dedicated to flowers are more varied. During his life he published just one work, *Trovas*. He became a great improviser, which won him a sympathetic audience in bohemian circles, and cultivated a satirical tone.

Bernardo Joaquim da Silva Guimarães was born in Ouro Preto, Minas

Gerais, on August 15, 1825, and returned to die there on March 10, 1884. He graduated from the School of Law in São Paulo and was an active participant in the Epicurean Society, for which he served as mentor.

He made his literary debut with a collection of poetry, *Cantos da solidão*, but was also a prolific novelist, widely read in Brazil. His *Poesias* appeared next, followed by *Novas poesias* and *Folhas de outono*.

Bernardo Guimarães was a poet who interiorized the world and had a tendency to exalt Nature and life. His versification is fluid, melodic, and tends to be very pictorial. He has a unique way of describing landscapes. In the city, he never hesitated to evoke, with nostalgia, the countryside and Nature (see for example, "Cenas do sertão").

He benefited considerably from his reputation as a satirist and knew how to create humorous poems, especially those his companions referred to as being called "bestiological" – an absurd genre of mocking, hermetic, meaningless verses. His famous obscene poem "Elixir do pajé" circulated in clandestine editions.

Aureliano José Lessa was born in Diamantina, Minas Gerais, in 1828, and died in Serro, Minas Gerais, on February 21, 1861. His literary production was collected in *Poesias póstumas*. Aureliano Lessa was a companion of Alvares de Azevedo and Bernardo Guimarães in their unbridled Byronism. He cultivated melancholy verse, punctuated with black humor, self-irony, and jocosity.

Casimiro de Abreu

Casimiro José Marques de Abreu was born in Barra de São João, in what was then the province of Rio de Janeiro, on January 4, 1839. He died on October 18, 1860, in Nova Friburgo, Rio de Janeiro, at twenty-one years of age. The illegitimate son of a Portuguese merchant, he was encouraged to pursue a career in business and left for Lisbon in 1853. Upon returning to Rio de Janeiro in 1854, he began dividing his life between business and poetry. In 1859, at the age of twenty, he published *Primaveras*. Shaped in the romantic mold, he knew how to bring the simplicity of adolescent emotions to his verses. His poetry dealt with his longing for his homeland ("Canção do exílio") and for his home ("No lar"), or with reminiscences of childhood ("Os meus oito anos"). He captured the picturesque side of Nature with colorful language.

Casimiro de Abreu also cultivated a more sentimental lyric poetry, in which one can see the theme of "love and fear." In the poem "Amor e medo" he confesses his desire for love and reveals his inability to realize that dream. Although nurtured by idealizations very similar to those of Alvares de Azevedo, Abreu's lyric poetry wears a more carnal mask, closer to the reality of his feelings, but Azevedo's dramatic force is much stronger and deeper.

The poetry of Casimiro de Abreu enjoyed great popularity in Brazil. His vocabulary is basic, the sentiments that he expresses are not complex, and his phrases are formed with crystalline simplicity. A poem like "Os meus oito anos" has become part of the collective memory of the nation because of the melodic fluidity of its verses.

Thematically, Casimiro de Abreu, in spite of his light and naive tone, is one of the interpreters of the melancholy that had taken possession of Brazilian romantic poets. In the introduction to *Primaveras*, he recognizes that his poems contain "unique manifestations of reflection and study," but also admits the importance of feelings: "it is the heart that overflows over the eternal theme of love."

The son of a Portuguese man, having spent time in Portugal, Casimiro was surely influenced by the Portuguese Romantics. However, his psychological predisposition was opposed to Portugal, since he lived in an environment in rebellion against that nation. Curiously enough, he is one of the best observers of the Nature that surrounded Brazilian Romanticism. In reality, Casimiro de Abreu gave voice to the sufferings of the century, the nostalgia, the unhappiness of love, the longing for the homeland, and the threat of imminent death, without, however, complicating those themes.

Fagundes Varela

Luís Nicolau Fagundes Varela was born on August 17, 1841, in Santa Rita do Rio Claro, in what was then the province of Rio de Janeiro, and died on February 18, 1875, in Niterói, Rio de Janeiro.

The work of Fagundes Varela is vast, and is divided into several thematic groupings. For example, the patriotic zeal that was so insistent in the first romantic writers is treated with notable fervor in his work. He began his career influenced by several literary movements, assimilating both Byronic inclinations and the Indianism of Gonçalves Dias. Even the social poetry of the final phase of Brazilian Romanticism eventually influenced some of his work.

Fagundes Varela was also touched by religious inspiration, as is evident in one of his most famous works, *Anchieta ou o evangelho nas selvas*, in which he describes the role of the missionary José de Anchieta in the colonization of Brazil. This is a long, confused, and thematically deficient poem, written in blank verse.

However, Fagundes Varela stands out for his clear descriptions of the flora and fauna of Brazil, and is, perhaps, the most pictorial of the romantic poets.

Noturnas, his first work, shows the influences of his predecessors, Gonçalves Dias, Alvares de Azevedo, and Casimiro de Abreu. From time to time it also foreshadows the *condoreirismo* of Castro Alves – a very eloquent form of expression, daring in its use of similes and metaphors, of social concerns, the most important of which was the issue of Abolition.

Technically, Fagundes Varela adopted more regular rhythms, decasyllabic and roundel meters drawn from popular tradition, which mark him as a transitional figure between Romanticism and Parnassianism.

Cantos e fantasias is regarded as his most successful work. In this book, curiously, he is at his very best in "Cântico do Calvário," a poem based on a real event, the death of his son. Through the use of blank verse, he is able to bring to life the drama of his loss and communicate the pain of the child's death.

The general tone of *Cantos e fantasias* reflects the poet's situation as he confronts the difficulties of his life. Yet it also reveals that religion is his consolation. Spiritualist poetry is what gave meaning to his life. It is important to point out that in the "Cântico do Calvário," Fagundes Varela approaches the theme of death in impersonal tones, tones of transcendence, of reflection on the destiny of man beyond this world.

He went on to publish *Cantos meridionais* and *Cantos do ermo e da cidade*. However, it is in *Anchieta ou o evangelho nas selvas* that he expanded upon his religious feelings; he wrote it when he left the city where he had problems with alcoholism and a bohemian lifestyle, taking refuge in the countryside.

In the poetry of Fagundes Varela, the urban vision is never in conflict with his rural heritage. He knew how to deal with these two poles of culture, presenting them through the eyes of a brilliant and imaginative poet, faithful to the portrait of the landscape.

Having produced a large and uneven body of work, his poetry seems to be the point where ideas typical of Romanticism merged with the painful expression of a life full of repeated failures.

Fagundes Varela also dedicated himself to the exaltation of his homeland, especially in *O estandarte auriverde* and *Vozes da América*. In *O estandarte auriverde*, he writes topical poetry, expressing his opposition to England's role in the Christie Question, halting the importation of slaves, and to all the English meddling in the affairs of Brazil's Second Empire. This theme was popular in his day, and Fagundes Varela in his own way gave voice to the soul of the people. It should be noted that he lived during a period in which patriotism was flourishing and there was great concern for social problems. The war with Paraguay (1864–1870) left deep scars on the Brazilian sensibility.

Vozes da América, on the other hand, contains poems of liberal inspiration ("Napoleão," for example), and prefigures the participatory fervor of Castro Alves and his imitators.

Finally, Fagundes Varela also turned his attention to the question of slavery, as we see in the poem "Mauro, O escravo."

Castro Alves and the third generation of romantic poets

Eventually, tearful sentimentalism lost its ability to move readers. An influx of new political and social ideas, along with the tumultuous process of national affirmation, which included both political agitation and the war with Paraguay, came to motivate a new language within Romanticism.

The fiery, declamatory poems of Victor Hugo found an echo in young Brazilian students, especially those studying law in the city of Recife. The *hugoanista* style quickly swept up the poet, orator, polemicist, and thinker Tobias Barreto de Meneses (1839–1889), whose works were soon forgotten despite the best efforts of the influential critic and historian Sílvio Romero. However, the emotional and high-flown poetry of Antônio Frederico de Castro Alves embodied to perfection the literary current closest to Hugo, generating a truly original style in Brazilian Romanticism, *Condoreirismo*.[1]

Castro Alves was born on March 14, 1847, in Curralinho, Bahia, and died in Salvador, Bahia, on June 6, 1871; he lived only twenty-four years. He gave a new voice to Romanticism, expressing an emphatic, optimistic, and confrontational vision of the world. He did not limit himself to poems demanding justice, poems in which the problem of slavery received special attention. He also included the accomplishments of civilization, like the book, the printing press, important social movements, and, as a good Romantic, the exaltation of liberty. The idea of progress also comes up frequently in his work, bringing to his verses the dynamism that propelled the nineteenth-century mentality and which motivated his French master, Victor Hugo. He was ambitious, with a sense of the monumental and the cosmic. Everything was oratorial, using hyperbolic rhetorical devices, and the public loved it.

Castro Alves quickly learned how to conquer an audience. His gifts of communication were extraordinary. He enjoyed great success when he visited Rio de Janeiro, encouraged by Machado de Assis. He was also received enthusiastically in São Paulo. Public opinion quickly welcomed

---

[1] Editors' note: the name of this movement refers to the Andean condor, a frequent image in the poetry of Castro Alves and his disciples; for these writers, the condor was an emblem of Americanism, of liberty, of free-ranging social concerns, and of verse that consistently sought emotional heights. (D. T. Haberly)

the fervent message of this new poet. However, to this day, critics complain of verbal excesses in certain poems by Castro Alves, claiming that, had he controlled the rhetorical avalanche a bit more, he would have produced a more enduring corpus of social poetry.

Castro Alves's abolitionist poetry contains great moments of humanitarian inspiration, but his poetic flights are at times impaired by the grotesqueness of certain images and by the redundancy of many similes. In spite of this, his poem "O navio negreiro," highly dramatic (in terms of narrative) and even deeply moving, enjoyed great popularity.

In the work of Gonçalves Dias, it was the plight of the Indian that was strategically employed in order to establish a national ideology. His heroism was the material for fiction or idealization. In Castro Alves's political rhetoric, the slave was used to defy the most powerful social class, the slave-owning large landowners. In a society based upon slavery, Alves made the slave a hero.

Very much involved in the pursuit of love, Alves also produced some of the most beautiful lyric poems of his literary school. His lyricism deserves special recognition because it culminates in real passion, at a time when love was no more than a topic for idealization. Casimiro de Abreu and Alvares de Azevedo associated love with the sensation of fear and they turned the possibility of love into a state of suffering. With Castro Alves we see a different treatment of this theme. His passion was born of his amorous encounters and carnal experiences. "Adormecida," for example, drips sensuality as he plays with the images of a flower and a sleeping woman. "Boa noite" reviews the different women that passed through his life. Reading this poem, one cannot help but notice the force of the amorous inspiration. In other compositions, Castro Alves allows the reader to leap from the dark regions of defeat to the bright world of realized dreams. In the works in which he recalled his unfulfilled aspirations and frustrated desires, Castro Alves still gave his poems the force of a positive and accomplishing disposition. He was far removed from the second generation of Romantics, who were characterized as the voices of dejection, contemplative idleness, and unhappiness.

Even in his poems of great breadth it is possible to point out moments of sublime artistic realization. In "Cachoeira de Paulo Afonso," for example, "Crepúsculo sertanejo" stands out because of its rhythmic texture and the descriptive charm of its natural setting.

Some bibliographic data will help to clarify what Castro Alves accomplished. The great love of his life, the actress Eugênia Câmara, whom he met in Recife and who accompanied him to Rio de Janeiro and São Paulo, left an indelible mark on his poetry. He challenged the moral attitudes of an incredibly conservative and prejudiced society by presenting himself in public with his mistress. The play *Gonzaga ou a Inconfidên-*

cia Mineira (1875) was written for Eugênia. In 1868 he left with her for São Paulo, where he enrolled in his third year of law school. That very same year she abandoned him. Soon after, he had an accident while hunting and wounded his foot. He was taken to Rio, operated on and could not return to Bahia until 1870. He had a few more opportunities to appear in public, but illness spread throughout his body and he soon died. The illness that he suffered and the limitations to which he was subject did not depress him, but they did bring touches of melancholy to his work.

He published *Espumas flutuantes* during his lifetime. Several books were published posthumously: *Gonzaga ou a Inconfidência Mineira*, *A cachoeira de Paulo Afonso*, *Vozes d'Africa*, and *Os escravos*. *Espumas flutuantes* is considered by some critics and historians, among them Antônio Soares Amora (*O Romantismo*, *A literatura brasileira*) as marking the end of Brazilian Romanticism. The book is also one of the masterpieces of that Romanticism.

Castro Alves's social poetry became outdated as Brazil moved beyond many of the problems of his time. His *"hugoanismo,"* and particularly that of his disciples, infected Brazilian poetry, deeply affected by the Paraguayan war, with a superabundance of declamatory phrases, antitheses, and masculine rhymes; this infection disfigured poetic discourse, giving it an undesirable oratorical tone.

However, his lyrical poetry, fully exalting emotion and strongly sensual, continues to be among the best Brazil has produced. Not only does it reflect his personal life, but also one finds, as the result of stylistic and thematic contamination, a whole series of romantic archetypes, taken from such immediate predecessors as Alvares de Azevedo, Casimiro de Abreu, and Fagundes Varela.

Sousândrade

Among the Brazilian Romantics, there is one isolated figure who is difficult to classify: Joaquim de Sousa Andrade, who signed himself Sousa Andrade, Sousa-Andrade, or Sousândrade. The use of the rare proparoxytone accent in the name "Sousândrade" lends an air of strangeness even to the name of the poet.

Sousândrade was born in Alcântara, Maranhão, on July 4, 1833, and died in São Luís, Maranhão, on April 20, 1902, after a period of sickness and abandonment. It is said that, deranged and a pauper, he was publicly stoned.

He was a republican who had lived in Europe and had moved to New York in order to educate his daughter. With the advent of the Republic, he began to design a new flag for the state of his birth, with three colors – white, black, and red – symbolizing the three races that formed Brazil. His first work, *Harpas selvagens* (1857) is still imbued with the tedium and pessimism of the era. However, *Guesa errante: poema americano* (1866) reveals a bizarre and innovative poet.

The novelty of Sousândrade's poetry lies in its disconcerting structure. Far removed from the typical sentimentality of the age, he achieves a certain imagistic objectivity through the fusion of different signs and of different languages, and through the stunning formation of neologisms.

His reintroduction into Brazilian literature is due in part to Fausto Cunha, who mentioned him in *A literatura brasileira* (1968), organized by Afrânio Coutinho. However, those mainly responsible are Augusto de Campos and Haroldo de Campos, who published an anthology of his work, accompanied by an interpretative essay: *Re-visão de Sousândrade*. Unfortunately, the anthology, by focusing on the high points of Sousândrade's poetry, makes it impossible to study all the different phases of his inspiration. These phases were irregular and asymmetrical and, at the end of his life, provide evidence of his steady decline.

Brazilian poetry from 1878 to 1902
Massaud Moisés

Although romantic poetry continued to be cultivated during the 1870s, it was showing signs of weariness, and a new poetic discourse began to emerge in reaction to it. In 1870, Sílvio Romero (1851–1914) published a series of articles – later collected in the fourth volume of the third edition of his *História da literatura brasileira* (5 vols., 1943) – in *Crença*, a Recife newspaper. In those articles, Romero attacked "the exaggerated *sentimentalism* and the decrepit *Indianism* of the *Harpejos poéticos* of Santa Helena Magno, the stentorian *Hugoanism* of Castro Alves' *Espumas flutuantes*, the *subjectivist* lyricism and the *pretentious humor* of the *Falenas* of Machado de Assis." This reaction against Romanticism rapidly acquired republican and anti-monarchist overtones, visible as early as 1872 in the *Névoas matutinas* (Rio de Janeiro) of Lúcio de Mendonça (1854–1909).

While not the direct causes of these changes, the erotic poetry of Charles Baudelaire (1821–1867), the 1865 Coimbra Question (a dispute between hardened Romantics and the academic generation of Coimbra, known for its revolutionary ideas), and the secretive realist lectures given at the Lisbon Casino in 1871 all greatly stimulated the poetic metamorphosis taking place in Brazil during the 1870s.

The year 1878 was a true watershed. Inspired by what he called "philosophical conceptualism" and "scientific poetry,"[1] Sílvio Romero published his *Cantos do fim do século* in Rio de Janeiro. The fact that Romero's poetry did not completely match the postulates he had set forth in 1870 was duly noted by Machado de Assis (1839–1908) in "A nova geração" (published in the *Revista Brasileira*, Rio de Janeiro, no. 2, Dec. 1, 1879), his famous study summing up the new generation. In spite of

---

[1] Strongly influenced by the belief that science was the means to solve all human problems, "scientific poetry" was practiced by those poets who thought that they could alter the human condition through their verses. They proposed a socially committed poetry and looked down on the vague expression of an individual's state of mind.

Machado's comments, Romero's message was echoed in the works of several other, lesser poets, notably José Isidoro Martins Júnior (1860–1904). Martins Júnior is known both for the "scientific poetry" he put into practice in *Visões de hoje* (1881) and for his proselytizing pamphlet *A poesia científica: escorço de um livro futuro* (1883).

The leading slogans and concepts of this period are "realism," the "new poetry," the veneration of the idea, and the alliance between poetry and science. The so-called "New Idea" quickly developed a political context, identifying liberty as the "Muse of the Strong," exalting the Republic, advocating Abolition, espousing Socialism, and struggling against the monarchy. Lúcio de Mendonça collected his political compositions from 1873 to 1889 in *Vergastas* (1889). Thus what Valentim Magalhães (1859–1903) dubbed "The Civic Muse or School of the Jackal" in his *A literatura brasileira* (1896) took the center of the stage. One of the best examples is *O régio saltimbanco* (1877), by Antônio da Fontoura Xavier (1856–1922), a pamphlet attacking the monarchy and Pedro II in alexandrine verses. On the other hand, the erotic strain in the poetry of the period, Baudelairean in its origins, is evident in the poems of Francisco Antônio Carvalho Júnior (1855–1879), collected in *Escritos póstumos/Parisina* (1879), as well as in many other works.

Also in 1878, the "Battle for Parnassus" was waged in the pages of the *Diário do Rio de Janeiro*. On one side were the followers of "old Romanticism"; on the other, the adherents of the "New Idea," who repudiated "dull, cold, wan lyricism," took justice as their cause, and followed the "modern ideal [that] has science as its center." In 1880, Augusto de Lima (1859–1934), who had already embraced scientific or realist poetry (see his *Contemporâneas* [1887], *Símbolos* [1892], *Poesias* [1909]), mocked romantic lyricism in the São Paulo *Revista de Ciências e Letras*.

Without realizing or intending it, the adepts of the "New Idea" were in fact perpetuating the romantic aesthetic, merely inverting its terms. Their iconoclastic ardor, essentially subjective rather than scientific or rational, was similar to the early Romantics' aversion to the ideas of Neoclassicism. This can be seen in the *Lira dos verdes anos* (1878) of Teófilo Dias (1854–1889), which exudes romantic lyricism from the title on; that lyricism slowly diminished, of course, but never completely disappeared in Dias's subsequent works (*Cantos tropicais* [1878], *Fanfarras* [1882]), in which one can see foreshadowings of the Parnassian renovation of poetry.

Other foreshadowings of the advent of Parnassianism can be found in the years that followed 1878, as a theory of poetry centered on a veneration for science was replaced by doctrines and practices that were strictly aesthetic in character. In the works of Antônio Cândido Gonçalves Crespo (1846–1883), a Brazilian poet who emigrated to Portugal and later came to be included in that nation's literature (*Miniaturas* [1871], *Noturnos* [1882]), and of Luís Guimarães (1845–1898) (*Sonetos e rimas* [1880]), the search for formal perfection as a counterbalance to the romantic tendency toward careless verse and an intellectual effort to avoid romantic sentimentality both became apparent.

This literary current remained nameless until the Portuguese writer Fialho de Almeida (1857–1911) referred to Luís Guimarães as a "Parnassian" in his preface to the second edition of Guimarães's *Sonetos e rimas* (1886). The popularization of this term as a label for the new poetic modality thus dates from 1886. Nonetheless, it is known that from 1882 on the Brazilian critic Tristão de Alencar Araripe Júnior (1848–1911) was aware of the term Fialho de Almeida later applied.

At the same time, other works of poetry hinted at the new winds that were blowing in the 1880s. *Sinfonias*, by Raimundo Correia (1859–1911), and *Meridionais* and *Sonetos e poemas*, by Alberto de Oliveira (1857–1937) show evidence of the gradual rejection of romantic excesses and simultaneous resistance to scientific poetry. By 1888, when Olavo Bilac (1865–1918) published his *Poesias* in São Paulo, one can say that Parnassianism had defined itself and come to dominate Brazilian letters.

What were the Parnassian writers trying to do? Their sources were *Le Parnasse contemporain, recueil de vers nouveaux*, published in Paris in three volumes, in 1866, 1869, and 1876 respectively. These volumes contained the poems of Théophile Gautier, Théodore de Banville, Leconte de Lisle, and others. Like their French models, the Brazilian Parnassianists adopted the principle of "Art for Art's Sake" and the veneration of form. They turned their backs on historical and social reality; they rejected romantic individualism and sought the dispassion that would allow them to make the poem an object derived from the ancient classical past. Craft and erudition took the place of inspiration. "Profissão de fé" (1886), the poem that opens Olavo Bilac's *Poesias*, firmly based on Gautier's Parnassian decalogue "L'Art" (*Emaux et camées* [1852]), is a lapidary summation of the aims of his generation. Bilac here proposes, among other things, an aesthetic program:

> Seduz-me um leve relicário
>   De fino artista.
> Invejo o ourives quando escrevo:
>   Imito o amor
> Com que ele, em ouro, o alto-relevo
>   Faz de uma flor.
>
>   ....
>
> Por isso, corre, por servir-me,
>   Sobre o papel

> A pena, como em prata firme
>   Corre o cinzel.
>   ....
>
> Torce, aprimora, alteia, lima
>   A frase; e, enfim,
> No verso de ouro engasta a rima,
>   Como um rubim.
>
> Quero que a estrofe cristalina,
>   Dobrada ao jeito
> Do ourives, saia da oficina
>   Sem um defeito:
>   ....
>
> Assim procedo. Minha pena
>   Segue esta norma.
> Por te servir, Deusa serena,
>   Serena Forma!

> [I am seduced by the delicate reliquary of a fine artist.
> I envy the goldsmith when I write:
> I imitate the love with which he works in gold
> to make the contours of a flower.
>   ....
>
> For this reason, my pen runs over the paper to serve me
> as the chisel runs in solid silver.
>   ....
>
> It turns, improves, heightens, polishes
> the phrase; and finally
> In the golden verse it sets the rhyme
> as a ruby.
>
> I want the crystalline strophe
> Duplicated with the skill of the goldsmith
> To come out of the workshop
> without a defect:
>   ....
>
> This is how I proceed.
> My pen follows this principle.
> To serve you, serene goddess
> of the serene form!][2]

As always, there is considerable distance between theory and practice. The adherents of this extreme formalism rarely achieved their ideal of

---

[2] As the essay has stated, the Parnassian poets focused their efforts on form first. The translations included here paraphrase the poems and their vocabulary as closely as possible, but do not reproduce their forms.

poetry as sculpted marble, valid for its style alone and free from sentiment and subjectivity. When they did achieve that ideal, they wound up banishing poetry from their verses, unwittingly replacing it with insipid metrical prose. Most of the time, they created artifacts whose highly polished form encases emotions – particularly emotions related to love poetry – whose romantic antecedents are readily recognizable. Thus one gets the feeling that, when these writers managed to create works worthy of being termed poems, the sculptured form of those works actually facilitated their expression of the emotions they were so energetically trying to banish from poetry. In short, these writers were still Romantics (if we define Romanticism as the centrality of the poet's voice and emotions) who expressed themselves with rigorous metrical perfection. Due to this combination of sentiment and form, they were Romantics who were more controlled than those of the generations between 1836 and 1878, but they were not more inspired as a result: their focus on form often constrained or distorted the emotional flow of their poems, above all when form was applied unimaginatively or badly; this is most evident in the works of those successors and disciples who lacked originality.

Among the fairly large number of Parnassian adherents, four names stand out. The first is Alberto de Oliveira, whose long life – eighty years – produced an extensive poetic opus. In addition to *Meridionais* and *Sonetos e poemas*, he published *Canções românticas* and *Versos e rimas*; he then collected these and other books of verse into four series, published under the title of *Poesias completas*. The volume *Póstuma* appeared after his death. Alberto de Oliveira lived the longest of the Parnassian poets and, perhaps for that reason, was one of the most productive during his fifty years of literary activity. Three separate styles appear during that long period: romantic lyricism predominates in the first of these, represented by his early books, particularly *Meridionais*; the second, visible in the *Livro de Ema* and *Por amor de uma lágrima* (both from 1912), shows evidence of symbolist influence; the third, Parnassian style, found in the largest number of poems and persisting over the longest period, is present in all of his other works.

It is noteworthy that the volume *Canções românticas*, which displays its aesthetic affiliation even in its title, reveals a temperament, a propensity that Parnassian formalism stifled or camouflaged. This is why critics have seen in him, and not just on the basis of his early works, "an elegiac poet – continuously forced to exercise Parnassian objectivity" (Eugênio Gomes, "Alberto de Oliveira"), or a "Romantic in disguise" (Geir Campos). In reality, like the other Parnassian poets, Alberto de Oliveira did clothe his romantic lyricism in sculpted bronze. However, unlike them, he carried the doctrine of dispassion and the veneration of mythology and classicism to extremes; as a result, he often chose stylistic solutions which impoverished – if not obscured – the meaning of his verse. This led him to create poems that seem to be versified prose, like the well-known "Vaso grego" in *Sonetos e poemas*. In such works, his vision is that of the sculptor or the painter of still-lifes, seeing the world as an infinite landscape of forms which do not necessarily carry meaning. Here Oliveira achieves the Parnassian ideal of true art, but in so doing irrevocably destroys his link to true poetry. Objectivity, poorly conceived and poorly practiced, dragged even his narrative or topical verse down to the level of poetic journalism devoid of feeling.

In general, however, there is a lyric pulse beating beneath the cloak of formalism. And, contrary to what one might expect, given the Parnassian tendency toward sensuality, particularly based on mythological situations, one can glimpse a tendency, like that of the Romantics, toward the platonic sentiment. When Oliveira does occasionally try his hand at the sensual, his inaptitude is evident in the bad taste of the images and the situations he creates; examples include the third sonnet of the third canto of *Alma em flor* (1905) and "A camisa de Olga" in *Versos e rimas*. Elsewhere he tried to cultivate a sensuality based on chance, derived primarily from books he had read rather than from real experiences; an example is "Um átomo," found in the *Livro de Ema*.

In any case, over time it is emotion which predominates in Oliveira's poetry, even though he confesses that he is striving to hide it (see "Confidência," in *Versos e rimas*). The evolution of his verse shows that Parnassian formal rigor, taken literally, implied violence against true poetry. This contradiction, resistant to the strategies of intellect and sensibility alike, characterized the whole Parnassian movement; Oliveira, who became a kind of prototype of the movement, suffered from all its limitations and inconsistencies. Not even his late realization of all this, which can be seen from the very beginning of the last series of *Poesias*, is enough to redeem his opus. Error had already produced irreversible effects, the result of a doctrine defensible as theory but inoperable, when strictly applied, in practice. A craftsman of supreme ingenuity – more so than any of his contemporaries – Alberto de Oliveira is the prime example, in Brazilian literature, of useless sacrifice to the goddess of Form.

Raimundo Correia left a much smaller body of work than did Alberto de Oliveira – *Primeiros sonhos*, *Sinfonias*, *Versos e versões*, and *Aleluias*; selected poems from these works were collected in *Poesias*. That work, unlike that of Oliveira, is marked by heterodoxy. Correia's adherence to Parnassianism seems the result of a misunderstanding, the result of fashion or of the literary environment in which he was educated. That Correia was aware of his mistake is clear from an undated letter, written to his friend Rodolfo Leite Ribeiro and included in his *Poesia completa e prosa*; in it he declared that he felt " completely destroyed by the ill effects of this school they call Parnassian, whose crippled and ricketic creations show all the signs of decadence and appear condemned, from birth, to death and oblivion . . . The course that you are pointing out to me is the one I should have followed, the one I unfortunately stopped following. The sun of the future is going to rise from the territory to which you are headed, not from the territory through which the rest of us have so far wandered."

Correia realized too late that he was bound, however schismatically, to Parnassian doctrine. He would have done better to listen to his inner voices, which called him to other solutions, solutions not always adopted because he had not yet fully considered his attachment to Parnassianism. The trajectory of Correia's work clearly expresses this fundamental ambiguity; that same ambiguity, however, sometimes produced first-rate poetry as a result of the psychic tension and the existential drama that inform it. It is therefore understandable that Agripino Grieco, a critic not given to easy praise (quite the opposite, in fact), came to consider Correia "the best of the Parnassians," and that Manuel Bandeira, a poet and essayist of great importance, included him among the "greatest poetic artists in our language." The fact is that Raimundo Correia was unquestionably the richest source of poetry in Brazilian Parnassianism, despite the limitations this literary tendency imposed – its quest for dispassion, formalism, and objectivity.

Raimundo Correia's first work, *Primeiros sonhos*, is romantic in nature; this is not surprising, given the persistence of romantic values throughout the second half of the nineteenth century. Nonetheless, alongside less vibrant poems, characterized by the timidity and imitativeness to be expected given the author's age – these are "the first fruits of youth," as he observes in the preface to this volume – one finds other works which foreshadow the author's trademark style and indicate his literary affiliations. Examples are the sonnet "A idéia nova," and "Epicédio," filled with a pessimism akin to that of the Portuguese poet Antero de Quental.

However, the impact of Parnassianism, all in all, overwhelmed these personal tendencies. Correia's second collection of poetry, *Sinfonias*, conformed to the new literary fashion, but did so in a way that saved it from the formalist artificialism then in vogue. Correia was able, perhaps better than any of his contemporaries, to achieve the perfect balance between his poetic form – which was lapidary and classical without being sculptural – and his personal conflict, which had a larger human and aesthetic dimension. The book opens with a very well-known poem, "As pombas," inevitably included in every anthology of Brazilian verse. In a poetic climate of melancholy, of *carpe diem*, of "Never More," the writer somehow emblematizes his skeptical vision of reality, a vision instantly communicated to the reader's sensibility; it is as if the reader thereby catches a glimpse of the collective consciousness of the whole Brazilian people or of a surface that mirrors an ageless archetype. A *topos* of nostalgia, the poem in one stroke fuses concrete reality and the tormented ego of the poet, making the feelings expressed universal. A number of other poems in this book are in the same key, evidence that it is here – in the transmission of this cosmic pain and in the formal perfection in which it is clothed – that the central source of Correia's poetry lies. One can see, as well, that the poet's melancholy move toward Nature, as if the latter were a prolongation of the ego, or vice versa, finally assumes the character of mysticism – in some ways the inversion of the despair the pain of melancholy generates. This eagerness to believe, despite his somewhat less ephemeral certainty, links Raimundo Correia to Antero de Quental and the Brazilian Cruz e Sousa, for whom art was a channel to – or even a substitute for – a transcendence denied or not yet attained.

Correia's *topos* of melancholy is also structured as an antithesis between the poet's ego and his masks, creating an anguished expressionism; this can be seen in one of Correia's best poems and one of the best poems of the period, "Mal secreto," written in a pure symbolist style reminiscent of Cruz e Sousa:

> Se a cólera que espuma, a dor que mora
> N'alma e destrói cada ilusão que nasce,
> Tudo o que punge, tudo o que devora
> O coração, no rosto se estampasse;
>
> Se se pudesse, o espírito que chora,
> Ver através da máscara da face,
> Quanta gente, talvez, que inveja agora
> Nos causa, então piedade nos causasse!
>
> Quanta gente que ri, talvez, consigo
> Guarda um atroz, recôndito inimigo,
> Como invisível chaga cancerosa!
>
> Quanta gente que ri, talvez existe,
> Cuja ventura única consiste
> Em parecer aos outros venturosa!

> [If the anger that froths, the pain that lives
> in the soul and destroys each illusion that is born,
> All that it pierces, all that the heart devours
> Is imprinted on the face;

If one could see the spirit that cries
inside the mask that is the face,
How many people, perhaps, who cause us envy now,
Would cause us pity instead!

How many people who laugh, perhaps,
Keep inside an atrocious, concealed enemy
Like an invisible cancerous wound!

How many people who laugh, perhaps exist,
Whose only good fortune consists
in appearing fortunate to others!]

This sort of desperation, ethical and philosophical in character, is not only non-existent in Parnassianism (a consequence of the movement's hide-bound aestheticism), but is rare indeed in Brazilian literature as a whole. It endured throughout Raimundo Correia's whole career, even though titles like *Sinfonias* or *Aleluias* suggest a festive joy incompatible with the nihilism of Antero de Quental or Promethean suffering. It was here that Correia found his own way of being a poet, and it is this that sets him apart from the other Brazilian Parnassianists and ties him to the greatest of our poets – particularly to Cruz e Sousa and, in some ways, to Augusto dos Anjos. (The works of Augusto dos Anjos are discussed in Chapter 11.) In short, Symbolism was Correia's true vocation, and his poetry moved rapidly toward it; this can be seen in "Plenilúnio," which appears the product of a true Symbolist, a Symbolist whose adherence to that movement is not superficial but, rather, congenital. When Correia fulfilled his vocation, he created one of the most mature and intense bodies of poetic work produced during the last quarter of the nineteenth century.

The poetic works of Olavo Brás Martins dos Guimarães Bilac, played in a similar key, include *Panóplias*, *Via Láctea*, and *Sarças de fogo*, which were collected in *Poesias*; the second edition of *Poesias* added *Alma inquieta*, *As viagens*, and *O caçador de esmeraldas*. The volume *Tarde* was published posthumously.

In 1907, when he was crowned "The Prince of Brazilian Poets," Olavo Bilac achieved the height of fame. However, because he was the incarnation of Parnassianism, in all of its irreconcilable contradictions, Bilac also became the favorite target for those disaffected with Parnassianism, most notably in the attacks mounted by the participants in the *modernista* [modernist] movement against the defenders of Parnassus. The fact is that Bilac, perhaps more than any of his contemporaries, fell into the trap his famous "Profissão de fé" set: by temperament and taste, he was a romantic writer of amorous lyrics, but he wound up writing a didactic hymn in which he proclaimed his willingness to die " in the cause of Style" and to fight for "the Serene Form." Bilac navigated between two fatal extremes – obedience to sentiment, to the feelings he possessed, thereby denying the dispassion and formalism Parnassianism required, or holding fast to his profession of faith and necessarily repressing his amorous and lyrical instincts. When Olavo Bilac managed to achieve harmony between his innermost inclinations, romantic in nature, and his conscious choice to seek "Art for Art's Sake," he became one of the clearest and most musical poetic voices of his time.

In Bilac's less harmonious moments, peripheral themes were the rule. Some were borrowed, in the name of objectivity, from Brazilian history (O caçador de esmeraldas), from classical antiquity (Rome, Nero, and so on), and from other authors (Goethe, Calderón, Bocage). When emotion is present in these works, it either appears foreign, derived from his external source, or seems suffocated, constrained by the straitjacket of form; the "I" of the poem never establishes an empathetic link to the topic that inspired it. Even a poem designed to be resonantly patriotic, like O caçador de esmeraldas, all in all becomes no more than a rhymed account of the colonial expedition of Fernão Dias Paes Leme.

In the same way, when Bilac chose Greek or Roman scenes permeated with sensuality as his inspiration – like "O julgamento de Frinéia," "Satânia," or "A tentação de Xenócrates" – the fidelity with which he portrays the scene highlights its artificiality. Despite the solemnity and sheen of his language, the polish and clarity of his verses, the sensuality is artificial, insincere. The eroticism of the situations he presents never arouses the poet, and therefore is not communicated to the reader. Finally, this sensuality belongs to these historical events, not to the poet; it is a secondhand sensuality, the result of an *imitatio* of classical texts rather than a transfiguration of the poet's own experience. While a poet less constrained by doctrinal devotion and more attuned to his inner self could have managed to identify himself with these scenes from the past or to project his experiences upon them, Bilac cannot do so; he remains a spectator.

Nevertheless, there are some poems by Bilac that show another, different facet, one characterized by internal vibrancy and existential scope. In such works, as if casting aside sterile and marmoreal formalism, Bilac reaches heights which set him apart from others of his generation and which make him the equal of the greatest lyric poets of the Brazilian tradition. This facet, sometimes latent and sometimes explicit in the poet's literary itinerary, reaches its climax in Via Láctea, a series of thirty-five sonnets and the fruit of toil and inspiration. Despite the presence of less felicitous poetic solutions within the work, it is obvious that this kind of Dante's Vita Nuova best captures and communicates lyrical and amorous emotions when it is most concrete in its form, its strophes of model simplicity. The ambience of these poems recalls the world of a troubadour singing songs of a love shaped by real sensuality, a restrained love, encased in the code of vasselage and harmonically linked to the obsessive confession of amorous conquest. The poet was attentive here, as nowhere else in his works, to the romantic and Platonic underpinnings of his vision of the world, symbolized by the recurrence of the word "star," referring here to a guide or a prefiguration of death.

Probably the product of a real experience, the breaking-off of Bilac's engagement to Alberto de Oliveira's sister, *Via Láctea* escaped inauthenticity thanks to its imaginative transfiguration of this sentimental episode and the verbal polish applied to its recounting. In effect, one senses the pulse of life deep inside the poet and the formal refinement used to express that pulse; this unity of feeling and expression is typical of the best lyric poetry. Going back to Camões and Bocage (to whom he refers as "dear master"), Bilac here identified himself with a tradition dating back to troubadour poetry and reached the apogee of his poetic inspiration, producing one of the most dense and melodious works of Brazilian Parnassianism.

Via Láctea was the climax of Bilac's inspiration; it was a special moment in the career of an able craftsman endowed with refined poetic sensibility, a moment in which feeling and form were fused. Bilac would never again attain the same intensity and plenitude. The fact is that his lyre was dominated by the two outermost strings, representing overflowing emotion and formal rigidity; when Bilac managed to avoid these two extremes, he proved himself to be a lyric poet of rare quality. *Via Láctea* expresses this unstable equilibrium between the two poles of his work, an equilibrium also attained in other poems, like "Nel mezzo del camin ..." from *Sarças de fogo*:

> Cheguei. Chegaste. Vinhas fatigada
> E triste, e triste e fatigado eu vinha.
> Tinhas a alma de sonhos povoada,
> E a alma de sonhos povoada eu tinha ...
>
> E paramos de súbito na estrada
> Da vida: longos anos, presa à minha
> A tua mão, a vista deslumbrada
> Tive da luz que teu olhar continha.
>
> Hoje, segues de novo ... Na partida
> Nem o pranto os teus olhos umedece,
> Nem te comove a dor da despedida.

E eu, solitário, volto a face, e tremo,
Vendo o teu vulto que desaparece
Na extrema curva do caminho extremo.

[I arrived. You arrived. You came exhausted
And sad, and sad and exhausted I came.
Your soul was full of dreams,
And I had a soul full of dreams . . .

And we stopped suddenly in the road
of life: long years, your hand held
in mine. My eyes were dazzled by the light
contained in your eyes.

Today, you set off again . . .
No tears your eyes moisten,
Nor are you moved by the pain of leaving.

And I, alone, turn my face and tremble,
Seeing your shadowy form disappear
In the distant curve of the most distant road.]

Much of the rest of his opus, however, gives the impression that Bilac was writing verse out of habit or in response to the literary environment of the *belle époque*. This changes when, in *Tarde*, a mournful requiem, he recaptures something of the flame that had emanated from youth and from ardent feelings of love. Yet this was the time for disenchanted philosophizing ("Os monstros"), for repentance, for reassessing his values. Like a disillusioned Rilke, in the poem "A um poeta," Bilac offered advice that disowns the exaggerated formalism of his "Profissão de fé." Now it was time to sum up his life, a time darkened by the wings of Schopenhauer's pessimism ("O ideal é morto") and by old age and death ("Introibo!" and "Fructidoro"). With one more step, the poet, bound down by melancholy, entered the space of Symbolism in "Sinfonia."

Bilac's last poems brought to an end one of the most lively and controversial reigns in Brazilian poetry. His lyrics sought to achieve universality through formal correctness and emotions carefully screened and approved by reason, but he often fell into "Art for Art's Sake" in works stripped of emotion or suffocated by the corset of metrical perfection. Bilac embodied the very dilemma that troubled all Parnassians: by rigidly respecting formalism and objectivity, he created poems that were correct but cold; when, on the other hand, he allowed his emotions to pour out, he deviated from the established aesthetic code. When he managed to overcome this impasse, by reconciling these two inclinations, or reconciling intellect and intuition, or even reconciling the classical Apollonian and the romantic Dionysian, the result was verse of high lyrical voltage. During such moments, Bilac reached levels that justify the prestige he continues to enjoy among readers and critics.

In addition to Oliveira, Correia, and Bilac, traditionally considered the principal poets of Parnassianism, we must examine the works of a few of their multitude of disciples. We shall begin with Vicente de Carvalho (1886–1924), who is equal to those three writers. He began his career with *Ardentias*, followed by *Relicário* (1888). Those two works, after extensive editing and rewriting, were republished under the title *Versos da mocidade*. It would have been better to have abandoned these poems to oblivion, since they contain verses which, as the author observes in his preface, are "vulgar and unforgivable." Not even the rigorous and heavy editing he gave these poems could save them from being, in general, "unforgivable verses," sins of his youth.

These early works do, however, allow us to better understand Carvalho's position within the Parnassian context. Profoundly romantic, these poems accentuate the ambiguity with which poets of the era adopted the aesthetics of dispassion and formalism. In the preface to *Versos da mocidade*, Carvalho recalled, as if in an act of penitence, that in a prologue for another writer's book, written in 1887, he had said that he preferred "the enigmatic and moving nightingale from *Menina e Moça* to the showy peacocks of Parnassianism." Carvalho added that he had not understood "the kind of art that makes the beauty of the phrase the sole value of the verse." In the same preface, however, he transcribed a section from another prologue – to *Ementário* (1908), by Gustavo Teixeira (1881–1937) – in which he affirmed that "in poetry, expression is everything; with the condition, of course, that it is the expression of something that is alive and beating within the verse."

Carvalho's adherence to Parnassianism, then, was late and superficial, as well as contradictory; this explains his moderate formalism, which served to express openly romantic emotions. His later books make this clear, starting with the title of the first of them: *Rosa, Rosa de amor, Poemas e canções* (this volume contains the earlier book as well), *A voz do sino*. In these works he produced the best of his fantasy, attaining the originality and balance that justify his fame. His verse is that of a pure aesthete: romantic emotion, lyrical and amorous, clothed in a compatible form and without the petrifying excesses found in orthodox Parnassian poetry. He was a poet of Nature, of a living Nature, with an acute sense of the plasticity and musicality of things; the sea was his favorite theme. A poet of the sea unlike any other in Brazilian poetry, Carvalho was moved by a "lucid pantheism," – in the words of Euclides da Cunha, who wrote the preface to *Poemas e canções* – and produced poems filled with the simplicity of song and litany (see the "Cantigas praianas").

The harmonious reconciliation of form and content to the point where they become indistinguishable, the product of synesthesia in which one can hear echoes of Baudelaire's correspondences, brings the poet close to symbolist poetry. This musicality derived from Nature, one of Carvalho's basic characteristics, reached its climax in "O pequenino morto" (from *Poemas e canções*), due to the fluidity of a mournful rhythm in combination with the painful emotions caused by the death of a very young daughter.

Whether confronting the dead child or Nature itself, Vicente de Carvalho did not restrain the mysticism that dominated a writer who professed "the sweet religion of nature" ("Carta a V. S.," in *Poemas e canções*). It is logical, therefore, that he would have moved from this mysticism to write about religious themes, as in the "Canções praianas" or in *A voz do sino*. In the same way, Carvalho spontaneously moved toward the master of Portuguese poetry, Camões; this can be seen in "Velho Tema," a series of five sonnets clearly influenced by the Portuguese master. In his very best works, Carvalho harmonized the various tendencies of his temperament and let his deepest feelings pour out, but not without first transforming those feelings through imagination. He was Platonic in his vision of Nature, very like Camões in his expression of the "disorder of the world," a romantic who did not disregard form, but who never made form an end in itself. Only the lack of deeper and more original insight keeps Carvalho from standing head and shoulders above his contemporaries.

In addition to Vicente de Carvalho, other poets adhered to the Parnassian code during the period between 1878 and 1902. One of these was Bernardino Lopes (1859–1916), the author of *Cromos* (1881), *Pizzicatos* (1886), *Dona Carmen* (1894), *Brasões* (1895), *Sinhá flor* (1899), *Val de lírios* (1900), *Helenos* (1901), *Patrício* (1904), and *Plumário* (1905). "Syncretistic Parnassian" is perhaps the label that best suits this poet. B. Lopes, as he signed himself, was an original. Romantic, Parnassian, and symbolist tonalities flow together in his works, in varying combinations. His poetic diction was that of Portugal, but he cultivated rustic themes and even came to "sing the praises of industrialization" (Poem LI of *Cromos*), thereby adopting a modern attitude that complemented his inclination toward the bucolic. In his works, once can see traces of a poetry of daily life which recalls the verses of the Portuguese poet Cesário Verde and foreshadows the poetry of the Modernists of 1922. B. Lopes was a poet without drama or history – despite the bohemian lifestyle that may have contributed to his early death. A sybarite, his poems exhale an optimistic, festive, almost carnivalesque sensuality, born of personal experience (his love for a prostitute), but which he transposed to other settings – to a refined Europe of viscountesses and archduchesses, or to an

Orient filled with concubines and much more. His poetry is colored by a voluptuous plasticity, an aesthetic hedonism with shades of Góngora, all of which leads one to think that B. Lopes might best be classified as an Impressionist. A craftsman working in verse, fascinated by feminine beauty, he stood out among his contemporaries for these reasons; but he wasted himself in the disorderly world in which he sought his inspiration, and thus failed to leave a body of work equal to his undeniable poetic gifts.

A woman deserves special recognition for having achieved the objectives of Parnassianism in a balanced way: Francisca Júlia da Silva (1874–1920). Francisca Júlia published two books, *Mármores* (1895) and *Esfinges* (1903). Both of these books, along with previously unpublished works, were edited by Péricles Eugênio da Silva Ramos as *Poesias* (1961). At a distance from both the frigid formalism of the Parnassians and the adjoining heresy of symbolist aesthetics, Francisca Júlia used verse as the necessary host – in biological terms – for the ideas or feelings which possessed her. As the titles of her books suggest, the tension of form corresponds to emotional struggle. Filled with mysticism, her pen shakes with repressed emotions – emotions set free only when, as it were, she is besieged by the demons of Symbolism. As a result of all this, she produced some of the best sonnets of Brazilian Parnassianism, sonnets in which the word, rigorously pared down to its essence, recovers the dispassion the movement professed; but that dispassion is understood correctly, in these works, not as the absence of emotion but rather as the control of emotion. Her sonnets express a deep-rooted anguish which is both aesthetic and psychological. When Francisca Júlia was more at peace within herself, or when she was under the spell of Parnassian orthodoxy or symbolist heresy, her works are less convincing – but her remarkable control of form is constant.

Another woman of distinction is Júlia Cortines Laxe (1868–1948), the author of *Versos* (1894) and *Vibrações* (1905). She stands out among her contemporaries because of her philosophical concerns, something rare indeed in Parnassian poetry. Venceslau de Queirós (1865–1921) also deserves mention. He wrote *Goivos* (1883), *Versos* (1890), *Heróis* (1898), *Sob os olhos de Deus* (1901), and *Rezas do Diabo* (1939). His work follows a trajectory that begins in Romanticism, passes through Parnassianism, and ends up in Symbolism. Sebastião Cícero de Guimarães Passos (1867–1909) should also be mentioned. He was the author of *Versos de um simples* (1891) and *Horas mortas* (1901), works characterized by a hedonistic lyricism that shrinks from nothing – even from the idea of death. There is also Júlio Salusse (1872–1948), who wrote *Neurose azul* (1895) and *Sombras* (1901), a writer known primarily for a single sonnet, "Cisnes." For years this work was an obligatory selection for any anthology, due to its tone of vague melancholy expressed in simple verses that were easy to memorize. And there are so many others, some of whom, like José Albano (1882–1923) and Luís Delfino (1834–1910), should appear in later sections of this history, since their works were published after 1902 and therefore fall into the era of the *belle époque*, a period notable for its blend of various poetic tendencies.

The Parnassian aesthetic was at the height of its power when reactions against it appeared; those reactions were very different from Parnassianism in their literary expression, but were sharply identical in their ideology. Between 1883 and 1887, José Joaquim de Campos da Costa de Medeiros e Albuquerque (1867–1934) produced a series of poems later collected under the title of *Canções da decadência* (Rio Grande do Sul, either Pelotas, undated, or Porto Alegre, dated 1889). These were significant because they called attention to the literary movements taking place in France during the 1880s. These new tendencies coalesced during the next few years, until 1893, when João da Cruz Sousa (1861–1898) published two books, *Missal* and *Broquéis*, and began the symbolist movement in Brazil.

Turning against the Parnassian aesthetic and renouncing Positivism, which served as the basis for realist theories of art, Symbolism in some ways recaptured romantic ideas. It proclaimed a subjective vision of art and of the world. Yet, because of advances in philosophy and psychology, as well as a general cultural context in which faith in science as a universal panacea was retreating in the face of doubts raised everywhere, the Symbolists were able to take that visit to its limits.

Instead of being content with romantic descriptions of the surface levels of the ego, levels expressed through emotion, the Symbolists explored the deepest regions of the psyche in search of what would later be generally described as the "unconscious" or the "subconscious." In order to express the contents of these deepest regions, they had to find new methods – a new language, based on a psychological grammar and with an equivalent lexicon, and the use of neologisms, archaic words, and all kinds of written representations. This led them to the symbol, which they understood as the power of suggestion, of the verbal representation of internal vibrations reachable only through flashes of insight like bolts of lightening in the darkness.

In addition, poetry returned to its old soulmate, music. Verlaine had already advised this in his "Art poétique" (1874): "Da la musique avant toute chose . . ." Also, following in the footsteps of Baudelaire, the Symbolists practiced "correspondences" and the most unexpected synesthesias. With these instruments, probing the inner world ended up revealing what Jung would call the "collective unconscious." This is the source of the symbolist preference for popular or folkloric themes, collective in origin and effect, for esoteric themes, or for Medieval and mystical themes. Free verse emerges, and the stifling formalism of the Parnassians is rejected – but the Symbolists did not lose sight of formal perfection, synonymous with beauty.

Most suitable for cold and misty climes, in Brazil Symbolism developed primarily in the south; it began in Santa Catarina and Paraná, but later was centered in Rio de Janeiro, at that point the cultural capital of the country. Cruz e Sousa, the founder of Brazilian Symbolism, was from Santa Catarina.

Cruz e Sousa was born in Desterro (now Florianópolis) in 1861. His father was a slave, but his mother had been freed. His formal education never went beyond secondary school. He made his literary debut in Desterro in 1885, co-authoring *Tropos e fantasias*, a collection of brief narratives and prose poems, with Virgílio Várzea (1863–1941). In 1893 he published *Broquéis*, a collection of poems in verse, and *Missal*, a collection of poems in prose. A collection of prose poems, *Evocações*, a collection of poems in verse, *Faróis*, and his *Últimos sonetos* appeared after Cruz e Sousa's death in 1898.

In *Tropos e fantasias*, Cruz e Sousa appeared torn between socially conscious, declamatory Romanticism and simple topical poetry. With the publication of *Broquéis* and *Missal*, Cruz e Sousa not only introduced Symbolism in Brazil, he also began his own poetic maturation, a process that would make him one of the best – if not the best – of his generation, and one of the greatest figures of Brazilian verse.

In these works, alongside Parnassian formalism, we can see the new techniques this emerging symbolist aesthetic would explore – alliteration, the use of capital letters, lexical and syntactical exoticism, musicality. That musicality moves in a sequence that begins as a murmuring litany but ends in symphonic ecstasy, as if born of some instinctive alliance of classical music and the barbaric harmonies of the poet's African ancestors. Cruz e Sousa is already a visualist and an impressionist, excited by synesthesia, "correspondences," and allegories, all hidden within a forest of symbols.

This aesthetic refinement was joined to a sensuality that derived, in part, from his courtship of Gavita, whom Cruz e Sousa called his "Black Nun," his "Nubian Woman," but which was also engulfed in spirituality and mysticism. Soon, however, anguish occupies the realm of his soul, probably as a result of his color, and drags him into the morbid and ambiguous situations the poet glorified under the sign of rebellion and despair. Cruz e Sousa's verses were guided by a baroque sinuosity of form and an extravagant choice of words, echoing the influence of Baudelaire's poetry. There is a certain nervousness in the poet's language during this phase, as if he were trying to fuse the cosmic and the personal, the banal with the tragic, thereby transforming poetry into a kind of record of his soul and of his marginal existence within a prejudice-ridden society.

The next phase in Cruz e Sousa's development, the period of *Faróis* and *Evocações*, make clear his suffering over his father's death and his wife's madness. The predominant tone is one of rebellion; his aestheticism gives way to tragedy, his mind becomes a stage filled with horrors, where the ghosts of the dead, omens, funerals, tedium, and decay act out a pantomime. In "Emparedado," from *Evocações*, one of the most unique texts in the Portuguese language and the epitome of this period of desperation, openly espousing Symbolism and bringing to mind a tormented and tragic Van Gogh who wrote poetry rather than painted, Cruz e Sousa writes: "I bore, like corpses lashed to my back and incessantly and interminably rotting, all the empiricisms of prejudice, the unknown layers of long-dead strata, of curious and desolate African races that Physiology had doomed forever to nullity with the mocking papal laughter of Haeckel!" (trans. D. T. Haberly, *Three Sad Races*).

Cruz e Sousa's last years, recorded in *Últimos sonetos*, are marked by a certain resignation and faith, a phase in which Christian *caritas* replaced Kierkegaardian despair. The anguish of being "walled in" gave way to spirituality. Cruz e Sousa achieved, in this book, the goal he had set forth in the opening poem of *Broquéis*, "Antífona": his verse is now free of a certain formal conventionalism he had picked up from Parnassianism, and free of a limiting aestheticism; his metaphors here are of fluid transparency, resulting in the total fusion of form and content. Cruz e Sousa thus had attained the symbolist ideal of exploring the outer limits of the semantic and musical content of words. He had reached the summit of his capacity to create ideas, producing some of the best sonnets in the Portuguese language.

Cruz e Sousa's existential drama is perhaps the result of religious preoccupations intensified by his status as a black man in a racist society. He hungered for something beyond, for exile, for a utopia, for a transcendental and nirvana-like paradise precisely in order to compensate for the stigma of being a social pariah compelled to struggle against the prejudice and incomprehension of his society; that prejudice and incomprehension increased as his extraordinary poetic talent became more widely recognized. In his works, the central battle was between the forces of Good and Evil, between the Spirit and the Flesh, between Error and Truth – all capitalized, as symbolist dogma dictated – and his verses expressed a convulsive desperation that came very close to madness.

This real-life existential drama of tragic proportions, which no other member of his generation shared, was transmuted by Cruz e Sousa's imagination into "dor fingida" ["feigned pain"]. This, together with his masterful control of form, a control guided by a sense of balance and propriety and capable of producing verses that expressed his convulsive inner world, made Cruz e Sousa the most important Brazilian symbolist and certainly one of the greatest poets in Brazilian literature; it also made him the equal of his European contemporaries, as the French critic Roger Bastide pointed out in a study comparing Cruz e Sousa to the masters of French and German Symbolism.

Diametrically opposed to Cruz e Sousa is Alphonsus de Guimaraens, the pen name adopted by Afonso Henriques da Costa Guimarães (1870–1921). The titles of his books attest to this difference: *Setenário das dores de Nossa Senhora, Câmara ardente, Dona Mística*, and *Kyriale. Pauvre lyre*, a collection of poems in French, and the *Pastoral aos crentes do amor e da morte* were published posthumously. Aside from a slight attraction to Parnassian formalism, the occasional influence of Cruz e Sousa, and even the production of humorous and social verse, the poetry of Alphonsus de Guimaraens revolves around a limited repertoire of themes. The passage of time refined those themes, perhaps making them more diaphanous in their expression, but did not modify the essence that gave them life.

Two thematic extremes support Alphonsus de Guimaraens's vision of the world: love and death. Generally appearing together, these themes reveal his fundamental tendency to explore amorous lyricism and mysticism. In his work these two themes are inextricably bound together; one leads to the other, one implies the other. Quite possibly autobiographical in origin (as a young man, the poet was in love with a cousin, Constança, who died in adolescence), Guimaraens's love poetry is colored by mysticism: the woman (Constança) appears as a saint or an angel, wearing a halo of spirituality. That spirituality is of Christian or Platonic–Christian origin, and vibrates with slight hints of eroticism.

The mystical poetry of Alphonsus de Guimaraens is that of a believer in agony, the same agony the Spaniard Miguel de Unamuno described, who suffers crises of faith in every small action of daily life, a sort of Christian Existentialism *avant la lettre*. The poet never loses sight of the idea or the sensation of death, a preoccupation perhaps founded on his loss of Constança; his feelings of love are transformed and shaken by his vision of the impossibility of love and his belief in the inexorable end of all things. The vicious circle in which the poetry of Alphonsus de Guimaraens moves is centered on his obsessive preoccupation with death, death occasionally transformed into the ecstasy of love or combined with that ecstasy. The only possible escape from this agony is death, which darkens the poet's days and his verses.

Guimaraens's poetry is that of a believer in Christianity, and death for him implied both liberation and the beginning of a new journey, one that would lead to the sexual consummation denied him in life. Personal experience and Christian eschatology are thus joined, the lover and the believer both attain fulfillment – the first because he achieves transcendental union with the Beloved, the second because he sees God face to face. This preoccupation with death explains the hopeless vision of existence that runs through Guimaraens's poems, a vision identified with a series of motifs of pain; it is not hard to see the impact, on that vision, of the pessimistic philosophy of Schopenhauer, along with the *Imitation of Christ* and the Bible, particularly the Book of Ecclesiastes.

This is the verse of a "Decadent" immersed in sensations of chaos, degeneration, and destruction; his vivid dreams of the afterlife, informed by a Platonism that harks back to the Middle Ages, are his only release. This central emphasis on the Medieval is one of the key characteristics of Guimaraens's Symbolism. It influenced both the form of his poetry, seen in his use of archaic meters like "rimances," "cantigas e voltas," and sonnets; it also influenced content, as Guimaraens sought to create the sort of poetry a troubadour would have written for his lady, a poetry filled with Medievalism and incense and immersed in chamber music. The diction he employed was very Portuguese, reinforced by the notable absence of references to Brazilian reality.

It is not surprising that Guimaraens turned his back on the landscape of Brazil. He was living in a world of dreams, illusions, abstractions, and memories, conversing with his fantasies and his yearnings for transcendence. This self-referentiality, however, did not lead to poetry that was hermetic or merely confessional; it was, rather, transformed by his imagination into verses that resonated both musically and visually. Guimaraens was, finally, "the recluse of Mariana," a small city in the interior of the state of Minas Gerais where he spent most of his life; his only human contact was with the kindred souls he found in literature – like Camões, Antero de Quental, and Antônio Nobre, among Portuguese writers, as well as the French poet Verlaine and the Brazilian Cruz e Sousa.

Alphonsus de Guimaraens stands out because of the subtlety of his expression and the delicacy of the emotions he dealt with. He shaped his poems as if he were composing liturgies or Gregorian chants. His verses resonate indelibly in the minds of his readers as the most translucent poetry created during the last twenty years of the nineteenth century.

Symbolist poetry had hundreds of adherents scattered through Brazil. Even after 1902, many of these remained faithful to the credo of Verlaine and Rimbaud; new Symbolists, guided by the same aesthetics, made their debuts. The poets that came to Symbolism after 1902 will be considered in a later chapter. Among the older poets, however, the first we will look at – because of chronology and because of his quality as a poet – is Emiliano Perneta (1866–1921). Perneta was the author of *Músicas* (1888), *Carta à Condessa d'Eu* (1889), *Ilusão* (1911), and *Setembro* (1934), along with several plays and prose works. His earliest pieces, in *Músicas*, blend Parnassian, romantic, and symbolist aesthetics, but show his characteristic sensualism and classicism and his heroic vision of existence. In *Ilusão*, he has completely assimilated Symbolism and Decadentism, but without giving up his highly geometric verse and his Hellenic philosophy of life, a philosophy based upon concerns that were not simply aesthetic. He thereby attains an equilibrium or, better, a dialectical tension between the concrete and the abstract, between reality and dream. Perneta's dialectic also includes, on one side, eroticism, a pagan view of Nature, Epicureanism, anticlericalism, decadent skepticism; on the other lie his praise of illusion, of solitude, of the ivory tower, of nirvana. The dialectic, as well, pairs the civilized and the primitive, sensualism and idealism, even the intuitive beauty of poetry and dark feelings about the human condition. This dialectic justifies Perneta's importance within the symbolist movement in Paraná, his home state, and in Brazil as a whole. *Setembro*, a book containing poems written between 1897 and 1920, suggests that Perneta the man had managed to find the peace he had sought for so long; however, it also provides evidence that, freed from the tension which had earlier both consumed and nourished him, he was less of a poet.

Perhaps the most authentic representative of the mystical vein in Brazilian Symbolism was Auta de Sousa (1876–1901). *Horto* (Natal, 1900), which contains the poems she wrote just before her death from tuberculosis, is a kind of intimate diary, a breviary of asceticism interrupted by death. This is more a poignant human document than a spontaneously symbolist work of literature; it is the creation of a more ingenuous Santa Teresa de Jesus whose sorrowful religious fervor never allowed her to even approach erotic ecstasy.

A similar figure is Manuel Azevedo da Silveira Neto (1872–1942), author of the elegiac *Antônio Nobre* (1900), and *Luar de hinverno* (1900). In Silveira Neto's works, mysticism is allied to the cult of Death, to the search for nirvana, to melancholy, to sadness; the poet's ego expands to the level of the cosmic. Like Cruz e Sousa and the Portuguese Antônio Nobre, Silveira Neto cultivated the uncommon as a vehicle for his embittered emotionalism; he did so with the patience of an artist in pursuit of perfection, as if Symbolism, in his hands, could be purified of all traces of Parnassianism by achieving the transparency of music and defining itself in ethical terms. The result is a sort of baroque pre-modern hermeticism. *Ronda crepuscular* (1923) shows Silveira Neto in decline; calm has replaced the sorrowful anguish seen in *Luar de hinverno*, bourgeois tranquillity has replaced the fevered agitation of youth.

Another facet of Symbolism – its esoteric, occultist, alchemical side – can be found in the works of Dario Veloso (1869–1937), from *Efêmeras* (1890) to *Atlântida* (1938). The last is an epic poem praising the submerged continent of Atlantis and Brazil, which was, according to the poet, destined to be a sort of Pythagorean Fifth Empire. Veloso's other works include *Alma penitente* (1897), *Esotéricas* (1900), *Hélicon* (1908), *Rudel* (1912), *Horto de Lísis* (1922), and *Cinerário* (1929).

The lyricism of Mário Pederneiras (1868–1915) is largely bourgeois in nature, with an additional interest in the daily events of domestic life and in the bucolic. Pederneiras was the author of *Agonia* (1900), *Rondas noturnas* (1901), *Histórias do meu casal* (1906), *Ao léu do sonho e à mercê da vida* (1912), and *Outono* (a collection of verses written in 1914 but published posthumously in Rio de Janeiro in 1921). In these works, beginning with *Histórias do meu casal*, and in the face of the overwhelming influence of Cruz e Sousa, Pederneiras suddenly began using free verse, often in a prose-like structure. Free verse was widely utilized after 1922, but was introduced into Brazilian literature in 1900 by Adalberto Guerra Duval (1872–1947) in his *Palavras que o vento leva . . .*, published in Brussels.

In the same year, 1900, Francisco Mangabeira (1879–1904) published *A tragédia épica* in Bahia. Its theme is the war in Canudos, which Euclides da Cunha (1886–1909) would immortalize, two years later, in his *Os sertões* [*Rebellion in the Backlands*]. Mangabeira's poem is written in strong and sharp verses, with the force of an epic, that cut to the quick; it reflects the Satanism of Baudelaire and anticipates the poetry of Augusto dos Anjos and, even, that of Surrealism.

These poets – and there are so many others who cannot be mentioned here – bring to a close this chapter in Brazilian literature, the poetry produced between 1878 and 1902. As we have seen, the verse of this period was guided by three influential currents: Realist poetry, impregnated with scientific ideas and echoing the context of the 1870s, a decade marked by the increasingly bitter struggle over Abolition and by the beginnings of the process that would lead, in 1889, to the Republic; Parnassian poetry; and symbolist poetry, aesthetic by nature and rather marginal in terms of the social reality of the period.

The Brazilian theatre up to 1900
Severino João Albuquerque

.

The colonial period

Although there may have been occasional representations for the enter-tainment of the colonists in the half-century that followed the Portuguese conquest of Brazil in 1500, no record of theatrical activity exists until the Jesuits, who came to the colony in 1549, resorted to the theatre as a tool in their effort to educate the settlers and convert the Indians to the Catholic faith. The kind of theatre the Jesuits practiced in Brazil profited from their previous experience with the art form in Portugal. The new environment, however, required an overall simplification of their performances. As a result, the colonial Jesuit theatre marked a departure from the scholarly texts and ponderous productions they were known to stage in Portugal.

The major figure of the Jesuit theatre in Brazil is José de Anchieta (1534–1597). Born in the Spanish Canary Islands but educated in Portugal, at the age of sixteen Anchieta joined the Society of Jesus, which in 1553 sent him to Brazil, where he was to stay for the rest of his life. In the forty-four years he spent in Brazil as a teacher, missionary, and advocate of Indian rights, Anchieta proved to be a prolific writer of chronicles, letters, sermons, poems, and plays; he is also the author of a Tupi grammar and dictionary. Whereas Anchieta wrote tragedies in Latin for the benefit of his fellow Jesuits, his more important legacy, the *autos*, are in Portuguese, Spanish, and Tupi, and sometimes a combination of two or three of those languages. From the beginning, Anchieta understood that if he was to succeed in his didactic effort to convert the Indians and propagate the faith, the natives' language had to be used. The choice of languages and the length of each play depended on the audience, occasion, and exigencies of the particular situation.

Anchieta's *autos* are characterized by brevity, directness, and simplicity of expression; although indebted to the techniques contributed by the Portuguese Renaissance playwright Gil Vicente (c.1465–c.1536), the Jesuit's works include major innovations in form and content. Adapting his theatre to the background of the audience, Anchieta represents historical and contemporary figures along with religious motifs and allegorical characters drawn from Western and indigenous mythologies. The *arte menor*, with a *redondilha* pattern, is the predominant verse form. Written with performance in mind – often to celebrate a special occasion such as the feast of a saint, the arrival of a religious relic, or the visit of a civilian or ecclesiastical dignitary – his *autos* reveal a remarkable feeling for spectacle, calling for the use of body paint, native costumes, song and dance, fights, torches, and processions. Anchieta's productions were very simple and straightforward; stage props were hardly used, much depended on mere suggestion and, since there were no formal theatres in the colony, his *autos* were performed in churchyards, small town *praças*, and Indian villages, often with the tropical forest as backdrop. The actors were all male, for the most part local residents and natives who lived in the missions; children took part in choruses and processions. Women were not allowed on the stage at that time and, at any rate, the Jesuits deliberately avoided female roles in their plays; when such a role occurred (as for example, that of Ingratidão [Ingratitude] in *Na vila de Vitória* [written about 1586]), male actors crossdressed.

Anchieta began writing *autos* at the request of the Jesuit superior in Brazil, Father Manuel da Nóbrega (1517–1570), who felt the need to counteract the excesses he saw in the plays that were then being put on inside churches. Only two short passages remain of Anchieta's first such piece, the *Auto de pregação universal* (written about 1567; published 1672), considered by many critics to be the first dramatic text written in Brazil, although there are references to a 1564 *Auto de Santiago*, of which no copy has survived. Apparently a long work – Anchieta's first important biographer, Father Simão de Vasconcelos, mentions a three-hour-long production – *Pregação universal* derives its title from the fact that, being in Tupi and Portuguese, the *auto* should appeal to natives and settlers alike, and that it was suitable to be performed in different parts of the colony, provided that names of individuals and references to local events and geography were changed.

Of the Anchieta *autos* that have survived in their entirety, two longer works, *Auto representado na festa de São Lourenço* (written about 1583) and *Na vila de Vitória* merit special attention as they include some of the best moments of Anchieta's theatre. Like a number of the remaining *autos*, they are multilingual (the former is in Tupi, Portuguese, and Spanish, and the latter in Portuguese and Spanish), strongly dependent on allegory, and present an interesting combination of serious and comical elements. However, they differ from the other *autos* not only in length and structure but also for departing from the prevailing representation of the central struggle in which the forces of Good and Evil do battle with predictable means and results. In *São Lourenço* there is evident collaboration between the opposing sides as the angels, having defeated the devils, send the latter to torment Décio and Valeriano, the Roman emperors who ordered the torture and murder of the saints celebrated in the *auto*. Thanks to the occasional use of farcical elements both plays show some degree of sympathy for the devils. Moreover, in *São Lourenço*, the choice of the devils' names reveals a political motive, since Guaixará, Aimbiré, and Saravaia were Indian chiefs whom the Portuguese denounced as traitors for their support of the French; thus, the defeat that awaits the devils served as an obvious message to the mostly indigenous audiences.

Although Anchieta's theatre was first and foremost an instrument of indoctrination, it had undeniable dramatic qualities. In adapting the *auto* form to a new environment, Anchieta consistently drew on indigenous elements, thus contributing the first known effort toward a Brazilian theatre. His struggle to change governmental policy and influence the attitudes of his audiences makes him a precursor of political theatre in Brazil; it is noteworthy that Anchieta's work deeply influenced some of the more important playwrights of the 1950s, who returned to the *auto* as the preferred form for their committed theatre.

However, just as theatrical activity prior to the arrival of the Jesuits was virtually nonexistent in Brazil, so too for a long period after Anchieta's death the theatre in the colony came to a virtual standstill. As a matter of fact, the 200 years following the demise of the Jesuit playwright are distinguished by an almost complete absence of dramatic pursuits. At least two factors should be considered in this regard. First, the Society of Jesus was now putting less value on the theatre as an instrument of religious instruction, a policy change that reflected the new emphasis on exploration of the interior prompted by frequent French and Dutch attacks on the coastal areas. Second, after a long period in which they were denied an opportunity to try their talents, secular playwrights were not quite ready to fill the gap created by the Jesuit withdrawal from the scene. Thus, following Anchieta's death, there was for a time a return to the sporadic pattern of light theatre for the entertainment of the colonists that had marked the pre-Jesuit era.

A third consideration is that whatever was performed in those days either was never committed to print or their printed copies have not survived. Unlike their Spanish counterparts elsewhere in Latin America, the Portuguese banned printing machines in Brazil until 1808. In addition to the limitations posed by a strict censorship, having a manuscript printed in Europe involved a very high commitment of funds. Moreover, the lack of interest in books among a public that was vastly illiterate and more concerned about surviving in a hostile environment meant such meager financial return that even those plays which may have been deemed printworthy remained unpublished.

Perhaps because it viewed Anchieta's *autos* as nothing more than tools in the missionary effort, the Society of Jesus did not have them printed; it was not until late in the nineteenth century that his plays began to appear in print, and then only through the efforts of dedicated non-religious critics. As a matter of fact, Anchieta's plays have reached us only because the notebooks containing the manuscripts in his (as well as others') handwriting were sent to the Vatican as part of the canonization paperwork initiated shortly after his death.

Nor, aside from a few occasional references, was a proper record of performances kept during the period. Formal theatres were not built and regular theatre groups were not formed until the second half of the eighteenth century. Since Portugal and, consequently, Brazil were under Spanish domination between 1581 and 1640, the first half of the seventeenth century saw a number of plays performed in Spanish for the benefit of an elite associated with the colonial administration. Although there are no records of their having been staged, two such plays may have been the comedies *Hay amigo para amigo* and *Amor, engaños y celos* by the poet and playwright Manuel Botelho de Oliveira (1636–1711), who included them in his multilingual volume of poetry, *Música do Parnaso*, and thus became the first published Brazilian playwright, just as he was the first Brazilian to publish a book of poetry. However, Botelho de Oliveira's theatrical talent was scant; the poet himself calls his two plays "descantes cômicos" ["musical comedies"] and hints that they are included in *Música do Parnaso* only so that his book could claim to comprise all genres. Verbose, slow-paced, and encumbered by the conventions of *cultismo*, *Hay amigo para amigo* and *Amor, engaños y celos* were poor imitations of *No hay amigo para amigo* and *La más constante mujer* by the Spanish playwrights Francisco de Rojas Zorrilla (1607–1648) and Juan Pérez de Montalbán (1602–1638), respectively. Spanish in language, theme, and technique, Botelho de Oliveira's two plays have no connection with the realities of the colony (Gomes, "Manuel Botelho de Oliveira," 259–62; Sousa, "Declínio do teatro jesuítico," 105–6).

Equally distant from the Brazilian experience were the representative works of the eighteenth century: *O Parnaso obsequioso* (1768), a drama set to music, by the important poet and political activist, Cláudio Manuel da Costa (1729–1789); and the three-act verse comedy *Amor mal correspondido* (1780) by Luís Alves Pinto (1719–1789), apparently the first play to be staged that was written in Portuguese by a Brazilian-born playwright. Both of these works were associated with areas (the former with Minas Gerais, the latter with Pernambuco) located at considerable distances from Rio de Janeiro which, although not yet the capital city, was quickly gaining importance as the political and cultural center of the colony.

In a series of pastoral letters and prohibitions the church denounced dramatic pieces as sinful and, following the expulsion of the Jesuits from Brazil in 1759, further dissociated itself from theatrical activity. This opened the way for the creation around the colony of numerous "Casas de Ópera" ["Opera Houses"], also known as "Casas de Comédia" ["Comedy Houses"] – small, modest playhouses offering little in the way of comfort and for the most part featuring adaptations of Molière, Calderón, Goldoni, and Metastasio, often directed by immigrant impresarios, and performed by mulattoes who were not embarrassed by what was then a highly disreputable activity. In addition to the so-called "teatro de vivos" ["theatre of the living" – i.e., performances by real people], a puppet theatre tradition evolved in the colony, as it did in Portugal. Ironically, the major name of the very popular Portuguese "opera" tradition (so called because it involved singing, the use of puppets, and farcical elements), and indeed of all eighteenth-century Portuguese theatre, was the Brazilian-born Antônio José da Silva, "O Judeu" ["The Jew"] (1705–1739), whose family left his native Rio de Janeiro for Lisbon when he was eight years old. The family move was highly unfortunate not only for the future of the Brazilian theatre but also for the playwright himself, as he was hanged and burned by the Inquisition at the age of thirty-four. Antônio José is more properly studied with the Portuguese theatre since he spent most of his life in Portugal and his works – all written in that country – reflect on Portuguese rather than Brazilian society.

In all likelihood, the first building erected to function as a theatre in Brazil was the Teatro da Praia, located in the city of Salvador, Bahia. As is the case with a number of the "Casas," very little is known about the Teatro da Praia, other than the year it opened (1760) and the titles of a few plays staged there. Equally poorly documented is the existence of "Casas" in Vila Rica, Mariana, Sabará, and Tijuco in the then prosperous province of Minas Gerais. More facts are on record about the Teatro do Padre Ventura, a small house located in the center of Rio de Janeiro and named after the colorful Catholic priest who was at once its director, maestro, dancer, and set designer. Although not built specifically as a theatre, the Teatro do Padre Ventura predates the Teatro da Praia by a few years; it appears to have been in operation from around 1750 until it burned down in 1769. The gap created by the destruction of Father Ventura's playhouse was filled by the construction, in 1770, of a new and more sophisticated "Casa de Opera" under the sponsorship of Luís de Almeida Portugal, Marquis of Lavradio and Viceroy of Brazil between 1769 and 1779, a long-time theatre enthusiast. This "Casa" was better known as Teatro de Manuel Luís, after its Portuguese-born manager, Manuel Luís Ferreira, a protegé of the viceroy. Ferreira formed one of Brazil's first permanent theatre groups (two members of the company were extremely popular: the singer Joaquina da Lapa, better known as "Lapinha," and the actor José Inácio da Costa, known to the public as "Capacho"), and in the 1790s invited to Rio de Janeiro the first foreign company ever to perform in Brazil; this group was led by the distinguished Portuguese actor and director António José de Paula. Other foreign companies followed, most of them practitioners of the forms – the Italian opera and the French melodrama – that were to hold sway over audiences for much of the next century.

There is documented evidence of the existence of "Casas" in the provinces as well: theatres were operating in Recife (1772), Cuiabá (1790), Porto Alegre (1794), São Paulo (1795), and Salvador (1798). However, most of the activity took place in the capital of the colony. In spite of a 1780 royal decree that banned women from the stage and otherwise limited theatrical activity, more playhouses opened as Rio de Janeiro gained prominence. The theatre acquired more vitality when that decree was lifted in 1800 and, very especially, after the Napoleonic Wars forced the Portuguese court to move to Brazil in 1808.

The nineteenth century

Like most other activities, the theatre profited considerably from Rio de Janeiro's new status as the seat of the Portuguese Empire. Within a few years of the arrival of the royal family, the city had a first-class theatre to meet the entertainment demands of the large, fairly sophisticated court: with the support of the royal family, the Portuguese impresario Fernando José de Almeida, better known as Fernandinho (?–1829), planned and built the Real Teatro de São João, named in honor of Prince Regent João. From its opening night on October 12, 1813, the Real Teatro became a catalyst for theatrical activity in Brazil, attracting foreign companies and later, under the direction of João Caetano dos Santos (1808–1863), encouraging the production of Brazilian plays.

Reconstruction began shortly after the Real Teatro burned down in March of 1824, so that it reopened in December of the same year, as the Imperial Teatro de São Pedro de Alcântara, in honor of Brazil's new Emperor, Pedro I. The building was to undergo two other politically determined name changes: first, in 1831, to Teatro Constitucional Fluminense, when the Emperor left for Portugal amid a growing patriotism and sentiment in favor of legality and a constitutional government;

and later, in 1838, again to São Pedro de Alcântara, as part of the campaign for the early accession of Pedro II to the throne.

Public demand for entertainment caused an increase in dramatic output and theatrical activity in mid nineteenth-century Brazil. Several new theatres came into existence in the provinces as well as in Rio de Janeiro. Comedy, farce, burlesque, melodrama, tragedy, and opera were being written and staged in spite of the inauspicious creation, in 1843, of the Conservatório Dramático Brasileiro [National Theatre Institute], which functioned as the government office in charge of theatre censorship until it was abolished in 1864. Such was the level of its involvement that no less than 228 plays were censored in 1845. However, the institution of censorship had begun to hinder the Brazilian theatre long before the by-laws of the Conservatório Dramático were approved. In the 1820s and 1830s, for example, a series of decrees regulated several aspects of theatrical activity; nor was theatre censorship discontinued following the demise of the Conservatório or the fall of the Empire (Sousa, "A censura teatral," 309, 311, 321).

No figure represents this period better than João Caetano dos Santos. One of the two most important names in the nineteenth-century Brazilian theatre (the other being the playwright Luís Carlos Martins Pena [1815–1848]), João Caetano was not an author, but an actor, impresario, and director of the first Brazilian acting company; that company made its debut in the Teatro Niteroiense, in the city of Niterói, on December 2, 1833, presenting a play of unknown authorship, *O príncipe amante da liberdade ou a independência da Escócia.* João Caetano's career was, however, more closely linked with the Teatro de São Pedro: it was there that he began his liaison with the actress Estela Sezefreda (1810–1874), who was later to become his wife; it was there that he made his debut as a professional actor in 1831 (the theatre was known then as the Constitucional Fluminense); and in 1834 he moved his company from Niterói to its stage. For the next three decades, in spite of several fallings-out and two major fires (in 1851 and 1856), he always managed to return to the São Pedro as actor, manager, and director of the company that had virtually achieved the status of a national theatre. João Caetano's association with that stage continues, as the theatre that still operates in the same location in the center of Rio de Janeiro has been named after him.

By all accounts an extraordinary actor, João Caetano was for several decades the model who inspired other Brazilian actors. Squarely in the Romantic tradition, he was an unschooled genius who rose to enormous acclaim. However, his success resulted at least in part from the need of the public of a fledgling nation to see local talent on a par with the foreign actors who performed in the theatres of Rio de Janeiro. Catering, perhaps, to the taste of a still largely Portuguese audience, he favored Portuguese melodramas, or translations or adaptations of French tragedies and historical plays.

João Caetano introduced many innovations to the Brazilian stage, including a new concept of performance which, as he explains in his *Reflexões dramáticas* (1837) and *Lições dramáticas* (1862), called for the elimination of the declamatory tone and exaggerated gestures which were a staple of the theatre of his time. He profited considerably from his association with the French director Emile Doux (1798–1876), who came to Brazil from Portugal and began working with the Brazilian actor in 1851. Late in his career, in order to perpetuate his innovations, João Caetano drew on his own resources to fund the creation of an acting school, the Escola Dramática, and to establish a competition to reward talented new playwrights.

Composed in the early years of his career, *Reflexões dramáticas* is little more than an adaptation, in very abridged form, of François Riccoboni's 1750 *L'Art du théâtre*, which João Caetano knew in Spanish translation (Prado, *João Caetano e a arte do ator*, 3). Written a quarter-century later and published one year before the author's death, *Lições dramáticas* is more than an enlarged version of his early book. In this ambitious work João Caetano draws on his extensive stage experience to write a textbook intended to be adopted in the Escola Dramática. The book also profits from João Caetano's firsthand observation of the *Comédie Française* and French Conservatory during an 1860 European tour. Appended to the *Lições* was a "Memória," or proposal, addressed nominally to the Marquis of Olinda (Pedro de Araújo Lima, Head of the Imperial Cabinet) but in reality to Pedro II (to whom the book is dedicated), outlining a plan for the creation of the Escola Dramática and making the case for state sponsorship of a national theatre and a national company like those of France and Portugal.

Although João Caetano is intimately associated with the inception of the two kinds of drama that dominated the nineteenth-century Brazilian stage, the Romantic theatre and the *comédia de costumes* [comedy of manners], he staged few Brazilian plays throughout his career, a setback for the creation of a national repertory. Perhaps the impresario in him spoke louder than the nationalist man of the theatre; at any rate, his failure to carry the banner of the national theatre was especially unfortunate because he, more than any of his contemporaries, was in a privileged position to stir others to the cause.

Nevertheless, it is generally accepted that Brazil's romantic theatre began on March 13, 1838, in the Teatro Constitucional Fluminense, when João Caetano staged and performed the title role in *Antônio José ou o poeta e a Inquisição* by Domingos José Gonçalves de Magalhães (1811–

1882), the Viscount of Araguaia. Magalhães has been credited with the introduction of Romanticism in Brazil by means of a journal, *Niterói: Revista Brasiliense*, and a book of poems, *Suspiros poéticos e saudades*, both published in Paris in 1836. A truly representative figure of this period of transition, Magalhães was a consul who lived mostly in Europe yet professed a staunch nationalism, the aristocrat and conservative politician who played the unlikely role of standard-bearer for a new school, the self-described romantic playwright whose plays adhere strictly to the neoclassical model.

Although there seems to be little reticence in Magalhães's claim that *Antônio José* is a Brazilian tragedy which treats of a national subject, the work's Portuguese plot, locale, and characters say otherwise. Moreover, Magalhães's treatment of the intrigue that led to the execution by the Inquisition of the eighteenth-century playwright does not comply with the requirements of the tragic mode. Nor can it be said that *Antônio José* was the first Brazilian romantic play to be staged, since it was preceded by a production, also by the João Caetano company, of the *Prólogo dramático*, by Manuel de Araújo Porto Alegre (1806–1879); that performance took place in the Teatro Constitucional Fluminense on December 2, 1837. This short play is a nationalist musical allegory in which a youth named Brazil resists all attempts to lead him away from the path to freedom and happiness. A poet, actor, architect, and, later, diplomat, Porto Alegre was an esteemed member of Rio de Janeiro's intellectual elite who is best remembered for his painting of the São Pedro's stage curtain. However, for all of Porto Alegre's connections, the staging of his *Prólogo dramático* had none of the publicity, anticipation, and care associated with the opening performance of *Antônio José*. Magalhães's prestige and his conscious effort to identify his play with the beginning of Brazil's romantic theatre were so persuasive that historians of Brazilian drama have persisted in incorrectly ascribing precedence to *Antônio José*.

Magalhães's second play, *Olgiato* (1841), received less attention than *Antônio José*, although it too was performed by João Caetano's company (without its leader) in the Teatro São Pedro, where it opened on September 7, 1839. The date represents an obvious attempt to capitalize on the seventeenth anniversary of the young nation's Independence. *Olgiato* presents the same essential problems that afflict Magalhães's first play: a supposedly romantic work that follows neoclassical dictates, a "tragedy" that does not qualify as such, and, above all, a "Brazilian" play set outside the country. Although romantic in their focus on the past (*Olgiato* takes place in fifteenth-century Milan and *Antônio José* in eighteenth-century Portugal), Magalhães's plays avoid the national past, be it the pre-Conquest days or the struggle for independence during the colonial period.

Nor are the subjects more national in the works of other Romantic poets who, like Magalhães, also wrote for the theatre. The most important of these poets are Antônio Gonçalves Dias (1823–1864), Manuel Antônio Álvares de Azevedo (1831–1852), and Casimiro de Abreu (1839–1860). It is especially ironic that the former, a distinguished student of Indian cultures and Brazil's foremost Indianist poet, chose to set his plays in foreign lands. Of Gonçalves Dias's four dramatic works, only *Leonor de Mendonça* is deserving of critical attention for its balanced depiction of a doomed love affair in sixteenth-century Portugal. The playwright had high hopes for this tragedy, clearly influenced by Almeida Garrett's *Frei Luís de Sousa* (Lisbon, 1844); with it he intended to bring to the Brazilian theatre the renovation which Garrett's play had introduced to the Portuguese stage a few years earlier. However, Gonçalves Dias was unable to interest João Caetano or any other producer in staging *Leonor de Mendonça*, probably because the play's ponderous language gives it a definitely untheatrical quality; it also steers clear of the *dramalhões*, the melodramatic works that were so much in favor at the time. In spite of the work's staging shortcomings, the playwright contributed a number of reflections on the theatre, in a prologue to *Leonor de Mendonça* that is regarded as a key document of nineteenth-century Brazilian dramatic theory.

The other three plays by Gonçalves Dias do not bear much scrutiny. Two of them (*Patkull, Beatriz Cenci*) were written in Portugal when the poet was twenty years old. Like the later *Boabdil*, they betray the author's inexperience and uncritical absorption of themes dear to European Romanticism – although it remains unclear whether he was familiar with Shelley's *The Cenci*. Following the Conservatório Dramático's banning of *Beatriz Cenci* and the repeated failures of his attempts to see his plays staged, Gonçalves Dias abandoned the theatre for good, pursuing his vastly more successful poetic career.

João Caetano is also connected with the start of another important kind of theatre in nineteenth-century Brazil, the *comédia de costumes*. Although he himself never performed in any such plays, and would only admit them as lighter fare in a double bill, it was his company that staged Brazil's first comedy of manners, Martins Pena's *O juiz na roça*, later *O juiz de paz na roça* [*A Rural Justice of the Peace*, 1948]. The one-act comedy was first performed as a complement to a longer, serious drama, Francisco Martínez de la Rosa's *A conjuração de Veneza*, on October 4, of that pivotal year of 1838, in the Teatro de São Pedro. The production launched at the peak of his creative power the career of Brazil's most accomplished author of the *comédia de costumes*. Unlike Gonçalves de Magalhães, Gonçalves Dias, and virtually every other Brazilian dramatist of his century, Martins Pena wrote solely for and about the theatre. In only a decade and a half of dramatic productivity, the country's first truly major playwright composed twenty-two comedies and six dramas, one of which was left unfinished; in less than two years as drama critic for Rio de Janeiro's *Jornal do Comércio*, he wrote a respectable series of articles later gathered in the volume *Folhetins: a semana lírica* (1965).

In contrast to his comedies, Martins Pena's serious dramas are rather mediocre theatre. Still, deserving of mention among them are *Itaminda ou o guerreiro de Tupã*, the only one which deals with a national subject, and Martins Pena's sole verse play, *Vitiza ou o Nero de Espanha*, the only serious drama by him to be performed during the playwright's lifetime, and the only one of his texts in which João Caetano performed.

The situation with the playwright's comedies was, of course, altogether different. With the advent of Martins Pena and the creation of the *comédia de costumes* – the two events virtually indistinguishable – Brazilian theatre finally came of age; at long last there could be no doubt as to the truly national quality of the theatre. Martins Pena became a very popular playwright (nine new plays were produced in 1845 alone) as the audiences immediately related to his comedies because of the colloquial language and the easily recognizable situations and realistic depictions of contemporary scenes and people he brought to the stage. Martins Pena's works so pleased the theatregoing public that by 1846 demand for his plays had far surpassed the playwright's ability to put out anything but hurriedly produced farces.

At their best, however, Martins Pena's comedies display an originality and directness of expression never matched in the Brazilian theatre. In addition to *O juiz de paz na roça*, two works that premièred in 1844, *O Judas em sábado de Aleluia* (1846) and *Os irmãos das almas* (1847), perhaps best exemplify the short duration (all but four of the twenty-two comedies have one act), quick pace, pithy dialogue, and remarkable timing of Martins Pena's comedies. Among the longer comedies, only the three-act *O noviço* (1853), first performed in 1845, retains the best features of Martins Pena's shorter works. Although laughter never ceases to be the primary goal, the comedies include a certain degree of social criticism. Through one or several characters, both short and long comedies denounce some form of iniquity: for example, a corrupt judicial system, dishonest businessmen and flirtatious women, predatory foreigners, theft, and adultery are criticized in the figures of the title characters, Antônio, Maricota, Gainer, Jorge, and Ambrósio, in *O juiz de paz na roça*, *O Judas em sábado de Aleluia*, *Os dous ou o inglês maquinista*, *Os irmãos das almas*, and *O noviço*, respectively. Perhaps as a result of the influence of Gil Vicente, Molière, and Antônio José, Martins Pena showed considerable skill in his use of satire to present character types such as, for example, the proponents of hydrotherapy, allopathy, and homeopathy in

Os três médicos (presented 1845; published 1956); the satire was especially mordant when criticism was aimed at persons of lesser social rank, as the music-lover in *O diletante* (presented 1845; published 1846); (Lyday, "Satire in the Comedies of Martins Pena," 64, 66–8). However, this kind of farcical satire is essentially a comedy of situations rather than characters; its dramatic conventions (disguises, characters in hiding, mistaken identities, near-tragedies, happy ending, etc.) and one-act structure left no room or time for character development.

Literary history has given Martins Pena the credit that is due him as the playwright who established the *comédia de costumes* and thus gave Brazilian drama the new form that distinguished it completely from the theatre that preceded him. He had a sure instinct for what theatregoers would accept with enthusiasm; the documentary value and the Brazilianness of his comedies have been acknowledged by numerous critics of his century as well as of our own. Although his followers and imitators never matched the quality of his comedies, the tradition Martins Pena initiated has become one of the most vibrant elements of the theatre in Brazil.

The second half of the nineteenth century saw a distinct drop in the quality, although certainly not in the number, of plays presented. The generation that followed Martins Pena favored a kind of realist drama that became known as *teatro de tese* [thesis play] or *teatro de casaca* [dress-coat theatre – so called because of the attire actors wore on stage]. However, in spite of a professed social concern, most dramatists of this school were unable to steer clear of melodrama or of inferior comedies. Foremost among the playwrights who came to the fore in the third quarter of the nineteenth century were Joaquim Manuel de Macedo (1820–1882) and José Martiniano de Alencar (1829–1877).

The realist period of Brazilian theatre starts with the production of Macedo's *O primo da Califórnia* (1858) in the Teatro Ginásio Dramático on April 12, 1855. By this time the Ginásio Dramático (formerly Teatro São Francisco de Paula, the new name an obvious imitation of the Théâtre Gymnase, which was closely associated with French realist theatre) was gaining prominence over the Teatro de São Pedro, as the thesis play replaced the *dramalhões*. Moreover, just as the acting company of João Caetano had been of fundamental importance for the romantic theatre, a newly formed group, based in the Ginásio Dramático and headed by the impresario Joaquim Heliodoro (1848–?) and the noted actress Maria Velluti (1827–?), was central to the *teatro de casaca*. Other important names associated with the Ginásio Dramático were the stage director Emile Doux (who had previously worked with João Caetano) and the actors Furtado Coelho (1831–1900) and Velluti's husband, Joaquim Augusto (1825–1873).

O primo da Califórnia stands out among Macedo's fifteen plays for its exposure of the Brazilian bourgeoisie's hypocrisy, lax morals, corrupted values, and fascination for things foreign. The same is true of two later works, both premiered in the Ginásio Dramático, *Luxo e vaidade* (presented 1860; published 1860) and *A torre em concurso* (presented 1861; published 1863). In 1878, toward the end of his career, Macedo wrote his own stage adaptation of his hugely successful 1844 novel, *A moreninha* – its third dramatic rendition in as many decades. Although the protagonist is a young woman, Carolina, her portrayal has none of the incisive criticism of the oppression of women in nineteenth-century Brazil seen in some other works by Macedo – as for example, in plays as diverse as *O cego* (presented 1849; published 1849) and *O fantasma branco* (presented 1851; published 1856). Several generations of historians of the Brazilian theatre have ignored Macedo's relatively strong stand on the issue. Those critics who do examine his female characters only make passing references to the plight of women in imperial Brazil, as they seem more interested in pointing out that so many of Macedo's plays have a happy ending, marriage having been the ultimate goal of the female protagonist. Albeit true, such facts cannot obscure the playwright's vehement denunciation of the unfavorable conditions which women had to face in Brazil at that time. In spite of his stand against the oppression of women, Macedo was reluctant or unwilling to tackle the issue of slavery. Although it is true that the first black character to be treated with dignity on the Brazilian stage appeared in a play by Macedo (Mendes, *A personagem negra no teatro brasileiro*, 37), that play – *O cego* – does not deal with slavery. It was left for Macedo's contemporary and fellow novelist, José de Alencar, to introduce the issue on the Brazilian stage.

Alencar was a prominent lawyer and conservative politician who served briefly in the imperial Cabinet as Minister of Justice. His political nationalism was matched in literature by a well-thought-out program that he hoped would foster the creation of a true Brazilian fiction. Although a number of his novels belong in the romantic tradition, as a playwright Alencar soon realized that if he wanted to educate the public on the evils of contemporary society, he had to write realist drama. His plays are nevertheless essentially romantic in form and, although supposedly realistic in content, their plots frequently defy verisimilitude. The problem becomes particularly serious in the works that examine prostitution and slavery, for melodrama quickly takes over, with the entirely bad tyrannizing the entirely good until the very end, when vice is punished and virtue finally rewarded.

In spite of his stated goal of revitalizing the Brazilian theatre, Alencar was much less successful as a playwright than as a novelist. His dramas are highly artificial pieces in which characters speak in sermons, and moralizing rather than psychological analysis prevails; his comedies, for the most part, lack the flow and spontaneity of Martins Pena's and even Macedo's works. Alencar's best-known dramas, *As asas de um anjo* (presented 1858; published 1860) and *Mãe* (presented 1860; published 1862), both of which premiered in the Ginásio Dramático, fail to vindicate the oppressed individuals they are supposed to defend. In the former, several characters who function as mouthpieces for the playwright lash out at, rather than sympathize with, the plight of Carolina, a Brazilian version of Dumas *fils*'s Marguerite Gautier in *La Dame aux Camélias* (1852), a play which had a monumentally successful run in Brazil in 1856; moreover, Carolina's eventual marriage to Luís is more punishment than reward, since the husband-to-be determines that theirs will be a sexless marriage. In its turn, *Mãe* is marred by an unbearably sentimental combination of motherhood and slavery. The sublime qualities of the slave Joana seem to undermine the pro-Abolition message, as it might be logical to argue that an institution that breeds such noble behavior is worth preserving (Araripe Júnior, *Literatura brasileira: José de Alencar*, 71). Joana's essential goodness and repeated acts of self-denial in effect deprive her character of all credibility. Nor is it likely that her final sacrifice for Jorge will make things easier for the apparently white medical student who turns out to be her son. Joana's suicide at the play's end only reinforces one of the slave-holder's most cherished images, that of the slave as the paradigm of blind devotion.

Alencar's most successful comedy, *O demônio familiar* (presented 1857; published 1858), also touches on the issue of slavery but manifests a troubling position on the matter because the institution of slavery is never unambiguously condemned. Moreover, Eduardo, the *raisonneur*, or character who voices the play's thesis, states at the end that by freeing Pedro he is in fact punishing the young slave who is the devil of the title. No effort is made to mask the fact that the point of view is that of the master, and, while the play does suggest that slavery has a deleterious effect, Pedro is presented in such a negative light that the spectator is led to believe that the victims of the institution are Eduardo and his family rather than Pedro and the other slaves.

In his quest for the renewal of the Brazilian theatre Alencar had high hopes for a historical drama, *O jesuíta* (1875) [*The Jesuit*], which he wrote on commission for João Caetano in 1861. After a falling-out between the two men, the renowned actor refused to play the title character. The matter was complicated further by the censors of the Conservatório Dramático, who deemed the play unacceptable; this incident in effect put an end to Alencar's dramatic career. When *O jesuíta* was finally produced in 1875, casting problems and political and religious opposition led to audience indifference and the production closed after only three shows. Alencar took a column in the daily, *O Globo*, in which he blamed the dismal failure on an ignorant public and on parts of the Brazilian intelligentsia. Some of Alencar's statements alienated his former admirer and fellow *Globo* writer, the distinguished abolitionist Joaquim Nabuco (1849–1910), and thus began one of the most acrimonious debates in nineteenth-century Brazil; this debate is fully documented in Afrânio Coutinho's *A polêmica Alencar-Nabuco* (1965).

In spite of the problems outlined above, one must be careful not to judge Alencar too harshly. His shortcomings as a dramatist must be weighed against the difficulties in adapting the thesis play to mid nineteenth-century Brazilian taste. For all practical purposes, he was the pioneer of social protest on the Brazilian stage, and he was the first major Brazilian playwright to include black protagonists in his works. In spite of Alencar's conservative posture, his plays *were* seen as anti-slavery statements, and, however distorted the reasons, for a while he became an unlikely champion of the cause of Abolition on the Brazilian stage, receiving as much attention as other playwrights who were more rightfully associated with the anti-slavery movement, such as Agrário de Meneses (1834–1863), Paulo Eiró (1836–1871), Rodrigo Otávio (1839–1882), and Apolinário Porto Alegre (1844–1904).

Whereas Brazil's romantic theatre was dominated by poet–playwrights, the most influential dramatists of the realist period were novelists. In addition to Macedo and Alencar, the celebrated novelist Joaquim Maria Machado de Assis (1839–1908) also wrote for the theatre. Although he is better remembered for his perceptive theatre criticism than for his plays, the young Machado had high expectations for his theatre. However, his good friend Quintino Bocaiúva's remark that Machado's pieces were more suited to be read than staged seems to have made an impression on the aspiring playwright. Machado's own critical acumen, too, must have played a part in his decision to dedicate more and more time to his narratives. Yet he never gave up the theatre altogether, and his last play appeared only two years before his death. Bocaiúva's comment, which soon became a critical commonplace, was as tactful as it was correct. For Machado's plays are short, subdued exercises in irony, sobriety, and understatement, with little action and much dialogue – sketches, as it were, of the elegant novelistic scenes he would produce in the future.

In addition to translations of works by Beaumarchais, Musset, Sardou, and other dramatists, Machado wrote sixteen original plays, a number of which are one-acts. The plays are comedies about the love tribulations of cosmopolitan, upper-middle-class characters who have very little about them that is distinctly Brazilian. Two notable exceptions are *Quase ministro* (1864), an ironic commentary on the fleeting nature of political loyalty, which he wrote at the request of an all-male amateur group, and

Tu, só tu, puro amor (1880), a historical drama written for a private celebration of the tricentennial of the death of the Portuguese poet Luís de Camões (c. 1525–1580). More often, as in two of the more interesting pieces, *Desencantos* (1861) and *Lição de botânica* (1906), the plot concerns the machinations of well-off women (often widows) and their suitors, leading in the end to the predictable marriage proposal and a moral lesson on some unsanctioned aspect of female social behavior.

The next playwright to show distinctive merit was Joaquim José da França Júnior (1838–1890), whose plays provide a transition between Martins Pena's *comédia de costumes* and Artur Azevedo's theatre. A lawyer by training, and a fine *cronista* with a keen sense of observation, França Júnior quickly absorbed the attitudes of his contemporaries and appears to have been absolutely sincere in his criticism of the morals prevalent in the late Brazilian Empire. França Júnior's theatre offers a good example of quality that improves with time; the last three of his surviving plays are by far the best work in a career that had begun two decades earlier.

The playwright was at his absolute best when portraying the corrupt politics of the second half of the nineteenth century, as in two of the last plays, *Como se fazia um deputado* (presented 1882; published 1882) and *Caiu o ministério!* (presented 1882; published 1884). By the time he wrote these works, França Júnior had outgrown the one-act format of the vast majority of his early plays. With the ampler time provided by a three-act comedy, in both these pieces he could better expose dishonest politicians and the system that fostered them. In *Como se fazia um deputado*, provincial politicians scheme to send one of their own to the Chamber of Deputies in Rio de Janeiro. The play depicts the overall stagnation brought about by liberals and conservatives in their efforts to stave off any kind of reform, for – despite the different names – both parties were formed of wealthy, reactionary landowners who fought with equal resolve to preserve the *status quo*. The productions at the Teatro Recreio Dramático drew large audiences who came for the highly successful satire and eminently faithful reproduction of the political process – so faithful in fact that the imperial censors demanded that the present tense of the original title, *Como se faz* . . ., be changed to a past form, *Como se fazia* . . .

In *Caiu o ministério* the setting has changed to the nation's capital but the fraudulent ways depicted in the previous work are essentially the same in the machinations that accompany the formation and retention of a new Cabinet. Conselheiro Brito, the man who has been charged with putting together the *ministério*, is beleaguered by newcomers who are as full of ambition as they are devoid of scruples. The new Cabinet soon collapses in the wake of a scandal involving Mr. James, a deceitful Englishman who plans, with the support of Brito's wife, to build a dog-powered railway system to the top of the Corcovado mountain in Rio de Janeiro. The crafty Englishman had by then developed into a type whereby playwrights criticized at once the exploitative foreigner and the Brazilian fascination with imported things and ideas, however absurd or outrageous: the type had made previous appearances in such works as Martins Pena's *Os dous ou o inglês maquinista*, Macedo's *A torre em concurso*, and an early work by França Júnior, *O tipo brasileiro*.

As doutoras (presented 1889; published 1932), the last of França Júnior's extant plays, examines another pressing issue of late nineteenth-century Brazil, that of women's role in society. Premiered only a few months before the Republic was instituted, the play reflects women's growing self-confidence and dissatisfaction with their status. While it provides an accurate portrayal of recent professional advances by Brazilian women, *As doutoras* ultimately succumbs to the predominant conservatism of the times, as its happy ending shows the female protagonists, physician Luísa Praxedes and lawyer Carlota de Aguiar, abdicating their professional gains and returning to the more traditional roles of mother and housewife in order to save their marriages.

França Júnior's good-humored examinations of the inner workings and limitations of the late empire gave way to the hugely popular format of song, dance, and light comedy that became known as *teatro ligeiro* or *teatro de revista*. Tired of the thesis play, theatregoers now demanded to be entertained rather than preached at. The impact and permanence of the genre were such that the Brazilian theatre bypassed the naturalist period, then prevalent in other parts of the world. Artistically, however, the new formula had little merit, as the web of comic possibilities found in the best plays of Martins Pena and França Júnior seemed lost, replaced by the standard characters, thin plots, and stock situations of their successors' derivative works.

The *teatro ligeiro* evolved from a number of sources, from the Brazilian *comédia de costumes* to the English music-hall, from Italian *burletta* to American vaudeville and French cabaret and can-can, and from parodies of foreign dramas to the *revistas de ano*, or satirical sketches of the previous year's most important events. A Portuguese import, the *revista do ano* had made its debut on the Brazilian stage in 1860 with *As surpresas do Senhor José da Piedade* by a little-known public employee named Justino de Figueiredo Novais (1829–1877), but it would be two more decades until the mode really met with success. Parodies of Offenbach's operettas were also enormously popular, particularly those staged by the director Jacinto Heller (1834–1909) and the actor Correia Vasques (1839–1892). By the 1880s theatrical activity had shifted from the stately houses of previous decades to a number of more informal spaces, located mostly in the nation's capital, bearing such names as Alcazar (the most successful of them all) and Varietés. In keeping with the turn-of-the-century fascination with all things Parisian, many actors and especially actresses were either French-born, French-speaking, or had dubious claims to French origin.

The most important name associated with the *teatro de revista* is undoubtedly that of Artur Nabantino Gonçalves de Azevedo (1855–1908). The author who was to become Brazilian theatre's most beloved figure, Artur Azevedo wrote his first major successful comedy (*Amor por anexins* [presented 1872; published 1872]) at the age of fifteen. Although he was also a prolific author of light verse, short stories, and newspaper columns, Azevedo is revered for his indefatigable work on behalf of a national theatre and for the faithful reproduction of an era in a body of some 200 original plays as well as translations, adaptations, and parodies of foreign dramatic works. In the former capacity, Azevedo was one of the most vocal advocates of the construction of Rio de Janeiro's Teatro Municipal (which he did not live to see completed) and, in spite of illness, he was responsible in the last months of his life for the ambitious project of staging fifteen Brazilian plays of "national repertoire" caliber as part of the Centennial Exposition of 1908. As to the latter capacity, Azevedo was always resentful of the poor reception his attempts at serious drama had among critics and audiences alike. His serious works include two anti-slavery plays, *O liberato* (presented 1881; published 1881) and *O escravocrata* (co-authored with Urbano Duarte [1855–1902]; 1884); performances of the latter piece were banned by the imperial censors. Azevedo often complained about being stereotyped as an author of frivolous *revistas* and he reacted strongly at the suggestion that he was responsible for the turn-of-the-century decline of the Brazilian theatre (Magalhães Júnior, *Arthur Azevedo e sua época*, 154–5). Be that as it may, a number of his *revistas* are masterpieces of the genre and, as a whole, they constitute invaluable sociocultural documentation of his time.

Similarly, important social records are two series of contributions, *O ano que passa* and *Teatro a vapor*, to Rio de Janeiro's daily newspapers, devised by Azevedo as an alternative to exorbitant production costs: the former are "cenas ilustradas" or drawings of dramatic scenes, published in *O País* from February to November, 1907, in lieu of the *revista de ano* for that year; and the latter are 105 humorous vignettes or comedies-in-a-nutshell (named *Teatro a vapor* because of their nature of rapidly sketched, quick-paced, short scenes), which he published almost every week in *O Século* between 1906 and 1908 (Moser, "Artur Azevedo's Last Dramatic Writings," 23–6).

It is noteworthy that some of Azevedo's most celebrated works were parodies of French operettas. Charles Lecoq's *La fille de Madame Angot* and *La pétite mariée* were given a Brazilian identity and became the hugely popular *A filha de Maria Angu* (presented 1876; published 1876) and *A casadinha de fresco* (presented 1876; published 1876), while Offenbach's *La belle Hélène* was converted into *Abel, Helena* (presented 1877; published 1877). In addition, one should keep in mind that several of Azevedo's works are adaptations (*O dote* [presented 1907; published 1907], for example, is a dramatic rendition of a short story by Júlia Lopes de Almeida [1862–1934]) and many of his *revistas* were composed in partnership: with Tomás Lino d'Assumpção (1844–1902) he authored his first attempt in the genre, *O Rio de Janeiro em 1877* (presented 1878; published 1883); with Aluísio Azevedo (1857–1913), his younger brother and exponent of Brazil's naturalist novel, he wrote *Fritzmac* (presented 1889; published 1889) and the timely *A República* (presented 1890); with José de Toledo Piza (1869–1910) he composed an excellent *revista-burletta*, *O mambembe* (presented 1904; published 1956); and with his good friend Francisco Moreira Sampaio (1851–1901), a fine playwright in his own right, Azevedo penned some of his more successful *revistas*, including *Cocota* (presented 1885; published 1885), *O bilontra* (presented 1886; published 1886), *O carioca* (presented 1886; published 1887), and especially the work credited with establishing the genre, *O mandarim* (presented 1884; published 1884).

Among the *revistas* of Azevedo's sole authorship, *O tribofe* (presented 1892; published 1892) deserves critical scrutiny not only for its intrinsic merit but also because Azevedo, with the assistance of three competent musicians, Nicolino Milano, Assis Pacheco, and Luiz Moreira, rewrote some of its scenes into his masterpiece, *A capital federal* (presented 1897; published 1897), perhaps the most popular Brazilian play of all time, and the first Brazilian play ever to be performed abroad (Lisbon, 1906) (Gonçalves, *Dicionário histórico e literário do teatro no Brasil*, I: 330). Better than any other play of the period, *A capital federal* reflects a compact that seemed to exist between the practitioners of the *teatro de revista* and their public. Its enormous success speaks of a commonly held wide-eyed fascination for the tokens of civilization (fashionable stores, fine restaurants, comfortable hotels, race tracks, and so on) that were beginning to be felt in the capital city of the young republic. In the best tradition of Martins Pena, the play depicts a family of honest country folk who are taken advantage of by wily city dwellers such as Lola the Spanish *cocotte* and Figueiredo the self-styled impresario of attractive mulatto women. After a series of mishaps the bumpkins finally find Gouveia, their daughter's fiancé, in search of whom they had come to Rio de Janeiro. The play ends happily, with the family's return to their native state of Minas Gerais and a grand finale in praise of the virtues of country people. Its characters are mostly *comédia de costumes* veterans (the rustic *fazendeiro*, the crafty man-about-town, the innocent young woman), but new types were added, most importantly the nosey *mulata*, Benvinda, who does have a precursor, Felisberta, in França Júnior's *Direito por linhas tortas* (presented 1870; published 1871), and who generated a myriad of imitations in the following decades.

Although it was not the first play to focus on the illusory charms of the nation's capital (José de Alencar's *O Rio de Janeiro: verso e reverso* [presented 1857; published 1857] and França Júnior's *Direito por linhas tortas* readily come to mind), Azevedo's work captured so well the spirit of the city that it remains (even after the countless imitations that inevitably followed) the unsurpassed dramatic portrayal of the former capital city. Its vibrant scenes, credible characters, perfect pace, and delicious verbal wit combine with the lively music into a cohesive unit rightfully seen as a climax of Brazil's *teatro de revista*.

A unique place in the history of Brazilian drama is held by José Joaquim de Campos Leão, better known by his assumed name of Qorpo-Santo (1829–1883), who lived in provincial isolation in Rio Grande do Sul, apparently oblivious of the theatrical scene of the nation's capital. Although he spent most of his adult life fighting a misguided judicial system that accused him of mental illness, Qorpo-Santo still managed to compose his seventeen extant plays in several, all-too-brief periods of tranquillity which he enjoyed in 1866. Largely ignored by theatre directors, critics, and historians until the mid 1960s, Qorpo-Santo was nevertheless the theatrical genius who, had his plays been produced, might have raised Brazilian drama to theretofore unknown heights.

Qorpo-Santo's plays are short satires populated by characters who often bear such odd names as Rapivalho, Miguelítico, Impertinente, Truquetruque, Perna de Galinha, and Espertalínio da Porciúncula. His theatre as a whole constitutes a wry indictment of his contemporaries, a satirical commentary on the pedantry of the Second Empire, and a truly subversive alternative to the commercially successful and officially sanctioned theatre of his time. Because of a general disregard for spatial and chronological consistency, and the numerous instances of disjunction and irrationality in his works, Qorpo-Santo is rightly seen by most contemporary Brazilian critics as a precursor of the Theatre of the Absurd. Those traits are more readily noticeable in his best works, *Mateus, Mateusa, As relações naturais*, and *Eu sou vida, eu não sou morte*, written, respectively, on May 12, 14, and 16, 1866. Qorpo-Santo was also the first Brazilian playwright to portray homosexuals (Tamanduá and Tatu, in *A separação de dois esposos*) and to allow actors and directors latitude in the staging of his plays. Perhaps because he seemed to sense that future generations would be more likely to understand and value his art, Qorpo-Santo printed his own works in a small press he purchased for that purpose. One of his projects was a multi-volume *Enciclopédia*, the fourth installment of which includes the texts of the seventeen plays. The now extremely rare volumes illustrate his peculiar notions about spelling as well as other idiosyncrasies.

Due to his isolation and the scorn of his contemporaries, Qorpo-Santo, unlike Martins Pena, had no imitators or followers. He remained virtually unknown for more than half a century after his death, and the first staging of his plays did not take place until 1966, 100 years after they were written (Aguiar, *O homens precários*, 245–50). The Brazilian theatre thus remained in the grip of the *comédia de costumes* which, along with the *teatro de revista*, resonated well into the twentieth century. That genre's hold was too tight to be relaxed even by such auspicious developments as the opening of new theatres and the advent of younger playwrights and innovative acting companies. In fact, the twentieth century would be almost half over before the conventions of the previous century gave way to genuine changes.

[6]

Brazilian fiction from 1800 to 1855
Mary L. Daniel

Prose fiction is without a doubt the "sleeper" of the literary genres in Brazil during the first half of the nineteenth century. In fact, it may be said that, with the exception of Teresa Margarida da Silva e Orta's *Máximas de virtude e formosura, ou Aventuras de Diófanes* (published in the second half of the eighteenth century), Brazilian fiction was born, and experienced a rather sickly infancy, during the period 1830–1855. It remains for the second half of the nineteenth century to raise this "late bloomer" among the literary genres in Brazil to its place of glory with the works of José de Alencar and Machado de Assis. Among the reasons typically given (Salles, *Primeiras manifestações da ficção na Bahia*, 8) for the lethargy in the development of Brazilian fiction are the preference among writers and the public for the prestigious poetic genre, the lingering of the neoclassical influence, the popularity of ecclesiastical and oratorical rhetoric, the immediate appeal of combative prose, and a simple lack of editors disposed to experiment with publication of an unproven genre. The public attention to events surrounding Brazil's Independence from Portugal and the pressure of immediate political and social concerns left little time for speculative writing (Paranhos, *História do romantismo no Brasil*, 36), though paradoxically the city of Rio de Janeiro had become a cultural center through the presence there of the Portuguese royal court, gaining a press in 1808 and publishing its first newspapers in 1813.

It would appear that Portuguese translations of French and English fictional works satisfied the Brazilian public until approximately 1840. Chateaubriand's *Atala* circulated as early as 1819 in translated form in Bahia, home of the Royal Medical School and of Brazil's most avid reading public of the period, and it is estimated (Cândido, *Formação da literatura brasileira*, 121) that by mid century over 150 European novels were available in Portuguese in Brazil (with half being translated between 1830 and 1854); Portuguese and North American fiction joined the flow after 1835. Beginning in 1836, Villeneuve & Co. offered translated short stories from various European countries in serial (*folhetim*) form at reasonable prices; full-length novels by Walter Scott, James Fenimore Cooper, and others were offered from 1837; other publishers joined the trend in 1838. Since the *folhetim* form of publication is fundamental to both long and short fiction in Brazil during the first half of the nineteenth century, it deserves special attention, both from the point of view of the history of journalism and from the perspective of the development and demands of literary tastes among the Brazilian reading public. At least one scholar believes that the literary history of Brazil can be antedated by at least ten years if one takes as point of reference the newspapers and journals of the time instead of published books themselves (Barbosa Lima Sobrinho, *Os precursores*, 15).

The *folhetim* (French *feuilleton*), of solid European antecedents, made its appearance in nascent Brazilian newspapers as a series of pages distinct from the "literary" pages of these journals, which were dedicated principally to poetry. A commentary from *A Epoca Literária*, one such journal, makes it clear that the presumed public for the serial fiction presented in the *folhetims* was female:

> Since the majority of women don't care for politics, science, *belles lettres*, and art, which is what these . . . journals deal with mostly, but are very attached to pleasant, sentimental literature, they feel deprived of full benefit of their subscription if the newspaper does not contain its *literary spice*, which consists of *folhetim* novels, reviews (*revistas*), short pieces (*crônicas*), and "scrapbook" items (*álbuns*), which are written especially for them.   (Salles, *Primeiras manifestações*, 12)

The *folhetim*, then, may be considered not only a vehicle for serial presentation of popular fiction which might subsequently be published in book(let) form, but also as the matrix for the very short fictional essay form known as the *crônica*, which developed into a major genre in Brazilian letters in the late nineteenth and twentieth centuries (see below). The early nineteenth-century *folhetim*, in its heavily sentimental appeal, was in harmony with the fairly sensationalist trend of most newspapers of the period; later in the century, as journalism became somewhat more objective, the *folhetim* began to lose favor among readers. In its heyday, it was ideally suited to the structure and tone of incipient Brazilian fiction, for the episodic nature, suspenseful chapter endings, and heightened emotional content of most early novels and novelettes benefited from an equally episodic, chapter-by-chapter mode of publication.

A key factor in the close link between fiction and journalism during the first half of the nineteenth century in Brazil is the fact that professional journalism was not yet mature; therefore, creative writers themselves founded and published journals and tooled them to their own tastes. Thus, publishers and writers were very often the same people, and literary tastes were developed in the reading public itself by a process of interaction with them. Polemics leading to organized literary criticism were also aired in the pages of newspapers during the period in question.

It is interesting to note that not all the journals which may be called "Brazilian" were actually published in Brazil. The earliest of the nineteenth-century journals – Hipólito da Costa's *Correio Brasiliense* (1808–1822) – circulated from London; *O Panorama* (an eight-page weekly published from 1837 to 1858 and directed partly by Alexandre Herculano) was published in Lisbon; and the short-lived *Niterói* (1836), founded by Brazilians Porto Alegre, Gonçalves de Magalhães, and Torres-Homem, went to press in Paris though its reading public was largely in Brazil.

Three centers of literary journalistic production predominate within Brazil itself during the first half of the nineteenth century: Rio de Janeiro (the "court," or administrative capital), Salvador da Bahia (former administrative capital, home of the medical school, and cultural center of the northeastern region), and Recife (capital of the province of Pernambuco and center of legal studies). The most influential journals published in these three centers and in the newly emerging urban and cultural nucleus of São Paulo are, in general chronological order:

Rio de Janeiro

Aurora Fluminense (founded in 1827 and published by Evaristo da Veiga)

Jornal do Comércio (recreated from an earlier journal in 1827 and publishing fictional contributions from 1837)

O Beija-flor (1830–1831)

O Chronista (perhaps the single most important organ in literary terms, published during the period 1836–1839 by a series of journalistic fiction writers, including Justiniano José da Rocha, Josino Nascimento da Silva, and Firmino Rodrigues da Silva)

O Jornal dos Debates (1837–1838)

O Diário do Rio (whose literary section began in 1837)

O Gabinete de Leitura (a family journal founded in 1837)

A Revista Nacional e Estrangeira (founded by journalistic fiction writer João Manuel Pereira da Silva and two colleagues, and published from 1839 to 1841)

Salvador da Bahia

O Guaicuru (1843–1845)

O *Musaico* (1844–1847)
O *Crepúsculo* (1845–1847)
O *Romancista* (1846–1847)
O *Ateneu* (1849–1850)
A *Epoca Literária* (1850–1851)

Recife

O *Carapuceiro* (a satiric journal edited by Lopes Gama from 1832 to 1847)

São Paulo

O *Farol Paulistano* (founded in 1827)

Mention has already been made of the popularity of short fictional works translated from French or English and published in various of the above journals during the first half of the nineteenth century. Identifying the first authentically *Brazilian* piece of fiction is difficult, as is shown by the varied opinions of critical commentators such as Massaud Moisés, Antônio Soares Amora, Brito Broca, Alexandre Barbosa Lima Sobrinho, David Salles, Mário da Silva Brito, Antônio Cândido, Haroldo Paranhos, and Wilson Martins, for such identification depends largely on the commentator's definition of genre. Concepts of novel, novelette, story, chronicle, epistle, melodrama, episode, etc., are vague, especially in the days of nascent fiction, and our brief overview of the first half of the nineteenth century does not propose a rigorous definition of terms or subdivision of fictional genres; we seek an inclusive, unpolemic presentation focusing on the broader qualities of the fictional works in question.

David Salles has spoken of the challenge of creating or adapting models for any "new" literary form, such as Brazilian fiction in the early nineteenth century, and suggests a certain initial copying of European treatises on morality and historical chronicles with an eye to simulating verisimilitude within a supposedly Brazilian setting. The most obvious models identified by Salles (*Primeiras manifestações*, 17–31) are:

(1) the "black novels," or novellas, and moral tales by authors such as Marmontel, with complex plots to simulate life and bring out its uncontrollable mystery; plots should develop by means of unforeseen coincidences in a linear series and should be punctuated by moral commentaries; the average length of such pieces would be from ten to thirty pages, and the tenor of the works would emphasize the tension between good and evil, with corresponding antithetical stock character types and use of Nature; traditional moral values should be upheld by this type of fiction;

(2) fiction evolved from the *theatre of customs*, depicting life in a more leisurely way through use of dialogue and description of social ambience; there is in this sort of fiction a role for humor, with less concern for moralization and fast plot development and more interest in the manner of life of the moment; usually having an urban focus, these works point up an observable dichotomy between traditional patriarchal models and new middle-class values and lifestyles.

Massaud Moisés notes (*História da literatura brasileira*, II: 57) that, following the European taste, fiction of a mysterious/fantastic nature was the first to capture the imagination of the Brazilian public, followed by the historical novel, which would ultimately become more enduring. Simultaneously with the historical novels appeared the sentimental fiction of troubled courtships, much in vogue throughout the romantic period. Wilson Martins has remarked (*História da inteligência brasileira*, II: 248) on the imprecise boundary existing between historical essays and novels having a historical basis during the early decades of the romantic period, and credits the success of both among the reading public to the heightened Brazilian interest in the study of history attendant upon political independence and the nationalism of early imperial days.

The first fictional work published in Brazil in the nineteenth century appears to be *Statira e Zoroastes*, a 58-page novelette of allegorical, moralizing character, authored by Lucas José de Alvarenga (1768–1831). Three years later, an anonymous novelette running to 50 pages in length and entitled *Olaya e Júlio ou A periquita* was published in *O Beija-flor*, occupying three numbers of the magazine. Both these works appeared in Rio de Janeiro, as did the majority of other fictional creations published in the decade of the 1830s.

João Manuel Pereira da Silva (1817–1897), an author–publisher of somewhat Lusitanian tastes and with a penchant for historiography, published during the biennium 1837–1838 numerous short stories in *O Jornal dos Debates*; the best-known of these are "Luísa," "Um último adeus," "Uma aventura em Veneza," and "As catacumbas de São Francisco de Paula." Several of his other stories appeared in the *Jornal do Comércio* between 1837 and 1849; of these, the most widely known appears to have been "O aniversário de D. Miguel em 1828" (published in 1839), a work showing Miguel, absolutist aspirant to the Portuguese throne, as a despot, and seeking to endear the more liberal D. Pedro I to the Brazilian public. Other journalists cultivating the genre of the historically oriented short story in the later 1830s were Justiniano da Rocha (1812–1862), Josino do Nascimento da Silva (1811–1886), Firmino Rodrigues da Silva (1815–1879), Francisco de Paula Brito (1809–1861), Vicente Pereira de Carvalho Guimarães (1820–?), João José de Sousa e Silva Rio (1810–1885), and Luís Carlos Martins Pena (1815–1848), a writer better-known for his comic plays. Martins Pena published several short stories in the *Correio das Modas* and *O Gabinete de Leitura* between 1839 and 1840, as did Sousa e Silva Rio, and others. Simultaneously, Pereira e Silva published "Uma paixão de artista," which he called a short story, and *Religião, amor e pátria*, referred to as a novelette. There appeared in *folhetim* form in *O Comércio* in 1839 a story (or novelette) attributed variously to Justiniano da Rocha (1812–1862) and Joaquim Norberto de Sousa e Silva (1820–1891) and entitled *Assassinos misteriosos, ou A paixão dos diamantes*; it was subsequently republished as a separate *folheto* of twenty-nine pages, while Pereira da Silva's story, "O aniversário de D. Miguel em 1828," yielded thirty-four in *folheto* form. Clearly, a degree of ambiguity as to just which genre was being published failed to concern either the author–publishers or their increasingly avid public of readers.

After a decade of uncertain starts, prose fiction in Brazil seems to tread a firmer course beginning in about 1840. In addition to shorter fiction of the type described above, such as Sousa e Silva's story "As duas órfãs" (1841), works of considerably greater length begin to appear. Two general thematic trends may be observed in works published during the first half of the decade, and to a degree in subsequent years: the continuing fascination with historical subjects, sometimes treated in melodramatic fashion, and the more domestic interest in Brazilian customs and sentimental themes. Some works, as we shall see, managed to incorporate elements of both trends.

The historical trend, though not warranting the rubric of "historical novel," is seen in a couple of anonymously published short novels appearing in the *Despertador Brasileiro* in 1839. These are *Virgínia, ou A vingança de Nassau* (subtitled *História brasileira*) and *O rapto malogrado*, bearing the same subtitle; the authorship of the first of these novels, based on the Dutch occupation of 1638, was subsequently attributed to Sousa e Silva. In 1840, Pereira da Silva published in *Jornal do Comércio* his short historical novel *Jerônimo Corte Real*, republished in book form twenty-five years later by the Livraria Garnier. At about the same time, Inácio Pires de Morais Sarmento published two short novels – *Francisco Luís de Sousa* and *O cavaleiro da Cruz* – in *O Museu Universal*, while José Rufino Rodrigues de Vasconcelos brought out *O homem misterioso*, a rather melodramatic work, and Sousa e Silva saw his novel *O sedutor* published in the *Despertador Brasileiro* (1840). Morais Sarmento, of Portuguese birth and with a strong historical penchant, published in *O Brasil* (1840) a historical novel entitled *João Pires da Bandeira, ou o alferes d'Afonso V*, while the Brazilian Francisco Adolfo de Varnhagen (1816–1878) was publishing in *O Panorama* (Lisbon) the novel *O descobrimento do Brasil – crônica do fim do século XV*.

The mid-1840s show a continuation of historical interest through fictional works with the appearance of one of the better-known novels of the day, *Um roubo na pavuna* (1843), authored by Luís da Silva Alves de Azambuja Susano (1791–1873), and the *Romances históricos* of Miguel Maria Lisboa, Barão of Japurá (1809–1881). The Portuguese Vicente Pereira de Carvalho Guimarães brought out several short historical novels in his magazine O *Ostentor* between 1845 and 1846, showing a nascent interest in Indianist themes; these serially published works are: *Jerônimo Barbalho Bezerra, A Guerra dos Emboabas, A cruz de pedra*, and *Os jesuítas na América*. The intention of this Lusitanian writer to emphasize the truly Brazilian character of these works is shown by the general title *Romanceiro brasílico* chosen for them.

Antônio Gonçalves Teixeira e Sousa (1812–1861), best known for his composition of what many critics consider the first full-length sentimental novel of customs in Brazil, *O filho do pescador*, was obviously attracted as well by the vehicle of the historical novel. Between 1847 and 1851 he serially published two such works: *Tardes de um pintor, ou Intrigas de um jesuíta*, criticized by some as a "false historical novel," and *Gonzaga, ou a Conjuração de Tiradentes*. The first of these works prefigures several lower-class marginal character types later used to advantage by Manuel Antônio de Almeida (1831–1861) in his *Memórias de um sargento de milícias* [*Memoirs of a Militia Sergeant*], and his favorable presentation of black and mestizo characters reveals a certain historical candor. Finally, in the tradition of short historical novels prior to the works of José de Alencar, which will serve to expand the genre after mid century, we find Alves de Azambuja Susano's 58-page novel dealing with a valid agricultural theme, *O Capitão Silvestre e Frei Veloso, ou A plantação do café no Rio de Janeiro* (1847).

The sentimental novel of picturesque local customs, focusing on the contemporary Brazilian scene and related to the "theatre of customs" of Martins Pena and other dramatists, began its surge of popularity in approximately 1840. O *Chronista* published in 1839 an anonymous short novel entitled O *homem de recursos, ou O noivado na rocha*, appearing in serial form, but it was the triennium 1843–1845 which saw the definitive launching of the sentimental novel. The four works which may be said to constitute the foundation of this sub-genre are Teixeira e Sousa's *O filho do pescador*, Gonçalves de Magalhães's *Amância* (1844), and two novels by Joaquim Manuel de Macedo (1820–1882): *A moreninha* and *O moço loiro*. Macedo, who wrote more than twenty novels in all, followed his initial successes with two more novels of the same order before the end of the decade – *Os dois amores* (1848) and *Rosa* (1849) – and is generally considered the father of the genre. Let us observe the salient qualities of his first novel, *A moreninha*, which invariably serves as the point of comparison for subsequent novels in the same vein.

Wilson Martins, who offers plot summaries and developmental outlines for all four of the above-mentioned works in Volume II of his *História da inteligência brasileira*, has remarked that *A moreninha* reflects the Brazilian public's interest in looking at itself, observing its customs, and trying to delineate its character. As creator of both the urban and social novel in Brazil, Macedo shows the tension between rural and city life; *A moreninha* itself supports the idea, later defended also by Alencar, that true love flourishes best in the country, and there is an obvious attempt to reproduce fairly natural dialogue between the characters. The authentically Brazilian brunette beauty and the *moleque* (mischievous slave boy) make their literary debut in this work, to be widely developed in later works by Alencar and other writers. Against the background of a patriarchal society, *A moreninha* contains a subtle appeal for a more equal education for women than was generally available at the time. There is, for example, a reference to British feminist Mary Wollstonecraft, mother of Mary Shelley (author of *Frankenstein*). Coincidentally, Wollstonecraft's *Vindication of the Rights of Woman* (1792) had been translated into Portuguese and published in Recife in 1832 by Dionísia Gonçalves (1809–1885), better known by her pseudonym, "Nísia Floresta"; such was the success of that work that it was republished in Porto Alegre in 1833.

The popularity of *A moreninha* is attested to by the appearance of a second edition of the work one year after its publication and by the author's offering of his second novel, *O moço loiro*, in that same year, in gratitude to his "feminine public" for its enthusiastic reception of his first novel. *O moço loiro* bears a slightly sharper edge of social commentary than *A moreninha*, caricaturing certain urban customs in a style similar to that of Martins Pena and documenting the style of life of the period.

The second half of the decade of the 1840s saw an increasing proliferation of sentimental novels of customs, not only in Rio de Janeiro but in Salvador da Bahia and other urban centers as well. A short enumeration of some of the best-known novels published at the time will serve to show the focus on young love prevalent in these works, as well as the continuing importance of journals and periodicals as the vehicle for initial publication of fictional works. In 1846 Teixeira e Sousa brought out *As fatalidades de dois jovens* in Rio and José Bernardino de Moura published *Uma reparação sublime* in Niterói. In the same year several novels appeared in serial form in Bahia: *O amante assassino*, published anonymously in *O Ateneu*, was later attributed to Mariano de Santa Rosa de Lima; Frei Manuel de São Caetano Pinto published *Emílio* in *O Crepúsculo*, in which journal appeared also Manuel Carigé Baraúna's *Eugênia* and *Júlia*, while Ambrósio Ronzi brought out *Cena da vida baiana* and Augusto Victorino Alves Sacramento Blake (1827–1903), best known for his extensive bio-bibliographical studies of colonial and nineteenth-century literature, published his novel *Dous casamentos* in *O Musaico*. In 1847 Nísia Floresta, best known for a non-fictional work entitled *Conselhos à minha filha* (1845) and for her positivistic and abolitionist essays, published a pair of novels in Rio de Janeiro; these are *Daciz, ou A jovem completa* and *A lágrima de um caeté*, both of a rather didactic nature. As mentioned earlier, Macedo himself launched a pair of somewhat moralistic novels in the biennium 1848–1849, and in those years there appeared also Carlos Augusto Cordeiro's novel, *Os amores de Carlos e Clara*, and Firmino Coelho do Amaral's *O calouro namorado* (published in *O Ateneu*). The decade ended with the appearance of at least four novels in the year 1850; Mariano de Santa Rosa de Lima returned to the pages of *O Ateneu* with *O legado da hora extrema* and *Amores de uma criatura sem dentes*, while in Pernambuco, Antônio Vitrúvio Pinto Bandeira Acióli de Vasconcelos published *Taliorato*, and in Niterói, Nísia Floresta brought out her last novel, *Dedicação de uma amiga*.

The decade of the 1850s began rather inauspiciously with the publication of several melodramatic works: José Higino Sodré Pereira da Nóbrega's *O assassínio e o adultério* (1851), Justino de Figueiredo Novais's *Os dois loucos* (1851), Caldre Fião's *O corsário* (1851), and Macedo's *Vicentina* (1853). The scene brightened, however, with the appearance in Maranhão of *A cigana brasileira*, a novel of customs authored by João Clímaco Lobato, and by the publication by "Um brasileiro" (*Correio Mercantil*, [1853]) of a series of *folhetins* bearing the title *Memórias de um sargento de milícias*. The latter work, whose author was soon discovered to be Manuel Antônio de Almeida (1831–1861), was republished in book form in 1854–1855; though the public of its day received it with general apathy because of its break with popular romantic literary conventions, it has since become popular because of its earthiness, rollicking good humor, and documentary value as a mirror of urban life in Rio de Janeiro during the period of the Regency.

The *Memórias de um sargento de milícias*, unique among Brazilian fiction works of the period in question by virtue of its having been translated into English, is structurally similar to the comedies of customs being staged by Martins Pena during the same time-frame. Reflecting in its rather picaresque character the episodic nature of a genre long popular in Europe but on the wane in favor of more melodramatic forms, *Memórias de um sargento de milícias* is a memorialistic work whose raw material seems to have been largely furnished to Almeida by one Antônio César Ramos, a militia sergeant in Rio de Janeiro. Vidigal, the policeman in this novel tracing the rise of a poor boy to a life of solid prosperity through fair means or foul, is drawn from Miguel Nunes Vidigar (1745–1843), who was César Ramos's commander and a fairly sympathetic figure as fictionally portrayed. The prototype of the *agregado*, or factotum, in

Brazilian literature appears in this work, though its development awaits the pen of Machado de Assis later in the century. Though the characters of this novel are not developed in psychological depth, they join to comprise a colorful gallery of social types in Balzacian fashion. *Memórias de um sargento de milícias* is, in short, the most realistic of Brazilian fictional works written before 1870.

Mention was made at the beginning of this chapter of the rather tenuous nature of the fictional genre in Brazil during the first half of the nineteenth century and of the ascendancy of poetry, drama, and journalism during the same period. A similar comment may be made with reference to the fiction writers of the period; with the exception of Macedo, none of the novelists and short-story writers continued firmly in the fictional tradition. Martins Pena, for example, always preferred the theatre and realized his most important works in drama. Pereira da Silva was essentially a historiographer, while Justiniano da Rocha clearly showed his primary devotion to journalism. Nísia Floresta made her most lasting contribution to Brazilian letters in the genre of the personal essay, while Gonçalves de Magalhães and several others were primarily poets. The true fictional vocations in Brazil develop only in the second half of the nineteenth century.

The Brazilian novel from 1850 to 1900
David T. Haberly

Brazilian novels and short stories of the second half of the nineteenth century reflected the complex and infinitely larger fictions which served as the basis of Brazilian society as a whole during the period. The most basic of those fictions, that Brazil was a progressive and essentially European nation which happened to find itself on the other side of the Atlantic, was an article of faith among the miniscule Brazilian elite – those who could read and write, those who voted, those who controlled government, economics, and society.

It has been estimated that those actively involved in cultural and political matters at the time of Independence in 1822 numbered about 20,000, out of a population of some 4 million. By 1871, when the total population had reached 10 million, only 147,621 children were enrolled in primary schools, and only 9,389 attended secondary schools. Ten years later, in 1881, only 147,000 Brazilians – out of a total population of around 13 million – were qualified to vote. To talk of progress, of politics, of literature during the nineteenth century, therefore, is inevitably to talk about this small elite; the other Brazilians, perhaps 97 or 98 percent of the population, remained outside what the elite defined as the mainstream of national society, isolated from politics, from culture, and from meaningful progress, by poverty, illiteracy, and racial discrimination. This last factor was of particular importance, for Brazil's population remained overwhelmingly non-white throughout most of the century.

The traditional, consensus history of Brazilian fiction from 1850 to 1900 is part of the national fiction, reflecting the belief that Brazil's culture and society were inextricably linked to Europe – and, in particular, to France. The history of prose fiction in Brazil has usually been described, therefore, as roughly parallel to that of France, allowing for a few delays due to the slow passage of ideas and styles across the Atlantic: the development of romantic fiction in the 1840s and 1850s; the triumph of Romanticism in the works of José de Alencar; the emergence of Realism;

and, in the last decades of the century, the triumph of Zola's Naturalism.

There are, however, several basic problems with this chronology. It is very difficult indeed to find any Brazilian novel from this period which conforms to the standard definitions of European or North American Realism; and the genre thus appears, at least superficially, to have moved directly from Romanticism to Naturalism. Moreover, the greatest Brazilian novelists of the period – José de Alencar, Joaquim Maria Machado de Assis, and Aluísio Azevedo – do not fit neatly into any of the recognized European schools of fiction.

This brief survey attempts to resolve at least some of these problems by suggesting a rather different chronology and structure for nineteenth-century Brazilian fiction, based upon the simple reality that the nation's culture during the period, whatever the beliefs and fantasies of the elite who wrote and read that fiction, was *not* that of Europe. Brazilians did read European fiction, and they were influenced by what they read, but the development of Brazilian fiction followed in its own path, with its own rules, and internal traditions and influences and the needs and expectations of national readers were at least as important as foreign models.

By 1850, prose fiction still had not established itself as a central genre in Brazilian literature. There were several reasons for this. First, the nation lacked a tradition of fiction; the two colonial works that can be tentatively classified as novels, *Compêndio narrativo do peregrino da América* (1728) by Nuno Marques Pereira (1652?–1728?) and *Máximas de virtude e formosura (Aventuras de Diófanes)* (1752) by Teresa Margarida da Silva e Orta (1711?–1787?), do not appear to have been influential in the nineteenth century. Secondly, while translations of European fiction, sold in relatively inexpensive editions or serialized in periodicals, were readily available to the Brazilian elite, these imported literary artifacts contained, deeply embedded in both their form and their content, a vision of a world very different from the intensely traditional, slave-owning, semi-feudal society of Brazil. The dichotomy between foreign models and national reality became critical only when Brazilians began to try their hands at writing works of fiction set in their own country and describing their own reality, and can readily be seen in three inter-related social issues of key importance to fiction: marriage patterns among the Brazilian elite, the concept of favor, and literacy.

In nineteenth-century Brazil, virtually all upper-class marriages were carefully arranged financial and social alliances, and represented the acceptance of family obligation rather than the free exercise of personal choice; contemporary treatises on family life preached that mutual tolerance and respect were about all that even the most fortunate married couples could realistically expect. Because the Brazilian legal system normally required the equal distribution of estates among multiple heirs, a common strategy for keeping large family holdings as intact as possible was endogamy – it was relatively common for men to be married to their aunts, nieces, first and second cousins, or widowed sisters-in-law.

If the vision of marriage as the triumph of romantic love found in much foreign fiction was alien to Brazilian writers and readers, so too was the assumption that individuals possessed some measure of control over their own destinies. For the elite, as for virtually all free Brazilians, the central organizing principle of society was not merit, but favor, and the institution which controlled access to favor and distributed its benefits was the extended family of relatives, godparents, and dependents or *agregados*. Intelligence, education, strength of character, goodness, diligence, devotion to duty – all of the virtues which graced the heroes and heroines of foreign fiction were virtually meaningless as determinants of success or failure in Brazil. What counted in this rigid and hierarchical society, rather, was the ability to obtain favor from those above and to distribute favor to those below, and that ability was almost entirely dependent upon birth and marriage.

Many Brazilian intellectuals, in the period around 1850, were convinced that the ideology implicit in foreign prose fiction made the genre itself inherently dangerous, even subversive. Illiteracy offered a defense against this danger; at the middle of the century, perhaps only about 20 percent of Brazilian men could read and write their own names – much less read a novel. While many readers of fiction in Europe or North America were female, at least 90 percent of Brazilian women were completely illiterate in 1850. Throughout the nineteenth century, therefore, most Brazilian novels were written by men to be read by other men; the point of view is almost invariably that of the male protagonist and/or narrator. In addition, the predominantly male audience for prose fiction allowed novelists to include material which would have been unthinkable in European or North American fiction. An early example is the famous episode of the hemorrhoids in *A moreninha* (1844), a sentimental novel by Joaquim Manuel de Macedo (1820–1882). At the end of the century, Brazilian novelists went considerably beyond Zola in their treatment of sexuality; the 1926 English translation of Aluísio Azevedo's *O cortiço [A Brazilian Tenement]* had to be heavily censored for North American audiences, and Adolfo Caminha's explicit novel of homosexual love, *Bom-Crioulo*, first published in 1895, was not translated into English (as *The Black Man and the Cabin Boy*) until 1982.

The first nineteenth-century Brazilians to create works of prose fiction thus faced the daunting task of adapting the genre to a new reality and to new readers. The novels of Joaquim Manuel de Macedo (1820–1882), among the very earliest Brazilian attempts at the genre, exemplify some of the problems inherent in this enterprise. Macedo wanted to write sentimental accounts of adventure and romance, but could not place his characters – utterly unexceptional young Brazilians of the elite, exactly like most of his readers – in situations which seriously challenged established social norms. The hero and heroine of *A moreninha*, for example, are closely linked by class and family friendship, and it is almost painfully obvious from their first introduction that they are destined to marry. Macedo tries very hard to suggest that their love is in some way exceptional, the product either of destiny or of free choice, but he is careful to have that love properly ratified, at the end of the novel, by a good deal of shuttling back and forth by other characters as the two families negotiate and approve the marriage.

Quite another approach was taken by Manuel Antônio Alvares de Azevedo (1831–1852) in his *Noite na taverna*, first published posthumously in 1855 and reprinted a number of times in the course of the nineteenth century. These brief narratives, written sometime after 1848, when Alvares de Azevedo entered the Faculty of Law at São Paulo, are among the very earliest Brazilian short stories; they are also the most popular and most influential examples of the genre before Machado de Assis. *Noite na taverna* has generally been described as just the sort of Byronic fantasy of exotic immorality, populated by fabulously beautiful and depraved women, that we might expect an adolescent boy to invent as an escape from classes in canon law and from a small and very provincial town. Yet, while nothing in the setting of *Noite* suggests that it takes place in Brazil, I would suggest that this popular and influential text is, in its own curious way, at least as faithful to the reality of Brazilian upper-class life as *A moreninha* – but faithful to the darkest side of that reality. Slavery, the central fact of Brazilian society, meant absolute power over other human beings, and that power was exercised, at least some of the time, through sexual aggression and violence. Almost every slave-owning family in Brazil had its oral histories of cruelty and perversion, and even the bizarre events described in *Noite na taverna* pale when compared to real events in those histories. Nor is it any accident that the one crime punished in *Noite* is incest, the fearful secret of many families of the elite – not the legal, church-sanctioned marriages between first cousins or between uncles and nieces, but the seduction or rape of slave women by their white half-brothers.

The *Memórias de um sargento de milícias* [*Memoirs of a Militia Sergeant*] by Manuel Antônio de Almeida (1831–1861) is the first important Brazilian novel published after 1850. The *Memórias*, published under the pseudonym of "Um brasileiro" ["A Brazilian"], were serialized in a Rio de Janeiro newspaper in 1853, and appeared in two volumes in 1854–1855. The text is rooted in two very different European prose traditions: semi-picaresque, satirical English novels of the eighteenth century, like those of Fielding and Smollett, which Almeida and other Brazilians read in French translation; and the early romantic *costumbrismo* of Spain and Portugal – generally sympathetic, even nostalgic, descriptions of local customs and traditions imperilled by modernization. The action of the *Memórias* takes place in Rio de Janeiro during the last days of Portuguese colonial rule, almost a half-century before the novel's publication, and Almeida describes a wide range of popular celebrations, customs, and beliefs, many of which had almost disappeared by 1853. This chronological distance is reinforced by social distance as well; most of the characters in the novel are Portuguese immigrants to Brazil, members of the tiny urban middle class of barbers, bailiffs, seamstresses, and soldiers – the social group from which Almeida himself came, but one considerably removed from most of his readers. Much of the interest of the text derives from the tension between Almeida's *costumbrista* nostalgia for simpler and more authentic times, on the one hand, and his sarcastic, irreverent, and highly intrusive narrator.

That narrative voice is perhaps Almeida's most significant contribution to prose fiction in nineteenth-century Brazil; variations of this voice appear in Alencar's urban novels and in most of Machado de Assis's major works. The narrator, of course, moves the plot along and maintains suspense through a careful mix of revelation and reticence, but in Almeida's novel, as in its successors, this particular narrative voice has other vital functions as well. Almeida's narrator is highly sophisticated, as well as extremely patronizing toward all the characters – particularly the female characters – and events he describes; he is carefully designed to convince upper-class male readers that he is one of them. Once that identification is established, the narrative voice serves as the sole guarantor of the authenticity and truthfulness of the text, independent of the perceived realism of the people and events described. Moreover, the narrative voice controls his readers' reactions to the text, carefully explaining how they are to react to individual twists and turns in the plot and to the characters he describes and satirizes.

Almeida's *Memórias* present a highly unsentimental vision of the nature of nineteenth-century Brazilian society; that vision is far indeed from that found in the European romantic novel or in Macedo's fiction. Lust is the basis of most relationships, while love is a rather pathetic emotion, largely out of place in this society. As Almeida's stupid, headstrong, and utterly worthless hero blunders through life, steadfastly refusing to do anything positive, he is protected and rescued, again and again, by a safety net endlessly stitched together by the almost nameless group of elderly men and women who conspire, in various largely amoral ways, to control his fate. As the narrator notes, "in that day (and they do say it is a defect of our own time) the use of influence and the mutual obligations between parent and godparent, or godparents to each other, were a veritable mainspring in the whole machinery of society" (*Memoirs*, trans. L. L. Barrett, 228). Almeida's humble militia sergeant and, by extension, all Brazilians, were pawns in a conspiracy of "influence and . . . mutual obligations." This conspiracy, in fact, *is* the *Memórias* and both forms its entirely Brazilian message and creates its plot; and its various participants serve as the narrator's agents in developing and advancing the action.

It has been suggested that the nineteenth-century Brazilian novel would have developed along quite different lines had Almeida not died in a shipwreck in 1861; however, there is no evidence that he produced any prose fiction between 1853 and his death. In fact, by 1861, José Martiniano de Alencar (1829–1877) had completely transformed both the nature and the status of fiction in Brazil.

Alencar, a member of a powerful political family from the province of Ceará, was a central figure in Pedro II's Empire. His first novel, *Cinco minutos*, was serialized in a Rio de Janeiro newspaper early in 1856. *Cinco minutos* is set among the elite of Rio de Janeiro, but its aims and techniques are very different from those of Macedo's novels. Alencar set out to write a best-seller as suspenseful, exciting, and potentially scandalous as any imported work; its plot – the courtship and eventual marriage of the aristocratic but temporarily impoverished narrator and the beautiful and wealthy young woman he encounters by chance, a relationship entirely independent of external pressures and family constraints – certainly sold a lot of newspapers, but was utterly improbable within the context of nineteenth-century Brazil.

Alencar attempted to use several different strategies to overcome the inherent implausibility of his narrative. First, he adopted the chatty, familiar narrator found in Almeida's *Memórias* and in his own regular newspaper column of gossip and social commentary. Alencar's fictional narrator is an apologist rather than a satirist, but he serves the same function as a primary guarantor of the essential truth of the text. Alencar also developed and expanded the rudimentary framing devices Macedo had used in his early novels, endeavoring to convince the reader that *Cinco minutos* is a factual account of real events, narrated by one of the protagonists. Third, like both Macedo and Almeida, Alencar provided a great deal of verifiably accurate detail in his realistic descriptions of Rio de Janeiro. Finally, Alencar explicitly and implicitly embedded a highly conservative ideology within his text. That ideology stressed the importance of maintaining the traditional values of Brazilian society, as Alencar defined them (patriotic fervor, thrift, simplicity of life-style, hard work, courage in the face of adversity, love of family, marital trust and fidelity), despite the dangerous attractiveness of amoral European capitalism and "foreign ways and customs."

Early in 1857, Alencar suddenly interrupted the serialization of his second, quite similar fiction of contemporary urban life, *A viuvinha*, and began writing and publishing something radically new and different – *O guaraní*, his first *indianista* [Indianist] novel. This text was instantly and enormously popular among the nation's readers. Set in the forests of Brazil in the early seventeenth century, *O guaraní* recounts the love of Peri, the most noble of all Indians, and Cecília, the blonde and beautiful daughter of a Portuguese colonizer. This chronological and physical setting, at once patriotically Brazilian and completely outside the personal experience of Alencar and his readers, freed the novelist from the inherent conflicts between European models and the reality of contemporary Rio de Janeiro. The freedom Alencar found in the wholly new and alien reality he created in *O guaraní* encouraged him to move beyond mere narration and begin constructing a highly original mythology of national genesis. At the end of the novel, both the Indian and the Portuguese forces are destroyed in a great conflagration; only Cecília and Peri survive, and while Alencar does not insist that these most perfect examples of Europe and Indian America will mate and repopulate Brazil, he does leave that option open for the reader to choose.

Iracema [*Iracema, the Honey-Lips: A Legend of Brazil*], Alencar's masterpiece and the most popular of all of his novels, goes even further in establishing the Brazilian creation-myth; its intensely allegorical plot and rhapsodic language set *Iracema* entirely apart from other nineteenth-century novels of Europe or North America. Iracema, the Indian princess whose name is an anagram of America, falls in love with Martim, a Portuguese explorer; the couple, consistently described as "The Virgin of the Land" and "The Warrior from the Sea," have a child, Moacir, whose name – Alencar tells us in his notes to the novel – means "Child of Pain." Weakened by childbirth, Iracema dies – as, Alencar implies, Indian America must die – leaving Moacir, the symbolic product of all the pain of the Conquest and the first true Brazilian, in the care of his Portuguese father.

During his long and productive career, Alencar produced one more Indianist fantasy, *Ubirajara*. He also wrote two long novels of Brazilian history, *As minas de prata* and *A guerra dos Mascates*. In 1870, Alencar invented the Brazilian regionalist novel with *O gaúcho*; this was followed by several other popular and influential novels set in various areas of the nation's interior. Alencar never personally visited most of these locales, using guide-books, the accounts of foreign travelers, and his own prodigious imagination to create his settings and his characters; virtually none of his readers had been outside the coastal cities, and Alencar was therefore free to create landscapes, social patterns, and characters almost at will.

Despite the success of his Indianist, regionalist, and historical novels, Alencar did not give up his struggle to create viable fictional representations of contemporary Brazilian life. The results of his efforts, from *A viuvinha* to *Senhora*, are a very mixed bag, and it is clear that Alencar never achieved the control and self-assurance he found in distant geographical and chronological settings. His most interesting urban novels, *Lucíola* and *Senhora*, deal with important social problems (prostitution and arranged marriages, respectively) and we can see Alencar endeavoring, through his themes and his detailed descriptions of clothes, furniture, and other cultural artifacts, to move toward the realism of Balzac, whom he greatly admired. At the same time, however, Alencar's analysis of Brazilian society was deeply flawed: the central problem, he insisted, was not slavery, which he strongly supported, or feudalism, which he idealized; rather, the root of all evil was the pursuit of uninherited wealth. Moreover, no matter how immoral his major characters might at first appear, in Alencar's hands they always turned out to have hearts of gold and to deserve the often contradictory and implausible happy endings he still felt obligated to provide.

Alencar's influence on the development of the nineteenth-century Brazilian novel cannot be overestimated; he nationalized the genre and made it respectable, he established its peculiar mix of detailed realistic description and romantic ideology, and he largely created its major sub-genres. His successors, particularly in the 1860s and 1870s, necessarily worked within the forms and structures Alencar had created. Their focus, with few exceptions, was the regionalist novel, a sub-genre which has dominated much of Brazilian fiction since Alencar. Virtually every major novelist in the thirty years which followed the publication of Alencar's *O gaúcho* wrote at least one regionalist novel – Machado de Assis and Raul Pompéia are the only well-known exceptions – and the enduring popularity of Regionalism can be seen in twentieth-century writers like Graciliano Ramos, Raquel de Queiroz, Jorge Amado, and even João Guimarães Rosa.

Brazilian and foreign critics have found it difficult to agree on a single definition of Regionalism as practiced during the period from about 1870 to the first decade of the twentieth century; the nature of two other sub-genres Alencar created or significantly refined, the Indianist novel and the historical novel, both of which became considerably less important components of Brazilian fiction after about 1880, has also been the subject of considerable discussion. In reality, however, these three sub-genres had a great deal in common, and can in fact be viewed as manifestations of a single impulse in Brazilian society and culture.

Regionalism, Indianism, and the historical novel all represented a movement away from contemporary, urban civilization toward something seen as more original, more authentic, more "ingenuous" – a word very often used both by regionalist novelists and by critics. This movement could be geographical (from the coastal cities to the backlands, from the central coast to the distant far south or to the even more distant Amazon); it could be historical. either recreating past events or describing societies, like those of Indians or mestizos or backwoodsmen, which survived into the present but which represented a way of life that had long since disappeared from the coastal cities; it could be ethnological, describing, in minute detail, the mores of populations defined in nineteenth-century raciological theories of race as considerably lower on the evolutionary scale than the urbanized elite of European descent.

There are a number of explanations for this movement. First, the idealization of the primitive, the ingenuous, was a standard component of romantic ideology, an ideology which continued to dominate most of Brazilian prose fiction throughout this period. Second, Brazilian writers, from Alencar on, felt strongly that it was their responsibility – again, a very romantic responsibility – to create a national literature and a national culture; Regionalism, Indianism, and historical fiction all could be seen as contributing to nationalism by their emphasis upon local landscapes and customs. Many writers after Alencar, however, were also determined to use fiction to document the character and establish the importance of their own specific regions – the south, the Amazon, the western interior, the backlands of the northeast. At the level of novelistic strategy, as well, all of these authors had learned from Alencar – and, perhaps, from Almeida's use of local color, a historical setting, and lower-class characters in his *Memórias de um sargento de milícias* – that upper-class urban readers were prepared to accept as real and believable almost anything with which they were not personally familiar. Finally, these three related sub-genres also represented a very clear movement away from the omnipresence of Africa in nineteenth-century coastal Brazil – to Indian Brazil, before the arrival of Africans and their descendents, or to regions and times in which those of African descent were not present.

Regionalism – and from now on I include in this term the last examples of both Indianist and historical fiction – after Alencar can be divided into three reasonably coherent groupings: romantic Regionalism of the period from about 1865 to about 1880; the regionalist movement Brazilians call *Naturalismo* [Naturalism], which also had an urban component and which reached its height in the period between 1881 and about 1895; and folkloric Regionalism, which began in the 1890s and continued well into the twentieth century.

The first important romantic Regionalist after Alencar was Bernardo Guimarães (1825–1884), a classmate and friend of Álvares de Azevedo. Guimarães wrote his first historical novel, O ermitão de Muquém, in 1858, but it did not appear until 1869; he went on to produce other historical and Regionalist novels set in the area of Minas Gerais, an Indianist novel, and Brazil's only important abolitionist novel, A escrava Isaura. Most of these works follow fairly closely in Alencar's footsteps, although Guimarães was a considerably weaker novelist. His characters are stereotypical representatives of pure Good or pure Evil, and his plots are rarely convincing. These flaws are particularly evident in A escrava Isaura, a novel which may have been influenced by Harriet Beecher Stowe's Uncle Tom's Cabin and, perhaps, by Dion Boucicault's 1861 play, The Octoroon. While Guimarães's text appears to attack slavery, his beautiful and angelic heroine is far from a typical slave; she is educated and highly cultured, and her "skin is like the ivory of a keyboard . . ." (Guimaraẽs, A escrava Isaura (1968), 24). In fact, A escrava Isaura is not really an abolitionist novel at all; it is an utterly unrealistic Indianist novel in which the Noble Savage – like Iracema a symbolic archetype of feminine goodness and suffering – happens to have African genes and happens to wind up marrying a millionaire; there is no evidence that the novel in any way changed the attitudes of the Brazilian slave-owners who bought and read Guimarães's text.

João Franklin da Silveira Távora (1842–1888) was from Alencar's home province of Ceará; like Guimarães, he began writing novels just as Alencar was transforming the Brazilian novel, but his major works date from the decade of the 1870s. In his pseudonymous essays entitled Cartas a Cincinato, Távora violently criticized Alencar for unrealistic descriptions of the interior and its inhabitants and for failing to focus on the need to create strong regional literatures as a precondition for a national literary culture. Despite his vehemence and sarcasm, many of Távora's complaints had considerable validity; but Távora's own attempts at fiction, centered on regional history and customs and on the problem of rural banditry, lack the vitality, imagination, and self-confident control of the material found even in Alencar's lesser works.

The last important romantic Regionalist was Viscount Alfredo d'Es-cragnolle Taunay (1843–1899), a noble of the imperial court. Taunay was an extremely uneven narrator, and only one of his novels is read today. That text, Inocência [Innocencia, 1889 and Inocencia, 1945], was one of the most popular novels of the century. It is considerably superior to other regionalist novels of its time, in large measure because Taunay relies more on dialogue – and most of the characters actually do sound like backwoodsmen rather than refined aristocrats – and less on the detailed description of the minutiae of rural life. The melodramatic plot of tragic love and the figure of Inocência, the teenage peasant girl who is as much a Noble Savage as Iracema or Isaura, however, come straight from late eighteenth-century French Romanticism.

The conservative, static quality of romantic Regionalism, far closer to Chateaubriand than to Balzac and Flaubert, may well have appealed to the Brazilian elite precisely because that elite was beginning to realize, in the course of the 1870s, that its Brazil – the Brazil of the court and the coastal cities – was changing in fundamental ways. The Empire had survived its first armed conflict since Independence, the Paraguayan War of 1865–1870 (the relative lack of importance of this conflict to the elite is suggested by the fact that no serious fiction was written about it), but in the 1870s Pedro II became involved in serious conflicts with the church and with the military, two of the pillars of his rule. A group of young aristocrats founded the Republican party in 1870, campaigning against the monarchy, against slavery, and against the special privileges the Catholic church had long enjoyed in Brazil. For the next two decades, these three issues preoccupied and deeply divided the Brazilian elite. Many members of that elite, most notably José de Alencar, were strongly opposed to even the very gradual process by which Brazil abolished slavery; the 1871 Law of the Free Womb freed all slaves born after its passage (not immediately, but when they became twenty-one) and the Law of the Sexagenarians (1885), as its name implies, freed slaves when they reached retirement age. Full Abolition, without compensation for slave-owners, was not accomplished until May 13, 1888, and the Empire fell eighteen months later. A relatively repressive military dictatorship followed the proclamation of the Republic in November of 1889, and elections were not held until 1894.

The movement Brazilians call *Naturalismo* was in large measure a response to these changes and conflicts, and to the elite's disquiet about the future of the nation. While it is possible to trace some elements of the movement to foreign sources, specifically the novels of the Portuguese Realist Eça de Queiroz and the naturalist novels and theories of Zola, much of *Naturalismo* developed from these national concerns and from the traditions Alencar and the romantic Regionalists had established. These factors clearly differentiate *Naturalismo* from European and North American Naturalism. While certain aspects of the Brazilian movement appeared new and shocking, in particular its almost obsessive focus on, and detailed description of, sexual relationships, I would argue that the movement is both a thematic and stylistic continuation of romantic Regionalism – but with a new and very different ideological basis. That intensely pessimistic ideology proclaimed three central truths, which appear in virtually all *naturalista* works: the consequences of change, at the level of society or of the individual, are certain to be negative; sexual desire is the single most powerful and controlling human emotion; and genetic heredity and environmental conditioning entirely determine character and behavior. While *naturalista* novelists sometimes claimed, at the surface level of the text, to be proponents of social reforms, their underlying message defines all change as dangerous and demonizes those seen as actual or potential agents of change – Brazilians of African descent (particularly mulattoes), and immigrants from Portugal.

While literary historians have traditionally regarded the publication of *O mulato* in 1881 by Aluísio Azevedo (1857–1913) as the beginning of *Naturalismo*, its roots can be traced back to the 1860s and 1870s. *As vítimas algozes*, a collection of short novels, was published in 1869 by Macedo – who was still writing fiction, although long since overshadowed by Alencar. This work is typical of much of literary Abolitionism in Brazil; Macedo argues, and seeks to exemplify with his astonishingly melodramatic and blood-thirsty tales, that slaves are in fact human beings, but that the environment of slavery has transformed them into wild beasts intent upon the physical and moral destruction of their white masters. The only solution, according to Macedo, is to abolish slavery and thereby separate Whites from their violent and immoral chattels. The same sort of virulent hostility toward Brazilians of African descent, more obviously based on genetics and without the veneer of Abolitionism, is evident in Tristão de Alencar Araripe Júnior's *O reino encantado*, which attacks both Blacks and religious fanaticism. Something similar can also be seen in two early novels by Herculano Marcos Inglês de Sousa (1853–1918), *O cacaulista* and *O coronel sangrado*. Inglês de Sousa's contemporaries greatly admired his ponderous *O missionário*, but the two earlier works now seem much more interesting. Both are regionalist at heart, focusing on life in the Amazon, but Inglês de Sousa's setting is the small city of Óbidos, carved out of the forests on the edge of the great river. A central figure in the two linked novels is the mulatto Lieutenant Ribeiro – reflecting a generalized concern among the Brazilian elite about potential competition from ambitious mulattoes and black freedmen.

Many of these strands came together in *O mulato*, published in 1881 by Aluísio Azevedo. It is considerably inferior, as a novel, to Inglês de Sousa's earlier *O coronel sangrado*, but it became immediately and enormously popular. Azevedo's fame as a *Naturalista* is somewhat ironic. He published eleven novels between 1879 and 1895, the year he obtained a position in the Brazilian diplomatic corps and gave up fiction for good. Only four of those novels – *O mulato*, *Casa de pensão*, *O homem*, and *O cortiço* – conform to the model of *Naturalismo*; most of the rest are romantic pot-boilers of the worst sort. Azevedo's ability, throughout his career, to move effortlessly from *Naturalismo* to Romanticism suggests how relatively slight were the differences between the two in his eyes.

O mulato is set in the northeastern city of São Luís do Maranhão. Azevedo inherited Regionalism's focus on the collective and its passion for detail; his major revision of the regionalist tradition is his intensely negative view of the backwardness and pettiness of São Luís society. The plot, in many ways less interesting to Azevedo than the setting, draws heavily on both *A escrava Isaura* and *Inocência*, influences which help to explain its popularity. The hero, Raimundo, is highly educated and appears to be entirely white; when he returns from Europe to São Luís, he is virtually the only person in the city who does not know the complex and violent family history that will determine his destiny: his mother was a slave, tortured and killed by his father's white wife, who then conspired in her husband's murder in order to become the lover of a local cleric. Raimundo, almost intolerably pure and innocent, is seduced by his white cousin, Ana Rosa, who did not marry at fifteen or sixteen and therefore suffers from hysteria. The villainous cleric and a Portuguese immigrant conspire to kill Raimundo after Ana Rosa becomes pregnant, and his death causes her to abort. Despite all this mayhem, Azevedo finds a happy ending; when we last see Ana Rosa, several years after the crime, she has married the immigrant and has finally found fulfillment in sex and maternity.

Azevedo presents his novel as an attack on racial prejudice. The subtexts, however, are very different: the dangers of educating mulattoes and allowing them to rise in society; the fear that such mulattoes would be sexually attractive to white women; the concern, expressed in José de Alencar's pro-slavery speeches, that Abolition and legal equality would reveal the skeletons in the closet of every upper-class Brazilian family; the view that those of African descent, regardless of appearance or culture, were potential catalysts for violence and immorality. São Luís, however much Azevedo appears to criticize it, is nonetheless a stable society before Raimundo's arrival; stability can be restored only by his violent removal, and Ana Rosa's bliss at the end of the novel proves that restoration.

O cortiço is Azevedo's masterpiece and one of the most influential novels of the century. It is set in the slums of Rio de Janeiro, a self-contained world largely cut off from the rest of the city and the nation – as much a distinct and distinctive region, in fact, as São Luís do Maranhão or the backlands of *Inocência*. Azevedo's description of this setting and its inhabitants is powerful and convincing, but his plot is far more melodramatic than realistic. João Romão, the greedy Portuguese immigrant who owns the slum, conspires to marry into the traditional elite – represented by the weak and decadent Miranda family. Romão succeeds, but only by destroying everyone he touches. This emphasis upon the upwardly mobile immigrant as a catalyst for change and, therefore, for destruction, continues themes present in *O mulato*; it is particularly ironic, however, since Azevedo's father was in fact a Portuguese immigrant. Perhaps in an effort to balance the scales, Azevedo does present one very positive immigrant character, the honest, innocent, hard-working Jerônimo, but Jerônimo's character and life are ruined by his contact with Rita Bahiana, a mulatto – the other pre-determined agent of destruction and self-destruction in *naturalista* fiction.

The success of *O mulato* encouraged other Brazilian writers to try their hands at *Naturalismo*, but only a few of their works are readable today. Perhaps the most popular of these novels in its own time, *A carne* (1888) by Júlio Ribeiro (1845–1890), now seems more laughable than shocking in its detailed, openly pornographic account of an aristocratic and educated young woman who becomes a nymphomaniac after seeing the half-naked, muscular bodies of her father's slaves. Raul Pompéia's *O Ateneu*, a far more interesting and enduring work, also appeared in 1888, the year in which slavery was abolished. Pompéia, born in 1863, committed suicide on Christmas Day in 1895. *O Ateneu* is less a novel than a series of vignettes and brief episodes based on Pompéia's own experiences in a very similar boarding school in Rio de Janeiro. It was viewed by his contemporaries as a *naturalista* work, a judgment repeated by José Veríssimo and Mário de Andrade; other critics have defined it as something entirely new and original in nineteenth-century Brazilian fiction, frequently classifying it as "impressionistic" rather than realistic or *naturalista*. My own feeling is that it is best viewed as an essentially *naturalista* text, written by a young man who was not at all sure how to write a novel. It is a collection of sketches of places and people, very similar to the drawings Pompéia produced to illustrate the text, unified by the author's vengeful hatred of all those who had tormented him as a boy, by his obsession with homosexual and heterosexual lust, and by his desire to satirize Pedro II's Empire as a hollow shell of noble ideas and trite phrases; the boarding school is the Empire, its director a pretentious and venal wind-bag, its inhabitants brutish, perverted, and cruel. The school's final destruction by fire and, it is suggested, by the flames of lust, is at once the author's fictional revenge and a metaphor for the fundamental political and social changes Pompéia hoped the Republic would bring.

By about 1890, the *naturalista* vogue began to fade, at least among readers in Rio de Janeiro; the great changes of Abolition and the end of the Empire had occurred, but – contrary to the predictions of *Naturalismo* – the traditional elite had survived and was no longer interested in reading about its potential destruction by immigrants and non-Whites. As a result, some of the most interesting late examples of the movement, works clearly struggling to move beyond the facile determinism and stereotyping of Azevedo, were largely ignored. One of these works, *Luzia-Homem*, by Domingos Olímpio Braga Cavalcanti (1850–1906), describes the struggle for survival of the inhabitants of the northeastern interior during a devastating drought; the central character, a strong, almost masculine young woman destroyed by Nature and by the lust of men, is one of the most complete and memorable heroines of Brazilian literature. Another authentic and believable heroine is the title-character of *Dona Guidinha do Poço* by Manuel de Oliveira Paiva (1861–1892), a work which was not published until 1952.

Perhaps the best novelist of *Naturalismo* was Adolfo Caminha (1867–1897). He published only two novels, *A normalista* (1892) and *Bom-Crioulo*; the latter is one of the most remarkable novels published anywhere during the nineteenth century. Like Alencar in *O guaraní* and *Iracema*, Caminha here moves beyond stereotypical characterization and descriptive detail into the realm of myth – but his myth is of Brazil's destruction rather than its creation. Aleixo, the cabin boy on a Brazilian merchant ship, is as innocent – and as weak – as any romantic heroine. Aboard the ship, a world of homosexually sadistic officers and brutalized seamen, Aleixo is seduced by Amaro – a fugitive slave whose homosexuality is portrayed as the almost inevitable result of the degradation he has experienced on the plantation from which he fled and on the ship. The love of Aleixo and Amaro – and it is described as love – is presented in very explicit terms, but it can survive only in the isolation of the ship. When the two return to land, Aleixo is again seduced – this time by an aging, syphilitic Portuguese prostitute. Maddened by jealousy, Amaro kills Aleixo. Reflecting themes introduced in Azevedo's *O mulato* and *O cortiço*, Caminha here allegorizes Brazil – white Brazil – as pure and helpless, caught between the degradation of the nation's non-white population and the amoral decadence of European immigrants; like Aleixo, white Brazil will inevitably be destroyed in the process.

After the relatively brief popularity of *Naturalismo*, much of Brazilian prose fiction returned to something very similar to the romantic Regionalism of the 1860s and 1870s. In the last decades of the century, a number of writers again sought to find and describe the authentic Brazil they wanted to believe survived in the interior and in regions far removed from the central coast. This revived Regionalism was more interested in local color, folklore, and dialect, and many of its works are no more than brief vignettes of peasant life. The major precursor of this local-color, folkloric Regionalism was Apolinário Porto Alegre (1844–1904), a writer from Rio Grande do Sul whose works appeared during the decade of the 1870s. There is also an almost palpable undercurrent of desperation in this flight from the cities, whose populations were rapidly swelling as freedmen left the plantations and as European immigrants poured in, to worlds untouched by Abolition, the Republic, immigration, or technological progress. The most influential works of the authors of folkloric Regionalism – Afonso Arinos (1868–1916), Valdomiro Silveira (1873–1941), João Simões Lopes Neto (1865–1916), Alcides Maia (1878–1944), Afrânio Peixoto (1876–1947), and Xavier Marques (1861–1942) – appeared well after the turn of the century, and are therefore outside the scope of this chapter; their thematic and technical roots, however, lie entirely in the nineteenth century. Their works are invaluable as snapshots, however idealized and impressionistic, of ways of life that have since disappeared, but as Lúcia Miguel-Pereira noted (*Prosa de ficção de 1870 a 1920*), they were all essentially tourists – looking in from the outside, unable to get inside their characters or to understand fully the realities of poverty and rural life.

As this discussion of romantic Regionalism, *Naturalismo*, and local-color Regionalism suggests, relatively few novelists after Alencar described life in the major cities of the nation, the cities in which most readers lived. This began to change, in the very last decades of the century, but few authors dedicated themselves exclusively to the urban novel. One example of this process is Taunay, who concentrated on urban novels after *Inocência*, but who never wrote anything else as good, or as popular, as that early work. Another example is the astonishingly prolific Henrique Maximiano Coelho Neto (1864–1934), who published sixteen novels and collections of short stories between 1891 and 1900 and who went on producing fiction, at about the same rate, well into the 1920s. In part because of the pressures imposed by Coelho Neto's desire for commercial success as a writer, the character and quality of his work varied tremendously: he wrote legends based entirely upon his always fertile imagination, Regionalist fiction closer to Romanticism than to the local-color school, novels of urban life that struggle toward Realism but never quite attain it, historical fiction about recent events, and attempts at *Naturalismo* that never quite ring true, perhaps because of Coelho Neto's basic optimism about life and about Brazil. The best of the urban novelists who began publishing after about 1890, in my own view, is a figure who is still largely ignored or minimized in the standard histories of Brazilian literature – Júlia Lopes de Almeida (1862–1934). Lopes de Almeida, the only important female novelist between the eighteenth century and the publication of Raquel de Queiroz's *O quinze* in 1930, produced a series of carefully drawn family chronicles, beginning with *A família Medeiros* (probably first published in 1892), that come closer than any other Brazilian texts to the standard model of European Realism. One of her contemporaries, the critic Nestor Vítor, described her as not really Brazilian and suggested that "the obvious care Sra. D. Júlia Lopes takes to write correctly makes her style a bit like what one so often finds with the handwriting of women in general and schoolteachers in particular, who try so hard not to break any rules that their script becomes more or less devoid of character" (cited by Miguel-Pereira, *Prosa de ficção*, 270). While this patronizing judgment has often been repeated, the truth is that Lopes de Almeida is almost the only writer of her generation who did not over-write dreadfully; perhaps because she was a woman, she saw and described reality objectively, without the distorting lenses of Romantic optimism or *naturalista* pessimism.

Joaquim Maria Machado de Assis (1839–1908) stands apart from all other Brazilian writers of prose fiction in the nineteenth century. Indeed, there are no comparable writers in all of Latin America before Jorge Luis Borges – a writer whom Machado in many ways resembles, particularly in his use of certain symbolic structures (the mirror, for example) and of highly unreliable and self-conscious narrators. Machado's uniqueness was in some measure the product of his extraordinary life; he is one of only a handful of examples of extreme upward social mobility within the rigid and hierarchical Empire. Machado was a mulatto, born and raised on a large estate near what is today the center of Rio de Janeiro. His father was a mulatto freedman, employed as an artisan by the wealthy and noble family which owned the estate; he was probably also related to that family. Machado's mother was Portuguese, and was employed, both before and after her marriage, by the same family. Machado probably attended the small school the family ran for its children and the children of its dependents, but we know very little about his childhood, his education, or his early life. In 1859, when he was twenty, Machado was working as a proofreader and producing his first literary texts – including poetry in French, which he had picked up somewhere along the way. No one could have predicted, in that year, that the talent and the driving ambition of this quite dark-skinned mulatto, a frail epileptic who stuttered badly and was terribly nearsighted, would make him Brazil's greatest writer, a high-ranking civil servant, and the first president of the Brazilian Academy of Letters.

Machado rose rapidly in Brazilian society, after about 1860, by creating and constantly refining the character he played, at least in public, for the rest of his life: an urbane, witty, and utterly refined gentleman, married to a Portuguese woman of good family. The public Machado was always perfectly dressed and perfectly mannered, erudite but never pretentious, generous with his friends, and endlessly helpful to younger writers. So successful was he in the creation of this fictional Machado that we struggle, largely in vain, to discern the Machado behind the mask; his contemporaries, it is clear, accepted the character as the man, and generally perceived him as both upper-class *and* white.

Machado began writing prose fiction rather late in his career, after he had largely accomplished his far more difficult and complex self-fictionalization. His first four novels (*Ressurreição*, *A mão e a luva* [*The Hand and the Glove*], *Helena* [*Helena*], and *Iaiá Garcia* [*Yaya Garcia*]) were set, like all of his works, in Rio de Janeiro. These early fictions are superficially romantic, influenced by the urban novels of Macedo and Alencar, but it is obvious that Machado was fundamentally uncomfortable with the tradition those novels had established. His vision of Brazilian society and of the human condition was far darker than that of his predecessors, and he found it very difficult indeed to bring his characters to the happy endings Brazilian readers had come to expect. These novels were widely read and admired, however, and, after the death of José de Alencar in 1877, Machado was generally recognized by his contemporaries as the greatest living Brazilian novelist.

Machado's theory and practice of prose fiction underwent fundamental changes after the publication of *Iaiá Garcia*, the most overtly anti-romantic of the early novels, in 1878. The first of his mature masterpieces, *Memórias póstumas de Brás Cubas* [*Epitaph of a Small Winner*], was published in 1881. It is hard to imagine two more different works than these novels, published only three years apart. *Memórias póstumas* is composed of dozens of short, almost fragmentary chapters; it is certainly possible to follow the plot despite this almost kaleidoscopic fragmentation, but it is often difficult to determine the exact relationship between a given chapter and the development of the plot. The sardonic, garrulous narrator, Brás Cubas, is already dead as he begins his narrative; he would rather not, he informs us, tell us the mechanics of the process he used to create the text we are reading, but he does speculate at considerable length about the process of literary creation in general. The story Brás Cubas wants to tell us is a sad one, of infidelity, failed love, failed ambition. His text, however, is often extremely funny; for example, one chapter, entitled "The Venerable Dialogue of Adam and Eve," consists of several pages of punctuation marks. The text is objective and realistic in its descriptions of people, places, and social patterns, but it also includes remarkable excursions into the fantastic and the philosophical, excursions which allow the narrator to present his ideas – which we may or may not be supposed to take seriously – on the nature of time, of history, of the human self, of the cosmos.

Machado went on to produce four more novels: *Quincas Borba* [*Philosopher or Dog*], *Dom Casmurro* [*Dom Casmurro*], and the two narratives of Counselor Ayres (*Esaú e Jacó* [*Esau and Jacob*] and *Memorial de Aires* [*Counselor Ayres' Memorial* and *The Wager: Aires' Journal*]). None is exactly like *Memórias póstumas* – Machado never repeated himself; but each is a *tour de force* in its own right. Equally impressive are Machado's short stories, some of which have been translated into English in *The Psychiatrist, and Other Stories* and *The Devil's Church and Other Stories*.

Machado's contemporaries, readers and critics alike, generally read these texts simply as works of fiction – enjoying the humor and the pathos, identifying intensely with characters very like themselves. During the decades since Machado's death, however, we have come to understand that these intensely readable fictions are also carefully constructed to be read on a number of different levels. The best example of Machado's multiplicity, perhaps, is *Dom Casmurro*, in which a lonely middle-aged man tells us the story of his life – his love for his childhood sweetheart, Capitu, whom he managed to marry but who later betrayed him with his best friend. That, at least, is how the novel was read from its publication in 1900 until 1960, when an American critic, Helen Caldwell, discovered that, embedded in Dom Casmurro's narrative, half-hidden in both what he says and what he leaves unsaid, is an equally moving and absolutely contradictory second narrative – the story of an innocent woman destroyed by her husband's insane jealousy: *The Brazilian Othello*. Both of these narratives – Dom Casmurro's story, as Machado presents it, and Capitu's story, which Machado almost certainly intended us to construct ourselves from the materials he provided – are coherent and convincing. Machado's point, in fact, is that the real events of life – as opposed to fiction – are far too complex and ambiguous to be interpreted and understood, even by those who experience them.

Machado's solution, then, to the conflict between form and reality in Brazilian fiction was to create both new narrative forms and a new reality those forms could be used to describe. The created universe of Machado's stories and novels shared certain details with nineteenth-century Rio de Janeiro, but it was entirely his own, a universe he could form and deform as he wished. It is this perception of the fictive world as an independent reality which most sharply differentiates Machado from his predecessors and contemporaries. Many of Machado's major novels and stories were written well after the Empire ended on November 15, 1889. Almost all of those texts, however, are set in an earlier period, between about 1850 and 1889. Machado's last novel, *Memorial de Aires*, published a year before his death, has as its central theme the process of letting go – of illusions, of life, of creating texts. The diary Counselor Aires writes, however, describes real and fictional events in 1888 – including the Abolition of slavery – and part of 1889. The Counselor's text, symbolic of all of Machado's texts, trails off into blank silence at some point in September – two months before the Empire fell. One interpretation of Machado's message here, I believe, is that his fictions depended, for their very existence, upon the multiple fictions of the Empire itself – the society and culture which had required Machado to fictionalize himself as a precondition for his success, and which had accepted without question that first and most extraordinary of all his fictional creations. Machado understood that the novelist's task, in nineteenth-century Brazil, was not to use fiction to describe reality, but to produce fictions within the context of a larger fiction; that realization allowed him to move beyond the formal and thematic constraints of the traditional novel to create the greatest masterpieces of Brazilian literature.

[8]

Brazilian fiction from 1900 to 1945
Mary L. Daniel

The twentieth century opened in Brazil with an atmosphere of intense political and economic interest but without a corresponding intensity in a literary manifestation. In the Amazonian area, Brazil's "last frontier," the rubber boom which had begun around 1860 was nearing its peak, focusing both public interest and international speculation upon the "exotic rainforest." The abolition of slavery in 1888 had resulted in large-scale appeals by the Brazilian government to certain foreign nations for the immigration of families with agricultural experience, bringing to Brazil thousands of Italian, German, and (after 1908) Japanese families. On the political scene, the advent of the Republic in 1889 had brought a decade of opportunism, austerity, factional unrest, and general disappointment to the country and, as the century turned, Brazilian intellectuals were in the throes of intense national self-examination in an attempt to discover whether Brazil was indeed in a period of progress or of decadence and whether the nation merited any kind of confidence at home or abroad. Reactions ranged from euphoric admiration (Afonso Celso, *Por que me ufano do meu país*, 1900) to pessimistic condemnation (Euclides da Cunha, *Os sertões*, 1902 [*Rebellion in the Backlands*]). Essayists throughout Brazil found their most fertile field of endeavor in the analysis of national strengths and weaknesses and the attempt to identify solutions to the latter. The perennial presence of national self-consciousness in Brazilian thought as the twentieth century began to run its course may be verified in the writings of essayists such as Alberto Torres (*O problema nacional brasileiro* [1914]), Monteiro Lobato (*Idéias de Jeca Tatu* [1919]), and Paulo Prado (*Retrato do Brasil* [1928]). Its pervasiveness in the genre of prose fiction will be observed throughout the present chapter.

Within the field of Brazilian letters, the first decade of the twentieth century seemed more like twilight than dawn. Machado de Assis, the master of psychological Realism who had delineated and exemplified the fictional sub-genres of novel, short story, and *crônica* since the 1860s, died

157

in 1908, leaving no literary "heir apparent." Aluísio Azevedo, the paragon of sociological Realism, wrote no novels after the turn of the century though he lived until 1913. The poetic scene is somewhat brighter than the fictional during the first two decades of the twentieth century, for poets of both the Parnassian (Olavo Brás Martins dos Guimarães Bilac, Alberto de Oliveira, Raimundo Correia) and symbolist (Alphonsus de Guimaraens, Vicente de Carvalho) schools continued productive careers. Theatre was in a weaker state in Brazil than either fiction or poetry as the twentieth century dawned, for the urban turn-of-the-century Brazilian public was far more enthusiastic about European operas than about standard theatrical presentations, especially "home-grown" dramas, and production of the latter responded to demand. The burgeoning of both fiction and poetry in twentieth-century Brazil begins as the First World War ends, and is undiminished to the present time.

Alfredo Bosi (*História concisa da literatura brasileira*, 340–3) has suggested the fairly continuous presence in Brazilian literature of a tension between *centrifugal* and *centripetal* concerns in the first half of the twentieth century. The centrifugal force involves the awareness and adaptation of new philosophical and literary currents emanating from Europe, while the centripetal implies a focus on essentially Brazilian themes and traditions. It would seem that the same inward–outward fluctuation may be perceived *within* the centripetal field of concern, manifesting itself in the dynamic balance between the national and the regional, particularly after approximately 1930 and especially in the fictional genre. The duality may be extended one step further within both the more cosmopolitan national and the regional themes: in this case, the centrifugal force implies a broad sociological scope, while the centripetal suggests a more introspective psychological focus. Brazilian fiction from 1900 to 1945 evolves from vestigially naturalistic Regionalism, through a nationalistic phase colored by the challenge of European Futurism, progressing finally to a definitively Brazilian Modernism. The latter is then at liberty to discover its own internal distinctives in a new Regionalism based not on scientific models but on the more warmly human concerns of the social sciences, with occasional forays into the field of morose personal introspection.

The late 1890s had been a period of intense concentration on pathological themes in Brazilian fiction, largely under the sign of European Realism/Naturalism and with both rural and urban contexts. Of the writers whose debut occurred during the decade of the 1890s, the most influential in terms of the twentieth century was Henrique Maximiano Coelho Neto (1864–1934), whose ambitious, though unrealized, plan was to create a historical mural of Brazil through his novels. Among his more than 120 fictional works, 11 of which were published in 1898 alone, there is considerable irregularity of quality but an undeniable brilliance in the weaving of words, and a pioneer step in the direction of what in mid twentieth century might be called "Magical Realism" through the confluence of the fantastic and the naturalistic. Though some of his best novels, notably *A capital federal, Miragem, Inverno em flor, A conquista,* and *O morto,* precede the historical period considered in the present chapter, Coelho Neto's marked prestige throughout the first two decades of the current century is evidenced by the popularity surrounding publication of the novels *Tormenta, Turbilhão, A esfinge* (1908), and *O rei negro,* as well as the short story collection *Banzo* (1913); revealing elements of normal and abnormal psychology within both urban and regional geographic settings, these works show an evident attempt to incorporate elements of black and backland dialectal Portuguese within the author's flow of elegant prose and to validate human types rarely treated as individuals in earlier Brazilian prose fiction. Coelho Neto was nominated for the Nobel Prize in literature by the Brazilian Academy of Letters in 1932, but criticized for his verbosity by subsequent generations.

Four turn-of-the-century novelists dedicated themselves primarily to the presentation, though not necessarily the full development, of female protagonists. These are Domingos Olímpio (1850–1906), Lindolfo Rocha (1862–1911), Júlia Lopes de Almeida (1862–1934), and Afrânio Peixoto (1876–1947), considered "minor novelists" within the context of Brazilian fiction both in terms of total literary production and influence on future generations. Domingos Olímpio, writing from within the context of the northeastern Brazilian drought cycle, made the most lasting impression of the four through his creation of the tough and tender manual laborer Luzia in *Luzia-Homem* (1903). Possessing physical and psychological qualities considered typically "masculine" and "feminine," this protagonist embodies the anguish of a woman who, through the force of circumstance and free choice, does not fit the mold prescribed for her sex. Lopes de Almeida, in her novels *A família Medeiros* (1894), *Memórias de Marta* (1899), *A falência* (1901), *A intrusa* (1908), *A herança* (1909), and *A Silveirinha* (1914), and the short story collection *Ânsia eterna* (1903), depicts urban customs of the period and reflects colloquial debates surrounding the two main issues of national interest: the Republic and Abolition. Rocha depicts a well-known prostitute of the Brazilian *sertão* against the backdrop of gold prospectors and local customs in *Maria Dusá* (1910). Peixoto, the most prolific of the four, reflects the gentle sentimentality of Lopes de Almeida in his novels *Fruta do mato* (1920), *Uma mulher como as outras* (1928), and *Sinhazinha* (1929), among other works, developing both urban ambiences and those of the rural area of his native Bahia.

In the genre of the short story, at least two writers accompanied Afrânio

Peixoto and Júlia Lopes de Almeida in the depiction of what Peixoto called "Society's Smile." These are J. J. Medeiros e Albuquerque (1867–1934) and João do Rio (pseudonym of Paulo Barreto, 1881–1921). Reflecting, in the style of Maupassant, the decadent dandyism of turn-of-the-century (sub)urban bourgeois society, both writers also cultivated journalism and the novel. Medeiros e Albuquerque's short story collections cluster in the first decade of the century (*Mãe tapuia* [1900], *Contos escolhidos* [1907], *Um homem práctico* [1908]) and during the last decade of his life (*O assassinato do general* [1926], *Se eu fosse Sherlock Holmes* [1932], *O umbigo de Adão* [1934]). The best of João do Rio's stories and chronicles are found in *Dentro da noite* (1910), *A mulher e os espelhos* (1911), *Rosário de ilusão* (n.d.), and *A correspondência de uma estação de cura* (1918).

Simultaneous with the genteel, perhaps "dilettantish," fiction of urban and rural manners which proliferated during the first two decades of the twentieth century in Brazil there existed two other general types of fiction within the period sometimes denominated as "pre-Modernism." The first, and more numerous, of the two is a specifically Regionalist fiction, typically short, depicting the geography and traditional customs of areas of Brazil as diverse as Rio Grande do Sul, the interior of São Paulo, Minas Gerais, Goiás, Bahia, and Amazonia. The second, and more serious, fictional type is that of polemic novels and stories, set within a distinctive and identifiable geographic framework but emphasizing the psycho-philosophical content in focus rather than the incidental. Among the writers of short regional fiction, the extreme south of Brazil (especially the state of Rio Grande do Sul) is represented by Simões Lopes Neto (1865–1916) and Alcides Maia (1878–1944), the state of São Paulo by Valdomiro Silveira (1873–1941), Minas Gerais by Afonso Arinos (1868–1916) and Godofredo Rangel (1884–1951), Goiás by Hugo de Carvalho Ramos (1895–1921), Bahia by Xavier Marques (1861–1942), and the Amazonian area by Alberto Rangel of Pernambuco (1871–1945) and Gastão Cruls of Rio de Janeiro (1888–1959), both of whom devoted a considerable portion of their fictional output to the tropical rainforest area to which their careers had taken them. The more polemic, and better-known, writers who exemplify the "fiction of ideas" of the first two decades of the century are José Pereira da Graça Aranha (1868–1931), José Bento Monteiro Lobato (1882–1948), and Afonso Henriques de Lima Barreto (1881–1992).

Simões Lopes Neto is the best known of the early twentieth-century *gaúcho* Regionalists. His two most widely circulated volumes of short stories – *Contos gauchescos* (1912) and *Lendas do Sul* (1913) – incorporate the *persona* of Blau Nunes, an Indian cowboy who acts as narrative *alter ego* of the author in describing and reacting in the first person to episodes and customs of rural life in the far southern border region. Alcides Maia traces numerous short impressions of the sometimes brutal, sometimes lyric life of the *pampa* in his novel *Ruínas vivas* (1910) and two collections of short stories: *Tapera* (1911) and *Alma bárbara* (1922). Valdomiro Silveira cultivates a special interest in the *caboclo* or *caipira* backland dwellers of southern central Brazil, showing both the integration of human beings and Nature, and the social interaction of individuals; his short story collections *Os caboclos* (1920), *Nas serras e nas furnas* (1931), and *Mixuangos* (1937) utilize the colloquial speech of uneducated backlanders for the narrative voice of the stories themselves. Afonso Arinos, considered the father of twentieth-century Regionalism by virtue of the early publication of his best-known collection of stories (*Pelo sertão*, [1898]), focuses on the miners and outlaws of central Brazil, who figure also in his novels *Os jagunços* (1898) and *O mestre de campo* (1918). His younger compatriot, Godofredo Rangel, was stimulated in his writing through a lengthy correspondence with Monteiro Lobato and shows rural life in the central plateau area of Brazil through a gently ironic prism in his novelettes *Vida ociosa* (1920), *Falange gloriosa* (n.d.), and *Os bem casados* (n.d.), and the short story collection *Os humildes* (1944). Hugo de Carvalho Ramos, best known for his collection of short stories *Tropas e boiadas* (1917), adds a sober note of description of human exploitation within the context of rural Goiás, foreshadowing future developments in the genre of regionalist fiction after 1930. The local color of Afro-Brazilian customs in the context of northeastern sugar plantations predominates in the long and short fiction of Bahian writer Xavier Marques, author of the novels *Jana e Joel* (1899), *Pindorama* (1900), *O sargento Pedro* (1902), *O feiticeiro* (1922), and *As voltas da estrada* (1930), and the short-story collections *Praieiros* (1902) and *A cidade encantada* (1919). Though the Amazonian region of Brazil produced no "native son" in the way of a Regionalist fiction writer in the early twentieth century, two authors from other areas of the country wrote of Amazonia on the basis of their prolonged residence there. Alberto Rangel, a disciple of Euclides da Cunha, depicts the domination of human beings by the natural vicissitudes of the tropical rainforest in his only collection of short stories, *Inferno verde* (1904), a work that profoundly affected the Brazilian public's awareness and interpretation of its northern region. Gastão Cruls, writing nearly two decades later, adds a somewhat more individualizing psychological texture to his depiction of Amazonia in the short story collections *Coivara* (1920), *Ao embalo da rede* (1923), and *História puxa história* (1938), and the novel *A Amazônia misteriosa* (1925).

The cutting edge of polemic fiction in twentieth-century Brazil comes in 1902 with the publication of *Canaã* [*Canaan*, 1920] by José Pereira da

Graça Aranha, the only widely read novelistic work by an author whose natural penchant lay in the area of analytical essays and lectures and whose most constant thematic preoccupation was the character and destiny of Brazil in the face of competing ethnic, sociological, political, and philosophical explanations and programs. The appearance of *Canaã*, referred to frequently as "Brazil's first ideological novel," in the same year as Euclides da Cunha's incriminating sociological analysis of governmental suppression of the messianic colony of Canudos in the interior of the state of Bahia (*Os sertões*), brought to the Brazilian public a double dose of serious concentration on the confrontation of cultures and value systems within the national territory of a multi-ethnic population. The inherent pessimism of Euclides da Cunha, based on an essentially deterministic view of cultural development, is counterbalanced somewhat by the eclectic perspective presented in Graça Aranha's novel. *Os sertões*'s underlying anguish also penetrates *Canaã*, which merits our attention in spite of its stylistic irregularities, and which manages to synthesize much of the turn-of-the-century debate surrounding Brazil's future.

Set in the interior of the eastern central state of Espírito Santo, an area of considerable Swiss and German immigration during the late nineteenth century, *Canaã* focuses on Brazil as "promised land" for its inhabitants; four contrastive opinions are expressed through the vehicle of conversations between and among the main masculine characters of the novel, two of whom are native Brazilians and two recent German immigrants. One of the immigrants, Lentz, represents a fundamentally Nietzschean approach to a country perceived as primitive and underdeveloped because of its inferior and racially mixed population, a country in dire need of direction from a superior Aryan race of immigrants; the other German, Milkau, incorporates a Tolstoyan idealism and tenderness which sees Brazil as a virgin Canaan where European antagonisms can be forgotten and many races can experience a new beginning in their inter-relationship. Among the Brazilians who dialogue with each other and with the immigrants, Pantoja and his circle represent the kind of blind nationalism that sees no defect in Brazil, while Paulo Maciel (the probable *alter ego* of Graça Aranha himself) sees a difficult future for his country and would prefer to "flee" to a Europe possessing a clear sense of identity; yet Maciel perceives in rather abstract fashion that Brazil is in the process of developing its destiny as a mulatto society which will inevitably "whiten" in accordance with new patterns of immigration.

If the dialogues of *Canaã* may be said to gravitate around the dialectic of Utopianism, the narrative and descriptive portions of the novel constitute an irregular mixture of pathological naturalistic episodes (e.g., the eating of an illegitimate newborn by a herd of peccaries) and ethereal symbolistic descriptions of Nature and dream sequences. In its dynamic confluence of contrastive opinions and literary techniques it synthesizes the moment in Brazilian intellectual and literary history in which it appeared, an extremely self-conscious time in which most of the centrifugal and centripetal forces mentioned earlier were in full interplay.

Considerably more pessimistic than Graça Aranha in his evaluation of Brazil's development and human potential is José Bento Monteiro Lobato, whose pragmatic experience in the area of agriculture in the state of São Paulo and concern for the sane exploration of Brazil's mineral resources (particularly iron ore and petroleum) led him to think in national terms while, at the same time, creating several volumes of short fiction based on pathetic and sometimes grotesque episodes of individual existence among the inhabitants of Brazil's rural south. An extremely lucid writer, Monteiro Lobato surrounded his volumes of short stories with ample epistolary and essayistic commentaries, to friends and to the general public, in the form of journalistic publication, and was a pioneer in the area of expansion of Brazil's national publishing houses in order to provide for more effective distribution of literary works produced within its borders. It was a well-known fact that as prolific a fiction writer as Coelho Neto, still active at the time Monteiro Lobato began his career, published his novels in Portugal and that Brazilian publishing houses were usually controlled by European interests. An interesting sidelight of Monteiro Lobato's lifelong concern with the stimulation of the Brazilian reading public and the ready availability of books for its consumption is the fact that he himself wrote more than twenty volumes of fiction for children, most of which continue as staple items of children's literature at the end of the twentieth century.

The most polemic of Monteiro Lobato's three main short story collections (*Urupês, Cidades mortas, Negrinha*) is the first, *Urupês*, for in it he concretized for the Brazilian imagination the figure of the sluggish, ignorant, and vegetating *caipira* [backlander] of southern Brazil in the person of Jeca Tatu. In direct confrontation with, and negation of, the "Noble Savage" created by José de Alencar in the person of Peri (1857) and the numerous and picturesque "peasant" types appearing in turn-of-the-century regionalist fiction, Monteiro Lobato counterposes the figure of Jeca, who embodies all that is inferior in the apathetic rural population of Brazil. Invariably following the "line of least resistance" and most comfortable in a squatting position, Jeca takes no initiative and has no ideas; all the great historical events of late nineteenth- and early twentieth-century Brazil mean nothing to him, for culture and inventiveness are the preserve of the urban population, largely mulatto and ambitious. Several years after publishing *Urupês* (whose title means "toadstools," symbol of human vegetation), a volume of stories in which episodes of pathetic lives, abused children, vengeance, superstition, and parasitism abound within the context of an abundant and hospitable natural setting, the author offered a published reevaluation of his negative interpretation of the *caipira* type, stating that further study had convinced him that the *jecas* of Brazil were not so much to be despised as to be pitied, for their apparently congenital apathy was in fact the result of poor health, diet, and sanitation and the blame was to be laid at the doorstep of the government, which should undertake a national campaign of public health. Thus Monteiro Lobato added one more cause to his agenda of polemics and joined Euclides da Cunha, Graça Aranha, and Lima Barreto in the multifaceted scrutiny of the nature of Brazil's socio-ethnic character and future in the context of the twentieth century.

The two other main collections of short stories by Monteiro Lobato – *Cidades mortas* and *Negrinha* – continue the focus on rural life already observed in *Urupês*, though the focus shifts somewhat to small-town settings in depleted agricultural lands. It is estimated that, through the author's conscious incorporation of common rural colloquial vocabulary in the majority of his stories, more than seventy "new" terms worked their way into the official national lexicon of Brazilian Portuguese.

Influenced by a period of residence in the United States in the 1920s, Monteiro Lobato added to his fiction a full-length novel of futuristic fantasy: *O choque das raças ou o presidente negro* (1926), in which he projects the election of a black president in the US by virtue of the greater fertility and higher birth-rate of black Americans; the impact of the event is offset, however, by the White-inspired tactic of sterilizing Blacks via the use of radiation! Ever the pessimist yet always the indefatigable planner, Monteiro Lobato may perhaps be viewed as a forerunner of the very Modernism he so loyally opposed in Brazil within a half-dozen years of his own most popular works of fiction being published.

Afonso Henriques de Lima Barreto, the third of the polemic novelists in Brazil's phase of self-examination during the first two decades of the twentieth century, uses as his literary context the city of Rio de Janeiro and its middle- to lower-class suburbs. A child of the very ambience he portrays, Lima Barreto reflects the frustrations of persons of lower-class background and/or mulatto heritage whose cultural preparation and dreams exceed the achievement level permitted them by the still-stratified society in which they live. Though the focus of his works is invariably the personal drama of the protagonists, it may be said that he recreates literarily the Rio de Janeiro of 1890–1910 in a manner reminiscent of Machado de Assis a generation earlier.

The principal novels of Lima Barreto – *Recordações do escrivão Isaías Caminha*, *Triste fim de Policarpo Quaresma* [*The Patriot*], *Numa e a ninfa*, *Vida e morte de M. J. Gonzaga de Sá*, and *Clara dos Anjos* (composed in 1904 but published posthumously in 1948) – evidence wide use of symbolic names to elevate their protagonists of both sexes to the level of archetypes. Isaías [Isaiah] Caminha, in spite of his prophetic name, cannot make a successful career in journalism, and Lima Barreto's first published novel turns into an invective against that profession. Policarpo Quaresma bears in his name the dual note of suffering implicit in the identity of Polycarp, an early Christian martyr, and the liturgical season of *Quaresma* [Lent]; his poet friend and guitar teacher, Ricardo Coração dos Outros [Heart of the Others], is a sympathetic and popular type based on the northeastern Brazilian poet Catulo da Paixão Cearense. A super-patriot, Policarpo consciously seeks to incorporate into his own personality and career all the essential qualities of "Brazilianness," from mastery of the guitar to that of the Tupi-Guarani language, exposing himself to ridicule and suspicion from nearly all who know him because of his exaggerated nationalism and high-flown aspirations. When his scientific agricultural projects also fail, Quaresma turns to patriotic political involvement on the side of the government to help protect the new Republic against its detractors; once again he is victimized, of course, and ultimately becomes "martyred" by the very nation he so blindly idolized. *Triste fim de Policarpo Quaresma* is the perfect companion piece to Alberto Torres's essay volume, O *problema nacional brasileiro*, published one year before Lima Barreto's novel.

While most of the characters in *Policarpo Quaresma* are fairly sympathetic and the protagonist's progressive lunacy is gently and humorously developed, another of Lima Barreto's novels published the same year (1915), *Numa e a ninfa*, is a fierce political satire, most of whose personages (supposed by some commentators to be drawn from life, *à clefs*) are cynical, dishonest, and stupid. *Vida e morte de M. J. Gonzaga de Sá*, published by Monteiro Lobato's editorial house in 1919, is the most Machadian of Lima Barreto's novels; its protagonist, whose name is prototypically Lusitanian, is a skeptical, Voltairean type whose perambulations through the city of Rio de Janeiro afford ample opportunity for the presentation of multiple *quadros de costumes*, as well as philosophical commentary on a variety of issues; the work constitutes a balanced satire against certain governmental figures and policies and is much better wrought than its predecessor of four years earlier.

Clara dos Anjos, the author's earliest and most carelessly written work and the only one of his novels published posthumously, shows the same symbolism of names mentioned above. The gentle protagonist, mulatta Clara, is sexually abused by the white villain of the story and, through her, Lima Barreto gives vent to his rage and indignation in the face of socio-ethnic inequality. Clara is one of the few strongly developed female protagonists in the author's work, whose complement of full-length novels is accompanied by numerous short stories and *crônicas* bearing essentially the same charge of piquantly negative assessment of Brazilian urban and suburban life in the early twentieth century.

As the winds of European Futurism began to reach Brazil from 1915 to the early 1920s and a new generation of writers appeared in the newly emerging industrial and cosmopolitan center of São Paulo, the three "polemic" fiction writers we have just considered showed widely fluctuating reactions to the nascent wave of what was beginning to call itself Brazilian Modernism. Graça Aranha, always adverse to static syntheses, hailed the new generation enthusiastically and defended its iconoclastic stance before the Brazilian Academy of Letters ("O espírito moderno" [1924]). Lima Barreto, caught between a deep attachment to traditions and a steadfast opposition to their sometimes stifling effect, tended to view the "new wave" of literary experimentation with suspicious eyes, though his death just a few months after the Modern Art Week in 1922 prohibited him from actually reading full-fledged modernist works. It was Monteiro Lobato, who might have appeared to be the "proto-martyr" of renewal movements in Brazil because of his declared opposition to the *status quo*, who turned out to be the most stolid enemy of Modernism, seeing it as a superficial and "foreign" imitation of the authentic Brazilian modernization *he* had sought to bring about in the country's economy, educational system, and literary life during the decade of 1910–1920, without a great deal of success. So, to the already existing polemic over Brazil's true character was added the debate as to which *generation* best understood, and could properly interpret, that identity.

Though the stage was set both politically and culturally for the emergence of São Paulo as the new center of national leadership by the early 1920s as well as for a "new look" in literary styles and values, various heterogeneous strands may be observed in the field of fiction which indicate that this genre would be slower to follow vanguardist tendencies than was the poetry of the same period. In Pernambuco, for example, Mário Sete (1886–1950) produced a series of picturesque, sentimental novels and short stories (*Senhora de engenho* [1921], *O palanquim dourado* [1922], *A filha de Dona Sinhá* [1924], *O vigia da casa-grande* [1924]) with traditional regionalistic themes, while in Rio de Janeiro Adelino Magalhães (1887–1969) cultivated what may be best described as impressionistic stories and chronicles (*Visões, cenas e perfis* [1918], *Tumulto da vida* [1920], *Inquietude* [1922], *A hora veloz* [1926], and later collections) which frequently verge on the pornographic. Although his short fiction may be considered vaguely akin to some of Coelho Neto's experimentation in longer prose, or seen as a possible prototype for surrealist fiction, Adelino Magalhães did not flow into the mainstream of the Modernism which was nascent at the time of publication of his early stories and left no literary "heir apparent" among younger writers.

In general terms, the modernist movement in Brazil may be seen as the most overt manifestation of the process of intellectual fermentation evident from around 1915 and corresponded to the wider wave of vanguardist reexamination of traditional values, styles, and methodologies accompanying the onset of the First World War throughout western Europe and the Americas. The search for new political and cultural answers resulted, within the Brazilian context, in a melding of influences derived from European Futurism and strong nationalistic impulses. By the early 1920s, São Paulo emerged as the vanguard center of Brazilian cultural life in its musical, artistic, and literary manifestations, for it was the area least bound by long-standing cultural traditions, as well as attracting the lion's share of foreign industrial development. The Modern Art Week held in São Paulo's Municipal Theatre early in 1922 served as a catalyst for numerous young artists, musicians, and writers (especially poets), though it shocked the general public by its unconventionality and brought down the ire of leading Brazilian writers concerned with propriety and more evolutionary methods of change and progress. Though fiction was the literary genre least represented in the recitations, concerts, and expositions of Modern Art Week itself, the iconoclastic urban focus of the modernist movement in both its cosmopolitan and nationalistic perspectives would soon be reflected in the new prose to be produced in the vicinity of São Paulo, radiating from there to the remainder of Brazil. Encompassing the period 1922–1945, Modernism may be subdivided into three segments, which together comprise the subject matter of the remainder of the present chapter. During the first half-dozen years (1922–1928) relatively little prose fiction results from the movement, though this is precisely the period of most intense production of poetic works as well as of polemic essays, and of the positioning of various aesthetic and political stances within the movement (e.g., *Verde-amarelismo*, *Anta*, *Pau-Brasil*, *Antropofagia*). The second phase of Modernism, extending from approximately 1928 until the late 1930s, is dominated by the surge of regionalist fiction of a predominantly socio-economic nature in northeastern, central, and southern Brazil, with the parallel though secondary flow of a more psychologically based fiction from several urban centers. The last half-dozen years of Modernism's dominance in Brazilian letters (late 1930s through the Second World War) incorporate serious theatrical works and a solid body of literary criticism within the movement, while the dual fictional trends of regionalistic and psychological works initiated in the 1930s continue vigorous and unabated.

Although the stylistic and thematic iconoclasm of the Modernists of the "first generation" (1922–1928) is most amply reflected in their poetry, the same qualities are reflected in the fiction of the three writers most representative of the São Paulo literary scene of the early 1920s. These are Oswald de Andrade (José Oswald de Sousa Andrade: 1890–1954), Mário de Andrade (1893–1945), and Antônio de Alcântara Machado (1901–1935). In the triumphal spirit of the initial wave of Modernism, these authors set aside the traditional tenets of "proper writing" in favor of a kind of *bricolage* (especially in the case of the two Andrades) based on spontaneity, jovial and chaotic intertextuality, and the creation of new hybrid fictional forms. Time-honored concepts of plot and character development were consciously violated, and linguistic experimentation used as an arm of protest against both European propriety and sentimental Brazilian nationalism ("Tupi or not Tupi, that is the question!" – Oswald de Andrade, *Manifesto antropófago* [1928]). Protagonists disintegrate into Protean figures (e.g., Macunaíma, João Miramar) who are in a constant process of formation and "becoming" as they absorb influences from near and far, symbols of the vigorous "young" Brazil and its cosmic race of people envisioned by the new writers from São Paulo. The result of such conscious application of literary license and systematic iconoclasm was a small group of fictional works whose aim was to change the face of Brazilian letters, though historical perspective shows that their reach exceeded their grasp and that the very authors who launched the program of literary renovation of the early 1920s became considerably more traditional themselves by the early 1930s and came to criticize their earlier "excesses."

Oswald de Andrade, the most aggressively irreverent of the first modernist generation, began rather inauspiciously with a proposed trilogy of novels, to be entitled "Trilogia do exílio" (a title later changed to *Os condenados*); its volumes, as eventually published, were *Alma* (1922), *A estrela de absinto* (1927), and *A escada vermelha* (1934). The composition of the trilogy was interrupted by the publication of Oswald's two most influential, perhaps "notorious," works of fictional narrative: *Memórias sentimentais de João Miramar* and *Serafim Ponte Grande*. Both are telegraphic, episodic works consisting of montages of travel narratives, sensorial and philosophical impressions, fragments of verse and letters, and parodic prefaces arranged in what might be called "cubist" style; both "antinovels" offer a carnivalization of a series of traditional literary forms in juxtaposition, including the initial copyright of the text ("May be translated, reproduced and deformed in all languages" – *Serafim Ponte Grande*). *Memórias sentimentais de João Miramar* shows a vague chronological line of development through the episodes in the life of its protagonist – a kind of parodic *Bildungsroman* in fragmentary form. *Serafim Ponte Grande* is even more heterodox in its hybridization, and is constructed in larger narrative blocks made up of chunks of various possible kinds of books. Following the publication of all of the above works, Oswald embarked upon a phase of lesser aesthetic and greater social concern, offering a mini-mural of segments of São Paulo society (e.g., Japanese immigrants) not previously treated in Brazilian fiction, in the two-volume series *Marco zero*, composed of *A revolução melancólica* (1943) and *Chão* (1945). The focus of subsequent critical interest upon Oswald's more "revolutionary" works is shown by the fairly recent translation of *Serafim Ponte Grande* into English [*Seraphim Grosse Pointe*].

Mário de Andrade, the "pope" and prime systematic theoretician of Brazilian Modernism in all its ramifications (see *A escrava que não é Isaura* [1925], *Aspectos da literatura brasileira* [1943], *O baile das quatro artes* [1943], *O empalhador de passarinho* [n.d.]), cultivated both long and short fictional genres. His three collections of short stories – *Primeiro andar* (1926), *Belazarte* (1934), and *Contos novos* (posthumous, 1947) – show a high level of concern with the social dramas of the anonymous citizens of urban centers and reflect the athor's essential tenderness and warmth toward the "little people" around him. It is not for his short stories that he is best known, however, but for his two full-length novels, *Amar, verbo intransitivo* (1927) [*Fräulein*] and *Macunaíma* [*Macunaíma*]. The first of these novels, called an "idílio" by its author, is fairly conventional in its language and style though its subject matter is quite unconventional, treating in a light-hearted yet Freudian manner the career of a German "governess" whose main charge is to give young Brazilian men their sexual initiation. The best-known of Mário's fictional works is without a doubt *Macunaíma*, referred to by its author as a "rapsódia," which is at once a compendium of ribald humor and an encyclopedia of the multiple ethnic and linguistic influences which have resulted in the development of Brazilian national character as perceived in the cosmopolitan modernist light of the mid-1920s. Subtitled *O herói sem nenhum caráter* [*The Hero With No Character At All*], *Macunaíma* traces the career of the protagonist of the same name, a black Amerindian who turns white upon bathing in a pool of magical green water in the Amazonian rainforest where he was born. He finds his way to São Paulo in search of the tribal amulet which has been stolen and resold to a rich Italian businessman and which he must restore to his tribe; before recovering the amulet, however, Macunaíma is exposed to the wide gamut of urban culture, including the telephone, the Stock Exchange, and Italo-Brazilian speech patterns. Via a series of magical techniques, he traces a circuitous path around the other regions of Brazil, enriching his peripatetic existence with the folkloric legends and wisdom of each of them in addition to his own inherited and acquired cultural "baggage." His mission fulfilled at last, he returns to his native rainforest, where he is transformed into the constellation Ursa Major; his story is transmitted by a verbose parrot to a researcher who subsequently visits the area! Seen as myth or as symbol of the collective Brazilian unconscious imagination, Macunaíma undergoes constant changes throughout the course of the work, never achieving a fixed or definable character; he remains always in a state of flux, amorphous, and immature, yet with an increased "wisdom of the streets" that sharpens his erotic and mischievous tendencies in the context of urban pressures.

Mário de Andrade's intent in the creation of *Macunaíma* was not the crystallization of a single, unified Brazilian literary language or character delineation but rather the heterogeneous confluence of all the main ethnic, historical, and linguistic threads which had converged in the Brazilian national territory over the centuries since before the arrival of the first Europeans, in what may appear to readers late in this century as a *tour de force* of Magical Realism, whose influence extends across the decades and over national boundaries in the subsequent fictional literature of South America.

Antônio de Alcântara Machado, younger compatriot of the Andrades of São Paulo, turned his attention more specifically to the neighborhoods of his native city, spanning the social gamut from lower to upper-middle class and probing the collective psychology of immigrant (especially Italian) and Brazilian-born populations in their dynamic interaction within Brazil's most rapidly developing metropolis of the 1920s. Adopting, like Oswald and Mário de Andrade, the colloquial language of narration and the dialectal linguistic idiosyncrasies of his protagonists, Alcântara Machado is credited with projecting into national literature the figure of the Italo-Brazilian of all socio-economic classes. Though he left one incomplete novel, *Mana Maria*, the author was much more at home in the genre of the short story. His three collections – *Pathé-Baby* (1926), *Brás, Bexiga e Barra Funda*, and *Laranja da China* – show him moving from a telegraphic, almost cinematographic, style of narration in the earliest series, which combines themes and impressions from European travels with those of Brazilian experience, to a somewhat calmer though still animated mode of presentation in the two later collections, whose themes are drawn almost exclusively from the São Paulo urban surroundings. The short stories composed immediately preceding his death were subsequently collected and published posthumously under the title *Cavaquinho e saxofone* (1940). Of the three *paulista* fiction writers just examined, Alcântara Machado shows the most gentle sense of humor and the greatest propriety in presentation of subject matter, corresponding to a gradual distancing from the more flamboyant aspects of modernist fiction seen in the early 1920s.

While the intellectual and cultural world of São Paulo seethed with new trends and tensions, the outlying regions of Brazil continued in a phase of relative "hibernation" as far as prose fiction is concerned during the first two-thirds of the decade of the 1920s. A certain gentle, picturesque Regionalism continued to prevail in the far south, where the tradition of Simões Lopes Neto and Alcides Maia was being carried on by Roque Callage (1888–1931), in his short story collections *Terra gaúcha* (1914), *Terra natal* (1920), *O drama das coxilhas* (1923), and *Quero-quero* (1927), and by Darci Azambuja (1903–1970), in the collections *No galpão* (1925) and *Contos riograndenses* (1928); there too a younger *gaúcho* writer named Ciro Martins (b. 1908) had published his first novelette, *Sem rumo* (1917), though more than a decade would elapse before the continuation of his fictional production in the novelette *Enquanto as águas correm* (1930), the short story collection *Campo fora* (1934), and the novels *Mensagem errante* (1942) and *Porteira fechada* (1944). The far north of Brazil, almost always the area farthest removed from the heartbeat of national life, saw the publication of the Amazonian novel *Deserdados* (1921) by Carlos de Vasconcelos (1881–1923), while in the central region Ranulfo Prata (1896–1942) brought out the novel *Dentro da vida* (1922), whose plot concerns life in a leprosarium in Minas Gerais. Modernism, in spite of its dynamically nationalistic component, had not "caught fire" in the provinces; a new wave of Regionalism, based on the sociocultural uniqueness of each of Brazil's diverse *mini-pátrias* yet set within the political context of national life and the awareness of regional inequities and interdependence, was yet to come. It came in the late 1920s, as the first generation of São Paulo Modernism was beginning to turn from primarily aesthetic concerns to programs of political action, and it came from Brazil's "oldest" cultural region, the northeast.

In February of 1926, exactly four years after the Semana de Arte Moderna in São Paulo, sociologist Gilberto Freyre convened the Primeiro Congresso Brasileiro de Regionalismo in Recife. This Northeastern Regionalist Congress, which involved the participation of writers, politicians, musicians, artists, artisans, medical doctors, and various other professionals, served as a catalyst for "consciousness-raising" concerning northeastern traditions, values, problems, and worth. In general terms, the far-reaching effects of the stimulus thus afforded may be compared with those of the Modern Art Week on the southern cosmopolitan intellectual and cultural scene. Its theoretical base is found in Gilberto Freyre's *Manifesto regionalista*, and the wave of artistic, musical, and literary works (including poetry, fiction, and drama) that resulted from the regionalistic awareness so awakened dominates the decade of the 1930s in Brazil and extends, in the case of writers such as Jorge Amado (b. 1912) and Raquel de Queiroz (b. 1910), to the present. Not only the northeast, but other areas of Brazil as well, embarked upon a period of renewed creative vigor, reflected in the nation-wide upsurge of literary publication noted throughout the 1930s and on through the period of the Second World War.

The Regionalism, or "Neorealism," of the 1930s and 1940s (and even later) in Brazil differs from the regionalistic Realism/Naturalism of the late nineteenth century primarily in its distancing from the scientific, deterministic mode of observation and narration and its implicit assumption of a commitment of solidarity between author/narrator and protagonist (whether individual or collective). Brazil's main twentieth-century regionalist fiction writers (José Américo de Almeida (1887–1980), Raquel de Queiroz, José Lins do Rego (1901–1957), Graciliano Ramos (1892–1953), Jorge Amado, and others) describe settings, problems, and persons about which they do in fact care, and their works are frequently tinged with both bittersweet memories of their own past and suggestions for sociopolitical reform involving widespread revolutionary activity on the local, national, and international level. There seems to be a direct correlation between the index of natural problems of a given region (e.g., the periodic and devastating droughts, or *secas*, of the northeast) and the volume of its regionalistic literary and artistic production; parallels may be seen in the case of the United States of the same period, a territory as vast and with as many distinctive regions as Brazil, in which the most vigorous literary output came precisely from the southern region (e.g., William Faulkner, Tennessee Williams, Erskine Caldwell, John Steinbeck, etc.) with its decadent plantations, "dustbowl" tragedies, and generally adverse circumstances. The influence of Brazilian Regionalism is seen directly in Portuguese literature beginning in the late 1930s, with an outpouring of Regionalist fiction from writers such as Miguel Torga, Alves Redol, Ferreira de Castro, and Carlos de Oliveira.

In the same year that Mário de Andrade published *Macunaíma*, José Américo de Almeida, who had already brought out a volume of regionalistic essays entitled *A Paraíba e seus problemas* in 1922, launched the subgenre of the Northeastern novel with *A bagaceira*, a work detailing the suffering of families displaced by cyclical droughts. Almeida returned to the Regionalistic fiction scene several years later with the novels *O boqueirão* (1935) and *Coiteiros* (1936), which deal with the problem of backland banditry (*cangaço*), a subject second only to the drought in terms of frequency of appearance in subsequent Regionalist fiction in Brazil in general.

Two years after the publication of *A bagaceira*, the "literature of the drought" in the northeast gained yet another novel – *O quinze* by Raquel de Queiroz of Ceará. This work is based specifically on the devastating *seca* of 1915 and focuses on the interaction of several families in their struggle for survival, with special emphasis given to the self-abnegation of

women. Raquel, the first of her sex to be admitted to the Brazilian
Academy of Letters (1977), maintained her effort in the genre of the full-
length novel through the decade of the 1930s, though subsequently she
came to prefer the vehicle of the short *crônica*, in which she remains
active. Her political involvement and concerns are patent in three novels
published within a decade of her initial work: *João Miguel* (1932),
Caminho de pedras, and *As três Marias* [*The Three Marias*]; all three deal
with the personal and collective dramas of northeastern men and women
who are incarcerated or are under persecution for "subversive" activities
and whose human value is being put to the test.

An interesting sidelight to the Northeastern drought cycle is its impact
on regionalist literature of other areas of Brazil, for the very *retirantes*
[refugees] who flee the *seca* in one area also appear as protagonists of
fictional works in other regions of the country. A case in point is the novel
A selva (1930) [*Jungle*] by Ferreira de Castro (1898–1974), a Portuguese
novelist who spent about a decade of his formative years in the Amazonian region of Brazil during the height of the rubber boom there (1910–
1919). At the outset of his career as a regional novelist of his own country,
he published what has become the best-known fictional depiction of the
northern region of Brazil, which has been translated into over a dozen
languages. The protagonists of *A selva* include an expatriate Portuguese
youth who has taken refuge in Brazil for political reasons and large
numbers of *retirantes* from the state of Ceará who are traveling up the
Amazon as contract laborers for a rubber company, in search of work to
support their families in the northeast. Ferreira de Castro presents in an
easily flowing journalistic style the geographical and sociological panorama of diverse ethnic groups and socio-economic classes thrown
together in the involuntary sub-society created by the rubber boom, with
its exploitation of the powerless and its unexpected mobility for the lucky.
Also in focus are the perception of Brazilians and their country by the
Portuguese (via the peripatetic career and impressions of the Lusitanian
expatriate), the rise and fall of the rubber boom (as viewed from the onset
of its decline around 1914), the linguistic idiosyncrasies of lower-class
northeasterners, the vast botanical vocabulary of the Amazonian region,
the awe-inspiring impact of a colossal rainforest upon those newly
arrived, and the hope of eventual human understanding and justice across
the boundaries of class, race, and social status. Destined originally for the
Portuguese reading public, *A selva* has become a Brazilian classic in its
own right; its impact may be compared with that of *La vorágine*, by the
Colombian José Eustasio Rivera (1924) and *Doña Bárbara*, by the
Venezuelan Rómulo Gallegos (1929).

In the early 1930s, two northeastern Brazilian fiction writers brought to
the sub-genre of the social novel a psychological overtone of essentially

pessimistic quality; these authors are the Alagoan Graciliano Ramos and the Paraíban José Lins do Rego, whose works find a general parallel in North American fiction of the period in the novels of William Faulkner. Of the two, Graciliano has achieved the greater international public, his works having been translated into twelve languages to date.

The four novels of Graciliano Ramos – *Caetés*, *São Bernardo*, *Angústia* [*Anguish*], and *Vidas secas* [*Barren Lives*] – were published in quick succession when the author was already in his forties and reveal in their misanthropy Graciliano's acknowledged debt to Dostoyevsky, Machado de Assis, and Eça de Queiroz. *Caetés*, the least sociological of the four, underlines self-interest as the key motivation of human existence; its first-person narration (Graciliano's favorite narrative mode) shows the increasingly cynical reflections of João Valério, a "cultured *sertanejo*" vegetating in a stifling provincial existence, as he attempts to recreate fictionally the world of the extinct Caeté Indian tribe only to find himself a savage soul covered by a thin veneer of modern social propriety. *São Bernardo* focuses upon the recollections of hard-hearted landowner Paulo Honório, whose self-assertive rise from poverty to wealth would form the grist of a picaresque novel were it not so devastatingly humorless. Social justice miscarries at every turn in Graciliano's world of the decadent sugar-growing aristocracy of the northeast, whether the point of view depicted be that of the "haves" (as in the case of the owner of the São Bernardo plantation) or the "have-nots" presented in the author's last two novels, the most widely read of his works.

Angústia utilizes the "stream of consciousness" technique for its first-person narration, the mind being that of Luís da Silva, who was raised in a *fazendeiro* family (see Carlos de Melo, protagonist of Lins do Rego's "Sugar Cane Cycle," especially *Menino de engenho*) but, because of the vicissitudes of the *seca* and other circumstances of life, finds himself traumatically transferred into the busy life of an urban capital city (Maceió), with which he feels unable to cope. The meandering, patchwork mixture of recall and on-going narration of recent events is the product of a deranged mind, making *Angústia* the most interesting of the author's novels in terms of structure since the work "ends" shortly before it "begins." The interplay of distant and recent past serves to underscore the character of the two contrastive worlds in which the narrator has functioned, as well as the crushing effect of society's pressure on a psychologically fragile human being. The tragic love triangles already present in Graciliano's earlier novels reappear in *Angústia*, though in each case the fatal results differ: suicide of the husband in *Caetés* and of the wife in *São Bernardo* and attempted or real murder (depending on the reader's interpretation of the novel, since the narrator–protagonist is insane) in *Angústia*.

The whirling, almost hypnotic, style of *Angústia*'s narration is replaced by a stark, terse delivery in *Vidas secas*, a work whose structure may be variously referred to as a series of vignettes, a collapsible novel, or a group of interrelated stories possessing the same nucleus of protagonists, and whose point of view is that of an omniscient though variable third person. In this work the reader accompanies and observes the five members of an impoverished *retirante* family – husband Fabiano, wife Vitória, anonymous older and younger sons, and dog Baleia – during their trek through the backlands in search of work and a fixed point of residence. Through the elevation of Baleia, factotum of the family, to a level of consciousnesses explored in indirect free style, and the self-depreciation of Fabiano, a *cabra* capable of only rudimentary thoughts and virtually no verbal communication, Graciliano underscores the marginal human level of awareness of these *jecas* of the northeast and the disparity between the two worlds of urban and rural existence. The cyclic nature of the *seca* determines human life, and the future looks as problematic as the past for the protagonists of *Vidas secas*.

If Graciliano Ramos appears as a "loner" depicting other "loners" to create a gallery of frustrated failures in the Machadian tradition, albeit within a distinctly northeastern context, José Lins do Rego reflects a clearly collective consciousness stimulated by assiduous contacts with sociologist Gilberto Freyre and fellow northeastern novelists (especially José Américo de Almeida and Raquel de Queiroz) and artists. Lins do Rego's fiction is generally memorialistic, incorporating innumerable elements from his own childhood on a sugar plantation and acquaintance with the backland bandits called *cangaceiros* in the northeast. The world recalled and recreated in the author's novels is the one depicted in the genre of the sociological essay by Gilberto Freyre's *Casa grande e senzala* (1933), and Lins do Rego stands as being at once the most prototypical and most diversified of the northeastern regionalist writers.

The major portion of Lins do Rego's novelistic production is encompassed in his "Sugar Cane Cycle," a series of five sequential novels published in the same number of years and containing essentially the same group of protagonists, members of four generations of a family of plantation owners and their extended households. The individual novels of this series are *Menino de engenho* [*Plantation Boy*], *Doidinho*, *Bangüê*, *Moleque Ricardo*, and *Usina*; several years later (1943) the author published *Fogo morto*, which is tangentially related to the aforementioned works and may be considered a "postscript" to the cycle. The single most salient protagonist in the "Sugar Cane Cycle" is Carlos de Mello, the *menino de engenho* who incorporates the author's own childhood experiences and impressions of plantation life, who goes away to school in the second novel of the cycle, returns to take over management of the plantation in *Bangüê* and, through his own ineptness and the nature of changing economic patterns in the larger world, is forced to sell out to a large sugar refinery (*Usina*) to remain solvent. Carlos's black childhood playmate, Ricardo, dominates the volume that bears his name, following an adolescent path that leads to the metropolis of Recife, labor strikes, and a sentence in prison; his career is taken up again in the first section of *Usina*, where he is seen in a homosexual relationship on the prison island (there are echoes of Raul Pompéia's *O Ateneu* in both *Doidinho* and *O moleque Ricardo*), from whence he is released to return to his home plantation to attempt re-entry into a formerly familiar environment now in the throes of change. In *Fogo morto* a neighboring landowner, aging and in ill health, is caught in the "cross-fire" of backland bandit raids and government reprisals as his plantation sinks into economic decadence. All in all, a depressing picture! The "Sugar Cane Cycle" traces northeastern Brazilian plantation life, in both its economic and cultural aspects, from the turn-of-the-century days immediately following the abolition of slavery up to the latter 1920s, with the advent of industrialization, multinational corporations, and ultimately economic depression at all levels. There is throughout the series an almost fatalistic sense that things will inevitably get worse, that a way of life traditionally Brazilian is being forced into a process of change in spite of itself in order to conform to internationally imposed patterns, and that the micro-economic is powerless against the macro-economic.

Having said that, we may well wonder what is so compelling in the "Sugar Cane Cycle." The answer lies partly in the documentary quality of this essentially memorialistic series and partly in its accessibility. The fiction of Lins do Rego in this cycle plays the same role as the regionalist poetry of Jorge de Lima, the sociological essays of Gilberto Freyre, and the art of Cândido Portinari in capturing and preserving a way of life on the wane; it partakes likewise of the same exuberant, earthy quality, the same depth of human warmth, the same tropical sensorial perception, the same inherent simplicity – in short, a lusty mix of diverse qualities presented in a straightforward manner. Lins do Rego tends to favor linear narratives with minimal plots, wide use of soliloquies at the expense of dialogue, a three-part segmentation of novels, generous inclusion of folkloric depictions and *quadros de costumes* of domestic plantation life (especially in *Menino de engenho*), and the creation (or recollection, since most of the cycle is based on the author's own experience) of quintessential human figures from the patriarchal northeast, such as Coronel José Paulino, the stern yet generous *fazendeiro*; the roving storytellers, syncretistic practitioners, and quixotic types who circulate among the plantations; and the numerous ex-slaves, black wet-nurses, and mulatto offspring of *fazendeiros* who comprise the heterogeneous "extended families" of the sugar plantations.

The drought refugees, or *retirantes*, who dominate the works of José

Américo de Almeida and Raquel de Queiroz and reappear in those of Graciliano Ramos and Ferreira de Castro, are secondary in the novels of Lins do Rego; when they do appear, as in *Usina*, it is as a menace to the economic well-being of the plantation poor, for they are seen as parasites on the most vulnerable segment of the *fazenda* population. Another segment of society also appearing in the ambivalent role of victimizer/victimized in Lins do Rego's works are the *cangaceiros*, or backland bandits, who constitute the main human nucleus of two other related novels: *Pedra Bonita* and *Cangaceiros*. These works bring into focus the twin curses of economic depravation and Sebastianistic superstition upon the socio-psychological consciousness of the rural poor; constituting a sequential pair, if not a full "cycle," these two novels reflect the atavistic concerns of Euclides da Cunha (*Os sertões*) concerning northeastern messianism and the forces that drive the uneducated into lives of violence and religious fanaticism.

Moving outside the geographically circumscribed area of the rural northeast, Lins do Rego published four more novels, these with a character more psychological than sociological. They are *Pureza* [*Pureza*], *Riacho doce* (1939), *Água-mãe* (1941), and *Eurídice* (1947). The first is set in a "generic" semi-rural town, the second along the northeastern coast, and the last two in the city of Rio de Janeiro. Exploring the mental aberrations and interpersonal relations of individuals without reference to their "geo-social" context, these novels lack the symbiotic cohesiveness of Lins do Rego's more telluric works.

The most optimistic, flamboyant, and internationally popular of the northeastern Regionalists, with translations in thirty-three languages and a fairly constant presence on the "best-seller" lists of Brazil, is Jorge Amado. Author of approximately twenty novels, half of which were published within the chronological scope of the present chapter, Amado debuted as a fiction writer in 1932 and continues to be productive at the time of writing. It is fair to say that, in terms of success among the members of the reading public, this author has discovered the "magic formula" of an appealing three-way mix of politics, sex, and local color, presented in colloquial language and with a great deal of lyrical sentiment and humanitarian subjectivity, characteristics which endear him, if not to analytical literary critics concerned with integrity and stylistic excellence, certainly to the masses of average readers, who find him the most accessible of all Brazilian fiction writers.

To date Jorge Amado has published the following novels:
O país do Carnaval (1932)
Cacau (1933)
Suor (1934)
Jubiabá [*Jubiabá*]

Mar morto [*Sea of Death*]
Capitães da areia
Terras do sem fim [*The Violent Land*]
São Jorge dos Ilhéus (1944)
Seara vermelha
Os subterrâneos da liberdade (1954)
Gabriela, cravo e canela [*Gabriela, Clove and Cinnamon*]
Os velhos marinheiros (a pair of novelettes) [*Home is the Sailor* and *The Two Deaths of Quincas Wateryell*]
Os pastores da noite [*Shepherds of the Night*]
Dona Flor e seus dois maridos (1966) [*Dona Flor and her Two Husbands*]
Tenda dos milagres (1970) [*Tent of Miracles*]
Tereza Batista cansada de guerra (1972) [*Tereza Batista: Home from the Wars*]
Tieta do agreste (1977) [*Tieta the Goat Girl*]
Farda, fardão, camisola de dormir (1979) [*Pen, Sword, Camisole*]
Tocaia Grande (1984) [*Showdown*, 1988]
O sumiço da santa (1988)

Though fully half of Jorge Amado's novels were published after the period being treated in this chapter, his thematic and stylistic tendencies remain the same; the only noteworthy alteration is that after the mid 1950s his fiction becomes considerably less political and partisan than before and comes to rely increasingly upon the components of sex, humor, and local color for its impact and popularity.

Amado's first novel, *O país do Carnaval*, reflects the ferment of conflicting ideological currents around the time of the revolution of 1930 and the beginning of the Getúlio Vargas regime. His following five works, published in as many years, show increasing maturity as he begins to grapple with the Regionalist themes closest to his heart: the cycle of cocoa-growing in the southern half of the state of Bahia and the lives of the urban poor in the northeastern port cities (especially Salvador). Of these pieces, Fred Ellison (*Brazil's New Novel*, 102) has said: "The story pattern of the novels is generally that of *Cacao*, in which the workers, after long enduring their economic servitude, are driven to collective action in a strike or some act of violence." *Cacau* is the crudest of the series in stylistic terms and *Mar morto* the most poetic. *Suor* is presented in fairly journalistic fashion, while both *Jubiabá* and *Mar morto*, the most fully developed of the Amado novels of the 1930s, explore in more dramatic tones the lives of fishermen, prostitutes, sailors, stevedores, circus entertainers, Afro-Brazilian fetish priests, small shopkeepers, and sundry other human types inhabiting the docks and alleys of Salvador da Bahia. Though Amado tends to group his characters in somewhat simplistic fashion into "exploiters" and "exploited," he possesses a humanitarian warmth that rarely condemns even the most commercial of businessmen, such as the owners of a bakery whose employees declare a strike in *Jubiabá* or the Arab contrabanders in *Mar morto*. Amado is most sympathetic, of course, with those perceived as underdogs, such as the pre-delinquent dock waifs of *Capitães da areia*, struggling young black men like boxer Antônio Balduíno of *Jubiabá* (who gains nearly super-human proportions), and the venerable old *pai-de-santo* Jubiabá of the same novel. There is a strong sense of collectivity about the micro-societies depicted in Amado's novels, for they are well developed and possess their own unwritten "laws" for lauded and proscribed behavior, though these may differ considerably from the standard laws of the wider society around them. Yet there exists mobility and the possibility of mutual comprehension between the "inner" and "outer" groups, as exemplified in characters such as the good priest of *Capitães da areia* and the doctor and school teacher of *Mar morto*, who are thoroughly integrated into the micro-society which they serve though from higher class backgrounds themselves. Couched in a fluid, "oral" style reminis-cent of the storytelling techniques of illiterate northeasterners, these novels are replete with songs, ballad poetry, and refrains which, though bordering on the repetitive, serve to lend cohesion and a folkloric quality to the texts.

After a hiatus of five years in his novelistic production, Jorge Amado brought out in the early to mid 1940s three works related to various aspects of the cocoa economy of his native state and the problems of those cast adrift in the *sertão* (echoes of the *seca* literature already described) by the rise and fall of the cocoa market at both the national and international level. These novels are *Terras do sem fim*, one of the author's best literary accomplishments; *São Jorge dos Ilhéus*, named after one of the two main cocoa ports of southern Bahia; and *Seara vermelha*, influenced by Euclides da Cunha's sociological vision in *Os sertões*. *Terras do sem fim* focuses upon land wars between cocoa barons in southern Bahia, showing a fairly multi-faceted presentation of several *fazendeiros* and overcoming the simplistic character delineation of his earlier cocoa novels. *São Jorge dos Ilhéus* casts the formerly triumphant landowners in the role of those exploited by capitalist exporters, who play the cocoa market to their own advantage and the disadvantage of the producers. In *Seara vermelha*, we see *retirantes* roving far from their rural northeastern lands in search of economic survival as far south as São Paulo; of the author's novels of the 1940s, this is the most irregular, suffering from the "grafting-on" of a chapter of political propaganda toward the end.

The inherent paradox of Jorge Amado's novels of the 1930s and 1940s is that, while believing himself to be a Marxist protest novelist, the author succeeded in idealizing the urban lower classes of the Brazilian northeast to the point of making them appear to be living a nearly perfect existence already as they work together and celebrate nightly at the sessions of their local *candomblé* congregation. While the economic change and "progress" form part of a semi-abstract dream (e.g., school teacher Dulce in *Mar morto*) in several of the novels, scenes of collective protest seem to be artificially orchestrated by professionals from the "outside" and superimposed upon the *real* life of the local people, which continues its colorful traditional pattern. The omniscient narrator meanders at will through the minds of his protagonists and secondary characters, dropping maturely developed thoughts of socio-economic theory ("Well did he know that...") amidst otherwise erotic impulses and instincts. Such is the "festive Marxism" of the Jorge Amado of the 1930s and 1940s. It is perhaps this very predictable mixture of the doctrinal and the delightful that satisfies the wide public that the author enjoys to the present.

In addition to the half-dozen "pillars" of Brazilian Regionalism presented above, another five lesser-known fiction writers of the 1930s and 1940s also merit at least cursory attention because of their contribution to the field of regionalistic fiction. In the Amazonian region, João Peregrino Jr. (b. 1898) produced a series of short story collections presenting scenes of life in the interior of the state of Pará; these are *Puçanga* (1929), *Matupá* (1933), and *Histórias da Amazônia* (1936). Abguar Bastos (b. 1912) follows an essentially sociological approach to the same region in three short novels: *Amazônia que ninguém sabe* (1931; republished under the title *Terra de Icamiaba* in 1934), *Certos caminhos do mundo* (1936), and *Safra* (1937). In northeastern Brazil, Amando Fontes (1899–1967) of Sergipe published a pair of novels depicting the tragic results of the traumatic urbanization of rural drought refugees – poverty, prostitution, tuberculosis, and lack of adaptation – constituting what might be considered a semi-sequel to Graciliano Ramos's *Vidas secas* in terms of plot development, though preceding the latter work in dates of publication; these novels are *Os corumbas* and *Rua do Siriri*. In central Brazil, Amadeu de Queirós (1873–1955) of southern Minas Gerais offered a half-dozen short novels – *Praga de amor* (1927), *Sabina* (1928), *O intendente do ouro* (1937), *A voz da terra* (1938), *O quarteirão do meio* (1944), and *João* (1945) – depicting in generally melancholic tone the inevitable transformation of the city of São Paulo and the manner of life of rural residents of the São Paulo–Minas Gerais border area. Within the State of São Paulo itself, Tito Batini (b. 1904) depicts the collective life of Italian immigrants, railroad workers, and other lower-class inhabitants of small towns in the interior, in the novels *E agora, que fazer?* (1941), *Entre o chão e as estrelas* (1943), and *Filhos do povo* (1945).

While Regionalism is without a doubt the "majority" trend within

Brazilian fiction in the period from 1930 to 1945, especially in the northern half of the country, another more introspective, urban, and "universal" tendency may be observed, particularly in fiction in the southern half of Brazil – the "other side of the coin" of Brazilian fiction from the Great Depression to the end of the Second World War.

The best-known and best-loved of the "cosmopolitan" novelists of Brazil is Erico Veríssimo (1905–1975), a *gaúcho* whose career included several years of residence in the United States as Director of Cultural Affairs for the Pan American Union. His literary production, consisting chiefly of novels, spans four decades and may be divided into three areas of thematic concern, only the first of which is demonstrated in his fictional works prior to the year 1945.

Erico Veríssimo evidences his primary socio-psychological concern related to the cycle of human life involved in adolescence, maturity, the aging process, and the personal interaction of individuals within a rather genteel middle-class urban ambience, touched incidentally by current events of a national and international nature (e.g., the Spanish Civil War), in his first five novels, which form a cycle in which the same nuclear group of young persons serve as protagonists, developing through their formative years and eventually finding their place in various professions and life settings or (rarely) becoming "misfits" within society. The novels of this cycle are *Clarissa* (1933), *Música ao longe*, *Caminhos cruzados* [*Crossroads*], *Um lugar ao sol*, and *Saga* (1940), of which the middle three are the strongest in terms of thematic–stylistic consistency. Pertaining to the same general area of individual and interpersonal concern, but independent of the cycle and of each other in plot and character development are three other novels: *Olhai os lírios do campo* [*Consider the Lilies of the Field*], *O resto é silêncio* [*The Rest is Silence*], and *Noite* [*Night*]. The author's strong humanitarian urge continues in evidence in this trio of novels, as does his essentially pictorial narrative style ("painting with words"), though certain structural innovations not present in his earlier cycle assert themselves in the 1940s, including the "point–counterpoint" arrangement of the interwoven plot–character strands of *O resto é silêncio* and the alternation of linear narrative and surrealistic subconscious sequences in *Noite*. Of extra-literary interest in these novels, which are as a group considerably more mature than those of the early to mid 1930s, is the persistent questioning of the professional role and social responsibility of individuals such as medical doctors (*Olhai os lírios do campo*) and especially writers (*O resto é silêncio*); what, for example, is the degree of guilt of a novelist (Veríssimo's own *porta-voz*, Tônio Santiago, in this case) in the suicide of one of his readers as a result of a self-induced fantasy relationship with a fictional character in one of his works? The weight of "being one's brother's keeper" remains a constant throughout the author's literary production, to surface most especially in works composed during the last decade of his life.

Erico Veríssimo's second and third areas of thematic concentration, though lying chronologically outside the domain of this chapter, merit at least a brief mention here. Inspired by the idea of a regionalistic literature on a scale far larger than the historically circumscribed socio-economic type produced in the remainder of Brazil, he published between 1949 and 1962 a panoramic historical epic of southern Brazil, covering the period from 1750 to 1945 and subdivided into three volumes of unequal length. The trilogy itself bears the title O tempo e o vento and consists of the following segments:

O continente [Time and the Wind], covering the period 1750–1893 and constituting both the lion's share of the trilogy's historical content and its best stylistic presentation;

O retrato, continuing the panorama through the end of the decade of the 1920s but with a narrower geographic scope;

O arquipélago, covering the Vargas period in Brazilian politics and consisting largely of ideological dialogues.

Although the same three families continue in their multiple generations through all three volumes of the trilogy, representing the microcosm of ethnic and political components active in the evolution of gaúcho society over the centuries, it is the first volume of the series that stands, along with O resto é silêncio and Olhai os lírios do campo, as distinctly superior to the remainder of the epic.

During the final decade of his life, Erico Veríssimo continued to expand his literary vision from the socio-psychological emphasis of his early work through the historical regionalistic sweep of his trilogy to an even broader international scope; this previously apolitical author, moved by increasing indignation concerning excesses of dictatorial power, war, political repression, and governmental corruption throughout the world of the 1960s, penned three diverse works in which his innate humanitarian vision is tinged with the ironic edge of disillusionment. These novels are O Senhor Embaixador (1965) [His Excellency, the Ambassador], O prisioneiro (1967), and Incidente em Antares. The first deals with diplomatic intrigue among members of the international ambassadorial community in Washington, D.C., the second with race relations among detainees in a Vietnamese prisoner-of-war camp, and the third with the events and collective state of mind in Brazil following the "Revolution" of 1964. Erico Veríssimo, always a balanced stylistic borrower–innovator, utilizes in the last of his novels elements of surrealistic "Magical Realism" strongly suggestive of Gabriel García Márquez's Cien años de soledad, published just four years earlier, and his Antares plays the same fictional role as Márquez's Macondo.

Erico Veríssimo is the most diversified and cosmopolitan of the southern, urban-based Brazilian fiction writers of the period 1930–1945. However, several other novelists and short-story writers of the states of Rio de Janeiro, Rio Grande do Sul, and Minas Gerais also merit critical attention for their role in the development of a body of essentially non-regionalistic fiction echoing a renewal of introspective, neo-spiritualistic (i.e., neo-Catholic), and ethical concerns emerging in Brazilian intellectual circles in the late 1930s and early 1940s, and to the contribution of this group of writers will be dedicated the final pages of this chapter. In general terms, it may be said that the writers from the interior state of Minas Gerais tend to be the most psychologically introspective and those from the urban area of Rio de Janeiro the most concerned with ethics and the small dramas of the urban life of "little people," with the *gaúchos* combining elements of both trends and the *paulistas* being conspicuously absent from consideration (though Antônio de Alcântara Machado, mentioned earlier in this chapter, might have evolved in this direction had he lived).

The most overtly moralizing and quantitatively prolific of these southern writers is *carioca* novelist Otávio de Faria (b. 1908), author of a thirteen-volume cycle of novels entitled *Tragédia burguesa*, fewer than half of which were published during the late 1930s and early to mid 1940s, and the remainder in subsequent decades. The individual volumes of this loosely interrelated series are *Mundos mortos* (1937), *Os caminhos da vida* (1939), *O lodo das ruas* (1942), *O anjo de pedra* (1944), *Os renegados* (1947), *Os loucos* (1952), *O senhor do mundo* (1957), *O retrato da morte* (1961), *Angela ou As areias do mundo* (1963), *A sombra de Deus* (1966), *O cavaleiro da Virgem* (1970), *O indigno* (1973), and *O pássaro oculto* (1977). Dealing preferentially with the religious and sexual dramas of adolescents, Faria's novels are strongly reminiscent of those of French Catholic fiction writers such as Mauriac, Bloy, and Bernanos but suffer from a certain monotony of style and theme due in part to their cyclic nature.

Partaking simultaneously of Erico Veríssimo's cosmopolitanism and Otávio de Faria's preoccupation with sin, grace, and the human condition is *carioca* novelist José Geraldo Vieira (1897–1977). His first novel, *A mulher que fugiu de Sodoma*, deals with the internal drama of a compulsive gambler and his second, *Território humano*, with introspective elements drawn from his own life. His best-known novel, *A quadragésima porta*, is a "contrapuntal" work set in Paris and offering a multifaceted glimpse into numerous lives of nationals and expatriates during the decades of the 1920s and 1930s, while *A túnica e os dados* is structured according to ecclesiastical Holy Week liturgy (compare Erico Veríssimo's *O resto é silêncio*, set entirely within the twenty-four-hour period from sundown on Good Friday to the evening of Easter Saturday). *Terreno baldio* (1961) is a sort of *Bildungsroman*, while *Paralelo 16:*

Brasília (1967) attempts to recreate the psycho-sociological ambience unique to Brazil's newly constructed capital city. Reflecting a consistent preoccupation with the balance and interplay in human consciousness of inner and outer worlds of perception, José Geraldo Vieira produced perhaps the most carefully crafted literary style of his generation.

A third novelist of the general Rio de Janeiro bay area, Cornélio Pena (1896–1958), shows in his four short novels a pronounced moroseness and somewhat metaphysical quality usually identified with the fiction of Minas Gerais, where coincidentally he spent his formative years. His *Fronteira* [*Threshold*] figures as one of the first novels of atavistic introspection in Brazil, a sub-genre to be explored several decades later by Autran Dourado and Adonias Filho. His later novels – *Dois romances de Nico Horta* (1939), *Repouso* (1948), *A menina morta* (1954) – continue the same ontological reflection and searching, but are less widely read than his initial work.

Minas Gerais novelist Lúcio Cardoso (1913–1968) began his literary career under the aegis of Regionalism, publishing two novels – *Maleita* (1933) and *Salgueiro* (1935) – on the subject of rural populations suffering illness and famine in the area of Bahia bordering his own state. He proceeded to reveal his true literary identity, however, as an introspective novelist with *A luz no subsolo* and *Mãos vazias*, works which explore morbid psychological states and processes. It is in this vein that he produced several novels in the decade of the 1940s – *O desconhecido* (1940), *Dias perdidos* (1943), *Inácio* (1945), *A professora Hilda* (1945), and *O anfiteatro* (1946) – and a later work which proved to be his most widely read novel: *Crônica da casa assassinada*. This last work, his most complex in fictional texture, explores hallucinatory states of consciousness in what may best be described as a "Freudian Catholic" manner and is a *tour de force* of psycho-sociological decadence.

Gaúcho novelist and short-story writer Dionélio Machado (1898–1986) explores the world of psychological introspection at the level of the personal dramas of the "little people" who populate urban centers such as Porto Alegre. His best-known novel is *Os ratos*, which utilizes the historical present to follow the mental ruminations of a young lower-class father during a period of approximately twenty-four hours as he faces the dilemma of inability to pay the milkman and the threat of no further milk delivery for his small child. Machado's other works include the short story collection *Um pobre homem* (1927) and the novels *O louco de Cati* (1942), *Desolação* (1944), and *Passos perdidos* (n.d.), in addition to two works published at wide intervals much later in his life but not considered part of the main *corpus* of his novelistic prose.

An introspective novelist who does not share the pessimism inherent in the works of Faria, Pena, Cardoso, and Machado is the *mineiro* Ciro dos

Anjos (b. 1906), whose three novels – *O amanuense Belmiro*, *Abdias* (1945), and *Montanha* (1956) – share a calm mood and a warmth of human kindness in their depiction of the thoughts and interaction of middle-class urban characters in the capital city and smaller towns of Minas Gerais as they absorb the influences of events occurring at the local and national level of society. *O amanuense Belmiro*, the author's best work, utilizes the pretext of diary memoirs to elucidate the narrator–protagonist's reflections on his own inner psychological processes and the circle of the friends around him as they relate to him and to each other; a fiction of self-contemplative analysis, this novel evokes the genteel irony of much of Machado de Assis's work, though its self-deprecation is of a generally happier tone.

Though full-length novels rather than short stories seem to be the fictional vehicle of choice among the southern Brazilian writers of the period 1930–1945, at least three authors of predominantly short fiction deserve mention at this juncture; they are the *mineiros* João Alphonsus (1901–1944) and Aníbal Machado (1894–1964) and the *carioca* Marques Rebelo (pseudonym of Edi Dias da Cruz, 1907–1973).

João Alphonsus, son of Symbolist poet Alphonsus de Guimaraens, shows great empathy for the tragi-comic aspects of the life of the residents of urban lower-class neighborhoods, a sensitivity that extends on a number of occasions to domestic animals such as cats and chickens and foreshadows the perspective of another *mineiro*, whose literary debut occurred in 1946 and therefore falls outside the chronology of this chapter but whose fiction changed the course of twentieth-century Brazilian letters: João Guimarães Rosa. João Alphonsus offered in the course of his short literary career three volumes of short stories – *Galinha cega* (1931), *Pesca de baleia* (1942), and *Eis a noite* (1943) – as well as two short novels, the latter of which explores socio-psychological aspects of life at a tuberculosis sanitarium in Minas Gerais: *Totônio Pacheco* (1934) and *Rola-Moça* (1938).

Like João Alphonsus, Aníbal Machado participated actively in the *mineiro* modernist groups that accompanied the evolution of the movement from its beginnings in São Paulo in the early 1920s, though his own literary debut came considerably later. His principal collection of short stories is *Vida feliz* (1944), to which were added a half-dozen narratives to form the larger work *Histórias reunidas* (1959). Aníbal's best-known stories are "A morte da porta-estandarte" and "Tati, a garota," two of the most frequently anthologized in modern Brazilian fiction. Several of his stories verge on the genre of the apologue in their use of personified objects to reflect human psychological states and social interaction. The tone of his narratives echoes the pathetic humor already observed in the works of João Alphonsus but, although the tragi-comic human condition remains much the same in the two writers, Aníbal Machado's perspective seems lighter, sometimes even puckish in its smile.

Of *carioca* birth and *mineiro* education, Marques Rebelo (Edi Dias da Cruz) carries on into the third quarter of the twentieth century the tradition of urban fiction already exemplified by Manuel Antônio de Almeida, whose biography he wrote, and Lima Barreto. Although he authored at least five full-length novels, Marques Rebelo's literary preference clearly falls to the genre of the short story, in which he has proven to be one of Brazil's most popular writers. His human focus is the lower-middle-class population of the modest neighborhoods on the north side of Rio de Janeiro, reflected not only in his choice of subject matter (the small private dramas of anonymous people) but also in the very colloquial linguistic style in which his short narratives are couched and his wide use of dialogue to enhance the intimacy of his readers with the fictional characters before them. As a writer committed to regular journalistic publication, he may also be considered a key figure in the mid twentieth-century surge of importance and popularity of the very short fictional genre known as the *crônica*, which combines elements of the personal essay with those of fiction. Among his short story collections are *Oscarina* (1931), *Três caminhos* (1933), and *Stela me abriu a porta* (1942); his novels include *Marafa* (1935), *A estrela sobe* (1938), and a later three-part novel in diary form entitled *O espelho partido*, consisting of the three volumes *O trapicheiro* (1959), *A mudança* (1962), and *A guerra está em nós* (1968), offering a fragmented, panoramic view of the Rio de Janeiro of the 1930s. He is the most jauntily ironic of the three writers of short fiction just considered, and within the broad scope of this chapter may be said to incorporate both the centrifugal and centripetal tendencies brought to bear upon Brazilian fiction during the first half of the twentieth century.

In conclusion, it may be instructive to remember that the literacy rate of Brazilians increased from 25 percent in 1920 to 43 percent in 1940. While the fiction writers of the early 1920s could count on a public of no more than one quarter of the Brazilian population, those of the early 1940s had a potential of nearly one half of that population as their readership; this fact may be related to the upsurge of publication already observed during the decade of the 1930s, placing fiction in the strongest position among the literary genres in terms of its impact on the public by the 1940s. We have observed the strongly sociopolitical tenor of the lion's share of Brazilian fiction, particularly the northeastern regionalist novels, during the years 1930–1945 (the "Vargas Period" in Brazilian politics), so may presume a mutually supportive relationship between writers and public during those years. The same relationship continues to the present, for example, in the case of Brazil's most popular novelist of the twentieth century, Jorge Amado.

As the midpoint of the decade of the 1940s approached, nevertheless, a change in authorial style and intent began to manifest itself on the Brazilian fictional scene. A new generation of authors emerged with vigorous individual personalities, wider acquaintance with contemporary trends in international philosophical thought, and a passion for the crafting of unique and original styles of writing. A serious new formal concern took hold of Brazilian fiction, corresponding generally to the Neo-Modernism of the "Generation of '45" in poetry, and two new giants of both long and short prose fiction – João Guimarães Rosa and Clarice Lispector – began to advance on the Brazilian literary scene, along with a number of other solid young writers.

Brazilian prose from 1940 to 1980
John Gledson

Any pattern which the literary historian discerns in the last half-century of Brazilian prose-writing is bound to be somewhat speculative and imposed on a very heterogeneous mass of material, but three conclusions at least seem inescapable, and can act as preliminary markers.

First, no-one can doubt that the political events of the 1960s and 1970s – the military coup of 1964, the ensuing repression, and censorship (gradually removed in the 1970s) – had a profound effect on the manner of, and the subject-matter tackled by, many writers. Perhaps it would be truer to say that the whole period, one of widespread and often traumatic change in all spheres, not simply political, changed the whole climate in which authors wrote. On the most immediate level, writers had to battle with censors: if, like Antônio Callado (b. 1917), they had already established a reputation, this could mean a cat-and-mouse game of novels printed then impounded, then allowed again (as happened with *Bar Don Juan*, his novel about middle-class guerrillas); in other cases, like that of *Zero* by Ignácio de Loyola Brandão (b. 1936) it could mean banning and even publication abroad (though for obvious reasons this was not such a frequent outlet as is the case in Spanish America). More important than such dramatic "cases," censorship also meant a general clamp-down and curtailing of possibilities. On a deeper level, the imposed silence, and the events of the 1960s themselves, produced the sensation that nothing could, or should, be the same again: when censorship was lifted, fiction looked very different. There was a spate of novels and stories, hardly removed from documentaries, which tried to tell "the real story," and some of these achieved an immense popularity, leading to what was described as a kind of Brazilian "Boom," very different, however, from its Spanish American model. Some of this fiction was doubtless opportunist, yet if such topics as violence, urban squalor, drugs, and terrorism sold books, this was also a reflection of a country that had not only passed though military dictatorship, but an economic boom (followed by a slump in the wake of the 1973 oil crisis) which changed the whole country, city and interior. Indeed, in the long term the importance of such changes as the vast growth in population, above all in such cities as São Paulo, Belo Horizonte, and Brasília (founded in 1959, and now with a population over a million), the accompanying growth of a large if precarious middle class with higher educational expectations, and the large-scale exploitation of the country's interior, including the Amazon basin, may give the military regime, for all its importance, a relatively minor role in a vast process which inevitably transformed literature along with almost everything else.

Secondly, the instruments at the service of writers have changed and diversified immensely throughout this period. 1956 is often cited as the *annus mirabilis*: João Guimarães Rosa (1908–1967) published his great novel *Grande sertão: veredas* [*The Devil to Pay in the Backlands*] in that year, as well as his equally experimental series of long stories, *Corpo de baile*. Typically, critics tell us that the novel begins "The Nuclear Age of Brazilian fiction" (Fausto Cunha, *Situações da ficção brasileira*, 27), or that later novelists write under Guimarães Rosa's shadow, affected by a kind of "anxiety of influence." On the other hand, a successful novelist and short-story writer like Rubem Fonseca (b. 1925) can tell us in refreshingly iconoclastic terms that all talk of a "tradition" in this sense is an illusion (*Feliz ano novo*, 143). The truth lies somewhere in between. On the one hand, Guimarães Rosa's experimentation, partly because it was so radical in all its aspects, did awaken many writers to unsuspected possibilities. There were imitations, but it is probably in the stylized oral language of *Ópera dos mortos* [*The Voices of the Dead*], by Autran Dourado (b. 1926), in the ignorance and brutality conveyed by the eponymous narrator in the novel *Sargento Getúlio* [*Sergeant Getúlio*] by João Ubaldo Ribeiro or even in the torrential and immensely evocative prose (however individual) of the memoirs of Pedro Nava (1903–1984) that the liberating effect of Guimarães Rosa's style can be found – in each of these cases, on writers with sufficient maturity to adopt, adapt, and create. Seen in this perspective, as above all a matter of fictional experimentation, the influence of Guimarães Rosa is part of a wider phenomenon, as evident, for instance, in the ascetic brevity of short stories by Dalton Trevisan (b. 1925), or in the lyrical and abstract intensity of Clarice Lispector (1920–1977) – in recent years, audiences have become more used to such things, as writers have become more skilled at combining them with readability. Genres, too, remain healthily fluid and various – if, primarily for reasons of space, I have concentrated on the novel in what follows, this is not entirely to the exclusion of the short story, which has retained a considerable popularity (and indeed had a kind of "Boom" of its own in the 1970s). Memoirs, too, remain among the most important products of the period: and it is only space that prevents discussion of such masters of the *crônica*, or short newspaper piece, as the poets Manuel Bandeira and Carlos Drummond de Andrade, or Rubem Braga (b. 1913), a journalist of genius who explicitly refused to write in any other form.

The third undoubted trend of the period is a growing literary public. This is a general phenomenon reflected at all levels, whether in the very large sales achieved by Jorge Amado (b. 1912), in the *succès de scandale* of some of the works published in the 1970s, or the ability of some writers – João Ubaldo Ribeiro, Rubem Fonseca, for example – to dedicate themselves to fiction as a career, in recent years; or at stylistic level, in the colloquial Brazilian language so effortlessly employed as the dominant part of a wider register, and which in its way reflects that same public's habits and expectations. Nor should it be forgotten that some writers have had considerable success with genres such as detective thrillers (Rubem Fonseca) or science fiction (Marcelo Paiva [b. 1959]). Even if the best-seller lists relatively seldom contain many Brazilian titles, this is part of an encouraging (if fitful) process of "normalization" – if one can call it that when so much of it is new in the Brazilian context.

The world has changed; writers have changed their view of their own art; the reading public has changed – all these processes, inseparable in any case, have moved forward in different ways and at different paces. Real, constructive change, however, seems to have concentrated in two decades, the 1950s and the period from about 1975 (when censorship began to be lifted) to around 1985. It is on these periods, and especially on the former, in which it is possible to gain greater historical perspective, that this chapter will concentrate. It is worth mentioning at this point, however, how singularly this contrasts with Spanish America, where the 1960s were so crucial. For this, we may safely blame political events and their tragic repercussions.

In the 1940s, one could perhaps have been excused for thinking that very little had changed at all: those, like José Lins do Rego (1901–1957) or Jorge Amado, who had established themselves in the 1930s, continued to publish – the former, in fact, produced perhaps his finest novel, *Fogo morto* (1943), significantly his most distanced view of the sugar-plantation world of *Menino de engenho*, in this decade, as did Amado his two linked works, *Terras do sem fim* and *São Jorge dos Ilhéus*: his increasing militancy in the communist cause led to the more simplistic *Seara vermelha*. Some writers who began to publish at this time, such as Bernardo Elis (b. 1915) (*Ermos e gerais* [1944]), Herberto Sales (b. 1917) (*Cascalho* [1944]), Josué Montello (b. 1917) (*Janelas fechadas* [1941], *A luz da estrela morta* [1946]) are essentially continuers of this realist tradition in one context or another – very often they are regionalist in the sense of bringing to the reader's note a social milieu, usually impoverished and exploitative, sufficiently removed from the reader's experience to be exotic: in Sales's case, the diamond workings of the Bahian hinterland, in Elis's, the backlands of Mato Grosso, in Montello's, his native state of Maranhão, whose history and present he has continued to portray in more recent works.

In 1947, and quite against the grain, Murilo Rubião (b. 1916) published the first of his collections of stories in the fantastic vein, *O ex-mágico* [*The Ex-Magician and Other Stories*]: he has remained faithful to himself in two later collections, *Os dragões e outros contos* and *O convidado*. It would be fair to say that only the last of these had a wide impact on the public, something which is a comment on a literary climate still dominated by Realism, and not on the quality of his work. Rubião's stories are close in spirit to (though more pessimistic than) Cortázar and Arreola: by unblinkingly putting abnormal chains of events into operation in a "normal" world, he shows its essential abnormality.

Realism, then, in one form or another, continued to dominate the literary scene into the 1950s, and indeed showed itself capable of extension and renewal, perhaps most significantly in the work of Erico Veríssimo (1905–1975) and Jorge Amado. Veríssimo published his ambitious historical trilogy, covering 200 years of the history of Rio Grande do Sul, *O tempo e o vento* (*O continente*, *O retrato*, and *O arquipélago*). Although at first sight a glorification of the *gaúcho* homeland and its heroes, Veríssimo's work is in fact, as Flávio Loureiro Chaves points out (*Erico Veríssimo*), humanist and demythifying in its bias (emphasizing, for instance, the role of women as guarantors of continuity in the family, rather than of male heroism), and portrays the change from a predominantly rural to an urban society, with the resulting adjustment and confusion of value systems. This liberal position is one which he has courageously maintained in later works like *Incidente em Antares*, a condemnation of political violence and corruption. Veríssimo is a traditional narrator, very successful (and popular) as such.

More successful still is Jorge Amado, who in 1958 published the book which marked a very important change in his development, *Gabriela, cravo e canela* [*Gabriela, Clove and Cinnamon*]: in such later works as *Dona Flor e seus dois maridos* [*Dona Flor and her Two Husbands*], *Tereza Batista cansada de guerra* [*Tereza Batista: Home from the Wars*], and *Tieta do agreste* [*Tieta*], he has exploited the new dimension of popularity discovered within this book. Nor is this popularity a simple phenomenon, reducible to Amado's evident skill as a storyteller, for instance, or to his ability to spice his novels with judicious doses of sex, violence, local color, and his own variety of humor. *Gabriela* owes its huge success, as novel and later as television soap-opera, to more than that. It presents an optimistic view of the Brazilian nation, overcoming the power of the *coronéis* and the backward, patriarchal society they represent, highly attractive at this time of developmentalist enthusiasm under the Kubitschek presidency. The central love-plot is surrounded by others which show how the rule of the gun is being replaced by a new, more urban dispensation, represented above all by Mundinho, the ambitious *carioca* businessman turned local politician, but also by most of the population of Ilhéus itself, on the point (in 1925, when the novel is set) of having its cocoa opened up to the world's commerce. The story of Gabriela and Nacib plays out this same optimistic story on a more mythical level: the novel could be described as a twentieth-century *Iracema* with a happy ending. The immigrant, petit-bourgeois bar-owner meets the spirit of the *sertão*, and finally discovers that he cannot do without her.

It is impossible to deny Amado's great importance in the history of modern Brazilian fiction: along with Veríssimo (and especially in *Gabriela*), he represents a moment of relative stability and hope, and he succeeds in giving it a more "Brazilian" flavor (where Veríssimo deals with a superficially less "typical" area, the south), however much of a folkloric wish-fulfillment that "Brazil" might be. Some equally Brazilian critics – Alfredo Bosi (*História concisa da literatura brasileira*) or Walnice Nogueira Galvão, for instance – have been less enthusiastic, and pointed up his ingrained sexism and color bias. This latter, in particular, might seem paradoxical in a writer who is in a sense so committed to black culture, and whose *Tenda dos milagres* [*Tent of Miracles*], for instance, is an account of racial discrimination in Salvador, whose hero is a mulatto doctor. Nevertheless, the amply documentable truth is that Amado is the happy or unwitting victim of the paternalism and the condescending racial views of such as Gilberto Freyre, who are willing to admire Blacks from above. This places considerable limitations on the extent to which he can be called a Realist, or his status as a progressive writer, both titles he would claim for himself. He continues to occupy a perhaps irresolvably ambiguous place in Brazilian writing, at one moment touted for the Nobel Prize, at the next accused of not writing serious books at all. Perhaps this is best summed up in an old gibe, which has its flattering side – he is often referred to as the "García Márquez dos pobres."

It is often forgotten that the 1950s saw the publication of the last, by then posthumous, work of the greatest novelist of the 1930s, Graciliano Ramos (1892–1953): his account of the year he spent in prison during the Vargas regime, *Memórias do cárcere*. "A cadeia não é um brinquedo literário" ["Prison is not a literary plaything"], Ramos says at one point, and not the least fascinating part of this often painful masterpiece is the way in which the writer questions his own position, as he encounters people far removed from his own social sphere and character – for instance, the guards and fellow-prisoners on the Ilha Grande, the infamous "colônia correcional" to which he was sent for the second part of his confinement. The staccato style, whose sarcasm is always ready to turn on the author himself, deliberately not flinching at the most humiliating or horrifying events, forces the reader to question many myths and "givens" – the position of the writer in a society in which illiteracy is so common being one of them.

Much important writing of the 1940s and 1950s tended to concentrate on worlds more familiar to middle-class, urban readers: domestic milieus, family dramas, existential crisis. The series of novels by Otávio de Faria (1908–1984), collectively entitled *Tragédia burguesa*, and published between 1944 and 1979, is one example, but one which fails to live up to the high ambition of its title, partly hamstrung by the author's intolerant religious views, which determine much of the structure of the novels. At times, in fact, the "spiritual" nature of crises, especially if seen in a religious light, begins to look strained – the case, for instance, of *Abdias* (1945) by Ciro dos Anjos (b. 1906), in which the sympathetic irony of his earlier *O amanuense Belmiro* breaks apart into a sexual obsession with a teenager on the part of the protagonist, alternately comic and desperately serious in the anguish it causes in a mature, married man.

Much more successful in expressing the doubts and struggles of a younger generation, in an urban context, were writers who themselves formed part of that generation. Perhaps the best and most revealing of these was Fernando Sabino (b. 1923) with his *O encontro marcado* [*A Time to Meet*], a semi-autobiographical novel, centering like *O amanuense Belmiro* on a group of *mineiro* intellectuals, but set in the late 1930s and the 1940s: its lively, alternately serious and ironic treatment of the hero, its easy, colloquial language, and realistic account of the process of growing up, of marriage, career, and so on, were an important advance. Antônio Cândido describes novels like this, *Ciranda de pedra* by Lygia Fagundes Telles (b. 1923), and *O braço direito* by Otto Lara Resende (b. 1922) as "the solid middle path" ("A nova narrativa," 206), and this seems a fair description of their indispensable role in dramatizing the everyday experiences of their own readership. Fagundes Telles is the author of numerous collections of stories and novels spanning more than three decades. They are normally set in the world of the *paulista* bourgeoisie; while this social background is always strongly implicit, however – and is extended to cover political involvement in *As meninas* [*The Girl in the Photograph*] – her most frequent and dominating concerns remain the frustrations and betrayals of her heroes and (more frequently) heroines in their struggles to fulfill themselves.

On a different level of intensity, and undoubtedly the finest and most influential representative of the fiction of existential crisis in an urban context, is Clarice Lispector. Her *Perto do coração selvagem*, published when she was only twenty-four, already displays many of the features of her work as a whole. It centers on a lone female protagonist and her struggle to reach the "savage heart" of unmediated feeling. Her works of fiction, and particularly her novels, court failure because, in their concentration on inner states and on the impossibility of true communication between human beings, they come very near to dispensing with plot. Indeed, it is in some ways inaccurate to categorize her as an urban writer at all, since her settings are not all urban, and certainly the social background is not where her interest as a writer is focused. However, in *Laços de família* [*Family Ties*] – a collection of stories first published in part as *Alguns contos* in 1952 – and in *A Legião Estrangeira* [*The Foreign Legion*], the setting of the middle-class apartment blocks of Rio de Janeiro frequently provides an anchorage for the intense emotions and crises which her heroines undergo. Similarly, it would be a travesty of such a masterpiece as "A imitação da rosa" (*Laços de família*) to say that it is a description of a nervous breakdown, which overtakes the childless Laura, the conventional wife of a man who is happiest "doing things men do, like talking about what goes on in the newspapers." On the contrary, by revealing something of what it is like to *be* Laura, in her "absurd" conflict with herself over whether to give or keep some roses, Lispector permanently shifts our perceptions, revealing danger and beauty in ordinary objects. In such later novels as *A maçã no escuro* [*The Apple in the Dark*] and *A paixão segundo G.H.*, it is easy to feel that she has been overambitious: in the first, the protagonist, Martim, has committed an unspecified crime which supposedly frees him from social constraints, and sets out on the existential quest to discover the nature of life – all this in peculiarly abstract setting, and recounted in language which often seems equally abstract and difficult to grasp unless in terms of philosophical Existentialism itself, which plainly provided her with the framework needed for the creation of longer works. Lispector's faults are emphatically also her virtues: even at her most seemingly pretentious, she remains capable of sudden depths and illuminations, of unforgettable moments of interior drama. It is this which has made her such an influential writer; it should also be said that she – along with Fagundes Telles in a different way – brought to an end the notion of specifically "female" writing with its own, limited province.

Two of the most powerful novels of the 1950s were by writers of a rather earlier generation, who were already established figures – *A menina morta*, by Cornélio Pena (1896–1958), and *Crônica da casa assassinada*, by Lúcio Cardoso (1913–1968). They bear comparison, too, in that both writers were members of a group with spiritual interests and Catholic sympathies and, more significantly still, perhaps, that for both these masterpieces they chose the world of the *casa-grande*, the plantation house of the interior, shown at the beginning of its decline in Pena's novel, set in the late 1860s, and in its final collapse in *Crônica*. *A menina morta* has been described as the best novel about slavery to have been written in Brazil, and certainly, in that it brings psychology and the evocation of atmosphere into a world too often treated with only the crudest Realism, that is so. More importantly, it explores the system itself; the struggles within the owning family, and in particular the attempt to create a "female" world of opposition to male tyranny and the power of economic reality (symbolized by the dead girl of the title), set up tensions which Pena's solemn, slow-moving style is peculiarly equipped to explore. Cardoso's novel likewise explores tensions within a rural oligarchic family: its picture of decadence is more colorful than Pena's, involving transvestism and incest; principally, however, Cardoso reveals himself to be a master of a complex narrative structure, involving the use of diaries, letters, confessions, etc., from some ten characters with different points of view in and out of the family. The tragedy which the novel gradually unfolds is caused at bottom by the clash between the traditional Meneses family and the fascinating Nina, a woman from Rio who marries into a family she thought was still rich, and inevitably accelerates its destruction.

Rather different in their focus are the novels of Adonias Filho (b. 1915), likewise set in the interior, this time in the area surrounding Ilhéus in southern Bahia, from where Jorge Amado also comes. Adonias's first novel, *Os servos da morte*, was followed by *Memórias de Lázaro* [*Memories of Lazarus*] and *Corpo vivo*; his fiction inhabits a nightmare world of murder, madness, and violence, which is partly that of the uncivilized interior of the country, in part that of unredeemed humankind itself. His plots move in a whirlwind of terrible events, sometimes told in a Faulknerian manner, from conflicting viewpoints resolved at the end. If one gets less illumination from them than from Faulkner, however, it is because they are too monochrome. The intention is partly to operate on a mythical level, something which unfortunately his style cannot always sustain.

In aims, if not in ultimate achievement, Adonias Filho and João Guimarães Rosa may be compared. Both use the *sertão* as a setting for existential drama and, in both, interest in plot is closely related to interest interest in myth. Their first books were also published in the same year, 1946. However, in Rosa, the lessons of Modernism have been learnt much more thoroughly, and indeed assimilated in a strikingly original way. His use of language is central to his ambition and achievement: through the use of neologisms, of onomatopoeia, of portmanteau words, of strange grammatical combinations (adjectives and even verbs carrying diminutives), and by a staccato syntax in which main verbs are often not present at all, or are replaced by gerunds, and which is intended in part to imitate oral delivery, he removes the reader into his own fictional realm. The world of the *sertão*, separate though reflecting the larger world, is essential to this provisional removal, this suspension of disbelief, and almost all his fiction is set there. Yet, as he also tells us, "the *sertão* is the world," and the state of suspension into which Rosa's language lifts us ("The Third Bank of the River," to cite the title of one of his stories) is intended in the end to restore a kind of innocence of perception, and spiritual awareness, not to be found in less poetic fiction.

He published *Sagarana* [*Sagarana*], his first book of (long) short stories when it had been ten years in gestation, and then waited another ten years until publishing the collection of (longer) stories (later published in pairs) entitled *Corpo de baile*, and *Grande sertão: veredas*. *Sagarana* already displays most of the features of this extraordinarily individual writer: his settings in the distant *sertão* of Minas Gerais, with its rough inhabitants; his stylization of their oral, anecdotal manner, coupled with an apparently contradictory (because sophisticated) awareness that this is "just" fiction; his frequent use of children and animals as central characters. His plots are no less unconventional; where they do move to a crisis, that, too, can surprise and subvert normal categories. The last story in *Sagarana*, "A hora e vez de Augusto Matraga," illustrates the point: the final shoot-out between the hero and the bandit-leader Joãozinho Bem-bem (Well-Well, or Bang-Bang? – a typically creative and ambiguous proper name) is in fact a reconciliation of an urge toward violence and the Christian duty of the defense of the weak.

Grande sertão: veredas is undoubtedly Rosa's masterpiece. It is an extended (450-page) monologue, "spoken" by Riobaldo, now a retired *jagunço* [bandit], and it is his character and obsessions which give the novel its unity, along with the plot itself, which concerns the struggle between two bandit groups, originating in the murder of the leader of the single gang of which they originally formed part; accompanying this almost "Western"-type plot is the story of Riobaldo's passionate and guilt-ridden relationship with his companion Diadorim, and his worry about a pact he has made with the Devil – of whose objective existence he is not, however, convinced. Toward the beginning of the novel especially, Rosa shifts back and forth in time and space, through Riobaldo's memory – the extraordinary lyrical power of such episodes as the encounter with the "child" (who later turns out to be Diadorim), which give great pleasure in their own right, nevertheless gradually build up a complex world of references which, when the narrative becomes more linear and the reader's task easier, fit into place as part of the reader's "crossing"; *travessia* is the word with which the novel ends.

As critics are increasingly coming to recognize, the aim of Guimarães

Rosa's fiction is primarily spiritual: throughout his life, he was attracted to such doctrines as Platonism and spiritualism. One could argue that, for all the immense detail of the *sertão* setting, it remains a wonderful backdrop for a quite consciously universal drama concerning the nature of love, of Evil (the real substance behind Riobaldo's fear of the Devil), and of the aim of life itself. This may explain in part why, in spite of its success and the critical acclaim which (with some exceptions) greeted it, its influence is not easily quantified. Stimulatingly, however, Silviano Santiago ("Vale quanto pesa," 34) suggests that Riobaldo's ignorant speech, directed at his more educated listener and asking to be corrected at the same time as it is certain of its own voice, subverts the tradition in which the power of speech and writing was held exclusively by a cultivated minority: it is for this reason that such critics as Angel Rama (*La novela en América Latina*, 224, etc.) have paralleled Rosa to José María Arguedas and Juan Rulfo. It is worth emphasizing that he dramatizes the tension between educated and colloquial levels of speech (on a comic level, in the marvellous character of Zé Bebelo), and that is why his example is so fruitful, and doubtless more pervasive than the examples given toward the beginning of this chapter.

In retrospect, the 1950s will surely be seen as one of the most important decades in Brazilian literary history, and not only because of *Grande sertão: veredas*. The Realism of the 1930s and 1940s revealed further latent possibilities, in terms of its popularity, its capacity of adjustment to urban middle-class settings, and even in its ability to question its own status, within its own conventions. The two crucial works in this respect are perhaps *Memórias do cárcere* and *Gabriela, cravo e canela*, and in contrasting them, one with its embarrassing honesty and direct appeal to an experience no reader would want to share, the other with its comfortable, complicitous appeal to the reader and closeness to myth, the edges and the dangers, as well as the virtues, of what had come to be accepted as mainstream fiction begin to emerge. It is here that, independently of the quality of their work, the experimental fiction of Guimarães Rosa and Clarice Lispector reveals its historical importance. Because they explored regions of linguistic and psychological experience, and, indeed, in part because of their high ambitions which transcend literature in a spiritual or metaphysical sense, they offered other possibilities to writers in the more rebellious and conflict-ridden 1960s and 1970s. The assumption of shared experience on which earlier Realism was based began to disappear.

The most significant area which remained, by and large, ignored in 1960, was that of the large cities and in particular the masses of the urban underprivileged, whose numbers were growing so spectacularly during the whole period with which this chapter deals – Angel Rama (*La novela*, 160) notes that, even in Latin American terms, Brazilian writers were relatively late to rise to this challenge. The model came from an unexpected quarter, the city of Curitiba, capital of Paraná, south of São Paulo, where Dalton Trevisan published privately, during the 1950s, small volumes of short stories, which reveal the irrational violence, the meanness, frustration, and sexual hang-ups of a host of minor characters – tramps, prostitutes, civil servants, small shopkeepers, etc.: his Joões and Marias, as they have been called. They are bleakly pessimistic tales, told with an economy which never satisfied their author, and which he would continually pare down even further. Trevisan, in his own chosen way as conscious a stylist as Guimarães Rosa, is his complete opposite, not only in his chosen milieu, but in the materialism and pessimism of his moral outlook. He has always preferred the short story as a genre (and the shorter the better, it seems – many are no more than three or four pages long). It proved to be a very successful experiment: when he was first published outside Curitiba, with *Novelas nada exemplares*, and even more with *Cemitério de elefantes*, he achieved considerable popularity, establishing a kind of literary myth around that least likely of places, the middle-sized provincial city. Later volumes (some with suggestive titles) include *Morte na praça*, *O vampiro de Curitiba*, *Desastres do amor*, and *A guerra conjugal* – these and later collections still concentrate on the same environment. At the same time, two other writers who concentrated on Rio de Janeiro found the short story a congenial form for the laconic and "camera-eye" presentation of urban alienation and marginalization. *Malagueta, Perus e Bacanaço* by João Antônio (b. 1937) reveals a world of stunted existences, often using the urban slang of his characters to increase our sense of their authenticity. Rubem Fonseca started, in such collections as *Os prisioneiros* (1963) and *A coleira do cão*, in rather similar vein, portraying, from within, the drop-outs of the city – failed professional boxers (in "A força humana"), and so on.

The 1960s and early 1970s were a difficult period for Brazilian writers, and one which, as has been said, unfortunately corresponded to the so-called *Boom* of the Latin American novel. As Antônio Cândido perfectly accurately says ("A nova narrativa," 199), the Brazilians were largely a symbolic presence in this phenomenon: the names of Guimarães Rosa and Lispector were often cited, but they were less often read and understood outside Brazil, something which admittedly is partly the result of their very individual styles. But of course the *Boom* reached Brazil as it did everywhere else in the world, and produced a sense of inadequacy, obscurely bound up with political frustration, and expressed in, for instance, Callado's *Bar Don Juan*. There was a desire to produce the Great Brazilian Novel, or to be the Guimarães Rosa of the 1960s, which produced some works in which the conception, perhaps inevitably, was grander than the achievement. An example, excellently analyzed by Daphne Patai (*Myth and Ideology in Contemporary Brazilian Fiction*, 143–66), is *Pessach: a travessia* (1967) by Carlos Heitor Cony (b. 1926) (in which Rosa-like intentions can perhaps be detected in the title): the rather obvious plot, concerning the forced and then willing commitment of a writer to the revolutionary cause, carries a mythical dimension, concerning the writer as Moses, prophet and leader, which points to, while failing to embody, the real gap which in fact separated writer from people, and Brazil from revolution. Callado's *Bar Don Juan*, previously mentioned, is a more effective, because more critical, treatment of the same question – published some four years later than *Pessach*, it already evinces disillusionment with the crazily idealistic and at times self-serving middle-class guerrillas. The same author's *Quarup* operates on a wider canvas, and contains an admirable account of the events of March and April 1964 in the northeast of Brazil, where repression of the organized sugar-workers was particularly brutal: here, he draws on his experiences as a journalist in the region, and in other parts, on his knowledge of the Amazon area and of Indians. However, the attempt to draw this heterogeneous material into a single unity, centering on the priest Padre Nando, who eventually rides off to join a band of guerrillas, is much less successful.

One has the impression that, caught by political events, such writers were all too anxious to identify literary success with the ability to encapsulate them in a grand vision. A further example is *A pedra do reino*, by Ariano Suassuna (b. 1927) an attempt to resuscitate the world of the ballads (the so-called *literatura de cordel*) of the northeast in a kind of Magical Realism, but which founders on the romantic schemes of the self-consciously quixotic narrator for a new, harmonious, political dispensation equally removed from left and right; a failure ultimately recognized by Suassuna's later decision to give up writing altogether.

Such works are perhaps best interpreted as the immediate effects of the political crisis, which (aside from *Quarup*, which has excellent parts) are unlikely to survive it. This may partly have to do with the generation to which these writers belong: without exception, they were experienced, with books already published in the 1950s – it may be that they thought that this time of crisis was the moment to produce a great summation, whereas the reverse was probably the truth. In a similar way, the novels and stories of José J. Veiga (b. 1915), *A hora dos ruminantes* [*The Three Trials of Manirema*], *A máquina extraviada* [*The Misplaced Machine and other Stories*], and *Sombras de reis barbudos*, usually set in small interior towns, but with Orwellian fantasies about take-over by alien organizations, ultimately fail to use the experience of *Os cavalinhos de Platiplanto* to sufficient effect – as was to be noticed by Davi Arrigucci Jr.

in the 1970s ("Jornal, realismo, alegoria," 80), allegory, while to some extent a necessary ploy, did not always work. Similarly, as Veiga's work perhaps also demonstrates, Magical Realism was a dangerous formula, in part because the "magical" parts too often, and too obviously, carry the "real" meaning.

The most unexpected product of this period came from an earlier generation still. In the early 1970s, Pedro Nava published the first in his ultimately six-volume, 2,500-page series of memoirs, entitled *Baú de ossos* – the five remaining volumes were published at more or less regular intervals through the 1970s and early 1980s finishing with *O círio perfeito* in 1983. Nava was a member of the Minas modernist group of which Carlos Drummond de Andrade was the unofficial leader, but had published virtually nothing literary until these memoirs: he was a distinguished doctor, with an amateur's interest in literature, or so it seemed. In a manner somewhat parallel to those of Guimarães Rosa, the reader is immediately struck by the linguistic exuberance of these works, though in a different register: neologisms are less frequent, and the syntax is more conventional, but the joy taken in lists, in technical terms, in obscenities, etc., is contagious, and the books are enlivened by a rumbustious humor, a delight in anecdote and characterization, and a natural sense of the drama of a situation. A more illuminating parallel, in fact, as Davi Arrigucci Jr. suggests (*Enigma e comentário*, 67–112), is Gilberto Freyre, whose mixture of patrician pride and awareness of the more intimate and even sordid aspects of family life Nava updates. Perhaps, in a sense, this is the great Brazilian novel others wanted to write: for the memoirs are not only his own, but those of his parents' and grandparents' families, extending principally through three states and cities, Ceará in the northeast, Minas, and Rio de Janeiro.

If, from one perspective, the enthusiasm with which Nava's work was greeted compensated for a moment of collective self-doubt, a sense that the younger generation, impeded by censorship, were unable to produce works of more universal relevance, from another, this recourse to history, and to a less varnished version of it, had its own appropriateness. In another context, this return to the past perhaps explains the turn taken in the late 1960s by Autran Dourado, who had already published several works, including the ambitious and Faulknerian *A barca dos homens*, in which the pursuit and killing of the innocent and half-idiot Fortunato reveals the tensions within a small island community; although the setting of this novel is Brazilian, its focus lies much more in the existential conflicts and compromises of the main characters. In 1967, he published *Opera dos mortos*, perhaps the best, though the most somber, novel of the decade. In it, the world of Cornélio Pena and Lúcio Cardoso, and the stylized oralism of Guimarães Rosa come together: Dourado has come to the town of Duas Pontes, where much of his later fiction – *O risco do bordado* [*Pattern for a Tapestry*], *Novelário de Donga Novais* – is set, and whose duality indicates something of how the roads from this small backwater of an interior town in the south of Minas lead to the interior and the exterior, in the geographical, social, and psychological senses of those words. The cast is reduced to a minimum – Rosalina, the last scion of the founder family of the town, unmarried, and cut off from the community; Quiquina, the black family servant, the dumb but all-seeing guardian of the house; and Juca Passarinho, the irresponsible, potentially violent Jack-of-all-trades who arrives in the town, and produces a plot of sexual attraction and jealousy which ends in the destruction of Rosalina's sanity. The hooting of the first car to come to Duas Pontes ends the story, but it is essentially about the past as an impasse, and in the three characters, who represent the three main elements in traditional Brazilian rural society – the masters, the slaves, and the *agregados* or retainers – we see how they interact, without ever understanding one another, to work their own destruction. In this novel as in *Os sinos da agonia*, set in eighteenth-century Minas, Dourado aims at a simplicity of plot akin to myth, but which also has important links with history.

There are certain parallels between the fiction of Dourado and that of Osman Lins (1924–1978), a northeasterner of similar age. Both began writing in the world of Existential and social concerns characteristic of the 1950s (Lins with *Os gestos*, *O visitante*, *O fiel e a pedra*), but plainly outgrew it, and set out to create a literary world which would be more independent: both are very conscious craftsmen. It is no accident that Lins is the author of an important work of criticism, *Guerra sem testemunhas*, which situates the Brazilian writer within his or her often frustrating and humiliating context. Significantly, he decides that, above all, the writer should be aware of such limitations, and should dedicate himself to exploring their possibilities: "Limitations are not necessarily limitations in the usual sense, but a strength." As with his fellow *pernambucano* João Cabral de Melo Neto, who proclaims much the same aesthetic in a poetic context, this can send him in apparently strange directions: to an admiration for Medieval art, for instance, given form in one of the stories of the first collection in which his artistic experimentalism is given full rein – *Nove, novena* – "Retábulo de Santa Joana Carolina." His most ambitious and experimental creation is *Avalovara*, in which he bases the structure of the novel on a palindromic Latin phrase and so allows the reader to read the novel in any way he or she pleases, following the relationship of the narrator with three women, one of whom is denoted only by a symbolic sign.

It is impossible to bring this account of the most recent period of Brazilian prose-writing to a confident close: the variety of work produced since the beginning of the end of censorship in the mid 1970s, makes generalization a dangerous business. Yet it is plainly a crucial period, remarkable for its radical questioning if for nothing else, and one in which Brazilian writing has come closer to its Spanish American counterpart, in achievement as well as in technique and theme. Amidst the welter of material, I shall pinpoint certain books – books, in general, rather than authors – who seem to define the period, at least provisionally. A guide is provided by Silviano Santiago's theory that fiction since 1964 has become more aware of the problem of power, not only in the immediate political sense, but in such areas as the family, relations between the sexes in general, and even in language, and that what masquerades as a carnival of "alegria" (he takes the word from a sharply satirical song by Caetano Veloso) is in fact more self-aware, willing, and able, to take risks than anything that precedes it ("Poder e alegria," *passim*).

An excellent starting-point is *A festa* [*The Celebration*] by Ivan Angelo (b. 1936) – it is a remarkably self-assured work, the more surprisingly so given its closeness in time to the events it describes. Like much of the fiction published at this time, it has considerable political content. Angelo himself has said in an interview that the incentive to return to fiction was given him by a trip to Europe in 1972, the experience of democracy there, and an encounter with Fernando Gabeira (b. 1943), the former urban guerrilla now turned author in his turn – *O que é isso, companheiro?* (1982) is a classic account of the kidnapping of the West German ambassador in 1969, amongst other things, and perhaps Brazil's best contribution to "testimonial" literature. In a sense, *A festa* continues the tradition of such novels as *O amanuense Belmiro* and *O encontro marcado* – set in Belo Horizonte, it lovingly satirizes the habits of the intellectual minority, their friends and partners. Now, they are into drugs, sex (including homosexuality) is more open, religion is closer to being a thing of the past; the text is littered with everyday swear-words. Quite deliberately, however, it goes beyond the limited Realism of such predecessors, in the (fictional) event which begins the novel, the arrival in the city of a large group of northeastern peasants fleeing from drought, and a subsequent riot. This is given a focus by the political context: the events of the novel, involving a wide variety of people, not all of them middle-class, take place on the sixth anniversary of the 1964 military coup, thus at the height of the repression, during the presidency of General Garrastazu Médici. Torture, along with the social distinctions which, in the end, it respects, is one of the novel's themes. Angelo's political message is, however, by no means obvious: while much of his position seems familiarly libertarian, there is also a real fear of a kind of reverse to this coin, leading to irrationalism and violence.

Plainly, this *is* a realist novel, and as such an ambitious one: Belo Horizonte is Brazil in a nutshell, and the various characters represent classes and generations. No doubt it is this very ambition which causes doubts, expressed in the fragmentary "Before the Celebration," often by someone called "The Writer" – and in the fragmentary structure of the novel itself. Both the ambition and the doubts are obvious features of the period in general: it is no accident that the 1970s also witnessed a boom in short-story writing, but many novels, like *A festa*, refuse to produce, or feel themselves incapable of producing, an ambitious synthesis. Angelo's next book, *A casa de vidro* [*The Tower of Glass*] is a series of short stories which aim, nevertheless, to form a whole – the book is subtitled "Cinco histórias do Brasil." Perhaps the most extreme case is Ignácio de Loyola Brandão's *Zero*, apparently a series of jumbled fragments set in an urban desert in a fictional country called "América Latíndia": in a sense, this is the proof that large ambition and fragmentation are natural if paradoxical bedfellows – in part, this is a healthy reaction against what in retrospect seemed like the naiveté of the previous decade and generation.

It is not surprising that the desire to confront the sources of power in fiction should have produced works which are themselves confrontational in one sense or another – the increased presence of the marginalized poor is itself an indication of that. The most celebrated example is perhaps Rubem Fonseca's story "Feliz ano novo," which opens his collection of that name, published (and banned) in 1975. In it, one of a gang of robbers recounts, in a matter-of-fact tone which is not the least shocking aspect of the story, a violent assault on a party in middle-class Rio de Janeiro, which results in unnecessary murder, rape, and defilement. One can see why Fonseca is so annoyed by versions of literary history which insist too much on tradition. For him, Realism comes before anything else, and that Realism, given the polarization of Brazilian society, can have nothing comforting about it: "I'm writing about people piled up in the city while technocrats sharpen the barbed wire" (*Feliz ano novo*, 143). In his later work, such as the highly successful *A grande arte* [*High Art*], he has written more conventional thrillers, which cannot unfortunately always be defended from the charge of exploiting the violence which in "Feliz ano novo" blew open so many hatches.

Curiously, Clarice Lispector's last work, published posthumously in the year of her death, approaches this same confrontation, though from a highly individual standpoint. *A hora da estrela* [*The Hour of the Star*] comes to grips with the dehumanizing world of poverty, without compromising the author's honesty, in two ways. First, she dramatizes her own distance from the subject (typically, she had earlier proclaimed that it was not something one ought to write about – one ought to do something about it), by creating a rather antipathetic and sarcastic male narrator, Rodrigo S. M. Having done this, she is free to explore the tawdry world of physical and spiritual deprivation of her heroine, Macabéa, a passive victim of the version of "culture" put out by Rádio Relógio, and the self-satisfied machismo of her dreadful boyfriend, Olímpico. This is the almost comic world of Manuel Bandeira's "Tragédia brasileira" – the sordid and untranscendent life of the poor, given depth by Clarice's control of her own pity and anger.

In such novels as *Armadilha para Lamartine* by Carlos Sussekind (b. 1933) and *Lavoura arcaica* by Raduan Nassar (b. 1935), we witness confrontation within the family, and in particular a questioning of the power of the father. The contexts are very different, however, though both books are plainly autobiographical to a degree: the first is set against a very detailed and precise background, middle-class Rio de Janeiro in the mid 1950s, the second in an immigrant family of Mediterranean origin whose social surroundings are almost totally ignored. Both examine extremely painful and potentially destructive relations between fathers and sons, in the first case leading to the son's internment in a mental hospital – a place also used as a metaphor of the extremes to which a polarized social situation can drive one in *Quatro olhos* by Renato Pompeu (b. 1941). In a later book, *Um copo de cólera*, Nassar examines an equally violent relationship between husband and wife: typically, too, in this period of questioning of established values, he allows the reader to imbibe the male point of view for nine-tenths of the novel, only to subvert it to the point of positing his narrator's madness in its last part.

Inevitably, in a new situation which many writers see, whether they use the phrase or not, as "capitalismo selvagem," some of the old traditions of Brazilian literature can only survive if they adapt: two examples, those of Regionalism and Indianism, can serve to illustrate this, through works by Antônio Torres (b. 1940) (*Essa terra* [*The Land*]), and Darcy Ribeiro (b. 1922) (*Maíra* [*Maíra*]), respectively. The former takes the world of *Vidas secas*, where the city is still over the horizon, into the 1970s when mass emigration from the northeast, where the novel is set, to São Paulo, is a dominant, and where the resulting family and personal tensions end in the suicide of the main character, Nelo. In *Maíra*, Ribeiro uses his considerable anthropological experience to evoke the world of a still un-"civilized" Indian tribe in loving detail, but (as was always the case with the best Indianism) he also shows this as a doomed world, threatened by all kinds of religious, economic, and cultural factors. Like Nelo, Isaías/Avá is torn between two worlds and in the end unable to bridge them.

Technically, all of these works are to some degree experimental, though the best writers have managed to combine an intelligently self-critical stance with readability: particularly good examples would be *A festa* itself, João Ubaldo Ribeiro's *Sargento Getúlio* (published rather earlier, in 1971) – in which the extraordinary violence of the speech of the eponymous hero, which owes something to Guimarães Rosa, reveals surprising self-doubt at the end – or Silviano Santiago's *Em liberdade*, which dramatizes Graciliano Ramos's life after his arrest, and uses it as an example of the difficulties of an artist who really did try to break the mold, the unspoken contract with the reader within which so much fiction operates uncritically.

To risk a final generalization: one thing which seems to link these novels, along with others that could have been mentioned, is a desire to make readers aware of language as a social phenomenon, which can tell us more about the characters than they themselves can. This is often the reason for narrations which subvert themselves (or each other, where more than one narrator is involved, as is frequent). Indeed language, in this sense, is usually an offensive weapon. A certain air of politeness and complicity, deliberately exploited by Machado de Assis, is disappearing, and Brazilian fiction, with remarkable skill and variety, is exploring a country with a sense of permanent tension and crisis. It is not surprising if daring is often dogged by fear.

The Brazilian short story
K. David Jackson

Contributing to the encounter of multiple cultural and literary sources in the Brazilian short story, reflecting its Latin American identity, is an a-historical, oral tradition of tales and legends from Amerindian, African, and European origins that came to be reflected in popular literature and folklore. While encompassing this folkloric background, a historical account of the modern Brazilian short story can be divided profitably into three chronological stages of development. The first extends from its nineteenth-century romantic origins and realist practices, dominated by Joaquim Maria Machado de Assis (1839–1908), to pre-modernist currents before 1922. Modernism, a second phase centered in the 1920s and 1930s, provided new aesthetic criteria crucial for the development of the modern story. Its national, artistic program, based on Brazilianized language and the rediscovery of national reality, continues to guide story writers. Contemporary and postmodern trends – with a sharp popular, urban, socio-political orientation filtered through complex, highly referential narrative strategies for which the short story has become a preferred form – constitute a third phase leading from the 1950s and 1960s to the 1990s. Common to the three phases of development are stylistic and thematic currents in Brazilian writing, such as *Regionalismo* [Regionalism], race, social and psychological analysis, dialectal and expressive differences in Brazilian language, and formal experimentation. A brief overview of each stage will serve as a frame of reference for our historical, interpretive survey.

Indigenous, popular, and folkloric narratives of Amerindian, African, or European origins contribute to an autochthonous vein in the Brazilian narrative tradition and bear on the development of the modern short story. Their influence on short narrative in Brazil parallels that of diverse traditional or folkloric forms (such as the morality tale, fable, saga, etc.) on narrative traditions imported from Europe. The roots of indigenous material in the Brazilian short story are to be found in legends and narratives from Indian cultures, transcribed by researchers such as João Barbosa Rodrigues (1842–1909), José Vieira Couto de Magalhães (1837–1898), and Basílio de Magalhães (1874–1957). Popular stories of Iberian or African origin have also been collected by Lindolfo Gomes (*Contos populares*), Sílvio Romero (*Contos populares do Brazil*), João Ribeiro (*O folk-lore*), and others. Câmara Cascudo's *Dicionário do folclore brasileiro* catalogues narrative folkloric themes (including the well-known "Saci Pererê," "Iara," "Negrinho do Pastoreio," "Lobishomem," "Gata Borralheira," and "Pedro Malasarte") and popular stories related either to the Iberian oral tradition, particularly ample in the *literatura de cordel* [chap-books] of the northeast, or to indigenous sources. The tradition of the oral folk narrative remains alive in the cultures of Brazil's interior, although its appearance in the modern short story is sporadic and often limited to regional fiction.

Building a solid tradition in the nineteenth century, the written Brazilian short story is acknowledged to have begun with the publication in 1841 of the short narrative entitled "As duas órphãs," by Joaquim Norberto de Sousa e Silva (1820–1891). The romantic tales of the grotesque and macabre by Alvares de Azevedo (1831–1852) in *Noite na taverna*, with multiple narrators in the tradition of the *Decameron*, represents an artistic point of departure for the short story in Brazil. Poe and Maupassant are frequently mentioned as models by Brazilian authors of the times. The most polished Brazilian contributions to the form are achieved between 1882 and 1906 in the formal perfection of Machado de Assis. The short story spreads to pre-modernist trends, represented by the regionalist, symbolist, *fin-de-siècle*, and impressionistic schools of the late nineteenth and early twentieth centuries.

The modernist aesthetic of the 1920s dramatically transformed the short story by introducing fragmented discourse, techniques of montage related to the cinema, altered visions of reality, telegraphic communication, a colloquial Brazilianized language, and other avant-garde trends. As a consequence of modernist experimentation, Brazilian short story writing has been assigned by analysts to interrelated narrative categories suggesting realist/historical, formal, or subjective approaches: (1) the break with the past and depiction of a fundamentally different world, (2) the practice of radical or experimental forms in the expression of a difference of perception, and (3) subjective, self-referential, or interiorized consciousness in narration. The advances of *Modernismo* [Modernism] underlie and shape the development of the contemporary short story and continue to affect postmodern writers. Walnice Nogueira Galvão asserts that the short story as practiced in Brazil can only be understood "in the last 60 years" ("Cinco teses sobre o conto," 168).

Since the 1960s short stories have been produced in industrial proportions in Brazil, streaming off the presses in volumes and anthologies arranged by author, by region, by year, by theme, by sex, or in public and private contests. The postmodern short story has become one of the most widely practiced forms in Brazilian literature, a fact Elódia Xavier attributes to the appeal of its fragmentary, discontinuous view of life (*O conto brasileiro*, 17–28). Postmodern trends consolidate and advance the aesthetic gains of Modernism, joined to contemporary pop, urban, and other narrative strategies. Short stories have acquired a structural sophistication that draws the reader into the narrative space, illustrated by Osman Lins's use of graphic signs, for example. The newness of the modern story, its perceived relationship to the journalistic *crônica* and the T.V. *novela*, practiced by, among others, Sérgio Porto and Chico Anísio, also contribute to its current popularity in Brazil.

Some inventive, versatile writers have challenged the traditional limits of short fiction by mixing it with other modes of writing, between prose and poetry, as seen in "Versiprosa" (1967) by Carlos Drummond de Andrade (1902–1987), *Retratos-Relâmpago* (1973) by Murilo Mendes (1901–1975), and *Ave, palavra* (1970) by João Guimarães Rosa (1908–1967). While historically the tradition of realistic narration has been quantitatively more representative of stories published in Brazil, it is thought to have lost much of its earlier creative force and vitality, while some of the very best stories are the work of aesthetic innovators. Noting the change of emphasis, Fábio Lucas ("O conto no Brasil moderno") considers recent stories to be characterized more by a state of spirit than by plot, abandoning the realistic documentation of society in favor of the realism of discourse. A symptomatic thematic trend, noted by Lucas, is the exploitation of repressive violence as a theme, related to post-1964 social forces.

Brazilian contributions to the theory of the short story by its authors are few and unsystematic, yet illustrate a diversity of opinion and approach. Machado de Assis affirms that it is a difficult mode despite its apparent ease, and that the result is a lack of public credibility. Exercising his usual wit, Machado states that stories are always superior to novels because, if both are mediocre, the former at least have the advantage of being short. With Modernism, Mário de Andrade revolutionized the definition of the short story: according to his famous statement, a short story is whatever the author calls a short story. Guimarães Rosa played on the difference in meaning between *estória* and *história*, or story and history, by stating that the story, strictly speaking, should be against history; the short story should be more similar to the anecdote. In recent years, Brazilian university scholars have also begun to interpret the short story and its theories (Luiz Costa Lima, Galvão, Lucas, Gilberto Mendonça Teles, Nádia Gotlib, João Alexandre Barbosa, Benedito Nunes, *et al.*).

Contrasting with its distant origin in community memory is the modern short story's dependence on the publishing mass market of newspapers and magazines. An inherent tension in the story, according to Galvão ("Cinco teses," 169), is the contradiction between free play of the imagination, essential to the ancient act of telling, full of magic, and the prose form suitable for newspapers or journals, in which the story becomes information or news. Interpreters of the short story have accepted this dichotomy in establishing theoretical models for the form in Brazil. Reflecting the case of Machado de Assis, Mário de Andrade (1893–1945) ("Contos e contistas," 7–10) suggests that stories should first be published in journals and only after achieving lasting value be printed in books. Galvão divides production into two categories: (1) the *conto de atmosfera* [story of atmosphere], privileging aesthetics over *Realismo* [Realism], and (2) the *conto enquanto anedota* or *conto de enredo* [story as anecdote, or story with plot], drawn from events or situations presented as reality. The dichotomy is reflected in André Jolles's (*Einfache Formen, Legende, Sage, Mythe, Prätsel, Spruch, Kasus, Memorabile, Mächen, Witz*) division of the short story into two types: the simple, or marvelous tale, and the artistic, or narrative frame. The first category, in each case, represents the oral tradition and use of imagination, escaping from or displacing the reality of observation, while the second reflects the realistic form required by the cultural mass market of nineteenth-century bourgeois society. Xavier (*O conto brasileiro*) also notes a general polarization since the 1920s into either introspective or social themes, which can interact. Further refining this dynamic, Costa Lima ("O conto na modernidade brasileira," 175, 182) categorizes Brazilian short stories into (1) *conto de marcação teatral* [reality depicted theatrically], or (2) *anedota da concreção* [facts turned into narrative]. Costa Lima finds the strength of the modern short story to lie in the superimposition of innovative and imaginative narrative techniques on a renewed, questioning observation of national reality.

In terms of its reflection of national reality, the Brazilian short story follows the typology Alfredo Bosi uses to describe the tension between the hero and his social world in the novel, proceeding from a lesser to a greater degree of tension: (1) populist, regional, or neo-regional; (2) resistance to forces of Nature or society; (3) psychological, subjective, or interiorized; and (4) mythic or metaphysical transmutation of reality (*História concisa da literatura brasileira*, 432–5). The latter category includes a line of invention based on poetic and linguistic materials, transformed to produce a style comparable to abstractionism in painting and music. This progression would also be suitable for a chronological description of the evolution of the short story in Brazil, as it progressed from dependency on exterior models to autonomous expression of national literature, capable of accompanying or even influencing world trends.

In the span of approximately 150 years, Brazil has contributed to world literature two undisputed masters of the short story, Joaquim Maria Machado de Assis and João Guimarães Rosa, who stand above the historical and stylistic lines of development of the form in Brazil.

Joaquim Maria Machado de Assis, Brazil's celebrated mulatto novelist of Rio de Janeiro and founder of the Academy of Letters, wrote more than two hundred stories, known for their thematic subtlety and technical perfection. Less than twenty have ever appeared in English translation (see *The Psychiatrist and Other Stories*; *The Devil's Church and Other Stories*). His earliest examples, printed in the *Jornal das Famílias*, are of a Romantic nature, consisting of moralistic love stories and parlor intrigues. They were collectively published under the titles *Contos fluminenses* and *Histórias da meia noite*. *Papéis avulsos* is the first volume to contain stories in the vein of psychological realism that characterizes Machado's writings after 1880. It is the first of five titles containing a total of sixty-three stories, representing the majority of his best work. The other four are *Histórias sem data*, *Várias histórias*, *Páginas recolhidas*, and *Relíquias de casa velha*. His uncollected stories have since been published in numerous anthologies.

Machado's stories analyze the subtleties and contradictions of human nature and motivation with an ironic and skeptical eye, transforming the ambiguities of his characters' speech and behavior into questions and mysteries for the reader. Averse to naturalistic interpretations of society and behavior, Machado portrays a more complex character, going beyond public conformity and surface behavior to explore psychological depths, in which the nature of characters and events is tenuous, ambiguous, or mysterious. A technique of suggestion, implication, or intimation at the service of emotional or intellectual suspense, within an ironic frame of reference, constitutes a stylistic shorthand through which Machado evidences his modernity as a writer.

Although description of the exterior world is limited, Machado's stories nevertheless contain abundant implicit criticism of social and class structures in Brazil during the period of the Second Empire (1840–1890) and the early years of the Republic. In his middle-class characters, the author subtly reveals a psychology dominated by the negative side of human behavior: exploitation of others, self-interest, corruption, parasitism, sadism, pretentiousness, vanity, envy, and other reprehensible motives, hidden only slightly beneath the mask of acceptable social behavior or disguised in unquestioned values of the times. Machado's humor and irony emphasize the futility and absurdity of human conflicts and machinations in view of the illusory nature of reality and the inexorable passing of time, through which experience is ultimately converted into illusion. Machado's pessimism and skepticism serve the aesthetic moralism of his narratives, creating an ironic sympathy for many of his characters.

Often Machado's deepest meanings result from complex narrative strategies in which he dialogues with the reader. "O segredo do Bonzo" (in *Papéis avulsos* [1882]) ["The Bonzo's Secret," in *The Devil's Church and Other Stories*], for example, is identified as a lost chapter in sixteenth-century Portuguese author Fernão Mendes Pinto's incredible novelesque account of Asian adventures, *Peregrinação* (1614), a work whose truthfulness has been questioned. Machado exploits the literary reception of Mendes Pinto's narrative autobiography in his own story. The unnamed narrator, traveling in "Bungo," relates the deceitful philosophy of an outcast Bonzo (Buddhist priest), who has discovered that public opinion or belief is more forceful than actual reality. His disciples learned to insinuate ideas into the minds of the masses for their own benefit. After describing a series of increasingly unbelievable examples, in which the masses are convinced that a disciple can do something which in fact he cannot do, the narrator abruptly and subtly implies, in the story's final line, that the reader has likewise been duped into following this outrageous tale to the end. Thus, all are victims of the Bonzo, resembling the deceived public of Fuchéu, and of the art of narration as well. Machado makes use of this exotic tale to draw parallels critical of Brazilian society of his day.

Psychological analysis is an essential ingredient in Machado's stories. In "A cartomante" (1884) from *Várias histórias* (1896), a fortune-teller sustains a young man's unrealistic and self-servingly optimistic interpretation of a note of invitation suddenly received from the man who is his business partner and husband of his lover. Thus, assured of the innocence of the impending encounter, and against his logical inclinations, he proceeds unknowingly to the scene in which he and his lover are murdered. In "Missa do galo" (1894) in *Páginas recolhidas* (1899), ["Midnight Mass," in *The Psychiatrist and Other Stories*], the narrator reflects on a puzzling incident in his youth. While waiting to attend midnight mass, he spent an evening in a drawing-room alone with a young wife, D. Conceição, whose husband was often away. The only action in this story is found in the nuances, suggestiveness, symbolism, and tone of the dialogue between the two characters, now reexamined by a mature male narrator for its unsuspected erotic and psychological subtleties.

The depth of Machado's questioning of social and psychological conventions is illustrated by his irony and skeptical humor. In "O alienista" (1881–1882) in *Papéis avulsos* (1882) ["The Psychiatrist," in *The Psychiatrist and Other Stories*], a psychiatrist examines the citizens of his small community and, observing that all inevitably suffer from some kind of mental illness or abnormality, concludes that it is he who should be isolated from society. He is thus the last to be confined in his own

The Brazilian short story

asylum. In "A igreja do Diabo" (1883) ["The Devil's Church," in *The Devil's Church and Other Stories*], Satan plans to exploit those who are outwardly virtuous but inwardly hypocritical. He is conquered, however, by an inexplicable group of men who are outwardly criminals but who consistently practice good deeds. God Himself provides the explanation: "It's the eternal human condition." Machado de Assis joins philosophical and psychological sublety with technical mastery in his finest stories.

João Guimarães Rosa published seventy-nine stories in *Sagarana* [*Sagarana*], *Primeiras estórias* [*The Third Bank of the River and Other Stories*], *Tutaméia: terceiras estórias*, and *Estas estórias* (posthumous). His interest in language and myth resulted in an intensified prose, characterized by rhythmic units, alliteration, onomatopeia, rhymes, unusual syntax, archaic or neological vocabulary, poetic devices, fusion of styles, etc. According to Benedito Nunes ("Guimarães Rosa"), Guimarães Rosa writes by discovering and accumulating new meanings in the common way words are used, culminating in the creation of open relationships based on an autonomous world of language. While disguised as realistic or regionalistic narratives of the rugged land and lives of Minas Gerais's *sertão*, laying bare its Medieval, popular, and folkloric roots, the stories' ultimate purpose is to probe philosophical questions of the nature and meaning of reality, language, existence, ethics, and religion. These questions arise directly from the language and experiences of people similar to his characters, among whom Guimarães Rosa lived for several years after receiving his medical degree. In the stories, as in the novel *Grande sertão: veredas* (1956) [*The Devil to Pay in the Backlands*], the musicality of the language of the *sertão*, with its intensified semantic charge, is transformed into a mythopoetic discourse.

"A terceira margem do rio" (in *Primeiras estórias*) ["The Third Bank of the River," in *The Third Bank of the River and Other Stories*], for example, is at once a Regionalist story of a family in the interior and a metaphysical questioning of the mysterious, archetypal forces of life. Characters are identified only by kinship terms, and the story is narrated by the youngest son, whose father without warning builds an "ark," bids the family farewell, and departs in his canoe to the middle of the river flowing by the village. There he can be seen to remain timelessly, as if in another realm of existence. The family's attempts to contact him and provide for his needs are futile, and finally abandoned. While recounting each relative's fortune in consequence of the father's seemingly absurd act, the young narrator sacrifices his own independence by devoting his story, and with it his life, in an attempt to understand its meaning and reestablish contact with the lost father. Guimarães Rosa associates the flow of the river with the meaning of existence, a puzzle whose sudden, strange manifestation disrupted this family's life.

"Famigerado" (in *Primeiras estórias*) illustrates the primacy of linguistic play in ostensibly realistic stories of the *sertão*. A proud leader of a band of marauders in the *sertão* approaches a settler, displaying a gentility of manners and politeness of speech only slightly masking his murderous inclinations, obvious to the settler. His true objective, concealed in manners of speaking and face-saving circumlocutions, is to ask the meaning of a word without yielding his absolute authority or appearing to be uneducated, without the settler even being able to acknowledge – according to the rules of the game – the existence of a question. The erudite and crafty settler, in order to protect his life, plays the game to perfection, carefully choosing the narrative strategy he uses to define the meaning of "famigerado." The story is at once a parody of the "Western" and a meditation on the dialectic of knowledge/ignorance and of Good/ Evil where it might be least expected, in the vast labyrinths of Brazil's *sertão*.

One of the most difficult writers in Brazilian literature, Guimarães Rosa enriches the short story by infusing it with meaning on many interacting levels at once, employing a synthetic linguistic spectrum encompassing biblical and classical themes and references fused with the creative, popular speech of the Brazilian *sertão*. Nunes affirms Guimarães Rosa's essential originality to lie in the creation of an autonomous world of language, a universe of interior linguistic space.

Massaud Moisés (*História da literatura brasileira*, v: 493) observes a boom in the production of the short story itself in the last decades of the nineteenth century, which he compares to the 1950s, on the part of authors mainly known for their longer prose works. For these Post-romantics, Realists, Naturalists, or *belle-époque* writers, Poe, Maupassant, and European movements continued to serve as models. Early examples include the ultra-romantic stories of Franklin Távora (1842–1888) and Bernardo Guimarães (1825–1884). The latter, mixing Realism and idealism, denounced injustices of slavery and promoted the mulatto and mestizo in the story of an attack against the *quilombo* [hidden communities of ex-slaves] in *Lendas e romances*. Alfredo d'Escragnolle Taunay (1843–1899) painted the Brazilian landscape with scientific observation, creating regionalist characters ("Juca, o tropeiro") in his *Histórias brasileiras* (1874), as did Apolinário Porto Alegre (1844–1904) in *Paisagens*. The step from Realism to Naturalism can be seen in the themes of anticlericalism and adultery in *Demônios* by Aluísio de Azevedo (1857–1913), and in the victory of Nature over man in the naturalist, scientific scenes of the Amazon by Inglês de Sousa (1853–1918) (*Contos amazônicos*, [1893]). The stories of Raul Pompéia (1863–1895), published in magazines under the rubric *Microscópicos*, could more accurately be called sketches connecting naturalist observation with a personal impressionism.

The Brazilian short story

In the late nineteenth and early twentieth centuries, the short story developed a particularly Brazilian type of character and plot through descriptive, psychological, or folkloric regional prose. Regionalism refers to geographically and culturally distinct regions, including the Amazon, northeast, and central *sertão* [interior geographical area], and to stock characters, such as the São Paulo *caipira* [regional folk and popular character] and the *gaúcho* of the south. Linked to Post-romanticism, early regionalist prose lacked the psychological, mythical, linguistic, and poetic expression that has come to be associated with Guimarães Rosa and other masters of the style. Two writers gave shape to the organized regionalist program that was to become one of the most dominant currents in contemporary Brazilian writing. Valdomiro Silveira (1873–1941) initiated the folkloric portraits of poor people from the interior of São Paulo state as early as 1891, when his story "Rabicho" appeared in the *Diário de São Paulo*. His stories exploit the pathetic and tragic passions of *paulista* society, illustrated by the settler in "Camunhengue" (1920) in *Os caboclos* who contracts leprosy and withdraws from family and society in desperation. Afonso Arinos de Melo Franco (1868–1916) described the regional *mineiro* [from Minas Gerais] character in *Pelo sertão* (1898), joining the elegant style of the historical novel to a more precise though surface description and visualization of the agrarian habits and moral character of the *sertanejo*. Both writers were interested in transcribing the flavor of regional speech and introduced dialect into their stories. João Simões Lopes Neto (1865–1916) documents the epic stories of the *gaúcho* in an artistic style that faithfully reflects legends and folklore, while integrating harmonically an oral style with the characters, language, and plots of *gaúcho* culture. Readers interested in obtaining a more exact knowledge of national reality could turn to stories of other regions, such as the fresh account of troops in Goiás (*Tropas e boiadas*) by Hugo de Carvalho Ramos (1895–1921), the Amazon scenes in *Inferno verde* by Alberto Rangel (1871–1945), the picturesque stories of Bahia (*Simples histórias*) by Xavier Marques (1861–1942) or the prolix *gaúcho* (*Tapera*) of Alcides Maia (1878–1944).

The poem in prose influenced the short story through its mixture of ultra-romantic, decadentist, and symbolist aesthetics, illustrated by João da Cruz e Sousa (1861–1898) in *Tropos e fantasias* (1885, with Virgílio Várzea). The symbolist story developed in the hands of César Câmara de Lima Campos (1872–1929), Luiz Gonzaga Duque Estrada (1862–1911), and Nestor Vítor (1868–1932). Lima Campos, author of *Confessor supremo*, specialized in the language of morbid, dramatic, fleeting impressions, while Gonzaga Duque achieved a special balance between fable and poetic language (*Horto de mágoas*). Together they founded several important literary and cultural magazines, including *Fon-Fon* (1908). With *Signos*, Nestor Vítor explores social questions through interior monologue and decadent aesthetic labyrinths. An avid practitioner of the short story in this phase is Artur de Azevedo (1855–1908), who brought theatrical expression, humor, and a popular voice to themes of the "human comedy" conveyed through the anecdote. His "possible," "ephemeral," and "out of date" stories also conveyed stylistic innovations, such as telegraphic repartee in the dialogues and the exploitation of explosive, iconoclastic humor. "Plebiscito," from *Contos fora da moda*, reveals the dynamics of a Brazilian family, not without a dose of almost malicious political humor, in the guise of an innocent question at the dinner table. A son asks his father what the word "plebiscite" means. While it is obvious to the reader that the master of the house does not know the answer, he refuses to admit this shortcoming and parlays the question into a challenge to his patriarchal authority. Style and language suffer comic manipulation at the service of established social values, with the infusion of political satire.

Cosmopolitan, urban prose of the *belle époque* is the métier of João do Rio (Paulo Barreto, 1881–1921), bohemian man of carioca letters whose life and art imitated each other in polished phrases. His stories (*Dentro da noite*, *A mulher e os espelhos*, *Rosário da ilusão*) advanced the decadent climate through themes of sexual degeneracy, morbidity, sadism, perversion, delirium, etc., narrated with a mixture of luxury and horror. "O Bebê de Tarlatana Rosa," his best-known story, is a macabre carnival adventure in which an upper-class gentleman and his circle descend into the lower-class dance halls of Rio de Janeiro for the sake of having a popular, degenerate experience. There, he is fascinated with a mysterious woman costumed as a rose-colored baby, who becomes the object of his inflamed, erotic desires. He accepts her one condition that he never remove her mask. After fleeing through darkened streets to a rendezvous, unable to resist temptation, he tears off the "baby's" mask, revealing only a horrifying wound in place of a nose. Other writers sharing the cultivated, mundane atmosphere of the times include J. Medeiros e Albuquerque (1867–1934) and Júlia Lopes de Almeida (1862–1934).

Henrique M. Coelho Neto (1864–1934) is the most prolific premodernist writer, author of some nineteen volumes of short stories published between 1891–1928. Coelho Neto absorbed many of the literary currents of his time, from urban and *sertanejo* works to bohemian Decadentism, while exploring themes of morbid sentiment and melodrama, from *boudoir* dramas to social cases of "philosophic" madness. Nurtured by Maupassant and Portuguese authors such as Camilo Castelo Branco (1825–1890), the twelve stories of *Urupês* [*Brazilian Short Stories*], by Monteiro Lobato (1882–1948), gained instant popularity through themes combining macabre, satiric humor with tragi-comic, pathetic, and ridiculous situations. His writings are also tinged by a taste for science fiction, an interest in language, and children's literature, with plots derived from his observation of life in the interior of São Paulo state. Over the years, *Urupês* has sold more copies than any other book of short stories in Brazil. Afonso Schmidt (1890–1964), largely ignored by criticism, made a living from his prolific writings. His stories depicted the rural or popular settings of the pathetic lives of socially marginal figures.

Advancing a current of social and cultural criticism perhaps implicit in Machado de Assis yet which matures only in the modernist story, Afonso Henriques de Lima Barreto (1881–1922), also a mulatto, makes of his writings an instrument of social criticism and revolt. The novelesque antihero Policarpo Quaresma is his demented patriot, the tragi-comic mask of an unflattering sociopolitical portrait. His one volume of stories, *Histórias e sonhos*, ranges from political satire to psychological investigation. His widely anthologized story, "O homem que sabia javanês," unmasks the ignorance and arrogance of Brazil's diplomatic aristocracy through the story of a youth who decides to improve his lot in life by becoming a specialist in Javanese. Naturally, he never learns the language but restricts his knowledge to a few entries in the encyclopedia and a half-dozen words, aided by the certainty that those limited resources would far exceed anyone else's knowledge of such an exotic place and topic. He suffers a scare when appointed as tutor for an elderly diplomat, but fortunately the old man's powers of learning prove extremely limited. After narrowly avoiding an encounter with a Javanese sailor, our expert finally achieves his goal through connections, being assigned to the Oceanic division of the Foreign Office as Brazil's representative in Europe. Lima Barreto humorously yet sharply criticizes an intellectual bureaucracy in which knowledge is the only superfluous ingredient. In his social satire, Lima Barreto may be viewed as a precursor of modernist trends.

The beginnings of a formally experimental style can be seen in Adelino Magalhães (1887–1969) (*Casos e impressões*), viewed by some critics as the precursor of the fragmentary style practiced by modernist authors of the 1920s. Magalhães's short prose fragments are poeticized impressions, with links to the aphorism and to imagism. His works can be connected with the later creative prose aphorisms and poetic sketches of Aníbal Machado, Murilo Mendes (1901–1975), and Guimarães Rosa.

The period of literary Modernism extending from 1922 to 1945 gave birth to the contemporary Brazilian short story and has continued to dominate the concept and production of short fiction for more than sixty years. Among its marks of modernity are the development of urban prose, use of Brazilianized rather than Portuguese norms, fragmented discourse, narrative and structural techniques derived from cinematography or cubistic geometry, introduction of colloquial style, linguistic multiplicity reflecting a radically changing social reality, and the use of humor, parody, and irony in social criticism.

São Paulo, with its Modern Art Week in 1922, was the center of literary modernization. Modernist groups formed in the states, adapting modernist techniques and values to the depiction of regionalist language and social life. Regionalist and realistic prose styles were transformed by modernist language and narration, leading to a wide variety of practices – including psychological, intimist, colloquial, and poetic – still applicable to the contemporary Brazilian short story. Modernist authors questioned national values with humor and satire, while drawing moral and existential portraits of the Brazilian character. Narrative style is marked by simple and direct language, paradox, irony, skepticism, myth, and metaphor. Experimental approaches foreshadowed practices that came to dominate postmodern writing, such as self-conscious narration, literary referentiality, and graphic variation. Representative modernist story writers are discussed below.

A catalyst of Brazilian Modernism in São Paulo primarily known for his novel *Macunaíma*, poetry, correspondence, literary criticism, and folklore, Mário de Andrade (1893–1945) was also the unrecognized master of the early modernist short story. Mário de Andrade published two volumes of stories during his lifetime, *Primeiro andar*, whose stories date from 1918, and *Belazarte*. Other major stories appeared posthumously in *Contos novos*. Mário de Andrade brought greater latitude to the conception and realization of the short story. Some creative, often avant-garde, touches he introduced include giving a character a number rather than a name (in "Primeiro de Maio") and having a character consciously refer to "Mário de Andrade" as his author. According to Costa Lima ("O conto na modernidade brasileira," 175–81), Mário's stories treat socially conventional situations and characters committed to the social taboos of a repressed society. Within these situations, employing symbols and even moments of epiphany, Mário de Andrade unmasks the underlying social mechanisms with the eye and understanding of a humanist.

In "O Peru de Natal" ["The Christmas Turkey" in *Contos novos*], an adolescent narrator relates the almost ritual preparation of the Christmas dinner in his lower-middle-class family in São Paulo soon after his father's death. The young man, who cultivates the reputation of an eccentric in his family, carefully constructs his emancipation from the continued stifling presence of his father and his code of self-denial, which had guided the family in its careful and self-conscious position in society, while expressing at the same time the youth's concern for family unity. The young narrator subtly takes advantage of a rite of passage, the Christmas turkey, a symbol of pleasure and plenty repressed by the old man's lingering hold over the household. By convincing his mother and aunts to eat the turkey with an enthusiasm meant to celebrate the efforts of his father's long years of labor, the ensuing feast acquires unconscious cannibalistic imagery and a celebratory, cathartic effect. The dinner perhaps symbolizes the eucharistic consumption of the world of the lost father. In the victory of the feast, the youth achieves his independence in a ritual passage to adulthood.

In his short life, Antônio de Alcântara Machado (1901–1935) developed the urban short story of the Italian immigrant in São Paulo of the 1920s. Along with the new reality in language and customs, Alcântara Machado also brought a different structure and speech to short fiction in *Brás, Bexiga e Barra funda*, *Laranja da China*, and two posthumous books, *Mana Maria* and *Cavaquinho e saxofone*. Based on picturesque, anecdotal, and humorous observations of the life of the new Italian *paulistas*, whom Bosi (*História concisa*, 421–2) has called "traditional families in decline," Alcântara Machado converts the stories of family dramas into a more profound presentation of the human relationships underlying adaptation to a new society, language, and values. The narrator belongs to the community and relies on dialogue, often reflecting pronunciation, to tell his story. Sensitive and ironic, the author's snapshots of characters such as "Gaetaninho" reveal the innocence and tragic charm of modernization. Although deaf, Gaetaninho plays soccer with companions on the immigrants' street, fantasizing of one day owning a car. He invents a funeral for Aunt Filomena in his dreams so that he can dress elegantly and ride in the car with his family. Filomena and the family are shocked by this affront to their social values. Ironically, Gaetaninho is struck and killed by a streetcar while chasing a soccer ball. He is carried to the cemetery in the very first car, while his rival Beppino shows up in a superb red suit. In Alcântara Machado's stories, the sentimental or tragic themes are subordinated to modernist speech, adaptation to new social values, and the documentary intention. They universalize the early culture of industrialization and urbanization in Brazil's largest city.

Further experimentation along the lines of popular syntax and colloquial language is found in Mário Neme's *Donana sofredora* and *Mulher que sabe latim*. The style continues to be a strong influence on the contemporary short story.

Although well known as a modernist author since the 1920s, the works by the *mineiro* Aníbal Machado (1894–1964) have been relatively neglected by critics, perhaps because of their widely separated publication (1944; 1959), in spite of his active role in modernist literary groups in Rio de Janeiro over the years. His stories contain expressionistic language and description with ties to symbolist musicality and surrealist otherworldliness. Imaginative and often dreamlike, his stories poetically relate the influence of unforeseen natural forces on the characters.

Aníbal Machado's "A morte da porta-estandarte" (in *Vida feliz*) is considered a classic of the modernist short story. Set during Carnival in Rio de Janeiro, the narrative explores the complex, almost instinctual forces of race, celebration, love, jealousy, and violence – as if Aníbal, paradoxically, were describing naturalistic theories using poetic language. The young mulatto woman chosen as standard-bearer to carry the pennant for her samba school will be parading her beauty and feminine appeal along the avenues, while her boyfriend, lost among the vast throng, must search for her by spotting the floating, moving banner held high above the crowd. This symbol of her presence, furthered by the catalyst of the mob and the black youth's romantic fears and obsessions, leads inevitably to a tragic finale, associated with the destructive forces inherent in Carnival. The standard-bearer is murdered, an act conveyed to the reader/observer only by the piercing scream, lost in the pandemonium, and the fall of the pennant. When the youth recovers from his trancelike possession and unwitting act, he is left to mourn his loss and tragic fate. The high drama of Aníbal's story is accompanied by a fluid, musical language that mirrors and intensifies his themes.

The *mineiro* João Alphonsus (1901–1944) continues the lyrical, colloquial style of Modernism in *Galinha cega* and *Pesca da baleia*. Son of symbolist poet Alphonsus de Guimaraens, João Alphonsus contributed to early modernist literary magazines along with Pedro Nava, Carlos Drummond de Andrade, and others, while publishing his best-known story, "Galinha cega," in the *paulista* review *Terra Roxa e Outras Terras* in 1926. Alphonsus transposes human feelings to the animal realm, projecting a psychology of irony and skepticism applied to everyday situations. Exploiting personification, the narrator relates not only the hen's inner feelings of liberty in her new owner's yard but her Existential meditations on the requisites for happiness: freedom and corn. The story, however, unveils the "darker side of life," beginning with her subjugation by the rooster's instinctual urges and her subsequent blindness. This weakness, or deviation from the norm for her species, singles her out for suffering and death, in spite of her owner's cares. Whether as a "football" for malicious, cruel youths or as prey for the possum that finally kills and defeathers her, the blind hen symbolizes the inexorable, natural decay of goodness and happiness.

Oscarina, the first volume of stories by Marques Rebelo (Edi Dias da Cruz) (1907–1973), followed by *Três caminhos*, represents modern urban prose of Rio de Janeiro. Stylistically, Rebelo follows a line of realistic narrative exemplified by Manuel Antônio de Almeida (1831–1861), Lima Barreto, and others, dominated by irony and objectivity. Rebelo wrote deceptively simply stories in colloquial language about the sufferings and frustrations of working-class neighborhoods of Rio de Janeiro. He documented the confrontation of tradition with the competition and bureaucracy engendered by modernization. Rebelo's stories are often about memories of childhood or daily life in a less complicated past. More lyrical and nostalgic than the usual social realism of the 1930s, the stories also maintain a distinction between the narrator and social reality in their structure. In "Circo de coelhinhos" the young narrator juxtaposes the arrival of two angora rabbits with the picaresque adventures and childhood tricks of Silvino, who is later struck by an ice truck and critically injured. Silvino's touching death is paralleled by the unexplained demise of the rabbits, both events serving as a rite of passage for the narrator.

Combining an interest in scientific theories in vogue in the 1920s with imaginative, unorthodox writing, Gastão Cruls (1888–1959) brought the relationship between fiction and reality into question. Inexplicable coincidences between fictional characters or events and what is recognized within fiction as "reality" lead Cruls to a metaliterary vein, reflected in major Spanish American writers such as Borges and Cortázar. Cruls's *A criação e o criador* (1928) and *Vertigem* (1938), however, remain unexplored by critics and undiscovered by the reading public. His fascination with the Amazon region, leading to his participation in the 1928 exploration by Cândido Rondon (1865–1968) into the interior of the Amazon, also became a dominant theme in his fiction, as seen in *Coivara* (1920), *Ao embalo da rede*, and *Amazônia misteriosa* (1925) [*The Mysterious Amazonia: A Brazilian Novel*]. In his short story "Meu sósia" (*História puxa história*), the narrator notices that his own research and creative interests in the Amazon are being copied by a mysterious double, who withdraws from a library the exact list of books required for the narrator's study. When the double avoids contact with the narrator and, fleeing the library, is run over by a car, the question of identity or reality is led to a perplexing, indeterminate conclusion. Cruls's story could be compared to the avant-garde fiction of Portuguese Modernist Mário de Sá-Carneiro (1890–1916).

Graciliano Ramos (1892–1953) is heir to a style of critical Realism sharply applied to Brazilian social reality, formally demanding while expressing a tragic sense of life. His ties to Modernism are found in colloquial northeastern language, folkloric themes, synthetic expression, and psychological questioning. Ramos's short stories (*Histórias de Alexandre*

[1944], Histórias incompletas, Insônia) are lesser known than his novels and memoirs, yet reflect a similar knowledge of the sociological and linguistic reality of the northeast in their portrayal of sertanejo life and customs. According to Osman Lins ("O mundo recusado"), Ramos's short fiction was largely written in the late 1930s, between the conclusion of his work as a novelist and the beginning of his books of memoirs. One should note that many of the chapters of the novel Vidas secas (1938) [Barren Lives], were first successfully published as independent stories. "Baleia," the story of the death of a dog, is narrated by Baleia the dog herself, since she is more verbal than Fabiano or his family. "A apresentação de Alexandre e Cesária" (1938), folk stories of the northeast, followed the children's story "A terra dos meninos pelados" (1937). The "Alexandre" stories illustrate a link between contemporary fiction and oral traditions; Graciliano notes in the preface that the stories are "not original," having derived from the folklore of his region. Lins's study, however, details the narrative artifices with which Graciliano crafted the folk tale into fiction with his own marks upon it.

Other Modernists who were not known principally for their stories also contributed to the genre, including Ribeiro Couto (1898–1963), Rodrigo Melo Franco de Andrade (1898–1969), Orígenes Lessa (1903–1986), Carlos Drummond de Andrade (1902–1987), and Erico Veríssimo (1905–1975).

In addition to João Guimarães Rosa, principal directions in the creative development of the short story in Brazil, carrying advances of Modernism into new dimensions, are represented by authors Clarice Lispector, Osman Lins, Dalton Trevisan, Murilo Rubião, Rubem Fonseca, and Lygia Fagundes Telles. These writers may be considered representative of major thematic or stylistic trends or categories that, under the aegis of modernist innovation, continue to dominate the contemporary Brazilian short story. These are (1) psychological/mythical/poetic, (2) linguistic/ formal innovation, (3) grotesque miniatures, (4) magical realism, (5) "pop"/social fiction, and (6) women's writing. While useful for purposes of classification, the characteristics of these broad trends are shared to a certain degree by all contemporary Brazilian writers.

Author of six collections of stories, Clarice Lispector (1920–1977) treats urban, feminist, and psychological themes that tie her work to the modernist movement and contribute to her position (with Guimarães Rosa) as a pivotal, revolutionary figure in contemporary Brazilian narrative. Lispector's works have been widely translated in recent years, and she is the subject of increasing international attention. The short story was particularly suited to Lispector's "lyrical" writing, focused around epiphanies, or sudden moments of intense insight or awareness of the human condition. Lispector approaches psychological, feminist, or Existential themes through language, symbol, and epiphany. By techniques of disarming language, Lispector carries her stories to levels of meaning and expression which there are no conventional words to express. Often lacking conventional plots, her stories concentrate on ontological themes of language, consciousness, and being, in a juncture of psychological and existential motifs. Benedito Nunes (*Clarice Lispector* "Retrato de um intelectual brasileiro") notes her style of "wearing down words," in an attempt to grasp what language cannot express and arrive at a meaning about which there are no more words. Her philosophical themes are structured in an interiorized, highly poetic narrative, in which characters struggle to know themselves, rejecting their social roles and routines in favor of a more authentic but often painful personal existence. The path to awareness in her works is often not clearly delineated, but often apparently directionless, ambiguous, and indeterminate. The reader is left uncertain not only about what is happening but also about its significance and ultimate development. By disguising philosophical themes in everyday language and situations and by creating internal, poetic discourse to express the struggle for being, Lispector transformed the short story after 1960.

"O búfalo" (*Laços de família*) [*Family Ties*], whose meaning is the subject of much debate, represents one of her most mysteriously metaphorical expressions of epiphany. A sole female protagonist (who is never named but only identified as a woman) finds herself at the zoo during springtime, searching blindly for an object to receive the hate she had directed toward a male who rejected and abused her. Experiencing an unexpected and uncontrollable catharsis, the woman flees from the collapse of her world and the crisis of its values, having lost every system of support that she had so carefully and trivially constructed to maintain her existence. Now reduced to weakness and emptiness, the woman undergoes a kind of death and rebirth, encountering at the zoo a new reading of themes of love, hate, loneliness, violence, and self-renewal while surrounded by "rites of Spring" enacted by the animals. The last of these that she encounters is an enormous black male water buffalo with impressive horns. The blackness, a heart of darkness, hypnotizes the woman, who is freed from the cycle of love and hate during the moment she and the buffalo stare into each other's eyes. The woman experiences an epiphany, "looking without eyes," revealing to her the forces of life. Transcending her experience, she confronts life for the first time as a result of her moment of crisis.

Psychological, mythical, and intimist fictional worlds also characterize another of Brazil's major authors of the short story, Autran Dourado (b.

1926). A *mineiro*, Dourado preserves a taste for Regionalism combined with baroque design and complexity. His works experiment with multiple narrative points of view, show a preference for stream of consciousness or other interior narrations, and are cast in hermetic symbolism. Lucas considers that Dourado writes the same infinite story throughout his career, uniting memories of childhood, expressing the myths, poetry, and passion of things past, with the dramatic, metaphysical consciousness of death (Lucas, "O conto no Brasil moderno," 126–7). Beginning in 1955 with *Três histórias na praia*, Dourado's works include *Nove histórias em grupos de Três*; *Solidão, solitude*; *Armas & corações* and *As imaginacões pecaminosas*. Illustrating Dourado's narrative innovation, the story "Os gêmeos" (in *As imaginações pecaminosas*) is structured as a musical dialogue between two characters on the theme of childhood tunes and dances. The "music" grows into a crescendo of dramatic, psychological revelation.

Other authors who continue the psychological, mythical, or poetic themes of Modernism include Breno Accioli (1921–1966), who creates an atmosphere of madness in *João Urso*. Samuel Rawet (1929–1984) (see Xavier, *O conto brasileiro*) investigates intellectually the adaptation of Jewish immigrants to their new environment, their existential dilemmas, and the author's relation to the text (*Contos do imigrante, Diálogo, O terreno de uma polegada quadrada*). The juxtaposition of memory and reality is a dominant theme in Luiz Vilela (b. 1942) (*No bar, Tarde da noite*, and *O fim de tudo*). Memory and the subconscious appear mixed with cinematography and Surrealistic flashes in *O cego e a dançarina* by João Gilberto Noll (b. 1947), one of the most important names in the contemporary story.

An innovative writer in whom the culture of Brazil's northeast and his native Pernambuco is present, Osman Lins conceived of narration as a conscious use of words within a structure of forms crossing traditional borders, well illustrated in the nine narratives of *Nove, novena [Nine, Novena]*. Different planes of experience – including characters, objects, situations, plots, and meanings – are brought together in openly Structural models that depend on the linguistic organization of the story. As author, Lins is not telling, rather writing, and meaning is to be found in the organization of his materials. Lins invents a series of identifying signs placed throughout his texts – circles, squares, rectangles, vertical lines, and other typographical marks – to symbolize the planes of discourse and serve as a key to their structure. The reader is thus drawn into the actual creative process. In "Um ponto no círculo," for example, a masculine and a feminine character monologue around the axle of a common experience, and in "O pentágono de Hahn" graphic symbols coordinate a collage of memories, experiences, and anxieties.

Accompanying the structural design is an intense verbal virtuosity that invents with a poetic imagination, full of hidden meanings built into allegories, metaphors, and symbols. In his story with a religious, mystical aura, "Retábulo de Santa Joana Carolina," Lins achieves a lyrical intensity not only through the multiple planes of monologues, dialogues, and impressions stemming from the destitute creatures of the northeast but also from the alliterative, culturally rich chain of names drawn from the land and its distinguishing morphology. In spite of the Realism of his characters, setting, and situation, Lins presents the reader with what João Alexandre Barbosa ("Nove, novena novidade") terms a musical, atonal narrative. It is composed of linguistic and typographical signs and of dissonant planes of discourse and meaning. Through an intense critical view of themselves, characters achieve an inner force of being. Lins's world, filtered through a poetic imagination and enhanced with innovative narrative techniques, represents the fullest development of psychological simultaneity in Brazilian fiction.

Experimentation with narrative structure represents a continuing modernist influence on the contemporary story, as seen in Autran Dourado. Others who reflect the same influence include Ricardo Ramos (b. 1929) (*Circuito fechado*), who works with a numbered sequence of linked stories in a parody of capitalist mass consumption, and Ivan Angelo (b. 1936) (*A casa de vidro*) [*The Tower of Glass*], whose five stories of Brazil present different viewpoints on the problem of national history and social reality.

Using techniques of defamiliarization and grotesque humor, Dalton Trevisan (b. 1925) has revolutionized the short story by negating any established order or values, while unmasking the primacy of human imperfection and malice in personal and social relationships. Trevisan is a prolific writer, author of some twenty volumes of stories spanning twenty-five years. *Novelas nada exemplares*, a title that deforms Cervantes, defines his fictions as unexemplary tales, a kind of inverted and perverted moral fable designed for the middle class of Curitiba, the provincial capital of Paraná. Trevisan explores themes including exploitation, cruelty, triviality, and meanness that reveal the uncontrollable, abject fantasies, impulses, and desires underlying and determining the dark side of human conduct. His minute stories constitute the psychosocial drama of modern urban society viewed in the negative. While his particular mixture of irony and pessimism is carried to shocking extremes of degradation and disgust in its portrayal of human nature, Trevisan makes a significant contribution to the short story through his approach to understatement and stylistic miniaturization (*O vampiro de Curitiba* [*The Vampire of Curitiba and Other Stories*]).

Trevisan's stories seem to have become progressively shorter and more concise, projecting his mastery of the ellipsis and scenic fragmentation to the genre as a whole. His use of the diminutive within simple, declarative sentences belies a highly sculptured style that produces a climate of degrading intimacy, scarcely disguising a gallery of horrors. Trevisan organizes his stories around paradigmatic fictional nuclei representing serious social, psychological, or existential situations which nevertheless, given their basic absurdity, contain elements of parody, humor, and fantasy. Also deepening the fictional context of his work is Trevisan's extensive recourse to literary referentiality, from classical mythology to world literature, converting his text into a rhetorical mural of quotations, allusions, and references. His constant incorporation of literary references produces a climate of parody, on the one hand, and universal meanings, on the other.

"Penelope" (in *Novelas nada exemplares*) for example, recasts the classical myth of the clever, patient, and faithful wife in the Brazilian middle-class setting of a retired couple. In the culminating years of a life of labor and devotion, an unexpected, perverted challenge strikes the couple, in the form of an anonymous letter left under the door once each week containing the single work "cuckold." At first dismissing or avoiding the persistent letter, the husband undergoes a metamorphosis carrying him to deceit, deception, and violence. He assassinates his loyal wife before coming to the belated realization of her innocence and his irreplaceable loss.

Weaving eternal myths into modern urban reality, while compacting the simple, explosive force of language into increasingly synthesized thematic nuclei, Trevisan stands alone in modern Brazilian literature as the prophet of the enormously destructive powers of modernization, conveyed through a minimalist fictional style.

João Antônio (b. 1937), following the tradition of picaresque critiques of popular urban classes found in Manuel Antônio de Almeida, Lima Barreto, and Trevisan, portrays the popular culture and the sufferings of the working class, bohemian neighborhoods of São Paulo where he grew up (*Malagueta, perus e bacanaço; Leão de chácara* [1975]). Slums, snooker, popular music, and marginalization are the principal themes. This vein of popular fiction alternates between the authentic reproduction of voices from São Paulo's oppressed underworld and the tendency to create picturesque, documentary social documents related to the journalistic chronicle and detective fiction. The story "Frio" (1963) traces an episode in the miserable life of a ten-year-old boy who lives in the slums near Sorocabana and delivers "packages" for his protector Paraná. The reader shares the impressions, simple desires, dangers, and adventures of this boy as he crosses the city on foot, avoiding the police, sleeping in a junkyard in Pompéia. An evocative vignette of innocent lives without a present or a future, "Frio" also illustrates João Antônio's reply to the Brazilian "economic miracle" of the years of dictatorship (1964–1985).

Other examples of this school include Otto Lara Resende (b. 1922), who concentrates on themes of crime and conflict (*Boca do inferno, As pompas do mundo*), and Flávio Moreira da Costa (b. 1942), who narrates the world of the *malandro* [rogue, scoundrel] using marginal speech from different regions of the country (*Malvadeza Durão*).

Unlike in Spanish America, Magical Realism was little practiced in Brazil, forming instead a natural part of surrealistic touches or poeticization applied to modernist narrative techniques. Aníbal Machado could be considered a precursor of the style through the influence of myth (*Histórias reunidas*). In *O ex-mágico* [*The Ex-Magician and Other Stories*], Murilo Rubião (b. 1916) became the first to create a small repertoire of allegorical stories blending quotidian and otherworldly description, mixing reality with fantasy. These were followed by *A estrela vermelha, Os dragões e outros contos, O convidado*, and *O pirotécnico Zacarias*. Appealing to biblical esotericism, Rubião produces enigmatic, foreboding, and symbolic tales of primordial enchantment, with touches of science fiction and the Absurd. According to Jorge Schwartz (*Murilo Rubião*), the modernity of Rubião lies not in the production of tension or rational doubt itself, typical of a category of fantastic literature, but rather in the juxtaposition of incompatible realities. In the tradition of Kafka, Rubião draws the reader into a self-conscious universe whose absurdity is no longer perplexing in itself.

In "O ex-mágico da taberna minhota" the hero appears full-grown, without birth or childhood, endowed with magical powers. The animals that constantly appear as a result of his slightest gestures contribute to an increasing feeling of alienation and sadness. He attempts suicide, but his magical powers sustain and frustrate him. On hearing that life as a civil servant is like a slow suicide, he joins the Secretaria de Estado. Over the years, he comes to regret this choice and feels the consequences of the loss of magic. Now he simply repeats the gestures of a magician, leading others to think that he is crazy, while he dreams of the enchantment of a magical world to which he had once belonged. "Os dragões" is an allegory with strong sociopolitical overtones. The arrival of dragons in a small provincial town is met with dismay by civil and church leaders, who insist on catechism and alphabetization. Although integrating themselves into the town's life, the dragons suffer discrimination and persecution. After the last one flees, the townspeople attempt to attract the hundreds of dragons who are waiting to enter other towns of the land, but to no avail. None will consider living there again.

José J. Veiga (b. 1915) paints an atmosphere of alienation in fantasies and fables of Brazilian life carried to the absurd (*Os cavalinhos de Platiplanto*; *A máquina extraviada*) [*The Misplaced Machine and Other Stories*]. "A máquina extraviada" is presented as an oral tale relating the arrival of a monstrous machine, assembled in front of City Hall in a small Brazilian town. As it has no instructions, no function, and no one knows how to operate it, the strange machine acquires the status of an icon, rivaling religious devotion. Men are hired to keep it shiny, and one worker's leg is sacrificed to the machine's anonymous appetite. Its magic will last only as long as it remains socially useless.

The "divine fables" of Moacyr Scliar (b. 1937) construct Orwellian social allegories with simplicity, magic, and humor in stories of Jewish immigrants in Rio Grande do Sul (*Histórias de médico em formação*; *O carnaval dos animais* [*Carnival of the Animals*]; *A balada do falso Messias* [*The Ballad of the False Messiah*]; *A massagista japonesa*; *O olho enigmático*). His characters react against social institutions and bureaucracy, constituting a judgment of Brazilian reality according to the values of Jewish thought.

Garcia de Paiva (b. 1920) experiments with magical realities related to science fiction in *Os Planelúpedes* and further experiments with techniques of film montage in the orthography of popular speech in *Dois cavalos num Fuscazul*. Elias José (b. 1936) also works in the style of Magical Realism, juxtaposing oneiric fantasies to the absurdity of daily life (*A mal amada*, *Um pássaro em pânico*, *O grito dos torturados*).

A *mineiro* residing in Rio de Janeiro, Rubem Fonseca (b. 1925) has capitalized on the themes of urbanization and militarization of Brazilian society, beginning in *Os prisioneiros*. Influenced by detective fiction and by the electronic gadgetry of North America, Fonseca depicts the crime, violence, degradation, and exploitation dominating the underworlds of Rio de Janeiro. Although participating in a category of Brazilian writing known as "literature of the dictatorship," Fonseca has more complex literary, social, and Existential interests. While painting a broad social mural, Fonseca condemns the bourgeois order and its shocking effects on human attitudes and relationships. He has been criticized, however, for his imitation in fiction of the high levels of violence, brutality, and inhumanity witnessed in city life. According to this argument, the reader who is shocked and repelled by a mirror image of the most sordid events engendered by urban, bourgeois capitalism is at the same time captivated by the compelling, best-selling mystery style. Lucas ("O conto no Brasil moderno," 143–5) affirms, in this regard, that the reader's fascination with plot is soon balanced by the author's philosophical or ideological questioning and informed by his intertexual and metalinguistic references. Fonseca transforms the modern city into a symbolic universe, with its own language, myth, art, and religion. The self-conscious narratives explore a new urban world of belief and symbol.

Fonseca is a master of plot in establishing interacting episodes and characters, achieved through both linguistic and thematic dexterity. *Lúcia McCartney, Feliz Ano Novo,* and *O cobrador* reveal the dual dimensions of Fonseca's style: the horror and brutality of urban life, on the one hand, and the aesthetic reflexivity of an ironic writer who incorporates a literary and cultural tradition into his urban chronicles. Through Fonseca's technical art, the reader perceives an implied distance between the real and the ideal, amoral and moral, or animal and human spheres of existence.

Popular, social, and political short fiction has a wide following in contemporary Brazil, perhaps traceable to the years of military dictatorship, although the style has roots in different phases of national literature. State violence has engendered a reflection in post-1964 literature preoccupied with social violence, imprisonment, and torture. In Ivan Angelo's *A casa de vidro: cinco histórias do Brasil,* Brazil itself is a large prison with walls of glass. Citizens who pass by on their way to work become immune to increasingly abject scenes of torture and suffering enacted, as it were, for their entertainment and as a warning. Ideological repression and gratuitous violence as themes appear in stories by a wide range of writers, including Wander Piroli (b. 1931), who in the 1960s published his insouciant *A Mãe e o filho da mãe;* Garcia de Paiva (*Dois cavalos num fuscazul*); Modesto Carone (b. 1937) (*Aos pés de Matilde*); Manoel Lobato (b. 1925) (*Flecha em repouso*); Júlio Gomide (*Liberdade para os pirilampos*); Mafra Carbonieri (b. 1935) (*Arma e bagagem*), and others.

Brazilian popular fiction takes multiple directions. Roberto Drummond (b. 1937) is the creator of a "pop" style carried toward the realm of fantasy (*A morte de D. J. em Paris*). Edilberto Coutinho (b. 1938) explores the social institution of Brazilian *futebol* [soccer] in *Maracanã, Adeus – onze histórias de futebol,* mixing humor and satire with experiments with typographical form in the use of parallel columns. Caio Abreu (b. 1948) explores satire and the Absurd (*O ovo apunhalado, Pedras de Calcutá, Morangos mofados*). Humor dominates cultural satire in works by actor Chico Anísio (b. 1931) (*O enterro do anão, Feijoada no Copa, Teje preso*), representing the confluence of the story with the situation drama, journalistic chronicle, and T.V. *novela.* João Ubaldo Ribeiro (b. 1940) (*Livro de histórias*) unites the strong Regionalism of Bahia with allegorical fantasies and satire of historical and social traditions.

Although Clarice Lispector also advances feminist perspectives in the Brazilian story, Lygia Fagundes Telles (b. 1923) began her literary career with two books of short stories, *Praia viva* and *O cacto vermelho,* exploring the theme of moral and economic adjustment of women to modern society in the urban atmosphere of São Paulo. Comparable to Lispector's scathing indictment of "family ties," Telles's stories consider family relationships and extended childhood to be obstacles to individual development and liberation. Social norms and conventions, exacerbated by authoritarianism and tradition, restrict and enclose female protagonists. They must face the anachronism of a bourgeois environment that no longer possesses the wealth or coherence to relate to rapid social change. Telles reveals her interest in narrative technique by abandoning psychological realism for shifting levels and points of view, introducing stylistic and structural innovations into a feminist social critique (*Seminário dos ratos*) [*Tigrela and Other Stories*].

The roots of the short stories by women in Brazil can be traced to Júlia Lopes de Almeida (1862–1934), considered the Brazilian George Sand. Several women writers of short fiction played a significant role in Modernism. Eneida de Morais (1903–1971), who was active in a modernist group in Belém, Pará, and later, in Rio de Janeiro, and São Paulo, militated for the Brazilian Communist Party. Imprisoned by the Vargas regime, Eneida, as she was known, became an advocate of women's rights. Her stories were collected in *Alguns personagens*. Adalgisa Nery (b. 1905), married to the modernist painter Ismael Nery until his death in 1936, devoted herself to literature and politics in the 1950s. A poet and novelist, Adalgisa published stories from 1943 (*Og*). A popular writer of novels and children's literature, Dinah Silveira de Queiroz (1910–1983) also wrote short stories. Helena Silveira (1911–1988), a journalist from São Paulo, contributed to the urban story.

Nélida Piñón (b. 1936), a major novelist, is perhaps the most established female author in Brazil today (*Tempo das frutas, Sala de armas, O calor das coisas*). While using dense language with multiple narrative levels, Piñón treats feminist themes, among the broad interests of her fiction. In "Colheita" (in *Sala de armas*), Piñón shares the solitude of a woman whose husband abandons their familiar village and family life in a superfluous but irresistible search for independence in the wider world. After his return, she finds the dignity and maturity to affirm the value of her simple existence, for which the husband must prove himself worthy. Julieta de Godoy Ladeira (b. 1935) writes satirically of problems of the urban middle class, with increasingly revolutionary solutions (*Passe as férias em Nassau, Dia de matar o patrão, Era sempre feriado nacional*). Hilda Hilst (b. 1930) illustrates what Costa Lima ("O conto na modernidade brasileira") terms *anedota de concreção*: abandoning of the frame of reference in favor of the realism of discourse. Her *Ficções* allegorize historical reality with multiple techniques of the imagination. Other female authors of importance include Eliza Lispector (192?–1989), Vilma Guimarães Rosa (b. 1931), Judith Grossmann (b. 1931), and Rachel Jardim (b. 193?).

Edla van Steen (b. 1936) is both author (*Antes do amanhecer, Até sempre*) and anthologist of recent feminist fiction (*O conto da mulher brasileira*). Her story "As desaventuras do João" ["The Misadventures of João" (in *Antes do amanhecer*)] is constructed as a simple dialogue between a couple who suddenly and briefly reinitiate an old passion. Through "surface" dialogue, Steen draws a subtle psychological portrait of the different inner worlds at play, while questioning the effects of time and change. Active voices in contemporary feminism include Sônia Coutinho (b. 1939), Tânia Faillace (b. 1939), Zulmira Ribeiro Tavares (b. 1930), Joyce Cavalcante (b. 1949), and Márcia Denser (b. 1949). In *Animal dos motéis*, Denser denounces the capitalist industry of pleasure, an environment in which women are objects of false luxury. Her character Diana is the liberated intellectual whose battleground is the Brazilian version of the motel.

Metaliterary play, the ironic grotesque, parody, and intertextuality can be counted among very many contemporary trends characterizing the postmodern short story. Silviano Santiago (b. 1936) advances metaliterary play (*O banquete*, *O olhar*) through what Lucas calls the "story-essay" ("O conto no Brasil moderno," 161). "O banquete" (1970), citing the case of André Gide, discusses writing as a "digestion of influences," a game in which the cannibalistic author eventually consumes his characters and, in return, may finally be served at the reader's banquet. "Labor Dei" (in *O banquete*), a title reflecting an interlinguistic and cultural pun based on an American holiday, takes place in an amusement park, where a Ferris wheel inverts the direction of the story's language. Dialogue is cast as popular theatre, in which the hero's autobiography is presented in the guise of a first-grade essay, with touches of the Absurd. Santiago parodies the social taboos of nineteenth-century Realism, in this case Eça de Queiroz's novel *O primo Basílio*, in "Perigo no uso de recursos não-científicos na Labiologia." His conscious use of linguistic parody reduces his narrations to the level of logical irrationality. Metaliterary touches in the postmodern story may also be seen in Flávio Aguiar's parody of Clarice Lispector (*Os caninos do vampiro*) and in the dense minitexts of Eric Nepomuceno (*Contradança*).

In *As peles frias*, Haroldo Maranhão (b. 1929) creates highly dramatic situations bordering on the Surreal, combining a subtle, rational critique of social values with grotesque humor and linguistic play. Maranhão's energized texts exemplify the postmodern style, through their self-consciousness, literary referentiality, and linguistic deformations of reality. These narrative tools serve to undermine the dominant cultural code by means of their pervasive irony on all levels of writing. There is a neo-baroque quality to Maranhão's intertextual parody, a system of language whose ultimate effect is to question the relationship between a specific language or discourse and the reality it pretends to encompass. The text itself becomes aware of the role of language and narrative in giving shape to reality. The ensuing play between history and fiction both produces a comic, surreal tension and poeticizes narrative language.

In "O leite em pó da bondade humana" (As peles frias), Maranhão's deformation of Keats's verse serves as a motif for a session of torture perpetrated by the military dictatorship. Realistic narration cedes to dreamlike unreality and, passing the threshold of pain, to poetic reverie and utopian vision preceding death. The grotesque inherent in human nature is invoked in "O defunto e o seu melhor bocado" (As peles frias), where a coffin has to be constructed to fit the exaggerated dimensions of the rigid members of the deceased, a subject of considerable consternation and irreverence. The absurdity of social conventions in Haroldo Maran-hão's stories is subjected to a panorama of textual play.

The short story occupies an important place in modern Brazilian litera-ture, and, in the last one hundred years, Brazilian authors have made a substantial contribution to the form. Specifically Brazilian contributions to the story spring from the singular nature of national reality. Selected features include the following: synthesis of African, European, and Amerindian folk and traditional material; myth or indigenous folk tales; regional characters and speech; colloquial language and dialects; docu-mentation of customs and sociohistorical moments; experimentation with discontinuous and poetic narrative structures; the psychological and existential portrait of the Brazilian character; the expressive possibilities and inventiveness afforded by the Brazilian Portuguese language; and the subtle analysis of the motivation, values, and relationships underlying a social world that seems deceptively familiar to the European or American reader, but that in fact embodies a decisive difference. The very diversity of Brazilian stories reflects the complexion and dynamics of the country: its people and character, geography and culture, colonial past and modern present. Along with Machado de Assis and Guimarães Rosa, many Brazilian writers will be read and remembered as being among the great international authors of the short story.

Brazilian poetry from 1900 to 1922
Marta Peixoto

Positioned between the rise of Parnassianism and Symbolism in the last two decades of the nineteenth century and the drastic innovations of Modernism in 1922, the period from 1900 to 1922 brought no dramatic changes of direction to Brazilian poetry. This period, which many literary historians agree to label "pre-Modernism," yielded more remarkable prose narratives – by Lima Barreto (1881–1922), Graça Aranha (1868–1931), Euclides da Cunha (1866–1909) – than poetry.

An absence of sustained quality in the works of poets who began writing in that period did not mean an absence of poetry. Much verse was in fact produced, read, and recited. Parnassianism (usually dated from 1882 with the publication of *Fanfarras* by Teófilo Dias (1857–1889)) and Symbolism (dated from 1893 with *Broquéis* and *Missal* by Cruz e Sousa (1861–1898)) continued into the new century. Major figures of established reputation were still alive and writing, such as the Parnassians Olavo Bilac (1865–1918), Raimundo Correia (1859–1911), Alberto de Oliveira (1857–1937), Vicente de Carvalho (1866–1924), and Francisca Júlia (1874–1920), and the Symbolist Alphonsus de Guimaraens (1870–1921). The younger poets starting out in those styles – the so-called neo-Parnassians and neo-Symbolists – did so as contemporaries of their masters, sometimes under their auspices. Symbolism never set down roots as firmly as Parnassianism, and the reign of the latter was tenacious. Otto Maria Carpeaux reminds us that in Brazil the sequence of movements did not follow the European one, where Symbolism supplanted the earlier Parnassianism: "the two great poets of Brazilian Symbolism, Cruz e Sousa and Alphonsus, did not manage to prevail, succumbing to a hostile environment. Parnassianism, outliving itself, continued; and when it was in turn defeated, the victory belonged to Modernism . . ." (*Pequena bibliografia crítica da literatura brasileira*, 216). Yet why the persistence of Parnassianism? Alfredo Bosi suggests that its appeal for the educated and semi-educated elite rested on its ornate Formalism relying on pre-established patterns. As the Parnassian poet who speaks in Manuel Bandeira's famous parodic poem "Os sapos" announces: "Reduzi sem danos / A formas a forma" (*Poesia completa e prosa*, 158) ["I reduced form to molds, with no damage"]. For Bosi, "there is an ingrained academicism in the spiritual attitude of the Parnassian poet. The same themes, the same words, the same rhythms come together to create a literary tradition that acts *a priori* upon the artistic sensibility, limiting or even abolishing originality: it is enough to consider, in this golden age of the Brazilian Academy of Letters, the immense vogue of the descriptive, or narrative–descriptive, or didactic–allegorical sonnet, a phenomenon one Modernist labelled 'sonnetococcus brasiliensis'. . ." (*O Pré-Modernismo*, 19–20).

Symbolism might not have attracted the exclusive devotion and superior performance of most poets in Brazil but so many were receptive to its echoes and reverberations that Andrade Muricy in his three-volume *Panorama do movimento simbolista brasileiro* was able to include 105 poets, many of whom began publishing in the 22-year period under discussion. In fact, Parnassian and symbolist poetics became intertwined in actual practice, despite the sense some poets had, as we see from their polemics, that the two styles were contrary and inimical. Confluence was the norm rather than the exception. Many young poets beginning their careers, such as Gilka Machado and Raul de Leoni, can only be labelled, if they must be labelled, Parnassian Symbolists. Even the Parnassian masters in many of their poems – Alberto de Oliveira in "Ave Maria! Na montanha," Raimundo Correia in "Plenilúnio," Vicente de Carvalho in "Pequenino morto" and "Sugestões do Crepúsculo," Olavo Bilac in "Surdina" – assimilate a symbolist musicality, a fondness for liturgical and funereal rites, and for crepuscular and nocturnal landscapes. The Symbolists, in turn, some of whom had begun as Parnassians, retained a preference for the sonnet, for rare words and rare rhymes ("semens" and "delirium-tremens," for instance, in Manuel da Silveira Neto [1872–1942]). The prestige of the European was common to both Parnassians and Symbolists, merely changing from the cult of Greek and Roman antiquity in Parnassianism to a symbolist mania for France, which made several poets write in French and assume French names. (This mania extended, of course, beyond Symbolists, poetry, and Brazil, and was a widespread trait of the dependent cultural life of Latin America at the time.) Both Parnassians and Symbolists in Brazil cultivate a sonorous, eloquent verse, despite Verlaine's advice to take eloquence and wring its neck. This declamatory tone is not surprising, given the vogue, which lasted through these two decades and beyond, of reciting poetry in French and Portuguese, often with great dramatic flair, in the literary *salões*.

The terms themselves, Parnassianism and Symbolism, inevitable as they seem in any discussion of the period, are fraught with difficulties.

They carry echoes of the originating European schools, and obscure the different shapes each took upon arriving in Brazil. The point of origin for Brazil was not only France and Belgium, but also Portugal. Antônio Nobre, Eugênio de Castro, Antero de Quental, and Cesário Verde, along with still other Portuguese poets, were much read in Brazil at the time. Moreover, Symbolism especially, even in France, was not single but multiple, encompassing such diverse tendencies as Decadentism and mysticism, and the disparate poetry of Baudelaire, Laforgue, Verlaine, Maeterlinck, to mention only a few of the poets whose influence reached Brazil. However, these complexities are beyond the scope of this essay. It should be mentioned in passing, however, that Brazilian Parnassianism lacked the emotional containment that was one of the precepts of its French proponents, and was perhaps even in France more operative in theory than in practice. The Brazilian Parnassians, as Manuel Bandeira points out, while discarding "a certain coy and weepy tenderness. . .so indiscreetly perceptible in the love lyrics of the Romantics" (*Antologia dos poetas brasileiros da fase parnasiana*, 17), did not feel obliged to renounce sentimentality. Only Francisca Júlia, taken to be the greatest woman poet of Parnassianism, followed to the letter the French principle of *impassibilité*, becoming famous for her "virile verses," as more than one critic put it. In her sonnet "Musa impassível" (*Esfinges* [1903]) she exhorts:

> Musa! um gesto sequer de dor ou de sincero
> Luto jamais te afeie o cândido semblante!
> (*Panorama da poesia brasileira*, III, 249)

> [Muse! Let no gesture of pain or sincere grief
> Ever mar your pure features!]

The freer play of sentiment in most Brazilian Parnassians brings them closer to the emotional delicacies or spasms of Symbolism. It is illustrative of the poetic confluences of the times that even the impassive Francisca Júlia embraced a mystical symbolism in her later years.

In the early career of Manuel Bandeira (1886–1968) we have a perfect example of one poet's response to this confluence of aesthetic currents. In his literary memoirs, *Itinerário de Pasárgada*, he tells about his cautious development from neo-Parnassian and neo-Symbolist into a modernist poet. Bandeira's keen sensitivity and passionate devotion to poetic craft make this precise and personal account of poems he read and wrote an invaluable contribution to the understanding of the period. Bandeira's two collections from those decades, *A cinza das horas* (1917) and *Carnaval* (1919), would by themselves have made him a poet to be remembered had they not been overshadowed by his later modernist accomplishments.

Other poets who began to publish in these two decades also went on to greater feats, and were "lost," as it were, to the period: Cecília Meireles, Mário de Andrade, Jorge de Lima, Cassiano Ricardo. An exception is Paulo Menotti del Picchia (1892–1988). His *Juca mulato* (1917), notable for a sentiment-drenched attention to the Brazilian people and environment, attempted in poetry a Regionalism that had its more effective contemporary practitioners in prose fiction. Although he continued to write poetry, *Juca mulato* remained his best-regarded poetic text. He went on to be a main participant in the modernist movement, and later founded one of its splinter groups, "Verde Amarelo."

The choice of poets for the following individual commentary is weighted toward those whom later generations found readable, rather than those who were at the time especially admired, but subsequently forgotten. Martins Fontes (1884–1937), Amadeu Amaral (1875–1929), Hermes Fontes (1888–1930), Mário Pederneiras (1868–1915): the minor poets of these decades are legion. It is not surprising, of course, that the poets later found valuable were mostly uncelebrated at the time, since Modernism introduced such radical changes in the notions of form, beauty, and the poetic. Many of these poets died young: of the six discussed below, four died in their thirties. Had they lived longer, some would undoubtedly have moved on to Modernism, as did Bandeira and others of their talented contemporaries.

Marcelo Gama (1878–1915) published two books of poetry which were posthumously gathered, along with previously uncollected poems, in *Via-sacra e outros poemas*. Despite the religious ring of "via sacra," which repeats the title of his first book, some of Gama's poems offer a refreshing departure from the high seriousness and *de rigueur* idealizations of neo-Symbolists and neo-Parnassians alike.

"Mulheres" (1909) is perhaps Gama's best poem. It narrates the *flânerie* of a poet who watches elegant women promenade in a downtown avenue. "Pela simples razão de eu ser viril e poeta /. . ./ olho as mulheres todas / com o mais impertinente interesse de esteta" (*Via Sacra e outros poemas*, 139) ["For the simple reason of being virile and a poet, I look at all the women with the most impertinent aesthetic interest"]. He imagines promises of erotic pleasure in the women's visual surfaces, and recalls their more or less virtuous reputations. His probing gaze is innocent of specific seductive intentions though not of poetic designs. He thinks of the women as "maravilhoso assunto / de um poema intenso, em que ando a meditar" (p. 140) ["a marvelous topic for an intense poem I have been considering"]. Akin to other *fin-de-siècle* dangerous females, these spider-women weave a web of temptations. Their seductive menace for the poet is translated into the sharp glints and angles of their bodies: "pupilas fatais de basilisco," "cabelos ígneos," "toda cortada em vértices e arestas," "cotovelos pontudos," "cintilação metálica de seus olhos," "fina fria flexível e ferina / como as espadas de Damasco" (pp. 139–46) ["fatal pupils of a basilisk," "fiery hair," "all faceted in sharp angles and edges," "pointy elbows," "the metallic scintillation of her eyes," "thin, cold, flexible, and cruel like the swords of Damascus"]. In one of the few extended commentaries on Marcelo Gama, Sebastião Uchoa Leite has recently detected in this poem traces of the ironic colloquialism found in the works of Corbière and Laforgue, a quality usually absent from Brazilian Symbolism. He argues convincingly that the poem anticipates the revolution in tone and diction that the 1920s would bring to Brazilian poetry ("Marcelo Gama," 99–107). Elements of parody and humor, in an ample lexicon including slang and foreign words, establish a context where even the commonplaces of the then current poetic diction gain a self-critical edge.

José Albano (1882–1923) was known to his contemporaries more for his peculiar and abrasive presence as a person than for his anachronistic poetry, which revives the lyric traditions of the Portuguese sixteenth century. Born in Fortaleza and educated in Europe (England, Austria, France), possessor of an exceptional talent for languages, when Albano returned to Brazil he found himself at odds with his country and his time. He loved his native language but not in its modern form. He modelled his poetry after that of Camões and idolized the supposed purity of an archaic Portuguese. In "Ode à língua portuguesa" he vows to preserve its "antigo estilo": "Língua minha dulcíssima e canora / que em mel com aroma se mistura" (*Rimas* [1966], 86) ["My language, most gentle and melodious, where honey and aroma mingle"]. During his lifetime, his poetry was privately printed in Barcelona and Fortaleza in small, elegant editions. Despite his cultivation of Renaissance poetic forms, meters, and lexicon, critics now agree that Albano was much more than a composer of clever pastiches. His deeply felt obsession with a glorious age of the Portuguese lyric resulted in poetry, especially sonnets, of impressive poetic quality. Manuel Bandeira, who contributed to establishing Albano's reputation by organizing and introducing a collection of his poems (*Rimas de José Albano* [1948]), singles out one of his sonnets as a poem "which sounds indeed like a posthumous poem of Camões" (*Apresentação da poesia brasileira*, 109). I quote another of his sonnets:

> Mata-me, puro Amor, mas docemente,
> Para que eu sinta as dores que sentiste
> Naquele dia tenebroso e triste
> De suplício implacável e inclemente.
>
> Faze que a dura pena me atormente
> E de todo me vença e me conquiste,

Que o peito saudoso não resiste
E o coração cansado já consente.

E como te amei sempre e sempre te amo,
Deixa-me agora padecer contigo
E depois alcançar o eterno ramo.

E, abrindo as asas para o etéreo abrigo,
Divino Amor, escuta que eu te chamo,
Divino Amor, espera que eu te sigo.

(Rimas [1966], 214)

[Kill me, pure Love, but sweetly,
so that I may feel the pain you felt
on that sad and gloomy day
of implacable and merciless torture.

Make harsh sorrow torment me
and vanquish me entirely,
for my breast is worn with longing
and my weary heart gives in.

Since I have loved you and will love you always,
let me now suffer by your side,
to merit later the eternal bough.

Spreading wings toward the heavenly shelter,
Divine Love, listen as I call,
Divine Love, wait and I will follow.]

Pedro Kilkerry (1885–1917) also had to wait for a later poet to claim for him his rightful recognition. He belonged to a group of second-generation Symbolists in Salvador gathered around the magazine *Nova Cruzada*. He published only in periodicals, leaving no book. Although he was mentioned in histories of literature and samples of his work were offered in anthologies, only in 1970 did his complete work become available in book form, painstakingly compiled and enthusiastically introduced by Augusto de Campos. Campos argues persuasively that Kilkerry deserves to be considered a precursor of the modernist movement, despite his scant literary production: only thirty-five poems and four fragments of poetic prose, along with a few other prose pieces. According to Campos, "Kilkerry brings to Brazilian Symbolism an experimentalism otherwise absent, and a new and very modern conception of poetry as synthesis and condensation, a poetry without redundancy, of daring metaphoric jolts, and at the same time of extraordinary verbal functionalism" (*Revisão de Kilkerry*, 29). Campos also points to an unusual absence of sentimentality, giving as an example the wry ending of the poem "É o silêncio," where "saudade," that obligatory topos of the Portuguese lyric tradition, takes on macabre and ironic colorations:

Vês? Colaboram na saudade a aranha,
Patas de um gato e asas de um morcego.
$\qquad\qquad\qquad$ (*Revisão*, 119)

[See? They collaborate in love-sickness:
The spider, a cat's paws and a bat's wings.]

Kilkerry's twisted syntax, hermetic metaphors, and illogical progressions have led critics to suggest for him a Mallarmean affiliation (hence, of course, the interest of the concrete poet Augusto de Campos). Yet he also has moments of accessible lyricism, where disconcertingly animated objects observe the observing subject:

É o silêncio, é o cigarro e a vela acesa.
Olha-me a estante em cada livro que olha.
E a luz nalgum volume sobre a mesa . . .
Mais o sangue da luz em cada folha.
$\qquad\qquad$ ("E o silêncio," *Revisão*, 117)

[It's the silence, the cigarette, and the candle's gleaming.
The bookshelf stares at me in each staring book.
And the light upon a volume on the table
With the blood of light spreading on each page.]

E eu magro espio . . . e um muro, magro, em frente
Abrindo à tarde as órbitas musgosas
– Vazias? Menos do que misteriosas –
Pestaneja, estremece . . . O muro sente!
$\qquad\qquad\qquad$ ("O muro," *Revisão*, 90)

[I, bony, look, and a bony garden wall
Opens to the evening its mossy sockets
– Empty? Less than mysterious –
Blinking, trembling! The garden wall feels!]

Gilka Machado (1893–1980) published her first volume of poetry, *Cristais partidos*, at the age of twenty-two and achieved immediate renown, even notoriety, because of an explicit female eroticism. Although in 1933 she was voted "the greatest woman poet of Brazil" in a contest sponsored by the magazine *O Malho*, her poetic production soon came to a halt. Although she lived a long life, her last collection of poetry (excluding anthologies) dates from 1938. She gradually slipped from public view and died all but forgotten.

She is rarely mentioned in literary histories of Brazil but recent interest in women's artistic production has brought her work under new scrutiny. It is not, it seems to me, for its aesthetic effectiveness that we will reread her poetry, but for the historical interest of its bold inscription of a female desire pressing against forces that would deny its existence. "Ser mulher," from *Cristais partidos*, reads in part:

> Ser mulher, vir à luz trazendo a alma talhada
> para os gozos da vida, a liberdade, e o amor . . .
>
> Ser mulher, e oh, atroz, tantálica tristeza!
> ficar na vida qual uma águia inerte, presa
> nos pesados grilhões dos preceitos sociais!
>
> *(Poesias completas, 56)*
>
> [To be a woman, to be born bearing a soul
> made for the pleasures of life, freedom and love . . .
>
> To be a woman, and oh, atrocious, tormenting sadness!
> to inhabit life as an inert eagle, caught
> in the heavy shackles of social rules!]

Whether in strict meter and rhyme, or in a freer polymetric verse, her rather wordy poetic cadences rely, like those of many of her contemporaries, on a liberal use of loosely applied adjectives and on the decorative rare word. The tone is exalted and declamatory. Apostrophes abound. A desirous female "I" lays claim to representative status ("Sou mais que uma mulher – sou a Mulher!" [p. 70] ["I am more than a woman – I am Woman!"]) and celebrates with exhibitionist verve her own aroused sensibilities and the charms of the beloved. Natural elements often take the place of one of the sexes in Gilka Machado's erotic exchanges:

> E não podes saber do meu gozo violento
> quando me fico, assim, neste ermo toda nua
> completamente exposta à Volúpia do Vento.
>
> (p. 93)
>
> [And you cannot know of my violent pleasure
> when I stand naked in this deserted place,
> completely exposed to the Voluptuous Wind!]

Even bolder representations of eroticism occur without projections onto Nature, as in the sequence "O grande amor," which celebrates in turn the loved one's hair, voice, mouth, hands, eyes, and tongue. In this female Eros tinged with masochism, pleasure contains a foreboding of unavoidable betrayal.

The antithetical glorifications that coexist in Gilka Machado's poetry – of erotic pleasure and of devotion to the spiritual – are brought to the fore in the titles of the four collections that followed her first book: *Estados d'alma*, *Mulher nua*, *Meu glorioso pecado* (1928), and *Sublimação* (1938). An anthology of 1931 bears the title *Carne e alma*. In Gilka Machado, flesh and soul are not so much rivals as collaborators. We see this in the opening lines of one of her sonnets:

> Eu sinto que nasci para o pecado
> Se é pecado na terra amar o Amor.
>
> *(Poesias completas, 51)*

[I feel that I was born to sin
If it is a sin on this earth to long for Love.]

The teasing detour from "Sin" to the pursuit of an ideal ("amar o Amor")
suggests a mutual enhancement in sexual abandon and devotion to the
spiritual.

Raul de Leoni (1895–1926) cultivated a different voluptuousness, "a
volúpia inútil de pensar" ["the useless voluptuousness of thought"] of his
poems, inclined toward skeptical philosophical reflection. His first publication, a long poem dedicated to Olavo Bilac, recently deceased, *Ode a um
poeta morto* (1919), suggests neo-Parnassian preferences. Here the poet as
a transtemporal being assumes many avatars from classical Greek to
modern times but retains a plastic and sensuous predilection for the
beauty of the world which his words reflect.

> Toda a emoção, que anda nas cousas, fala,
> Nos seus diversos tons e reflexos e cores,
> Pela tua palavra irisada de opala,
> Feita de irradiações e de finas tessituras.
> (*Luz mediterrânea* [1915], 16)

[All the emotions hidden in things speak
In their various tones and shimmers and colors
Through your words iridescent like opals,
Made of fine textures and irradiations.]

Leoni's only book, *Luz mediterrânea*, transposes his native tropical light
into the more prestigious landscapes of the Mediterranean. Frequent
references to ancient Greek philosophy, to Florence, to the Italian
Renaissance bear witness to his admiration for Mediterranean culture. In
a fantasy common to the elite of his time, he imagines for himself a
European lineage, including an alternative birthplace for his soul. The
opening poem of the collection, "Pórtico," begins:

> Alma de origem ática, pagã,
> Nascida sob aquele firmamento
> Que azulou as divinas epopéias,
> Sou irmão de Epicuro e de Renan.
> (p. 29)

[My pagan soul has an Attic origin,
born under those blue skies
that colored the divine epics,
I am a brother of Epicurus and Renan.]

Luz mediterrânea, published in the very year when the Modernists of
1922 opened new vistas for Brazilian literature, reached its eleventh
edition in 1965, attesting to a continued audience for a poetry that clings
to an aesthetics which the Modernists set out to replace. Perhaps mainly in

recognition of Leoni's verbal elegance, he was well received by the "moderns" as well as by the "ancients." For Alfredo Bosi, his poems "endure amid the widespread perishability of pre-Modernist poetry"; he admires Leoni's clarity of expression and his "artist's hand capable of verses of superb visualization and rhythm" (*O Pré-Modernismo*, 35). Andrade Muricy points to the "irradiation of Symbolism" in Leoni's poetry (*Panorama*, III: 194). In poems such as "Crepuscular," "Torre morta do ocaso," and "A hora cinzenta," crepuscular and misty landscapes translate inner states. In Leoni, we once again find neo-Parnassianism and neo-Symbolism coexisting peacefully side by side.

Augusto dos Anjos (1884–1914) is the strangest and most remarkable of the poets to be considered here. Born and raised on a faltering sugar plantation in the state of Paraíba, he studied law in Recife and moved to Rio de Janeiro in 1910, where he earned his living as a school teacher. His only book, *Eu*, was practically unnoticed at the time. Subsequent editions in the 1920s brought him more recognition, yet the Modernists of 1922 failed to notice the linguistic inventiveness of his poetry. He found favor with the reading public before attaining critical acclaim – a surprising favor, given his acerbic poeticizing of a universe in decay. Reprints and new editions continued to appear, gradually including previously uncollected poems. By 1982, *Eu* reached its thirty-fifth edition.

It is fitting that these two decades that saw the criss-crossing, if not merging, of contrary poetic styles should culminate in this most heterogeneous text. *Eu* has been labelled neo-Parnassian, neo-symbolist, premodernist, and even derivative of an earlier Romanticism. The imprint of the scientific realist poetry of the 1870s, of Decadentism, of Naturalism, of the Baroque, and a coincidence with German Expressionism have also been detected. However, it is more expeditious to skirt these labels and focus on the peculiar combinations that energize Anjos's poetic language.

In Recife, Augusto dos Anjos came in contact with the then fashionable materialist and evolutionist doctrines (Comte, Haeckel, Darwin, Spencer). He incorporated into his poems a scientific and philosophical vocabulary ("psicogenética," "moléculas," "monismo," "moneras," "ontogênese," "filogênese," "vitellus"), at his best deriving from those words strangely incantatory effects. His anguish about human life – he read Schopenhauer early on – projects outward onto a vast cosmos: human beings who march in sorrow toward death share the fate of a whole universe of sentient forces that form temporary conjunctions only to disintegrate again. The vicissitudes of matter and energy, their generation and decay, gain a theatrical pathos: "o choro da Energia abandonada," "a dor da Força desaproveitada," "o soluço da forma ainda imprecisa" ("O lamento das coisas" [1963], 181) ["the weeping of abandoned Energy," "the pain of wasted Forces," "the sob of still shapeless form"]. Ferreira Gullar points out that at the heart of Augusto dos Anjos's tormented poems there is a conflict between the scientific theories he evokes and the distress they arouse in him: "His theoretical perspective understands life as a material phenomenon subject to the implacable laws of nature; his affective disposition takes this as a tragedy, suffers it, rebels against it, tries to overcome it in aesthetic creation. Lugubrious death and deterioration pervade his work, generating a peculiar and original poetic language" ("Augusto dos Anjos", 51).

In Anjos, a pleasure in rhetorical density – antitheses, hyperboles, sonorous words, majestic rhythms (he used mainly a strongly accented ten-syllable line) – contrasts sharply with his dark themes: the horrified and fascinated witnessing of the decomposition of life. As critics often mention, this contrast bears the imprint of Baudelaire's aesthetics of decay, as it appears in "La charogne." "O verme – este operário das ruínas" (*Eu* [1963], 60) ["the maggot, that builder of ruins"] is a frequent protagonist. A grim teleology that culminates in decay, reminiscent of Brás Cubas's famous dedication of his book to a maggot in Machado de Assis's *Memórias póstumas de Brás Cubas* (1881), can be seen in the concluding stanzas of the sonnet "O deus-verme":

> Almoça a podridão das drupas agras,
> Janta hidrópicos, rói vísceras magras
> E dos defuntos novos incha a mão . . .
>
> Ah! Para ele é que a carne podre fica,
> E no inventário da matéria rica
> Cabe aos seus filhos a maior porção!
>
> (*Eu* [1963], 63)
>
> [He lunches on rotten bitter fruit
> and dines on dropsical cadavers.
> He gnaws on scrawny innards
> and swells the hands of those who have just died . . .
>
> Ah! It is for him that the flesh will rot
> And in the legacy rich matter leaves behind
> His descendants receive the greatest share.]

In this fascinated observation of the spectacle of life devouring life, Augusto dos Anjos reveals a curious kinship to Machado de Assis.

Despite its title, *Eu* does not celebrate the power of the "I," who occupies a convergence of negative forces devoid of power: he is sombre, solitary, buffeted by anguishing hallucinations, hounded by bad luck.

> Eu, filho do carbono e do amoníaco,
> Monstro de escuridão e rutilância,
> Sofro, desde a epigênesis da infância,

A influência má dos signos do zodíaco.
("Psicologia de um vencido," *Eu* [1963], 60)

[I, born of carbon and ammonia,
Monster of darkness and radiance,
I suffer, since the epigenesis of infancy,
The wicked influence of the Zodiac signs.]

Eu sou aquele que ficou sozinho
Cantando sobre os ossos do caminho
A poesia de tudo quanto é morto!
("O poeta do hediondo," *Eu* [1963], 20)

[I am the one who stayed on alone,
Singing over bones strewn by the roadside
The poetry of everything that is dead!]

As he wanders through cemeteries and leper colonies, the "I" is not so much an individual as a depersonalized victim of life harboring its own corrosive forces.

Tal uma horda feroz de cães famintos,
Atravessando uma estação deserta,
Uivava dentro do *eu*, com a boca aberta,
A matilha espantada dos instintos!
("As cismas do destino," *Eu* [1963], 68)

[Like a ferocious pack of hungry dogs
Crossing a deserted station,
Howling inside the "I," mouths agape,
The astonished horde of instincts!]

He is also a sensitive receiver of messages of suffering radiating from all animate and inanimate matter: "Vinha-me às cordas glóticas a queixa das coletividades sofredoras" (p. 82) ["The lament of suffering collectivities came to my vocal chords"]. Even his moderately optimistic *credo* requires the annihilation of the "I":

Creio, perante a evolução imensa,
Que o homem universal de amanhã vença
O homem particular que eu ontem fui!
("Ultimo credo," *Eu* [1963], 90)

[I believe, given the enormity of evolution,
That the universal man of tomorrow will triumph
Over the particular man I used to be!]

Anjos's sweeping rhetoric at times includes colloquial inflections and the lexicon of daily life. A parallel de-idealization affects his themes. Along with fateful energy, microscopic germs, and busy maggots, everyday suffering creatures populate his poems: stray dogs, a caged bird, a sheep about to be slaughtered, drunks, prostitutes, the sick. As Ferreira Gullar argues, this is a significant innovation in the stylized and "literary" poetry of his time, fixated on versions of the sublime. Dos Anjos's greatest literary descendant, João Cabral de Melo Neto (b. 1920), alludes to this kinship in stanzas that describe Augusto dos Anjos ("O sim contra o sim," *Serial* [1961]) in terms perfectly applicable to many of Cabral's own poems: "o timbre fúnebre," "dureza de pisada," "geometria de enterro" (*Poesias completas*, 61) ["the funereal timbre," "the harshness of step," "the geometry of burial"]. I would also point to another less obvious but important similarity. Although the first person pronoun *eu* all but disappears in Cabral, the implicit lyric subject shares the depersonalized nature of Dos Anjos's *eu*, and its capacity for projecting inner conflicts outward onto a tortured world and registering in an arresting and concrete language harsh lives and the inroads of death.

From among the poets whose careers began and ended in these two decades, Anjos alone left his mark on later poetry and elicited a substantial body of critical commentary. His grim yet powerful poetic language is perhaps the only major achievement those poets have left us. Yet it would be wrong to slight the minor achievements. The first twenty years of the twentieth century wrote, read, and recited lyric poetry with enthusiasm. This devotion to the genre certainly fueled its radical reconsideration and the more dazzling poetic achievements of the following decades.

Brazilian poetry from Modernism to the 1990s
Giovanni Pontiero

With the advent of Modernism, intellectual and cultural life in Brazil found new impetus. The pioneers of the movement launched a programme of reform and renewal. They defended artistic freedom and encouraged innovation. Even sixty years later, the excitement they had engendered had scarcely abated. Modernism was officially launched in February 1922 at São Paulo's Teatro Municipal with the participation of writers, artists, and musicians. Three separate programmes included lectures outlining the movement's objectives, readings of prose and poetry reflecting the new aesthetics, and musical recitals. The exhibition of cubist and expressionist works of art displayed in the theatre foyer aroused hostile reactions before the public even entered the auditorium. Graça Aranha (1868–1931), an established writer who achieved lasting fame with his best-selling novel *Canaã* (1902) [*Canaan*], gave the inaugural lecture entitled "A emoção estética na arte moderna". Expressing unequivocal support for the radical changes proposed by younger artists working in various media, Graça Aranha's provocative statements enraged die-hard traditionalists and aroused some skepticism even amongst the Modernists themselves. With suitably opulent rhetoric he welcomed this "Maravilhosa aurora!" ["Wondrous dawn"] with its "pinturas extravagantes, esculturas absurdas, música alucinada, poesia aérea e desarticulada" (*Espírito moderno*, 1925) ["extravagant paintings, absurd sculptures, hallucinated music, vague, disarticulated poetry"]. The poet Menotti del Picchia (1892–1989) expounded modernist ideals. Mário de Andrade (1893–1945), the movement's guiding spirit, read extracts from *Paulicéia desvairada* [*Hallucinated City*] and his scornful dismissal of bourgeois values provoked heckling and jeering, and when Ronald de Carvalho (1893–1935) recited *Os sapos* [*The Toads*], parodying the literary establishment, the outraged audience became hysterical. The poem had been written by Manuel Bandeira (1886–1968), who pledged his support from Rio de Janeiro and, although he was older than

247

most of the movement's pioneers, his verses of *Libertinagem* (Rio de Janeiro, 1930) [Debauchery] crystallized to perfection the mood and objectives of Modernism.

Menotti del Picchia announced that Modernism would be militant and uncompromising in its war against intransigent purists and outdated canons of taste. Arcadia and its myths belonged to the past. Modernists would banish Parnassian and post-romantic influences, and create new values in art and literature attuned to the twentieth century. The editorial of the first issue of *Klaxon* (São Paulo, May 15, 1922) called on all participants to pursue artistic forms that would be "atual" ["up-to-date"] rather than simply "novo" ["new"]. This was an age of jazz, fast cars, the Charleston, and motion pictures, in short, the era of *Klaxon*. The new aesthetics would capture the euphoria of the times as industrialization and technological progress began to transform urban Brazil.

The modernist programme had not been formulated overnight. Isolated factors had set the process of change in motion long before intellectuals and artists started to exchange ideas and clarify their aims. The poet, playwright, and novelist, Oswald de Andrade (José Oswald de Sousa Andrade; 1890–1954) had witnessed the impact of Marinetti's Futurism, launched in Europe in 1909, and he established contact with avant-garde poets in Paris who had abandoned traditional concepts of poetry in favour of free verse and internal harmony. Upon returning to Brazil in 1912, he soon began to publish his own experiments with free verse, which predictably scandalized Parnassians and Symbolists alike and aroused their hostility. Some Brazilian Modernists subsequently argued that Marinetti's influence had been overstated, but the Italian poet's *Manifesto tecnico*, published in Milan, in May 1912, undoubtedly provided them with most of their key images and themes – electric light, ventilators, aeroplanes, workers' rights, engines, factory chimneys, dynamos, and mechanics – even if they stopped short of the Italian poet's stated conviction that modern art should embody "violence, cruelty and injustice" (futurist manifesto, published in *Le Figaro*, February 20, 1909).

Luís de Montalvor (1891–1947) and Ronald de Carvalho (1893–1935) launched a short-lived magazine *Orpheu*. The only two numbers to appear were published in March and June 1915. The main objective of *Orpheu* was to bring the achievements of the European Avant-Garde to the attention of the Brazilian intelligentsia and to provide a platform for young writers and artists with new ideas. By 1917, the movement's pioneers, Oswald and Mário de Andrade, were actively collaborating in their determination to create a more favorable climate for experimentation in every sphere of creative art. Political events and social changes at home and abroad convinced them that the moment had come to publicize their aims. There were enough frustrated writers and artists living and working in São Paulo by 1920 to support their programme. The workers' strikes in the city had encouraged other minority groups to voice their grievances, and the forthcoming celebrations to mark the centennial of Brazilian Independence (September 1822) seemed an opportune date to launch a Modernist manifesto.

The heroic phase of Brazilian *Modernismo* [Modernism] was aggressive and strident. The movement's pioneers stressed the need to penetrate the spirit of contemporary life rather than simply portray its externals. They expressed their contempt for earlier literary movements and resented European influences, especially those imported from Portugal and France. Henceforth, Brazilian artists would export rather than import ideas. The art they envisaged would be multifaceted and even arbitrary: "polimorfo, onipresente, inquieto, cômico, irritante, contraditório, invejado, insultado, feliz" (*Klaxon*) ["polymorphous, omnipresent, restless, comic, irritable, contradictory, envied, reviled, joyful"]. Writers and poets would forge a new language that would merge literary and colloquial forms with the utmost freedom and individuality. Stereotyped images of Brazil and Brazilians would disappear as artists began to reassess the country's history and traditions, its ethnic complexity, and the impact of accelerating immigration. Mário de Andrade paid homage to his beloved São Paulo, the nerve cell of Brazil:

> São Paulo! comoção de minha vida . . .
> (*Paulicéia desvairada*, "Inspiração," l.1)
>
> [São Paulo! tumult of my life . . .]

Art and artists could only hope to survive by adapting to an inevitable process of change. The pioneers of Modernism found beauty and excitement in this new age of machines and technology. Only later would they begin to question and fear the more negative aspects of progress.

Initially, the provocative slogans of the Modernists were more readily digested than the aesthetics they were trying to define. Oswald de Andrade scandalized his critics with a colorful portrait of his personal "Futurist poet," while the poet in question, Mário de Andrade, systematically demolished the poets revered by previous generations – Raimundo Correia (1859–1911), Alberto de Oliveira (1857–1937), and Olavo Bilac (1865–1918) – in a series of analytical essays entitled: "Mestres do passado". Only the Symbolists could claim to have influenced the new poetry. In another explanatory essay, *A escrava que não é Isaura*, Mário de Andrade insisted that Modernist poets were not concerned with Nature and reality but with their own individual responses to the world around them.

The influence of Marinetti's Futurism was played down even further. Any inspiration from Europe, the Modernists argued, had been much more diffuse: Verhaeren's *Villes tentaculaires*, the cubist experiments of Apollinaire, Max Jacob, André Salmon, Blaise Cendrars, and Jean Cocteau, the Dadaism of Tzara, Francis Picabia, and Paul Dermée. This eclecticism is apparent in the "poetic polyphony" exploited by Mário de Andrade in the verses of *Paulicéia desvairada*. Echoes of the European Avant-Garde are also present in Oswald de Andrade's improvised lyrics and in the zany descriptions of Guilherme de Almeida (1890–1969). Oswald de Andrade invents verbs to create his own whimsical world in "Bengaló" (in *Poesias reunidas* [1966]):

> O piano fox trota
> domingaliza
> (lines 6–7)
>
> [The piano fox-trots
> Sundayizes]

and Almeida creates sonorous rhythms in his onomatapoeic "Samba" (in *Poesia vária* [1947]):

> estronda / rebenta / retumba / ribomba
> (lines 9–12)
> [booming / rolling / roaring / rumbling]

Modernism with its jesting and polemics soon caught the public imagination. The São Paulo poets joined forces with visual artists who shared this desire for reform and renewal: the painters Anita Malfatti, Di Cavalcanti, Tarsila do Amaral, and John Graz, the sculptors Vítor Brecheret and W. Haeberg, and the architects Antônio Moya and George Przirembel.

Contacts were also established with artists and writers resident in Rio de Janeiro who shared the movement's ideals. The latter met in bookshops and cafés where they avidly discussed their work, exchanged the latest novelties from Europe, and read their poems to each other. In Rio de Janeiro, Renato Almeida (1895–1981), Ronald de Carvalho, Sérgio Buarque de Holanda (1902–1982), and Manuel Bandeira soon became familiar faces at these lively gatherings. Ronald de Carvalho's *Epigramas irônicos e sentimentais* (1922) [Ironic and Sentimental Epigrams] also celebrated "happiness and freedom," and Bandeira devised his own bacchanalian pleasures in the poems of *Carnaval* (1919) [*Carnival*].

The poets united under the banner of Modernism soon began to define their own positions. Heated debate led to conflicts and several defections within their ranks. Oswald de Andrade, the most dynamic and outspoken of the movement's pioneers, set out his own ideals in *Manifesto da poesia pau-brasil* published in the *Correio da Manhã* on March 18, 1924. He wanted a poetry capable of portraying the real Brazil, a lyricism in the flowering, "Agil e cândida. Como uma criança" ["agile and innocent. As a child"] and totally devoid of artifice; "A Poesia para os poetas. Alegria dos que não sabem e descobrem" ["Poetry for poets. The happiness of those who prefer discovering to knowing"]. The modern poet envisaged by Oswald de Andrade would shun the past and strive for "A síntese . . . O equilíbrio . . . A invenção . . . Uma nova perspectiva" ["Synthesis . . . Equilibrium . . . Invention . . . A new perspective"], thus ensuring the utmost individuality. He himself led the way with taut, epigrammatic poems which captured the national scene, life on the sugar plantations, provincial landmarks, the Brazilian Carnival, and the pulsating rhythms of urban life. Restless and versatile, Oswald de Andrade's moods fluctuate between outrageous satire and quiet lyricism, between collo-quial parody and Impressionist description:

> Lá fora o luar continua
> E o trem divide o Brasil
> Como num meridiano.
> ("Noturno," *Poesias reunidas* [1945])
>
> [Outside the moonlight persists
> And the train divides Brazil
> Like a meridian.]
>
> ("Nocturne")

He exercised a profound influence over his contemporaries. Menotti del Picchia, Guilherme de Almeida, Sérgio Milliet (1898–1966), Ribeiro Couto (1898–1963), and Ronald de Carvalho all shared Oswald de Andrade's interest in discovering the spiritual core of Brazil. They probed its folklore and customs and evoked Brazil's historical landmarks: Ouro Preto, Congonhas do Campo, Bahia, Recife, Sabará. They tried to define the Brazilian character, its mestizo roots and unmistakable colloquial-isms. These traits are embodied in Bandeira's personal "Evocação do Recife," in which he defends "a língua errada do povo / língua certa do povo" (lines 67–8) ["the ungrammatical language of the people / the authentic language of the people"].

Brazil and Brazilians become the burning question in the modernist manifestos launched by dissident groups. *Terra Roxa e outras terras*, published in São Paulo in January 1926, promised a new phase of literary activity which would entertain as well as instruct with a wide range of prose and poetry faithful to the so-called "espírito moderno" ["modern spirit"]. Ronald de Carvalho spoke for all Modernists when he urged: "Cria o teu ritmo e criarás o mundo" ["Create your rhythm and you will create the world"]. In another explosive editorial in the *Revista de Antropofagia*, launched in São Paulo on May 1, 1928, Oswald de Andrade extolled Primitivism. Censuring the vices of what passes for a civilized, Christian society, he argued "O espírito recusa-se a conceber o espírito sem corpo" ["The spirit refuses to conceive the spirit without its body"], and he defended spontaneous instinct as the one cohesive factor in any assessment of Brazil's social, economic, and cultural evolution. The anthropophagists were out to celebrate life. They rejected the oppressive theories of Freud and advocated a reality "sem complexos, sem loucura, sem prostituições" ("Manifesto antropófago," *Revista de Antropofagia*, 1) ["without complexes, without madness, without prostitutions"].

These sentiments are expressed somewhat more coherently in the last important modernist manifesto of the 1920s, *Manifesto do Verde-amarelismo ou de Escola da Anta* (May, 1929). The intellectuals and poets who united under this banner included Menotti del Picchia, Cassiano Ricardo (1895–1974), Raul Bopp (1898–1984), Plínio Salgado (1895–1975), and Cândido Mota Filho (1897–1977). Like the anthropophagists, they preached a new spirit of nationalism rooted in Brazil's primitive civilizations; an age dominated by the Tupi Indians and joyfully free of all religious precepts and philosophical theories; a race notable for its spontaneity as opposed to arid intellectualism. The *Verdeamarelistas* opposed all rhetoric, both verbal and conceptual, and urged creative artists to be creative without any discussion.

The manifestos had debated every aspect of Brazilian culture. It was now time for Brazilian artists and poets to assert their individuality with confidence. The verses of Menotti del Picchia's *República dos Estados do Brasil* (1928), Raul Bopp's *Cobra Norato* (1931), and Cassiano Ricardo's *Borrões de verde e amarelo* (1926), all drew inspiration from "primitive telluric forces." They interpreted the myths of Amazonia, and re-worked popular legends of African and Indian origin. Mysterious spirits and deities are invoked in these poems – Tangolomongo, Mula-de-Padre, and Pai-da-Mata, the goddesses Iaiá and Janaína often in a language as impenetrable as the strange rituals they describe. Cassiano Ricardo speaks for all the anthropophagists when he speaks of an earthly paradise:

> Brasil cheio de graça
> Brasil cheio de pássaros
> Brasil cheio de luz
>   ("Martim Cererê")
>
> [Brazil full of grace
> Brazil full of birds
> Brazil full of light]

This exploration of primitive Brazil inevitably led to renewed interest in the various customs and traditions throughout different regions. In Minas Gerais in central Brazil, Carlos Drummond de Andrade (1902–1987) launched *A Revista* in mid 1925 with other young poets who valued their provincial roots. Drummond's first book of poems, *Alguma poesia*

(1930), captures the atmosphere and pace of provincial life in "Igreja," "Sesta," and "Romaria," poems noteworthy for their colloquialism and wry observations in keeping with the *mineiro* temperament. In Rio de Janeiro, a spiritually exiled Bandeira portrayed and interpreted the Pernambuco of his childhood in the verses of *Libertinagem*. Poets and artists living in the northeast agreed with the Pernambucan historian and sociologist Gilberto Freyre (1900–1987) that provincial values would outlive the materialism of the industrialized cities in the south. The "creative soul" of Brazil was firmly entrenched in remote towns and settlements untouched by progress. Provincial life inspired the popular verses of Ascenso Ferreira (1895–1965), a compromise between speech and song which Bandeira described as "genuine northeastern rhapsodies which faithfully reflect the soul, one moment playful, the next nostalgic, of the inhabitants of the sugar plantations" ("Apresentação da poesia brasileira" in *Ensaios literários*). Drawing on the folklore of the people, he conjured up the Brazilian interior with its: "*mocambos*," "*mangues*," "*moleques*," "*mulatos*," "*cajueiros*," "*mangabas*," and "*caiporas*," ["shacks," "mangroves," "black urchins," "mulattos," "cashew trees," "mangaba fruits," and "jungle sprites"]. In the manner of Bopp, Ferreira uses the rhythms of Afro-Brazilian folklore to evoke a world of secret rites:

> Sertão! – Jatobá!
> Sertão! – Cabrobó!
> – Cabrobó!
> – Ouricuri!
> – Exu!
> – Exu!
> ("Sertão," *Poesias completas* [1971])

In a quieter vein, Joaquim Cardozo (1897–1978) also conjured up the unmistakable atmosphere of the northeastern provinces in *Imagens do nordeste*. His lyrical evocations of the old cities of Olinda and Recife probe the region's colonial past and explore tranquil settings unchanged by time and progress.

Southern Brazilians, too, had their own unmistakable world – the pampas. The poets associated with the *Revista Verde*, launched at Cataguazes in September 1927, were also anxious to "abrasileirar o Brasil" ["brazilianize Brazil"]. Guilhermo César (b. 1908), Enrique de Resende (1899–1973), Rosário Fusco (1910–1977), Francisco Peixoto (b. 1909), and Ascânio Lopes (1906–1929) used their poetry to portray the gaucho's harsh existence and inner solitude. The communities they describe are almost feudal, their lives dominated by the mysterious forces of Nature, their physical resilience matched by a defiant stoicism. The dominant note is one of human solidarity: the aphorisms have all the solemnity of messianic prophesies. These qualities are present in the early verses of Augusto Meyer (1903–1970) and Tasso da Silveira (1895–1968), especially in the latter's *Alegorias do homem novo* (1926), which combine local colloquialisms with archaic Portuguese expressions.

The mid 1930s saw a gradual change of mood and expression in Brazilian poetry. A number of poets began to express dissatisfaction with the histrionics and rabid nationalism of some of their contemporaries. Lesser talents were composing free verse under the banner of Modernism without any real grasp of the movement's objectives. The entire group of *Festa* poets urged a return to a poetry of introspection dealing with universal themes. Poets like Tasso da Silveira, Adelino Magalhães (1887–1969), Andrade Muricy (1895–1984), and Murilo Araújo (1894–1980) voiced their support for the manifesto, but its aims were most effectively illustrated by poets who were independently moving in the same direction: for example, Bandeira and Drummond de Andrade, who were disciplined craftsmen from the outset. Augusto Frederico Schmidt (1906–1965) spoke for the entire *Festa* group when he declared:

> Não quero mais o Brasil
> Não quero mais geografia
> nem pitoresco.
> ("Poema," *Poesias escolhidas* [1946])

> [I no longer want Brazil
> I no longer want geography
> however picturesque.]

Schmidt's spiritual disquiet and brooding meditations about life and death in the verses of *Canto da noite* (1934) [*Night Song*] were to find more vigorous expression in the poetry of Jorge de Lima (1895–1953), especially in *A túnica inconsútil* (1938) and in the Surrealist visions of *A poesia em pânico* by Murilo Mendes (1901–1975), which was published in the same year as Schmidt's verses. Meanwhile women poets like Cecília Meireles (1901–1964) and Henriqueta Lisboa (1904–1985) expressed the same existential preoccupations with greater simplicity and restraint. Remarkable for their control and musicality, Lisboa's intimate lyrics were the fruit of a rigorous process of reduction to essentials. Sentiment overrules sentimentality when she confides: "A vida me enganhou mas foi sábia na sua essência" ("Humildade" in *Lírica* [1958]) ["Life betrayed me but was essentially wise"].

This inner tranquillity is even more pronounced in the lyrical verse of Meireles, whose key collections – *Viagem* (1939), *Vaga música* (1942), *Mar absoluto* (1945), and *Retrato natural* (1949), were to consolidate her reputation as the greatest woman poet in the Portuguese language. Like most of her contemporaries in the immediate postmodernist phase, Meireles pays tribute to earlier generations of Portuguese and Brazilian poets, including all the great names of Parnassianism and Symbolism whom militant Modernists had arbitrarily dismissed. Independent of any specific school or program, this prolific and versatile poet composed verses in traditional meters and in free verse with equal assurance. In his *Ensaios literários*, Bandeira defined her poetry as "timeless, diaphanous and crystalline," with its distilled emotions and subtle interrogations. Her lyricism is comparable with that of Bandeira himself: utter simplicity combined with depth and an almost unbearable pathos:

> Eu canto porque o instante existe
> e a minha vida está completa.
> Não sou alegre nem sou triste:
> sou poeta.
> ("Motivo," *Obra poética* [1958])

> [I sing because the instant exists
> and my life is complete.
> I am neither happy nor sad:
> I am a poet.]

Stark poems of self-analysis are common to all the major Brazilian poets of the 1930s and 1940s. The exuberance and optimism of the early Modernists subsided into quiet reflection occasionally tinged with humour. In Rio Grande do Sul, Mário Quintana (b. 1906) forged "Um poema sem outra angústia que a sua misteriosa condição de poema" ["A poem without any anguish other than its mysterious condition of being a poem"], while Dantas Mota (1913–1974) mourned the decline of rural settlements in his native Minas Gerais with lyric poems characterized by *saudade* and elegiac evocations. The themes are more varied in urban poets like Dante Milano (b. 1899) and Vinícius de Moraes (1913–1980). The latter's "Saudade de Manuel Bandeira" in *Poemas, sonetos e baladas* (1946) expresses his debt to Bandeira, "o poeta lúcido . . . ascético . . . áspero" ["the lucid . . . ascetic . . . austere poet"], whose moral integrity, erudition, and discipline made him the ideal confidant and mentor for so many younger poets.

Bandeira's lasting influence was also acknowledged by Carlos Drummond de Andrade in his "Ode no cinqüentenário do poeta brasileiro." The salient qualities attributed to Bandeira in this poem: "violenta ternura . . . infinita polícia . . . gravidade simples . . . sofrimento seco" ["violent tenderness . . . infinite refinement . . . simple sobriety . . . parched suffering"] set the seeds of Drummond's own perceptive account of human alienation. Drummond steadily progressed from the whimsical gaucherie of "Poema de sete faces" and "A balada do amor através das edades" to the disquieting sentiments of "Congresso Internacional do Medo" as the shadows of war and repression started to loom in the late 1930s. A quest for modernity was gradually replaced by a need for eternity, and the edgy, restless rhythms of his early poetry gradually yielded to the serene lyricism of *Claro enigma* (1951).

Drummond's erudition, his powers of self-appraisal and his constant striving for new inventions and refinements in terms of language and meaning, and his clear precepts about the craft and function of poetry soon singled him out as the most accomplished Brazilian poet of modern times. The enemy of mystification, he warned his fellow poets:

> Não dramatizes, não invoques,
> não indagues. Não percas tempo em mentir.
> . . .
> Não forces o poema a desprender-se do limbo.
> Não colhas no chão o poema que se perdeu.
> Não adules o poema. Aceita-o
> como ele aceitará sua forma definitiva e concentrada
> no espaço.
> ("Procura da poesia," *Nova reunião*)

> [Don't dramatize, don't invoke,
> don't probe. Waste no time telling lies.
> . . .
> Don't force the poem to escape from limbo.
> Don't retrieve the poem lying on the floor.
> Don't flatter the poem. Just accept it
> as it accepts its final, concentrated form
> in space.]

Deep convictions shape the very structure of Drummond's poems. Nagging uncertainties and relentless interrogations give substance and sharpness to his observations of the world around him. A poet for other poets and for ordinary men, Drummond even at his most pessimistic inspires confidence and transforms his very negations into something poetically positive. His influence is perceptible in the work of nearly every poet associated with the Generation of 1945, a productive crop of heterogeneous poets who retained their individuality while pursuing common objectives.

The Generation of 1945 unanimously acknowledged the need to express the aspirations and concerns of a world much altered by a second World War: Bueno de Rivera (b. 1911) described the poet of his time:

> periscópio raro
> nas lagoas turvas
> ("A volta dos megatérios," *Mundo submerso* [1944])

[a rare periscope
in turbid waters]

A similar function is performed by Tiago de Melo (b. 1926) in the role of poet–catalyst:

> Unindo os extremos da vida
> e mostrando a verdade
> como uma fruta aberta.
> ("A fruta aberta," *A lenda da rosa* [1956])

> [Uniting the extremes of life
> and showing the truth
> like an open fruit.]

The critical essays of the period stressed the need for discipline and research. Fernando Ferreira de Loanda (b. 1924), in collaboration with Ledo Ivo (b. 1924) and Darcy Damasceno (b. 1922), launched the first number of the *Revista Orpheu* (Spring 1947), a journal offering a wide range of new poems both traditional and experimental and invariably characterized by clarity, professionalism, and a vigilant craftsmanship, which banished any suggestion of facile improvisation. Hermeticism was rejected by most of these poets in favour of a poetic diction that would appeal to a wider public, an important factor if artists and writers were to identify with the political and social issues of the day. Mauro Mota (1911–1984), for example, became much admired for his intimate descriptions of ordinary things and people, which, although highly personal, are never obscure. He transforms an umbrella into "uma grande rosa negra, que se abre sobre mim na chuva" ["a huge black rose that opens above me in the rain"] and interprets the barking of a dog as "um latido ancestral" ["an ancestral wail"] capable of unleashing "a fome do tempo" ["the hunger of time"].

This "grave ofício de poeta" ["serious profession of being a poet"] is upheld by practiced theoreticians like Péricles Eugênio da Silva Ramos (b. 1919) and Domingos Carvalho da Silva (b. 1915). The latter opposes any romantic vision of the poet at work:

> Meu verso é a minha vida prática,
> salário e suor do meu rosto
> ("O Poeta," *Poemas escolhidos* [1956])

> [My verse is my practical life,
> my wages and the sweat of my brow.]

Geir Campos (b. 1924), Paulo Mendes Campos (b. 1922), Stella Leonardos (b. 1923), and José Paulo Moreira da Fonseca (b. 1922) are all conscious "artesãos da palavra" ["artisans of the word"]. They share a preference for adjectives such as "lógico," "lúcido," "sereno," "claro," "essencial" ["logical," "lucid," "serene," "clear," "essential"]. Their common goal is neatly phrased by Moreira da Fonseca:

> Quando tudo te parece perdido
> escuta a vida.
> ("Renascimento," *Poesias* [1949])

> [When all seems lost
> listen to life.]

Human malaise is probed with a clinical eye. Bueno de Rivera unravels: "a vida noturna do espírito" ["the nocturnal life of the spirit"], while Moreira da Fonseca attempts to reconstruct the pieces of his "espelho quebrado em 68 fragmentos, tentando espelhar um rosto desolado" ["mirror shattered into 68 fragments, trying to mirror a desolate face"].

There are echoes of Drummond's battle with the powers of Good and Evil ("Poema de purificação") in works such as *Mapa azul da infância* by Marcos Konder Reis (b. 1922), in *Caminhos de Belém* (1962) by Afonso Félix de Sousa (b. 1925), and in *Canto para as transformações do homem* (1964) by Moacyr Félix (b. 1926) in which "todas as luas são tristes e ferem diariamente o homem e seu abraço" ["all the moons are sad and daily wound man and his embrace"]. Ledo Ivo touches upon the central paradox of man's existence when he wryly observes:

> O universo é o sonho de Deus
> e Deus é o sonho dos homens.
> ("O sonho," *Uma lira dos vinte anos* [1962])

> [The universe is the dream of God
> and God is the dream of men.]

The spiritual corrosion of the times often creates a sense of personal guilt in these poets. Paulo Mendes Campos confides:

> . . . meus pais não souberam impedir
> Que o sorriso se mudasse em zombaria
> E um coração em coisa fria.
> ("Sentimento de Tempo," *Poemas* [1979])

> [. . . my parents were unable to prevent
> That my smile should turn to scorn
> My ardent heart into something cold.]

In contrast, Darcy Damasceno impartially defines the formidable challenge confronting the poets of his generation:

> Entre a loucura e a infância
> Plantar o humano e o trágico
> aos pés da eternidade.
> ("Poema," *Poemas* [1946])

[Between madness and infancy
To plant the human and tragic
At the feet of eternity.]

João Cabral de Melo Neto (b. 1920) has been rightly acclaimed as the most creative and individual poet to have emerged from the Generation of 1945. While many of his contemporaries showed signs of returning to traditional themes and techniques, he experimented further in his pursuit of mathematical precision. The order and permanence Cabral invokes in *Pedra do sono* (1942), and *O engenheiro* (1945), became the hallmark of his own poetics:

> Procura a ordem
> que vês na pedra:
>   nada se gasta
>   mas permanece.
> ("Pequena ode mineral," *Poemas reunidos* [1945])

> [Pursue the order
> you observe in the stone:
>   nothing is lost
>   yet it endures.]

In *Psicologia da composição* (1947), he compares the composing of poetry to "delírio, transe, tumulto" ["delirium, trance and tumult"]. A fierce struggle with words and concepts is inevitable – "tentando / salvar da morte os monstros / germinados em seu tinteiro" ["trying / to rescue from death the monsters / germinated in his inkwell"] – before the poet ultimately achieves stark simplicity. Powerful emotions are rigorously controlled. Complex issues are conveyed by means of essentialized, sharply defined images: stone, sun, tree, desert. Cabral's poetic diction is uncompromisingly austere:

> O engenheiro sonha coisas claras:
>   . . .
> o engenheiro pensa o mundo justo,
> mundo que nenhum véu encobre.
>   ("O engenheiro")

> [The engineer dreams of transparent things:
>   . . .
> the engineer believes the world to be sound,
> a world no veil conceals.]

Subsequent books of poetry betray a deepening concern with the harsh social conditions in his native Pernambuco. The drama of the Brazilian interior or *sertão* and the plight of the *sertanejos* stricken by drought and famine is narrated without emphasis or contrivance in poems like

"Paisagem do capibaribe" and "Congresso no polígono das secas," and, most memorably of all, in *"Morte e vida severina"* (1956), a dramatic poem based on a traditional nativity play. His later poems reveal even greater concentration and precision. In *Uma faca só lâmina* (1955) the key images "uma bala enterrada no corpo . . . um relógio pulsando em sua gaiola . . . uma faca íntima . . . lâmina cruel" ["a bullet buried in the body . . . a watch pulsating in its cage . . . an intimate knife . . . cruel blade"] constitute the living mechanism which gives Cabral de Melo Neto's poetry its muscular agility. Like Drummond before him, Cabral opened up exciting new paths for others to follow. Cabral's poetry made considerable impact throughout the 1960s and 1970s, and his influence extended beyond Brazil to Portugal and Spain. His innovations would be respected even by the Concrete poets who were generally critical, if not entirely hostile, in their appraisal of the Generation of 1945.

Concrete poetry was launched in São Paulo in 1952 when Décio Pignatari (b. 1927), Augusto de Campos (b. 1931), and Haroldo de Campos (b. 1929) published the first issue of *Noigandres* with some startling innovations – non-figurative poems with geometric features. The enigmatic title *Noigandres* had been culled from the Provençal troubadour Arnaut Daniel and used by Pound in his *Cantos*. The Concrete poets would replace conventional "discursive" syntax with ideograms. Subjective expression would become objective and aim for the immediate communication achieved by newspaper headlines or strip cartoons. The Concrete poem would be released from a strictly literary context and become integrated with other art forms – music, painting, architecture, and the graphic arts in general.

By 1955, *Concretismo* [Concretism] had gained momentum. *Noigandres* 2 appeared and Concrete poets read and displayed their spatial poems at a music festival held at São Paulo's Teatro de Arena. The movement's pioneers had also established close links with experimental artists and poets in Europe, such as Eugen Gomringer in Germany, whose *Constellations* harmonized with the aesthetics of the Concretists.

The following year, the first national exhibition of Concrete Art was organized at the Museu de Arte Moderna in São Paulo. Ronaldo Azeredo (b. 1937), Ferreira Gullar (b. 1930), and Wlademir Dias Pino (b. 1927) displayed their poems alongside the work of avant-garde painters and sculptors. *Noigandres* 3 was published to coincide with the exhibition. Its success encouraged the promoters to transfer the exhibition to Rio de Janeiro, where it was well attended and enthusiastically reviewed in the literary supplement of the *Jornal do Brasil*. The supplement also published the poems of José Lino Grunewald (b. 1931), Reinaldo Jardim (b. 1926), and the veteran poet Pedro Xisto (b. 1901), as examples of the latest graphic techniques.

Noigandres 3 put Concrete poetry into perspective. Influences could be traced back to the early experiments of the Brazilian symbolist poet Joaquim de Sousa Andrade (1833–1902), to the modernist inventions of Oswald de Andrade, and more recently to the sparse verses of João Cabral de Melo Neto. The main influences from abroad were Mallarmé's *Un coup de dés*, Apollinaire's *Calligrammes*, Pound's *Cantos*, the minimalist techniques of e. e. cummings, and Joyce's word montages. Carrying these experiments further, the Concrete poets explored the artistic potential of "words in space," either in isolation or in association, either in black and white or in colour. With the publication of *Noigandres 4* in 1958, Concrete poets began to diversify their techniques by composing "code-poems," "semiotic poems," or "poems without words." Augusto de Campos experimented with ideograms and "popcretas," which departed from any conventional use of syntax; Haroldo de Campos obliterated the frontiers between prose and poetry and broadened the function of semantics. The printed word became something mobile and magnetic, subject to unexpected vibrations and sudden metamorphoses. Poems were constructed like mantras or phonic talismans, and important links were established with the musical experiments of composers like Boulez, Stockhausen, Berio, and Ponge.

By 1959, the poets associated with *Noigandres* could justly claim to be at the forefront of an international movement. That same year, their work was shown and debated at a Concrete exhibition in Stuttgart, organized by Max Bense, while in Munich the arts journal *Nota* devoted a special issue to the Brazilian Avant-Garde. The following year the movement's achievements were publicized even further afield with a large-scale exhibition at the Museum of Modern Art in Tokyo.

A new anthology of poetry and criticism, *Invenção* (1962–1968), edited by Décio Pignatari, and his *Teoria da poesia concreta* (1956) published in collaboration with Augusto and Haroldo de Campos, outlined the movement's role in changing contemporary attitudes to poetry. The word-object had been stripped to bare essentials. Enigmas had been replaced by verbal choreography, and words, whole or fragmented, were now seen as germ-syllables exploding and expanding on the blank page as they progressed toward concreteness. The permutations on these basic principles seemed infinite. They ranged from Décio Pignatari's *meta-poema* or "poem about a poem," constructed from the word "Terra":

ra	terra	ter
rat	erra	ter
rate	rra	ter
rater	ra	ter
raterr	a	ter
raterra	ter	

```
araterra      ter
raraterra      te
rraraterra      t
erraraterra
t er ra ra t e rra
```

to José Lino Grunewald's digital poem "Cinco":

```
1
22
333
4444
c i n c o
```

The movement's critics deplored the absence of any emotional texture in these experiments but there are clear undertones of prurience and satire respectively in the following "mini-poems" by Décio Pignatari:

> abrir as portas
> abrir as pernas
> cobrir as corpos
>
> [to open doors
> to open legs
> to cover bodies]

> = a pátria é a família
>   (com televisão)
>   amplificada
>
> = [the fatherland is the family
>   (with television)
>   amplified]

Predictably, divisions and defections soon occurred within the ranks of Concretism and, by the 1960s, critics were already discussing Post-Concrete aesthetics. New theories about the nature and function of poetry were aired and new manifestos launched. The most radical of these was *Poesia Praxis* [Praxis Poetry] launched by Mário Chamie (b. 1933) in *Lavra Lavra* (1962). The Praxist poet would replace the *palavra-coisa* [word-object] of Concretism with the *palavra-energia* [word-energy], the maximum action expressed with a minimum of words. Chamie argued that concretist theories had become too turgid. An excess of technical jargon scarcely helped to promote communication. By contrast, the Praxis poet would create poems capable of being aesthetically and semantically transformed, even manipulated, with the reader's participation.

Poesia Praxis rejected all canons and dogmas and found inspiration in some fact or emotion without recourse to conventional themes. The new poetry would probe words, explore potential meanings and contradictions, and invite the reader to share the experience. Chamie's factual observations in the following poem are deliberately devoid of any emotion:

> dependo do fichário
> do ponto de meu ônibus
> do contrato
>
> dependo da poupança
> do meu imposto
> de minha taxa
> do nome no cadastro
> ("Dependência," *Lavra Lavra* [1962])

> [I depend on the filing cabinet
> on my bus stop
> on my contract
>
> I depend on my savings
> on my taxes
> on my rates
> on the name in the register]

The tone adopted here is disarmingly neutral but the poets who mustered under the banner of *Poesia Praxis* developed Chamie's manifesto with striking individuality. *Poesia Praxis* was carried a stage further by Alvaro de Sá (b. 1935) and Moacy Cirne (b. 1943) who developed their own variant: *Poema Processo* [Poem-Process] – a process influenced by recent developments in electronics and computers and intended to *sanitize* Concretism. Alvaro de Sá introduced the novel idea of codifying the existing alphabet by replacing each letter with a geometrical symbol (e.g., "a" = a triangle; "b" = a rectangle surrounded by a circle, etc.). Poets like Antônio Carlos Cabral, Armando Freitas Filho, Camargo Meyer (b. 1941), Carlos Rodrigues Brandão (b. 1940), Clodomir Monteiro (b. 1939), José de Oliveira Falcón (b. 1940), Lauro Juk, and Mauro Gama (b. 1938) are all "word designers" in the Chamie mould, but they strike a wide variety of moods. There is drama and horror in the "Balada da corda bamba" by Arnaldo Saraiva, in which he contemplates the onslaught of time and man's capacity for self-destruction. The reader's thoughts flap and flutter in harmony with the movement of the bat itself in "Amorcegação" by Clodomir Monteiro, while Yvonne Gianetti Fonseca beats out the robust rhythms of indigenous ceremonies in "Natureza morta ou trópico."

Rio de Janeiro and São Paulo soon became the Meccas for the Brazilian Avant-Garde. Both cities offered suitable outlets for exhibiting and publishing the latest innovations. In more remote centres, smaller groups of avant-garde poets were obliged to work in greater isolation with considerably less publicity. Nonetheless, interesting experiments in art and literature continued to emerge from the various regions of Brazil, both north and south. Minas Gerais produced its own Avant-Garde with the publication of *Revista Tendência* (1957–1962), edited by the critic Fábio Lucas. As the title of the journal makes clear, this enterprise set trends rather than establishing a specific movement or school. Like Mário Chamie's Praxis poetry, the *Tendência* manifesto also rejected dogmas while inviting dialogue. Contacts were made with São Paulo's Concretists and Post-Concretists and an exchange program of lectures and seminars set up. Competitions were organized to attract new talent and prize-winners had their entries published in the literary supplement of the *Estado de Minas*.

The poets Affonso Avila (b. 1928) and Affonso Romano de Sant'Anna (b. 1937) became the dominant forces in this group. Avila's *Cartas do solo* (1961) and *Frases feitas* (1963), examined alongside the parodic testimonies of Romano de Sant'Anna, illustrate the salient qualities of their inventive structures and linear precision. Seriousness goes hand in hand with self-parody in the work of these poets. Torn between self and society, Romano de Sant'Anna has to conciliate both roles:

> Eu
>> moderno poeta, e brasileiro
>> com a pena e pele ressequidas ao sol dos trópicos,
>> quando penso em escrever poemas
>> – aterram-me sempre os terrais problemas.
>>> ("Rainer Maria Rilke e eu")

> [I
>> modern poet, and Brazilian
>> with my suffering and skin parched by the sun of the tropics,
>> when I think of writing poems
>> I am always terrified by terrestrial problems.]

He is a poet not only fearful of existence, but uncertain about the validity of literature itself. In "Elaborando as perdas" the poet is shaken by the thought that "a literatura talvez não seja mais que uma finada flor" ["perhaps literature is nothing but a withered flower"].

The *Revista Tendência* expanded under two new headings: *Vereda* [Path] and *Ptyx* [the symbolic conch or shell]. Technically, these are further variations of the same formulae. The visual–spatial patterns of Libério Neves (b. 1935) can be readily identified with Post-Concretism while the "minimalist" compositions of Dirceu Xavier (b. ?) are reminiscent of the Japanese haiku:

> as dores que o mundo dá
> são fáceis de se sentir

difíceis de se contar.
                    ("Fragmento")

[the sorrows the world gives
are easy to feel
difficult to narrate.]

Cryptic and self-deprecating, these poets address themselves to the central task of struggling with words and meaning. José Paulo Gonçalves da Costa (b. ?) sums up the caution and skepticism of his contemporaries:

sei pouco de filosofia
sei nada de religião.
sei lá se sou poeta!

conheço sim, palavras
profundas, vigorosas, violentas
– capazes de morte e amor
num só instante.

basta-me possuí-las
dizê-las não é preciso,
tão pouco que se acredite.
                    ("As palavras")

[I know little about philosophy.
I know nothing about religion.
Who knows if I'm a poet!

Yes, I know words
deep, vigorous, violent
– capable of death and love
in a single instant.

I need only possess them
no need to say them,
for they are scarcely believed.]

Alongside various groups and movements, individual poets came to the fore without any clear affiliations or commitments. They were not indifferent to the theories and reforms of the Avant-Garde but chose to remain independent and eclectic. Lindolf Bell (b. 1938) took poetry to the streets, to stadiums, factories, student unions, and working-men's clubs in the form of *Catequese poética* [Poetic catechism]. He printed poems on T-shirts which he defined as *corpoemas* [body poems], designed poster-poems, and engraved poems on large stones. This was poetry for the people which he displayed anywhere and everywhere like graffiti. Ferreira Gullar who was instrumental in propagating Concretism and Post-Concretism, dissociated himself from both groups in the early 1960s and turned to popular poetry. The Mayakovsky credo that "There is no revolutionary art without revolutionary form" had made a deep impression on Brazilian writers and poets and convinced them of the need for greater political involvement. In "Coisas da terra" Gullar boldly asserts: "Todas as coisas de que falo são de carne" ["All the things of which I speak are made of flesh"]. His interest in social issues becomes much more accentuated in subsequent collections until the poem becomes "uma bandeira" ["a banner"]. The verses of *Poema sujo* (1977) also reveal his deep attachment to his provincial roots. The mercurial Walmir Ayala (b. 1933) represents another common phenomenon in the 1960s and 1970s, namely, the re-emergence of a talented and versatile poet whose later work reflects the influence of successive postmodernist trends. From the late 1950s, Ayala also made a valuable contribution as critic, essayist, and anthologist.

Some of the most interesting poets in the 1970s and 1980s have been described as "poetas novos à moda antiga" ["new poets in the old style"]. The description would suit Paulo Bonfim (b. 1926) from São Paulo and two influential poets from Rio Grande do Sul, Carlos Nejar (b. 1939) and Armindo Trevisan (b. 1933). Nejar's Odyssean poems have a timeless quality. His native pampas create a symbolic arena for trenchant human dramas. His gaucho antiheroes, exploited and forsaken, exemplify "a condição de não ser homem" ["the condition of not being human"]. The gauchos and the land they inhabit are indistinguishable in a transfigured landscape where love, human and divine, becomes "a mais alta constelação" ["the highest constellation"]. Trevisan, too, moves with the same ease from intimate regional scenes to the universal symbols of contemporary culture, as in his deeply moving "Acalanto para Marilyn Monroe."

From the 1940s there has been an upsurge in the number of women writing poetry. Notable for their individuality and assured technique are Renata Pallottini (b. 1931), Olga Savary (b. 1933), Hilda Hilst (b. 1930), Ilka Brunhilde Laurito (b. 1925), Idelma Ribeiro de Faria (b. 1924), Lupe Cotrim Garaude (b. 1933), Adélia Prado (b. 1936), and Marly de Oliveira (b. 1935). Pallottini's admirable sonnets combine subtlety and power. Here is a poet who can justly claim "Tenho um ritmo fértil a latejar-me nas têmporas" ["I have a fertile rhythm throbbing in my temples"]. The spontaneous warmth and intimacy in these women poets is never allowed to degenerate into tasteless effusions. The qualities they themselves value are discipline and restraint. Lupe Cotrim Garaude speaks for all these women when she describes herself as being:

> . . . solitária e precisa
> nas coisas irresolúveis
> – desnudada em nitidez
>   ("Clara manhã")

[. . . alone and precise
amidst irresolvable things
– stripped down to clarity]

They shun any sentimentality or fatuous confidences and, as Marly de Oliveira reminds us, "uma fera" ["a wild beast"] lurks beneath this calm exterior. She sums up the common pursuit of all the women poets of her generation in two short lines:

Poesia é caminho, única vertigem
além do amor, da anunciação
("Invocação de Orpheu")

[Poetry is a path, the only vertigo
beyond love or annunciation]

To conclude, it is important to note the wider contributions made by nearly all the poets in this survey to Brazilian culture in general. Like the precursors of Modernism, they have excelled as poets, critics, essayists, translators, and dramatists. They have propagated the values of Brazilian art and literature as lecturers, journalists, and diplomats throughout Europe and North America. Many of their poems have been set to music by composers of both classical and popular music. Most of all, they have set standards of literary excellence which provide sound guidance for those who will succeed them. The battles of the Generation of 1922 were not fought in vain. The artistic integrity and freedom to experiment they achieved have lost none of their momentum.

The Brazilian theatre in the twentieth century
Severino João Albuquerque

The first three decades of the twentieth century witnessed the continued prevalence of the comedy of manners, with only slight attention being paid to the symbolist and psychological plays of Goulart de Andrade (1881–1936), Roberto Gomes (1882–1922), and Paulo Gonçalves (1897–1927). Rio de Janeiro's uncontested role as national center of theatrical activity was reinforced by the stagings of the important but short-lived Teatro da Exposição Nacional (1908) and Teatro da Natureza (1916), and by the opening of its grand Teatro Municipal in 1909. Although there was a significant increase in the number of Brazilian plays written and performed, there was nevertheless little improvement in the overall quality of the theatre, as producers and authors adhered to the hackneyed but commercially safe formulae of the comedy of manners and musical revues. Burlettas continued to draw large audiences; one of the more successful of these plays was *Forrobodó* (produced in Rio de Janeiro in 1911) by Carlos Bettencourt (1890–1941) and Luiz Peixoto (1889–1973), with music by the immensely successful composer of popular music and theatre scores, Chiquinha Gonzaga (Francisca Hedwiges Neves Gonzaga [1847–1935]).

The better-known playwrights of the time, such as Cláudio de Souza (1876–1954) and João do Rio (Paulo Barreto [1881–1921]), continued the spirit of earlier generations but did not break new ground. Without the hallmarks of Martins Pena's and Artur Azevedo's geniuses, their twentieth-century followers failed to give convincing theatrical representation to new situations and character attributes, unable as they were to steer clear of nostalgia and naive nationalism. Even the most successful plays of the period, such as, for example, João do Rio's *A Bela Madame Vargas* (performed 1912; published, 1912), Souza's *Flores de Sombra* (1916; 1919), *Onde Canta o Sabiá* (1921; 1950) by Gastão Tojeiro (1880–1965), and *Ministro do Supremo* (1921; 1940) by Armando Gonzaga (1889–1954), are but pleasing interludes amidst the overwhelming mediocrity and did not improve the quality of subsequent works.

In its turn, the serious drama remained for the most part ignored, vastly outnumbered as it was by the *comédias* and *revistas* heavily favored by the public. In terms of quality, it was as unconvincing as the comedy, as is so readily apparent in the works of two playwrights who authored both comedies and serious dramas, Henrique Coelho Neto (1864–1934) and Viriato Correia (1884–1967). While theatrical talent is considerably depleted in the latter, the former does present some good qualities, such as concern for the plight of women and an interest in Afro-Brazilian themes but these are for the most part overwhelmed by the negative aspects – superficiality, weak construction, and, above all, grandiloquence – so that the appeal of his plays remains sporadic at best. In drama, as in every other literary genre he practiced, Coelho Neto was an extremely prolific author, one who seemed to value output to the detriment of quality.

The theatre of the period revolved around a number of national companies run by dedicated impresarios, such as Gomes Cardim (1864–1932) and Pascoal Segreto (1868–1920), and led by extremely popular actors who often doubled as managers, most notably Apolônia Pinto (1854–1937), Leopoldo Fróes (1882–1932), Abigail Maia (1887–1981), Itália Fausta (1887–1951), Jaime Costa (1897–1967), and Procópio Ferreira (1898–1979). Their emergence was extremely important for it meant a growing recognition and public support of the national theatre in its competition with foreign companies and playwrights. In such a state of affairs, however, the stage director had very little control over the production. Plays were written specifically for these actors, characters were designed to suit certain peculiarities of their acting, and their strengths and weaknesses influenced the choice of repertoire for an entire company whose survival often depended on the continued popularity of its star. While they could occasionally side-step convention, these actors had a diction and bearing that would seem outdated even to some of their contemporaries; however, their long, successful careers provide further evidence of the resilience of nineteenth-century tradition.

Along with a number of well-known theatre professionals of the time, several of these actors formed what later became known as the Grupo Trianon, named after Rio de Janeiro's Teatro Trianon, where some of the most triumphal successes of the twentieth-century comedy of manners were staged after it opened in 1915. Other members of the group included the playwrights Tojeiro, Gonzaga, Correia, Ernani Fornari (1899–1964), and Oduvaldo Viana (1892–1972). Ironically, Viana contributed to Trianon's demise, as the decline of the group's influence was set off by the emergence of a new house, aptly named Teatro Rival, which opened in 1934 with the staging of Viana's best work, *Amor* (1934). Directed by the playwright, the production made famous the actress Dulcina de Moraes (b. 1911) and occasioned the formation of the important Companhia Dulcina-Odilon.

Long associated with the Praça Tiradentes area of Rio de Janeiro, the revues had their heyday in the 1930s and 1940s. Numerous new productions opened every year and some theatres, the Recreio and the São José among them, became the exclusive domain of the genre. Adding more samba, glitter, and raciness to its nineteenth-century precursor, the modern *revista* achieved such a degree of popularity that at one point it was seen as a serious threat to the survival of mainstream theatre. Cleverly produced by such managers as Jardel Jércolis (1895–1945), Geysa Bôscoli (1907–1978), Carlos Machado (1908–1991), and Walter Pinto (b. 1913), the revues employed an array of talent, thus drawing to the nation's capital a multitude of actors, many of whom had served their apprenticeship in the circus. The major names included Aracy Cortes (Zilda de Carvalho Espíndola, 1904–1986), Oscarito (Oscar Teresa Dias, 1906–1970), Dercy Gonçalves (b. 1907), Grande Otelo (Sebastião de Souza Prata, 1915–1993), and Mara Rúbia (b. 1918). These and several other names were catapulted to national fame in the 1950s when they appeared in enormously popular *chanchadas*, a film style that borrowed many conventions of the revue, thus reviving in another medium the then declining genre.

The extended influence and enormous popularity of such long-drawn-out nineteenth-century practices deferred by a half-century the coming of modernity to the stages of Brazil. Addicted as they were to the predictability and proven success of Feydeau's dated techniques, Brazilian theatre practitioners did not care to learn about the work of the more important European stage directors; as late as the mid 1930s only a handful of intellectuals and avant-garde dramatists were familiar with the contributions of Copeau, E. Gordon Craig, Appia, Stanislavsky, and Meyerhold. However, perpetuating the belief in the superiority of foreign art, the public still demanded to be exposed to European theatre. They were of course accustomed to dictating choice of repertoire but their taste showed little discrimination; thus, visiting vaudeville companies such as the French Ba-ta-clan (featuring the "bombshell" Mistinguett) and the Spanish Velasco enjoyed tremendous success while playwrights such as Shaw, Chekhov, and Strindberg remained virtually ignored.

Moreover, the otherwise revolutionary Modern Art Week of 1922 had little immediate impact on the theatre, even though it took place in São Paulo's Teatro Municipal (which had opened in 1911) and its events included a good deal of theatricality – as in poetry recitals and the deliberate attempts to shock the bourgeoisie. Although historians of Brazilian drama have traditionally preferred to stress the fact that the Week ignored the theatre, it is now clear that several of its participants had a keen interest in the art form and did indeed exert far-reaching influence on the subsequent theatrical scene (Prado, "O teatro"). Mário de Andrade (1893–1945), the leading name in Brazilian Modernism, wrote two unjustly neglected avant-garde plays, *Moral Quotidiana* (1925) and *Café: Tragédia Secular* (1942); more recently, however, some of his narratives have been successfully adapted to the stage, including *O Banquete* (by Camila Amado) and *Macunaíma* (by Antunes Filho), the latter undoubtedly the most important theatrical event of the 1970s. Another of the Week's organizers, the essayist and novelist José Pereira da Graça Aranha (1868–1931), had had a play, *Malazarte* (1911), staged in Paris in 1911 (Faria, "Graça Aranha e o teatro"); Antônio de Alcântara Machado (1901–1935), the noted author of *crônicas* and short stories, wrote perceptive pages (included in *Terra Roxa e Outras Terras* [1926] and *Cavaquinho e Saxofone* [1940]) on the situation of the Brazilian theatre in the 1920s. While modernist painters such as E. di Cavalcanti (1897–1976) and Lula Cardozo Ayres (1910–1987) designed settings for the Companhia Procópio Ferreira and the Teatro de Brinquedo, the architect Flávio de Carvalho (1899–1973) activated the highly original if short-lived Teatro de Experiência, whose production of the avant-garde *Bailado do Deus Morto* was closed down by the police after only three performances in late 1933 (Dória, *Moderno teatro brasileiro*, 7, 30, 44–5). Also in 1933, another play written for the Teatro de Experiência, *O Homem e o Cavalo* (1934), by the prominent Modernist, Oswald de Andrade (José Oswald de Sousa Andrade [1890–1954]), was dealt with even more harshly and its performance forbidden on its opening night.

Oswald's enormous creative energy and the spread of his interests led to a strong involvement with the theatre, but his influence was not to be felt until much later, since his most important plays – *O Homem e o Cavalo*; *A Morta* and *O Rei da Vela* (both 1937) – although available in print, were not performed in the 1930s; *O Rei da Vela*, for example, was not staged until Teatro Oficina's milestone production in 1967. While Oswald's theatre uses expressionist and Brechtian techniques and, in content, borrows from Marx, Freud, and Nietzsche, it is anchored in a thoroughly Brazilian frame of reference. Above all, it is a radical application of the notion of a cultural and literary "cannibalism" or selective importation of ideas which he put forth in his *Manifesto Antropófago* of 1928.

Written in 1933, the three-act *O Rei da Vela* (which is dedicated to Alvaro and Eugênia Moreyra, "for struggling to raise the abandoned child that is the Brazilian theatre") constitutes a devastating denunciation of crass capitalism through a portrait of a new class, the moneyed bourgeoisie, as it replaces the bankrupt landowners and coffee barons. Through characterization and scathing satire, the play depicts both groups as equally corrupt and unscrupulous. The upper-class characters' struggle to preserve their standard of living reveals their moral and financial decadence. The bourgeoisie is guilty on two counts, for prostituting itself in exchange for the aristocracy's name and tradition, and also for aligning itself with foreign interests. The intelligentsia does not fare much better, as its representative, Pinote, is a writer who peddles his dubious talents to the rich. That such a world does not hold a place for love is confirmed by Oswald's recasting of the famous Medieval love story of Abelard and Heloïse. In *O Rei da Vela* the suitor is a predatory member of the *nouveau riche* with two equally insidious incarnations: Abelardo I, the usurer, and Abelardo II, the self-proclaimed Socialist. When Abelardo I becomes Abelardo II nothing besides his name is different, the point being that no substantive change will occur until the socio-economic structure undergoes radical transformation. Abelardo is intent on buying the tradition of distinction associated with Heloísa's family name, while the bride and her relatives see the courtship as an opportunity to regain their squandered fortune. At the play's end money's preeminence is reaffirmed as each side attains its goal and both classes lose, while foreign capital, represented by an American businessman, Mr. Jones, asserts its control of the Brazilian economy.

In *O Homem e o Cavalo* the anti-bourgeois revolution has won and is now in control of the entire world. Its nine tableaux of cosmic proportions (the play was meant to be performed in a soccer stadium or to be filmed) and corrosive satire document the new regime's attempts to correct the inequities of the old order by destroying the myths perpetuated by capitalism and Christianity. With its revolutionary form and message, propagandistic monologues, large cast of characters (from Cleopatra and Jesus Christ to the ironically misnamed Mister Byron and Lord Capone), and diversity of settings (the boat of Saint Peter, an interplanetary airport, the Derby at Epsom, the largest socialist factory in the world, Heaven, and so on), Oswald's play is in many ways reminiscent of Mayakovsky's 1918 *Mystery-Bouffe* (Clark, "Oswald and Mayakovsky"). Its main thrust is a denunciation of past and present evils of capitalism, along with the celebration of a new era in which the peasant's horse, representative of the economic exploitation of the past, is replaced by the new symbol of proletarian liberation, the horse-power evocative of the collectively owned industries of the future.

A Morta, Oswald's most hermetic play, includes elements of Expressionism, Surrealism and Brecht's epic theatre. The work recasts another famous pair of literary lovers, Dante and Beatrice, as O poeta [The Poet] and Beatriz; these two and the Hierofante [Hierophant] are the only characters to appear in all three scenes of the one-act play. Each scene takes place in a different locale visited by the Poet in his search for an Art that is both beautiful and committed to social change. The three scenes ("The nation of the individual"; "The nation of grammar"; "The nation of anaesthetic") illustrate the major threats (lack of commitment; norms; death of the senses) facing the artist in bourgeois society. In his journey the

Poet learns that Art, in order not to be the dead being of the title, must seek vitality and renewal in commitment and revolution. At the play's end, the Poet finally finds liberation when he comes to understand the true meaning of Art as an endeavor in the service of social ends. He then sets fire to the entire scene, symbolically destroying the old myths created by the bourgeois mind-set.

Just as the Hierophant was the interpreter of sacred mysteries in ancient Greece, in Oswald's play it anticipates events and explains situations in addresses (such as the opening and closing monologues) much in line with the Brechtian distantiation effect. The text includes several other instances of avant-garde techniques such as narrative or epic style, episodic development, character split between puppet and actor, and movement of actors among the audience.

Oswald's revolutionary dramatic texts thus dispel the prevalent notion that Brazilian Modernists held the theatre in low esteem. The publication and performance fortunes of his works as well as of those of his colleagues in the movement suggest that other factors were at work. Ruthless censorship, a public weaned on fatuous comedies of manners, and a conservative theatrical establishment combined to keep Oswald's texts away from the stages; to the detriment of the Brazilian theatre, for three decades his works would be restricted to the realm of literature.

Innovation came late to the theatre proper, and rather unevenly, in spasmodic spurts, until it finally and unequivocally asserted itself in 1943 with the powerful bursting onto the scene of Nelson Rodrigues (1912–1980). While the traditionalists insisted on staging the simpler, less provocative depictions of life found in those ever-popular holdovers from the nineteenth century, the Modernists, who were generally younger, believed that the theatre must reflect the enormous changes that were already taking place in every aspect of the social order. They insisted that the theatre had to adapt to a vastly changed society that had developed other channels of entertainment and public debate, with the phenomenal success of radio, film, recorded music, and soccer. Comedies and revues were associated with the slave-holding monarchy; they were woefully inadequate for a rapidly modernizing republic, at a time when the old, land-holding aristocracy was dying out and, following the Revolutions of 1930 and 1932, being replaced by a liberal, urban, more educated middle class.

The renewal of the 1940s, was preceded by a number of important efforts such as the Batalha da Quimera and the Teatro de Brinquedo. The former was but one of the attempts made by Renato Viana (1894–1953) to create an artistically valid theatre in Brazil. Working in Rio de Janeiro with two noted Modernists, the composer Heitor Villa-Lobos (1887–1959) and the poet Ronald de Carvalho (1893–1935), Viana, a playwright, actor, and director, envisioned the Batalha as a group whose immediate aim was to introduce expressionist theatre onto the Brazilian stage. Their first production, Viana's *A Ultima Encarnação de Fausto*, staged in 1922, met with adverse public and critical reaction. Undaunted by this and other failures, Viana displayed his boundless enthusiasm and energy in other endeavors such as São Paulo's Colméia (1924), Rio de Janeiro's Caverna Mágica (1927), Teatro de Arte (1932), and Teatro-Escola (1934), and Porto Alegre's Escola Dramática (1942) and Teatro Anchieta (1944). From 1948 until his death in 1953 he chaired Rio de Janeiro's Escola Dramática, later renamed Escola de Teatro Martins Pena (Dória, "Semana de 22," 58–61).

The brainchild of another participant of the Modern Art Week, Alvaro Moreyra (1888–1964), and his wife Eugênia Moreyra (1899–1948), the Teatro de Brinquedo began, as its name suggests, as a diversion for a select group of upper-class intellectuals who had tired of the mediocre theatre of the time. The group was inspired by avant-garde French directors, especially Copeau, with whose work, in the Théâtre Vieux Colombier, Alvaro had become familiar during a visit to Paris. Formed in the nation's capital in 1927, the Teatro de Brinquedo soon achieved unexpected success with plays such as A. Moreyra's *Adão, Eva e Outros Membros da Família* (1922), which opened in the Cassino Beira-Mar in November of that year. Their second production was somewhat less successful; staged in late 1927, *Espetáculo do Arco da Velha* combined skits, poetry, singing, circus acts, and a remarkable use of pantomime. Following a series of well-received performances in São Paulo in early 1928, the group disbanded upon their return to Rio de Janeiro. Much like its short-lived 1937 reincarnation (under the new name of Companhia de Arte Dramática), the Teatro de Brinquedo was poorly structured and organized and its repertoire limited to a few plays. These and other problems may have been related to the group's amateur status or perhaps to the absence of a clearly defined aesthetic agenda. However, its shortcomings notwithstanding, the Teatro de Brinquedo did make a lasting contribution: it gave amateur groups a newfound sense of purpose and relevance, and it helped to form a more knowledgeable core of theatre-goers who would be more receptive to the work of Os Comediantes and other groups of the late 1930s and 1940s.

An important event in the early 1930s was the emergence as a major playwright of Joracy Camargo (1898–1973), who had been associated with the Grupo Trianon and, more recently, with the Teatro de Brinquedo. In a marked departure from the trivialities of his Trianon contributions, the ground-breaking *Deus lhe Pague* (1933) reflects, albeit timidly, the inspiration of the Russian Revolution and its vibrant economic plans. Introducing Karl Marx's name (but not quite his ideas) onto the Brazilian stage, Camargo played with the public's curiosity about communism and with the belief that the then recent crash of the New York Stock Exchange had signaled the demise of stagnant capitalism. Curiously, the work and its author were widely perceived as being sympathetic to Marxism in spite of some clearly conservative ideas expressed in the play and the famous likening of Communism to an ineffective and harmless straw toy.

Deus lhe Pague was enormously popular from its first performance, in São Paulo's Teatro Boa Vista on December 30, 1932. Three decades later it had had more than 10,000 performances (Magaldi, *Panorama do teatro brasileiro*, 187); Procópio Ferreira alone played the main role more than 3,200 times (*Depoimentos*, I, 99). The play achieved such a huge success not only because of the novelty of its theme but also because it was written specifically for Procópio, who was the biggest box-office draw of the time. The social criticism, however, is tame and done in naive terms and for the most part in a somewhat confused manner. The two main characters, Mendigo and Outro, are reminiscent of Um and Outro in *Adão, Eva e Outros Membros da Família*. Although their dialogue touches on major issues, from love and old age to philosophy and economics, a true debate never takes place, for Outro is nothing but a foil for the old man's ideas. The protagonist's quandary seems to derive from the predicament of the wealthy, but often personally frustrated, capitalist. Unhappy with the world of finances, and unable to commit himself in unselfish love, Mendigo leads a double life, co-habiting with a beautiful young woman named Nancy in an elegant home and, unbeknown to her, begging in the streets to finance their luxurious life-style.

It is often, and correctly, held against *Deus lhe Pague* that the allegory is too obvious, the ideas superficial, the situations inconsistent, the melo-drama unbearable, and that the play deals in puerile style with philosophical questions and social conditions that are considerably more complex than Camargo made them. The charges are equally right with regard to the didactic tone, but we have to acknowledge the fact that the playwright was faced with the problem of what note to strike in areas totally uncharted for the Brazilian theatre. If sometimes the language sounds pompous, if the posturing comes directly from the classroom, or if the play ultimately collapses beneath the burden of its many flaws, we need to remember the novelty in Brazilian theatre, and the urgency of the issues the playwright was addressing, in the early 1930s. Although Camargo's play is hopelessly dated, his subject matter remains extremely relevant as contemporary Brazilian society has made very little progress in the resolution of its essential contradictions and inequities.

In the wake of *Deus lhe Pague*'s success, Joracy Camargo enjoyed a long career in the theatre, not only as a very prolific playwright but also as a director and producer; he later served as president of the Sociedade Brasileira de Autores Teatrais (SBAT). Created in 1917, the SBAT was instrumental in the passing of legislation concerning the rights of actors and playwrights, granting legal statute to performance contracts and regulating copyright and royalty standards. Its role was strengthened with the creation in 1937 of the Associação Brasileira de Críticos Teatrais and the Serviço Nacional de Teatro (SNT), an agency of the Ministry of Education, which at that time was headed by a distinguished intellectual, Gustavo Capanema (1900–1985). The SNT's first director was a playwright of some note, Abadie de Faria Rosa (1889–1945), who had earlier chaired the SBAT. Through several administrations and name changes, the Theatre Institute (SNT; later an arm of the Ministry of Culture called Fundação Nacional de Artes Cênicas, or FUNDACEN) has been a strong promoter of a genuine Brazilian theatre, subsidizing productions of new plays as well as classics, encouraging the growth of a children's theatre, offering incentives for the formation of acting companies and construction of new theatres, and publishing an impressive array of fine theatre material, from the long-overdue definitive editions of the complete works of the country's most important nineteenth-century dramatists to the award-winning texts in its annual monograph and original play contests. Although it has made several attempts at establishing its Companhia Dramática Nacional, the Theatre Institute has been unable to maintain a permanent company. However, this has turned out to be a far from unfortunate development, for it facilitated the survival of existing companies and the creation of new groups, both professional and amateur. The latter in particular have been vitally important to the development of twentieth-century Brazilian theatre. The efforts of Renato Viana and Alvaro and Eugênia Moreyra started to pay off in the late 1930s and early 1940s, with the emergence of several influential amateur groups.

The Teatro do Estudante do Brasil (TEB) was created in 1938 by one of the greatest promoters of the theatre in Brazil, Paschoal Carlos Magno (1906–1980). The TEB was important not only for discovering young acting talent, most notably Cacilda Becker (1921–1969) and Sérgio Cardoso (1925–1972), but also for bringing the theatre to the people in the nation's capital as well as in tours around the country, performing on trucks and boats, sometimes in villages where a play had never before been staged. With a conviction seldom seen among the country's acting companies, the TEB performed Western classics as well as Luso-Brazilian works, from Sophocles and Shakespeare to Gil Vicente and Gonçalves Dias. Noteworthy among the numerous other endeavors of the energetic Paschoal are the hugely successful theatre festivals he organized around the country, the Teatro do Estudante gathering in 1947, and the opening of the 100-seat Teatro Duse in his own Rio de Janeiro residence in 1952.

A parallel development was the emergence of important amateur groups in other parts of the country. In 1941 Waldemar de Oliveira (1900–1977) created the highly successful Teatro de Amadores de Pernambuco, an offshoot of the Grupo Gente Nossa, which Samuel Campelo (1889–1939) had started a decade earlier. Following his creation of the Grupo de Teatro Experimental de São Paulo in 1939, Alfredo Mesquita (1907–1986) served as director (from 1948 to 1969) of the influential Escola de Arte Dramática (EAD) – later incorporated into the University of São Paulo – whose acting company is credited with introducing to Brazil the works of Beckett, Ionesco, and Pinter, as well as the concept of arena theatre (*Depoimentos*, II, 31; Prado, *Apresentação do teatro brasileiro moderno*, 198); one of the EAD's most energetic instructors was the Portuguese-born Luís de Lima (b. 1929), who emphasized the importance of mime on the stage. Other important student groups of the 1940s were the Grupos de Teatro Universitário; Rio de Janeiro's was led by Jerusa Camões (b. 1917) and São Paulo's by Décio de Almeida Prado (b. 1917), who was later to become, along with Sábato Magaldi (b. 1927) and Yan Michalski (1932–1990), one of the nation's foremost theatre critics of the century.

The most lasting contribution of these amateur groups has been the promotion of the stage director to the pivotal position in a production. Before their formal view of the theatre became prevalent, audiences and playwrights alike accepted without much question that valid stagings could be erected around prosaic texts and histrionic actors. Thanks to the work of directors such as Mesquita, Oliveira, and the TEB's Esther Leão (b. 1902) and Maria Jacintha (b. 1910), the quality of acting and of production as a whole reached a level considerably higher than was previously known. Nowhere is this more evident than in the collaboration of another amateur group, Rio de Janeiro's Os Comediantes, with the Polish director Zbigniew Ziembinsky (1908–1978), who emigrated to Brazil in 1941. In many ways the continuation of the Moreyras' Teatro de Brinquedo, Os Comediantes was founded in 1938 by Brutus Pedreira (1904–1964), Tomás Santa Rosa (1909–1956), Luiza Barreto Leite (b. 1912), Agostinho Olavo (1919–1988), and others. Although initially more interested in foreign drama (they started with a production of Pirandello's *Così è se vi Pare*, in a Portuguese version entitled *A Verdade de Cada Um*), the group heeded the advice of Louis Jouvet – who was temporarily residing in Rio de Janeiro – to stage a Brazilian text (Dória, *Moderno teatro*, 75–8, 83–5), settling on Nelson Rodrigues's *Vestido de Noiva* [*The Wedding Dress*]. Ziembinsky's staging of Rodrigues's work marks the beginning of modern theatre in Brazil, more than twenty years after the Modern Art Week fermented the other areas of aesthetic expression. With this highly innovative production (premiered in Rio de Janeiro's Teatro Municipal on December 28, 1943), the Brazilian theatre finally came to terms with the symbolist and expressionist experiments it had ignored earlier in the century. While Oswald de Andrade's potential revolution remained in print and Joracy Camargo's innovation was limited to subject matter, it was left for the team of Rodrigues, Ziembinsky, Santa Rosa, and Os Comediantes to usher in the renovation in acting, sound and lighting, and scenic design.

That *Vestido de Noiva* evolved into the seminal work of twentieth-century Brazilian theatre was due to a number of factors, foremost among them Ziembinsky's staging and the universality of Nelson Rodrigues's vision. The highly stylized production used a multi-level stage divided into three planes standing for reality, memory, and hallucination. The events represented on the latter two levels are a projection of the protagonist's inner self as she experiences a moment of crisis, and do not always reflect what happens on the level of reality. The frequent shifting of the action among the three levels, the elimination of the conventional use of time (except on the level of reality), and the use of distortion and exaggeration suggest the state of flux and confusion of our psychic processes, as well as the conflicts that arise from the disparate perceptions generated by the different components of the mind. Central dualities such as illusion and reality, and fact and fantasy, appear in constant clash as the moribund Alaíde attempts to comprehend her inner crisis. When her condition deteriorates she confuses parts of her past with her imaginary world, which includes a prostitute, Madame Clessy, who gradually leads Alaíde to acknowledge repressed desires and to face the true source of her crisis, which is a conflict with her sister Lúcia over Pedro, the man both women love. Clessy and the characters who only exist on the mental levels disappear when Alaíde dies toward the end of Act III; as a result the layers of memory and hallucination fade away, and reality finally becomes the only experience (Clark and Gazolla, *Twentieth-Century Brazilian Theatre*, 57–60).

Nelson Rodrigues's subsequent plays confirm that the core of his art is an ability to generate theatrical metaphors by mobilizing all the resources of the stage – visual and verbal. Critics have broken the body of Rodrigues's drama into distinct phases. While Sábato Magaldi follows the playwright's terminology and groups the works under "psychological plays," "mythical plays," and "Rio de Janeiro tragedies" (*Nelson Rodrigues*, 1), Hélio Pelegrino divides Rodrigues's theatre into two major phases ("A obra e *O Beijo no Asfalto*," 9–13). The first period, which he calls "mythological cycle" or "mythical comedies," is comprised of the works in which the unconscious mind is explored, whether on a personal or collective level. In addition to *Vestido de Noiva*, this cycle includes *Album de Família* (1967; 1946), *Anjo Negro* (1948; 1948) and other plays that often recall the theatre of Eugene O'Neill. The later works constitute the second phase, which Pelegrino has categorized as the "human comedies" because of the more realistic portrayal of characters and situations, in plays such as *Boca de Ouro* (1960; 1960), *O Beijo no Asfalto* (1961; 1961), and *Toda Nudez Será Castigada* (1965; 1966). In general, however, it can be said that, regardless of cycles and phases, Rodrigues's theatre bears the stamp of Freudian and Jungian psychology as the playwright delves into the unconscious and subconscious strata of the psyche, often presenting his characters as archetypes of human misery and conflict (Clark and Gazolla, *Twentieth-Century Brazilian Theatre*, 53). Throughout Rodrigues's theatre, the playwright's perfect command of the language of his medium accounts for a striking combination of poetry and vulgarity as he portrays a violently prejudiced patriarchal society, in the process exposing – with a mixture of fascination and disgust – all manner of sexual repression, perversions, and taboos.

Following the acclaim accorded Nelson Rodrigues's works, it was finally evident to Brazilian playwrights, directors, and audiences that subject matter could be controversial and characters, complex; that chronology could be disregarded and dialogue, spontaneous; and that settings could be immaterial and lighting, suggestive. Among the many paradoxes attending his career, Rodrigues cherished the role of theatrical innovator as much as he did that of Brazil's reactionary *extraordinaire*; in addition, he was a staunch supporter of the military government of the 1960s and 1970s despite the consistent harassment he faced from a ruthless censorship throughout his career. Yet from such paradoxes – and a profoundly human vision – he fashioned a rich body of work likely to stand as the most enduring of twentieth-century Brazilian theatre.

Ziembinsky's collaboration with Nelson Rodrigues and Os Co-mediantes inspired a new generation of playwrights and theatre-goers and opened the door to other groups and stage directors; thanks to his creative energy and daring sense of innovation, Brazilian *mise-en-scène* finally hit its stride. Soon there came along an impressive roster of other European stage directors and set designers such as the Polish Zygmunt Turkow (1922–1970), the Belgian Maurice Vaneau (b. 1926), and the Italians Aldo Calvo (b. 1911), Bassano Vaccarinni (b. 1914), Gianni Ratto (b. 1916), Ruggero Jacobbi (1919–1981), Alberto d'Aversa (1920–1969), Adolfo Celi (1922–1986), Luciano Salce (b. 1922), and Flaminio Bollini (1924–1978). Before long their ideas were in control of the best that was done in Brazilian theatre; the nation's performing arts are deeply indebted to these individuals for the guidance that expedited the renovation of the 1940s and 1950s. Most of these names were associated at one point or another with the Teatro Brasileiro de Comédia (TBC), a São Paulo group which was as full of innovative energy as Rio de Janeiro's Os Comediantes and just as much of an aesthetic milestone.

Created in 1948 by the Italian–Brazilian industrialist Franco Zampari (1898–1966), the TBC confirmed what was becoming clear ever since the success of the Teatro de Brinquedo and the Teatro do Estudante do Brasil: that the ailing commercial theatre would be salvaged by the new ideas and talent of the amateur groups. No other event in twentieth-century Brazilian theatre better underscores the significance of the collaboration between student, amateur, and professional theatre than the formation of the TBC. Rejecting the prima donna system prevalent in earlier professional companies, the group was fortunate to be able to draw talent from the local, highly respected Escola de Arte Dramática as well as from Rio de Janeiro's most successful amateur groups. After the TBC turned professional in 1949, the possibility of being involved in an aesthetically valid commercial theatre brought to São Paulo such directors and actors as Ziembinsky, Jacobbi, Sérgio Cardoso, Cacilda Becker, and Jardel Filho (1927–1983). Under Zampari's guidance, Salce, Celi, Ratto, and others staged remarkable productions at the Rua Major Diogo theatre, popularizing in Brazil the works of, among others, Pirandello, García Lorca, O'Neill, Arthur Miller, and Tennessee Williams, and launching or consolidating a number of distinguished acting careers, such as those of Paulo Autran (b. 1922), Cleide Yáconis (b. 1923), Sérgio Britto (b. 1923), Tônia Carrero (b. 1928), Raul Cortez (b. 1931), Italo Rossi (b. 1932), Walmor Chagas (b. 1933), Glauce Rocha (1933–1971), and Teresa Raquel (b. 1939).

Catering to the preference of its predominantly bourgeois audiences, the TBC presented mostly foreign drama during its heyday (1948–1958). In the meantime, while hoping that the contemporary Brazilian theatre would catch up with the recent developments, the group looked back to the romantic playwright Antônio Gonçalves Dias (1823–1864), whose *Leonor de Mendonça* (1847) received at long last the careful production that it deserved. In those early years the TBC did, however, stage a small number of works by contemporary Brazilian dramatists, most of which were poorly received. It seems that Brazil's playwrights were slow in rising to the occasion, ill equipped as they were to meet the expectations created by the artistry of Os Comediantes, Ziembinsky, Nelson Rodrigues, and the Zampari group. A contemporary Brazilian author singled out by the TBC during that period was Abílio Pereira de Almeida (1906–1977), whose social comedies were big box-office draws since their themes were of immediate concern to the bourgeois audiences. However, even the best of his works staged by the Zampari group, *Paiol Velho* (1951; 1953) and *Santa Marta Fabril S.A.* (1955; 1955), are superficial treatments of potentially affecting situations and already ring rather hollow only a few decades after being written.

It was not until its last phase (which lasted from 1958 until the group's demise in 1964) that the TBC added more Brazilian plays to its repertoire, including works by such leading contemporary playwrights as Jorge Andrade (Aluízio Jorge Andrade Franco [1922–1984]), Alfredo Dias Gomes (b. 1922), and Gianfrancesco Guarnieri (b. 1934). However, as most critics agree, by then the TBC was in frank artistic decline and heavily in debt, to a great extent because of Zampari's poor managerial skills and disastrous involvement with the Vera Cruz Film Studios; the gloomy financial picture had been compounded by the unwise decision to open a TBC sister-house in Rio de Janeiro. Moreover, Zampari was no longer at the helm, with the artistic direction now in the hands of such *metteurs-en-scène* as Antunes Filho (José Alves Antunes Filho [b. 1929]) and Flávio Rangel (1932–1988), whose ideas on the theatre stood miles apart from the TBC's original tenets. Finally, by that time the big names had left the company to start groups of their own, thus occasioning one of the most significant legacies of the TBC – the spawning of a number of important professional groups such as the Companhias Nydia Lícia–Sérgio Cardoso, Tônia–Celi–Autran, Cacilda Becker, and the Teatro dos Sete; talent schooled in the TBC also fed the incipient Brazilian television of the 1950s and 1960s.

The above-mentioned companies, as well as other groups not originated in the TBC (notably Dulcina–Odilon, Henriette Morineau–Artistas Unidos, Maria Della Costa–Sandro Polloni–Teatro Popular de Arte), offered a mixed fare of commercial and artistic theatre. The commercial side of these endeavors was a major factor in the success of the urban sophisticated comedy of the 1950s. Partly a regression to the comedies of manner of earlier decades, partly a catching-up with the best commercial theatre in the United States and Europe, the cosmopolitan comedies of Henrique Pongetti (1898–1979), Raymundo Magalhães Júnior (1907–1982), Pedro Bloch (b. 1914), Millôr Fernandes (b. 1924), and João Bethencourt (b. 1924) often presented themes and locales not intrinsically Brazilian. José da Silveira Sampaio (1914–1964), in turn, satirized the foibles and travails of his fellow *cariocas* in *A Incoveniência de Ser Esposa* (1948; 1961), *Flagrantes do Rio* (1951; 1968), and other plays, while Guilherme Figueiredo (b. 1915) achieved artistic as well as commercial success in Brazil and abroad with his updatings of the plots and language of Aesop, Plautus, Aristophanes, and other authors of classical Antiquity, most notably in *Um Deus Dormiu lá em Casa* (1949; 1957) [*A God Slept Here*] and *A Raposa e as Uvas* (1953; 1958). Figueiredo and Pongetti also wrote children's theatre, a genre that hit its stride in the 1950s with the creation, in 1951, of Rio de Janeiro's Tablado by Maria Clara Machado (b. 1921), the greatest figure in children's theatre in Brazil, whose best and most beloved work remains *Pluft, o Fantasminha* (1953; 1957). Other important names in this genre are Lúcia Benedetti (b. 1914), Stella Leonardos (b. 1923), and Tônio Carvalho (b. 1944).

In its turn, the popular theatre experienced a major boost with the creation in 1953 of the Teatro de Arena de São Paulo. Under the guidance of José Renato (Renato José Pécora [b. 1926]), a graduate of the Escola de Arte Dramática, several young actors formed a group with the resolve of steering clear of the prevalent socially alienated theatre. Rejecting the TBC for representing all the wrongs of the bourgeois theatre (grandiose, often wasteful productions, with the proscenium theatre and alienating texts entailing physical as well as ideological distance from the public), the company adopted a concept that, harking back to the early theatre and also the circus, had been previously put to use in the Soviet Union, Western Europe, and the United States, where it became known as "theatre-in-the-round" or "arena stage." This model enabled the Arena to stage low-budget productions that began to galvanize a younger, more socially aware audience for whom the theatre became a means of political expression at a time of nationwide heated debate over the merits of quick industrialization dependent on foreign capital.

In 1956 Gianfrancesco Guarnieri and Oduvaldo Viana Filho (Vianinha; 1936–1974) joined the group when the Arena absorbed the Teatro Paulista do Estudante, and shortly afterwards Augusto Boal (b. 1931) also associated himself with the company upon returning to Brazil after studying drama at Columbia University. Having initiated a series of ground-breaking Seminários de Dramaturgia [Drama Workshops] for the cast and the general public, Boal was named artistic director of the company. Under Boal, the Arena was the most important theatre group in the country until its demise in 1971 following his imprisonment, torture, and exile. In addition to introducing the Brechtian model to the Brazilian stage, Boal developed a valuable set of acting exercises as well as the Arena's own acting method, the "sistema coringa": in stark contrast to the star system, this "Joker system" required actors to switch roles so that every actor would play all roles, even the smallest parts; the key figure was the Joker, who functioned as narrator and commentator, encouraging the public to see the play critically rather than involving themselves emotionally in the represented action.

As an exile in Argentina, Peru, Portugal, and France, Boal continued experimenting with innovative techniques such as "teatro-jornal" ["newspaper theatre"], "teatro invisível" ["invisible theatre"], and "teatro foro" ["courtroom theatre"]. His theoretical works are among the best writings on the theatre ever to appear in Latin America. In *Teatro del Oprimido y otras poéticas políticas* (1974) [*Theatre of the Oppressed*], the highly original poetics of a theatre for the liberation of the oppressed, Boal takes to task most of the Western theatre, from Aristotle to bourgeois drama, for shunning political commitment, siding with the ruling class, and ignoring the masses. Drawing from Brechtian theory as well as from the ideology of the pedagogical method developed by Paulo Freire (b.

1921), Boal counters what he denounces as Aristotle's age-long artistic and political intimidation of the audience by arguing that all theatre is necessarily political, and that the spectator must be made conscious of his or her oppression in order to become a protagonist in the liberation process.

Critics point out distinct periods in the history of the Teatro de Arena de São Paulo (Dória, *Moderno teatro*, 164–5; Boal, *Teatro do Oprimido*, 185–97). Slight differences in terminology aside, the company experienced four phases. The first emphasized foreign realist drama as the group attempted to put into practice the ideas discussed in their Drama Workshops. The second phase, which paid attention to Brazilian social drama, launched the playwriting careers of, among others, Guarnieri and Vianna Filho with the unequivocal successes of *Eles Não Usam Black Tie* (1958; 1959) and *Chapetuba Futebol Clube* (1959; 1959), respectively; in addition to Guarnieri and Vianinha, the cast now included such gifted young actors as Milton Gonçalves (b. 1933), Flávio Migliaccio (b. 1934), and Nelson Xavier (b. 1941), who were joined later by Paulo José (b. 1937), Dina Sfat (1938–1989), and many others. The third, and perhaps least relevant, stage attempted to impart a Brazilian character to such classics of the Western theatre as Machiavelli's *La Mandragola*, Lope de Vega's *El Mejor Alcalde El Rey*, and Molière's *Tartuffe*.

The fourth period introduced the "Joker system" as the group experimented with a new formula of a Brazilian musical steeped in Brechtian praxis. This phase also confirmed Boal's talent as a dramatist (intimated in earlier works such as *Revolução na América do Sul* [1960]), given the acclaim accorded *Arena Conta Zumbi* (1965; 1970) and *Arena Conta Tiradentes* (performed 1967), two plays he co-authored with Guarnieri, welcoming, as always, the input of the cast. It was the playwrights' goal in staging colonial history to pitch their public into the colonial mood by having The Joker reinterpret history, thus destroying the myths perpetuated by the Luso-Brazilianist perspective of the ruling classes. Moreover, the public was expected to see in the struggle of both heroes of the colonial past a call for action against the latter-day oppressor, the military regime then in control of the nation. The *Arena Conta* performances bespoke the authors' and director's visceral sense of theatricality. In their hands, the plays drew an immediate responsiveness from the audiences, who played a vital role in the productions, reacting as they did to the intense experience while the vibrant music of Edu Lobo (b. 1937) resonated on the almost naked stage. At a time of dwindling civil liberties, attending the performances became an act of political protest for the public that packed the Arena playhouse (*Zumbi* ran for eighteen months in São Paulo alone).

Guarnieri's co-authorship of the *Arena Conta* musicals had been preceded by the plays that established him as the most committed playwright of the time. *Eles Não Usam Black Tie* develops around the conflict between Otávio, a long-time union activist, and his son, Tião, over striking at the plant where both men work. Only the slum-dwelling, working-class characters – represented by Otávio – adhere to principle and loyalty, while the city people, although never seen on stage, are presented as corrupt and – because of the implication that they have influenced Tião's decision to cross the picket lines – corrupting. *A Semente* (1961; 1961) also depicts the world of factory workers and their families. Here they face organized repression of their struggle for better pay and safer working conditions. A longer and ideologically more sound work than *Black Tie*, *A Semente* delves deep into the dilemmas besetting Agileu, a communist union leader who must reconcile all sorts of personal needs and domestic dramas with his adamantly impartial devotion to the cause he has espoused. Introducing to the Brazilian stage Marxist protagonists (more than a quarter-century after *Deus lhe Pague*) and an honest concern for the plight of the poor, *Black Tie* and *A Semente* became Guarnieri's compassionate, meticulously crafted, and profoundly affecting paean to the working people of Brazil.

The most distinguished name among African-Brazilian playwrights is Abdias do Nascimento (b. 1914), the tireless promoter of black theatre in Brazil and founder in 1944 of the important Teatro Experimental do Negro (TEN). The TEN was instrumental in training black actors and theatre technicians, encouraging the writing of plays that reflect black culture, and raising the consciousness of both Blacks and Whites about the existence of racism in Brazil's much-touted "racial democracy." The best plays commissioned by the group were later published in an anthology edited by Nascimento, *Drama para Negros e um Prólogo para Brancos* (1961). The acting careers launched by the TEN include those of Aguinaldo Camargo (1915–1952), Zeni Pereira (b. 1925), and Ruth de Souza (b. 1929). Among the most notable black actors and actresses in contemporary Brazilian theatre are Grande Otelo, Milton Gonçalves, Antônio Pitanga (b. 1939), and Zezé Mota (b. 1944).

The trend toward genuine stage representation of the people of Brazil facilitated the emergence of another hallmark of the 1950s and early 1960s, a strong regionalist theatre. Giving the Brazilian theatre several superlative plays and launching a number of important playwriting careers, this mostly northeastern phenomenon belied the notion that, in matters of the stage during this period, as Rio de Janeiro and São Paulo went, so went the rest of the nation. Seldom has the Brazilian theatre scene accorded a new play the attention paid to the *Auto da Compadecida* [*The Rogue's Trial*] by Paraíba-born Ariano Suassuna (b. 1927). The enormous impact of its premiere (by the Teatro Adolescente, under the direction of

Clênio Wanderley) in Recife's Teatro Santa Isabel on September 11, 1956, was duplicated during its tour of the south the following year. The work is deeply rooted in Medieval miracle plays, *commedia dell'arte*, Gil Vicente, and Calderón. In addition, some Brechtian elements are blended with the rich traditions of the circus, *cordel* [folk narrative], and *sertanejo* culture that are so familiar to the playwright. This fusion of fable and reality, in which Jesus Christ and the Virgin coexist with humble peasants and *cangaceiros* [rural bandits], makes way for a few masterstrokes of ingenuity, such as casting a black actor as Christ. That the *Auto da Compadecida* became a contemporary classic was due not only to the simplicity of story line, mixed with the subtle and highly affecting treatment of powerful universal issues of human nature, but also to the ability of Suassuna's theatre to transcend mockery and become a profoundly pertinent social and anticlerical criticism.

The *auto* form lended itself well to Suassuna's art, with a strong social component adroitly added to the religious frame prevalent in Anchieta's colonial theatre. This is equally true of works by other northeastern playwrights who have turned to, and often adapted, the traditional form as a vehicle for the expression of social and political protest. Another preeminent example of this trend is *Morte e Vida Severina: Auto de Natal Pernambucano* (1956) by Pernambuco-born João Cabral de Melo Neto (b. 1920). The intention to moralize, however, is not so conspicuous in *Morte e Vida* as it is in *Compadecida*, and verse has replaced the lively dialogue of Suassuna's play. The social concern is nevertheless a central feature of Cabral de Melo's *auto*. Fleeing from the drought-ridden, parched *sertão* [backlands] in search of a better life in the coastal city of Recife, the protagonist witnesses along the way widespread misery and disease, which are linked to the outrageously unfair income distribution and lack of land reform in the northeast of Brazil. By virtue of his name, the most frequent among the poor peasants of the region, Severino is a northeastern Everyman, a representative of his fellow victims of economic exploitation and political oppression. As the title's word sequence suggests, he is also the individual who must undertake a parallel journey from despair to hope. The moment of change occurs during the focal point of the play – an *auto*-within-the-*auto* which depicts the birth of an infant in a slum in the *mangues* [swamps] of Recife. Blending political and religious elements (the premature, emaciated child is born to a woman named Maria and a man named José, who is a carpenter by trade), this modern-day Nativity among the destitute prefigures a new age of equality and justice. Under the direction of Silnei Siqueira (b. 1934), another graduate of the Escola de Arte Dramática, *Morte e Vida Severina* was produced in 1965 by the Teatro da Universidade Católica de São Paulo, with music by Chico Buarque (Francisco Buarque de Holanda, b. 1944); widely acclaimed in Brazil and Europe, the production was awarded first prize in the 1966 Nancy Theatre Festival in France.

Other Pernambuco-born dramatists of note are Joaquim Cardozo (1897–1978), José Carlos Cavalcanti Borges (1910–1983), Osman Lins (1924–1978), and, especially, Hermilo Borba Filho (1917–1976), who wrote original plays as well as theatre history and criticism, devoting particular attention to popular dramatic traditions such as the Christmas pageant of *bumba-meu-boi* and the *mamulengo* puppet theatre. An early champion of the theatre of Suassuna and other young playwrights, the tireless Hermilo also helped to create the Teatro do Estudante de Pernambuco (1946) and the Teatro Popular do Nordeste (1957), which in turn influenced the formation of Recife's Movimento Popular de Cultura (MPC) and Rio de Janeiro's Centro Popular de Cultura (CPC). The MPC, led by another tireless promoter of the theatre, Luiz Mendonça (b. 1931), was created during the Miguel Arraes administration, while the latter functioned as the theatre extension of the União Nacional dos Estudantes (UNE). Inspired by the Cuban Revolution, the peasant movement of the northeast, UNE's radical politics, Paulo Freire's literacy project, and even some issues debated initially in the Theatre Workshops of the Teatro de Arena, both MPC and CPC rejected the capitalist orientation of bourgeois theatre, favoring instead collective creation and spare productions in improvised theatres such as shantytowns, factories, sugar mills, community centers, and school yards.

Many regionalist playwrights turned their attention to the farce, a genre in which Suassuna also excelled, not so much because the views and stories of his early years in the *sertão* remained the wellspring of his theatre but because of his familiarity with the classics of the genre, such as Plautus's *Aulularia*, of which *O Santo e a Porca* (1964) is a highly effective adaptation, as evidenced in its first production (by the Teatro Cacilda Becker, under Ziembinsky's direction, in 1958). Noteworthy farces by dramatists from other parts of Brazil include *A Farsa da Esposa Perfeita* (1959; 1960) by Edy Lima (b. 1921) from Rio Grande do Sul, who was a member of the Arena group, and *O Santo Milagroso* (1963; 1967) by Lauro César Muniz (b. 1938) from São Paulo, who also attended the Escola de Arte Dramática.

Although long-time Rio de Janeiro residents, two dramatists born in the northeast wrote important regionalist plays. Raquel de Queiroz (b. 1910), who is from Ceará, is the author of *Lampião* (1954; Rio de Janeiro, 1953) and *A Beata Maria do Egito* (1958; 1958) while Dias Gomes, who is originally from Bahia, has produced several works in this vein. Although his first dramatic pieces (written for Procópio Ferreira and Jaime Costa) date back to the 1940s, Dias Gomes interrupted his playwriting career during most of the 1950s while he worked for radio and television stations.

The relevant phase of Dias Gomes's theatre starts with *O Pagador de Promessas* [*Payment as Pledged*], which opened on July 29, 1960, in the Teatro Brasileiro de Comédia – the same house, fittingly enough, which had seen an earlier generation redefine the Brazilian theatre. Although the building was the same, the TBC had gone through a radical ideological transformation that included the staging of Brazilian plays genuinely concerned with the plight of the people. The production marked the directorial debut of Flávio Rangel at the TBC and established the reputation of Leonardo Villar (b. 1923) and Natália Timberg (b. 1929) as major performers.

Due to a highly effective presentation of local color (including a game of *capoeira* and several instances of religious syncretism), main characters, and language, *O Pagador de Promessas* stands as the absolute paradigm of Brazilian regionalist drama. Dias Gomes's merit as a playwright lies in the fact that he is able to incorporate these elements and still present us with a universally valid work. The simple plot line centers around a poor farmer's attempt to fulfill a promise he has made in return for the cure of his donkey Nicolau. Zé do Burro, the protagonist, is an uncomplicated man who does not distinguish between Catholic saints and *candomblé* deities and thus cannot understand why he is denied entrance in the Church of Santa Bárbara in Salvador, where he has promised to deliver the full-scale cross he has carried on his back for several miles. Zé is unable to relate to the urban mind-set (lack of communication is a central theme of the play) and he becomes the victim of church intolerance and exploitation at the hands of politicians, businessmen, and a sensationalist press; even his marriage is suddenly at risk, for his wife, Rosa, who has accompanied him, is seduced by a local pimp.

While Padre Olavo, the parish priest, is undeniably intransigent, Zé too is himself inflexible in his views and resolve to keep his promise. In this respect he represents the Individual who must assert his autonomy before the overwhelming and insensitive forces of an Institution, or of Society as a whole. When the Bishop proposes to relieve Zé of his obligation, the peasant declines the offer. This uncompromising stance becomes Zé's *hamartia* [tragic flaw] and the protagonist thus assumes an almost tragic stature; the play also includes other elements of classical tragedy such as the unities of time, action, and place, a five-part structure, and a denouement which involves the unforeseen death of the hero (Lyday, "The Theater of Alfredo Dias Gomes," 222; Rosenfeld, *O mito e o herói no moderno teatro brasileiro*, 52–4, 58–62, 73–5). The end of *O Pagador de Promessas* reinforces the portrayal of the protagonist as a Christ figure and establishes Zé do Burro as the unwitting leader of a nascent popular revolt when, ironically, his dead body is carried on the cross and into the church he was not allowed to enter in life.

Dias Gomes has written other intriguing regionalist plays. The fourteen-scene *A Revolução dos Beatos* (1962) is a satire of the fanaticism and political and commercial exploitation surrounding the controversial figure of Padre Cícero Romão Batista (1844–1934), who was excommunicated for disobedience and unsubstantiated claims of miracles worked in Juazeiro do Norte, in the northeastern state of Ceará. The thirteen-scene *O Berço do Herói* (1965), which takes place in a fictional town in the interior of the state of Bahia, was banned outright from the stage by the government censors. Like *A Revolução dos Beatos, O Berço do Herói* represents a marked departure from the mostly serious tone and classical structure of *O Pagador de Promessas*; the concern for individual freedom in a capitalist society is nonetheless as central to *O Berço* as it is to *O Pagador*. Moreover, like several of the plays that followed *O Pagador de Promessas, O Berço do Herói* departs from the Realism of the 1960 play by including split stages, multi-media experiments and such Brechtian techniques as distantiation and breaking the action into numerous short scenes that advance the narrative style.

O Berço do Herói sets its premise like a timebomb and then proceeds to poke intermittent fun at the situations which unravel as the protagonist – who was believed to have died a hero's death at war – returns home to the town which had derived considerable economic prosperity from its native son's posthumous fame. When the rather unheroic details of Cabo Jorge's desertion become known, those who stand to lose most from his return arrange for his murder. As in *O Pagador de Promessas* and *A Revolução dos Beatos*, secondary characters provide much of the local color in *O Berço do Herói*; they are essentially stereotypes but they perform the important function of representing the insensitive forces of society fighting to perpetuate a corrupt establishment (Clark and Gazolla, *Twentieth-Century Brazilian Theatre*, 95).

Other important Dias Gomes plays, although not in the regionalist vein, are two works set among the poor in modern-day Rio de Janeiro. *A Invasão* (1962) vividly depicts the actions of a group of dispossessed people as they attempt in vain to avert the indignities entailed by inadequate housing. Very different in tone and form is *Doutor Getúlio, sua Vida e sua Glória* (1968), written (in a combination of prose and popular verse) with the poet Ferreira Gullar (José Ribamar Ferreira, b. 1930). A sympathetic portrayal of the one-time dictator, the play adroitly juxtaposes the lives of slum-dwelling members of a samba school and the career of the populist politician, which will be the theme of the pageant the samba group is rehearsing for the next Carnival parade.

Dias Gomes's interest in historical drama also appears in *O Santo Inquérito* (Rio de Janeiro, 1966). Although different from *Doutor Getúlio* in form, technique, setting, and historical time, *O Santo Inquérito* also succeeds as an examination of an episode of the national past. To a large extent because of the strong characterization of its protagonist, Branca Dias, the work is as triumphant a celebration of individual freedom within intolerant society as *O Pagador de Promessas*. The 1966 play, however, includes an element absent in *Doutor Getúlio* and *O Pagador*, for it alludes through allegory to the political situation of the mid-1960s in Brazil. Through the depiction of an investigation by the Holy Office in eighteenth-century Paraíba, the play seeks to raise the public's awareness of the suppression by the military of all forms of dissent.

Dias Gomes has given the national stage a number of memorable characters and plot lines and, despite his considerable difficulties with official censorship throughout his career, some of his plays stand among the most important in twentieth-century Brazilian theatre. Three of his dramatic works have had phenomenal success in other media as well: the film version of *O Pagador de Promessas* was awarded the first prize in major international film festivals (including Cannes, in 1962), while *O Berço do Herói* and *Odorico, o Bem-Amado* (1963), a satire of corrupt and hypocritical Brazilian politicians, achieved tremendous popularity as *telenovelas*. In fact, the Globo Network adaptation of *O Berço do Herói* (entitled *Roque Santeiro*, 1985–1986) became the most popular program of all time on Brazilian television.

Another important playwright of the 1950s and early 1960s is the Niterói-born Antônio Callado (b. 1917), whose *Pedro Mico* (1957; 1957), a compelling drama about life in the slums of Rio de Janeiro, in many ways parallels Guarnieri's *Gimba, o Presidente dos Valentes* (1959; 1959). Callado's interest in Regionalism and political theatre merged in *Forró no Engenho Cananéia* (1964). He has also written plays about the plight of Brazilian Indians (*Frankel* [1955]). Like several other white playwrights, such as Zora Seljan (b. 1918), Callado has a strong interest in African-Brazilian theatre. He has authored several plays on black themes, four of which are gathered in *A Revolta da Cachaça: Teatro Negro* (1983).

Jorge Andrade is São Paulo's foremost regionalist playwright. His play *A Moratória* (1956) opened the five-year period of greatest success in the Brazilian theatre that also included the premieres of *Auto da Compadecida*, *Eles Não Usam Black Tie*, and *O Pagador de Promessas*. The work of the quintessential *paulista* dramatist, Andrade's theatre chronicles the history of the São Paulo coffee aristocracy in a ten-play cycle the playwright later entitled *Marta, a Árvore e o Relógio*. The plays gathered in *Marta, a Árvore e o Relógio* comprise eight previously published works rearranged to suit historical chronology and two new pieces, *As Confra-*

rias and *O Sumidouro*, written specifically to serve as the Cycle's prologue and epilogue, respectively (Moser, "Jorge Andrade's São Paulo Cycle," 17–23). Furthermore, as Andrade readied the texts for the 1970 volume he rewrote some scenes and added references to passages and characters in other plays of the Cycle, deftly working new, relevant material into a complex and diverse tapestry that includes tragedy (*Pedreira das Almas* [1960]) as well as comedy (*Os Ossos do Barão* [1964]), and social history (*Vereda da Salvação* [1965]) as well as autobiography (*Rasto Atrás* [1967]). Infused with the traditions of Andrade's native state – the playwright himself was a descendant of rich coffee planters – the São Paulo Cycle is a vividly re-created panorama of a particular time (from late eighteenth to mid twentieth centuries), place (the mostly rural state of São Paulo), and circumstance (origin, heyday, and decadence of the rural oligarchy in the course of several generations).

Dedicated to Alfredo Mesquita, who was the playwright's professor and mentor at the Escola de Arte Dramática, *A Moratória* is probably Jorge Andrade's finest hour. Everything that was admirable about his later work is present here: the compassion, the delight in resilience, the unsentimental reverence for the past. The three elements symbolically alluded to in the title of the Cycle are also to be found in *A Moratória*: the tenacious woman, the attachment to the land, the love of family in spite of generation conflicts and economic debacle. The play's first production (Teatro Maria Della Costa, São Paulo, 1955) featured the direction of Gianni Ratto and launched the career of Fernanda Montenegro (b. 1929), who played the role of Lucília. Ratto made outstanding use of a divided stage, which, as specified in the sidetext, allowed for the action to take place concurrently in 1929 and 1932, with each set depicting the conse-quences for a coffee planter's family of the momentous political and economic changes then occurring in Brazil.

The other pinnacle in Jorge Andrade's career was *Vereda da Salvação*. That its first production (by the TBC, in 1964, under the direction of Antunes Filho) was the last in the group's history has considerable significance in modern Brazilian theatre, not only because it closes the TBC chapter but, most importantly, because it places the poor centerstage in Jorge Andrade's theatre. In a marked departure from the decadent rural oligarchy of earlier plays, *Vereda* gives preeminence to the peasants, a group heretofore virtually ignored by the playwright. More extensively victimized by the economic disaster and deprived of such relief options as moratoria, marriage to rich immigrants, or nostalgia for a happier past, the tenant farmers react to loss in ways radically different from those of their former employers. Mirroring the real-life episode the play is based on, the sharecroppers turn to religious fanaticism as their only hope for redemption. Furthermore, again as in the actual events in the village of

Catulé, their dreams are destroyed by police intervention and the ensuing final massacre of the peasants suggests that, however different the economic picture, violent repression remains a central element in the way the Brazilian elites respond to social unrest.

Emphasis on collective action as seen in *Vereda da Salvação* and other Brazilian plays of the 1950s and early 1960s was hardly acceptable to the military regime installed in April of 1964. The armed forces and the conservative civilians who assumed control of the political process had a visceral distrust of the CPC, MPC, and popular theatre in general. However, in spite of such repressive measures as the closing-down of the CPC and MPC, the period of creativity which had characterized the Brazilian theatre since about 1955 did not come to a sudden halt immediately after the military coup. In its first years the regime was relatively moderate and somehow the theatre continued to thrive. Texts whose contestatory nature was transparent were still allowed to be staged. One example of this reluctant tolerance was the 1965 production of *Liberdade, Liberdade* (1965). Created by Millôr Fernandes and Flávio Rangel, the show was a collage of text and music extolling individual freedom and democratic rule throughout Western civilization; without making too many direct references to the situation in Brazil, the authors left it for the public to draw the not-too-difficult analogy. Co-produced by Teatro de Arena and Grupo Opinião, *Liberdade, Liberdade* had a long run in Rio de Janeiro before embarking on a triumphant tour of the country.

Opinião was started in Rio de Janeiro in 1964 under the leadership of Armando Costa (1933–1984), João das Neves (b. 1934), Ferreira Gullar, Oduvaldo Viana Filho, and other former members of the CPC. The group took its name from the successful musical by the same title (1965). *Opinião* was staged by Boal in December of 1964, with text by Vianinha, Costa, Boal, and Paulo Pontes (1940–1976), music by Zé Keti and João do Valle, and featuring the noted singers Nara Leão (1942–1989) in the Rio de Janeiro production, and Maria Bethânia (b. 1944) in the staging of the play the following year in São Paulo. *Opinião*, along with the already-mentioned *Arena Conta* plays, was part of the musical trend that prevailed between 1964 and 1968 as the theatre cautiously tested its adversaries. The use of popular music – Brazil's eminently national cultural expression – created a common idiom of spontaneous interaction which facilitated the ideological complicity between theatre and theatre-goers (Schwarz, "Cultura, 1964–1969," 81; Damasceno, *Cultural Space and Theatrical Conventions in the Works of Oduvaldo Viana Filho*, 143, 159).

It soon became apparent, however, that the rule of exception would last much longer than the period of transition it was initially thought to be.

The resulting impasse of democracy and culture was deftly conveyed in another enormously successful Opinião production, the aptly titled *Se Correr o Bicho Pega, se Ficar o Bicho Come* (1966), which was staged in 1966 under the direction of Gianni Ratto (formerly of the TBC) with an impressive cast led by Vianinha, Odete Lara (b. 1929), Agildo Ribeiro (b. 1932), and Hugo Carvana (b. 1937). The authors, Vianinha and Ferreira Gullar, were particularly inspired in their selection of the farce to refer allegorically to the political atmosphere of the time. They were equally fortunate in adapting Brechtian techniques to the popular themes, and song and verse form, of the *cordel* tradition in order to present a clever, often hilarious, plot that builds up to a dramatic impasse symbolic of the political closure (the "beast" of the title) of the mid 1960s.

Opinião thus marked the emergence as a major playwright of Viana Filho, a former member of the CPC whose career had started in the Arena Workshops, and whose first play, *Chapetuba Futebol Clube*, was staged by the São Paulo group in 1959. The triumphs and the burdens of the Brazilian theatre during the military regime come together in the career of Vianinha, who continued to write steadily throughout the dictatorship until his untimely death in 1974. His plays are bound together by some unifying themes: middle-class alienation, conflict of generations, the challenges of economic survival and political activism.

Vianinha's political commitment is evident from the beginning of his career. In 1964, the year of the military take-over, his play *Quatro Quadras de Terra*, a passionate denunciation of social injustice in rural Brazil, received the prestigious Latin American Theatre Award from Cuba's Casa de las Américas. In 1968, the year of the radicalization of the regime, another of his plays, *Papa Highirte*, sparked a serious controversy within the Brazilian government itself, as one of its agencies, the Serviço Nacional de Teatro – unaware of the author's identity, since manuscripts were submitted anonymously – awarded the play first prize in its annual Concurso Nacional de Teatro, and honored the publication contract to which all first-prize winners are traditionally entitled. The Justice Department's reaction was as adamant as it was swift: all but a few copies were apprehended, a nationwide ban – not lifted until 1979 – was imposed on performances of the play, and the annual contest itself was discontinued until 1974, when, ironically, the entire process was repeated, with Vianinha again taking first prize (for *Rasga Coração*), the SNT again honoring the publication contract (actually deferred until 1980), and the Justice Department again imposing a nationwide ban – as with that of *Papa*, not lifted until 1979 – on productions of the work (Michalski, *O palco amordaçado*, 71, 84, 89, 94).

In vivid flashbacks, *Papa Highirte* depicts the brutal workings of a Latin American dictator who, while now in exile, still plots to regain power and to resume the imposition on his people of the atrocities portrayed or mentioned in the play. On the other hand, *Rasga Coração*, finished only weeks prior to the author's death, has none of *Papa Highirte*'s energetic candor. Vianinha's last play provides a tender commentary on the nature of the Brazilian national character while casting a sympathetic, if somewhat cynical, eye at the country's political scene between 1930 and 1970.

While there are similarities between *Papa Highirte* and *Rasga Coração*, the differing attitudes toward autocratic rule expressed therein are significant enough to identify the two plays as vehicles for the opposing strategies employed by the playwright to give theatrical configuration to repression. Thus, while violence is rather graphic and torture figures prominently in *Papa Highirte*, aggression in *Rasga Coração* is quietly accepted as a necessary element of the political struggle. Moreover, while in *Papa Highirte* the victims are presented as uncompromising idealists at the hands of a ruthless dictatorship, in *Rasga Coração* the oppressed falter in their commitments. The play's central figure, Manguari Pistolão, a former political activist who had been at odds with his father, now expects his son Luca to submit to repression. Like his father before him, Luca will not abide by the rules of the establishment (illustrated in his case by a ban on long hair in the classroom), drops out of school, and moves out of his parents' home. By portraying three generations struggling between idealism and security, protest and acceptance, *Rasga Coração* points to a cyclical pattern, of conformity prevailing over resistance to repression, in Brazilian politics from the Revolution of 1930 to the early 1970s.

Vianinha's switch from the Realism of his first works to the heightened quality that informs *Rasga Coração* helped allay his own misgivings about the onesidedness that blemishes earlier works such as *Quatro Quadras de Terra*. Moreover, the almost oneiric aura around *Rasga Coração* is commensurate with the playwright's sympathy for the older generation of left-wing activists. For, while the father–son conflict appears prominently in Vianinha's dramaturgy, from such early plays as *Os Azeredos mais os Benevides* to such later works as *A Longa Noite de Cristal* (Guimarães, *Um ato de resistência*, 69–71, 76–7, 119–22), it is not until his very last play that Vianinha takes a definite stand and sides with the older generation of leftists, which he calls "o revolucionário" ["the Revolutionary"] as opposed to the merely "novo" ["New"] of the younger rebels. Thus, *Rasga Coração* rejects, as inefficient, characters who represent a wide range of political attitudes, from the "novo antigo" ["the old New"] of Castro Cott, the *Integralista* [member of the Brazilian Fascist Party] of the 1930s, to the "novo anárquico" ["the new Anarchy"] of Lord Bundinha, the Anarchist of the 1930s, and Luca, the hippie of the early 1970s. Seen under a considerably more favorable light is Luca's father, Manguari, a representative of the communist activists of the 1930s and 1940s and, apparently thanks to a good deal of compromising, a survivor of much political repression.

Each generation depicted in *Rasga Coração* includes a politically conscious character who embodies the belief held by the playwright, toward the end of his career, that, given the realities of Brazil's culture and national temperament, some degree of moderation is essential for success-ful participation in that country's politics. Thus, just as in the 1930s Manguari's restraint is favored over Castro Cott's exuberance, in the 1970s the moderate Camargo Moço prevails over the uncompromising Luca. The thrust of Vianinha's last play owes much of its powerfulness to the credibility of the character Camargo Moço. It is mostly due to his caution during the student rebellion that Camargo Moço, in marked contrast with the wayward Luca, can come through as the constructive element in the represented conflict. Ironically, Luca (named after Luís Carlos Prestes [1898–1990], who was for several decades the respected leader of the Brazilian Communist Party) is hardly the image of the "Cavaleiro da Esperança" ("Knight of Hope," as Prestes was known) and Camargo Moço, rather than Manguari Pistolão's son, is presented as the embodiment of hope in the fight against those who advocate the perpetuation of Brazil's unfair socio-economic system.

A third important theatre group, Oficina, shared the limelight with Arena and Opinião for most of the 1960s. The company, founded in São Paulo in 1958, was led by José Celso Martínez Correa (b. 1937), who at first cultivated links with Boal and the Arena group and, later, with an influential director and acting teacher, the Russian-born Eugênio Kusnet (1898–1975). For the best part of fifteen years, as he directed the Oficina in one revolutionary staging after the other, Zé Celso came to personify a genuine belief in the vindication of an avant-garde theatre in urban Brazil. The group's eclectic repertoire included Brazilian as well as foreign plays; among the latter, Gorky's *The Petit Bourgeois* and *Enemies*, Max Frisch's *Andorra*, and Brecht's *Galileo* and *In the Jungle of the Cities*. Their most successful undertaking, however, was the staging in 1967 of Oswald de Andrade's *O Rei da Vela*, with the main roles played by the other three principals of the group, Renato Borghi (b. 1937), Fernando Peixoto (b. 1937), and Itala Nandi (b. 1942). The remarkable production was based on a *tropicalista* notion of Brazilian reality which emphasized the assimilation by Brazilians themselves of a foreign, grotesquely exotic view of the country. By theatrically distorting a cultural distortion the group turned Oswald's text into a landmark spectacle of caustic humor and savage aggressiveness. Oficina's reclaiming of Oswald's play parallels another major restoration of the 1960s, that of the theatre of Qorpo-Santo (José Joaquim de Campos Leão, 1829–1883), whose short, unusual, highly satirical works began to be staged one hundred years after their composition.

Because Oficina subscribed to most of the tenets of Artaud's Theatre of Cruelty, their productions were widely misunderstood by a large segment of the public. There was a generalized perception among bourgeois theatre-goers that Zé Celso and Oficina meant to provoke the most negative response to the spectacle with an arrogant disregard for the mental and physical well-being of the audience. In sum, it was widely believed that Oficina subscribed to the notion that theatre is theatre at its best when it is most extreme and disruptive.

What the group did, however, was to call the theatre into question while still working within its framework. As their subsequent productions showed, Oficina's highly unorthodox approach still included an absolute love of the theatre. Works such as the collage *Gracias, Señor* (produced in 1972) illustrate the group's view of acting as an intense, almost religious, experience through which a generation's feeling of profound discontentment could be expressed. There was thus created around Oficina an aura of countercultural redemption, which was at least in part responsible for the group's problems. Zé Celso's task became increasingly difficult as the hard-line regime coupled intolerance with violence in their dealings with the arts, until it was no longer possible to keep the Oficina in operation. The group disbanded after the 1973 production of Chekhov's *Three Sisters*. The following year Zé Celso was arrested by the military and released after intense pressure from the international artistic community. Forced into exile, he left for Portugal and later, Mozambique, where for several years he was involved in the practice of revolutionary theatre and film.

Zé Celso's only production outside the Oficina in the 1960s was *Roda Viva* (1967) by Chico Buarque (b. 1944), which opened in Rio de Janeiro's Teatro Princesa Isabel in January of 1968. The staging, seemingly designed to jolt the spectators out of their political passivity, included a good deal of crudity and aggressiveness, which in turn elicited a violent backlash from the extreme right. With tacit government approval, the paramilitary forces of the infamous Comando de Caça aos Comunistas (CCC) attacked the cast when the play was staged in São Paulo, virtually destroying the Teatro Ruth Escobar in July of 1968. The violence was repeated during the Porto Alegre run in September, and performances of *Roda Viva*, one of the most controversial works in all of Brazilian theatre, were interrupted shortly thereafter when the federal censors invoked vague notions of "national security" to ban the play from the stages.

After the promulgation of the Fifth Institutional Act [AI-5] in December of 1968, the scope of theatrical activity in Brazil was severely limited. Nevertheless, the theatre came to represent resistance to the military dictatorship. Whereas financial dictates forced a number of dramatists (including such prestigious names as Dias Gomes and Vianinha) to turn to television scriptwriting, other theatre professionals were undaunted by the clampdown and continued to struggle, although their efforts were almost certain to win for them the censor's muzzle. For much of the next decade, Brazilian playwrights were presented with crises of enormous proportions to which to respond – the many faces of repression, from censorship to persecution, arrests and torture, denial of subsidies, closing down of theatres, and even arson. With the severe curtailment of the freedom of the press, the theatre had a unique contribution to make, and not only because many of its people were at the forefront of the resistance. In spite of the arrests and torture experienced by Boal, Zé Celso, and many others, Brazilian theatre professionals countered the victimization with an art form that was often as urgent as the confrontations on the streets. Realizing the potential of their experiences, several playwrights set out to offer a forceful political commentary conveyed by effective dramatizations of the plight of the disenfranchised. A number of plays of the period depict the lives of those whom the oppressor has determined to be "marginal": the unemployed, prostitutes, pimps, thieves, homosexuals. Among the authors of this mode are Antônio Bivar (b. 1940), José Vicente (b. 1943), Timochenko Wehbi (b. 1943), Fernando Melo (b. 1945), and, above all, Plínio Marcos (Plínio Marcos de Barros, b. 1935).

Delving into the world of the underclasses for his first plays in the mid and late 1960s, Plínio Marcos was treading paths theretofore left unexplored by Brazilian playwrights. With their emphasis on sex, money, and violence, Marcos's plays depict a world with its own social structure and its own notion of success as an achievement that is strictly dependent on crass exploitation and extreme disaffection. As portrayals of self-contained communities with their own inflexible mores and rules, Marcos's plays are revealing in an unforeseen manner. They speak eloquently about how the self-destructive behavior of the oppressed reveals the ampler societal forces that dictate it. The crudity and directness of the speech, the fact that the characters are losers, belie the artistry involved in the theatrical depiction of a kind of subject about which most potential spectators could hardly crave more detail.

As victims of a system which mercilessly rejects the financially deprived, Marcos's characters have learned almost instinctively to rely on violence as the only leverage. Their personal interactions are thus marked by physical aggression. Likewise, vulgarity and abrasiveness are the forces that drive Marcos's dialogue. In his most potent plays the characters reject evasiveness to state without hesitation what they want from other people; in doing so they beleaguer those around them with an abundant use of foul language. Paco and Tonho, the hustlers in *Dois Perdidos numa Noite Suja* (produced 1966) [*Two Lost in a Filthy Night*], are deprived of elaborate language and reduced to sheer instinct. Like Berrão in *Homens de Papel* (1967; 1978) and Giro in *Abajur Lilás* (1975), Vado in *Navalha na Carne* (produced 1967) has a single impetus, having the situation well in hand. In *Dois Perdidos*, Paco's ruling preoccupation is to persuade Tonho to cooperate in an armed robbery in which he, Paco, will be in charge. Both before and after the hold-up, the two men angrily try to outwit each other, as they observe violent verbal and non-verbal rituals of control and submission. Violence climaxes toward the end when Tonho rebels against his room-mate's relentless provocations in an explosion of fury that ends with his brutal murder of Paco.

With Augusto Boal, Plínio Marcos was the playwright most seriously affected by the military-imposed censorship. Of all the art forms, the theatre was the most frequently and seriously harassed by the military government between 1968 and 1979, for the armed forces identified as one of their strongest opponents the alliance between college students, labor unions, and theatre groups. Actors, directors, playwrights, and those associated with the theatre in general were major targets of the Federal Police, who interpreted any expression of dissent as an act of treason and a threat to national security. Careers were often ruined or seriously damaged due to problems with the censorship division of the Ministry of Justice, whose officials were particularly wary of the theatre because the ever present possibility of improvisation during a performance made it a highly effective awareness-raising vehicle.

Among the actions taken by the censors to harass playwrights and theatre professionals was, of course, the immediate prohibition of a text that was submitted to them for approval. As the censors became more intolerant, outright prohibition was slowly dropped in favor of a more sophisticated tactic. They would approve the submitted text, allow rehearsals, let the company incur sometimes considerable debts to produce the play, and then, on opening night, hours or even minutes before curtain time, word would come to the theatre that the play was unacceptable. This kind of action caused the financial ruin in 1973 of the producers of Chico Buarque and Ruy Guerra's *Calabar: O Elogio da Traição*, reputedly the most expensive production in Brazilian theatre until that date. Less frequently, the production was allowed to run one or two nights, only to be closed down, with no further explanations than a reference to excessive use of foul language, the regime's favorite justification for rejecting a work deemed politically unacceptable. As time went by, this strategy dismantled a few of the best theatre groups, closed down for good a number of traditional theatres in Rio de Janeiro and São Paulo, and ruined some very promising careers. By 1973, due to such serious financial losses, and to the imprisonment, torture, and criminal prosecution of prominent playwrights such as Augusto Boal, the relevant sectors of the Brazilian theatre had been virtually paralyzed (Peixoto, "Como transmitir sinais de dentro das chamas"), forced as they were to function in the margins and interstices of whatever little cultural life there remained.

There was more than a little poignancy in the fact that fine dramatists, all with a series of important works behind them, had to wait to get their new plays considered (and more often than not, banned) by intolerant government censors. However, beleaguered by censorship tribulations – and yet, at the same time, reinvigorated with fresh talent – the Brazilian theatre in the early 1970s entered a new period of transition that was as stimulating as it was strenuous. As for the new talent, the scope of dramatic expression – irate, sarcastic, discouraged – reflects a growing helplessness. No other work illustrates this period better than the monologue, *Apareceu a Margarida* [*Miss Margarida's Way*], by Roberto Athayde (b. 1949). The monologue convention proves to be ideally suited to Athayde's denunciation of repression, as the phenomenally successful work subverts the conventions of the genre with the development of an implicit conflict between the repressive teacher and her fifth-grade students. Athayde's monologue is a deft representation of repression because, if on one hand it reaffirms the addresser's full control of the situation, on the other hand it openly challenges the assumption that Dona Margarida does not have to contend with dissension on stage.

Apareceu a Margarida presents a considerable amount of verbal violence from the authoritarian teacher, who is, of course, assured that there will be no retaliation from the other side. Although, as the playwright, directors, and actresses who have performed the title role attest, audience participation varies widely in different performances of the play (Unruh, "Language and Power in *Miss Margarida's Way* and *The Lesson*," 135n), spectators take the opportunity to react to Dona Margarida's repression, and often choose to intervene verbally. Because, as Unruh explains, the structure of Athayde's play "exploits the captive situation of a group of people who have paid to see a performance and are then harangued, preached to, humiliated, seduced and provoked," the audience can fathom "the experience of life under absolute and arbitrary power"; moreover, "by placing [the audience] in a situation where the easiest alternative is not to respond at all, Miss Margarida forces them to experience the price of silence in an authoritarian context" (p. 133). With the cessation of the verbal violence near the end of the play, three points seem to be beyond dispute: first, that Dona Margarida's power is gained only at the expense of the students' free expression; second, that the woman's power is maintained only because of her incessant, sophisticated verbal assault on the students; and third, that the firmness of Dona Margarida's control of the class is directly proportional to her awareness of language's enormous coercive power.

As time went by, the political climate turned more and more hostile to the theatre and, as a result, plays became increasingly indirect. This trend became known as "teatro de metáforas" ["theatre of metaphors"] or "teatro de ocasião" ["theatre of circumstances"], a kind of survival tactic adopted by dramatists who did not want to quit altogether during the darkest years of the military dictatorship. Repression had led playwrights to dense metaphor and excessive symbolism to the detriment of comprehension, as is the case with two self-referential works, Guarnieri's *Um Grito Parado no Ar* (performed 1973), and *Pano de Boca* (1974) by Fauzi Arap (b. 1939). Another consequence of the increased repression was the appearance of a kind of ethereal theatre best represented by the Teatro Ipanema, which opened in Rio de Janeiro in the late 1960s. Led by actors and directors Rubens Correa and Ivan de Albuquerque, Ipanema staged foreign pieces by Chekhov and Arrabal but their major successes were two works by young Brazilian playwrights, José Vicente's *Hoje é Dia de Rock* and *A China é Azul* by José Wilker (b. 1944). Both works, produced in 1971 and 1972, respectively, were seen by a vast number of mostly young people who were tantalized by the sound track, pacifist message, and highly poetical visual conception presented on stage.

If some major works managed to be staged against all odds (such as *Apareceu a Margarida* in 1973), the banning of other important plays such as Buarque and Guerra's *Calabar*, Guarnieri's *Ponto de Partida* (1976; 1976), and *Patética* (1980; 1978) by João Ribeiro Chaves Neto (b. 1945) at the time they would have been staged robbed the works of their dramatic urgency. Both *Patética* and *Ponto de Partida* reflect on the 1975 death under torture of the journalist Wladimir Herzog in the São Paulo facilities of the Army's Division of Internal Operations. The more successful of the two works, *Patética* was one of the more objectionable plays to the Brazilian censors in two decades of military rule. The winner of the 1977 Best Play Award of the Serviço Nacional de Teatro, *Patética* met with the same fate that had awaited two earlier laureates, Vianinha's *Papa Highirte* and *Rasga Coração*. The work was immediately banned by the Ministry of Justice and the Theatre Institute failed to honor the publication clause of the award. The play was published in 1978 by a distinguished publication house traditionally supportive of progressive causes; however, in keeping with the censors' considerably stronger suspicion of the theatre, the first performance of *Patética* was not permitted until 1980.

In an effective exploration of the interaction of different levels of experience, Chaves Neto's play involves a destitute circus troupe portraying critical moments of the lives of an immigrant Jewish family whose son, Glauco Horowitz, an investigative journalist, at one point in the play conducts a video interview with the circus star, Joana da Criméia. The Horowitz family is soon subjected to the painful realization that by escaping to Brazil they were not completely free from the oppression that drove them out of Europe. Summoned to a military office to clarify some vague charges involving his name, Glauco is arrested, interrogated, tortured, and killed inside the army headquarters.

After a biased military investigation reaffirms the official report of Glauco's death as suicide by hanging, members of the panel scold the torturers for their carelessness and then proceed to falsify evidence before handing the corpse over to the Horowitz family. As the play ends, the actors, no longer playing the roles pertaining to the Horowitz case, worry again about their own financial situation following the imminent closing of the circus. Exiting down the steps from the stage to the orchestra, the troupe members direct their eyes, and the spectator's, toward the stage, where on the otherwise empty space a spotlight shows Glauco's body hanging from a rope. Staring at the corpse, the actors (and often the audience) unite their voices in a final, sung protest against the institution of torture and the regime which thrives on it.

In spite of the efforts of Eugênia Moreyra in the 1920s and 1930s, and Raquel de Queiroz and Patrícia Galvão (1910–1962) in the 1950s, it was not until the late 1960s and early 1970s that women playwrights emerged as forces to contend with. Isabel Câmara (b. 1940) and Consuelo de Castro (b. 1946) have a deep concern for, and a clear understanding of, the people they write about; the candor with which their characters reveal themselves is proof of that in plays such as Câmara's *As Moças* (1969; 1973), and Castro's *Caminho de Volta* (1974; 1976) and *Aviso Prévio* (1987) [*Walking Papers*]. Castro's work is particularly provocative when the dramatic focus is set on the role women played in the political struggle of the late 1960s; such is the case with *À Prova de Fogo* (written in 1968 but banned from the stage until 1974; 1977) and *À Flor da Pele* (1969; 1971).

In her theatre, Leilah Assunção (Maria de Lourdes Torres de Assunção, b. 1943) ventures into a hostile, violent, male-dominated culture to depict male and female characters who are alienated and helpless, as in *Jorginho, o Machão* (1970; 1977) and *Roda Cor de Roda* (1975; 1977). In *Fala Baixo Senão Eu Grito* (1969; 1977), her best work to date, Assunção was influenced by the vogue of the two-character play which dominated the Western theatre for much of this period. These plays depict the intense and sometimes brutal relations of two individuals who, for all the differences between them, are complementary selves and therefore cannot exist apart from each other; in the Brazilian theatre, Marcos's *Dois Perdidos* and Vicente's *O Assalto* (1970; 1970) are two of the more successful theatrical explorations of the destructiveness that seems to constitute an inextricable part of those relationships.

The unnamed man who one fine night enters Mariazinha's modest boarding-house room in *Fala Baixo Senão Eu Grito* is a projection of the less repressed component of the lonely woman's personality. That the stranger's bursting into Mariazinha's meager world reflects her own desire for change is stressed by the fact that the door had been left unlocked and that the man's speech and attitudes often echo Mariazinha's feelings. The sexual aspect of the welcomed intrusion is manifested by the pervasive penetration imagery, ranging from the man's very entering of the room to his suggestive profanities and threats of physical violence. The man, or Mariazinha's mental picture of him, next leads the woman on a planned route to personal liberation that includes an intense verbal barrage and two dreamy romps. Prancing around the unpretentious room while he turns the furniture as well as the rest of her world upside down, the visitor verbally bombards the startled Mariazinha with his mock auction of the woman's material possessions. Although she is slow to react to the upheaval, Mariazinha joins the man's demolition of the room at the key moment when she herself attacks the wardrobe which, like the other scant furniture items, she considered to be part of her family. The ravage is finally completed when Mariazinha overcomes her hesitation and helps with the destruction of one last item, the grandfather clock which she revered as her father.

The momentary paralysis that afflicts Mariazinha following the cathartic process gives way to movement again as the woman joins the intruder in long, imaginary trips that take her out of her enclosed world. As they drift about the city of São Paulo, the dialogue reveals Mariazinha's preoccupation with death and suicide. Moreover, as Margo Milleret has pointed out, "it is during these excursions that Mariazinha realizes her desires for material wealth, beauty, and sexual liberation by acting out episodes in the lives of three make-believe women"; still, although the man senses the futility in Mariazinha's flights of fancy, "he has nothing to offer in exchange for her fantasies of a glamorous life and security" ("Entrapment and Flights of Fantasy in Three Plays by Leilah Assunção," 52). Nevertheless, he pursues his aims in other areas of Mariazinha's life. In a key moment in the woman's attempted liberation, the stranger assists her as she struggles to overcome her inability to swear. In the role of language-teacher-cum-consciousness-raiser, the visitor succeeds in helping Mariazinha verbalize raw emotion for the first time in a life of restraint and self-denial.

The next step in the liberation process entails Mariazinha's admission of never having experienced sexual pleasure; however, the man falls short of complete success, since, as he is about to convince the woman to follow him out of her lifeless room and into the real world – this time in earnest – Mariazinha, overcome by her fears, starts calling for help and the lights go out around them, signalling the would-be liberator's failure to terminate his charge's attachment to the inside world's protectiveness. A long-delayed fulfillment of the title's threat, Mariazinha's desperate scream attests to the renewed strength of her self-denial and confirms the increasingly violent expedients used by her suppression mechanism in quelling her desire for self-liberation.

By the mid 1970s the links between text and performance were not quite broken, but certainly badly strained. Thanks to the contribution of several new, talented theatre groups (such as the highly influential Asdrúbal Trouxe o Trombone), the fascination with performance continued. However, as the winds of political change slowly began to blow, playwrights again reclaimed the word sign as the vital component of the spectacle. This shift is best illustrated by one of the more successful plays of the decade, Chico Buarque and Paulo Pontes's *Gota d'Água* (performed 1975). In the important preface to the printed text of *Gota* the playwrights insist on the prevalence of verbal language over *mise-en-scène* and emphasize that adequate communication with the public is essential if national culture and a concern for the welfare of the people of Brazil are to replace the foreign trends and savage capitalism that had taken over Brazilian society.

In a time of social unrest and political uncertainty, this Third-World *Medea* – with its exceptional characterization, pertinent denunciation of real-estate speculation, and superb depiction of populist tactics – becomes a genuine Brazilian political drama. The inclusion of samba, *candomblé*, and other elements intrinsic to Brazilian culture adds considerably to the work's impact. The music is vibrant and the songs help to delineate character, advance plot, and distill dramatic moments.

When *Gota* opened in 1975, its success vindicated the central idea of Buarque and Pontes: that the enormous power of Greek tragedy could be revealed to contemporary Brazilian audiences by presenting Euripides' *Medea* in the form of a conflict between greed and loyalty in the slums of Rio de Janeiro. The adaptation of the Greek classic was enormously rewarding for Buarque and Pontes. Its immediate impact on the audiences made possible the long-sought reconciliation of stage and public. The play afforded the playwrights the opportunity to develop a number of exciting notions about theatre (also evident in Buarque's *Ópera do Malandro* [1978; 1978]), creating a dramatic style of their own and expanding and refining the possibilities of musical theatre in Brazil.

With *abertura* or greater political openness in the late 1970s, the prospect of major changes in the Brazilian theatre, for the first time since the clampdown of AI–5, came of age. Prominent figures such as Boal and

Zé Celso, who had been in exile, could now return to Brazil. Ruth Escobar (b. 1936), a Portuguese émigrée, redoubled her valiant efforts to abolish censorship altogether and improve the quality of productions. Other important actors and producers were confident enough to undertake significant new endeavors, such as the 1978 opening of Sérgio Britto's Teatro dos Quatro in Rio de Janeiro. The National Theatre Institute implemented the highly successful Projeto Mambembe designed to encourage theatre attendance. In the franker atmosphere fostered by *abertura*, wider room was allowed for dramatic treatment of both current social problems and some darker episodes of the military regime. Major works such as *Calabar* and *Rasga Coração* were finally staged and Plínio Marcos's important works from the 1960s were published, *Dois Perdidos numa Noite Suja* for the first time and *Navalha na Carne* for the second time, although for all practical purposes the 1979 edition is the first one the reading public had access to, since the first edition (1968) was apprehended shortly after publication. In addition to primary texts, previously banned works of criticism were also published in the late 1970s and early 1980s, such as Fernando Peixoto's collections of essays, Yan Michalski's and Sônia Khéde's studies of censorship and the theatre, and two seminal works by Augusto Boal, *Teatro do Oprimido* and *Técnicas latino-americanas de teatro popular*, both first published in Spanish while the author was in exile in Buenos Aires.

The early *abertura* period also saw the first edition and/or staging of several poignant denunciations of a central fact of the military regime – the long shadow of torture. Jorge Andrade's *Milagre na Cela* was premiered in 1978, Vianinha's *Papa Highirte* and Mário Prata's *Fábrica de Chocolate* in 1979, and Chaves Neto's *Patética* and Dias Gomes's *Campeões do Mundo* in 1980. In the wake of the political liberalization, Brazilian drama was able to steer clear of the "teatro de metáforas" that so considerably restricted the artistic eloquence of many playwrights. Drawing from then recently available testimonies of former guerrilla fighters such as Fernando Gabeira's *O Que é Isso, Companheiro?* and Alfredo Syrkis's *Os Carbonários*, these uncensored dramatic portrayals of the most repressive years of Brazil's military dictatorship depict torture with a kind of realism that had been largely absent from the Brazilian stage for most of the 1970s.

In spite of these auspicious developments, the Brazilian theatre did not regain its previous vitality immediately after the political reforms of the late 1970s and early 1980s. The scarcity of major new plays during the post-*abertura* period can in part be explained by the different experiences of those more directly affected by censorship during the military regime. With the political liberalization, Boal returned to Brazil for the first time in eight years to lecture and conduct workshops in Rio de Janeiro and São

Paulo in November, 1979. Since then he has visited Brazil several times while still maintaining his residence and professional activities in France, where for several years he has directed a Center for the Theatre of the Oppressed. At the invitation of the government of the state of Rio de Janeiro during the Brizola administration, Boal ran a "Fábrica de Teatro Popular" ["Popular Theatre Workshop"] aimed at bringing the theatre to those who are usually not in contact with it. Still, while he was in Brazil during the 1985 season to produce his new play, *O Corsário do Rei* (1985), Boal was denounced for having lost touch with the "Brazilian experience."

Plínio Marcos, in his turn, wrote a new play, *Madame Blavatsky* (São Paulo, 1987), in which he chose to keep away from "teatro engajado" ["committed theatre"] and, as a matter of fact, from the Brazilian experience altogether. Also, much to everyone's surprise, Marcos avoided the use of foul language in the play. This is of course very ironic, because when he finally had the chance to use *palavrões* and freely write on the plight of the oppressed, the playwright chose to use acceptable language and to focus on a nineteenth-century foreign figure. Marcos now practices a sort of cosmic religion which has drawn him to mystic figures such as Helena Petrovna Blavatsky (1831–1891), the Ukrainian feminist and advocate of the occult who in 1875 helped found the Theosophical Society in New York City. Marcos insists that his interest in mysticism is by no means recent, and reminds his critics that in the 1960s Dom Hélder Câmara had already detected the religiosity underlying his early plays. Whether or not he is a recent convert, Marcos seems to have adopted a more ascetic lifestyle; in keeping with his moral views, the playwright shunned commercial distribution of the text of his latest play, which he had printed in a small press. The slim books were then sold in the streets of São Paulo by the playwright himself and a group of friends. The play, which had opened in August, 1985, in the teatro Aliança Francesa, under the direction of Jorge Takla, was received favorably by both critics and theatre-goers. Walderez de Barros, Marcos's ex-wife, gave a bravura performance in the title role, which earned her both the Molière and Mambembe awards in São Paulo as Best Actress of 1985.

Boal and Marcos may have been forced to stay away too long, from the country and from the theatre scene, respectively, and, as some of their critics believe, their best work may indeed be behind them, but judging by their latest plays, their careers are hardly over. Both playwrights are still recovering from the experience of exile and ruthless censorship of their works. Those who gave *O Corsário do Rei* and *Madame Blavatsky* a negative reception may have been guilty of stereotyping. After all, one cannot expect every Plínio Marcos play to be about the oppressed lower classes, or every Boal play to be an application of his "técnicas de teatro."

Since *O Corsário do Rei*, Boal has directed a critically acclaimed production of Racine's *Phèdre* which opened in February, 1986, in Rio's Teatro de Arena, with the superb Fernanda Montenegro in the title role, and in 1987 his staging of Argentinean playwright Griselda Gambaro's *La Malasangre* was selected by *Veja* magazine as one of the best plays of Brazil's 1987 theatre season.

Another aspect of the state of the theatre in Brazil in the 1980s has to do with the challenges and accomplishments of different generations. While the older playwrights, Boal, Marcos, Guarnieri, Dias Gomes, have chosen to distance themselves from the 1960s and 1970s, and are still adapting to a new state of affairs where censorship is no longer the major impediment, the new generation of playwrights, most of them too young to be writing in the 1960s and early 1970s, but who nevertheless grew up in an atmosphere of oppression under the dictatorship, they too are striving to overcome the ghost of censorship, and have yet to convey their experience in outstanding contributions to the Brazilian theatre. Still, their plays have established a major trait of the Brazilian theatre in the 1980s, the shift away from political commitment and social protest, and toward a more intense interest in examining the individual experience, often returning to childhood and adolescence in search of answers and solace.

However, there have been signs of enormous talent among the younger playwrights. Perhaps the two most promising of these authors are Naum Alves de Souza (b. 1942) and Maria Adelaide Amaral (b. 1942). *A Aurora da Minha Vida* (performed 1981), the best of Naum's works to date, reveals the playwright's remarkable sensitivity for the mostly uneventful lives of a large segment of the Brazilian population. In *No Natal a Gente Vem te Buscar* (1979; 1982) Naum revisits his troubled childhood, and the result is a moving play with several brilliant scenes involving thwarted hopes and unfulfilled yearnings in a family of Brazilian provincials. With *A Aurora da Minha Vida*, *No Natal a Gente Vem te Buscar*, and *Um Beijo, um Abraço, um Aperto de Mão* (1984; 1986) Naum has shaped "a genuinely dramatic cycle of memoirs, simultaneously ironic, painful and mystic, in which he attempts to come to terms with the ghosts of his childhood and youth" (Michalski, *O teatro sob pressão*, 86). The poignancy of Naum's plays is hinged on the idea of wasted possibilities and unconscious cruelties; their sadness comes from the way the playwright alludes to our losses and our unawareness of the significance of the things we love most until they are gone forever. A prize-winning playwright and also an accomplished director and stage settings designer (he was responsible for the superb visual concepts of Antunes Filho's 1978 staging of *Macunaíma*), Naum possesses one of the most distinctive voices in the Brazilian theatre today and as such deserves a lot more critical attention than he has so far received.

Maria Adelaide Amaral's theatre, like Naum's, avoids the political sphere. Her plays reveal a profound interest in the problems of professional middle-class men and women living in the big cities of contemporary Brazil. *De Braços Abertos* (performed 1984), her most successful work to date, is a psychological study of a liberated woman, Luísa, as she searches for a mature lover in contemporary São Paulo. Although educated and successful, the three men with whom she becomes involved are insecure and destructive, woefully unprepared to accept a new reality in which Brazilian women, emotionally and intellectually fortified by a better understanding of their social and political situation, demand to be treated as equals; *De Braços Abertos* was voted "Best Play" of the 1984 season by the São Paulo Association of Theatre Critics, and Amaral received the Mambembe award for Distinguished Playwright of the Year. Disaffection in its most intense contemporary aspects constitutes the central concern of Amaral's art and she has dealt with it in a variety of forms. In addition to plays, she has also written perceptive novels depicting the lives of the same kinds of disaffected characters, sometimes, as in *Luísa: Quase uma História de Amor* (1986), revising dramatic material and adapting it to narrative conventions.

Another promising young playwright is Júlio César Conte (b. 1955). Head of the group, Do Jeito que Dá, based in Rio Grande do Sul, Conte achieved critical and popular acclaim with his *Bailei na Curva* (1984), which opened in 1983 in Porto Alegre, where it was seen by more than 60,000 people in one year before it had an equally successful run in Rio de Janeiro, and went on national tour. Fast-paced, good-humored, often sarcastic, *Bailei na Curva*, spanning a twenty-year period, looks at the experiences of a group of urban characters, all of them children at the time of the 1964 coup, and tracks their growing up in the 1960s, 1970s, and early 1980s. They have weathered the currents of repression and economic difficulties to find the bittersweet personal accommodations the play seems to celebrate. Using very little in the way of props and decor, *Bailei na Curva* depends to a large extent on the acting talent of the members of Do Jeito que Dá, as the cast is required not only to represent different characters at different ages, but also to sing and dance on stage. The play also depends heavily on audience empathy, although this is not to say that only those who were teenagers in the 1960s and 1970s can relate to the twenty-one short scenes that form *Bailei na Curva*. However, the most remarkable feature of Conte's play is that its emphasis on individual experience departs from the social concerns of the committed theatre of the 1960s and 1970s. In spite of the moving tribute to Pedro, the only character who, like his father before him, became involved in the resistance to the regime, and, we are told, "disappeared" and died in prison, the play seems to be a compassionate, forgiving look at those who, perhaps ignoring their conscience, chose to keep on moving along on the safer road, so that they would not "bailar na curva" (idiomatic Portuguese for becoming the "odd man out").

The banner of politically committed theatre was carried in the 1970s and 1980s by authors such as João das Neves, Chico de Assis, César Vieira (Edibal Almeida Piveta, b. 1931), Carlos Henrique Escobar (b. 1933), and Carlos Queiroz Telles (b. 1936). Both Neves and Assis trace their commitment to their heady days with Grupo Opinião. Neves's *O Último Carro* (1976; 1976) and Escobar's *A Caixa de Cimento* (1979; 1978) constitute compelling allegories about a situation of extreme repression and despair, while Assis's *Missa Leiga* (performed 1972), performed in an abandoned factory (the original setting – a church – was rejected by the censors), compounds the atmosphere of repression by a deft exploration of the scenic space. Telles, in his turn, has resorted to episodes of colonial history, as in *Frei Caneca* (1972; 1973), in order to speak metaphorically about the present. Working with the group União e Olho Vivo, Vieira has drawn from history as well as popular theatre traditions to craft – in plays such as *O Evangelho segundo Zebedeu* (1971; 1975) and *Morte aos Brancos* (1984; 1987) – a potent commentary on the violent political and cultural repression that undergirds Brazilian society.

A number of experimental ensemble theatre groups must be given credit for the revitalization of Brazil's theatre in the late 1970s and 1980s. In addition to voicing the concerns of a new generation that wished to distance itself from the production system as well as the issues that preoccupied theatre practitioners of the 1950s and 1960s, these new groups are characterized by an enormous creative energy and devotion to their art that more than compensate for their lack of financial resources. Deprived of access to traditional houses by the rampant real-estate speculation of the early and mid 1970s they have had to find and adapt new acting spaces; as a result, their productions depend on a good deal of improvisation. Such adverse conditions have contributed to the short life span that unfortunately has become another trait of this type of theatre. Moreover, even the more successful among them are not very concerned about keeping a record of their productions, leaving scant material for the theatre researcher to work with.

The most important of these groups was the trend-setting Asdrúbal Trouxe o Trombone, created in Rio de Janeiro in 1974. Led by Hamilton Vaz Pereira (b. 1951) and featuring such actors as Regina Casé and Luís Fernando Guimarães, the group's best production has been the collective work, *Trate-me Leão* (performed 1977), a sequence of short scenes that examine problems of adolescence and youth – again, concern with the individual is prevalent over the social element. Of the many groups that proliferated in the wake of Asdrúbal, in addition to the above-mentioned

Do Jeito que Dá and União e Olho Vivo, the following are worthy of special attention. Tá na Rua, formed in 1979 in Rio de Janeiro, as its name indicates, specializes in street performance and describes its work as an endless rehearsal; the group is led by Amir Haddad, who had earlier applied similar notions in his work with another salient group, A Comunidade. The Teatro do Ornitorrinco, created in São Paulo in 1977 and directed by Luiz Roberto Galizia until his untimely death in February of 1985, has been led since then by Cacá Rosset (b. 1954); in addition to their own experimental productions, Ornitorrinco performs an eclectic repertoire ranging from Jarry to Brecht, and from Molière (their adaptation of *Le Malade Imaginaire* was featured in Joseph Papp's 1990 Festival Latino in New York Ciry) to Alberto Boadella; Ornitorrinco's daring production of Boadella's *Teledeum* in 1987 occasioned an incident that sent shock waves through Brazil's artistic community because it reactivated the censorship mechanism, thus belying the civilian government's assurances of freedom of artistic expression.

The most accomplished of the theatre groups in Brazil from the late 1970s to the 1990s was the São Paulo-based Grupo Teatro Macunaíma, led by Antunes Filho (José Alves Antunes Filho [b. 1929]), who is presently the foremost stage director in the country. Originally called Pau Brasil, the group derived its current name from Mário de Andrade's modernist narrative (1928), which they staged in 1978. The work – adapted for the stage by Jacques Thiériot – has since been performed with enormous success not only in Brazil but also in several international festivals and tours of Europe and the Americas. Under the meticulous direction of Antunes Filho, the Macunaíma ensemble unleashed the energy of the keystone text of Brazilian Modernism, in many ways paralleling Grupo Oficina's earlier return to another Modernist milestone, Oswald de Andrade's *O Rei da Vela* in 1967. Antunes's production captured the vitality of Brazilian folklore and captivated the public with its "celebration of magic and ritual, native dance and music, instinctual liberation, and in general the Brazilian collective imagination" (George, "The Staging of *Macunaíma* and the Search for National Theatre," 51).

The career of Antunes Filho, from his early days with the TBC in the 1950s and 1960s (initially as assistant director and, later, as director of works such as Jorge Andrade's *Vereda da Salvação* in 1964) to the repertory concept he brought to São Paulo's Teatro Anchieta in 1984, epitomizes the best elements of contemporary theatre in Brazil. As director of the Center for Theatre Research of São Paulo's Serviço Social do Comércio (SESC), Antunes contributed immensely to the renovation of the Brazilian theatre in the 1980s through the training of new talent and the adaptation to Brazilian reality of innovative techniques of experimental ensemble theatre. In a manner uncharacteristic of the Brazilian theatre, preparations for each new production take several months; in true ensemble fashion, total dedication is expected of the cast, who must participate in the painstaking research of the text as well as in the lengthy and exacting rehearsals.

Grupo Macunaíma's significance is compounded by the fact that they were instrumental in setting a major trend of the period, the stage adaptation of texts belonging to other literary genres, or the restaging of plays from other periods. Thus, Antunes's group has staged two collages of Nelson Rodrigues's plays from the 1940s, 1950s, and 1960s: *Nelson Rodrigues: O Eterno Retorno*, a *tour de force* including scenes from four of Nelson's most demanding works, was premiered in 1981, and *Nelson 2 Rodrigues*, with scenes from *Album de Família* and *Toda Nudez Será Castigada*, opened in 1984. That same year they ventured outside the Brazilian theatre for the first time to present a highly provocative staging of *Romeo and Juliet*. In May of 1986, with Raul Cortez in the title role, the group opened *Augusto Matraga*, a stage rendition of "A Hora e a Vez de Augusto Matraga," the last short story in *Sagarana* (1946) by João Guimarães Rosa (1908–1967). In 1989 they went back to Nelson, this time with another collage, *Paraíso Zona Norte*, with scenes from the plays *A Falecida* and *Os Sete Gatinhos*.

Another important *paulista* group is Núcleo Pessoal do Victor, led by Celso Nunes, a director with an impressive record prior to the formation of Victor, whose name was derived from their 1975 production of Roger Vitrac's play with the same title. In 1979 the group staged, to wide acclaim, Carlos Alberto Soffredini's *Na Carrera do Divino*, a celebration of the disappearing *caipira* culture of southeastern Brazil, which is in some ways an attempt to return to an earlier, less challenging stage of life. In 1983 Pessoal do Victor staged Alcides Nogueira's adaptation of *Feliz Ano Velho*, Marcelo Rubens Paiva's best-selling autobiography (1982), with considerable critical and popular success. Because Paiva's book, written in his early twenties, following an accident that paralyzed him from the waist down, goes back to his teenage years as he meditates on the meaning of life and chance, this play too is part of the already-mentioned tendency to focus on the individual rather than the social, and to return to childhood and youth in search of solace. *Feliz Ano Velho* was the recipient of numerous awards, among them Best Play of 1983 from the Instituto Nacional de Artes Cênicas and also from the Associação Paulista de Críticos de Arte.

Other successful stage renditions of other genres include Grupo Jaz-o-Coração's 1978 adaptation of *Triste fim de Policarpo Quaresma* (1915), the celebrated satirical novel by Lima Barreto (1881–1922); José Possi's 1979 rendition of *Um sopro de vida* (1978), a posthumously published novella by Clarice Lispector (1925–1977) in which autobiography and fiction are inextricably interwoven; Rubens Correa's stage version of Manuel Puig's novel *El beso de la mujer araña* for the Teatro Ipanema in 1981; Gilberto Carneiro's 1987 staging of *Lúcia McCartney*, one of the pieces in the foremost collection of short stories of the 1970s, *Feliz Ano Novo* by Rubem Fonseca (b. 1925), which was banned for most of the decade; Ulysses Cruz's 1988 rendition of *Corpo de baile* (1956), Guimarães Rosa's collection of seven novellas by the same title; and Boal's 1988 production of *O encontro marcado*, a stage version of the 1956 novel of coming of age by Fernando Sabino (b. 1923) – another instance of the period's trend to portray youths in search of answers. In 1989 Virginia Woolf's *Orlando* was given a vibrant staging by Bia Lessa, with script by Sérgio Sant'Anna (b. 1941), who had earlier contributed a provocative addition to the blurring of the genres with his novel *A tragédia brasileira* (1987). Even the rarely traveled route of film to stage was attempted in the 1980s, with success, by film director Arnaldo Jabor's 1987 staging of his *Eu te Amo* (1981).

Finally, as part of the trend to reevaluate Nelson Rodrigues's theatre, another influential group, the Londrina-based Grupo Delta de Teatro, under the direction of José Antônio Teodoro, restaged as a musical Rodrigues's *Toda Nudez Será Castigada* (1965), one of the main characters of which is a sexually confused youth. The recipient of several awards, including Best Theatre Group in 1985, Delta has since performed in the United States (in New York's 1986 Festival Latino) and in Portugal, where their work was enthusiastically received in 1987. Other noteworthy groups of the period are: São Paulo's Boi Voador and Forrobodó, Rio de Janeiro's Pessoal do Despertar and Pessoal do Cabaré, Londrina's Proteu, and Porto Alegre's Tear.

Perhaps no single individual contributed more to the revitalization of the *mise-en-scène* in the 1980s and early 1990s than Gerald Thomas (b. 1954). Critics have been left to find their own labels for his unique, often controversial productions, the most remarkable aspect of which is the paramount importance of the visual design, created by his wife Daniela Thomas (b. 1958). Born in Brazil and educated in England, Gerald Thomas served his apprenticeship in London's street theatre scene in the 1970s and in New York's La Mama Experimental Theater in the early 1980s. Influenced by the staging notions of Robert Wilson, minimalist art, and contemporary opera, Gerald Thomas has mastered the substitution of visual metaphor for verbal imagery in works such as *Eletra com Creta* (performed 1985), *Carmem com Filtro* (1986), and *Carmem com Filtro 2* (1990). Shunning narrative for images that speak to a collective unconscious, he too has joined the trend to adapt other genres to the stage, with his highly original production of Kakfa's *The Trial* in 1987.

Equally original is the contribution of Denise Stoklos (b. 1950), who, like Thomas, performed in London in the 1970s and in New York's La Mama in the 1980s. Stoklos creates a kind of theatre that pleases even the most demanding of critics, as befits an artist whose strong background in pantomime has not prevented the incorporation of the verbal sign in her inimitable work. Winner of the 1986 Mambembe and 1987 Associação Paulista de Críticos de Arte Best Actress awards, Denise has performed in a number of solo plays, such as Dacia Mariani's *Mary Stuart* (1987), her own adaptation of *Hamlet* (1988), and *Casa* (1990), that seek to strip acting of its numbing conventions and let the body speak for itself. The sets are stark, the stage virtually empty except for the commanding presence of the artist, whose approach shares a good deal with performance art and can be traced to the most essential aspects of the theatre – hence Stoklos's characterization of her work as Teatro Essencial.

The 1980s also witnessed the emergence of a combination of performance art and improvisation comedy called "teatro do besteirol" (from "besteira" or "foolishness"), whose immediacy is at the same time its greatest strength and its major drawback. Performing almost always in duos, besteirol artists such as Miguel Falabella and Guilherme Karam, and Pedro Cardoso and Felipe Pinheiro, draw on current politics and middle-class concerns for their irreverent routines. Puppet theatre also showed telltale signs of enormous vitality in the 1980s; such strength was especially evident in the contributions of Belo Horizonte's Grupo Giramundo, Rio de Janeiro's Contadores de Estórias, Porto Alegre's Cem Modos, and São Paulo's XPTO. The latter group has been particularly successful in borrowing from the extremely fertile tradition of the circus, as has another innovative *paulista* group, Circo-Grafitti.

Now, more than fifty years after Ziembinsky's revolutionary staging of Nelson Rodrigues's *Vestido de Noiva*, it is evident that its clarion call to a new age of the Brazilian theatre was heeded, leaving behind an era of bombastic actors and mediocre playwrights and their repetitive comedies of manners. On the other hand, it is likewise clear that the new age that *Vestido* heralded came to pass not much more than a decade and a half later, with the spotlight turning from companies such as Os Comediantes and the Teatro Brasileiro de Comédia to Regionalist theatre (Suassuna, Dias Gomes, Jorge Andrade) and politically committed groups such as Arena, Opinião, and Oficina. It was out of these three groups that there evolved the major names (Guarnieri, Boal, Vianinha, José Celso) that were to lead the Brazilian theatre during the turbulent period that followed the military coup of 1964. In spite of the overwhelming odds posed by strict censorship, persecution and detention of leading figures, and other repressive measures, the Brazilian theatre managed to maintain a certain quality and dignity that carried it through the longest and most serious crisis in its history to date. Following the nation's return to democracy, the older generation of playwrights have felt the need to rethink the artistic expression of their political commitment, while the younger dramatists, who are often associated with vibrant new groups, prefer to emphasize individual experience over social commitment. The new guard has not turned its back on the best elements of the nation's theatre tradition, as witness the several revivals of Nelson Rodrigues's plays (undertaken most prominently by Grupo Macunaíma's leader, Antunes Filho, himself a product of the traditional TBC), nor have they limited their efforts to a strictly dramatic sphere, borrowing, in some cases with considerable success, from other genres and art forms. The generational turnover is now a reality, but the odds faced are formidable, among them a deteriorating economy and the deep penetration of television in a country with a high illiteracy rate. Undaunted, the younger set continue their struggle to revitalize the Brazilian stage. Their endeavors include the forging of a new relationship between the theatre and a younger audience who are receptive to experiments with pantomime, circus elements, performance art, and improvisational comedy. In doing so, in only a few years they have already left an imprint on the contemporary stage, thus making a substantial contribution to the effort to reshape the theatre of Brazil in the late 1980s and early 1990s.

[14]

Brazilian popular literature (the *literatura de cordel*)
Candace Slater

Side by side, and often intertwined, with the work of Brazil's best-known novelists, playwrights, and poets, popular literature has played a primary role in the nation's cultural life over many centuries. "Popular" is used here to mean of and by the people. It refers to prose, poetry, and theatre produced and consumed primarily by persons of limited means and education, operating on a local and, sometimes, regional basis, as opposed to that created by educated individuals writing for themselves and for a literate national and international audience.

A good deal of Brazilian popular literature is primarily or exclusively oral. It includes a wealth of Medieval Portuguese and often pan-European dramatic forms, such as puppet theatre and Christmas pageants, as well as a variety of proverbs, folktales, and legends, a number of which have all but disappeared in Spain and Portugal. Not infrequently, these Iberian transplants have fused with other, equally varied, and deeply-rooted African and indigenous traditions. From time to time, one can also detect further borrowings from the various immigrant groups (German, Japanese, Syrian and Lebanese, Italian, and Jewish, among others) which have found a home over the centuries in Brazil.

In addition to this myriad of oral traditions, many of which have yet to be systematically collected and studied, there is also a large and vibrant printed literature known as the *literatura de cordel*. Significant both in its own right and as an ongoing source of inspiration for a variety of educated authors, the *cordel* has become of increasing interest over the last few decades not only to scholars but also to a more general public.

Heir to a ballad and broadside tradition found throughout most of Medieval Europe, the "stories on a string" (the name refers to the cord on which the little booklets were customarily suspended for display) arrived with the first colonists. These pamphlet stories, called *folhetos* or, more colloquially, *folhetes*, continued to be imported from Lisbon to Rio de

Janeiro in the decades following Independence in 1822. Then, in the second half of the century, a new sort of *cordel* literature began emerging in the vast, arid northeastern interior.

The rise of a regional *cordel* with distinctive formal and thematic features had various practical causes. The dramatic growth of the backlands' subsistence farmer population and the concomitant rise of a series of rotating open-air markets was certainly one. Equally important were the appearance of a growing number of secondhand printing presses which provided a local means of production for the pamphlets, and the existence of a strong tradition of oral poetic improvisation on which would-be *cordel* authors could draw.

The significance of the *repentista* or poet–improviser in the emergence of a recognizably northeastern and Brazilian *cordel* cannot be underestimated. *Sextilhas*, those generally septasyllabic six-line stanzas constituting the *repentista*'s stock-in-trade, quickly replaced the prose and decasyllabic verses of Iberian pamphlet literature as semi-literate poets began producing a wide array of journalistic accounts, religious fables, comic escapades, and love and adventure stories which might feature regional figures such as the northeastern bandits known as *cangaceiros*. The presence of the *repentista* tradition is also obvious in the *folheto* writers' frequent use of additional metrical forms associated with improvisation (the ABC, the *martelo agalopado*, the *galope à beiramar*) and their fondness for printed versions of what were supposedly oral contests or *pelejas* between the most celebrated poet–improvisers of the day. Although not all *cordel* authors were *repentistas* and not all *repentistas* were authors, a number of individuals did indeed ply both trades and a special camaraderie existed between the two.

If the northeastern pamphlet stories were unlike their Portuguese forebears in a number of important respects, they also stood apart in some ways from other New World descendants of the same ballad and broadside. The *cordel* diverges, for instance, from the Mexican *corrido*, in its close reliance on traditional folktales called *trancosos* as much as or more than on topical, journalistic themes. Moreover, not only are *folhetos* usually longer than *corridos*, but their musical component is considerably less important. Although the vendor might deliver his verses to the tune of a rustic violin, instrumental accompaniment was not essential to his performance. "Books" rather than broadsides, the best-known *cordel* stories were often associated with individual authors both admired and envied for their command over the written word. "In the old days," *cordel* poet Manuel Camilo dos Santos (1905–1987) explains, "the rancher always set an extra place at the table for the *cordel* writer. His star shone much brighter than that of the *repentista* who does not create a story from start to finish but goes jumping like a cricket from one theme to the next" (interview, Campina Grande, Paraíba, March 6, 1978).[1]

Despite the existence of individual differences, the great majority of *folheto* writers followed a common model. After an initial invocation to the Muse (or, sometimes, God), the poet would switch to the third-person narrative only to revert to the "I" form in a conclusion emphasizing the story's moral. Often, the first letter of each line of the last stanza or stanzas formed an acrostic of the author's name.

Cordel authors generally employed a mix of self-consciously literary and unmistakably regional and colloquial language. Although the poetry is often little more than a vehicle for action, some stories reveal flashes of intense lyricism. Images such as that of a dazzling if distinctly aeroplane-like Mysterious Peacock (the name of a particularly famous *folheto*) are memorable. So are comparisons such as that of love with a drop of water that extinguishes the desire for vengeance. (The latter appears in the *folheto* version of *Romeo and Juliet* by João Martins de Ataíde.) Moreover, although *cordel* poets routinely deal in stereotypes, a number of their characters reveal appealing idiosyncrasies. The minor role of the heroine's old aunt in Ataíde's *Uma noite de amor* (n.d.), for instance, does not keep *folheto* buyers from remembering her with enthusiasm.

> Um dia a tia Diná
> Disse: querida sobrinha
> Sei que não amas ao duque
> Tua sorte é igual à minha
> Uni-me a quem não amava
> E vivo sempre sozinha.
>
> [One day her Aunt Diná said,
> Dear niece, I know
> you don't love the duke.
> Your fate is the same as mine
> because I married someone
>   I didn't love
> and for this reason, I live alone.]

Early *cordel* poets found inspiration not only in the Muse, but also in the prospect of escaping the harsh routine of subsistence agriculture. Instead of tilling the fields from dawn to dusk like the vast majority of their customers, they spent their days traveling from fair to fair. Often barely literate themselves, they would chant (rather than sing) verses written by themselves and others for a largely illiterate public. Attracted

---

[1] All interview material cited here and in subsequent pages was recorded by the author of this essay in 1977–1978 and 1987.

by the poet's presentation, and by appealing cover illustrations – usually rustic block prints or photographs not necessarily related to the subject matter – *folheto* buyers would often take their purchase to a literate member of the community, such as the landowner or *coronel*, who would read them aloud for the group. In the absence of formal schooling, a good number of backlands inhabitants taught themselves to read via the *literatura de cordel*. Having learned the best-known stories by heart, they would proceed to painstakingly decipher the printed page. Dog-eared pamphlets in which a succession of owners have laboriously copied the letters beneath each line of print bear testimony to the *cordel*'s practical, pedagogic, as well as entertaining, journalistic, and moralizing function.

In the Iberian peninsula, and indeed much of Europe, the chap-books served as a catch-all for a wide array of subject matter. Written by a variety of authors for different segments of the population, these pamphlets were often united by little other than their physical form. They are thus different from the northeastern *cordel*, whose very particular regional and class identity is unmistakable.

The relative uniformity of the *folheto* in no way negates the existence of sizable differences among poets. Those possessing a little more education and money, as well as a more effective network of social relations, might succeed in obtaining their own printing presses. Possession of these generally secondhand or artisanal presses put them in a position to buy manuscripts by other poets, to which they frequently affixed their own name. Sometimes, the real writer's name was omitted unintentionally; on other occasions the identifying acrostic was purposefully altered. Thus the celebrated *folheto* publisher, Leandro Gomes de Barros (1865–1918), and his successors, João Martins de Ataíde (1880–1959), and José Bernardo da Silva (1901–1972), appear as the authors of not only their own stories but also many hundreds of others which they almost certainly did not write.

As one might expect, the most important *cordel* presses were located in cities. Yet, although the port of Recife quickly became the most important *folheto* center in Brazil (Leandro Gomes de Barros and João Martins de Ataíde were based there), the *cordel* remained firmly associated with the backlands. Not only were the great majority of *folheto* buyers from the interior, but most *folhetos* revealed an underlying moral vision closely associated with a rural agricultural society. Time and again, the story focuses on the partnership between an individual and a divine, or human, other. In the face of a challenge to this alliance, the first party demonstrates either *firmeza* [constancy] or *falsidade* [double-dealing]. Depending on the nature of the protagonist's response, reward (material prosperity and, often, a happy marriage) or retribution (ridicule, material loss, and even death) ensues. The story then concludes with an implicit, if not explicit, reassertion of the underlying moral code.

The identity of parties in question may vary. Most frequently, the protagonist is of inferior social status. On occasion, however, the person tested is a member of the elite. Then too, while the partner to the moral alliance is often a human patron, this second slot is sometimes filled by God. No matter what the identity of the actors, however, the great majority of traditional, northeastern *folhetos* reveal the basic six-step pattern diagrammed below:

pact → test → response → counter-response → judgment → pact reasserted
→ response

Northeastern *folhetos* began circulating in quantity during the 1880s and reached their heyday in the 1950s. Successful *cordel* stories routinely sold tens, and even hundreds, of thousands of copies. In contrast, the works of educated authors customarily appeared in very limited editions. For example, the renowned *modernista* poet, Manuel Bandeira (1886–1964), whose 1930 "Vou-me embora para Pasárgada" ["Pasárgada"] provides the inspiration for more than one best-selling *folheto* version of a trip to a magical kingdom called "São Saruê," frequently found himself obliged to finance the publication of his own books.

Although the advent of radio and movies led some observers to predict the *cordel*'s imminent demise, poets cheerfully incorporated material gleaned from these sources into their works. Moreover, the same people who would listen to a radio or watch a film, or, later, television program, would often purchase a *folheto* version of what they had already seen or heard. This was true of journalistic, as well as fictional, themes. In 1954, specially chartered aeroplanes delivered pamphlet versions of the suicide of President Getúlio Vargas to points throughout the northeast. Like their forebears who had taken *folhetos* with them to the Amazon during the Rubber Boom, immigrants from the northeast brought the *cordel* with them in their exodus to the burgeoning cities of the industrial south after the Second World War.

In the 1960s and increasingly in the 1970s, a series of developments dramatically decreased *folheto* sales. The large-scale conversion of subsistence farmers into waged laborers radically eroded the traditional market system of rotating weekly fairs on which the poet had always depended. "In the past if things didn't go well in Timbaúba, I was always able to do something about it the next day in Bezerros or Limoeiro," explains the poet Severino Borges. "Today, no. If things don't go well in Timbaúba, I don't eat all week" (interview, Timbaúba, Pernambuco; March 2, 1978).

The rising cost of printing supplies, transportation, and lodging, and the imposition of "floor taxes" in the municipal markets placed a further drain on poets' always limited resources. The widescale introduction of the transistor radio into the backlands in the 1960s, the construction of new highways, and the expanding urban labor market gave people access to a previously distant outside world. Contact with this larger universe often placed in question a code of beliefs to which *folheto* writers and buyers had previously, at least in theory, subscribed. At the same time, their once relatively isolated "folk culture" became an object of increasing interest to an educated middle class. As a result, the *cordel*, once the almost exclusive province of the poor and illiterate, began to find a new market not just in politically active intellectuals eager to communicate with the rural masses, but also in tourists enamored of local color, and students completing high school civics assignments. At the same time, an increasing number of Brazilian and foreign scholars in a variety of disciplines – literature, communications, history, sociology, and anthropology, among others – started to study the *literatura de cordel* systematically.

We have already noted that the *cordel* was never uniform. The existence of a basic six-step challenge pattern in no way precluded often sizable differences based on factors such as place of residence and level of education, as well as temperament and writing style. Today, however, these divisions are considerably more marked than in the past. The *folhetos* for sale in contemporary marketplaces tend to be a mixture of now-classic love and adventure stories and newer, almost exclusively journalistic pieces which may depart markedly from their forebears both in terms of style and underlying structure. Incorporating urban themes and an unmistakably urban vocabulary, they often eschew any clearcut moral. Their authors are increasingly apt to speak as individuals with their own opinions rather than as mouthpieces for the community and the ethical code to which all of its members ostensibly adhere.

The longstanding division between northern and southern *cordel* has greatly intensified. At present, the *cordel* is a pale shadow of its former self in the northeast. Although *folhetos* continue to appear in urban marketplaces and a handful of vendors still make the rounds of backlands fairs, most have diversified their wares to include secondhand magazines as well as items such as school supplies, articles of clothing (socks, belts, handkerchiefs), and similar sundries. "If today I had to depend on the *folheto* to feed my children," says Edson Pinto da Silva, Recife's biggest vendor, "I would die of hunger. Even as it is, things aren't going well. And so I am thinking of leaving the profession for something else. Children's underwear, for instance. I like poetry much more than underwear, you understand, but it certainly doesn't sell" (interview, Recife, Pernambuco, August 12, 1987).

The great majority of present-day northeastern poets are middle-aged or older. Although these individuals continue to write stories, many find themselves unable to publish. The large presses of the past have disappeared and the few *cordel* writers who continue to see their stories into print are either owners of small, rustic presses or graphic artists as well as authors. A number of the sons of well-known northeastern *folheto* writers are presently painters and printmakers in the urban south. These young people have left their birthplace for Rio de Janeiro and São Paulo because conditions for popular art forms such as the *cordel* are generally more favorable in southern cities than they are back home. Municipal funding (at least, in Rio de Janeiro), as well as private sector and public foundation support has insured a continued stream of stories. The prestige of the exotic, as well as a desire in at least some cases to reach the *folheto*'s traditional public, has spurred the emergence of new poets who may be neither from the northeast nor from the lower classes. Teachers, politicians, pastoral workers, and radio personalities are among the authors of today's stories in verse. At the same time, poets who were born in the northeast but who by this time may have lived for three or four decades in Rio or São Paulo have taken to writing *folhetos* with a decidedly southern flavor. Even when their stories follow the traditional six-step pattern, they are easily distinguishable from the classics which were once their models. "Today is different," explains Apolônio Alves dos Santos (b. 1926), who moved to Rio from the northeast only to return home almost forty years later. "And so, poetry is changing too. Because, you know, we poets have to accompany the times" (interview, Rio de Janeiro, August 16, 1987).

For over a hundred years now, a wide variety of Brazilian writers have looked with interest to the *literatura de cordel*. Pioneer studies of the *cordel* by poet–novelist Celso de Magalhães (1849–1879), novelist José de Alencar (1829–1877), and philologist Sílvio Romero (1851–1914), appeared in the second half of the nineteenth century. Members of literary societies of the period, such as the Escola do Recife and Padaria Espiritual of Fortaleza often collected ballads and *folhetos*. Some of these individuals went on to incorporate *cordel* themes, if not bits and pieces of actual *folhetos*, into regionalist novels. Domingos Olímpio's *Luzia-Homem* (1903) and Franklin Távora's *O cabeleira* (1876) are two of the most obvious examples.

The interest in the *cordel* as a poetic form and its appropriation and transformation by educated authors continued into the twentieth century. While some modern writers find inspiration in specific *cordel* stories, others make less direct, though no less significant, use of *folhetos* and the larger ballad tradition which lies behind them. Still others, whom one would not normally associate with popular culture or the northeast, have looked to the *cordel* for a number of quite varied reasons. Unlike the majority of nineteenth-century examples, who, with the exception of Alencar, tend to be literary figures of primarily regional importance, the examples offered below are nationally and internationally acclaimed authors.

The first set of writers, composed exclusively of northeasterners tend, like the nineteenth-century Naturalists, to have grown up in close contact with folk and popular traditions including the *literatura de cordel*. Some of these individuals, most notably José Lins do Rego (1901–1957) and Jorge Amado (b. 1912), were influenced by the *regionalista* movement of the late 1920s and 1930s, closely associated with the Recife-based sociologist, Gilberto Freyre (1900–1987). These early Regionalists sought to affirm the value of local, often rural, realities in the face of what its adherents saw as the overly urban and "internationalist" direction of the vanguard representing *Modernismo* or Brazilian Modernism. Other, somewhat younger authors, such as Alfredo Dias Gomes (b. 1922) and Ariano Suassuna (b. 1927), might be considered Regionalists as well.

Works by these individuals may simply employ the *cordel* as a source of local color. Quite often, however, *cordel* themes and formulae are integral to the text. The author may borrow one or another personage from the *folheto* tradition, play on its stylistic or thematic features, or utilize actual snippets of one well-known story or another.

Ariano Suassuna's three-act *Auto da Compadecida* [*The Rogues' Trial*], for instance, is a contemporary reworking of Medieval morality plays which draws on folk themes which form the basis for at least three readily recognizable *folhetos*. The first story, that of the burial of a dog, appears in Leandro Gomes de Barros's *O dinheiro* (n.d.). The second, the tale of a money-excreting horse appears in a *folheto* by the name of *O cavalo que defecava dinheiro* (n.d.), most probably also by Leandro. The third, a pointed illustration of the negative effects of arrogant behavior entitled *O castigo da soberba* (n.d.), may be Leandro's as well. In addition to these specific texts, Suassuna also relies on a number of more general *cordel* conventions.

The play's lead character is a rogue named João Grilo [John Cricket] who recalls a large number of similar picaresque figures in Brazilian as well as Iberian pamphlet literature. Like the João Grilos, Pedro Mala-sartes, and Pedro Quengos who make an appearance in numerous northeastern folktales, he delights in showing up the foibles of his supposed social superiors through his quick wit. Like his *cordel* counterparts, Suassuna's protagonist is both petty and cruel upon occasion, as when he refuses to forget that the baker's wife fed her dog meat fried in butter in a moment when he went hungry. Scurrilous and often funny, his willingness to take advantage of those gullible enough to trust him highlights the poverty and injustice of his own existence.

In contrast, however, to the *cordel* author, who regularly invites readers to delight in the details of how the rogue's hypocritical social superiors get their come-uppance, Suassuna stages a Judgment scene in which the Cricket, who has just died in an encounter with a backlands bandit, is resuscitated and repents of his past misdeeds. Thus, although the play, like the *folhetos* on which it draws, possesses a clear moral message, Suassuna's protagonist is much more complex and more endearing than the great majority of his *cordel* counterparts, who remain gadflies to the end. In addition, the playwright's conception of divine figures such as Christ and the Virgin Mary is notably different from that of *folhetos*. Not only is the Christ of this modern *auto* a black man, but both he and Mary reveal a human, forgiving quality largely alien to the stern saints of the *cordel*.

The influence of the northeastern *folheto* is also clear in a number of the novels of Jorge Amado, who for over half a century has produced novels with an unmistakably regional flavor. Perhaps the single most obvious example of his allegiance to popular culture is his *Tereza Batista cansada de guerra* [*Tereza Batista: Home from the Wars*], which looks to both the *cordel* and Afro-Brazilian religious traditions in terms of theme and structure. Amado's Tereza, a woman from the backlands whose adventurous spirit allows her to overcome all odds, recalls the Medieval Iberian ballad heroine called the *Donzela Guerreira* or Warrior Maiden. (The author's titular "cansada de guerra," literally, "tired of war," is clearly meant to suggest this traditional heroine.)

The novel's positive treatment of the sensual Tereza, however, makes her very different from the overwhelming majority of *folheto* prostitutes, who are cast in a decidedly negative light. Although the *cordel* author initially pictures these figures as leading enviable lives of luxury, they inevitably end up sick, poor, and despised. More often than not, the story concludes with the protagonist herself counseling readers not to follow her sorry example. "Estas dores que hoje sofro" says the unhappy protagonist of João Martins de Ataíde's *A vida de uma meretriz* (n.d.):

> É justo que sofra elas.
> Estas lágrimas que derramo
> Serão em paga daquelas
> Que fiz gotejar dos olhos
> Das casadas e das donzelas.

> [These pains which I suffer today are just,
> and these tears I shed are in payment for others
> that I caused to flow from the eyes
> of married women and virgins.]

Yet, if Amado's Tereza is certainly not characteristic of *folheto* prostitutes in her overt enjoyment of her own sexuality, her unfailing courage does recall a number of the strong-willed *folheto* protagonists collectively known as *mulheres valentes* [valiant women]. Her unswerving loyalty to a personal code of ethics is similarly *cordel*-like. Surrounded by hypocrites and cowards, she does not hesitate to fight and suffer for what she believes.

Amado consciously calls attention to the presence of the *cordel* tradition throughout the novel. The book actually begins with a comparison of Tereza's life to a *folheto* story. "Peste, fome e guerra, morte e amor," asserts the author in an epithet, "a vida de Tereza Batista é uma história de cordel." ["Plague, famine, war, love and death, Tereza Batista's life is a street (*cordel*) ballad."] The book's primary divisions are given multiple, *folheto*-like subtitles. The initial section, for example, is called "A Estreia de Tereza Batista no Cabaré de Aracaju ou O Dente de Ouro de Tereza Batista ou Tereza Batista e o Castigo do Usuário" ["Tereza Batista's debut at the Aracaju cabaret or Tereza Batista's gold tooth or Tereza Batista and how she gave the moneylender his due"]. In the concluding chapter, "A Festa do Casamento de Tereza Batista ou A Greve do Balaio Fechado na Bahia ou Tereza Batista Descarrega a Morte no Mar" ["Tereza Batista's wedding celebration or the 'Closed Basket' strike in Bahia or Tereza Batista dumps Death into the ocean"], the narrator reports that Tereza's marriage has been immortalized in a *folheto*.

The author attempts to reinforce the reader's sense of his tale's allegiance to the *cordel* and the folk and popular culture with which it is associated in various other ways. Illustrations resembling stylized woodcuts, by the Bahian artist, Carybé, are clearly meant to recall the rustic covers of many *folhetos*. Amado likewise incorporates a number of *cordel* forms into his prose. One portion of the book is divided into brief sections, each beginning with subsequent letters of the alphabet in a pointed imitation of the oral improvisational ABC form often utilized by *cordel* poets. Moreover, the supposed author of the verses commemorating Tereza's marriage is none other than the well-known Bahian *folheto* author, Rodolfo Coelho Cavalcante (1919–1984). Rodolfo, one should note, would later compose a *cordel* version of Amado's novel. In his version of the story, Tereza does not live happily ever after, but rather, in good *folheto* fashion, repents of the life of prostitution into which her poverty has forced her. She then dies and lives on as a saint in the memory of the people. ("Tereza no nosso século" remarks the poet, "foi a Pecadora-Santa, / foi a Santa Pecadora." "Tereza was the sinner saint and saintly sinner of our times.")

In addition to authors such as Suassuna and Amado, who make direct use of the *cordel* within their work, there are also others who draw on popular poetry in a more diffuse, though no less noteworthy, manner.

Among the most important representatives of this second group of writers are João Guimarães Rosa (1908–1967), João Cabral de Melo Neto (b. 1920), and Osman Lins (1924–1978). Like both Amado and Suassuna, all three of these authors were born in the northeast (Guimarães Rosa on his family's ranch in the interior of Minas Gerais, Cabral and Lins in the Pernambucan capital of Recife) and, thus, grew up with the *literatura de cordel*. They nonetheless stand apart from our earlier examples in their often extremely cosmopolitan and, in some cases, markedly experimental style, as well as in their predilection in some instances for non-northeastern subject matter. Although regional elements are present in virtually all of Guimarães Rosa's highly inventive prose, Cabral and Lins wholly abandon these in a significant portion of their work.

Like Amado's Tereza Batista, the figure of Diadorim in João Guimarães Rosa's monumental *Grande sertão: veredas* [*The Devil to Pay in the Backlands*] suggests the Medieval Warrior Maiden, as well as her more contemporary, *cordel* counterparts. Despite the absence here of the *folheto* techniques which Amado so conspicuously utilizes, Guimarães Rosa throughout his novel draws on that broader northeastern folk tradition in which the *cordel* has its roots. His heroine, for instance, is ultimately closer than Tereza Batista to the original prototype in her concealment of her sexual identity during prolonged engagement in martial combat. Also, like her *folheto* sisters, Diadorim is both loyal and chaste. The narrator's vision of the world as a stage in which Good and Evil battle – though not his ultimate recognition of this battle's complex humanity – is also reminiscent of the *literatura de cordel*.

An indirect and yet significant relationship to the *cordel* can be seen in the work of the poet João Cabral de Melo Neto. In his widely acclaimed *Morte e vida severina* (1956) [*Death and Life of a Severino*], the poet makes use of a variety of northeastern folk-literary traditions, including the ballad and broadside. Subtitled *Auto de Natal pernambucano* [*A Pernambucan Christmas Play*] the poem invites oral performance. (Indeed, a later edition of the work places it among other "poemas em voz alta" or "poems to be read aloud.")

The protagonist of *Morte e Vida*, the long-suffering Severino, introduces himself to the reader as one of the *amarelinhos* (little hungry ones or, literally, little yellow ones) who appear time and again in *folhetos*. Like a number of his *cordel* counterparts, he finds himself forced to flee drought in the backlands only to encounter repeated injustice in both countryside and city. Although the poet clearly takes a dim view of a social system which produces countless Severinos, he ends, like the *folheto* writer, with a statement of faith. Life, suggests Cabral, is indeed worth living

mesmo quando é assim pequena
a explosão, como a ocorrida;
mesmo quando é uma explosão
como a de há pouco, franzina;
mesmo quando é a explosão
de uma vida severina

[even when the explosion
like that which has occurred is this small,
even when it is an explosion
like this recent, rickety one,
even when it is the explosion
of a Severino-like life].

Echoes of the *cordel* as well as of a more general regional folk and popular literary tradition are similarly visible in the work of Osman Lins. As one would expect, they are most obvious in his overtly regionalist plays, *Lisbela e o prisioneiro* and *Guerra do "Cansa cavalo,"* both of which are set in the northeast and employ unmistakably regional figures and language. They also appear, however, in a more subtle and interesting manner in the prose piece "Retábulo de Santa Joana Carolina," which is part of the collection, *Nove, novena: narrativas* (1966).

This extremely beautiful description of the life of a poverty-stricken northeastern schoolteacher (based on the author's maternal grandmother) contains clear echoes of that class of *cordel* stories known to authors and their audiences as *martírios* ["sufferings" or "martyrdoms"]. A play of voices, the "Retábulo" consistently counterpoints individual and cosmos in its presentation of a series of a dozen "mysteries." In her unfailingly valiant responses to repeated trials, Joana is very much like a *folheto* heroine. The sense of the marvelous, if not the miraculous, which infuses everyday experience throughout the narrative is also highly reminiscent of the *literatura de cordel*. The conclusion, in which the protagonist assumes her place amidst dozens of other poor northeasterners whose proper names also connote flora and fauna (Prados, Pumas, Figueiras, Azucenas, Pereiras, Jacintas, Rosas, Leões, and Margaridas) emphasizes the emblematic, and thus once again *folheto*-like, nature of the prose.

Finally, there are authors whom one would not normally associate with either the northeast or folk traditions who have nonetheless drawn on the *literatura de cordel*. Good examples of this third group are Mário de Andrade (1893–1945), Antônio Callado (b. 1917), and Clarice Lispector (1925–1977). In contrast to the writers we have considered up to this point, these individuals are rarely northeasterners. Of the examples cited, only one – Clarice Lispector – actually lived in the northeast for an extended time. (Ukrainian by birth, Clarice spent part of her childhood in

Recife. She then moved south with her family, however, and went on to spend much of her adult life abroad.)

Mário de Andrade's ties to the *literatura de cordel* take the form of a discussion of *folhetos* about the northeastern outlaws called *cangaceiros* (the term comes from the rifle slung like a yoke or *canga* over the gunman's back), entitled "O romanceiro de Lampeão" (1932). The essay, which focuses on diverse *cordel* presentations of the famous and infamous bandit known throughout the backlands as Lampeão or "Lampião" emphasizes the importance of popular traditions to modernist writers and thinkers. Its subsequent inclusion in *O baile das quatro artes* (1943), a volume containing essays on a wide variety of subjects, calls attention to the role of folk forms in defining the *brasileiridade* or "Brazilianness" which was one of the hallmarks of the early phases of Brazilian *Modernismo* [Modernism]. Mário's interest in *folhetos* and his enthusiasm for the ambiguous *cordel* outlaw belies easy classifications of *Modernismo* as exclusively urban and southern. For Mário, as for many of his fellow Modernists, the *cordel* is as much "art" as Chopin's music, English architecture, and the paintings of Cândido Portinari.

Antônio Callado's attachment to the *literatura de cordel* is obvious in his two-act play, *Forró no Engenho Cananéia*. Written after a stint as a journalist in the state of Pernambuco, *Forró* is atypical of this author's works in its strongly regional flavor, but much like them in its unmistakable political dimension. Callado's play underscores the acute interest in popular culture – particularly that of the vast, poor, and still relatively isolated northeast – which numerous artists and intellectuals developed in the early 1960s. ("We wanted to be able to speak the language of the people," the politically committed contemporary poet, Ferreira Gullar, [b. 1930], explains in a personal interview in Rio de Janeiro, November 24, 1977.) Because the region was, and to this day remains, the stronghold of the traditional landowning system, northeastern folk forms became a national idiom for expressing protest and the desire for reform. This interest did not disappear with the military coup that ousted leftist president João Goulart but, if anything, intensified and grew more diverse. "We had to understand where we had erred," says anthropologist Antônio Augusto Arantes. "We had to understand the people because the people weren't with us in 1964" (interview, Campinas, São Paulo, December 14, 1977).

Finally, it is initially hard to imagine any author farther removed from popular culture than Clarice Lispector. The intensely cosmopolitan and introspective character of her fiction initially appears at odds with the quintessentially regional and action-oriented *literatura de cordel*. Nevertheless, the author's last, and for many critics finest, work, *A hora da estrela* [*The Hour of the Star*] begins with a plethora of subtitles that mimic the *folheto* tradition. Here the author describes the narrative which follows as, among other things, a "lamento de um blue" ["blues lament"], "um assovio no vento escuro" ["a whistle in the dark wind"], "o direito ao grito" ["the right to shout"], and, most significantly for our purposes, an "história lacrimogênica de cordel" ["a tearful *cordel* story"].

Clarice does not return directly to the *cordel* at any time in this novel about the Northeasterner, Macabéa, a homely typist who ekes out a miserable existence in Rio de Janeiro. Nevertheless, perhaps more than any other of the works cited in this discussion, the book captures the spirit of the *literatura de cordel*. Like a long line of semi-literate *folheto* writers, this supremely sophisticated author acknowledges both the crippling reality of poverty and the transformative power of the imagination. Macabéa's love of words and the reality they alternately veil and illumine transcends the limits of her cramped life in a run-down rooming-house. It is even stronger than her need for human love and companionship, as she cannot bring herself to stop asking annoying semantic questions of an erstwhile boyfriend who responds by breaking off with her in bewildered disgust. ("Macabéa, you're a hair in my soup!" he exclaims.) Lispector's sheepish, Coca-Cola-loving heroine embodies the desire not just to speak out against oppression, but to change the world through poetry. Like the countless *folheto* heroes and heroines whom the *cordel*-like title page recalls, Macabéa exhibits *firmeza*. Passive at first glance, her fascination with a world beyond her own minuscule existence makes her in the long run the rebel which her name implies.

The *Hora da estrela* is thus a reminder that, although the word is rendered memorable in the hands of its most skilled and passionate artisans, the true source of its power remains that broader human experience which is and will always be the property of all. Like so many other classics of Brazilian literature, it bears witness to the enduring creative force of popular culture and of the *literatura de cordel*. "Why do all these professors come around here now asking us questions?" muses *cordel* poet Francisco de Souza Campos (b. 1926):

> Well, I don't know for sure, but I suppose it's because there are so many people in this world who have an education and yet who still can't write a single verse. Then you have the poet, a poor devil who never went to school, who has trouble scraping together a few coins for bread or busfare, and he sits down and writes a story that leaves everybody marveling. So to my way of thinking, all these people want to understand just how the poet makes his stories. They are all itching to know how such a miracle occurs.
>
> (Interview, São Lourenço da Mata, Pernambuco, March 1, 1978)

Literary criticism in Brazil
K. David Jackson

The practice of literary criticism in Brazil is characterized historically by the high quality and vitality of critical debate and its importance to national literary, intellectual, cultural, and political life. A progressive development of critical self-awareness is interconnected with foundations and concepts of national history and culture. Dependent on literary creation, on one hand, and archival or legal documents, on the other, critical writing forms a strong and prolific tradition, recently documented in Wilson Martins's two-volume history of Brazilian literary criticism (*A crítica literária no Brasil*) and six-volume history of the Brazilian intelligentsia (*História da inteligência brasileira*), and further described in a wide bibliography of essays on the nature and theory of criticism in Brazil. Cosmopolitan thinkers in a South American context, exemplary founding figures of criticism from the nineteenth century established parameters of intellectual debate, from agnostic and revolutionary to orthodox and traditional, that to a great extent continue to shape the contemporary interchange of critical ideas. The continuing broad social and intellectual influence of critical debate today can be inferred from its prominence in journalistic literary supplements and its continuing relevance to national issues, as well as its growing role in universities and research.

Historical approaches to Brazilian criticism traditionally emphasize exemplary figures and fundamental texts within a chronological framework. Writings of major figures in criticism, starting in the nineteenth century from the Romantics to Sílvio Romero (1851–1914) and Araripe Júnior (1848–1911), can be read both chronologically, drawing on their relationships with literary movements and periods, and thematically, following the evolution and development of their philosophical foundations. In a third sense, these writings extend beyond themselves to establish a critical mass of texts guiding a historical sense of criticism and shaping ways of thinking critically. A body of fundamental texts forms the *corpus* of a Brazilian critical canon, marking its historical and intellectual boundaries.

329

Intertwined with chronology and a canon of selected texts are two overarching concepts identified as persistently characterizing and delimiting the scope of critical thought in Brazil: cosmopolitanism and the sense of nationality. The first deals with international sources, models, and values that made possible the theoretical and philosophical foundations of critical ideas in a colonial society. Cosmopolitan influence shaped the baroque, neoclassical, and romantic periods. Following nineteenth-century Positivism, the principal international critical currents reaching Brazil included Symbolism and aestheticism, European avant-garde movements, Freudianism, and Primitivism (1920s); Marxism and Existentialism (1930s and 1940s); the Anglo-American "New Criticism" ("Generation of 1945"); Germanic or Spanish linguistic circles and phenomenology (1960s); French Structuralism and semiotics (1970s); Poststructuralism and deconstruction (1980s), in addition to philosophical, psychological, and linguistic schools. Using intertextual methods, aesthetic criticism was influenced by stylistics, poetics, and the other arts, while the relationship of literature to history and society was studied in Marxist theory or the works of Walter Benjamin and the Frankfurt School. In the study of morphology, derived from Russian Formalists and French semanticists, Structuralists produced intertextual studies of parody and language, a current leading to Lévi-Strauss and later to psychoanalytic studies and Derridean deconstruction. Deconstructivist critics formulated radical revisions of modernist literary and cultural values. Beginning around 1957, the São Paulo Concrete Poetry movement brought language, translation, and theories of the international artistic and literary Avant-Gardes into the national literary debate, with a polarizing effect on critical debate. A polemical climate opposing aesthetic Formalism to Marxist social criticism dominated critical inquiry from 1950 to 1980, when it was eclipsed by postmodern concerns.

The view of literature as an expression of the sense of nationality, the other founding concept of Brazilian criticism, developed during the romantic period from the convergence of literary history with literary historiography and the idea of national literature. From early on, criticism was bound to political nationalism. Benedito Nunes points out (in "Literary historiography") an inherent conceptual complexity in the instinct of nationality, in that its first literary codification during the romantic period was drawn from the whole colonial age, when national literature was imagined to exist, but had no effective reality. Throughout the long colonial period, Brazilian literature developed from different cultural, ethnic, linguistic, and literary traditions. Its Western legacy was primarily from the classical world, Portugal, and France, while texts that found its multicultural nationality are self-referential chronicles, epics, and myths of discovery. The sense of nationality in this context is always potentially ephemeral, timeless, mysterious, mythical, and incomplete. Intellectual culture had been transplanted in Brazil, while modified by national sentiment and foreign trends, and developed both as a reflection and a distortion of its original models. Concepts of nationality in literature are ultimately concerned with questions of identity, legitimacy, and authenticity. The present essay traces these two overarching concepts in selected critical texts drawn from the historical range of critical thought in Brazil.

Cosmopolitanism and the sense of nationality, natural and complementary companions in a post-colonial society, inevitably produce contradictions and tensions that accompany the development of critical thinking in Brazil. Critical tensions between the two concepts add to the complexity and dynamics of critical thought. First, given the import of political independence from Portugal, the cosmopolitan and the national were considered to be antagonistic currents, whether interpreted in terms of universal versus particular, center versus periphery, artificial versus natural, or foreign versus native. A further tension between cosmopolitanism and nationality arises in the importation of exterior models for analysis of national themes, resulting in a double sense of inadequacy because of the lack of Brazilian philosophy or theory, on the one hand, and the absence of definitive criteria for the definition of authentic or legitimate nationality, on the other. For the first reason, Sílvio Romero dedicated an uncommonly large part of his *História da literatura brasileira* to the philosophy of Tobias Barreto of the Recife school. In the second case, modernist author Mário de Andrade transformed lack of character into one of the principal attributes of a definitive sense of national identity in *Macunaíma*, synthesized in the refrain "Ai! Que preguiça!" ["Ai! I'm bushed!"]. The recourse to cosmopolitan sources for critical currents and ideas, while natural in a country without intellectual traditions or institutions where French culture and language represented an ideal, itself produced a resonance in criticism because of the changes, subtle or radical, undergone by European ideas when brought to the vastly different Brazilian context. Additionally, the idea of imported or derivative culture cultivated arguments of national deficiency, making possible strategies for self-criticism and correction aimed at rescuing national culture from an impasse which had historical roots but was conceptually self-imposed and perpetuated as a theme of criticism. As a corollary, nationalist criticism is often considered to have accepted too unquestioningly the unity and coherence of its cosmopolitan models, while doubting its own critical authority. Theories of national difference, analyzing questions of legitimacy and authenticity, constitute an enduring line of critical debate.

The history of criticism in Brazil can be conceived of in large periods or epochs. The colonial background, especially the Brazilian baroque style, laid foundations for national ideas that were codified only during Romanticism. Historiographic accounts of the New World depicted the land's magical, Utopian qualities, as writing began to break with its European models. The Brazilian Baroque, epitomized by the rational and ornate sermons of the Jesuit Antônio Vieira (1608–1697), first published in Portugal in 1907–1909 and in Brazil in 1943–1945, was an early example of a European aesthetic that took strong root in Brazil. Similarly, Arcadist poets prefigured political independence with themes of Nature and the Indian, while altering their European models, as seen in O Uraguai by Basílio da Gama (1741–1795), published in Lisbon in 1769. The association of literature with political nationalism and cultural identity, created by Romanticism, later became increasingly an enduring criterion of value. Criticism defined the instinct of nationality in the cultural sources of Brazilian writing, whether in the idealization of the Noble Savage, the slave, the pioneer, or through perceived superlative qualities of the land, people, and Nature. Modern literary historiography continues to reflect the heritage of the nineteenth-century romantic period, including European traveler–scholars. Foreign commentators on Brazilian literature in this period include Friedrich Bouterwek (1765–1828), Simonde de Sismondi (1773–1842), Ferdinand Denis (1798–1890), and Almeida Garrett (1799–1854). Notable Brazilian contributors include José Inácio de Abreu e Lima (1794–1869), Ferdinand Wolf (1796–1866), Domingos Gonçalves de Magalhães (1811–1882), Francisco Adolfo de Varnhagen (1816–1878), Pereira da Silva (1817–1897), and Joaquim Norberto de Sousa e Silva (1820–1891).

A second moment, in the late nineteenth and early twentieth centuries, is dominated by the scientific Naturalism, also termed agnostic evolutionism, of Sílvio Romero and by deterministic theories of race, culture, and milieu following Darwin and Spencer. Romero applied his scientific critical spirit, in the sense of the day, to propose another effective reality for Brazilian nationality, opposed to the Romantics, substituting the mulatto for the Indian or caboclo. Truths of scientific analysis are seen as critical tools to correct the national defects and inferiorities assumed by Naturalistic principles: a population deteriorated by miscegenation, subservient dependence on foreign goods and ideas that culminated in a false identity, and lack of inner convictions and determination. Positivism derived from Comte and Taine, with its motto of order and progress, provided a pervasive model that would underlie subsequent concepts of modernization and social change. In contrast, Machado de Assis and José Veríssimo brought aesthetic critieria to the expression of nationality, supplanting or modifying naturalistic outlooks with broader literary, social, and psychological bases to support the sense of nationality. Symbolist criticism was represented by Nestor Vítor (1868–1932), João Ribeiro (de Andrade Fernandes) (1860–1934), and Graça Aranha (1868–1931), whose philosophical essays (*A estética da vida*; *O espírito moderno*) on the inchoate modern spirit provided a theory for early Modernists.

Essayists of the late nineteenth century cite the need for systematic, scientific, or doctrinaire criticism as a fundamental ingredient of a developing national literature. In "O ideal do crítico" Machado de Assis (1839–1908) cites, as a purpose of criticism, the improvement of the quality of a new literature, based on the necessary principles of sincerity, solicitude, and justice. In Machado's essay, criticism further benefits from qualities of coherence, systematization, independence, impartiality, tolerance, moderation, urbanity, tact, and perseverance. Applied criticism depends exclusively on the critic's moral conscience, and the objective is impartial truth. Armed with this self-tutelage, the ideal critic should search out the spirit and soul of a book, which is then analyzed according to laws and rules of beauty. Within this formula, Machado applies to literary criticism criteria of ethics, aesthetics, and nationality, which he understands as an intimate and interior sentiment of time and place, conveyed through universal rules and practices of art.

Machado de Assis's 1873 essay on the "O instinto da nacionalidade" underlies subsequent critical reflections on a theme that remains fundamental in national thought and letters to the present. Machado considers that national touches can give shape and independence to a nascent but ill-formed literature in need of a basis for invention. He distinguishes between a local color of national tradition in customs of the interior and the capital cities, with their mixture of European influences; likewise, his society differed across time. What best confirms Brazil's complex nationality for Machado, however, is observation and analysis of passions and character, in his opinion a rare quality little-developed by authors. The Indian, a prime symbol of nationality for the Romantics, is for Machado as much universal as Brazilian, one of many sources in the dichotomy of barbarous or civilized antecedents to nationality, along with social customs and the splendor of Nature. Machado further considers that a nationalistic spirit is not limited to local themes, and he notes that even unquestionably Brazilian authors wrote on universal subjects, even borrowed from other literatures: what makes Shakespeare an essentially English poet, he argued, is not British territory or history. Rather than theme, which may be remote in time and place, Machado finds a certain intimate sentiment that connects an author to a particular time and nationality. His sense of nationality is more interior than exterior.

A principal interpreter of the critical method of Sílvio Romero, Antônio Cândido sees in the contradictions and revolutionary potential of his criticism the reflection of a complex, disturbed, and discordant society, a nervous image of the country, seemingly in flagrant contradiction with the objective and scientific methods with which Romero wished to approach critical activities (*O método crítico de Sílvio Romero*, 240). Writing on "A função da crítica" (in Cândido, *Sílvio Romero*), Romero promotes criticism as a remedy for a weak and derivative national literature. Scientific criticism is all the more necessary, in his view, to correct and attack an atmosphere suffocated by the preconceptions and falsities of a poor, banal national spirit, corrupted by Portuguese and French ideas. Criticism should be composed therefore of purity, truth, nobility of convictions, and faith in itself. Similarly, the nation should seek to be cultured, free, and original. This relationship between criticism and nationality invokes a prescription, in Romero's terms, for writing with passion, and herein the contradiction: his is a strong criticism serving the country's future with a higher reason, unappreciated by the nationalistic formulae and illusions of Romanticism. Acting as doctor, soldier, or biological scientist, Romero attacks all barriers to enlightened development and national self-realization. The critic's passionate role crosses into the creative realm through its dramatic sense of reform and epic purpose, as an adjunct to the earlier sense of nationality.

Romero's essay on "A psicologia nacional" (1881), based on positivistic theory, also evidences the influence of Machado de Assis's earlier essay, "O instinto." The instinct of nationality is also for Romero a spirit of the time, deficient in education and imitative of foreign influences, primarily as a consequence of race, but nevertheless an original, popular, and spontaneous spirit related to ethnography, generalized as a national spirit. Making use of Positivism, he defines political and social evolution as a revolutionary process by which the strongest devour the weakest in a natural social selection. Contradictorily, Romero supports the idea of an autonomous regional, multiple, and decentralized Brazil in which the national soul is the sum of widely diverse, lively provincial customs. Perhaps foreseeing the future, Romero warns against the compressive, uniformizing centralism emanating from the capitals, since the national soul lies in the ethnography of a diverse land and peoples.

José Veríssimo (1857–1916), author (*Cenas da vida amazônica* [1886]) and critic (*História da literatura brasileira*), while sharing a view of Brazilian literature as weak and imitative and advancing a sense of national sentiment as subtle and undefinable, rejects the naturalist school and promotes a systematic definition of the historicity of texts employing aesthetic above national criteria. In the essay "A literatura nacional e os estudos literários" (1894), Veríssimo relates the value of literature to spiritual, literary, and scientific culture. Defending critical independence, Veríssimo affirms that the literary work does not depend on schools or theories. The intimate sense of nationality, rather, must be joined to the idea of individual talent, understood as taste and opinion joined to keen observation and sincerity of purpose. In this sense, Machado de Assis, who avoids nationalist themes or settings, would better represent his time and place than the formulaic novels of Aluísio de Azevedo, best represented by *O homem*, whose social and psychological pathology is determined by precepts of the naturalist school. Veríssimo values the relationship between a writer's historical moment and the representation of national or human aspirations, which he recognizes in the fecundity and vigor of the Romantics. He considers both author and critic to be free, independent, and eclectic writers to be judged in accord with the faithful observation and representation of their circumstances and environment.

The modernist movement begun in the 1920s effectively changed the historical appreciation of the past, particularly through a sense of intellectual autonomy and through analysis of society by the developing social sciences. The latter are represented by *Retrato do Brasil* by Paulo Prado (1869–1943); *Casa grande e senzala* by Gilberto Freyre (1900–1987); *Raízes do Brasil* by Sérgio Buarque de Holanda (1902–1982); *A cultura brasileira* by Fernando de Azevedo (b. 1894) and *História da literatura brasileira; seus fundamentos econômicos* (1938) by Nelson Werneck Sodré (b. 1911) and *Formação da sociedade brasileira*. Creative writers also developed critical perspectives. Modernists sought out the autochthonous, folkloric roots of national life and letters, motivated by a resurgence of scholarship on questions of cultural identity leading to a critical, and at times ideological, examination of national values. Individual literary interpretations based on cultural, historical, sociological, or aesthetic considerations were informed by an often eclectic mixture of European schools of thought. In the modernist sense of nationality, following Nunes, Brazil's supposed defects became superiorities. Emphasis on Brazil's diverse folk traditions and ethnic make-up produced a vital sense of national culture, evidenced in such composite literary personages as Juca Mulato, Jeca Tatu, and Macunaíma. Modernists were, in effect, redefining Brazil through compression, reduction, and centralization of culture, rooted in a sense of nationality conceived and directed by the urban intelligentsia that it served. If during the modernist period international critical and philosophical currents became Brazilianized, at the same time what was defined as national cultural reality was cast as an object of study or data for scientific research or collection and was later placed at risk as one of the goods of modernization. As a consequence of the Modernists' centralizing thought, culture and literature emerged as a coherent and perhaps self-sufficient system that, in itself, provided a source of national originality and critical innovation that would profoundly influence contemporary Brazil.

During the modernist period, criticism became a tool in the declaration of the aesthetic independence of national life. Many Modernist authors were also critics, as is the case of Ronald de Carvalho (1893–1935), who published a brief history of Brazilian literature (*Pequena história da literatura brasileira*), Manuel Bandeira (1886–1968), and Sérgio Buarque de Holanda, who published anthologies of national poetry. Oswald de Andrade's "Manifesto da poesia pau-brasil" (1924) ["Manifesto of Pau-Brasil Poetry" and "Manifesto antropófago" (1928) ["Cannibal Manifesto"] also contain cultural and social criticism. Mário de Andrade's letters and essays, particularly *A escrava que não é Isaura* (1924), are prime sources for creative theory and analysis, drawing on European sources such as Apollinaire's "L'esprit nouveau," with a sense of national expression based on Primitivism, myth, and folklore. His essay "O movimento modernista" (1942) is a retrospective recognition of the parallel roles of criticism and creation in a movement that served vanguardist cosmopolitanism and fervent nationalism simultaneously. Mário's negative appraisal resurrects contradictions between method and nationality formulated earlier by Romero. Mário characterizes the period as self-consuming, a destructive convulsion of the sense of nationality, called Brazilian reality. Extreme attitudes of protest and revolt inspired by European avant-garde movements faithfully reflect the negativity of their own moment, in his opinion, through the loss of legitimacy and "autophagic self-destruction" of São Paulo's traditional aristocracy. On the positive side, Mário reconstitutes Brazilian reality in three principles that fuse scientific and creative trends: aesthetic research, artistic intelligence, and creative consciousness. Using ideas rooted in Veríssimo, Mário calls for critical individualism and rejection of literary schools. He recalls the time as one of a contradictory and continuous state of celebration, in which the Brazilian world was created anew through the metaphor of cannibalist consumption. If the advent of Modernism was a historical inevitability, it was nevertheless played out with unquestioned vitality. Thus, in his dual roles of modernist creator and critic, Mário de Andrade promoted theoretical analysis of national culture as a symbolic system, joining aesthetic independence to critical nationality.

Oswald de Andrade, in his retrospective essay "O caminho percorrido" (1944) in *Ponta de lança*, represents a contrast in the use of criticism for a polemical and rhetorical defense of modernist aesthetics. He identifies a divided national critical legacy in Machado de Assis and Euclides da Cunha (1866–1909): the pessimism of a condemned society and a mystic or messianic populism, respectively. Also underlying his essay is a sense of national history as potentiality, an illogical process whose meaning is the sum of unclear events. Adopting a nationalist point of view, Oswald legitimizes modernist qualities of subversion and rebellion by allying them with a historical chronology of popular revolt, beginning with the political independence movement of Vila Rica. The historical significance of each moment further lies in its ties with the economic "revolutions" of gold and coffee. Thus Oswald defends the notion of a subjective nationality, economically based, expressed in the struggle for unrealized goals and in language that links radical aesthetics with economics and technology, within a scheme of national evolution and progress.

Under Oswald's program, the independent intellectual or critic struggles against the grain of a condemned society, while ironically giving voice to inchoate popular and prophetic national aspirations. Through Jorge Amado and others, the people for the first time become characters in the Brazilian novel, as one of the fruits of native Primitivism that was in his opinion the modernist movement's pivotal innovation. For Oswald, the "Cannibal Manifesto"'s metaphor of consumption, as part of that Primitivism, prefigured the economic crisis of 1929 and the political revolution of 1930, and its intellectuals paid a price for their advanced political program found in the "Cannibal Magazine"'s second "dentition" (edition), addressing issues including divorce and abortion. A confluence of aesthetics and ideology describes Oswald's Neo-romantic and Avant-Garde view of the artist as fighter for the modernization and salvation of society, who still maintained a posture of ingenuous "hospitable joviality" or cordiality then considered endemic to the sense of nationality.

Critical writing became a professional activity during this period, led by the eminent and prolific Catholic critic Alceu de Amoroso Lima (1893–1983), who used the pseudonym of Tristão de Athayde. A national critical production was advanced by Alvaro Lins (1912–1970; *Jornal de Crítica*), Sérgio Milliet (1898–1966; *Diário Crítico*), Agripino Grieco (1888–1973; editor of the *Boletim de Ariel*), and Otto Maria Carpeaux (1900–1978; *História da literatura ocidental*). Lúcia Miguel-Pereira (1903–1959) added a feminine voice to criticism, with an analysis of the development of the Brazilian novel in *Prosa de ficção*. Although neglected, Patrícia Galvão (1910–1962) reinvigorated a renovating current of cultural and literary criticism through journalism in radical or ephemeral publications such as *Vanguarda Socialista* (1945–1946). Intellectual and critical orientations were documented in *Testamento de uma geração* by Edgard Cavalheiro (1911–1958) and Mário Neme's *Plataforma da Nova Geração*. From the 1940s, literary supplements became prime vehicles for critical activity, later illustrated by Mário Faustino (1930–1962) in the *Jornal do Brasil*.

The foundations of critical change following the fading of Modernism around 1945 range from the internationalism of Carpeaux to an intense reinforcement of the canons of Brazilian literature. The canon is newly codified in historical series, represented in the 1960s by *Manifestações literárias da era colonial* by José Aderaldo Castello (b. 1921), *O Romantismo* by Antônio Soares Amora (b. 1917), *O Realismo* by João de Almeida Pacheco, *O Simbolismo* by Massaud Moisés (b. 1928), *O Pré-modernismo* by Alfredo Bosi (b. 1936), and *O Modernismo* by Martins (b. 1921). Coutinho began the volumes of *A literatura no Brasil* (1956), Mário da Silva Brito (b. 1916) published the first volume of *História do Modernismo brasileiro*, and Alfredo Bosi his *História concisa da literatura brasileira*, leading to Martins's *História da inteligência brasileira* and Moisés's five-volume *História da literatura brasileira* (1980s). These canonical treatises were complemented and counterbalanced by rich theoretical and interpretive essays.

Afrânio Coutinho (b. 1911) and Antônio Cândido (b. 1918) are among leading voices in critical theory and a strong influence on the formal poetics of João Cabral de Melo Neto (b. 1920) and his school, after 1945. Coutinho expanded the scope of Brazilian literature and its claims of originality by dating the first signs of nationality from the moment of Brazil's discovery and by revaluing the Baroque in the literary origins of what he termed a "fortunate tradition" (*A tradição afortunada*). Giving equal privilege to theories of political and aesthetic autonomy, Coutinho introduced Anglo-American New Criticism to Brazil. His essay on "O instinto da nacionalidade" (1959), expanding on Machado de Assis, posits a universality within Machado's intimate sense of nationality, operating through forms of acculturation or assimilation that absorb foreign elements into a new Brazilian totality. Coutinho's theory of the universal in the national, reminiscent of the cannibalist metaphor, draws on the critical background and currents of the Western tradition to enrich a national identity that itself inscribes a plural world of vast and substantial cultures. Coutinho's nationalism looks inward and can be said to create sophisticated but closed forms by borrowing from cosmopolitan aesthetic tradition, translating and "transfiguring great masters and models" into thought and language so singular that only Brazilians can feel and understand them (*Conceito de literatura brasileira*).

Antônio Cândido, an avid reader of Romero and Veríssimo, joins the Romerian tradition, linking literature and society to aesthetic bases of criticism and a humanistic culture. Cândido's *Formação da literatura brasileira*, contrary to Coutinho, identifies the first dense configuration of national expression in mid eighteenth-century descriptions of Nature, character, and rhetoric, initiating the struggle for acculturation in a land of weak literary sensibilities. Certain traits of nationality may be responsible for privileging the selection and aesthetic treatment of literary themes, although the resulting works function as autonomous entities ruled by their special characteristics. In the neoclassical Arcadists, Cândido finds a model for harmonizing nationality and expression, through the assimilation and reworking of classical forms and themes from the Western tradition. An inverse formulation of the sense of national identity is found in Cândido's essay "Dialética da malandragem," an analysis of Manuel Antônio de Almeida's novel *Memórias de um sargento de milícias* (1854–1855), in which the roguish hero personifies a hierarchical society whose structural similarity to the European masks a fundamental difference in function. Its characters operate according to picaresque relationships in an inverted morality, passing freely between spheres of order and disorder. In this sense, Cândido defined a dystopic national character through a subtle reflection in aesthetic form of society functioning to produce advantage, of which Macunaíma is one of the later incarnations. Cândido's essay posits the difference of Brazilian culture from its models as a distinctive although critical national trait.

Extensive contemporary production has broadened and refined the critical, aesthetic, and ideological judgments of literary history, while reflecting the modern theoretical crisis in literary historiography, as descriptive prose is questioned by new concepts of language and textuality. Any account of recent criticism must of necessity be highly selective and incomplete. Major contributors to dominant critical trends, from semiotics, feminism, deconstruction, intertextuality, and metalanguage to ideological, aesthetic, textual, formal, or other eclectic positions, include Aracy Amaral (b. 1930), Augusto de Campos (b. 1931), Haroldo de Campos (b. 1929), Walnice Nogueira Galvão (b. 1937), Luiz Costa Lima (b. 1937), Telê Porto Ancona Lôpez (b. 1938), José Guilherme Merquior (1941–1990), Benedito Nunes (b. 1929), Leyla Perrone-Moisés (b. 1934), Affonso Romano de Sant'Anna (b. 1937), Silviano Santiago (b. 1936), Roberto Schwarz (b. 1938), and Flora Sussekind (b. 1955), among others. Brazilian literary scholarship, as well as writing, draws from cosmopolitan trends of criticism which are interwoven in the national context with popular and indigenous culture. The temporal model of production faces an alternate syncretic model characterized by rupture with tradition and emphasizing a dysphoric rather than euphoric sense of nationality, in terms proposed by Haroldo de Campos ("Da razão antropofágica"). Criticism itself has become an autonomous topic of critical writing. Theoretical foundations of critical thinking have become greatly enhanced in an interpenetration of national and cosmopolitan values, while the symbolic and critical whole of "Brazilian culture" as a limit to criticism is being redrawn in view of postmodern and transnational models of critical thinking.

Recent criticism has expanded the scope of Brazilian critical thought in relation to theory and nationality by a thorough participation in transnational currents, characterized by the autonomy and self-referentiality of criticism as a field, and including a reappraisal of the nature of Brazilian or Latin American national identity and writing. Brazilian critics have sought to reformulate and to restate the principal thematic lines and questions of national criticism, within the context of theoretical and conceptual advances. Recent lines of investigation include texts and editions, advanced by the Instituto de Estudos Brasileiros and the UNESCO Archives project and women's studies in literature and criticism (see Gotlib, A mulher na literatura). Distinguished critical essays incorporate or expound on cosmopolitan currents, while addressing the question of tradition versus innovation. The debate on imitative versus authentic in national literary expression is constantly reshaped through the blend of national and transnational thinking.

Aesthetic, philosophical, and artistic critical currents are represented by Benedito Nunes and Aracy Amaral. Uniting philosophy with aesthetic criticism and language, Nunes analyzes Brazilian literary modernity, its relationship to the European vanguards, its specificity in Brazil, and its literary and philosophical backgrounds. Oswald, canibal defends the suggestive philosophical tenets of Oswald de Andrade's "cannibal movement" as a theory touching ethnic substrata of national civilization in an inversion, or subversion, of European influences. One of the first critics of Clarice Lispector, Nunes analyzes the relationship between her near-mystical view of reality and the drama of language designed to express what seems to surpass words. In interdisciplinary and intertextual studies of aesthetic expression, Aracy Amaral integrates modernist literature and the plastic arts in her books on Tarsila do Amaral, the Modern Art Week, and Blaise Cendrars in Brazil.

No longer limited by nationality, Brazilian critics are also active in transnational currents. Augusto de Campos's "anticriticism" connects neovanguardist practices with syncretic reconstruction of literary innovation as a tradition in the intellectual essay. Redefining tradition in terms of novelty and invention, Campos recovered and interpreted the works of "lost" authors whose works demand a reevaluation of aesthetics: Sousândrade, Kilkerry, Pagu. One of few critics to work with music and plastic arts, Campos introduced the indeterminacy of composer John Cage into critical prose. The late José Guilherme Merquior wrote on the history of European literary and intellectual culture, in the framework of the evolution and analysis of critical ideas, which he applied to Brazilian authors. Luiz Costa Lima's concept of "control" of historical imagination is a broad theory applied to literature, culture, and philosophy in European and Brazilian literatures since the Renaissance. The idea of control is not overt, but rather seeks to define a border or limit to the possibilities of imaginative construction, inherent in the expressive context of any historical moment or period, captured in its fundamental building blocks and mode of thought. The theory conceives of the literary imagination, and subsequent writing, as subject to unstated limits exercised by formative conditions of culture, both literary and extraliterary. Silviano Santiago explores the concept of "in between" to define the space of Latin American writing, redefining positions of cosmopolitanism and nationality through a spatial form of intertextuality. Neither totally derivative nor self-contained, the "in between" narrative is capable of influencing and revitalizing previously hegemonic literatures.

Readdressing the theme of inadequacy in national character, its status as a copy or imitation of foreign models, and its search for authenticity, ingeniously treated by Cândido, Roberto Schwarz analyzes different critical perspectives in "Nacional por subtração" in *Que horas são?* ["Brazilian Culture: Nationalism by Elimination"]. Schwarz identifies a fundamental problem in the historical insistence on harmony and homogeneity and Nature and cultural life, as found in Romero, as criteria of authenticity in a country whose social and economic relationships were defined by disequality on every level. The crisis of imitation, for Schwarz, is rather a symptom of other kinds of deficiencies endemic to the old colonial system and its forms of cultural expropriation, polarized into elite and slave groups. Rather than opposition, Schwarz discerns an occult dynamic of interdependence between model and copy, borne out by two literary theories of cultural production originating in Brazil. Oswald de Andrade's "Antropofagia" inverts the equation of dependency through local Primitivism that regenerates culture through a Utopian metaphor of consumption. Secondly, the theorization of an original cultural voice for Latin America, neither totally indigenous nor totally derivative, becomes an antidote for the question of imitation. Essays by Santiago and Haroldo de Campos elaborate the "space in between" or the "dialogue and difference" that constitute the creative power of the periphery over central cultures through the growth of alternate paradigms. Schwarz's examples illustrate how contemporary criticism considers the question of national identity as a critical construct to be studied within its own historical evolution.

Leyla Perrone-Moisés, in an analysis of the methodology of comparative literature ("Literatura comparada: intertexto e antropofagia" [1982] *Flores da escrivaninha*), makes a case for the reformulation and resolution of historical questions of cosmopolitanism and nationality, separating the problem from its political context. Given that Brazilian letters were created under a colonial "anxiety of influence," manifested historically either by cultural deficiency or self-sufficiency in comparison with "superior" cosmopolitan literatures, Perrone-Moisés proposes a theoretical resolution involving open criticism and the aesthetics of reception, grounded in Oswald de Andrade's theory of cultural cannibalism in "Antropofagia." If metropolitan cultures of origin were themselves made up of shifting relationships between national and foreign elements, the insistence upon national cultural independence and originality would be based on an illusion, or false problem. Perrone-Moisés prefers the metaphor of nationality as absorption and transformation, grounded in the "Manifesto antropófago" of 1928, in order to redefine literary tradition in terms of receptivity and critical choice. She sees in the cannibal metaphor of ritual devouring a form of intertextuality, beyond notions of influence or originality, that subjects tradition to a constant redefinition and reexamination through the constantly changing relationship between self and other. Perrone-Moisés places Oswald de Andrade's manifesto alongside other critical theories of tradition and originality proposed by Bakhtin, Tinianov, Kristeva, and Borges.

Constructing a transnational view of literary innovation in the critical essay, Haroldo de Campos developed the concept of dialogue and difference (in the sense of Derrida) in the Brazilian tradition, both through the aesthetics of a rupture of genres and a critical, dystopic nationalism, reinforced by the recovery of neglected authors such as Sousândrade and Oswald de Andrade. Experimental art, privileging aesthetic invention as an instigator of national advancement, can act as an agent of difference. As a creative writer, Campos illustrates the orienting role of criticism in contemporary composition. In essays favoring open works or art within a synchronic canon of literary history (A arte no horizonte do provável), Campos was a precursor of Umberto Eco. Campos's selection was composed of aesthetically original and thematically critical expressions of nationality, grounded in the baroque tradition of Gregório de Matos and extending to the neo-vanguard movement of Concrete Poetry. This broad temporal scope, translated into aesthetic theory, led Campos to revalue Brazil's baroque heritage in contemporary forms of writing, while postulating the tenets of national postmodernity as postutopian writing. Campos further represents a new stage in the fusion of creator and critic: his activity as translator, from the Bible, Dante, and Goethe to Mallarmé, Joyce, and Pound, informs his own poetic works, uniting linguistic creativity with the elaboration of universal themes of literary traditions. Criticism and translation share a new linguistic and textual basis for creation, raising national poetic expression to the level of cosmopolitan art in a world context, where all traditions serve the ends of national poetic production. The result, in terms of national expression, is poetry for exportation whose universality lies both within and beyond a sense of nationality defined by Campos as invention, thus joining in a transnational context aesthetic independence with the classic Romerian ideal of a "cultured, free, and original" national literature.

If Modernism altered the reading of the past, transnational and postmodern criticism in Brazil reinvented the tradition as a critical construct, subjecting it to ever more rigorous modes of analysis. It remains to be seen whether this vigorous and serious critical apparatus will achieve an effective reality in national life comparable to that of its romantic predecessors.

The essay: architects of Brazilian national identity
Thomas E. Skidmore

For more than a century Brazilian intellectuals have agonized over their country's national identity. Until the 1950s they attempted to capture its essence by relying on colorful language and historical allusions. Building on a paradoxical combination of faith and doubt, they wrestled especially with the troublesome question of how racial intermixture had affected the Brazilian character. Such a preoccupation had been common among elite thinkers of Latin America since the late nineteenth century, when the theories of white racial superiority arrived with the prestige conferred by North Atlantic "science." The questions remained constant. Who are we? How have we become this way? Does a racially mixed people have a future in the "civilized" world?

This chapter focuses on some of the most influential Brazilian writers who have taken up these themes. They all tried to define Brazil's national identity in both a cultural and a political dimension. For each historical period, the context is sketched and the focus turns to one or two of the period's most widely read books on Brazilian national identity. All of these works went through numerous printings and are still read in Brazil.

The years from 1870 to 1889 saw the Brazilian empire in decline. Despite Brazilian victory in the Paraguayan War (1865–1870), Emperor Dom Pedro II faced increasing opposition at home from a republican movement. In 1889 the higher military, endorsing republican ideology, deposed the only genuine monarchy that nineteenth-century Latin America had ever produced. These years also saw the rapid rise of coffee as Brazil's chief export, restricted largely to the south central areas, especially the states of Rio de Janeiro, Minas Gerais, and São Paulo. This shifted the Brazilian economy southward and, along with the decline of sugar and cotton, contributed to the rapid economic decline of the northeast, whose sugar economy had fueled the prosperity of colonial Brazil.

Virtually all observers branded Brazilian literature of the era as

345

unoriginal and uninteresting, modeled largely on that of Paris. In the realm of ideas, Brazilian thinkers were powerfully influenced by social Darwinism and by French Positivism. Overlaying both was a vague liberalism – especially from France and England – which had been an important trademark of Brazilian politics since Independence in 1822.

Outsiders in these years tended to see Brazil as little more than a tropical appendage of Europe. Sanitation was primitive, even in the largest cities, and epidemic diseases such as yellow fever were common. It had been the last country in the Americas to abolish slavery (1888). Against this backdrop Brazilian intellectuals struggled to define their country's national identity. One of the pioneers was the combative intellectual and literary critic, Sílvio Romero (1851–1914).

Romero, born in the frequently drought-stricken northeastern state of Sergipe, fought his way up to become a major literary critic in the national capital of Rio de Janeiro. His *História da literatura brasileira* was the first comprehensive overview of Brazilian literary history by a Brazilian. In it he discussed Brazilian national character at length.

Romero described himself as a Social Darwinist, arguing that race and environment were the keys to understanding artistic creation. An incurable polemicist, he often contradicted himself to score a debating point. Yet his inconsistencies had another, more fundamental explanation. Looking at Brazil through the lens of Social Darwinism did not lead to comfortable speculation. Describing himself as "always inspired by the ideal of an autonomous Brazil, independent in politics and even more so in literature" (Romero, *História*, I, xxiv), Romero argued that Brazil "could never be creative and up to date in adapting European doctrines and schools of thought to the Brazilian social and literary world, unless Brazilians first understood the state of thought in the Old World and had a clear idea of our own past and present" (I, 11).

Romero, like all educated Brazilians of his era, was highly sensitive to the question of race. (The 1872 census showed the population to be only 38% white, a figure which varied between 44% and 55% in the censuses from 1890 to 1980.) He was virtually alone, however, in acknowledging that Brazilians were fundamentally a racially mixed people. "Every Brazilian is a *mestiço*, if not in blood, then in ideas. The initial contributing factors were the Portuguese, the Negro, the Indian, the physical environment and imitation of foreigners" (I, 4), he explained. What was the link to the Brazil of the 1880s? "We have an unhealthy population, which leads a short, sickly, and unhappy life" (I, 46), a plight that Romero saw as having resulted from the massive use of slaves. "The white man, the coldhearted author of so many crimes, took everything he could from the Indian and the Negro and then discarded them like useless objects. He was helped by his son and collaborator, the *mestiço*, who succeeded him, assuming his color and his power" (I, 55).

Romero thought the African had contributed much more than the Indian to the creation of the new nationality. "The African race has had an enormous influence in Brazil, second only to the European; it has penetrated our intimate life and shaped in great part our everyday psychology" (I, 89). Romero then gave his argument a twist unique in his day: "The Negro, who does not exist in most Spanish American republics, has enabled us to distinguish ourselves from them in a highly positive way" (I, 53).

Romero was a prolific literary critic and commentator on culture and politics. He delighted in attacking establishment politicians and self-important local literati. His most remembered literary judgment was also his least felicitous: a scathing criticism of Machado de Assis for having failed to create any memorable fictional personages (*Machado de Assis*). However, he was closer to the mark in excoriating the Brazilian reading public as apathetic. Brazil, he said, was still living on "second- or third-hand" European ideas (*História*, I, 102).

Yet Romero never surrendered his emotional commitment to his country. He urged his readers to be confident. He ended the prologue of his *História* with a characteristic declaration: "Literary independence and scientific independence, both reinforcing Brazil's political independence – that is my life's dream. They are the triple challenge for the future. We must be confident!" (I, xxvi).

In fact, Romero's language was ambiguous enough to be read in two ways. Pessimistic Brazilians could choose to believe the determinist theories he outlined, while the optimists could fix on his nationalist championing of Brazil's cultural originality. The optimists could also take reassurance from his argument (to which he himself was not always faithful) that Brazil's population would inevitably become whiter. Romero thought that European immigrants, who began flocking to Brazil in the late 1880s, would accelerate this "whitening" process. Romero himself was on balance an optimist, notwithstanding his nervous references to determinist theories. It was probably this very optimism that attracted so many readers then and since.

After the army deposed Emperor Dom Pedro II in 1889 and declared a Republic, the first two presidents came from among the victorious generals. The leaders of the Republican party, who had furnished the ideological rationale for the army's coup, did not gain power until 1894, when a São Paulo politician was elected the first civilian president. The Republicans' first decade saw a series of armed threats to the new regime. In 1893, for example, naval officers favoring a return of the monarchy seized control of a fleet in the Rio de Janeiro bay, threatening to close the port if their demands were not met. They eventually surrendered, but not before fomenting considerable political disruption. The nervous republican government banned monarchist candidates from running for office and imposed censorship on the small but articulate movement urging a return to royal rule.

Another monarchist challenge soon provided the venue for a literary classic that became another landmark analysis of Brazil's national identity. It was the 1896 rebellion at Canudos, in the backlands of the vast northeastern state of Bahia. A messianic community had formed, refusing to acknowledge local government authority. An army column was sent to subdue them, but the rebels withstood it. The rebels finally fell, massacred to the last man (some women and children survived) by army reinforcements.

Euclides da Cunha (1866–1909), a young former army officer turned journalist, was sent by a leading São Paulo newspaper to cover the rebellion at Canudos, 1,000 miles to the north. He arrived in time to witness the final massacre. Deeply moved by the rebels' courage, he wrote a series of stirring newspaper dispatches describing the backlanders' epic struggle against overwhelming odds. He then expanded his coverage into what became an instant classic, Os sertões [Rebellion in the Backlands].

What kind of book was it? The first quarter was a detailed essay on the interaction of man and environment in the semi-arid sertão region, explained according to the science of the day. This gave many Brazilian readers their first real look at the drought-ridden northeastern backlands. In addition to applying the latest geological and climatological wisdom of the day, Euclides repeated the views of leading European spokesmen for scientific racism, such as Gumplowicz and Lapouge. "A mixing of highly diverse races is usually prejudicial," he argued, adding that "miscegenation carried to an extreme brings retrogression" (Os sertões [1985], 174). The person of mixed blood "is a degenerate who lacks the physical energy of his savage ancestors, and does not have the intellectual distinction of his civilized ancestors" (p. 175).

The final three-quarters of the book recounted the army's campaign to subdue the rebels. Euclides saw the latter's courage and cunning as dramatically demonstrating man's potential in the sertão, a perception that seemed to contradict his earlier acceptance of scientific racism.

He described the drama on two levels. One was the military battle. Euclides depicted the insurgents' skill in using their environment against the army – luring the soldiers into ambushes in unfamiliar country, watching them cut to ribbons by the cacti and poisoned by eating nonedible plants they had never before seen. As for the vainglorious and incompetent army officers Euclides described, no reader could fail to see the divergence between the reality of hostile Bahia and the fantasy world of the War Ministry in Rio de Janeiro.

On another level his book indicted the very people of mixed blood whose courage he admired. Euclides attributed their rebellion largely to the emotional instability of the *sertanejos*, personified in the "atavistic" personality of their renegade leader and ex-priest, Antônio Conselheiro. Here Euclides expressed the elite's worry – articulated earlier by Sílvio Romero – about the connection between the biology of miscegenation and the process of nation-building. If race mixing created instability, how long would it take to achieve a stable national identity?

These two levels of analysis led to two different conclusions. The first was the urgent need for political reform, which followed from the hair-raising accounts of army incompetence, itself reflecting the elite's willful and uncomprehending neglect of the interior. The second conclusion was a note of encouragement about Brazil's racial mix, which followed from the discovery of a noble struggle for freedom on the part of non-Whites (although this was at the same time called into question by Euclides's acceptance of scientific racism).

Os sertões, an indictment of the elite (the only book buyers), received immediate critical acclaim in Rio de Janeiro. Why? In part it was Euclides's scathing criticism of the army; many intellectuals resented the military repression of the 1890s, with its censorship and martial law. However, the answer probably lies mostly in Euclides's ability to tap the elite's guilt about how little their ideal of Brazilian nationality related to their country's actual condition, *without* questioning all their basic social assumptions.

This interpretation is borne out by the favorable reaction of the literary critics. Virtually all discussed the racial question. The critics were as equivocal on the key questions as Euclides had been. Several agreed that the connection between ethnic and social integration was crucial. None was willing to conclude that Brazil's fate was hopeless. And none was clear-sighted enough to point out the inconsistencies at the heart of Euclides's analysis (*Os sertões: juízos críticos*).

The difficulties caused for the Republicans by events such as the rebellion at Canudos were exacerbated by the government's own lack of cohesion. Republican leaders often failed to agree on the presidential succession. Balloting was routinely fraudulent, especially in the interior, with local party machines commonly delivering suspiciously huge majorities for their candidates. Such fraud disillusioned many of the younger political elite, who yearned for the respectability of West European political systems.

Further aggravating the political malaise were increasing regional economic disparities. The southern central region took an increasing economic lead, fueled by streams of immigrants from Italy, Spain, Germany, and Japan. Liberalism continued to prevail in official discourse, much to the frustration of its critics. Yet the press overflowed with eloquent attacks on the liberal ideals supposedly enshrined by the

Republic. Brazilian reality, charged the dissenting politicians and law professors, was a parody of democratic, representative government. The dissenters demanded political reforms to bring Brazilian government into line with the country's economic and social realities. For some this meant replacing electoral democracy with a "strong" government that would lift Brazil above the painful realities of its illiteracy, misery, and empty rhetoric. The most influential writer of this view was Francisco José de Oliveira Vianna (1883–1951).

A lawyer–historian from the state of Rio de Janeiro, Vianna was described by contemporaries as mulatto, a possible key to his preoccupation with the role of race in Brazilian history. In 1910, Vianna began publishing a stream of newspaper articles and books, gaining steadily in influence among his elite readers. In 1916 he won a professorship at the Law Faculty in Rio de Janeiro, but preferred to spend most of his time across the bay in Niterói, the capital of his native state of Rio de Janeiro. *Populações meridionais do Brasil* was Vianna's first major book.

This two-volume work began by praising "the great Ratzel" and describing Gobineau, Lapouge, and Ammon, the European high priests of scientific racism, as "mighty geniuses." Vianna described himself as seeking to "define the social character of our people, as realistically as possible, in order to establish our differences from other peoples, especially the great European peoples" (*Populações* [1952] I, 13). Brazilians studied themselves too little, he argued, and thus suffered "innumerable illusions" about their capacities (I, 19). What Brazilians needed was "a cool, detached analysis" laying bare "the special tendencies of our mentality and our character" (I, 22). He asked how Brazil's racially mixed population would fare in the modern world and whether Brazil could remain a unified country, given its vast regional differences.

On first reading, Oliveira Vianna sounded much like Sílvio Romero or Euclides da Cunha. He thought Brazil was in danger internationally, and he saw national self-examination as a crucial first step toward collective action. Like Romero and Euclides he accepted the authority of foreign racialist theoreticians. What, then, did he add that was new?

One element was a romanticized picture of colonial Brazil. Vianna thought the Portuguese who had come to America were "the most eugenic" because, "by the laws of social anthropology those who emigrate are strong and rich in courage, imagination and will power" (I, 114). By a stroke of the pen he had rehabilitated the oft-denigrated early settlers. These courageous male Lusitanians had come to the new exotic land without their women, explained Vianna. "Plunged into tropical splendor, their nerves dulled by the intense sun, they were attracted to those vast and primitive breeding grounds which were the plantation slave quarters." There they found "the languid and tender Indian woman"

along with the "passionate, loving, prolific, and seductive" Negro woman
(I, 101). Thus was born the *mestiço*.

Vianna escaped the absolute categories of the scientific racists by
arguing that the African slaves had come from varying tribes – some
"highly loyal," others "ferocious," or "virile and brave." The offspring of
white unions with such varied slaves also varied. Some *mestiços* were
"inferior," while others inherited the psychic and even somatic features of
the "superior" race. "From the texture of his hair to the color of his skin,
from the morality of his feelings to the vigor of his intelligence," the
superior *mestiço* "has a perfectly Aryan appearance" (I, 153). So Oliveira
Vianna was able to reassure his worried, race-conscious readers that,
through historical luck and the nature of early Portuguese settlement,
Brazil was steadily getting whiter.

He saw this felicitous race-mixing as having facilitated Brazil's great
westward expansion of the seventeenth and eighteenth centuries. Miraculously, in Vianna's account, the "Aryanized" *mestiços* joined white
"nobility" to secure Brazil's claim to its western reaches which had once
belonged to the Spanish crown.

Vianna found other virtues in Brazil's ethnic history: "Our people
mixed and melded without any overt ethnic battles" (I, 392). He made no
mention of the many bloody slave revolts or of the equally bloody
campaigns to exterminate the runaway slave communities. Here Vianna
was echoing a theme of Sílvio Romero – that in Brazil the African
influence had evolved in a uniquely beneficial way. Thus was the myth of
Brazil's "non-violent" past given one of its classic formulations.

Vianna also thought contemporary Brazil was in political danger. He
believed Brazil had erred in uncritically adopting nineteenth-century
European liberal institutions. It had thereby failed to insure "authority"
and "national unity" (I, 429). Brazil had survived, but only because the
populations of the Southern center – the heroes of Vianna's book – saved
it from a tremendous catastrophe "by their conservative spirit and by their
moderate and cautious temperament" (I, 435).

The Spanish American republics had not, in Vianna's view, been so
lucky when they imported European liberalism. Unlike the Brazilian
statesmen, the nation builders in Argentina and Chile "faced populations
that were constantly conspiring and fighting." Brazil was saved by the
"natural aversion to violence" of its southern peoples (I, 434–5). Thus the
nineteenth century, like the centuries before it, had a happy ending – all
wrapped in the language of racial improvement, the lingua franca of
Vianna's readers. Starting from similar premises, he had emerged with a
far more optimistic message than Euclides da Cunha.

However, Vianna saw the lesson of Brazilian history as its failure to
have created a strong state. Brazilian nationality now needed "mass,

form, fiber, nerve, skeletal structure and character." Above all, it needed "a centralizing state with a powerful, dominating and unifying national government" (I, 429). Vianna rapidly became the spokesman *par excellence* for the anti-liberal critics of Brazil's malfunctioning electoral system. Later, during the dictatorship of Getúlio Vargas (1937–1945) he got the opportunity to apply his nostrums when he helped fashion the corporatist laws that institutionalized the strong state he advocated.

Paulo Prado (1869–1943) belonged to one of São Paulo's most prominent families, sustained by a fortune in coffee plantations. He was a noted aesthete and patron of the arts who had largely financed the famous São Paulo Modern Art Week in 1922. In 1928 he published *Retrato do Brasil*, a slim volume which cast a gloomy pall over the debate about national character.

His "portrait," which opened with the famous phrase "In a radiant land lives a sad people," analyzed Brazilian character in terms of the three vices (lust, greed, and melancholy) which had supposedly resulted from the combination of a "man set free in the wilderness with the sensual Indian" (*Retrato* [1962] 3, 22). This produced "our primitive mixed-blood populations" (p. 27). The Brazilian was "a new man" heading either toward his "fateful triumph" or toward "disillusionment and disaster" in realizing "his historical and geographical destiny" (p. 127). The solution, for Prado, was whitening – "the so-called Aryanization of the Brazilian is a fact of everyday observation. Even with one-eighth Negro blood the African appearance completely fades away. Since the colonial era the Negro has been slowly disappearing" (pp. 159–60). Here was an even more confident endorsement of whitening than Romero or da Cunha had ever made. It reflected the increasing optimism on this front felt by the Brazilian elite.

Yet the book's overall tone made Brazil's heritage sound debilitating and its negative effects on Brazilian personality inescapable. The combination of the amoral Portuguese, the seductive climate, and the pliant Indian-African character seemed to disqualify Brazil from the modern industrial world. In his postscript, however, Prado confidently cited avant-garde US sociologists, who had begun to emphasize environment over race as an explanation for social behavior. In the end Prado saw Brazil's problem as essentially political. He denounced his country's "petty politics" and its local "oligarchies" (p. 178). He repeated the then current lamentations that Brazil had failed to exploit her great natural resources. Neglect was everywhere – public hygiene, transportation, education, in virtually every sphere of social policy. "In a country which has practically everything, we import everything: from fashions – ideas and clothes – to broom handles and toothpicks" (p. 174). Prado, intending to shock his readers, saw only two ways out of Brazil's disorganization and stagnation. It would take war or revolution to cure a sick Brazil.

The Republic that had arrived via a military coup in 1889 collapsed in another coup in 1930. As in the 1890s, the military handed over power to a new generation of civilians, led by Getúlio Vargas, a former governor of Rio Grande do Sul. The prolonged attempt at democratic reform after 1930 led to yet another military coup in 1937, led this time by the incumbent president himself, as Vargas installed an eight-year dictatorship (called the *Estado Novo*, following Portuguese corporatist nomenclature and ideology). State and local government power was sharply reduced, creating the strong centralizing force Oliveira Vianna had urged.

Economically Brazil fared well. Although the world crash of 1929 led to a rapid loss of foreign exchange reserves and a sharp drop in export income, Brazilian industry expanded rapidly to supply many products previously imported. The Second World War, which Brazil entered in 1942 on the Allied side, was another economic stimulus, as US demand for strategic material helped Brazil rebuild its foreign exchange reserves. Meanwhile, state intervention in the economy grew, reflecting the corporatist centralization of the Vargas dictatorship. The pace of industrialization accelerated in São Paulo, now Brazil's largest city and rapidly becoming the leading industrial center in the developing world.

Culturally these years were highly creative. The 1920s and 1930s produced many attempts to define Brazil's national identity, much influenced by the intense literary innovation of *Modernismo* [Modernism] (not to be confused with the movement of the same name in Spanish America). Scholars and publishers rushed to republish the rich descriptions of Brazil bequeathed by foreign travelers of earlier centuries, often with notes and commentary.

The Vargas dictatorship also created new centralized cultural institutions, such as the Instituto Nacional do Livro, which subsidized distribution of government-sponsored cultural magazines, and radio programs. The vigor and originality of the modernist movement gave legitimacy to the dictatorship's claim to be promoting Brazilian national culture.

These years also saw the United States begin to challenge France as the predominant foreign cultural influence in Brazil. North American popular culture, fed by an increasing flood of US radio programs, phonograph records, and Hollywood films, established a fascination among city-dwelling Brazilians. This contest for the country's cultural allegiance formed the backdrop for the emergence of the historian–sociologist Gilberto Freyre, the most famous twentieth-century interpreter of Brazilian national identity.

Freyre (1900–1987) was born in Recife, capital of the state of Pernambuco, in the heart of the traditional sugar-cane economy of the northeast. He came from a distinguished family and pursued an atypical education by attending an American high school in Recife and then traveling to the

US for his college degree at Baylor, a Baptist university in Texas. This experience significantly shaped the young Brazilian's view of his native culture. Freyre then attended graduate school at Columbia University in New York, studying with the noted anthropologist Franz Boas, who had become one of the first outspoken opponents of the scientific racism that still dominated academic thought in the North Atlantic world and Latin America. His five years of study in the US, mostly in the South with its Jim Crow laws and violent racism, deeply influenced Freyre, giving him a permanent point of reference in his future interpretations of Brazil. At Columbia he wrote a master's paper, *Vida social no Brasil nos meados do século* XIX [*Social Life in Brazil in the Middle of the Nineteenth Century*], containing many of the themes he was to make famous in *Casa grande e senzala* [*The Masters and the Slaves*].

Casa grande e senzala was a social history of the slave-plantation world of northeastern Brazil in the sixteenth and seventeenth centuries when sugar furnished the productive base for Brazil's multiracial society. Freyre sympathetically (and graphically) depicted the intimate personal relations between the planter families and their slaves. In picturing this intensely patriarchal ethos, Freyre dwelt on the many ways in which the African (and, to a much lesser extent, the Indian) influenced the planters' life-style in food, clothing, and sexual behavior.

Freyre began by assuming that Brazil's history differed significantly from the United States, the only other comparable slave-holding society in the Western hemisphere. As he noted in the preface to the first edition, "Every student of patriarchal regimes and of Brazil's slave-holding economy should become acquainted with the 'deep south'" (*Casa grande*, xi).

Casa grande presented a society in which every Brazilian, from aristocrat to pedlar, reflected a polyglot culture. Here Freyre clearly followed Sílvio Romero, whose influence he frequently acknowledged. Freyre further argued that the Portuguese in Brazil had long since lost any chance to be "pure" Whites, since the Portuguese themselves were of dubious white lineage, having for centuries mixed with their Moorish conquerors.

Freyre saw the Portuguese as uniquely equipped to colonize the tropics. He noted that "race consciousness virtually did not exist among the cosmopolitan and plastic-minded Portuguese" (p. 2). The Portuguese colonist was "a Spaniard without the militant flame or the dramatic orthodoxy of the *conquistador* of Mexico and Peru, an Englishman without the harsh profile of the Puritan. He was the compromiser, without absolute ideals or fixed prejudices" (p. 197). Furthermore, the Portuguese used "the natives, chiefly the women, as more than mere labor; they became the elements to create the family" (p. 24). Freyre was thus led to his famous conclusion that "Brazil has the most harmonious race relations" in the Americas (p. 88).

Freyre had thereby turned on its head the long-familiar and painful question of whether generations of race mixing had done irreparable damage. Brazil's ethnic jumble, he argued, was an immense asset. He showed how recent research in nutrition, anthropology, medicine, psychology, sociology, and agronomy had rendered racist theory obsolete and had pointed up new villains – insufficient diet, impractical clothing, and disease (especially syphilis), too often undiagnosed and untreated. He cited studies by Brazilian scientists showing that it was the Indian and the Negro who had contributed to a healthier diet and a more practical style of dress in Brazil.

Equally important for the book's sustained impact was its frank description of the intimate history of patriarchal society. While this incurred the criticism of some academic critics abroad and conservative readers at home, it appealed to Brazilian readers because it explained the origin of their personalities and culture. At the same time, they were getting the first scholarly examination of Brazilian national character that unambiguously told them they could be proud of their racially mixed tropical civilization. Its social vices, which Freyre freely acknowledged, could be attributed, he argued, primarily to the slave-holding monoculture dominating the country until the late nineteenth century. The supposedly evil consequences of miscegenation came not from race-mixing itself, but from the unhealthy relationship of master and slave under which it had most often occurred.

Freyre wrote two successor volumes to *Casa grande e senzala: Sobrados e mucambos* [*The Mansions and the Shanties*], which focused on the transition to an urban culture in the eighteenth and early nineteenth century, and *Ordem e progresso* [*Order and Progress*], which painted a panorama of the elite's self-image in the first several decades of the twentieth century. These volumes carried forward Freyre's portrait of the patriarchical ethos inherited from the colonial era. Although rich in historical detail and insight, neither had the impact of *Casa grande e senzala*.

Freyre's writings did much to focus attention on the inherent value of the African as the representative of a civilization in its own right. Freyre thus furnished, for those Brazilians ready to listen, a rationale for a multiracial society in which the component "races" – European, African, and Indian – could be seen as *equally* valuable. The practical effect of his analysis was *not*, however, to promote racial egalitarianism. Rather, it served to reinforce the elite's well-established goal of "whitening" by showing graphically that the (primarily white) elite had gained valuable cultural traits from their intimate contact with the African and Indian.

Yet his analysis did answer a question preoccupying the elite: was white supremacy of the United States' variety the only path to progress in the modern world? By implication (which few readers could miss), Freyre answered in the negative. He depicted a Brazil which was superior in human terms. It was the US that had chosen the destructive path of legal segregation, to be maintained only by repression.

Raízes do Brasil by Sérgio Buarque de Holanda (1902–1982) was closer in format and approach to Paulo Prado's *Retrato do Brasil* than to the work of either Oliveira Vianna or Gilberto Freyre. It was an elegant essay drawing on literary and historical sources, without Freyre's vast range of information or Oliveira Vianna's narrowly focused social history. Like both, however, it emphasized the colonial era.

Buarque de Holanda's title revealed his orientation. Portugal has created "the present shape of our culture – any other influence had to conform to that shape." The role of miscegenation? The "mixture with indigenous or foreign races has not made us as different from our overseas ancestors as we would sometimes like to think" (*Raízes* [1956], 30). Unfortunately for those who wanted economic development, Brazil did not get the worker prototype (such as supposedly went to New England), but get-rich-quick adventurers. The Portuguese "wanted to extract enormous riches from the soil without making great sacrifices" (p. 50). They also showed "extraordinary social flexibility," and revealed a "complete, or almost complete, lack of racial pride, at least that kind of obstinate and uncompromising pride that typifies the northern peoples." Furthermore, the Portuguese were, compared to Spanish, "incomparably gentler, better able to accommodate social, racial and moral discord" (p. 51). They were notably lacking in the "martial spirit." Brazilians don't yearn for the "prestige of a conquering country and . . . are notorious for abhorring violent solutions." Brazil was "one of the first nations to abolish the death penalty in law, having abolished it long before in practice" (p. 260). Buarque de Holanda thought the Brazilian could be summed up in the Portuguese word "cordial," which he equated with affability, hospitality, and generosity.

Raízes do Brasil presented an interesting gloss on the national identity motif. The author virtually discarded race as an explanatory concept. Instead he constructed a collective personality for the Portuguese, Spanish, and English, then generalizing about comparative national development. Unlike Freyre, Buarque de Holanda said virtually nothing about the African or the Indian, nor did he look closely at the non-European elements in Brazilian culture. In fact, Buarque de Holanda contributed little that was new to the portrait of national identity which we have seen emerging. He reinforced Gilberto Freyre's image of the Portuguese as racially tolerant and Oliveira Vianna's image of them as the bequeathers of a flawed political legacy.

An essential feature of Buarque de Holanda's society was "an invasion of the public by the private, of the state by the family" (p. 103). It led to a "slackness of social structure" and a "lack of organized hierarchy." In short, a "lack of cohesion in our social life" (p. 18). He also believed, with Oliveira Vianna, that Brazil was adrift. The Brazilians, he announced, "are still exiles in our own land" (p. 15). Both authors wanted to rouse their readers to undertake radical reforms, although the nature of their reforms differed sharply.

Buarque de Holanda worried about Brazil's political future. In the Brazil of the mid 1930s opinion was polarizing, as both left and right preached extremism. He had personally witnessed the rise of Fascism while living in Germany. The descent into the Brazilian dictatorship of 1937–1945 was imminent. Like Paulo Prado in *Retrato do Brasil*, he aimed his erudite text at the elite whom he hoped to rouse in defense of a democratic Brazil.

The two decades after the end of the Vargas dictatorship in 1945 (which was ended by another military coup) brought a return to electoral democracy and constitutional government, although in a political culture that remained deeply authoritarian. In the electoral era that followed, Vargas became the eventual beneficiary, returning to power in 1951 as a popularly elected president. Pursuing increasingly nationalistic policies, he collided with conservative landowners, São Paulo businessmen, anticommunist military, and the United States government. Faced with the threat of yet another military coup in 1954, he committed suicide, throwing the conservative enemies of his populist policies on the defensive for another decade.

The first widely read essayist on Brazilian identity to appear after 1945 was Vianna Moog (1906–1988), a novelist and literary critic from Brazil's southernmost state of Rio Grande do Sul. In 1955 he published *Bandeirantes e pioneiros* [*Bandeirantes and Pioneers*], a direct and detailed comparison of cultural archetypes in Brazil and the US. This perhaps reflected his country's recent wartime experience, when a Brazilian army division had fought alongside the US Fifth Army, helping to drive Nazi troops from Italy in 1944–1945.

Moog's message was implicit in his book's title. The first word, *bandeirantes*, referred to the get-rich-quick explorers who roamed Brazil's interior in the seventeenth and eighteenth centuries. These rude adventurers incarnated all the supposed Iberian defects: contempt for manual labor, a fixation on Europe, irresponsible eroticism, and an extreme individualism. The title's second word, *pioneiros*, incarnated all the supposed North American virtues: respect for the dignity of labor, an urge to break with the past, a belief in the moral perfectibility of man, and a keen sense of community.

Moog started with the image of the Brazilian as "an indolent, congenitally melancholy man, the product of three sad races whom fate has joined on American soil" (*Bandeirantes* [1961], 107). This sounded like Paulo Prado. However, Moog challenged that authority, arguing that in fact "there is no real proof for the congenital sadness of the Indian, the Negro, the Portuguese" (p. 108).

He then contrasted the archetypes – the *bandeirante* and the pioneer – that held the answer to Brazil's relative backwardness. The *bandeirante* disdained work, sought quick riches, and lived only to return to Europe. It was these traits, passed on to modern-day Brazilians, that held back Brazilian progress. Meanwhile, the pioneer, heir of the New England colonists, valued work and sought to build for the morrow. These cultural traits, Moog argued, made it possible for "the United States, a continent younger and smaller than Brazil, to achieve virtually miraculous progress, while Brazil, with a history a hundred years older than the United States, is still the uncertain land of the future" (p. 9).

To compare Brazil with the US was not new, as we have seen. Thoughtful Brazilians had done it more frequently as the United States' economic lead over Brazil increased in the late nineteenth and early twentieth centuries. Yet no widely read writer had posed the question as boldly as Moog.

What made his book accessible to a wide public was its didactic style (and its frequent oversimplification of social science theory). He rebutted racist determinism by citing academic authorities who claimed to have discredited it scientifically. To clinch his case, Moog recounted several notorious Yankee misadventures in Brazil. One was Henry Ford's ambitious rubber plantation project of the 1930s and 1940s in the Amazon, which failed despite enormous investment and abundant technical expertise from the north. Ford's failure to understand the psychology of Brazilian workers and the limitations of plantation agriculture in the rainforest (laterite soils leaching out, etc.) doomed his project from the start. If Whites were superior, asked Moog, why did an entrepreneurial genius such as Henry Ford fail so ignominiously? Moog's second example was a colony founded by United States Confederate émigrés in the Amazon valley. Two generations after their arrival in the late 1860s they had virtually disappeared into the marginal jungle population. Again, Moog asked, where was white superiority – especially since these were Whites from the Old South, bastion of Aryan supremacy?

Moog went on to give his readers a witty, documented case against racist theory. He argued that Brazil's lack of racial discrimination "may have been a positive factor, and may become one of Portuguese-Brazilian culture's best legacies, despite the high price Brazilians have paid and may still have to pay for it" (p. 47). It was an echo of Freyre but in more explicit terms.

Moog refuted other deterministic explanations for Brazil's failure to progress at the US pace. The defeatists had pointed out, for example, that Brazil's river system did not constitute an easy inland transportation network. Many of the major rivers were broken by waterfalls, making them unnavigable. Others ran only tortuously toward the ocean. Brazil also lacked coal. How could it industrialize without the vital resources that had fueled development in North America? Moog dismissed these liabilities by arguing that "history can tell us more about social facts than can the reductionist theories of geographic, ethnic, biological, or economic determinism" (p. 106). By history, he meant the collective psychologies created since colonization.

Like his forerunners in interpreting Brazilian national character, Moog had a larger purpose than simply to explain. He wanted to rouse his readers to change the country. He longed to lift Brazil closer to the US performance. However, this could only happen if there were a "reform of the spirit," a call echoing Paulo Prado's message. Moog wanted Brazil to undertake a "major collective self-examination" (p. 250). Yet he added a message that no predecessors had offered. He pointed to the United States, long taken as the superior example, as a model of how *not* to develop.

Thus Moog's book served to reassure his Brazilian readers. They were right to compare Brazil to the United States. They were right to conclude the United States was far ahead in material progress. Yet they should know that Brazil was achieving progress, while the United States would have to slow down to regain its humanity. If Brazil lacked discipline, the United States lacked a human dimension. Moog's language bore little relation to the anguish of Oliveira Vianna or Paulo Prado. However, it did resemble Freyre's message. In fact, it was Freyre's vindication of the Portuguese as the progenitors of a new tropical civilization that gave Moog the justification to write his optimistic tract.

For all their differences, these essayists from Sílvio Romero to Vianna Moog had constructed an evolving myth, which became steadily more optimistic (with some back-sliding) through the years. It began with a vision of the Portuguese colonizer as a sensuous, pragmatic improviser, unlike the rigid Spanish *conquistador* or the intolerant English Puritan. The indulgent Portuguese character had helped to soften slavery, according to this view, and thus to save Brazil from either North American racism or Indo-America's caste societies. Equally important, argued most of the twentieth-century essayists before the 1950s, Brazil's population was steadily becoming whiter. Brazil had reached the modern world with the most humane society in the Americas. Whether it would know what to do with that humanity, they argued, was the unanswered question.

After the 1950s the context for the dialogue over Brazil's national identity shifted, as the rise of modern social science created a major new

359

intellectual force in Brazil. Although a few anthropologists and sociologists had begun field research in the 1920s, the institutional bases for the social sciences only began to be consolidated in the 1950s (Corrêa, *História da antropologia no Brasil*). Scholars now had a new perspective that could undercut the literary-style essay so long popular.

In 1959 a psychology professor had published the initial edition of the first book-length survey of Brazilian writing on national identity (Leite, *O caráter nacional brasileiro*). It marked a new era as the diagnosticians became more self-conscious in methodology and less naive in assumptions.

The dialogue now attracted anthropologists, especially those willing to move beyond conventional field-work on indigenous peoples to generalize about the fundamentals of Brazilian civilization. Prominent among such scholars who emerged in the late 1940s was Darcy Ribeiro (b. 1922), an academic anthropologist who helped plan the creation of the new University of Brasília in the late 1950s. Later a top adviser to President João Goulart (1961–1964), he was forced into exile in 1964 when the military overthrew Goulart, an heir to the populist politics of Getúlio Vargas. During his years of exile (primarily in Spanish America), Ribeiro wrote a multi-volume study of "civilization in the Americas," devoting one installment to Brazil (*As Américas e a civilização*).

Ribeiro did not restrict his message to academic audiences. On his return from exile he again plunged into politics, allying closely with the populist politician Leonel Brizola who twice won the governorship of Rio de Janeiro state in the 1980s. Ribeiro's solution to the dilemma of Brazil's development was one of the most overtly political of any of the writers discussed here. (Gilberto Freyre was a federal deputy in the 1946 Congress and later strongly supported the military coup of 1964.) Having been one of Goulart's most radical advisers in 1963–1964, he now relentlessly attacked the economic and political establishment and called for Brazilian scholars to "see as our fundamental task the study of the social revolution needed to overcome backwardness and dependency" (*As Américas* [1988] 11). Ribeiro praised Euclides da Cunha and Sílvio Romero for their pioneering insights and credited Oliveira Vianna and Gilberto Freyre with significant contributions, despite the former's "racism" and "colonialist vision," and the latter's "reactionary" nostalgia for the era of slavery (p. 12).

In his schema of world history Ribeiro placed the Brazilians among the "New Peoples," produced by the combination of "very disparate ethnic branches such as the indigenous, the African, and the European" (p. 58). He saw Brazil's "historico-cultural configurations," especially the "colonial slave-based domination," as crucial in "dehumanizing" the Negro and the Indian and in producing elite theories which drew on "European parascientific publications" about race and climate to create "learned justifications for backwardness and national poverty" (pp. 74–5, 131, 156). What these theories had failed to see was "the role of colonial plundering and patronal exploitation" (p. 157). For Ribeiro the only "morally defensible position" for a Brazilian intellectual was to recognize his/her society as "unjust, violent, and backward" and "demand a revolution" (p. 165).

Ribeiro typified a generation of prominent academic intellectuals (including Florestan Fernandes, Celso Furtado, and Antônio Cândido) radicalized by confrontation with Brazil's deep social inequalities, the unrelenting conservatism of its elite, and the repeated intervention of its military. All saw their country's redemption to lie in radical political change from the left, although they differed on the preferred leadership. Like Paulo Prado half a century earlier, they saw a political shock as the therapy needed to shake Brazil out of its historic impasse.

Roberto da Matta (b. 1936) was another anthropologist who moved from the study of the Indian to the study of the wider Brazilian society. Da Matta, like Freyre, had studied in the US and took that country as his reference point in analyzing Brazil. He enthusiastically embraced a combination of structuralist and symbolic approaches in writing a diagnosis of "the Brazilian dilemma" in his *Carnavais, malandros e heróis* [*Carnivals, Rogues and Heroes*].

Da Matta found the essence of Brazilian character to lie in the structural relationships and accompanying values bequeathed by the highly hierarchical society of early modern Portugal and its slave-holding American colony. He analyzed the Freyre-type myth of his country's harmonious racial evolution (incarnated in the "fable of the three races") as the persistent rationale for what he frankly termed "our racism" (*Relativizando* [1981], 58). It was "the most reactionary prism" of Brazilian history because it presented that past as a "'history of races' and not of men" (p. 60). This "myth of the three races" has long furnished "the basis for a political and social plan for the Brazilian, i.e., 'whitening' as the goal to be pursued" (p. 69).

What were the sources of this "racismo à brasileira" (p. 68)? Like Darcy Ribeiro, Da Matta pointed to the colonial past as crucial in shaping Brazil's modern identity, but he emphasized more the profoundly "anti-individualist" and "anti-egalitarian" value system and social structure bequeathed by the Portuguese crown and church (p. 74). "The critical feature of our entire system is its profound inequality. In this system there is no need to segregate the mestizo, the mulatto, the Indian, and the Negro because the hierarchies guarantee the superiority of the White as the dominant group" (p. 75).

Da Matta rejected Freyre's argument that Portuguese colonization had been "essentially more open and humanitarian," arguing instead that any easy intimacy of inter-racial relations had been possible only because "here the White and the Negro each had a fixed and unambiguous place within a well-established hierarchical totality" (p. 79). The misplaced focus on each of the "three races," argued Da Matta, has "delayed our understanding of ourselves as a society marked by a unique social structure and a specific culture" (p. 85). He found Darcy Ribeiro to have succumbed to the traditional reliance on "race" as an explanatory category, thus invalidating, in Da Matta's view, his attempt to classify Brazilians as one of the "new peoples" (p. 85).

Da Matta's approach resembled that of Freyre in frequently evoking the intimate tone and texture of fundamental social relations, as in his famous analysis of the imperious locution used to address social inferiors: "Sabe com quem está falando?" ["Do you realize who you're talking to?"]. Also like Freyre (who wrote frequently for newspapers and magazines), Da Matta sought a wide audience and was able to use the essayist's newest medium, television, in "Os brasileiros," a ten-part TV series of short portraits of key national traits. Like Darcy Ribeiro, Da Matta saw Brazilian society as desperately needing change, but he saw the solution to lie in adopting more egalitarian values, a process more profound than mere political change. In this he was closer to Moog than he was to the radical leftist intellectuals of whom Darcy Ribeiro was a leading example.

Finally, both Darcy Ribeiro and Roberto da Matta shared the modern social scientist's rejection of the racist assumptions so long common in elite dialogue on national identity. By the late 1970s thoughtful Brazilians faced growing evidence (based on official census data) that non-Whites were systematically disadvantaged (as measured by differentials in income, employment, education, life expectancy, infant mortality, etc.) in their society (Lovell, *Desigualdade racial no Brasil contemporâneo*; Fontaine, *Race, Class and Power in Brazil*). Yet the "fable of the three races," along with the myth of Brazil's "racial democracy" persists (Skidmore, "Fato e mito"). The pre-1960 architects of Brazil's self-image constructed a national identity that has resisted the attacks of both theory and fact. Moreover, if the role of race in that construct has only begun to be demystified, the role of gender is equally in need of critical exploration. As one leading Brazilian scholar of women's studies has noted, it may be "through studies of race and gender" that "we will finally get the answer to that eternal question, 'What country is this?'" (Heloísa Buarque de Holanda, "Os estudos sobre mulher e literatura no Brasil," 88).

The Brazilian and the Spanish American literary traditions: a contrastive view

J. G. Merquior

The early texts of Iberian America as a whole could hardly be literature *of* the New World; they were, rather, literature *about* the newly discovered and gradually occupied lands that stretched from New Spain (today's Mexico) to the river Plate basin. To our modern eyes these chronicles of conquest, beginning with the first inventories (the letters of Columbus and of Pero Vaz de Caminha, for example) have long seemed out of place within the canon of Iberian American literature, since they lack the conventional marks of both nationality – their authors, of course, were Europeans almost to a man – and literariness; with a few exceptions, they are marginal to the sacred triad – epos, drama, and the lyric – which defines the core of literature in the aesthetic sense. Yet one should avoid anachronism. After all, until the age of Voltaire, "literature" retained a primarily *cognitive* rather than aesthetic meaning; that is, literature meant learning rather than a body of imaginative works. This is precisely what these early colonial writings are: accounts of acquaintance, of a learning process. Besides, these texts are by no means devoid of literary value. Literary historians used to stress the coarse and unclassical, "Gothic" character of most such chronicles. Yet some of them – in the Brazilian case, beginning with Caminha's letter of 1500 – evince rhetorical skills worthy of the best humanist writing of the Renaissance.

Is it possible to find significant differences between the Spanish and Portuguese American literatures of conquest and, later, of colonization? On a topical basis, yes. To begin with, the main Portuguese texts, like the catechetic *Diálogo sobre a conversão do gentio* (1557) of the Jesuit Manuel da Nóbrega (1517–1570), the *História* (1576) of Pero de Magalhães Gândavo (fl. 1570), or the works of Nóbrega's disciple, Father José de Anchieta (1534–1597), all belong to the *later* sixteenth century. When Alonso de Ercilla (1534–1594) published the first part of one of the earliest poems on an American subject, the epic *La Araucana*, in 1569, Bento Teixeira (1564?–?), the author of its Luso-Brazilian counterpart, was still a boy; Teixeira's *Prosopopéia*, a Camonian epyllion celebrating the deeds of the brothers Jorge and Duarte Coelho in mastering Pernambuco (just as Ercilla sang in praise of the conquest of Chile), was printed no earlier than 1601.

More importantly, Portuguese settlement, which never encountered Amerindians of high material culture, offered no ground for the passionate pleading of a Bartolomé de Las Casas (1474–1566) or the mestizo ambivalence of El Inca Garcilaso de la Vega (1539–1616), whose *Comentarios reales* (1609) couched a vindication of Indian virtues in a humanist *sermo nobilis*. In short, Portuguese America did not give rise to any classic of the *leyenda negra*; and when the greatest of all baroque preachers, Antônio Vieira (1608–1697), resumed the defense of the Indians, around the middle of the seventeenth century, he – unlike Las Casas – did so more through exhortation than through denunciation.

Vieira's theology was, by the way, criticized by the sharpest mind in all of colonial verse, the Mexican Sor Juana Inés de la Cruz (1648–1695). The best *criollo* poetry produced in the far more modest intellectual climate of Salvador or Recife (in comparison to Mexico City) was very different indeed from that of Sor Juana. Although scholars such as Segismundo Spina are certainly right in pointing out the quality of the religious poems of the outstanding Brazilian colonial poet, Gregório de Matos (1623?–1696), it is in his satirical and erotic pieces that Gregório remains unrivalled. And albeit he was as familiar as Sor Juana with Quevedo, and with Góngora, Gregório wrote – unlike her, or, for that matter, Vieira – as a *culteranista* virtuoso rather than as a disciple of *conceptismo*.

There was a further discrepancy between the two incipient literary traditions. As Sérgio Buarque de Holanda has shown in his classic study, *Visão do paraíso* (1959), the Portuguese mind proved far less utopian than the Spanish one. Perhaps because of the absence of large pools of native Amerindian labor, the geographical dispersal of colonists in an economy based on sugar, the prevalence of a down-to-earth commercial approach to the colony, or the much later arrival of crown and church personnel, the masters of Brazil climbed down from the lofty dreams of high-minded Spanish *conquistadors*. At any rate, in Portuguese America the vision of El Dorado tended to be restrained, as can be seen in the *Grandezas do Brasil* (written in 1618) of Ambrósio Brandão, in the first general history of Brazil, completed in 1627 by the Franciscan friar Vicente do Salvador (1564–1636?), or in a later Jesuit text, the *Cultura e opulência do Brasil por suas drogas e minas* (1711) of Father André João Antonil (1650–1721?); the tone of all of these, beneath their professed aims of exaltation and celebration, is often surprisingly realistic and even debunking. Even the chiliastic prophetism of Vieira was not Brazil-centered: the focus of his neo-Sebastianist fervor remained Portuguese rather than American.

Can we relate this divergence in Iberian ethos to the colonial fate of such phenomena as the Baroque and Neoclassicism? One wonders. In the visual arts, Portugal delayed long in yielding to the Baroque, and in fact did so only under John V, in the first half of the eighteenth century. Many works of baroque literature, whether major texts, like the *Nova floresta* (1706–1728) of the Portuguese Manuel Bernardes (1644–1710), or just a minor example, like the *Música do Parnaso* (1705) of the Brazilian Botelho de Oliveira (1636–1711), were not published until the first decades of the new century. Nonetheless, Portuguese writers were already producing baroque masterpieces by 1620; one example is *Corte na aldéia* (1619), by Franciso Rodrigues Lobo (1580?–1622?), a work highly praised by no less than Gracián. Moreover, Portuguese conceptualism was to be the glory of the Braganza Restoration which began in 1640.

The striking contrast as concerns the colonies was that, while extraordinary texts in verse and prose – Vieira's sermons, or Sor Juana's *Primero sueño*, for example – were created in Iberian America under the sign of the Baroque, as soon as baroque models gave way to Neoclassicism the literary landscape of Spanish America became relatively barren, whereas the mining towns of Brazil produced a first-rate poetical harvest – the Arcadian lyricism of the late eighteenth century. The Arcadian chief shepherds were Cláudio Manuel da Costa (1729–1789), Tomás Antônio Gonzaga (1744–1810?), Manuel Inácio da Silva Alvarenga (1749–1814), and José Basílio da Gama (1741–1795), who also penned the fine and strongly lyricized epic poem *O Uraguai* (1769). With Metastasio instead of Góngora for a paradigm, these poets not only surpassed their Portuguese predecessors and contemporaries, but also had no peer in Mexico or Lima. Moreover, their copy-cat academies, no matter how small by European standards, planted the roots of a literary culture in a systematic sense. In so far as normal literary activity requires a modicum of textual exchange and a sustained output, with at least embryonic forms of a public and of critical reactions, the Brazilian Arcadians were the first significant group of conscious writers in the Americas.

Nativist undertones underlying the classic motifs of Arcadian alienation enhance the charm of the lyricists of the mining region of Minas Gerais. However, a full-blooded assertion of Americanism combined with neoclassical ideals came only much later, during the age of Spanish American Independence, in the writings of Andrés Bello (1781–1865). In Brazil, the whole period stretching from 1800 to 1840 was dominated by publicists of neoclassical-cum-Enlightenment upbringing, the background also shared by the Minas Gerais poets and by Bello. Verse output of lasting value in Brazil during this period dwindled to little more than the Rousseaunian lyricism of Father Antônio Pereira de Sousa Caldas (1762–1814), though the expression of self and sentiment reached new heights in the colorful, Chateaubriandesque oratory of Father Francisco de Monte Alverne (1784–1859), a preacher at the imperial court during the reign of Pedro I (1822–1831); Monte Alverne also taught philosophy to the rather pedestrian founders of Brazilian Romanticism, Domingos José Gonçalves de Magalhães (1811–1882) and Manuel José de Araújo Porto Alegre (1806–1879).

The rise of Romanticism in the now Balkanized nations of Spanish America, beginning in the 1840s, brought two major changes. First, French influences replaced Iberian literary models. Second, the literary initiative shifted from the north of Hispanic America to the river Plate region. Brazil certainly shared in the first of these changes – but its early Romanticism, programmatically launched in Paris in 1836 by the mediocre Gonçalves de Magalhães, flourished in the traditional center of literary activity, Rio de Janeiro, often under the direct sponsorship of the imperial court. The greatest Argentinean Romantics, Esteban Echeverría (1805–1851) and Domingo Faustino Sarmiento (1811–1888), spent a long time in dangerous opposition to the *supercaudillo* Rosas, who was overthrown in 1852. In sharp contrast, the leaders of Brazilian Indianist Romanticism, the poet Antônio Gonçalves Dias (1823–1864) and the novelist José de Alencar (1829–1877), were born in the 1820s and were, respectively, a professor at the Imperial Secondary School (and, later, a researcher in Europe funded by the Emperor) and a very prominent conservative politician. Echeverría's Lamartinean poems, "Elvira" (1832) and "La cautiva" (1837), may nowadays seem somewhat dated, whereas Gonçalves Dias's short "I-Juca-Pirama" (1851) is simply the best *poem*, in the strong poematic sense, produced in Portuguese during the whole of the nineteenth century. Yet Echeverría, besides becoming an influential theorist of Romanticism in his posthumous *Fondo y forma de las obras de imaginación*, left a jewel of romantic Realism (the novella *El matadero*, written in 1839–1840) and widely read essay, *El dogma socialista* (1846). Now, if we put this together with that great book of 1845, Sarmiento's *Facundo*, we shall readily infer that early Argentinean Romanticism held social views largely more advanced than its Brazilian equivalent – something only to be expected, given the differences in the respective social structures of the two countries, even well before the invasion of the pampas by European immigrants.

In reality, though, things were more complex. Echeverría may have been, like his Spanish counterpart, Espronceda, a Romantic bard with utopian Socialist leanings. However, recent research has shown that the political ideas of Alencar, notably those expressed in his treatise on representative government, were fairly radical within the context of the liberalism of the age; on the other hand, Sarmiento's positions became distinctly conservative forms of liberalism at the end of his life. Argentinean Romanticism was just more conspicuously libertarian because of the fight against Rosas's autocracy, while in Brazil the first great Romantics – aside from naive *costumbristas* like the playwright Luís Carlos Martins Pena (1815–1848) or the comic novelist Manuel Antônio de Almeida (1831–1861; *Memórias de um sargento de milícias* [1854–1855]) – made their mark through well-wrought icons of imaginative literature, like Gonçalves Dias's "poesia americana" or Alencar's skillful blend of epic and romance in *O guaraní* (1857). In short, by mid-century there was no Brazilian *Facundo* – but then there was no *Iracema* (1865) in Spanish either.

However, the next stage – the final period of Romanticism, starting with the Paraguayan War (1865–1870) – almost reversed the contrast. For then it was that southern Spanish American Romanticism produced a functional equivalent of Alencar's Indianism: the gaucho epic, *Martín Fierro* (1872 and 1879), by José Hernández (1834–1886). Moreover, Indianism itself made a late comeback in Spanish America with Juan Zorrilla de San Martín's *Tabaré* (written in 1879, first published in 1888). Now while the spirit of gaucho and Indianist literature clearly went against the grain of the progressive, civilization-or-barbarism ideology of *Facundo*, Brazilian Romanticism was taking precisely the other path: it turned "social" in a progressive sense, most spectacularly in the abolitionist odes of Antônio de Castro Alves (1847–1871). The latter's "O navio negreiro" (1868) harnessed Hugoan eloquence and radical liberalism, dealing with the one issue about which the patriarch of Brazilian Romanticism, José de Alencar, was truly conservative: the question of slavery.

What about the next big wave – Spanish American *Modernismo*? Once more the focus of literary innovation shifted, this time northward to Mesoamerica, as the Nicaraguan Rubén Darío (1867–1916) came to the fore, followed by his fellow poets in Mexico (Manuel Gutiérrez Nájera [1859–1895], Amado Nervo [1870–1919], José Juan Tablada [1871–1945]), all born between 1855 and 1871. With Darío as the new Góngora, Spanish American letters overtook their Spanish models. In Brazil, by contrast, the tropical Belle Époque at the end of the nineteenth century was marked by the total cultural hegemony of Rio de Janeiro. A late romantic revolt by northern Brazilian writers against Rio de Janeiro's control, a revolt led by João Franklin da Silveira Távora (1842–1888) in the 1870s, quickly faded out, although some philosophical prose and verse was produced by the "German" school in the northeastern city of Recife under the leadership of Tobias Barreto (1839–1889).

Modernismo churned out luxury literature in an age of elite consumption – the high-end market of the upper classes in the growing capital cities of Spanish America. Like Parnassian poetry in Brazil, *Modernismo*'s stock-in-trade was fine craftsmanship. Roger Bastide shrewdly remarked that verse goldsmiths like the Brazilian Alberto de Oliveira (1857–1937) conquered status by dint of style, winning public recognition as star performers in strenuous artistic competition among themselves. Brazilian Belle Époque writers were often of humbler social origins than their romantic predecessors. People like Alencar or Castro Alves (or the great mid-century lyricists Manuel Antônio Alvares de Azevedo [1831–1852], Casimiro de Abreu [1839–1860], and Luís Nicolau Fagundes Varela [1841–1875]) came from the upper class, but most Parnassian poets and Naturalist novelists of Brazil were of bourgeois origin, and certainly viewed literary achievement as a means to improve their social status.

One wonders whether such a perspective also applies, and to what extent, to the Spanish American Post-romantics. Widely imitated *Modernistas* like Darío or Leopoldo Lugones (1874–1938) lived off journalism or diplomacy or both – and official jobs often came as a reward for literary glory. In his Parnassian–symbolist ivory tower, Darío, the friend of Verlaine, polished bold new verses, borrowing foreign words, depicting exotic scenery in daring meters. His prestige as a nomadic poet in Madrid, Paris, or Buenos Aires established a new paradigm: the poet as craftsman rather than romantic bard. Despite all the worth of their work, the era's genuine Romantics, like the Cuban José Martí (1853–1895) or the Afro-Brazilian João da Cruz e Sousa (1861–1898), did not shape the main direction of poetic diction as Darío and Lugones managed to do. Martí did not wish his *Versos sencillos* (1891) to "decir lo raro" ["tell the rare"] – the very opposite of the *modernista* recipe. Cruz e Sousa, the finest Brazilian lyricist since Gonçalves Dias, wrote with a Novalis-like depth far removed from the verbal coquetry and the technical fireworks that were the trademarks of *Modernismo*. Yet Darío's own evolution, from *Azul* (1888) to *Cantos de vida y esperanza* (1905), is strikingly paralleled by the development of the darling of Brazilian Parnassians, Olavo Bilac (1865–1918), from *Poesias* (1888) to *Tarde* (1919).

This primacy of Spanish American voices in verse did not extend to fiction. It has often been noted that Spanish America, today the mother of so many gifted novelists, has no Galdós in its past. There was indeed no Naturalist boom in Hispanic American letters, scarcely anything comparable to the Brazilian mix of lip-service to Zola and social satire along the lines of the Portuguese Eça de Queiroz; that mix overwhelmed Brazilian fiction after the publication of *O mulato* (1881), by Aluísio Azevedo (1857–1913). Nor was there as effective an instance of *écriture artiste*, of pent-up impressionist narrative, as the 1888 *O Ateneu* of Raul Pompéia (1863–1895).

Above all, as Carlos Fuentes has noted, Spanish American produced no writer of prose fiction at the level of Joaquim Maria Machado de Assis

(1839–1908). To be sure, the Brazilian Naturalists themselves, on the average poor writers even when they were good narrators, can hardly be compared to Machado. It is also true that Machado stood isolated, respected yet misunderstood; his eminence, unlike that of Darío, bred no swarm of imitators. Machado, whom his contemporaries and even his entourage at the fledgling Brazilian Academy of Letters mistook for a drawing-room skeptic, a South American Anatole France, evinced the utmost depth, cunning, and originality in his mature work, beginning around 1880. Injecting his wry Schopenhauerian pessimism into novels and short stories adrift from the main types of nineteenth-century fiction, Machado achieved a baffling blend of Realism with the maverick Menippean thrust of his beloved English models, Swift and Sterne. A tropical Gogol writing with Chekhovian reticence, he displayed a lust for language as well as a taste for moral deflation and psychological *chiaroscuro* which are utterly modern – indeed, far more modern than his North American contemporary Henry James. Yet his nimble prose remained buried in Portuguese, and even today it is doubtful whether most translations capture the full verbal zest of this most allusive and elusive of nineteenth-century masters.

The lack of a clear stylistic focus and international standing also kept other Brazilian writers, much younger than Machado and writing in the first two decades of the twentieth century, from enjoying the kind of visibility Darío's *Modernismo* had achieved. Nevertheless, three extremely influential figures stand out: Euclides da Cunha (1866–1909), Afonso Henriques de Lima Barreto (1881–1922), and Augusto dos Anjos (1884–1914). The tortured verses of dos Anjos, an idiosyncratic yet best-selling poet, twisted Parnassian forms and symbolist techniques into something approaching Expressionism. Like Lugones's *Lunário sentimental* (1909), dos Anjos's volume of verse, somewhat misleadingly entitled *Eu* (1912), employs scientific terminology; but its mood is the grimmest cosmic pessimism rather than the Laforguean irony of Lugones. Lima Barreto, a mulatto whose novels were published between 1909 and 1919, was a living rebuff to the sophisticated, Parnassian aloofness of Brazilian literati. Lima's *engagé* stance was alien to the amenities of the kind of literature produced by the self-satisfied members of the Brazilian Academy of Letters.

As for Euclides da Cunha (1866–1909), the other leading *engagé* writer of the Brazilian Belle Époque, his work – most notedly his unique and monumental masterpiece, *Os sertões* (1902) – is an astonishing crucible in which positivist scientism, Jacobin republicanism, and high-voltage *écriture artiste* are fused. Lima Barreto and Euclides both conceived of writing as a social mission, a nationalist enterprise against backwardness (in the case of Euclides) or oppression (Lima Barreto).

Euclides da Cunha's writings on the Amazon and other continental issues made him known to Spanish Americans. He was basically – like his two great predecessors as journalists, the late Romantic Joaquim Nabuco (1849–1910) and the Parnassian orator Rui Barbosa (1849–1923) – a product of what Roque Maciel de Barros has felicitously dubbed "the Brazilian Enlightenment": the big movement of ideas, derived mainly from Positivism, which rescued Brazilian literature from the intellectual innocence of Romanticism. Comte and Spencer, Renan and Haeckel inspired critics, historians, and essayists. Da Cunha's ideas, like his cyclopean style, are closer to this climate of thought than to his contemporary José Pereira da Graça Aranha (1868–1931), a reader of Nietzsche and of the Scandinavian playwrights. Graça Aranha often seems akin to the spirit of El Ateneo in Mexico – a trend of thinking leading from Positivism to Neo-Idealism, and from Renan to Bergson. Yet Graça Aranha's vitalist aestheticism is also reminiscent of another reader of Renan, the Uruguayan José Enrique Rodó (1871–1917). While Euclides da Cunha shared the universalist progressivism of the Argentinian essayist José Ingenieros (1877–1925), Graça Aranha fell somewhere between scientism and *fin-de-siècle* Idealism. Indeed, the fact that Rodó was the leading Spanish American thinker of that time, just as Darío was its quintessential artist, provides us with another striking contrast. For if we take Euclides da Cunha to be the central Brazilian intellectual of this period – which he was – then it should be clear that Brazilian thought was dealing with values more telluric than anything found in Rodó's *Ariel*, published in 1900, two years before *Os sertões*.

The years from 1915 to 1940 are generally described as the age of Avant-Garde poetry and of the social and regionalist novel in Spanish American literature. Vicente Huidobro (1893–1948) launched *Creacionismo* in Buenos Aires in 1916. Poetry rebelled against mimesis. Ortega y Gasset, in 1925 (*The Dehumanization of Art*), listed Mallarmé – along with Debussy, Pirandello, and the Dadaists – as a dehumanizer of art. Huidobro and the *Ultraístas* made a virtue of this and longed for a pure poetry, as free from feeling and eroticism as from logic or meter. Metaphor should break anthropocentric shackles; verse ought to avoid description, even of inner realms. In practice, however, the best avant-garde poetry of Spanish America was not in thrall to this dour diet. César Vallejo (1892–1938) was often boldly experimental in both rhythm and lexicon, but *Trilce* (1922) was also starkly referential lyricism, socially as well as psychologically. The same can be said of the Afro-Cuban verse of Nicolás Guillén (b. 1902) after 1930; and Pablo Neruda (1904–1973), along with Vallejo the central voice of the period, went as far as to speak of "impure" poetry (a socially and politically committed poetry, oblivious to formal refinement). Modern Spanish American verse had indeed opted for a "residence on earth." Between them, Vallejo and Neruda had destroyed the ivory tower Darío himself had ended up undermining – and in the process, the poetic initiative had once more moved to southern Spanish America, notwithstanding the high-quality work of a few Mesoamerican *Postmodernistas* like Ramón López Velarde (1888–1921).

All in all, Brazilian modern poetry took a different course. Daring departures from standard language were generally avoided. Although there were early contacts with both Italian and French Futurism, the Brazilian avant-garde movement turned out to be a moderate Modernism (in the European, not the Spanish, sense). Early modern verse in São Paulo and Minas Gerais, especially that in the form of snapshot-poems (the "poema piada" or "joke poem," for example), seemed to follow the primitivist, anti-decadent, and objectivist line exemplified by Blaise Cendrars and his cubist–futurist *Kodak*. However, this was not to last, and modern verse soon groped toward ampler kinds of expression. Selective Surrealism and free verse remained common, as did, of course, the usual blend of tones and of high and low, "poetic" and prosaic, subject matter. Yet extensive use of experimental language, wild metaphors, and typographical gimmicks was rare. Manuel Bandeira (1886–1968) was a central figure; yet he was far closer to Xavier Villaurrutia (1903–1950) than to Huidobro. Even Murilo Mendes (1901–1975), a committed Surrealist, refrained from automatic writing and eschewed avant-garde posturing. Neo-romantics like Augusto Frederico Schmidt (1906–1965; *Pássaro cego* [1930]) and Cecília Meireles (1901–1964; *Viagem* [1939]) were considered as modern as Mário de Andrade (1893–1945) or Carlos Drummond de Andrade (1902–1987), the greatest name in Brazilian modern verse. Drummond started as a shy Cubist, an epigrammatic closet ironist; then he wrote Neruda-like odes on solidarity (*Sentimento do mundo* [1940]). However, after a classic of social lyricism – *A rosa do povo* (1945), the Brazilian parallel to Vallejo's *Poemas humanos* (1939) – Drummond classicized his style in the meditative, baroque poems of *Claro enigma* (1951). One is reminded, to some extent, of Borges's development from *Fervor de Buenos Aires* (1923) to *Elogio de la sombra* (1969).

Brazilian Modernism challenged the primacy of Rio de Janeiro, as avant-garde sects in São Paulo and Recife openly defied the authority of the Academy; Modernism itself broke out in São Paulo in 1922. Roughly speaking, this tropical Avant-Garde preferred a technically moderate literature of modernization to the fierce cultural rejectionism of their European elders. Mário de Andrade and Drummond were ambivalent about the city, seeing it as a source of liberation as well as alienation; their basic feeling about social modernity is distinctly unlike that of T. S. Eliot. Moreover, Brazilian modern poets seem quite "romantic," in that they created a truly inward-looking lyric; Bandeira and Drummond were much more deeply subjective than Brazil's Romantics, Bilac, or Augusto dos Anjos. They were personal poets, whereas the European and North American heads of the modern movement (Pound or Eliot, or Valéry and Montale – not to mention Fernando Pessoa) were great sculptors of *personae*. The process in modern poetry since Rimbaud which Hugo Friedrich (*The Structure of Modern Poetry*) called de-subjectifying was hardly at work as a defining aspect of Brazilian poetry in the early twentieth century.

Thus the triangle formed by the focal works of Huidobro, Vallejo, and Neruda is very different, as a magnetic field, from the more traditional growth of modern verse in Brazil. The Hispanic South Americans prolonged the experimental thrust present in Darío, making it more radical. The Brazilians stayed closer to traditional lyric discourse, once it had been shorn of Parnassian ornament and symbolist incantation. Thus they naturally returned to classical forms, including the sonnet.

Let us turn to narrative prose. Pessimism and a taste for the grotesque, those specialities of river Plate culture, were deployed in the Poe-like short stories of Horacio Quiroga (1878–1937) and the bizarre political fictions of Roberto Arlt (1900–1942; *Los siete locos* [1929]). While the idealization of the gaucho reached its climax in *Don Segundo Sombra* (1926), by Ricardo Güiraldes (1886–1927), Macedonio Fernández (1874–1952), an odd *porteño* mix of Unamuno and Chesterton, produced masterpieces of philosophical semi-fiction. However, the tone of Spanish American fiction as a whole was set by the novel of the Mexican Revolution and the tales of *Indigenismo*. Here we find a fair degree of convergence with developments in Brazil. The narrative flashes, the economical staccato rhythms of *Los de abajo* (1915), the archetypal novel of the 1910 Mexican Revolution by Mariano Azuela (1873–1952), are not so different from the technique used by the Brazilian Graciliano Ramos (1892–1953) in *Vidas secas* (1938). On the whole, social protest was more potent amidst the Andean *Indigenistas*, but two great novels of social realism, one from Colombia and the other from Venezuela, powerfully restated Sarmiento's dilemma – civilization of barbarism: *La vorágine* (1924) by José Eustasio Rivera (1889–1928) and *Doña Bárbara* (1929) by Rómulo Gallegos (1884–1969). In Brazil, social Regionalism was also ideologically heterogeneous. The novels of José Lins do Rego (1901–1957), culminating with *Fogo morto* (1943), painted the decline of rural patriarchs. Yet Graciliano Ramos and Jorge Amado (b. 1912), strong presences in the 1930s and 1940s, were Marxists or *marxisants*. Social realism, on the other hand, implied by its very nature the survival of Regionalism, and so regions such as Rio Grande do Sul or Minas Gerais enhanced their own literary traditions. While Brazilian Regionalists lacked anything like *Indigenismo* for a cause or a basis, the fiction boom of the 1930s generally mirrored the stylistic moderation of most modern verse. As in Spanish America, the social novels of Brazil were written in a kind of low-key Naturalism – Naturalism minus Zola, as it were. Innovative literary language in prose was confined to the rhapsodies of the São Paulo Avant-Garde, like Mário de Andrade's *Macunaíma* (1928) or *Serafim Ponte Grande* (1933) by Oswald de Andrade (1890–1954) – although neither author stuck with this ludic, parodistic style in other narrative texts.

Finally, a few words about the essay during the years that followed the First World War. *Modernismo* in Spanish America had been the age of Rodó and El Ateneo. In the following period, Spanish American thought went far beyond *Arielismo*. It did so chiefly in two countries: Mexico and Peru. The two key concepts were the utopian *raza cósmica* of José Vasconcelos (1881–1959) and the Indoamerica of Raúl Haya de la Torre (1895–1981). What set all this apart from *Arielismo*'s paeans to "Latin" culture as opposed to an alleged Anglo-Saxon materialism and philistinism was the dramatic stress on telluric values, and on miscegenation as both struggle and redemption. In Brazil, too, the racial mix was legitimized. However, the legitimization came by way of social history, from the historical–anthropological frescoes of Gilberto Freyre (1900–1987), rather than from the prophetism of Vasconcelos or Haya de la Torre. A great writer himself, Freyre inspired the nostalgic Regionalism of José Lins do Rego and the Afro-Brazilian poems of Jorge de Lima (1895–1953). Yet by far the leading Brazilian essayist was Mário de Andrade. Devising a flexible program of national synthesis, playing the critical superego to poets like Bandeira and Drummond, promoting modern composers and the preservation of colonial sites, campaigning for the right to aesthetic research, and gently inducing the moderns to be social-minded without being dogmatic, Mário remained, until his untimely death in 1945, *the* man of letters of Brazilian Modernism. The stature of the Mexican Alfonso Reyes (1889–1959) in Spanish America was, perhaps, somewhat similar; but while the spirit of Reyes's humanism belongs to the pre-modern family of ironists like Gide or Thomas Mann, Mário wrote in the restless vein of the moderns. Few texts could be more different from the serenity of Reyes's *Visión de Anáhuac* (1917) than the harlequinesque tone and the direct, lively moral concern of Mário's writings on art, music, and literature.

Presumably a good way to epitomize the next era in Spanish American letters, roughly the years from about 1940 to 1965, would be to call it "The Age of Borges." Although Borges's international reputation dated from rather late, starting with the accolades of French critics during the rise of Structuralism, the old Avant-Gardist now reaped the fruits of his transformation into one of the world masters of the short story. Yet

Borges's growing if belated glory was in a sense the culmination of the shift of literary focus from northern and western Spanish America to the river Plate, for it was in this last area that fiction first began to eschew social realism. The move toward freer and more inward-looking forms stretches back to *Historia de una pasión argentina* (1937), by Eduardo Mallea (1903–1982), and to *Adán Buenosayres* (1948) by Leopoldo Marechal (1900–1970), a novel whose impact had to wait for the post-war years; its satirical treatment of the intelligentsia and use of stream-of-consciousness technique were harbingers of future developments. This tendency toward pessimism and subjectivity was to receive further support from Uruguayan writers like Juan Carlos Onetti (b. 1909) and Mario Benedetti (b. 1920). The gloomiest vision, though, appeared in the chilly novel of Ernesto Sábato (b. 1911), *Sobre héroes y tumbas* (1961); the *descensus ad infernos* with which Sábato closes his fresco of the twilight of classical Peronism seems to illustrate what Theodor Adorno called "participation in the darkness," reckoning it the gist of modern art.

However, the essential point is, of course, that Sábato's heady cocktail of melancholy, metaphysics, and melodrama was above all an exercise in allegory – and allegory was very much the hub of the new fiction. Naturally, symbolization was never quite absent from much of previous Spanish American narrative, as is patently the case in *Don Segundo Sombra* or *Doña Bárbara*. Yet now hidden, polysemic meanings began to shape plot and language, harnessing the techniques of Kafka, Joyce, and Faulkner. *El señor presidente* (1946), the great dictatorship novel by Miguel Angel Asturias (1899–1974), is redolent with allegory, as are the finest works of Juan Rulfo (b. 1918) or José Lezama Lima (1912–1977). Yet good, artistic fiction-writing – artistic to a degree uncommon in the average social or *indigenista* novel – also resorted to allegory without indulging in too much obscurity. The masterpieces of Alejo Carpentier (1904–1980) explored "lo real maravilloso" ["Magical Realism"] of the Caribbean past in a basically clear, objective way. Regarding Surrealism as a structural given of Latin American society, Carpentier managed to avoid both the drabness of the document and the arbitrariness of free-wheeling fantasy. Again, Borges's metaphysical juggling, in his tersely written short stories, is obviously miles away from any poetics of darkness; rather, it is a luminous art, a kind of narrative *conceptismo* – and the same can be said of Julio Cortázar (1916–1984), the next Argentinian master of the fantastic tale.

How, in comparison, did Brazilian fiction evolve? The traditional craft of middle-brow fiction continued to thrive, but Brazilians also borrowed from modern European and North American masters. Clarice Lispector (1925–1977) responded to Lawrence and Woolf, Adonias Filho (b. 1915) and Autran Dourado (b. 1926) to Faulkner, João Guimarães Rosa (1908–

1967) to Mann's mythologizing and Joyce's word-coining; there was a Kafkaesque atmosphere in the short stories of Dalton Trevisan (b. 1925) or José J. Veiga (b. 1915). Generally speaking, Regionalism declined. In its wake there was some parting of ways, so that whereas some new novelists chose a kind of clever "reportage" novel, others went for highly technical narrative. The postmodernist years also saw the rise of female novelists – Lispector first and foremost; but also Dinah Silveira de Queiroz (1910–1983) and Lygia Fagundes Telles (b. 1923).

Antônio Cândido's remark (*Introducción a la literatura del Brasil*) that Brazilian Regionalism was for quite a long time weaker than its Hispanic counterpart led the great critic to notice a paradox: when the Brazilian regionalist novel finally reached a high level, thanks to an injection of social realism, the genre was on its way out in other areas, like the river Plate countries. As for the next stage of Brazilian fiction, dominated by Guimarães Rosa, Cândido prefers to talk of "super-regionalism." There is doubtless a need to conceptualize the difference, for Rosa's novellas in *Corpo de baile* and the novel *Grande sertão: veredas* (both published in 1956) lifted Regionalism to a truly Gnostic level. Rosa conceived of the modern novel as a subtle mix of epic and lyric. Indeed, his playful vocabulary and malleable syntax strongly poeticized his stories without in any way interfering with his keen sense of plot and character; like Borges, Rosa never spurned suspense. A deeply religious mind, Rosa was peerless in his depictions of the Brazilian landscape yet often fathomed the mystery of evil and the deepest recesses of the soul. At the time of his death in 1967, Rosa had become, in Brazilian letters, what Borges was in the Spanish American world – the central writer. Through him, Brazilian modern literature at last entered the age of radical Formalism, paying the price of hermeticism which goes with it.

This tendency toward hermeticism is also found in Clarice Lispector. In her work, the introspective novel of religious torment, typified by writers like Cornélio Pena (1896–1958) and Lúcio Cardoso (b. 1913), became an abstract, poignant text written in nervous, quivering prose – a lyricization of narrative writing as intense as, albeit very different from, that of Guimarães Rosa. Finally, hermeticism was also a general effect of the orphic epic of a modern poet whose best efforts came around 1950: Jorge de Lima. Myth and archetype, wrought in spell-binding stanzas of Surreal cultism, made de Lima's *Invenção de Orfeu* (1952) something very different from the concise, direct lyricism of Bandeira or even the complex but far more accessible late poems of Drummond. Just as Rosa freed Brazilian artistic fiction from the last remnants of conventional Realism and careless writing, Jorge de Lima broke with the transparency of neo-romantic poetry.

The obvious counterpart of *Invenção de Orfeu* and its progeny, on the

Hispanic side, was not the erstwhile avant-garde verse of Huidobro, the wry Realism of Vallejo, or the neo-romantic Muse of Neruda. Rather, it was the poetry of Octavio Paz (b. 1914), from "Piedra de sol" (1957) to *Blanco* (1967), because it was here that the concept and practice of the modern *poem* as such overcame the traditional episodism, the customary occasionalism of the romantic or *modernista* lyric. Just as Darío, with his wide influence, became the new Góngora of the Hispanic world, Paz became the new Darío – but with a major difference: a conspicuous *deepening* of philosophical preoccupations. So the second hegemonic force in Hispanic literature in the modern age turned out to be, together with the ludic shadow of Borges, the poetics of Paz. The last Surrealist, Paz pitted poetry against history. His essay (*El arco y la lira* [1957]) started to praise poetical revolt ("the tradition of dissention") over and above the myth of revolution. This is not the place to discuss, even briefly, his profound rethinking of Mexican culture, from *El laberinto de la soledad* (1950) to *Posdata* (1970); nor his shrewd study of Sor Juana, a model of critical perceptiveness, a healthy remove from the "methodological pestilence" of our time. Nowadays Paz the liberal essayist, of late more important than Paz the poet, occupies the place once held by Ortega y Gasset as the leading ideological agitator of the Hispanic world.

Octavio Paz's achievement was to enshrine aestheticism as the core of Spanish American poetics, and some of the very best poets of the 1980s and 1990s began as his conscious heirs. However, Paz's controlled Surrealism was not the only course open to poets writing in the 1950s. Some adopted an unabashed sentimental and colloquial style, or produced vigorous *engagé* verse; others shaped classicist rather than more popular discourses, while in Chile Nicanor Parra (b. 1914) launched the concept of the *antipoem*. In Brazil, the main trends were similar, up to a point. João Cabral de Melo Neto (b. 1920; *Psicologia da composição* [1947], *Uma faca só lâmina* [1956]) developed an antipoetry of his own, with an almost puritanical insistence on clear denotation and lucid composition. Cabral's favorite poets – Ponge, Marianne Moore, Crabbe – are all adept at skillful description, far from pathos and generalities. He has written the best Brazilian poetry since Drummond, and, like Drummond, has been able to face the task of producing social lyrics (as in *O rio*, 1954) without surrendering to facile rhetoric. Yet Cabral's antipoetry, unlike Parra's, is not satirical but phenomenological. His obstinate plea for verbal honesty is an ethics as consistent as – yet vastly different from – Paz's ontological poetics.

The Brazilians with whom Paz came in contact – rather late in their respective, independent careers – were the brothers Haroldo de Campos (b. 1929) and Augusto de Campos (b. 1931), founders of *Concretismo* [Concretism] in São Paulo. Launched in the mid 1950s, Concrete Poetry abandoned verse and operated through typographical devices akin to the visual arts. Expression was as much repudiated as mimesis. The *Concretos* appreciated Cabral's objectivism, his "engineering" approach to writing, but they also had the highest regard for Oswald de Andrade (1890–1954), the most experimental of the 1922 Modernists, and the closest to the "Kodak" technique used in French poetry prior to Surrealism. Technically, *Concretismo* presented two main aspects: on the one hand, there was a will to integrate non-verbal signs into the poem; on the other, an exploration of the materiality of signifiers. *Concretismo* did well to react against the stale neo-Parnassian work of the poets of the Generation of 1945, including virtuosi like Ledo Ivo (b. 1924), but it is not surprising that the movement quickly brought about other reactions in turn, notably from another São paulo poet–critic, Mário Chamie, who fathered a rival movement centered around the magazine *Praxis*.

In any event, by 1960 Brazilian literature was torn between two incompatible tendencies. There was the vatic neo-Cultism of the later Jorge de Lima and the cool, objectivist quatrains of Cabral, the two major influences on the new verse – both largely alien to Spanish American trends at the same time, despite all the common denominators in terms of Surrealism or "antipoetry." Together these forces meant a triumph of *poematic* form, as opposed to the looser poetic formats of the *modernista* tradition in Bandeira, Drummond, Murilo Mendes, or the neo-Romantics. At the same time, there were now two formalist regimes: one conservative (the neo-Parnassians of the Generation of 1945), the other radically experimental (the new Avant-Garde represented by *Concretismo* and its diaspora). Again, there was no proper equivalent in Spanish America. In prose, too, it would be difficult to find a Spanish American analogue to the negative mysticism of Lispector (*Laços de família* [1960]), or to the super-regionalism of Guimarães Rosa. The main axis of Brazilian *Modernismo* – the balance between modernized, subjective poetry and the neorealist social novel – had clearly lost its dominance among creative writers. Social Regionalism underwent enormous changes, most noticeable in Jorge Amado's evolution into a novelist of the erotic Picaresque, a process which started with *Gabriela, cravo e canela* (1958). Moreover, as if to corroborate these changes on the literary scene, the period from 1940 to 1960 also saw the arrival of something sadly missing from the early modern literature of Brazil – play-writing. In the witty classical comedies of Guilherme Figueiredo (b. 1915), the nostalgic Regionalism of Jorge Andrade (1922–1984) or Ariano Suassuna (b. 1927), the militant social drama of Gianfrancesco Guarnieri (b. 1934), and the powerful Freudian melodramas of Nelson Rodrigues (1912–1980), who deployed an uncanny gift for writing deeply illuminating rhetorical kitsch plays about middle-class motives and morality, modern Brazil at last got a dramatic literature worthy of its poetry and fiction.

It is customary to date the last stage of Spanish American literature from the Cuban Revolution. This is only a relative truth. In terms of intellectual prestige, the fictions of Borges were what started the so-called *Boom*. If Darío was the first among Spanish American writers to shape the direction of literary taste in Spain, Borges was the first writer from the hemisphere to be acknowledged as the peer of leading Europeans. Indeed, the first decades of the postmodern era could well be called the "Age of Beckett and Borges." However, the point is that Borges began writing his *ficciones* a quarter of a century before Fidel Castro's victory, and they of course owe nothing to the spirit of left-wing radicalism. However, in terms of popularity it is undeniable that the *Boom* was linked to novels by intellectual fellow-travelers of the Cuban Revolution, most notably Gabriel García Márquez (b. 1928). One might even sum up the major pattern in Spanish American letters since the mid 1960s as a combination of the acute technical self-awareness of Borges, Carpentier, or Paz and a determination to renew the ideal of *engagé* literature.

García Márquez's *Cien años de soledad* (1967) became the best-selling epitome of the new novel with a loose radical or libertarian intent. Macondo and its generations of Buendías are painted with a narrative skill making the utmost profit from humor, hyperbole, and allegory, not to mention the subtle parodies of Carpentier and Borges. *Cien años* is a distinctly "modern" book, yet not a bit difficult. The same applies to the earlier novel by Guillermo Cabrera Infante (b. 1929), *Tres tristes tigres* (1963), where parody and language play take the place of García Márquez's artistry in plot-building, or to the ironical pop fiction of Manuel Puig (b. 1939), beginning with *La traición de Rita Hayworth* (1968). These comic novelists are best characterized as eminent representatives of what John Barth has famously dubbed the literature of replenishment (in *The Atlantic*, 245 (Jan. 1980), 65–71) – Postmoderns who, like Pynchon in the United States, make a mockery of the old dichotomies of the modernist tradition: Realism/the fantastic, form/content, high literature/popular genres, pure art/*engagé* writing, and so on.

Be that as it may, even before the world success of *Cien años de soledad* the supposedly monolithic ideological facade of the *Boom* was beginning to crack. Attempts to keep the *Boom* in the orbit of Castroism were already being challenged in the 1960s, when the fine Uruguayan critic Emir Rodríguez Monegal launched a journal in Paris, *Mundo Nuevo*, in open defiance of the ideological orthodoxy recommended by Cuba's *Casa de las Américas*. The subsequent ideological evolution of many writers confirmed this departure from communist allegiance, most conspicuously in the work of the Peruvian Mario Vargas Llosa (b. 1936). A novelist of solid craftsmanship, Vargas Llosa first made his mark as a powerful social critic with great technical skill, as in *La casa verde* (1966), and he was one of the first to write a book-length analysis of García Márquez's achievement. Yet, after a couple of comic novels published in the 1970s, Vargas Llosa disengaged himself from the dogmas of left-wing radicalism to become the major example – along with Octavio Paz – of a great Latin American intellectual with clear radical origins who arrives at a conscious and consistent liberal standpoint.

Such evolution, it goes without saying, can hardly please everyone in a region like Latin America, where the intelligentsia remains predominantly Marxist if no longer Leninist. Liberal convictions are of course no more a guarantee of literary value than radical belief. However, Vargas Llosa's ideological change certainly did not prevent him from writing a masterpiece, *La guerra del fin del mundo* (1981), a creative fictional reprise of Euclides da Cunha's heroic subject in *Os sertões*. The handling of the plot and the character delineation are worthy of Guimarães Rosa, and these, along with Vargas Llosa's consummate ability in deploying narrative points of view, makes *La guerra* the best Spanish American novel of the decade.

According to the Mexican critic José Joaquín Blanco (*Crónica de la poesía mexicana* [1977]), the vogue of psychoanalysis in Latin American bourgeois culture since 1970 has undermined the credibility of oneiric poems: in an age of generalized psychological suspicion, the romantic aspirations of visionary writing are no longer convincing. Blanco thinks that, under these circumstances, poets no longer seek "the lasting crystallization of the sublimated moment" but, rather, "the passing expression of current life." Sometimes this will to desacralize the poem has worked very well. Nevertheless, in other instances the idea of a deliberately prosaic and colloquial poetry – even when resorting to the authority of Pound, as in the *engagé* verse of the Nicaraguan priest Ernesto Cardenal (b. 1925) – seldom rises above the level of tedious enumeration; exchanging a Nerudian rhetoric of invective for documentary effects is no warrant of poetic accomplishment. In any case, in view of the desacralizing bent of several influential poets in the two decades since 1970, some critics have spoken of a schizoid pattern in Spanish American letters, formed by the coincidence of hermetic (that is, experimental) fiction and prosaic, accessible verse. This is not entirely true, however, since the "demotic" trend has certainly not engulfed all poetry since around 1970, and postmodern fiction, even when experimental, is not necessarily hermetic.

Let us now turn for the last time to Brazil, and gauge both convergence and divergence. The first thing to be noted is a relative poverty. There was no Brazilian *Boom*, and the Spanish American *Boom* cannot be explained away, as some Brazilians have suggested, as due solely to the preferences of French critics in combination with the dynamics of the North American book trade. The creative exuberance of Spanish American narrators since Cortázar cannot be reduced to the wonders of marketing or to critical diktats. It is a fact, however regrettable, that the performance of Brazilian verse since João Cabral and of Brazilian fiction since Guimarães Rosa has been generally less powerful or less convincing than the Spanish American authors. Yet there have been significant developments between 1965 and 1990. In poetry, one should not overlook the achievements of post-1945 verse, most notably in the work of Marly de Oliveira, nor the literarization of popular music, from the bossa nova onwards; this latter trend, which began with a former Modernist–Romantic, Vinícius de Moraes (1913–1980), has rightly inserted song-writers like Chico Buarque de Holanda (b. 1944) and Caetano Veloso among the new poets. Caetano led *Tropicalismo*, a typical late 1960s cocktail of pop art and avant-garde expression. There was an undeniable persistence of avant-garde poetry, of beyond-verse experiments. Nevertheless, still more characteristic of the postmodern period was the surge of anti-*Concretismo* texts, from the *Poema sujo* (1975) of Ferreira Gullar (b. 1930) and the return to poematic length in Affonso Romano de Sant'Anna, to the so-called "marginal poetry," a pop Minimalism led by Cacaso (Antônio Carlos de Brito [b. 1944]), Francisco Alvim, and Chacal. The "marginals" were in fact reacting, as belated crypto-Romantics, against the two major forces in Brazilian poetry after Modernism: the Neocultism of Jorge de Lima and the objectivism of Cabral. The best guide to alternative literature, critic Heloísa Buarque de Holanda, identifies a "post-tropicalist" trend in the 1970s, represented by maverick authors like Jorge Mautner and Paulo Leminski. At basically the same time, avant-garde fictions were turning tropicalist, as in Márcio Souza's "feuilleton," *Galvez, Imperador do Acre* (1977) or "tougher" as in Ignácio de Loyola Brandão's *Zero* (1975).

Brutalism and Minimalism tended to prevail in many fictional texts, in contrast to the more urbane ways of the Spanish American Postmoderns. The generals were blamed for the rudeness of the new Brazilian literature. Yet there were generals, or other similar forms of authoritarianism, almost everywhere else, so this hardly explains the Brazilian difference. Yet some writers, notably Rubem Fonseca (b. 1925), a master of the short story, managed to put coarse language and sordid situations to good literary use. The authoritarian decades naturally saw the rise of protest novels, beginning with *Quarup* (1967) by Antônio Callado. There was also an unexpected return to *sertanejo* Regionalism, reminiscent of the strongest social realism of the 1930s. A solid body of fiction about immigrant families and modern problems also developed, including the short stories of Moacyr Scliar (b. 1937), the novel *Lavoura arcaica* (1975) by Raduan Nassar (b. 1935), and the sage-like *A república dos sonhos* (1984) by Nélida Piñon (b. 1936), a former avant-garde narrator who evolved from hermetic *nouveaux romans* to more linear plots and clearer structures. Some of the very best prose of these years was found in memoirs, like those of the modernist physician Pedro Nava (1903–1984) – a true master of Brazilian prose – or the ex-guerrilla Fernando Gabeira. Darcy Ribeiro, in *Maíra* (1976), proved that a social scientist could become a creative writer in an age of fictional scarcity. Fortunately fiction became opulent again with the magnificent mock epic, *Viva o povo brasileiro* (1984), by João Ubaldo Ribeiro (b. 1940), an engrossing, hero-less historical saga, written in a sapid, sumptuous prose, in which sharp satire alternates with deep lyricism. Meanwhile, two very recent books of poetry, Ruth Villela's *Beira vida* and Pedro Paulo Sena Madureira's *Rumor de facas*, both published in 1989, provide clear evidence that verse, in a significant, non-trivial sense, has survived.

Spanish American literature is a misleading concept, largely a construct of academics writing from outside and in general institutionally tempted to think of the Third World as a homogeneous entity, of Latin America as a monolith, and of Spanish America as a unity rather than a complex whole. To be sure, since the days of Andrés Bello there has been many an effort to use culture to overcome a Balkanized polity; literary Bolivarianism has never been far away. Yet efforts are not achievements, and in the end national or regional traditions have been at least as important as supposed common elements and unifying factors. Few critics have protested the homogenizing approach to Latin American letters, though Mário Bene-detti has eloquently warned that while Latin American writers normally share a concern for the continent's common fate, each belongs to a *national* context with its own past and present; that context is more than a mere superficial differentiation within a larger, more essential identity. After all, nobody talks of Australian and Canadian literatures as mere specifications of the same matrix; why should we do otherwise for such a huge and highly diversified subcontinent as Latin America, or even for its Hispanic majority? Geographical contiguity, which has in fact long been cancelled by isolation rather than constant contact, is no substitute for cultural continuity. A less lazy conceptual disposition would put more stress on plurality and difference than is currently done. Now if this seems valid for Spanish-language literature from Buenos Aires to Mexico City, it is all the more so in the case of Brazil, a vast country which for quite a long time focused on cultures across the Atlantic and which has shown little interest – aside from occasional spells of warfare – in its neighbors; these, of course, returned the compliment by completely ignoring Brazilian culture. Small wonder, then, that any comparison of the Brazilian and Spanish American literary traditions reveals as many divergences as similarities. In the past, all in all, literary developments in Brazil were rarely linked to those in the Andes, in Mesoamerica, or even in the Plate region – any more than developments in those areas themselves were linked.

On the other hand, there *is* no denying that national literary reactions to the elements common to all Latin American bourgeoisies – the cluster of cultural links with Western Europe, the inevitable and persistent mimesis of modern culture – did indeed share much ground, creating, at the very least, a number of functional equivalents between local responses to common European models which these literatures adapted as well as adopted. Even so, the fact that similar adaptations often took place at different stages in each literary tradition proves that contrast could well hide beneath likeness. Nowadays, however, as the law of the world is increasing interdependency, cultural interaction within Latin America is bound to grow. Latin American unity lies in the future, and fortunately enough it will be one more case of convergence within diversity. As cultural history never tires of teaching us, contact often thrives on contrast, and vice versa.

Bibliography

Bibliography of general bibliographies of Spanish American literature
Hensley C. Woodbridge

This bibliography attempts to list with brief comments many of the most important general bibliographies and dictionaries in the field of Spanish American literature. The major portion is arranged by country and sometimes by region. There is a classified arrangement within each country usually by literary genres and topics. It is hoped that each entry has been described in such detail that it can be easily located. The annotations are intended to show the scope of the item with an occasional evaluation of its accuracy, up-to-dateness, and general usefulness.

It will be noticed that the majority of these items have been published in the last two decades. Library catalogs (Peru's *Biblioteca nacional*, for example) are being made available on an international basis, a greater attempt has been made to cover periodical literature on a current basis (*Hispanic American Periodical Index*), more and more bibliographies of literary genres are appearing. While not part of this bibliography more and more outstanding author bibliographies have appeared and are being planned.

Current bibliographies and periodical indexes

Bibliografía de publicaciones japonesas sobre América latina en 1974– (title also in Japanese), Tokyo, Instituto iberoamericano de la Universidad de Sofía, 1975–.
    Classified bibliography of Japanese publications on Latin America. It is the current source for Japanese translations of Latin American authors and Japanese criticism of them.
"Bibliografía hispánoamericana," *Revista Hispánica Moderna*, 1–15 (1934–1947).
"Bibliografía hispánica," *Revista Hispánica Moderna*, 16–22 (1948–1956).
"Bibliografía hispanoamericana," *Revista Hispánica Moderna*, 23–32 (1956–1966); 33–35, nos. (1967–1969).
    For almost thirty-five years this was the fullest bibliography of its kind. It is a classified bibliography that includes dissertations and book reviews as well as books and articles. It contains more than 80,000 numbered items.

This is an adaptation of a bibliography that appeared in Paula Covington, ed. *Latin America and the Caribbean: A Critical Guide to Research Sources* (Westport, Conn.: Greenwood Press, 1992). Greenwood Press is an imprint of Greenwood Publishing Group, Inc.

Bibliography of general bibliographies

Bibliographie der Hispanistik in der Bundersrepublik Deutschland, Osterreich und der deutschprachigen Schweiz, comp., Titus Heydenreich, ed. Christoph Strosetski, Frankfurt-am-Main, Veruert. Editionen der Iberoamericana. Reihe II. Bibliographische Reihe, 4, 1978–1981; Reihe 5, 1982–1986. Both vols., 1988; 1987–1989, 1990. (170 pages.)

Volumes contain sections devoted to Latin American literature written by individuals in the German-speaking areas of Europe regardless of where their material was published.

Bibliographie latine-américaine d'articles, Paris, Institut d'Hautes Etudes de l'Amérique latine, 1975– .

Semi-annual. Some of the approximately 3,500 yearly items deal with Hispanic American literature.

Bulletin bibliographique Amérique latine: analyse des publications françaises et recherche bibliographique automatisée sur le fichier FRANCIS, 1– (1981–). Semi-annual. Excellent current source for studies on Latin America published in France by the French.

Columbus Memorial Library. *Index to Latin American Periodicals. Humanities and Social Sciences*, Boston: G. K. Hall, 1–2 (1961–1962); Metuchen, N.Y.: Scarecrow Press, 3–10, 2 (1963 June 1970).

Index to Latin American Periodical Literature 1929–1960, 8 vols., Boston, G. K. Hall, 1962. First supplement with the same publisher is for 1961–1965, 1968, 2 vols. The *Index* for 1966–1970, 1980, 2 vols., has the same publisher.

These indexes are a reproduction of the periodical part of the dictionary catalog of this library.

Handbook of Latin American Studies, 1– (1935–), 1936– , vols. I–XIII, Cambridge, Mass., Harvard University Press, 1936–1951; vols. XIV–XL were published in Gainesville, University of Florida Press, 1951–1978; vols. XLI– are published in Austin, University of Texas Press, 1979– .

Vols I–XXV contain a selective annotated bibliography of important *belles lettres*, literary history, and literary criticism that appeared during the year covered. The literatures of certain areas or periods are selected and annotated by experts in the field. With vol. XXVI, the section devoted to literature appears in the Humanities volume, which now alternates with a volume devoted to the social sciences. Bibliographies regardless of subject usually appear in the "General Works" section of each volume. Despite its selectivity it has long been and continues to be an essential reference source in the field of Latin American literature.

Hispanic American Periodicals Index, 3 vols., (1970–1974), Los Angeles, University of California Latin American Center, 1975– . Current volumes index approximately 200 journals, many of which are not indexed elsewhere. Essential current classified bibliography for authors and movements.

Indice Español de Humanidades, Madrid, Instituto de Información y Documentación en Ciencias Sociales y Humanidades (ISOCO [y] Centro Nacional de Información Documentación, 1, no. 1 (Jan.–June 1978–).

The first issue reproduces the contents pages of 171 journals published in 1976. Key-word index allows the user to locate material on a given topic or author.

Leavitt, Sturgis E., Madaline W. Nichols, and Jefferson Rea Spell. *Revistas hispano-*

americanas: índice bibliográfico 1843–1935, Santiago de Chile, Fondo Histórico y Bibliográfico José Toribio Medina, 1960. (xiv, 589 pages.)

A classified index of 30,107 items found in slightly more than 50 files of periodicals published in Spanish America.

MLA International Bibliography of Books and Articles on the Modern Languages and Literatures, MLA, 1956– .

From 1921 to 1955 covered publications of the United States. Material on Latin American literature beginning with the 1969 edition has appeared in volume II of the bibliography. Recent volumes are arranged by periods within country.

Romanische Bibliographie, Tübingen, Max Niemeyer, 1965– . Biennial, 1967– .

Formerly appeared annually as a supplement to the *Zeitschrift für romanische Philologie*, 1875/1876–1879; no volumes for 1923; volumes exist for 1940–1950, 1951–1955, 1956–1960; from 1961–1962 continues with two years to a volume. Classified arrangement by region. Includes citations to book reviews. Recent volumes contain author index, reviewer index, and subject index.

The Year's Work in Modern Language Studies, Cambridge, Modern Humanities Research Association. Annual volumes for 1931–1939, 1950– . Vol. XI covers 1940–1949. Brief critical annotations are provided. Author and subject indexes.

Bibliographies (general)

Bellini, Giuseppe. *Bibliografía dell'ispanoamericanismo italiano: contributi critici*, Universitario degli Studio di Venezia, Seminario di Letterature Iberiche e Iberoamericane, Milan: Cisalpino, 1981. (100 pages.)

1,191 Italian contributions to the study of Latin American literature published between 1940 and 1980 are listed, whether published in the form of a book or as an article in a periodical. Unfortunately no pagination is given for the items included.

Bibliografía general de la literatura latinoamericana, ed. Jorge C. Andrade, Paris, UNESCO, 1972. (1987 pages.)

Each of the three chronological periods compiled by four outstanding scholars is divided into "Bibliografías generales," "Bibliografías regionales," and "Historias generales."

Bryant, Shasta M. *Selective Bibliography of Bibliographies of Hispanic American Literature*, 2nd. edn., expanded and revised, Austin, University of Texas Press, Institute of Latin American Studies, 1976. (x, 100 pages.)

Almost two-thirds of the 662 entries are author bibliographies; almost all are annotated.

Buxo, José Pascual, and Antonio Melis (eds.). *Apuntes para una bibliografía crítica de la literatura hispanoamericana*, I, *Historias literarias*, Centro di Ricerche per l'America Latina, Ricerche Letterie, 3, Florence, Valmartina, 1973. (vii, 133 pages.)

Critical evaluations of 144 histories of Latin American literature as well as of the literature of the individual countries.

Forster, Merlin. "Spanish-American literary bibliography – 1967," *Modern Language Journal*, 53 (1969), 85–9.

Foster, David William. "Spanish-American literary bibliography, 1968," *Modern*

Language Journal, 53 (1969), 550–4.

"Bibliografía literaria hispanoamericana 1977–1978–1979, 1982–1983–1984," *Revista Iberoamericana*, 46 (1980), 591–664; 51 (1985), 347–53.

Annotated bibliographies of reference works published during the years covered by the article's title.

Johnson, Harvey L. "Spanish-American literary bibliography, 1969–1970, 1972–1974," *Modern Language Journal*, 55 (1971), 306–11; 56 (1972), 365–72; *Hispanófila*, 54 (1975), 61–68, 69–78; 64 (1978), 93–9.

"Spanish-American literary bibliography – 1962–1966," *Hispania*, 46 (1963), 557–60; 47 (1964), 766–71; 48 (1965), 856–64; 49 (1966), 793–99; *Modern Language Journal*, 51 (1967), 402–8.

Johnson, Harvey L., and David William Foster. "Bibliografía literaria hispanoamericana 1976," *Revista Iberoamericana*, 44 (1978), 221–9.

Lozano, Stella, *Selected Bibliography of Contemporary Spanish-American Writers*. Latin American Bibliography Series, 8, Los Angeles University of California Latin American Studies Center, 1979. (v, 149 pages.)

Material published during the brief period 1974–1978, "except for the women writers, in which case material is listed regardless of date" (p. iii).

Mundo Lo, Sara de. *Index to Spanish American Collective Biography*, 4 vols., Boston, G. K. Hall, 1981–1985. Vol. I: *The Andean Countries*, 1981. (496 pages – Chile, Bolivia, Ecuador, Peru, Colombia, and Venezuela.) Vol. II: *Mexico*, 1982. (xxx, 378 pages.) Vol. III: *The Central American and Caribbean Countries*, 1984. (xxxiii, 360 pages.) Vol. IV: *The River Plate Countries*, 1985. (xxxi, 388 pages. Argentina, Uruguay, and Paraguay.)

One of the most extraordinary reference works of the 1980s, which provides an index to biographical studies published in books. The annotations for each volume almost always list the biographies included. The index is to biographies in collections; book-length biographical studies do not appear.

Okinshevich, Leo. *Latin America in Soviet Writings: A bibliography*, ed. Robert G. Carlton, 2 vols., Baltimore, Md., Johns Hopkins University Press, 1966. Vol. I: 1917–1958. Vol. II: 1959–1964.

Items 2784–3407 (I, 159–91) and items 3412–4423 (II, 186–223) list literary criticism, histories of literature, and translations of Latin American authors.

Rela, Walter. *Guía bibliográfica de la literatura hispano-americana desde el siglo xix hasta 1970*, Buenos Aires, Pardo, 1971. (613 pages.)

Classified unannotated bibliography of 6,023 items.

Spanish American Literature: A selected bibliography 1970–1980, (title also in Spanish), Montevideo AS, 1982. (231 pages.)

Its 1,502 items could serve as a supplement to the preceding item.

Schnepl, Ryszard, and Kryzsztof Smolana (eds.) "Cultura," in *Bibliografía de Publicaciones sobre América Latina en Polonia 1945–1977* (title also in Polish), Varsovia, Biblioteca Nacional, Instituto de Historia, Academia de Ciencias en Polonia, Sociedad Polaca de Historiadores [y] Sociedad Polaca de Estudios Latinoamericanos, 1978, 100–13.

Many of items 628–732 include Latin American literary works translated into Polish, along with their Polish reviews. Spanish titles are given for works in Polish.

Zubatsky, David S. *Latin American Authors: An annotated guide to bibliographies*, Metuchen, New York, Scarecrow Press, 1986. (ix, 332 pages.)

An indispensable guide to bibliographies of Latin American authors which "includes citations that appear in periodicals, books, dissertations, and *Festschrift* volumes" (p. v).

Black Authors

Bansart, Andrés. *El negro en la literatura hispanoamericana (bibliografía y hemerografía)*, Colección de bolsillo, 2, Valle de Sartenejas, Venezuela, Editorial de la Universidad Simón Bolívar, 1986. (113 pages.)

661 items that deal chiefly with the "Presencia del descendiente de negroafricanos en la literatura hispanoamericana" (p. v).

Jackson, Richard L. *The Afro-Spanish American Author: An annotated bibliography of criticism*, N.Y., Garland, 1980. (xix, 129 pages.)

Jackson, an outstanding expert on Afro-Spanish American authors, has divided this well-annotated bibliography of 562 items into general bibliographies, general studies, anthologies, and authors.

The Afro-Spanish American Author II: *The 1980s: An annotated bibliography of recent criticism*, West Cornwall, Conn., Locust Hill Press, 1989. (xxviii, 154 pages.)

A supplement with the same arrangement as the previous volume.

"Studies in Caribbean and South American literature: an annotated bibliography," *Callaloo*, 10– (1987–   ).

One of its sections is "Afro-Hispanic literature," which has been compiled by a variety of individuals. The bibliography for 1990 is divided into newly published and translated works, interviews, general studies, studies on poetry, studies on fiction, studies on drama, and studies on individual authors.

Williams, Lorna V. "Recent works on Afro-Hispanic literature," *Latin American Research Review*, 22:2 (1987), 245–54.

Critical evaluation of four important works in this field.

Dictionaries and Handbooks

Becco, Horacio Jorge. *Diccionario de literatura hispanoamericana: autores*, Textos Huemul, Buenos Aires, Huemul, 1984. (313 pages)

Brief biographical sketch followed by a listing of the author's works with pertinent bibliographical details.

Bhalla, Alok. *Latin American Writers: A bibliography with critical and biographical introductions*, New York, Envoy, 1987. (174 pages.)

Each of the eighteen biographical sketches of twentieth-century Spanish American writers is provided with a bibliography of the author's works, a bibliography of his books or anthologies of his works in English translation, as well as a bibliography of criticism of the author in English. The volume's printer has no accent marks.

Forster, David William. *Handbook of Latin American Literature*, 2nd. edn., New York, Garland, 1992. (820 pages.)

Brief histories of the literatures of the different countries are provided. Each literary historical sketch is followed by an extremely brief bibliography. More than a dozen individuals contributed to this volume. This edition has articles on the principal Hispanic groups in the US, films, and in paraliterature.

Klein, Leonard S. (ed.) *Latin American Literature in the Twentieth Century: A guide*, New York, Ungar, 1986. (x, 278 pages.)

Based on the Latin American entries in *Encyclopedia of World Literature in the Twentieth Century* (5 vols. Ungar, 1981–1984). Contains "13 national and regional surveys . . ., 92 individual articles on major writers. . . An appendix with articles on Afro-Cubanism, Magic realism and Modernismo" (back cover). Though published in 1986 no mention is made of García Márquez's winning of the Nobel Prize in 1982. The signed biographical–critical articles usually provide bibliographies of the authors' works as well as critical studies.

Reichardt, Dieter, *Lateinamerikanische Autores: Literatur-lexikon und Bibliographie der deutschen Ubersetzungen*, Tübingen, Erdman, 1972. (719 pages.)

This German biographical dictionary of Latin American authors is arranged by country and is a valuable source for their German translations.

Shimose, Pedro (ed.) *Diccionario de autores iberoamericanos*, Madrid, Ministerio de Asuntos Exteriores, 1982. (459 pages.)

Includes Spanish, and Latin, American as well as Chicano authors.

Solé, Carlos A., and María Isabel Abreu (eds.) *Latin American Writers*, 3 vols., New York, Charles Scribner's Sons, 1989.

Numerous authorities provide biographical–critical sketches of 172 authors in articles ranging from 2,500 to 10,000 words. The selected bibliography is divided into first editions, modern editions, English translations, biographical and critical studies, and bibliographies.

Drama

Acuña, René. *El teatro popular en Hispanoamérica: una bibliografía anotada*, Mexico, Universidad Nacional Autónoma de México, 1979. (114 pages.)

Despite its title not all items are annotated, some are obviously known second-hand. Contains 380 items on Hispanic American popular theatre. Also has a section of 141 items on Spain's popular theatre.

Allen, Richard. *Teatro hispanoamericano: una bibliografía anotada/Spanish American Theatre, an Annotated Bibliography*, Boston, G. K. Hall, 1987. (633 pages.)

Arranged by country. Provides brief plot summaries and critical comment. Locates at least one copy in the United States.

Becco, Horacio Jorge. *Bibliografía general de las artes del espectáculo en América latina*, Paris UNESCO, 1977. (118 pages.)

Classified bibliography of 1,797 items, many of them on the theatre.

Carpenter, Charles A. "Modern drama studies: an annual bibliography," *Modern Drama*, 17–34 (1974–1991), continued by Rebecca Cameron *et al.*, 35–(1992–   ).

Records "current scholarship, criticism, and commentary that may prove valuable to students of modern dramatic literature" (*Modern Drama*, 18 [1975], 61). "Spanish" section later changed to "Hispanic"; it covers drama of Spain, Portugal, Brazil, and Spanish America, regardless of language.

"Latin American theater criticism, 1966–1974: some addenda to Lyday and Woodyard," *Revista Interamericana de Bibliografía*, 30 (1980), 246–53.
Praises Lyday and Woodward (below) and adds 97 items.

"Spanish-American drama" in *Modern Drama Scholarship and Criticism, 1966–1980: An international bibliography*, University of Toronto Press, 1986. 193–210.

Hebblethwaite, Frank P. *A Bibliographical Guide to the Spanish American Theater*, Basic Bibliographies, 6, Washington, Pan American Union, 1969. (viii, 84 pages.)
Classified bibliography "on the history and criticism of the Spanish American theatre in its entirety... It is not a compilation of dramatic works, nor of studies concerning individual authors, plays or playhouses" (p. vi). Many items are annotated.

Hoffman, Herbert H. *Latin American Play Index*, vol. I *1920–1962*, Metuchen, NJ, Scarecrow, 1984. (v, 147 pages.)

Latin American Play Index, vol. II *1962–1980*, Metuchen, NJ, Scarecrow, 1983. (iv, 131 pages.)
These volumes provide data on 3,300 plays by more than 1,000 dramatists who have written or write in Spanish, French, or Portuguese.

Jones, Willis Knapp. *Behind Spanish American Footlights*, Austin, University of Texas Press, 1966. (xvi, 609 pages.)
Volume is now dated but was for some time the standard history of Spanish American drama.

Lyday, Leon F., and George W. Woodyard. *A Bibliography of Latin American Theater Criticism 1940–1974*, Guides and Bibliographic Series, 10, Austin, University of Texas Press, Institute of Latin American Studies, 1976. (xvii, 243 pages.)
Many of the 2,360 items are annotated.

Neglia, Erminio, and Luis Ordaz. *Repertorio selecto del teatro hispanoamericano contemporáneo*, 2nd edn., rev. and enlarged, Tempe, Center for Latin American Studies, Arizona State University, 1980. (xix, 110 pages.)
Lists contemporary dramatists alphabetically with country. It includes many anthologies.

"Recent publications, Materials received and current bibliographies," *Latin American Theater Review*, 3– (1969–   ).
Published in each issue of the *Review*, this bibliography is the best current source of data on recently published plays, as well as on critical studies of the Latin American theatre.

Toro, Fernando de, and Peter Roster. *Bibliografía del teatro hispanoamericano contemporáneo (1900–1980)*, 2 vols. Editionen der Iberoamericana Reihe, 2, Bibliographische Reihe, 3, Frankfurt, Vervuert, 1985.
Most complete biography yet published of the contemporary Spanish American theatre. Vol. I is a classified bibliography of 6,952 items, while vol. II ("Crítica," "Libros originales") is a classified bibliography of 3,132 items. It is unfortunate that there is no index.

Trenti Rocamora, José Luis. *El repertorio de la dramática colonial hispanoamericana*, Buenos Aires, ALEA, 1950. (110 pages.)
Deals with the published drama of the colonial period; in a supplement, reference is made to unpublished texts preserved in repositories.

Essays

Los ensayistas (University of Georgia), 1– (1976–   ).
    Publishes at irregular intervals bibliographies of studies on Spanish American essayists.
Horl, Sabine. *Der Essay als literarische Gattung in Lateinamerika*, Frankfurt, Lang, 1980. (xiii, 100 pages.)
    Classified bibliography of 722 items.

Fiction

Balderston, Daniel. *The Latin American Short Story: An annotated guide to anthologies and criticism*, Bibliographies and Indexes in World Literature, 34, New York, Greenwood Press, 1992. (xx, 529 pages.)
    This classified, partially annotated, bibliography is divided into anthologies with their contents usually given, and criticism. The annotations are extremely useful. The three indexes – of authors, critics, and titles – should make this easy to use.
Becco, Horacio Jorge. "Antologías del cuento hispanoamericano: notas para una bibliografía" in *Narradores latinoamericanos 1929–1979*, vol. II, Memoria del XIX Congreso del Instituto Internacional de Literatura Iberoamericana, 2, Caracas, Centro de Estudios Latinoamericanos Rómulo Gallegos, 1980, 287–327.
    Valuable for its listing of 350 anthologies of the Spanish American short story, pp. 293–327.
Becco, Horacio Jorge, and David William Foster. *La nueva narrativa hispanoamericana: bibliografía*, Buenos Aires, Pardo, 1976. (226 pages.)
    Unannotated list of 2,257 items on the "new" novel and short story. Lists the works, translations, and criticism of fifteen authors in its first part. The second is "Referencias generales," and the third is "Referencias nacionales."
Brower, Keith H. *Contemporary Latin American Fiction: An annotated bibliography*, Pasadena, Salem Press, 1989. (218 pages.)
    A classified annotated bibliography of material in English on twenty-three authors.
Foster, David William. *The Twentieth-Century Spanish American Novel: A bibliographical guide*, Metuchen, N.J., Scarecrow, 1975. (227 pages.)
    Provides ". . . a working bibliography on the criticism pertaining to the 56 Spanish-American novelists most commonly studied in the U.S. . ." (p. vi). This unannotated bibliography includes "Basic monographic studies on the Spanish-American novel" and divides the material on authors in much the same way as the preceding item.
Foster, Jerald. "Towards a bibliography of Latin American short story anthologies," *Latin American Research Review*, 12:2 (1977), 103–8.
    Critically annotated bibliography of over fifty items. Includes anthologies of Latin American short stories in English translation.
Luis, William (ed.), *Modern Latin-American Fiction Writers: First series*. Dictionary of Literary Biography, 113, Detroit, Mich., Gale Research, 1992. (404 pages.)
    Excellent introduction to the life and work of thirty Latin American fiction

writers. Specialists on individual authors first provide a listing of the author's works along with their English translations, if any; a biographical–critical sketch, often well-illustrated, follows. The bibliography, depending on the author, may be divided into interviews, bibliographies, biographies, and references.

Luis, William and Ann González. *Modern Latin American Fiction Writers. Second series*. Dictionary of Literary Biography, 145. Detroit Mich.: Gale Research, 1994. (413 pages.)

Format for thirty-nine authors the same as preceding item.

Matlowsky, Bernice. *Antologías del cuento hispanoamericano: guía bibliográfica*, Monografías bibliográficas, 3, Washington, Pan American Union, 1950. (48 pages.)

Alphabetizes seventy-five annotated items, by author or editor, and provides an author index.

Meehan, Thomas C. "Bibliografía de y sobre la literatura fantástica," *Revista Iberoamericana*, 46: 110–11 (Jan.–June 1980), 243–54.

Ocampo de Gómez, Aurora M. *Novelistas iberoamericanos contemporáneos: obras y bibliografía crítica. Primera parte*, Cuadernos del Centro de Estudios Literarios, 2, 4, 6, 9, 11, (5 parts) Mexico, Universidad Nacional Autónoma de México, 1971–1981.

Provides dates and nationality of important contemporary novelists, lists their works and critical studies about them.

Zeitz, Eileen M., and Richard A. Seybolt. "Hacia una bibliografía sobre el realismo mágico," *Hispanic Journal*, 3:1 (1981) 159–67.

Provides a bibliography of general critical studies on Magical Realism, and studies on seven specific authors.

Poetry

Anderson, Robert Roland. *Spanish American Modernism: A selected bibliography*, Tucson, University of Arizona Press, 1970. (xxii, 167 pages.)

Provides data on critical studies on seventeen authors of this period. Individual index for each author. Extremely useful for period covered.

Celma Valero, María Pilar. *Literatura y periodismo en las revistas del fin de siglo: estudio e índices (1888–1907)*, Madrid, Ediciones Jucar, 1991. (898 pages.)

Index to twenty Spanish journals of the period which provides data on publications, within them, by Rubén Darío, Amado Nervo, Ricardo Jaimes Freyre, Julián del Casal, José Santos Chocano, and others.

Hoffman, Herbert H. *Hoffman's Index to Poetry: European and Latin American poetry in anthologies*, Metuchen, N.J., Scarecrow, 1985. (xiii, 672 pages.)

Indexes poems from these areas found in almost 100 anthologies. There are indexes both of title and of first lines.

Sefamí, Jacobo. *Contemporary Spanish American Poets: A bibliography of primary and secondary sources*, Bibliographies and Indexes in World Literature, 33, New York, Greenwood Press, 1992. (xix, 245 pages.)

Data are provided concerning the book-length publications of eighty-five poets born between 1910 and 1952. This classified bibliography is followed by a list of bibliographies on the authors, and then critical studies divided into books and dissertations, essays, reviews, interviews. Probably more useful for more recent poets than for the better-established ones.

Emilia de, Zuleta (ed.) *Bibliografía anotada del modernismo*, compiled and annotated by Hilda Gladys Fretes and Esther Bárbara, technical work by Hebe Pauliello de Chocolous, Cuadernos de la Biblioteca, 5, Mendoza, Universidad Central de Cuyo, Biblioteca Central, 1970 [c. 1973]. (138 pages.)

Annotates 245 items. Emphasis is on the movement rather than individual authors.

Women authors

Cortina, Lynn Ellen Rice. *Spanish-American Women Writers*, New York, Garland, 1983. (xi, 292 pages.)

Arranged by countries. Provides the author's dates and lists her publications.

Corvalán, Graciela N. V. *Latin American Women Writers in English Translation: A bibliography*, Latin American Bibliography Series, 9, Los Angeles, California University, Latin American Studies Center, 1980. (iv, 109 pages.)

Data provided on 282 women writers whose works have either been translated into English or for whom there are critical or biographical studies in English.

Cypess, Sandra Messinger, David R. Kohut, and Rachelle Moore. *Women Authors of Modern Hispanic South America: A bibliography of literary criticism and interpretation*, Metuchen, N.J., Scarecrow, 1989. (xii, 159 pages.)

Divided into general studies and then arranged by country. Provides critical studies on 169 women authors.

Knaster, Meri. "Literature, mass media, and folklore" in M. Knaster (ed.), *Women in Spanish America: An annotated bibliography from pre-Conquest to contemporary times*, Boston, G. K. Hall, 1977, 39–94.

Items 160–414 of this extremely selective annotated list deal with women writers of this area.

Marting, Diane E. (ed.) *Spanish American Women Writers: A bio-bibliographical source book*, New York, Greenwood Press, 1990. (xxvi, 645 pages.)

Escritoras de Hispanoamérica. Una guía bio-bibliográfica, ed., prol. and rev. of Spanish edn. by Montserrat Ordóñez, Bogotá, Siglo Veintiuno Editores, 1990. (638 pages.)

Each of the fifty articles on individual women authors is divided into biography, major themes, survey of criticism, and a bibliography of the author's works and works about the author. There are also two essays: "Indian women writers of Spanish America" and "Latina Writers in the US." There are three appendixes as well as title and subject indexes.

Bibliographies by country

Argentina

Bibliographies

Becco, Horacio Jorge. *Bibliografía de bibliografías literarias argentinas*, Basic Bibliographies, 9, Washington, OAS, 1972. (92 pages.)

Excellent source for author and genre bibliographies.

Bibliografía argentina de artes y letras, 1–50 (1959–1971).

Invaluable for period covered. Classified, sometimes annotated, bibliography of books and articles that deal with folklore, art, theatre, literature, journalism, geography, biography, and history.

Foster, David William. *Argentine Literature: A research guide,* 2nd edn., revised and enlarged, New York, Garland, 1982. (xliii, 778 pages.)

Fullest bibliography of critical studies on Argentinian literature. General references are divided into thirty sections. The sections devoted to seventy-three authors are divided into bibliographies, critical monographs and dissertations, and critical essays.

Dictionary

Diccionario de la literatura latinoamericana: Argentina, 2 vols., Washington, Pan American Union, 1960–1961.

The material on each author is divided into two sections: the first is a biographical and critical sketch; the second is a bibliography of his or her separately published works and critical studies dealing with them.

Organbide, Pedro, and Roberto Yalmi. *Enciclopedia de la literatura argentina,* Buenos Aires, Sudamericana, 1970. (639 pages.)

Provides biographies and critical comments on Argentinian authors. Most entries are signed by one of the nineteen contributors and many include very brief bibliographical data on material about the author.

Prieto, Adolfo. *Diccionario básico de literatura argentina,* Biblioteca Argentina Fundamental, Buenos Aires Centro Editor de América Latina, 1968. (159 pages.)

Besides brief biographies of important authors there are entries on literary works and movements. No bibliography of critical studies provided.

Drama

Ferdis, Rubén. *Diccionario sobre el origen del teatro argentino,* Buenos Aires, Alberto Kleiner Ediciones, 1988. (104 pages.)

Martínez, Martha. "Bibliografía sobre teatro argentino (1955–1976)," *Ottawa Hispánica,* 5 (1983), 89–100.

The 122 entries do not include studies on individual dramatists; they deal only with the Argentinian theatre.

Pepe, Luz E., and María Luisa Punte. *La crítica teatral argentina (1880–1962),* special issue of *Bibliografía Argentina de Artes y Letras,* 27–8 (1966), 6–78.

Classified bibliography of the Argentinian theatre (including the circus, puppets, children's theatre, etc.) for the period covered.

Poppa, Tito Livio. *Diccionario teatral del Río de la Plata,* Buenos Aires, Carro de Tespis, 1961. (104 pages.)

Includes dramatists from the beginning of the Argentinian theatre through the 1950s, as well as data on theatres, theatrical groups, etc.

Zsyas de Lima, Perla. *Diccionario de autores teatrales argentinos (1950–1980),* Buenos Aires, Editorial Rodolfo Alonso, 1981. (188 pages.)

Provides brief biographical sketches of the dramatists of the period and a list of their published works, as well as data on the performances of their plays.

History

Arrieta, Rafael Alberto (ed.) *Historia de la literatura argentina*, 6 vols., Buenos Aires, Ediciones Peuser, 1958–1960.

Library catalog

Universidad de Buenos Aires. *Bibliografía argentina: catálogo de materiales argentinos en las bibliotecas de la Universidad de Buenos Aires*, 7 vols., Boston, G. K. Hall, 1980.

"The catalog comprises approximately 110,000 author cards for books and pamphlets found in 17 central and 56 departmental libraries of the University of Buenos Aires' Faculties, Schools, and Institutes" (p. xi).

Literary periodicals

Salvador, Nélida. "Revistas literarias argentinas (1893–1940): aporte para una bibliografía," *Bibliografía Argentina de Artes y Letras*, 9, pt. 2 (1961), 45–115.

An important source for data on Argentinian literary journals for the period covered.

Poetry

Frugoni de Fritzsche, Teresa. *Indice de poetas argentinos*, Guías bibliográficas, 8. Universidad de Buenos Aires, Facultad de Filosofía y Letras, Instituto de Literatura Argentina "Ricardo Rojas," 1963–1968. 4 parts.

Alphabetical by author; titles in chronological order.

González Castro, Augusto. *Panorama de las antologías argentinas*, Buenos Aires, Colombo, 1966. (293 pages.)

Extensively annotated bibliography of poetry anthologies published mainly between 1939 and 1937.

Prodoscini, María del Carmen. *Las antologías poéticas argentinas, 1960–1979*, Universidad de Buenos Aires, Facultad de Filosofía y Letras, Instituto de Literatura Argentina "Ricardo Rojas," 1971. (32 pages.)

Evaluates the almost twenty poetry anthologies listed in her "Bibliografía de las antologías poéticas" (pp. 6–7).

Short stories

Ardisone, Elena. *Bibliografía de antologías del cuento argentino*, Colección Cuadernos de biblioteca, 12, Buenos Aires, Centro de investigaciones bibliotecológicas, EUDEBA, 1991. (153 pages.)

Chertudi, Susana. *El cuento folklórico y literario regional*, special issue of *Bibliografía Argentina de Artes y Letras*, 16 (1962), 1–35.

Women authors

Cattarossi Arana, Nélida María. *Primer diccionario de escritoras y plásticas de Mendoza*, Buenos Aires, Inca, 1985. (63 pages.)

Bolivia

Bibliographies

Arze, José Roberto. "Ensayo de una bibliografía biográfica boliviana," in *Bio-bibliografía boliviana, 1978*, La Paz, Amigos del Libro, 1980. (71 pages.) Reprinted as *Ensayo...*, La Paz, Amigos del Libro, 1981, 203–72.

Lists 367 biographies, autobiographies, memoirs, and collected biographies.

Costa de la Torre, Arturo. *Catálogo de la bibliografía boliviana: libros y folletos 1900–1963*, vol. I, La Paz, Universidad Mayor de San Andrés, 1966. (1254 pages.) Vol. II deals with other subjects.

Brief biographies of 3,003 authors; each followed by a chronological listing of the author's separately published works.

Ortega, Julio. "Manual de bibliografía de la literatura boliviana," *Cuadernos Hispanoamericanos*, 263–4 (1972), 657–71.

Divided into history and literary criticism, anthologies and literary collections, bibliographical works and Bolivian catalogs, Bolivian periodicals and newspapers, and general sources.

"Bibliografía selecta de la literatura de Bolivia," *Revista de Crítica Literaria Latinoamericana*, 1 (1975), 159–60.

Classified and annotated.

Dictionaries

Guzmán, Augusto. *Biografías de la literatura boliviana: biografía, evaluación, bibliografía*, Enciclopedia Boliviana, Cochabamba, Amigos del Libro, 1982. (307 pages.)

(ed.) *Diccionario de la literatura latinoamericana: Bolivia*, Washington, Pan American Union, 1957. (xi, 121 pages.)

The material on each author is divided into two sections: a biographical–critical sketch followed by a bibliography of the author's separately published works and critical studies on them.

Ortega, José, and Adolfo Cáceres Romero. *Diccionario de la literatura boliviana*, La Paz, Amigos del Libro, 1977. (337 pages.)

Provides data on authors since 1825 when Bolivia became independent. Includes a brief biography, a list of works, and a bibliography of criticism.

Drama

Soria, Mario T. "Bibliografía de teatro boliviano del siglo xx" in *Teatro boliviano en el siglo* xx, La Paz, Biblioteca Popular Boliviana de "Ultima Hora," 1980. 211–26.

Plays, often with incomplete bibliographical data, are arranged in chronological order under the name of the dramatist. Pp. 227–30 are a valuable list of articles and essays on the Bolivian theatre and dramatists.

Fiction

Echeverría, Evelio. "Panorama y bibliografía de la novela social boliviana," *Revista Interamericana de Bibliografía*, 27 (1977), 143–52.

>The bibliography (pp. 149–52) is divided into 1904–1952 and 1952–1979.

Paz Soldán, Alba María. "Indice de la novela boliviana (1931–1978)," *Revista Iberoamericana*, 52 (Jan.–March 1986), 311–20.

>Within each decade, arranged alphabetically by novelist.

Poppe, René. *Indice del cuento minero boliviano*, Cuadernos de Investigación, La Paz, Instituto Boliviano de Cultura, Instituto Nacional de Historia y Literatura, Departamento de Literatura, 1979. (16 pages.)

>*Indice de los libros de cuentos bolivianos*, *Primera parte*, Cuadernos de Investigación, 2, La Paz, Instituto Boliviano de Cultura, Instituto Nacional de Historia y Literatura, 1979. (13 pages.)

>Useful lists of Bolivian short stories.

History

Finot, Enrique. *Historia de la literatura boliviana*, 5th. edn., La Paz, Gisbert, 1981. (588 pages.)

>Fullest history of Bolivian literature with no notes and no bibliography of critical studies. Contains two appendixes: Mesa, José de, and Teresa Gilbert, "El período colonial" and Vilela, Luis Felipe, "Los contemporáneos."

Caribbean region

Coll, Edna. *Las Antillas*, Río Piedras, Universidad de Puerto Rico, Editorial Universitaria, 1974. (418 pages.)

>Bibliographical dictionary of novelists of Cuba, Puerto Rico, and the Dominican Republic.

Fenwick, M. J. *Writers of the Caribbean and Central America: A bibliography*, 2 vols., New York, Garland, 1992.

>Besides the Spanish-speaking countries of Central America and the Caribbean, it includes Venezuela and Colombia as well as the numerous former British, Dutch, and French colonies in the Caribbean. Only the barest bibliographical details are given and the poor proofreading makes it a set to be used with extreme caution.

Herdeck, Donald E., *et al. Caribbean Writers: A bio-bibliographical encyclopedia*, Washington, Three Continents, 1979. (943 pages.)

>Part IV, "Spanish language literature from the Caribbean" deals with the writers of Cuba, the Dominican Republic, and Puerto Rico, with bibliographies of critical studies on the literature of these areas.

>There are brief essays on the literatures of each of the countries or areas included. An attempt has been made to list the important works of all the authors

covered. However, many more entries could be added to the biographical–critical bibliographies.

Perrier, José Luis. *Bibliografía dramática cubana, incluye a Puerto Rico y Santo Domingo*, New York, Phos, 1926. (115 pages.)

The authors of the three areas appear in one alphabetical list; no critical studies of the authors and their works are given.

Central America

Arellano, Jorge Eduardo. "Bibliografía general de la literatura centroamericana," *Boletín Nicaragüense de Bibliografía y Documentación*, 29 (1979), 1–5.

Fifty-five unannotated items divided into reference works, anthologies, and critical studies.

Diccionario de la literatura latinoamericana: América Central, Washington, Pan American Union, 1963.

Vol. I is for Costa Rica, El Salvador, and Guatemala; vol. II is for Honduras, Nicaragua, and Panama. Also contains a somewhat dated "Bibliografía de la literatura centroamericana," II, 281–92.

The material on each author is divided into two sections: a biographical–critical sketch followed by a bibliography of the author's separately published works and critical studies on them.

Chile

Bibliographies

Bibliografía chilena de obras en el exilio. Lista parcial. 1973–1985, Santiago, Comité Pro-Retorno de Exiliados Chilenos, Servicio de Extensión de Cultura Chilena (SEREC), 1986. (34 folios. Mimeographed.)

637 items that include works by exiled Chilean authors. Because of difficulties in obtaining works by these authors, the list is not exhaustive and the bibliographical entries are often incomplete.

Biblioteca Nacional de Chile. *Referencias críticas sobre autores chilenos*, 1–9 (1968–1974); *Referencias . . . chilenos. Con apéndice sobre autores españoles e iberoamericanos*, 10– (1975–   ).

Volume 17, for 1982, was published in 1991. It is an outstanding bibliography – the only one of its kind in Latin America – of critical and biographical studies on Chilean, Spanish American, and Latin American authors published in Chilean periodicals and leading newspapers. It is great pity that it is so late in appearing.

Foster, David William. *Chilean Literature: A working bibliography of secondary sources*, Boston, G. K. Hall, 1978. (xxii, 236 pages.)

Divided into two main divisions. "General References" has twenty-eight sections. The bibliographies of the forty-six authors are divided into bibliographies, critical books and theses, and critical essays. Index of critics.

Jofre, Manuel Alcides. *Literatura chilena en el exilio*, Santiago, [Biblioteca Nacional de Chile?], 1983. (74 folios. Mimeographed.)

Material, regardless of genre, is arranged chronologically by author. Here too many of the items listed are known to the compiler second-hand and there are many incomplete items for this reason.

Rojas Piña, Benjamín. "Bibliografía de la literatura chilena, 1967–1968," *Revista Chilena de Literatura*, 1 (1970), 97–117.

"Bibliografía de la literatura chilena, 1969–1970," *Revista Chilena de Literatura*, 2–3 (1970), 215–39.

Classified bibliographies that often provide the contents of the works cited.

Dictionaries

Diccionario de la literatura latinoamericana: Chile, Washington, Pan American Union, 1958. (234 pages.)

The material on each author is divided into two sections: a biographical–critical sketch followed by a bibliography of the author's separately published works and critical studies on them.

Rojas, Luis Emilio. *Biografía cultural de Chile*, 2nd. edn., Santiago, Gong Ediciones, 1988. (343 pages.)

Includes biographies of authors.

Smulewicz, Efraín. *Diccionario de la literatura chilena*, 2nd edn., Santiago, Editorial Andrés Bello, 1984. (xviii, 494 pages.)

Contains numerous errors.

Drama

Durán Cerda, Julio. *Repertorio del teatro chileno. Bibliografía, obras, inéditas y estrenadas*, Publicaciones del Instituto de Literatura Chilena, Serie C: Bibliografías y Registros, 1, Santiago, Instituto de Literatura Chilena, 1962. (247 pages.)

Essential bibliography on the Chilean theatre that lists 1,710 plays, as well as important studies on the theatre in Chile since 1910.

Fiction

Castillo, Hómero, and Raúl Silva Castro. *Historia bibliográfica de la novela chilena*, Charlottesville, Bibliographical Society of the University of Virginia, 1961. (214 pages.)

Provides data on Chilean novels and short story collections.

Goić Cedomil. "Bibliografía de la novela chilena del siglo xx," *Boletín de Filología* (Universidad de Chile), 14 (1962), 51–168.

Excludes short stories and anthologies. Lists 1,232 items written chiefly between 1910 and 1961.

Guerra-Cunningham, Lucia. "Fuentes bibliográficas para el estudio de la novela chilena (1843–1960)," *Revista Iberoamericana*, 42:96–7 (1976), 601–19.

Classified bibliography of general studies on the Chilean novel.

Lastra, Pedro. "Registro bibliográfico de antologías del cuento chileno, 1876–1976," *Revista de Crítica Literaria Latinoamericana*, 5 (1977), 89–111.

Chronological arrangement. Indicates contents of anthologies.

Roman-Lagunas, J. "La novela chilena: estudio bibliográfico," 2 vols., diss., University of Arizona, 1985. (752 pages.)

Extremely important bibliography of the Chilean novel. The second chapter is a classified bibliography of general studies in the field. Chapter 3 is an annotated bibliography of special topics and Chapter 4 is a bibliography of twenty-nine novelists. The classified bibliographies for some of these authors are the fullest now available.

Villacura Fernández, Maúd. "Bibliografía de narradores chilenos nacidos entre 1935–1949," *Revista Chilena de Literatura*, 4 (1973), 109–28.

Lists books and short stories published in anthologies, periodicals, and newspapers, both Chilean and foreign, as well as translations, between 1956 and 1970.

History

Silva Castro, Raúl. *Panorama literario de Chile*, Santiago, Editorial Universitaria, 1961. (570 pages.)

Library catalog

Welch, Thomas L. *Catálogo de la colección de la literatura chilena en la Biblioteca Colón*, Documentation and Information Series, 7, Washington, Secretaría General, Organization of American States, 1983. (ix, 154 pages.)

Lists works by and about Chilean authors, and about Chilean literature, in the Columbus Library.

Poetry

Escudero, Alfonso M. "Fuentes de consulta sobre los poetas románticos chilenos," *Aisthesis*, 57 (1970), 295–307.

Provides biographical and critical material on nine Chilean romantic poets.

Colombia

Bibliography

Orjuela, Héctor H. *Fuentes generales para el estudio de la literatura colombiana, Guía bibliográfica*, Publicaciones de Instituto Caro y Cuervo, Serie bibliográfica, 7, Bogotá, Instituto Caro y Cuervo, 1968. (xl, 863 pages.)

Classified, often annotated, bibliography of Colombian literature. Locates copies in US and Colombian libraries.

Dictionaries

García Prada, Carlos. *Diccionario de la literatura latinoamericana. Colombia*, Washington, Pan American Union, 1959. (ix, 179 pages.)

The material on each author is divided into two sections: a biographical–critical sketch followed by a bibliography of the author's separately published works and critical studies on them.

Madrid Malo, Nestor. "Ensayo de un diccionario de la literatura colombiana," *Boletín Cultural y Bibliográfico*, 7(1964), 401–5, 613–18, 823–8, 1004–11, 1183–94, 1377–86, 1615–21; 9 (1966), 1766–74, 1973–82, 2206–16, 2430–7; 10 (1966), 630–7; 10 (1967), 530–8, 817–25; 10: 11 (1967), 84–91; 12:5 (1969), 69–81.

    Biographies of Colombian authors, A–C.

Sánchez López, Luis María. *Diccionario de escritores colombianos*, 3rd. edn., enlarged and revised, Bogotá, Plaza & Janes Editores, 1978. (547 pages.)

    Despite its size, it provides only the barest biographical data and omits dates of authors' works.

Drama

Orjuela, Héctor H. *Bibliografía del teatro colombiano*, Publicaciones del Instituto Caro y Cuervo, Serie bibliográfica, 10, Bogotá, Instituto Caro y Cuervo, 1974. (xxvii, 312 pages.)

    Lists plays written by Colombians as well as critical studies on Colombian dramatists and their works.

González Cajigao, Fernando. "Adiciones a la *Bibliografía del teatro colombiano*" in *Materiales para una historia del teatro en Colombia*, Bogotá, Instituto Colombiano de Cultura, 1978, 690–713.

Vitoria Bermúdez, Xorge. "Indice biobibliográfico de autores colombianos de teatro hasta el siglo XIX," *Logos* (Cali), 10 (1974), 7–22.

    Provides few bibliographical details, gives the date of the first performance for the plays listed. Covers period between 1610 and 1900.

Fiction

Mena, Lucile Inés. "Bibliografía anotada sobre el ciclo de la violencia en la literatura colombiana," *Latin American Research Review*, 13:3 (1978), 95–107.

    Lists seventy-four novels of the period and annotates thirty-five critical studies that deal with the Colombian novel of "violencia."

Porras Collantes, Ernesto. *Bibliografía de la novela en Colombia: con notas de contenido y crítica de las obras y guías de comentarios sobre los autores*, Publicaciones del Instituto Caro y Cuervo, Serie bibliográfica, 11, Bogotá, Instituto Caro y Cuervo, 1976. (xix, 888 pages.)

    Bibliographical data on 2,326 novels published through 1974. Lists of pseudonyms as well as a title index and a chronological index are provided.

Williams, Raymond L. "La novela colombiana 1960–1974: una bibliografía," *Chasqui*, 5:3 (1976), 27–39.

    Bibliographical data on 149 Colombian novels.

History

Gómez Restrepo, Antonio. *Historia de la literatura colombiana*, 2nd. edn., 4 vols., Bogotá, Imprenta Nacional, 1945–1946.

    Combination literary history and anthology. Stops with nineteenth century.

Poetry

Cobo Borda, J. G. "La nueva poesía colombiana: una década. 1970–1980," *Boletín Cultural y Bibliográfico*, 16: 9–10 (1979), 75–122.

Orjuela, Héctor H. *Las antologías poéticas de Colombia: estudio y bibliografía*, Publicaciones del Instituto Caro y Cuervo, Serie bibliográfica, 6. Bogotá, Instituto Caro y Cuervo, 1966. (xii, 514 pages.)

Provides data on 389 anthologies. Lists authors for each volume and locates at least one copy in a library either in the United States or in Colombia.

Bibliografía de la poesía colombiana, Publicaciones del Instituto Caro y Cuervo, Serie bibliográfica, 9, Bogotá, Instituto Caro y Cuervo, 1971. (xxii, 486 pages.)

Data provided on the principal books and pamphlets or translations of each poet, as well as anonymous poetry. Translations are listed under the name of the Colombian translator.

Women authors

Solari, M. "Ecriture féminine dans la Colombie contemporaine," diss., University of Toulouse, 1982. (335 pages.)

Provides bio-bibliographical data on the most representative women prose-writers of Colombia, for the period 1950–1980.

Costa Rica

Bibliography

Dobles Segreda, Luis. "Novela, cuento y artículo literario" and "Teatro," in *Indice bibliográfico de Costa Rica*, San José, Lehmann, 1934, IV, 3–378, 385–429.

Kargleder, Mary, and Warren H. Mory. *Bibliografía selectiva de la literatura costarricense*, San José, Editorial Costa Rica, 1978. (109 pages.)

Bibliography of Costa Rican literature from 1869 through 1976. No references to material published in anthologies, journals, or newspapers unless they have been separately published. Translations are listed under the name of the translator if the individual is Costa Rican.

Dictionary

Diccionario de la literatura latinoamericana: América Central, Washington, Pan American Union, 1963, I, 2–39.

The material on each author is divided into two sections: a biographical–critical sketch followed by a bibliography of the author's separately published works and critical studies on them.

Short story

Menton, Seymour. "Indice bibliográfico del cuento costarricense," in his *El cuento costarricense: estudio, antología y bibliografía*, Antologías Studium, 8, México, Andrea, Lawrence, University of Kansas Press, 1964, 163–82.

This outstanding study on the Costa Rican short story has a bibliography of stories published in anthologies, short story collections, and in magazines.

Portuguez de Bolaños, Elizabeth (ed.) "Bibliografía" in *El cuento en Costa Rica: estudio, bibliografía y antología*, San José, Lehmann, 1964, 309–40.

Classified bibliography of the Costa Rican short story and of Costa Rican novels that have "cuadros costumbristas."

Cuba

Bibliographies

"Bibliografía de la crítica literaria cubana, 1959–1983: la crítica," *Revista de Literatura Cubana*, 3:5 (1985), 132–40.

Includes Cuban criticism of both Cuban and non-Cuban authors.

"Bibliografía de la literatura cubana," *Revista de Literatura Cubana*, 1 (1983), 101–31.

Books, articles, and book reviews that deal with Cuban literature and were published in 1981. The first part is for the seventeenth–nineteenth centuries, the second deals with twentieth-century Cuban literature.

Casal, Lourdes. "A bibliography of Cuban creative literature: 1958–1971," *Cuban Studies Newsletter*, 2:2 (1972), 2–29.

Divided by literary genres. It includes works both by Cubans living in Cuba and by those living outside Cuba. Also includes translations of Cuban works.

"Classified bibliography," *Cuban Studies/Estudios Cubanos*, 1– (1970–   ).

Each issue of this semi-annual journal has a classified bibliography with sections on literature and language.

Fernández, José B., and Roberto G. Fernández. *Indice bibliográfico de autores cubanos, diáspora, 1959–1979, Bibliographical Index of Cuban Authors: Diaspora, 1959–1979*, Miami, Ediciones Universal, 1984. (106 pages.)

Classified bibliography of the literary and linguistic works of Cuban exiled writers.

Foster, David William. *Cuban Literature: A research guide*, Garland Reference Library of the Humanities, 511, New York, Garland, 1985. (522 pages.)

Critical references on ninety-eight Cuban authors preceded by a classified bibliography and general references on Cuban literature.

Rolo, Lázaro. "Bibliografía de la crítica literaria cubana," *Revista de Literatura Cubana*, 3:5 (1985), 373–93.

181 items.

Black authors

Bibliografía de temas afrocubanos, Havana, Biblioteca nacional José Martí, 1986. (581 pages.)

Trelles y Govín, Carlos Manuel. "Bibliografía de autores de la raza de color, de Cuba," *Cuba Contemporánea*, 43 (1927), 30–78.

Divided into material on black writers during the period of slavery, those after the slavery period, periodicals published by Blacks, and works of all kinds by Whites about Blacks.

Dictionaries

Instituto de Literatura y Lingüística de la Academia de Ciencias de Cuba. *Diccionario de la literatura cubana*, 2 vols., Havana, Letras Cubanas, 1980–1984.

An indispensable source for the study of Cuban authors, cultural institutions, and literary journals. Each author entry includes a biographical sketch, a chronological listing of the author's works, and a bibliography of critical and biographical studies about the author. Cuban exile authors are omitted and a certain political bias is noticeable with the omission of a writer of the status of Guillermo Cabrera Infante. It must rank along with the dictionaries for Mexican and Venezuelan literature as one of the best such dictionaries produced in Latin America.

Maratos, Daniel C., and Marnesha Hill. *Escritores de la diáspora cubana: manual biobibliográfico* (title also in English), Metuchen N.J., Scarecrow Press, 1986. (391 pages.)

Biographies are given in both English and Spanish. The author's bibliography is divided into works published outside Cuba and critical studies on the author.

Martínez, Julio A. (ed.) *Dictionary of Twentieth-Century Cuban Literature*, New York, Greenwood Press, 1990. (xii, 537 pages.)

Preface describes volume thus: "useful, one-volume companion to contemporary Cuban literature, this dictionary provides, in a single alphabetical sequence, ready reference information on contemporary Cuban creative writers on the island or in exile as well as essays on literary genres and movements" (p. ix). Biographical and critical sketches of the authors are followed by a bibliography of their published books and one of secondary sources.

Drama

Armenteros Toledo, Marta B. *Festivales de teatro de La Habana: 1980–1984: boletín bibliográfico*, Havana, Biblioteca Nacional José Martí, 1987. (86 pages.)

Inerarity Romero, Zayda. "Ensayo de una bibliografía para un estudio del teatro cubano hasta el siglo XIX," *Islas*, 36 (May–Aug. 1970), 151–71.

Classified annotated bibliography of 100 items that the author considers to be the principal bibliographical sources for the study of the Cuban theatre.

Palis, Terry L. "Annotated bibliographical guide to the study of Cuban theater after 1959," *Modern Drama*, 25 (1979), 391–408.

"The 121 entries include books and articles which contain bibliographical information on contemporary Cuban theatre or critical studies concerning the effect of the Cuban cultural revolution on the nature of the dramatic activity there, and a list of seventy-four plays, written, staged, and published after 1955 . . ." (p. 392).

Rivero Múñiz, José. *Bibliografía del teatro cubano*, Havana, Biblioteca Nacional José Martí, 1957. (120 pages.)

Based on the library that once belonged to Francisco de Paula Coronado. Authors range from the early 1800s to the 1950s. It includes unpublished manuscripts as well as published dramatic works.

Skinner, Eugene R. "Research guide to post-Revolutionary Cuban drama," *Latin American Theatre Review*, 7:2 (1974), 59–68.

Divided into bibliographies, articles and books, and reviews. Attempts to provide "a specialized guide to post-Revolutionary Cuban theatre" (p. 59).

Fiction

Abella, Rosa. "Bibliografía de la novela publicada en Cuba, y en el extranjero por cubanos, desde 1959 hasta 1965," *Revista Iberoamericana*, 32 (1966), 307–11.

  Lists data on seventy-six novels by Cubans, regardless of place of publication.

Casal, Lourdes. "The Cuban novel, 1959–1969: an annotated bibliography," *Abraxas*, 1 (1970), 72–92.

  Briefly summarizes seventy-seven novels and sometimes provides critical studies on them.

Menton, Seymour. "Bibliography" in his *Prose Fiction of the Cuban Revolution*, Latin American Monographs, 37, Austin, University of Texas Press, 1975, 287–317.

  Outstanding classified and partially annotated bibliography of Cuban novels, short-story anthologies and short stories by Cubans in exile, as well as foreign prose fiction of the Cuban Revolution. This volume is the finest treatment of the prose fiction of the Cuban Revolution in English and probably in any language.

Sánchez, Julio C. "Bibliografía de la novela cubana," *Islas*, 3 (Sept.–Dec. 1960), 321–56.

  Lists 800 titles.

History

Henríquez Ureña, Max. *Panorama histórico de la literatura cubana*, 2 vols., Havana, Edición Revolucionaria, 1967.

Remos y Rubio, Juan J. *Historia de la literatura cubana*, 3 vols., Miami, Mnemosyne, 1969.

  Reprint of 1945 edition.

Library catalog

Figueras, Myriam. *Catálogo de la colección de la literatura cubana en la Biblioteca Colón*, Documentation and Information Series, 9, Washington, Secretaría General, Organization of American States, 1984. (x, 114 pages.)

  Classified bibliography divided into eight sections with author and title indexes.

Poetry

Bibliografía de la poesía cubana en el Siglo XIX, Havana, Biblioteca Nacional José Martí, Departamento de Colección Cubana, 1965. (89 pages.)

  Chronological list of 1,111 separately published works of poetry by Cubans, regardless of place of publication.

Montes Huidobro, Matías, and Yara González. *Bibliografía crítica de la poesía cubana (exilio 1959–1971)*, Colección Scholar, Madrid, Playor, 1973. (138 pages.)

  In addition to providing bibliographical data on the works of poetry by

Cubans outside Cuba, many of the comments on these works are review-length. The annotation to *Cinco poetisas cubanas* occupies pp. 20–3.

Dominican Republic

Bibliographies

Olivera, Otto. *Bibliografía de la literatura dominicana (1960–1982)*, Lincoln, Nebr. Society of Spanish and Spanish-American Studies, 1985. (86 pages.)
  Classified bibliography of 1,181 entries with a section on periodical publications and index.

Romero, Guadalupe. "Bibliografía comentada de la literatura dominicana," *Eme Eme*, 3:14 (1974), 104–56.
  173 annotated entries divided into anthologies, bibliographies, critical studies, and literary histories.

Waxman, Samuel Montefiore. *A Bibliography of the Belles-Lettres of Santo Domingo*, Cambridge, Mass., Harvard University Press, 1931. (31 pages.) Supplemented by Vetilio Alfau Durán, *Clío*, 198 (1956), 154–61. Reprinted as *Apuntes de bibliografía dominicana en torno a las rectificaciones hechas a la obra del prof. Waxman*, Ciudad Trujillo, Editorial Dominicana, 1956, (8 pages). Reviewed and supplemented by Pedro Henríquez Ureña and Gilberto Sánchez-Lustrino, *Revista de Filología Española*, 21 (1934), 293–309.

Dictionaries

Contin Aybar, Néstor. *Historia de la literatura dominicana*, 4 vols., San Pedro de Macorís, Universidad Central del Este, 1982–1986.
  Despite its title this is a bio-bibliographical dictionary of Dominican authors, arranged within chronological periods. One wonders at the omission of Juan Bosch.

Tarazona Hijo, Enrique. *Guía biobibliográfica. 123 escritores dominicanos vivos–1983*, [Santo Domingo, Alfa y Omega, 1983]. 139.
  Provides a brief biographical sketch for each author as well as a list of the authors' works. Excludes critical studies.

Fiction

Alfau Durán, Vetilio. "Apuntes para la bibliografía de la novela en Santo Domingo," *Anales de la Universidad de Santo Domingo*, 23 (1958), 203–24; 24 (1958), 405–35; 26 (1960), 87–100.
  Covers A–F. Includes brief biographies of authors and, often, summaries of the novels, with occasional critical comments taken from reviews or critical studies.

History

Henríquez Ureña, Max. *Panorama histórico de la literatura dominicana*, 2nd. edn., Santo Domingo, Colección Pensamiento Dominicano, 1966. (337 pages.)

Poetry

Alfau Durán, Vetilio. "Apuntes para la bibliografía poética dominicana," *Clio*, 122 (1965), 34–60; 123 (1968), 107–19; 124 (1969), 53–68; 125 (1970), 50–77.

After providing a bibliography of critical studies and anthologies of Dominican poetry, works are arranged alphabetically by author.

Ecuador

Bibliographies

Bibliografía de autores ecuatorianos, [Quito] Biblioteca Nacional de Ecuador, 1978. (474 pages.)

Classified bibliography based on the collection of the country's national library.

Rolando, Carlos. *Las bellas letras en el Ecuador*, Guayaquil, Imprenta y Talleres Muncipales, 1944. (xxi, 157 pages.)

An important bibliography that could have been greatly improved.

Dictionaries

Barriga López, Franklin, and Leonardo Barriga López. *Diccionario de la literatura ecuatoriana*, Colección Letras del Ecuador, 103–4, 106–8, 2nd edn., rev. and enlarged, 5 vols., Guayaquil, Cultura Ecuatoriana, Núcleo del Guayas, 1980.

Includes biographies of Ecuadorian authors as well as having entries on institutions and corporations interested in culture. It gives titles and dates of an author's works and sometimes cites critics. However, there are no bibliographies of critical studies on individual authors.

Diccionario de la literatura latinoamericana: Ecuador, Washington, Pan American Union, 1962. (xi, 172 pages.)

The material on each author is divided into two sections: a biographical–critical sketch followed by a bibliography of the author's separately published works and critical studies on them. Contains a helpful, though now dated, "Bibliografía de las letras ecuatorianas" (pp. 167–72).

Drama

Luzuriaga, Gerardo. "Bibliografía del teatro ecuatoriano," *Cultura* (Ecuador), 5:13 (May–Aug. 1982), 227–32.

Bibliografía del teatro ecuatoriano 1900–1980, Quito Cultura Ecuatoriana, 1984. (131 pages.)

Provides a bibliography of reference works for the study of Ecuadorian literature and drama of the period covered, a bibliography of published or performed plays, and critical references on Ecuadorian drama and dramatists.

History

Barrera, Isaac J. *Historia de la literatura ecuatoriana*, 4 vols. in 1, Quito, Cultura

Ecuatoriana, 1960.
   Fullest history of Ecuadorian literature.

El Salvador

Dictionary

Diccionario de la literatura latinoamericana: América Central, Washington, Pan American Union, 1963, I, 141–84.
   The material on each author is divided into two sections: a biographical–critical sketch followed by a bibliography of the author's separately published works and critical studies on them.

History

Toruño, Juan Felipe. *Desarrollo literario de El Salvador: ensayo*, San Salvador, Ministerio de Cultura, Departamento Editorial, 1958. (440 pages.)
Gallegos Valdés, Luis. *Panorama de la literatura salvadoreña*, 2nd edn., San Salvador, UCA Editores, 1989. (483 pages.)
   Probably the fullest history of Salvadoran literature.

Guatemala

Dictionaries

Albizúrez Palma, Francisco. *Diccionario de autores guatemaltecos*, Colección Guatemala, 13, Serie José Joaquín Pardo, 1, Guatemala, Tipografía Nacional, 1984. (96 pages.)
   Provides brief biographical sketches along with the authors' works and their dates. Includes material on anonymous works.
Diccionario de la literatura latinoamericana: América Central, Washington, Pan American Union, 1963, I, 86–136.
   The material on each author is divided into two sections: a biographical–critical sketch followed by a bibliography of the author's separately published works and critical studies on them.

Fiction

Ciruti, Joan. "The Guatemalan novel: a critical bibliography," Ph.D. diss. Tulane University, 1959. (263 pages.)
   Pages 106–253 are a critical bibliography of the Guatemalan novel that annotates 558 novels.
Menton, Seymour. "Los señores presidentes y los guerrilleros: The new and the old Guatemalan novel (1976–1982)," *Latin American Research Review*, 19:2 (1984), 93–117.
   Divided into critical commentary and criticism on the novels of the period (pp. 93–110), and a chronological, briefly annotated list of the eighty-four novels published between 1955 and 1982 (pp. 110–17).

History

Albizúrez Palma, Francisco, and Catalina Barrios y Barrios. *Historia de la literatura guatemalteca*, 3 vols., Guatemala, Editorial Universitaria de Guatemala, 1981–1987.

    Extensive history with excellent pertinent bibliographies by Lourdes Bendfeldt Rojas.

Honduras

Dictionaries

Argueta, Mario R. *Diccionario de escritores hondureños*, n.p., n.p., 1986. (110 pages.)

    Provides extremely short biographical sketch along with a listing of the author's works and their dates. Only for very important authors is any attempt made at a critical evaluation.

Diccionario de la literatura latinoamericana: América Central, Washington, Pan American Union, 1963, II, 138–83.

    Material on each author is divided into two sections: a biographical–critical sketch followed by a bibliography of the author's separately published works and critical studies on them.

González, José. *Diccionario de autores hondureños*, Tegucigalpa, Editores Unidos, 1987, 7–83. Pp. 85–120 are a glossary of literary terms by S. Turaiev.

    Both this and Argueta, *Diccionario* (above), should probably be consulted for the authors of this country. On the whole, González provides fuller data on the writers than Argueta. Both must be used with care. They provide different birthdates; González lists but one book by Murillo Soto, whereas Argueta lists three.

History

Paredes, Rigoberto, and Manuel Salinas Paguada. *Literatura hondureña*, Tegucigalpa, Editores Unidos, 1987. (300 pages.)

    Eleven essays by different specialists in this field.

Mexico

Bibliographies

Foster, David William. *Mexican Literature: A bibliography of secondary sources*, 2nd. edn., enlarged and updated, Metuchen, N.J., Scarecrow, 1992. (x, 686 pages.)

    General studies are divided into twenty-eight sections. Data are provided on eighty Mexican authors. The section on each author is divided into bibliographies, critical monographs and dissertations, and critical essays.

"Historia literaria," *Bibliografía Histórica Mexicana* (Colegio de México), 1– (1967–).

    This annual includes chiefly histories and anthologies of Mexican literature as well as biographies of authors. Literary criticism is excluded.

Dictionaries

Agras García de Alba, Gabriel. *Biobibliografía de los escritores de Jalisco*, Serie bibliográficas, 9, 2 vols. to date, Mexico, Universidad Nacional Autónoma de México, Instituto de Investigaciones Bibliográficas, 1980– . (Vol. I: *A*, cxxvii, 622 pages; vol. II: *B*, cx, 147 pages.)

This and Aranda Pamplona, *Bibliografía*, and Montejano y Aguinaga, *Bibliografía* (both below) are regional bio-bibliographical dictionaries. Each provides biographical data on the writers as well as a list of the published works and bibliography of critical studies on them. Each is preceded by lengthy prefatory material.

Aranda Pamplona, Hugo. *Biobibliografía de los escritores del estado de México*, Serie bibliografías, 5, Mexico, Universidad Nacional Autónoma de México, Instituto de Investigaciones Bibliográficas, 1978. (105 pages.)

Lara Valdez, Josefina. *Diccionario bibliográfico de escritores contemporáneos de México*, Mexico, 1988. (247 pages.)

Brief biographical sketches of writers born between 1930 and 1950, along with data on their published books.

Montejano y Aguinaga, Rafael. *Biobibliografía de los escritores de San Luis Potosí*, Serie bibliografías, 6, Mexico, Universidad Nacional Autónoma de México, Instituto de Investigaciones Bibliográficas, 1979. (lxxx, 439 pages.)

Ocampo de Gómez, Aurora M., and Ernesto Prado Velázquez. *Diccionario de escritores mexicanos*, Mexico, Universidad Nacional Autónoma de México, 1967. (xxvii, 442 pages.)

Extraordinarily useful bio-bibliographical dictionary of Mexican writers. For each author, a biographical sketch is provided, as well as a listing of the author's works and of critical studies about this individual.

Ocampo de Gómez, Aurora M. (ed.) *Diccionario de escritores mexicanos: siglo XX. Desde las generaciones del Ateneo y novelistas de la Revolución hasta nuestros días*, Mexico, Universidad Nacional Autónoma de México, 1988– . (Vol. I, A-Ch.)

Format the same as previous entry.

Drama

Lamb, Ruth S. *Mexican Theatre of the Twentieth Century: Bibliography and study*, Claremont, Calif., Ocelot, 1975. (143 pages.)

Except for the introductory essay, this appears to be a facsimile reproduction of her *Bibliografía del teatro mexicano del siglo XX* (Mexico, Andrea, 1962, 143 pages).

Includes a bibliography of the Mexican twentieth-century theatre arranged by author, a critical bibliography, or texts of plays.

Monterde García Icazbalceta, Francisco. *Bibliografía del teatro en México*, Monografías Bibliográficas Mexicanas, 28, Mexico, Monografías Bibliográficas Mexicanas, 1933. (lxxx, 649 pages.) Reprinted: Bibliography and Reference Series, 369, New York, Burt Franklin, 1970.

Extensive bibliography of plays by and about Mexicans by both Mexicans and those of other nationalities.

Essay

Polasky, Sulema Laufer. "Bibliografía selecta anotada sobre la crítica de cinco ensayistas mexicanos," Ph.D. diss., University of Cincinnati, 1983. (222 pages.)

Useful bibliography – even though there are numerous omissions and bibliographical inconsistencies which should have been corrected – of Antonio Caso, Samuel Ramos, José Vasconcelos, Alfonso Reyes, and Octavio Paz as essayists in the fields of philosophy, sociology, and psychology.

Fiction

Hoffman, Herbert H. *Cuento mexicano index*, Newport Beach, Headway, 1978. (600 pages.)

This set indexes 7,230 short stories by 490 Mexican authors born after 1870 or so. All books analyzed have been published since 1945. The compiler refers to these books only by numbers keyed to a "List of books analyzed"; complete pagination would have been helpful.

Iguiniz, Juan B. *Bibliografía de novelistas mexicanos: ensayo biográfico, bibliográfico y crítico*, Monografías Bibliográficas Mexicanas 3, Mexico, Monografías Bibliográficas Mexicanas, 1926. (xxxv, 432 pages.)

Provides brief biographical data for important authors. Lists authors' books but no critical studies.

Leal, Luis. *Bibliografía del cuento mexicano*, Colección Studium, 21, Mexico, Andrea, 1958. (162 pages.)

Indexes stories found in books, anthologies, newspapers, and magazines up to 1957.

Rutherford, John. *An Annotated Bibliography of the Novels of the Mexican Revolution of 1910–1917 in English and Spanish*, Troy, N. Y. Whitston, 1972. (180 pages.)

Locates copies in Mexican libraries. Volume is in both English and Spanish.

History

González Peña, Carlos. *History of Mexican Literature*, tr. Gusta Barfield Nance and Florence Johnson Dunstan, 3rd. edn., Dallas, Southern Methodist University Press, 1968. (540 pages.)

Standard history of Mexican literature; lacks footnotes and bibliography.

Historia de la literatura mexicana desde los orígenes hasta nuestros días, 15th. edn., Mexico, Editorial Porrúa, 1984. (362 pages.)

Periodical lists and indexes

Forster, Merlin H. *An Index to Mexican Literary Periodicals*, Metuchen, N.J., Scarecrow, 1966. (276 pages.)

Indicates the literary genre of 4,036 articles found in 16 journals published during the period 1920–1960.

Nicaragua

Dictionaries

Arellano, Jorge Eduardo. "Diccionario de las letras nicaragüenses. Primera entrega: escritores de la época colonial y el siglo XIX," *Cuadernos de Bibliografía Nicaragüense*, 3–4 (1982). (144 pages.)

Bio-bibliographical dictionary of 100 Nicaraguan writers of the colonial period and of the nineteenth century. Extremely useful study for the period covered.

Cerutti, Franco. "Datos para un futuro diccionario de escritores nicaragüenses (primera parte)," *Revista del Pensamiento Centroamericano*, 168–9 (July–Dec. 1980), 1–16; "(segunda parte)," *ibid.*, 172–3 (July–Dec. 1981), 6–17.

Bio-bibliographical and critical sketches are provided for sixteen authors. Bibliographies include critical studies.

Diccionario de literatura latinoamericana: América Central, Washington, Pan American Union, 1963, II, 185–236.

Material on each author is divided into two sections: a biographical–critical sketch followed by a bibliography of the author's separately published works and critical studies on them.

History

Arellano, Jorge Eduardo. *Panorama de la literatura nicaragüense*, 5th. edn., Managua, Nueva Nicaragua, 1986. (197 pages.)

Extremely useful for the bibliographical data provided. Includes "bibliografía fundamental" and a "Fichero de autores nicaragüenses," a bibliography by and about contemporary Nicaraguan writers.

English translations

Woodbridge, Hensley C. "Una bibliografía de la literatura nicaragüense en inglés," *Boletín Nicaragüense de Bibliografía y Documentación*, 8 (Nov.–Dec. 1975), 1–5; 18 (1977) 84–97.

The first part is a bibliography of English translations of Nicaraguan authors with the exception of Rubén Darío; the second part is a bibliography of Rubén Darío in English translation. An attempt has been made to identify the Spanish title of as many translations as possible.

Panama

Bibliography

King, Charles A. "Apuntes para una bibliografía de la literatura de Panamá," *Revista Interamericana de Bibliografía*, 14 (1964), 262–302.

Classified by literary genres.

Dictionary

Diccionario de la literatura latinoamericana: América Central, Washington, Pan American Union, 1963, II, 238–80.

Material on each author is divided into two sections: a biographical and critical sketch followed by a bibliography of the author's separately published works and critical studies on them.

History

Miró, Rodrigo. *La literatura panameña: origen y proceso*, 7th. edn., Panama, Litho Editorial Chen, 197. (336 pages.)

History of Panamanian literature from 1502 on. Longest section deals with this country's literature from 1903 to 1970. Contains a bibliography.

Poetry

Miró, Rodrigo. *Bibliografía poética panameña*, Panama, Imprenta Nacional, 1942. (61 pages.)

Provides bibliographical data on Panamanian and foreign authors. There is also a chronological listing of titles.

Short story

El cuento en Panamá (estudio, selección, bibliografía), Panama, n.p., 1950, 191–201.

Divided into "Autores nacionales," "Libros de material vario, que incluyen cuentos," and "Novelas de tema o ambiente panameño."

Paraguay

Bibliographies

Fernández-Caballero, Carlos F. S. *The Paraguayan Bibliography: A retrospective and enumerative bibliography of printed works of Paraguayan authors*, 2 vols., vol. I: *Aranduka ha kuatianee paraguai rembiapocure*, Washington, Arandú, 1970; vol. II, *Paraguai tai hume: tove paaguai arandú taisarambi ko yuy apere*, Amherst, Seminar on the Acquisition of Latin American Literary Materials, University of Massachusetts Library, 1975. (221 pages.)

Provides bibliographical data on almost 4,000 separately published works written either by Paraguayans or about Paraguay and published between 1724 and 1974.

Jones, David Lewis. "Literature" in *Paraguay: A bibliography*, New York, Garland, 1979, 372–415.

Certain portions, especially on better-known authors, would appear to be very selective. Divided into general studies, individual authors before 1935, and individual writers after 1935.

Vallejo, Roque. *Antología de la prosa paraguaya*, vol. I, *Generación del 900*, Colección Centauro, Asunción, Pueblo, 1973. (154 pages.)

Brief biographies of twenty-nine Paraguayan authors followed by biographical and critical studies.

Dictionary

Pérez Mavievich, Francisco. *Diccionario de la literatura paraguaya (primera parte)*, Biblioteca Colorados Contemporáneos, 7, Asunción, América, 1983. (291 pages.)

Covers authors A–Cuento. Provides a biography, an evaluation of the author's works, and a bibliography of material by and about the author. Articles are provided on literary genres, that on the Paraguayan short story covers pp. 157–291.

History

Centurión, Carlos R. *Historia de las letras paraguayas*, 3 vols., Buenos Aires Editorial Ayacucho, 1947–1951.

History of Paraguayan literature through the first half of the twentieth century.

Peru

Bibliographies

Foster, David William. *Peruvian Literature: A bibliography of secondary sources*, Westport, Conn., Greenwood, 1981. (xxix, 324 pages.)

The first section is a classified bibliography of general studies on Peruvian literature and is divided into twenty-four sections. The second section provides data on critical studies on thirty-eight authors.

Fuentes Benavides, Rafael de la. "Autores del primer siglo de la literatura peruana," *Boletín Bibliográfico* (Biblioteca de la Universidad de San Marcos), 9.12, 3–4 (1939), 268–332; 10.12, 1–2 (1940), 81–133.

Bio-bibliographical dictionary of sixteenth- and seventeenth-century Peruvian authors, through the letter "F."

Pease, Franklin G. Y. "Literatura y lingüística" in *Perú: una aproximación bibliográfica*, Mexico, Centro de estudios Económicos y Sociales del Tercer Mundo, 1979, 186–205.

Rodríguez Rea, Miguel Angel. *El Perú y su literatura. Guía bibliográfica*, Lima, Pontificia Universidad Católica del Perú, 1992. (251 pages.)

The 628 items are divided into "Historias generales," "Antologías y compilaciones," "Diccionarios," "Bibliografías y hemerografías," "Ensayos, estudios y crítica," "Miscelánea," "Indice onomástico," and "Indice temático." The annotations usually provide the contents of the volume or some other indication of the item's coverage.

Sánchez, Luis Alberto, *et al. Contribución a la bibliografía de la literatura peruana*, Lima, Universidad Nacional Mayor de San Marcos, 1969. (279 pages.)

Contains 1,965 annotated references.

Tauro, Alberto. "Bibliografía peruana de literatura." *Boletín de la Biblioteca Nacional*, 13–14:19–20 (1957–1959), 109–298. Reprinted Lima, [Villanueva], 1959. (194 pages.)

Classified bibliography of 2,097 items that lists principally works on Peruvian literature that have appeared since 1931.

Dictionaries

Arriola Grande, Maurilio. *Diccionario literario del Perú: nomenclatura por autores*, 2nd. edn., rev. and enlarged, 2 vols., Lima, Universo, 1983.

Includes some non-Peruvians who have written about Peru's history and literature. Provides a brief biography, critical note, and an evaluation of each author. Lists no references about the author.

Romero de Valle, Emilia. *Diccionario manual de literatura peruana y material afines*, Lima, Universidad Nacional Mayor de San Marcos, Departamento de Publicaciones, 1966. (356 pages.)

She gives less data on individual authors than Arriola Grande. However, she provides data on literary movements in Peru, journals, and newspapers, which are all ignored by Arriola Grande.

Drama

Natella, Arthur A., Jr. "Bibliography of the Peruvian theatre, 1946–1970," *Hispanic Journal*, 2:2 (1981), 141–7.

"The list includes works which have been presented on the Peruvian stage, published, or both" (p. 141).

Reverte Bernal, Concepción. "Guía bibliográfica para el estudio del teatro virreinal peruano," *Historiografía y Bibliografía Americanistas*, 29 (1985), 129–50.

Principal bibliographical source for the study of the theatre in colonial Peru. It is classified and annotated.

Fiction

Rodríguez Rea, Miguel Angel. "El cuento peruano contemporáneo; índice bibliográfico," I, "1900–1930," *Lexis*, 7:2 (1983), 287–309; II, "1931–1945," *Lexis*, 8:2 (1984), 249–73; III, "1946–1950," *Lexis*, 10:2 (1986), 237–50; IV, "1951–1955" *Lexis*, 13:1 (1989), 135–51; V, "1956–1960," *Lexis*, 15:2 (1991), 233–51.

Provides data on 250 titles.

Vidal, Luis Fernando. "Las antologías del cuento en el Perú," *Revista de Crítica Literaria Latinoamericana*, 1:2 (1974), 121–38.

Provides contents of forty-nine anthologies published between 1908 and 1975.

Villanueva de Puccinelli, Elsa. *Bibliografía de la novela peruana*, Lima, Biblioteca Universitaria, 1969. (xii, 88 pages.)

Besides listing the works of Peruvian novelists, Villanueva de Puccinelli provides a chronology.

History

Higgins, James. *A History of Peruvian Literature*, Liverpool Monographs in Hispanic Studies, 7, Wolfeboro, N. J., E. Cairns, 1987. (379 pages.)

A scholarly, up-to-date, useful history of Peru's literature, in English.

Sánchez, Luis Alberto. *La literatura peruana: derrotero para una historia cultural del Perú*, 5 vols., Lima, Ediciones de Ediventas, 1965–1966.

Outstanding history with a useful "Apreciaciones sobre fuentes bibliográficas para una historia de la literatura peruana" of 662 items: v, 1671–753.

Library catalog

Biblioteca Nacional del Perú. *Catálogo de autores de la colección peruana*, 6 vols., Boston, G. K. Hall, 1979.

"... it includes catalog cards for Peruvian imprints and for publications about Peru from 1553 through 1977 which are found in the National Library" (p. vii).

Poetry

Cabel, Jesús. *Bibliografía de la poesía peruana 65/79*, [Lima], Amaru, [1980]. (143 pages.)

Lists Peruvian poets published either in Peru or abroad. Volume divided into books, anthologies, *plaquetas*, and a supplement. Includes 1,249 titles.

Bibliografía de la poesía peruana 80/84, [Lima, Biblioteca Universitaria, 1986]. (45 pages.)

Includes 352 titles.

[Jara, Umberto.] "Libros de poesía publicados entre 1980–1989," *Debate*, 11:58 (Nov.–Dec. 1989), 67–8.

Lists 147 titles.

Monguio, Luis. "Contribución a la bibliografía de la poesía peruana (1915–1950)" in his *La poesía postmodernista peruana*, Berkeley, University of California Press, 1954, 207–39.

Provides data on 151 titles.

Rodríguez Rea, Miguel Angel. "Poesía peruana del siglo xx," *Hueso Húmero*, 7 (Oct.–Dec. 1980) 133–50; 8 (Jan.–March 1981), 132–49; 9 (April–June 1981), 148–58; 14 (July–Sept. 1982), 186–204.

This four-part bibliography covers 1901–1920, 1921–1930, 1931–1935, and 1936–1940, and includes data on 483 works of poetry by Peruvians, regardless of the place of publication.

Puerto Rico

Bibliographies

Bravo, Enrique R. *An Annotated Selected Puerto Rican Bibliography: Bibliografía puertorriqueña selecta y anotada*, New York, Urban Center of Columbia University, 1972, 60–84.

Bilingual bibliography with a classified literature section.

Foster, David William. *Puerto Rican Literature: A bibliography of secondary sources*, Westport, Conn., Greenwood, 1982. (324 pages.)

The first section is a classified bibliography of general studies on Puerto Rican literature. The second part provides bibliographies of critical studies on eighty Puerto Rican authors.

Hill, Marnesba D., and Harold B. Schleifer. *Puerto Rican Authors: A bibliographic handbook*, Metuchen, N.J., Scarecrow, 1974. (267 pages.)

Bilingual bio-bibliographical dictionary of Puerto Rican authors that lists their works but extremely few biographical and critical references.

Pedreira, Antonio S. *Bibliografía puertorriqueña (1493–1930)*, foreword by Francesco Cordasco, Bibliography and Reference Series, 496, New York, Burt Franklin, 1974, 487–558.

Originally published in 1932. A classified bibliography on literary history that may occasionally prove useful.

Vivó, Paquita. *The Puerto Rican: An annotated bibliography*, New York, Bowker, 1973, 113–46, 215–16.

Useful annotations on Puerto Rican literature, literary history, and criticism in periodicals.

Dictionaries

Rivera de Alvarez, Josefina. *Diccionario de literatura puertorriqueña*, Río Piedras, La Torre, 1955. (499 pages.)

After a "Panorama histórico de la literatura puertorriqueña" (pp. 1–161), there is a bio-bibliographical dictionary of Puerto Rican authors. It also includes entries on Puerto Rican cultural institutions.

Drama

Gonzáles, Nilda. *Bibliografía del teatro puertorriqueño (siglos XIX y XX)*, Río Piedras, Editorial Universitaria, 1979. (xx, 223 pages.)

Extremely useful bibliography of the Puerto Rican theatre, as well as criticism concerning it. Includes data on both published and unpublished plays, as well as information on certain performances.

Fiction

Quiles de la Luz, Lillian. "Indice bibliográfico del cuento en la literatura puertorriqueña (1843–1963)" in *El cuento en la literatura puertorriqueña*, Río Piedras, Editorial Universitaria, 1968, 141–293.

Extensive bibliography of the Puerto Rican short story as found in books, anthologies, and periodicals.

History

Cabrera, Francisco Manrique. *Historia de la literatura puertorriqueña*, Río Piedras Editorial Cultural, 1986. (364 pages.)

A standard history appearing in many editions.

Rivera de Alvarez, Josefina. *Historia de la literatura puertorriqueña*, 2 vols., San Juan, Editorial del Departamento de Instrucción Pública, 1969.

  Fullest history of Puerto Rican literature with extensive bibliographical data.

Literatura puertorriqueña: su proceso en el tiempo, Madrid, Partenón, 1983. (953 pages.)

  Gives biographical sketches and historical survey.

United States

Chicano literature

Eger, Ernestina N. *A Bibliography of Criticism of Contemporary Chicano Literature*, Chicano Studies Library Publications, 5, Berkeley, University of California, Chicano Studies Library Publications, 1982. (xxi, 295 pages.)

  An excellent classified bibliography that lists books, articles, reviews, and dissertations, published or written on this subject chiefly between 1960 and 1979.

Foster, Virginia Ramos. "Literature" in David William Foster (ed.), *Sourcebook of Hispanic Culture in the United States*, Chicago, American Library Association, 1982, 86–111.

  Seventy-six well-annotated items in a classified bibliography.

Martínez, Julio A., and Francisco A. Lomeli (eds.). *Chicano Literature: A reference guide*, Westport, Conn., Greenwood, 1985. (xii, 492 pages.)

  The biographical–critical artis on Chicano authors written by several dozen specialists are followed by a listing of the authors' most important works and of their critical studies. There are also articles on various literary genres.

Trujillo, Roberto G., and Andrés Rodríguez. *Literatura Chicana: Creative and Critical Writings through 1984*, intro. Luis Leal, Oakland, Calif., Floricano, 1985. (xi, 95 pages.)

  The 783 items are divided by literary genres. Besides the usual types of material that one would expect to find, the compilers include data on Chicano literary periodicals, and video and sound recordings.

Cuban-American literature

Lindstrom, Naomi E. "Cuban American and Continental Puerto Rican Literature" in David William Foster (ed.), *Sourcebook of Hispanic Culture in the United States*, Chicago, American Library Association, 1982, 221–45.

  Classified well-annotated bibliography of sixty-one items.

Uruguay

Bibliographies

Rela, Walter. *Fuentes para el estudio de la literatura uruguaya, 1835–1968*, [Montevideo], Banda Oriental, 1969. (134 pages.)

  Classified unannotated bibliography of 930 items.

Literatura uruguaya: bibliografía selectiva (title also in English), Special Studies, 26, Tempe, Arizona State University, Center for Latin American Studies, 1986. (86 pages.)

The first part of this work is "Referencias críticas" which deals with general studies and is a classified bibliography of critical studies, bibliographies, anthologies, etc. The second part provides data on the book-length works of close to 100 authors and on book-length critical studies on their works.

Welch, Thomas L. *Bibliografía de la literatura uruguaya*, Washington, Organization of American States, 1985. (xii, 502 pages.)

Lists 9,239 items by Uruguayan authors in the Columbus Memorial Library. It has a title index. Unlike most of the preceding works, Welch includes translations of these authors if they are in this library.

Dictionaries

Diccionario de literatura uruguaya, 2 vols., Montevideo, Arca-Credisol, 1987.

This is an excellent national literary dictionary comparable to those that exist for Cuba, Peru, Mexico, and Venezuela. More than fifty critics have collaborated to produce this work. The material on each author is divided into a biographical–critical sketch, a list of the author's works, and one of critical studies on the author. The individual sketches run from one to five pages.

Rela, Walter. *Diccionario de escritores uruguayos*, Montevideo, Ediciones de la Plata, 1986. (397 pages.)

Rela provides a biographical sketch of each author; his critical comments are quotations from literary critics. These bio-bibliographical sketches range from one to seven pages. The bibliographical data adds little to that found in his *Literatura uruguaya: bibliografía selectiva* (above).

Drama

Rela, Walter. *Repertorio bibliográfico del teatro uruguayo, 1816–1964*, Colección Medusa, Montevideo, Editorial Síntesis, 1965. (35 pages.)

Unannotated classified bibliography.

Diccionario de autores teatrales uruguayos, Montevideo Proyección, 1988. (138 pages.)

Pages 5–33 are a "Breve historia del teatro uruguayo. S. XIX–XX." A bio-bibliographical dictionary of Uruguayan dramatists.

Fiction

Englekirk, John E., and Margaret M. Ramos. *La narrativa uruguaya: estudio crítico-bibliográfico*, University of California Publications in Modern Philology, 80, Berkeley University of California Press, 1967. (338 pages.)

Provides data on 525 novels and 7,000 short stories by 265 authors. Quotations from critics are provided for many of these works; copies are located in nine US, Spanish, and Uruguayan libraries.

History

Capítulo oriental: la historia de la literatura uruguaya, Montevideo, Centro Editor de América Latina, 1968–1969. (45 fascicles.)

A different scholar deals with each different topic of Uruguayan literature. The last fascicle is an index to the complete work.

Literary journals

Barite, Mario, and María Gladys Ceretta. *Guía de revistas culturales uruguayas 1895–1985*, Montevideo, Ediciones "El Galeón," 1989. (101 pages.)

Bibliographical data such as frequency, names of important contributors, and place of publication are provided for 239 literary journals published during these 90 years in Uruguay.

Women poets

Moratorio, Arsinoe. "La mujer en la poesía del Uruguay (Bibliografía 1879–1969)," *Revista de la Biblioteca Nacional* (Montevideo), 4 (Dec. 1970), 43–63.

Presents data on the works of women poets published in book form as well as reprints and translations of their books. Works under each poet are arranged chronologically.

Venezuela

Afro-Venezuelan literature

Ramos Guédez, José Marcial. "Literatura afrovenezolana" in *Bibliografía afrovenezolana*, Serie Bibliográfica, 2, Caracas, Instituto Autónomo Biblioteca Nacional y de Servicios de Bibliotecas, 1980, 99–106.

Items 858–936 are an unannotated listing of material by black Venezuelans or material that discusses how Blacks are presented in Venezuelan literature.

Bibliographies and surveys

Becco, Horacio Jorge. *Fuentes para el estudio de la literatura venezolana*, 2 vols., Caracas, Centauro, 1978.

Valuable classified bibliography of 1,860 items.

Bibliografía de bibliografías venezolanas: literatura (1968–1979), Caracas, Editorial Andrés Bello, 1979. (62 pages.)

Classified bibliography of 250 items.

Cardozo, Lubio. *Bibliografía de literatura merideña*, Merida, Universidad de los Andes, Facultad de Humanidades y Educación, Escuela de Letras, Centro de Investigaciones Literarias, 1967. (91 pages.)

Bibliography indexes 275 books by writers from the state of Merida.

Lovera de Sola, Roberto J. "La literatura venezolana en 1971," *Montalbán*, 1 (1972), 548–84.

"La producción literaria en 1972," *Libros al Día*, 1:10 (1976), 21–8.
"Producción literaria 1971. Bibliografía fundamental," *Libros al Día*, 1:15 (1976), 2–28.
    Excellent survey of Venezuelan *belles lettres* for the years covered.
Niño de Rivas, María Lys. "Escritores actuales de Venezuela, una bibliografía," *ARAISA*, 1975, 349–82.
    Lists works published in the 1960s and early 1970s. Often indicates literary genre.
Villasana, Angel Raúl. *Ensayo de un repertorio bibliográfico venezolano*, 6 vols., Colección Cuatricentenario de Caracas, Caracas, Banco Central de Venezuela, 1969–1979.
    Includes works published in Venezuela or about Venezuela between 1808 and 1950. Concentrates on works of literature, history, and those of a general nature.

Dictionary

Diccionario general de la literatura venezolana (autores), 2 vols. Mérida, Editorial Venezolana, Consejo de fomento, Consejo de publicaciones, Universidad de los Andes, 1987.
    Wherever possible, for each author there is given a brief biographical sketch, a critical note, and a listing of the author's published books and works about the author. This is an outstanding bio-bibliographical dictionary.

Drama

Greymont, Sally J. "Hacia una bibliografía del teatro venezolano colonial," *Latin American Theatre Review*, 8:2 (1975) 45–9.
    Includes works that refer to pre-Columbian, colonial, and folk theatre, as well as to colonial dramatists.
Rojas Uzcátegui, José de la Cruz, and Lubio Cardozo. *Bibliografía del teatro venezolano*, Mérida, Instituto de Investigaciones Literarias "Gonzalo Picón Febres," 1980. (199 pages.)
    Most extensive bibliography of the Venezuelan theatre from 1801 to 1978.

Fiction

Bibliografía de la novela venezolana, Caracas, Universidad Central de Venezuela, Facultad de Humanidades y Educación, Escuela de Letras, Centro de Estudios Literarios, 1963. (71 pages.)
    Data provided on 324 titles by 187 authors whose works were published between 1842 and 1962.
Larrazábal Henríquez, Osvaldo, *et al. Bibliografía del cuento venezolano*, Caracas, Universidad Central de Venezuela, Facultad de Humanidades y Educación, Instituto de Investigaciones Literarias, 1975. (315 pages.)
    Data provided on 3,311 short stories by 332 authors.

Bibliography of general bibliographies

History

Picón Salas, Mariano. *Estudios de literatura venezolana*, Caracas, Ediciones EDIME, 1961 (320 pages.)
Essays on individual authors follow the general literary history of the country.

Periodical index

Ziona Hirshbein, Cesia. *Hemerografía venezolana 1890–1930*, Caracas, Universidad Central de Venezuela, Facultad de Humanidades y Educación, Instituto de Estudios Hispanoamericanos, 1978. (574 pages.)
Useful classified index of literature that appeared in Venezuelan journals.

Poetry

Becco, Horacio Jorge, and Alberto Amengual. "Antologías poéticas americanas y venezolanas en el siglo XIX," in *Memoria del III Simposio de docentes e investigadores de la literatura venezolana*, vol. I, Mérida, Universidad de los Andes, Facultad de Humanidades y Educación, Instituto de Investigaciones Literarias "Gonzalo Picón Febres," 1981, 238–49.
Divided between Spanish American poetry anthologies and Venezuelan ones. Gives bibliographical details for each volume and lists Venezuelan writers included.

Sembrano Urdaneta, Oscar. *Contribución a una bibliografía general de la poesía venezolana en el siglo XX*, Caracas, Universidad Central de Venezuela, Facultad de humanidades y Educación, Escuela de Letras, 1979. (367 pages.)
Includes data on 2,068 volumes of poetry by 747 authors. Provides critical studies on Venezuelan poets.

Women authors

La mujer en las letras venezolanas. Homenaje a Teresa de la Parra en el año internacional de la mujer, 5–26 octubre de 1975, Caracas, Congreso de la República, 1976. (176 pages.)
Extensive bibliography of Venezuelan women authors.

Translations

Brazilian (Portuguese)

Wogan, Daniel S. *A literatura hispano-americana no Brasil 1877–1944: bibliografía de crítica, história, literária e traduções*, Baton Rouge, Louisiana State University Press, 1948. (98 pages.)
Critical studies are briefly annotated and are arranged in chronological order. Translations are arranged by author.

English

Christensen, George K. "A bibliography of Latin American plays in English translation," *Latin American Theatre Review*, 6:6 (1973), 29–30.

Attempts to list both published and manuscript translations of plays. Extremely incomplete.

Freudenthal, Juan R., and Patricia M. Freudenthal. *Index to Anthologies of Latin American Literature in English Translation*, Boston, G. K. Hall, 1977. (xxxvi, 199 pages.)

Indexes almost 120 books and issues of periodicals devoted to Latin American literature in translation. It is unfortunate that no attempt is made to provide the original title in Spanish or Portuguese.

Hulet, Claude L. *Latin American Prose in English*, Basic Bibliographies, 1, Washington, Pan American Union, 1964. (191 pages.)

Divided by literary genre and then, within each genre, by country.

Latin American Poetry in English Translation, Basic Bibliographies, 2, Washington, Pan American Union, 1965. (182 pages.)

Arranged by country. Spanish or Portuguese titles are often provided.

Shaw, Bradley A. *Latin American Literature in English Translation: An annotated bibliography*, New York University Press, for Center for Inter-American Relations, 1976. (x, 144 pages.)

Arranged by genre and then by country. Includes only books and anthologies and almost always gives the title in the original language.

Latin American Literature in English 1975–1978, supplement to *Review* (New York, Center for Inter-American Relations), 24 (1979). (23 pages.)

Provides data on 111 annotated entries that supplement and update previous item. Entries are arranged alphabetically by author or editor and are divided into anthologies, individual works, additions to the original volume, and reprints published before 1975.

Wilson, Jason. *An A to Z of Latin American Literature in English Translation*, London, Institute of Latin American Studies, 1990. (35 pages.)

Provides a bibliography of books (chiefly fiction and poetry) translated into English. The original Spanish or Portuguese title is often given.

Bibliography of bibliographies

Cordeiro, Daniel Raposo. *A Bibliography of Latin American Bibliographies: Social Sciences and Humanities*, Metuchen, N.J., Scarecrow, 1979. (vii, 272 pages.)

Gropp, Arthur E. *A Bibliography of Latin American bibliographies*, Metuchen, N.J., Scarecrow, 1968. (ix, 515 pages.)

A Bibliography of Latin American Bibliographies. Supplement, Metuchen, N.J., Scarecrow, 1971. (xiii, 277 pages.)

Latin American Bibliographies Published in Periodicals, 2 vols., Metuchen, N.J., Scarecrow, 1976.

Loroña, Lionel. *A bibliography of Latin American Bibliographies, 1982–1983. Annual report*, Bibliography and Reference Series, 10, Madison, Wis., Seminar on the

Acquisition of Latin American Library Materials, 1984. (27 pages.)

Bibliography of Latin American and Caribbean Bibliographies: Annual report, 1984–1985, Bibliography and References Series, 15, Madison, Wis., Seminar on the Acquisition of Latin American Library Materials, 1986. (128 pages.)

Bibliography of Latin American and Caribbean Bibliographies: Annual report, 1985–1986, Bibliography and References Series, 17, Madison, Wis., Seminar on the Acquisition of Latin American Library Materials, 1986. (54 pages.)

A Bibliography of Latin American Bibliographies, 1980–1984: Social Sciences and Humanities, Metuchen, N.J., Scarecrow, 1987. (223 pages.)

Bibliography of Latin American and Caribbean Bibliographies: Annual report, 1986–1987, Bibliography and References Series, 20, Madison, Wis., Seminar on the Acquisition of Latin American Library Materials, 1987. (64 pages.)

Bibliography of Latin American and Caribbean Bibliographies: Annual report, 1987–1988, Bibliography and References Series, 23, Madison, Wis., Seminar on the Acquisition of Latin American Library Materials, 1988. (68 pages.)

Bibliography of Latin American and Caribbean Bibliographies: Annual report, 1988–1989, Bibliography and References Series, 25, Madison, Wis., Seminar on the Acquisition of Latin American Library Materials, 1989. (66 pages.)

Bibliography of Latin American and Caribbean Bibliographies: Annual report, 1989–1990, Bibliography and References Series, 27, Albuquerque, N.M., Seminar on the Acquisition of Latin American Library Materials, 1990. (48 pages.)

Bibliography of Latin American and Caribbean Bibliographies, 1985–1989: Social Sciences and Humanities, Metuchen, N.J., Scarecrow, 1992.

Bibliography of Latin American and Caribbean Bibliographies: Annual report, 1990–1991, Bibliography and References Series, 30, Albuquerque, N.M., Seminar on the Acquisition of Latin American Library Materials, 1992. (125 pages.)

Bibliography of Latin American and Caribbean Bibliographies: Annual report, 1991–1992, Bibliography and References Series, 3, Albuquerque, N.M., Seminar on the Acquisition of Latin American Library Materials, 1992.

Piedracueva, Haydée. *A Bibliography of Latin American Bibliographies, 1975–1979: Humanities and Social Sciences*, Metuchen, N.J., Scarecrow, 1982. (329 pages.)

Williams, Gayle Ann. *Bibliography of Latin American and Caribbean Bibliographies: Annual report, 1992–1993*, Bibliography and References Series, 34, Albuquerque, N.M., Seminar on the Acquisition of Latin American Library Materials, 1993. (81 pages.)

All of these have a classified arrangement with author and subject indexes. They are particularly excellent for providing a more or less current bibliography on authors, literary subjects and national bibliography as well as periodical indexes.

Argentina

Geoghegan, Abel Roidolfo. *Bibliografía de bibliografías argentinas, 1807–1970*, Buenos Aires Casa Pardo, 1970. (130 pages, plus 36 pages of advertisements.)
Classified bibliography by subject.

Colombia

Giraldo Jaramillo, Gabriel. *Bibliografía de bibliografías colombianas*, 2nd. edn., corrected and updated Rubén Pérez Ortiz, Publicaciones del Instituto Caro y Cuervo, Serie Bibliográfica, 1, Bogotá, Instituto Caro y Cuervo, 1960. (xvi, 204 pages.)
  Classified bibliography by subject.

Cuba

Fernández Robaina, Tomás. *Bibliografía de bibliografías cubanas: 1859–1972*, Havana, Biblioteca Nacional "José Martí," Departamento de Hemeroteca e Información de Humanidades, 1973. (340 pages.)
  Classified annotated bibliography with author–subject and periodical–title index.

Dominican Republic

Bibliografía de la bibliografía dominicana, Ciudad Trujillo, Roques Román, 1948. (66 pages.)
  Classified bibliography.

Mexico

Millares Carlo, Agustín, and José Ignacio Montecón. *Ensayo de una bibliografía de bibliografías mexicanas (la imprenta, el libro, las bibliotecas, etc.)*, Biblioteca de la II Feria del Libro y Exposición Nacional del Periodismo, Mexico, D.F., 1943. (xvi, 224 pages.)
Ensayo de una bibliografía de bibliografías mexicanas (La imprenta. . .). Adiciones, III Feria del Libro y Exposición Nacional del Periodismo y I de Cine y Radio, Mexico, D.F., 1944. (46 pages.)
  Though dated, these are still the fullest and most accurate of such bibliographies dealing with Mexico. Classified with excellent indexes.

Peru

Lostaunau Rubio, Gabriel. "Literatura" in *Fuentes para el estudio del Perú (bibliografía de bibliografías)*, Lima, Imprenta y encuadernación Herrera Márquez, 1980, 287–317.
  Divided into "Obras generales," "Poesía," "Teatro," "Cuento y novela," "Literatura infantil," and "Publicaciones periódicas literarias."

Uruguay

Musso Ambrosi, Luis Alberto. *Bibliografía de bibliografías uruguayas, con aportes a la historia del periodismo*, Montevideo, 1964. (vii, 102 pages.)
  Classified bibliography of 637 items. Indexed.

Catalogs of Latin American collections of the United States

Florida

Gainesville University libraries. *Catalog of the Latin American Collection*, 13 vols., 1st supplement, 7 vols. 1979.

    Close to 210,000 cards are reproduced.

Texas

University of Texas library. *Catalog of the Latin American Collection*, 31 vols., Boston, G. K. Hall, 1969. 1st supplement, 5 vols., 1971; 2nd supplement, 3 vols., 1973; 3rd supplement, 8 vols., 1975; 4th supplement 3 vols., 1977.

Bibliographic Guide to Latin American Studies, 1979– , Boston, G. K. Hall, 1980– .

    "... serves as an annual supplement..." (p. ix) to the catalogs of the University of Texas Library. It "consists of publications cataloged by the Latin American Collection (LAC) of the University of Texas, with additional entries from the Library of Congress for thorough subject coverage" (p. iv).

Tulane University

Tulane University Library. *Catalog of the Latin American Library of the Tulane University Library, New Orleans*, 10 vols., Boston, G. K. Hall, 1970. 1st supplement, 2 vols., 1973; 2nd supplement, 2 vols., 1975; 3rd supplement, 2 vols., 1978.

    These catalogs of three outstanding Latin American collections are extremely valuable bibliographical resources.

Volume 1: Discovery to Modernism

Chapter 1: A brief history of the history of Spanish American literature

The following represents more of a "works consulted" list than a bibliography proper. In the case of the anthologies, Beatriz González Stephan's book (*La historiografía literaria del liberalismo hispanoamericano del siglo XIX*) has a more complete list. I include here only the ones that I have been able to work with at Yale's extensive Latin American collection. The same holds for the precursors and the works of literary criticism listed. Since criticism, not literature, is the object of study of this chapter, there are very few annotations to these entries. The bibliography proper, like the others in this work, is selective and annotated. The reader is also encouraged to consult the bibliographies of chapters on literary criticism and the essay. Entries are listed chronologically unless otherwise stated.

Precursors (Bibliographers and bibliophiles)

Beristain de Souza, José Mariano. *Bibliotheca hispanoamericana septentrional; ó, Catálogo y noticia de los literatos, que ó nacidos, ó educados, ó florecientes en la América septentrional española, han dado a luz algún escrito, ó lo han dejado preparado para la prensa*, Mexico, A. Valdés, 1816–1821; recent edn., Mexico, Editorial Fuente Cultural, 1947.

  Prologue addressed "To Ferdinand VII, Catholic King of Spain and the Indies." Wishes to show enlightenment of Mexico, and that Spain has not been tryannical nor did it come to America for only gold and silver.

Tapia y Rivera, Alejandro. *Biblioteca histórica de Puerto Rico, que contiene varios documentos de los siglos XV, XVI, XVII y XVIII*, Puerto Rico, Imprenta de Márquez, 1954.

Odriozola, Manuel de. *Colección de documentos literarios del Perú*, Lima, A. Alfaro, 1863–1867.

García Icazbalceta, Joaquín. *Bibliografía mexicana del siglo XVI. Primera parte. Catálogo razonado de libros impresos en México de 1539 á 1600. Con biografías de autores y otras ilustraciones. Precedido de una noticia de la introducción de la imprenta en México*, Mexico, Andrade & Morales, 1886; modern edn., prepared by Agustín Millares Carlos, Mexico, Fondo de Cultura Económica, 1954.

  Says that he began his work in 1846. There was later a dispersal of Mexican collections that have led to the appearance of rare works in catalogues of rare editions. He adds that while he has called it *Primera parte* he has no intention of writing others, though "whomever does it will render a great service to letters and to the fatherland" (p. viii).

Medina, José Toribio. *Bibliotheca americana. Catálogo breve de mi colección de libros relativos a la América Latina; con un ensayo de bibliografía de Chile durante el período colonial*, Santiago, Typus authoris, 1888.

List of his own considerable collection.

Bibliotheca hispanoamericana, 1493–1810, vol. 1: *1493–1600*, Santiago, Fondo Histórico y Bibliográfico José Toribio Medina, 1958.

Facsimile edition of volume published 1898–1907. Fundamental to map the circulation of books and the evolution of editorial activities. Entries have detailed annotations.

Anthologies

(1824–1928)

La lira argentina, o colección de las piezas poéticas, dadas a luz en Buenos Ayres durante la guerra de su independencia, Buenos Aires, 1824; modern edn. by Pedro Luis Barcía, Buenos Aires, Academia Argentina de las Letras, 1982.

El Parnaso Oriental, ó Guirnalda poética de la República Uruguaya, 2 vols., Buenos Aires, Imprenta de la Libertad, 1835; modern edn. by Gustavo Gallina, Montevideo, Imprenta "El Siglo Ilustrado," 1927.

Gutiérrez, Juan María (ed.). *América poética. Colección escojida de composiciones en verso escritas por americanos en el presente siglo*, Valparaíso, Imprenta del Mercurio, 1846.

Ortiz, José Joaquín (ed.). *El Parnaso granadino; colección escojida de poesías nacionales por JJO*, Bogotá, Imprenta de Ancízar, 1848.

Ureta, J. M. (ed.). *Lira patriótica del Perú. Colección escojida de poesías nacionales desde la proclamación de la independencia hasta el día*, Lima, Imprenta de D. Fernando Velarde, 1853.

Borda, José Joaquín (ed.). *La lira granadina. Colección de poesías nacionales, escojidas y publicadas por JJB i José María Vergara i Vergara*, Bogotá, Imprenta de "El Mosaico," 1860.

Palma, Ricardo. *Dos poetas (Don Juan María Gutiérrez y Doña Dolores Ventenilla)*, Valparaíso, G. Helfmann, 1861.

Polo, José Toribio (ed.). *El Parnaso peruano; ó repertorio de poesías nacionales antiguas y modernas, precedidas del relato y biografía de su autor*, Lima, J. E. del Campo, 1862.

Giraldez, Tomás (ed.). *La guirnalda argentina. Poesías de jóvenes argentinos*, compiled T. Giraldez, Buenos Aires, Imprenta de La Bolsa, 1863.

Cortés José Domingo. *Inspiraciones patrióticas de la América Republicana*, compiled by J. D. Cortés, Valparaíso, Imprenta de la Patria, 1864.

Mistura para el bello sexo. Repertorio de canciones y yaravíes cantables, antiguos y modernos, para recreo del bello sexo, Arequipa, Imprenta de Francisco Ibáñez, 1865.

Molestina, Vicente Emilio (ed.). *Lira ecuatoriana. Colección de poesías líricas nacionales*, selected and arranged with biographical notes by V. E. Molestina, Guayaquil, Calvo & Cia., 1866.

Corona poética ofrecida al pueblo peruano el 28 de julio de 1866, Lima, Imprenta dirigida por J. R. Montemayor, 1866.

Molestina, Vicente Emilio (ed.). *Literatura ecuatoriana. Colección de antigüedades literarias, fábulas, epigramas, sátiras y cuadros de costumbres nacionales*, selected and arranged with biographical notes by V. E. Molestina, Lima, Alfaro & Cia., 1868.

Cortés, José Domingo (ed.). *Parnaso peruano*, Valparaíso, Imprenta Albin de Cox & Taylor, 1871.

    Interesting prologue about the state of national letters.

Corpancho, Godofredo (ed.). *Lira patriótica, o colección escogida de poesías sobre asuntos patrióticos para ejercicios de declamación*, Lima, 1873.

Palma, Ricardo (ed.). *Lira americana; colección de poesías de los mejores poetas del Perú, Chile y Bolivia*, Paris, Bouret et fils, 1873.

Cortés, José Domingo (ed.). *Parnaso arjentino; poesías líricas*, Santiago, Imprenta A. Bello, 1873.

    Has a prologue and biographical notes.

Castellanos, José (ed.). *Lira de Quisqueya. Poesías dominicanas*, chosen by J. Castellanos with biographical notes on the authors, Santo Domingo, Imprenta de García Hermanos, 1874.

Cortés, José Domingo (ed.). *América poética; poesías selectas americanas con noticias biográficas de los autores coleccionados*, París, A. Bouret, 1875.

Poetisas americanas, ramillete poético del bello sexo hispanoamericano, Paris, Bouret et fils, 1875. It also says "Mexico, Librería de A. Bouret e hijo," but the book was printed in Paris.

Rojas, José María (ed.). *Biblioteca de escritores venezolanos contemporáneos*, arranged, with biographical notes by J. M. Rojas, Caracas, Rojas Hermanos, 1975. It also says "Paris, Jouyet et Roger Editeurs"; modern edn., prologue Manuel Alfredo Rodríguez, Caracas, Concejo Municipal del Distrito Federal, 1975.

Cortés, José Domingo (ed.). *Prosistas americanos. Trozos escojidos de literatura coleccionados i extractados de autores mejicanos-uruguayos-bolivianos-ecuatorianos-cubanos-venezolanos-peruanos-chilenos-arjentinos-colombianos-americanos*, Paris, Tipografía La Hure, 1875.

    The front-matter contains curious facts about the editor.

Dr. Laso de los Vélez (ed.). *Poetas de la América Meridional. Colección escogida de poesías de Bello, Berro, Chacón, Echeverría, Figueroa, Lillo, Madrid, Maitin, Mármol, Navarrete y Valdés*, Havana, Alejandro Chao/Barcelona, Gaspar Homededeu, 1875. Printed in Barcelona.

Magariños Cervantes, Alejandro (ed.). *Album de poesías coleccionadas con algunas breves notas por AMC*, Montevideo, Imprenta de la Tribuna, 1878.

    Card at Yale's Sterling Memorial Library reads: "Biblioteca Americana publicada en París por Don Alejandro Magariños Cervantes. For volumes in the Yale Library belonging to this collection see individual titles under MC,A, 1825–1893," but only his novels appear.

Sama, Manuel María (ed.). *Poetas puerto-riqueños*, Producciones en verso, escogidas y coleccionadas por D. José M. Monge, D. Manuel M. Sama y D. Antonio Ruiz Quiñones. Precedidas de un prólogo por D. José M. Monge, Mayagüez, M. Fernández, 1879.

"Yaravíes quiteños," Congrès International des Americanistes, 4th session, Madrid, 1881. *Actas de la cuarta reunión*, Madrid, 1882–1883.

Menéndez Pelayo refers to Jiménez de Espada as "nuestro primer americanista."

García Salas, José María (ed.). *El Parnaso centroamericano (primera parte)*, Guatemala, Ministerio de Educación Pública, 1962; originally published in Guatemala, Imprenta de Pedro Arenales, 1882.

Lagomaggiore, Francisco (ed.). *América literaria; producciones selectas en prosa y verso*, compiled by F. Lagomaggiore, Buenos Aires, Imprenta de "La Nación," 1883.

Coronado, Martín (ed.). *Literatura americana. Trozos escogidos en prosa y en verso. Originales de autores nacidos en América Latina*, 2 vols., Buenos Aires, but it says, "Imp. Paul Dupont 1884 – París."

Riva Palacio, Vicente (ed.). *El Parnaso mexicano. J. Joaquín Fernández Lizardi. Su retrato y biografía con el juicio crítico de sus obras y poesías escogidas de varios autores*, gen. ed. Sr. Gral. C. VRP, Mexico, Librería La Ilustración, 1885.

Añez, Julio, (ed.). *Parnaso colombiano; colección de poesías escogidas*, first study of D. José Rivas Groot, Bogotá, Librería Colombiana, Camacho Roldán & Tamayo, 1886–1887.

Substantial introduction.

Parnaso venezolano, Serie 1 vol. 1: *Curaçao, 1887–90*, [Venezuela].

A poet per volume; the first is Bello.

Uriarte, Ramón (ed.). *Galería poética centro-americana. Colección de poesías de los mejores poetas del Centro*, preceded by brief biographical information and critical reviews of each of the authors included; 2nd. edn., Guatemala, Tip. "La Unión," 1888.

Pío Chavez, Manuel, and Manuel Rafael Valdivia. *Lira arequipeña. Colección de las más selectas poesías de los vates antiguos y modernos*, Arequipa, M. P. Chaves, 1889; modern edn., Artemio Peraltilla Díaz, Lima, Editorial El Sol, 1972.

Estrada, José Manuel (ed.). *Lira argentina; recopilación de poesías selectas de poetas argentinos*, Buenos Aires, P. M. Carballido & Cia., 1989.

Figueroa, Pedro Pablo (ed.). *Prosistas y poetas de América moderna*, Bogotá, Casa Editorial de J. J. Pérez, 1891.

Already includes Rubén Darío.

Calcaño, Julio (ed.). *Parnaso venezolano; colección de poesías de autores venezolanos desde mediados del siglo xviii hasta nuestros días*, with introductory section on the origin and progress of poetry in Venezuela by J. Calcaño, vol. 1, Caracas, Tip. "El Cojo," 1892. First volume.

Mera, Juan León (ed.). *Antología ecuatoriana. Cantares del pueblo ecuatoriano*; compilation J. L. Mera, with introductory essay, and notes on colloquial language, Academia Ecuatoriana, Quito, Imprenta de la Universidad Central del Ecuador, 1892.

Vigil, José María (ed.). *Poetisas mexicanas, siglos XVI, XVII, XVIII y XIX*, Antología formada por encargo de la Junta de Señoras correspondiente de la Exposición de

Chicago, Mexico, Oficina Tipográfica de la Secretaría de Fomento, 1893, modern edn., Ana Elena Díaz Alejo and Ernesto Prado Velázquez, Universidad Nacional Autónoma de México, *c.* 1977.

Mistura para el bello sexo. Canciones y yaravíes, novísima compilación, Arequipa, Imprenta de La Bolsa, 1893.

Romagosa, Carlos (ed.). *Joyas poéticas americanas. Colección de poesías escogidas. Originales de autores nacidos en América,* Córdoba, Argentina, Imprenta La Minerva, 1897.

    Includes poetry in Spanish, English, Portuguese, and French, with translations into Spanish.

Ugarte, Manuel (ed.). *La joven literatura hispanoamericana. Antología de prosistas y poetas,* Paris, Librería Armand Colin, 1906.

    I have only seen this third edition, which indicates that the book sold well.

Parnaso venezolano. Selectas composiciones poéticas coleccionadas por CBA, with essay on development and current status of lyrical poetry in Venezuela by Sr General Pedro Arisimendi Brito. Barcelona and Buenos Aires, 1906; enlarged edn., Juan González Camargo, Barcelona, Maucci, 1917?

La nueva lira criolla; guarachas, canciones, décimas y cantares de la guerra, 6th edn., enlarged, Havana, La Moderna Poesía, 1907.

Donoso, Armando (ed.). *Parnaso chileno,* expanded by Baronesa de Wilson, Barcelona, Maucci, 1910.

Ortiz, Alberto (ed.). *Parnaso nicaragüense; antología completa de sus mejores poetas,* Barcelona, Maucci, 1912.

García Calderón, Ventura (ed.). *Parnaso peruano,* compiled V. G. Calderón, Barcelona, Maucci, 1914.

Bazil, Oswaldo (ed.). *Parnaso dominicano; compilación completa de los mejores poetas de la República de Santo Domingo,* Barcelona, Maucci, [*c.* 1915].

Méndez Pereira, Octavio (ed.). *Parnaso panameño,* prologue and biographies by O. Méndez Pereira, Panama, Tip. el Istmo, 1916.

Donoso, Armando (ed.). *Pequeña antología de poetas chilenos contemporáneos,* Santiago, Ediciones de Filosofía, Arte y Literatura, 1917.

Bazil, Oswaldo (ed.). *Parnaso antillano; compilación completa de los mejores poetas de Cuba, Puerto Rico y Santo Domingo,* Barcelona, Maucci, [1918?].

    Prologue dated, "Barcelona, 17 de noviembre de 1916."

Oyuela, Calixto (ed.). *Antología poética hispano-americana; con notas biográficas y críticas,* 5 vols., Buenos Aires, A. Estrada & Cia., 1919–1920.

Del Valle, Adrián (ed.). *Parnaso cubano; selectas composiciones poéticas,* expanded edn. Barcelona, Maucci, 1920.

    Prologue dated "Habana, julio de 1906."

Caro Grau, Francisco (ed.). *Parnaso colombiano. Nueva antología esmeradamente seleccionada,* 3rd. edn., Barcelona, Maucci, n.d. Prologue signed 1920.

Bolívar Coronado, Rafael (ed.). *Parnaso costarricense; selección esmerada de los mejores poetas de Costa Rica,* Barcelona, Maucci, [1922?].

Brissa, José (ed.). *Parnaso ecuatoriano. Antología de las mejores poesías del Ecuador,* selected by J. Brissa, Barcelona, Maucci, n.d.

    Yale stamp indicates 1929 acquisition.

Pagano, José León (ed.). *El Parnaso argentino; poesías selectas,* with 21 illustrations,

5th. edn., Barcelona, Maucci, 191?

"La poesía americana," an essay by Juan María Gutiérrez serves as prologue.

Esteva, Adalberto A. (ed.). *El parnaso mexicano; antología completa de sus mejores poetas con numerosas notas biográficas*, 2 vols., notes by A. A. Esteva and José Pablo Rivas, Barcelona, Maucci, 191?

Erazo, Salvador (ed.). *Parnaso salvadoreño; antología esmeradamente seleccionada de los mejores poetas de la República del Salvador*, Barcelona, Maucci, n.d.

Donoso, Armando (ed.). *Nuestros poetas. Antología chilena moderna*, prologue and notes Armando Donoso, Santiago, Nascimento, n.d.

Torres Rivera (ed.). *Parnaso puertorriqueño. Antología esmeradamente seleccionada de los mejores poetas de Puerto Rico*, Barcelona, Maucci, [1921].

Artucio Ferreira, Antonio (ed.). *Parnaso uruguayo, 1905–1922*, Barcelona, Maucci, 1992.

De Vitis, Machael Angelo (ed.). *Parnaso paraguayo; selectas composiciones poéticas*, Barcelona, Maucci, [1925].

Porta Mences, Humberto (ed.). *Parnaso guatemalteco (1750–1928)*, with biographical and bibliographical notes. Guatemala, C. A. [Tip. Nacional], 1928.

Literary criticism (Alphabetical order)

Amunátegui, Gregorio Víctor. *Informes presentados al decano de la Facultad de Humanidades sobre la Historia de la literatura colonial de Chile (1541–1810), por S. S. Gregorio V. Amunátegui i B. Vicuña Mackenna*; bound together with J. T. Medina, *Historia de la literatura colonial de Chile*, Santiago, El Mercurio, 1878.

Amunátegui, Miguel Luis. *Vida de Don Andrés Bello*, Santiago, printed by Pedro G. Ramírez, 1882.

   Don José Joaquín de Mora. Apuntes biográficos, Santiago, Imprenta Nacional, 1888.

Amunátegui y Solar, Domingo. *Bosquejo histórico de la literatura chilena. Período colonial*, Santiago, Imprenta Universitaria, 1918.

Bachiller y Morales, Antonio. *Apuntes para la historia de las letras, y de la instrucción pública de la Isla de Cuba*, 3 vols., Havana, Imprenta de P. Massana, 1859–18961; modern edn. Havana, Academia de Ciencias de Cuba, Instituto de Literatura y Lingüística, 1965.

Barros Arana, Diego. *Bibliotheca americana. Collection d'ouvrages inédits ou rares sur l'Amérique*, 3 vols., Paris, A. Franck, 1862–1864.

   The only work published appears to have been *Purén indómito*, the epic poem by Captain Fernando Alvarez de Toledo.

Bartres Jáuregui, Antonio. *Literatura americana. Colección de artículos*, Guatemala, Tip. de "El Progreso," 1879.

Blanco-Fombona, Rufino (ed.). *Autores americanos juzgados por los españoles*, Paris and Buenos Aires, Casa Editorial Hispano-americana, 1913.

   An interesting "Dos palabras por vía de introducción. . ."

Echeverría, Esteban. *Obras completas de D. Esteban Echeverría*, Buenos Aires, C. Casaralle, Imprenta y Librería de Mayo, 1870–1874.

Fernández Guerra y Orbe, Luis. *D. Juan Ruiz de Alarcón y Mendoza, Obra premiada en público certámen de la Real Academia Española*, Madrid, Rivadeneyra, 1871.

Figueroa, Pedro Pablo. *Miscelánea biográfica americana (estudios históricos, críticos y literarios)*, Santiago, Imprenta de la Unión, 1888.

Fombona Palacio, Manuel. *Poetas españoles y americanos*, 2nd. edn., Caracas, Librería Española de L. Puig Ros, 1881.

García Icazbalceta, Joaquín. *Francisco Terrazas y otros poetas del siglo* XVI, Madrid, Ediciones J. García Turranzas, 1962.

García Icazbalceta, Joaquín, (ed.). *México en 1554*, by Cervantes de Salazar, Francisco, 3 Latin dialogues translated by J. García Icazbalceta, notes by Julio Jiménez Rueda, Universidad Nacional Autónoma de México, 1952.

García Merou, Martín. *Confidencias literarias*, Buenos Aires, Imprenta Casa Editora "Argos," 1893.
  Spicy literary gossip.

Gutiérrez, Juan María. *Estudios histórico-literarios*, selection, prologue and notes Ernesto Morales, Buenos Aires, Angel Estrada & Cia., 1940.

"Noticias sobre un libro curioso y rarísimo, impreso en América al comenzar el siglo XVII," *Revista del Río de la Plata*, 6:21 (1873), 86–105.
  About Diego de Dávalos's *Miscelánea Austral*.

Lastarria, José Victoriano. *Recuerdos literarios; datos para la historia literaria de la América española i del progreso intelectual en Chile*, 2nd. edn., Santiago, M. Servat, 1885.

Lastarria, prologue and selection Luis Enrique Délano, Mexico, Ediciones de la Secretaría de Educación Pública, 1944.

Medina, José Toribio. *Historia de la literatura colonial de Chile*, Santiago 1878; bound with Gregorio V. Amunátegui and B. Vicuña Mackenna, *Informes presentados al decano de la Facultad de humanidades sobre la Historia de la literatura colonial de Chile (1541–1810)*, (see above).

Mera, Juan León. *Ojeada histórico-crítica sobre la poesía ecuatoriana desde su época más remota hasta nuestros días*, 2nd. edn., followed by new appendixes, Barcelona, Imprenta de J. Cunil Sala, 1893; modern edn. by Raúl Silva Castro, Santiago, 1968.

Oyuela, Calixto. *Estudios y artículos literarios*, Buenos Aires, Imprenta de P. E. Coni e hijos, 1889.

Estudios literarios, prologue Alvaro Melián Lafinur, 2 vols., Buenos Aires, Academia Argentina de Letras, 1943.

Oyuela, Calixto (ed.). *Trozos escogidos de la literatura castellana desde el siglo XII hasta nuestros días (España y América)*, Buenos Aires, A. Estrada, 1885.

José Mármol. Poesías escogidas, Buenos Aires, Agencia General de Librería y Publicaciones, 1922.

Sosa, Francisco. *Escritores y poetas sudamericanos*, Mexico, Oficina Tip. de la Secretaría de Fomento, 1890.

Torres Caicedo, José María. *Ensayos biográficos y de crítica literaria sobre los principales publicistas, historiadores, poetas y literatos de América Latina*, 3 vols., Paris, Guillaumin & Cia., 1863–1868.

Ensayos biográficos y de crítica literaria sobre los principales poetas y literatos hispano-americanos. Primera serie, vol. II, París, Librería de Guillaumin & Cia., 1863.

Ensayos biográficos y de crítica literaria sobre los principales publicistas, historia-

dores, poetas y literatos de la América Latina. Segunda serie, Paris, Baudry, Librería Europea, Dramard-Baudry & Cia., Sucesores, 1868.

Ugarte, Manuel. *Las nuevas tendencias literarias*, Valencia, F. Sempere & Cía., 1908 (?).

Vergara y Vergara, José María. *Historia de la literatura en Nueva Granada. Parte Primera. Desde la conquista hasta la independencia (1538–1820)*, Bogotá, Imprenta de Echeverría nos., 1867.

Wilson, Baronesa de. *El mundo literario americano. Escritores contemporáneos. Semblanzas. Poesías. Apreciaciones. Pinceladas*, 2 vols., Barcelona, Maucci, 1903.

Newspapers and magazines

La Biblioteca Americana o Miscelánea de Literatura, Artes i Ciencias. Por una sociedad de americanos, London, G. Marchant, 1823.

Directed by Andrés Bello.

El repertorio Americano, 1–4 (Oct. 1826 – Aug. 1827), London, Bossanges, Barthés & Lowell, 1826–1827.

Also directed by Andrés Bello, this was the most influential of the two journals.

Revista Española de Ambos Mundos, 1–4 (1853–1855), Madrid, Est. Tip. de Mellado.

Directed by Alejandro Magariños Cervantes (1825–1893).

Revista del Rio de la Plata; periódico mensual de historia y literatura de América, Buenos Aires, Imprenta de Mayo, 1871–1877.

Directed by Juan María Gutiérrez.

El Museo de Ambas Américas, 1–3: 1–36 (1842), Valparaíso.

Founded, in Valparaíso, Chile, by Colombian García del Río.

Revista de Santiago, 1 (April 1848), Santiago, Imprenta Chilena.

Directed by Lastarria.

Revista de Buenos Aires. Memoria y noticias para servir a la historia antigua de la República Argentina, edited and published by the founders of the *Revista de Buenos Aires*, Buenos Aires, Imprenta de Mayo, 1865.

Directed by J. M. Gutiérrez.

Correo de Comercio, 1, Buenos Aires, Real Imprenta de Niños Expósitos, 1810–1811.

Archivo americano y espíritu de la prensa del mundo, 1 (June 12, 1843).

Revista del Río de la Plata; periódico mensual de historia y literatura de América, Buenos Aires, Imprenta de Mayo, 1871–1877.

Revista chilena, 1–16 (Jan. 1875 – June 1880), Santiago, J. Núñez, 1875–1880.

Miguel Luis Amunátegui is one of the editors.

Literary histories (Alphabetical order)

Anderson Imbert, Enrique. *Historia de la literatura hispanoamericana*, 2 vols., Mexico and Buenos Aires, Fondo de Cultura Económica, 1954.

Spanish American Literature. A history, tr. John V. Falconieri, 2 vols., Detroit, Wayne State University Press, 1963; 2nd edn., revised and updated by Elaine Malley, 1969.

Arrom, José Juan. *Esquema generacional de las letras hispanoamericanas. Ensayo de un método*, Bogotá, Instituto Caro y Cuervo, 1963; 2nd. edn., 1977.

Aubrun, Charles V. *Histoire des lettres hispano-américaines*, Paris, Armand Colin, 1954.

Bazin, Robert. *Histoire de la littérature américaine de langue espagnole*, Paris, Hachette, 1953.

Bellini, Giuseppe. *Historia de la literatura hispanoamericana*, Madrid, Castalia, 1985.

Coester, Alfred. *The Literary History of Spanish America*, New York, Macmillan, 1916.

Díez-Echarri, Emiliano, and José María Roca Franquesa. *Historia de la literatura española e hispanoamericana*, 2nd edn., Madrid, Aguilar, 1966.

Franco, Jean. *An Introduction to Spanish American Literature*, Cambridge University Press, 1969.

Gallo, Uro, and Guiseppe Bellini. *Storia della litteratura ispanoamericana*, Milan, Nuova Accademia Editrice, 1958.

   Gallo wrote the first three parts, and Bellini the fourth and last.

Goic, Cedomil. *Historia y crítica de la literatura hispanoamericana: Epoca colonial*, Barcelona, Editorial Crítica, Grupo Grijalbo, 1988.

Hamilton, Carlos. *Historia de la literatura hispanoamericana*, New York, Las Américas, 1961.

Henríquez Ureña, Pedro. *Literary Currents in Hispanic America*, Cambridge, Mass., Harvard University Press, 1945.

   Historia de la cultura en la América Hispánica, Mexico, Fondo de Cultura Económica, 1947.

   Las corrientes literarias en la América Hispánica, Mexico, Fondo de Cultura Económica, 1949.

Lazo, Raimundo. *Historia de la literatura hispanoamericana*, Mexico, Editorial Porrúa, vol. I, 1965; vol. II, 1967.

Leal, Luis. *Breve historia de la literatura hispanoamericana*, New York, Knopf, 1971.

Leguizamón, Julio A. *Historia de la literatura hispanoamericana*, 2 vols., Buenos Aires, Editoriales Reunidas, 1945.

Madrigal, Luis Iñigo (ed.). *Historia de la literatura hispanoamericana*, Madrid, Cátedra, 1982.

Menéndez y Pelayo, Marcelino. *Antología de poetas hispanoamericanos*, published by the Real Academia Española de la Lengua, vol. I: *México y América Central*, Madrid, Est. Tipográfico "Sucesores de Rivadeneyra," 1893.

Rodríguez Monegal, Emir (ed.). *The Borzoi Anthology of Latin American Literature: From the time of Columbus to the twentieth century*, 2 vols., New York, Knopf, 1977.

Sánchez, Luis Alberto. *Nueva historia de la literatura americana*, Buenos Aires, Ediciones Ercilla, 1937.

Shimone, Pedro. *Historia de la literatura latinoamericana*, Madrid, Playor, 1989.

Torres Ríoseco, Arturo. *The Epic of Latin American Literature*, Los Angeles, University of California Press, 1942; published in Spanish as *La gran literatura iberoamericana*, Buenos Aires, Emecé, 1945.

Valbuena Briones, Angel. *Literatura hispanoamericana*, Madrid, Gili, 1962; published as 4th volume of Angel Valbuena Pratt's *Historia de la literatura española*, Barcelona, Gili, 1963.

Secondary bibliography

Ardao, Arturo. *Génesis de la idea y el nombre de América Latina*, Caracas, Centro de Estudios Rómulo Gallegos, 1980.

Study of Torres Caicedo and others, with an anthology of relevant texts.

Campra, Rosalba. "La búsqueda de categorías críticas en el siglo XIX: *Escritores y poetas sudamericanos* de Francisco Sosa," *Filología* (Instituto de Filología y Literaturas Hispánicas "Dr. Amado Alonso"), 22, 2 (1987), 27–43.

Lucid and informative on Sosa's 1890 project, a book of essays on various South American authors that would reveal and promote the existence of a Latin American literature.

"Las antologías hispanoamericanas del siglo XIX: proyecto literario y proyecto político," *Casa de las Américas*, 162 (1987), 37–46.

Ground-breaking article revealing the importance, from a critical, historical, and political point of view, of poetry anthologies in nineteenth-century Spanish America.

Carilla, Emilio. "El primer biógrafo de Alberdi (José María Torres Caicedo)," *Thesaurus* (Boletín del Instituto Caro y Cuervo), 43:1 (1988), 1–11.

Informative on literary relations among Latin Americans in Paris during the middle of the nineteenth century.

"José María Torres Caicedo, 'descubridor' de la literatura argentina," *Thesaurus* (Boletín del Instituto Caro y Cuervo), 44:2 (1989), 334–68.

Completes information in previous article.

Carpentier, Alejo. "Literatura y conciencia política en América Latina" in *Tientos y diferencias. Ensayos*, Universidad Nacional Autónoma de México, 1964; available in English as "Literature and political awareness in Latin America" in Doris Meyer (ed.), *Lives on the Line. The testimony of contemporary Latin American authors*, Berkeley, University of California Press, 1988, 21–30.

Strong on relations among Latin American writers during the nineteenth century, and the interaction of literature and politics.

Cordero, Luis Agustín. *Nicolás Antonio, bibliógrafo americanista*, Lima, Universidad Nacional Mayor de San Marcos, Seminario de Historia Rural Andina, 1980.

About the famed collector and bibliographer.

Fernández Moreno, César, (ed.). *América latina en su literatura*, Mexico, Siglo XXI/ UNESCO, 1972.

Important essays by António Cândido, Haroldo de Campos, Rubén Bareiro Saguier, José Luis Martínez, and others on topics of relevance to question of Latin American literary history.

Latin America in its Literature, ed. Ivan A. Schulman New York, Holmes & Meier, 1980.

Flitter, Derek. *Spanish Romantic Literary Theory and Criticism*, Cambridge University Press, 1991.

Excellent background to origins of Romanticism in Spain, with useful information for Latin America.

González Echevarría, Roberto. "Nota crítica sobre *The Borzoi Anthology of Latin American Literature*, de Emir Rodríguez Monegal" in his *Isla a su vuelo fugitiva;*

ensayos críticos sobre literatura hispanoamericana, Madrid, Porrúa, 1983, 227–34.

On Rodríguez Monegal's conception of Latin American literary history.

The Voice of the Masters: Writing and authority in modern Latin American literature, Austin, University of Texas Press, 1985.

Reassessment of conception of literature in relation to issue of cultural identity in Latin America.

"Reflections on *Espejo de paciencia*," *Cuban Studies*, 16 (1986), special issue on "The emergence of Cuban nationality," ed. Enrico Mario Santí, 101–22.

On the founding of Cuban literature and the publication of the first edition of the renaissance epic *Espejo de paciencia*.

"Reflexiones sobre *Espejo de paciencia*," *Nueva Revista de Filología Hispánica* (El Colegio de México), 35:3 (1987), 571–90.

Myth and Archive: A theory of Latin American narrative, Cambridge University Press, 1990.

An attempt to write the history of Latin American narrative from the perspective of its relations with non-literary forms of discourse.

González-Stephan, Beatriz. *La historiografía literaria del liberalismo hispanoamericano del siglo XIX*, Havana, Casa de las Américas, 1987.

Best study to date on the history of Latin American literary historiography.

Losada, Alejandro. *Los modos de producción cultural en América Latina 1840–1970*, São Paulo, Ed. Graal, 1980.

Attempt at redefinition of cultural production in Latin America using Marxist-derived approach.

"Bases para un proyecto de una historia social de la literatura en América Latina (1780–1970)," *Revista Iberoamericana*, 114–15 (1981), 167–88.

Derived from previous item, more focused on literature.

Paz, Octavio. *Los hijos del limo: del romanticismo a la vanguardia*, Barcelona, Seix Barral, 1974.

Modern poetry as reaction against modernity.

Children of the Mire: Modern poetry from Romanticism to the Avant-Garde, tr. Rachel Phillips, Cambridge, Mass., Harvard University Press, 1974.

Pizarro, Ana (ed.). *Hacia un historia de la literatura hispanoamericana*, Mexico, El Colegio de México/Universidad Simón Bolívar, 1987.

Essays on Latin American literary history from sociological perspective.

Rama, Angel. *La ciudad letrada*, Hanover, N.H. Ediciones del Norte, 1984.

Retells history of Latin American literature by considering evolution of lettered elites.

Rodríguez Monegal, Emir. *El otro Andrés Bello*, Caracas, Monte Avila, 1969.

Fundamental study with emphasis on Bello's exile in London, where he published his great journals and absorbed the romantic spirit.

Sarlo Sabajanes, Beatriz. *Juan María Gutiérrez: historiador y crítico de nuestra literatura*, Buenos Aires, Editorial Escuela, 1967.

Most complete study of one of the founders of Latin American literature.

Shumway, Nicolas. *The Invention of Argentina*, Berkeley, University of California Press, 1991.

Creation of national myths in Argentina and the relation of this process to literature.

Suberscaseaux, Bernardo. *Cultura y sociedad liberal en el siglo XIX: (Lastarria, ideología y literatura)*, Santiago, Editorial Aconcagua, 1981.
    Best study of literary activity in nineteenth-century Chile.

Tauro, Alberto. *Manuel Odriozola: prócer, erudito, bibliotecario*, Lima, Universidad Nacional Mayor de San Marcos, 1964.
    Study of Peruvian scholar and librarian.

Chapter 2: *Cultures in contact: Mesoamerica, the Andes, and the European written tradition*

Primary and secondary sources

Books

Acuña, Rene, and Robert Carmack. *Título de los señores de Totonicapán*, Universidad Nacional Autónoma de México.
    Quiché-Maya history from origins to mid fifteenth century.

Adorno, Rolena. *Guaman Poma: Writing and resistance in colonial Peru*, Austin, University of Texas Press, 1986. Guaman Poma's appropriation of European literary and intellectual culture.
    Cronista y príncipe: la obra de Felipe Guaman Poma de Ayala, Lima, Pontificia Universidad Católica, 1989. A study of Guaman Poma's writing that probes his Andean concerns somewhat more deeply than does the author's English-language monograph (*Guaman Poma: Writing and resistance*).

Adorno, Rolena (ed.). *From Oral to Written Expression: Native Andean chronicles of the early colonial period*, Latin American Series, 4, Syracuse University, Maxwell School of Citizenship and Public Affairs, 1982. Essays on Titu Cussi Yupanqui, Juan de Santacruz Pachacuti Yamqui, Guaman Poma de Ayala, and the Huarochirí traditions.

Alva Ixtlilxóchitl, Fernando de. *Nezahualcoyotl Acolmiztli*, ed. Edmundo O'Gorman, Mexico, Gobierno del Estado, 1972.
    Obras históricas, ed. Edmundo O'Gorman, Serie de historiadores y cronistas de Indias, 4, 2 vols., Universidad Nacional Autónoma de México, 1975–1977.
    Historia de la nación chichimeca, ed. Germán Vázquez Chamorro, Madrid, Historia 16, 1985.

Alvarado Tezozomoc, Hernando. *Crónica mexicana escrita hacia el año de 1598* [1598], ed. Manuel Orozco y Berra, Mexico, Editorial Leyenda, 1944.
    Reprint of the 1878 edition.
    Crónica mexicayotl [1609], tr. Adrián León Instituto de Investigaciones Históricas, Primera Serie Prehispánica, 3, Universidad Nacional Autónoma de México, 1975.
    Reprint of the 1949 edition.

Arguedas, José María (tr.). *Canciones y cuentos del pueblo quechua*, Lima, Huascarán, 1949.
    Tupac Amaru Kamaz Taytanchisman. Haylli-Taki. A Nuestro Padre Creador Tupac Amaru. Himno-Canción, Lima, Salqantay, 1962.
    Dioses y hombres de Huarochirí, Lima, Museo Nacional de Historia e Instituto de

Estudios Peruanos, 1966.

First Spanish translation of the Huarochirí manuscript, bio-bibliographical essay on Avila by Pierre Duviols.

Arguedas, José María, and Francisco Izquierdo Ríos. *Mitos, leyendas y cuentos peruanos*, Lima, Ministerio de Educación Pública, 1947.

Arias Larreta, Abraham. *Literaturas aborígenes. Azteca. Incaica. Maya-Quiché*, Los Angeles, Sayari, 1951.

Arrom, José Juan. *Mitología y artes prehispánicas de las Antillas*, Mexico, Siglo Veintiuno Editores, 1975.

Asturias, Miguel Angel, and J. M. González de Mendoza (eds. and trans.). *Popol-vuh o Libro del consejo de los indios quichés*, Buenos Aires, Editorial Losada, 1965.

A very literary translation of the *Popol Vuh*, based on the French version by Georges Raynaud.

Barrera Vázquez, Alfredo (ed. and trans.). *El libro de los cantares de Dzitbalché*, Serie Investigaciones, 9, Universidad Nacional Autónoma de México, Instituto Nacional de Antropología, 1965.

Transcription of Yucatec Maya text with Spanish translation.

Baudot, Georges. *Utopía e historia en México. Los primeros cronistas de la civilización mexicana (1520–1569)* [1977], tr. Vicente González Loscertales, Madrid, Espasa-Calpe, 1983.

Early Franciscan missionary activity and ethnographic writings in New Spain.

Bethell, Leslie (ed.). *The Cambridge History of Latin America*, vol. I and II: *Colonial Latin America*, Cambridge University Press, 1984.

Includes essays on pre-Columbian Mesoamerica and the Andes (Miguel León-Portilla, John V. Murra), the trauma of conquest (Nathan Wachtel), native societies under colonial rule (Charles Gibson), and colonial literature and intellectual life (Jacques Lafaye).

Bierhorst, John. *Cantares mexicanos: Songs of the Aztecs*, Stanford University Press, 1985.

Bilingual Nahuatl/English edition of prehispanic *Cantares*. Accompanied by *A Nahuatl-English Dictionary and Concordance to the "Cantares Mexicanos."*

Borgia Steck, Francisco. *El primer colegio de México*, Mexico, Centro de Estudios Franciscanos, 1944.

Brief history of the Colegio de Santacruz de Tlaltelolco.

Brasseur de Bourbourg, Charles Etienne. *Rabinal-Achi ou le drame-ballet du tun*, Colletion de Documents dans les Langues Indigènes, 2, pt. 2, Paris, Arthus Bertrand, 1862.

Sole available version of the complete text of the Rabinal Achi.

Brinton, Daniel G. *Aboriginal American Authors and Their Productions: Especially those in the native languages. A chapter in the history of literature*, Philadelphia, D. G. Brinton, 1883.

The first introduction, in English, to the verbal culture of native American peoples as literature.

Brinton, Daniel G. (ed.). *The Güegüence; a comedy ballet in the Nahuatl-Spanish dialect of Nicaragua*, Philadelphia, D. G. Brinton, 1883.

The Annals of the Cakchiquels, Philadelphia, D. G. Brinton, 1885.

Ancient Mexican Poetry, Philadelphia, D. G. Brinton, 1887.

First publication of the literature of pre-Columbian Mexico; selections from the ms. of the *Colección de Cantares Mexicanos*, discovered by Vigil in the Biblioteca Nacional de México in 1880.

Burkhart, Louise. *The Slippery Earth: Nahua-Christian moral dialogue in sixteenth-century Mexico*, Tucson, University of Arizona, 1989.

The ideological confrontation between Nahua and Christian beliefs, based on the study of doctrinal texts in Nahuatl.

Carmack, Robert M. *Quichean Civilization: The ethnohistoric, ethnographic and archaeological sources*, Berkeley and Los Angeles, University of California, 1973.

Survey of Quiché and Quiché-related texts and sources.

The Quiché Mayas of Utatlán: The evolution of a highland Guatemala kingdom, Norman, University of Oklahoma, 1981.

The development and decline of prehispanic Quiché society and culture based on native sources.

Caso, Alfonso. *El pueblo del sol*, Mexico, Fondo de Cultura Económica, 1953.

Classic study of Aztec culture.

Chang-Rodríguez, Raquel. *La apropiación del signo: tres cronistas indígenas del Perú*, Tempe, Arizona State University, Center for Latin American Studies, 1988.

The account of Titu Cussi Yupanqui and the chronicles of Joan de Santacruz Pachacuti Yamqui and Felipe Guamán Poma de Ayala.

Chimalpahin Quauhtlehuanitzin, Domingo de San Antón Muñón. *Relaciones originales de Chalco Amaquemecan*, ed. and tr. Silvia Rendón, Mexico, Fondo de Cultura Económica, 1965.

Spanish translation of various *relaciones* of Chimalpahin.

Octava relación, ed. and tr. José Rubén Romero Galván, Universidad Nacional Autónoma de México, 1983.

Chimalpahin's eighth *relación*, translated from Nahuatl into Spanish.

Clendinnen, Inga. *Ambivalent Conquests: Maya and Spaniard in Yucatan, 1517–1570*, Cambridge University Press 1987.

Intercultural contact between Spaniards and Mayas in Yucatan.

Cline, Howard F. (ed.). *Guide to Ethnohistorical Sources, Part Two, Handbook of Middle American Indians*, vol. XIII, Austin, University of Texas Press, 1973.

Fundamental reference work, particularly on missionary writings.

Cline, Howard F., Charles Gibson, and H. B. Nicholson (eds.), *Guide to Ethnohistorical Sources, Part Three, Handbook of Middle American Indians*, vol. XIV, Austin, University of Texas Press, 1975.

Survey and census of native Middle American pictorial manuscripts.

Guide to Ethnohistorical Sources, Part Four, Handbook of Middle American Indians, vol. XV, Austin, University of Texas Press, 1975.

Fundamental reference work on colonial prose manuscripts of Middle America.

Covarrubias, Sebastián de. *Tesoro de la lengua castellana o española* [1611, 1674], ed. Martín de Riquer, Barcelona, S. A. Horta, 1943.

Dictionary and cultural reference source indispensable to Spanish and Spanish colonial studies.

Craine, Eugene R., and Reginald C. Reindorp. *The Códex Pérez and the Book of Chilam Balam of Maní*, Norman, University of Oklahoma, 1979.

English translation of lowland Maya historical traditions.

Durán, Fray Diego de. *Historia de las Indias de Nueva España y islas de tierra firme*, 2 vols., Mexico, Editora Nacional, 1951.

Durand-Forest, Jacqueline de. *L'Histoire de la vallée de Mexico selon Chimalpahin Quauhtlehuanitzin: (du XIe au XVIe siècle), troisième relation de Chimalpahin Quauhtlehuanitzin*, 2 vols., Paris, L'Harmattan, 1987.

Duverger, Christian. *La conversion des Indiens de Nouvelle Espagne*, Paris, Seuil, 1987.

Includes text of Sahagún's *Coloquios*.

Duviols, Pierre. *La destrucción de las religiones andinas (conquista y colonia)* [1971], tr. Albor Maruenda, Universidad Nacional Autónoma de México, 1977.

Ecclesiastical campaigns against native religion in colonial Peru, emphasising techniques of acculturation and suppression of nativist movements.

Edmonson, Munro S. (ed.). *Sixteenth-Century Mexico: The work of Sahagún*, Albuquerque, University of New Mexico, 1974.

Anthology of essays by noted scholars on Sahagún and his works.

Supplement to the Handbook of Middle American Indians, vol. III: *Literatures*, Austin, University of Texas Press, 1985.

Nahuatl, Yucatec Maya, Tzotzil, Quiché, and Chorti (Maya) colonial traditions are surveyed by noted scholars.

Edmonson, Munro S. (trans.). *The Ancient Future of the Itza. The Book of Chilam Balam of Tizimin*, Austin, University of Texas Press, 1982.

English translation of a classic lowland Maya text.

Heaven-born Mérida and Its Destiny: The Book of Chilam Balam of Chumayel, Austin, University of Texas Press, 1986.

Farfán, José Mario Benigno. *El drama quechua Apu Ollantay*, Publicaciones Runa-Simi 1, Lima, 1952.

Farriss, Nancy. *Maya Society under Colonial Rule: The collective enterprise of survival*, Princeton University, 1984.

The Yucatec Maya during the colonial period. See chapter on Maya elites and appendix on sources.

Garibay, Angel María. *Historia de la literatura náhuatl, Primera parte (Etapa autónoma: de c. 1430 a 1521), Segunda parte: El trauma de la conquista (1521–1750)* [1953–4], 2nd edn., 2 vols., Mexico, Porrúa, 1971.

Extraordinary survey of Nahuatl and Spanish-language traditions; classification based on traditional Nahua types and European genres.

Garibay, Angel María (ed. and trans.). *Poesía náhuatl*, 3 vols., Universidad Nacional Autónoma de México, 1964–1968.

Monumental bilingual Spanish/Nahuatl edition and translation of the two major collections of prehispanic Nahuatl lyric, the *Cantares mexicanos* and the *Romances de los señores de la Nueva España*. Vol. 1 includes Pomar's *Relación* (1582).

Gibson, Charles. *The Aztecs under Spanish Rule: A history of the Indians of the Valley of Mexico, 1519–1810*, Stanford University, 1964.

Classic study of the native societies of central Mexico under Spanish rule.

Goody, Jack. *The Domestication of the Savage Mind*, Cambridge University Press, 1977.

Volume 1

The acquisition of literacy by oral societies.

Goody, Jack (ed.). *Literacy in Traditional Societies*, Cambridge University Press, 1968.

Includes Ian Watt and Jack Goody's influential essay on "The consequences of literacy."

Gruzinski, Serge. *La Colonisation de l'imaginaire: sociétés indigènes et occidentalisation dans le Mexique espagnol, xvie–xviiie siècle*, Paris, Gallimard, 1988.

Transformation of memory and diffusion of European beliefs through introduction of alphabetic writing in indigenous Mexican society under colonialism.

Guaman Poma de Ayala, Felipe. *Nueva corónica y buen gobierno*, eds. John V. Murra, Rolena Adorno, and Jorge L. Urioste, 3 vols., Madrid, Historia 16, 1987.

Second, revised edition of one published in 1980 (Mexico, Siglo Veintiuno Editores), translation of Quechua texts by Urioste, new introductory essays.

Guillén Guillén, Edmundo. *Versión Inca de la conquista*, Lima, Milla Batres, 1974.

Eye-witness accounts of the conquest wars of 1532–1536 by survivors of the Inca armies.

Gutiérrez Estévez, Manuel. *Biografías y confesiones de los indios de América*, Arbor: Ciencia, Pensamiento y Cultura, 515–16 (1988), 9–244.

Studies on Amerindian biographical and autobiographical writing and confessional testimony, colonial to contemporary times.

Harrison, Regina. *Signs, songs, and memory in the Andes: Translating Quechua language and culture*, Austin, University of Texas, 1989.

A major contribution to the study of the problems of cultural translation and the oral traditions of Ecuadorian Quichua (particularly women's songs) of the Andes.

Hemming, John. *The Conquest of the Incas*, London, Macmillan, 1970.

The conquest of Tawantinsuyu, the developing relations between Spaniards and Andeans, and the fate of survivors of the Inca royal house.

Horcasitas, Fernando. *El teatro náhuatl: épocas novohispana y moderna. Primera parte*, prologue Miguel León-Portilla, Monografías del Instituto de Investigaciones Históricas, Serie de Cultura náhuatl, Monografías, 17. Universidad Nacional Autónoma de México, 1974.

Jákfalvi-Leiva, Susana. *Traducción, escritura, y violencia colonizadora: un estudio de la obra del Inca Garcilaso de la Vega*, Latin American Series, 7, Maxwell School of Citizenship and Public Affairs, Syracuse University, 1984.

El Inca Garcilaso's theories of language and literary translation.

Karttunen, Frances, and James Lockhart. *The Art of Nahuatl Speech: The Bancroft dialogues*, UCLA Latin American Center Publications, 65, Los Angeles, University of California, 1987.

Nahuatl texts and English translations of *huehuehtlahtolli* dialogues.

Keen, Benjamin. *The Aztec Image in Western Thought* [1971], New Brunswick, N.J., Rutgers University, 1985.

Classic study of colonial Mexican historiographic and intellectual culture.

Klor de Alva, J. Jorge, H. B. Nicholson, and Eloise Quiñones Keber (eds.), *The Work of Bernardino de Sahagún: Pioneer ethnographer of sixteenth-century Aztec Mexico*, Albany, Institute for Mesoamerican Studies, and Austin, University of Texas Press, 1988.

Studies on Sahagún by noted scholars.

Lara, Jesús (ed. and trans.). *Tragedia del fin de Atawallpa*, Cochabamba, Bolivia, Imprenta Universitaria, 1957.

La literatura de los quechuas: ensayo y antología [1969], 4th. edn., La Paz, Editorial "Juventud," 1985.

Survey and anthology of Quechua-language traditions classified as poetry, theatre, the *relato*; historical works excluded.

León-Portilla, Miguel. *Literaturas precolombinas de México*, Mexico, Pormaca, 1964.

Study of verbal cultural production of ancient Mexico as literature, amplified in the English version, *Precolumbian Literatures of Mexico*, Norman, University of Oklahoma, 1969.

Literatura del México antiguo. Los textos en lengua nahuatl, Caracas, Biblioteca Ayacucho, 1978.

The author's most comprehensive collection of Nahuatl texts in Spanish translation.

Toltecayotl. Aspectos de la cultura Náhuatl, Mexico, Fondo de Cultura Económica, 1980.

Nahua concepts and methods of preserving history.

Literaturas de Anáhuac y del Incario, la expresíon de dos pueblos del sol, Mexico, SEP/Universidad Nacional Autónoma de México, 1982.

Pre-Columbian cultural productions of Mesoamerica and the Andes taken from colonial texts.

Los franciscanos vistos por el hombre nahuatl: testimonios indígenas del siglo XVI, Serie de Cultura Nahuatl Monografías, 21, Universidad Nacional Autónoma de México, 1985.

The Broken Spears: The Aztec account of the conquest of Mexico, tr. Lysander Kemp, Boston, Beacon Press, 1962.

Aztec Thought and Culture: A study of the ancient Nahuatl mind, tr. Jack Emory Davis, Norman, University of Oklahoma, 1963.

León-Portilla, Miguel (ed.) *Visión de los vencidos: Relatos indígenas de la Conquista*, tr. A. Garibay, Universidad Nacional Autónoma de México, 1959.

Indigenous American accounts of the Spanish conquests.

León-Portilla, Miguel (ed.). *Cantos y crónicas del México antiguo*, Madrid, Historia 16, 1986.

Selected texts in Spanish of Nahua cultural expression with an informative introduction to the field of study.

León-Portilla, Miguel (ed. and trans.). *Coloquios y doctrina cristiana: los diálogos de 1524*, Universidad Nacional Autónoma de México y Fundación de Investigaciones Sociales, A.C., 1986.

Spanish translation of the Nahuatl text of the *Coloquios*; includes Sahagún's Spanish version and facsimile of the original manuscript.

Lienhard, Martin. *La voz y su huella*, Havana, Casa de las Américas, 1990.

The most comprehensive recent treatment of oral and written traditions in Latin America from the pre-Columbian through the colonial and contemporary periods.

Testimonios, cartas y manifiestos indígenas, Caracas, Biblioteca Ayacucho, 1992.

A major compilation of examples of written, dictated or spoken texts that form part of the emerging *corpus* of indigenous American textuality.

Liss, Peggy K. *Mexico under Spain, 1521–1556: Society and the origins of nationality*, University of Chicago Press, 1975.

Spanish ideologies of colonialism in New Spain and the origins of Mexican identity.

Lockhart, James. *The Nahuas after the Conquest*, Stanford University Press, 1992.

A monumental social and cultural history of the Indians of central Mexico from the sixteenth to the eighteenth century, based heavily on indigenous-language sources.

Lockhart, James, and Stuart B. Schwartz. *Early Latin America. A history of colonial Spanish America and Brazil*, Cambridge University Press, 1983.

López-Baralt, Mercedes. *El mito taíno: raíz y proyecciones en la Amazonía continental*, Río Piedras, Puerto Rico, Huracán, 1977.

Taino mythology collected by Pané and its relationship to Arawak traditions of the Amazonian region.

Icono y conquista: la Crónica de Indias ilustrada como texto cultural, Madrid, Hiperión, 1988.

A semiotic study of the iconographic text of the *Nueva corónica y buen gobierno*.

MacCormack, Sabine. *Religion in the Andes: Vision and imagination in early colonial Peru*, Princeton, Princeton University, 1991.

A monumental study of sixteenth- and seventeenth-century European theorizing and Andean thinking about religion and religious conversion in the Andes.

Mace, Carroll Edward. *Two Spanish-Quiché Dance-dramas of Rabinal*, Tulane Studies in Romance Languages and Literatures, 3, New Orleans, Tulane University, 1970.

Quiché and Spanish versions of two contemporary dance-dramas with an introduction emphasizing pre-Columbian and colonial antecedents.

Mannheim, Bruce. *The language of the Inka since the European invasion*, Austin, University of Texas Press, 1991.

The first synthetic history of the Quechua language and the social and political forces that have influenced it; indispensable for placing literary and written documents in social and chronological context.

Martín, Luis. *The Intellectual Conquest of Peru: The Jesuit College of San Pablo, 1568–1767*, New York, Fordham University, 1968.

The first Jesuit foundation in Spanish America and its activity in colonial Peru.

Martínez, José Luis. *Nezahualcóyotl: vida y obra*, Mexico, Fondo de Cultura Económica, 1972.

The life and work of the pre-Columbian Acolhua lord and poet Nezahualcóyotl; helpful for studying Alva Ixtlilxochitl.

Mediz Bollo, Antonio (ed.). *Libro de Chilam Balam de Chumayel*, Biblioteca del Estudiante Universitario, 21, 4th edn., Universidad Nacional Autónoma de México, 1979.

Reprint of 1941 edition of the Spanish translation of the Chumayel text.

Meneses, Teodoro L. (ed. and trans.). *Teatro quechua colonial: antología*, Lima, Ediciones Edubanco, 1983.

443

Anthology of colonial Quechua drama, including the *Tragedia del fin de Atahualpa*.

Monterde, Francisco. *Teatro indígena prehispánico (Rabinal Achi)*, Biblioteca del Estudiante Universitario, 71, Universidad Nacional Autónoma de México, 1955.
A Spanish translation of the *Rabinal Achi*.

Muñoz Camargo, Diego. *Historia de Tlaxcala*, ed. Germán Vázquez Chamorro, Madrid, Historia-16, 1987.

Ocaranza, Fernando. *Capítulos de la historia franciscana*, 2 vols., Mexico, 1933–1934.
El imperial colegio de indios de la Santa Cruz de Santiago Tlaltelolco, Mexico, 1934.
History and documents concerning the Colegio.

Ong, Walter J. *Orality and Literacy: The technologizing of the word*, London and New York, Methuen, 1982.
Impact of writing and print culture on traditional thought and expression in the West.

Ortiz, Fernando. *Contrapunteo cubano del tabaco y el azúcar* [1940], Caracas, Biblioteca Ayacucho, 1978.
Introduction of the concept of transculturation.

Ortiz Rescaniere, Alejandro. *De Adaneva a Inkarrí (una visión indígena del Perú)*, Lima, Retablo de Papel, 1973.

Ossio, Juan M. *Ideología mesiánica del mundo andino*, Lima, Ignacio Prado Pastor, 1973.
Essays on native Andean spiritual beliefs and ideologies.

Pané, Fray Ramón. *Relación acerca de las antigüedades de los indios*, ed. José Juan Arrom, 8th. edn., Mexico, Siglo Veintiuno Editores, 1988.
Revised and expanded version of 1974 edition; includes appendices on the Tainos.

Pease, Franklin G. Y. *El Dios creador andino*, Lima, Mosca Azul, 1973.
Andean religion approached through the concept of the creator god, from pre-Columbian Viracocha to Inkarrí of colonial and contemporary times.

Porras Barrenechea, Raúl. *Los cronistas del Perú (1528–1650) y otros ensayos*, ed. Franklin Pease G. Y., Lima, Banco del Crédito del Perú, 1986.
Classic study of historiography on the Andes and the Spanish conquest of its peoples; includes the 1948 monograph on Guaman Poma.

Pupo-Walker, Enrique. *Historia, creación y profecía en los textos del Inca Garcilaso de la Vega*, Madrid, José Porrúa Turanzas, 1982.
Valuable reflections on *La Florida del Inca*.

Quiroga, Pedro de. *Coloquios de la verdad* [1563], ed. Julián Zarco Cuevas, Seville, Tip. Zarzuela, 1922.
Dialogues on the hardships of colonization on the colonized, written by a Spanish priest.

Ravicz, Marilyn Ekdahl (ed.). *Early Colonial Religious Drama in Mexico: From Tzompantli to Golgotha*, Washington, Catholic University of America Press, 1970.
English translations of colonial religious dramas in Nahuatl with a general introduction to the topic.

Recinos, Adrián (ed. and trans.). *Popol Vuh: Las antiguas historias del Quiché*, Mexico and Buenos Aires, Fondo de Cultura Económica, 1947.

Memorial de Sololá. Título de los señores de Totonicapán, tr. Dionisio José Chonay, Mexico and Buenos Aires, Fondo de Cultura Económica, 1950.

Crónicas indígenas de Guatemala, Guatemala, Editorial Universitaria, 1957.

Spanish translations of *títulos* and indigenous chronicles of the highland Maya.

Recinos, Adrián, and Delia Goetz (trans.). *The Annals of the Cakchiquels*, Norman, University of Oklahoma, 1953.

Ricard, Robert. *The Spiritual Conquest of Mexico*, tr. Leslie Byrd Simpson, Berkeley and Los Angeles, University of California, 1966.

Classic study of missionary methods of Mendicant friars from 1523 to 1572, based on missionary outlook.

Rivet, Paul, and Georges de Créqui-Monfort. *Bibliographie des langues aymará et kicua*, vol. 1, Paris, Institut d'Ethnologie, 1951.

Fundamental inventory of Quechua-language writings of the colonial period.

Roys, Ralph L. (tr. and ed.). *The Book of Chilam Balam of Chumayel*, Washington, Carnegie Institution, 1933.

Critical translation of the most famous of the *Books of Chilam Balam*. A second edition was published by the University of Oklahoma (1967).

Sahagún, Fr. Bernardino de. *Florentine Codex: Book 12: The conquest of Mexico*, no. 14, part XIII, ed. Arthur J. O. Anderson and Charles E. Dibble, 2nd. edn., Santa Fe, School of American Research and University of Utah, 1975.

Aztec version of the conquest of Mexico.

Florentine Codex: General history of the things of New Spain, tr. and ed. Arthur J. O. Anderson and Charles E. Dibble, Monographs of the School of American Research, 14, Santa Fe, School of American Research and University of Utah, 1982.

The revised, authoritative edition, in English translation, of the *Historia general de las cosas de Nueva España*.

Salomon, Frank. *Native Lords of Quito in the Age of the Incas: the political economy of North Andean chiefdoms*, Cambridge University Press, 1986.

Political and economic relations of northern Andean societies before the Spanish invasion. Useful preface on native and European chronicle traditions.

Salomon, Frank and George L. Urioste. *The Huarochirí Manuscript: A testament of ancient and colonial Andean religion*, Austin, University of Texas Press, 1991.

A landmark English–Quechua edition of the Huarochirí myths and tales, revealing the Andean cultural landscape and its deeper assumptions.

Scharlau, Birgit (ed.). *Bild-Wort-Schrift*, Tübingen, G. Narr-Verlag, 1989.

Image/word/writing: essays on modes of native American verbal and pictorial communication in pre-conquest and colonial times.

Scharlau, Birgit, and Mark Münzel. *Qellqay. Mündliche Kultur und Schrifttradition bei Indianern Lateinamerikas*, Frankfurt, Campus-Verlag, 1986.

Oral traditions transcribed in colonial times and their relation to traditional and pre-conquest forms of record-keeping.

Schroeder, Susan. *Chimalpahin and the kingdoms of Chalco*, Tucson, University of Arizona Press, 1991.

An important study of the Nahuatl-language chronicler and the mentality of the Nahuas in the early colonial period.

Spalding, Karen. *Huarochiri: An Andean society under Inca and Spanish Rule*, Stanford University, 1984.

Changes in Andean society from pre-Inca times to the late eighteenth century in the province of Huarochirí.

Stern, Steve J. *Peru's Indian Peoples and the Challenge of Spanish Conquest: Huamanga to 1640*, Madison, University of Wisconsin, 1982.

The creation of colonial society in Huamanga and the changes in the labor system as a consequence of native resistance.

Street, Brian V. *Literacy in Theory and Practice*, Cambridge University Press, 1984.

Szemiński, Jan. *Un Kuraca, un dios y una historia (Relación de antigüedades de este reyno del Pirú por don Juan de Santa Cruz Pachacuti Yamqui Salca Mayhua)*, Serie monográfica de antropología social e historia, 2, Jujuy, Argentina, Universidad de Buenos Aires, 1987.

Andean thought in its colonial historical circumstances, in the writings of Pachacuti Yamqui.

Taylor, Gerald (ed. and trans.). *Ritos y tradiciones de Huarochirí del siglo XVII*, Lima, Instituto de Estudios Peruanos and Instituto Francés de Estudios Andinos, 1987.

Translation into Spanish of the Huarochirí manuscript with biographical study of Avila by Antonio Acosta.

Tedlock, Barbara. *Time and the Highland Maya*, Albuquerque, University of New Mexico, 1982.

An ethnographic study of the concepts of Quiché time based on documentary sources and personal apprenticeship to a Quiché diviner.

Tedlock, Dennis. *The Spoken Word and the Work of Interpretation*, Philadelphia, University of Pennsylvania, 1983.

Theoretical questions and interpretative problems pertinent to orality and oral poetics.

Tedlock, Dennis (ed. and trans.). *Popol Vuh, A Mayan Book of Myth and History*, New York, Simon & Schuster, 1985.

Translation and commentary on "The Mayan Book of the Dawn of Life," utilizing knowledge of contemporary Quiché culture.

Titu Cussi Yupanqui, Diego de Castro. *Ynstrucción del Ynga don Diego de Castro Titu Cussi Yupanqui...*, ed. Luis Millones Santa Gadea, Lima, El Virrey, 1985.

Todorov, Tzvetan. *The Conquest of America: The question of the other*, tr. Richard Howard, New York, Harper Colophon, 1985.

An essay on communication and conquest and sixteenth-century European (Spanish) attempts to understand alterity.

Urioste, George (tr.). *Hijos de Pariya Qaqa: la tradición oral de Waru Chiri*, Latin American Series, 6, Syracuse University, Maxwell School of Citizenship and Public Affairs, 1983.

Quechua transcription and Spanish translation of the Huarochirí manuscript.

Vega, El Inca Garcilaso de la. *Comentarios reales de los Incas, primera y segunda partes* [1609, 1617], in *Obras completas del Inca Garcilaso de la Vega, II–IV*, ed. Carmelo Sáenz de Santa María, Biblioteca de Autores Españoles, 133–5, Madrid, Atlas, 1963–1965.

Royal Commentaries of the Incas and General History of Peru, tr. Harold V. Livermore, 2 vols., Austin, University of Texas Press, 1966.

Volume 1

Wachtel, Nathan. *Sociedad e ideología: ensayos de historia y antropología andinas*, Lima, Instituto de Estudios Andinos, 1973.

Includes a comparative essay on El Inca Garcilaso de la Vega and Felipe Guaman Poma de Ayala.

The Vision of the Vanquished: The Spanish conquest of Peru through Indian eyes, 1530–70 [1971], tr. Ben and Siân Reynolds, New York, Harper & Row, 1977.

Ethnohistorical study of the trauma of conquest, and resistance to the processes of acculturation in the Andes.

Wolf, Eric. *Sons of the Shaking Earth: The people of Mexico and Guatemala – their land, history, and culture*, University of Chicago, 1959.

A classic synthesis of Mesoamerican peoples and culture.

Zamora, Margarita. *Language, Authority, and Indigenous History in the Comentarios reales de los incas*, Cambridge University Press, 1988.

Language as rhetorical strategy and aspect of the process of cultural integration in the first part of the *Comentarios reales*.

Shorter pieces

Acosta, Antonio. "Estudio biográfico sobre Francisco de Avila," in Taylor (ed. and trans.), *Ritos y tradiciones de Huarochirí del siglo XVII*, Lima, Instituto de Estudios Peruanos e Instituto Francés de Estudios Andinos, 1987, 553–616.

Avila's life and relations with the Huarochiri community.

Adorno, Rolena. "La *ciudad letrada* y los discursos coloniales," *Hispamérica*, 48 (1987), 3–24.

Morisco and Andean protests against cultural suppression in Spain and the viceroyalty of Peru.

"Nuevas perspectivas en los estudios literarios coloniales hispanoamericanos," *Revista de Crítica Literaria Latinoamericana*, 28 (1988), 11–28.

Examination of new trends in colonial literary studies.

Albó, Xavier. "Jesuitas y culturas indígenas, Perú 1568–1606: Su actitud, métodos y criterios de aculturación," *América Indígena*, 36:3,4 (1966), 249–308, 395–445.

Jesuit missionary activity, and responses by colonized natives.

Ballesteros Gaibrois, Manuel, "Relación entre fray Martín de Murúa y Felipe Guaman Poma de Ayala" in Roswith Hartman and Udo Oberem (eds.), *Estudios americanistas, 1: libro jubilar en homenaje a Hermann Trimborn*, 2 vols., Collectanea Instituti Anthropos, 20, St. Augustin, Hans Yolker und Kulturen, Anthropos Institut, 1978–1979, I, 39–47.

"Dos cronistas paralelos: Huaman Poma y Martín de Murúa (Confrontación de las series reales gráficas)," *Anales de Literatura Hispanoamericana*, 9:10(1981), 15–66.

Barrera Vázquez, Alfredo, and Sylvanus Griswold Morley (eds. and trans.). "The Maya chronicles" in *Contributions to American Anthropology and History*, Carnegie Institution of Washington, 1949, 1–85.

Critical study and English translation of Maya chronicles in the Books of Chilam Balam of Mani, Tizimin, and Chumayel.

Bode, Barbara. "The Dance of the Conquest of Guatemala" in B. Bode (ed.), *The Native Theatre in Middle America*, Middle American Research Institute Publica-

447

tion, 27, New Orleans, Tulane University, 1961, 204–92.

Detailed study of the Dance of the Conquest of Guatemala with Spanish text, musical score, and census of existing manuscripts.

Brotherston, Gordon, "Continuity in Maya writing: new readings of two passages in the *Book of Chilam Balam of Chumayel*" in Norman Hammond and Gordon R. Wiley (eds.), *Maya Archaeology and Ethnohistory*, Austin, University of Texas Press, 1979, 241–58.

An analysis of the survival of Maya traditions despite successive invasions of foreigners.

Edmonson, Munro S. "Quiché literature" in Edmonson (ed.), *Supplement to the Handbook of Middle American Indians*, vol. III: *Literatures*, gen. ed. V. R. Bricker, Austin, University of Texas Press, 1985, 107–32.

A survey of Quiché cultural production organized according to genre and century.

Edmonson, Munro S., and Victoria R. Bricker. "Yucatecan Mayan literature" in Edmonson (ed.), *Supplement*, vol. III (see preceding entry), 44–63.

Analysis of structures and genres of Yucatec Maya written traditions.

Farfán, José María Benigno "Poesía folklórica quechua," *Revista del Instituto de Antropología* (Tucumán), 2 (1942), 531–625.

Gibson, Charles. "The Aztec aristocracy in colonial Mexico," *Comparative Studies in Society and History*, 2 (1959–1960), 169–96.

Ranks and roles of native aristocracy in colonial Mexico.

"A survey of Middle American prose manuscripts in the native historical tradition" in Cline *et al.* (eds.), *Guide to Ethnohistorical Sources, Part Four. Handbook of Middle American Indians*, vol. XV, (see above), 311–21.

Gibson, Charles, and John B. Glass, "A census of Middle American prose manuscripts in the native historical tradition" in Cline *et al.* (eds.), *Guide*, vol. XV (see above), 322–400.

Indispensable census of Mesoamerican historical writings.

Glass, John B. "Annotated references" in Cline *et al.* (eds.), *Guide*, vol. XV (see preceding entry), 537–724.

Annotated listing of the works cited in Cline, Gibson, and Nicholson (eds.), *Guide, Part Three* and *Guide, Part Four* (see above). All pertinent editions and translations through 1968–1969.

González Echevarría, Roberto. "José Arrom, autor de la *Relación acerca de las antigüedades de los indios* (picaresca e historia)" in his *Relecturas: estudios de literatura cubana*, Caracas, Monte Avila, 1976, 17–35.

Valuable reflection on writing and colonialism.

Harrison, Regina. "Modes of discourse: the *Relación de antigüedades deste reyno del Pirú* by Joan de Santacruz Pachacuti Yamqui Salcamaygua" in Adorno (ed.), *From Oral to Written Expression*, (see above) 65–99.

Language patterns in the ritual Quechua discourses recorded by Santacruz Pachacuti.

Imbelloni, José. "La tradición peruana de las cuatro edades del mundo en una obra rarísima impresa en Lima en el año 1630," *Anales de Arqueología y Etnología*, 5 (1994), 55–94. Comparison of historical traditions in Pachacuti Yamqui, Guaman Poma, and Spanish ecclesiastical writers.

Jiménez Moreno, Wigberto. "Síntesis de la historia precolonial del valle de México," *Revista Mexicana de Estudios Antropológicos*, 15, primera parte (1954–1955), 219–36.

Summary of the ethnic histories of Central Mexico for pre-Conquest times.

"La historiografía tetzcocana y sus problemas," *Revista Mexicana de Estudios Antropológicos*, 18 (1962), 81–5.

Prehistoric and colonial periodization of historiography on Texcoco.

Klor de Alva, J. Jorge. "Spiritual conflict and accommodation in New Spain: toward a typology of Aztec responses to Christianity" in George A. Collier, Renato I. Rosaldo, and John D. Wirth (eds.), *The Inca and Aztec States (1400–1800): Anthropology and history*, New York, Academic Press, 1982, 345–66.

Klor de Alva, J. Jorge (trans.). "The Aztec–Spanish dialogues (1524)," *Alcheringa*, 4:2 (1980), 52–193.

English translation of the Nahuatl text of the *Libro de los coloquios*.

Kubler, George. "The Quechua in the colonial world" in *Handbook of South American Indians*, vol. II: *Andean Civilizations*, Washington, Smithsonian Institution, 1946; rpt. New York, Cooper Square Publishers, 1963, 331–410.

Basic reference work on cultural structure and change in Andean society under Spanish colonial rule.

León-Portilla, Miguel. "Testimonios nahuas sobre la conquista espiritual," *Estudios de Cultura Nahuatl*, 11 (1974), 11–36.

Includes the study of *nepantlism*.

"Nahuatl literature" in Edmonson (ed.), *Supplement*, (see above), 7–43.

Survey of written traditions in Nahuatl and pre-Columbian survivals in colonial productions.

Leinhard, Martin. "La crónica mestiza en México y el Perú hasta 1620: apuntes para su estudio histórico-literario," *Revista de Crítica Literaria Latinoamericana*, 9 (1983), 105–15.

Hypotheses about historiographic production by native and mestizo writers.

"La épica incaica en tres textos coloniales (Juan de Betanzos, Titu Cussi Yupanqui, el Ollantay), *Lexis*, 9:1 (1985), 61–85.

López-Baralt, Luce. "Crónica de la destrucción de un mundo: la literatura aljamiado-morisca," *Bulletin Hispanique*, 82 (1980), 16–58.

Morisco written cultural traditions in Spain during the sixteenth century.

MacCormack, Sabine. "Pachacuti: miracles, punishments, and Last Judgment. Visionary past and prophetic future in early colonial Peru," *American Historical Review*, 93 (1988), 960–1006.

Andeans' persistence in interpreting the world according to their own dynamic cultural experience.

"Atahualpa y el libro," *Revista de Indias*, 48:184 (1988), 693–714.

The clash between oral and literate cultures in the historiography on the confrontation of the Inca prince with the written word; English version: "Atahualpa and the book," *Dispositio*, 14:36–8 (1989), 141–68.

Mannheim, Bruce. "*Una nación acorralada*: Southern Peruvian Quechua language planning and politics in historical perspective," *Language and Society*, 13:3 (1984), 291–309.

History of colonial linguistic policy in Peru.

"On the sibilants of colonial southern Peruvian Quechua," *International Journal of American Linguistics*, 54:2 (1988), 168–208.

    Includes a survey of colonial-period Quechua texts.

Mignolo, Walter D. "La historia de la escritura y la escritura de la historia" in Merlin H. Forster and Julio Ortega (eds.), *De la crónica a la nueva narrativa mexicana: coloquio sobre literatura mexicana*, Oaxaca, Mexico, Oasis, 1986, 13–28.

    How sixteenth-century historians understood the writing of history, with a discussion of León-Portilla's *Toltecayotl* (1980, see above).

"La lengua, la letra, el territorio (o la crisis de los estudios literarios coloniales)," *Dispositio*, 10 (1986), 137–61.

    Critique of received notions about colonial literature and current scholarly trends.

"Anahuac y sus otros: la cuestión de la letra en el Nuevo Mundo," *Revista de Crítica Literaria Latinoamericana*, 28 (1988), 29–53.

    Theoretical formulation for the study of written, oral, and mixed written/oral cultural productions of the early colonial period.

Muñoz Camargo, Diego. "Descripción de la ciudad y provincia de Tlaxcala" in René Acuña (ed.), *Relaciones geográficas del siglo XVI: Tlaxcala, t.IV*, Universidad Nacional Autónoma de México, 1984.

Pachacuti Yamqui Salcamayhua, Joan de Santacruz. "Relación de antigüedades deste reyno del Pirú" in Francisco Esteve Barba (ed.), *Crónicas peruanas de interés indígena*, Biblioteca de Autores Españoles, 209, Madrid, Atlas, 1968, 281–319.

Pease, Franklin G. Y. "Introducción" in Felipe Guamán Poma de Ayala, *Nueva corónica y buen gobierno*, ed. Franklin Pease G. Y., Caracas, Biblioteca Ayacucho, 1980, ix–lxix.

    Comprehensive introduction to Guaman Poma, his world, and his work.

Pomar, Juan Bautista. "Relación de Tezcoco" in *Nueva colección de documentos para la historia de México*, ed. Joaquín García Icazbalceta, 5 vols., Mexico, Imprenta de Francisco Díaz de León, 1886–1892, III, 1–69.

    A subsequent edition appears in Garibay (ed. and trans.), *Poesía náhuatl* (see above), 149–219.

"Relación de la ciudad y provincia de Tezcoco" in René Acuña (ed.), *Relaciones geográficas del siglo* XVI: *México*, t. III, Universidad Nacional Autónoma de México, 1986.

Rowe, John Howland. "Inca culture at the time of the Spanish Conquest" in *Handbook of South American Indians,* vol. II: *Andean Civilizations,* ed. Julian H. Steward, Washington, Smithsonian Institution, 1946; rpt. New York, Cooper Square Publishers. 183–330.

    Basic study and ethnographic description of Inca culture based on sixteenth-century sources.

"The Incas under Spanish colonial institutions," *Hispanic American Historical Review*, 37 (1957), 155–99.

    Survey of Spanish colonial institutions which most directly affected the natives of the Andes.

Roys, Ralph L. "Guide to the Codex Pérez," *Contributions to American Anthropology and History*, Washington, Carnegie Institution, 1949.

"The prophecies of the Maya Tuns or Years in the Books of Chilam Balam of

Tizimin and Maní," *Contributions to American Anthropology and History*, Washington, Carnegie Institution, 1949.

Roys, Ralph L. (ed. and trans.) "The Maya Katun prophecies of the Books of Chilam Balam, Series 1," *Contributions to American Anthropology and History*, Washington, Carnegie Institution, 1960.

Study and translation of the prophetic literature in the Yucatec Maya language and European script.

Salomon, Frank. "Chronicles of the impossible: notes on three Peruvian indigenous chroniclers" in Adorno (ed.), *From Oral to Written Expression* (see above), 9–39.

The cultural complexities of colonial native Andean writers.

Scharlau, Birgit. "Abhangigkeit und Autonomie: die Sprachreflexionen des Inca Garcilaso de la Vega" in Hans-Josef Niederehe (ed.), *Akten des Deutschen Hispanistentages Wolfenbüttel, 28.2. – 1.3.1985*, Hamburg, Helmut Buske, 1986, 235–53.

El Inca Garcilaso's ideas on language and their relationship to linguistic traditions of sixteenth- and seventeenth-century Spain.

"Mündliche überlieferung-Schriftlich gefasst: zur 'Indianischen Historiographie' im kolonialen Peru," *Komparatistische Hefte*, 15–16 (1987), 135–45.

The oral traditions "put into writing" in the historiography of colonial Peru.

"Escrituras en contacto: el caso del México colonial" in *Actes du XVIIIème Congrès International de Linguistique et Philologie Romanes*, Tübingen, Niemeyer, 1989.

The transition from pictographic to alphabetic writing in early colonial Mexico.

Schroeder, Susan. "Chimalpahin's view of Spanish ecclesiastics in colonial Mexico" in Susan E. Ramírez (ed.), *Indian-Religious Relations in Colonial Spanish America*, Latin American Series, 9, Maxwell School of Citizenship and Public Affairs, Syracuse University, 1989, 21–38.

"Indigenous sociopolitical organization in Chimalpahin" in Herbert Harvey (ed.), *Land and Politics in the Valley of Mexico*, Albuquerque, University of New Mexico, 1991, 141–62.

Solano, Francisco de. "El intérprete: uno de los ejes de la aculturación," in *Terceras jornadas americanistas de la Universidad de Valladolid: estudios sobre política indigenista española en América*, Universidad de Valladolid, 1975, 265–78.

Roles of the native interpreter in colonial times.

Spalding, Karen. "The colonial Indian: past and future research perspectives," *Latin American Research Review*, 7:1 (1972), 47–76.

Issues in the study of native societies in Spanish America with emphasis on the Andean.

Szemiński, Jan. "Las generaciones del mundo según don Felipe Guamán Poma de Ayala," *Histórica*, 7:1 (1983), 69–109.

Andean concepts of creation, divinity, and time, in Guaman Poma's *Nueva corónica*.

"De la imagen de Wiraqucan según las oraciones recogidas por Joan de Santa Cruz Pachacuti Yamqui Salcamaygua," *Histórica*, 9:2 (1985), 247–64.

Analysis of ritual texts on the concept of deity in Santa Cruz Pachacuti.

Tedlock, Barbara "On a mountain in the dark: encounters with the Quiché Maya culture hero" in Gary H. Gossen (ed.), *Symbol and Meaning beyond the Closed Community: Essays in Mesoamerican ideas*, Studies on Culture and Society, 1, SUNY-Albany, Institute for Mesoamerican Studies, 1986, 125–138.

    Symbols of resistance in native dance-dramas.

Tedlock, Dennis. "Hearing a voice in an ancient text: Quiché Maya poetics in performance" in Joel Sherzer and Anthony C. Woodbury (eds.), *Native American Discourse: Poetics and rhetoric*, Cambridge University Press, 1987, 140–75.

    Analysis of a speech from the Rabinal Achi.

Vázquez, Juan Adolfo. "The field of Latin American Indian literatures," *Latin American Indian Literatures*, 1:1 (1977), 1–33.

    Bibliographic essay on pre-Columbian, colonial, and contemporary cultural traditions of Mesoamerica, South America, and the Caribbean.

The author wishes to thank Dennis Tedlock and Wayne Ruwet, and also Birgit Scharlau, Susan Schroeder, Walter Mignolo, and Osvaldo Pardo for their helpful comments.

Chapter 3: The first fifty years of Hispanic New World historiography: the Caribbean, Mexico, and Central America

Primary sources

Casas, Fray Bartolomé de las. *Brevísima relación de la destrucción de las Indias*, ed. André Saint-Lu, Madrid, Cátedra, 1987.

    The Spanish Colonie, New York, Readex Microprint Corporation, 1966. Reprint of the 1583 English version of the *Brevísima relación de la destrucción de las Indias*, based on the French translation by Jacques de Miggrode.

Columbus, Christopher. *Textos y documentos completos*, ed. Consuelo Varela, 2nd edn., Madrid, Alianza Editorial, 1984.

    Diario de a bordo, ed. Luis Arranz, Madrid, Historia 16, 1985.

    The Voyages of Christopher Columbus, tr. and ed. Cecil Jane, London, The Argonaut Press, 1930.

    Spanish texts and English versions of Columbus's journals and others' accounts of the four voyages.

    Journals and Other Documents on the Life and Voyages of Christopher Columbus, tr. and ed. Samuel Eliot Morison, New York, The Heritage Press, 1963.

    English versions of Columbus's journals, others' accounts of the voyages, plus important letters by Columbus.

    Diario of Christopher Columbus's First Voyage to America, 1492–1493, tr. Oliver Dunn and James E. Kelley, Jr., Norman, University of Oklahoma Press, 1989.

    The most recent, and bilingual, edition of Columbus's diary with a helpful concordance.

Cortés, Hernán. *Cartas de relación*, ed. Mario Hernández, Madrid, Historia 16, 1985.

    Letters from Mexico, tr. Anthony R. Pagden, New York, Grossman Publishers, 1971.

    Authoritative translation of all of Cortés's major letters, including the first.

Fernández de Oviedo, Gonzalo. *Historia general y natural de las Indias*, ed. Juan Pérez de Tudela Bueso, Biblioteca de Autores Españoles, 117, 5 vols., Madrid,

Ediciones Atlas, 1959.

Sumario de la natural historia de las Indias, ed. Manuel Ballesteros, Madrid, Historia-16, 1986.

Natural History of the West Indies, tr. and ed. Sterling A. Stoudemire, University of North Carolina Studies in the Romance Languages and Literatures, 32, Chapel Hill, University of North Carolina Press, 1959.

Translation of *Sumario de la natural historia de las Indias*, with useful annotations.

López de Gómara, Francisco. *Cortés: The life of the Conqueror by his secretary*, tr. and ed. Lesley Byrd Simpson, Berkeley, University of California Press, 1964.

An excerpted translation of the second part of the author's *Historia general de las Indias*.

Mártir de Anglería, Pedro. *Décadas del Nuevo Mundo*, ed. Luis Arocena, Buenos Aires, Bajel, 1944.

De orbe novo. The Eight Decades of Peter Martyr d'Anghera, tr. and ed. Frances Augustus MacNutt, 2 vols., New York and London, G. P. Putnam's Sons, 1912.

Núñez Cabeza de Vaca, Alvar. *Naufragios*, ed. E. Pupo-Walker, Madrid, Castalia, 1993.

Castaways, tr. Frances López-Morillas, ed. E. Pupo-Walker, Berkeley, University of California Press, 1993.

Best translation.

Rodríguez Freyle, Juan. *The Conquest of New Granada*, tr. William C. Atkinson, London, The Folio Society, 1961.

Secondary sources

(Works cited or germane to the study of early New World historiography; see the bibliographical essays at the end of Volume 1 of the *Cambridge History of Latin America* for historical sources *per se*.)

Books

Alegría Ricardo E. *Apuntes en torno a la mitología de los indios taínos de las Antillas Mayores y sus orígenes suramericanos*, Barcelona, Centro de Estudios Avanzados de Puerto Rico y el Caribe, 1978.

Contains a study of Pané's work and comparison of Taíno with South American myths.

Arrom, José Juan. *Mitología y artes prehispánicas de las Antillas*, Mexico, Siglo Veintiuno Editores, 1975.

Contains important interpretations of Taíno myths.

Esquema generacional de las letras hispanoamericanas. Ensayo de un método, 2nd. edn., Bogotá, Instituto Caro y Cuervo, 1977.

Useful scheme of Latin American historiography and literature.

Austin, J. L. *How to do things with Words*, Cambridge, Mass., Harvard University Press, 2nd. edn., 1975.

Austin's classic 1955 lectures on speech-act theory.

Bataillon, Marcel. *Erasmo y España. Estudios sobre la historia espiritual del siglo XVI*,

tr. Antonio Alatorre, 2nd. edn., Mexico, Fondo de Cultura Económica, 1966.
    Authoritative study of the influence of Erasmus in Spain.
Boorstin, Daniel J. *The Discoverers*, New York, Random House, 1985.
    Provides excellent background information on Columbus's voyages and
    thought.
Carbia, Rómulo D. *La crónica oficial de las Indias Occidentales*, Ediciones Buenos
    Aires, 1940.
    Study of the official chronicle and chronicler in the New World.
Carpentier, Alejo. *El arpa y la sombra*, Mexico, Siglo Veintiuno Editores, 1979.
    Trenchant historical novel on Columbus's life and writings.
Casas, Bartolomé de las. *Historia de las Indias*, ed. Agustín Millares Carlo, 3 vols.,
    Mexico, Fondo de Cultura Económica, 1951.
    Las Casas's global history of the Indies, with a preliminary study by Lewis
    Hanke.
Curtius, Ernst Robert. *European Literature and the Latin Middle Ages*, tr. Willard R.
    Trask, Bollingen Series, Princeton University Press, 1973.
    Fundamental source on rhetorical forms and topics.
Díaz del Castillo, Bernal. *Historia verdadera de la conquista de la Nueva España*, ed.
    Miguel León-Portilla, 2 vols., Madrid, Historia 16, 1984.
    Famed version of the conquest of Mexico as recounted by a soldier of Cortés's
    infantry in a well-annotated edition.
    The Discovery and Conquest of Mexico, 1517–1521, tr. A. P. Maudley, intro. Irving
    A. Leonard, New York, Farrar, Straus, Giroux, & Cudahy, 1956.
    Excerpted translation of the *Historia verdadera*.
Elliott, J. H. *The Old World and the New: 1492–1650*, Cambridge University Press,
    1970.
    Crucial study of the New World's impact on the Old.
Esteve Barba, Francisco. *Historiografía indiane*, Madrid, Gredos, 1964.
    Overview of early New World historiography.
Feuter, Eduard. *Historia de la historiografía moderna*, tr. Ana Maria Ripullone,
    Buenos Aires, Nova, 1953.
    Contains a survey and incisive discussions of Spanish and New World
    historiography.
Friede, Juane, and Benjamin Keen (eds.). *Bartolomé de las Casas in History: Toward
    an understanding of the man and his work*, Dekalb, Northern Illinois University
    Press, 1971.
    See especially article by Venancio D. Carro on the Spanish theological–
    juridical renaissance and its relationship to Las Casas's thought.
Gerbi, Antonello. *Nature in the New World: From Christopher Columbus to Gonzalo
    Fernández de Oviedo*, tr. Jeremy Moyle, Pittsburgh University Press, 1985.
    The most extensive studies of Mártir and Oviedo available in English.
Goic, Cedomil (ed.). *Historia y crítica de la literatura hispanoamericana*, vol. 1 *Epoca
    colonial*, Páginas de Filología, Barcelona, Editorial Crítica, Grupo Grijalbo,
    1988.
    Compilation of significant previously published articles on colonial themes
    and authors, with excellent bibliographical information.
Hanke, Lewis. *Bartolomé de las Casas: An interpretation of his life and writing*, The

Hague, Malrtinus Nijhoff, 1951.

A comprehensive study by the author of many worthy works on Las Casas.

Henríquez Ureña, Pedro. *Literary Currents in Hispanic America*, Cambridge, Mass., Harvard University Press, 1949.

Important analysis of the emergence of a Latin American culture, beginning with Columbus.

Hogden, Margaret T. *Early Anthropology in the Sixteenth and Seventeenth Centuries*, Philadelphia, University of Pennsylvania Press, 1964.

Detailed background on early travel accounts and ethnographies.

Iñigo Madrigal, Luis (ed.). *Historia de la literatura hispanoamericana*, vol. 1, Madrid, Cátedra, 1982.

Contains fine original articles on New World culture, historiography, and historiographers.

Johnson, Julie Greer. *Women in Colonial Spanish American Literature: Literary images*, Contributions in Women's Studies, 43, Westport, Conn., Greenwood Press, 1983.

Discusses myth of Amazons in chapter on women in early historical writings.

Leonard, Irving A. *Books of the Brave*, ed. Rolena Adorno, Berkeley, University of California Press, 1992.

Classic history of the impact of novels of chivalry in the New World.

León Portilla, Miguel (ed.). *Visión de los vencidos. Relatos indígenas de la Conquista*, 10th. edn., Mexico, Universidad Nacional Autónoma de México, 1984.

See the "Relación de 1528," a text contemporaneous to our period.

López Baralt, Mercedes. *El mito taíno: raíz y proyecciones en la Amazonía continental*, Río Piedras, Puerto Rico, Huracán, 1976.

Detailed study of the myths presented by Pané and their South American antecedents.

Menéndez Pidal, Ramón. *La lengua de Colón*, Madrid, Austral, 1942.

Features essay on Colombus's linguistic background.

Morison, Samuel Eliot. *Admiral of the Ocean Sea: A life of Christopher Columbus*, 2 vols., Boston, Little, Brown & Co., 1942.

Basic source on Columbus's life and voyages with detailed information on navigation.

O'Gorman, Edmundo. *The Invention of America*, Bloomington, Indiana University Press, 1961.

Path-breaking study of how European writers invented, rather than discovered, America.

Cuatro historiadores de Indias, Mexico, Sepsetentas, 1979.

O'Gorman's important introductions to his editions of Mártir, Oviedo, Las Casas, Acosta. Pagden, Antony R. *The Fall of Natural Man: The American Indian and the origins of comparative ethnology*, Cambridge University Press, 1982.

Detailed analysis of the debates on the American Indians.

Pastor, Beatriz. *Discurso narrativo de la conquista de América*, Havana, Casa de las Américas, 1983.

Extensive, innovative treatment of colonial *lettres* from a literary and ideological perspective. A revised edition has published by Ediciones del Norte, Hanover,

N.H., 1987. (The references in this chapter are to the 1983 edition.)

Prescott, William H. *History of the Conquest of Mexico and History of the Conquest of Peru*, New York, The Modern Library, n.d.

The venerable romantic history of the conquests.

Pupo-Walker, Enrique. *La vocación literaria del pensamiento histórico en América; desarrollo de la prosa de ficción: siglos* XVI, XVII, XVIII, y XIX. Madrid, Gredos, 1982.

Innovative methodology and analyses of the emergence of fiction in Latin America from the sixteenth to the nineteenth centuries.

Rodríguez Freyle, Juan. *El carnero*, ed. Dario Achury Valenzuela, Caracas, Biblioteca Ayacucho, 1979.

History of New Granada, including proto-literary tales.

Salas, Alberto Mario. *Tres cronistas de Indias: Pedro Mártir de Anglería. Gonzalo Fernández de Oviedo. Bartolomé de las Casas*, Mexico, Fondo de Cultura Económica, 1959.

Still the fundamental source of information on the life and writings of these authors.

Sánchez Alonso, Benítez. *Historia de la historiografía española*, 3 vols., Madrid, Consejo Superior de Investigaciones Científicas, 1941–1950.

Contains a useful outline of the characteristics and texts of colonial historiography.

Todorov, Tzvetan. *The Conquest of America: The question of the other*, tr. Richard Howard, New York, Harper & Row, 1984.

Suggestive methodology and audacious analyses of texts, with a focus on the Indians.

Wilgus, Curtis A. *The Historiography of Latin America: A guide to historical writing 1500–1800*, Metuchen, N.J., Scarecrow, 1975.

A thorough annotated bibliography of major and minor texts of the period.

Articles

Alvarez López, Enrique. "La historia natural en Fernández de Oviedo," *Revista de Indias*, 17: 69–70 (1957), 541–601.

An examination of Oviedo's contributions to the natural sciences by the noted natural historian.

Avalle Arce, Juan Bautista. "Las hipérboles del padre Las Casas," *Revista de la Facultad de Humanidades*, Universidad Autónoma de San Luis Potosí, 1 (1960), 33–55.

Admirable stylistic analysis of Las Casas's *Brevísima relación*

Carreño, Antonio. "*Naufragios*, de Alvar Núñez Cabeza de Vaca: una retórica de la crónica colonial," *Revista Iberoamericana*, 140 (1987), 499–516.

Fine rhetorical analysis of the chronicles; comparison of the Picaresque and *Naufragios*.

Elliott, J. H. "The mental world of Hernán Cortés," *Transactions of the Royal Historical Society*, 17 (1967), 41–58.

An admirable examination of Cortés's intellectual underpinnings.

"Cortés Velázquez and Charles V," introduction to Anthony R. Pagden, *Letters from Mexico*, New York, Grossman Publishers, 1971, xi–lxvii.

Masterful introduction to historical background and narrative strategies of Cortés's letters.

Frankl, Victor. "Hernán Cortés y las tradición de las Siete Partidas," *Revista de Historia de América*, 53–4 (1962), 9–74.

Pioneering analysis of Cortés's *First Letter*.

González Echevarría, Roberto. "José Arrom, autor de la *Relación acerca de las antigüedades de los indios* (picaresca e historia)" in his *Relecturas: estudios de literatura cubana*, Caracas, Monte Avila, 1976, 17–35.

"Humanismo, retórica y las crónicas de la conquista" in his *Isla a su vuelo fugitiva*, Madrid, José Porrúa Turanzas, 1983, 9–25.

Invernizzi Santa Cruz, Lucia. "Naufragios e infortunios: discurso que transforma fracasos en triunfos," *Dispositio*, 11, 28–9 (1986), 99–111.

Lafaye, Jacques. "Les miracles d'Alvar Núñez Cabeza de Vaca (1527–1536)," *Bulletin Hispanique*, 64 (1962), 136–53.

Lagmanovich, David. "Los *Naufragios* de Alvar Núñez como construcción narrativa," *Kentucky Romance Quarterly*, 25:1 (1978), 27–37.

Lewis, Robert E. "Los *Naufragios* de Alvar Núñez: historia y ficción," *Revista Iberoamericana* 120–1 (1982), 681–94.

The preceding four articles are important studies of *Naufragios* from a literary perspective.

MacLeod, Murdo J. "Self-promotion: the *relaciones de méritos y servicios* and their historical and political interpretation," unpublished paper read at the "Book of the Americas" conference, Brown University, Providence, Rhole Island, June 1987.

A unique description of the form, content, and context of the *relación* in Mesoamerica.

Mignolo, Walter D. "El metatexto historiográfico y la historiografía indiana," *Modern Language Notes*, 96 (1981), 358–402.

Interesting examination of the genres of history and chronicle in New World historiography from a modern theoretical stance.

Molloy, Sylvia. "Alteridad y reconocimiento en los *Naufragios* de Alvar Núñez Cabeza de Vaca," *Nueva Revista de Filología Hispánica*, 35:2 (1987), 425–49.

A nuanced, innovative treatment of apology and autobiography in *Naufragios*.

Olschki, Leonardo. "What Columbus saw on landing in the West Indies," *Proceedings of the American Philosophical Society*, 84 (1941), 633–59.

Founding study of Columbus's reactions in the *Diario* to the natural and human aspects of the New World.

Otté, Enrique. "Aspiraciones y actividades heterogéneas de Gonzalo Fernández de Oviedo, cronista," *Revista de Indias*, 18:71 (1958), 9–61.

Commercial and political activities of Oviedo.

Palm, Erwin W. "España ante la realidad americana," *Cuadernos Americanos*, 38:2 (1948), 135–67.

Medieval influences in Columbus's *Diario*.

Pupo-Walker, Enrique. "Pesquisas para una nueva lectura de los *Naufragios* de Alvar Núñez Cabeza de Vaca," *Revista Iberoamericana*, 140 (1987), 517–39.

"Notas para la caracterización de un texto seminal: los *Naufragios* de Alvar Núñez

Cabeza de Vaca," *Nueva Revista de Filología Hispánica*, 38:1 (1990), 163–96.
    Two crucial studies that do justice to the multiple aspects of *Naufragios*.
Vásquez, Josefina Zoraida. "El indio americano y su circunstancia en la obra de
    Oviedo," *Revista de Indias*, 17:69–70 (1957), 433–519.
    Fundamental to a nuanced understanding of Oviedo's positions on the Indians.
Zamora, Margarita. "'Todas son palabras formales del Almirante': Las Casas y el
    Diario de Colón," *Hispanic Review*, 57 (1989), 25–41.
    Las Casas's interventions in Columbus's *Diario*.

Chapter 4: Historians of the conquest and colonization of the New World: 1550–1620

Primary sources

Acosta, José de. *Historia natural y moral de las Indias* [1590], ed. Edmundo
    O'Gorman, Mexico, Fondo de Cultura Económica, 1962.
Alva Ixtlilxóchitl, Fernando de. *Historia de la nación chichimeca* [1608–1625?], ed.
    Germán Vázquez Charmono, Madrid, Historia 16, 1985.
Casas, Fray Bartolomé de las. *Historia de las Indias* [1527–1562], ed. Agustín Millares
    Carlo, 3 vols., Mexico, Fondo de Cultura Económica, 1951.
    History of the Indies, tr. and ed. André M. Collard, New York, Harper Torch-
    books, 1971.
        An abridged edition.
Cieza de León, Pedro de. *El señorio de los Incas* [155?], ed. Manuel Ballesteros,
    Madrid, Historia 16, 1985.
    Historia del descubrimiento y conquista del Perú, ed. Carmelo Sáenz de Santa
    María, Madrid, Historia 16, 1986.
    La crónica del Perú [1553], ed. Manuel Ballesteros, Madrid, Historia 16, 1984.
    The Incas, tr. Harriet de Onís, ed. Victor Wolfgang von Hagen, Norman, University
    of Oklahoma Press, 1959.
        Edited translation of the *Crónica del Perú*.
Díaz de Guzmán, Ruy. *La Argentina* [1612], ed. Enrique de Gandía, Madrid, Historia
    16, 1986.
Díaz del Castillo, Bernal. *Historia verdadera de la conquista de la Nueva España*, ed.
    Miguel León-Portilla, 2 vols., Madrid, Historia 16, 1984.
    The Discovery and Conquest of Mexico, 1517–1521, tr. A. P. Maudley, intro. Irving
    A. Leonard, New York, Farrar, Straus, Giroux, & Cudahy, 1956.
        An excerpted translation of Bernal's long work.
Durán, Fray Diego de. *Historia de las Indias de Nueva España e islas de tierra firme*
    [1570–1581], ed. Angel María Garibay, 2 vols., Mexico, Porrúa, 1967.
    The Aztecs, tr. and ed. Doris Heyden and Fernando Horcasitas, New York, Orion,
    1964.
        Abridged and illustrated edition.
Guaman Poma de Ayala, Felipe. *El primer nueva corónica y buen gobierno* [1615], ed.
    John V. Murra and Rolena Adorno, 3 vols., Mexico, Siglo Veintiuno Editores,
    1980.
Herrera y Tordesillas, Antonio de. *Historia general de los hechos de los castellanos en*

las islas y tierra firme del mar océano [1601–1615], ed. and notes, Mariano Guesta Domingo, 4 vols., Universidad Complutense de Madrid, 1991.

Inés de la Cruz. "Fundación del convento de San José" [1625], ms., Archivo del Convento de San José de México. (See also Muriel, *Cultura femenina novohispana*, and Sigüenza y Góngora, *Parayso occidental*, below.)

Landa, Diego de. *Relación de las cosas de Yucatán* [1566], ed. Miguel Rivera, Madrid, Historia 16, 1985.

Yucatan Before and After the Conquest, tr. and notes William Gates, New York, Dover Publications, 1978.

Reprint of a limited 1937 edition.

López de Gómara, Francisco. *Historia general de las Indias y la conquista de México* [1552], ed. Jorge Gurria Lacroix, 2 vols., Caracas, Biblioteca Ayacucho, 1979.

Cortés: The life of the Conqueror by his secretary, tr. and ed. Lesley Byrd Simpson, Berkeley, University of California Press, 1964.

Translation of the second part of Gómara's history.

Mariana de la Encarnación. "Relación de la fundación del Convento antiguo de Santa Teresa" [1641], Perry-Castañeda Library, University of Texas, Austin, MS G 79. (See also Muriel, *Cultura femenina novohispana*, and Arenal and Schlau, *Untold Sisters*, below.)

Chronicle of the Founding of the Ancient Convento de Santa Teresa, tr. Amanda Powell, 1989; excerpts from the original Spanish, translated, in Arenal and Schlau, *Untold Sisters*, 368–74 (below).

Motolinía, Fray Toribio de. *Historia de los indios de la Nueva España* [1541?], ed. Edmundo O'Gorman, Mexico, Porrúa, 1969.

Motolinía's History of the Indians of New Spain, tr. Francis Borgia Steck, Washington, Academy of American Franciscan History, 1951.

Annotated edition with a bio-bibliographical study.

Pachacuti Yamqui, Juan de Santacruz. "Relación de antigüedades deste reino del Perú" [1613], in Francisco Esteve Barba (ed.), *Crónicas peruanas de interés indígena*, Biblioteca de Autores Españoles, 209, Madrid Atlas, 1968, 281–319.

Sahagún, Fray Bernardino de. *Historia general de las cosas de Nueva España* [1577], ed. Alfredo López Austin and Josefina García Quintana, 2 vols., Mexico, Alianza Editorial Mexicana, 1989.

Florentine Codex: General history of the things of New Spain, tr. and ed. Charles E. Dibble and Arthur J. O. Anderson, Santa Fe: School of American Research, and University of Utah, 1950–1982.

Contains the only complete paleography of the Nahuatl text.

Suárez de Peralta, Juan. *Tratado del descubrimiento de las Indias* [1589], ed. Federico Gómez de Orozco, Mexico, Secretaría de Educación Pública, 1949.

Tezozomoc, Hernando Alvarado. *Crónica mexicana* [1598], ed. Manuel Orozco y Berra, Mexico, Porrúa, 1975.

Titu Cussi Yupanqui, Diego de Castro. *Relación de la conquista del Perú* [1570], Lima, Biblioteca Universitaria, 1973.

Valdivia, Pedro de. *Cartas de relación de la conquista de Chile* [1545–1552], ed. Mario Ferreccio Podesta, Santiago, Editorial Universitaria, 1970.

Vega, Garcilaso Inca de la. *Comentarios reales de los Incas* [1609], ed. Angel Rosenblat, Buenos Aires, Emecé, 1943.

Historia general del Perú [1617], 2 vols., Buenos Aires, Peuser, 1959.

Royal Commentaries of the Incas and General History of Peru, tr. Harold V. Livermore, 2 vols., Austin, University of Texas Press, 1966.

Excellent translation of the entire work.

Zárate, Agustín de. *Historia del descubrimiento y conquista del Perú*, ed. Jan M. Kermeni, Lima, Imprenta D. Miranda, 1944.

The Discovery and Conquest of Peru, tr. J. M. Cohen, Baltimore, Penguin Books, 1968.

Includes Books I to IV of Zárate's history.

Secondary sources

Books

Adorno, Rolena (ed.). *From Oral to Written Expression: Native Andean chronicles of the early colonial period*, Latin American Series, 4, Syracuse University, Maxwell School of Citizenship and Public Affairs, 1982.

Contains articles on Guamán Poma, Pachacuti Yamqui, and Titu Cussi Yupanqui.

Guamán Poma de Ayala: Writing and resistance in colonial Peru, Austin, University of Texas Press, 1986.

Indispensable multidisciplinary treatment of the work.

Arenal, Electa, and Stacey Schlau. *Untold Sisters: Hispanic nuns in their own works*, Albuquerque, University of New Mexico Press, 1989.

Contains excerpts of *vidas* in both Spanish and English.

Arrom, José Juan. *Certidumbre de América*, Havana, Anuario Bibliográfico, 1959.

Contains a landmark study of the term "creole."

Bacigalupo, Marvyn Helen. *A Changing Perspective: Attitudes toward creole society in New Spain (1521–1610)*, London, Tamesis Books, 1981.

Well-documented analysis of the idea of the creole.

Bethell, Leslie (ed.). *Colonial Spanish America*, Cambridge University Press, 1987.

Contains key historical articles by Elliott and others.

Blanco, José Joaquín. *La literatura en la Nueva España. Conquista y Nuevo Mundo*, Mexico, Cal y Arena, 1989.

Contemporary literary history from a Mexican perspective.

Burkholder, Mark A., and Lyman Johnson. *Colonial Latin America*, Oxford University Press, 1990.

A useful and up-to-date concise history of the period.

Chang-Rodríguez, Raquel (ed.). *Prosa hispanoamericana virreinal*, Barcelona, Borrás Ediciones, 1978.

Contains articles on El Inca Garcilaso and others.

Clendinnen, Inga. *Ambivalent Conquests: Maya and Spaniard in Yucatan, 1517–1570*, Cambridge University Press, 1987.

History treating Diego de Landa's era in the peninsula.

Elliott, J. H. *Imperial Spain 1459–1716*, New York, St. Martin's Press, 1963.

Definitive study of economic, social, and intellectual history.

Elliott, J. H. (ed.). *Poder y sociedad en la España de los Austrias*, Barcelona, Editorial

Crítica, 1982.

Collects important articles reflecting historical debate on the seventeenth century.

Florescano, Enrique. *Memoria mexicana. Ensayo sobre la reconstrucción del pasado: época prehispánica – 1821*, Mexico, Mortiz, 1987.

A consideration of the changing idea of a national past.

Franco, Jean. *Plotting Women: Gender and representation in Mexico*, New York, Columbia University Press, 1989.

Contains important chapters on colonial women writers.

Goic, Cedomil (ed.). *Historia y crítica de la literatura hispanoamericana: época colonial*, Barcelona, Editorial Crítica, 1988.

Contains a section of articles on El Inca Garcilaso.

Gonzalbo Aizpuru, Pilar. *Las mujeres en la Nueva España: educación y vida cotidiana*, Mexico, El Colegio de México, 1987.

Studies women's education in Mexican convents and homes.

González Echevarría, Roberto. *Myth and Archive: A theory of Latin American narrative*, Cambridge University Press, 1990.

Crucial treatment of the legal roots of colonial narrative.

Israel, J. I. *Race, Class and Politics in Colonial Mexico: 1610–1670*, Oxford University Press, 1975.

Discusses the formation of mestizo, mulatto and creole groups.

Lafaye, Jacques. [1974]. *Quetzalcóatl y Guadalupe: la formación de la conciencia nacional en México*, 2nd. edn., Mexico, Fondo de Cultura Económica, 1985.

A cultural history of Mexican identity.

Quetzalcóatl and Guadalupe: the formation of Mexican National Consciousness 1531–1813, University of Chicago Press, 1974.

Lavrin, Asunción (ed.). *Sexuality and Marriage in Colonial Latin America*, Lincoln, University of Nebraska Press, 1989.

Collects articles on the colonial family structure.

Leonard, Irving A. *Books of the Brave: being an account of books and men in the Spanish Conquest and settlement of the sixteenth-century New World*, Cambridge, Mass., Harvard University Press, 1949.

Classic study of the novels of chivalry and the chronicles.

Baroque Times in Old Mexico: Seventeenth-century persons, places, and practices, Ann Arbor, University of Michigan Press, 1959.

Highly entertaining cultural history of the period.

León-Portilla, Miguel, and Angel María Garibay (eds.). *The Broken Spears: The Aztec account of the conquest of Mexico*, tr. Lysander Kemp, Boston, Beacon Press, 1962.

Aztec prose and poetry of the sixteenth century.

Maravall, José Antonio. *Culture of the Baroque: Analysis of a historical structure*, tr. Terry Cochran, Minneapolis University of Minnesota Press, 1986.

Meticulous study of seventeenth-century society in Spain.

Martín, Luis. *Daughters of the Conquistadores: Women of the viceroyalty of Peru*, Albuquerque, University of New Mexico Press, 1983.

Social history of both family and convent cultures.

Méndez, María Agueda (ed.). *Catálogo de textos marginados novohispanos. Inquisi-*

ción Siglos XVIII y XIX. Mexico, Archivo General de la Nación/El Colegio de México/Universidad Nacional Autónoma de México, 1992.
> Invaluable catalog of texts confiscated by the Inquisition in Mexico.

Muriel, Josefina. *Cultura femenina novohispana*, Mexico, Universidad Autónoma de México, 1982.
> Extensive descriptions and excerpts of women writers.

Picón-Salas, Mariano. *De la Conquista a la Independencia: tres siglos de historia cultural hispanoamericana*, Mexico, Fondo de Cultura Económica, 1944.
> Includes a seminal study of baroque literature in America.

A Cultural History of Spanish America, from Conquest to Independence, tr. Irving A. Leonard, Berkeley, University of California Press, 1962.

Pupo-Walker, Enrique. *Historia, creación y profecía en los textos del Inca Garcilaso de la Vega*, Madrid, José Porrúa Turanzas, 1982.
> Discusses El Inca Garcilaso's use of renaissance historiography.

La vocación literaria del pensamiento histórico en América; desarrollo de la prosa de ficción: siglos XVI, XVII, XVIII y XIX, Madrid, Gredos, 1982.
> Collection of essays, including discussion of Garcilaso.

Ross, Kathleen. *The Baroque Narrative of Carlos de Sigüenza y Góngora: A New World Paradise*, Cambridge University Press, 1993.
> Discusses the relevance of Sigüenza y Góngora's works to the early fiction and historiography of Spanish America.

Sigüenza y Góngora, Carlos de. *Parayso occidental*, Mexico, Juan de Ribera, 1684.
> Contains excerpts of work by Inés de la Cruz.

Todorov, Tzvetan. *The Conquest of America: The question of the other*, tr. Richard Howard, New York, Harper Colophon, 1985.
> Controversial treatment of cultural signs and conquest.

Varner, John Grier. *El Inca: The life and times of Garcilaso de la Vega*, Austin, University of Texas Press, 1968.
> An authoritative and readable biographical study.

Zamora, Margarita. *Language, Authority, and Indigenous History in the Comentarios reales de los incas*, Cambridge University Press, 1988.
> Studies the importance of philology in the *Comentarios*.

Zapata, Roger A. *Guamán Poma, indigenismo y estética de la dependencia en la cultura peruana*, Minneapolis, Institute for the Study of Ideologies and Literature, 1989.
> Analyzes Guaman Poma's text and its modern reception in Peru.

Articles

Adorno, Rolena. "Discourses on colonialism: Bernal Díaz, Las Casas and the twentieth-century reader," *Modern Language Notes*, 103:2 (March 1988), 239–58.
> Studies Bernal Díaz as an *encomendero* opposed to Las Casas.

"Arms, letters and the native historian in early colonial Mexico" in René Jara and Nicholas Spadaccini (eds.), *1492–1992: Re-discovering colonial writing*, Minneapolis, Prisma Institute, 1989, 201–24.

"The warrior and the war community: constructions of the civil order in Mexican

Conquest history," *Dispositio*, 15: 36–8 (1989), 225–46.

Two discussions of Alva Ixtlilxóchitl's work.

Beverley, John. "Barroco de estado: Góngora y el gongorismo" in his *Del Lazarillo al Sandinismo: estudios sobre la función ideológica de la literatura española e hispanoamericana*, Minneapolis, Institute for the Study of Ideologies and Literature, 1987, 77–97.

Studies the baroque era from a Marxist perspective.

Castro-Klarén, Sara. "Dancing and the sacred in the Andes: from the *Taqui-Oncoy* to 'Rasu-Niti'," *Dispositio*, 15:36–8 (1989), 169–85.

Analysis of Andean cultural responses to colonization.

Concha, Jaime. "La literatura colonial hispano-americana: problemas e hipótesis," *Neohelicon*, 4:1–2 (1976), 31–50.

Socio-cultural approach to El Inca Garcilaso and others.

Gandía, Enrique de. "Introducción" to his edition of Díaz de Guzmán, *La Argentina*, cited above, 7–48.

Provides a complete if tendentious history of the work.

González-Echevarría, Roberto. "José Arrom, autor de la *Relación acerca de las antigüedades de los indios* (picaresca e historia)" in his *Relecturas: estudios de literatura cubana*, Caracas, Monte Avila, 1976, 17–35.

Important essay on the *relación* and the picaresque.

"Humanismo, retórica y las crónicas de la conquista" in his *Isla a su vuelo fugitiva*, Madrid, José Porrúa Turanzas, 1983, 9–25.

Treats the rhetorical background of Bernal Díaz's work.

Hanke, Lewis. "Bartolomé de las Casas, historiador," preliminary study to the edition of Las Casas, *Historia de las Indias*, cited above, ix–lxxxvi.

Indispensable study of the work's sources and politics.

Lavalle, Bernard. "El Inca Garcilaso de la Vega" in Luis Iñigo Madrigal (ed.), *Historia de la literatura hispanoamericana: época colonial*, Madrid, Cátedra, 1982, 135–43.

Brief bio-bibliographical essay.

León-Portilla, Miguel. "Introducción" to his edition of Bernal Díaz del Castillo, *Historia verdadera*, cited above, vol. A, 7–58.

An excellent survey of the work and its significance.

MacCormack, Sabine. "Atahualpa and the book," *Dispositio*, 15:36–8 (1989), 141–68.

Analyzes Andean versions of the Atahualpa-Pizarro encounter.

Mariscal, Mario. "Prólogo" to his edition of Tezozomoc, *Crónica mexicana*, México: Universidad Nacional Autónoma de México, 1943, ix–xlvi.

Useful survey of the indigenous aspects of the text.

Mignolo, Walter D. "Cartas, crónicas y relaciones del descubrimiento y la conquista" in Luis Iñigo Madrigal (ed.), *Historia de la literatura hispanoamericana: época colonial*, Madrid, Cátedra, 1982, 57–116.

Suggestive typological analysis of colonial texts.

Moraña, Mabel. "Barroco y conciencia criolla en Hispanoamérica," *Revista de Crítica Literaria Latinoamericana*, 14:28 (1988), 229–51.

Discusses the problem of dependency in the *Barroco de Indias*.

Myers, Kathleen, "Autobiographical writing in Spanish American convents, 1650–1800: a bibliographical essay" in her *Word from New Spain: The spiritual autobiography of Madre María de San José (1656–1719)*, Liverpool University Press, 1993, 209–14.

    Useful discussion of work on the writing of colonial religious women.

O'Gorman, Edmundo. "Prólogo" to his edition of José de Acosta, *Historia natural*, cited above, xi–liii.

    The most complete analysis available of Acosta's text.

  "Estudio introductorio" to his edition of Alva Ixtlilxóchitl, *Obras históricas*, vol. I, Mexico, Universidad Nacional Autónoma de México, 1975, 1–257.

    Exhaustive study of the author's complete works.

Simpson, Leslie Byrd. "El siglo olvidado de México," appendix to Woodrow Borah, *El siglo de la depresión en Nueva España*, Mexico, Secretaría de Educación Pública, 1975, 141–54.

TePaske, John J., and Herbert S. Klein. "The seventeenth-century crisis in New Spain: myth or reality?" *Past and Present*, 90 (1981), 116–35.

    Controversial study of economic cycles in New Spain.

Vázquez, Germán. "Introducción" to his edition of Alva Ixtlilxóchitl, *Historia de la nación*, cited above, 7–41.

    Survey of current historical approaches to the work.

Chapter 5: Historians of the colonial period: 1620–1700

Primary sources

Avila, Francisco de. *Dioses y hombres de Huarochirí; narración quechua recogida por Francisco de Avila*, tr. José María Arguedas, Lima, Museo Nacional de Historia y el Instituto de Estudios Peruanos, 1966.

Calancha, Antonio de la. *Corónica moralizada de la provincia del orden de San Augustín Nuestro Padre*, Barcelona, P. Lacavalleria, 1638.

  Crónicas agustinas del Perú, 2 vol., Madrid, Consejo Superior de Investigaciones Científicas, 1972.

Cobo, Bernabé. *Historia del Nuevo Mundo*, Seville, E. Rasco, 1890–1895.

Fernández de Piedrahita, Lucas. *Historia general de las conquistas del Nuevo Reino de Granada*, Antwerp, J. T. Verdussen, 1688.

  Noticia historial de las conquistas del Nuevo Reino de Granada, Bogotá, Editorial Kelly, 1973.

Núñez de Pineda y Bascuñán, Francisco. *Cautiverio feliz del maestro de campo, jeneral Don Francisco Núñez de Pineda y Bascuñán, y razón individual de las guerras dilatadas del reino de Chile*, Santiago, Imprenta del Ferrocarril, 1863.

  El cautiverio feliz, ed. Angel González, Santiago, Zig-Zag, 1974.

  The Happy Captive, tr. William C. Atkinson, London, The Folio Society, 1977.

Ovalle, Alonso de. *Histórica relación del reyno de Chile*, Rome, F. Cavallo, 1646.

  Histórica relación del reino de Chile, Santiago, Instituto de Literatura Chilena, 1969.

  An Historical Relation of the Kingdom of Chile, Rome, F. Cavallo, 1649.

Rodríguez Freyle, Juan. *Conquista i descubrimiento del Nuevo reino de Granada de las Indias Occidentales del mar Océano, i fundación de la ciudad de Santa Fé*, Bogotá, Pizano & Pérez, 1859.

Volume 1

El Carnero, Bogotá, Editorial Bedout, 1973.

The Conquest of New Granada, tr. William C. Atkinson, London, The Folio Society, 1961.

Ruiz de Montoya, Antonio. *Conquista espiritual hecha por los religiosos de la Compañía de Jesús en las provincias del Paraguay, Paraná, Uruguay, y Tape*, Madrid, Imprenta del Reyno, 1639.

Conquista espiritual hecha por los religiosos de la Compañía de Jesús, Bilbao, Corazón de Jesús, 1892.

Sigüenza y Góngora, Carlos de. *Glorias de Querétaro*, Mexico, Bernardo Calderón, 1680.

Teatro de virtudes políticas que constituyen un príncipe, Mexico, Bernardo Calderón, 1680.

Parayso Occidental, plantado y cultivado en su magnífico Real Convento de Jesús María, Mexico, Juan de Ribera, 1684.

Infortunios que Alonso Ramírez natural de la ciudad de S. Juan de Puerto Rico padeció, assí en poder de Ingleses Piratas, Mexico, Bernardo Calderón, 1690.

Libra astronómica y philosófica, Mexico, Bernardo Calderón, 1690.

Mercurio volante con la noticia de la recuperación de las provincias del Nuevo México, Mexico, Bernardo Calderón, 1693.

Piedad heroyca de Don Fernando Cortés, Mexico, Librería Religiosa, 1898.

Alboroto y motín de los indios de México, ed. Irving A. Leonard, Mexico, Talleres graficos del Museo Nacional de Arqueología, Historia, y Etnografía, 1932.

The Misadventures of Alonso Ramírez, tr. Edwin H. Pleasants, Mexico, Imprenta Mexicana, 1962.

Seis obras, ed. William Bryant, Caracas, Biblioteca Ayacucho, 1984.

Simón, Pedro. *Noticias historiales de las conquistas de tierra firme en las Indias Occidentales*, Cuenca, D. de la Yglesia, 1627.

Historial de la expedición de Pedro de Ursúa al Marañón y de las aventuras de Lope de Aguirre, Lima, Sanmartí, 1942.

The Expedition of Pedro de Ursúa and Lope de Aguirre in Search of El Dorado and Omagua in 1560–1, tr. William Bollaert, New York, Burt Franklin, 1971.

Solís, Antonio de. *Historia de la conquista de México*, Madrid, Imprenta de Bernardo de Villadiego, 1684.

Historia de la conquista de México, Mexico, Porrúa, 1978.

The History of the Conquest of Mexico, London, H. Lintot, 1753.

Torres, Bernardo de. *Crónica de la provincia peruana de los ermitaños de San Augustín Nuestro Padre*, Lima, Imprenta de Julián Santos de Saldaña, 1657.

Villarroel, Gaspar de. *Gobierno eclesiástico-pacífico y unión de los dos cuchillos, pontificio y regio*, Madrid, Domingo García Morras, 1656–7.

Gobierno eclesiástico pacífico, Quito, Ariel, 1975.

Secondary sources

Books

Anadón, José. *Pineda y Bascuñán, defensor del araucano: vida y escritos de un criollo chileno del siglo XVII*, Santiago, Editorial Universitaria Seminario de Filología

Hispánica, 1977.

    Biographical study of Pineda y Bascuñán; good reference source.

Arocena, Luis. *Antonio de Solís, Cronista indiano: Estudio sobre las formas historiográficas del barroco*, Buenos Aires, Editorial Universitaria, 1963.

    Classic study of Solís and his work as *cronista mayor*.

Bethell, Leslie (ed.). *The Cambridge History of Latin America*, vol. 1: *Colonial Latin America*, Cambridge University Press, 1984.

    General study of political, social, economic, and institutional history of Latin America.

Carbia, Rómulo D. *La crónica oficial de las Indias Occidentales*, Ediciones Buenos Aires, 1940.

    Historical overview of the establishment and development of the *crónica mayor*.

Carilla, Emilio. *La literatura barroca en Hispanoamérica*, New York, Anaya, 1972.

    General overview of the Spanish American Baroque.

Casas de Faunce, María. *La novela picaresca latinoamericana*, Madrid, Editorial Planeta, 1977.

    History of picaresque genre in Latin American literature.

Chang-Rodríguez, Raquel. *Violencia y subversión en la prosa colonial hispanoamericana, siglos XVI y XVII*, Madrid, José Porrúa Turanzas, 1982.

    Valuable study of social and political dimensions of *El Carnero*, *Cautiverio feliz*, and *Infortunios de Alonso Ramírez*, among others.

Herman, Susan. *The "Conquista y descubrimiento del Nuevo Reino de Granada," Otherwise Known as "El carnero": The "Corónica," the "Historia," and the "Novela,"* diss., Yale University, 1978.

    Most complete study to date on discursive typologies in this text.

Jara, René, and Nicholas Spadaccini (eds.). *1492–1992: Re-discovering colonial writing*, Minneapolis, The Prism Institute, 1989.

    A collection of essays examining the colonial experience through a wide array of historical writings.

Leonard, Irving A. *Don Carlos de Sigüenza y Góngora: A Mexican savant of the seventeenth century*, Berkeley, University of California Press, 1929.

    First important study on Sigüenza as Mexico's principal intellectual of the late colony.

    Baroque Times in Old Mexico. Seventeenth-century persons, places, and practices, Ann Arbor, University of Michigan Press, 1959.

    Fundamental study of literary culture of baroque Mexico.

Mason, Margaret L. *Literary and Historical Aspects of Rodríguez Freile's "El carnero,"* diss., University of Kentucky, 1980.

Morales Pradilla, Próspero. *Los pecados de Inés de Hinojosa*, Bogotá, Plaza & Janés, 1986.

    Recent novel based on reported exploits in *El carnero* of Inés de Hinojosa.

Pollard, Dennis. *Rhetoric, Politics, and the King's Justice in Pineda y Bascuñán's "Cautiverio feliz,"* diss., University of Michigan, 1986.

    In-depth study of discursive typologies and political intentions within *Cautiverio feliz*.

Pupo-Walker, Enrique. *La vocación literaria del pensamiento histórico en América;*

desarrollo de la prosa de ficción: siglos XVI, XVII, XVIII, y XIX, Madrid, Gredos, 1982.

Highly original investigation of literary qualities of colonial historiography.

Ross, Kathleen. *Carlos de Sigüenza y Góngora's "Parayso Occidental": Baroque narrative in a colonial convent*, diss., Yale University, 1985.

Only complete investigation to date of one of Sigüenza's lesser-known works.

The Baroque Narrative of Carlos Sigüenza y Góngora: A New World Paradise, Cambridge University Press, 1994.

A superb study of the overall relevance of Sigüenza y Góngora's works. She focuses on the *Paraíso occidental*.

Vidal, Hernán. *Socio-historia de la literatura colonial hispanoamericana: tres lecturas orgánicas*, Minneapolis, Institute for the Study of Ideologies and Literature, 1985.

Typical example of sociological study of literature and historiography of colonial Spanish America.

Articles

Alstrum, James. "The real and the marvelous in a tale from *El Carnero*," *Kentucky Romance Quarterly*, 29 (1982), 115–24.

Examination of literary features of Juana García's episode; parallels drawn with modern writers, especially Alejo Carpentier.

Arrom, José J. "A contrafuerza de la sangre, o un 'caso ejemplar' del Perú virreinal," *Kentucky Romance Quarterly*, 23 (1976), 319–26.

Seminal study of a tale from Bernardo de Torres's *Crónica de la provincia peruana*.

"Carlos de Sigüenza y Góngora: relectura criolla de los *Infortunios de Alonso Ramírez*," *Thesaurus*, 42 (1987), 23–46.

A careful textual analysis of *Infortunios* carried out in light of extant scholarship; examines differences between historicist and rhetorical readings.

Benso, Silvia. "La técnica narrativa de Juan Rodríguez Freyle," *Thesaurus*, 32 (1977), 95–165.

Long monograph summarizing stylistic tendencies of Freyle.

Bost, David H. "From conflict to mediation: humanization of the Indian in *Cautiverio feliz*," *South Eastern Latin Americanist*, 29 (1985), 8–15.

Study of the characterization of the Indian in Pineda's work.

Burrus, E. J. "Sigüenza y Góngora's efforts for readmission into the Jesuit order," *Hispanic American Historical Review*, 33 (1953), 387–91.

Typical example of biographical scholarship on colonial figures.

Carilla, Emilio. "Literatura barroca y ámbito colonial," *Thesaurus*, 24 (1969), 417–25.

General overview of literary and artistic trends of the Baroque in Latin America.

Chang-Rodríguez, Raquel. "Apuntes sobre sociedad y literatura hispanoamericanas en el siglo XVII," *Cuadernos Americanos*, 33 (1974), 131–44.

Excellent synopsis of major authors and texts of the seventeenth century.

"El 'Prólogo al lector' de *El carnero*: guía para su lectura," *Thesaurus*, 29 (1974), 177–81.

Interpretation of the prologue as way of understanding intentions of author.

Cummins, J. S. "*Infortunios de Alonso Ramírez*: 'A just history of fact'?" *Bulletin of Hispanic Studies*, 61 (1984), 295–303.

Historicist reading of *Infortunios*.

Foster, David William. "Notes toward reading Juan Rodríguez Freyle's *El carnero*: the image of the narrator," *Revista de Estudios Colombianos*, 1 (1986), 1–15.

Focuses on the goals of the narrator as key to understanding intention of work.

Gimbernat de González, Ester. "Mapas y texto: para una estrategia del poder," *Modern Language Notes*, 95 (1980), 388–99.

A study of the text as a document of power and persuasion.

Giraldo Jaramillo, Gabriel. "Don Juan Rodríguez Freyle y *La Celestina*," *Boletín de Historia y Antigüedades*, 27 (1940), 582–6.

One of the first to examine the literary currents within *El carnero*.

González, Aníbal. "*Los infortunios de Alonso Ramírez*: picaresca e historia," *Hispanic Review*, 51 (1983), 189–204.

Fine example of contemporary critical theories applied to Spanish American colonial historiography.

González Echevarría, Roberto. "José Arróm, autor de la *Relación acerca de las antigüedades de los indios* (picaresca e historia)" in his *Relecturas: estudios de literatura cubana*, Caracas, Monte Avila, 1976, 17–35.

Crucial for understanding the literary and juridical significance of the *relación*.

Hamilton, Roland. "El Padre Bernabé Cobo y las lenguas indígenas de América," *Lexis*, 2 (1978), 91–6.

Linguistic study of Cobo's *Historia del Nuevo Mundo*.

Johnson, Julie Greer. "Picaresque elements in Carlos de Sigüenza y Góngora's *Los infortunios de Alonso Ramírez*," *Hispania*, 64 (1981), 60–7.

Comparison of *Infortunios* with *Lazarillo de Tormes* and *Guzmán de Alfarache*.

Lagmanovich, David. "Para una caracterización de *Infortunios de Alonso Ramírez*," *Sin nombre*, 2 (1974), 7–14.

Brief examination of different narrative tendencies within this work.

Leal, Luis. "El *Cautiverio feliz* y la crónica novelesca" in Raquel Chang-Rodríguez (ed.), *Prosa hispanoamericana virreinal*, Barcelona, Hispam, 1978, 113–140.

Examination of novelesque traits of *Cautiverio feliz*.

MacCormack, Sabine. "Antonio de la Calancha: un agustino del siglo XVII en el Nuevo Mundo," *Bulletin Hispanique*, 84 (1982), 60–94.

Shows influence of Augustin's *City of God* on Calancha's writings.

"'The heart has its reasons': predicaments of missionary Christianity in early colonial Peru," *Hispanic American Historical Review*, 65 (1985), 443–66.

Exhaustive treatment of different patterns of evangelism in early colonial Peru.

Martinengo, Alessandro. "La cultura literaria de Juan Rodríguez Freyle," *Thesaurus*, 19 (1964), 274–99.

Traditional source and influence study.

Ortiz, Gloria M. "Juan Rodríguez Freyle: su actitud ante la mujer en *El carnero*" in Justina Ruiz de Conde *et al.* (eds.) *Essays in Honor of Jorge Guillén on the Occasion of his 85th Year*, Cambridge, Mass., Abedul, 1978, 52–63.

Looks at Rodríguez Freyle's legendary views of women.

Pérez Blanco, Lucrecio. "Novela ilustrada y desmitificación de América," *Cuadernos americanos*, 41 (1982), 176–95.

Refutes the assertion that *Infortunios* resembles a picaresque novel; claims that the Greek novel had more influence on its literary composition.

Pupo-Walker, Enrique. "*El carnero* y una forma seminal del relato afrohispano" in Reinaldo Sánchez (ed.), *Homenaje a Lydia Cabrera*, Miami, Editorial Universal, 1978, 251–7.

Importance of Juana García to later fiction of African influence.

"La reconstrucción imaginativa del pasado en *El carnero* de Rodríguez Freyle," *Nueva Revista de Filología Hispánica*, 27 (1978), 346–58.

Brilliant analysis of literary disposition of *El Carnero* with focus on presence of *La Celestina*.

Ramos, Demetrio. "The chronicles of the early seventeenth century: how they were written," *The Americas*, 27 (July 1965), 41–53.

Historical study of the tension between historians of the Crown and priests.

Ross, Kathleen. "'*Alboroto y motín de México*': una noche triste criolla," *Hispanic Review*, 56 (1988), 181–90.

Lucid study of this somewhat neglected text; read against the horizon of sixteenth-century "classics," such as Hernán Cortés.

Sibirsky, Saúl. "Carlos de Sigüenza y Góngora (1645–1700): la transición hacia el iluminismo criollo en una figura excepcional," *Revista Iberoamericana*, 32 (Jan. – Dec. 1966), 195–207.

Useful overview of Sigüenza's main works.

Stoetzer, O. Carlos. "Historia intelectual del período colonial," *Inter-American Review of Bibliography*, 29 (1979), 171–96.

Bibliographical assessment of major periods of Latin American history; useful history of educational institutions.

Tomanek, Thomas J. "Barrenechea's *Restauración de la Imperial y conversión de almas infieles* – the first novel written in Spanish America," *Revue des Langues Vivantes*, 40, (1974), 257–68.

Only study of little-known text.

Zamora, Margarita. "Historicity and literariness: Problems in the literary criticism of Spanish American colonial texts," *Modern Language Notes*, 102 (1987), 334–46.

An important re-assessment of critical approaches to Spanish American historiography.

Chapter 6: Colonial lyric

Because the lyric in colonial Latin America is essentially part of Golden Age Spanish poetry, the basic scholarly and bibliographical works should be consulted, as well as critics such as Dámaso Alonso, R. O. Jones, Rafael Lapesa, Fernando Lázaro Carreter, Antonio Rodríguez Moñino, Elias Rivers, Arthur Terry, Bruce Wardropper, Edward M. Wilson, and others.

Modern anthologies

Chang Rodríguez, Raquel, and R. de la Campa. *Poesía hispanoamericana colonial:*

historia y antología, Madrid, Alhambra, 1985.

Convenient, if somewhat conventional anthology, with informative introductions and bibliographies.

Méndez Plancarte, Alfonso (ed.) *Poetas novohispanos. Primer siglo (1521–1621)*, notes A. Méndez Plancarte, Mexico, Universidad Nacional Autónoma de México, 1942.

Poetas novohispanos. Segundo siglo (1621–1721), Mexico, Universidad Nacional Autónoma de México, 1944.

Elegant and informative anthology by one of the most authoritative specialists in the field.

General studies

Alonso, Dámaso. "Influjo de Góngora en el siglo XVII y el XVIII: en la América española" in his *Góngora y el Polifemo*, Madrid, Gredos, 1961, 240–4.

Provides useful clarifications.

Arenal, Electa, and Stacey Schlau. *Untold Sisters: Hispanic nuns in their own works*, Albuquerque, University of New Mexico Press, 1989.

Groundbreaking and authoritative.

Arrom, José Juan. *Esquema generacional de las letras hispanoamericanas. Ensayo de un método*, 2nd. edn., Bogotá, Instituto Caro y Cuervo, 1977.

Chapters on colonial literature are best in the book.

Beverly, John. "Sobre Góngora y el gongorismo colonial," *Revista Iberoamericana*, 114–15 (1981), 33–44.

Attempt at Marxist interpretation of Colonial Baroque.

Buxó, José Pascual. *Góngora en la poesía novo-hispana*, Mexico, Universidad Nacional Autónoma de México, 1960.

Somewhat mechanical but useful tally of Gongorine figures copied by poets in New Spain.

Carilla, Emilio. *El gongorismo en América*, Facultad de Filosofía y Letras de la Universidad de Buenos Aires, 1946.

Still useful for some of its information.

Carpentier, Alejo. "Problemática de la actual novela latinoamericana" in his *Tientos y diferencias*, Mexico, Universidad Nacional Autónoma de México, 1964, 5–46.

Major statement on the baroqueness of Latin American literature.

Cheesman Jiménez, Javier. "Nota sobre Cristóbal de Arriaga Alarcón, poeta de la Academia Antártica," *Boletín del Instituto Riva-Agüero*, 1 (1951), 341–8.

Though Arriaga is a very minor poet, this article furnishes useful information about poetic activity in late sixteenth-century Lima.

Colombí-Monguió, Alicia de. "Las visiones de Petrarca en la América virreinal," *Revista Iberoamericana*, 120–1 (1982), 563–86.

On translations of Petrarch's Canzone 323 by Enrique Garcés, Diego Dávalos y Figueroa, and Juan de Guevara. Superb analysis of difference in the interpretation of *imitatio* between renaissance and baroque poets.

Durán, Manuel, and Roberto González Echevarría. *Calderón y la crítica: historia y antología*, Madrid, Gredos, 1976.

Some of the articles included are relevant to baroque poetics.

Volume 1

El Barroco en América. XVII *Congreso del Instituto Internacional de Literatura Iberoamericana*, vol. 1, Madrid, Ediciones Cultura Hispánica del Centro Iberoamericano de Cooperación, 1978.

Contains many articles on both the Colonial baroque and the contemporary Neo-Baroque, some of which are good.

Gilman, Stephen. "An introduction to the ideology of the Baroque in Spain," *Symposium*, 1 (1946), 82–107.

Crucial for history of ideas.

González Echevarría, Roberto. "El 'monstruo de una especie y otra': *La vida es sueño*, III, 2,725," *Co-Textes* (Centre d'Etudes et Recherches Sociocritiques, Université Paul Valéry, Montpellier), 3 (1982), 27–58.

On key figure in baroque poetics.

Celestina's Brood: continuities of the Baroque in Spain and Latin America, Durham, Duke University Press, 1993.

Essays on Golden Age and colonial baroque literature in Spain and Latin America.

Henríquez Ureña, Pedro. "La cultura y las letras coloniales en Santo Domingo" in Emma Susana Speratti Piñero (ed.), *Obra crítica*, prologue Jorge Luis Borges, Mexico, Fondo de Cultura Económica, 1960, 331–444.

Strong on details of early years of Spanish Empire in America.

Hesse, Everett W. "Calderón's popularity in the Spanish Indies," *Hispanic Review*, 23 (1955), 12–27.

Details on performances.

Leonard, Irving A. *Books of the Brave: being an account of books and of men in the Spanish Conquest and settlement of the sixteenth-century New World*, Cambridge, Mass., Harvard University Press, 1949.

Remains the standard work on the circulation of books in colonial Latin America.

Baroque Times in Old Mexico: Seventeenth-century persons, places, and practices, Ann Arbor, University of Michigan Press, 1959.

Unsurpassed account of poetic activity in seventeenth-century Mexico.

Lezama Lima, José. *La expresión americana*, Havana, Instituto Nacional de Cultura, 1957.

Daring and influential statements on the centrality of the Baroque in Latin American culture.

Menéndez y Pelayo, Marcelino. *Antología de poetas hispano-americanos. Publicada por la Real Academia Española*, vol. 1: *México y América Central*, Madrid, Est. Tipográfico "Sucesores de Rivadeneyra," 1893.

Still a formidable introduction, in spite of author's annoying paternalism and other prejudices.

Miró Quesada, Aurelio. *El primer virrey-poeta en América (Don Juan de Mendoza y Luna, Marqués de Montesclaros)*, Madrid, Gredos, 1962.

The Marquis was viceroy of New Spain and then of New Castille, where he was a cultural promoter and a minor poet.

Osorio Romero, Ignacio. *Floresta de gramática, poética y retórica en Nueva España (1521–1767)*, Mexico, Universidad Nacional Autónoma de México, 1980.

Bibliography of books and treatises on grammar, poetics, and rhetoric imported to New Spain or printed there.

Parker, Alexander A. *"Polyphemus and Galatea*: A study in the interpretation of a baroque poem" in Luis de Góngora, *Polyphemus and Galatea*, tr. Gilbert F. Cunningham, Austin, University of Texas Press, 1977.

Thorough and authoritative introduction to baroque poetics.

Paz, Octavio. *Los hijos del limo: del romanticismo a la vanguardia*, Barcelona, Seix Barral, 1974.

Major statement on the modern history of Spanish-language poetry.

Children of the Mire: Modern poetry from Romanticism to the Avant-Garde, tr. Rachel Phillips, Cambridge, Mass., Harvard University Press, 1974.

Picón Salas, Mariano. *De la Conquista a la Independencia: tres siglos de historia cultural hispanoamericana*, Mexico, Fondo de Cultura Económica, 1944.

Excellent account of the "Barroco de Indias," linking poetry to other arts.

A Cultural History of Spanish America. From Conquest to Independence, tr. Irving A. Leonard. Berkeley, University of California Press, 1962.

Reyes, Alfonso. "Letras de la Nueva España" in his *Obras completas*, vol. XII, Mexico, Fondo de Cultura Económica, 1983, 279–395.

Elegant and pedagogically useful.

Roggiano, Alfredo. *En este aire de América*, Mexico, Editorial Cultura, 1966.

About Gutierre de Cetina, Juan de la Cueva, and Eugenio de Salazar.

"Poesía renacentista en la Nueva España," *Revista de Crítica Literaria Latino-americana*, (Lima), 14:28 (1988), 69–83.

Revises and expands work on Eugenio de Salazar.

Ross, Kathleen. "'Alboroto y motín de México': una noche triste criolla," *Hispanic Review*, 56 (1988), 181–90.

Although focused on prose, article makes original contribution to our understanding of the transition from Renaissance to Baroque in New World literature.

Ryan, Hewson A. "Una bibliografía gongorina del siglo XVII," *Boletín de la Real Academia Española*, 33:140 (Sept. – Dec. 1953), 427–67.

Important for understanding of "gongorismo en América."

Sabat de Rivers, Georgina. *Estudios de literatura hispanoamericana: Sor Juana Inés de la Cruz y otros poetas barrocos de la colonia*, Barcelona, Promociones y Publicaciones Universitarias, S:S., 1992.

Authoritative essays on colonial poets.

Sarduy, Severo. "El barroco y el neobarroco" in *América Latina en su literatura*, ed. and intro. César Fernández Moreno, Mexico, Siglo Veintiuno Editores UNESCO, 1972, 167–84.

Influential statement on relations between modern Latin American neo-baroque literature and the Baroque.

"The Baroque and the Neobaroque" in *Latin America in Its Literature*, tr. Mary G. Berg, London, Holmes & Meier Publishers, 1980, 115–32.

Schons, Dorothy. "The influence of Góngora on Mexican literature during the seventeenth-century," *Hispanic Review* 7 (1939), 22–34.

Still one of the best pieces on the subject.

Tauro, Alberto. *Esquividad y gloria de la Academia Antártica*, Lima, Huascarán, 1948.

Valuable still for some of its information on Peruvian poetic activity at the turn from the sixteenth to the seventeenth century.

Terry, Arthur. "A note on metaphor and conceit in the Siglo de Oro," *Bulletin of Hispanic Studies*, 31 (1954), 91–7.

Superb analysis of key concepts of seventeenth-century poetics.

"The continuity of renaissance criticism: poetic theory in Spain between 1535 and 1650," *Bulletin of Hispanic Studies*, 31 (1954), 27–36.

Poetic theory from sixteenth-century proponents of *mimesis*, following Aristotle's *Poetics*, to advocates of metaphor, who follow the *Rhetoric*. Essential for Colonial Baroque.

Varela, Consuelo. "La obra poética de Hernando Colón," *Anuario de Estudios Americanos*, 40 (1983), 185–201.

Eighteen poems in Spanish and one in Latin by the Discoverer's son, with a good introduction.

Weckmann, Luis. *La herencia medieval de México*, Mexico, El Colegio de México, 1984.

Wide-ranging and rich in detail, with useful information on popular poetry.

Wilson, Edward M. "The four elements in the imagery of Calderón," *Modern Language Review*, 31 (1936), 34–47.

Classic article on the functioning of baroque imagery, indispensable for understanding poets like Matías de Bocanegra and Sor Juana Inés de la Cruz.

Romancero

Mejía Sánchez, Ernesto. *Romances y corridos nicaragüenses*, Mexico, Imprenta Universitaria, 1946.

Well-informed anthology, with excellent introduction. contains modern *romances* that hark back to the Middle Ages.

Menéndez Pidal, Ramón. *Los romances de América y otros estudios*, Buenos Aires, Espasa-Calpe Argentina, 1943.

Title essay is a classic on the subject.

Romancero colombiano. Homenaje a la memoria del Libertador Simón Bolívar en su primer centenario: 1783–1883, Bogotá, Imprenta de La Luz, 1883.

Contains *romances* signed by poets like Rafael Núñez, Teodoro Valenzuela, and Ricardo Carrasquilla, covering the sweep of Bolívar's life.

Reynolds, Winston A. *Romancero de Hernán Cortés; estudio y textos de los siglos XVI y XVII*, Madrid, Ediciones Alcalá, 1967.

The author's exhaustive research only yielded nine *romances*. Good study and anthology.

Simmons, Merle E. *The Mexican Corrido as a Source for the Interpretive Study of Modern Mexico (1870–1950)*, Bloomington, Indiana University Press, 1957.

Briefly outlines evolution of *corrido* from *romance* and then studies modern Mexico in light of the latter.

Simmons, Merle E. *A Bibliography of the Romance and Related Forms in Spanish America*, Bloomington, Indiana University Press, 1963.

The standard reference.

Cancionero peruano del siglo XVII, ed. Raquel Chang-Rodríguez, Lima, Pontificia

Universidad Católica del Perú, 1983.
Good edition of mostly ephemeral courtly poetry, with informative introduction to seventeenth-century poetry in Peru.
"Flores de baria poesía," prólogo, edición, crítica e índices de Margarita Peña, Mexico, Universidad Nacional Autónoma de México, 1980.
Excellent edition of this 1577 manuscript, with an important introduction.

Authors

ANONYMOUS

Cornejo Polar, Antonio (ed.). *Discurso en loor de la poesía. Estudio y edición*, Separata de la Revista *Letras* (Lima), 68–9 (1964).

AMARILIS

Texts

"Epístola a Belardo" in Chang-Rodríguez and de la Campa, *Poesía hispanoamericana colonial*, above, 196–204.
Good text, introduction, and some notes.

Secondary

Sabat de Rivers, Georgina. "Amarilis: innovadora peruana de la epístola horaciana," *Hispanic Review*, 58 (1990), 455–67.
Useful overview of tradition of Horatian epistle, and how Amarilis alters that tradition.

BERNARDO DE BALBUENA

Texts

La grandeza mexicana y compendio apologético en alabanza de la poesía, estudio preliminar de Luis Adolfo Domínguez, 2nd. edn., Mexico, Porrúa, 1975.
Until recently the most accessible edition, contains reliable information and text.
Grandeza mexicana, edición crítica de José Carlos González Boixo, Rome, Bulzoni Editori, 1988.
Excellent edition with up-to-date information.
Siglo de oro en las selvas de Erífile, edición, introducción y notas de José Carlos González Boixo, Xalapa, Mexico, Clásicos Mexicanos Universidad Veracruzana, 1989.
Now the standard edition.

Secondary

Entrambasaguas, Joaquín de. "Los sonetos de Bernardo de Balbuena," *Revista de Letras* (Universidad de Puerto Rico en Mayagüez), 1:4 (1969), 483–504.

Studies the eleven sonnets included in *Siglo de Oro en las selvas de Erífile*, and one that appeared in the preliminaries of a book by someone else. Persuasive on the value of Balbuena as lyric poet.

Fucilla, Joseph G. "Bernardo de Balbuena's *Siglo de Oro* and its sources," *Hispanic Review*, 15:1 (1947), 101–19.

The sources are Virgil, Petrarch, El Inca Garcilaso, Boscán, and Gálvez de Montalvo.

Horne, John van. *El Bernardo of Bernardo de Balbuena. A study of the poem with particular attention to its relation to the epics of Boiardo and Ariosto and to its significance in the Spanish Renaissance*, Urbana, University of Illinois Press, 1927.

The first, and still the best, critical edition, the source of all authoritative ones.

Bernardo de Balbuena. Biografía y crítica. Guadalajara, Imprenta Font, 1940.

Most authoritative information on Balbuena.

Rama, Angel. "Fundación del manierismo hispanoamericano por Bernardo de Balbuena," *The University of Dayton Review*, 16:2 (1983), 13–22.

Perceptive on conceits, and particularly on emblems.

Roggiano, Alfredo. "Instalación del barroco hispánico en América: Bernardo de Balbuena" in Raquel Chang – Rodríguez and Donald A. Yates (eds.), *Homage to Irving A. Leonard. Essays on Hispanic art, history and literature*, East Lansing, Michigan State University Latin American Studies Center, 1977, 61–74.

Good on context.

Rojas Garcidueñas, José. *Bernardo de Balbuena. La vida y la obra*, Mexico, Instituto de Investigaciones Estéticas, Universidad Nacional Autónoma de México, 1958.

Conventional life and works very dependent on van Horne.

GUTIERRE DE CETINA

Texts

Cetina, Gutierre de. *Sonetos y madrigales completos*, ed. Begoña López Bueno, Madrid, Cátedra, 1981.

Best edition with ample biographical and bibliographical information.

Secondary

Peña, Margarita. "Poesía de circunstancias: dos epístolas en un cancionero novohispano," *Anuario de Estudios Americanos*, 36 (1979), 503–30.

Transcription and commentary of epistles, contained in *Flores de baria poesía*, exchanged by Baltazar del Alcázar and Gutierre de Cetina. Excellent on relations of Cetina with poetic activity in New Spain.

MATÍAS DE BOCANEGRA

Text

"Canción a la vista de un desengaño" in Alfonso Méndez Plancarte (ed.), *Poetas novohispanos, Segundo siglo (1621–1721)*, Mexico, Universidad Nacional Autónoma de México, 1944, 93–101.

Secondary

Colombí-Monguió, Alicia de. "El poema del padre Matías de Bocanegra: trayectoria de una imitación," *Thesaurus*, 36 (1981), 1–21.

  Traces sources of "Canción" back through Petrarch's *Canzone delle visione* through Fray Luis, Quevedo, and Calderón.

"La 'Canción famosa a un desengaño' del Padre Juan de Arriola, S. I. (texto y contexto imitativos)," *Anuario de Letras* (Mexico), 20 (1982), 215–49.

  Imitations of Bocanegra's "Canción" in the eighteenth century.

JUAN DE LA CUEVA

Capote, Higinio. "La epístola quinta de Juan de la Cueva," *Anuario de Estudios Americanos*, 9 (1952), 597–616.

  Transcription and commentary of Cueva's epistle, written in Mexico, and containing a long description of Mexico City that could be an antecedent of Balbuena's *Grandeza mexicana*.

DIEGO DÁVALOS Y FIGUEROA

Texts

Dávalos y figueroa, Diego. *Miscelánea austral*, Lima, Antonio Ricardo, 1602.

Secondary

Cisneros, Luis Jaime. "Sobre literatura virreinal peruana (asedio a Dávalos y Figueroa)," *Anuario de Estudios Americanos* (Seville), 12 (1955), 219–52.

  Detailed account of poetic activity in Peru at the end of the sixteenth, and beginning of the seventeenth, century.

Cheesman Jiménez, Javier. "Un poeta de la Academia Antártica: Antonio Falcón de Villarroel," *Letras Peruanas. Revista de Humanidades* (Lima), 1:3 (1951), 71–2.

  Falcón de Villarroel considered founder of Academia Antártica.

Colombí-Monguió, Alicia de. *Petrarquismo peruano: Diego Dávalos y Figueroa y la poesía de la Miscelánea Austral*, London, Tamesis Books, 1985.

  The best book ever written on colonial Latin American poetry.

Lohmann Villena, Guillermo. "El licenciado Francisco Falcón (1521–1587). Vida, escritos y actuación en el Perú de un procurador de indios," *Anuario de Estudios Americanos*, 27 (1970), 131–94.

  About an uncle of Antonio Falcón de Villarroel, founder of the Academia Antártica; contains interesting information about cultural life in viceregal Peru.

Lohman Villena, Guillermo. "Enrique Garcés, descubridor del mercurio en el Perú, poeta y arbitrista," *Anuario de Estudios Americanos* (Seville), 5 (1948), 439–82.

  Well-documented and absorbing biographical article on Garcés, who, besides his metallurgical exploits, translated Petrarch and Camoens into Spanish while in Peru.

HERNANDO DOMÍNGUEZ CAMARGO

Texts

Obras, ed. Rafael Torres Quintero, estudios de Alfonso Méndez Plancarte, Joaquín
  Antonio Peñalosa, y Guillermo Hernández del Alba, Biblioteca de Publicaciones
  del Instituto Caro y Cuervo, 15, Bogotá, Instituto Caro y Cuervo, 1960.
  The standard edition.
Antología poética, prólogo, selección y notas de Eduardo Mendoza Varela, Medellín,
  Colombia, Bedout, 1969.
  Popular edition.
Obras completas, ed. Giovanni Meo Zilio, Caracas, Biblioteca Ayacucho, 1986.
  Best easily available edition.

Secondary

Carilla, Emilio. "Domínguez Camargo y su 'Romance al Arroyo de Chillo'," and "Las
  Obras completas de Domínguez Camargo" in his *Estudios de literatura hispa-
  noamericana*, Bogotá, Instituto Caro y Cuervo, 1977, 15–43.
  First essay links famous "Romance" to a passage in Góngora, second is an
  informative review of the *Obras*.
Diego, Gerardo. "La poesía de Hernando Domínguez Camargo en nuevas vísperas,"
  Thesaurus, 16:2 (1961), 281–310.
  Reminisces about his "discovery" of Domínguez Camargo in 1927, and praises
  his poetry.
Gimbernat de González, Ester. "Apeles de la re-inscripción: a propósito del *Poema
  heróico* de Hernando Domínguez Camargo," *Revista Iberoamericana*, 53:140
  (1987), 569–79.
  On the use of emblems in the *Poema* and the relationship of Domínguez
  Camargo's poetry to painting.
Loveluck, Juan. "Lectura de un texto barroco: un romance de Domínguez Camargo"
  in *El barroco en América: XVII Congreso del Instituto Internacional de Literatura
  Iberoamericana*, vol. I, Madrid, Ediciones Cultura Hispánica, 1978, 289–95.
  Gloss of the "romance," analyzing its stylistic features.

JUAN DE ESPINOSA MEDRANO, EL LUNAREJO

Texts

*Apologético en favor de Don Luis de Góngora principe de los poetas lyricos de Espana,
  contra Manvel de Faria y Sovsa, Cauallero Portugues, que dedica Al Exm. S. Don
  Lvis Mendez de Haro, Dvqve de Olivares, sv avtor el D. Ivan de Espinosa
  Medrano, Colegial Real en el insigne Seminario de S. Antonio el Magno,
  Cathedratico de Artes y Sagrada Theologia en el: Cura Rector de la Santa Iglesia*

BIBLIOGRAPHY

Cathedral de la Ciudad del Cuzco, cabeça de los Reynos del Peru en el nuevo Mundo. Año de 1662, Lima, Imprenta de Iuan de Queuedo y Zarate, 1662.
Extremely rare first edition. Copy at Yale University's Beinecke Library,
García Calderón, Ventura. "Juan de Espinosa Medrano. *Apologético en favor de D. Luis de Góngora,*" *Revue Hispanique*, 65 (1925), 397–538.
First modern edition of the *Apologético*, based on 1694 edition, with interesting introduction.
Apologético, selección, prólogo y cronología Augusto Tamayo y Vargas, Caracas, Biblioteca Ayacucho, 1982.
Best available edition. Contains other works by Espinosa Medrano.

Secondary

Cisneros, Luis Jaime. "Relectura del *Lunarejo: el 'Can del Cielo'*," *Lexis* (Pontificia Universidad Católica del Perú), 4:2 (1980), 171–7.
Corrects errata in modern editions.
Cisneros, Luis Jaime. "La polémica Faria-Espinosa Medrano: planteamiento crítico," *Lexis* (Pontificia Universidad Católica del Perú), 11:1 (1987), 1–62.
Valuable information, but the debatable conclusion is that the *Apologético* was an academic exercise in rhetoric, because it refutes only part of Faria's critique of Góngora.
Cisneros, Luis Jaime, and Pedro Guibovich Pérez, "Juan de Espinosa Medrano, un intelectual cuzqueño del seiscientos: nuevos datos biográficos," *Revista de Indias*, 48:182–3 (1988), 327–47.
Summarizes all the documentary evidence about Espinosa Medrano, and provides fresh information drawn from archives.
Giordano, Jaime. "Defensa de Góngora por un comentarista americano," *Atenea* (Revista Trimestral de Ciencias, Letras y Artes, Universidad de Concepción, Chile), año 38: 152:393 (July–Sept. 1961), 226–41.
Early piece on recent reappraisal of Espinosa Medrano.
González Echevarría, Roberto. "Poética y modernidad en Juan de Espinosa Medrano, el 'Lunarejo'," *Revista de Estudios Hispánicos* (University of Puerto Rico), Special issue *Letras coloniales*, ed. Mercedes López Baralt, año 19 (1992), 221–37.
English version in González Echevarría, *Celestina's Brood*.
Study of *Apologético* based on the first edition and recent views of the Baroque.
Howell, Susana. "Una nueva lectura del *Apologético*, de Espinosa Medrano," *Revista de Archivos Bibliotecas y Museos* (Madrid), 82:3 (July–Sept. 1979), 583–91.
Good insights into relationship of *Apologético* to modern poetics.
Hopkins, Eduardo. "Poética de Espinosa Medrano en el *Apologético en favor de D. Luis de Góngora,*" *Revista de Crítica Literaria Latinoamericana* (Lima), 4:7–8 (1977–1978), 105–18.
Interesting observations about rhetoric.
Jammes, Robert. "Juan de Espinosa Medrano et la poésie de Góngora," *Caravelle. Cahiers du Monde Hispanique et Luso-Brésilien*, 7 (1966), 127–42.
Good information on debates about Góngora, with questionable interpretation of *Apologético*.
Núñez Cáceres, Javier. "Propósito y originalidad del *Apologético* de Juan de Espinosa

478

Medrano," *Nueva Revista de Filología Hispánica* (El Colegio de México), 32:1 (1983), 170–5.

Asserts that polemical disposition of *Lunarejo*, like that of Sor Juana and Sigüenza y Góngora had the purpose of proving that Americans were not barbarians.

SOR JUANA INÉS DE LA CRUZ

Texts

El sueño, edición y prosificación e introducción y notas del Dr. Alfonso Méndez Plancarte, Mexico, Imprenta Universitaria, 1951.

Extremely useful edition, with prose version of the "Primero sueño."

Obras completas de Sor Juana Inés de la Cruz, edición, prólogo y notas de Alfonso Méndez Plancarte, Mexico and Buenos Aires, Fondo de Cultura Económica, 1952.

Still the standard edition.

Poesía, teatro y prosa, edición y prólogo de Antonio Castro Leal, Mexico, Porrúa-Colección de Escritores Mexicanos-, 1985.

Most accessible edition, without notes.

Obras completas, prólogo de Francisco Monterde, Mexico, Porrúa, 1977.

Popular edition of complete works.

Inundación castálida, edición, introducción y notas de Georgina Sabat de Rivers, Madrid, Clásicos Castalia, 1982.

The best edition, offers detailed and reliable information on the first publication of Sor Juana's poetry.

A Woman of Genius. The intellectual autobiography of Sor Juana Inés de la Cruz, tr. Margaret Sayers Peden, photographs by Gabriel North Seymour, Salisbury, Conn., Lime Rock Press, 1982.

Excellent translation of the "Respuesta a Sor Filotea."

A Sor Juana Anthology, tr. and intro. Alan S. Trueblood, foreword Octavio Paz, Cambridge, Mass., Harvard University Press, 1988.

The best English translations of Sor Juana's poetry, with a superb introduction.

Secondary

Bénassy-Berling, Marie-Cécile. *Humanisme et réligion chez Sor Juana Inés de la Cruz: la femme et la culture au XVII siècle*, Paris, Publications de La Sorbonne, 1982.

Best overall study of Sor Juana and her intellectual milieu, from a sympathetic and well-informed Catholic perspective.

Durán, Manuel. "El drama intelectual de Sor Juana y el antiintelectualismo hispánico," *Cuadernos Americanos*, 4 (July–Aug. 1963), 238–53.

Still one of the best articles on Sor Juana's intellectual dilemmas.

Gates, Eunice Joiner. "Reminiscences of Góngora in the works of Sor Juana Inés de la Cruz," *PMLA*, 54 (1939), 1041–58.

Remains an important study, from which many have profited.

Johnson, Julie Greer. "A comical lesson in creativity from Sor Juana," *Hispania*, 71 (1988), 441–4.

Sees "Ovillejos" as a critique of conventional view of women in poetic tradition.

Leonard, Irving A. "The 'encontradas correspondencias' of Sor Juana Inés de la Cruz: an interpretation," *Hispanic Review*, 23 (1955), 33–47.

Links poetic devise of pitting contraries to Sor Juana's intellectual predicament.

Luciani, Frederick. "Anamorphosis in a sonnet by Sor Juana Inés de la Cruz," *Discurso Literario*, 5:2 (1986), 423–32.

Exemplary close reading of a Sor Juana sonnet.

"El amor desfigurado: el ovillejo de Sor Juana Inés de la Cruz," *Texto Crítico* (Lima), 34–5 (1986), 11–48.

One of the best articles on Sor Juana; a brilliant analysis of "Ovillejos."

"The burlesque sonnets of Sor Juana Inés de la Cruz," *Hispanic Journal*, 8:1 (1986), 85–95.

The best comprehensive analysis of Sor Juana's burlesque sonnets.

"Octavio Paz on Sor Juana Inés de la Cruz: the metaphor incarnate," *Latin American Literary Review*, 15:30 (1987), 6–25.

Sensitive and insightful critique of Paz's book on Sor Juana.

Paz, Octavio. *Sor Juana Inés de la Cruz, o las trampas de la fe*, Barcelona, Seix Barral, 1982.

Not only the best book on Sor Juana, but one of the very best on colonial poetry.

Sor Juana or, The Traps of Faith, tr. Margaret Sayers Peden, Cambridge, Mass., Harvard University Press, 1988.

Perelmúter Pérez, Rosa. *Noche intelectual: la oscuridad idiomática en el "Primero sueño,"* Mexico, Universidad Nacional Autónoma de Mexico, 1982.

Detailed analysis of poetic technique in "Primero sueño."

Sabat de Rivers, Georgina. *El "Sueño" de Sor Juana Inés de la Cruz: tradiciones literarias y originalidad*, London, Tamesis Books, 1977.

Best overall study of sources of "Primero sueño."

Sabat de Rivers, Georgina. "Sor Juana: la tradición clásica del retrato poético" in Merlin H. Foster and Julio Ortega (eds.), *De la crónica de la nueva narrativa mexicana. Coloquio sobre literatura mexicana*, Mexico, Oasis, 1986, 79–93.

Excellent disscussion of traditional background of Sor Juana's portrait poems.

Terry, Arthur. "The tenth muse: recent work on Sor Juana Inés de la Cruz," *Bulletin of Hispanic Studies*, 66:2 (1989), 161–6.

Incisive overview.

DIEJO DE MEXÍA DE FERNANGIL

Texts

Primera parte del Parnaso Antártico, de obras amatorias, con las 21 Epístolas de Ovidio, i el in Ibin, en tercetos. Dirigidas a do Iuan Villela, Oydor en la Chancillería de los Reyes. Por Diego Mexia, natural de la ciudad de Sevilla; i residente en la de los Reyes, en los riquissimos Reinos del Piru. Año 1608. Con Privilegio; En Sevilla. Por Alfonso Rodríguez Gamarra.

There is a facsimile edition, with introduction, by Trinidad Barrera, Rome, Bulzoni Editori, 1990.

Secondary

Pociña, Andrés. "El sevillano Diego Mexía de Fernangil y el humanismo en Perú a finales del siglo XVI," *Anuario de Estudios Americanos*, 40 (1983), 163–84.

MATEO DE ROSAS OQUENDO

Texts

Sátira hecha por Mateo Rosas de Oquendo a las cosas que pasan en el Pirú, año de 1598, estudio y edición crítica por Pedro Lasarte, Madison, The Hispanic Seminary of Literary Studies, 1990.
Excellent edition and introduction.

Secondary

Leal, Luis. "Picaresca hispanoamericana: de Oquendo a Lizardi" in Andrew P. Debicki and Enrique Pupo-Walker (eds.), *Estudios de literatura hispanoamericana en honor a José J. Arrom*, Chapel Hill, North Carolina Studies in the Romance Languages and Literatures, 1974, 47–58.

SIGÜENZA Y GÓNGORA, CARLOS

Texts

Poemas, recopilados y ordenados por Irving A. Leonard, con un estudio preliminar de E. Abreu Gómez, Madrid, Talleres Tipográficos de G. Sáez, 1931.
Excellent edition and introduction.

Secondary

Leonard, Irving A. *Don Carlos de Sigüenza y Góngora: A Mexican savant of the seventeenth century*, Berkeley, University of California Press, 1929.
Still the most authoritative and well-written introduction to Sigüenza.

FRANCISCO DE TERRAZAS

Texts

Poesías, edición, prólogo y notas de Antonio Castro Leal, Biblioteca Mexicana, 3, Mexico, Librería de Porrúa Hermanos, 1941.
Standard edition.

Secondary

García Icazbalceta, Joaquín. *Francisco de Terrazas y otros poetas del siglo XVI*, Madrid, Biblioteca Tenanitle/Ediciones José Porrúa, 1962.

Collected from Icazbalceta's complete works, essay was written in 1883. Summary of the little that is known about Terrazas, cites long passages from his incomplete epic poem *Nuevo mundo y conquista*.

JUAN DEL VALLE Y CAVIEDES

Texts

Obras completas, ed. Daniel R. Reedy, Caracas, Biblioteca Ayacucho, 1984.

Most available edition.

Obra completa, edición y estudios de María Leticia Cáceres, Luis Jaime Cisneros, and Guillermo Lohmann Villena, Lima, Banco de Crédito del Peru, 1990.

Now the standard edition.

Juan del Valle y Caviedes. Obra poética I. Diente del Parnaso (Manuscrito de la Universidad de Yale), edición, introducción y notas de Luis García Abrines Calvo. Jaén, Diputación Provincial de Jaén, 1993.

Changes the reading of many poems and adds heretofore unknown information about poet.

Secondary

Cáceres, María Leticia. *La personalidad y obra de D. Juan del Valle y Caviedes*, Arequipa, Imprenta Editorial El Sol, 1975.

Conventional life and works, but with interesting information about editions.

Luciani, Frederick. "Juan del Valle y Caviedes: *El amor médico*," *Bulletin of Hispanic Studies*, 64 (1987), 337–48.

Though focused on theatre, one of the best pieces on Caviedes in general.

Reedy, Daniel D. *The Poetic Art of Juan del Valle y Caviedes*, Chapel Hill, University of North Carolina Press, 1964.

Most up-to-date life and works.

Torres, Daniel R. "*Diente del Parnaso* de Caviedes: de la sátira social a la literaria," *Mester*, 18 (1989) 115–21.

Argues that satire of doctors is also an indirect statement on poetics.

Chapter 7: Epic poetry

Abbreviations:

BL/YU = Beinecke Library, Yale University
BRC/UPR-RP = Biblioteca Regional del Caribe, Universidad de Puerto Rico, Río Piedras
HSA = Hispanic Society of America, New York
LL/IU = Lilly Library, Indiana University
NL = Newberry Library, Chicago
NYPL = New York Public Library

Primary sources

Alvarez de Toledo, Fernando. *Purén indómito*, ed. Diego Barros Arana, Biblioteca Americana, Collection d'Ouvrages Inédits ou Rares sur l'Amérique, Paris, Librairie A. Franck Leipzig, A. Franck'sche Verlags-Buchhandlung, 1862.
   First edition of the original manuscript in the Biblioteca Nacional in Madrid.
Balbuena, Bernardo de. *El Bernardo, o Victoria de Roncesvalles. Poema heroyco*, Madrid, Diego Flamenco, 1624.
   First edition. In HSA.
El Bernardo, Biblioteca Ilustrada de Gaspar & Roig, Madrid, Imprenta de Gaspar & Roig, 1852.
   A complete edition of the work.
Barco Centenera, Martín del. *Argentina y conquista del Río de la Plata*, Lisbon, Pedro Craasbeck, 1602.
   First edition.
La Argentina. Poema histórico, estudios de Juan María Gutiérrez y Enrique Peña, Buenos Aires, Talleres de la Casa Jacobo Preuser, 1912.
   A facsimile reprint of the 1602 first edition.
Belmonte Bermúdez, Luis de. *La Hispálica*, ed. Santiago Montoto, Seville, Imprenta y Libreria de Sobrino de Izquierdo, 1921.
   An excellent contribution to our knowledge of the literary work of Belmonte Bermúdez.
Carvajal y Robles, Rodrigo de. *Poema heroyco del asalto y conquista de Antequera*, Ciudad de los Reyes, Geronymo de Contreras, 1627.
   First edition.
Poema del asalto y conquista de Antequera, ed. Francisco López Estrada, Anejo IX del *Boletín de la Real Academia Española*, Madrid, Imprenta de la Real Academia Española, 1963.
   An excellent edition based on the 1627 Lima first edition.
Castellanos, Juan de. *Primera parte de las elegías de varones ilustres de Indias*, Madrid, Viuda de Alonso Gómez, 1589.
   First edition. In LL/IU.
Domínguez Camargo, Hernando, *San Ignacio de Loyola, fundador de la Compañía de Jesús. Poema heroyco*, Madrid, Joseph Fernández de Buendía, 1666.
   First edition. In HSA.
San Ignacio de Loyola, fundador de la Compañía de Jesús. Poema heroico, prologue Fernando Arbeláez, Bogotá, Empresa Nacional de Publicaciones, Editorial ABC, 1956.
Obras, Rafael Torres Quintero (ed.), estudios de Alfonso Méndez Plancarte, Joaquín Antonio Peñalosa y Guillermo Hernández de Alba, Biblioteca de Publicaciones del Instituto Caro y Cuervo, 15, Bogotá, Instituto Caro y Cuervo, 1960.
   The edition and accompanying studies are magnificent. The correct edition of the complete works of Domínguez Camargo.
Dorantes de Carranza, Baltasar. *Sumaria relación de las cosas de la Nueva España, paleografía de José María de Agreda y Sánchez*, Mexico, Imprenta del Museo Nacional, 1902.

An account of the legitimate descendants of the *conquistadores* and the first Spanish settlers.

Ercilla y Çúñiga, Alonso de. *La Araucana* [Pt. 1], Madrid, Pierres Cossin, 1569.
First edition. In HSA.

Primera, segunda y tercera partes de la Araucana, Pedro Bellero, 1597.
One of the two editions which were printed in 1597.
In LL/IU.

Escobar y Mendoza, Antonio. *Nueva Jerusalén María Señora, poema heroyco. Parte segunda*, Mexico, Imprenta de la Bibliotheca Mexicana, 1759.
An account of the life, virtues, and miracles of the Virgin Mary. In LL/IU; JCBL/BU.
Microfilm in BRC/UPR-RP.

Escoiquiz, Juan de. *México conquistada*, 3 vols., Madrid, Imprenta Real, 1798.
A poem about the conquest of Mexico written by the tutor of Ferdinand VII, who was also Canon of Zaragoza.

Hojeda, Fray Diego de, *La Christiada*, Seville, Diego Pérez, 1611.
First edition. In HSA.

La Christiada, ed. Mary Helen Patricia Corcoran, Washington, Catholic University of America Press, 1935.
A modern edition based on Manuscript 8312 of the Biblioteca del Arsenal of Paris.

La Cristiada, prologue Rafael Aguayo Spencer, 2 vols., Lima, Editorial PTCM, 1947.
An edition prepared to divulgate the work.

Lobo Lasso de la Vega, Gabriel de, *Cortés valeroso y Mexicana* [Pt. 1], Madrid, Pedro Madrigal, 1588.
First edition. In HSA.

Mexicana, ed. José Amor y Vázquez, Biblioteca de Autores Españoles, 232, Colección Rivadeneira, Real Academia Española, Madrid, Ediciones Atlas, 1970. (Contains "Primera parte de Cortés valeroso.")
A modern edition based on the first edition; includes a carefully documented preliminary study.

Mendoza y Monteagudo, Juan de. *Las guerras de Chile*, Santiago, n.p., 1888.
The only known edition of this seventeenth-century poem.

Miramontes Zuázola, Juan de. *Armas antárticas*, ed. Jacinto Jijón y Caamaño Quito, 1921.
A reprint of the first edition prepared by Coronel Zegarra.

Armas antárticas, prólogo y cronologia de Rodrigo Miró, Caracas, Biblioteca Ayacucho, 1978.
A modern edition of the early seventeenth-century poem, which has no indication of publication place and date.

Oña, Pedro. *Arauco domado*, ed. José Toribio Medina, edición crítica de la Academia Chilena correspondiente a la Real Academia Española, Santiago, Imprenta Universitaria, 1917.
The best edition of this work by Oña.

Oviedo y Herrera, Luis Antonio de. *Vida de Santa Rosa de Santa María, natural de Lima, y patrona del Perú. Poema heroico*, Madrid, Juan García Infancón, 1711.

Together with *Nueva Jerusalén María Señora*, an example of a sacred epic with a feminine character. In LL/IU.

Pané, Fray Ramón. *Relación acerca de las antigüedades de los indios. Primer tratado escrito en América*, ed. José Juan Arrom, Mexico, Siglo XXI Editores, 1974.

Peralta Barnuevo Rocha Benavides, Pedro de. *Lima fundada o conquista del Perú*, Lima, Francisco Sobrino y Bados, 1732.
    First edition. In LL/IU.

Piñero Ramírez, Pedro. *Luis de Belmonte y Bermúdez. Estudio de La Hispálica*, Serie Primera, 5, Seville, Publicaciones de la Diputación Provincial de Sevilla, Sección Literatura, 1976.
    A study of the life and work of Belmonte Bermúdez.

Reyna Zeballos, Miguel. *La eloquencia del silencio. Poema heroyco*, Madrid, Diego Miguel de Peralta, 1738.
    A work dedicated to King Philip V's confessor; an example of the literary taste of the era.
    First edition. In LL/IU.

Ruiz de Alarcón y Mendoza, Juan. *Comedias*, ed. Juan Eugenio Hartzenbusch Biblioteca de Autores Españoles, 20, Madrid, Imprenta de Rivadeneira, 1852.
    The authorized edition.

Ruiz de León, Francisco. *Hernandía, Triumphos de la fe y gloria de las armas españolas. Poema heroyco*, Madrid, Imprenta de la Viuda de Manuel Fernández, y del Supremo Consejo de la Inquisición, 1755.
    First edition. In LL/IU.

Saavedra y Guzmán, Antonio de. *El peregrino indiano*, Madrid, Pedro Madrigal, 1599.
    First edition. In LL/IU; NYPL.

Sáenz de Ovecuri, Diego. *Thomasiada al Sol de la Iglesia, y su Doctor Santo Thomas de Aquino*, Guatemala, Joseph Pineda Ybarra, 1667.
    A good sampler of poetic meters with which the author sings to St. Thomas Aquinas.
    First edition. In LL/IU.

Sigüenza y Góngora, Carlos. *Oriental planeta evangélico*, Mexico, Doña María de Benavides, 1700.
    There is no modern edition, as far as is known.
    First edition. In HSA.

Solís, Antonio de. *Historia de la conquista de México, población y progresos de la américa Septentrional, conocida por el nombre de Nueva España*, Madrid, Imprenta de Bernardo Peralta, 1732.
    One of the several editions of Solís's history that circulated in the seventeenth and eighteenth centuries.
    In LL/IU.

Terrazas, Francisco de. *Poesías*, ed. Antonio Castro Leal, Biblioteca Mexicana, 3, Mexico, Librería de Porrúa Hermanos, 1941.
    An edition of all the poems attributed to Terrazas, including the fragments of *Nuevo Mundo y Conquista* consulted by Dorantes de Carranza.

Vaca Alfaro, Enrique. *Festejos del Pindo, sonoros concentos del Helicón [. . .] Poema Heróico*, Cordoba, Andrés Carrillo de Paniagua, 1662.

An example of the peninsular sacred epic, written in praise of the Very Holy Conception of Mary.

First edition. In HSA.

Valdés, Rodrigo de. *Poema heroyco hispano-latino panegyrico de la fundación, y grandezas de la [. . .] ciudad de Lima*, Madrid, F. Garabito de León y Messía, 1687.

An example of an epic poem in a bilingual, Latin–Spanish edition.

First edition in BL/YU.

Villagrá, Gaspar Pérez de. *Historia de la Nueva México*, Alcalá, Luys Martínez, 1610.

First edition in LL/IU; NL; NYPL.

History of New Mexico [Alcalá, 1610], tr. Gilberto Espinosa, intro. and notes F. W. Hodge, Los Angeles, The Quivira Society, 1933.

A modern translation of the poem into a foreign language.

Xufré del Aguila, Melchor. *Compendio historial del descubrimiento, conquista y guerra del Reyno de Chile, con otros dos discursos*, Lima, Francisco Gómez Pastrana, 1630.

First edition of all the known work of Xufré del Aguila.

Secondary sources

Books

Beristáin y Souza, José Mariano. *Biblioteca hispanoamericana septentrional* [1521–1850], vols. I–IV, 3rd. edn., Mexico, Ediciones Fuente Cultural, 1947.

The best bibliographical catalog of colonial Mexican writers.

Blanco, José Joaquín. *La literatura en la Nueva España. Conquista y Nuevo Mundo*, Mexico, Cal y Arena, 1989.

An essay lacking a systematic bibliography.

Caravaggi, Giovanni. *Studi sull'epica ispanica del Rinascimento*, Istituto di Letteratura Spagnola e Ispano-Americana, 25, Universita di Pisa, 1974.

A collection of magnificently documented essays about the Hispanic epic.

Chevalier, Maxime. *L'Arioste en Espagne (1530–1650). Recherches sur l'influence du "Roland Furieux"*, Institut d'Etudes Ibériques et Ibéroaméricaines de l'Université de Bordeaux, 1966.

A fundamental study for the understanding of the transmission of the renaissance epic. Documented and erudite.

Cuesta Mendoza, Antonio. *Historia eclesiástica de Puerto Rico colonial*, vol. I: 1508–1700, Ciudad Trujillo, Ed. Imprenta Arte y Cine, 1948.

An historical review of the Puerto Rican church and its principal leaders. A somewhat antiquated tone.

Descubrimiento y conquista de América. Cronistas, poetas, misioneros y soldados. Antología, ed. Margarita Peña, Clásicos Americanos, 14, Mexico, SEP/Universidad Nacional Autónoma de México, 1982.

An anthology of chronicles of the Indies.

Deyermond, Alan D. *Historia de la literatura española, vol. I: La Edad Media*, tr. Luis Alonso López, Letras e Ideas, Instrumenta 1, 5th edn., Barcelona, Ariel, 1979.

A good historical overview and correct critical judgments regarding Medieval literature.

Volume 1

Diccionario Porrúa de historia, biografía y geografía de México, 2 vols., 3rd. edn., Mexico, Porrúa, 1964.

A good reference work.

Flores de baria poesía, ed. Margarita Peña, Seminario de Literatura Española, Facultad de Filosofía y Letras, Mexico, Universidad Nacional Autónoma de México, 1980.

A book of miscellaneous Petrarchan-style lyrics gathered in Mexico in 1577.

Gallardo, Bartolomé José. *Ensayo de una biblioteca española de libros raros y curiosos*, ed. M. R. Barco del Valle and J. Sancho Rayón, vols. I–IV, Madrid, Imprenta y Fundición de Manuel Tello, 1889.

A fundamental catalog of pre-nineteenth-century Spanish and Spanish American authors.

Geigel Sabat, Fernando A. *Balduino Enrico*, Barcelona, Editorial Araluce, 1934.

A study of the siege of the city of San Juan, Puerto Rico, in 1624 by General Balduino Enrico. Bernardo de Balbuena is mentioned.

Medina, José Toribio. *Biblioteca hispano-americana. (1493–1810)*, vols. I and II, Santiago 1898.

A catalog of writers associated with Spanish America.

Mejía Sánchez, Ernesto. *Gaspar Pérez de Villagrá en la Nueva España*, Cuadernos del Centro de Estudios Literarios, Mexico, Universidad Nacional Autónoma de México, 1971.

Previously unknown facts about the personality of Pérez Villagrá.

Menéndez Pidal, Ramón. *La epopeya castellana a través de la literatura española*, Buenos Aires, Espasa-Calpe Argentina, 1945.

A study of the principal moments in the Castilian epic and its influence on the ballad and drama.

Menéndez y Pelayo, Marcelino. *Historia de la poesía hispanoamericana*, ed. Enrique Sánchez Reyes, vol. II, Santander, Consejo Superior de Investigaciones Científicas, 1948.

An obligatory reference work. Contributions important in their time.

Pierce, Frank. *La poesía épica del Siglo de Oro*, tr. J. C. Cayol de Bethencourt, Biblioteca Románica Hispánica, 2, Estudios y Ensayos, 2nd. edn., Madrid, Gredos, 1968.

The most systematic and documented study of the subject. A required reference work.

Rojas Garcidueñas, José. *Bernardo de Balbuena. La vida y la obra*, Estudios de Literatura, Instituto de Investigaciones Estéticas, Mexico, Universidad Nacional Autónoma de México, 1958.

The biography of Balbuena and a critical analysis of his work.

Vila Vilar, Enriqueta. *Historia de Puerto Rico (1600–1650)*, prologue Francisco Morales Padrón, Seville, Escuela de Estudios Hispanoamericanos, 1974.

Contains references to Bernardo de Balbuena.

Articles

Diego, Gerardo. "Un verso de Domínguez Camargo" in Cedomil Goic (ed.), *Historia y crítica de la literatura hispanoamericana,* vol. 1: *Epoca colonial*, Páginas de Filología, Barcelona, Editorial Crítica, Grupo Grijalbo, 1988, 241–2.

One poet discovers another in a penetrating and lucid essay.

Goic, Cedomil. "Alonso de Ercilla y la poesía épica" in C. Goic (ed.), *Historia y crítica de la literatura hispanoamericana*, vol. I: *Epoca colonial*, Páginas de Filología, Barcelona, Editorial Crítica, Grupo Editorial Grijalbo, 1988, 196–215.
An invaluable study. It contains a bio-bibliography of Ercilla and critical studies of Ercilla, epic authors, and texts.

González Echevarría, Roberto. "Reflexiones sobre *Espejo de paciencia*, de Silvestre de Balboa," offprint of *Nueva Revista de Filología Hispánica*, 35:2 (1987), 571–90.
It revives the polemics surrounding Balboa and his poem.

Wogan, Daniel. "Ercilla y la poesía mexicana," *Revista Iberoamericana*, 3:6 (1941).
A study tracing the influences of Ercilla on the Mexican epic of the sixteenth to the nineteenth centuries.

Chapter 8: Spanish American theatre of the colonial period

Primary sources

Acevedo, Francisco de. *El pregonero de Dios y Patriarca de los pobres*, ed. Julio Jiménez Rueda, Textos de literatura mexicana, 3, Mexico, Imprenta Universitaria, 1945.
A well-prepared edition.

Arrom, José Juan, and José Rojas Garcidueñas (eds.). *Tres piezas teatrales del Virreinato*, Mexico, Universidad Nacional Autónoma de México, Instituto de Investigaciones Estéticas, 1976.
Contains carefully edited texts and excellent introductions.

Bramón, Francisco. *Auto del triunfo de la Virgen y gozo mexicano*, ed. Agustín Yáñez Textos de literatura mexicana, 1, Mexico, Imprenta Universitaria, 1945.
A well-prepared edition.

Brinton, Daniel G. (ed.). *The Güegüence; a comedy ballet in the Nahuatl-Spanish dialect of Nicaragua*, Brinton's Library of Aboriginal American Literature, 3, Philadelphia, D. G. Brinton, 1883.
Still the most authoritative study and text of the play.

Bryant, William C. (ed.). "La *Relación de un ciego*, pieza dramática de la época colonial," *Revista Iberoamericana*, 44 (1978), 569–75.
First modern printing of text, with introduction and notes.

Centeno de Osma, Gabriel. *El pobre más rico, comedia quechua del siglo XVI*, ed. José M. B. Farfán and Humberto Suárez Alvarez, Monumenta Linguae Incaicae, 2, Lima, Editorial Lumen, 1938.
A facsimile of the Quechua manuscript with a Spanish translation.

Cid Pérez, José, and Dolores Martí de Cid (eds.). *Teatro indio precolombino*, Madrid, Aguilar, 1964.
An annotated anthology, with thorough introduction and analyses of texts.

Teatro indoamericano colonial, Madrid, Aguilar, 1973.
An anthology with introduction and analyses of texts.

Cornyn, John H., and Byron McAfee (eds.). "Tlacahuapahualiztli," *Tlalocan*, I (1944), 314–51.
An edition of the Nahuatl text with English translation.

Cruz, Sor Juana Inés de la. *Obras completas*, ed. Alfonso Méndez Plancarte and Alberto G. Salceda, Biblioteca Americana, 18, 21, 27, 32, Mexico, Fondo de Cultura Económica, 1951–1957.
Volumes III and IV devoted to Sor Juana's theatre: contain well-annotated texts and excellent introductions.
Poems, tr. Margaret Sayers Peden, Binghamton, N. Y., Bilingual Press/Editorial Bilingüe, 1985.
Includes facing Spanish/English texts from *loa* to *El divino Narciso*.
Cueto y Mena, Juan de. *Obras*, ed. Archer Woodford, Bogotá, Instituto Caro y Cuervo, 1952.
A well-annotated edition.
González de Eslava, Fernán. *Coloquios espirituales y sacramentales*, ed. José Rojas Garcidueñas, Colección de escritores mexicanos, 74, 75, Mexico, Porrúa, 1958.
Excellent edition of González de Eslava's complete theatrical works.
Hunter, William A. (ed. and trans.). *The Calderonian Auto Sacramental "El Gran Teatro del mundo": An edition and translation of a Nahuatl version*, New Orleans, Tulane University, Middle American Research Institute, 1960.
A study and Spanish translation of a mid seventeenth-century Nahuatl version of Calderón's *auto*.
Jiménez Rueda, Julio (ed.). *Sufrir para merecer*, Boletín del Archivo General de la Nación (Mexico), 20 (1949), 379–459.
A largely unedited transcription of original manuscript.
Johnson, Harvey Leroy (ed.). *An Edition of "Triunfo de los Santos", With a Consideration of Jesuit School Plays in Mexico Before 1650*, diss., Philadelphia, University of Pennsylvania, 1941.
Carefully annotated edition with thorough introduction.
Llamosas, Lorenzo de las. *Obras*, ed. Rubén Vargas Ugarte, Clásicos peruanos, 3, Lima, 1950.
Include's Llamosas's *zarzuela*, marred by editor's deletions and minus *loa* and *sainete* that originally accompanied it.
Llanos, Bernardino de. *Egloga por la llegada del padre Antonio de Mendoza representada en el colegio de San Ildefonso (siglo XVI)*, tr. and ed. José Quiñones Melgoza, Mexico, Universidad Nacional Autónoma de México, Instituto de Investigaciones Filológicas, 1975.
Spanish translation of Latin original, with excellent introduction and notes.
Diálogo en la visita de los inquisidores, representado en el Colegio de San Ildefonso (siglo XVI), y otros poemas inéditos, tr. and ed. José Quiñones Melgoza, Mexico, Universidad Nacional Autónoma de México, Instituto de Investigaciones Filológicas, 1982.
Spanish translation of Latin original, with excellent introduction and notes.
Meneses, Teodoro L. (ed. and trans.). *Teatro quechua colonial: antología*, Lima, Ediciones Edubanco, 1983.
New Spanish translations of Quechua plays, including first edition of *El rapto de Proserpina* by Espinosa Medrano.
Ocaña, Diego de. *Comedia de Nuestra Señora de Guadalupe y sus milagros*, ed. Teresa Gisbert, Biblioteca Paceña, Cuadernos de teatro, 1, La Paz, Alcaldía Municipal, 1957.

Well-prepared edition.

Orbea, Fernando de. *Comedia nueva: la conquista de Santa Fe de Bogotá*, Bogotá, Publicaciones del Ministerio de Educación de Colombia, 1950.

Unedited transcription of original manuscript.

Ravicz, Marilyn Ekdahl (ed.). *Early Colonial Religious Drama in Mexico: From Tzompantli to Golgotha*, Washington, Catholic University of America Press, 1970.

Well-annotated English versions of Nahuatl plays; contains excellent introduction.

Ripoll, Carlos, and Andrés Valdespino (eds.). *Teatro hispanoamericano: antología crítica*, vol. I, New York, Anaya-Book Co., 1972.

Interesting selection of well-annotated texts.

Rojas Garcidueñas, José (ed.). *Autos y coloquios del siglo* XVI, Biblioteca del Estudiante Universitario, 4, Mexico, Ediciones de la Universidad Nacional Autónoma, 1939.

Useful edition of colonial Mexican plays; intended for student rather than scholarly use.

Valle y Caviedes, Juan del. *Obra completa*, ed. Daniel R. Reedy, Caracas, Biblioteca Ayacucho, 1984.

Thorough and scholarly edition of Valle y Caviedes's works.

Vargas Ugarte, Rubén (ed.). *De nuestro antiguo teatro: colección de piezas dramáticas de los siglos* XVI, XVII, *y* XVIII, Biblioteca Histórica Peruana, 4, Lima, Universidad Católica del Perú, Instituto de Investigaciones Históricas, 1943.

Indispensable volume of rare colonial plays, some marred by editor's deletions.

Secondary sources

Books

Anderson-Imbert, Enrique. *Crítica interna*, Madrid, Taurus, 1961.

Includes chapter on Bramón's *Los sirgueros de la Virgen*.

Arias Larreta, Abraham. *Literaturas aborígenes de América: azteca, incaica, maya, quiché*, 10th. edn., San José, Costa Rica, Editorial Indoamérica, 1976.

Good source of information on pre-Conquest indigenous drama.

Arrom, José Juan. *Estudios de literatura hispanoamericana*, Havana, 1950.

Includes essays on early Cuban letters and colonial *entremeses*.

Historia del teatro hispanoamericano: época colonial, 2nd. edn., Mexico, Ediciones de Andrea, 1967.

Still the best synthesis of colonial Spanish American theatre; some references no longer up to date.

Arróniz, Othón. *Teatros y escenarios del siglo de oro*, Biblioteca Románica Hispánica, Estudios y Ensayos, 260, Madrid, Gredos, 1977.

An invaluable history of theatres and stagecraft in Golden Age Spain and colonial New Spain.

Teatro de evangelización en Nueva España, Mexico, Universidad Nacional Autónoma de México, 1979.

Good synthesis of the theme; contains in appendix previously unpublished

Egloga pastoril by Juan de Cigorondo.

Ballinger, Rex Edward. *Los orígenes del teatro español y sus primeras manifestaciones en la Nueva España*, diss., Universidad Nacional Autónoma de México, Mexico, 1951.

Includes text of Nahuatl/Spanish *Loa satírica.*

Bocanegra, Mathias de. *Jews and the Inquisition of Mexico: The great auto de fe of 1649*, tr. and ed. Seymour B. Liebman, Lawrence, Kans., Coronado Press, 1974.

Contemporary account of auto de fe; offers insight on mass spectacle in colonial Mexico.

Camacho Guizado, Eduardo. *Estudios sobre literatura colombiana, siglos* XVI–XVII, Bogotá, Ediciones Universidad de los Andes, 1965.

Useful mainly for its reproduction of Fernández de Valenzuela's *Laurea crítica.*

Díaz del Castillo, Bernal. *Historia verdadera de la conquista de la Nueva España*, Colección "Sepan Cuantos. . .," 5, Mexico, Porrúa, 1960.

Chronicles mass spectacle in sixteenth-century Mexico.

Garibay K., Angel María. *Historia de la literatura náhuatl*, Biblioteca Porrúa, 1, 5, Mexico, Porrúa, 1953–1954.

A fundamental source of information; contains chapters devoted to pre-Conquest drama and missionary theatre.

Horcasitas, Fernando. *El teatro náhuatl: épocas novohispana y moderna*, Instituto de Investigaciones Históricas, Serie de Cultura Náhuatl, Monografías, 17, Mexico, Universidad Nacional Autónoma de México, 1974.

An authoritative history, with an anthology of Spanish versions of Nahuatl theatre and a descriptive list of manuscripts.

Johnson, Julie Greer. *Women in Colonial Spanish American Literature: Literary images*, Contributions in Women's Studies, 43, Westport, Conn., Greenwood Press, 1983.

Contains chapter on women in colonial drama.

Leal, Rine. *La selva oscura: historia del teatro cubano desde sus orígenes hasta 1868*, vol. I, Havana, Editorial Arte y Literatura, 1975.

Excellent, well-documented study, particularly useful for information on African element in early Cuban theatre.

Leonard, Irving A. *Baroque Times in Old Mexico: Seventeenth-century persons, places, and practices*, Ann Arbor, University of Michigan Press, 1959.

Classic study, particularly useful for information on circulation of European books in Spanish colonies.

Lohmann Villena, Guillermo. *El arte dramático en Lima durante el Virreinato*, Publicaciones de la Escuela de Estudios Hispanoamericanos de la Universidad de Sevilla, 12, Madrid, 1945.

A comprehensive history based on archival documents, some of which are reproduced in appendix.

María y Campos, Armando de. *Guía de representaciones teatrales en la Nueva España*, Colección La Máscara, 1, Mexico, B. Costa/Amic Editor, 1959.

Lists known theatrical representations in New Spain by year and reviews documents pertinent to colonial Mexican theatre.

Monterde, Francisco. *Cultura mexicana: aspectos literarios*, Mexico, Editora Intercontinental, 1946.

Contains chapter on Sor Juana's secular theatre.

Oeste De Bopp, Marianne. *Influencia de los misterios y autos europeos en los de México (anteriores al Barroco)*, Mexico, 1952.

Formal and thematic comparison of early Mexican religious theatre with that of Europe.

Olavarría y Ferrari, Enrique de. *Reseña histórica del teatro en México, 1538–1911*, Biblioteca Porrúa, 21, 3rd. edn., Mexico, Porrúa, 1961.

An updated edition of magisterial history of Mexican theatre, first compiled in the late nineteenth century.

Paz, Octavio. *Sor Juana, or, The Traps of Faith*, tr. Margaret Sayers Peden, Cambridge, Mass., Harvard University Press, 1988.

Important study of Sor Juana's life and works, as well as of colonial Mexican culture.

Pedro, Valentín de. *América en las letras españolas del Siglo de Oro*, Buenos Aires, Sudamericana, 1954.

Overview of Golden Age Spanish plays set in New World.

Pérez, María Esther. *Lo americano en el teatro de sor Juana Inés de la Cruz*, Torres Library of Literary Studies, 20, Eastchester, N.Y., Eliseo Torres, 1975.

Useful study of Sor Juana's theatre; ranges beyond narrow theme suggested by title.

Pla, Josefina. *El teatro en el Paraguay*, Colección Camalote, 1, 2nd. edn., Asunción, Diálogo, 1967.

Slender but pithy volume, especially useful for information on Jesuit theatre in Guarani language.

Reyes, Alfonso. *Letras de la Nueva España*, Colección Tierra Firme, 40, Mexico, Fondo de Cultura Económica, 1948.

Contains chapters on missionary and Creole theatre.

Ricard, Robert. *La conquête spirituelle du Mexique*, Travaux et Mémoires de l'Institut d'Ethnologie, 20, Université de Paris, 1933.

Classic study of the theme, with much useful information on missionary theatre.

The Spiritual Conquest of Mexico, tr. Leslie Byrd Simpson, Berkeley and Los Angeles, University of California, 1966.

Rojas Garcidueñas, José. *El teatro de Nueva España en el siglo XVI*, SepSetentas, 101, 2nd. edn., Mexico, Secretaría de Educación Pública, 1973.

An updated edition of the 1935 original; an overview of authors, texts, theatrical trends.

Saz, Agustín del. *Teatro hispanoamericano*, vol. I, Barcelona, Editorial Vergara, 1963.

A useful history of Spanish American theatre through the nineteenth century.

Schilling, Hildburg. *Teatro profano en la Nueva España*, Mexico, Universidad Nacional Autónoma de México, 1958.

An invaluable history based on archival materials, some of which are reproduced in appendix.

Shergold, N. D. *A History of the Spanish Stage from Medieval Times until the End of the Seventeenth Century*, Oxford, Clarendon Press, 1967.

Useful for the literary and historical contextualization of colonial Spanish American theatre.

Sten, María. *Vida y muerte del teatro náhuatl*, SepSetentas, 120, Mexico, Secretaría de Educación Pública, 1974.

A synthesis of pre-Conquest drama and presence of indigenous element in Mexican theatre through twentieth century.

Suárez Radillo, Carlos Miguel. *El teatro barroco hispanoamericano: ensayo de una historia crítico-antológica*, 3 vols., Madrid, José Porrúa Turanzas, 1981.

A thorough history of Spanish American theatre from approximately 1600 to 1750, with excerpts from plays.

Torres-Ríoseco, Arturo. *Ensayos sobre literatura latinoamericana*, Berkeley, University of California Press, 1953.

Contains chapters on indigenous theatre, González de Eslava, and Sor Juana.

Trenti Rocamora, J. Luis. *El teatro en la América colonial*, Buenos Aires, Editorial Huarpes, 1947.

A history of colonial theatre in North and South America, with emphasis on Argentina.

Weber de Kurlat, Frida. *Lo cómico en el teatro de Fernán González de Eslava*, Universidad de Buenos Aires, Facultad de Filosofía y Letras, 1963.

A useful, full-length study of a largely overlooked playwright.

Articles

Arrom, José Juan. "Cambiantes imágenes de la mujer en el teatro de la América virreinal," *Latin American Theater Review*, 12:1 (1978), 5–15.

Relates portrayal of female characters to successive periods and movements in colonial theatre.

Arrom, José Juan, and José Manuel Rivas Sacconi. "La *Laurea crítica* de Fernando Fernández de Valenzuela, primera obra teatral colombiana," *Thesaurus*, 14 (1959), 161–85.

First modern printing of text, with introduction and commentary.

Betancourt, Helia. "El protocolo de Julián Bravo (1599): primer contrato de una agrupación teatral en América," *Latin American Theater Review*, 19:2 (1986), 17–22.

The text of the contract of an emigré Spanish theatre group in Lima.

Daniel, Lee A. "The *loa*: one aspect of the Sorjuanian mask," *Latin American Theater Review*, 16:2 (1983), 43–50.

A useful introduction to Sor Juana's eighteen *loas*.

Dauster, Frank. "De los recursos cómicos en el teatro de Sor Juana," *Caribe*, 2:2 (1977), 41–54.

An analysis of comic technique in Sor Juana's *comedias* and *sainetes*.

Hanrahan, Thomas. "El tocotín, expresión de identidad, *Revista Iberoamericana*, 36 (1970), 51–60.

An analysis of the use of the *tocotín* in colonial Mexican drama, with emphasis on Jesuit theatre.

Henríquez Ureña, Pedro. "El teatro de la América española en la época colonial," Emma Susana Speratti Piñero (ed.), *Obra crítica*, Mexico, Fondo de Cultura Económica, 1960, 698–718.

An excellent synthesis of colonial Spanish American theatre.

Hesse, Everett W. "Calderón's popularity in the Spanish Indies," *Hispanic Review*, 23 (1955), 12–27.

Observations based on compiled list of known performances of Calderón's plays in the colonies (included as appendix).

Hunter, William A. "The seventeenth-century Nahuatl *entremés* 'In ilamatzin ihuan in piltontli'," *Kentucky Foreign Language Quarterly*, 5 (1958), 26–34.

Description of and commentary on this unedited *entremés*.

Icaza, Francisco A. de. "Cristóbal de Llerena y los orígenes del teatro en la América española," *Revista de Filología Española*, 8 (1921), 121–30.

First modern printing of Llerena's *entremés*, with introduction and commentary.

Jiménez Rueda, Julio (ed.). "Documentos para la historia del teatro en la Nueva España," *Boletín del Archivo General de la Nación* (Mexico), 15 (1944), 101–44.

The text of a series of documents relating to civil and ecclesiastical control of theatre in colonial Mexico.

Johnson, Harvey L. "Nuevos datos para el teatro mexicano en la primera mitad del siglo XVII," *Revista de Filología Hispánica*, 4 (1942), 127–51.

Excerpts from and commentary on the *actas* of the municipal council of Mexico City relating to theatre (1601–1643).

"Noticias dadas por Tomás Gage, a propósito del teatro en España, México y Guatemala (1624–1637)," *Revista Iberoamericana*, 8 (1944), 257–73.

Eyewitness observations on colonial theatre excerpted from Thomas Gage's *A New Survey of the West Indies* (1648).

Jones, Willis Knapp. "Women in the early Spanish American theatre," *Latin American Theater Review*, 4:1 (1970), 23–34.

Discusses the gradual appearance of actresses on colonial stages.

Leonard, Irving A. "Notes on Lope de Vega's works in the Spanish Indies," *Hispanic Review*, 6 (1938), 277–93.

Offers documentary evidence of Lope's popularity in colonies.

Luciani, Frederick. "Juan del Valle y Caviedes: *El Amor Médico*," *Bulletin of Hispanic Studies*, 64 (1987), 337–48.

Relates Valle y Caviedes's *baile* to his larger body of satirical verse.

Lyday, Leon F. "The Colombian theatre before 1800," *Latin American Theater Review*, 4:1 (1970), 35–50.

A survey of colonial Colombian theatre.

Meneses, Teodoro L. "Ciertas reminiscencias de algunos clásicos en el monólogo de Yauri Ttito del drama quechua *El pobre más rico*: contribución a la datación de esta pieza," *Sphinx*, 4, 10–12 (1940), 119–23.

Finds possible sources in Góngora and Calderón and argues for seventeenth-century dating of play.

Merrim, Stephanie. "Narciso *desdoblado*: Narcissistic stratagems in *El divino Narciso* and the *Respuesta a sor Filotea de la Cruz*," *Bulletin of Hispanic Studies*, 64 (1987), 111–17.

Fine example of new critical direction in Sor Juana scholarship.

Oeste de Bopp, Marianne. "Autos mexicanos del siglo XVI," *Historia Mexicana*, 3 (1953), 112–23.

Synthesizes presence of indigenous element in missionary theatre.

Parker, Alexander A. "The Calderonian sources of *El divino Narciso* by Sor Juana
Inés de la Cruz," *Romanistisches Jahrbuch*, 19 (1968), 257–74.
  Indispensable for the understanding of the literary context of Sor Juana's *auto*.
Paso y Troncoso, Francisco del. "Comédies en langue naualt" in *Congrés Inter-
national des Américanistes (XIIe session tenue a Paris en 1900)*, Paris, Ernest
Leroux, Editeur, 1902, 309–16.
  Contains French translation of anonymous Nahuatl *entremés*.
Pasquariello, Anthony M. "The *entremés* in sixteenth-century Spanish America," *The
Hispanic American Historical Review*, 32 (1952), 44–58.
  An overview of *entremeses* by González de Eslava and Llerena.
"The evolution of the *loa* in Spanish America," *Latin American Theater Review*,
3:2 (1970), 5–19.
  A synthesis of the development of the genre from the sixteenth through the
eighteenth centuries.
"The seventeenth-century interlude in the New World secular theater" in Raquel
Chang-Rodríguez, Donald A. Yates (eds.), *Homage to Irving A. Leonard: Essays
on Hispanic art, history and literature*, East Lansing, Michigan State University,
Latin American Studies Center, 1977, 105–13.
  An overview of interludes by Sor Juana and Valle y Caviedes.
Reverte Bernal, Concepción. "Guía bibliográfica para el estudio del teatro virreinal
peruano," *Historiografía y Bibliografía Americanistas*, 29 (1985), 129–50.
  Lists primary and secondary bibliographical sources on Peruvian theatre
through eighteenth century.
Reynolds, Winston A. "El demonio y Lope de Vega en el manuscrito mexicano
*Coloquio de la nueva conversión y bautismo de los cuatro últimos reyes de
Tlaxcala en la Nueva España*," *Cuadernos Americanos*, 163 (1969), 172–84.
  Finds important sources in Lope de Vega.
Ricard, Robert. "Sur *El divino Narciso* de Sor Juana Inés de la Cruz," *Mélanges de la
Casa de Velázquez*, 5 (1969), 309–29.
  An analysis and source-study of Sor Juana's *auto*.
Rojo, Grínor, and Kathleen Shelly. "El teatro hispanoamericano colonial" in Luis
Iñigo Madrigal (ed.), *Historia de la literatura hispanoamericana*, vol. I, Madrid,
Cátedra, 1982, 319–52.
  A synthesis of colonial theatre from the sixteenth through the eighteenth
centuries.
Trexler, Richard C. "We think, they act: clerical readings of the missionary theatre in
16th century New Spain" in Steven L. Kaplan (ed.), *Understanding Popular
Culture: Europe from the Middle Ages to the nineteenth century*, Berlin, Mouton,
1984, 189–227.
  Interesting analysis of early Spanish ethnographers in colonial Mexico as
"creators" of culture.

Chapter 9: Viceregal culture

Alberro, Solange. *Del gachupín al criollo. O de cómo los españoles de México dejaron
de serlo*, Mexico, El Colegio de México, 1992.
Arenal, Electa and Stacey Schlau (eds.) *Untold Sister: Hispanic Nuns in Their Own*

Works, Albuquerque, University of New Mexico Press, 1989.

Arte y mística del barroco, Mexico, Consejo Nacional para la Cultura y las Artes, 1994.

Astuto, Louis Philip. *Eugenio Espejo: reformador ecuatoriano de la Ilustración (1747–1795)*, Mexico, Fondo de Cultura Económica, 1969.

Barreda y Laos, Felipe. *Vida intelectual de la colonia*, Lima, L. I. Rosso, 1937.

Bartolache, José Ignacio (ed.) *Mercurio Volante* (1772–1773).

Benavides, Alfredo. *La arquitectura en el Virreinato del Perú y la Capitanía General de Chile*, 3rd. edn., Santiago, Andrés Bello, 1988.

Beristain y Souza, José Mariano. *Bibliotheca hispano-americana septentrional*, Amecameca: Tip. del Colegio Católico, 1883–1897.

Bernard, Carmen, and Serge Gruzinski. *De l'idolatrie. Une archéologie de sciences religieuses*, Paris, Seuil, 1988.

Brading, David. *The First America: The Spanish monarchy, creole patriots, and the liberal state, 1492–1867*, Cambridge University Press, 1991.

Burke, Marcus. *Pintura y escultura en Nueva España: el barroco*, Mexico, Grupo Azabache, 1992.

Busto, José Antonio del. *Reseña histórica del arte colonial peruano*, Lima, Pontificia Universidad Católica, 1983.

Caldas y Tenorio, Francisco José (ed.) *Semanario del Nuevo Reino de Granada*, 3 vols., Bogotá, Editorial Minerva SA, 1942.

Cardozo Galué, Germán, *Michoacán en el siglo de las luces*, Mexico, El Colegio de México, 1973.

Carreño, Alberto María. *La real y pontificia Universidad de México, 1536–1865*, Mexico, Universidad Nacional Autónoma de México, 1961.

Castañeda, Carmen. *La educación en Guadalajara durante la colonia, 1555–1821*, Guadalajara, El Colegio de Jalisco and El Colegio de México, 1984.

Cervantes de Salazar, Francisco. *Mexico en 1554*, Mexico, Universidad Nacional Autónoma de México, 1964.

Cevallos-Candau, Javier, *et al. Coded Encounters: Writing, gender, and ethnicity in colonial Latin America*, Amherst, University of Massachusetts Press, 1994.

Chiaramonte, José Carlos. *La Ilustración en el Río de la Plata*, Buenos Aires, Puntosur Editores, 1989.

Cruz de Amenaba, Isabel. *Arte y sociedad en Chile, 1550–1650*, Santiago, Editorial de la Universidad Católica de Chile, 1986.

Dumbar Temple, Ella. *La universidad: libros de posesiones de cátedras y actos académicos*, Lima, Comisión Nacional del Sesquicentenario de la Independencia del Perú, 1974.

Eguiara y Eguren, J. J. *Prólogos a la bibliotheca americana*, Mexico, Fondo de Cultura de México, 1944.

Elliot, John H. *The Old World and the New, 1492–1650*, Cambridge University Press, 1972.

Esteve Barba, Francisco. *Historiografía indiana*, Madrid, Gredos, 1964.

   Historia General de América. vol. XXVII: *Cultura virreinal*, ed. Antonio Ballesteros, Barcelona, Salvat, 1965.

Fernández del Castillo, Francisco (compiler). *Libros y libreros en el siglo XVI*, Mexico: Archivo General de la Nación y Fondo de Cultura Económica, 1982.

Friede, Juan. *La censura española del siglo XVI y los libros de historia de América*, Mexico, Editorial Cultura, 1959.

Furlong, Guillermo. *Bibliotecas argentinas durante la dominación hispánica*, Buenos Aires, Editorial Huarpes, 1944.

Matemáticos argentinos durante la dominación hispánica, Buenos Aires, Editorial Huarpes, 1945.

La cultura femenina en la época colonial, Buenos Aires, Editorial Kapelusz, 1951.

Historia social y cultural del Río de la Plata, 1536–1810, 2 vols., Buenos Aires, Tipografía Editora Argentina, 1969.

Gallegos Rocaful, José María. *El pensamiento mexicano en los siglos XVI y XVII*, Mexico, Centro de Estudios Filosóficos, 1951.

García Ayluardo, Clara, and Manuel Ramos Medina (eds.) *Manifestaciones religiosas en el mundo colonial americano*, vol. I: *Espiritualidad barroca colonial. Santos y demonios en América*, Mexico, Universidad Iberoamericana, 1993.

García Izcabalceta, José. *Bibliografía mexicana del siglo XVI*, ed. Agustín Millares Carlos, Mexico, Fondo de Cultura Económica, 1954.

Gerbi, Antonelli. *La naturaleza de las Indias Nuevas. De Cristóbal Colón a Gonzalo Fernández de Oviedo*, tr. Antonio Alatorre, Mexico, Fondo de Cultura Económica, 1978.

Gisbert, Teresa, *Iconografía y mitos indígenas en el arte*, La Paz, Librería Gisbert, 1980.

Gómez Hurtado, Alvaro, and Francisco Gil Tovar. *Arte virreinal de Bogotá*, Bogotá, Villegas Editores, 1987.

Gonzalbo Aizpuru, Pilar. *Historia de la educación en la época colonial: el mundo indígena*, Mexico, El Colegio de México, 1990.

Historia de la educación en la época colonial: la educación de los criollos y la vida urbana, Mexico, El Colegio de México, 1990.

González Casanova, Pablo. *El misoneísmo y la modernidad cristiana en el siglo XVIII*, Mexico, El Colegio de México, 1948.

Gruzinski, Serge. *La colonisation de l'imaginaire. Sociétés indigenes et occidentalisation dans le Mexique espagnol, XVIe–XVIIe siècles*, Paris, Gallimard, 1988.

Guijo, Gregorio de. *Diario*, Mexico, Editorial Porrúa, 1952.

Hanke, Lewis. *Aristotle and the American Indians. A study in race prejudice in the modern world*, Bloomington, University of Indiana Press, 1975.

Henríquez Ureña, Pedro. *Literary Currents in Hispanic America*, Cambridge, Mass., Harvard University Press, 1945. In Spanish: *Historia de la cultura en la América Hispana*, Mexico, Fondo de Cultura Económica, 1947.

Hernández de Alba, Guillermo. *Documentos para la historia de la educación en Colombia (1540–1653)*, Bogotá, Patronato Colombiano de Artes y Ciencias, 1969.

Jacobsen, J. V. *Educational Foundations of the Jesuits in Sixteenth Century New Spain*, Berkeley, University of California Press, 1938.

Jiménez Rueda, Julio. *Historia de la cultura en México: El virreinato*, Mexico, Editorial Cultura, 1950.

Johnson, Julie Greer. *The Book in the Americas: The role of books and printing in the development of culture and society in colonial Latin America*, Providence, Rhode Island, The John Carter Brown Library, 1988.

Kelemen, Pál. *Baroque and Rococo Art in Latin America*, 2 vols., New York, Dover, 1967.

Lanning, John Tate. *Academic Culture in the Spanish Colonies*, New York, Oxford University Press, 1940.

The University in the Kingdom of Guatemala, Ithaca, Cornell University Press, 1955.

Eighteenth Century Enlightenment in the University of San Carlos de Guatemala, Ithaca, Cornell University Press, 1956.

León, Nicolás. *Bibliografía mexicana del siglo XVIII*, 5 vols., Mexico, Imp. de F. Díaz de León, 1902–1908.

Leonard, Irving A. *Books of the Brave: Being an account of books and men in the Spanish Conquest and settlement of the sixteenth century New World*, Cambridge, Mass., Harvard University Press, 1949.

Baroque Times in Old Mexico, Ann Arbor, University of Michigan Press, 1959.

Don Carlos de Sigüenza y Góngora. Un sabio mexicano del siglo XVII, Mexico, Fondo de Cultura Económica, 1984.

León Pinelo, Antonio de. *El paraíso en el Nuevo Mundo*, 2 vols., Lima, Imprenta Torres Aguirre, 1943.

Lewis, Robert E. *The Humanistic Historiography of Francisco López de Gómara (1511–59)*, Ann Arbor, University of Michigan Press, 1987.

Lohmann Villena, Guillermo. *Juan de Matienzo: Autor del "Gobierno del Perú." Su personalidad y obra*, Seville, Escuela de Estudios Hispano-Americanos, 1966.

López-Baralt, Mercedes (ed). *Iconografía política del Nuevo Mundo*, Río Piedras, Universidad de Puerto Rico, 1990.

Luna Díaz, Lorenzo M. *et al. La Real Universidad de México: Estudios y textos*, 2 vols., Mexico, Universidad Nacional Autónoma de México, 1987.

Malagón Barceló, Javier, and José M. Ots Capdequi. *Solórzano y Pereira y la política indiana*, 2nd. edn., Mexico, Fondo de Cultura Económica, 1983.

Marzal, Manuel M. *La transformación religiosa peruana*, Lima, Pontificia Universidad Católica del Perú, 1983.

Maza, Francisco de *et al. Cuarenta siglos de plástica mexicana*, Mexico, Editorial Herrero, 1970.

Medina, José Toribio. *Cosas de la colonia: apuntes para la crónica del siglo XVIII en Chile*, Santiago, Fondo Histórico y Bibliográfico José Toribio Medina, 1952.

Historia de la imprenta en los antiguos dominios españoles de América y Oceanía, Santiago, Fondo Histórico y Bibliográfico, 1958.

Melquíades, Andrés Martín. *Los recogidos: nueva visión de la mística española: 1500–1700*, Madrid, Fundación Universitaria Española, 1975.

Mercurio Peruano de historia, literatura, y noticias públicas, Lima, 1791–1795.

Miranda, José. *España y Nueva España en la época de Filipe II*, Mexico, Universidad Nacional Autónoma de México, 1962.

Moreno Navarro, Isidoro. *Los cuadros del mestizaje americano: estudio antropológico del mestizaje*, Madrid, José Porrúa Turanzas, 1973.

Mugaburu, José and Francisco. *Chronicle of Colonial Lima. The diary of Joseph and Francisco Mugaburu, 1640–1697*, tr. and ed. Robert Ryal Miller, Norman, University of Oklahoma Press, 1975.

Muriel, Josefina. *Cultura femenina virreinal*, Mexico, Universidad Nacional Autónoma de México, 1982.

Navarro, Bernabé. *Cultura mexicana moderna en el siglo XVIII*, Mexico, Universidad Nacional Autónoma de México, 1964.

Otero, Gustavo A. *La vida social del coloniaje: S. XVI, XVII, XVIII*, La Paz, 1975.

Pagden, Anthony. *The Fall of the Natural Man: The American Indian and the origins of comparative Ethnology*, Cambridge University Press, 1982.

   Spanish Imperialism and the Political Imagination, New Haven, Yale University Press, 1990.

Pereira Salas, Eugenio. *Historia del arte en el reino de Chile*, Buenos Aires, Ediciones de la Universidad de Chile, 1965.

Perez-Marchand, Monelisa. *Dos etapas ideológicas del siglo XVIII en Mexico a través de los papeles de la Inquisición*, Mexico, Universidad Autónoma Nacional de México, 1945.

Picón-Salas, Mariano. *A Cultural History of Spanish America: From Conquest to Independence*, tr. Irving A. Leonard, Berkeley, University of California Press, 1962.

Rojas Abrigo, Alicia. *Historia de la pintura en Chile*, Santiago, Talleres de Impresos Vicuña, 1981.

Romero, José Luis. *Latinoamérica: las ciudades y las ideas*, Mexico, Siglo Veintiuno Editores, 1976.

Salas, Alberto M. *Tres cronistas de Indias*, Mexico: Fondo de Cultura Económica, 1986.

Santa Cruz y Espejo, Javier Eugenio. *Primicias de la cultura en Quito*, Quito, Archivo Municipal, 1947.

Sartori, Marco. *Arquitectura y urbanismo en Nueva España, Siglo XVI*, Mexico, Grupo Azabache. 1992.

Sebastián, Santiago. *El barroco iberoamericano: mensaje iconográfico*, Madrid, Ediciones Encuentro, 1990.

Shafer, Robert Jones. *The Economic Societies in the Spanish World, 1763–1821*, Syracuse, New York, Syracuse University Press, 1958.

Solórzano y Pereira, Juan. *Política indiana* [1648], Madrid, Compañía Ibero-Americana de Publicaciones, 1930.

Torre Revello, José. *El libro, la imprenta y el periodismo en América durante la dominación española*, Buenos Aires, Publicaciones del Instituto de Investigaciones Históricas, 1940.

Toussaint, Manuel. *Colonial Art in Mexico*, Austin, University of Texas Press, 1967.

Tovar de Teresa, Guillermo. *Pintura y escultura del Renacimiento en México*, Mexico, INAH, 1979.

   México barroco, Mexico, SAHOP, 1981.

   Pintura y escultura en Nueva España, 1557–1640, Mexico, Grupo Azabache, 1992.

Trabulse, Elías. *Ciencia y religión en el siglo XVII*, Mexico, El Colegio de México, 1974.

   Historia de la ciencia en México, Mexico, Conacyt, Fondo de Cultura Económica, 1983.

Válcarcel, Luis E. *Ruta cultural del Perú*, Lima, Editorial Cultura Ecléctica, 1939.

Vargas, O. P. José María. *La cultura de Quito colonial*, Quito, Editorial "Santo Domingo," 1941.

Vargas Lugo, Elisa. *México barroco: vida y arte*, Mexico, Salvat, 1993.
Vargas Ugarte, Rubén. *Historia de la iglesia en el Perú*, 5 vols., Lima and Burgos, 1953–1961.
Viqueira Albán, Juan Pedro. *¿Relajados o reprimidos? Diversiones públicas y vida social en la ciudad de México durante el siglo de las luces*, Mexico, Fondo de Cultura Económica, 1987.
Weckman, Luis. *La herencia medieval en México*, 2 vols., Mexico, Comex, 1984.
Zavala, Silvio. *El mundo americano en la época colonial*, Mexico, Editorial Porrúa, 1967.

Articles

Fernández de Recas, Guillermo S. "Libros y libreros de mediados del siglo XVII en México," *Boletín de la Biblioteca Nacional de México*, 12:1–2 (1961).
Furlong, Guillermo, "León Pinelo y su Paraíso en el Nuevo Mundo" in *Nacimiento y desarrollo de la filosofía en el Río de la Plata*, Buenos Aires, G. Kraft, 1952.
Lavallé, Bernard. "Las 'doctrinas' de frailes como reveladoras del incipiente criollismo sudamericano," *Anuario de Estudios Americanos*, 36 (1979), 447–65.
Lavrin, Asunción. "Misión e historiografía de la iglesia en el período colonial americano," *Anuario de Estudios Americanos*, 41:2 (1989), 11–54.
Malagón Barceló, Javier. "The role of the letrados in the colonization of the Americas," *The Americas*, 18:2 (1961), 1–17.

Chapter 10: *The eighteenth century: narrative forms, scholarship and learning*

Primary sources

Acosta Enríquez, José Mariano. *Sueño de sueños*, prologue and selection Julio Jiménez Rueda, Mexico, Universidad Nacional Autónoma de México, 1945.
  Well-prepared edition.
Alcedo y Bejarano, Antonio de. *Diccionario geográfico-histórico de las Indias occidentales o América*, 5 vols., Madrid, Benito Cano (other printers for vols. II–V), 1786–1789.
  Fairly inaccessible today.
Diccionario geográfico-histórico de las Indias occidentales o América, vols. CCV–CCVIII, ed. Ciriaco Pérez-Bustamante, Madrid, Biblioteca de Autores Españoles, 1967.
  Important re-edition with thorough introductory essay.
Alegre, Javier. *Historia de la Compañía de Jesús en Nueva España, que estaba escribiendo el P. Francisco Javier Alegre al tiempo de su expulsión*, [1767], 3 vols., Mexico, Carlos María Bustamante, 1841–1842.
  Important source for historians.
Memorias para la historia de la provincia que tuvo la compañía de Jesús en Nueva España [1771], ed. J. Jijón Caamaño, 2 vols., Mexico, Porrúa, 1940–1941.
  Compendium of the *Historia*.
Historia de la provincia de la Compañía de Jesús de Nueva España, eds. Ernest J.

Burrus y Félix Zubillaga, 4 vols., Rome, Institutum Historicum S. J., 1956.
Excellent edition with copious annotations.

Alzate, José Antonio. "Elogio histórico del doctor don José Ignacio Bartolache," *Gacetas de la literatura de México*, 4 vols., Puebla, Oficina de Hospital de San Pedro, 1831, I, 405–13.
Eulogy published August 3, 1790, less than two months after Bartolache's death.

Arrate y Acosta, José Martín Félix de. *Llave del Nuevo Mundo, Antemural de las Indias Occidentales (La Habana descripta: noticias de su fundación, aumentos y estado)* [1761], Havana, Sociedad Económica de Amigos del País, 1830.
Intro. (i–xv) by Pedro Pascual Sirgado y Zequeira (unsigned). Well-prepared edition.

Llave del Nuevo Mundo, ed. Julio J. Le Riverend Brusone, Mexico, Fondo de Cultura Económica, 1949.
Introductory essay discusses evolution of Cuban historiography and reflects nationalistic impulse behind much of early Latin American literary history.

Llave del Nuevo Mundo, Antemural de las Indias Occidentales, Havana, Comisión Nacional Cubana de la UNESCO, 1964.
Well-prepared edition.

Arzáns de Orsúa y Vela, Bartolomé. *Historia de la villa imperial de Potosí* [1705–1736], ed. Lewis Hanke and Gunnar Mendoza, 3 vols., Providence, R. I. Brown University Press, 1965.
Excellent edition; introductory studies are indispensable for students of Arzáns.

Tales of Potosí, tr. Frances M. López-Morillas, ed. R. C. Padden, Providence, R. I., Brown University Press, 1975.
Informative introduction and selected tales delightfully translated, making Hanke/Mendoza edition accessible to English-speaking readers.

Azara, Felix de. *Apuntamientos para la historia natural de los quadrúpedos del Paraguay y Río de la Plata*, 2 vols., Madrid, 1802.
Text had appeared in French in 1801 (*Essais sur l'Histoire Naturelle des Quadrupèdes de la Province du Paraguay*, 2 vols., Paris, 1801).

Apuntamientos para la historia natural de los Páxaros del Paraguay y del Río de la Plata, 3 vols., Madrid, 1802–1805.
Well-prepared edition.

Voyages dans l'Amérique Méridionale, ed. C. A. Walckenaer, notes by G. Cuvier and M. Sonnini, 4 vols., Paris, 1809.
French edition which served as source for later Spanish translations.

Descripción e historia del Paraguay y del Río de la Plata, 2 vols., Madrid, 1847. (Vol. I: *Descripción*; vol. II: *Historia*.)
Published posthumously by Azara's nephew; better known in Spanish as *Viajes por la América meridional*.

Geografía física y esférica de las provincias del Paraguay y Misiones guaraníes, Anales del Museo Nacional de Montevideo, 1904.
Edition based on 1790 manuscript in the Biblioteca Nacional de Montevideo.

Viajes por la América meridional, 2 vols., Madrid, Espasa-Calpe, 1941.
Useful edition.

Memoria sobre el estado rural de Río de la Plata y otros informes, Buenos Aires, Bajel, 1943.

Useful edition which includes lengthy bio-bibliographical introduction by Julio César González.

Bartolache, José Ignacio. *Lecciones matemáticas que en la Real Universidad de México dictaba Josef Ignacio Bartolache . . . primer quaderno*, Mexico, Imprenta de la Biblioteca Mexicana, 1769.

Key source.

El Mercurio Volante con Noticias Importantes y Curiosas sobre Varios Asuntos de Física i Medicina, 1–16 (Oct. 17, 1772 – Feb. 10, 1773), Mexico, Imprenta de D. F. de Zúñiga.

Considered by many to be America's first medical journal.

Mercurio Volante (1772–1773), intro. Roberto Moreno, Mexico, Universidad Nacional Autónoma de México, 1979.

Very useful introduction and complete text of 1772–1773 publication.

Beristaín de Souza, José Mariano. *Biblioteca hispanoamericana septentrional*, [1816], 3 vols., Mexico, Universidad Nacional Autónoma de México, 1980.

Well-prepared facsimile edition of this important bibliographical source.

Bueno, Cosme. *Disertaciones geográficas y científicas*, Vol. 3, 1–260 in Manuel de Odriozola (ed.), *Documentos literarios del Perú*, Lima, 1872.

Key source.

Geografía del Perú virreinal (siglo XVIII), ed. Daniel Valcarcel, Lima, Instituto de Historia de la Universidad de San Marcos, 1951.

Includes descriptions relating to modern-day Peru only.

Buffon, Georges-Louis Leclerc. *Natural History*, 10 vols., London, 1947.

Key source for the debate on New World nature and civilization.

Caldas, Francisco José de. *Semanario del Nuevo Reyno de Granada*, [1807–1808], rpt., Paris, Librería Castellana, 1849.

Re-edition of the original, with brief biographical preface and index of issues.

Campillo y Cosío, José del. *Nuevo sistema de gobierno económico para la América: con males y daños que le causa el que hoy tiene, de los que participa como España: y remedios universales para que la primera tenga considerables ventajas, y la segunda mayores intereses*, Madrid, Imprenta de B. Cano, 1789.

Classic eighteenth-century economic study; divided into two parts dealing with problems and suggested remedies.

Carrió de la Vandera, Alonso. *El lazarillo de ciegos caminantes . . . en Gijón, en la Imprenta de la Rovada. Año de 1773*, Lima, 1776.

First edition which gave rise to widespread confusion regarding date and place of publication, and identity of author.

El lazarillo de ciegos caminantes, ed. Martiniano Leguizamón, Buenos Aires, Biblioteca de la Junta de Historia y Numismática Americana, 1908.

Leguizamón's chapter divisions provided basis for future editions.

El lazarillo de ciegos caminantes, ed. Emilio Carilla, Barcelona, Labor, 1973.

Well-prepared edition with introduction and copious notes.

El lazarillo de ciegos caminantes, ed. A. Llorente Medina, Caracas, Biblioteca Ayacucho, 1985.

Well-prepared edition with introductory study, chronology, and appendixes of

Carrió de la Vandera's other extant works.

El lazarillo. A guide for inexperienced travelers between Buenos Aires and Lima, tr. Walter D. Kline, Bloomington, Indiana University Press, 1965.

Edited translation with foreword by Irving A. Leonard and glossary of Spanish terms.

Castillo y Guevara, Francisca Josefa de la Concepción del. *Afectos espirituales*, 2 vols., Bogotá, Biblioteca Popular de Cultura Colombiana/Ministerio de Educación, 1942.

Carefully prepared edition.

Mi Vida, Bogotá, Biblioteca Popular de Cultura Colombiana/Ministerio de Educación, 1942.

Carefully prepared edition of the spiritual autobiography.

Obras completas, intro. Darío Achury Valenzuela, 2 vols., Bogotá, Banco de la República, 1968.

Excellent edition with exhaustive introductory study by the foremost scholar of Madre Castillo's works.

Caulín, Fray Antonio. *Historia coro-gráphica. Natural y evangélica de la Nueva Andalucía*... [1779], ed. Pablo Ojer, Caracas, Academia Nacional de la Historia/ Fuentes para la Historia Colonial de Venezuela, 1966.

Carefully prepared edition.

Cavo, Andrés. *Los tres siglos de México*..., ed. Carlos María Bustamante, Mexico, L. Abadiano y Valdés, 1836–1839.

Bustamante added explanatory notes from Alegre's history of the Jesuits and a "Suplemento" covering the years 1767–1820.

Los Tres Siglos de Méjico, Mexico, Imprenta de J. R. Navarro, 1852.

Reprint of earlier edition.

Clavijero, Francisco Javier. *Storia antica del Messico*, 4 vols., Cesena, Italy, Gregorio Biasini, 1780–1781.

First edition, in Italian.

Storia della California, 2 vols. in one, Venice, M. Fenzo, 1789.

Published posthumously.

Historia antigua de Mégico, tr. from Italian José Joaquín de Mora, 2 vols., London, R. Ackermann, 1826.

There are numerous re-editions of this Spanish translation.

Historia de la antigua o Baja California..., tr. from Italian Nicolás García de San Vicente, Mexico, Imprenta del Museo Nacional de Arqueología, Historia y Etnografía, 1933.

Useful translation.

Historia antigua de México, primera edición del original escrito en castellano por el autor..., ed. Mariano Cuevas, 4 vols., Mexico, Porrúa, 1945.

Important source.

Historia antigua de México, ed. Mariano Cuevas, 4 vols., Mexico, Porrúa, 1964.

Amplified and revised reprint of the 1945 edition.

Historia antigua de México, ed. Rafael García Granados, 2 vols., Mexico, Editora Nacional, 1970.

Well-prepared edition.

The History of Mexico, tr. from Italian Charles Cullen, 2 vols., London, G. G. J. &

J. Robertson, 1787.

Excellent translation.

The History of Mexico, 3 vols., Philadelphia, Budd Bartram/T. Dobson, 1804.

The first of many re-editions of the 1787 Cullen translation.

The History of (Lower) California, tr. and ed. Sara E. Lake and A. A. Gray, Stanford University Press, 1937; California, Manessier Publishing Company, 1971.

Useful translation.

The History of Mexico, intro. Burton Feldman, 2 vols., New York Garland, 1979.

Extremely useful recent re-edition of the 1787 Cullen translation.

Conde y Oquendo, Francisco Javier. *Discurso sobre la elocuencia. El Album Mexicano, periódico de literatura, arte y bellas letras*, Mexico, Ignacio Cumplido, 1849, I, 380–85, 454–7.

Excerpts of Conde y Oquendo's previously unpublished treatise on oratory.

Disertación histórica sobre la aparición de la portentosa imagen de María Sma. de Guadalupe de México, 2 vols., Mexico, Imprenta de la Voz de la Religión, 1852.

First edition of the essay begun in 1794 to refute Bartolache's writings on the Virgin of Guadalupe.

Durand, José (ed.). *Gaceta de Lima*, 2 vols. [1756–1762, 1762–1765], Lima, COFIDE, 1982.

Valuable primary source with well-researched prologue.

Eguiara y Eguren, Juan José de. *Prólogos a la "Biblioteca Mexicana,"* ed. Federico Gómez de Orozco, Mexico, Fondo de Cultura Económica, 1944.

First Spanish translation of the prologues, published as bilingual edition.

Biblioteca mexicana, tr. from Latin Benjamín Fernández Valenzuela, intro. Ernesto de la Torre Villar and Ramiro Navarro de Anda, Mexico, Universidad Nacional Autónoma de México, 1986–1990.

Extensive publishing project, unsurpassed as a source.

Fonseca, Onofre de. *Historia de la milagrosa aparición de Nuestra Señora de la Caridad. Patrona de Cuba y de su Santuario en la Villa del Cobre*, Santiago de Cuba, Escuela Tipográfica "Don Bosco," 1935.

Onofre's manuscript dates from 1703, but was lost and later rewritten by Bernardino Ramírez in 1782.

Gamarra y Davalos, Juan Benito Díaz de. *Tratados. Errores del entendimiento humano. Memorial ajustado. Elementos de filosofía moderna*, ed. José Gaos, Mexico, Universidad Nacional Autónoma de México, 1947.

Selections and translations from Díaz de Gamarra's writings with a useful introduction, chronology, and bibliography.

Gumilla, José. *El Orinoco ilustrado*, intro. Constantino Bayle, S. J. Madrid, Aguilar, 1945.

Lively travel narrative.

Haenke, Thaddeaus Peregrinus. *Descripción del Reyno de Chile*, intro. de Agustín Edwards, Santiago, Nascimento, 1942.

Useful source.

Humboldt, Alejandro de. *Cartas americanas*, tr. Marta Traba, ed. Charles Minguet, Caracas, Biblioteca Ayacucho, 1980.

Letters written from America, most of them after 1800; extensive chronology and bibliography.

Volume 1

Humboldt, Alexander von. *Political Essay on the Kingdom of New Spain*, tr. John Black, ed. Mary Maples Dunn, New York, Knopf, 1972.

> Abridged; useful for English-speaking reader.

Juan, Jorge, and Antonio de Ulloa. *Relación histórica del viaje a la América Meridional . . .*, Madrid, Antonio Marín, 1748.

> First edition of Juan and Ulloa's descriptive treatise on South American flora, fauna, cities, and inhabitants. An important source.

Dissertación histórica, y geográphica sobre el meridiano de demarcación entre los dominios de España, y Portugal, y los parages por donde passa en la América Meridional, conforme a los tratados, y derechos de cada estado, y las mas seguras, y modernas observaciones, Madrid, Antonio Marín, 1749.

> Discusses Spanish/Portuguese borders in the New World.

Noticias secretas de América sobre el estado naval, militar, y político de los reynos del Perú y provincias de Quito . . ., London, Imprenta de R. Taylor, 1826.

> First edition of the manuscript, "Discurso y reflecciones políticas sobre los reynos del Peru," intended by its authors for limited circulation. Key source.

A Voyage to South America, tr. John Adams, 2 vols., London, John Stockdale, 1806.

> Classic English translation of the *Relación histórica*.

A Voyage to South America, intro. Irving A. Leonard, New York, Knopf, 1964. (The John Adams translation, abridged.)

> Carefully prepared edition which includes primarily selections describing eighteenth-century life in the Spanish colonies; of interest for English-speaking reader.

Discourse and Political Reflections on the Kingdoms of Peru [1749], tr. John J. Tepaske and Besse A. Clement, intro. John J. Tepaske, Norman, University of Oklahoma Press, 1978.

> Carefully prepared translation based on manuscript copy of the *Noticias secretas*; slightly edited, with an excellent introductory study.

León y Gama, Antonio de. *Descripción histórica y cronológica de las dos piedras que con ocasión del nuevo empedrado que se está formando en la plaza principal de México, se hallaron en ella el año de 1790* [1792], ed. Carlos María de Bustamante, 2nd. edn. Mexico, Imprenta del Ciudadano Alejandro Valdés, 1832.

> Important edition of León y Gama's attempt to decipher the meaning of the Sun Stone and Statue of Coatlicue.

Llano Zapata, José Eusebio. *Memorias histórico-físicas-apologéticas de la América Meridional*, ed. Ricardo Palma, biographical intro. Manuel de Mendiburu, Lima, Imprenta y Librería de San Pedro, 1904.

> Well-prepared edition of manuscript presented to Charles III in 1761. This first volume deals with historical and scientific topics; other two volumes on flora and fauna have apparently been lost.

Mier Noriega, Fray Servando Teresa de. *Historia de la Revolución de Nueva España, antiguamente Anahuac . . .*, 2 vols., London, Imprenta de Guillermo Glindon, 1813.

Memorias, ed. Antonio Castro Leal, 2 vols., Mexico, Porrúa, 1946; 2nd. edn., 1971.

> First published in 1856.

Ideario político, ed. Edmundo O'Gorman, Caracas, Biblioteca Ayacucho, 1978.

> Very useful volume, bringing together letters, speeches, memoranda; excellent

prologue and bibliography.

Molina, Juan Ignacio. *Compendio de la historia geográfica, natural y civil del reyno de Chile*, Madrid, Don Antonio de Sancha, 1788 (Part I), 1795 (Part II).

Originally written in Italian; key source.

The Geographical, Natural, and Civil History of Chili, 2 vols., London, Longman, Hurst, Rees, & Orme, 1809.

Excellent translation with notes and appendix.

Morell de Santa Cruz, Pedro Agustín. *Historia de la isla y catedral de Cuba*, preface Francisco de Paula Coronado, Havana, Imprenta "Cuba Intelectual," 1929.

Useful edition and introductory essay. Morell de Santa Cruz's history contains text of Balboa's *Espejo de paciencia*.

Moxó, Benito María de. *Cartas mejicanas* [1805], 2nd. edn., Genoa, Tip. de Luis Pellas, 1837.

Useful point of comparison with Clavijero; well-prepared edition.

Muñoz, Juan Batista. "Memoria sobre las apariciones y el culto de Nuestra Señora de Guadalupe de México. Leída en la Real Academia de la Historia por su individuo supernumerario Don Juan Bautista Muñoz" in *Memorias de la Real Academia de la Historia*, vol. V, Madrid, 1817, 205–24.

Text of Muñoz's address on the historiographical sources for the Guadalupan cult.

Historia del nuevo mundo [1793], intro. José Alcina Franch, Mexico, Aguilar, 1975.

Carefully prepared edition of this key source.

Mutis, José Celestino. *Flora de la real expedición botánica del Nuevo Reino de Granada*, Madrid, Cultura Hispánica, 1963.

Very difficult to locate.

Archivo epistolar, ed. Guillermo Hernández de Alba, 2 vols., Bogotá Editorial Kelly, 1968.

Very complete collection of Mutis's vast correspondence.

Olavide y Jáuregui, Pablo de. *El evangelio en triunfo o Historia de un filósofo desengañado*, 8th. edn., 4 vols., Madrid, Don Josef Doblado, 1808.

Standard edition of text.

Obras dramáticas desconocidas, ed. Estuardo Núñez, Lima Biblioteca Nacional del Perú, 1971.

Carefully prepared edition of previously unpublished works.

Obras narrativas desconocidas, ed. Estuardo Núñez, Lima, Biblioteca Nacional del Perú, 1971.

Carefully prepared edition of previously unpublished works.

Oviedo y Baños, José de. *Historia de la conquista y población de la provincia de Venezuela*, Madrid, Gregorio Hermosilla, 1723.

Very difficult to locate.

Historia de la conquista y población de la provincia de Venezuela, Caracas, Domingo Navas Spínola, 1824.

Very difficult to locate.

Historia de la conquista y población de la provincia de Venezuela, ed. Cesáreo Fernández Duro, Madrid, Biblioteca de los Americanistas, 1885.

Annotated edition which includes indexes of personal names and appendix of documents.

Historia de la conquista y población de la provincia de Venezuela, ed. Caracciola Parra León, Analectas de historia patria, Caracas, Parra León Hnos./Editorial Sur América, 1935.

Excellent prologue by Parra León.

Historia de la conquista y población de la provincia de Venezuela, New York, Paul Adams/Scribner's, 1940.

Deluxe facsimile of the 1824 edition, with introduction by Adams, maps, photographs, and index. Re-issued following year in slightly less lavish format.

Historia de la conquista y población de la provincia de Venezuela, intro. Guillermo Morón, Biblioteca de Autores Españoles, Historiadores de Indias, 107 Madrid, Ediciones Atlas 19.

Well-prepared edition.

Historia de la conquista y población de la provincia de Venezuela, Caracas, Homenaje al Cuatricentenario de la Fundación de Caracas/Barcelona, Ariel, 1967.

Facsimile reproduction of 1824 Domingo Navas Spínola edition. The introduction by Pedro Grases includes an extensive bibliography.

The Conquest and Settlement of Venezuela, tr. and intro. Jeannette Johnson Varner, prologue John Lombardi, Berkeley, University of California Press, 1987.

Excellent edition of special interest for English-speaking readers with detailed introductory study, complete bibliography, and glossary.

Pauw, Cornelius de. *Recherches philosophiques sur les Américains*, 3 vols., London, 1771.

Important source for debate on New World civilization.

Raynal, Guillaume-Thomas. *A Philosophical and Political History of the Settlements and Trade of the Europeans in the East and West Indies*, tr. J. O. Justamond, 3rd. edn., 6 vols., London, 1798.

Key source for the debate on New World civilization.

Reynel Hernández, Marcos. *El peregrino con guía y medecina universal del alma*, 1750–1761.

Spiritual autobiography; very difficult to locate.

Ribera, Nicolas Joseph de. *Descripción de la isla de Cuba*. Intro and notes Hortensia Pichardo Viñals, Havana, Instituto Cubano del Libro, 1973.

Well-prepared edition.

Robertson, William. *The Works of William Robertson D. D.*, 8 vols., Oxford, 1825.

Key source for debate on New World natural history and civilization.

Santa Cruz y Espejo, Francisco Javier Eugenio de. *Escritos del Dr. Francisco Javier Eugenio Santa Cruz y Espejo*, prologue, and notes Federico González Suárez, 2 vols., Quito, Imprenta Municipal, 1912.

Far-ranging collection of many previously unpublished writings.

El nuevo Luciano de Quito, 1779, ed. and notes by Aurelio Espinosa Pólit, prologue Isaac J. Barrera, Quito, Imprenta del Ministerio de Gobierno, 1943.

Well-prepared annotated edition.

Primicias de la Cultura de Quito (1792), Quito, Unión Nacional de Periodistas del Ecuador, 1944.

Carefully prepared edition of the prospectus and only seven issues which were published.

Primicias de la Cultura de Quito, Publicaciones del Archivo Municipal, 23, Quito, Archivo Municipal, 1947.
> Facsimile edition.

Escritos médicos, comentarios e iconografía, Quito, Imprenta de la Universidad, 1952.
> Well-prepared collection of Espejo's writings on medical topics, some of them previously unpublished; includes "Reflexiones médicas" and "Memoria sobre el corte de Quinas."

Primicias de la Cultura de Quito, Quito, Publicaciones del Museo de Arte e Historia de la Municipalidad de Quito, 29, 1958.
> Useful edition.

Obra educativa, ed. Philip L. Astuto, Caracas, Biblioteca Ayacucho, 1981.
> Carefully prepared volume which includes *El nuevo Luciano de Quito, Marco Porcio Catón*, and *La ciencia blancardina*.

Obras escogidas, intro. Hernán Rodríguez Castelo, 2 vols., Guayaquil, Clásicos Ariel, n.d.
> Includes bibliographical references.

Ulloa, Antonio de. *Noticias americanas: entretenimientos phísico-históricos, sobre la América Meridional y Septentrional oriental . . .*, Madrid, Manuel de Mina, 1772.
> Key source for natural history of Spanish America.

Unanúe, José Hipólito. *Observaciones sobre el clima de Lima*, Madrid, 1815.
> Key source; difficult to obtain.

Obras científicas y literarias, 3 vols., Barcelona, Serra Hnos. & Russell, 1914.
> Important volume which brings together Unanúe's many diverse writings and includes an introductory biographical study.

Urrutia y Montoya, Ignacio José de. *Obras*, 2 vols., Havana, Imprenta El Siglo xx/ Academia de la Historia de Cuba, 1931.
> Well-prepared edition.

Velasco, Juan de. *Historia del reino de Quito en la América Meridional* [1789–1791], ed. Aurelio Espinosa Pólit, 2 vols., Puebla, Mexico, Biblioteca Mínima Ecuatoriana, 1960.
> The definitive edition of Velasco's work and basis for subsequent re-editions.

Historia del reino de Quito en la América Meridional, ed. Alfredo Pareja Diezcanseco, Caracas, Biblioteca Ayacucho, 1981.
> Very useful edition which includes chronology and bibliography.

Secondary sources

Books

Achury Valenzuela, Darío. *Análisis crítico de los "Afectos espirituales,"* Bogotá, Biblioteca de Cultura Colombiana, 1962.
> Exhaustively detailed study of Madre Castillo's *Afectos*; text of each *Afecto* is followed by a commentary on its language, structure, sources and place within the larger work.

Actas del simposium CCL aniversario nacimiento de Joseph Celestino Mutis, ed. Paz Martín Ferrero, Cadiz, Diputación Pcial. de Cadiz/Editorial La Voz, 1986.

Several articles of interest on Mutis, pharmacological science, and scientific expeditions, although site of symposium (Cadiz) leads to focus on Spanish Enlightenment.

Aldridge, A. Owen. *The Ibero-American Enlightenment*, Urbana and Chicago, University of Illinois, 1971.

Key collection of essays on the Enlightenment in Spain, Latin America and Anglo-America.

Arcila Farias, Eduardo. *Reformas económicas del siglo XVIII en Nueva España.* vol. I: *Ideas económicas, comercio y régimen de comercio libre;* vol. II: *Industria, minería y Real Hacienda*, Mexico, SepSetentas, 1974; rpt., *El siglo ilustrado en América. Reformas económicas del siglo XVIII en Nueva España*, Caracas, Ed. del Ministerio de Educación, 1955.

Important background on Bourbon economic reforms.

Arciniegas, Germán. *Latin America: A cultural history*, New York, Knopf, 1968. (Tr., *El continente de siete colores*, Sudamericana, 1965).

Classic work for English-speaking readers, now somewhat dated.

Arenal, Electa, and Stacey Schlau. *Untold Sisters: Hispanic nuns in their own works*, Albuquerque, University of New Mexico Press, 1989.

Includes selected excerpts from writings of several eighteenth-century Latin American nuns (with brief introductory remarks and English translation).

Arias Divito, Juan Carlos. *Las expediciones científicas españolas durante el siglo XVIII*, Madrid, Cultura Hispánica, 1968.

Wealth of information on scientific expeditions, in particular the botanical expedition to New Spain.

Arrom, José Juan. *Esquema generacional de las letras hispanoamericanas. Ensayo de un método*, Bogotá, Instituto Cara y Cuervo, 1963.

A classic literary history which includes references to many eighteenth-century writers, even if the generational scheme is less persuasive now than when first proposed.

Certidumbre de América; estudios de letras, folklore y cultura, 2nd. edn., Madrid, Gredos, 1971.

Important collection of essays, including Arrom's study of the legend of the Virgen del Cobre of Cuba.

Batllori, Miguel, S. J. *El Abate Viscardo. Historia y mito de la intervención de los Jesuitas en la independencia de Hispanoamérica*, Caracas, Instituto Panamericano de Geografía e Historia, 1953.

Useful background on historical consequences of Jesuit expulsions.

Bernal, Ignacio. *A History of Mexican Archaeology: The vanished civilizations of Middle America*, London, Thames & Hudson, 1980.

Chap. 4, "The Age of Reason (1750–1825)," discusses Clavijero and León y Gama.

Bobb, Bernard E. *The Viceregency of Antonio María Bucareli in New Spain, 1771–1779*, Austin, University of Texas Press, 1962.

Valuable historical background.

Brading, David. *The First America: The Spanish monarchy, creole patriots, and the liberal state, 1492–1867*, Cambridge University Press, 1991.

Impressive and far-reaching cultural history; mentions a number of important eighteenth-century writers.

Buechler, Rose Marie. *Gobierno, minería y sociedad: Potosí y el "Renacimiento" borbónico 1776–1810*, 2 vols., La Paz, Biblioteca Minera Boliviana, 1989; tr. & revised edn., *The Mining Society of Potosí. 1776–1810*, Syracuse University Press, 1981.

   Exhaustively detailed study which provides valuable background for reading of Arzan's *Historia*.

Bueno, Salvador. *Historia de la literatura cubana*, 3rd. edn., Habana, Editora del Ministerio de Educación/Editora Nacional de Cuba, 1963.

   Mentions eighteenth-century Cuban writers not often included elsewhere.

Burkholder, Mark A. *Politics of a Colonial Career: José Baquijano and the Audiencia of Lima*, Albuquerque, University of New Mexico; 1980; Wilmington, Del., Scholarly Resources, 1990.

   Well-researched political biography of a creole Bourbon aristocrat.

Calderón Quijano, José Antonio (ed.). *Los virreyes de Nueva España en el Reinado de Carlos IV*, 2 vols., Escuela de Estudios Hispano-Americanos de Sevilla, 1972.

   Valuable historical background; each chapter dedicated to a different viceroy.

Cardozo Galué, Germán. *Michoacán en el Siglo de las Luces*, Mexico, El Colegio de México, 1973.

   Fairly limited focus; interesting appendix of documents from Michoacan archives.

Carilla, Emilio. *El libro de los misterios: "El lazarillo de ciegos caminantes,"* Madrid, Gredos, 1976.

   Key work in which Carilla synthesizes and expands on his numerous articles on *El lazarillo*.

Cassirer, Ernst. *The Philosophy of the Enlightenment*, tr. Fritz C. A. Koelln and James P. Pettegrove, 1951; rpt., Boston, Beacon Press, 1955.

   Classic study on the Enlightenment.

Chiaramonte, José Carlos. *Pensamiento de la Ilustración. Economía y sociedad iberoamericanas en el siglo XVIII*, Caracas, Biblioteca Ayacucho, 1979.

   Essential anthology of eighteenth-century thinkers, with the *caveat* that Chiaramonte tends to overemphasize importance of peninsular thinking and ignores some Latin American figures.

Deck, Allan F. *Francisco Javier Alegre: A study in Mexican literary criticism*, Rome and Tucson, Jesuit Historical Institute, 1976.

   Key resource for any study of Alegre.

Decorme, Gerard. *La obra de los jesuitas mexicanos durante la época colonial (1752–1767)*, 2 vols., Mexico, Antigua Librería Robredo de José Porrúa & Hijos, 1941. (Vol. I: *Funciones y obras*; vol. II: *Las misiones.*)

   Exhaustively researched study.

Defourneaux, Marceliu. *Pablo de Olavide ou l'Afrancesado (1725–1803)*, Presses Universitaires de Paris, 1959.

   Life and works study focusing on French influences; useful bibliography.

Domínguez Ortiz, Antonio. *Sociedad y estado en el siglo XVIII español*, Barcelona, Ariel, 1976.

   Useful historical background.

García-Pabón, Leonardo. *Espacio andino, escritura colonial y patria criolla: la historia de Potosí en la narrativa de Bartolomé Arzans*, diss., University of Minnesota, 1990.

Valuable addition to Arzans bibliography which proposes that the *Historia* provides a space for representation of creole consciousness.

Gerbi, Antonello. *The Dispute of the New World. The history of a polemic, 1750–1900*, tr. Jeremy Moyle, revised and enlarged edn., University of Pittsburgh Press, 1973. Trans. of *La disputa del Nuevo Mondo: storia de una polemica 1750–1900*, Milan and Naples, Riccardo Ricciadi Editore, 1955.

Fascinating cultural history.

Hanke, Lewis. *Bartolomé Arzáns de Orsúa y Vela's "History of Potosi,"* Providence, R.I., Brown University, 1965.

Very important reference; appendix contains English translation of Arzans's chapter headings and extensive bibliography.

Henríquez Ureña, Max. *Panorama histórico de la literatura cubana*, Havana, Editorial Arte y Literatura, 1978.

Very good overview of early Cuban Literature.

Hernández Luna, Juan. *José Antonio Alzate: estudio biográfico y selección*, Mexico, Secretaría de Educación Pública, 1945.

Useful introduction and anthology, although it does not include Alzate's best-known writings (for example, the essay on cochineal dyes or the description of Xochicalco).

Lafaye, Jacques. *Quetzalcóatl and Guadalupe: The formation of Mexican national consciousness 1531–1813*, University of Chicago Press, 1974. (Trans. *Quetzalcóatl et Guadalupe*, Paris, Gallimard, 1974.)

Absorbing cultural history.

Lafuente, Antonio, and Antonio Mazuecos. *Los caballeros del punto fijo: ciencia, política y aventura en la expedición geodésica hispanofrancesa al virreinato del Perú en el siglo XVIII*, Madrid, Serbal/Consejo Superior de Investigaciones Científicas, 1987.

Lavish volume with fine reproductions of maps and documents from Juan and Ulloa's geodesical expedition.

Lanning, John Tate. *Academic Culture in the Spanish Colonies*, London and New York, Oxford University Press, 1940.

Classic essays (originally delivered as a series of lectures) which include references to a number of eighteenth-century thinkers.

The University in the Kingdom of Guatemala, Ithaca, N.Y., Cornell University Press, 1955.

Classic study of academic culture in colonial Guatemala.

The Eighteenth-Century Enlightenment in the University of San Carlos de Guatemala, Ithaca, N.Y., Cornell University Press, 1956.

Classic study of learning and ideas in a Spanish colonial university.

Lazo, Raimundo. *La literatura cubana. Esquema histórico (desde sus orígenes hasta 1966)*, Havana, Editora Universitaria, 1967.

Useful source for eighteenth-century Cuban writers.

Historia del la literatura hispanoamericana. El período colonial (1492–1780), Havana, Instituto de Libro, 1968.

Brief mentions of Madre Castillo, Alegre, Clavijero, Alzate.

Lezama Lima, José. *La expresión americana*, Madrid, Alianza Editorial, 1969.
Fascinating essay on Latin American culture, though it contains little mention of the eighteenth century.

Lockhart, James, and Stuart B. Schwartz. *Early Latin America: a history of colonial Spanish America and Brazil*, Cambridge University Press, 1983.
Valuable historical background.

Lohmann Villena, Guillermo. *Pedro de Peralta. Pablo de Olavide*, Lima, Biblioteca Hombres del Perú, 1964.
Life and works studies of two important figures from colonial Peru.

López Segrera, Francisco. *Los orígenes de la cultura cubana (1510–1790)*, Havana, Unión de Escritores y Artistas de Cuba, 1969.
Fairly general essay which argues that the eighteenth century brought necessary conditions for development of Cuban culture.

Luque Alcaide, Elisa. *La educación en Nueva España en el siglo XVIII*, Escuela de Estudios Hispano-Americanos de Sevilla, 1970.
Detailed history, with separate chapters devoted to education of Creoles, women, Indians.

Maneiro, Juan Luis, and Manuel Fabri. *Vidas de mexicanos ilustres del siglo XVIII*, ed. Bernabé Navarro, Mexico, Universidad Nacional Autónoma de México, 1956.
Essential source for study of eighteenth-century Mexico.

Maza, Francisco de la. *El guadalupanismo mexicano*, Mexico, Porrúa & Obregón, 1953.
Very complete history of the legend of the Virgin of Guadalupe.

Méndez Plancarte, Gabriel (ed.). *Humanistas de siglo XVIII*, Mexico, Universidad Nacional Autónoma de México, 1941.
Anthologized fragments of works by Mexican Jesuits; another essential source for study of eighteenth-century Mexico.

Menéndez y Pelayo, Marcelino. *Historia de la poesía hispanoamericana*, 2 vols., Madrid, Librería General de Victoriano Suárez, 1911 (I), 1913 (II). References in the text are from II.

Miranda, José. *Humboldt y México*, Mexico, Universidad Nacional Autónoma de México, 1962.
Well-researched study which includes introduction on eighteenth-century Mexico.

Morales Borrero, María Teresa. *La Madre Castillo: su espiritualidad y su estilo*, Bogotá, Instituto Caro y Cuervo, 1968.
Compares style of the *Afectos* and the *Vida*.

Morner, Magnus (ed.). *The Expulsion of the Jesuits from Latin America*, New York, Knopf, 1965.
Useful collection of essays.

Morón, Guillermo. *José de Oviedo y Baños*, Caracas, Fundación Eugenio Mendoza, 1958.
Argues that the literary value of Oviedo y Baños's work lies in its epic impulse, descriptive passages, and anecdotes.

Muriel, Josefina. *Cultura femenina novohispana*, Mexico, Universidad Autónoma de México, 1982.
Muriel's study of women in colonial Mexico stands, along with studies by

Lavrin, Arenal, and Schlau, as an essential source on this topic.

Myers, Kathleen. *Becoming a Nun in Seventeenth-Century Mexico: An edition of the spiritual autobiography of María de San Joseph (Volume 1)*, diss., Providence, R.I., Brown University, 1986.
    A valuable source on late seventeenth- and early eighteenth-century convent writing.

Navarro, Bernabé. *Cultura mexicana moderna en el siglo XVIII*, Mexico, Universidad Nacional Autónoma de México, 1983.
    Essential work for understanding evolution of modern thinking (which Navarro distinguishes from European enlightened thinking) in Mexico.

Onís, Carlos W. de. *Las polémicas de Juan Bautista Muñoz*, Madrid, José Porrúa Turanzas, 1984.
    Intellectual history which discusses polemic between Muñoz and Clavijero.

Onís, Harriet de (ed.). *The Golden Land*, New York, Knopf, 1948.
    Translated fragments of eighteenth-century works; of interest to English-speaking readers despite frequent bibliographic inaccuracies.

Pupo-Walker, Enrique. *La vocación literaria del pensamiento histórico en América; desarollo de la prosa de ficción: siglos XVI, XVII, XVIII, y XIX*, Madrid, Gredos, 1982.

Rama, Angel. *La ciudad letrada*, Hanover, N.H. Ediciones del Norte, 1984.
    Intriguing study of language and writing in the Spanish colonies.

Rodríguez Castelo, Hernán (ed.). *Letras de la Audiencia de Quito (Período Jesuítico)*, Caracas, Biblioteca Ayacucho, 1984.
    Anthology with useful introduction; devotes a chapter to spiritual writers and another to sacred orators.

Romero, José Luis (ed.). *Pensamiento político de la emancipación*, 2nd. edn., 2 vols., vol. I: *1790–1809*; vol. II: *1810–1815*, 1977; Caracas, Biblioteca Ayacucho, 1985.
    Excellent source on eighteenth-century writers and thinkers.

Ronan, Charles. *Francisco Javier Clavigero S. J. (1731–1787). Figure of the Mexican Enlightenment: His life and works*, Chicago, Loyola University Press, 1977.
    Exhaustively researched bio-bibliographical study.

Saínz, Enrique. *La literatura cubana de 1700 a 1790*, Havana, Letras Cubanas, 1983.
    Valuable reference for identifying little-known eighteenth-century Cuban writers.

Sánchez, Luis Alberto. *La literatura peruana: derrotero para una historia espiritual del Perú*, 2 vols., Lima, "La Opinión Nacional," 1929.
    Useful for identifying little-known eighteenth-century Peruvian writers.

Sarrailh, Jean. *L'Espagne eclairée de la seconde moitié du XVIIIe siècle*, Paris, Librairie C. Klincksieck, 1964; Spanish trans., *La España ilustrada de la segunda mitad del siglo XVIII*, Mexico, Fondo de Cultura Económica, 1957.
    Classic study of Spanish Enlightenment.

Shafer, Robert Jones. *Economic Societies in the Spanish World (1763–1821)*, Syracuse, N.Y., Syracuse University Press, 1958.
    Useful background.

Soto Paz, Rafael (ed.). *Antología de periodistas cubanos*, Havana, Empresa Editora de Publicaciones, 1943.
    Useful source on early Cuban periodicals.

Stolley, Karen. *"El lazarillo de ciegos caminantes": un itinerario crítico*, Hanover, N.H., Ediciones del Norte, 1992.
> Analysis of narrative strategies employed by Carrió de la Vandera.

Tavera Alfaro, Xavier. *El nacionalismo en la prensa mexicana del siglo XVIII*, Mexico, Club de Periodistas de México, 1963.
> Discusses importance of periodical literature in disseminating enlightend thought in pre-Independence Mexico.

Temple, William Edward. *José Antonio Alzate y Ramírez and the "Gacetas de literatura de México": 1768–1795*, diss., Tulane University, 1986.
> Exhaustively researched study of Alzate's life and works.

Toribio Medina, José. *La imprenta en Bogotá (1739–1821)*, Santiago, Imprenta Elzeviriana, 1904.
> Key bibliographic source.

La imprenta en la Habana (1707–1810). Notas bibliográficas, Santiago, Imprenta Elzeviriana, 1904.
> Key bibliographic source.

La imprenta en Quito (1760–1818), Santiago, Imprenta Elzeviriana, 1904.
> Key bibliographic source.

Notas bibliográficas referentes a las primeras producciones de la Imprenta en algunas ciudades de la América Española (1754–1823), Santiago, Imprenta Elzeviriana, 1904.
> Key bibliographical source.

Valcárcel, Daniel. *La rebelión de Túpac Amaru*, Mexico, Fondo de Cultura Económica, 1947.
> Valuable historical background.

Valle, Enid Mercedes. *La obra narrativa de Pablo de Olavide y Jáuregui*, diss., University of Michigan, 1987.
> Most complete reading of Olavide's narrative works to date.

Vargas, Fray José María. *Historia de la cultura ecuatoriana*, Quito, Editorial Casa de la Cultura Ecuatoriana, 1965.
> Useful for identifying eighteenth-century Ecuadorian writers.

Whitaker, Arthur Preston. *The Huancavelica Mercury Mine*, Cambridge, Mass., Harvard University Press, 1941; rpt., Westport, Conn., Greenwood Press, 1971.
> Useful historical background for reading Arzans.

Whitaker, Arthur Preston (ed.). *Latin America and the Enlightenment*, intro. Federico de Onís, 2nd. edn., 1942; Ithaca, Cornell University Press, 1961.
> Classic collection of essays.

Articles

Anderson, Benedict. "Creole pioneers" in *Imagined Communities*, revised edn., 1983; London and New York, Verso, 1991, 47–65.
> Argues that key role in growth of nationalism was played by creole government functionaries and provincial publishers.

Antoni, Claudio G. "Women of the early modern period. A late baroque devotional writer: Madre Castillo," *Vox Benedictina*, 4:2 (1987), 155–68.
> Brief introduction, with translated excerpts from *Mi vida*.

Arcila Farias, Eduardo. "Ubicación de Oviedo y Baños en la historiografía" in *Cuatro ensayos de historiografía*, Caracas, Ministerio de Educación, 1957, 33–9; rpt. in Germán Carrera Damas (ed.), *Historia de la historiografía venezolana*, Caracas, Universidad Central de Venezuela, 1961, 45–8.

Well-researched essay on relationship between Oviedo y Baños and the erudite school of historiography.

Astuto, Philip L. "Eugenio Espejo: A man of the enlightenment in Ecuador," *Revista de Historia de América*, 44 (1957), 369–91.

Well-researched article.

"Eugenio Espejo: crítico dieciochesco y pedagogo quiteño," *Revista Hispánica Moderna*, 34:3–4 (1968), 513–22.

Very useful article for background and textual analysis; points to Espejo's use of the dialogue to set forth his pedagogical theories in *El nuevo Luciano* and *La ciencia blancardina*.

Bataillon, Marcel. "Introducción a Concolorcorvo y a su itinerario de Buenos Aires a Lima," *Cuadernos Americanos*, 111:4 (1960), 197–216.

Of fundamental importance; argues definitively against possibility of an Indian author and discusses the split or double narrator.

Beerman, Eric. "Eugenio Espejo and La Sociedad Económica de los Amigos del País de Quito" in Alberto Gil Novales (ed.), *Homenaje a Noël Salomon: Ilustración española e independencia de América*, Barcelona, Universidad Autónoma de Barcelona, 1979, 381–7.

Useful historical background on the "societies of friends" in general and Espejo's role in founding Quito's society.

Betrán, Antonio. "La priora de Santa Rosa de Santa María, una monja fuera de lo común," *México Desconocido*, 181 (1992), 68–70; in English, 23–4.

Given inaccessibility of María Anna Agueda de San Ignacio's writings and paucity of critical studies, a useful – if very basic – introduction.

Beuchot, Mauricio. "La ley natural como fundamento de la ley positiva en Francisco Xavier Alegre," *Dieciocho*, 14:1–2 (1991), 124–9.

Fairly dense discussion of philosophical principles in Alegre.

Bose, Walter B. L. "*El lazarillo de ciegos caminantes* y su problema histórico," *Labor de los Centros de Estudio* (La Plata), 2, 24:3 (1941) 219–87.

Bose is a historian of the colonial postal system who provides valuable background for the text.

Brown, Laura, and Felicity Nussbaum. "Revising critical practices. An introductory essay" in Brown and Nussbaum (eds.), *The New Eighteenth Century*, New York, Methuen, 1987, 1–22.

Cogent introductory essay which calls for an interdisciplinary critique of ideology in eighteenth-century studies.

Buesa Oliver, Tomás. "Sobre Cosme Bueno y algunos de sus coetáneos," *Homenaje a Fernando Antonio Martínez*, Bogotá, Instituto Caro y Cuervo, 1979, 332–72.

Well-researched article which discusses Bueno, Azara, Alcedo, Carrió de la Vandera.

Calvo, Abel. "Feijóo y su concepto de la conquista española de América" in *Fray Benito Jerónimo Feijóo y Montenegro: estudios reunidos en conmemoración del IIo centenario de su muerte (1764–1964)*, Universidad de la Plata, Facultad de

Humanidades y Ciencias de la Educación 1965, 281–92.
Identifies Feijóo's essays of greatest interest to eighteenth-century Latin American writers.

Carilla, Emilio. "Feijóo y América" in *Fray Benito Jerónimo Feijóo y Montenegro: estudios reunidos en conmemoración del IIo centenario de su muerte (1764–1964)*, Universidad de la Plata, Facultad de Humanidades y Ciencias de la Educación 1965, 293–310.
Enumerates essays which mention America.

Cody, W. F. "An index to the periodicals published by José Antonio Alzate y Ramírez," *Hispanic American Historical Review*, 33 (1953), 442–75.
Useful bibliographic resource.

Crocker, Lester. "The Enlightenment: what and who?" *Studies in Eighteenth-Century Culture*, 17 (1987), 335–47.

Defourneaux. "Pablo de Olavide: l'homme et le mythe," *Cahiers du Monde Hispanique et Luso-brésilien*, 7 (1966), 167–78.
Biographical study.

Espín Lastra, Alfonso. "Biblioteca General de la Universidad Central Sección de libros coloniales que pertenecen a la Universidad de San Gregorio Magno y luego a la Biblioteca del doctor Eugenio Espejo," *Cuadernos de Arte y Poesía* (Quito), 9, (1960), 107–47.
Well-researched bibliographical study of Santa Cruz y Espejo.

Galindo y Villa, Jesús. "El enciclopedista Antonio Alzate." *Memorias de la Academia "Antonio Alzate,"* 54 (1934), 1–14.
Well-researched essay on Alzate's life and works.

Garza G., Baudelio. "Análisis de tres aspectos de una obra narrativa de Pablo de Olavide," *Cathedra* (Facultad de Filosofía y Letras de la Universidad de Monterrey), 2 (1975), 39–56.
Structural analysis of "El incógnito o el fruto de la ambición."

Gimbernat de González, Ester. "El discurso sonámbulo de la Madre Castillo," *Letras Femeninas*, 13:1–2 (1987), 42–52.
Analysis of autobiographical subject in *Mi vida*.

Goic, Cedomil. "La novela hispanoamericana colonial" in Luis Iñigo Madrigal (ed.), *Historia de la literatura hispanoamericana*, vol. 1: *Epoca colonial*, Madrid, Cátedra, 1982, 369–406.
Useful discussion of a number of eighteenth-century works, although the characterization of these colonial narratives as "novels" may strike the reader as problematic.

González del Valle, Francisco. "Un trabajo inédito del Padre José Agustín Caballero. *El curso de Filosofía Electiva*, introducción," *Revista Cubana*, 17:2 (1943), 143–61.
Of historical and bibliographical interest.

González Stephan, Beatriz. "The early stages of Latin American historiography" in René Jara and Nicholas Spadaccini (eds.), *1492–1992: Rediscovering colonial writing*, Minneapolis, Minn., Prisma Institute, 1989, 291–322.
Useful essay, with specific mentions of Eguiara and Llano y Zapata.

Grases, Pedro. "La historia de la provincia de Venezuela de José de Oviedo y Baños (1723)" in *De la imprenta en Venezuela*, Caracas, Ediciones de la Facultad de

Humanidades y Educación, 1979.

Written on the occasion of the re-editing of Oviedo y Baños's history; useful overview of work's publication history.

Johnson, Julie Greer. "Feminine satire in Concolorcorvo's *El lazarillo de ciegos caminantes*," *South Atlantic Bulletin*, 45:1 (1980), 11–20; rep. in Julie Greer Johnson, *Women in Colonial Spanish American Literature: Literary images*, Westwood, Conn., Greenwood Press, 1983, 87–114.

Discusses representation of women in *El lazarillo*.

"*El nuevo luciano* and the satiric art of Eugenio Espejo," *Revista de Estudios Hispánicos*, 23:3 (1989), 67–85.

Well-researched article which provides useful introduction to Espejo's life and satiric works.

Karsen, Sonja. "Alexander von Humboldt in South America: From the Orinoco to the Amazon," *Studies in Eighteenth-Century Culture*, 16 (1986), 295–302.

Fairly general overview which discusses Humboldt's 1799–1804 travels with Bonpland to South America.

Kerson, Arnold L. "José Rafael Campoy and Diego José Abad: two enlightened figures of eighteenth-century Mexico," *Dieciocho*, 7:2 (1984), 130–45.

Discusses these two particular figures within more general context of community of Jesuit writers and scholars in eighteenth-century Mexico.

Lafaye, Jacques. "Conciencia nacional y conciencia étnica en la Nueva España: un problema semántico" in James W. Wilkie, Michael C. Meyer, Edna Monjón de Wilkie (eds.), *Contemporary Mexico: Papers of the IV International Congress of Mexican History*, Berkeley, University of California Press/Mexico, El Colegio de México, 1976, 38–46.

Discusses ambiguity of term "nación" in pre-Independence period, with particular mention of Clavijero and Eguiara.

"Literature and intellectual life in colonial Spanish America" in Leslie Bethell (ed.), *The Cambridge History of Latin America*, vol. II: *Colonial Latin America*, Cambridge University Press, 1984, 663–704.

Well-researched background study. Eight volumes planned.

Lemmon, Alfred E. "The Mexican Jesuit expulsos of 1767: theological and philosophical writings," *Xavier Review* (New Orleans), 1:1–2 (1980–1981), 53–7.

Mentions Clavijero, Landivar, Abad, Alegre, Cavo, Guevara, and Bazoazabal.

Leonard, Irving. "Pedro de Peralta: Peruvian polygraph (1664–1743)," *Revista Hispánica Moderna*, 39 (1968), 690–9.

Life and works essay which includes an intriguing mention of Peralta's marginalia to *Lima fundada* (695).

Le Riverend Brusone, Julio J. "Comentario en torno a las ideas sociales de Arrate." *Revista Cubana*, 17:2 (1943), 326–41.

Focus on Arrate's economic arguments regarding slavery in Cuba.

"Carácter y significación de los tres primeros historiadores de Cuba," *Revista Bimestre Cubana*, 65:1–2–3 (1950), 152–80.

Discusses Urrutia y Montoya and Arrate.

"Notas para una bibliografía cubana de los siglos XVII y XVIII," *Universidad de la Habana*, 29–30 (1950), 128–231.

Brusone provides annotated transcriptions of the entries pertaining to Cuban writers in Beristaín's *Biblioteca*, with a brief introductory note and some documents included in appendixes.

Lerner, Isaías. "The *Diccionario* of Antonio de Alcedo as a source of enlightened ideas" in A. Owen Aldridge (ed.), *The Ibero-American Enlightenment*, Urbana and Chicago, University of Illinois Press, 1981, 71–93.

Well-researched article which includes excellent bibliographical notes and many interesting quotes from the *Diccionario*'s entries.

"Sobre dialectología en las letras coloniales: el vocabulario de Antonio de Alcedo," *Sur*, (Jan.–Dec. 1982), 117–29.

Another carefully researched article by Lerner.

Lohmann Villena, Guillermo. "La biblioteca de un peruano de la Ilustración: el contador Miguel Feijó de Sosa," *Revista de Indias*, 174 (1984), 367–84.

Inventory of an eighteenth-century personal library.

Macera Dall'Orso, Pablo. "Bibliotecas peruanas del siglo XVIII" [1962] in *Trabajos de historia*, 4 vols., Lima, Instituto Nacional de Cultura, 1977, I, 283–312.

Well-researched article documenting the difficult material conditions limiting eighteenth-century Peruvian libraries and describing several private, university, and religious libraries.

"Lenguaje y modernismo peruano del siglo XVIII" (1963) in *Trabajos de historia*, 4 vols., Lima, Instituto Nacional de Cultura, 1977, II, 9–77.

Dense and well-researched article which argues ideological significance of linguistic developments in colonies.

"El indio y sus intérpretes peruanos del siglo XVIII" [1964] in *Trabajos de historia*, 4 vols., Lima, Instituto Nacional de Cultura, 1977, II, 303–16.

Article attempts to explain the lack of interest in indigenist studies in eighteenth-century Peru.

"El indio visto por los criollos y españoles" in *Trabajos de historia*, 4 vols., Lima, Instituto Nacional de Cultura, 1977, II, 317–24.

Continuation of previous article.

Marañón, Gregorio. "Vida y andanzas de don Pablo de Olavide" in Manuel Cisneros (ed.), *Seis temas peruanos*, Madrid, Espasa-Calpe, 1960, 99–113.

Bio-bibliographical study.

Margáin, Carlos R. "Don Antonio León y Gama (1735–1802). El primer arqueólogo mexicano. Análisis de su vida y obra" in *Memorias del Primer Coloquio Mexicano de Chistoria de la Ciencia*, 2 vols., Mexico, Sociedad Mexicana de Historia de la Ciencia y la Tecnología, 1964, II, 149–83.

Definitive study to date of León y Gama.

Martín, Juan Luis. "José Martín Félix de Arrate y Mateo de Acosta, el primero que se sintió Cubano," *Revista de la Biblioteca Nacional*, (Havana), 1:4 (1950), 32–60.

Family history with annotated bibliography of Arrate's sources.

Mazzara, Richard A. "Some picaresque elements in Concolorcorvo's *El lazarillo de ciegos caminantes*," *Hispania*, 46:2 (1963), 323–7.

Straightforward essay which discusses master/slave relationship and vagabondage theme.

McPheeters, D. W. "The distinguished Peruvian scholar Cosme Bueno 1711–1798," *Hispanic American Historical Review*, 35:4 (1955), 484–91.

Useful introduction to Bueno's life and works, with special focus on the

Descripciones de provincias.

Minguet, Charles. "Alejandro de Humboldt ante la Ilustración y la independencia de Hispanoamérica" in Alberto Gil Novales (ed.), *Homenaje a Noël Salomon: Ilustración española e Independencia americana*, Universidad Autónoma de Barcelona, 1979, 69–79.

Valuable overview of Humboldt's writings on Latin America.

"América hispánica en el Siglo de las Luces," *Cuadernos Americanos*, 1:1 (1987), 30–41.

Argues that effects of Enlightenment can be seen in late eighteenth century.

Moreno, Rafael. "Creación de la nacionalidad mexicana," *Historia Mexicana*, 12 (1963), 531–51.

Fairly general article, with focus on Alzate and Bartolache's refutation of European charges of American inferiority.

"La concepción de la ciencia en Alzate," *Historia Mexicana*, 13 (1964), 346–78.

Notes encyclopedic character of Alzate's publications.

Moreno, Roberto. "José Antonio de Alzate y los virreyes," *Cahiers du Monde Hispanique et Luso-brésilien*, 12 (1969), 97–114.

Underscores Alzate's polemical character.

"Ensayo biobibliográfico de Antonio de León y Gama," *Boletín del Instituto de Investigaciones Bibliográficas* (Mexico), 2 (1970), 43–135.

The most complete bio-bibliographical study of León y Gama to date.

"Las notas de Alzate a la *Historia antigua* de Clavijero," *Estudios de Cultura Nahuatl*, 10 (1973), 359–92.

Well-researched article which chronicles literary relationship between Alzate and Clavijero.

"El indigenismo de Clavijero y de Alzate" in *Estudios sobre la política indigenista española en América*, 3 vols., Seminario de Historia de América/Universidad de Valladolid, 1977, III, 43–52.

Persuasive argument that Neo-Aztecism is central to Mexican Enlightenment.

Morón, Guillermo. "José de Oviedo y Baños" in *Los cronistas y la historia*, Caracas, Ediciones del Ministerio de Educación, 1957, 85–155.

Very complete study, originally written as introduction to *Historia* for the Biblioteca de Autores Españoles edition.

Navarro, Bernabé. "Alzate, símbolo de la cultura Ilustrada Mexicana," *Memoria y Revista de la Academia Nacional de Ciencias*, 54 (1952), 85–97.

Reflects author's interest in modern philosophy as key element of Mexican Enlightenment.

Parra León, Caracciolo. "Oviedo y Baños: historia de Venezuela" in *Analectas de historia patria*, Caracas, Parra León Hnos., 1935, iv–xlvi.

Exhaustive study of Oviedo y Baños' life and works. Of great interest.

Perricone, Catherine R. "La Madre Castillo: mística para América" in Manuel Criado de Val (ed.), *Santa Teresa y la literatura mística hispánica. Actas del I Congreso Internacional sobre la Literatura Mística Hispánica*, Madrid, EDI, 1984, 1671–742.

Argues link between Madre Castillo's mystic writing and courtly love tradition.

Phelan, John Leddy. "Neo-Aztecism in the eighteenth century and the genesis of

Mexican nationalism" in Stanley Diamond (ed.), *Culture in History: Essays in honor of Paul Radin*, New York, Octagon, 1981, 760–70.

Analysis of attitudes of educated Creoles toward the Indians.

Planchart, Julio. "Oviedo y Baños y su *Historia de la conquista y población de la provincia de Venezuela*" in *Discursos*, Caracas, Tip. Americana, 1941, 5–57; rpt. in *Temas críticos*, Caracas, Ministerio de Educación Nacional, 1948, 207–48.

Careful reading of the *Historia* which begins by praising its "venezolanidad."

Portuondo, José Antonio. "Los comienzos de la literatura cubana (1510–1790)" in *Panorama de la literatura cubana*, Universidad de la Habana/Centro de Estudios Cubanos, 1970, 7–85.

Identifies Cuban writers often overlooked in more general literary histories.

Pupo-Walker, Enrique. "En el azar de los caminos virreinales: relectura de *El lazarillo de ciegos caminantes*" in his *La vocación literaria del pensamiento histórico en América*, Madrid, Gredos, 1982, 647–70.

Important essay which focuses on relationship to historiographical tradition and the role played by double narrator.

Real Díaz, José J. "Don Alonso Carrió de la Vandera, autor del 'Lazarillo de ciegos caminantes'," *Anuario de Estudios Americanos* (Seville), 13 (1956), 387–416.

Important study which put to rest speculation about Indian author.

Rivera-Rodas, Oscar. "Niveles diegéticos en las crónicas de Arzans," *Revista Iberoamericana*, 134 (1986), 2–28.

Persuasive article analyzing temporal framework of *Historia*.

Robledo Palomeque, Angela Inés. "La escritura mística de la Madre Castillo y el amor cortesano: religiones de amor," *Thesaurus*, 42 (1987), 379–89.

Standard "life and works" article, primarily based on *Mi vida*.

Ruiz Castañadea, María del Carmen. "La segunda *Gazeta de México* (1728–1739, 1742)," *Boletín del Instituto de Investigaciones Bibliográficas*, 2:1 (1970), 23–42.

Interesting background on an early Mexican gazette.

Soons, Alan. "An idearium and its literary presentation in 'El lazarillo de ciegos caminantes'," *Romanische Forschungen*, 91 (1979), 92–5.

Analysis of socio-historical issues raised in the text.

Tavera Alfaro, Xavier. "Periodismo dieciochesco," *Historia mexicana*, 2 (1952), 110–15.

Discusses Alzate's role in disseminating scientific and philosophical Enlightenment within evolving political climate of eighteenth-century Mexico.

Torre Revello, José. "Viajeros, relaciones, cartas y memorias. (Siglos XVII, XVIII y primer decenio del XIX)" in Ricardo Levene (ed.), *Historia de la nación Argentina*, vol. IV: *El momento histórico del virreinato del Río de la Plata*, Buenos Aires, Ateneo, 1940, 545–85.

Mentions Concolorcorvo and Félix de Azara.

Torres, Bibiano. "La epidemia de Matlalzahuatl de 1736–1739" in *Estudios sobre la política indigenista española en América*, 3 vols., Seminario de Historia de América/Universidad de Valladolid, 1975–1976, II, 189–95.

Historical background of epidemic mentioned by Alegre and Cavo which led to designation of Virgin of Guadalupe as patron saint of Mexico City.

Waldron, Kathy. "The sinners and the bishop in colonial Venezuela: the *Visita* of Bishop Mariano Martí, 1771–1784" in Asunción Lavrin (ed.), *Sexuality &*

Marriage in Colonial Latin America, Lincoln, Nebr., and London, University of Nebraska Press, 1989, 156–77.

Of particular interest because Martí's investigations reflect the more general eighteenth-century interest in enlightened reforms based on the methodical gathering of information.

Whilhite, John F. "The Enlightenment in Latin America: tradition versus change," *Dieciocho*, 3:1 (1980), 18–26.

Notes scientific and economic interests of many eighteenth-century writers.

Wilson, Iris Higbie. "Scientists in New Spain: the eighteenth century expeditions," *Journal of the West* 1:1 (1962), 24–44.

Fairly rudimentary overview of the Royal Scientific Expedition to New Spain and Malaspina's expedition to circumnavigate the globe; useful introduction for English-speaking readers to the climate of scientific expedition in eighteenth-century Latin America.

Zapata, Roger. "El 'Otro' del *Lazarillo*," *Dieciocho*, 13:1–2 (1990), 58–70.

Argues that Carrió de la Vandera's work reflects a colonialist vision which attempts to defend Spain's disintegrating colonial structures.

Chapter 11: Lyric poetry of the eighteenth and nineteenth centuries

More than any other period in the history of Latin American literature, the eighteenth century calls for a reading – and often a rediscovery – of primary texts, rather than a review of secondary sources, themselves scarce. The present essay and the following bibliography have been guided by that premise, which has been extended to the discussion of the much-neglected nineteenth-century lyric as well. There are excellent editions of some individual figures: Heredia (*Poesías completas*) and Olmedo (*Poesías completas*) – though as the dates suggest, they are due for review or at least to be made available in more accessible reprintings – and more recently Melgar (*Poesías completas*) and Pardo y Aliaga (*Poesías*); and Barcia (*La lira argentina*) has provided a superb text for an important anthology from the period. On the other hand, J. M. Gutiérrez's anthology *América poética* has never been reprinted. What is true for such figures whose importance is universally recognized, extends of course to lesser-known authors and the great mass of poetry dispersed in periodical publications or of still more difficult access, although Miranda and González Casanova (*Sátira anónima del siglo XVIII*), the facsimile of the *Mercurio Peruano* (1965) and the exemplary work of Hernández de Alba and Hernández Peñalosa (*Poemas en alabanza de los defensores de Cartagena de Indias en 1741*) testify to the feasibility of significantly expanding the body of texts. The field becomes all the broader and the scholarly needs all the more urgent, if, as I have argued, indigenous literature is to be reclaimed from the discipline of anthropology, the scientific expeditionaries accounted the acme of enlightenment letters, and, more generally, the division between verse and prose superseded. Unfortunately, I have been unable to pursue those directions within the present constraints, and the bibliography of primary sources represents, therefore, but a sampling of more or less accessible editions of the authors mentioned in the text. Note, however, that I do include nineteenth-century critical prose among primary sources, since, I believe, these texts must be studied in their own right for a proper assessment of

Romanticism, and not merely as a point of entrance to the poetry that is their concern.

With regard to the secondary sources, the situation is, if anything, more drastic than with respect to primary texts. The case of Gómez de Avellaneda, however, points the way forward. Long neglect was first addressed with modest results by Alzaga and Núñez (*Ensayo de diccionario del pensamiento vivo de la Avellaneda*) and Fontanella ("Mystical diction and imagery in Gómez de Avellaneda and Carolina Coronado") and even Cabrera and Zaldivar (*Homenaje a Gertrudis Gómez de Avellaneda*); Miller "Gertrude the Great" is more helpful. Then, at last, the major breakthrough by Kirkpatrick, *Las Románticas*; see also Harter, "Gertrudis Gómez de Avellaneda." The cases can be multiplied, as no-one, with the exception of Bello, has received proper critical attention (even Bello is most frequently the subject of study for his work in prose, but see Bareiro Saguier ["La poesía de Andrés Bello"], as well as the excellent discussion by Rivera-Rodas [*La poesía hispanoamericana del siglo xix*] cited in the text). In this light, I have focused a considerable portion of the bibliography on studies of English literature of a theoretical bent. It is becoming increasingly commonplace to declare that Latin American Romanticism is a separate phenomenon, incommensurable with European developments (a claim which, in itself, represents a romantic stance). This is true enough, if the point is not exaggerated, but it does not obviate the study of contemporaneous literatures elsewhere for an illumination of the contrasts as well as the commonalities. Moreover, much of the theoretical discussion in Anglo-American and continental literary studies over the past generation has arisen precisely from the reading of the eighteenth- and ninteenth-century literatures in those areas. To ignore these developments is even greater folly than to bring foreign theories to bear upon Hispanic literature without concern for the specificity of cultural context and literary tradition. The items included here are suggestive of the variety of reading strategies being explored elsewhere. I might add that if eighteenth- and ninteenth-century studies in Latin American letters are to adopt a more comparative approach, that effort might well begin closest to home through a reconsideration of the peninsular tradition, though to do so will mean overcoming the prejudices of the very period in question. Critical studies of eighteenth- and ninteenth-century peninsular literature are also in need of renewal and reinforcement but, particularly with respect to the eighteenth century, they are far in advance of Latin American criticism. The work of Sebold (e.g. *El rapto de la mente*) and Arce (*La poesía del siglo ilustrado*), along with that of Dérozier (*Manuel Josef Quintana et la naissance du libéralisme en Espagne*), Demerson (*Don Juan Meléndez Valdés y su tiempo*) and Polt (*Batilo*) mentioned in the present essay, provide a necessary base for Latin American studies of the period.

Primary sources (including anthologies)

Alegre, Javier. *Opúsculos inéditos latinos y castellanos del P. Francisco Javier Alegre (veracruzano) de la Compañía de Jesús*, Mexico, Imprenta de Francisco Díaz de León, 1889.

   Poetry of one of the leading figures of the neo-Latin school; includes his annotated translation of Boileau.

Amunátegui, Miguel Luis, and Gregorio Victor Amunátegui. *Juicio crítico de algunos poetas hispano-americanos*, Santiago, Imprenta del Ferrocarril, 1861.

A crucial measure of mid nineteenth-century taste, this early effort in the history of Latin American literary criticism commends itself for its valuable information, its continental scope, and its acute judgment, often at odds with the high acclaim received by the poets under study in their own national contexts.

Baralt, Rafael María. *Obras literarias publicadas e inéditas de Rafael María Baralt*, ed. and intro. Guillermo Díaz-Plaja, Biblioteca de Autores Españoles, 204, Madrid, Real Academia Española, 1967.

Prose and verse texts with an informative introduction by Díaz-Plaja.

Barcia, Pedro Luis. *La lira argentina o Colección de las piezas poéticas dadas a luz en Buenos Aires durante la guerra de su independencia* [Buenos Aires, 1824], Biblioteca de la Academia Argentina de las Letras, Serie Clásicos Argentinos, 25, Buenos Aires, Academia Argentina de las Letras, 1982.

Exemplary editorial presentation of a most important nineteenth-century anthology.

Bareiro Saguier, Rubén (ed.) *Literatura guaraní del Paraguay*, Biblioteca Ayacucho, 70, Caracas, Biblioteca Ayacucho, 1980.

Illuminating collection of indigenous literature.

Barrera Vásquez, Alfredo (trans. and ed.). *El libro de los cantares de Dzitbalché*, Serie Investigaciones, 9, Mexico, Instituto Nacional de Antropología, 1965.

A collection of Yucatec Mayan lyric poetry compiled in the eighteenth century; includes facsimiles and transcriptions of the original texts, translations, a brief introduction, and excellent notes.

Bello, Andrés. *Obra literaria*, ed. and intro. Pedro Grases, chronology Oscar Sambrano Urdaneta, Biblioteca Ayacucho, 50, Caracas, Biblioteca Ayacucho, 1985.

A widely accessible, annotated edition of the literary works of the outstanding intellectual figure of the early nineteenth century; the collection includes his complete poetry as well as valuable essays including literary criticism devoted to such figures as J. M. Heredia and J. J. Olmedo.

Bolívar, Simón. *Cartas del Libertador*, ed. Vicente Lecuna, 10 vols., Caracas, Lit. y Tip. del Comercio, 1929.

A fundamental source for the study of America in the Independence period.

Caro, José Eusebio. *Antología. Verso y prosa*, Biblioteca Popular de Cultura Colombiana, Bogotá, Editorial Iqueima, 1951.

A modern edition of one of the principal poets of the romantic period.

Carilla, Emilio (ed.). *Poesía de la Independencia*, Biblioteca Ayacucho, 59, Caracas, Biblioteca Ayacucho, 1979.

A good anthology based upon the findings of Carrilla, *La literatura de la independencia hispanoamericana*.

Castillo, Francisca Josefa del. *Afectos espirituales*, Clásicos colombianos, 2–3, 2 vols., Bogotá, Biblioteca Popular de Cultura Colombiana, 1942.

Devotional guide to the mystical path: a very important prose work; includes Madre Castillo's poetry.

Castillo Andraca y Tamayo, Fray Francisco del. *Obras de Fray Francisco del Castillo Andraca y Tamayo*, intro. and notes Rubén Vargas Ugarte, S. J. Clásicos peruanos, 2, Lima, Editorial Studium, 1948.

A fine edition of a very interesting eighteenth-century poet.

Cortés, José Domingo (ed.). *Poetisas americanas. Ramillete poético del bello sexo hispano-americano*, Paris and Mexico, Librería de A. Bouret & hijos, 1875.

The most extensive compilation of women's poetry in the nineteenth century: a treasure of little-studied and altogether forgotten names.

De la Campa, Antonio R., and Raquel Chang-Rodríguez. *Poesía hispanoamericana colonial. Historia y antología*, Madrid, Alhambra, 1985.

More an anthology than a literary history; nevertheless, the brief introductions to each writer are very informative and the selection of eighteenth-century authors is excellent.

Echeverría, Esteban. *Dogma socialista*, intro. Alberto Palcos, Biblioteca de Autores Nacionales y Extranjeros referente a la República Argentina, 2, Universidad Nacional de La Plata, 1940.

An invaluable collection of prose texts by Echeverría, J. M. Gutiérrez, and others.

"El matadero" y "La cautiva" de Esteban Echeverría, suivis de trois essais de Noé Jitrik, Annales littéraires de l'univérsité de Besançon, 103, Paris, Les Belles Lettres, 1969.

The edition of these important texts by Echeverría recommends itself for the inclusion of the valuable essays by Jitrik.

Edmonson, Munro S. "The songs of Dzitbalche: a literary commentary," *Tlalocan*, 9 (1982), 173–208.

Transcription and English translation of this eighteenth-century compilation of Mayan lyric poetry, with a brief but valuable commentary.

Falcao Espalter, Mario. *Antología de poetas uruguayos*, vol. 1, Montevideo, Claudio García, 1922.

Good selection but no critical apparatus.

Flores, Angel. *The Literature of Spanish America*, 5 vols., New York, Las Américas, 1966.

A standard anthology of particular use to the reader with limited command of Spanish, since extensive prose translations of passages are provided in the notes.

Gautier, Théophile. *Oeuvres complètes*, vol. XI, Geneva, Slatkine Reprint, 1978.

A major figure in French Romanticism; the volume includes his *Histoire du romantisme* (1884).

Ghiraldo, Alberto. *Antología americana*, 4 vols., Madrid, Renacimiento, 1923.

Not widely known, this collection offers nevertheless the best representative selection of any anthology of late eighteenth- and nineteenth-century prose and poetry.

Gómez de Avellaneda, Gertrudis. *Obras literarias*, vol. 1. *Poesías líricas*, intro. Nicasio Gallego, "Apuntes biográficos" by Nicomedes Pastor Díaz, Madrid, Rivadeneyra, 1869.

A collection of poetry compiled late in the career of the Cuban woman who had become the leading literary figure in Spain at mid-century; astonishingly under-studied.

Gutiérrez, Juan María (ed.) *América poética. Coleccion escojida de composiciones en verso, escritos por americanos en el presente siglo. Parte lírica*, Valparaíso, Imprenta del Mercurio, 1846.

The first continent-wide anthology of lyric poetry in Spanish America: this is a

Volume 1

text of the utmost importance that urgently demands reprinting in a critical edition.

Estudios biográficos y críticos sobre algunos poetas sud-americanos anteriores al siglo XIX, Buenos Aires, Imprenta del Siglo, 1865.

An inaugural investigation of colonial literature, including essays on Sor Juana, Aguirre, Lavardén, and Olavide, by the best Hispanic American literary critic of the nineteenth century.

Gutiérrez, Ricardo, and Olegario Víctor Andrade. *Selección de poemas. Ricardo Gutiérrez/Olegario Víctor Andrade*, Biblioteca Argentina Fundamental, 7, Buenos Aires, Centro Editor de América Latina, 1967.

Two estimable late nineteenth-century poets in a popular format.

Gutiérrez González, Gregorio. *Poesías*, Bogotá, Editorial de Cromos, 1926.

A collection by one of the best poets of the mid nineteenth century; no critical apparatus.

Heredia, José María. *Poesías completas. Homenaje de la Ciudad de la Habana en el centenario de la muerte de Heredia. 1839–1939*, Colección Histórica Cubana y Americana, 3, 2 vols., Municipio de la Habana, 1940.

A superb critical edition of the complete poetry of the most important poet of the period.

Hernández de Alba, Guillermo, and Guillermo Hernández Peñalosa (eds.). *Poemas en alabanza de los defensores de Cartagena de Indias en 1741*, Publicaciones del Instituto Caro y Cuervo, 50, Bogotá, Instituto Caro y Cuervo, 1982.

An excellent edition of poems, related documents, and introductory material.

Luz y Caballero, José de la. "Filósofos cubanos. El presbítero José Agustín Caballero," *Revista de Cuba*, 3 (1878), 481–91.

Reprint of the 1835 text (*Diario de la Habana*) of the eulogy of one Cuban philosopher by another; brief portrait of an intellectual era.

Manzano, Juan Francisco, and Gabriel de la Concepción Valdés. *Autobiografía, cartas y versos (Havana 1937)/Poesías completas de Plácido (Paris 1862)*, Nendeln, Kraus Reprint, 1970.

Better in prose than in verse, Manzano's account of his life as a slave in Cuba is a document of great importance for both social and literary history. His work is bound in this volume with a reprint of the 1862 edn. of the poetry of Plácido (see Valdés, *Los poemas más representativos de Plácido*).

Martí, José. *Obras completas. Edición conmemorativa del centenario de su natalicio*, ed. M. Isidro Méndez, Mariano Sánchez Roca, and Rafael Marquina, 2 vols., Havana, Editorial Lux, 1953.

A two-volume collection of the writings of the preeminent intellectual figure in Spanish American letters at the close of the nineteenth century.

Meléndez Valdés, Juan. *Obras en verso*, ed. John H. R. Polt and Georges Demerson, Colección de Autores Españoles del Siglo XVIII 28, Oviedo, Cátedra Feijoo-Centro de Estudios del Siglo XVIII, 1981–1983.

Exemplary critical edition.

Melgar, Mariano. *Poesías completas*, ed. Aurelio Miró Quesada, Estuardo Núñez, Antonio Cornejo Polar, Enrique Aguirre, and Raúl Bueno Chavez, Clásicos peruanos, 1, Lima, Academia Peruana de la Lengua, 1971.

Excellent critical edition.

525

Menéndez y Pelayo, Marcelino. *Antología de poetas hispano-americanos*, 4 vols., Madrid, Sucesores de Rivadeneyra, 1895.
   The largest selection in the most widely available anthology, compiled by an indefatigable researcher whose great erudition, Horatian taste, and colonialist prejudices have dominated scholarship in the field.
Mercurio peruano, facsimile edn., 6 vols., Lima, Biblioteca Nacional del Perú, 1965.
   A reprint of one of the most important periodical publications of the Latin American Enlightenment.
Miranda, José, and Pablo González Casanova (eds.). *Sátira anónima del siglo XVIII*, Letras Mexicanas, Mexico, Fondo de Cultura Económica, 1953.
   Very valuable anthology of anonymous poetry from Mexico with a useful introductory essay by González Casanova.
Navarrete, Manuel. *Poesías profanas*, Biblioteca del Estudiante Universitario, 7, Mexico, Ediciones de la Universidad Nacional Autónoma, 1939.
   An accessible collection from Mexico's most important poet at the close of the eighteenth century.
Ochoa, Anastasio de. *Poesías de un mexicano*, 2 vols., New York, Lanuza, Mendia, 1828.
   A collection of great importance.
Olmedo, José Joaquín. *Poesías completas*, ed. Aurelio Espinosa Pólit, Biblioteca Americana, Literatura Moderna, Poesía, Mexico, Fondo de Cultura Económica, 1947.
   Excellent edition including invaluable notes; the introductory essay is still the best text on Olmedo.
Pacheco, José Emilio (ed.). *La poesía mexicana del siglo XIX (antología)*, Mexico, Empresas Editoriales, 1965.
   A good selection of poetry made still better by the valuable introductory notes to each author in the anthology and a useful bibliography; Pacheco makes it clear nonetheless that he finds little interest in the period.
Pardo y Aliaga, Felipe. *Poesías de don Felipe Pardo y Aliaga*, ed., intro. and notes Luis Monguió, Berkeley, University of California Press, 1973.
   Excellent edition of an important mid nineteenth-century Peruvian poet, including a very informative introduction and comprehensive bibliography.
Peralta Barnuevo Rocha Benavides, Pedro de. *Lima fundada / o conquista del Peru, / poema heroico / en que se decanta / toda la historia del descubrimiento y sujecion de sus provincias / por D. Francisco Pizarro / Marqués de los Atabillos, inclito y primer gobernador de este vasto imperio* [1732], ed. Manuel de Odriozola, Colección de Documentos Literarios del Perú, 1, Lima, Establecimiento de Tipografía y Encuadernación de Aurelio Alfaro, 1863.
   An extremely long epic of the colonial history of Peru: highly representative of the meeting between baroque style and the newly developing Enlightenment spirit.
Quintana, Manuel José. "Noticia histórica y literaria de Meléndez" in Ferrer del Río (ed.), *Obras completas del Excmo. Sr. D. Manuel José Quintana*, Biblioteca de Autores Españoles, 19, Madrid, Imprenta de Hernando & Co., 1898, 109–21.
   Valuable critical reflections by the leading man of letters in Spain in the first quarter of the nineteenth century. N.B. Despite the title of the volume, BAE 19 is

by no means complete.

Poesías completas, ed. Albert Dérozier, Madrid, Clásicos Castalia, 16, Madrid, Castalia, 1980.

A superb edition with excellent introduction and notes of the complete poetry of the Spanish author with the most significant impact on the formation of Spanish American verse in the early nineteenth century. Quintana's fortunes have declined over the past century; his star will rise again.

Rivera, Jorge B. (ed.). *Poesía gauchesca*, prologue Angel Rama, Biblioteca Ayacucho, 29, Caracas, Biblioteca Ayacucho, 1977.

A fine anthology of gaucho poetry.

Rivera de Alvarez, Josefina, and Manuel Alvarez Nazario. *Antología general de la literatura puertorriqueña: prosa-verso-teatro*, vol. 1: *Desde los orígenes hasta el realismo y naturalismo*, Madrid, Ediciones Partenón, 1982.

Valuable collection with useful critical notes.

Rodríguez Castelo, Hernán (ed.). *Letras de la Audiencia de Quito (período jesuita)*, Biblioteca de Ayacucho, 112, Caracas, Biblioteca Ayacucho, 1984.

A fine collection including the complete poetry of Juan Bautista Aguirre. See the valuable introduction by the editor with an extensive section dedicated to Aguirre.

Salaverry, Carlos Augusto. *Salaverry, Poesía*, ed. Alberto Escobar, Biblioteca de Cultura, Lima, Universidad Nacional Mayor de San Marcos, Patronato del Libro Universitario, 1958.

A collection with a modest critical apparatus.

Sanfuentes, Salvador. *Obras escogidas de D. Salvador Sanfuentes*, Edición de la Academia Chilena, Santiago, Imprenta Universitaria, 1921.

Selection of work by an important nineteenth-century poet.

Santa Cruz y Espejo, Francisco Javier Eugenio de. *Obra educativa*, ed. Philip L. Astuto, Biblioteca Ayacucho, 89, Caracas, Biblioteca Ayacucho, 1981.

Includes the major texts of an important prose writer who articulates a transitional poetics in reaction to baroque style and scholastic method.

Shelley, Percy Bysshe. *Selected Poetry and Prose of Percy Bysshe Shelley*, ed. Carlos Baker, New York, Modern Library, 1951.

Accessible edition with an introduction by Baker.

Terralla Landa, Esteban. *Lima por dentro y fuera*, ed. Alan Soons, Exeter Hispanic Texts, University of Exeter, 1978.

Modern edition with glossary of this important satiric poem originally published in 1797.

Urbina, Luis G., Pedro Henríquez Ureña, and Nicolás Rangel. *Antología del centenario. Estudio documentado de la literatura mexicana durante el primer siglo de independencia. 1800–1821* [1910], Mexico, Porrúa, 1985.

The best critical anthology of any of the national literatures of this period, including, among other items of the greatest value, a substantial introduction by Urbina.

Ureña de Henríquez, Salomé. *Poesías completas. Edición conmemorativa del centenario de su nacimiento 1850–1950*, Biblioteca Dominicana, Serie I, vol. 4, Ciudad Trujillo, Impresora Dominicana, 1950.

The edition includes some prose by the author as well as an extensive introduction by Joaquín Balaguer and a critical bibliography.

Valdés, Gabriel de la Concepción (Plácido). *Los poemas más representativos de Plácido (edición crítica)*, eds. Frederick S. Stimson and Humberto E. Robles, Estudios Hispanófila, 40, Chapel Hill, N.C., Estudios Hispanófila, 1976.
Useful modern edition.

Varela, Juan Cruz. *Poesías*, intro. Manuel Mujica Láinez, Biblioteca de Clásicos Argentinos, 9, Buenos Aires, Estrada, 1934.
Comprehensive collection; a new critical edition is urgently needed.

Zequeira y Arango, Manuel de. *Poesías [de] Zequeira y Rubalcava*, Havana, Comisión Nacional Cubana de la UNESCO, 1964.

Secondary sources

Books

Abraham, Nicolas, and Maria Torok. *L'écorce et le noyau*, La Philosophie en effet, Anasémies, 2, Paris, Aubier-Flammarion, 1978.
A radical revision of Freud that provides a theoretical basis for the melancholic poem. One essay has appeared in Spanish: Abraham and Torok, "El duelo o la melancolía: introyectar-incorporar," translated by Marina Pérez de Mendiola, *Revista de Estudios Hispánicos*, 22:3 (1988), 93–107.

Abrams, M. H. *The Mirror and the Lamp: Romantic theory and the critical tradition*, Oxford University Press, 1953.
A seminal study of romantic poetics focusing on English literature.

The Correspondent Breeze: Essays on English Romanticism, New York, Norton, 1984.
Important collection of essays; see especially, "Structure and style in the greater romantic lyric" (pp. 76–108), originally published in 1965.

Alzaga, Florinda, and Ana Rosa Núñez. *Ensayo de diccionario del pensamiento vivo de la Avellaneda*, Collección Clásicos Cubanos, Miami, Ediciones Universales, 1975.
A thesaurus.

Arce, Joaquín. *La poesía del siglo ilustrado*, Madrid, Alhambra, 1981.
An essential study of eighteenth-century Spanish poetry.

Batllori, Miguel. *La cultura hispana-italiana de los jesuitas expulsos. Españoles-hispanoamericanos-filipinos*, Madrid, Gredos, 1966.
Invaluable study of the cultural contribution of the Jesuits.

Berruezo León, María Teresa. *La lucha de Hispanoamérica por su independencia en Inglaterra. 1800–1830*, Madrid, Ediciones de Cultura Hispánica, 1989.
Highly informative study of the interrelations of the many important Hispanic figures of the period who crossed paths in London.

Bloom, Harold. *The Anxiety of Influence. A theory of poetry*, New York, Oxford University Press, 1973.
The cornerstone of Boom's large-scale effort to revamp the theoretical conception of literary history.

Bravo Villasante, Carmen. *Una vida romántica: La Avellaneda*, Madrid, Cultura Hispánica, 1986.

Updated biography.

Brown, Marshall. *Preromanticism*, Stanford University Press, 1991.

An important, theoretically informed study, concentrating on English and German literature, that redefines the period.

Cabrera, Rosa M., and Gladys B. Zaldivar (eds.). *Homenaje a Gertrudis Gómez de Avellaneda. Memorias del simposio en el centenario de su muerte*, Miami, Ediciones Universal, 1981.

An uneven collection and surprisingly slender, given the magnitude of the subject; nevertheless, a first step in revitalizing studies of Gómez de Avellaneda.

Caceres Romero, Adolfo. *Nueva historia de la literatura boliviana*, vol. I: *Literaturas aborígenes (Aimara-Quecha-Callawaya-Guarin)*, La Paz and Cochabamba, Bolivia, Editorial los Amigos del País, 1987.

A valuable general introduction to the indigenous literatures of four language groups of Bolivia from pre-Columbian times to the present.

Carilla, Emilio. *La literatura de la independencia hispanoamericana (neoclasicismo y prerromanticismo)*, Editorial Universitaria de Buenos Aires, 1964.

An informative early survey, long a standard work in the field.

Cevallos Candau, Francisco J. *Juan Bautista Aguirre y el barroco colonial*, Madrid, Edi-6, 1983.

Comprehensive treatment.

Del Pino, Díaz, (ed.). *Revista de Indias*, 180 (1987).

Valuable special issue dedicated to the scientific expeditions of the Enlightenment period.

Demerson, Georges. *Don Juan Meléndez Valdés y su tiempo (1754–1817)*, Madrid, Taurus, 1971.

Important biography.

Dérozier, Albert. *Manuel Josef Quintana et la naissance du libéralisme en Espagne*, Paris, Les Belles Lettres, 1968.

Excellent biography, including important critical insights into the work of Quintana and the literature of the period.

Freud, Sigmund. *The Standard Edition of the Psychological Works of Sigmund Freud*, general ed. James Strachey, vol. XIV, London, Hogarth, 1957.

The volume contains, among other essays, "Mourning and melancholia" (1917).

Gilbert, Sandra M., and Susan Gubar. *The Madwoman in the Attic: The woman writer and the nineteenth-century literary imagination*, New Haven, Yale University Press, 1979.

A landmark study that adapts H. Bloom's theory of revisionism to the study of women's writing in the nineteenth century.

Henríquez Ureña, Pedro. *Literary Currents in Hispanic America*, [1945], New York, Russell & Russell, 1963.

The best one-volume literary history of Latin America.

Jiménez Rueda, Julio. *Letras mexicanas en el siglo XIX*, Mexico, Fondo de Cultura Económica, 1944.

Chapters 1–7 dedicated to the history of society and the arts of eighteenth-century Mexico: a good introduction.

Kernan, Alvin. *The Imaginary Library. An essay on literature and society*, Princeton

University Press, 1982.

    See the general theoretical argument of Chapter 1, concerning the social institution of literature, which is developed further in Kernan, *Printing Technology* (below).

Printing Technology, Letters and Samuel Johnson, Princeton University Press, 1987.

    A study of the impact of new technology and the widespread print culture on the formation of literature as a social institution and within it the figure of the romantic writer.

Kirkpatrick, Susan. *Las Románticas. Women writers and subjectivity in Spain, 1835–1850*, Berkeley, University of California Press, 1989.

    Perhaps the single best book of criticism in Hispanic studies in the area covered in this chapter. The discussion of Gómez de Avellaneda is outstanding.

La bótanica en la expedición Malaspina, 1789–1794. Pabellón Villanueva, Real Jardín Botánico, Oct.–Nov. 1989, Colección "Encuentros," Madrid, Turner, 1989.

    Fine collection of illustrated essays, scope exceeds indication of title.

Lara, Jesús. *La poesía quechua*, Mexico, Fondo de Cultura Económica, 1947.

    A valuable study. Includes a bilingual anthology.

Lindenberger, Herbert. *The History in Literature: On value, genre, institutions*, New York, Columbia University Press, 1990.

    A set of stimulating theoretical essays in the mode of the New Historicism on topics in Romanticism.

Losada, Alejandro. *La literatura en la sociedad de América Latina. Perú y el Río de la Plata 1837–1880*, Editionen der Iberoamericana, 3, Frankfurt, Klaus Dieter Vervuert, 1983.

    A challenging and theoretically sophisticated study.

Ortega y Gasset, José. *La deshumanización del arte y otros ensayos de estética*, Madrid, Revista de Occidente en Alianza Editorial, 1984.

    Important texts by Ortega, whose work had a formative impact on Latin American letters in this century.

Paz, Octavio. *Los hijos del limo. Del romanticismo a la vanguardia*, Biblioteca Breve, Barcelona, Seix Barral, 1974.

    The most influential study of Romanticism in Hispanic letters: a fascinating thesis, brilliantly argued, and the principal critical antagonist of my own essay. As I have contended, Paz misreads – or in fact leaves unread – eighteenth-century letters and in consequence offers a skewed vision of the nineteenth century.

Sor Juana Inés de la Cruz o las trampas de la fe, Mexico, Fondo de Cultura Económica, 1982.

    Excellent study of Sor Juana and the intellectual climate of colonial times.

Children of the Mire: Modern poetry from Romanticism to the Avant-Garde, tr. Rachel Phillips, Cambridge, Mass., Harvard University Press, 1974.

Sor Juana, or, The traps of Faith, tr. Margaret Sayers Peden, Cambridge, Mass., Harvard University Press, 1988.

Picón-Salas, Mariano. *Formación y proceso de la literatura venezolana*, Caracas, Editorial Cecilio Acosta, 1940.

    An informative history, especially useful for the eighteenth and nineteenth centuries.

Polt, John H. R. *Batilo. Estudios sobre la evolución estilística de Meléndez Valdés*, University of California Publications in Modern Philology, 119 Textos y Estudios del Siglo XVIII, 15, Berkeley, University of California Press, Oviedo, Centro de Estudios del Siglo XVIII, 1987.

The best study available of this fundamental peninsular poet.

Pratt, Mary Louise. *Imperial Eyes. Travel Writing and Transculturation*, London, Routledge, 1992.

An excellent book of detailed and theoretically sophisticated discussions of travel literature; a foundation upon which to rebuild the field of eighteenth- and nineteenth-century studies of Latin American letters.

Puig-Samper, Miguel Angel. *Crónica de una expedición romántica al Nuevo Mundo. La Comisión Científica del Pacífico (1862–1866)*, Madrid, Centro de Estudios Históricos/Consejo Superior de Investigaciones, Departamento de Historia de la Ciencia, 1988.

Meticulous study with many reproductions of relevant graphic art.

Rama, Angel. *La ciudad letrada*, Hanover, N.H. Ediciones del Norte, 1984.

Provocative discussion of the history of the relations between writing and power in Latin America.

Rivera-Rodas, Oscar. *La poesía hispanoamericana del siglo XIX (Del romanticismo al modernismo)*, Madrid, Alhambra, 1988.

The best study currently available of the early nineteenth century.

Sebold, Russell P. *El rapto de la mente. Poética y poesía dieciochescas*, Madrid, Editorial Prensa Española, 1970.

Fundamental reading in the discussion of eighteenth-century peninsular literature.

Siskin, Clifford. *The Historicity of Romantic Discourse*, New York, Oxford University Press, 1988.

An interesting theoretical argument.

Soler Cañas, Luis. *Negros, gauchos y compadres en el cancionero de la Federación (1830–1848)*, Buenos Aires, Instituto de Investigaciones Históricas Juan Manuel Rosas, 1958.

Good introduction to marginal figures in the poetry of the period.

Stafford, Barbara Maria. *Voyage into Substance: Art. science, nature and the illustrated travel account, 1760–1840*, Cambridge, MIT University Press, 1984.

An astonishingly comprehensive account.

Articles

Bareiro Saguier, Rubén. "La poesía de Andrés Bello: lectura actualizada del significado," *Revista Nacional de Cultura/Consejo Nacional de Cultura* (Caracas), 43:249 (1983), 144–60.

A fine study of Bello underlining the role of exile in his poetry.

Carullo, Sylvia G. "Una aproximación a la poesía afro-argentina de la época de Juan Manuel de Rosas," *Afro-Hispanic Review*, (1985), 15–22.

Informative.

Edmonson, Munro S., and Victoria R. Bricker. "Yucatecan Mayan literature" in M. S. Edmonson (ed.), *Supplement to the Handbook of Middle American Indians*, vol.

III: *Literatures*, gen. ed. Victoria Reifler Bricker, with the assistance of Patricia A. Andrews, Austin, University of Texas Press, 1985, 44–63.
Extremely useful introductory study.

Fontanella, Lee. "Mystical diction and imagery in Gómez de Avellaneda and Carolina Coronado," *Latin American Literary Review*, 19 (1981), 47–55.
Modest results.

González Echevarría, Roberto. "Albums, ramilletes, parnasos, liras y guirnaldas: fundadores de la historia literaria latinoamericana," *Hispania*, 75:4 (1992), 875–83.
Preliminary version of the study of Latin American literary historiography included in these volumes.

Gossen, Gary H. "Tzotzil literature" In M. S. Edmondson (ed.), *Supplement to the Handbook of Middle American Indians*, vol. III: *Literatures*, gen. ed. Victoria Reifler Bricker, with the assistance of Patricia A. Andrews, Austin, University of Texas Press, 1985, 64–106.
Extremely useful introductory study.

Griffith, Reginald Harvey. "The progress pieces of the eighteenth century." *Texas Review*, 5 (1920), 218–33.
An essay devoted to a sub-genre in eighteenth-century English poetry bearing upon Bello's famous *silvas*.

Grünfeld, Mihai. "Cosmopolitismo modernista y vanguardista: una identidad latinoamericana divergente," *Revista Iberoamericana*, 146–7 (1989), 33–41.
A fine essay suggesting a perspective that may be brought to bear on the eighteenth and nineteenth centuries with great profit.

Harter, Hugh A. "Gertrudis Gómez de Avellaneda" in Diane Marting (ed.), *Spanish American Women Writers: A bio-bibliographical source book*, New York, Greenwood Press, 1990, 210–25.
A valuable introduction to the author and the related criticism.

Johnson, Julie Greer. "*El nuevo luciano* and the satiric art of Eugenio Espejo," *Revista de Estudios Hispánicos*, 23:3 (1989), 67–85.
A fine essay that brings needed attention to the work of Santa Cruz y Espejo.

Leonard, Irving A. "A great savant of colonial Peru: Don Pedro de Peralta," *Philological Quarterly*, 12 (1933), 54–72.
A good biographical study of Peralta.

Martínez Baeza, Sergio. "La introducción de la imprenta en el Nuevo Mundo (los primeros impresos americanos: 1535–1810)," *Atenea*, 451 (1985), 81–98.
Succinct history of printing in colonial America, updating the classic study by José Toribio Medina.

Meehan, Thomas C., and John T. Cull. "'El poeta de las adivinanzas': Esteban de Terralla y Landa," *Revista de Crítica Literaria Latinoamericana*, 19 (1984), 127–57.
Much useful information about Terralla with a sympathetic critical review of *Lima por dentro y fuera*.

Miller, Beth K. "Gertrude the Great: Avellaneda, nineteenth-century feminist" in Beth Miller (ed.), *Women in Hispanic Literature: Icons and fallen idols*, Berkeley, University of California Press, 1983, 201–14.
A valuable step in the recuperation of one of the period's most important

writers.

Noriega, Julio E. "Wallparrimachi: transición y problematización en la poesía quechua," *Revista de Crítica Literaria Latinoamericana*, 133 (1991), 209–25.

An insightful study distinguishing between history and legend and reflecting on the ideological implications of the reception of Wallparrimachi.

Paravisini-Gebert, Lizabeth. "Salomé Ureña de Henríquez (1850–1897)" in Diana Marting (ed.), *Spanish American Women Writers: A bio-bibliographical source-book*, Westport, Conn; Greenwood Press, 1990.

Brief but valuable introduction in a very important reference source.

Rivers, Elias. "Góngora y el Nuevo Mundo," *Hispania*, 75 (1992), 857–61.

Overview of intertextual relations between Latin American and Peninsular Baroque.

Sacks, Peter M. *The English Elegy. Studies in the genre from Spenser to Yeats*, Baltimore and London, Johns Hopkins University Press, 1985.

Chapter 1 provides an excellent theoretical introduction to the elegy.

Sommer, Doris. "El otro Enriquillo," *Hispámerica*, 30 (1981), 117–45.

An excellent ideological analysis; a model for a needed study of the contemporary work of Zorrilla de San Martín. The essay was included in English ("The other Enriquillo") in her important book, *One Master for Another: Populism as patriarchal rhetoric in Dominican novels*, New York, Lanham, 1983.

Stolley, Karen. *"El Lazarillo de ciegos caminantes:" un itinerario crítico*, Hanover, N.H. Ediciones del Norte, 1992.

An excellent study of a crucial eighteenth-century text.

Zaldumbide, Gonzalo. "Estudio preliminar" in Juan Bautista de Aguirre, S.I. *Poesías y obras oratorias*, ed. Zaldumbide and Aurelio Espinosa Pólit, Clásicos Ecuatorianos, 3, Quito, Ediciones del Instituto Cultural Ecuatoriano, Imprenta del Ministerio de Educación, 1943.

A fine introduction to Aguirre in an edition that brought his poetry to public attention once again.

Chapter 12: Spanish American theatre of the eighteenth century

Primary sources

Barranca, José Sebastián (tr.). *Ollanta o La severidad de un padre y la clemencia de un rey*, Lima, Imprenta Liberal, 1868.

First Spanish translation of text.

Castillo Andraca y Tamayo, Francisco del. *Obras*, ed. Rubén Vargas Ugarte, Clásicos Peruanos, 2, Lima, Editorial Studium, 1948.

Includes *Mitrídates* and a selection of *loas*, *entremeses*, and *sainetes*.

Castro, José Agustín de. *Miscelánea de poesías sagradas y humanas*, 2 vols., Puebla, Mexico, P. de la Rosa, 1797.

Rare collection of works, deserving of modern edition.

Cid Pérez, José, and Dolores Martí de Cid (eds.). *Teatro indio precolombino*, Madrid, Aguilar, 1964.

An annotated anthology, with thorough introduction and analyses of texts.

Teatro indoamericano colonial, Madrid, Aguilar, 1973.

An anthology with introduction and analyses of texts.

El amor de la estanciera, Publicaciones del Instituto de Literatura Argentina, 4, no. 1, Buenos Aires, Imprenta de la Universidad, 1925.

First modern printing of play, preceded by "noticia" by Mariano G. Bosch.

Halty, Nuria, and Howard Richardson (tr.). "*Ollantay*," *First Stage*, 6 (1967), 12–36.

Useful English translation of text.

Lara, Jesús (ed. and tr.). *Tragedia del fin de Atawallpa*, Cochabamba, Bolivia, Imprenta Universitaria, 1957.

Spanish translation with thorough introduction.

Lohmann Villena, Guillermo (ed.). *Un tríptico del Perú virreinal: el Virrey Amat, el Marqués de Soto Florido y La Perricholi*, North Carolina Studies in the Romance Languages and Literatures, 15, Chapel Hill, University of North Carolina, 1976.

Text of *Drama de dos palanganas* prefaced by detailed study of historical context.

Markham, Clements R. (tr.). *Ollanta, An Ancient Inca Drama*, London, Trubner & Co., 1871.

First English translation of text.

Meneses, Teodoro L. (ed. and tr.). *Teatro quechua colonial, antología*, Lima, Ediciones Edubanco, 1983.

New Spanish translations of Quechua plays, with thorough introductions.

Pacheco Zegarra, Gabino (ed. and tr.). *Ollantai, drame en vers quechuas du temps des Incas*, Paris, Maisonneuve & Cie., 1878.

French translation of play.

Ollantay, drama quechua, Buenos Aires, Editorial Americana, 1942.

Well-respected Spanish translation of play.

Peralta Barnuevo, Pedro de. *Obras dramáticas*, ed. Irving A. Leonard, Santiago, Imprenta Universitaria, 1937.

Annotated edition with introduction.

Obras dramáticas cortas, ed. Elvira Ampuero *et al.*, Lima, Ediciones de la Biblioteca Universitaria, 1964.

Texts of short dramatic pieces prefaced by co-authored essays on Peralta Barnuevo.

Pita, Santiago de. *El príncipe jardinero y fingido Cloridano*, ed. José Juan Arrom, Havana, Consejo Nacional de Cultura, 1963.

Annotated edition with introduction.

Pleyto y querella de los guajolotes, Puebla, Mexico, Ediciones Teatro Universitario, 1958.

Unannotated edition with brief introduction; pamphlet form.

Ravicz, Marilyn Ekdahl (ed.). *Early Colonial Religious Drama in Mexico: From Tzompantli to Golgotha*, Washington, Catholic University of America Press, 1970.

Well-annotated English versions of Nahuatl plays; contains excellent introduction.

Ripoll, Carlos, and Andrés Valdespino (eds.). *Teatro hispanoamericano: antología crítica*, vol. 1, New York, Anaya-Book Co., 1972.

Interesting selection of well-annotated texts.

Sánchez, Luis Alberto (ed.). *Drama de los [sic] palanganas Veterano y Bisoño*, Lima,

Editorial Jurídica, 1977.

Annotated edition with introduction and appendix containing reproductions of pertinent historical documents.

Vargas Ugarte, Rubén (ed.). *De nuestro antiguo teatro: colección de piezas dramáticas de los siglos XVI, XVII y XVIII*, Biblioteca Histórica Peruana, 4, Lima, Universidad Católica del Perú, Instituto de Investigaciones Históricas, 1943.

Indispensable volume of rare colonial plays, some marred by editor's deletions.

Vela, Eusebio. *Tres comedias*, ed. Jefferson Rea Spell and Francisco Monterde, Mexico, Imprenta Universitaria, 1948.

Well-annotated edition with thorough introduction.

Secondary sources

Books

Arrom, José Juan. *Historia de la literatura dramática cubana*, Yale Romanic Studies, 23, New Haven, Yale University Press, 1944.

Excellent brief history; includes illustrations.

Historia del teatro hispanoamericano (época colonial), 2nd. edn., Mexico, Ediciones de Andrea, 1967.

Still the best synthesis of colonial Spanish American theatre; some references no longer up-to-date.

Barrera, Isaac J. *Historia de la literatura ecuatoriana*, Quito, Casa de la Cultura Ecuatoriana, 1960.

Massive history, with chapters on colonial theatre and brief selection of dramatic texts in appendix.

Bosch, Mariano G. *Teatro antiguo de Buenos Aires, piezas del siglo XVIII, su influencia en la educación popular*, Buenos Aires, El Comercio, 1904.

Contains mostly peninsular texts; some data on colonial playwrights and texts.

Historia del teatro en Buenos Aires, Buenos Aires, El Comercio, 1910.

Contains chapters on colonial period and brief selection of dramatic texts in appendix.

Descalzi, Ricardo. *Historia crítica del teatro ecuatoriano*, 6 vols., Quito, Casa de la Cultura Ecuatoriana, 1968.

Includes chapters on colonial theatre and brief selection of dramatic texts.

Gisbert, Teresa. *Teatro virreinal en Bolivia*, La Paz, Biblioteca de Arte y Cultura Boliviana, Dirección Nacional de Informaciones de la Presidencia de la República, 1962.

A very brief survey of Bolivian theatre of the colonial period.

Horcasitas, Fernando. *El teatro náhuatl: épocas novohispana y moderna*, Monografías del Instituto de Investigaciones Históricas, Serie de Cultura Náhuatl, 17, Mexico, Universidad Nacional Autónoma de México, 1974.

An authoritative history, with anthology of Spanish versions of Nahuatl theatre and descriptive list of manuscripts.

Johnson, Julie Greer. *Women in Colonial Spanish American Literature: Literary images*, Contributions in Women's Studies, 43, Westport, Conn., Greenwood Press, 1983.

Contains chapter on women in colonial drama.

Jones, Willis Knapp. *Behind Spanish American Footlights*, Austin, University of Texas Press, 1966.

Useful history of Spanish American theatre, organized by country.

Lohmann Villena, Guillermo. *El arte dramático en Lima durante el Virreinato*, Publicaciones de la Escuela de Estudios Hispanoamericanos de la Universidad de Sevilla, 12, Madrid, 1945.

A comprehensive history based on archival documents, some of which are reproduced in appendix; includes brief selection of texts.

María y Campos, Armando de. *Guía de representaciones teatrales en la Nueva España*, Colección La Máscara, 1, Mexico, B. Costa/Amic Editor, 1959.

Lists known theatrical representations in New Spain by year and reviews documents pertinent to colonial Mexican theatre.

Olavarría y Ferrari, Enrique de. *Reseña histórica del teatro en México, 1538–1911*, Biblioteca Porrúa, 21, 3rd. edn., Mexico, Porrúa, 1961.

An updated edition of magisterial history of Mexican theatre, first compiled in late nineteenth century.

Pla, Josefina. *El teatro en el Paraguay*, Colección Camalote, 1, 2nd. edn., Asunción, Diálogo, 1967.

Especially useful for information on Jesuit theatre in Guarani language.

Rela, Walter (ed.). *Breve historia del teatro uruguayo*, vol. 1, Buenos Aires, Editorial Universitaria, 1966.

Includes short introduction and selection of texts.

Reverte Bernal, Concepción. *Aproximación crítica a un dramaturgo virreinal peruano: Fr. Francisco del Castillo ("El Ciego de la Merced")*, Universidad de Cádiz, 1985.

Excellent critical analyses of Castillo's full-length plays and short theatrical pieces.

Rojas, Ricardo. *Un titán de los Andes*, Buenos Aires, Editorial Losada, 1939.

Synthesizes textual, archeological, and historical scholarship on *Ollántay* legend.

Sánchez, Luis Alberto. *El doctor Océano: estudios sobre don Pedro de Peralta Barnuevo*, Lima, Universidad Nacional Mayor de San Marcos, 1967.

Includes useful essay on Peralta Barnuevo's theatre.

Saz, Agustín del. *Teatro hispanoamericano*, vol. 1, Barcelona, Editorial Vergara, 1963.

A useful history of Spanish American theatre through the nineteenth century.

Schilling, Hildburg. *Teatro profano en la Nueva España*, Mexico, Universidad Nacional Autónoma de México, 1958.

An invaluable history based on archival materials; includes thorough analysis of Vela's *La pérdida de España*.

Suárez Radillo, Carlos Miguel. *El teatro barroco hispanoamericano: ensayo de una historia crítico-antológica*, 3 vols., Madrid, José Porrúa Turanzas, 1981.

A thorough history of Spanish American theatre from approximately 1600 to 1750, with excerpts from plays.

El teatro neoclásico y costumbrista hispanoamericano: una historia crítico-antológica, 2 vols., Madrid, Ediciones Cultura Hispánica, Instituto de Cooperación Iberoamericana, 1984.

A thorough history of Spanish American theatre from approximately 1750 to 1850, with excerpts from plays.

Trenti Rocamora, J. Luis. *El teatro en la América colonial*, Buenos Aires, Editorial Huarpes, 1947.

A history of colonial theatre in the Americas, with emphasis on Argentina.

Articles

Arrom, José Juan. "Cambiantes imágenes de la mujer en el teatro de la América virreinal," *Latin American Theater Review*, 12:1 (1978), 5–15.

Relates portrayal of female characters to successive periods and movements in colonial theatre.

Castagnino, Raúl H. "El teatro menor de Pedro de Peralta Barnuevo" in his *Escritores hispanoamericanos, desde otros ángulos de simpatía*, Buenos Aires, Nova, 1971, 103–15.

Descriptive summary of Peralta Barnuevo's short theatrical pieces.

Hesse, Everett W. "Calderón's popularity in the Spanish Indies," *Hispanic Review*, 23 (1955), 12–27.

Observations based on compiled list of known performances of Calderón's plays in the colonies (included as appendix).

Hills, Elijah Clarence. "The Quechua drama *Ollanta*," *Romanic Review*, 5 (1914), 127–76.

Indispensable study of *Ollántay*.

Johnson, Harvey L. "Loa representada en Ibagué para la jura del rey Fernando VI," *Revista Iberoamericana*, 7 (1944), 293–308.

Well-annotated text of *loa* with introduction.

"*La Historia de la Comberción de San Pablo*, drama guatemalteco del siglo XVIII," *Nueva Revista de Filología Hispánica*, 4 (1950), 115–60.

Well-annotated text of play with thorough introduction.

Leonard, Irving A. "An early Peruvian adaptation of Corneille's *Rodogune*," *Hispanic Review*, 5 (1937), 172–6.

Brief discussion of Peralta Barnuevo's *La Rodoguna*.

"El teatro en Lima, 1790–93," *Hispanic Review*, 8 (1940), 93–112.

List of performances drawn from archival material, with interpretative summary.

"The 1790 theater season of the Mexico City Coliseo," *Hispanic Review*, 19 (1951), 104–20.

List of performances drawn from archival material, with interpretative summary.

"The theater season of 1791–1792 in Mexico City," *Hispanic American Historical Review*, 31 (1951), 349–64.

List of performances drawn from archival material, with interpretative summary.

Lohmann Villena, Guillermo, and Raúl Moglia. "Repertorio de las representaciones teatrales en Lima hasta el siglo XVIII," *Revista de Filología Hispánica*, 5 (1943), 313–43.

Chronological listing of plays performed in Lima from 1563 to 1793.

Pasquariello, Anthony M. "Two eighteenth-century Peruvian interludes, pioneer pieces in local color," *Symposium*, 6 (1952), 385–90.
    Study of interludes by Peralta Barnuevo and Monforte y Vera.
"The evolution of the *loa* in Spanish America," *Latin American Theater Review*, 3: 2 (1970), 5–19.
    Study of evolution of genre based on analyses of individual texts.
"The evolution of the *sainete* in the River Plate area," *Latin American Theater Review*, 17: 1 (1983), 15–24.
    Study of evolution of genre based on analyses of individual texts.
Reverte Bernal, Concepción. "Guía bibliográfica para el estudio del teatro virreinal peruano," *Historiografía y Bibliografía Americanistas*, 29 (1985), 129–50.
    Lists primary and secondary bibliographical sources on Peruvian theatre through eighteenth century.
Spell, Jefferson R. "The theater in New Spain in the early eighteenth century," *Hispanic Review*, 15 (1947), 137–64.
    Historical study largely based on archival material.
Tamayo Vargas, Augusto. "Obras menores en el teatro de Peralta," *Revista Histórica* (Instituto Histórico del Perú), 27 (1964), 82–93.
    Useful study of Peralta Barnuevo's short dramatic pieces.
Trenti Rocamora, J. Luis. "La primera pieza teatral argentina," *Boletín de Estudios de Teatro* (Buenos Aires), 4 (1946), 224–34.
    Annotated text of *loa* by Fuentes del Arco with introduction.
"El teatro porteño durante el período hispánico," *Estudios* (Buenos Aires), 78 (1947), 408–34.
    A historical overview of colonial theatre in Buenos Aires.
"El teatro y la jura de Carlos IV en Arequipa," *Mar del Sur*, 1:5 (1949), 28–35.
    Annotated text of *entremés* with introduction.
Vargas Ugarte, Rubén. "Un coloquio representado en Santiago en el siglo XVIII," *Revista Chilena de Historia y Geografía*, 111 (1948), 18–55.
    Text of *Coloquio de la Concepción* with brief introduction.

Chapter 13: The nineteenth-century Spanish American novel

Primary sources

Acevedo Díaz, Eduardo. *Ismael* in *La Tribuna Nacional*, Buenos Aires, 1888.
    Nativa in *La Opinión Pública*, Montevideo, 1889–1890.
    El grito de gloria, La Plata, Ernesto Richelet, 1893.
Aguirre, Nataniel. *Juan de la Rosa – Memorias del último soldado de la independencia* in *El Heraldo de Cochabamba*, Cochabamba, 1885.
Alberdi, Juan Bautista. *Peregrinación de Luz del Día, o viaje y aventuras de la Verdad en el Nuevo Mundo*, Buenos Aires, C. Casavalle, 1871.
Altamirano, Ignacio Manuel. *Clemencia* in *El Renacimiento*, Mexico, 1869.
    El Zarco – episodios de la vida mexicana en 1861–63, Mexico, J. Ballescá & Cía., 1901.
    Clemencia tr. and ed. Elliot B. Scher and Nell Walker, Boston, D. C. Heath, 1944.
    El Zarco, the Bandit, tr. Mary Allt, New York, Duchnes, 1957; London, The Folio

Society, 1957.

Christmas in the Mountains, tr. and ed. Harvey L. Johnson, Gainesville, University of Florida Press, 1961.

Ancona, Eligio. *La cruz y la espada*, 2 vols., Paris, Rosa & Bouret, 1866.

Los mártires del Anáhuac, Mexico, José Bastiza, 1870.

Anonymous. *Jicotencal*, Philadelphia, Guillermo Stavely, 1826.

Aréstegui, Narciso. *El Padre Horán – escenas de la vida del Cusco* in *El Comercio*, Lima, 1848.

Argerich, Juan Antonio. *Inocentes o culpables*, Buenos Aires, El Courrier de la Plata, 1884.

Barbará, Federico. *El prisionero de Santos Lugares*, Buenos Aires, Las Artes, 1857.

Betancourt, José Ramón. *Una feria de la Caridad en 183. . .*, Havana, Soler, 1858.

Bilbao, Manuel. *El inquisidor mayor, o Historia de unos amores*, Lima, José María Manterola, 1852 (first part); Lima, Imp. del Correo, 1852 (second part).

Blest Gana, Alberto. *La aritmética en el amor – novela de costumbres*, Valparaiso, El Mercurio, 1860.

El pago de las deudas – novela de costumbres, Valparaiso, El Mercurio, 1861.

Martín Rivas – novela de costumbres político-sociales, Santiago, La Voz de Chile, 1862.

El ideal de un calavera – novela de costumbres, Santiago, La Voz de Chile, 1863.

Durante la reconquista – novela histórica, 2 vols., Paris, Garnier Hnos., 1897.

Martín Rivas tr. Mrs. Charles Witham, London, Chapman & Hall, 1916; New York, Knopf, 1918; New York, Gordon Press, 1977.

Bonó, Pedro F. *El montero – novela de costumbres* in *El Correo de Ultramar*, Paris, 1856.

Cabello de Carbonera, Mercedes. *Blanca Sol*, Lima, Carlos Prince, 1889.

Las consecuencias, Lima, Torres Aguirre, 1889.

El conspirador – autobiografía de un hombre público, Lima, La Voce d'Italia, 1892.

Cambacérès, Eugenio. *Pot-pourri – silbidos de un vago*, Buenos Aires, M. Biedma, 1882.

Música sentimental – silbidos de un vago, Paris, Hispano-Americana, 1884.

Sin rumbo – estudios, Buenos Aires, M. Biedma, 1885.

En la sangre in *Sud-América*, Buenos Aires, 1887.

Campo, Angel de (Micrós). *La Rumba* in *El Nacional*, Mexico, 1891.

Cané, Miguel. *Esther* in Alejandro Magariños Cervantes (ed.), *Biblioteca Americana* IV, Buenos Aires, Imp. de Mayo, 1858.

La familia de Sconner in Alejandro Magariños Cervantes (ed.), *Biblioteca Americana* IV, Buenos Aires, Imp. de Mayo, 1858.

Carrasquilla, Tomás. *Frutos de mi tierra*, Bogotá, Librería Nueva, 1896.

Cisneros, Luis Benjamín. *Julia, o Escenas de la vida de Lima*, Paris, Rosa & Bouret, 1861.

Edgardo, o Un joven de mi generación – romance americano-español, Paris, Rosa & Bouret, 1864.

Covarrubias, Juan. *Gil Gómez el insurgente, o La hija del médico – novela histórica mexicana*, Mexico, Manuel Castro, 1859.

La clase media – novela de costumbres mexicanas, Mexico, Manuel Castro, 1859.

La sensitiva, Mexico, Manuel Castro, 1859.

El diablo en México – novela de costumbres, Mexico, Manuel Castro, 1860.

Cuéllar, José Tomás de. *La linterna mágica*, 7 vols., Mexico, Ignacio Cumplido, 1871–1872 (includes: I: *Ensalada de pollos* II: *Historia de Chucho el Ninfo*, III: *Isolina la ex-figurante*, IV: *Las jamonas*, V–VI: *Las gentes que "son así,"* VII: *Gabriel el cerrajero o las hijas de mi papá*); *La linterna mágica*, 2nd. edn., 5 vols., Barcelona, Tip. Espasa & Cía., 1889–1890, (includes: *Los mariditos IV*); *La linterna mágica*, 3rd. edn., 19 vols., Santander, Blanchard, 1890–1892 (includes: *Los fuereños y la nochebuena VII, Las posadas XIX*).

Baile y cochino, Mexico, Filomeno Mata, 1886.

Delgado, Rafael. *La Calandria* in *Revista nacional de Letras y Ciencias*, Mexico, 1890.

Diaz, Eugenio. *Manuela* in *El Mosaico*, Bogotá, 1858.

Echeverría, José Antonio. *Antonelli* in *El Album*, Havana, 1839.

Estrada, Santiago. *El hogar en la pampa*, Buenos Aires, El Siglo, 1866.

Fernández de Lizardi, José Joaquín. *El periquillo sarniento*, 3 vols., Mexico, Alejandro Valdés, 1816 (incomplete); 5 vols., Mexico, Galván, 1830–1831 (complete).

Noches tristes, Mexico, Mariano de Zúñiga y Ontiveros, 1818 (incomplete); *Noches tristes y día alegre*, Mexico, Alejandro Valdés, 1819 (complete).

La Quijotita y su prima, 3 vols., Mexico, Mariano de Zúñiga y Ontiveros, 1818–1819.

Vida y hechos del famoso caballero don Catrín de la Fachenda, Mexico, Alejandro Valdés, 1832.

The Itching Parrot, tr. and ed. Katherine Anne Porter, Garden City, N.Y., Doubleday, Doran & Co., 1942.

Frías, Heriberto. *¡Tomochic!* in *El Demócrata*, Mexico, 1894 (incomplete); *¡Tomochic! – Episodios de la campaña de Chihuahua, 1892 – relación escrita por un testigo presencial*, Rio Grande City, Texas, Jesús T. Recio, 1894 (complete).

Galván, Manuel de Jesús. *Enriquillo*, Santo Domingo, Colegio de San Luis Gonzaga, 1879 (incomplete), *Enriquillo – leyenda histórica dominicana*, Santo Domingo, García Hnos., 1882 (complete).

The Cross and the Sword (Enriquillo) tr. and ed. Robert Graves, Bloomington, Indiana University Press, 1954; London, Gollancz, 1956.

Gamboa, Federico. *Suprema ley*, Paris and Mexico, Vda. de Ch. Bouret, 1896.

Metamorfosis, Tip. Nacional de la Ciudad de Guatemala, 1899.

Santa, Barcelona, Talleres Araluce, 1903.

García Merou, Martín. *Ley social*, Buenos Aires, M. Biedma, 1885.

Gómez de Avellaneda, Gertrudis. *Sab*, Madrid, Calle del Barco, 1841.

Guatimozín, último emperador de México, 4 vols., Madrid, D. A. Espinosa, 1846.

Cuauhtemac, the Last Aztec Emperor, tr. Mrs. Wilson W. Blake, Mexico, F. P. Hoeck, 1898.

Sab – Autobiography, tr. and ed. Nina Scott, Austin, Univeristy of Texas Press, in press.

Gorriti, Juana Manuela. *La quena* in *Revista de Lima*, Lima, 1845.

El tesoro de los incas in *Sueños y realidades*, II, Buenos Aires, Imp. de Mayo, 1865.

Grandmontagne, Francisco. *Teodoro Foronda – evoluciones de la sociedad argentina*, 2 vols., Buenos Aires, La Vasconia, 1896.

Groussac, Paul. *Fruto vedado – costumbres argentinas* in *Sud-América*, Buenos Aires, 1884.

Guerra, Rosa. *Lucía de Miranda*, Buenos Aires, Americana, 1860.

Gutiérrez, Eduardo. *Juan Moreira* in *La Patria Argentina*, Buenos Aires, 1879–1880.
Santos Vega, Buenos Aires, Imp. de la Patria Argentina, 1880.
Hormiga negra in *La Patria Argentina*, Buenos Aires, 1881.
El Chacho, Buenos Aires, N. Tomassi, 1886.

Gutiérrez, Juan María. *El Capitán de Patricios* in *El Correo del Domingo*, Buenos Aires, 1864.

Holmberg, Eduardo L. *Dos partidos en lucha – fantasía científica*, Buenos Aires, El Arjentino, 1875.

Hostos, Eugenio María de. *La peregrinación de Bayoán – novela*, Madrid, El Comercio, 1863.

Inclán, Luis G. *Astucia, el Gefe de los Hermanos de la Hoja, o los charros contrabandistas de la rama*, 2 vols., Mexico, Inclán, 1865.

Isaacs, Jorge. *María*, Bogotá, Gaitán, 1867.
María: A South American romance, tr. Rollo Ogden, New York and London, Harper & Brothers, 1890; rpt. ed. Ralph Hayward Keniston, New York, Ginn & Co., 1918; rpt., ed. John Warshaw, Boston, D. C. Heath, 1926.

Lapuente, Laurindo. *El Herminio de la Nueva Troya*, Buenos Aires, La Reforma Pacífica, 1857.

López, Lucio V. *La gran aldea – costumbres bonaerenses* in *Sud-América*, Buenos Aires, 1884.

López, Vicente Fidel. *La novia del hereje o La Inquisición de Lima*, Buenos Aires, Imp. de Mayo, 1854.
La loca de la guardia – cuento histórico, Buenos Aires, Imp. de Mayo, 1896.

Magariños Cervantes, Alejandro. *Caramurú*, 2 vols., Madrid, Aguirre & Cía., 1850 [1848].

Mansilla, Eduarda. *El médico de San Luis*, Buenos Aires, La Paz, 1860.
Lucía Miranda in *La Tribuna*, Buenos Aires, 1860.

Mármol, José. *Amalia*, 2 vols., Montevideo, Uruguayana, 1851 (incomplete), 8 vols., Buenos Aires, Americana, 1855 (complete).
Amalia: A romance of the Argentine, tr. Mary J. Serrano, New York, E. P. Dutton, 1919; rpt. 1944; rpt. New York, Gordon Press, 1977.

Matto de Turner, Clorinda. *Aves sin nido*, Lima, Carlos Prince, 1889.
Herencia, Lima, Matto Hnos., 1895.
Birds without a Nest – A story of Indian life and priestly oppression in Peru, tr. J. G. Hudson, London, Charles J. Thynne, 1904.

Mera, Juan León. *Cumandá o un drama entre salvajes*, Quito, J. Guzmán Almeida, 1879.
Cumandá, tr. and ed. Pastoriza Flores, New York, D. C. Heath, 1932.

Meza y Suárez Inclán, Ramón. *Mi tío el empleado*, Barcelona, L. Tasso Serra, 1887.
Don Aniceto el tendero, Barcelona, L. Tasso Serra, 1889.

Milla y Vidaurre, José (Salomé Jil). *La hija del adelantado*, Guatemala, Imp. de la Paz, 1866.
Los nazarenos, Guatemala, Imp. de la Paz, 1867.
El visitador, E. Goubaud & Cía., 1897.

Miró, José María. *La bolsa* in *La Nación*, Buenos Aires, 1891.

Mitre, Bartolomé. *Soledad*, La Paz, La Epoca, 1847.

Morúa Delgado, Martín. *Sofía*, Havana, Alvarez & Cía, 1891.

    La familia Unzúazu, Havana, La Prosperidad, 1901.

Nieto, Juan José. *Yngermina o La hija de Calamar – novela histórica, o recuerdos de la Conquista*, Kingston, Jamaica, R. J. de Córdoba, 1844.

Ocantos, Carlos María. *Quilito*, Paris, Garnier Hnos., 1891.

    Promisión, Madrid, I. Moreno, 1897.

Palma y Romay, Ramón de. *Una Pascua en San Marcos* in *El Album*, Havana, 1838.

Payno, Manuel. *El fistol del diablo* in *La Revista Científica y Literaria*, Mexico, 1845–1846.

    Los bandidos de Río Frío – novela naturalista humorística, de costumbres, de crímenes y de horrores, por Un Ingenio de la Corte, 2 vols., Barcelona, J. F. Parres & Cía., n.d. [1889–1891].

Picón Febres, Gonzalo. *El sargento Felipe* in *El Cojo Ilustrado*, Caracas, 1899.

Podestá, Manuel T. *Irresponsable*, Buenos Aires, La Tribuna Nacional, 1889.

Rabasa, Emilio. *La Bola*, Mexico, Alfonso E. López & Cía., 1887.

    La gran ciencia, Mexico, Alfonso E. López & Cía., 1887.

    El cuarto poder, Mexico, Spíndola & Cía., 1888.

    Moneda falsa, Mexico, Spíndola & Cía., 1888.

Reyles, Carlos. *Beba*, Montevideo, Dornaleche y Reyes, 1894.

Riofrío, Miguel. *La emancipada* in *La Unión*, Quito, 1863.

Sicardi, Francisco A. *Libro extraño*, 2 vols., Barcelona, El Anuario, n.d. (5 vols. Originally published in Buenos Aires, 1894–1903).

Sioen, Aquiles. *Buenos Aires en el año 2080*, Buenos Aires, Librería del Colejio, 1879.

Solar, Alberto del. *Contra la marea*, Buenos Aires, F. Lajouane, 1894.

Suárez y Romero, Anselmo. *Francisco*, New York, N. Ponce de León, 1880.

Viana, Javier de. *Gaucha*, Montevideo, A. Barreiro y Ramos, 1899 (incomplete); Montevideo, O. M. Bertani, 1913 (complete).

Villafañe, Segundo I. *Emilio Love*, Buenos Aires, Mackern & McLean, 1888.

    Horas de fiebre, Buenos Aires, Juan A. Alsina, 1891.

Villaverde, Cirilo. *El espetón de oro* in *El Album*, Havana, 1838.

    Cecilia Valdés in *La siempreviva*, Havana, 1839, (incomplete); *Cecilia Valdés o La loma del ángel*, Havana, Lino Valdés, 1839 (incomplete); New York, El Espejo, 1882 (complete).

    La joven de la flecha de oro in *La Cartera Cubana*, Havana, 1840.

    El guajiro in *Faro Industrial de La Habana*, Havana, 1842.

    El penitente in *Faro Industrial de La Habana*, Havana, 1844.

    The Quadroon or Cecilia Valdés – A romance of Old Havana, tr. Mariano J. Lorente, Boston, L. C. Page & Co., 1935.

    Cecilia Valdés, or Angel's Hill – A novel of Cuban customs, tr. and ed. Sydney G. Gest, New York, Vantage Press, 1962.

Yepes, José Ramón. *Iguaraya* in *La Revista Album de Familia*, Caracas, 1872.

Zeno Gandía, Manuel. *La charca – crónicas de un mundo enfermo*, Ponce, M. López, 1894.

Volume 1

Secondary sources

Books

Acevedo Escobedo, Antonio. *La ciudad de México en la novela*, Mexico, Secretaría de Obras y Servicios, 1973.

Examines the impact of modernization on Mexico City as represented in the Mexican novel.

Alegría, Fernando. *Historia de la novela hispanoamericana*, Mexico, Ediciones de Andrea, 1965.

Historical outline of the Spanish American novel, divided by periods and countries.

Nueva historia de la novela hispanoamericana, Hanover, N.H., Ediciones del Norte, 1986.

An eclectic and somewhat loose history of the Spanish American novel. Emphasis on the twentieth century.

Alonso, Carlos J. *The Spanish American Regional Novel: Modernity and autochthony*, Cambridge University Press, 1990.

An outstanding work on the *criollista* novel, particularly interesting for its views on the issues of modernity and autochthony.

Anderson, Benedict. *Imagined Communities: Reflections on the origin and spread of nationalism*, London and New York, Verso, 1983.

A provocative, concise study of nationalism as a cultural and literary phenomenon.

Anderson, Theodore. *Carlos María Ocantos, Argentine Novelist*, New Haven, Yale University Press, 1934.

A traditional study of the life, times and works of Ocantos.

Anderson Imbert, Enrique. *Estudios sobre escritores de América*, Buenos Aires, Raigal, 1954.

Includes excellent chapters on the nineteenth-century historical novel as well as on Isaacs's *María* and Galván's *Enriquillo*.

Arciniegas, Germán. *Genio y figura de Jorge Isaacs*, Buenos Aires, EUDEBA, 1967.

Useful introduction to the life and works of Jorge Isaacs.

Azuela, Mariano. *Cien años de novela mexicana*, Mexico, Botas, 1947.

The Mexican novel through the eyes of a Mexican novelist. Interesting notes on Ignacio Manuel Altamirano and Manuel Payno.

Bakhtin, Mikhail Mikhailovich. *The Dialogic Imagination*, tr. Caryl Emerson and Michael Holquist, ed. Michael Holquist. Austin, University of Texas Press, 1981.

A major, influential collection of essays, extraordinarily useful in answering the question: what is a novel?

Barbagelata, Hugo D. *La novela en Hispanoamérica*, Montevideo, El Libro Inglés, 1946.

A traditional global study of the Spanish American novel. Emphasis on the nineteenth century.

Barreda, Pedro. *The Black Protagonist in the Cuban Novel*, Amherst, University of Massachusetts, 1979.

A well-documented study with emphasis on the nineteenth-century Cuban novel.

Bibliografía de la novela venezolana, Caracas, Centro de Estudios Literarios, Universidad Central de Venezuela, 1963.

Lists titles by alphabetical and chronological order.

Blasi, Alberto O. *Los fundadores: Cambacérès, Martel, Sicardi*, Buenos Aires, Eds. Culturales Argentinas, 1962.

A solid study acknowledging Cambacérès, Miró (Martel), and Sicardi as the founders of the Argentinian modern novel.

Braudel, Fernand. *Civilization and Capitalism 15th–18th Century*, tr. Sian Reynolds, 3 vols. New York, Harper & Row, 1981–1984.

A major, influential historical study of the times that preceded industrial growth.

Brushwood, John S. *Mexico in its Novel: A nation's search for identity*, Austin, University of Texas Press, 1966.

Underscores the relationships between the novel and national identity in Mexico.

Genteel Barbarism: Experiments in analysis of nineteenth-century Spanish-American novels, Lincoln, Nebr., and London, University of Nebraska, 1981.

Includes structuralist studies of *Guatimozín, Amalia, Martín Rivas, María, Mi tío el empleado, Aves sin nido, Suprema ley, El sargento Felipe*.

Cabrera, Rosa M., and Gladys B. Zaldívar (eds.). *Homenaje a Gertrudis Gómez de Avellaneda. Memorias del simposio en el centenario de su muerte*, Miami, Ediciones Universal, 1981.

An important collection of articles on Avellaneda's works. Pieces by Julio Hernández-Miyares, Mildred B. Boyer, Alberto Gutiérrez de la Solana, and Concepción T.Alzola are among the best works on *Sab* and *Guatimozín*.

The Cambridge History of Latin America, III, IV, ed. Leslie Bethell, Cambridge University Press, 1985, 1986.

The best available collection of specialized historical works on nineteenth-century Latin America.

Cantonnet, María Ester. *Las vertientes de Javier de Viana*, Montevideo, Alfa, 1969.

Discusses Viana's literary production and his search for a Uruguayan national literature.

Carilla, Emilio. *El romanticismo en la América Hispánica*, 2 vols., Madrid, Gredos, 1967.

One of the most informative texts ever written on Spanish American Romanticism.

Carrillo, Francisco. *Clorinda Matto de Turner y su indigenismo literario*, Lima, Ediciones de la Biblioteca Universitaria, 1967.

A solid study of Matto de Turner's political and social views.

Castagnaro, R. Anthony. *The Early Spanish American Novel*, New York, Las Americas, 1971.

An excellent study of the nineteenth-century Spanish American novel.

Castillo, Homero, and Raúl Silva Castro. *Historia bibliográfica de la novela chilena*, Mexico, Ediciones de Andrea, 1961.

Alphabetical list of authors. It is not a history.

Castro Arenas, Mario. *La novela peruana y la evolución social*, Lima, Cultura y

Libertad, 1965.

A traditional social approach to the Peruvian novel.

Castro Leal, Antonio. *La novela del Méjico colonial* I, Mexico, Aguilar, 1964.

Provides detailed information on the Mexican historical novel.

Cometta Manzoni, Aida. *El indio en la novela de América*, Buenos Aires, Futuro, 1960.

A useful work studying the Indian as a principal character in the Spanish American novel. Emphasis on the nineteenth century.

Conde, Pedro. *Notas sobre el "Enriquillo,"* Santo Domingo, Taller, 1978.

An important commentary on the role played by Galván's *Enriquillo* in shaping a fictitious national identity in the Dominican Republic.

Cornejo Polar, Antonio. *La novela peruana: siete estudios*, Lima, Horizonte, 1977.

Includes a sweeping critique of Clorinda Matto de Turner's positivist attitude toward the Indian.

La formación de la tradición literaria en el Perú, Lima, Centro de Estudios y Publicaciones, 1989.

A powerful work emphasizing the relationships between national identity and literary tradition in Peru.

Cotarelo y Mori, Emilio. *La Avellaneda y sus obras*, Madrid, Tip. de Archivos, 1930.

Well documented, biographical and critical monograph on Gertrudis Gómez de Avellaneda's life and works. Questions Avellaneda's abolitionist sincerity.

Cueva, Agustín. *La literatura ecuatoriana*, Buenos Aires, Cedal, 1968.

Provides interesting critical comments on Mera's *Cumandá*.

Curcio Altamar, Antonio. *Evolución de la novela en Colombia*, Bogotá, Instituto Caro y Cuervo, 1957.

Studies the evolution of the Colombian novel since colonial times to 1965. A traditional work. Bibliography.

Díaz Arrieta, Hernán (Alone). *Don Alberto Blest Gana*, Santiago, Nascimento, 1940.

Studies Balzac's influence on Blest Gana's novels.

Englekirk, John E., and Margaret M. Ramos. *La narrativa uruguaya: estudio crítico-bibliográfico*, Berkeley and Los Angeles, University of California Press, 1967.

Includes a long introductory essay, and alphabetical lists of authors and secondary sources.

Englekirk, John E., and Gerald. E. Wade. *Bibliografía de la novela colombiana*, Mexico, Ed. Universitaria, 1950.

Alphabetical list of authors.

Figarola Caneda, Domingo. *Gertrudis Gómez de Avellaneda: biografía, bibliografía e iconografía*, Madrid, Sociedad General Española de Librería, 1929.

An in-depth study of Avellaneda's life and works.

Fishburn, Evelyn. *The Portrayal of Immigration in Nineteenth Century Argentine Fiction (1845–1902)*, Berlin, Colloquium, 1981.

Useful monograph studying the European immigrant as a literary character in nineteenth-century Argentina.

Flores, Angel. *Narrativa hispanoamericana 1816–1981: historia y antología*, 2 vols., Mexico, Siglo Veintiuno Editores, 1981.

Very useful. Includes bibliographical information on works by and about: José Joaquín Fernández de Lizardi, Esteban Echeverría, Eugenio Díaz, Cirilo Villaverde, Juana Manuela Gorriti, José Milla y Vidaurre, Alberto Blest Gana, Jorge

Isaacs, Nataniel Aguirre, Eugenio Cambacérès, Mercedes Cabello de Carbonera, Eduardo Acevedo Díaz, Clorinda Matto de Turner, Manuel Zeno Gandía, Emilio Rabasa, Tomás Carrasquilla, and Carlos Reyles.

Ford, Jeremiah D. M., and Maxwell I. Raphael. *A Bibliography of Cuban Belles-Lettres*, Cambridge, Mass., Harvard University Press, 1933.

> Very useful for nineteenth-century Cuban literature. Part I: bibliographies, dictionaries, histories of literature, and anthologies; part II: alphabetical list of authors; part III: anonymous or collective works; part IV: periodicals.

Foster, David William. *The Argentine Generation of 1880: Ideology and cultural texts*, Columbia, University of Missouri, 1990.

> The latest work on the literary production of the so-called *Generación del 80*.

Freire, Tabaré. *Javier de Viana, modernista*, Montevideo, Universidad de la República, 1957.

> Studies *modernista* features in Viana's literary production.

García, Germán. *La novela argentina: un itinerario*, Buenos Aires, Sudamericana, 1952.

> Clear and comprehensive study of the Argentinian novel. Emphasis on the twentieth century.

El inmigrante en la novela argentina, Buenos Aires, Hachette, 1970.

> An excellent work on the European immigrant as a main character in the Argentinian novel. Emphasis on the nineteenth century.

Garganigo, John F. *El perfil del gaucho en algunas novelas de Argentina y Uruguay*, Montevideo, Síntesis, 1966.

> Brief monograph on the gaucho as a character in some Argentinian and Uruguayan novels. Emphasis on the nineteenth century.

Javier de Viana, New York, Twayne's World Authors Series, 1972.

> A concise and excellent study of the life and works of Javier de Viana.

Girard, René. *La violence et le sacré*, Paris, Bernard Grasset, 1972.

> A major, influential anthropological work relevant to my definition of national identity as a feeling related to mimetic desire.

Glass, Elliot S. *México en las obras de Emilio Rabasa*, Mexico, Diana, 1974.

> Examines social life in Mexico through the works of Rabasa.

Goiĉ, Cedomil. *La novela chilena – los mitos degradados*, Santiago, Editorial Universitaria, 1968.

> An impressive analysis of eight Chilean novels. Emphasis on the twentieth century.

Historia de la novela hispanoamericana, Ed. Univ. de Valparaíso, 1972.

> Traces a development of the Spanish American novel according to generations.

Gómez Tejera, Carmen. *La novela en Puerto Rico*, San Juan, Universidad de Puerto Rico, 1947.

> A history of the Puerto Rican novel, organized by themes.

González, Manuel Pedro. *Trayectoria de la novela en México*, Mexico, Juan Pablos, 1951.

> An eclectic and somewhat arbitrary study of the Mexican novel.

González Echevarría, Roberto. *Myth and Archive: A theory of Latin American narrative*, Cambridge University Press, 1990.

> An outstanding work studying the origin and evolution of Latin American

narrative. It stresses the importance of European scientific discourse as a main source of the nineteenth-century Latin American novel.

González Stephan, Beatriz. *La historiografía literaria del liberalismo hispanoamericano del siglo* xix, Havana, Casa de las Américas, 1987.

Discusses the manipulative character of nineteenth-century Spanish American literary historiography.

Grases, Pedro. *La primera versión castellana de "Atala,"* Caracas, 1955.

A study of *Atala*'s influence on Spanish American Romanticism.

Guzmán, Augusto. *La novela en Bolivia 1847–1954*, La Paz, Juventud, 1955.

Provides useful information about Nataniel Aguirre's *Juan de la Rosa*.

Guzmán, Julia M. *Manuel Zeno Gandía: del romanticismo al naturalismo*, Madrid, Hauser y Menet, 1960.

Overview of Zeno Gandía's life and works.

Apuntes sobre la novelística puertorriqueña, San Juan, Coquí, 1969.

Mainly an interpretation of Manuel Zeno Gandía's works.

Hakala, Marcia. *Emilio Rabasa: novelista innovador mexicano en el Siglo* xix, Mexico, Porrúa, 1974.

Acknowledges Rabasa as the founder of the modern Mexican novel.

Halperin Donghi, Tulio. *El pensamiento de Echeverría*, Buenos Aires, Sudamericana, 1951.

A major work on Esteban Echeverría's ideas and their impact on the *Generación de 1837*.

Henríquez Ureña, Pedro. *Las corrientes literarias en la América Hispánica*, Mexico and Buenos Aires, Fondo de Cultura Económica, 1949.

A major study of the different literary currents in Spanish America.

Literary Currents in Hispanic America [1945], New York, Russell & Russell, 1963.

Hernández de Norman, Isabel. *La novela romántica en las Antillas*, New York, Ateneo Puertorriqueño, 1969.

A comprehensive study of the romantic novel in Cuba, Puerto Rico, and the Dominican Republic.

Hernández Sánchez-Barba, Mario. *Historia y literatura en Hispano-América (1492–1820): la versión intelectual de una experiencia*, Valencia, Castalia, 1978.

An intellectual history of colonial Spanish America. It stresses the literary importance of European scientific works during the eighteenth century.

Iguíniz, Juan B. *Bibliografía de novelistas mexicanos: ensayo biográfico y crítico; precedido de un estudio histórico de la novela mexicana*, Mexico, Monografías Bibliográficas, 1926.

Includes (1) a brief study of the Mexican novel, (2) a list of works on the Mexican novel, (3) biographical summaries, (4) an alphabetical list of authors.

Jiménez Rueda, Julio. *Letras mexicanas en el siglo XIX*, Mexico, Fondo de Cultura Económica, 1944.

Traditional study of nineteenth-century Mexican literature.

Kristal, Efraín. *The Andes Viewed from the City: Literary and political discourse on the Indian in Peru, 1848–1930*, New York, Peter Lang, 1987.

Studies the dialogue between the novel and social reform in Peru.

Levy, Kurt L. *Tomás Carrasquilla*, Boston, Twayne's World Author Series, 1980.

A clear and concise work on Carrasquilla's life and works.

Litchblau, Myron I. *The Argentine Novel in the Nineteenth Century*, New York, Spanish-American Printing Co., 1959.

This study includes chronological lists of (1) Argentinian novels of the nineteenth century, (2) bibliographical sources, (3) books and articles on individual authors and novels, (4) books and articles on the Argentinian novel in general. Descriptive, but extraordinarily useful.

Loveluck, Juan M. (ed.). *La novela hispanoamericana*, Santiago, Editorial Universitaria, 1963.

A collection of general works on the Spanish American novel.

Ludmer, Josefina. *El género gauchesco – un tratado sobre la patria*, Buenos Aires, Suramericana, 1988.

An in-depth study of the *gaucho* both as a literary character and a patriotic icon.

Luis, William. *Literary Bondage: Slavery in Cuban narrative*, Austin, University of Texas Press, 1990.

A solid work. Excellent chapters on Suárez y Romero's *Francisco*, Manzano's *Autobiografía*, and Villaverde's *Cecilia Valdés*.

Lyotard, Jean-François. *La condition postmoderne: rapport sur le savoir*, Paris, Minuit, 1979.

A major influential work, specially useful for its reflections on the different paradigms of knowledge.

Martínez, José Luis. *La expresión nacional: letras mexicanas del siglo XIX*, Mexico, Editorial Universitaria, 1955.

One of the most important works ever written on nineteenth-century Mexican letters.

Marting, Diane E. (ed.). *Women Writers of Spanish America: An annotated bio-bibliographical guide*, New York, Greenwood Press, 1987.

A massive bio-biographical work listing over 1,000 names. Provides biographical summaries and annotated entries.

McGrady, Donald. *La novela histórica en Colombia, 1844–1959*, Bogotá, Kelly, 1962.

A solid study of the historical novel in Colombia. Emphasis on nineteenth century.

Jorge Isaacs, New York, Twayne's World Author Series, 1972.

An excellent introduction to Isaacs's life and works.

Mejía Duque, Jaime. *Isaacs y María: el hombre y su novela*, Bogotá, La Carreta, 1979.

Illuminating analysis of the relationships between Isaacs's life and his *María*.

Meléndez, Concha. *La novela indianista en Hispanoamérica (1832–1889)*, Madrid, Librería y Casa Editorial Hernando, 1934.

Still a useful work. Comments on European and American sources related to *indianista* fiction. Emphasis on works by Avellaneda, Galván, and Mera. Bibliography.

Menton, Seymour. *Historia crítica de la novela guatemalteca*, Guatemala, Editorial Universitaria, 1960.

Devotes a chapter to José Milla's novels. Acknowledges *El visitador* as one of the best Spanish American historical novels of the period.

La novela colombiana: planetas y satélites, Bogotá, Plaza & Janés, 1978.

A solid study of ten Colombian novels. Emphasis on the twentieth century.

Morand, Carlos. *Visión de Santiago en la novela chilena*, Santiago, Aconcagua, 1977.
Examines the impact of modernization on Santiago de Chile as represented in the Chilean novel.

Navarro, Joaquina. *La novela realista mexicana*, Mexico, Compañía General de Ediciones, 1955.
A thorough study of the Mexican realist novel. Credits Emilio Rabasa with being the first of Mexico's realist writers.

Onega, Gladys S. *La inmigración en la literatura argentina, 1810–1910*. Santa Fe, Univ. Nacional del Litoral, 1965.
Studies European immigration as a main theme in the Argentinian novel.

Pérez-Firmat, Gustavo. *The Cuban Condition: Translation and identity in modern Cuban literature*, Cambridge University Press, 1989.
An outstanding work studying Cuban identity as the product of a self-concious recasting of foreign models.

Picón-Salas, Mariano. *De la Conquista a la Independencia: tres siglos de historia cultural hispanoamericana*, Mexico, Fondo de Cultura Económica, 1944.
An inspired and concise cultural history of Spanish America before Independence.
  A Cultural History of Spanish America: from Conquest to Independence, tr. Irving A. Leonard, Berkeley, University of California Press, 1962.

Poblete Varas, Hernán. *Genio y figura de Alberto Blest Gana*, Buenos Aires, EUDEBA, 1968.
An excellent introduction to the life and works of Blest Gana.

Porras Collantes, Ernesto. *Bibliografía de la novela en Colombia*, Bogotá, Instituto Caro y Cuervo, 1976.
An excellent annotated bibliography. Includes listing of works on individual authors and novels.

Portantiero, Juan Carlos. *Realismo y realidad en la narrativa argentina*. Buenos Aires, Procyón, 1961.
Focuses on realist traits in the Argentinian novel.

Portuondo, José Antonio. *Capítulos de literatura cubana*, Havana, Letras Cubanas, 1981.
A Marxist approach to Cuban literature. Chapters on Gertrudis Gómez de Avellaneda and Domingo Delmonte's group.

Prieto, Adolfo. *Proyección del rosismo en la literatura argentina*, Rosario, Argentina, Instituto de Letras, 1959.
Investigates the historical representation of Rosas's terror in Argentinian letters.

Pupo-Walker, Enrique. *La vocación literaria del pensamiento histórico en América: desarrollo de la prosa de ficción: siglos XVI, XVII, XVIII, y XIX*, Madrid, Gredos, 1982.
An outstanding work studying the literary and dialogic orientation of early historiographical discourse in Spanish America.

Rama, Angel. *La ciudad letrada*, Hanover, N.H., Ediciones del Norte, 1984.
Investigates the relationship between writing and urban development in Spanish America.

Ramos, Julio. *Desencuentros de la modernidad en América Latina: literatura y política en el siglo XIX*, Mexico, Fondo de Cultura Económica, 1989.

A concise and clear study questioning the coherence of Spanish American modernity through the works of José Martí and others.

Ratcliff, D. F. *Venezuelan Prose Fiction*, New York, Instituto de las Españas, 1933.

A traditional study of the Venezuelan novel.

Read, J. Lloyd. *The Mexican Historical Novel (1826–1910)*, New York, Instituto de las Españas, 1939.

Provides useful descriptions of plots and characters in the nineteenth-century Mexican historical novel. Bibliography.

Rivera, Jorge B. *El folletín y la novela popular*, Buenos Aires, Centro Editor de la América Latina, 1968.

Interesting monograph on the impact of European serialized novels on Latin American readers.

Rodríguez Monegal, Emir. *Eduardo Acevedo Díaz: dos versiones de un tema*, Montevideo, Eds. del Río de la Plata, 1963.

The best available work on Acevedo Díaz's novels.

El otro Andrés Bello, Caracas, Monte Avila, 1969.

A major study of Bello's life, times, and writings.

Rojas, Angel F. *La novela ecuatoriana*, Mexico and Buenos Aires, Fondo de Cultura Económica, 1948.

Includes an excellent chapter on Mera's *Cumandá*.

Rojas, Ricardo. *Historia de la literatura argentina*, 4th. edn., 9 vols., Buenos Aires, Guillermo Kraft, 1957.

A major work. Volume VIII studies the Argentinian novel during the nineteenth century.

Rusich, Luciano. *El inmigrante italiano en la novela argentina del 80*, Madrid, Playor, 1974.

Studies the theme of the Italian immigrant in the Argentinian novel.

Sánchez, Julio C. *La obra novelística de Cirilo Villaverde*, Madrid, De Orbe Novo, 1973.

A thorough sociological approach to Villaverde's works.

Sánchez, Luis Alberto. *Proceso y contenido de la novela hispanoamericana*, Madrid, Gredos, 1953.

A generational overview of the Spanish American novel. An important work.

Escritores representativos de América, Madrid, Gredos, 1963.

Includes interesting essays on Tomás Carrasquilla, Jorge Isaacs, and José Milla.

Santovenia, Emeterio S. *Personajes y paisajes de Villaverde*, Havana, Academia Nacional de Artes y Letras, 1955.

An interesting work. Villaverde emerges as the ideal chronicler of the Cuban nation.

Sarlo, Beatriz. *Juan María Gutiérrez: historiador y crítico de nuestra literatura*, Buenos Aires, Escuela, 1967.

A concise study of Juan María Gutiérrez's life and works.

Schwartz, Kessel. *A New History of Spanish American Fiction*, I, University of Miami Press, 1972.

Solid and well-documented study. Excellent bibliography of secondary sources.

Shaw, Bradly A. *Latin American Literature in English Translation: An annotated bibliography*, New York University, 1976.

> The most comprehensive bibliography of its kind. 624 items listed.

Silva Castro, Raúl. *Alberto Blest Gana*, Santiago, Zig-Zag, 1955.

> A lengthy, though somewhat disorganized, work on Blest Gana's life and literary production.

Panorama de la novela chilena (1843–1953), Mexico, Fondo de Cultura Económica, 1955.

> A traditional overview of the Chilean novel. Bibliography.

Sommer, Doris. *Foundational Fictions: The national romances of Latin America*, Berkeley, University of California Press, 1991.

> An excellent innovative work, revealing the complicity of the romantic love-story with Latin American nationalism, patriotic celebration, and programs of national consolidation.

Sosa, Enrique. *La economía en la novela cubana del siglo XIX*, Havana, Letras Cubanas, 1978.

> Examines the impact of plantation economy in Cuban society as represented in the nineteenth-century novel.

Suárez-Murias, Marguerite C. *La novela romántica en Hispanoamérica*, New York, Hispanic Institute in the United States, 1963.

> A useful, informative introduction to the romantic Spanish American novel.

Torres Rioseco, Arturo. *Bibliografía de la novela mejicana*, Cambridge, Mass. Harvard University Press, 1933.

> Alphabetical list of authors.

La novela en la América Hispana, Berkeley, University of California Press, 1939.

> One of the first global studies of the Spanish American novel. Emphasis on the nineteenth century.

Uslar Pietri, Arturo. *Breve historia de la novela hispanoamericana*, Caracas and Madrid, Edime, 1954.

> Emphasizes the importance of *costumbrismo*. Acknowledges Mármol's *Amalia* as the first true Spanish American novel.

Villanueva de Puccinelli, Elsa. *Bibliografía de la novela peruana*, Lima, Biblioteca Universitaria, 1969.

> Lists titles in alphabetical and chronological orders.

Viñas, David. *Literatura argentina y realidad política*, Buenos Aires, Jorge Alvarez, 1964.

> Studies the relationship between literature and politics in Argentinian society. Includes a powerful chapter on Mármol's *Amalia*.

Wallerstein, Immanuel. *The Modern World-System*, 2 vols., New York, Academic Press, 1974–1980.

> A major influential economic study of the origins and consolidation of the European world-economy.

Warner, Ralph E. *Historia de la novela mexicana en el siglo XIX*, Mexico, Antigua Librería Robredo, 1953.

> A traditional overview of the nineteenth-century Mexican novel.

White, Hayden. *Metahistory: The historical imagination in nineteenth-century*

Europe, Baltimore, Johns Hopkins University Press, 1973.

    A major influential work, particularly relevant to my views on the aprioristic relationship between a writer's desire for a given national project and the rhetorical model followed by his/her work.

Williams, Raymond Leslie. *The Colombian Novel 1844–1987*, Austin, University of Texas Press, 1991.

    An overview of more than one hundred works. Emphasizes the regional nature of the Colombian novel. Bibliography.

Williams Alzaga, Enrique. *La pampa en la novela argentina*, Buenos Aires, Angel Estrada & Cía., 1955.

    Studies country life in the Argentinian novel.

Yáñez, Mirta (ed.). *La novela romántica latinoamericacana*, Havana, Casa de las Américas, 1978.

    A collection of important pieces on the romantic Spanish American novel. Includes essays by Emilio Carilla, Pedro Henríquez Ureña, Fernando Alegría, Luis Alberto Sánchez, Julio A. Leguizamón, Alberto Zum Felde, Ezequiel Martínez Estrada, Noé Jitrik, David Viñas, Juan Carlos Ghiano, Enrique Anderson Imbert, Jaime Mejía Duque, Concha Meléndez, and others. Emphasis on *Facundo*, *María*, *Enriquillo*, and *El Zarco*.

Yepes Boscán, G. *La novela indianista en Venezuela*, Maracaibo, Venezuela, Universidad de Zulia, 1965.

    A descriptive study of the *indianista* novel in Venezuela. Emphasis on the nineteenth century.

Young, Robert J. *La novela costumbrista de "Cecilia Valdés,"* Universidad Nacional Autónoma de México, 1949.

    An interesting *costumbrista* reading of Villaverde's *Cecilia Valdés*.

Zamudio Zamora, José. *La novela histórica en Chile*, Santiago, Flor Nacional, 1949.

    A traditional work on the Chilean historical novel. Acknowledges Blest Gana's *Durante la reconquista* as the best Chilean historical novel.

Zum Felde, Alberto. *La narrativa en Hispanoamérica*, Madrid, Aguilar, 1964.

    Provides interesting notes on the particularities of the Spanish American novel.

Articles

Ainsa, Fernando. "'La tierra prometida' como motivo en la narrativa argentina," *Hispamérica*, 53–4 (1989), 3–23.

    Studies the theme of the promised land in the novels of Groussac, Ocantos, and others.

Alba-Buffill, Elio. "Loveira y Zeno Gandía: representantes del naturalismo en las Antillas" in *Estudios literarios sobre Hispanoamérica (homenaje a Carlos M. Raggi y Ageo)*, San José, Círculo de Cultura Panamericano, 1976, 85–96.

    Acknowledges Loveira's and Zeno Gandía's works as the first naturalist novels in the Caribbean.

Allen, Martha. "La personalidad literaria de Carlos Reyles," *Revista Iberoamericana*, 25 (1947), 91–115.

    An important article on Reyles's works.

Alvarez García, Imeldo. "La obra narrativa de Cirilo Villaverde," prologue to

Volume 1

Villaverde's *Cecilia Valdés*, I, Havana, Letras Cubanas, 1979.
An informative study of Villaverde's life, times, and works.

Anderson Imbert, Enrique. Prologue to Jorge Isaacs, *María*, ed. E. Anderson Imbert, Mexico and Buenos Aires, Fondo de Cultura Económica, 1951.
A thorough study of *María* with an interesting appendix.

"Notas sobre la novela histórica en el siglo XIX" in Arturo Torres-Rioseco (ed.), *La novela iberoamericana*. Albuquerque, University of New Mexico Press, 1952, 3–24.
Perceptive article on the nineteenth-century Spanish American novel.

Apter Cragnolino, Aída. "Ortodoxia naturalista, inmigración y racismo en *En la sangre* de Eugenio Cambaceres" in Raquel Chang-Rodríguez and Gabriella de Beer (eds.), *La historia en la literatura iberoamericana: memorias del XXVI Congreso del Instituto Internacional de Literatura Iberoamericana*, Hanover, N.H., Ediciones del Norte, 1989, 225–35.
A critique of Cambaceres's social prejudices in *En la sangre*.

Araya, Guillermo. Prologue to Alberto Blest Gana, *Martín Rivas*, 2nd. edn., Madrid, Cátedra, 1983.
Focuses on *Martín Rivas*'s treatment of Chilean history and society.

Arias, Augusto. Prologue to Juan León Mera, *Cumandá*, ed. A. Arias, Quito, Casa de la Cultura Ecuatoriana, 1948.
Provides interesting information about Mera and the background of *Cumandá*.

Arrieta, Rafael A. "Esteban Echeverría y el romanticismo en el Plata" in his *Historia de la literatura argentina*, II. Buenos Aires, Peuser, 1958, 19–111.
An excellent chapter on Echeverría and the emergence of romantic literature in the River Plate region.

Arrufat, Antón. "El nacimiento de la novela en Cuba," *Revista Iberoamericana*, 152–3 (1991), 747–57.
A socio-economic interpretation of the emergence of the Cuban novel.

Bancroft, Robert I. "*El Periquillo Sarniento* and *Don Catrín*: which is the masterpiece?" *Revista Hispánica Moderna*, 34 (1968), 227–41.
An engaging comparison of Lizardi's best two novels.

Barreda, Pedro. "Abolicionismo y feminismo en la Avellaneda: lo negro como artificio narrativo en *Sab*," *Cuadernos Hispanoamericanos*, 342 (1978), 613–26.
Comments on Avellaneda's abolitionist and feminist views.

Barrera, Trinidad. "Estudio preliminar," prologue to Juan León Mera, *Cumandá o un drama entre salvajes*, ed. T. Barrera, Seville, Alfar, 1989.
A lengthy and well-documented introduction to Juan León Mera's *Cumandá*.

Beane, Carol A. "Los contornos discursivos del Africa de *María*" in Raquel Chang-Rodríguez and Gabriella de Beer (eds.), *La historia en la literatura iberoamericana: memorias del XXVI Congreso del Instituto Internacional de Literatura Iberoamericana*, Hanover, N.H., Ediciones del Norte, 1989, 201–12.
A thorough critique of the episode of Nay and Sinar in Isaacs's *María*.

Beck, Phyllis Powers. "Eugenio Cambaceres: The vortex of controversy," *Hispania*, 56 (1963), 755–9.
Interesting note about the contradictory nature of Cambaceres's style.

Bello, Andrés. "*Bosquejo histórico de la constitución del gobierno de Chile durante el primer período de la revolución. Desde 1810 hasta 1814*, por Don José Victorino Lastarria" in *Obras completas* XIX, Caracas, Ministerio de Educación, 1957, 223–4. [*El Araucano*, January 7, 1848.]

"Colección de los viajes y descubrimientos que hicieron por mar los españoles desde fines del siglo XV" in *Obras completas* XIX, Caracas, Ministerio de Educación, 1957, 445–84. [*El Repertorio Americano III*, April 1827.]

"Modo de escribir la historia" in *Obras completas* XIX, Caracas, Ministerio de Educación, 1957, 229–42. [*El Araucano*, January 28, 1848.]

"Modo de estudiar la historia" in *Obras completas*, XIX, Caracas, Ministerio de Educación, 1957, 246. [*El Araucano*, February 7, 1848.]

"*La Araucana*, por Don Alonso de Ercilla y Zúñiga" in *Obras completas* IX, 2nd. edn., Caracas, Ministerio de Educación, 1981, 349–62. [*El Araucano*, February 5, 1841.]

Benarós, León. "Eduardo Gutiérrez: un descuidado destino," prologue to E. Gutiérrez's *El Chacho*, Buenos Aires, Hachette, 1960.

An excellent introduction to Gutiérrez's works.

Benítez-Rojo, Antonio. "Power/sugar/literature: toward a reinterpretation of Cubanness," *Cuban Studies*, 16 (1986), 9–31.

Studies the relationship between sugar and literature in the writings of Villaverde, Palma y Romay, Suárez y Romero, and other members of Domingo Delmonte's circle.

Blasi, Alberto. "Orígenes de la novela argentina: Manuel T. Podestá" in Alan M. Gordon and Evelyn Rugg (eds.), *Actas del Sexto Congreso Internacional de Hispanistas*, University of Toronto, 1980, 111–14.

Interesting note on Podesta's *Irresponsable*.

Borgeson, Paul W., Jr. "Problemas de técnica narrativa en dos *novellas* de Lizardi," *Hispania*, 3 (1986), 504–11.

Compares the narrative style of *Noche triste y día alegre* to *Don Catrin*'s.

Bremer, Thomas. "Historia social de la literatura e intertextualidad: funciones de la lectura en las novelas latino-americanas del siglo XIX (el caso del 'libro en el libro')," *Revista de Crítica Literaria Latinoamericana*, 24 (1986), 31–49.

Studies intertextuality in Mármol's *Amalia* and Isaacs's *María*.

Brown, Donald F. "Chateaubriand and the story of Feliciana in Jorge Isaac's *María*," *Modern Language Notes*, 62 (1947), 326–9.

About Chateaubriand's influence on Isaacs's *María*.

Brown, James W. "Heriberto Frías, a Mexican Zola," *Hispania*, 50 (1967), 467–71.

Compares Frías's method to Zola's.

Brushwood, John S. "Juan Díaz Covarrubias: Mexico's martyr novelist," *The Americas*, 10 (1958), 301–6.

Mostly a bio-bibliographical note.

"The Mexican understanding of Realism and Naturalism," *Hispania*, 43 (1960), 521–8.

Interesting article on the emergence of non-romantic fiction in Mexico.

"Heriberto Frías on social behaviour and redemptive woman," *Hispania*, 46 (1962), 249–53.

A sociological approach to Frías's *¡Tomochic!*

Bueno, Salvador. "Los temas de la novela cubana," *Asomante*, 4 (1960), 39–48.

Describes main thematic currents of the Cuban novel.

"El negro en *El Periquillo Sarniento*: antirracismo de Lizardi," *Cuadernos Americanos*, 183 (1972), 124–39.

Notices Lizardi's democratic views on the Negro.

"La narrativa antiesclavista en Cuba de 1835 a 1839," *Cuadernos Hispanoamericanos*, 451–2 (1988), 169–86.

A traditional study of the abolitionist narratives produced in Cuba during the period 1835–1839.

Burns, E. Bradford. "Bartolomé Mitre: The historian as novelist, the novel as history," *Revista Interamericana de Bibliografía*, 32 (1982), 155–267.

A brilliant article on Mitre's views on the role of the novel.

Cabrera Saqui, Mario. Prologue to Anselmo Suárez y Romero, *Francisco – el ingenio o Las delicias del campo*, Havana, Ministerio de Educación, 1947.

An excellent piece on Suárez y Romero's life and works.

Camurati, Mireya. "Blest Gana, Lukács y la novela histórica," *Cuadernos Americanos*, 197 (1974), 88–99.

A Lukácsian approach to Blest Gana's novels.

Cánepa, Gina. "Folletines históricos del Chile independiente y su articulación con la novela naturalista," *Revista de Crítica Literaria Latinoamericana*, 30 (1989), 249–58.

Studies the relationship between the early Chilean *feuilleton* and the naturalist novel.

Carlos, Alberto J. "*René, Werther* y *La nouvelle Héloise* en la primera novela de la Avellaneda," *Revista Iberoamericana*, 60 (1965), 223–38.

Notices European influences on Avellaneda's *Sab*.

Carricaburu, Norma. "Carnaval y carnavalización en la generación del 80," *Filología*, 1 (1987), 183–205.

A Bakhtinian reading of the literary production of the so-called *Generación del 80* in Argentina.

Castillo, Homero, and Raúl Silva Castro. "Algunas observaciones y notas sobre Eugenio Cambaceres," prologue to Cambaceres, *Obras completas*, ed. E. M. S. Danero Santa Fe, Castellví, 1956.

Provides useful information about Cambaceres's life and works.

Castro Leal, Antonio. Prologue to José Tomás de Cuéllar, *Ensalada de pollos – baile y cochino*, ed. A. Castro Leal, Mexico, Porrúa, 1946.

Provides interesting information about Cuéllar's life and works.

Colón Zayas, Eliseo R. "La escritura ante la formación de la conciencia nacional: *La peregrinación de Bayoán*, de Eugenio María de Hostos," *Revista Iberoamericana*, 140 (1987), 627–34.

A foundational reading of Hostos's novel.

Concha, Jaime. Prologue to Alberto Blest Gana, *Martín Rivas*, Caracas, Biblioteca Ayacucho, 1977.

A solid social approach to Blest Gana's *Martín Rivas*.

Cornejo Polar, Antonio. Prologue to Clorinda Matto de Turner, *Aves sin nido*, Havana, Casa de las Américas, 1974.

A solid, critical work on the limitations of Matto de Turner's views on the Indian.

Cros, Edmund. "Space and textual genetics: magical consciousness and ideology in *Cumandá*," *Sociocriticism*, 4–5 (1986–1987), 35–72.

> Relates Mera's conservative ideology to his magic treatment of the forest in *Cumandá*.

Cruz, Mary. Prologue to Gertrudis Gómez de Avellaneda, *Sab*, Havana, Arte y Literatura, 1976.

> Notices the influence of Victor Hugo's *Bug-Jargal* in Avellaneda's novel.

Danero, E. M. S. Prologue to Lucio V. López, *La gran aldea*, Buenos Aires, Albatros, 1939.

> Acknowledges *La gran aldea* as the first Argentinian modern novel.

Davis, Jack Emory. "Picturesque 'Americanismos' in the works of Fernández de Lizardi," *Hispania*, 54 (1961), 74–81.

> Notices picturesque traits in Lizardi's style.

"Algunos problemas lexicográficos en *El Periquillo sarniento*," *Revista Iberoamericana*, 23 (1968), 163–71.

> Deals with Lizardi's use of popular speech.

Delgado, Jaime. "El *Guatimozín* de Gertrudis Gómez de Avellaneda" in XVII *Congreso del Instituto Internacional de Literatura Iberoamericana*, Madrid, Centro Iberoamericano de Cooperación/Universidad Complutense de Madrid, 1978, 959–70.

> An important article on Avellaneda's *Guatimozín*.

Dellepiane, Angela B. "Ciencia y literatura en un texto de Eduardo L. Holmberg" in Keith McDuffie and Rose Minc (eds.), *Homenaje a Alfredo A. Roggiano*, Pittsburgh, IILI, 1990, 457–76.

> An interesting article on Holmberg's Darwinist novel *Dos partidos en lucha*.

Epple, Juan Armando. "Eugenio Cambaceres y el naturalismo en Argentina," *Ideologies and Literatures*, 3 (1980), 16–50.

> Thorough, interdisciplinary article on Cambacérès's Naturalism.

"Mercedes Cabello de Carbonera y el problema de la novela moderna en el Perú" in Silverio Muñoz (ed.), *Doctores y proscritos: la nueva generación de latinoamericanistas chilenos en U.S.A.*," Minneapolis, Institute for the Studies of Ideologies and Literatures, 1987, 23–48.

> Studies the emergence of the modern novel in nineteenth-century Peru. A sociological approach.

Etcheverry, José Enrique. "Historia, nacionalismo y tradición en la obra de Eduardo Acevedo Díaz" in Arturo Torrez-Rioseco (ed.), *La novela iberoamericana*, Albuquerque, University of New Mexico Press, 1952, 155–65.

> A nationalist reading of Acevedo Díaz's works.

Fivel-Demoret, Sharon Romeo "The production and consumption of propaganda literature: The Cuban anti-slavery novel," *Bulletin of Hispanic Studies*, 1 (1989), 1–12.

> Deals with *Sab*, *Francisco El ranchador*, and *Petrona y Rosalía* as abolitionist pamphlets.

Foster, David William. "Manuel T. Podestá's *Irresponsable*: Naturalism ideologically revised," *Romance Notes*, 3 (1987), 215–21.

> Interesting note on Podestá's manipulation of Zola's social ideas.

"*La gran aldea* as ideological document," *Hispanic Review*, 1 (1988), 73–87.

A solid article studying Lucio V. Lopez's novel as a critical text of its times.

Foucault, Michel. "Qu'est-ce qu'un auteur?" *Bulletin de la Societé Française de Philosophie*, 3 (1969), 73–104.

A major, influenial essay relevant to my views on discourse formation in Spanish America.

Fox-Lockert, Lucía. "Contexto político, situación del indio y crítica a la Iglesia de Clorinda Matto de Turner" in Keith McDuffie and Alfredo Roggiano (eds.), *Texto/Contexto en la literatura iberoamericana: memoria del XIX Congreso del Instituto Internacional de Literatura Iberoamericana*, Madrid, IILI, 1980, 89–94.

Focuses on Matto de Turner's discrepancies with the Catholic church.

Franco, Jean. "En espera de una burguesía: la formación de la intelligentsia mexicana en la época de la Independencia" in José Amor y Vázquez, A. David Kossoff, Geoffrey W. Ribbans (eds.), *Actas del VIII Congreso de la Asociación Internacional de Hispanistas*, Madrid, Istmo, 1986, 21–36.

Excellent study of the situation of the intellectual in Mexico's society during the 1820s. Contributes to a better understanding of Fernández de Lizardi's role as a writer.

Friol, Roberto. "La novela cubana en el siglo XIX," *Unión*, 4 (1968), 179–207.

The best available article on the nineteenth-century Cuban novel.

García Cabrera, Estela. "La Conquista y colonización a la luz de Manuel de Jesús Galván," *Horizontes*, 61 (1987), 5–12.

Note on Galván's *Enriquillo* as historical text.

Garrels, Elizabeth. "El 'espíritu de la familia' en *La novia del hereje*," *Hispamérica*, 46–7 (1987), 3–24.

A solid analysis of Vicente Fidel Lopez's novel as a family romance.

Godoy, Bernabé. "Lo permanente y lo transitorio en el *Periquillo*," *EtCaetera*, 2 (1951), 1–22.

A nationalist reading of Lizardi's *Periquillo*.

Goiĉ, Cedomil. "La novela hispanoamericana colonial" in Luis Iñigo Madrigal (ed.), *Historia de la literatura hispanoamericana*, vol. I: *Epoca colonial*, Madrid, Cátedra, 1982, 369–406.

A well-documented article on the fictional works that preceded *El Periquillo sarniento*.

González, Aníbal. "Turbulencias en *La charca*, de Lucrecio a Manuel Zeno Gandía," *MLN* (1983), 208–25.

The best available article on Zeno Gandía's *La charca*.

González, Eduardo. "American theriomorphia: the presence of *Mulatez* in Cirilo Villaverde and beyond" in Gustavo Pérez Firmat (ed.), *Do the Americas Have a Common Literature?* Durham, Duke University Press, 1990, 177–97.

Engaging race/gender reading of Villaverde's *Cecilia Valdés*.

González, Reynaldo. "Para una lectura historicista de *Cecilia Valdés*," *Casa de las Américas*, 129 (1981), 84–92.

A solid historicist reading of Villaverde's *Cecilia Valdés*.

González Cruz, Luis F. "Influencia cervantina en Lizardi," *Cuadernos Hispanoamericanos*, 286 (1974), 188–203.

Notices Cervantes's influence on Lizardi's *La Quijotita y su prima* and *Don Catrín de la fachenda*.

Gotschlich Reyes, Guillermo. "Grotesco y tragicomedia en *El ideal de un calavera* de Alberto Blest Gana," *Revista Chilena de Letras*, 29 (1987), 119–48.
Interesting reading of Blest Gana's novel as a tragi-comic piece.
Graña, Cecilia. "Buenos Aires en *Amalia*: la ciudad desierta," *Nueva Revista de Filología Hispánica*, 1 (1985–1986), 194–218.
Discusses Mármol's description of Buenos Aires.
Grass, Roland. "José López-Portillo y Rojas y la revolución agraria en México," *Cuadernos Americanos*, 146 (1966), 240–6.
Relates López-Portillo y Rojas's *La parcela* to the novels of the Mexican Revolution.
Guerra-Cunningham, Lucía. "Estrategias femeninas en la elaboración del sujeto romántico en la obra de Gertrudis Gómez de Avellaneda," *Revista Iberoamericana*, 132–3 (1985), 707–22.
Compares feminist strategies in Avellaneda's *Sab*, and *Dos mujeres*.
"La visión marginal en la narrativa de Juana Manuela Gorriti," *Ideologies & Literatures*, 2 (1987), 59–76.
Studies Gorriti's characters as marginal entities.
Henríquez Ureña, Max. "Influencias francesas en la novela de la América española" in Juan Loveluck (ed.), *La novela hispanoamericana*, Santiago, Editorial Universitaria, 1966, 145–52.
Studies French influences on the Spanish American novel.
Henríquez Ureña, Pedro. "Apuntaciones sobre la novela en América," *Humanidades*, 15 (1927), 133–46.
Indispensable commentaries on the emergence, development, and particularities of the Spanish American novel.
Jackson, Richard L. "Slavery, racism and autobiography in two early black writers: Juan Francisco Manzano and Martín Morúa Delgado" in William Luis (ed.), *Voices from Under. Black narrative in Latin America and the Caribbean*, Westport, Conn., Greenwood Press, 1984, 55–64.
Studies black liberation and social integration in Manzano's and Morúa Delgado's works.
Johnston, Marjorie C. "José Milla, reatratista de costumbres guatemaltecas," *Hispania*, 32 (1949), 449–52.
Presents José Milla as a *costumbrista* writer.
Knowlton, E. C. "China and the Philippines in *El Periquillo sarniento*," *Hispanic Review*, 30 (1962–1963), 336–47.
Interesting article about the influence of Juan González de Mendoza's Asiatic accounts on Lizardi's *Periquillo*.
Lagos-Pope, María Inés. "Estructura dual y sociedad patriarcal en *María*," *Revista de Estudios Colombianos*, 8 (1990), 12–20.
An important critique of Isaacs's views.
Laguerre, Enrique. Prologue to Manuel Zeno Gandía, *La charca*, Caracas, Biblioteca Ayacucho, 1978.
A useful introduction to Zeno Gandía's works. Bibliography.
Lamb, Ruth S. "The *Costumbrismo* of the Pensador Mexicano and Micrós," *The Modern Language Journal*, 35 (1951), 193–8.
Notices *costumbrista* traits in the works of Joaquín Fernández de Lizardi and

Angel de Campo.

Latcham, Ricardo A. "Blest Gana y la novela realista," *Anales de la Universidad de Chile*, 112 (1958), 30–46.
  Acknowledges Blest Gana as the father of the realist novel in Spanish America.

Lazo, Raimundo. Prologue to Cirilio Villaverde, *Cecilia Valdés*, ed. R. Lazo, Mexico, Porrúa, 1979.
  A crucial study of Villaverde's novel.

Leal, Luis. "*Jicotencal*, primera novela histórica en castellano," *Revista Iberoamericana* 49 (1960), 9–31.
  Excellent article on *Jicotencal* proposing Félix Varela as its author.

Leante, César. "*Cecilia Valdés*, espejo de la esclavitud," *Casa de las Américas*, 89 (1975), 19–25.
  Studies Cuban slave society in Villaverde's *Cecilia Valdés*.

Lewald, H. Ernest. "La Bolsa como símbolo y crónica en la literatura argentina," *Chasqui*, 2–3 (1983), 19–26.
  Studies the stock-market as literary theme in Argentinian literature.

Lewis, Bart L. "Literature and society: Madame de Staël and the Argentine Romantics," *Hispania*, 4 (1985), 740–6.
  Notices Madame de Staël's influence on the nineteenth-century Argentinian novel.

"Recent criticism of nineteenth-century Latin American literature," *Latin American Research Review*, 2 (1985), 182–8.
  A useful review-article.

Lipp, Solomon. "The popular novel in nineteenth-century Latin America," *Canadian Review of Comparative Literature*, 3 (1982), 406–23.
  Studies the emergence of the Latin American popular novel. Emphasis on Eduardo Gutiérrez's works.

López Michelsen, A. "Ensayo sobre la influencia semítica en *María*," *Revista de las Indias*, 62 (1944), 5–10.
  Underscores semitic influences on Isaacs's *María*.

Losada, Alejandro. "El surgimiento del realismo social en la literatura de América Latina," *Ideologies and Literatures*, 11 (1979), 20–55.
  Studies the emergence of social awareness in nineteenth-century Latin American literature.

Lozano, Carlos. "*El Periquillo sarniento* y la *Histoire de Gil Blas de Santillana*," *Revista Iberoamericana*, 40 (1955), 263–74.
  A thorough work studying the influence of *Gil Blas* on *El Periquillo*.

Luis, William. "*Cecilia Valdés*: el nacimiento de una novela antiesclavista," *Cuadernos Hispanoamericanos*, 451–2 (1988), 187–93.
  Provides useful information about the genesis of Villaverde's *Cecilia Valdés*

Madrigal, Luis Íñigo. "La novela naturalista hispanoamericana" in Ricardo Vergara (ed.), *La novela hispanoamericana: descubrimiento e invención de América*, Ed. Univ. de Valparaíso, 1973, 71–94.
  A comprehensive overview of the Spanish American naturalist novel.

Magnarelli, Sharon. "The love story: reading and writing in Jorge Isaacs' *María*" in her *The Lost Rib – Female Characters in the Spanish-American Novel*, London and Toronto, Bucknell University, 1985, 19–37.

An important feminist reading of *María*.

Marinello, Juan. "Americanismo y cubanismo literarios" in his *Ensayos* [1932], Havana, Arte y Literatura, 1977, 47–60.

A seminal essay stressing the paradoxical nature of Spanish American literature.

Martínez, Dámaso. "Nacimiento de la novela: José Mármol" in *Historia de la literatura argentina* I, Buenos Aires, Centro Editor de América Latina, 1980, 265–88.

Notices an influence of Mármol's *Amalia* in the French novel.

Martínez, José Luis. "Fernández de Lizardi y los orígenes de la novela en México" in *La expresión nacional*, Mexico, Editorial Universitaria, 1955, 7–26.

Excellent chapter on the nationalist importance of Lizardi's works.

Marún, Gioconda. "Relectura de *Sin rumbo*: floracíon de la novela moderna," *Revista Iberoamericana*, 135–6 (1986), 377–92.

Close reading of Eugenio Cambacérès's *Sin rumbo* as an early modernist novel.

Mathieu, Corina. "La presencia de Rosas en la literatura argentina," *Selecta*, 2 (1981), 152–5.

Interesting note on the treatment of Rosas in Argentinian literature.

McGrady, Donald. Prologue to Jorge Isaacs, *María*, ed. D. McGrady, Barcelona, Labor, 1970.

One of the most interesting and informative texts on *María*.

Mejía, Gustavo. Prologue to Jorge Isaacs, *Maria*, ed. G. Mejía, Caracas, Biblioteca Ayacucho, 1978.

A solid, interdisciplinary approach to *María*. Relates Isaacs's novel to the decadence of the traditional land-owner in nineteenth-century Colombia.

Menton, Seymour. "*Frutos de mi tierra* o *Jamones y solomos*," ed. S. Menton, prologue to Tomás Carrasquilla, *Frutos de mi tierra*, Bogotá, Instituto Caro y Cuervo, 1972.

One of best works available on *Frutos de mi tierra*.

Meyer, Elvira V. de. "El nacimiento de la novela: José Mármol" in *Historia de la literatura argentina*, I, Buenos Aires, Centro Editor de América Latina, 1967, 216–39.

An excellent chapter on Mármol's writings.

Mignolo, Walter D. "Aspectos del cambio literario (a propósito de la *Historia de la novela hispanoamericana* de Cedomil Goic," *Revista Iberoamericana*, 42 (1976), 31–49.

An excellent discussion of Goic's *Historia de la novela hispanoamericana*.

Miliani, Domingo. "Gonzalo Picón Febres," prologue to Gonzalo Picón Febres, *La literatura venezolana en el siglo* XIX, Caracas, Presidencia de la República, 1972.

An informative introduction to Picón Febres's life and works.

Millán, María del Carmen. Prologue to Angel de Campo, *Ocios y apuntes, y La rumba*, Mexico, Porrúa, 1958.

An important work. Observes the presence of multiple styles in *La rumba*.

Miller, Beth K. "Gertrude the Great: Avellaneda, nineteenth-century feminist" in Beth Miller (ed.), *Women in Hispanic Literature: Icons and fallen idols*, Berkeley, University of California Press, 1983, 201–14.

An engaging article studying Avellaneda as feminist.

Molloy, Sylvia. "Paraíso perdido y economía terrenal en *María*," *Sin Nombre*, 3 (1984), 36–55.
> An excellent reading of Isaacs's *María* as a circular text trying to preserve the past.

Moore, Ernest A. "Heriberto Frías and the novel of the Mexican Revolution," *Modern Language Forum*, 1 (1942), 12–27.
> Relates Frías's *¡Tomochic!* to the novel of the Mexican Revolution.

Moraña, Mabel. "*El Periquillo sarniento* y la ciudad letrada," *Revista de Estudios Hispánicos*, 3 (1989), 113–26.
> Interesting article studying Periquillo's relationship to the society of his times.

Navia Romero, Walter. "Introducción y análisis de *Juan de la Rosa*," prologue to Nataniel Aguirre *Juan de la Rosa*, ed. W. Navia Romero, Cochabamba, Bolivia, Los Amigos del Libro, 1969.
> A powerful work on Aguirre's *Juan de la Rosa*.

Novo, Salvador. Prologue to Luis G. Inclán, *Astucia, el jefe de los Hermanos de la Hoja, o Los charros contrabandistas de la Rama* 1 ed. S. Novo, Mexico, Porrúa, 1946.
> Provides useful information on the life and works of Inclán.

Nunn, Marshall. "Las obras menores de Cirilo Villaverde," *Revista Iberoamericana*, 14 (1948), 255–61.
> Useful article on Villaverde's novels other than *Cecilia Valdés*.

Onís, Federico de. "Tomás Carrasquilla, precursor de la novela moderna," prologue to T. Carrasquilla, *Obras completas*, 1, Madrid, EPESA, 1952.
> A solid study presenting Carrasquilla as a forerunner of the contemporary Spanish American novel.

Ordóñez, Montserrat. "Soledad Acosta de Samper: una nueva lectura," *Nuevo Texto Crítico*, 2 (1989), 49–55.
> A constructive reading of Acosta de Samper's novels.

Pagés Larraya, Antonio. Prologue to Eduardo L. Holmberg, *Eduardo L. Holmberg – cuentos fantásticos*, ed. A. Pagés Larraya, Buenos Aires, Hachette, 1957.
> Provides information about Holmberg's life and works.

Paz Soldán, Alba María. "Narradores y narración en la novela *Juan de la Rosa* de Nataniel Aguirre," *Revista Iberoamericana*, 134 (1986), 29–52.
> A solid study of *Juan de la Rosa* as a national program for nineteenth-century Bolivia.

Percas Ponseti, Helena. "Sobre la Avellaneda y su novela *Sab*," *Revista Iberoamericana*, 54 (1962), 347–57.
> Notices certain coincidences between Avellaneda and her character Carlota.

Pereda Valdés, Ildefonso. "El campo uruguayo a través de tres grandes novelistas: Acevedo Díaz, Javier de Viana y Carlos Reyles," *Journal of Inter-American Studies*, 8 (1966), 535–40.
> An interesting comparative study of Díaz's, Viana's, and Reyles's treatment of the Uruguayan countryside.

Perus Coinet, Françoise. "*María* de Jorge Isaacs o la negación del espacio novelesco," *Nueva Revista de Filología Hispánica*, 2 (1987), 721–51.
> A sweeping critique of Isaacs's *María*.

Picón Garfield, Evelyn. "Desplazamientos históricos: *Guatimozín, último emperador de Méjico* de Gertrudis Gómez de Avellaneda" in Raquel Chang-Rodrígez and Gabriella de Beer (eds.), *La historia en la literatura iberoamericana: Memorias del* XXVI *Congreso del Instituto Internacional de Literatura Iberoamericana*, Hanover, N.H., Ediciones del Norte, 1989, 97–107.

Focuses on Avellaneda's problematic characterization of Hernán Cortés in her *Guatimozín*. An important article.

Portuondo, Aleida T. "Vigencia política y literaria de Martín Morúa Delgado," *Círculo*, 9 (1980), 199–212.

An informative article on Morúa Delgado's life and works.

Puento, A. M. Eligio de la. Prologue to Ramón de Palma y Romay, *Cuentos cubanos*, Havana, Cultural, 1928.

A comprehensive and informative review of Palma y Romay's narrative works.

Prologue to Cirilo Villaverde, *Dos Amores*, Havana, Cultural, 1930.

The most important critical text on this novel.

Pupo-Walker, Enrique. "Relaciones internas entre la poesía y la novela de Jorge Isaacs," *Boletín del Instituto Caro y Cuervo*, 22 (1967), 45–59.

Interesting article on the relationships between Isaacs's *María* and his poetry.

Rama, Angel. "La modernización literaria latinoamericana (1870–1910)," *Hispamérica*, 35 (1983), 3–19.

Studies the impact of modernization on Latin American literature.

Ramírez, Oscar M. "Oligarquía y novela folletín: *En la sangre* de Eugenio Cambaceres," *Ideologies and Literatures*, 1 (1989), 249–69.

A sociological study of *En la sangre* as a serial novel in *El Sud-Americano*.

Ramos Escandón, Carmen. "The novel of Porfirian Mexico: a historian's source: problems and methods," *Ideologies and Literatures*, 3 (1981), 118–33.

A solid study of Mexican Realism during the *Porfiriato*.

Rela, Walter. Prologue to Carlos Reyles *Beba*, Montevideo, Barreiro y Ramos, 1965.

One of the most important works on Reyles's *Beba*.

Reyes, Alfonso. "El *Periquillo sarniento* y la crítica mexicana" in A. Reyes *Obras completas*, IV, Mexico, Fondo de Cultura Económica, 1956, 169–78.

A critique of Lizardi's works and popularity.

Reyes Nevares, Salvador. Prologue to Ignacio Manuel Altamirano, *Obras completas*, Mexico, Oasis, 1959.

Solid introduction to the life, times, and works of Altamirano.

Reyes Palacios, Felipe. Prologue to *El Periquillo Sarniento* in *Obras de José Joaquín Fernández de Lizardi*, VIII, Mexico, Universidad Nacional Autónoma de México, 1982.

A crucial study of Lizardi's *Periquillo*.

Rivera, Juan Manuel. "*La peregrinación de Bayoán*: fragmentos de una lectura disidente," *Revista de Crítica Literaria Latinoamericana*, 30 (1989), 39–55.

An interesting study of Hostos's novel as autobiographical fiction.

Rodríguez Coronel, Rogelio. Prologue to Ignació Manuel Altamirano, *El Zarco*, Havana, Casa de las Américas, 1976.

A Marxist approach to Altamirano's novel.

Rodríguez Monegal, Emir. Prologue to Eduardo Acevedo Díaz, *El grito de gloria*, ed. E. Rodríguez Monegal, Montevideo, Ministerio de Instrucción Pública, 1964.

One of the best works available on *El grito de gloria*.

Prologue to his edition of Eduardo Acevedo Díaz's *Nativa*, ed. E. Rodríquez
Monegal, Montevideo, Ministerio de Instrucción Pública, 1964.

> One of the best works available on *Nativa*.

"La novela histórica: otra perspectiva" in Roberto González Echevarría (ed.)
Historia y ficción en la narrativa hispanoamericana, Caracas, Monte Avila, 1984,
169–83.

> Includes interesting comments on Acevedo Díaz's historical novels.

Sacoto, Antonio. Prologue to Miguel Riofrío, *La emancipada*, Universidad de Cuenca,
1983.

> Provides useful information about Riofrío's liberal ideas.

"Mujer y sociedad en tres novelas ecuatorianas" in Raquel Chang-Rodríguez and
Gabriella de Beer (eds.), *La Historia en la literatura iberoamericana: memorias
del* XXVI *Congreso del Instituto Internacional de Literatura Iberoamericana*,
Hanover, N.H., Ediciones del Norte, 1989, 213–23.

> Includes an important commentary on Riofrío's *La emancipada*.

Saínz de Medrano Arce, Luis. "Historia y utopía en Fernández de Lizardi" in Raquel
Chang-Rodríguez and Gabriella de Beer (eds.), *La Historia en la literatura
iberoamericana: memorias del* XXVI *Congreso del Instituto Internacional de
Literatura Iberoamericana*, Hanover, N.H., Ediciones del Norte, 1989, 77–83.

> A utopian reading of the Saucheofú episode in Lizardi's *Periquillo*.

Salper, Roberta L. "La economía de latifundio y el nacimiento de la literatura nacional
en el Caribe," *Cuadernos Hispanoamericanos*, 429 (1986), 101–13.

> Links the emergence of national literatures in Cuba and Puerto Rico to
> plantation economy.

Schade, George D. "El arte narrativo en *Sin rumbo*," *Revista Iberoamericana*, 44
(1978), 17–29.

> Studies Cambacérès's style and literary techniques.

Schulman, Iván. "Reflections on Cuba and its antislavery literature," *Annals of the
Southeastern Conference on Latin American Studies*, 7 (1976), 59–67.

> Studies Domingo Delmonte's influence on abolitionist Cuban literature.

"Sociedad colonial, sociedad esclavista: La Habana de *Cecilia Valdés*" in Gilbert
Paolini (ed.), *La Chispa '87: Selected proceedings*, New Orleans, Tulane University 1987, 281–9.

> Examines the impact of slave society on Havana as represented in Villaverde's
> *Cecilia Valdés*.

Sklodowska, Elzbieta. "*María* de Jorge Isaacs ante la crítica," *Thesaurus*, 3 (1983),
617–24.

> Interesting article commenting on the many readings of *María*.

Solomon, Noel. "La crítica del sistema colonial de la Nueva España en *El Periquillo
sarniento*," *Cuadernos Americanos*, 138 (1965), 167–79.

> Studies Fernández de Lizardi as a liberal intellectual.

Sommer, Doris. "The other Enriquillo" in her *One Master for Another: Populism as
patriarchal rhetoric in Dominican novels*, New York, University Press of
America, 1983, 51–92.

> A brilliant, revisionist reading of Galván's *Enriquillo*.

"El mal de *María*: (Con)fusión en un romance nacional," *MLN*, 2 (1989), 439–74.

> One of the most outstanding articles ever written on *María*.

Spell, Jefferson Rhea. "The genesis of the first Mexican novel," *Hispania*, 14 (1931), 53–8.

Notices certain common traits between Periquillo and Fernández de Lizardi.

"A textual comparison of the first four editions of *El Periquillo sarniento*," *Hispanic Review*, 31 (1963), 134–47.

Lizardi's *Periquillo* seen through its different editions.

"New light on Fernández de Lizardi and his *El Periquillo sarniento*," *Hispania*, 4 (1963), 753–4.

Provides new information about Lizardi's life.

Subercaseaux, Bernardo. "Nacionalismo literario, realismo y novela en Chile (1850–1860)," *Revista de Crítica Literaria Latinoamericana*, 5 (1979), 21–32.

A nationalistic reading of Blest Gana's novels.

Tamayo Vargas, Augusto. Prologue to Narciso Aréstegui, *El Padre Horán*, 1, Lima, Universo, 1969.

Provides useful information about Narciso Aréstegui and his works.

Tanner, Roy L. "Dimensions of historic imagination: nineteenth-century Spanish American narrative," *Discurso Literario*, 1 (1986), 265–78.

Studies treatment of history in early Spanish American novels.

"La presencia de Ricardo Palma en *Aves sin nido*," *Hispanic Journal*, 1 (1986), 97–107.

Notices the influence of Palmas's *Tradiciones peruanas* on Matto de Turner's novel.

Tudisco, Blondet, and Antonio Tudisco. Introductory texts to Cirilo Villaverde, *Cecilia Valdés o La loma del angel*, New York, Las Américas, 1964.

Includes a biographical note on Cirilo Villaverde, a comprehensive description of the novel's characters, an interesting linguistic note, and a poor bibliography of Villaverde's works.

Velázquez, Rogerio M. "La esclavitud en la *María* de Jorge Isaacs," *Universidad de Antioquía*, 33 (1957), 91–104.

A critique of *María*'s paternalistic views on slavery.

Verbitsky, Bernardo. "Juan Moreira," prologue to Eduardo Gutiérrez, *Juan Moreira*, ed. María T. F. de Fritzche and Bernardo Verbitsky, Buenos Aires, EUDEBA, 1961.

A short commentary stressing the importance of *Juan Moreira* in Argentina's popular theatre.

Vidal, Hernán. "*Cumandá*: apología del estado teocrático," *Revista Latinoamericana de Crítica Literaria*, 6 (1980), 199–212.

A convincing reading of Juan León Mera's *Cumandá*.

Visca, Arturo Sergio. Prologue to Javier de Viana, *Gaucha*, Montevideo, Biblioteca Artigas, 1956.

Excellent study of Javier de Viana's characters in *Gaucha*.

Vogeley, Nancy. "Mexican newspaper culture on the eve of Mexican Independence," *Ideologies and Literatures*, 4 (1983), 358–77.

Emphasizes the cultural importance of journalism in Fernández de Lizardi's times.

"The concept of 'the people' in *El Periquillo sarniento*," *Hispania*, 3 (1987), 457–67.

Notices the presence of an early class conciousness in Lizardi's *Periquillo*.

Wade, Gerald, and John Englekirk. "Introducción a la novela colombiana," *Revista Iberoamericana*, 30 (1949–1950), 231–51.
  An informative article on the Colombian novel.
Warshaw, Jacob. Prologue to Jorge Isaacs, *María*, Boston, D. C. Heath, 1926.
  Considers Edgar Allan Poe one of the most influential writers on Isaacs.
Yáñez, Agustín. "Estudio preliminar," prologue to Agustín Yáñez (ed.), *El Pensador mexicano*, Mexico, Universidad Nacional Autónoma de México, 1962.
  A solid study stressing the importance of popular culture in Fernández de Lizardi's works.
Yunque, Alvaro. Prologue to Eduardo Gutiérrez, *Croquis y siluetas militares*, ed. Alvaro Yunque, Buenos Aires, Hachette, 1956.
  A detailed study of Gutiérrez's works from a social perspective.
Zavala, Iris. "Puerto Rico, siglo XIX: literatura y sociedad," *Sin Nombre*, 7 (1977), 7–26; 8 (1977), 7–19.
  A convincing description of Puerto Rican society and culture in the nineteenth century.

Chapter 14: The brief narrative in Spanish America: 1835–1915

Primary sources

Acevedo Díaz, Eduardo. *El combate de la trapera y otros cuentos*, ed. Angel Rama, Montevideo, Arca, 1965.
Alberdi, Juan Bautista. *Escritos satíricos y de crítica literaria*, ed. José A. Oría, Buenos Aires, Angel Strada & Cía., 1945.
Alonso, Manuel A. *El Gíbaro. Cuadro de costumbres de la Isla de Puerto Rico*, Barcelona, Juan Olivares Impresor, 1849.
Altamirano, Ignacio Manuel. *Paisajes y leyendas, tradiciones y costumbres de México*, Mexico Antigua Librería Robredo, 1949.
Alvarez, José Sixto (Fray Mocho). *Cuentos de Fray Mocho*, Buenos Aires, Biblioteca de Caras y Caretas, 1906.
Asencio Segura, Manuel. *Artículos, poesías y comedias*, Lima, Carlos Príncipe Impresor, 1885.
Bachiller y Morales, Antonio. *Tipos y costumbres de la isla de Cuba*, ed. Miguel de Villa, Havana, Librería M. Villa, 1881.
Benítez Rojo, A., and M. Beneditti (eds.). *Un siglio del relato latinoamericano*, Havana, Casa de las Américas, 1976.
  Contains prose works of José María Heredia.
Betancourt, José Victoriano. *Artículos de costumbres*, Havana, Publicaciones del Ministerio de Educación, 1941.
Caicedo Rojas, José. *Apuntes de ranchería y otros escritos escogidos*, Bogotá, Biblioteca Popular de Cultura, 1945.
Cárdenas Rodríguez, José María de. *Colección de artículos satíricos y de costumbres*, prologue Cirilo Villaverde, Havana, Consejo Nacional de Cultura, 1963.
Carrasquilla, Tomás. *Cuentos de Tomás Carrasquilla*, ed. Benigno A. Gutiérrez, Medellín, Colombia, Editorial Bedeout, 1956.

Carrión, Miguel de. *Inocencia*, Havana, Alberto Castillo, Editor, 1903.

Castellanos, Jesús. *De tierra adentro*, Havana, Imp. Cuba y América, 1906.

La conjura, Madrid, Revista Archivos, 1909.

A novel and several short stories.

Obras, 2 vols., Havana, Academia Nacional de Artes y Letras, 1915–1916.

Cuéllar, José Tomás de. *La linterna mágica*, ed. Mauricio Magdaleno, Mexico, Biblioteca del Estudiante Universitario, 1941.

Like most of his contemporaries, listed below, Cuéllar wrote primarily *costumbrista* sketches and a few lyrical narratives.

Ensalada de pollos y baile y cochino, ed. Antonio Castro Leal, Mexico, Porrúa, 1946.

Delgado, Rafael. *Cuentos y notas*, Mexico, Imprenta de V. Agüeros, 1902.

D'Halmar, Augusto. *La lámpara y el molino*, Santiago, Imprenta Nueva York, 1914.

Includes nine short stories.

Díaz Castro, Eugenio. *Novelas y cuadros de costumbres*, Bogotá, Biblioteca Popular Colombiana, 1985.

Echeverría, Esteban. *Antología de prosa y verso*, ed. Osvaldo Pellettieri, Buenos Aires, Editorial Belgrano, 1981.

Gerchunoff, Alberto. *The Jewish Gauchos of the Pampas*, Prudencio de Pereda, New York, Abelar-Schumann, 1955.

Gorriti, Juana Manuela. *Sueños y realidades*, 2 vols., La Revista de Buenos Aires, 1865.

Groot, José Manuel. *Historias y cuadros de costumbres*, Bogotá, Biblioteca Popular Colombiana, 1951.

Güiraldes, Ricardo. *Cuentos de muerte y de sangre*, Buenos Aires, Librería La Facultad, 1915.

Iglesia, Alvaro de la. *Tradiciones cubanas*, intro. Jesús Castellanos, Havana, Imprenta de Meresma y Pérez, 1911.

Lastarria, José Victoriano. *Antaño y Ogaño: novelas y cuentos de la vida hispano-americana*, Valparaíso, Imprenta del Mercurio, 1885.

Lillo, Baldomero. *Subterra. Cuadros mineros*, Santiago, Imprenta Moderna, 1904.

Sub sole, Santiago, Imprenta Universitaria, 1907.

Relatos populares, ed. J. S. González Vera, Santiago, Nacimiento, 1942.

The Devil's Pit and Other Stories, tr. Esther Dillon and Angel Flores, Washington, Pan American Union, 1959.

Lugones, Leopoldo. *La guerra gaucha*, Buenos Aires, Arnaldo Moen & Hnos., 1905.

Las fuerzas extrañas, Buenos Aires, A. Moen & Hnos., 1906.

Matto de Turner, Clorinda. *Tradiciones cuzqueñas y leyendas*, ed. José G. Cassió, Cuzco, Librería e Imprenta H. G. Rozas, 1917.

Mera, Juan León. *Novelitas ecuatorianas*, Quito, Casa de la Cultura Ecuatoriana, 1948.

Milla y Vidaurre, José (Salomé Jil). *El visitador*, Guatemala, Centro Editorial Universitaria, 1960.

Los nazarenos, Guatemala, Editorial José Pineda Ibarra, 1967.

Montalvo, Juan. *Narraciones*, ed. César E. Arroyo, Madrid, Imprenta A. Marzo, 1919.

Prosa narrativa, ed. Matilde Calvo Gárgano, Buenos Aires, Plus Ultra, 1966.

Obligado, Pastor S. *Tradiciones argentinas*, Barcelona, Montaner & Simón Editores, 1903.

Palma, Clemente. *Cuentos malévolos*, intro. Miguel de Unamuno, Barcelona, Salvat, 1904.

Palma, Ramón. *Cuentos cubanos*, ed. Eligio de la Puente, Havana, Cultural, 1928.

Palma, Ricardo. *Tradiciones peruanas*, ed. Edith Palma, 5th. edn., Madrid, Aguilar, 1964.
Contains the broadest selection of texts.
Cien tradiciones peruanas, ed. José M. Oviedo, Caracas, Biblioteca Ayacucho, 1977.
The best edition.

Palma, Ricardo. *The Knights of the Cape and Thirty-Seven other Selections from the "Tradiciones peruanas,"* tr. Harriet de Onís, New York, Knopf, 1945.

Pardo Aliaga, Felipe. *El espejo de mi tierra*, Lima, Imprenta José María de la Concha, 1840.

Payno, Manuel. *El fistol del diablo: novela de costumbres mexicanas*, ed. Antonio Castro Leal, Mexico, Porrúa, 1976.

Payró, Roberto. *Pago chico*, Buenos Aires, Rodríguez Gile, 1908.
Nuevos cuentos de pago chico, Buenos Aires, Imprenta Minerva, 1928.

Prieto, Guillermo. *Costumbres y fiestas de indios*, Mexico, Siglo Veintiuno Editores, 1842.
Musa callejera, Mexico, Imprenta Universitaria, 1940.

Riva Palacio, Vicente. *Cuentos del General*, Madrid, Librería Soler, 1896.

Roa Bárcena, José María. *Lanchitas*, Mexico, Imprenta de I. Escalante, 1878.

Rojas, Arístides. *Leyendas históricas de Venezuela*, Caracas, Imprenta de la Patria, 1890.

Sierra, Justo. *Cuentos románticos*, [1896] ed. Antonio Castro Leal, Mexico, Editorial México, 1934.

Tapia y Rivera, Alejandro. *Mis memorias. Puerto Rico cómo lo encontré y cómo lo dejo*, Río Piedras, Editorial Dil, 1979.

Vallejo, José J. (Jotabeche). *Obras de José J. Vallejo*, ed. Alberto Edwards, vol. I, Santiago, Biblioteca de Escritores de Chile, 1911.

Vergara y Vergara, José María. *Las tres tazas*, Bogotá, Ministerio de Educación, 1936.

Viana de, Javier. *Campo*, Montevideo, Barreiro Ramos, 1896.
Gurí y otras novelas, Montevideo, Barreiro y Ramos, 1901.
Macachines, Montevideo, Bertani, 1910.
Leña seca, Montevideo, Bertani, 1911.

Villaverde, Cirilo. *Cuentos de mi abuelo. El penitente*, New York, M. M. Hernández, 1889.

Wilde, Eduardo. *Trini y otros relatos*, Buenos Aires, EUDEBA, 1960.
Cuentos y otras páginas, ed. T. Frugoni de Fritzsche, Buenos Aires, Plus Ultra, 1965.

Secondary sources

Allen, Walter. *The Short Story in English*, New York, Oxford University Press, 1981.

Alonso, Carlos J. *The Spanish American Regional Novel: Modernity and autochthony*, Cambridge University Press, 1990.

A keen analysis of Latin America's problematic relationship with modernity.

Alva, Florencio (ed.). *Siemprevivas: los mejores cuentos de los mejores prosistas nacionales*, Buenos Aires, Otras Edits., 1924.

Contains texts not easily found in other anthologies.

Anderson Imbert, Enrique. *El arte de la prosa de Juan Montalvo*, Mexico, El Colegio de México, 1948.

The best comprehensive study of Montalvo.

Anderson Imbert, Enrique, and E. Florit. *Literatura hispanoamericana*, New York, Holt, Rinehart, & Winston, 1970.

References to "La Tísica" come from this source.

Anderson Imbert, Enrique, and Lawrence B. Kiddle (eds.). *Veinte cuentos hispano-americanos del siglo XX*, New York, Appleton-Century Crofts, 1956.

Outlines the development of the short story in Spanish America. Contains a wide selection of texts.

Aparicio Laurencio, Angel. *Trabajos desconocidos y olvidados de José María Heredia*, Madrid, Ediciones Universal, 1972.

Useful commentary on Heredia's prose works.

Ara, Guillermo. *Leopoldo Lugones*, Buenos Aires, Mandrágora, 1958.

A descriptive overview of Lugones's works.

Araya Orlandi, Julio, and Alejandro Ramírez. *Augusto D'Halmar: obras, estilo, técnica*, Santiago, Editorial El Pacífico, 1960.

A biographical and stylistic study.

Aurora, Shirley L. *Proverbial Comparisons in Ricardo Palma's Tradiciones Peruanas*, Berkeley, University of California Press, 1966.

A useful overview of analogical patterns.

Balderston, Daniel. *The Latin American Short Story: An annotated guide to antholo-gies and criticism*, Westport, Conn., Greenwood Press, 1992.

The most complete bibliography of the short story in Spanish America and Brazil.

Baquero Goyanes, Mariano. *El cuento español en el siglo XIX*, Madrid, CSIC, 1949.

Rich in factual information. It elucidates indirectly common features of peninsular and Spanish American *Costumbristas*.

Barba Salinas, Manuel (ed.). *Antología del cuento salvadoreño 1880–1955*, San Salvador Ministerio de Cultura, 1952.

The best general source for authors active at the turn of the century.

Barrera, Inés, and Eulalia (eds.). *Tradiciones y leyendas del Ecuador*, Quito, Imp. Nacional, 1947.

Combines different modalities of the brief narrative.

Bécquer, Gustavo A. *Obras completas*, Madrid, Aguilar, 1969.

Betancourt, José V. *Artículos de costumbres*, Havana, Publicaciones del Ministerio de Educación, 1941.

Benítez Rojo, A., and M. Benedetti (eds.). *Un siglo del relato latinoamericano*, Havana, Casa de las Américas, 1976.

Contains prose works of José María Heredia.

Borges, Jorge Luis. *El idioma de los argentinos*, Buenos Aires, M. Gleizer, 1928.

An ironic but revealing commentary on Wilde's texts and on Argentinian literature.

Borges, Jorge Luis and Betina Edelbergh. *Leopoldo Lugones*, Buenos Aires, Editorial Troquel, 1955.

Bueno, Salvador. *Policromía y sabor de costumbristas cubanos*, Santiago de Cuba, Universidad de Oriente, 1953.

Costumbristas cubanos del siglo XIX, Caracas, Biblioteca Ayacucho, 1985.

Extensive anthology of representative authors. Useful introduction; bibliographical material is incomplete.

Quotations of A. Bachiller y Morales, Francisco Baralt, and Luis V. Betancourt were taken from this anthology.

(ed.). *Antología del cuento en Cuba 1902–1952*, Havana, Ediciones del Ministerio de Educación, 1953.

References to J. Castellanos "La agonía de la Garza" are taken from this source.

The anthologies by this author contain the best selection of short stories produced around 1900. This one and *Cuentos cubanos* below are not well edited.

(ed.). *Cuentos cubanos del siglo XIX*, Havana, Artes y Literatura, 1975.

A comprehensive selection of authors. Not well organized.

Burgos, Fernando (ed.). *Antología del cuento hispanoamericano*, Mexico, Porrúa, 1991.

A good and broad selection of stories. Contains useful and reliable bibliographical information.

Carilla, Emilio. *El romanticismo en la América Hispánica*, 2 vols., Madrid, Gredos, 1967.

Useful for factual information, lacking in analytical content.

Castellanos, Jesús. *La agonía de la garza*, Havana, Artes y Letras, 1979.

Castro Rawson, Margarita (ed.). *El costumbrismo en Costa Rica*, San José, Editorial Costa Rica, 1966.

Contains an informative introductory study and a wide selection of texts. *Costumbrismo* was a prominent narrative form in Costa Rica, and this study is the most thorough investigation of the topic.

Coester, Alfred (ed.). *Cuentos de la América Española*, New York, Gin & Co., 1920.

Only in anthologies can one find *costumbrista* narratives that have not been reprinted in this century. This textbook contains a broad selection of *cuadros de costumbres* by Manuel Fernández Juncos, Francisco de Sales Pérez, Luis Orrego Luco, Clorinda Matto de Turner, and many others.

Colchie, Thomas (ed.). *Penguin Book of Latin American Short Stories*, London, Viking Press, 1992.

Most of the selections were written in the last fifty years.

Colford, William E. (ed.). *Classic Tales from Spanish America*, New York, Scribner's, 1962.

Correspondencia entre Sarmiento y Lastarria, 1844–1888, ed. María L. del Pino, Buenos Aires, Artes Gráficas Bartolomé Chiesino, 1954.

Dorn, Georgette M. *Latin America, Spain and Portugal, an Annotated Bibliography of Paperback Books*, Washington, Hispanic Foundation of the Library of Congress, 1971.

It covers a wide range of subject matter. Literary items are not numerous.

Duffey, Frank M. *The Early Cuadro de Costumbres in Colombia*, Studies in Romance

Languages, 26, Chapel Hill, University of North Carolina, 1956.

A comprehensive and well-organized study. It focuses on Colombian texts but much of what it uncovers applies to Spanish American *Costumbrismo*.

Echeverría, Amilcar (ed.). *Antología del cuento clásico centroamericano*, Guatemala City, Biblioteca de Cultura Popular, 1961.

Many of the texts selected are *cuadros de costumbres*. Six for each country.

Escobar, Alberto (ed.). *Cuentos y cuentistas*, Caracas, Librería Cruz del Sur, 1951.

Adequate selection of early Venezuelan short-story writers.

La narración en el Perú, Lima, Editorial Juan Mejía Baca, 1960.

An anthology, with a useful overview of its subject matter. Quite informative.

Antología general de la prosa en el Perú, 3 vols., Lima, Fundación del Banco Continental, 1986.

Includes a broad selection of texts. See also Escobar (ed.), *La narración en el Perú*.

Fabbiani, Mario (ed.). *Cuentos y cuentistas*, Caracas, Librería Cruz del Sur, 1951.

A fair selection of early Venezuelan short-story writers.

Flores, Angel (ed.). *Historia y antología del cuento y la novela en Hispanoamérica*, New York, Las Américas, 1959.

Offers a broad selection of stories and fragments of novels written mainly between 1816 and 1885. The bibliographical data is incomplete.

Spanish Stories: Cuentos españoles, New York, Bantam Books, 1960.

In spite of its title, includes stories by Ricardo Palma and Benito Lynch. Bilingual edition. This and the 2 volumes below are restricted to early forms of the short story in Latin America.

Flores, Angel, and Dudley Poore (eds.). *Fiesta in November; stories from Latin America*, Boston, Houghton Mifflin, 1942.

Contains stories by authors who started writing at the turn of the century, such as Eduardo Barrios (Chile), José Rubén Romero (Mexico), and Andrés Vaidelomar (Peru), among others.

Frank, Waldo (ed.). *Tales from the Argentine*, tr. Anita Brenner, New York, Fanar & Rinehart, 1930.

Contains stories by R. Güiraldes, R. Payró, Lucio V. López, Lugones, and Sarmiento.

García, Germán. *Roberto Payró: testimonio de una vida y realidad de una literatura*, Buenos Aires, Nova, 1961.

Garganigo, John F. *Javier de Viana*, New York, Twayne Series, 1972.

A well-organized and perceptive overview of Viana's works.

Ghiano, Juan Carlos. *El matadero de Echeverría y el costumbrismo*, Buenos Aires, EUDEBA, 1968.

An informative study.

González Echevarría, Roberto. *Myth and Archive: A theory of Latin American narrative*, Cambridge University Press, 1990.

A lucid and innovative analysis of the discourses that have converged in the Latin American narrative from colonial days to the present.

Güiraldes, Ricardo. *Obras completas*, Buenos Aires, Emecé, 1962.

Halperin Donghi, Renata (ed.). *Cuentistas argentinos del siglo XIX*, Buenos Aires, Editorial Universitaria, 1950.

Most of the stories selected were written in the *costumbrista* mode.

Holguín, Andrés (ed.). *Los mejores cuentos colombianos*, vol. 1, Lima, Editora Latinoamericana, 1959.
> Useful but poorly organized.

Irving, Washington. *The Life and Letters of Washington Irving*, ed. P. M. Irving, vol. 11, New York, G. P. Putnam's Sons, 1863.

James, Henry. *The Notebooks of Henry James*, New York, Oxford University Press, 1947.
The Ambassadors, New York, W. W. Norton & Co., 1964.

Jones, Willis K. (ed.). *Spanish American Literature in Translation*, 2 vols., New York, Frederick Ungar, 1963.
> Vol. 1 contains prose selections by Montalvo, Palma, Sarmiento, and C. Villaverde.

Kason, Nancy M. *Breaking Traditions: The fiction of Clemente Palma*, Lewisburg, Penn., Bucknell University Press, 1988.
> The best study on C. Palma.

Kingsley, M. B. *Estudio costumbrista de la obra de Facundo. José T. de Cuéllar*, Mexico, Universidad Nacional Autónoma de México, 1944.
> Describes almost all the short fiction produced by Cuéllar.

Lamb, Ruth (ed.). *Antología del cuento guatemalteco*, Mexico, Ediciones de Andrea, 1959.
> Well-organized and well-conceived. It offers a good selection of texts.

Lancelotti, Mario A. (ed.). *El cuento argentino, 1840–1940*, Buenos Aires, Editorial Universitaria, 1964.
> Broad selection of brief narratives of nineteenth-century texts. Poorly presented.

Lanuza, Eduardo. *Genio y figura de Roberto Payró*, Buenos Aires, EUDEBA, 1965.
> Life and works of Payró. It is an informative monograph.

Laplaces, Alberto. *Eduardo Acevedo Diaz*, Montevideo, Claudio García, 1931.
> General descriptive study.
(ed.). *Antología del cuento uruguayo*, 2 vols., Montevideo, C. García & Cía., 1943.
> The most complete source available.

Larra, Mariano J. *Artículos*, Barcelona, Editorial Plantea, 1966.

Lastra, Pedro. *El cuento hispanoamericano del siglo XIX*, Santiago, Editorial Universitaria, 1972.
> Informative and perceptive overview of the *costumbrista* narrative. Contains rare bibliographical entries.

Latcham, Ricard (ed.). *Antología del cuento hispanoamericano contemporáneo 1910–1956*, Santiago, Zig-Zag, 1958.
> It includes several texts (by country) seldom chosen for a book of this kind. Offers sketchy biographical and bibliographical data.

Leal, Luis. *Historia del cuento hispanoamericano*, [1966] Mexico, Ediciones de Andrea, 1971.
> Still the most useful book on this topic. In its second chapter summarizes the achievements of the main *costumbristas*. Contains a good deal of bibliographical information. The quotations from Alfonso Reyes regarding A. Nervo and from Jorge Borges on Lugones are taken from this book.

(ed.). *Antología del cuento mexicano*, Mexico, Ediciones de Andrea, 1957.
   A brief but representative *corpus* of *costumbrista* texts. Contains bibliographical information.

Levine, Suzanne J. *Latin America: Fiction and poetry in translation*, New York, Center for Interamerican Relations, 1970.
   It describes the content of each item. Often a good listing of bilingual editions.

Levy, Kurt L. *Vida y obra de Tomás Carrasquilla, genitor del regionalismo en la literatura hispanoamericana*, Medellín, Colombia, Editorial Bedout, 1958.
   Descriptive essay, mainly biographical.

Lida, María Rosa. *El cuento popular hispanoamericano y la literatura*, Buenos Aires, Editorial Losada, 1941.
   It documents the impact of folklore and classical legends on Spanish American fiction.

Lindo, Hugo (ed.). *Antología del cuento moderno centroamericano*, San Salvador, Universidad Autónoma de El Salvador 1959.
   The best source of its kind available.

López-Morillas, Juan. *El Krausismo español: perfil de una aventura intelectual*, Mexico, Fondo de Cultura, 1980.

Luque Muñoz, Henry (ed.). *Narradores colombianos del siglo XIX*, Bogotá, Instituto Colombiano de Cultura, 1976.
   Complements Holguín's anthology described above. Offers a good selection of well-known *Costumbristas*. Poorly edited.

Mancisidor, José (ed.). *Cuentos mexicanos del siglo XIX*, Mexico, Editorial Nueva España, 1947.
   Complements Leal's selection. See above.

Manzor, Antonio (ed.). *Antología del cuento hispanoamericano*, Santiago, Zig-Zag, 1940.
   Several romantic authors are represented. The description of authors and texts is deficient.

Marroquín Lorenzo, José María Rivas Groot. *Pax*, Bogotá, La Oveja Negra, 1986.
   Describes life and works of Rivas Groot, who collaborated in the preparation of this book.

Matlowsky, Bernice D. *Antologías del cuento hispanoamericano: guía bibliográfica*, *Monografías Bibliográficas*, 3, Washington, Unión Panamericana, 1950.
   A short bibliographical guide. Useful mainly for items printed before the Second World War. Contains items in English. Dated but thorough.

Mazlish, Bruce. *A New Science: the breakdown of connections at the birth of sociology*, New York, Oxford University Press, 1989.

Mazzei, Angel (ed.). *Treinta cuentos argentinos 1800–1940*, Buenos Aires, Editorial Guadalupe, 1968.
   Complements the anthology of Pagés Larraya described above.

Meléndez, Concha (ed.). *Antología de autores puertorriqueños. El cuento*, San Juan, Ediciones del Gobierno del Estado Libre Asociado de Puerto Rico, 1957.
   Costumbrismo was a prominent narrative form in Puerto Rican letters. It is well represented in this anthology.

Menton, Seymour (ed.). *El cuento costarricense: estudio, antología y bibliografía*, Mexico, Ediciones de Andrea, 1964.

The best general source. Well-organized, informative. Contains a perceptive commentary on Justo Sierra's story "Fiebre amarilla."

El cuento hispanoamericano, 2 vols., Mexico, Fondo de Cultura Económica, 1976.
The best-known anthology of its kind. Its scholarly apparatus is limited, and very few early short stories are included. A fair selection of authors writing around 1900. Contains some bibliographical information.

The Spanish American Short Story, Berkeley, University of California Press, 1980.
Includes texts by Carrasquilla, Echeverría, Lastarria, López Portillo, Lillo, Payno, Viana, and Zeledón, among others.
Widely used.

Mesonero Romanos, Ramón. *Obras completas*, Madrid, Renacimiento, 1925.

Miró Quezada, Luis. *Felipe Pardo Aliaga, 1806–1906*, Lima, Imprenta Lucero, 1906.
Biographical study of general interest.

Montesinos, José F. *Costumbrismo y novela: ensayo sobre el redescubrimiento de la realidad española*, Madrid, Editorial Castalia, 1960.
Although it focuses on peninsular *Costumbrismo* much of what it contains applies to Spanish American authors. A very sound study.

Montgomery, Clifford M. *Early Costumbrista Writers in Spain, 1750–1830*, Monographs in Romance Languages, Philadelphia, University of Pennsylvania, 1931.
It describes the initial stages of the *Costumbrismo hispánico*.

Nolasco, Sócrates (ed.) *El cuento en Santo Domingo*, 2 vols., Santo Domingo, Librería Dominicana, 1957.
Offers a broad range of texts from *Costumbristas* to contemporary forms. Not well-edited.

Onís, Harriet de (ed.). *Spanish Stories and Tales*, New York, Knopf, 1954.
Good selection of stories by Arturo Cancela, R. Gallegos, R. Güiraldes, and R. Palma, among others.

Oviedo, José Miguel. *Genio y figura de Ricardo Palma*, Buenos Aires, EUDEBA, 1965.
The best general study.

Oviedo, José Miguel. *Antología crítica del cuento hispanoamericano 1830–1920*, Madrid, Alianza Editorial, 1989.
Though brief, this is the best anthology available. Authors and texts are well documented. Its introductory study and the essays devoted to the first seven authors are perceptive and contain new biographical and bibliographical data.

Pagés Larraya, Antonio (ed.). *Veinte relatos argentinos, 1838–1887*, Buenos Aires, Editorial Plus Ultra, 1974.
Leading *Costumbristas* figure prominently in this anthology.

Picón Padilla, Eduardo (ed.). *Antología del cuento colombiano*, 2 vols., Bogotá, Ministerio de Educación Nacional, 1959.
Vol. 1 contains a good selection of early short stories.

Picón Salas, Mariano. *Formación y proceso de la literatura venezolana*, Caracas, Editorial Cecilia Acosta, 1940.
Chapter 11 characterizes *Costumbrismo* in Venezuela. Much of what the author says in that regard is applicable to other Spanish American countries.

A Cultural History of Spanish America: From Conquest to Independence, [1944] tr. Irving A. Leonard, Berkeley, University of California Press, 1962.
An impressive summary of the intellectual history of Spanish America.

(ed.). *Satíricos y costumbristas venezolanos*, 2 vols., Lima, Festival del libro venezolano, 1958.

The best source of its kind, with a perceptive introduction.

Poe, Edgar Allan. *The Works of Edgar Allan Poe*, vol. II, New York, Charles Scribners & Sons, 1914.

Reyes, Alfonso. *Obras completas*, 17 vols., Mexico, Fondo de Cultura, 1962.

Rivera Rivera, Modesto. *Concepto y expresión del costumbrismo en Manuel A. Alonso Pacheco*, San Juan, Instituto de la Cultura Puertorriqueña, 1980.

The best study on Alonso as a *Costumbrista*.

Rodó, José Enrique. *Escritos de la Revista Nacional de Literatura y Ciencias Sociales*, ed. José P. Segundo and J. A. Zubillaga, Montevideo, Ministerio de Instrucción Pública, 1946.

Rodríguez Monegal, Emir (ed.). *The Borzoi Anthology of Latin American Literature*, 2 vols., New York, Knopf, 1977.

Contains a few stories by authors writing around 1900.

Rojas, Manuel (ed.). *Los costumbristas chilenos*, Santiago, Zig-Zag, 1957.

The best selection of its kind available. Not well-edited.

Sanín Cano. *Letras colombianas*, Bogotá and Mexico City, Fondo de Cultura, 1944.

Describes the relevance of *Costumbrismo* in Colombian fiction and the continuity of that narrative modality in the twentieth century.

Sanz y Díaz, José (ed.). *Antología de cuentistas hispanoamericanos*, Madrid, Aguilar, 1964.

Offers early examples of romantic short fiction. Information on authors and bibliography is often incorrect.

Sayers Peden, Margaret. *The Latin American Short Story: A critical history*, Boston, Twayne, 1983.

A clear, well-written, but schematic, overview of this genre. It concentrates on twentieth-century authors.

Silva, José A. *Obras completas*, Bogotá, Banco de la República, 1965.

Silva Castro, Raúl (ed.). *Cuentistas chilenos del siglo XIX*, Santiago, Prensas de la Universidad de Chile, 1934.

The best selection of early forms of the short story.

Torres-Rioseco, Arturo (ed.). *Short Stories of Latin America*, tr. Zoila Nelken and Rosalie Torres-Rioseco, New York, Las Américas, 1963.

Selections by H. Quiroga and the Cuban Félix Pita Rodríguez are of special interest.

Turrell, Charles A., (ed.). *Spanish American Short Stories*, New York, MacMillan & Co., 1920.

Watson, Magda. *El cuadro de costumbres en el Perú decimonónico*, Lima, Universidad Católica del Perú, 1980.

The best study of *Costumbrismo* in Peru.

Wordsworth, William. *The Poetical Works of W. Wordsworth*, ed. Edward Dowjen, 3 vols., London, George Bell & Sons, 1823.

Zanetti, Susan (ed.). *Costumbristas de América Latina*, Buenos Aires, Centro Editor de América Latina, 1973.

Offers a large selection of texts by José Milla, Pardo Aliaga, and other prominent *Costumbristas*. Not well-edited.

Volume 1

Articles

Aristizábal, Luis H. "Las tres tazas: De Santa Fé a Bogotá, a través del cuadro de costumbres," *Boletín Cultural y Bibliográfico*, (Bogotá), 25 (1988), 61–79.

    A valuable study. It illustrates the linking of the *cuadro de costumbres* with graphic illustrations. Much of the bibliography is incomplete.

Arrom, Juan José. "Mitos taínos en las letras de Cuba, Santo Domingo y México" in his *Certidumbre de América; estudios de letras, folklore y cultura*, 2nd. edn., Madrid, Gredos, 1971.

    Offers a fair sampling of texts and some bibliographical data.

Barrenechea, Ana María. "Notas al estilo de Sarmiento," *Revista Iberoamericana*, 21 (1956), 275–94.

    Elucidates the eclectic style of Sarmiento. Indirectly it shows the impact of *Costumbrismo* on his most imaginative texts.

Barrera, Trinidad. "Introduction" to Juan León Mera, *Cumandá o un drama entre salvajes*, Seville, Ediciones Alfar, 1989, 9–66.

    It summarizes current scholarship on Mera.

Bello, Andrés. "Modos de estudiar la historia" in *Obras completas*, XIX, Caracas, Ministerio de Educación, 1957, 243–52.

Bueno, Salvador. "Introductory essay on Jesús Castellanos" in *Antología del cuento en Cuba*, Havana, Ediciones del Ministerio de Educación, 1953, 9–15.

    Contains sketchy information. Very little has been written on this gifted writer.

    "Costumbristas cubanos del siglo XIX" in *Temas y personajes de la literatura cubana*, Havana, Ediciones Unión, 1964, 51–73.

Cannizo, María. "The article of manners and customs in Puerto Rico," *Hispania*, 38 (1955), 472–5.

Castillo, Homero. "José V. Lastarria y el cuento chileno," *Symposium*, 13 (1959), 121–7.

    Documents the marginal status of the short story in the mid nineteenth century.

    "El mendigo, primer relato novelesco de Chile" *Quaderni Ibero-Americani*, 27 (1961), 158–64.

    A general commentary on this important text by Lastarria.

Castro Leal, Antonio. "Introduction" to Justo Sierra, *Cuentos románticos* Mexico, Editorial México, 1946.

    General overview of Sierra's short fiction.

D'Halmar, Augusto. "Cuento como cuento un cuento," *Atenea*, 25 (1948), 8–19.

    Revealing anecdotes about the creative process.

Dumas, Claude. "Montalvo y Echeverría: problemas de estética literaria en América Latina del siglo XIX," *Juan Montalvo en Francia. Annales Littéraires de l'Université de Besançon* (Paris), 190 (1976), 77–86.

    Places Montalvo in the context of polemics concerning the uniqueness of Spanish American literature.

Edberg, George J. "The Guatemalan José Milla and his *cuadros*," *Hispania*, 44 (1961), 666–74.

    A descriptive summary.

González Pérez, Aníbal. "El periodismo en las *Tradiciones peruanas* de Ricardo

Palma," *La Torre*, 5 (1988), 113–38.

    An excellent study of Palma's use of journalistic devices.

Jiménez Rueda, Julio. "Introduction" to José M. Roa Bárcena, *Relatos*, Mexico, Universidad Nacional Autónoma de México, 1955.

    Useful, though a very general discussion of Roa Bárcena's stories.

Kirkpatrick, Susan. "The ideology of *Costumbrismo*," *Ideologies and Literature*, 2:7 (1978), 28–34.

    A perceptive analysis of the diverse ideological currents which affected the *Costumbristas*.

Landarech, Alfonso María. "Itinerario del cuento salvadoreño" in *Estudios literarios*, San Salvador, Ministerio de Cultura, 1959, 22–32.

    A chronological review of authors and texts.

Leal, Luis. "José Tomás Cuéllar (Facundo)" in his *Breve historia del cuento mexicano*, Mexico, Ediciones de Andrea, 1956, 48–50.

    Overview of his fiction.

    "Dos cuentos olvidados de Vicente Riva Palacio," *Anales del Instituto de Investigaciones Estéticas*, Mexico, Universidad Nacional Autónoma de México, 27 (1958), 63–70.

    The stories discussed are "Los azotes" and "Un buen negocio."

    "Riva Palacio, Vicente" in his *Historia del cuento hispanoamericano*, Mexico, Ediciones de Andrea, 1971, 25–6.

    Summary of his fictional works.

Leslie, John K. "Problems relating to Sarmiento's *Artículos críticos y literarios*," *Modern Language Notes*, 61 (1946), 289–99.

    An inventory of short narratives and essays.

Lezama Lima, José. "Verba criolla" in his *Tratados de La Habana*, Madrid, Editorial Anagrama, 1971.

Loayza, Luis. "Palma y el pasado" in *El sol de Lima*, Lima, La Mosca Azul Editores, 1974, 89–115.

    Incisive information on Palma's use of history.

Marshall E. "Las obras menores de Cirilo Villaverde," *Revista Iberoamericana*, 14:28 (1948), 255–62.

    Documents Villaverde's production as a *Costumbrista*.

Moreno Fraginals, Manuel. "Anselmo Suárez Romero," *Revista de la Biblioteca Nacional José Martí*, 22 (1950), 28–42.

    A historical appraisal of Romero's texts.

Oría, José A. "Alberdi Figarillo: contribución al estudio de la influencia de Larra en el Río de la Plata," *Humanidades*, 25 (1936), 223–83.

    General but useful study of the reception of Larra's texts.

Osea, Mario. "Sobre siete cuentos maestros de la literatura chilena," *Atenea*, 25 (1948), 34–62.

    Focuses on texts of Federico Gana, D'Halmar, Barrios, and M. Latorre, among others.

Oviedo, José Miguel. "Juana Manuela Gorriti" in his *Antología crítica del cuento hispanoamericano. 1820–1920*, Madrid, Alianza Editorial, 1989, 89–90.

    Summarizes the limited scholarship available on Gorriti's short fiction.

Portuondo, José Antonio. "Jesús Castellanos escritor" in *Cuentos cubanos contem-*

poráneos, Mexico, Editorial Leyenda, 1946.

Pupo-Walker, Enrique. "Elaboración y teoría en los cuentos de Ricardo Güiraldes," *Cuadernos Hispanoamericanos*, 225 (1977), 165–72.

"El cuadro de costumbres, el cuento y la posibilidad de un deslinde," *Revista Iberoamericana*, 102–3 (1978), 1–15.

Disavows the formal links which supposedly exist between the short story and the *cuadro de costumbres*.

"Reflexiones para otras lecturas del relato costumbrista," *Revista de Estudios Hispánicos*, 2 (1990), 15–36.

Comments on the discursive interaction between the social sciences and the *costumbrista* narrative.

Rojas, Ricardo. "Vida y obras de Alberdi" in *La literatura Argentina*, III, Buenos Aires, Kraft Editores, 1920, 505–35.

Useful summary of life and works.

Scari, Robert M. "Ciencia y ficción en los cuentos de Leopoldo Lugones," *Revista Iberoamericana*, 30 (1964), 163–87.

Sedwick, Ruth. *Baldomero Lillo*, New Haven, Yale University Press, 1956.

An adequate global appraisal of Lillo's literary production.

Spell, Jefferson, R. "The *costumbristas* movement in Mexico," *PMLA*, 50 (1935), 290–315.

A thorough historical account of *Costumbrismo*.

Torres Manzo, Carlos. "Perfil y esencia de Rafael Delgado," *Cuadernos Americanos*, 40 (1953), 247–61.

Enumerates general features of Delgado's works.

Torriente, Loló de la. "Jesús Castellanos: un precursor," *El Mundo* (Havana) 61, (June 4, 1962), 20.

Vergara de Bietti, Noemí. "Eduardo Wilde, padre del humorismo argentino" in *Humoristas del 80*, Buenos Aires, Plus Ultra, 1976, 19–38.

This study links Wilde to stylistic devices used by *Costumbristas* who wrote in the manner of Roberto Payró and his followers.

Chapter 15: The Spanish American theatre of the nineteenth century

This bibliography does not include studies of individual dramatists. The interested reader should also consult such sources as the journals *Latin American Theater Review* and *Gestos*, and the *Handbook of Latin American Studies*.

Secondary sources

Arrom, José Juan. *Historia de la literatura dramática cubana*, New Haven, Yale University Press, 1944.

Earliest and best general introduction by the founder of Spanish American theatre studies in the United States.

Historia del teatro hispanoamericano: época colonial, 2nd. edn., Mexico, Ediciones de Andrea, 1967.

Although dealing primarily with the colonial period, provides invaluable background for understanding the nineteenth century.

Esquema generacional de las letras hispanoamericanas. Ensayo de un método, 2nd. edn., Bogotá, Instituto Caro y Cuervo, 1977.

The best effort to synthesize Spanish American literature within a generational structure.

Blanco Amores de Pagella, Angela. *Iniciadores del teatro argentino*, Buenos Aires, Ministerio de Cultura y Educación, 1972.

Useful critical commentary accompanied by a disorganized anthological selection of fragments.

Carella, Tulio. *El sainete criollo*, Buenos Aires, Hachette, 1967.

Excellent general introduction.

Castagnino, Raúl. *Literatura dramática argentina, 1717–1967*, Buenos Aires, Pleamar, 1968.

The best general history for the entire period.

Teatro argentino premoreirista. Buenos Aires, Plus Ultra, 1969.

Concise study of the regional popular theatre from 1717 through *Solané*.

Cruz, Jorge (ed.). *Teatro argentino romántico*, Buenos Aires, Ministerio de Cultura y Educación, 1972.

The introduction is a useful resumé; includes texts of two plays by Mármol and a translation of Hugo.

Dauster, Frank. *Historia del teatro hispanoamericano: siglos XIX y XX*, 2nd. edn., Mexico, Ediciones de Andrea, 1973.

The most up-to-date overview, although in need of revision.

Durán Cerda, Julio. *Panorama del teatro chileno, 1842–1959*, Santiago, Edit. del Pacífico, 1959.

Historical anthology including texts of Barros Grez and the active romantic movement.

Ghiano, Juan Carlos. *Teatro gauchesco primitivo*. Buenos Aires, Losange, 1957.

The most important texts of popular theatre from about 1780, with a polemical but intelligent introduction.

González Cajiao, Fernando. *Historia del teatro en Colombia*, Bogotá, Instituto Colombiano de Cultura, 1986.

A comprehensive history covering from pre-Columbian rituals through 1985.

González Freire, Natividad (ed.). *Teatro cubano del siglo XIX*, 2 vols., Havana, Editorial Arte y Literatura, 1975.

Includes the most representative works.

Jorge Lafforgue (ed.). *Teatro rioplatense (1886–1930)*, prologue David Viñas, Caracas, Biblioteca Ayacucho, 1977.

A revisionist Marxist approach and texts of plays from *Moreira* through the *grotesco*.

Leal, Rine. *Breve historia del teatro cubano*, Havana, Letras Cubanas, 1980.

Especially interesting because of its focus on the popular theatre.

La selva oscura, 2 vols., Havana, Editorial Arte y Literatura, 1975, 1982.

A massive history of Cuban theatre from the beginnings to 1902.

Leal, Rine (ed.). *Teatro bufo siglo XIX*, Havana, Editorial Arte y Literatura, 1975.

The editor's comments deal primarily with historical context and social and ethnic content and implications.

Teatro mambí, Havana, Letras Cubanas, 1978.

Six plays from the struggle for independence.

Comedias cubanas siglo XIX, 2 vols., Havana, Letras Cubanas, 1979.

Representative plays, including *sainetes*.

Luzuriaga, Gerardo, and Richard Reeve (eds.). *Los clásicos del teatro hispano-americano*, Mexico, Fondo de Cultura Económica, 1975.

Includes works by Gorostiza, Ascensio Segura, Barros Grez, and Sánchez, and *Juan Moreira*.

Magaña Esquivel, Antonio (ed.). *Teatro mexicano del siglo XIX*, Mexico, Fondo de Cultura Económica, 1972.

Six plays, from 1810 to 1847.

Magaña Esquivel, Antonio, and Ruth Lamb. *Breve historia del teatro mexicano*, Mexico, Ediciones de Andrea, 1958.

Well-documented study covering the pre-Hispanic period to 1958.

Marco, Susana, Abel Posadas, Marta Speroni, and Griselda Vignolo. *Teoría del género chico criollo*, Editorial Universitaria de Buenos Aires, 1975.

Sociological study of *sainete orillero*, untrustworthy in aesthetic judgments but informative.

Marial, José. *Teatro y país*, Buenos Aires, Agon, 1984.

Covers the period 1810–1983; quite detailed in coverage of the nineteenth century.

Mazzei, Angel. *Dramaturgos post-románticos*, Buenos Aires, Ministerio de Educación y Cultura, 1970.

The rural theatre and its transition into a less anti-social movement, with texts of *Moreira* and plays by Leguizamón and Granada.

Monasterios, Rubén. *Un estudio crítico y longitudinal del teatro venezolano*, Caracas, Universidad Central de Venezuela, 1974.

General history of a little-studied movement.

Morfi, Angelina. *Historia crítica de un siglo de teatro puertorriqueño*, San Juan, Instituto de Cultura Puertorriqueña, 1980.

Supersedes all previous work on Puerto Rican theatre; the appendix includes a play by Méndez Quiñones.

Morgado, Benjamin. *Histórica relación del teatro chileno*, Santiago, SEREC, 1985.

A general history.

Olavarría y Ferrari, Enrique de. *Reseña histórica del teatro en México, 1538–1911*, Biblioteca Porrúa, 21, 3rd. edn., Mexico, Porrúa, 1961.

Invaluable introduction to the nineteenth century by an active participant. First published in 1880, this is revised and augmented.

Ordaz, Luis (ed.). *El drama rural*, Buenos Aires, Hachette, 1959.

Historical anthology of the development of the rural drama.

Breve historia del teatro argentino, vols. I–VI, Buenos Aires, Editorial Universitaria, 1962–1963.

Excellent historical anthology devoted to the nineteenth and early twentieth centuries.

Teatro argentino, Buenos Aires, Centro Editor de América Latina, 1979–1980.

Anthology covering the nineteenth century and the twentieth through the *grotesco* of the 1930s. Vols. I through IV treat the nineteenth century through Sánchez, vol. VI is the *sainete*.

Pereira Salas, Eugenio. *Historia del teatro en Chile desde sus orígenes. . .*, Santiago, Universidad de Chile, 1974.

    Detailed information to about 1849.

Rela, Walter. *Teatro uruguayo, 1807–1979*, Montevideo, Ediciones de la Alianza, 1980.

    A good general introduction.

Reyes, Carlos José, and Maida Watson Espener. *Materiales para una historia del teatro en Colombia*, Bogotá, Instituto Colombiano de Teatro, 1978.

    A collection of articles covering the whole range of Colombian theatre.

Reyes de la Maza, Luis. *Cien años de teatro en México (1810–1910)*, Mexico, Secretaría de Educación Pública, 1972.

    A condensation of the prologues to Reyes de la Maza's invaluable series; a real social history of the theatre.

    Circo, maroma, y teatro. (1810–1910), Mexico, Universidad Nacional Autónoma de México, 1985.

    Detailed panorama of the whole century.

Ripoll, Carlos, and Andrés Valdespino. *Teatro hispanoamericano. Antología crítica: siglo XX*, New York, Anaya Book Co., 1973.

    The best general anthology of the period, with examples from Neo-classicism, Romanticism, *Costumbrismo*, the Puerto Rican *jíbaro* theatre, and three plays by Sánchez.

Rojas Uzcátegui, José de la Cruz. *Historia y crítica del teatro venezolano (siglo XIX)*, Mérida, Venezuela, Universidad de los Andes, 1986.

    Primarily detailed listings and resumés of plays, important because the material is virtually unknown.

El teatro en la Independencia: piezas teatrales, 2 vols., Lima, Comisión Nacional del Sesquicentenario de la Independencia del Perú, 1974.

    One of the few sources for early Peruvian theatre, this anthology includes a good deal of material not easily available elsewhere.

Chapter 16: The essay in Spanish South America: 1800 to Modernismo

Primary sources

Alberdi, Juan Bautista. *Obras completas*, 8 vols., Buenos Aires, La Tribuna Nacional, 1886.

    Although far from complete, this edition contains Alberdi's best known texts.

    Escritos póstumos, 16 vols., Buenos Aires, Imprenta Europea, 1895–1901.

    Essential work gathered mostly from Alberdi's lengthy European exile.

    Grandes y pequeños hombres del Plata, Paris, Garnier Hnos, 1912.

    A collection of essays anonymously edited. Particularly important as commentary on the presidencies of Mitre and Sarmiento, the Paraguayan War, and Mitre's *Historia del Belgrano* and *Historia de San Martín*.

    Las "Bases" de Alberdi, ed. Jorge M. Mayer [1852], Buenos Aires, Sudamericana, 1969.

    A first-rate critical edition of Alberdi's *Bases y puntos de partida para la organización política de la República Argentina* of 1852.

Artigas, José Gervasio. *Archivo Artigas*, 20 vols., Montevideo, Comisión Nacional Archivo Artigas, 1950–1981.

A staggering project, this attempt to collect all of Artigas's notes, speeches, letters and decrees, is still not complete.

José Artigas, documentos: compilación y prólogo, ed. Oscar H. Bruschera, Havana, Casa de las Américas, 1971.

A good, representative collection of Artigas's writings which for the most part allows Artigas to speak for himself.

Bello, Andrés. *Obras completas*, 15 vols. Santiago P. G. Ramírez, 1881–1893.

Although older and less complete than the following title, this remains an eminently useful edition of Bello's most significant works.

Obras completas, 22 vols., Caracas, Ediciones del Ministerio de Educación, 1951.

Major works and periods are introduced by short essays by a variety of scholars.

Obras literarias, ed. Pedro Grases, Caracas, Biblioteca Ayacucho, 1979.

Includes essays on literature as well as much of Bello's poetry. Grases's comments merit close attention.

Bilbao, Francisco. *Obras completas*, ed. Manuel Bilbao, 2 vols., Buenos Aires, Casa del Gobierno Provincial, 1865.

Still the most complete sampling of Bilbao's work. Some of his lesser-known religious works are only available in this edition.

El evangelio americano, ed. Alejandro Witker, Caracas, Biblioteca Ayacucho, 1988.

Includes a bibliography, the complete *Evangelio*, and excerpts from other works, including *La sociabilidad chilena*. The introductory essay by Witker, however, is tendentious and unreliable.

Bolívar, Simón. *Obras completas*, ed. Vicente Lecuna, 3 vols., Havana, Edición Lex, 1950.

Not really complete but close.

Escritos políticos, ed. Graciela Soriano, Madrid, Alianza Editorial, 1969.

Inexpensive anthology with a good introduction.

Selected Writings of Bolívar, 2 vols., ed. Vicente Lecuna and Harold A. Bierck, Jr., Caracas and New York, Colonial Press, 1951.

Best anthology of Bolívar's writings in English.

Echeverría, Esteban. *Dogma socialista* [1837], Buenos Aires, El Ateneo, 1947.

Also contains the complete text of *Ojeada retrospectiva sobre el movimiento intelectual en el Plata desde el año '37* of 1846.

Obras completas, ed. Juan María Gutiérrez 5 vols., [1870–1874], Buenos Aires, Ediciones Antonio Zamora, 1951.

Contains all of Echeverría's best-known texts plus a biographical essay by Juan María Gutiérrez.

Hernández, José. *Prosas de José Hernández*, ed. Enrique Herrero, Buenos Aires, Editorial Futuro, 1944.

Contains Hernández's famous biography of El Chacho (Angel Vicente Peñaloza) which is also an important attack on Sarmiento, Mitre, and Argentinian liberalism generally.

Artículos periodísticos de José Hernández, ed. Walter Rela, Montevideo, Editorial

El Libro Argentino, 1967.

A good sampling of Hernández's work as a journalist. Contains pieces from various periods in his career.

Lastarria, José Victorino. *Miscelánea histórica y literaria*, Valparaíso, Mercurio, 1855.

Obras completas, 14 vols., Santiago, Imprenta Barcelona, 1906–1934.

Arranged according to subject, e.g. parliamentary speeches, literary criticism, historical writing, etc.

Recuerdos literarios, ed. Raúl Silva Castro, Santiago, Zig-Zag, 1967.

One of several editions of Lastarria's most enduring work. Intelligent introductory essay by the editor.

Montalvo, Juan. *Siete tratados*, 2 vols., Paris, Garnier, 1930.

Includes an introduction by Rufino Blanco Fombona. Republished in Mexico by the Secretaría de Educación Pública in 1947 with an introduction by Antonio Acevedo Escobedo.

Las catilinarias, El Cosmopolita, El Regenerador, ed. Benjamín Carrión, Caracas, Biblioteca Ayacucho, 1977.

An excellent introduction to some of Montalvo's lesser-known works. The satirical *Catilinarias* were published over a period of time in Panama; *El Cosmopolita* and *El Regenerador* were magazines Montalvo edited and for the most part filled with his own prose. Good preliminary essay by Carrión.

Capítulos que se le olvidaron a Cervantes, 2 vols., Quito, Ediciones Sesquicentena, 1987.

One of the few complete versions of this posthumous work.

Diario, cuentos, artículos, páginas inéditas, 2 vols., Municipio de Ambato, 1987.

Extensive selection of Montalvo's less famous works; some overlap with *Las catilinarias*, above.

Geometría moral, Municipio de Ambato, 1987.

Good edition of one of Montalvo's best-known works. Includes a bibliography.

Selections from Juan Montalvo, tr. and ed. Frank MacDonald and Nancy Cook Brooks, Tempe, Arizona State University, Center for Latin American Studies, 1984.

While not particularly artful, these are among the few English translations available of Montalvo's work.

Moreno, Mariano. *Escritos de Mariano Moreno*, ed. Norberto Piñero, Buenos Aires, Biblioteca del Ateneo, 1896.

An early anthology that remains the most complete available. Has the complete text of the *Plan de operaciones*.

Sarmiento, Domingo Faustino. *Obras de D. F. Sarmiento*, 52 vols., Buenos Aires, Imprenta Mariano Moreno, 1895–1900.

Impressive collection of Sarmiento's work, although not complete. Includes letters, speeches, and major books.

Civilización y barbarie: vida de Juan Facundo Quiroga, ed. Raimundo Lazo [1845], Mexico Porrúa, 1977.

An inexpensive edition with a good introduction. Also worth consulting is the edition by Biblioteca Ayacucho, 1977, with an introductory essay by Noé Jitrik.

Secondary sources

Books

Anderson Imbert, Enrique. *El arte de la prosa en Juan Montalvo*, Mexico, El Colegio de México, 1948.
>One of the few extensive studies of Montalvo's work. Writing from a marked *estilística* perspective, Anderson concludes that Montalvo's genius lies more in his language than in his ideas.

Ardao, Arturo. *Espiritualismo y positivismo en el Uruguay*, Mexico, Fondo de Cultura Económica, 1956.
>Good analysis of Uruguayan Positivism and its mixed reception.

Assunçao, Fernando O., and Wilfredo Pérez, *Artigas: jefe de los orientales*, Montevideo, Próceres, 1982.
>The only volume to appear of what is supposed to be a five-volume biography. If subsequent volumes are as good as the first, this will be the definitive biography of Artigas.

Belaúnde, Víctor Andrés. *Bolívar and the Political Thought of the Spanish American Revolution*, 2nd. edn., Baltimore, The Johns Hopkins University Press, 1966.
>Good description of Bolívar's thought compared with intellectual currents elsewhere in Spanish America. The first edition of 1938 is available in Spanish as *Bolívar y el pensamiento de la revolución hispanoamericana*, Madrid, Editorial Cultura Hispana, 1959.

Bernstein, Harry. *Making an Inter-American Mind*, Gainesville, University of Florida, 1961.
>Primarily concerned with Pan-American developments. Some distortion of national movements.

Biblioteca de mayo: colección de obras y documentos para la historia argentina, 18 vols., Buenos Aires, Congreso de la Nación, 1960.
>An essential reprint of many of the most important documents of Argentinian history during the Independence period. Includes memoirs, reprints of newspapers, and government edicts.

Bunkley, Allison Williams. *The Life of Sarmiento*, Princeton University Press, 1952.
>A superb biography that holds its age very well. Exceptional guide not only to Sarmiento's life but also to the documents he left.

Cardozo, Efraím. *Apuntes de historia cultural del Paraguay*, Asunción, Universidad Católica Nuestra Señora de la Asunción 1985.
>A general cultural history that covers artistic, literary, and intellectual developments.

Carrión, Benjamín. *El pensamiento vivo de Montalvo*, Buenos Aires, Editorial Losada, 1961.
>Useful if mostly uncritical study of Montalvo's work.

Castellanos, Alfredo. *Vida de Artigas*, Montevideo, Medina Editor, 1954.
>Good, short biography with ample discussion of Artigas's major ideas.

Crawford, William Rex. *A Century of Latin American Thought*, 2nd. edn., Cambridge, Mass., Harvard University Press, 1961.
>A pioneering work marked by exceptional clarity. Good bibliography.

Davis, Harold Eugene. *Latin American Social Thought*, University Press of Washington, 1961.

> Mostly an anthology with good introductions and some bibliographical information. Some of the translations are the only ones available.

Latin American Thought: A historical introduction, Baton Rouge, Louisiana State University, 1972.

> An ambitious overview of pre-colonial to modern thought. Excellent bibliography. Devotes considerable attention to Christian and conservative thinkers – an area often neglected.

Demicheli, Alberto. *Artigas, el fundador: su proyección histórica*, Buenos Aires, Ediciones Depalma, 1978.

> Primarily concerned with Artigas's ideas on law and state.

Donoso, Ricardo. *Las ideas políticas en Chile*, Santiago, Universidad de Chile, 1967.

> Good outline history of political debates since independence.

Feinmann, Juan Pablo. *Filosofía y nación*, Buenos Aires, Editorial Legasa, 1982.

> Good essays on Moreno and Alberdi and their relation to European thought.

Francovich, Guillermo. *La filosofía en Bolivia*, La Paz, Juventud, 1966.

> A broad history that covers colonial times to the present.

Fuentes de la filosofía latinoamericana, Washington, Organization of American States, 1967.

> An early bibliography, still useful for materials published before 1965.

Fuenzalida Grandón, Alejandro. *Lastarria i su tiempo: su vida, obras e influencia en el desarrollo político e intelectual de Chile*, Santiago, Imprenta Cervantes, 1893.

> Republished in 1911 by Imprenta Barcelona, also in Santiago.
> Despite its age, this continues to be a useful biography.

Gandía, Enrique de. *Historia de las ideas políticas en la Argentina*, 5 vols., Buenos Aires, Depalma, 1960–1968.

> Although written from a markedly nationalist point of view, this is nonetheless a useful intellectual history of Argentina.

Gómez Robledo, Antonio. *Idea y experiencia de América*, Mexico, Fondo de Cultura Económica, 1947.

> An insightful interpretative essay with considerable historical information.

Grases, Pedro. *Estudios sobre Andrés Bello*, 2 vols., Barcelona, Seix Barral, 1981.

> Essays on a variety of topics. Anything written by Grases on Bello is necessary and fascinating reading.

Halperín Donghi, Tulio. *El pensamiento de Echeverría*, Buenos Aires, Sudamericana, 1951.

> Studies how Echeverría's ideas developed, how they relate to European thought, and how they fit into intellectual currents of the time.

Tradición política española e ideología revolucionaria de Mayo, Buenos Aires, EUDEBA, 1961.

> A superb study packed with information. Although the historical context is primarily Argentina, the book is an indispensable guide to ideas throughout Spanish America during the first years of independence. Also available in translation.

José Hernández y sus mundos, Buenos Aires, Sudamericana, 1985.

> Without question the most thorough and best-documented study ever done on

Hernández. Halperín's distaste for his subject, however, both as a man and as a nationalist icon, someties leads him to portray Hernández with undue negativity.

Politics, Economics and Society in Argentina in the Revolutionary Period, tr. Richard Southern, New York, Cambridge University Press, 1975.

Handbook of Latin American Studies, Washington, Hispanic Foundation, Library of Congress, published annually.

The best source in Spanish or English for information on recent publications on Latin America, all topics.

Henríquez Ureña, Pedro. *Literary Currents in Hispanic America*, Cambridge, Mass., Harvard University Press, 1945.

Historia de la cultura en la América Hispánica, Mexico, Fondo de Cultura Económica, 1947.

Two pioneering works in Spanish American literary history and criticism.

Ingenieros, José. *La evolución de la ideas argentinas*, 2 vols., Buenos Aires, Taller Gráfico Argentino de L. J. Rosso, 1918–1920.

Despite its age and liberal biases, this remains an exceptionally useful and readable work.

Jaramillo Uribe, Jaime. *El pensamiento colombiano en el siglo XIX*, Bogotá, Temis, 1964.

Jitrik, Noé. *Muerte y resurrección de Facundo*, Buenos Aires, Centro Editor de América, 1968.

Provocative essay on Sarmiento's work, the man Facundo, and the metamorphoses each has experienced in Argentinian intellectual life.

Jorrín, Miguel, and John D. Martz. *Latin American Political Thought and Ideology*, Chapel Hill, University of North Carolina Press, 1970.

Gives a social scientist's view of some of the texts and authors considered here.

Levene, Ricardo. *Ensayo histórico sobre la revolución de Mayo y Mariano Moreno*, 3 vols., Buenos Aires, Editorial Peuser, 1960.

A detailed and well-researched biography. Levene argues, unconvincingly, against the authenticity of the *Plan de operaciones*.

Los fundadores en la filosofía de América Latina, Washington, Organization of American States, 1970.

A sequel to the previous title, augmented and updated.

Masur, Gerhard. *Simón Bolívar*, 2nd. edn., Albuquerque, University of New Mexico Press, 1969.

Good biography with extensive bibliographical information.

Mata, G. Humberto. *Sobre Montalvo o desmitificación de un mitificador*, Cuenca, Cénit, 1961.

A collection of essays of varying quality dedicated to the debate Montalvo continues to inspire among his compatriots.

Mayer, Jorge M. *Alberdi y su tiempo*, EUDEBA, 1963.

A superb biography and also an extensive guide to the events and bibliography of the entire period.

Mead, Robert. *Breve historia del ensayo hispanoamericano*, Mexico, Studium, 1956.

A good outline of major essays and essayists. Includes some bibliographical information. Also available in a second edition under the title *Historia del ensayo hispanoamericano*, published in 1973 with the collaboration of Peter G. Earle.

Mijares, Augusto. *Lo afirmativo venezolano*, Caracas, Ediciones de la Fundación Eugenio Mendoza, 1963.

    Although primarily concerned with establishing positive national values, this book contains substantial information about intellectual debates of all sorts.

El Libertador, 2nd. edn., Caracas, Arte, 1965.

    A fine biography of Bolívar.

Murillo, Fernando. *Andrés Bello: historia de una vida y de una obra*, Caracas, Casa de Bello, 1986.

    A first-rate biography. Includes an extensive bibliography as well as a fine introduction by Pedro Grases.

Palacios, Alfredo L. *Esteban Echeverría*, Buenos Aires, La Tribuna Nacional, 1951.

    Good literary biography. Limited, and now dated, bibliography.

Pérez Vila, Manuel. *La formación intelectual de Bolívar*, Caracas, Sociedad Bolivariana de Venezuela, 1964.

    Describes the sources and experiences that inform Bolívar's thought.

Romero, José Luis. *Las ideas políticas en la Argentina*, Mexico, Fondo de Cultura Económica, 1946.

    A fundamental work, filled with information but marred by incomplete bibliographical references. Available in translation as:

A History of Argentine Political thought, tr. Thomas F. McGann, Stanford University Press, 1963.

Sala de Touron, Luica, Nelson de la Torre, and Julio C. Rodríguez. *Artigas y su revolución agraria*, Mexico, Siglo Veintiuno Editores, 1978.

    Although primarily concerned with economic matters, this book outlines not only Artigas's ideas on agrarian reform but also his attempts to realize them. Useful bibliography.

Salazar Bondy, Augusto. *Historia de las ideas en el Perú contemporáneo*, 2 vols., Lima, Francisco Moncloa Editores, 1965.

    Although primarily about twentieth-century intellectual life, this extensive history contains substantial information about earlier intellectual developments as well.

Shumway, Nicolas. *The Invention of Argentina*, Berkeley, University of California Press, 1991.

    Survey of intellectual developments in Argentina between 1800 and 1880 as they relate to nation formation. Extensive bibliography.

Subercaseaux, Bernardo S. *Cultura y sociedad liberal en el siglo XIX: Lastarria, ideología y literatura*, Santiago, Editorial Aconcagua, 1981.

    Both a superb intellectual biography of Lastarria as well as an indispensable guide to virtually every debate that took place during Lastarria's life. Good bibliography.

Zea, Leopoldo. *Dos etapas del pensamiento hispano-americano*, Mexico, El Colegio de México, 1949.

    An essential work. Particularly good on Spanish American Positivism.

El pensamiento latinoamericano, 2 vols., Mexico, Pormaca, 1965.

    Although considerably expanded, this entry covers much of the same ground as the previous title. Available in translation as:

The Latin American Mind, tr. James H. Abbott and Lowell Dunham, Norman,

University of Oklahoma Press, 1963.

Zum Felde, Alberto. *Proceso intelectual del Uruguay*, Montevideo, Editorial Claridad, 1941.

> Good, solid history. Useful, but now dated, bibliography.

Articles

Abellán, José L. "Introducción" in *Siete tratados: réplica a un sofista seudocatólico*, Madrid, Editora Nacional, 1977, 9–53.

> Although this edition contains only one of the *tratados*, the introductory essay provides a good overview of Montalvo's life and particularly of his appeal to Spanish writers as diverse as Valera and Unamuno.

Bader, Thomas. "Early positivist thought and ideological conflict in Chile," *The Americas*, 26 (April, 1970), 376–93.

> Good introduction with bibliography.

Rodó, José Enrique. "Montalvo" in Emir Rodríguez Monegal (ed.), *Obras completas*, Madrid, Aguilar, 1967, 589–627.

> A justly famous and lengthy essay originally published *c.* 1906.

Chapter 17: The essay of nineteenth-century Mexico, Central America, and the Caribbean

Primary sources

Fernández de Lizardi, José Joaquín. *Obras*, 10 vols., Mexico, Universidad Nacional Autónoma de México, 1963–1982.

> The standard edition of his works.

Hostos, Eugenio María de. *Moral social*, Santo Domingo, Imp. de García Hnos., 1888.
Obras completas, 20 vols., Havana, Obispo y Bernaza, 1939.

> References in the text are to this edition.

Martí, José. *Obras completas*, prologue M. Isidro Méndez, 2 vols., Havana, Lex, 1946.

> One of several editions of the complete works. References in the text are to this edition.

Obras completas, 2 vols., Havana, Centro de Estudios Martianos, 1983.

> The most recent and most standard edition of the complete works.

The America of José Martí: Selected writings, José de Onís, New York, Noonday, 1953.

> One of several translations of Martí's writings on the USA and Latin America.

Inside the Monster. Writings on the United States and American imperialism, tr. Elinor Randall, L. A. Baralt, J. de Onís, and R. H. Foner, ed. Philip S. Foner, New York, Monthly Review Press, 1973.

Our America: Writings on Latin America and the struggle for Cuban Independence, tr. Elinor Randall, J. de Onís, and R. H. Foner, ed. Philip S. Foner, New York, Monthly Review Press, 1977.

Ramírez, Ignacio. *Obras completas de Ignacio Ramírez*, 2 vols., Mexico, Editorial Nacional, 1952.

Rosa, Ramón. *Escritos selectos*, ed. R. Heliodoro Valle, Buenos Aires, W. M. Jackson, 1946.

A representative anthology with helpful notes and introduction. References to Rosa's work in the text are to this volume.

Sierra, Justo, *México, su evolución social*, 2 vols., Mexico and Barcelona, J. Ballescá & Cía., 1900–1902.

Obras completas del maestro Justo Sierra, 14 vols., Mexico, Universidad Nacional Autónoma de México, 1948.

The Political Evolution of the Mexican People, tr. C. Ramsdell, notes and intro. E. O'Gorman, prologue A. Reyes, Austin, University of Texas Press, 1969.

Valle, José Cecilio del. *Obras de José Cecilio del Valle*, compiled José del Valle and Jorge del Valle-Matheu, 2 vols., Guatemala City, Tip. Sánchez de Guise, 1929–1930; another *Obras* appeared in Tegucigalpa, Honduras, in 1914.

References in the text are to the 1929–1930 Guatemala edition.

El pensamiento vivo de José Cecilio del Valle, ed. and prologue Rafael del Valle, 3rd. edn., San José, Editorial Universitaria Centroamericana, 1982.

A good selection of Valle's most important essays. References in text are to this edition.

Varona, Enrique José. *Desde mi belvedere*, definitive edition, Barcelona, Maucci, 1917.

Obras de Enrique José Varona, Havana, Edición Oficial, 1936.

Incomplete edition of his complete works, but includes some major items such as *Estudios literarios y filosóficos, Violetas y ortigas*, etc.

Textos escogidos, interpretative essay and selection R. Lazo, Mexico, Porrúa, 1968.

Helpful introduction, bibliography, and representative selection. References in the text are to this edition.

Secondary sources

Books

Anuario del Centro de Estudios Martianos, Havana, Centro de Estudios Martianos, 1978– .

Annual bibliographic series continuing the *Anuario martiano* (see below).

Anuario martiano, Havana, Consejo Nacional de Cultura, 1969–1975.

Annual serial report on Martí bibliography.

Crawford, William Rex. *A Century of Latin American Thought*, 2nd. edn., Cambridge, Mass., Harvard University Press, 1961.

Originally published in 1944, this has become a standard reference in the field.

Davis, Harold Eugene *Latin American Thought: A historical introduction*, Baton Rouge, Louisiana State University Press, 1972.

Valuable concise summaries of minor as well as major thinkers and essayists.

Earle, Peter G., and Robert G. Mead. *Historia del ensayo hispanoamericano*, Mexico, Ediciones De Andrea, 1973.

Updated version of Mead's earlier *Breve historia*. Brief entries but very informative.

Fernández Retamar, Roberto, *Calibán, apuntes sobre la cultura en nuestra América*, Buenos Aires, Editoral la Pléyade, 1973.

Important for relationship between ideas of Martí, Rodó, and others of the late nineteenth century.

Ferrero Acosta, Luis. *Ensayistas costarricenses*, San José, Antonio Lehmann, 1971.
> One of the few studies on the subject; includes some material on nineteenth century.

Garfield, Evelyn Picón, and Ivan Schulman. *Las entrañas del vacío: ensayos sobre la modernidad hispanoamericana*, Mexico Ediciones Cuadernos Americanos, 1984.
> Chapter 4, pp. 79–96, contains some valuable information on Martí and his place in literary history.

González Obregón, Luis, Don. *José Joaquín Fernández de Lizardi*, Mexico, Botas, 1938.
> The bibliography of Lizardi's work in this study is especially valuable.

Hostos, Adolfo de. *Indice hemero-bibliográfico de Eugenio María de Hostos*, San Juan, Comisión Pro-celebración del Centenario de Hostos, 1940.
> Valuable for dating Hostos's many unpublished articles, newspaper pieces, etc.

Mañarch, Jorge. *Martí el apóstol*, 3rd. edn., Buenos Aires and Mexico, Espasa-Calpe, 1946.
> Probably the best-known of many basic studies of Martí. Other important studies include those of J. C. Ghiano, J. Marinello, E. Martínez Estrada, A. Iduarte, F. Lizaso, E. Roig de Leuchsenring.

Mantecón, José I., *et al. Bibliografía general de don Justo Sierra*, Mexico, Universidad Nacional Antónoma de México, 1969.
> Very valuable for exact dating of Sierra's works.

Stabb, Martin S. *In Quest of Identity: Patterns in the Spanish American essay of ideas, 1890–1960*, Chapel Hill, University of North Carolina Press, 1967.
> Though much of the study deals with the twentieth century, considerable analysis of late nineteenth century is included.

Vitier, Medardo. *Varona, maestro de juventudes*, Havana, Trópico, 1937.
> *Del ensayo americano*, Mexico, Fondo de Cultura Económica, 1945.
> Interpretive studies of leading nineteenth- and early twentieth-century essayists.

Yañez, Agustín. *Don Justo Sierra: su vida, sus ideas, y su obra*, Mexico, Universidad National Antónoma de México, 1962.

Zea, Leopoldo. *Dos etapas del pensamiento en Hispano américa: del romanticismo al positivismo*, Mexico, El Colegio de México, 1949.
> One of the truly classical studies of Spanish American thought of the nineteenth century.

Zum Felde, Alberto. *Indice crítico de la literatura hispanoamericana*, Vol II: *El ensayo y la crítica*, Mexico, Guaranía, 1954.
> Abundant material on major essayists such as Martí, Hostos, and Varona.

Articles

Ainsa, Fernando. "Hostos y la unidad de América Latina," *Cuadernos Americanos*, 3:16 (1989), 67–86.
> On Hostos's ideas of Latin American unity related to the utopian theme.

Cardenas, Eliana. "José Martí y la identidad latinoamericana," *Plural*, 125 (1981), 16–24.

Carpentier, Alejo. "Martí y Francia" in *La novela latinoamericana en vísperas de un nuevo siglo y otros ensayos*, Mexico, Siglo Veintiuno Editores, 1981.
Originally in *Casa de las Américas*, 87 (Nov.–Dec. 1974), 62–72.

Fernández Retamar, Roberto. "José Martí en los orígenes del antiimperialismo latino americano," *Casa de las Américas*, 25 (July–Aug. 1985), 3–11.
One of revolutionary Cuba's foremost literary spokesmen discusses Martí in the context of imperialism.

Fornet Betancourt, Raúl. "José Martí y el problema de la raza negra en Cuba," *Cuadernos Americanos*, 16 (July–Aug. 1989), 124–39.

Franco, Jean. "La heterogeneidad peligrosa: escritura y control social en vísperas de la independencia mexicana," *Hispamérica*, 12 (Apr.–Aug. 1983), 3–34.
Comments on Lizardi's ideology.

Guerra Cunningham, Laura. "Feminismo e ideología liberal en el pensamiento de Eugenio María de Hostos," *Cuadernos Americanos*, 16 (July–Aug. 1989), 139–50.

Lagmanovich, David. "Lectura de un ensayo 'Nuestra América' de José Martí, 11235–45" in Ivan A. Schulman, *Nuevos asedios al modernismo*, Madrid, Taurus, 1987.
Comments on this basic essay of Martí.

Merrell, Floyd. "Justo Sierra y la educación positivista de México," *Hispanófila*, 33 (May 1990), 67–78.

Ramos, Julio. "La escritura del corresponsal: lectura de las escenas norteamericanas de José Martí," *Escritura: Revista de Teoría y Crítica Literarias*, 6 (July–Dec., 1981), 329–53.
On Martí's reportage in North America.

Ripoll, Carlos, "Martí y el socialismo," paper from II Congreso Cultural de Verano del CCP y la Univ. de Miami, in Alba-Buffill, Elio, *et al.*, *José Martí ante la crítica actual*, Miami, Círculo de Cultura Panamericana, 1983.

Le Riverend Brusone, Julio J. "Los Estados Unidos: Martí, crítico del capitalismo financiero, 1880–9," *Casa de las Américas*, 24 (Sept.–Oct. 1983), 3–13.

Sacoto, Antonio. "El americanismo de Martí," *Cuadernos Americanos*, 258 (Jan.–Feb. 1985), 162–9.

Schulman, Ivan A. "Desde los Estados Unidos: Martí y las minorías étnicas y culturales," *Los Ensayistas*, 10–11 (Mar. 1981), 139–52.

Vogeley, Nancy. "The concept of 'the people' in *El Periquillo sarmiento*," *Hispania*, 70 (Sept. 1987), 457–67.
Though dealing with the novel, comments on Lizardi's emphasis on colloquial speech and lower classes.

Zea, Leopoldo. "Hostos como conciencia latinoamerica," *Cuadernos Americanos*, 16 (July–Aug. 1989), 49–57.

Chapter 18: The gaucho genre

Secondary sources

Books

Albarracín-Sarmiento, Carlos. *Estructura del Martín Fierro*, Amsterdam, John Benjamin, 1981.
   A delimitation of the time and space of the narration and of the events narrated, and an examination of the text's facticity and of its reception.
Anderson Imbert, Enrique. *Análisis del Fausto*, Buenos Aires Centro Editor de América Latina, 1969.
   Textual analysis of the poem on the basis of its genesis and its forms, as well as an assessment of the poem's readings.
Azeves, Angel. *La elaboración literaria del Martín Fierro*, Universidad de La Plata, 1960.
   Analyzes the sources and literary traditions of the poem. Commentary on some of its verses.
Con el Martín Fierro, Buenos Aires, Editorial Remitido, 1968.
   Outlines the gauchesque, epic, and picaresque antecedents of the poem. Notes for the teaching of the poem at university level.
Borello, Rodolfo A. *El poema Martín Fierro*, Mendoza, Ediciones Cuyo Hispánico, 1972.
   Argumental and formal analysis of the text and of the national elements it contains.
Hernández: poesía y política, Buenos Aires, Plus Ultra, 1973.
   A biography of Hernández, together with a textual and stylistic analysis of Martín Fierro. Includes a complete bibliography of editions of the poem and of critical studies current through 1973.
Borello, Rodolfo A., *et al. Trayectoria de la poesía gauchesca*, Buenos Aires, Plus Ultra, 1977.
   Four essays about the gaucho genre, its origins, and its characteristics, by Horacio J. Becco, Rodolfo Borello, Adolfo Prieto, and Félix Weinberg.
Borges, Jorge Luis. *Aspectos de la literatura gauchesca*, Montevideo, Número, 1950.
El Martín Fierro, Buenos Aires, Columba, 1953.
   Textual analysis of the two parts of the poem in relation with other gauchesque works. Borges's essays on the gaucho genre are an important element for understanding his literature.
Brumana, Herminia. *Nuestro hombre*, Buenos Aires, Rosso, 1939.
   Interesting for its author's feminine perspective in the analysis of Martín Fierro from the viewpoint of liberty and justice.
Cali, Américo. *Martín Fierro ante el derecho penal*, 2nd. edn., Buenos Aires, Abeledo-Perrot, 1979.
   Juridic analysis of the crimes committed and forms of legality enforced throughout the poem, as well as a judgment and absolution of the protagonist.
Canal-Feijóo, Bernardo. *De las "aguas profundas" en el Martín Fierro*, Buenos Aires, Fondo Nacional de las Artes, 1973.

Analysis of the text from the perspective of the biblical and Masonic symbolism that informs it.

Carreto, Andrés. *Ida y vuelta de José Hernández*, Buenos Aires, Corregidor, 1972.
Biography of José Hernández and a historical–political study of the poem.

Coni, Emilio A. *El gaucho. Argentina-Brasil-Uruguay*, Buenos Aires, Sudamericana, 1945.
Exhaustive and polemic study of the history of the gaucho, of the word "gaucho," and of gaucho literature from an anti-gaucho perspective.

Cortazar, Augusto Raúl. *Poesía gauchesca argentina. Interpretada con el aporte de la teoría folklórica*, Buenos Aires, Guadalupe, 1969.
Amply documents the oral and folkloric contributions to the constitution of the genre.

Chávez, Fermín. *José Hernández*, 2nd. edn., Buenos Aires, Plus Ultra, 1973.
Biography of the poet and an anti-liberal reading of the poem. Includes an appendix of various documents.

Fernández Latour de Botas, Olga. *Prehistoria de Martín Fierro*, Buenos Aires, Platero, 1977.
Documented analysis of the folkloric elements of the poem, from the perspective of sociocultural relations and of the gaucho's cultural patrimony.

García, Néstor. *Análisis socio-estructural de la obra de J. Hernández*, Universidad de Buenos Aires, 1972.
Textual analysis, informed by a reading of Lucien Goldmann's sociology of literature.

Halperín Donghi, Tulio. *José Hernández y sus mundos*, Buenos Aires, Sudamericana, 1985.
The most important and up-to-date biography of José Hernández as a journalist and as one of the formulators of a ruralist ideology in Argentina.

Leumann, Carlos A. *El poeta creador: cómo hizo Hernández "La vuelta de Martín Fierro,"* Buenos Aires, Sudamericana, 1945.
A study of the manuscripts of *La vuelta* and its variants, from the perspective of the creative process; compares Hernández to Dostoyevsky and Poe.

Losada Guido, Alejandro. *Martín Fierro: gaucho, héroe, mito*, Buenos Aires, Plus Ultra, 1967.
Examines the relations between sociohistorical context and authorial intention; analysis of the gaucho genre and of Martín Fierro as a mythic symbol.

Ludmer, Josefina. *El género gauchesco. Un tratado sobre la patria*, Buenos Aires, Sudamericana, 1988.
Constitution and history of the genre from the viewpoint of its tones and its relations to the law and the state, and as the foundation of a national tradition.

Lugones, Leopoldo. *El payador*, Buenos Aires, Otero & Cía., 1916.
Considers *Martín Fierro* as an epic poem of Greco-Roman ascendancy and as the Argentinian national book.

Lynch, John. *Juan Manuel de Rosas*, Buenos Aires, Emecé, 1984.
One of the most comprehensive historical studies of Rosas and the gauchos between 1829 and 1852.

Martínez Estrada, Ezequiel. *Muerte y transfiguración de Martín Fierro*, Buenos Aires and Mexico, 2nd. edn., 2 vols., Fondo de Cultura Económica, 1958.

Among the most important essays on the classic. Inaugurates a new brand of phenomenologic and psychoanalytic criticism of the text and its world.

Mujica Laínez, Manuel. *Vida de Aniceto el Gallo (Hilario Ascasubi)*, Buenos Aires, Emecé, 1943.

Vida de Anastasio el Pollo (Estanislao del Campo), Buenos Aires, Emecé, 1948.
These two biographies of important gauchesque writers are written in a form that is nearly novelistic and both are amply documented.

Pagés Larraya, Antonio. *Prosas de Martín Fierro*, Buenos Aires, Raigal, 1952.
Critical study and anthology of Hernández's journalistic and political writings which shed light on the poem.

Rama, Angel. *Los gauchipolíticos ríoplatenses. Literatura y sociedad*, Buenos Aires, Calicanto, 1976.
One of the most important studies of the gaucho genre and its transformation from political poetry to social poetry.

Rodríguez Molas, Ricardo. *Luis Pérez y la biografía de Rosas escrita en 1830*, Buenos Aires, Clío, 1957.
Critical and historical introduction preceding the text of one of the least-studied gaucho poets.

Historia social del gaucho, Buenos Aires, Marú, 1968.
History of the gaucho as a social class from colonial times until the time of the gaucho's transformation into a rural peon. Contains a valuable appendix of documents.

Rojas. Ricardo. *Historia de la literatura argentina*, vols. i and ii, Buenos Aires, Editorial Losada, 1948.
One of the first fundamental studies of the genre. Traces the connections between gaucho poetry and the poetry of the *payadores*, representatives of a popular conscience. Posits *Martín Fierro* as an epic song of democracy.

Romano, Eduardo. *Sobre poesía popular argentina*, Buenos Aires, Centro Editor de América Latina, 1983.
Distinguishes between popular, traditional, and "cultivated" poetry and defines the genre and its subsequent derivations in the tango and throughout twentieth-century literature.

Sansone de Martínez, Eneida. *La imagen en la poesía gauchesca*, Montevideo, Universidad de la República, 1962.
Analysis of the gaucho song, its different parts (presentation, challenge, and *payada*), and of the images presented in each.

Tiscornia, Eleuterio F. *La lengua de Martín Fierro*, Universidad de Buenos Aires, 1930.
The language of the classic text is studied as a function of dialectal variety and analyzed according to its vocabulary, morphology, and syntax, in order to discover in its imagery the psychological traits of the speakers.

Unamuno, Miguel de. *El gaucho Martín Fierro*, Buenos Aires, Americalee, 1967.
Examines the first part of *Martín Fierro* from a philological and social perspective to conclude that it is a symbol of Argentinian popular culture as well as of a Hispanic universality.

Various authors. *Martín Fierro. Un siglo*, Buenos Aires, Xerox Argentina, 1972.
Articles on the poem's fundamental critical sources; review of Hernández's life and work; appendix of documents with critical receptions of the text at the time

of its publication; complete up-to-date bibliography; and facsimile of the first edition of *Martín Fierro*.

Villanueva, Amaro. *Crítica y pico*, Santa Fe, Colmegna, 1945.

Analysis of the preludes of *Martín Fierro* as well as of other texts of the genre. Examines readings of *Fausto* from the time of its publication.

Weinberg, Félix. *Juan Gualberto Godoy: literatura y política*, Buenos Aires, Solar Hachette, 1970.

Study of Godoy's poem, *Carro*, along with an analysis of his gauchesque texts from the political and polemical perspective of the time.

Zorraquín Becú, Horacio. *Tiempo y vida de José Hernández (1834–1886)*, Buenos Aires, Emecé, 1972.

Important and well-documented political biography of the poet.

Articles

Borges, Jorge Luis. "La poesía gauchesca" in *Discusión*, Buenos Aires, Emecé, 1950.

Borges was one of the first critics to insist upon the conventional and literate aspects of the genre. A brief comparative history of gauchesque poetry.

Bunge, Carlos O. "El derecho en la literatura gauchesca" in *Estudios jurídicos*, Madrid, Espasa-Calpe, 1926.

One of the first essays to treat the juridic problems that are debated within the gaucho genre.

Ludmer, Josefina. "La lengua como arma. Fundamentos del género gauchesco" in Lía Schwartz and Isaías Lerner (eds.), *Homenaje a Ana María Barrenechea*, Madrid, Castalia, 1984.

Analyzes the emergence of the genre from the perspective of the various uses of voices and its oral tones.

Rama, Angel. "Prólogo" to *Poesía gauchesca*, Caracas, Biblioteca Ayacucho, 1977.

Analysis of the genre as a literary system and as the invention of an audience.

Volume 2: The twentieth century

Chapter 1: Modernist poetry

Primary sources

Agustini, Delmira. *El libro blanco*, Montevideo, Bertani, 1907.
  Cantos de mañana, Montevideo, Bertani, 1910.
  Los cálices vacíos, "Pórtico" by Rubén Darío, Montevideo, Bertani, 1913.
Casal, Julián del. *Hojas al viento*, Havana, El Retiro, 1890.
  Nieve, Havana, 1892.
  Bustos y rimas, Havana, La Habana Elegante, 1893.
Chocano, José Santos. *En la aldea*, Lima, Imprenta del Estado, 1895.
  Iras santas, Lima, Imprenta del Estado, 1895.
  Azahares, Lima, Imprenta del Estado, 1896.
  Selva virgen, Lima, Imprenta del Estado, 1898.
  El canto del siglo, Lima, La Industria, 1901.
  El fin de Satanás y otros poemas, Guatemala, Tipografía Nacional, 1901.
  Alma América: poemas indo-españoles, Madrid, Suárez, 1906.
  ¡Fiat lux!, Madrid, Pueyo 1908, and Paris, Ollendorff, 1908.
  Primacías de oro de Indias, Santiago, Siglo XX, 1934.
  Spirit of the Andes, tr. Edna Worthley Underwood, Portland, Maine, Mosher Press, 1935.
Darío, Rubén. *Abrojos*, Santiago, Cervantes, 1887.
  Canto épico a las glorias de Chile. Certamen Varela. Obras premiadas y distinguidas entre las novecientas noventa composiciones presentadas al certamen literario promovido en 1887 por el señor Don Federico Varela. Antología, Santiago de Chile, Imprenta Cervantes, 1887.
  "Rimas," in *Certamen Varela*, I, Santiago, Cervantes, 1887, 186–96.
  Azul. . . Valparaíso, Excélsior, 1888. 2nd. edn., Guatemala, La Unión, 1890; 3rd edn., Buenos Aires, La Nación, 1905.
  Los raros, Buenos Aires, Talleres de "La Vasconia," 1896.
  Prosas profanas y otros poemas, Buenos Aires, Coni, 1896. 2nd. edn., augmented, Paris/Mexico, Bouret, 1901.
  Cantos de vida y esperanza. Los cisnes y otros poemas, Madrid, Tipografía de la Revista de Archivos, Bibliotecas y Museos, 1905. 2nd. edn., Barcelona/Madrid, Granada, 1907; 3rd edn., Barcelona, Maucci, 1915.

Oda a Mitre, Paris, Eyméoud, 1906.

Opiniones, Madrid, Librería de Fernando Fe, 1906.

El canto errante, Madrid, M. Pérez Villavicencio, 1907.

El viaje e Nicaragua e Intermezzo tropical, Madrid, Ateneo, 1909.

Poema del otoño y otros poemas, Madrid, Ateneo, 1910.

Letras, Paris, Garnier Hnos., 1911.

Todo al vuelo, Madrid, Editorial Renacimiento, 1912.

Historia de mis libros, Buenos Aires, La Nación, 1913.

Canto a la Argentina y otros poemas, Madrid, Corona, 1914.

La vida de Rubén Darío escrita por él mismo, Barcelona, Maucci, 1915.

Lira póstuma, Madrid, Mundo Latino, 1918.

Eleven poems of Rubén Darío, tr. Thomas Walsh and Salomón de la Selva, intro. by Pedro Henríquez Ureña, New York, G. P. Putnam's Sons, 1916.

Selected Poems, tr. Lysander Kemp, prologue Octavio Paz, Austin, University of Texas Press, 1965.

Darío, Rubén, and Eduardo Poirier. *Emelina*, Valparaíso, 1887.

Díaz Mirón, Salvador. *Lascas*, Xalapa, Tip. del Gobierno del Estado, 1901.

Poemas, prologue Rafael López, Mexico, Cultura, 1918.

Eguren, José María. *Simbólicas*, Lima, La Revista, 1911.

La canción de las figuras, Lima, Tip. de la Penitenciaría, 1916.

Poesías: Simbólicas, La canción de las figuras, Sombra, Rondinelas, Lima, Amauta, 1929.

Gavidia, Francisco. *Versos y pensamientos*, San Salvador, Imprenta Nacional, 1884.

Libro de los azahares, San Salvador, Imprenta Nacional, 1913.

González Martínez, Enrique. *Preludios*, Mazatlán, Retes, 1903. Republished in *La hora inútil*, Mexico, Porrúa, 1916.

Lirismos, Mocorito, Sinaloa, La Voz del Norte, 1907. Republished in *La hora inútil*, Mexico, Porrúa, 1916.

Silenter, prologue Sixto Osuna, Mocorito, Sinaloa, La Voz del Norte, 1909.

Los senderos ocultos, Mocorito, Sinaloa, La Voz del Norte, 1911. 2nd. edn., prologue Alfonso Reyes, Mexico, Porrúa, 1915.

La muerte del cisne, Mexico, Porrúa, 1915.

El libro de la fuerza, de la bondad y del ensueño, Mexico, Porrúa, 1917.

Parábolas y otros poemas, prologue Amado Nervo, Mexico, Munguía, 1918.

La palabra del viento, Mexico, México Moderno, 1921.

El romero alucinado (1920–1922), Buenos Aires, Babel, 1923. 2nd. edn., with a critical note by Enrique Díez-Canedo, Madrid, Calleja, 1925.

Las señales furtivas (1923–1924), prologue Luis G. Urbina, Madrid, Calleja, 1925.

Poemas truncos, Mexico, Mundial, 1935.

Ausencia y canto, Mexico, Taller Poético, 1937.

El diluvio de fuego. El esbozo de un poema, Mexico, Abside, 1938.

Tres rosas en el ánfora, Mexico, El Nacional, 1939.

Bajo el signo mortal. . ., Mexico, Poesía Hispano-americana, 1942.

Segundo despertar y otros poemas, Mexico, Nueva Floresta, 1945.

Vilano al viento, Mexico, Stylo, 1948.

Babel, Mexico, Revista de Literatura Mexicana, 1949.

El nuevo Narciso y otros poemas, Mexico, Fondo de Cultura Económica, 1952.

González Prada, Manuel. *Minúsculas*, Lima, El Lucero, 1901.
  Presbiterianas, Lima, El Olimpo, 1909.
  Exóticas, Lima, El Lucero, 1911.
Gutiérrez Nájera, Manuel. *Poesías*, prologue Justo Sierra, Mexico, Oficina Impresora del Timbre, 1896.
  Obras inéditas de Gutiérrez Nájera, ed. Edwin K. Mapes, New York, Instituto de las Españas, 1939.
Herrera y Reissig, Julio. *Los peregrinos de piedra*, Montevideo, Bertani, 1909.
  Cilas alucinada y otras poesías, San José, Costa Rica, Alsina, 1916.
  Los éxtasis de la montaña y otros poemas escogidos, ed. Francisco González Guerrero, Mexico, Victoria, 1917.
  Los parques abandonados, Buenos Aires, América, 1919.
  Opalos, Buenos Aires, América, 1919.
Icaza, Francisco A. de. *Efímeras*, Madrid, Rivadeneyra, 1892.
  Lejanías, Madrid, Rivadeneyra, 1899.
  La canción del camino, Madrid, Rivadeneyra, 1905.
Jaimes Freyre, Ricardo. *Castalia bárbara*, Buenos Aires, 1899.
  Leyes de la versificación castellana, Buenos Aires, Coni, 1912.
  Los sueños son vida, Buenos Aires, Sociedad Cooperativa Editorial, 1917.
Lugones, Leopoldo. *Las montañas del oro*, Buenos Aires, Korn, 1897.
  Los crepúsculos del jardín, Buenos Aires, Arnaldo Moen & Hnos., 1905.
  Lunario sentimental, Buenos Aires, Arnaldo Moen & Hnos., 1910.
  Odas seculares, Buenos Aires, Arnaldo Moen & Hnos., 1910.
  El libro fiel, Paris, Piazza, 1912.
  El libro de los paisajes, Buenos Aires, Otero & García, 1917.
  Las horas doradas, Buenos Aires, Babel, 1922.
  Romancero, Buenos Aires, Babel, 1924.
  Poemas solariegos, Buenos Aires, Babel, 1928.
  Romances del Río Seco, Buenos Aires, Sociedad de Bibliófilos Argentinos, 1938.
Martí, José. *Ismaelillo*, New York, Thompson & Moreau, 1882.
  Versos sencillos, New York, Weiss, 1891.
  Obras reunidas, vol. XI: *Versos libres*, ed. Gonzalo Quesada y Aróstegui, Havana, Rambla & Bouza, 1913.
  Obras reunidas, vol. XVI: *Flores del destierro*, ed. Gonzalo de Quesada y Miranda, Havana, Molina, 1933.
  Major Poems: A bilingual edition, tr. Elinor Randall, ed., with intro, by Philip S. Foner, New York, Holmes & Meier, 1982.
Miró, Ricardo. *Preludios*, Panama, Moderna, 1908.
  La leyenda del Pacífico, Panama, La Unión, 1924.
  Caminos silenciosos, Panama, Nacional, 1939.
Molina, Juan Ramón. *Tierras, mares y cielos*, Tegucigalpa, Tip. Nacional, 1913.
Nervo, Amado. *Místicas*, Mexico, Escalante, 1898.
  Perlas negras, Mexico, Escalante, 1898.
  Poemas, Paris, Bouret, 1901.
  El éxodo y las flores del camino, Mexico, Impresora de Estampillas, 1902.
  Lira heroica, Mexico, Impresora de Estampillas, 1902.
  Los jardines interiores, Mexico, Díaz de Léon, 1905.

En voz baja, Paris, Ollendorff, 1909.

Serenidad, Madrid, Renacimiento, 1914.

Elevación, Madrid, Tip. Artística Cervantes, 1917.

Plenitud, Madrid, Tip. Artística Cervantes, 1918.

El estanque de los lotos, Buenos Aires, Menéndez, 1919.

La amada inmóvil, Madrid, Biblioteca Nueva, 1920.

Obras completas, vol. XXVII, *El arquero divino*, ed. Alfonso Reyes, Madrid, Biblioteca Nueva, 1922.

La hermana agua, Madrid, Hijos de M. G. Hernández, n.d.

Confessions of a Modern Poet, tr. Dorothy Kress, Boston, Bruce Humphries, 1935.

Plenitude, tr. William F. Rice, Los Angeles, J. R. Miller, 1928.

Othón, Manuel José. *Poemas rústicos*, Mexico, Aguilar Vera, 1902.

Reynolds, Gregorio. *Quimeras*, La Paz, Cochabamba, 1915.

Redención, poema cíclico, La Paz, Arno Hnos., 1925.

Sierra, Justo. *Poesías*, Mexico, Universidad Nacional Autónoma de México, 1949.

Silva, José Asunción. *Poesías*, prologue Miguel de Unamuno, Barcelona, Ortega, 1908.

Tamayo, Franz. *La prometheida o las oceánides*, La Paz, Imprenta Artística, 1917.

Nuevos Rubáyat, La Paz, Imprenta Artística, 1927.

Urbina, Luis G. *Ingenuas*, Paris/Mexico, Bouret, 1902.

Puestas del sol, Paris/Mexico, Bouret, 1910.

Lámparas en agonía, Mexico, Bouret, 1914.

Valencia, Guillermo. *Ritos*, Bogotá, Samper, 1899.

Catay, Bogotá, Cromos, 1929.

Translations of individual poems by modernist authors appear in the following works:

Allen, John Houghton (ed. and tr.). *A Latin-American Miscellany*, Dallas, Kaleidograph Press, 1943.

Blackwell, Alice Stone (tr.). *Some Spanish-American Poets*, with intro. and notes by Isaac Goldberg, New York, D. Appleton & Co., 1929; London, Oxford University Press, 1937, New York, Greenwood Press, 1968.

Cohen, John Michael (ed. and tr.). *The Penguin Book of Spanish Verse*, Harmondsworth and Baltimore, Penguin Books, 1956 (with plain prose translations of each poem); 3rd. edn., 1988 (with fewer Spanish American poets).

Craig, George Dundas (comp. and tr.). *The Modernist Trend in Spanish-American Poetry: A collection of representative poems of the modernist movement and the reaction, translated into English verse, with a commentary*, Berkeley, University of California Press, 1934.

Creekmore, Hubert (ed.). *A Little Treasure of World Poetry*, New York, Scribner, 1952.

Fitts, Dudley (ed.). *Anthology of Contemporary Latin American Poetry*, Norfolk, Conn., New Directions, 1942.

Flores, Angel (ed.). *An Anthology of Spanish Poetry from Garcilaso to García Lorca in English Translation with Spanish Originals*, Garden City, Anchor Books, 1961.

Goldberg, Isaac. *Studies in Spanish-American Literature*, New York, Brentano's, 1920.

Mexican Poetry: An anthology, Girard, Kans., Haldeman-Julius Co., 1925.

Johnson, Mildred Edith (tr.). *Spanish Poems of Love*, New York, Exposition Press, 1955.

Johnson, Mildred Edith (ed. and tr.). *Swans, Cygnets and Owl: An anthology of modernist poetry in Spanish America*, Columbia, University of Missouri Press, 1956.

Jones, Willis Knapp (ed.). *Spanish-American Literature in Translation: A selection of poetry, fiction, and drama since 1888*, New York, Frederick Ungar, 1963.

Paz, Octavio (ed. and intro.). *Anthology of Mexican Poetry*, tr. Samuel Beckett, preface by C. M. Bowra, Bloomington, Indiana University Press, 1958.

Strand, Mark (ed.). *New Poetry of Mexico*, New York, E. P. Dutton, 1970.

Translations from Hispanic Poets, New York, Hispanic Society of America, 1934.

Underwood, Edna Worthley (tr.). *Anthology of Mexican Poets from the Earliest Times to the Present Day*, Portland, Maine, Mosher Press, 1932.

Walsh, Thomas (ed.). *Hispanic Anthology: Poems translated from the Spanish by English and North American poets*, New York, G. P. Putnam's Sons, 1920.

Weisinger, Nina Lee, and Marjorie C. Johnston (eds. and trs.). *Los otros americanos*, Garden City, Doubleday, Doran & Co., 1934.

Secondary sources

Books

Abrams, Meyer Howard. *The Mirror and the Lamp: Romantic theory and the critical tradition*, London, Oxford University Press, 1971.

    Erudite study of English and German Romanticism that provides important background for understanding Modernism.

 Natural Supernaturalism: Tradition and revolution in romantic literature, New York, W. W. Norton, 1973.

    Studies the orthodox and heterodox beliefs that influenced the development of Romanticism in England and Germany. Important background for understanding Spanish American Modernism.

Abril, Xavier. *Eguren, el obscuro (el simbolismo en América)*, Cordoba, Argentina, Universidad Nacional de Córdoba, 1970.

    Emphasizes the symbolist roots of Eguren's poetry.

Alvar, Manuel. *La poesía de Delmira Agustini*, Seville, Escuela de Estudios Hispano-americanos, 1958.

    Traditional and somewhat dated overview of Agustini's poetry.

Anderson, Robert Roland. *Spanish American Modernism: A selected bibliography*, Tucson, University of Arizona Press, 1970.

    Provides data regarding critical studies on seventeen writers of the period.

Anderson Imbert, Enrique. *La originalidad de Rubén Darío*, Buenos Aires, Centro Editor de América Latina, 1967.

    Clear, thorough, and illuminating overview of the life and works of Rubén Darío.

Aparicio, Frances R. *Versiones, interpretaciones y creaciones: instancias de la traducción literaria en Hispanoamérica en el siglo veinte*, Gaithersburg, Md., Hispamérica, 1991.

    The chapter on Modernism focuses on Gutiérrez Nájera and Valencia; it perceptively and intelligently relates translation to the modernist search for a uniquely Spanish American language and style.

Ara, Guillermo. *Leopoldo Lugones*, Buenos Aires, Mandrágora, 1958.
Overview of Lugones's entire *opus*.

Becco, Horacio Jorge. *Leopoldo Lugones: bibliografía de su centenario (1876–1974)*, Buenos Aires, Culturales Argentinas, 1978.
Contains references to studies on the author, his life, and his work.

Bibliografía anotada del modernismo, ed. Emilia de Zuleta, comp. and annotated by Hilda Gladys Fretes and Esther Bárbara, Cuadernos de la biblioteca, 5, Mendoza, Universidad Central de Cuyo, Biblioteca Central, 1970.
Emphasis on the modernist movement rather than on individual authors.

Blanch y Blanco, Celestino. *Bibliografía martiana, 1954–1963*, Havana, Biblioteca Nacional "José Martí," Departamento de Colección Cubana, 1965.
Bibliography of items by and about Martí.

Bollo, Sarah. *Delmira Agustini en la vida y la poesía*, Montevideo, Cordón, 1963.
Brief introduction to Agustini's life, themes, and techniques.

Borges, Jorge Luis. *Leopoldo Lugones*, 2nd. edn., Buenos Aires, Pleamar, 1965.
Insightful and illuminating study of one literary giant by another.

Brushwood, John S. *Enrique González Martínez*, New York, Twayne, 1969.
Useful introduction to the life, times, and works of González Martínez.

Bula Píriz, Roberto. *Herrera y Reissig (1875–1910): vida y obra, bibliografía, antología*, New York, Hispanic Institute, 1952.
Interesting background to the life and works of Herrera.

Calinescu, Matei. *Five Faces of Modernity: Modernism, Avant-Garde, Decadence, Kitsch, Postmodernism*. Durham, Duke University Press, 1987.
Study of modernity and its various manifestations including Spanish American Modernism.

Carter, Boyd G. *En torno a Gutiérrez Nájera*, Mexico, Botas, 1960.
Introduction to life, times, and works of Gutiérrez Nájera.

Castillo, Homero (ed.). *Estudios críticos sobre el modernismo*, Madrid, Gredos, 1968.
Twenty-two of the most influential essays on Modernism written before 1967.

Charry Lara, Fernando (ed.). *José Asunción Silva, vida y creación*, Bogotá, Procultura, 1985.
A collection of forty-five important pieces on Silva, including essays by Smith, Bowra, Gicovate, Ghiano, Fogelquist, Roggiano, Schulman, Picon Garfield, Osiek, Castillo, Goldberg, Anderson, Gutiérrez Girardot, Orjuela, Loveluck, and Schanzer.

Davison, Ned J. *The Concept of Modernism in Hispanic Criticism*, Boulder, Col., Pruett, 1966. Translation into Spanish, *El concepto de modernismo en la crítica hispánica*, Buenos Aires, Nova, 1971.
Comprehensive review of the often contradictory assessments of Modernism made by modernists and critics up to 1966.

Del Greco, Arnold Armand. *Repertorio bibliográfico del mundo de Rubén Darío*, New York, Las Américas, 1969.
Extensive bibliography on Darío's life and works.

Díaz Plaja, Guillermo. *Modernismo frente a noventa y ocho*, Madrid, Espasa-Calpe, 1951.
Emphasizes and exaggerates the differences between Modernism and the

Generation of '98 at Modernism's expense.

Durán, Manuel. *Genio y figura de Amado Nervo*, Editorial Universitaria de Buenos Aires, 1968.

Good overview of Nervo's life, times, and works.

Ellis, Keith. *Critical Approaches to Rubén Darío*, University of Toronto Press, 1974.

A review of the many different ways Darío's work has been studied.

Faurie, Marie-Josèphe. *Le modernisme hispano-américain et ses sources françaises*, Paris, Centre de Recherches de l'Institut d'Études Hispaniques, 1966.

Study of French sources in keeping with early critical perspective on Modernism.

Fernández Retamar, Roberto. *Introducción a José Martí*, Havana, Casa de las Américas, 1978.

Series of essays on Martí's life and works that underscore his sympathies with the goals of Revolutionary Cuba.

Ferreres, Rafael. *Los límites del modernismo y del 98*, Madrid, Taurus, 1964.

Series of essays that highlights the similarities between Modernism and the Generation of '98.

Fiore, Dolores Ackel. *Rubén Darío in Search of Inspiration (Greco-Roman Mythology in His Stories and Poetry)*, New York, Las Américas, 1963.

Studies Darío's recourse to Greek and Roman mythology.

Forster, Merlin H. *Historia de la poesía hispanoamericana*, Clear Creek, Ind., The American Hispanist, 1981.

A clear and concise history of Spanish American poetry with a useful bibliography.

Gicovate, Bernardo. *Julio Herrera y Reissig and the Symbolists*, Berkeley, University of California Press, 1957.

A solid, informative early reading of Herrera's work within the context of symbolist beliefs and techniques.

Giordano, Jaime. *La edad del ensueño: sobre la imaginación poética de Rubén Darío*, Santiago, Editorial Universitaria, 1970.

Studies Darío's poetry in light of its symbolist roots, focusing on its search for profound realities through sound and image.

Glickman, Robert Jay. *Guillermo Valencia and the Poetic World of "Ritos": Interpretations based upon the use of a concordance*, Los Angeles, University of California, 1963.

Major study of the poetry of Valencia.

Glickman, Robert Jay (ed.). *The Poetry of Julián del Casal: A critical edition*, 2 vols., Gainesville, University Presses of Florida, 1978.

The second volume of notes provides valuable background to the specific poems and to Casal's work in general.

González, Aníbal. *La crónica modernista hispanoamericana*, Madrid, José Porrúa Turanzas, 1983.

Studies the modernist chronicles in their relation to philology and journalism, providing important background for modernist poetry as well.

La novela modernista hispanoamericana, Madrid, Gredos, 1987.

Studies modernist novels in terms of the interplay between commitment and art, underscoring the political sensitivity that contributed to the development of the modernist movement.

González, Manuel Pedro. *Fuentes para el estudio de José Martí: ensayo de bibliografía clasificada*, Bibliografía cubana, 1, Havana, Ministerio de Educación, Dirección de Cultura, 1950.

Extensive bibliography of items by and about Martí.

Grass, Roland, and William R. Risley. *Waiting for Pegasus: Studies of the presence of Symbolism and Decadence in Hispanic letters*, Macomb, Ill., Western Illinois University, 1979.

Collection of essays underscoring the links between Spanish and Spanish American Modernism and the symbolist movement.

Gutiérrez Girardot, Rafael. *Modernismo*, Barcelona, Montesinos, 1983.

Studies Hispanic literature of the turn of the century in terms of the sociocultural changes taking place.

Halty Ferguson, Raquel. *Laforgue y Lugones: dos poetas de la luna*, London, Tamesis Books, Ltd., 1981.

Studies the influence of Laforgue on Lugones.

Handelsman, Michael H. "Una bibliografía crítica de las revistas literarias del modernismo ecuatoriano (1895–1930)," in *El modernismo en las revistas literarias del Ecuador: 1895–1930. Ensayo preliminar y bibliografía*, Cuenca, Cultura Ecuatoriana, Nucleo del Azuay, 1981.

Studies the Ecuadorian journals of the modernist movement.

Henríquez Ureña, Max. *Breve historia del modernismo*, Mexico, Fondo de Cultura Económica, 1954.

Thorough history of the movement which gives careful attention to personal and literary context.

Hernández-Chiroldes, J. Alberto. *Los versos sencillos de José Martí (análisis crítico)*, Miami, Ediciones Universal, 1983.

A detailed, line-by-line analysis of *Los versos sencillos*.

Hulet, Claude L. *Latin American Poetry in English Translation*, Basic Bibliographies, 2, Washington, Pan American Union, 1965.

Arranged by country and author with titles of individual poems given.

Hurtado Chamorro, Alejandro. *La mitología griega en Rubén Darío*, Avila, La Muralla, 1969.

Studies Darío's recourse to Greek mythology.

Ingwersen, Sonya Anne. *Light and Longing: Silva and Darío: Modernism and religious heterodoxy*, New York, Peter Lang, 1987.

Examines the influence of occultism and other forms of heterodoxy upon Silva and Darío.

Irazusta, Julio. *Genio y figura de Leopoldo Lugones*, Buenos Aires, Editorial Universitaria de Buenos Aires, 1968.

The life and times of Lugones.

Jaimes Freyre, Mireya. *Modernismo y 98 a través de Ricardo Jaimes Freyre*, Madrid, Gredos, 1969.

Emphasizes Jaimes Freyre's symbolist roots from the perspective of an artificially strong division between Modernism and the Generation of '98.

Jiménez, José Olivio. *José Martí: poesía y existencia*, Mexico, Oasis, 1983.

Major study on Martí's life and poetry.

Antología crítica de la poesía modernista hispanoamericana, Madrid, Hiperión, 1985.
> Thoughtful, perceptive, and useful introductory notes, selection, and bibliography.

Jiménez, Juan Ramón. *El modernismo: notas de un curso*, ed. Ricardo Gullón and Eugenio Fernández Méndez, Mexico, Aguilar, 1962.
> The poet's influential statement on Modernism as an epoch.

Jirón Terán, José. *Bibliografía general de Rubén Darío (julio 1883–enero 1967)*, Publicaciones del Centenario de Rubén Darío, Managua, San José, 1967.
> Valuable for Central American publications on Darío.

Jitrik, Noé. *Leopoldo Lugones: mito nacional*, Buenos Aires, Palestra, 1960.
> Discusses Lugones and his search for an Argentinian literature.

Las contradicciones del modernismo: productividad poética y situación sociológica, Mexico, El Colegio de México, 1978.
> Using sociological and Marxist concepts, this study presents an analysis of key modernist characteristics.

Jrade, Cathy L. *Rubén Darío and the Romantic Search for Unity: The modernist recourse to esoteric tradition*, Austin, University of Texas Press, 1983. Augmented Spanish version, *Rubén Darío y la búsqueda romántica de la unidad: el recurso modernista a la tradición esotérica*, Mexico, Fondo de Cultura Económica, 1986.
> Study of the impact that esoteric tradition had both directly and indirectly upon the formation of the modernist *Weltanschauung* and upon Darío's poetic production.

Karsen, Sonja P. *Guillermo Valencia, Colombian Poet*, New York, Hispanic Institute in the United States, 1951.
> Overview of Valencia's life and poetry.

Kirkpatrick, Gwen. *The Dissonant Legacy of Modernismo: Lugones, Herrera y Reissig, and the voices of modern Spanish American poetry*, Berkeley, University of California Press, 1989.
> Studies Modernism's development and transformation – mostly through the poetry of Lugones – as it anticipates key features of the Avant-Garde.

Lorenz, Erika. *Rubén Darío: "Bajo el divino imperio de la música,"* tr. Fidel Coloma González, Managua, Ediciones "Lengua," 1960.
> Study of musicality in the poetry of Rubén Darío.

Lozano, Carlos. *Rubén Darío y el modernismo en España 1888–1920: ensayo de bibliografía comentada*, New York, Las Américas, 1968.
> Includes critical studies on, and contributions to Spanish journals by, Darío.

Magis, Carlos Horacio. *La poesía de Leopoldo Lugones*. Mexico, Ateneo, 1960.
> An analysis of Lugones's world-view and poetics and how they are manifested in the themes and techniques of his poetry.

Mapes, Erwin K. *La influencia francesa en la obra de Rubén Darío*, Managua, Publicaciones del Centenario, 1967.
> Spanish translation, from the French, of this classic study. It examines the influence of French texts upon Darío's literary production.

Marasso, Arturo. *Rubén Darío y su creación poética*, Buenos Aires, Kapeluz, 1954.
> Traces the "sources" of Darío's poetry in literature and in the plastic arts.

Martínez, José Luis (comp.). *La obra de Enrique González Martínez*, Mexico, Colegio Nacional 1951.

Collection of more than sixty articles published in honor of González Martínez on his eightieth birthday.

Matlowsky, Bernice D. *The Modernist Trend in Spanish–American Poetry: A selected bibliography*, Washington, Pan American Union, 1952.

Short and somewhat dated.

Núñez, Estuardo. *José María Eguren: vida y obra, antología, bibliografía*, New York, Hispanic Institute, 1964.

Summary of Eguren's life and categorization of poetic elements.

Orjuela, Héctor H. *"De sobremesa" y otros estudios sobre José Asunción Silva*, Bogotá, Instituto Caro y Cuervo, 1976.

Essays on Silva's works, literary relations, and the tenor of the times during which he wrote.

Osiek, Betty Tyree. *José Asunción Silva: estudio estilístico de su poesía*, Mexico, Ediciones de Andrea, 1968.

A stylistic analysis of the poetry of Silva along with a brief concordance and three critical essays by others.

José Asunción Silva, Boston, Twayne, 1978.

Introduction to the life, times, and works of Silva.

Pacheco, José Emilio. *Antología del modernismo (1884–1921)*, 2 vols., Mexico, Universidad Nacional Autónoma de México, 1978.

Insightful introduction which places Modernism within its social, cultural, and literary contexts.

Pasquel, Leonardo. *Bibliografía diazmironiana*, Colección suma veracruzano, Serie bibliográfica, Mexico, Citlaltépetl, 1966.

Incomplete bibliography of items by and about Salvador Díaz Mirón.

Paz, Octavio. *Los hijos del limo: del romanticismo a la vanguardia*, Barcelona, Seix Barral, 1974.

Essay on modern poetry that focuses on the underlying belief and poetic structures of Romanticism, Modernism, and the Avant-Garde. Essential reading.

Children of the Mire: Modern poetry from Romanticism to the Avant-Garde, tr. Rachel Phillips, Cambridge, Mass., Harvard University Press, 1974.

Pearsall, Priscilla. *An Art Alienated from Itself: Studies in Spanish American Modernism*, Romance Monographs, 43, University, Miss., Romance Monographs Inc., 1984.

Examines "modern" features within the work of Casal, Gutiérrez Nájera, and Darío.

Peraza Sarausa, Fermín. *Bibliografía martiana, 1853–1955*, Havana, Anuario Bibliográfico Cubano, 1956.

Massive bibliography of items by and about Martí.

Pérus, Françoise. *Literatura y sociedad en América Latina: el modernismo*, Havana, Casa de las Américas, 1976.

Statement on the applicability of Marxist theory to literary inquiry with two final chapters on Modernism and Darío.

Picón Garfield, Evelyn, and Iván A. Schulman. *"Las entrañas del vacío": ensayos sobre la modernidad hispanoamericana*, Mexico, Cuadernos Americanos, 1984.

Studies modernity as it appears in Spanish America and Spanish American literature.

Pino Saavedra, Yolando. *La poesía de Julio Herrera y Reissig: sus temas y su estilo*, Santiago, Prensas de la Universidad, 1932.

Traditional study of Herrera's themes and style.

Rama, Angel. *Rubén Darío y el modernismo (circunstancia socioeconómica de un arte americano)*, Caracas, Ediciones de la Biblioteca de la Universidad Central de Venezuela, 1970.

Studies the relationship between the formation of Modernism and Spanish America's entrance into the modern world economy.

Rubén Darío: el mundo de los sueños, Barcelona, Editorial Universitaria, Universidad de Puerto Rico, 1973.

Introduction by Rama and collection of prose pieces by Darío that underscore the importance to Darío of phenomena that lie outside the realm of the positive sciences.

Raymond, Marcel. *From Baudelaire to Surrealism*, London, Methuen, 1970.

Introduction to French romantic and symbolist poetics that provides important background to Spanish American Modernism.

Reyes, Alfonso. *Tránsito de Amado Nervo*, Santiago, Ediciones Ercilla, 1937.

Insightful if limited and dated study of Nervo's poetry by the Mexican writer.

Ripoll, Carlos. *Archivo José Martí repertorio crítico: medio siglo de estudios martianos*, New York, Eliseo Torres & Sons, 1971.

Important bibliography of studies on Martí.

Indice universal de la obra de José Martí, New York, Eliseo Torres, 1971.

Useful index to Martí's work.

Rodríguez Monegal, Emir. *Sexo y poesía en el 900*, Montevideo, Alfa, 1969.

From the perspective of turn-of-the-century Uruguay, its customs, prejudices, and sexual mores, Rodríguez Monegal presents a perceptive study of the poetry of Roberto de las Carreras and Delmira Agustini.

Rodríguez-Peralta, Phillis White. *José Santos Chocano*, New York, Twayne, 1970.

General introduction to the life and works of Chocano.

Rosenblaum, Sidonia Carmen. *Modern Women Poets of Spanish America*, Westport, Conn., Greenwood Press, 1978 (originally published in 1945).

Studies the life, times, and works of Agustini along with chapters on Mistral, Storni, and Ibarbourou.

Salinas, Pedro. *La poesía de Rubén Darío*, Buenos Aires, Editorial Losada, 1948.

Examines Darío's poetry in terms of his erotic longings and social concerns.

Schulman, Iván A. *Génesis del modernismo: Martí, Nájera, Silva, Casal*, Mexico, El Colegio de México, 1966.

Study of these four early Modernists and their contributions to the genesis of the modernist movement.

Símbolo y color en la obra de José Martí, Madrid, Gredos, 1970.

Exhaustive study of Martí's symbolism.

Schulman, Iván A., and Manuel Pedro González. *Martí, Darío y el modernismo*, with a prologue by Cintio Vitier, Madrid, Gredos, 1969.

Prologue by Vitier underscores Martí's "futurity." Articles by Schulman and González reaffirm Martí's essential role within Modernism.

Seluja, Antonio. *Julio Herrera y Reissig: vida y obra*, Montevideo, Ministerio de Educación y Cultura, 1984.
   A useful compendium of facts on the life and works of Herrera.
Siles Guevara, Juan. *Bibliografía preliminar de Ricardo Jaimes Freyre*, Cuadernos de bibliografía, 2, La Paz, Ministerio de Informaciones, Cultura y Turismo, 1969.
   Short bibliographic study.
Silva, Clara. *Genio y figura de Delmira Agustini*, Editorial Universitaria de Buenos Aires, 1968.
   Introduction to the figure of Agustini with "testimonials" and "opinions" by many friends, fellow authors, and critics.
Silva-Santisteban, Ricardo (ed.). *José María Eguren: aproximaciones y perspectivas*, Lima, Universidad del Pacífico, 1977.
   Collection of essays on the life and poetry of Eguren.
Skyrme, Raymond. *Rubén Darío and the Pythagorean Tradition*, Gainesville, University Presses of Florida, 1975.
   Studies the influences on Darío of Pythagorean notions that came primarily through French literature.
Smith, Mark I. *José Asunción Silva: contexto y estructura de su obra*, Bogotá, Ediciones Tercer Mundo, 1981.
   Overview of the life, times, and works of Silva.
Stephens, Doris. *Delmira Agustini and the Quest for Transcendence*, Montevideo, Ediciones Geminis, 1975.
   Presents provocative ideas about Agustini's world-view.
Sucre, Guillermo. *La máscara, la transparencia: ensayos sobre poesía hispanoamericana*, Caracas, Monte Avila, 1975.
   Insightful collection of essays on modernist and avant-garde poetry.
Taylor, Terry Oxford. *La expresión simbólica de Manuel Gutiérrez Nájera*, Madrid, Ediciones Maisal, 1977.
   Study of the beliefs and ideals of Gutiérrez Nájera evident in the symbols of his poetry.
Torres, Hernán (ed.). *Estudios, edición en homenaje a Guillermo Valencia*, Cali, Colombia, Carvajal, 1976.
   Collection of important articles on the poetry of Valencia including those written by Glickman, Valencia, Schulman, Olivera, Florit, Trueblood, Miller, Ayerbe Chaux, Arboleda Valencia, and Ramos. It also contains a brief bibliography by Torres.
Vela, Arqueles. *El modernismo: su filosofía, su estética, su técnica.* Mexico, Porrúa, 1972.
   Overview of the major features of modernist verse.
Vitier, Cintio. *Los versos de Martí: tres conferencias de Cintio Vitier*, Havana, Cuadernos Cubanos, n.d. [1968?].
   Insightful and perceptive introduction to Martí's three major collections of verse.
   Lo cubano en la poesía, Havana, Instituto del Libro, 1970.
   Contains two important chapters on Modernism, one on Martí and one on Casal.
Woodbridge, Hensley C. *Rubén Darío: A selective classified and annotated bibliogra-*

phy, Metuchen, N.J., Scarecrow Press, 1975.

Annotated bibliography on works for the most part published between 1950 and 1974.

Rubén Darío: bibliografía selectiva clasificada y anotada, Leon, UNAN, 1975.

Slightly enlarged Spanish version of English bibliography.

"Rubén Darío: bibliografía selectiva, clasificada y anotada, suplemento para los años 1974–1976," *Cuadernos Universitarios*, 2nd series, 20 (1977), 33–66.

"Rubén Darío: bibliografía selectiva, clasificada y anotada, suplemento II para los años 1975–1978," *Cuadernos de Bibliografía Nicaragüense*, 2 (1981), 70–92.

Yurkievich, Saúl. *Celebración del modernismo*, Barcelona, Tusquets, 1976.

Reexamines Modernism, Darío, Lugones, and Herrera y Reissig from the perspective of *la vanguardia*.

Articles

Alegría, Fernando. "Aporte de la mujer al nuevo lenguaje poético de Latinoamérica," *Revista/Review Interamericana*, 12 (1982), 27–35.

Discusses the relationship between the Avant-Garde and the poetry of Agustini, Mistral, Storni, and Ibarbourou.

Anderson, Robert Roland. "Naturaleza, música y misterio: teoria poética de José Asunción Silva," *La Torre*, 16 (1968), 201–14.

Introduction to Silva's literary theory.

Blanco Aguinaga, Carlos. "La ideología de la clase dominante en la obra Rubén Darío," *Revista de Filología Hispánica*, 29 (1980), 520–55.

Examines how the ideology of the ruling class appears in Darío's work.

"Lectura de 'Neurosis' de Julián del Casal," *Casa de las Américas*, 21 (1980), 48–56.

Provocative, "Marxist" reading of this famous poem.

Blasco, Javier. "Modernismo y modernidad," *Insula*, 42 (1987), 37.

Review article on recent publications on Modernism, especially those linking the literary movement with modernity.

Botelho Gosálvez, Raúl. "Ricardo Jaimes Freyre en el modernismo americano," *Cuadernos Americanos*, 156 (1968), 238–50.

Places Jaimes Freyre in the context of Modernism.

Camurati, Mireya. "Dos cantos al centenario en el marco histórico-social del modernismo en la Argentina," *Revista Iberoamericana*, 55 (1989), 103–27.

Interesting comparison of the poems by Lugones and Darío.

Cardwell, Richard A. "Darío and *El Arte Puro*: the enigma of life and the beguilement of art," *Bulletin of Hispanic Studies*, 47 (1970), 37–51.

Discusses the metaphysical base of Darío's work and the progressive erosion of Darío's faith in art as an absolute.

Cubeñas, José Antonio. "Presencia socio-cultural en la poesía de Rubén Darío," *Abside: Revista de Cultura Mexicana*, 41 (1977), 263–81.

Concludes that Darío writes *poesía comprometida*, which is responsive to the sociocultural changes occurring throughout the economically more advanced regions of Spanish America.

Debicki, Andrew P., and Michael J. Doudoroff. "Estudio preliminar" in Rubén Darío, *Azul. Prosas profanas*, Madrid, Editorial Alhambra, 1985.

Informative introduction to Darío's life, work, and aesthetics along with an important study of how his poetry developed in relation to the other arts.

Delgado, Washington. "Situación social de la poesía de Rubén Darío," *Cuadernos Hispanoamericanos*, 312 (1976), 575–89.

Discusses Darío's poetry in light of Spanish America's entrance into the world economy and the resulting optimism and cosmopolitanism.

Espina, Eduardo. "Julio Herrera y Reissig y la no-integrable modernidad de 'La Torre de las Esfinges'," *Revista Iberoamericana*, 55 (1989), 451–6.

Studies Herrera's break with traditional modernist discourse.

Fernández-Morera, D. "The term 'Modernismo' in literary history" in *Proceedings of the Xth Congress of the International Comparative Literature Association*, coordinating editor Anna Balakian, publication editor James J. Wilhelm, New York, Garland, 1985.

Seeks to clarify the ambiguities that arise regarding the term "Modernism" and delineates its relationship with other contemporaneous movements.

Ferreres, Rafael. "Acotaciones al modernismo," *Cuadernos Hispanoamericanos*, 383 (1982), 314–28.

Studies the Modernism of Spain.

Fontella, Lee. "Parnassian precept and a new way of seeing Casal's *Museo ideal*," *Comparative Literature Studies*, 7 (1970), 450–79.

Study of the influence of Parnassian aesthetics upon the conception and execution of *Mi museo ideal*, Casal's collection of sonnets depicting paintings by Gustave Moreau.

Gerdes, Dick, and Tamara Holzapfel. "'Las dos cabezas': lo erótico en función de lo ético," *Hispania*, 68 (1985), 49–54.

Holds that "Las dos cabezas" reflects the complexity of Valencia's artistic goals only if read in its entirety, with its epigraph and with "Judith y Holofernes."

González Echevarría, Roberto. "Modernidad, modernismo y nueva narrativa: *El recurso del método*," *Revista Interamericana de Bibliografía/Interamerican Review of Bibliography*, 30 (1980), 157–63.

Perceptive study of the impact of cultural values upon the formation of Modernism and of the latter upon Carpentier.

"Martí y su 'Amor de ciudad grande': notas hacia la poética de *Versos libres*" in *Isla a su vuelo fugitivo: ensayos críticos sobre literatura hispanoamericana*, Madrid, José Porrúa Turanzas, 1983.

Brilliant analysis of Martí's vision of poetry and its relatonship to action in the modern, post-Edenic world.

Gullón, Ricardo. "Pitagorismo y modernismo," *Mundo Nuevo*, 7 (1967), 22–32.

Examines the fundamental link between Pythagoreanism and Modernism.

"Ideologías del modernismo," *Insula*, 26:291 (1971), 1, 11.

Briefly outlines the "ideologies" that came to influence the development of Modernism, including anti-Naturalism, anti-Positivism, occultism, spiritualism, mysticism, cabalism, and Platonism.

Hamilton, Carlos. "Rubén Darío y Antonio Machado" in *XVII Congreso del Instituto Internacional de Literatura Iberoamericana, 1978*, Madrid, Ediciones Cultura Hispánica del Centro Iberoamericano de Cooperación, 1978, 759–71.

Underscores the similarities between the poetry of Rubén Darío and that of

Antonio Machado.

Herrero, Javier. "Fin de siglo y modernismo. La virgen y la hetaira," *Revista Iberoamericana*, 46 (1980) 29–50.

Shows how a realignment of values underlies modernist eroticism.

Higgins, James. "The rupture between poet and society in the work of José María Eguren," *Kentucky Romance Quarterly*, 20 (1973) 59–74.

Sees Eguren's rejection of society as a sophisticated statement of values.

Horányi, Mátyás. "Notas sobre el concepto de modernidad de Rubén Darío," *Revista Chilena de Literatura*, 1–3 (1970), 199–206.

Deals with Darío's *España contemporánea* and his own concept of modernity, especially as a basis for contrasting the intellectual life in Spain and Spanish America.

Jaimes Freyre, Mireya. "Universalismo y romanticismo en un poeta 'modernista': Ricardo Jaimes Freyre," *Revista Hispánica Moderna*, 31 (1965), 236–46.

Analyzes Jaimes Freyre's metrical innovations and musicality.

Jehenson, Myriam Yvonne. "Four women in search of freedom," *Revista/Review Interamericana*, 12 (1982), 87–99.

Focuses on Agustini, Ibarbourou, Mistral, and Storni.

Jensen, Theodore W. "Christian-Pythagorean dualism in Nervo's *El donador de almas*," *Kentucky Romance Quarterly*, 28 (1981), 391–401.

Examines Nervo's "Pythagoreanism."

Jiménez, José Olivio. "Un ensayo de ordenación trascendente en los *Versos libres* de Martí," *Revista Hispánica Moderna*, 34 (1968), 671–84.

Examines Martí's aesthetic, philosophic, and political agenda.

Jrade, Cathy L. "El significado de un vínculo inesperado: *Rayuela* y 'Tuércele el cuello al cisne'," *Revista Iberoamericana*, 47 (1981) 145–54.

Examines the relationship between Modernism and later Spanish American literature through Cortázar's citing of González Martínez's famous sonnet.

"El Modernismo y la Generación del '98: ideas afines, creencias divergentes," *Texto Crítico*, 14 (1988), 15–29.

Discusses the similarities and differences between Modernism and the Generation of '98 by examining poems by Amado Nervo and Antonio Machado.

"Socio-political concerns in the poetry of Rubén Darío," *Latin American Literary Review*, 36 (1990), 36–49.

Examines the generally overlooked presence of socio-political concerns in Darío's poetry, especially in his early works.

Karsen, Sonja. "El modernismo en Colombia: Guillermo Valencia: el poeta como traductor," *Thesaurus: Boletín de Instituto Caro y Cuervo*, 40 (1985), 349–61.

Focuses on Valencia and role of translation in the development of Modernism.

Kirkpatrick, Gwen. "The limits of *modernismo*: Delmira Agustini and Julio Herrera y Reissig," *Romance Quarterly*, 36 (1989), 307–14.

Studies the changing nature of Modernism through the poetry of Agustini and Herrera.

Leal, Luis. "Situación de Amado Nervo," *Revista Iberoamericana*, 36 (1970), 485–94.

Traces the ups and downs of Nervo's reputation.

Lima, Robert. "Cumbres poéticas del erotismo femenino en Hispanoamérica," *Revista de Estudios Hispánicos*, 18 (1984), 41–59.

Discusses erotic imagery and sexual desire in the poetry of Agustini, Mistral, Storni, and Ibarbourou.

McGuirk, Bernard. "On misreading Mallarmé: Rubén Darío and *The Anxiety of Influence*," *Nottingham French Studies*, 26 (1987), 52–67.

Explores how poetic influence works by examining the "Yo persigo una forma" and "Mes bouquins refermés sur le nom de Paphos."

Molloy, Sylvia. "Dos lecturas del cisne: Rubén Darío y Delmira Agustini" in Patricia Elena González and Eliana Ortega (eds.), *La sartén por el mango: encuentro de escritoras latinoamericanas*, Río Piedras, Puerto Rico, Ediciones Huracán, 1984.

Insightful examination of Agustini's relationship to her social and literary models.

"Ser y decir en Darío: el poema liminar de *Cantos de vida y esperanza*," *Texto Crítico*, 14 (1988), 30–42.

Brilliant analysis of this autobiographical poem and its many goals, especially its response to Rodó.

Montero, Oscar. "Las ordalias del sujeto: *Mi museo ideal* y *Marfiles viejos* de Julián del Casal," *Revista Iberoamericana*, 55 (1989), 287–306.

Studies Casal's "singularly modern" aesthetics by focusing on these two series of sonnets from *Nieve*.

Moretić, Yerko. "Acerca de las raíces ideológicas del modernismo hispanoamericano," *Philologica Pragensia*, 8 (1965), 45–53.

One of the first articles to recognize the importance of class and economy in the formation of Modernism.

Natella, Arthur, Jr. "Toward a definition of Latin American Modernism – debate and reconciliation," *Romanticism Past and Present*, 8 (1984), 23–38.

Places Modernism in the context of Romanticism.

Nougué, André. "Rubén Darío y el 98" *Cuadernos Hispanoamericanos*, 218 (1968), 302–15.

Holds that Darío is as "noventayochista" as Unamuno or Maeztu, as concerned with Spain's defeat as the Spaniards.

Ortega, Bertín. "Gutiérrez Nájera y sus contemporáneos: afrancesamiento vs. nacionalismo," *Texto Crítico*, 14 (1988), 118–26.

Shows that there is no inconsistency in Gutiérrez Nájera's interest in French literature and his nationalistic aspirations.

Ortega, Julio. "José María Eguren," *Cuadernos Hispanoamericanos*, 83 (1970), 60–85.

Useful introduction and overview of the poetry of Eguren.

Paraíso de Leal, Isabel. "Teoría y práctica del verso libre en Ricardo Jaimes Freyre," *Revista Española de Lingüística*, 12 (1982), 311–19.

Examines Jaimes Freyre's theory and practice of free verse.

Paz, Octavio. "El caracol y la sirena," in *Cuadrivio*, Mexico, Joaquín Mortiz, (1965), 11–65.

"The siren and the seashell" in *The Siren and the Seashell and Other Essays on Poets and Poetry*, tr. Lysander Kemp and Margaret Sayers Peden, Austin, University of Texas Press, 1976, 17–56.

Extraordinary essay on Darío's poetry, its musicality, its eroticism, and its relationship to its modern context.

"Literatura de fundación" in his *Puertas al campo*, Mexico, Universidad Nacional Autónoma de México, 1966, 11–19.

Essay on the "founding" of Spanish American literature.

Pedemonte, Hugo Emilio. "Las eglogánimas de Julio Herrera y Reissig," *Cuadernos Hispanoamericanos*, 60 (1964), 483–501.

Broad and informative introduction to Herrera's bucolic poetry.

Phillips, Allen W. "Antonio Machado y Rubén Darío," *Sin Nombre*, 2 (1971), 36–47.

Discusses the importance of Darío's presence in Madrid at the beginning of the twentieth century and the personal and literary friendship that developed between these two great poets.

"Cuatro poetas hispanoamericanos entre el modernismo y la vanguardia," *Revista Iberoamericana*, 55 (1989), 426–49.

Perceptive examination of the works of Lugones, Herrera, López Velarde, and Tablada and of the way they retain modernist characteristics at the same time that they anticipate features of the Avant-Garde.

Podesta, Bruno. "Hacia una conceptualización ideológica del modernismo hispano," *Cuadernos Americanos*, 195 (1974), 227–37.

Examines Modernism's reaction to or investigation of: Romanticism, Positivism, mysticism, orientalism, Pythagoreanism, and Nietzschean values.

Real de Azúa, Carlos. "El modernismo literario y las ideologías," *Escritura: Teoría y Crítica Literarias*, 2 (1977), 41–75.

Holds that Modernism did not have a fixed ideology but rather offered varying, at times contradictory, reactions to many diverse factors including economic growth, urbanization, and an increasing Europeanization of culture.

Rivera-Rodas, Oscar. "El discurso modernista y la dialéctica del erotismo y la castidad: un poema de Ricardo Jaimes Freyre," *Revista Iberoamericana*, 55 (1989) 43–62.

Focuses on "Voz extraña" by Jaimes Freyre.

Rivero, Eliana. "Poesía modernista y perspectiva ideológica: la 'Sonatina' de Rubén Darío," *Explicación de Textos Literarios*, 8 (1980), 51–8.

Studies the hierarchy of values that permeates "Sonatina."

Rodríguez-Peralta, Phyllis. "The Modernism of José María Eguren," *Hispania*, 56 (1973), 222–9.

Focuses on the modernist characteristics of Eguren's poetry.

Roggiano, Alfredo A. "Bibliografía de y sobre Leopoldo Lugones," *Revista Iberoamericana*, 53 (1962), 155–213.

Useful bibliography of works by and on Lugones.

"Modernismo: Origen de la palabra y evolución de un concepto" in Catherine Vera and George R. McMurray (eds.) *In Honor of Boyd G. Carter*, Laramie, University of Wyoming, 1981, 93–103.

Traces the development of the term "Modernism" and links it to features of modernity that began as early as the second half of the eighteenth century.

Rojas, Santiago. "Unidad temática y anecdótica en 'Los doce gozos' de Leopoldo Lugones," *Hispanófila*, 34 (1990), 29–42.

Detailed analysis of 'Los doce gozos' by Lugones.

Romero de Valle, Emilia. "Chocano en la Revolución Mexicana," *Letras: Organo de la Facultad de Letras y Ciencias Humanas de la Universidad Nacional Mayor de*

San Marcos, Lima, Perú, 78–9 (1967), 77–91.

Studies Chocano's involvement with the Mexican Revolution.

Salinas, Pedro. "El cisne y el buho" in Literatura española siglo xx, Madrid, Alianza Editorial, 1970, 46–66.

Famous article that emphasizes the differences between Darío's modernist swan and González Martínez's postmodernist owl.

"El problema del modernismo en España, o un conflicto entre dos espíritus" in Literatura española siglo xx, Madrid, Alianza Editorial, 1970, 13–25.

This 1941 article distinguishes between the formal innovations of modernist poetry and the seriousness of the Generation of '98.

Santí, Enrico Mario. "Ismaelillo, Martí, y el modernismo," Revista Iberoamericana, 52 (1986), 811–40.

Provides a reading of Ismaelillo that reconciles Martí's literary and political endeavors.

Schulman, Iván A. "José Martí frente a la modernidad hispanoamericana: los vacíos y las reconstrucciones de la escritura modernista," Revista Iberoamericana, 55 (1989), 175–92.

Considers Martí's writings in light of those elements that contributed to the modernization of Spanish America and Spanish American discourse.

Shaw, Donald L. "Modernismo: A contribution to the debate," Bulletin of Hispanic Studies, 46 (1967) 195–202.

One of the first articles to recognize the relationship between Spanish American Modernism and European Romanticism.

Siebenmann, Gustav. "Reinterpretación del modernismo" in Germán Bleiberg and E. Inman Fox (eds.), Pensamiento y letras en la España del siglo xx, Nashville, Tenn., Vanderbilt University Press, 1966, 497–511.

Reassertion of Salinas's and Díaz-Plaja's distinction between Modernism and the Generation of '98.

Smith-Soto, Mark I. "José Asunción Silva: The literary landscape," Kentucky Romance Quarterly, 29 (1982), 283–92.

Studies the influence of the literary Zeitgeist upon Silva's work.

"Lugones and Darío: towards a subversive genealogy," Romance Quarterly, 36 (1989), 189–94.

Shows the influence of Lugones's Las montañas del oro upon Darío's later poetic production.

Taylor, Terry O. "Manuel Gutiérrez Nájera: originality and the question of literary borrowings," Symposium, 27 (1973), 269–79.

Discusses Gutiérrez Nájera's unique and original response to Parnassian and decadent aesthetics.

Trueblood, Alan S. "Rubén Darío: the sea and the jungle," Comparative Literature Studies, 4 (1967), 425–56.

Article on Darío's sea poetry that illuminates the core of his poetic vision.

Valera, Juan. "Carta-Prólogo" in Rubén Darío, Azul... Madrid, Espasa-Calpe, 1937.

Extraordinarily perceptive early reading of Azul... by this Spanish novelist and critic.

Villena, Luis Antonio de. "El camino simbolista de Julián del Casal," INTI: Revista de Literatura Hispánica, 7 (1978), 35–48.

Examines the symbolist nature of Casal's poetry.

Vitier, Cintio. "En la mina martiana," prologue to Iván Schulman and Manuel Pedro González, *Martí, Darío y el modernismo*, Madrid, Gredos, 1969.

"Vallejo y Martí," *Revista de Crítica Literaria Latinoamericana*, 7 (1981), 95–8.
Short but illuminating piece on the similarities between Vallejo and Martí.

Yurkievich, Saúl. "Rubén Darío y la modernidad," *Plural*, 9 (1972), 37–41.
One of the first articles to focus on "modernity" as an important factor in the development of Darío's poetry.

Zavala, Iris M. "1898, Modernismo and the Latin American revolution," *Revista Chicano-Riqueña*, 3 (1975), 43–7.
Sees Modernism as part of the Latin American struggle for emancipation.

Chapter 2: Modernist prose

Primary sources

Darío, Rubén. *Azul. . .*, Valparaíso, Imprenta Excelsior, 1888.

Los raros, Buenos Aires, Talleres de "La Vasconia," 1896.

España contemporánea, Paris, Garnier, 1901.

Peregrinaciones, Paris, Librería de la viuda de Charles Bouret, 1901.

La caravana pasa, Paris, Garnier, 1902.

Tierras solares, Madrid, Tipografía de la Revista de Archivos, Bibliotecas y Museos, 1904.

El viaje a Nicaragua e Intermezzo tropical, Madrid, Imprenta de Bernardo Rodríguez, 1909.

El mundo de los sueños. Prosas póstumas, Madrid, Renacimiento, 1922.

El hombre de oro y La isla de oro, Santiago, Zig-Zag, 1937.

Díaz Rodríguez, Manuel. *Confidencias de Psiquis*, Caracas, El Cojo Ilustrado, 1897.

Cuentos de color, Caracas, Tip. de J. M. Herrera Irigoyen & Cía., 1899.

Idolos rotos, Paris, Garnier, 1901.

Sangre patricia, Caracas, Tip. J. M. Herrera Irigoyen & Cía., 1902.

Domínici, Pedro César. *El triunfo del ideal*, Paris, Librería de la Vda. de Ch. Bouret, 1901.

Dyonisios, Librería de la Vda. de Ch. Bouret, 1910.

Gómez Carrillo, Enrique. *Almas y cerebros*, Paris, Garnier, 1898.

El alma encantadora de París, Barcelona/Buenos Aires, Maucci, 1902.

De Marsella a Tokío. Sensaciones de Egipto, la India, China, y el Japón, Paris, Garnier, 1905.

El modernismo, Madrid, Editorial Francisco Beltrán, 1905.

El primer libro de las crónicas, Madrid, Mundo Latino, 1919.

Ciudades de ensueño: Constantinopla. Jerusalén. Atenas. Damasco. Nikko, Madrid, Espasa-Calpe, 1920.

La Grecia eterna, vol. xv of *Obras completas*, Madrid, Mundo Latino, 1920.

González Prada, Manuel. *Páginas libres*, Paris, Tip. de P. Dupont, 1894.

Horas de lucha. Lima, Tip. "El progreso literario," 1908.

Gutiérrez Nájera, Manuel. *Cuentos frágiles*, Mexico, Imprenta del comercio de E. Dublan & Cía., 1883.

Cuentos color de humo y Cuentos frágiles, Madrid, Biblioteca Andrés Bello, 1916.

Divagaciones y fantasías: crónicas de Manuel Gutiérrez Nájera, selected, with an introductory study and notes, by Boyd G. Carter, Mexico, Secretaría de Educación Pública, 1944.

Cuentos completos y otras narraciones, ed., with prologue and notes, by E. K. Mapes, introductory study by Francisco González Guerrero, Mexico, Fondo de Cultura Económica, 1958.

Cuentos y cuaresmas del Duque Job, ed. with intro. by Francisco Monterde, Mexico, Porrúa, 1972.

Larreta, Enrique. *La gloria de don Ramiro*, Madrid, V. Suárez, 1908.

The Glory of Don Ramiro: A life in the times of Philip II, tr. L. B. Walton, London, J. M. Dent & Sons, Ltd./New York, E. P. Dutton, 1924.

Lugones, Leopoldo. *La guerra gaucha*. Buenos Aires, Arnaldo Moen & Hnos., 1905.

Les fuerzas extrañas: Una vida en tiempos de Felipe Segundo, Buenos Aires, Arnaldo Moen & Hnos., 1906.

Martí, José. *Lucía Jerez (Amistad Funesta)*, New York, El Latino, Americano, 1885; published under the pseudonym Adelaida Ral.

Obras completas, collected and organized by Néstor Carbonell, 8 vols., Havana, Edición especial de "La Prensa," 1919–1920.

Obras completas, 27 vols., Havana. Editorial Nacional de Cuba, 1963–1965.

The America of José Martí: Selected writings, tr. José de Onís, intro. by Federico de Onís, New York, Noonday Press, 1953.

Inside the Monster: Writings on the US and American imperialism, tr. Elinor Randall, Luis A. Baralt, Juan de Onís, and Roslin Held Foner, ed. with intro. and notes by Philip S. Foner, New York. Monthly Review Press, 1975.

Our America: Writings on Latin America and the struggle for Cuban independence, tr. Elinor Randall, with additional translations by Juan de Onís and Roslin Held Foner, ed. with intro. and notes by Philip S. Foner, New York, Monthly Review Press, 1977.

On Education: Articles on educational theory and pedagogy, and writings for children from The Age of Gold. tr. Elinor Randall, ed. with intro. and notes by Philip S. Foner, New York, Monthly Review Press, 1979.

On Art and Literature: Critical writings, tr. Elinor Randall, Luis A. Baralt, Juan de Onís, and Roslin Held Foner, ed. with intro. and notes by Philip S. Foner, New York, Monthly Review Press, 1982.

Nervo, Amado. *El bachiller*, Mexico, Talleres de El Mundo, 1895.

Cuentos misteriosos, in *Obras completas*, vol. xx, ed. Alfonso Reyes, Madrid, Biblioteca Nueva, 1920–1922.

Prado, Pedro. *La reina de Rapa-Nui*, Santiago, Imprenta Universitaria, 1914.

Alsino, Santiago, Imprenta Universitaria, 1920.

Quiroga, Horacio. *Cuentos de amor, de locura y de muerte*, Buenos Aires, Cooperativa Editorial Limitada, 1917.

Reyles, Carlos. *La muerte del cisne*, Paris, Ollendorf, 1910.

El embrujo de Sevilla. Buenos Aires & Montevideo, Agencia General de Librería Publicaciones, 1927.

Rodó, José Enrique. "El que vendrá" in *La vida nueva*, vol. I, Montevideo, Dornaleche y Reyes, 1897.

Ariel. Montevideo, Dornaleche & Reyes, 1900.

Motivos de Proteo, Montevideo, J. M. Serrano & Cía., 1909.

El camino de Paros, Valencia, Editorial Cervantes, 1918.

Ariel, tr. Margaret Sayers Peden, prologue by Carlos Fuentes, foreword by James Symington, Austin University of Texas Press, 1988.

Sanín Cano, Baldomero. *La civilización manual y otros ensayos*, Buenos Aires, Babel, 1925.

Indagaciones e imágenes, Bogotá, Talleres de Ediciones de Colombia, 1926.

Silva, José Asunción. *De sobremesa*, Bogotá, Editorial Cromos, 1925.

Torres, Carlos Arturo. *Idola fori. Ensayo sobre las supersticiones políticas*, Valencia, F. Sempere & Cía., 1909.

Secondary sources

Books

Alonso, Amado. *Ensayo sobre la novela histórica. El modernismo en "La gloria de don Ramiro,"* Buenos Aires, Instituto de Filología, Imprenta y Casa Editora Coni, 1942.

The classic stylistic analysis of Larreta's novel.

Anderson Imbert, Enrique. *La originalidad de Rubén Darío*, Buenos Aires, Centro Editor de América Latina, 1967.

Araujo, Orlando. *La palabra estéril*, Maracaibo, Venezuela, Universidad del Zulia, 1966.

An ideological and stylistic study of the works of Manuel Díaz Rodríguez.

Ghiano, Juan Carlos. *Análisis de "La gloria de don Ramiro,"* Buenos Aires, Centro Editor, 1968.

Studies the sources and the style of Larreta's novel.

González, Aníbal. *La crónica modernista hispanoamericana*, Madrid, José Porrúa Turanzas, 1983.

Studies the modernist chronicles in their relation to philology and journalism.

La novela modernista hispanoamericana, Madrid, Gredos, 1987.

Views the Modernists' novels as attempts to reconcile art with political commitment.

Henríquez Ureña, Max. *Breve historia del modernismo*, Mexico, Fondo de Cultura Económica, 1954.

Documented history of the movement.

Ibieta, Gabriella. *Tradition and Renewal in "La gloria de don Ramiro,"* Potomac, Scripta Humanistica, 1986.

Studies the reception of Larreta's novel and compares Larreta's work to similar European historical novels.

Jiménez, José Olivio, *et al. Estudios críticos sobre la prosa modernista*, New York, Eliseo Torres, 1975.

An anthology of essays by various scholars on modernist prose.

Meyer-Minneman, Klaus. *Der spanischamerikanische Roman des Fin de siècle*, Tübingen, Max Niemeyer Verlag, 1979.

Broad-ranging erudite study that covers modernist as well as naturalist and creolist novels.

Olivares, Jorge. *La novela decadente en Venezuela*, Caracas, Editorial Armitano, 1984.
    An erudite study of works by three turn-of-the-century Venezuelan novelists: Díaz Rodríguez, Domínici, and Coll.

Orjuela, Hector H. *"De sobremesa" y otros estudios sobre José Asunción Silva*, Bogotá, Instituto Caro y Cuervo, 1976.
    A study of Silva's sources and themes.

Silva Castro, Raúl. *Pedro Prado (1886–1952)*, Santiago, Editorial Andrés Bello, 1965.
    Biographical–critical study of the author of *Alsino*.

Tyree Osiek, Betty. *José Asunción Silva*. Boston, Twayne, 1978.
    Studies the life and works of Silva.

Vaz Ferreira, Carlos. *Moral para intelectuales*, Montevideo, Imprenta el Siglo Ilustrado, 1920.
    Lecture notes from a course given by Vaz Ferreira in 1909.

Vitier, Cintio, and Fina García Marruz. *Estudios martianos*, Havana, Biblioteca Nacional "José Martí," 1969.
    A collection of essays about diverse aspects of Martí's life and work, but concentrating mainly on his prose.

Articles

Anderson Imbert, Enrique. "La prosa poética de José Martí: *Amistad funesta*" in *Estudios sobre escritores de América*. Buenos Aires, Editorial Raigal, 1954, 125–65.
    A stylistic study of Martí's novel.

González Echevarría, Roberto. "The Case of the Speaking Statue: *Ariel* and the magisterial rhetoric of the Latin American essay" in his *The Voice of the Masters; Writing and authority in Modern Latin American Literature*, Austin, University of Texas Press, 1985.
    Studies some of the rhetorical conceits used in Rodó's essay in the context of a theory of literary authority.

Henríquez Ureña, Max. "Influencias francesas en la novela de la América Hispana" in Juan Loveluck (ed.), *La novela hispanoamericana*, Santiago, Editorial Universitaria, 1969, 95–104.
    Lists French novels that may have served as sources for modernist novels.

Kronik, John. "Enrique Gómez Carrillo: Francophile propagandist," *Symposium*, 21 (Spring 1967), 50–60.
    Biographical–critical essay on the Guatemalan journalist.

Lastra, Pedro. "Relectura de *Los raros*" in Iván A. Schulman (ed.), *Nuevos asedios al modernismo*, Madrid, Taurus, 1987, 198–209.
    Studies the structural coherence of Darío's book of essays.

Lida, Raimundo. "Estudio preliminar" in Ernesto Mejía Sánchez (ed.), *Los cuentos completos de Rubén Darío*, with editor's notes. Mexico, Fondo de Cultura Económica, 1950.
    A stylistic approach to Rubén Darío's stories.

Loveluck, Juan. "*De sobremesa*, novela desconocida del modernismo," *Revista*

Iberoamericana, 31 (Jan.–June 1956), 17–32.

Notes the novel's importance in a broader Spanish American context, and analyzes it thematically and stylistically.

Martí, Jorge L. "Teoría y técnica novelística en *El embrujo de Sevilla*," *Hispania*, 51 (1968), 239–43.

Reads Reyles's novel in terms of his theories about the genre.

Meyer-Minneman, Klaus. "José Martí, *Amistad funesta*," *Romanistisches Jahrbuch*, 22 (1971), 306–18.

Analyzes Martí's novel in the context of decadentist fiction.

"La novela modernista hispanoamericana y la literatura europea de 'fin de siglo': puntos de contacto y diferencias" in Iván A. Schulman (ed.), *Nuevos asedios al modernismo*, Madrid, Taurus, 1987, 246–61.

Defines the genre of the modernist novel through a comparison with its French *fin-de-siècle* equivalent.

Phillips, Allen W. "El arte y el artista en algunas novelas modernistas" in *Temas del modernismo hispánico y otros estudios*, Madrid, Gredos, 1974, 261–93.

Notes the prevalence of "artist–heroes" in the modernist novel.

Picón Garfield, Evelyn. "*De sobremesa*: José Asunción Silva, el diario íntimo y la mujer prerrafaelita" in Iván A. Schulman (ed.), *Nuevos asedios al modernismo*, Madrid, Taurus, 1987, 262–81.

Studies Silva's use of the diary form in his novel and its source in Marie Bashkirtseff's *Journal* (1887).

Pupo-Walker, Enrique. "Notas sobre los rasgos formales del cuento modernista," *Anales de Literatura Hispanoamericana*, 1 (1973), 469–80.

Studies the formal traits of the modernist short story with a view toward its generic definition.

Roggiano, Alfredo A. "El modernismo y la novela en la América Hispana" in *La novela iberoamericana*. Albuquerque, N.M., Instituto Internacional de Literatura Iberoamericana, 1957, 24–45.

Comments on the Modernists' attempts to innovate in the novel.

Schulman, Ivan A. "Reflexiones en torno a la definición del modernismo" in Hornero Castillo (ed.), *Estudios críticos sobre el modernismo*, Madrid, Gredos, 1968.

Vitier, Cintio. "Sobre *Lucía Jerez*" *Diálogos* (Colegio de México), 87 (1979), 3–8.

Comments on the moralizing tendency found in Martí's novel.

Chapter 3: *The* Vanguardia *and its implications*

Primary sources

Adán, Martín. *La casa de cartón*, Lima, Talleres de Impresiones y Encuadernaciones "Perú," 1928.

The Cardboard House, tr. Katherine Silver, Saint Paul, Minn., Graywolf Press, 1990.

Arlt, Roberto. *El juguete rabioso*, Buenos Aires, Editorial Latina, 1926.

Los siete locos, Barcelona, Editorial Latina, 1929.

El jorobadito, Buenos Aires, Librerías Anaconda, 1933.

The Seven Madmen, tr. Naomi Lindstrom, Boston, David R. Godine, 1984.

Borges, Jorge Luis. *Fervor de Buenos Aires*, Buenos Aires, Imprenta Serantes, 1923.
  Luna de enfrente, Buenos Aires, Ediciones Proa, 1925.
  Selected Poems 1923–1967, ed. Norman Thomas di Giovanni, New York, Delacorte
    Press, 1972.
Brull, Mariano. *Poemas en menguante*, Paris, Le Moil & Pascali, 1928.
Cuadra, Pablo Antonio. *Poemas nicaragüenses 1930–1933*, Santiago, Nascimiento,
    1934.
Fernández, Macedonio. *No toda es vigilia la de los ojos abiertos*, Buenos Aires,
    Manuel Gleizer, 1928.
  Papeles de recienvenido, Buenos Aires, Cuadernos del Plata, 1929.
  Selected Writings in Translation, ed. Jo Anne Engelbert, Mansfield, Tex., Latitudes
    Press, 1984.
Ferreiro, Alfredo Mario. *El hombre que se comió un autobús*, Montevideo, La Cruz
    del Sur, 1927.
Garmendia, Julio. *La tienda de muñecos*, Paris, Editorial Excélsior, 1927.
Girondo, Oliverio. *Veinte poemas para ser leídos en el tranvía*, Argenteuil, France,
    Imprenta Coulouma, 1922.
  Calcomanías, Madrid, Espasa-Calpe, Imprenta Sucesores de Rivadeneyra, 1925.
  Espantapájaros (al alcance de todos), Buenos Aires, Ediciones Proa, 1932.
  En la masmédula, Buenos Aires, Losada, 1954.
González Lanuza, Eduardo. *Prismas*, Buenos Aires, J. Samet, 1924.
Gorostiza, José. *Muerte sin fin*, Mexico, Editorial Cultura, 1939.
  Poesía, Mexico, Fondo de Cultura Económica, 1964.
  Death Without End, tr. Laura Vallaseñor, Austin, University of Texas Press, 1969.
Guillén, Nicolás. *Motivos de son*, Havana, Rambla & Bouza, 1930.
  Sóngoro Cosongo. Poemas mulatos. Havana, Imprenta Ucar, García & Cía., 1931.
  West Indies Ltd., Havana, Imprenta Ucar, García & Cía., 1934.
  Man-making Words: selected poems of Nicolás Guillén, tr. Robert Márquez and
    David Arthur McMurray, Amherst, University of Massachusetts Press, 1972.
Hernández, Felisberto. *Fulano de tal*, Montevideo, José Rodríguez Riet, 1925.
  Libro sin tapas, Rocha, Imprenta La Palabra, 1929.
  La cara de Ana, Mercedes, Uruguay, 1930.
  La envenenada, Florida, Uruguay, 1931.
Hidalgo, Alberto. *Simplismo*, Buenos Aires: Sociedad de Publicaciones El Inca, 1925.
Hidalgo, Alberto, Vicente Huidobro, and Jorge Luis Borges. *Indice de la nueva poesía
    americana*, Buenos Aires, Sociedad de Publicaciones El Inca, 1926.
Huidobro, Vicente. *El espejo de agua*, Buenos Aires, Orión, 1916.
  Ecuatorial, Madrid, Imprenta Pueyo, 1918.
  Poemas árticos, Madrid, Imprenta Pueyo, 1918.
  Manifestes, Paris, Editions de la Revue Mondiale, 1925.
  Mío Cid Campeador, Madrid, Compañía Iberoamericana de Publicaciones, 1929.
  Altazor, Madrid, Compañía Iberoamericana de Publicaciones, 1931.
  Cagliostro, Santiago, Zig-Zag, 1934.
  Arctic Poems, tr. William Witherup and Serge Echeverría, Santa Fe, Desert Review
    Press, 1974.
  Altazor, or a voyage in a parachute, tr. Eliot Weinberger, Saint Paul, Minn.,
    Graywolf Press, 1988.

Huidobro, Vicente, and Hans Arp. *Tres novelas ejemplares*, Santiago, Zig-Zag, 1935.
On the cover, the title is *Tres inmensas novelas*.

Maples Arce, Manuel. *Andamios interiores*, Mexico, Editorial Cultura, 1922.
Poemas interdictos, Jalapa, Mexico, Ediciones de Horizonte, 1927.

Neruda, Pablo. *Veinte poemas de amor y una canción desesperada*, Santiago, Nascimento, 1924.
El habitante y su esperanza, Santiago, Nascimento, 1926.
Tentativa del hombre infinito, Santiago, Nascimento, 1926.
Residencia en la tierra: 1925–1931, Santiago, Nascimento, 1933.
Residencia en la tierra, vol. II: *1931–1935*, Madrid, Cruz & Raya, 1935.
Twenty Love Poems and a Song of Despair, tr. W. S. Merwin, London, Cape, 1969.
Residence on Earth, tr. Donald D. Walsh, New York, New Directions, 1973.

Novo, Salvador. *Ensayos*, Mexico, Talleres Gráficos de la Nación, 1925.
It includes "Ensayos de poemas," reprinted as *XX poemas*.
Return Ticket, Mexico: Editorial Cultura, 1928.

Oquendo de Amat, Carlos. *Cinco metros de poemas*, Lima, 1927.

Owen, Gilberto. *Novela como nube*, Mexico, Ediciones de Ulises, 1928.

Palacio, Pablo. *Débora*, Quito, Ecuador, 1927.
Un hombre muerto a puntapiés, Quito, Universidad Central de Quito, 1927.

Pasos, Joaquín. *Breve suma*, Managua, Editorial Nuevos Horizontes, 1945.

Ramos Sucre, José Antonio. *La torre de timón*, Caracas, Lit. y Tip. Vargas, 1925.

Silva Valdés, Fernán. *Agua del tiempo*, Montevideo, Pegaso, 1921.

Tablada, José Juan. *Un día. . .*, Caracas, Imprenta Bolívar, 1919.
Li-Po y otros poemas, Caracas, Imprenta Bolívar, 1920.

Torres Bodet, Jaime. *Margarita de niebla*, Mexico, Editorial Cultura, 1927.

Uslar Pietri, Arturo. *Barrabás y otros relatos*, Caracas, Lit. y Tip. Varcas [Vargas], 1928.

Vallejo, César. *Los heraldos negros*, Lima, [Imprenta Souza Ferreyra], 1918.
Trilce, Lima, Talleres Tip. de la Penitenciaría, 1922.
Poemas humanos, Paris, Les Éditions des Presses Modernes, 1939.
Trilce, tr. David Smith, New York, Grossman Publishers, 1974.
The Complete Posthumous Poetry, tr. Clayton Eshleman and José Rubia Barcia, Berkeley, University of California Press, 1978.

Vela, Arqueles. *El café de nadie*, Jalapa, Mexico, Ediciones de Horizonte, 1926.

Vidales, Luis. *Suenan timbres*, Bogotá, Editorial Minerva, 1926.

Villaurrutia, Xavier. *Nocturnos*, Mexico, Fábula, 1931.
Nostalgia de la muerte, Buenos Aires, Sur, 1938.

Westphalen, Emilio Adolfo. *Las ínsulas extrañas*, Lima, Bustamante & Ballivián, 1933.

Magazines and periodicals

Amauta (Lima), 1–32 (September 1926 to September 1930), Director, José Carlos Mariátegui.

Caballo Verde para la Poesía (Madrid), 1–4 (October 1935 to January 1936). Director, Pablo Neruda.

Cartel (Montevideo), 1–10 (December 1929 to March 1931). Directors, Julio Sigüenza and Alfredo Mario Ferreiro.

Contemporáneos (Mexico), 1–43 (June 1928 to December 1931).

> Founded by Bernardo Gastélum, Ortiz de Montellano, Torres Bodet, and Enrique González Rojo.

Creación (Madrid), 1–3 (April 1921 to February 1924). Director, Vicente Huidobro.

> Numbers 2–3 published in Paris with the title *Création*.

Favorables París Poema (Paris), 1–2 (June 1926 to October 1926). Directors, Juan Larrea and César Vallejo.

Flechas (Lima), 1–6 (October 1924 to December 1924). Directors, Federico Bolaños and Magda Portal.

Horizonte (Jalapa, Mexico), 1–10 (April 1926 to May 1927). Director, Germán List Arzubide.

Martín Fierro (Buenos Aires), 1–45 (February 1924 to November 1927). Director, Evar Méndez.

Los Nuevos (Bogotá), 1–5 (June–August 1925). Director, Felipe Lleras Camargo.

La Pluma (Montevideo), 1–19 (August 1927 to September 1931). Director, Alberto Zum Felde.

Prisma: Revista Mural (Buenos Aires), 1–2 (December 1921 to March 1922). Director not listed.

Proa (Buenos Aires), 1–2 (August 1922 to July 1923). Director not listed. Second series, 1–15 (August 1924 to January 1926). Directors, Borges, Brandán Caraffa, Ricardo Güiraldes, and Pablo Rojas Paz.

Revista de Avance (Havana), 1–50 (15 March 1927 to 15 September 1930). Founded by Juan Marinello, Jorge Mañach, Francisco Ichaso, Alejo Carpentier, and Martí Casanovas.

Trampolín-Hangar-Rascacielos-Timonel (Lima), 1–4 (1926–1927). Directors, Serafín Delmar and Magda Portal.

> Each issue had a different title, in the order indicated.

Ulises (Mexico), 1–6 (1927–1928). Directors, Xavier Villaurrutia and Salvador Novo.

Secondary sources

Books

Belluzzo, Ana María de Moraes (ed.). *Modernidade: vanguardas artísticas na América Latina*, Sao Paulo, Fundaçao Memorial na América Latina, 1990.

> Proceedings of a symposium on the Avant-Garde in Latin America, including Brazil.

Bradbury, Malcolm, and James McFarlane (eds.). *Modernism 1890–1930*, Harmondsworth, Penguin Books, 1976.

> Extremely useful collection of essays on the European movements and contexts.

Bueno, Raúl. *Poesía hispanoamericana de vanguardia*, Lima, Latinoamericana Editores, 1985.

> Semiotic analysis of avant-garde poetry.

Bürger, Peter. *Theory of the Avant-garde*, tr. Michael Shaw, foreword by Jochen Schulte-Sasse, Minneapolis, University of Minnesota Press, 1984.

A theoretical reconstruction of the social status of art in bourgeois society.

Burgos, Fernando (ed.). *Prosa hispánica de vanguardia*, Madrid, Orígenes, 1986.
Proceedings of a symposium on avant-garde Hispanic prose fiction.

Calinescu, Matei. *Faces of Modernity: Avant-garde, Decadence, Kitsch*, Bloomington, Indiana University Press, 1977.
A cultural approach to modernity.

Castañeda Vielakamen, Esther. *El vanguardismo literario en el Perú (estudio y selección de la revista Flechas)*, Lima, Amaru, 1989.
A study and anthology of *Flechas*, the earliest avant-garde journal.

Collazos, Oscar (ed.). *Los vanguardismos en la América Latina*, Havana, Casa de las Américas, 1970.
Selected essays on the *Vanguardia*.

Costa, René de (ed.). *Vicente Huidobro y el creacionismo*, Madrid, Taurus, 1975.
Useful collection of essays on *Creacionismo*.

Forster, Merlin H., and K. David Jackson. *Vanguardism in Latin American Literature: An annotated bibliographical guide*, Westport, Conn., Greenwood Press, 1990.
An indispensable selective bibliography of avant-garde writing and criticism.

González-Alcantud, José A. *El exotismo en las vanguardias artístico-literarias*, Barcelona, Anthropos, 1989.
Interdisciplinary study on the concept of the exotic in the Avant-Garde.

Howe, Irving (ed.). *Literary Modernism*, Greenwich, Conn., Fawcett, 1967.
Major essays on the idea of the modern.

Huizinga, Johan. *In the Shadow of Tomorrow*, London, Heinemann, 1936.

Mangone, Carlos, and Jorge Warley. *El manifiesto: un género entre el arte y la política*, Buenos Aires, Biblos, 1993.

Masiello, Francine. *Lenguaje e ideología: las escuelas argentinas de vanguardia*, Buenos Aires, Hachette, 1986.
Essential reading on the Argentinian Avant-Garde.

Micheli, Mario de. *Las vanguardias artísticas del siglo XX*, Madrid, Alianza Editorial, 1979.
A Marxist approach to the avant-garde movements.

Müller-Bergh, Klaus. *Poesía de vanguardia y contemporánea*, Madrid, Editorial La Muralla, 1983.
Brief overview of avant-garde and contemporary poetry.

Osorio T., Nelson. *El futurismo y la vanguardia literaria en América Latina*, Caracas, Centro de Estudios Latinoamericanos Rómulo Gallegos, 1982.
Study of the reception of Futurism in Latin America.

La formación de la vanguardia literaria en Venezuela (antecedentes y documentos), Caracas, Academia Nacional de la Historia, 1985.
A key book for the study of the Avant-Garde in Venezuela.

Manifiestos, proclamas y polémicas de la vanguardia literaria hispanoamericana, Caracas, Biblioteca Ayacucho, 1988.
Carefully documented gathering of programmatic and polemical avant-garde texts.

Paz, Octavio. *Los hijos del limo: del romanticismo a la vanguardia*, Barcelona, Seix Barral, 1974.
A classic on modern poetry and its relationship to the idea of the modern.

Children of the Mire: Modern poetry from Romanticism to the Avant-Garde, tr. Rachel Phillips, Cambridge, Mass., Harvard University Press, 1974.

Pérez Firmat, Gustavo. *Idle Fictions: the Hispanic Vanguard novel*, Durham, Duke University Press, 1983.

    Significant study on avant-garde fiction, primarily on Spanish and Mexican narrative.

Perloff, Marjorie. *The Futurist Movement: Avant-garde, avant guerre, and the language of rupture*, University of Chicago Press, 1986.

    Excellent chapter on the manifesto as art form.

Picon Garfield, Evelyn, and Iván A. Schulman. *"Las entrañas del vacío": ensayos sobre la modernidad hispanoamericana*, Mexico, Cuadernos Americanos, 1984.

    Essays on the notion of Spanish American modernity.

Poggioli, Renato. *The Theory of the Avant-Garde*, trans. from the Italian by Gerald Fitzgerald, Cambridge, Mass., Belknap/Harvard University Press, 1968.

    A classic book on the phenomenology of the Avant-Garde, devoted primarily to the sociology and ideology of the movements.

Río de la Plata (Paris), 4–6 (1987).

    Monographic issue on the 1920s in the River Plate region.

Russell, Charles. *Poets, Prophets, and Revolutionaries: the literary Avant-garde from Rimbaud through Postmodernism*, Oxford University Press, 1985.

    A judicious assessment of the history of the literary Avant-Garde and Neo-Avant-Garde.

Sarlo, Beatriz. *Una modernidad periférica: Buenos Aires 1920 y 1930*, Buenos Aires, Ediciones Nueva Visión, 1988.

    An interdisciplinary investigation of the cultural history of Buenos Aires in the 1920s.

Schneider, Luis Mario. *El estridentismo o una literatura de estrategia*, Mexico, INBA, 1970.

    Essential reading on Stridentism.

México y el surrealismo: (1925–1950), Mexico, Arte y Libros, 1978.

    Study of the reception of Surrealism in Mexico.

Schopf, Federico. *Del vanguardismo a la antipoesía*, Rome, Bulzoni, 1986.

    One of the best introductions to avant-garde poetry.

Schwartz, Jorge. *Vanguarda e cosmopolitismo na década de 20: Oliverio Girondo e Oswald de Andrade*, Sao Paulo, Editora Perspectiva, 1983.

    A study of the relationship of the Latin American and Brazilian Avant-Gardes in the 1920s.

Las vanguardias latinoamericanas: textos programáticos y críticos, Madrid, Cátedra, 1991.

    Another anthology of programmatic texts, including Brazil.

Sheridan, Guillermo. *Los 'Contemporáneos' ayer*, Mexico, Fondo de Cultura Económica, 1985.

    A major book on the *Contemporáneos*.

Sucre, Guillermo. *La máscara, la transparencia: ensayos sobre poesía hispanoamericana*, Caracas, Monte Avila, 1975.

    Perceptive readings of the major poets of the period.

Torre, Guillermo de. *Historia de las literaturas de vanguardia*, Madrid, Ediciones

Guadarrama, 1965.

The first history of the international Avant-Garde, originally published in 1925 and revised in 1965.

Unruh, Vicky. *Latin American Vanguards*, Berkeley, University of California Press, 1994.

Verani, Hugo J. *Las vanguardias literarias en Hispanoamérica (manifiestos, proclamas y otros escritos)*, Rome, Bulzoni, 1986; 2nd. edn., Mexico, Fondo de Cultura Económica, 1990; 3rd edn., Mexico, Fondo de Cultura Económica, 1995.

The first extensive anthology and study of the major manifestos and proclamations of the Avant-Garde. All manifestos quoted in this chapter are taken from this edition.

Verani, Hugo J. (ed.). *Narrativa vanguardista hispanoamericana*, selection and prologues Hugo Achugar & Hugo Verani, Mexico, Universidad Nacional Autónoma de México/Ediciones del Equilibrista, 1995.

Videla, Gloria. *El ultraísmo: estudios sobre movimientos poéticos de vanguardia en España*, Madrid, Gredos, 1963.

The first book-length study on Ultraism, mainly on the Spanish movement.

Videla de Rivero, Gloria. *Direcciones del vanguardismo hispanoamericano*, 2 vols., Mendoza, Argentina, Universidad Nacional de Cuyo, Facultad de Filosofía y Letras, 1990; 2nd edn., Pittsburgh, Instituto Internacional de Literatura Iberoamericana, 1994.

Meticulous study of avant-garde poetry and anthology of programmatic texts.

Weisgerber, Jean (ed.). *Les avant-gardes littéraires au XXe siècle*, Budapest, Akadémiai Kiadó, 1984. Vol. I: *History*. Vol. II: *Theory*.

The most comprehensive and informed discussion of the history and theory of the international Avant-Garde, sponsored by the Center for the Study of the Literary Avant-gardes in Brussels. Particularly valuable are the articles by Adrian Marino.

Wentzlaff-Eggebert, Harald. *Las literaturas hispánicas de vanguardia: Orientación bibliográfica*. Frankfurt: Klaus Dieter Vervuert, 1991.

Fundamental bibliography of Spanish and Spanish/American Avant-Garde documents and criticism.

Wentzlaff-Eggebert, Harald (ed.). *La vanguardia europea en el contexto latinoamericano*. Frankfurt: Klaus Dieter Vervuert, 1991.

Papers read in a colloquium in Berlin, including coverage of the Neo-Avant-Garde of the 1980s, and film.

Yurkievich, Saúl. *A través de la trama: sobre vanguardias y otras concomitancias*. Barcelona, Muchnik, 1984.

Suggestive re-examination of the Avant-Garde and related topics.

Articles

Abastado, Claude. "Introduction à l'analyse des manifestes," *Littérature* (Paris), 39 (Oct. 1980), 3–16.

Arellano, Jorge Eduardo. "El movimiento nicaragüense de vanguardia," *Cuadernos Hispanoamericanos*, 468 (June 1989), 7–44.

Burgos, Fernando. "La vanguardia hispanoamericana y la transformación narrativa,"

Nuevo Texto Crítico (Stanford), 2:3 (1989), 157–69.

Campos, Haroldo. "Superación de los lenguajes exclusivos" in César Fernández Moreno (ed.), *América Latina en su literatura*, Mexico, Siglo Veintiuno Editores, 1972, 279–300.

Correa Camiroaga, José. "La vanguardia y la literatura latinoamericana," *Acta Litteraria Academia Scientiarum Hungaricae* (Budapest), 17:1–2 (1975), 55–70.

Enzensberger, Hanz Magnus. "Las aporías de la vanguardia," *Sur* (Buenos Aires), 285 (Nov.–Dec. 1983), 1–23.

Fernández, Teodosio. "Sobre la imagen creacionista," *Cuadernos para la Investigación de la Literatura Hispánica* (Madrid), 8 (1987), 115–22.

Fernández Moreno, César. "Poesía tradicional y poesía de vanguardia," *Boletín de la Academia Argentina de Letras*, 23:89 (1958), 355–97.

Fernández Retamar, Roberto. "Sobre la vanguardia en la literatura latinoamericana" in *Para una teoría de la literatura hispanoamericana*, Mexico, Editorial Nuestro Tiempo, 1977, 135–39.

Flaker, Aleksandar. "Discriminations of the concept of *Avant-garde*" in *Proceedings of the 8th Congress of the International Comparative Literature Association*, vol. 1, Stuttgart, Kunst und Wissen – Erich Bieber, 1980, 925–28.

"Notes sur l'étude de l'avant-garde," *Revue de Littérature Comparée* (Paris), 56:2 (1982), 125–37.

Forster, Merlin H. "Latin American *Vanguardismo*: chronology and terminology" in *Tradition and Renewal*, Urbana, University of Illinois Press, 1975, 12–50.

Goić, Cedomil. "El surrealismo y la literatura iberoamericana," *Revista Chilena de Literatura* (Santiago), 8 (April 1977), 5–34.

Jitrik, Noé. "Papeles de trabajo: notas sobre la vanguardia latinoamericana," *Revista de Crítica Literaria Latinoamericana* (Lima), 8:15 (1982), 13–24.

Marino, Adrian. "L'avant-garde et la 'revolution' du langage poétique," *Cahiers Roumains d'Études Littéraires* (Bucharest), 2 (1975), 92–107.

"Essai d'une définition d'avant-garde," *Revue de l'Université de Bruxelles*, 1 (1975), 64–120.

Mignolo, Walter. "La figura del poeta en la lírica de vanguardia," *Revista Iberoamericana* (Pittsburgh), 118–19 (Jan.–June 1982), 131–48.

Monguió, Luis. "El vanguardismo y la poesía peruana" in *La poesía postmodernista peruana*, Berkeley, University of California Press, 1954, 60–86.

Müller-Bergh, Klaus. "El hombre y la técnica: contribución al conocimiento de corrientes vanguardistasa hispanoamericanas," *Revista Iberoamericana*, 118–19 (Jan.–June 1982), 149–76.

"De Agú y anarquía a la Mandrágora: notas para la génesis, la evolución y el apogeo de la vanguardia en Chile," *Revista Chilena de Literatura*, 31 (1988), 33–61.

Musacchio, Danièle. "Le surréalisme dans la poésie hispano-américaine," *Europe* (Paris), 46:475–6 (1968), 258–84.

Ortega, Julio. "La escritura de vanguardia," *Revista Iberoamericana*, no. 106–7 (Jan.–June 1979), 187–98.

Osorio T., Nelson. "*La tienda de muñecos* de Julio Garmendia en la narrativa de la vanguardia hispanoamericana," *Actualidades* (Caracas), 3–4 (1977–1978), 11–36.

Pacheco, José Emilio. "Nota sobre la otra vanguardia," *Revista Iberoamericana*, 106–

7 (Jan.–June 1979), 327–34.

Pizarro, Ana. "Vanguardismo literario y vanguardia política en América Latina," *El Pez y la Serpiente* (Managua), 24 (Summer 1981), 185–209.

"Sobre la vanguardia en América Latina. Vicente Huidobro," *Revista de Crítica Literaria Latinoamericana*, 8:15 (1982), 171–9.

Quiroz, Emiliano. "Manuel Maples Arce y sus recuerdos del estridentismo," and "La cultura en México," *¡Siempre!*, 483 (May 12, 1971), II.

Rama, Angel. "Medio siglo de narrativa latinoamericana (1922–1972)" in *La novela en América Latina*, Bogotá, Instituto Colombiano de Cultura, 1982, 99–202.

Rincón, Carlos. "Sobre la actualidad de la vanguardia," *Fragmentos* (Caracas), 3 (Feb. 1978), 60–73.

Rivera-Rodas, Oscar. "La estética de la modernidad en el lenguaje poético hispánico," *Revista de Estudios Hispánicos*, 24:3 (1990), 57–85.

Rodríguez Monegal, Emir. "El olvidado ultraísmo uruguayo," *Revista Iberoamericana*, 118–19 (Jan.–June 1982), 257–74.

Romero, Armando. "Ausencia y presencia de las vanguardias en Colombia," *Revista Iberoamericana*, 118–19 (Jan.–June 1982), 275–87.

Sarlo, Beatriz. "Vanguardia y criollismo: la aventura de *Martín Fierro*" in *Ensayos argentinos: de Sarmiento a la vanguardia*, Buenos Aires, CEDAL, 1983, 127–71.

Siebenmann, Gustav. "Modernismos y vanguardia en el mundo ibérico," *Anuario de Letras* (Mexico), 20 (1982), 251–86.

"César Vallejo y la vanguardia," *Hispania*, 72:1 (March 1989), 33–41.

Sucre, Guillermo. "Poesía hispanoamericana y conciencia del lenguaje," *Eco* (Bogotá), 198–200 (April–June 1978), 608–33.

Szabolcsi, Miklós. "Avant-Garde, Neo-Avant-Garde, Modernism: questions and suggestions," *New Literary History*, 3:1 (Autumn 1971), 49–70.

"La 'vanguardia' literaria y artística como fenómeno internacional," *Casa de las Américas*, 13:74 (Sept.–Oct. 1972), 4–17.

Unruh, Vicky. "Mariátegui's aesthetic thought: a critical reading of the Avant-Gardes," *Latin American Research Review*, 24:3 (1989), 45–69.

Verani, Hugo J. "Estrategias de la vanguardia" in Ana Pizarro (ed.), *América Latina: palabra, literatura y cultura*, vol. III, Sao Paulo, Fundação Memorial da América Latina, 1995, 75–87.

"Infrazioni dell'avanguardia" in Dario Puccini and Saúl Yurkievich (eds.), *Storia della civiltà letteria ispanoamericana*, Turin, UTET, in press.

Videla de Rivero, Gloria. "En torno al concepto de la 'vanguardia literaria' y sus matices en Hispanoamérica," *Revista de Literaturas Modernas* (Mendoza, Argentina), 21 (1988), 57–72.

Yurkievich, Saúl. "Los avatares de la vanguardia," *Revista Iberoamericana*, 118–19 (Jan.–June 1982), 351–66.

Chapter 4: *The literature of* Indigenismo

Primary sources

Alegría, Ciro. *El mundo es ancho y ajeno*, Santiago, Ercilla, 1941.

In order to bring traditional communities into the present, the Indian must become conversant with the ruling culture.

Broad and Alien is the World, New York, Farrar & Rinehart, 1941.

Alencar, José de. *Iracema, lenda do Ceará*, Río de Janeiro, Viana & Filho, 1865.

Tale of impossible love between an Indian maiden and a Spanish soldier.

Iracema, the Honey Lips, London, Bickers, 1886.

Aréstegui, Narciso. *El padre Horán, escenas de la vida del Cuzco*, Lima, Imprenta El Comercio, 1848.

Portrait of a lecherous priest, heavily laced with pungent political discourse concerning the Indians.

Arguedas, Alcides. *Raza de bronce*, La Paz, González & Medina, 1919.

A young Indian woman is raped and accidentally killed by the landowner's son and a group of his friends.

Arguedas, José María. *Agua*, Lima, Cía. de Impresiones y Publicidad, 1935.

Author's first collection of short stories showing the Indians' servile position.

Yawar Fiesta, Lima, Cía. de Imprenta y Publicaciones, 1941.

Arguedas's first novel. The expulsion of a community of Indians from their own lands.

Los ríos profundos, Buenos Aires, Editorial Losada, 1958.

Indian world seen through the eyes of a schoolboy from a *ladino* family.

Todas las sangres, Buenos Aires, Editorial Losada, 1964.

Complex and sensitive novel about the imperialist takeover of Peru.

El zorro de arriba y el zorro de abajo, Buenos Aires, Editorial Losada, 1971.

A combination of personal diaries and fiction outlining the destructive effects of foreign industrial exploitation.

Deep Rivers, tr. Frances Horning Barraclough, intro. by John V. Murra, afterword by Mario Vargas Llosa, Austin, University of Texas Press, 1978.

Asturias, Miguel Angel. *Leyendas de Guatemala*, Mexico, Ediciones Oriente, 1930.

Guatemalan folklore heavily imbued with the language of Surrealism and Asturias's unique brand of Magical Realism.

Hombres de maíz, Buenos Aires, Editorial Losada, 1949.

The dispossessed Indian returns to harvest the land after many mishaps. He is identified with the Mayan corn god, Hunahpú, and is portrayed as the begetter of a new breed: the men of maize.

Mulata de tal, Buenos Aires, Editorial Losada, 1963.

Uproarious dramatization of a fantastic folktale: a poor Indian trades off his wife to the devil in exchange for wealth.

Mulata, tr. Gregory Rabassa, New York, Delacorte, 1967.

Men of Maize, tr. Gerald Martin, New York, Dell Publishing, 1975.

Castellanos, Rosario. *Balún canán*, Mexico, Fondo de Cultura Económica, 1957.

Tense relationship between Indians and *ladinos* during the presidency of Lázaro Cárdenas as seen through the eyes of a young girl.

Oficio de tinieblas, Mexico, Mortíz, 1962.

Conflict of cultures in which the Indians resort to secret religious practices as a defense against the abuses of the *ladinos*.

The Nine Guardians, tr. Irene Nicholson, New York, Vanguard Press, 1960.

Castro, Carlo Antonio. "Che Ndu: ejidatario chinanteco," *La Palabra y el Hombre* (Xalapa, Mexico), 8 (1958), 401–26.

Tale of Indian hero who is receptive to the advantages of Western civilization.

Castro Pozo, Hildebrando. *Celajes de sierra*, Lima, Lib. Editorial J. Mejía Baca, 1916.

Short stories revealing the author's experiences after years of contact with Indian communities.

Echeverría, Esteban. "La cautiva," in his *Rimas*, Buenos Aires, Imprenta Argentina, 1837.

Centers on a legendary figure of nineteenth-century Argentina – the white woman who is captured by Indians and forced to become concubine to a chief.

Gallegos, Rómulo. *Canaima*, Barcelona, Casa Editorial Avaluce, 1935.

White man turns his back on Western world and joins Indian community.

Galván, Manuel de Jesús. *Enriquillo, leyenda histórica dominicana*, Santo Domingo, Imprenta de García Hermanos, 1882.

Love of Indian chief, Enriquillo – befriended by Bartolomé de las Casas – for his cousin Mencía, who is half Indian, half Spanish.

García Calderón, Francisco. *Le Pérou contemporain*, Paris, Dujartic et cie., 1907.

García Calderón, Ventura. *La venganza del cóndor*, Mexico, Editorial Mundo Latino, 1924.

Short stories inspired by author's experience as a frustrated prospector roaming through the Andes.

The White Llama, London, Golden Cockerel, 1939.

Gorriti, Juana Manuela. "Si haces mal no esperes bien," Revista de Lima, 1860.

Short story, describing the fatal attraction between half-siblings, which serves as model for Matto's *Aves sin nido*.

Graña, Ladislao. *Sé bueno y serás feliz*, Revista de Lima, vol. II, 1860.

The woeful tale of a kind, hard-working Indian, whose life is practically destroyed by a greedy governor.

Hernández, J. R. *Azcaxochitl o la flecha de oro: leyenda histórica azteca*, Mexico, Barbedillo, 1878.

Romantic idealization set in the fourteenth century at the time of Aztec rule.

Herrera, Flavio. *El tigre*, Guatemala, Editorial Popol-Vuh, 1934.

Indians are found to be riddled with insurmountable defects in this exuberantly baroque epic.

Icaza, Jorge. *Huasipungo*, Quito, Imprenta Nacional, 1934.

Indians revolt against unrelenting repression.

López Albújar, Enrique. *Cuentos andinos*, Lima, Imprenta de La Opinion Nacional, 1920.

Focus on the psychology and behavior of the Indian.

Nuevos cuentos andinos, Santiago, Ercilla, 1937.

The Peruvian judge and author is the first to create "flesh-and-blood" Indian characters.

López y Fuentes, Gregorio. *El Indio*, Mexico, Ediciones Botas, 1935.

Indians who come in contact with *ladinos* and learn their ways end up changing their character as well as their lives: they improve their position but stop thinking about their fellow Indians.

El Indio, Norman, Okla. Ernest Hermann Hespelt, 1940.

Matto de Turner, Clorinda. *Aves sin nido*, Lima, Imprenta del Universo de Carlos Prince, 1889.

A story of Indian life in nineteenth-century rural Peru as seen through the eyes of an upper-class *ladino* family.

Indole, Lima, Tipolitografía Bacigalupi, 1891.

Inspired by *El Padre Horán*, this novel lays bare the mechanisms of the seduction of women by priests.

Herencia, Lima, Imprenta Bacigalupi, 1893.

Brings about resolution to question of *mestizaje* raised in *Aves sin nido*.

Birds Without a Nest. A story of Indian life and priestly oppression in Peru, London, Charles J. Thynne, 1904.

Mendoza, Jaime. *En las tierras del Potosí*, Barcelona, Imprenta Viuda de Luis Tasso, 1911.

Eventful dramatization of the horrible working conditions in Bolivian tin mines.

Mera, Juan León. *Cumandá: o un drama entre salvajes*, Buenos Aires, Espasa-Calpe, 1951.

A pastiche of Chateaubriand's *René*. A beautiful Indian maiden falls in love with the son of a landowner, who becomes a priest.

Monteforte Toledo, Mario. *Entre la piedra y la cruz*, Guatemala, Editorial "El Libro de Guatemala," 1948.

Story of a poor and honest Indian who is schooled in the city and strays from the path and destiny of his people.

Pozas, Ricardo. *Juan Pérez Jolote. Biografía de un tzotzil*, Mexico, Fondo de Cultura Económica, 1948.

Portrait of a Tzotzil Indian's social life as he comes in contact with Western civilization.

Rodríguez, Alberto. *Donde haya Dios*. Buenos Aires, Lautaro, 1955.

Rubín, Ramón. *El callado dolor de los Tzotziles*, Mexico, Costa Amic, 1949.

Ladino society destroys the Indian and his way of life.

La bruma lo vuelve azul, Mexico, Fondo de Cultura Económica, 1954.

Realistic portrayal of Indians' identity crisis as they are torn between two cultures.

Sarmiento, Domingo Faustino. *Civilización i barbarie: vida de Juan Facundo Quiroga, aspecto físico, costumbres i ábitos de la República Argentina*, Santiago, El Progreso, 1845.

How savagery becomes an institution in Argentina during Rozas's regime.

Facundo: Life in the Argentine republic in the days of the tyrants, New York, Hurd & Houghton, 1868.

Scorza, Manuel, *Historia de Garabombo el invisible*, Barcelona, Planeta, 1972.

Stirring and humorous fictionalization of the real-life events of the Indian massacre perpetrated by government troops in Rancas, Peru, in 1962.

Redoble por Rancas, Barcelona, Planeta, 1970.

The community of Rancas is swallowed up by a zoomorphic fence that symbolizes the voracious Cerro de Pasco Corporation.

Cantar de Agapito Robles, Espluges de Llobregat, Plaza & Janes Editores, 1976.

Agapito, the hero of this saga, continues the struggle against oppression that begins to be told in the first installment of "La Guerra Silenciosa"; under his command, the rivers in the land begin to flow once again.

El Jinete insomne, Espluges de Llobregat, Plaza & Janes Editores, 1976.
   A portrait of the community of Yanacocha, Peru, in which reality and invention are freely mixed.
La tumba del relámpago, Mexico, Siglo XXI, 1979.
   Conclusion of "La Guerra Silenciosa" and a more blatant injunction than preceding works in the series; the author appears as a character in the action.
Torres y Lara, Jose T. (Itolararres). *La trinidad del Indio o costumbres del interior*, Lima, Imprenta Bolognesi, 1885.
   Acrimonious study of the "trinity" that exploits the Indian in a small Andean town: the priest, the judge, and the governor.
Wyld Ospina, Carlos. *La gringa*, Guatemala, Tip. Nacional, 1933.
   Tale of *criollo* life in which Indians appear merely as background color.
La tierra de los Nahuyacas, Guatemala, Editorial del Ministerio de Educación Pública, 1957.
   Striking and sympathetic portrayal of Kecchi Indians.
Zepeda, Eraclio. *Benzulul*, Xalapa, Mexico, Universidad Veracruzana, 1959.
   Collection of short stories written from the Indians' point of view.

Secondary sources

Books

Ahern, Maureen, and Mary Seale Vázquez. *Homenaje a Rosario Castellanos*, Spain, Albatross Hispanófila Ediciones, 1980.
   Good collection of essays providing biographical information as well as useful critical insights.
Brushwood, John S. *Mexico in its Novel: A nation's search for identity*, San Antonio, University of Texas Press, 1966.
   Enlightening study dwelling on the relationship between literature, culture, and economics.
Castelpoggi, Atilio. *Miguel Angel Asturias*, Buenos Aires, Ed. "La Mandrágora," 1960.
Cornejo Polar, Antonio. *Literatura y sociedad en el Perú: la novela indigenista*, Lima, Lasontay, 1980.
   The best and most lucid synthesis of *Indigenismo*. Lacks bibliography.
Los universos narrativos de José María Arguedas, Buenos Aires, Editorial Losada, 1981.
   An invaluable critical study of one of the key figures of Peruvian *Indigenismo*.
Escajadillo, Tomás G. "La narrativa indigenista: un planteamiento y ocho incisiones," doctoral diss., Universidad Nacional Mayor de San Marcos, 1971.
   Good synthesis of the theme; particularly useful for its categorizing system of the literature portraying the Indian.
Franco, Jean. *The Modern Culture of Latin America*, London, Pall Mall, 1967.
   Broad overview of Latin American culture in the twentieth century.
Harss, Luis. *Los Nuestros*, Buenos Aires, Sudamericana, 1978.
   Invaluable essays on key figures of twentieth-century Latin American literature including Asturias and J. M. Arguedas.

Kristal, Efraín. *The Andes Viewed from the City: Literary and political discourse on the Indian in Peru (1848–1930)*, New York, Bern, Frankfurt-am-Main, Paris, Peter Lang, 1987.

Authoritative study of Peruvian *Indigenismo* highlighting the nexus between the country's economic development and its literary production. Contains a good number of fresh insights that go against long-established opinions.

Lorand de Olazagasti, Adelaida. *El Indio en la narrativa guatemalteca*, San Juan, Puerto Rico, Editorial Universitaria, 1968.

Broad but useful overview of *Indianismo* and *Indigenismo* in Guatemala.

Mariátegui, José Carlos. *Siete ensayos de interpretación de la realidad peruana*, Lima, Amauta, 1928.

Classic and very important study; particularly useful for information on the social and political situation in Peru.

Seven interpretive essays on Peruvian reality, tr. Marjory Urquidi, Austin, University of Texas Press, 1971.

Martin, Gerald. *Miguel Angel Asturias, Hombres de Maíz, Edición crítica de las obras completas*, Paris and Mexico, Klincksieck, 1981.

Fully annotated critical study of this crucial novel preceded by informative essays written by Martin, Vargas Llosa, *et al*. Contains appendix, notes, glossary, and bibliography.

Meléndez, Concha. *La novela Indianista en Hispanoamérica (1832–1889)*, Madrid, Editorial Hernando, 1934.

Foundational study of *Indianismo* focusing on twenty-four novels.

Menton, Seymour. *Historia crítica de la novela guatemalteca*, Guatemala, Editorial Universitaria, 1960.

Useful and well-documented overview.

Ortega, Julio. *Ventura García Calderón*, Biblioteca Hombres del Perú, 37, Lima, Editorial Universitaria.

Rama, Angel. *Transculturación narrativa en América Latina*, Mexico, Siglo XXI, 1982.

Important study of *Indigenismo*, focusing on the work of José María Arguedas in the last chapters.

Rodríguez-Luis, Julio. *Hermeneútica y praxis del indigenismo: la novela indigenista de Clorinda Matto a José María Arguedas*, Mexico, Fondo de Cultura Económica, 1980.

A useful and extremely well-documented history of the movement in Peru.

Rojas, Ricardo. *Eurindia, ensayo de estética sobre las culturas americanas*, Buenos Aires, Editorial Losada, 1951.

Culture cannot be transplanted; Latin American genius withers because it identifies with Europe and not with its own roots which are in the land.

Sáenz, Jimena. *Genio y figura de Miguel Angel Asturias*, Buenos Aires, EUDEBA, 1974.

Studies the work of the Guatemalan Nobel Prize winner from a biographical perspective. Preceded by useful chronology.

Urrello, Antonio. *José María Arguedas: el nuevo rostro del indio. Una estructura mítico-poética*, Lima, Juan Mejía Baca, 1974.

Useful insights into the work of Peruvian author; ranges beyond narrow theme suggested by title.

Vargas Llosa, Mario. *Entre sapos y halcones*, Madrid, Ediciones Culturales Hispánicas del Centro Iberoamericano de Cooperación, 1978.

Insightful description of Arguedas's invention of reality. A look at violence and sexuality in his work.

Villoro, Luis. *Los grandes momentos del indigenismo en México*, El Colegio de Mexico, 1950.

Emphasis on sociological and ontological problems of Indians and mestizos.

Articles

Arias-Larreta, Abraham. "Definición del indigenismo peruano," *La Nueva Democracia* (1956), 36–42.

Overview of *Indigenismo* in Peru with emphasis on the country's political situation.

Bourricaud, François. "Algunas características originales de la cultura mestiza en el Perú contemporáneo," *Revista del Museo Nacional*, Lima, 23 (1954), 162–73.

The rise of the mestizo seen from a sociological and ethnological perspective.

Chang-Rodríguez, Eugenio. "El indigenismo peruano y Mariátegui," *Revista Iberoamericana*, 50 (1984), 367–93.

Thoroughly researched and documented. Mariátegui's process of conversion to *Indigenismo*.

Crumley de Pérez, Laura Lee. "*Balún canán* y la construcción narrativa de una cosmovisión indígena," *Revista Iberoamericana*, 50 (1984), 491–503.

Role of the author/narrator in the conception of the novel.

De Beer, Gabriella. "Ramón Rubín y *El callado dolor de los tzotziles*," *Revista Iberoamericana*, 50 (1984), 559–68.

Lucid analysis highlighting the "scientific" emphasis of Mexican post-Revolutionary novels that portray the Indian.

Kristal, Efraín. "Problemas filológicos e históricos en *Páginas libres* de Manuel González Prada," *Revista de Crítica Literaria Latinoamericana*, 11:23 (1986), 141–50.

Points out shortcomings of recent edition of *Páginas libres*, with a prologue by Luis Alberto Sánchez.

Lienhard, Martin. "La legitimación indígena en dos novelas centroamericanas," *Cuadernos Hispanoamericanos*, 414 (1984), 110–20.

Highly controversial and fascinating study of *Hombres de maíz* and *Balún canán*.

Menton, Seymour. "La novela del indio y las corrientes literarias" in D. Bleznick and Juan Valencia (eds.), *Homenaje a Luis Leal, Estudios sobre literatura latinoamericana*, Madrid, Insula, 1978.

Records and synthesizes presence of indigenous element in Latin American literature.

Moraña, Mabel. "Función ideológica de la fantasía en las novelas de Manuel Scorza," *Revista de Crítica Literaria Latinoamericana*, 17 (1983), 171–92.

Indispensable for understanding the role of fantasy in the fiction of the Peruvian author.

Portal, Marta. "Narrativa indigenista mexicana de mediados de siglo," *Cuadernos*

Hispanoamericanos, 298 (1975), 196–207.

Interesting analysis of Mexican authors whose work is in many ways a response to the reforms enacted by Lázaro Cárdenas.

Rodríguez Chicharro, César. "Carlo Antonio Castro: *Los hombres verdaderos*," *La Palabra y el Hombre* (Xalapa, Mexico), 11 (1959), 504–9.

Nexus between ethnology and literature as shown in Castro's novel.

Sánchez, Luis Alberto. "El indianismo literario, ¿tendencia original o imitativa?," *Revista Nacional de Cultura* (Jan–Feb. 1960), 107–17.

Distinction between *Indianismo* and *Indigenismo*.

Sommers, Joseph. "Changing views of the Indian in Mexican literature," *Hispania*, 47 (1964), 47–55.

The Mexican novel of the 1930s condemns the way Indians are plundered, but does so with a paternalistic attitude similar to Ventura García Calderón's in Peru. The Indian is prisoner of a culture which keeps him ignorant so he must be viewed from the outside by non-Indian narrators.

"El ciclo de Chiapas: nueva corriente literaria," *Cuadernos Americanos*, 133:2 (1964), 246–61.

Essential for understanding this very important literary current in Mexico.

"The indian-oriented novel in Latin America: new spirit, new forms, new scope," *Journal of Inter-American Studies*, 6:2 (1964), 249–65.

Fine example of new critical direction in scholarship regarding *Indigenismo*.

Tamayo, José Armando. "Persistencia del indigenismo en la narrativa peruana," *Cuadernos Hispanoamericanos*, 117–18 (1979), 367–77.

Literary *Indigenismo* from Aréstegui to Scorza.

Tauro, Alberto. "Antecedentes y filiación de la novela indianista," *Mar del sur* (Nov. 1948), 29–40.

Focus on early phases of Peruvian *Indigenismo*. Refers to *Aves sin nido* as the first "*indianista*" novel in Peru.

Urrello, Antonio. "Antecedentes al neoindigenismo," *Cuadernos Hispanoamericanos*, 286 (1974), 23–4.

How the child narrator of *Los ríos profundos* opens the reader's eyes to a new perspective of the Indian world.

Chapter 5: Afro-Hispanic American literature

Primary sources

Albornoz, Aurora de, and Julio Rodríguez-Luis (eds.). *Sensemayá: la poesía negra en el mundo hispanohablante*, Madrid, Orígenes, 1980.

Arozarena, Marcelino. *Canción negra sin color*, Havana, Ediciones Unión, 1966.

Artel, Jorge. *Tambores en la noche: 1931–1934*, Bogotá, Ediciones Bolívar, 1940.

Poemas con botas y banderas, Barranquilla, Ediciones Universidad del Atlántico, 1972.

Antología poética: 1931–1943, Bogotá, Ediciones Ecoe, 1979.

No es la muerte, es el morir, Bogotá, Ediciones Ecoe, 1979.

Ballagas, Emilio. *Cuaderno de poesía negra*, Havana, Imprenta "La Nueva," 1934.

Ballagas, Emilio (ed.). *Antología de la poesía negra hispanoamericana*, Madrid,

Bolaños & Aguilar, 1935.

Mapa de la poesía negra americana, Buenos Aires, Editorial Pleamar, 1946.

Barrios, Pilar. *Piel negra. Poesías (1917–1947)*, Montevideo, Nuestra Raza, 1947.

Mis cantos, Montevideo, Comité Amigos del Poeta, 1949.

Campo afuera, Montevideo, Publicaciones Minerva, 1959.

Bernard, Eulalia. *Ritmohéroe*, San José, Editorial Costa Rica, 1982.

Brindis de Salas, Virginia. *Pregón de Marimorena*, Montevideo, Sociedad Cultural Editora Indoamericana, 1946.

Cien cárceles de amor, Montevideo, Compañía Impresora, 1949.

Cabrera Infante, Guillermo. *Tres tristes tigres*, Barcelona: Seix Barral, 1968.

Three Trapped Tigers, tr. Suzanne Jill Levine, New York, Harper & Row, 1971.

Carpentier, Alejo. *Obras completas de Alejo Carpentier*, vol. 1, Mexico, Siglo Veintiuno Editores, 1983.

Cofiño López, Manuel. *Cuando la sangre se parece al fuego*, Havana, UNEAC, 1975.

Cyrus, Stanley (ed.). *El cuento negrista sudamericano. Antología*, Quito, Editorial Casa de la Cultural Ecuatoriana, 1973.

Díaz Sánchez, Ramón. *Mené* (1936), Caracas, Avila Gráfica, 1950.

Cumboto (1950), Santiago, Editorial Universitaria, 1967.

Cumboto, tr. John Upton, Austin, University of Texas Press, 1969.

Diez-Canseco, José. *Estampas mulatas*, Lima, Populibros Peruanos, 1967. Enlarged edn., Editorial Universo, 1973.

Duncan, Quince. *Una canción en la madrugada*, San José, Editorial Costa Rica, 1970.

Hombres curtidos, San José, Editorial Territorio, 1971.

Los cuatro espejos, San José, Editorial Costa Rica, 1973.

La rebelión pocomía y otros relatos, San José, Editorial Costa Rica, 1976.

La paz del pueblo, San José, Editorial Costa Rica, 1978.

Final de calle, San José, Editorial Costa Rica, 1979.

Estupiñán Bass, Nelson. *Canto negro por la luz. Poemas para negros y blancos*, Esmeraldas, Ediciones del Núcleo Provincial de Esmeraldas de la Casa de la Cultura Ecuatoriana, 1954.

Cuando los guayacanes florecían, Quito, Casa de la Cultura Ecuatoriana, 1954.

Timarán y Cuabú: cuaderno de poesía para el pueblo, Quito, Casa de la Cultura Ecuatoriana, 1956.

El paraíso, Quito, Casa de la Cultura Ecuatoriana, 1958.

El último río, Quito, Casa de la Cultura Ecuatoriana, 1966.

Senderos brillantes, Quito, Casa de la Cultura Ecuatoriana, 1974.

Las puertas del verano, Quito, Casa de la Cultura Ecuatoriana, 1978.

Toque de queda, Guayaquíl, Casa de la Cultura Ecuatoriana, 1978.

El desempate: cuaderno de poesía para el pueblo, Portoviejo, Editorial Gregorio, 1980.

Bajo el cielo nublado, Quito, Casa de la Cultura Ecuatoriana, 1981.

Las 2 caras de la palabra, Quito, Ediciones Contragolpe, 1982.

El crepúsculo, Quito, Editora Nacional, 1992.

Los canarios pintaron el aire de amarillo, Ciudadela El Olivo: Editorial Universitaria, Universidad Técnica del Norte, 1993.

When the Guayacans Were in Bloom, tr. Henry J. Richards, Washington, Afro-Hispanic Institute, 1987.

Pastrana's Last River, tr. Ian Isidore Smart, Washington, D.C., Afro-Hispanic Institute, 1993.

Franco, José Luciano. *La diáspora africana en el nuevo mundo*, Havana, Editorial Ciencias Sociales, 1975.

González, José Luis, and Mónica Mansour (eds.). *Poesía negra de América*, Mexico, Ediciones Era, 1976.

González Pérez, Armando (ed.). *Poesía afrocubana última*, Milwaukee, Center for Latin America, University of Wisconsin, 1975.

Guillén, Nicolás. *Motivos de son*, Havana, Rambla & Bouza, 1930.

Sóngoro Cosongo. Poemas mulatos, Havana, Imprenta Ucar, García & Cía., 1931.

West Indies, Ltd., Havana, Imprenta Ucar, García, & Cía., 1934.

Cantos para soldados y sones para turistas, Mexico, Editorial Masas, 1937.

El son entero: suma poética, 1929–1946, Buenos Aires, Pleamar, 1947.

La paloma de vuelo popular, elegías, Buenos Aires, Editorial Losada, 1958.

El diario que a diario, Havana, UNEAC, 1972.

La rueda dentada, Havana, Instituto Cubano del Libro, 1972.

Obra poética (1920–1972), 2 vols., Havana, Editorial Arte y Literatura, 1974.

Prosa de prisa, 1929–1972, 3 vols., Havana, Editorial Arte y Literatura, 1976.

Cuba libre; poems by Nicolás Guillén, tr. Langston Hughes and Ben Frederic Carruthers, Los Angeles, The Ward Ritchie Press, 1948.

Man-Making Words: Selected Poems of Nicolás Guillén, tr. Robert Márquez and David A. McMurray, Amherst, University of Massachusetts Press, 1972.

¡Patria o muerte! The Great Zoo and other poems by Nicolás Guillén, ed., tr., and intro., Roberto Márquez, New York and London, Monthly Review Press, 1972.

Tengo, tr. Richard J. Carr, Detroit, Broadside Press, 1974.

The Daily Daily, tr. Vera M. Kutzinski, Los Angeles, University of California Press, 1989.

Guirao, Ramón (ed.). *Orbita de la poesía afrocubana 1928–1937*, Havana, Imprenta Ucar, García & Cía., 1938.

Jiménez, Blas R. *Caribe africano en despertar*, Santo Domingo: Nuevas Rutas, 1984.

Latino, Simón (ed.). *Los mejores versos de la poesía negra*, Buenos Aires, Cuadernos de Poesía, n. 23, 1963.

Llorens Torres, Luis. *Sonetos sinfónicos*, San Juan de P. R., Compañía Editorial Antillana, 1914.

López Albujar, Enrique. *De la tierra brava; poemas afroyungas*, Lima, Editora Peruana, 1938.

Manzano, Juan Francisco. *Autobiografía, cartas y versos de Juan Fco. Manzano*, ed. José Luciano Franco, Havana, Municipio de La Habana, 1937.

Autobiografía de un esclavo, ed. Ivan Schulman, Madrid, Ediciones Guadarrama, 1975.

Poems by a Slave in the Island of Cuba, Recently Liberated; Translated from the Spanish, by Richard R. Madden, M.D., with the History of the early Life of the Negro Poet, Written by Himself; to which are prefixed two Pieces Descriptive of Cuban Slavery and the Slave Traffic, by Richard R. Madden, London, T. Ward & Co., 1840.

Reprint: ed. Edward J. Mullen, Hamden, Conn., Archon Books, 1981.

Martínez, Gregorio. *Canto de sirena*, Lima, Mosca Azul Editores, 1976.

Mondéjar, Publio L. (ed.). *Poesía de la negritud*, Madrid, Editorial Fundamentos, 1972.

Morales, Jorge Luis (ed.). *Poesía afroantillana y negrista: Puerto Rico, República Domínica, Cuba*, Río Piedras, Editorial Universitaria, Universidad de Puerto Rico, 1976.

Morejón, Nancy. *Amor, cuidad atribuida*, Havana, UNEAC, 1964.

 Grenada Notebook (Cuaderno de Granada), tr. Lisa Davis, bilingual edn., New York, Círculo de Cultura Cubana, 1984.

 Where the Island Sleeps Like a Wing. Selected Poetry by Nancy Morejón, tr. Kathleen Weaver, San Francisco, Black Scholar Press, 1985.

Morúa Delgado, Martín. *Sofía*, Havana, Imprenta de A. Alvarez & Cía., 1891.

 La familia Unzúazu, Havana, La Prosperidad, 1901.

Noble, Enrique (ed.). *Literatura afro-hispanoamericana: poesía y prosa de ficción*, Lexington, Mass., Xerox Publishing, 1973.

Obeso, Candelario. *Cantos populares de mi tierra*, Bogotá, Imprenta de Borda, 1877. Reprinted in Amir Smith Córdoba (ed.), *Vida y obra de Candelario Obeso*, Bogotá, Centro para la Investigación de la Cultura Negra, 1984.

Ortiz, Adalberto. *Juyunqo. Historia de un negro, una isla y otros negros*, Buenos Aires, Editorial Americalee, 1943.

 Camino y puerta de la angustia: poemas, Mexico, Islas, 1945.

 Tierra, son y tambor: cantares negros y mulatos, Mexico, La Cigarra, 1945.

 El animal herido. Poesía completa, Quito, Casa de la Cultura Ecuatoriana, 1959.

 El espejo y la ventana, Quito, Casa de la Cultura Ecuatoriana, 1967.

 La entundada y cuentos variados, Quito, Casa de la Cultura Ecuatoriana, 1971.

 Fórmulas, El vigilante insepulto, Tierra, son y tambor, Quito, Casa de la Cultura Ecuatoriana, 1973.

 La envoltura del sueño, Núcleo de Guayas, Casa de la Cultura Ecuatoriana, 1982.

 Juyungo. A classic Afro-Hispanic novel by Adalberto Ortiz, tr. Susan F. Hill and Jonathan Tittler, Washington, Three Continents Press, 1982.

Ortiz, Fernando. *Hampa afrocubana. Los negros brujos (Apuntes para un estudio de etnología criminal)*, Madrid, Libraría de F. Fé, 1906.

 Glosario de afronegrismos, Havana, Imprenta "El Siglo XX," 1924.

 Ensayos etnográficos, ed. Miguel Barnet and Angel Fernández, Havana, Editorial de Ciencias Sociales, 1984.

Palacios, Arnoldo. *Las estrellas son negras*, Bogotá, Editorial Iqueima, 1949.

 La selva y la lluvia, Moscow, Ediciones en Lenguas Extranjeras, 1958.

Palés Matos, Luis. *Tuntún de pasa y grifería: poemas afroantillanos*, San Juan: Biblioteca de Autores Puertorriqueños, 1937.

 Obras, ed. Margot Arce de Vásquez, Río Piedras: Editorial de la Universidad de Puerto Rico, 1984.

Pedrozo, Regino. *Nosotros*, Havana, Editorial Trópico, 1933.

 Antología poética (1918–1938), Havana, Municipio de la Habana, 1939.

Pereda Valdés, Ildefonso. *La guitarra de los negros*, Montevideo, n.p., 1926.

 Raza negra, Montevideo, n.p., 1929.

Pereda Valdés, Ildefonso (ed.). *Antología de la poesía negra americana*, Santiago, Ediciones Ercilla, 1936.

Preciado Bedoya, Antonio. *Jolgorio: poemas*, Quito, Casa de la Cultura Ecuatoriana,

1961.

Tal como somos, Quito, Ediciones Siglo XX, 1969.

De sol a sol, Quito, Círculo de Lectores, 1979.

Canción testimonial, Esmeraldas, Banco Central de Ecuador, 1986.

Ruiz del Vizo, Hortensia (ed.). *Black Poetry of the Americas*, 2 vols., Miami, Ediciones Universal, 1972.

Poesía negra del caribe y otras áreas, Miami, Ediciones Universal, 1972.

Salazar Valdés, Hugo. *Dimensiones de la tierra (1947–1952)*, Popayán, Colombia, Universidad del Cauca, 1952.

Toda la voz, Bogotá, Imprenta Nacional, 1958.

Pleamar: poemas, Cali, Departamento del Valle, 1975.

Rostro iluminado del Chocó, Cali, Impresión Feriva, 1980.

Santa Cruz Gamarra, Nicomedes. *Décimas*, Lima, Editorial Juan Mejia Baca, 1959.

Décimas, Lima, Editorial Juan Mejía Baca, 1960.

Cumanana: décimas de pie forzado y poemas, Lima, Editorial Juan Mejia Baca, 1964.

Canto a mi Perú, Lima, Libreria Studium, 1966.

Décimas y poemas: antología, Lima, Campodonico Ediciones, 1971.

Ritmos negros del Perú, Buenos Aires, Editorial Losada, 1971.

Santa Cruz Gamarra, Nicomedes (ed.). *La décima en el Perú*, Lima, Instituto de Estudios Peruanos, 1982.

Has a long, very detailed, historical introduction.

Sanz y Díaz, José (ed.). *Lira negra. Selecciones afroamericanas y españolas*, Madrid, Aguilar, 1945.

Sojo, Juan Pablo. *Nochebuena negra*, Caracas, Editorial General Rafael Urdaneta, 1943.

Temas y apuntes afro-venezolanos, Caracas, Tip. La Nación, 1943.

Toruño, Juan Felipe (ed.). *Poesía negra. Ensayo y antología*, Mexico, Obsidiana, 1953.

Truque, Carlos Arturo. *La Granizada y otros cuentos*, Bogotá, Editorial Espiral, 1953.

El día que terminó el verano y otros relatos, Bogotá, Instituto Colombiano de Cultura, 1973.

Valdés, Gabriel de la Concepción (Plácido). *Poesías completas*, ed. Sebastián Alfredo de Morales, Havana, Librería y Efectos de Escritorio, 1886.

Los poemas más representativos de Plácido, ed. Frederick Stimson and Humberto Robles, Chapel Hill, Estudios de Hispanófila, 1976.

Valdés Cruz, Rosa E. (ed.). *La poesía negroide en América*, New York, Las Américas, 1970.

Vasconcelos, José. *El Negrito Poeta Mexicano y sus populares versos*, ed. Nicolás León, Mexico, Imprenta del Museo Nacional, 1912.

Wilson, Carlos Guillermo (Cubena). *Cuentos del negro Cubena*, Guatemala, Editorial Landívar, 1977.

Pensamientos del negro Cubena, Los Angeles, n.p., 1977.

Chombo, Miami, Ediciones Universal, 1981.

Short Stories By Cubena, tr. Ian I. Smart, Washington, DC, Afro-Hispanic Institute, 1987.

Zapata Olivella, Juan. *Bullanguero: poesía popular*, Bogotá, Ediciones Tercer

Mundo, 1974.

Panacea: poesía liberada, Cartagena, Editora Bolívar, 1976.

La hamaca soñadora: poemarios infantiles, Cartagena, Heliografo Moderno, 1979.

El color en la poesía, Port-au-Prince, Haiti, Imprimérie Le Natal, 1982.

Historia de un joven negro, Port-au-Prince, Edición Haitiana Le Natal, 1983.

Pisando el camino de ébano, Bogotá, Ediciones Lerner, 1984.

Zapata Olivella, Manuel. *Tierra mojada*, Bogotá, Editorial Espiral, 1947.

La pasión vagabunda (relatos), Bogotá, Editorial Santa Fé, 1949.

He visto la noche (relatos), Bogotá, Editorial Andes, 1953.

Hotel de vagabundos (drama), Bogotá, Editorial Espiral, 1955.

La calle 10, Bogotá, Ediciones Casa de la Cultura, 1960.

Cuentos de muerte y libertad, Bogotá, Colección Narradores Colombianos de Hoy, 1961.

Corral de negros, Havana, Casa de las Américas, 1963. Published in 1967 as *Chambacú: corral de negros*, Medellín, Editorial Bedout. The two editions are not identical.

Detrás del rostro, Madrid, Aguilar, 1963.

En Chima nace un santo (1963); Barcelona, Seix Barral, 1964.

¿Quién dió el fusil a Oswald?, Bogotá, Editorial Revista Colombiana, 1967.

Changó, el gran putas, Bogotá, Editorial La Oveja Negra, 1983.

El fusilamiento del diablo, Bogotá, Editorial Plaza & Janes, 1986.

¡Levántate Mulato! Por mi raza hablará el espíritu, Bogotá, Rei Andes Ltda., 1990.

Changó, el gran putas, first critical edn., Bogotá, Rei Andes Ltda., 1992.

Chambacú: Black slum, tr. Jonathan Tittler, Pittsburgh, Penn., Latin American Literary Review Press, 1989.

A Saint is Born in Chimá, tr. Thomas Kooreman, Austin, University of Texas Press, 1991.

Secondary sources

Books

Aguirre, Mirta. *Un poeta y un continente*, Havana, Editorial Letras Cubanas, 1982.
  Collection of her essays on Guillén (1948–1979).

Angier, Angel. *Nicolás Guillén, notas para un estudio biográfico-crítico*, 2 vols., Santa Clara, Universidad Central de las Villas, 1962–1964.
  Detailed account of Guillén's biography and literary career to 1934 (vol. I) from 1934 to 1948 (vol. II).

Belrose, Maurice. *Présence du noir dans le roman vénézuélien*, Paris, Editions Caribéennes, 1981.
  Thorough survey of the image of Blacks and mulattoes from *Peonía* (1890) to *Cumboto* (1950).

Benítez Rojo, Antonio. *La isla que se repite: El Caribe y la perspectiva posmoderna*, Hanover, N.H., Ediciones del Norte, 1989. *The Repeating Island: The Caribbean and the postmodern perspective*, tr. James Maraniss, Durham, N.C., Duke University Press, 1992.
  Interesting attempt to theorize about "Caribbeanness" that suffers from its

neglect of race and gender issues.

Biblioteca Nacional "José Martí." *Bibliografía de Nicolás Guillén*, Havana, Instituto Cubano del Libro, 1975.

Bueno, Salvador. *El negro en la novela hispanoamericana*, Havana, Editorial Letras Cubanas, 1986.

> Examines "representative" nineteenth- and twentieth-century novels from historical, social, and political perspectives.

Caraballo, Vicente. *El negro Obeso. Apuntes biográficos y escritos varios*, Bogotá, Editorial ABC, 1943.

> Mostly anecdotal reconstruction of Obeso's life and the controversial circumstances of his death. Includes a brief analysis of his poetry.

Cartey, Wilfred. *Black Images*, New York, Teachers' College Press, Columbia University, 1970.

> Compares the image of Blacks in Hispanic and French Caribbean poetry. Extensive comments on Guillén, Palés Matos, and Ballagas.

Cobb, Martha K. *Harlem, Haiti and Havana. A comparative critical study of Langston Hughes, Jacques Roumain, and Nicolás Guillén*, Washington, Three Continents Press, 1979.

> Focuses on "influence relations" between these three writers.

Colloque Négritude at Amérique Latine (eds.). *Négritude et Amérique Latine*, Dakar, Senegal, Les Nouvelles Editions Africaines, 1974.

> Conference papers and transcriptions of panel discussions. Participants include Ildefonso Pereda Valdés, Nicomedes Santa Cruz, and Manuel Zapata Olivella.

Coulthard, Gabriel R. *Race and Colour in Caribbean Literature*, London, Oxford University Press, 1962. First published as *Raza y color en la literatura antillana* in 1958.

> Comparative, largely thematic analysis of anglophone, francophone, and Hispanic Caribbean texts from the nineteenth and twentieth centuries.

Cuadernos Hispanoamericanos, special issue on "Los negros en América," 451–2 (1988).

> Includes essays on Afro-Hispanic religion, music, literature, and history, from Cuba, Puerto Rico, Dominica, Peru, and Chile.

DeCosta, Miriam (ed.). *Blacks in Hispanic Literature: Critical essays*, Port Washington, N.Y., Kennikat Press, 1977.

> First attempt to structure a new critical framework for Afro-Hispanic literature.

Duncan, Quince. *El negro en la literatura costarriquense*, San José, Editorial Costa Rica, 1975.

> Brief introductory overview.

Duncan, Quince, and Carlos Meléndez (eds.). *El negro en Costa Rica*, San José, Editorial Costa Rica, 1972.

> Collection of literary, historical, anthropological, and sociological essays.

Ellis, Keith. *Cuba's Nicolás Guillén: Poetry and ideology*, University of Toronto Press, 1983.

> Attempts to show ideological consistency in Guillén poetry from *Motivos de son* to *El diario que a diario*.

Fernández de Castro, José Antonio. *El tema negro en las letras de Cuba (1608–1935)*, Havana, Editorial Mirador, 1943.

Studies the work of black writers and journalists from Manzano and Plácido to Guillén.

Fernández de la Vega, Oscar, and Alberto Pamies, *Iniciación a la poesía afro-americana*, Miami, Ediciones Universal, 1973.

Historical study of "black poetry" in Hispanic America. Useful reference work.

Fernández Retamar, Roberto. *El son de vuelo popular*, Havana, Editorial Unión, 1972.

Includes three essays on Guillén's poetry.

Fernández Robaína, Tomás. *Bibliografía sobre estudios afro-americanos*, Havana, Biblioteca Nacional "José Martí," 1968.

González Echevarría, Roberto (ed.). *Latin American Literary Review*, special issue on Hispanic Caribbean literature, 8 (1980).

Includes a detailed introduction (in part devoted to the Cuban *son*), and translations of Carpentier's *El milagro de Anaquillé* and "Histoire de lunes."

Habibe, Frederick Henrik. *El compromiso en la poesía afroantillana de Cuba y Puerto Rico*, Curaçao, 1985.

Analyzes Afro-Antillean poetry from the perspective of politically "compromised" literature. Offers detailed historical comments on early twentieth-century Cuba and Puerto Rico.

Jackson, Richard L. *The Black Image in Latin American Literature*, Albuquerque, University of New Mexico Press, 1976.

Surveys representations of Blacks in Afro-Hispanic poetry and fiction from the early nineteenth century to the present. Regards *mestizaje* as a particular manifestation of racism.

Black Writers in Latin America, Albuquerque, University of New Mexico Press, 1979.

Predominantly thematic, chronological survey of the development of black self-consciousness in the poetry and fiction of Afro-Hispanic writers since the eighteenth century. Laments the absence of a "black aesthetic" even in the contemporary texts.

The Afro-Spanish American Author. An annotated bibliography of criticism, New York, Garland, 1980.

The most extensive, though by no means complete, bibliography of Afro-Hispanic literature so far. A second volume is forthcoming.

Black Literature and Humanism in Latin America, Athens, University of Georgia Press, 1988.

Discusses selected novels by Artel, Ortiz, Manuel Zapata Olivella, Juan Pablo Sojo, and Cubena as "Afro-humanistic literature."

Jackson, Shirley M. *La novela negrista en Hispanoamérica*, Madrid, Editorial Pliegos, 1986.

Thorough, though mostly sociohistorical readings of a broad sampling of novels by and about Blacks.

Jahn, Jahnheinz. *A History of Neo-African Literature. Writing in two continents*, tr. Oliver Coburn and Ursula Lehrburger, New York, Faber & Faber, 1968.

Traces the development of diasporic literature until the 1960s. Insists that racial characteristics cannot be used as literary criteria.

Johnson, Lemuel A. *The Devil, the Gargoyle, and the Buffoon. The Negro as metaphor in Western literature*, Port Washington, N.Y., Kennikat Press, 1969.

Comparative study that concentrates on criticizing white writers for writing about Blacks. Includes some comments on Guillén.

Kutzinski, Vera M. *Against the American Grain: Myth and history in William Carlos Williams, Jay Wright, and Nicolás Guillén*, Baltimore, Johns Hopkins University Press, 1987.

Includes detailed comments on *El diario que a diario* and some of Guillén's early poems.

Sugar's Secret: Race and the erotics of Cuban Nationalism, Charlottesville, University Press of Virginia, 1993.

Provocative study of the significance of blackness, femininity, and masculinity to the formation of Cuban nationalist discourse since the early nineteenth century.

(ed.) *Callaloo*, special issue on Nicolás Guillén, 10 (1987).

Includes critical essays, translations of Guillén's poetry, and an "Afro-Cuban" play by Jay Wright.

Lewis, Marvin A. *Afro-Hispanic Poetry, 1940–1980. From slavery to "Negritud" in South American verse*, Columbia, University of Missouri Press, 1983.

Discusses selected poetry by Brindis de Salas, Barrios, Nicomedes Santa Cruz, Estupiñán Bass, Ortiz, Artel, Salazar Valdés, and Juan Zapata Olivella.

Treading the Ebony Path. Ideology and violence in contemporary Afro-Colombian prose fiction, Columbia, University of Missouri Press, 1987.

Analyzes selected novels and short fiction by Palacios, Truque, Artel, and Juan and Manuel Zapata Olivella.

Luis, William (ed.). *Voices From Under. Black narrative in Latin America and the Caribbean*, Westport, Conn., Greenwood Press, 1984.

Includes a detailed introduction as well as essays on Carpentier, Manzano, Morúa Delgado, Ortiz, Duncan, Isaacs, and López Albújar.

Literary Bondage: Slavery in Cuban Narrative, Austin, University of Texas Press, 1990.

Includes thorough examination of the autobiographical work of Manzano and Morúa, Delgado's second novel.

Mansour, Monica. *La poesía negrista*, Mexico, Ediciones Era, 1973.

Study and anthology of Afro-Hispanic poetry from the colonial era to the present that specifically distinguishes between *negrista* and *negritud* poetry.

Martínez-Estrada, Ezequiel. *La poesía afro-cubana de Nicolás Guillén*, Montevideo, Arca, 1966.

Emphasizes the European and socio-critical aspects of Guillen's early poetry.

Matos Moctezuma, Eduardo. *El Negrito Poeta Mexicano y el Dominicano*, Mexico, Porrúa, 1980.

Reprints of the poetry of José Vasconcelos and Manuel ("Meso") Mónica with brief historical introductions to each.

Morejón, Nancy (ed.). *Recopilación de textos sobre Nicolás Guillén*, Havana, Casa de las Américas, 1974.

Includes mostly essays with a Marxist approach to Guillén in order to

Volume 2

"balance" the "black" criticism of his work.

Nación y mestizaje en Nicolás Guillén, Havana, UNEAC, 1982.
>Traces the development of Guillén's cultural and political nationalism from his early poetry and newspaper articles to his most recent writings.

Moreno Fraginals, Manuel (ed.). *Africa en América Latina*, Mexico, Siglo Veintiuno Editores UNESCO, 1977.
>Ambitious collection of essays on the social and cultural history of Blacks in Latin America. Includes only one cursory essay on literature.

Notre Librairie, special issue on Afro-Hispanic culture, 80 (1985).
>Includes informative essays on Cuba, Puerto Rico, Brazil, Peru, Ecuador, Venezuela, and Colombia.

Pérez Firmat, Gustavo. *The Cuban Condition: Translation and identity in modern Cuban literature*, New York, Cambridge University Press, 1989.
>Includes provocative chapters on Fernando Ortiz and Nicolás Guillén.

Pereda Valdés, Ildefonso. *Linea de color (ensayos afro-americanos)*, Santiago, Ediciones Ercilla, 1938.
>Collection of essays on Blacks in the United States dedicated to Langston Hughes and Nancy Cunard.

Lo negro y lo mulato en la poesía cubana, Montevideo, Editorial Ciudadela, 1970.
>Comments on extensive selections of *negrista* poetry from Cuba.

Perera, Hilda. *Idapo: el sincretismo en los cuentos negros de Lydia Cabrera*, Miami, Ediciones Universal, 1971.
>Analyzes *Cuentos negros de Cuba* and *¿Por que?* as well as providing an overview of Cabrera's literary and anthropological works.

Piquet, Daniel. *La cultura afrovenezolana en sus escritores contemporáneos*, Caracas, Monte Avila, 1982.
>Detailed formal and historical analyses of *Cumboto*, *Pobre negro*, and *Canción de negros*.

Prescott, Lawrence. *Candelario Obeso y la iniciación de la poesía negra en Colombia*, Bogotá, Publicaciones del Instituto Caro y Cuervo, 1985.
>Comments on Obeso's poetry and its literary and historical context.

Richards, Henry J., and Teresa Cajiao Salas. *Asedios a la poesía de Nicomedes Santa Cruz*, Quito, Editorial Andina, 1982.
>Thematic, ahistorical readings of selected poems. Labels Santa Cruz as a social poet of "negritud."

Ruscalleda Bercedoniz, Jorge María. *Cuatro elementos sustanciales en la poesía de Nicolás Guillén*, Río Piedras, Universidad de Puerto Rico, Editorial Universitaria, 1975.
>Detailed, but limited, examination of the themes and style of all of Guillén's verse.

Sardinha, Dennis. *The Poetry of Nicolás Guillén. An introduction*, London, New Books Ltd., 1976.
>Useful, but limited, introduction to Guillén's poetic style. Includes a 1972 interview with the poet.

Smart, Ian I. *Central American Writers of West Indian Origin: A new Hispanic literature*, Washington, Three Continents Press, 1984.
>Extremely useful historical and literary overview with special focus on Costa Rica and Panama. Argues convincingly in favor of a pan-Caribbean literature.

Smith Córdoba, Amir (ed.). *Vida y obra de Candelario Obeso*, Bogotá, Centro para la Investigación de la Cultura Negra, 1984.

Collection of biographical and critical essays. Includes *Cantos populares de mi tierra* and "translations" of the poems into "proper" Spanish.

Torre, Rogelio de la. *La obra poética de Emilio Ballagas*, Miami, Ediciones Universal, 1977.

Useful comments on "Elegía de María Belén Chacón" and "Actitud" as "poemas de la dirección interior."

Tous, Adriana. *La poesía de Nicolás Guillén*, Madrid, Cultura Hispánica, 1971.

Focuses on Gillén's "inside view" of Cuban Blacks.

Williams, Lorna. *Self and Society in the Poetry of Nicolás Guillén*, Baltimore, Johns Hopkins University Press, 1983.

Surveys Guillén's work from a largely sociohistorical perspective.

Young, Ann Venture. *The Image of Black Women in Twentieth-Century South American Poetry*, Washington, Three Continents Press, 1987.

Limited thematic overview.

Zeñón Cruz, Isabelo. *Narciso descubre su trasero: el negro en la cultura puertorriqueña*, 2 vols., Humacao, Puerto Rico, Editorial Furidi, 1975.

Comprehensive study/anthology of the image of Blacks in Puerto Rican literature. Valuable reference work.

Articles

Jackson, Richard L. "Afro-Hispanic literature: Recent trends in criticism," *Afro-Hispanic Review*, 7 (1988), 32–5.

Kooreman, Thomas. "Integración artística de la protesta social en las novelas de Manuel Zapata Olivella," *Afro-Hispanic Review*, 6:1 (1987), 27–30.

Very useful overview with emphasis on changing themes and narrative strategies.

Molloy, Sylvia. "From serf to self: the autobiography of Juan Francisco Manzano," *MLN*, 104 (1989), 393–417.

Meticulous critical examination of the different versions of Manzano's autobiography and the extent of their ideological conditioning.

Mose, Kendrick E. A. "*Changó, el gran putas* y el negro en la novelística del Colombiano Zapata Olivella," *Afro-Hispanic Review*, 7 (1988), 45–8.

Thorough, imaginative reading, balanced between criticism of, and praise for, the novel.

Trelles, Carlos M. "Bibliografía de autores de la raza de color en Cuba," *Revista Cubana Contemporánea*, 43 (1927), 30–78.

Chapter 6: *The* criollista *novel*

Primary sources

Argentina

Manuel Gálvez (1882–1962)
  La maestra normal (1914)

Ricardo Güiraldes (1886–1927)
  Don Segundo Sombra (Buenos Aires, 1926)
Enrique Larreta (1875–1961)
  Zogoibi (1926)
Benito Lynch (1885–1951)
  Los carranchos de la Florida (1916)
  Raquela (1918)
  La evasión (1922)
  Las mal calladas (1923)
  El inglés de los güesos (1924)
  El romance de un gaucho (1930)
Roberto J. Payró (1867–1928)
  El casamiento de Laucha (1906)
  Pago chico (1908)

Chile

Eduardo Barrios (1882–1963)
  Gran señor y rajadiablos (1948)
  Tamarugal (1944)
Luis Durand (1895–1954)
  Frontera (1949)
  Siete cuentos (1955)
Mariano Latorre (1886–1955)
  Cuentos del Maule (1912)
  Zurzulita (1920)
  Chilenos del mar (1929)
Rafael Maluenda (1855–1963)
  Escenas de la vida campesina (1909)
Juan Marín (1900–1963)
  El infierno azul y blanco (Paralelo 53 sur) (1936)
  Naufragio (1939)
Ernesto Montenegro (1885–1967)
  Mi tío Ventura (1938)

Colombia

José Eustasio Rivera (1888–1928)
  La vorágine (Bogotá 1924)
César Uribe Piedrahita (1897–1951)
  Toá (1933)
  Mancha de aceite (1935)

Costa Rica

Luis Dobles Segreda (1891–1957)
  Rosa mística (1920)

Caña brava (1926)

Carmen Lyra (1888–1951) (pseudonym for María Isabel Carvajal)
   Los cuentos de mi tía Panchita (1920)
   Bananas y hombres (1931)

Cuba

Carlos Montenegro (1900–1953)
   Cuentos de la manigua (1941)
Luis Felipe Rodríguez (1888–1947)
   Cómo opinaba Damián Paredes (1916)
   La pascua de la tierra natal (1923)
   Ciénaga (1937)
   Marcos Antilla (1932)

Dominican Republic

Ramón Marrero Aristy (1913–1959)
   Over (1939)
Miguel Angel Monclús Brea (1893–1967)
   Cosas criollas (1927)
   Escenas criollas (1929)
Sócrates Nolasco (1884–1980)
   Cuentos del sur (1939)
   Cuentos cimarrones (1958)
José María Pichardo (1888–1964)
   Tierra adentro (1917)

El Salvador

Alberto Rivas Bonilla (1891–?)
   Andanzas y malandanzas (1955)
   Me monto en un potro (1943)
Salarrué (1899–1975) (pseudonym for Salvador Salazar Arrué)
   Cuentos de barro (1933)

Guatemala

Flavio Herrera (1892–1962)
   El tigre (1932)
   La tempestad (1934)
   Caos (1949)
Carlos Wyld Ospina (1891–1956)
   La gringa (1933)

Honduras

Marcos Carías Reyes (1905–1949)
  La heredad (1931)
  Trópico (1948)

Panama

José María Núñez (1894–?)
  Cuentos criollos (1947)
José Huerta (1899–?)
  Alma campesina (1930)

Puerto Rico

Abelardo Díaz Alfaro (1919)
  Terrazo (1947)
Enrique Laguerre (1906)
  La llamarada (1935)
  Solar Montoya (1941)
Miguel Meléndez Muñoz (1884–1966)
  Fuerzas contrarias (1905)
  Yuyo (1913)
  Cuentos del cedro (1936)
  Cuentos de la carretera central (1941)

Uruguay

Horacio Quiroga (1878–1937)
  Cuentos de la selva (1918)
  Anaconda (1921)
  Los desterrados (1926)
Carlos Reyles (1868–1938)
  El terruño (1916)
  El gaucho Florido (1932)
Enrique Amorim (1900–60)
  El paisano Aguilar (1934)
  La trampa del pajonal (1938)

Venezuela

Manuel Díaz Rodríguez (1868–1927)
  Peregrina o el pozo encantado (1921)
Rómulo Gallegos (1884–1969)
  La trepadora (1925)
  Doña Bárbara 1929)
  Cantaclaro
  Canaima (1935)

Pobre negro (1937)
El forastero (1945)
Sobre la misma tierra (1947)
La brizna de paja en el viento (1952)
José Rafael Pocaterra (1889–1955)
Vidas oscuras (1913)
Tierra del sol amada (1918)
La casa de los abuelos (1946)

Secondary sources

Books

Alonso, Carlos J. *The Spanish American Regional Novel: Modernity and autoch-thony*, Cambridge Studies in Latin American and Iberian Literature, 2, Cambridge University Press, 1990.
> A reexamination of the *novela de la tierra* from a contemporary critical perspective.

Araujo, Orlando. *Lengua y creación en la obra de Rómulo Gallegos*, 2 vols., Caracas, Ediciones En La Raya, 1977.
> The standard critical work on Gallegos's works.

Castillo, Homero. *El criollismo en la novelística chilena*, Mexico, Ediciones de Andrea, 1962.
> Mostly a study of the novels of Mariano Latorre.

Contreras, Francisco. *Le Mondonovisme*, Paris, Mercure de France, 1917.
> A collection of pieces advancing the new doctrine published by the author in *Le Mercure* (Paris).

Giberga, Eliseo. *El pan-americanismo y el pan-hispanismo*, Havana, Rambla & Bouza, 1916.
> An essay that represents the debate between the two doctrines.

Henríquez Ureña, Pedro. *Seis ensayos en busca de nuestra expresión*, Madrid, Babel, 1927.
> An essential collection of essays concerning literary expression in Latin America.

Hernández de Norman, Isabel. *La novela criolla en las Antillas*, New York, Plus Ultra, 1977.
> Examines mostly nineteenth-century works, but is a good background for a study of the *criollista* novel of the twentieth century.

Latcham, Ricardo. *El criollismo*, Santiago, Editorial Universitaria, 1956.
> A good survey of the concept and its literary manifestations.

Lugones, Leopoldo. *El payador*, Caracas, Biblioteca Ayacucho, 1979.
> A study of the wandering jongleur of the pampas.

Mallory, William E., and Paul Simpson-Housley (eds.). *Geography and Literature: A meeting of the disciplines*, Syracuse University Press, 1987.
> Essays exploring the literature–land connection.

Neale Silva, Eduardo. *Horizonte Humano: vida de José Eustasio Rivera*, Madison, University of Wisconsin Press, 1960.
> An essential critical work for any interpreter of Rivera's works. An unim-

peachable model of the life-and-works genre.

O'Gorman, Edmundo. *Meditaciones sobre el criollismo*, Centro de Estudios de Historia de México, 1970.

A meditation on the roots of *criollismo* in Mexico, which the author locates in the *barroco literario* of the colonial period.

Pérez, Trinidad (ed.). *Recopilación de textos sobre tres novelas ejemplares*, Havana, Casa de las Américas, 1971.

Useful compilation of essays and documents related to the three novels discussed.

Prieto, Adolfo. *El discurso criollista en la formación de la Argentina moderna*, Buenos Aires, Sudamericana, 1988.

A study of the relationship between *criollismo* and the creation and consolidation of the modern Argentinian state. Includes, as an appendix, an index to the important collection of *criollista* works that is housed at the Instituto Iberoamericano in Berlin.

Reyes, Alfonso. *Obras completas*, 12 vols., Mexico, Fondo de Cultura Económica, 1960.

A paramount figure in the debate about cultural autochthony.

Romano, Eduardo. *Análisis de Don Segundo Sombra*, Buenos Aires, Centro Editor de América Latina, 1967.

A thorough analysis of the text as an ideological and literary artifact.

Rubione, Alfredo (ed.). *En torno al criollismo: textos y polémica*, Buenos Aires, Centro Editor de América Latina, 1983.

A collection of documents surrounding a polemic on *criollismo* in Argentina.

Sarmiento, Domingo F. *Life in the Argentine Republic in the Days of the Tyrants: Or civilization and barbarism*, tr. Mary Mann, New York, Hafner Publishing Company, 1971.

The book that established the civilization versus barbarism paradigm; perhaps *the* essential book in Latin American letters of the nineteenth century.

Schärer-Nussberger, Maya. *Gallegos: el mundo inconcluso*, Caracas, Monte Avila, 1979.

The best book on Gallegos's *oeuvre*.

Shaw, Donald L. *Gallegos: Doña Bárbara*, London, Grant & Cutler, 1972.

A solid study of the novel in its literary and historical context.

Stabb, Martin S. *In Quest of Identity: Patterns in the Spanish American essay of ideas, 1890–1960*, Chapel Hill, University of North Carolina Press, 1967.

An influential examination of the essay of cultural definition in the twentieth century in Latin America.

Torres Rioseco, Arturo. *La novela en la América Hispana, University of California Publications in Modern Philology*, 21:2 (1939), 159–256.

Novelistas contemporáneos de América, Santiago, Nascimento, 1939.

These two works by Torres Rioseco together make up the first book-length study of the *novela de la tierra*.

Articles

Arrom, José Juan. "Criollo: definición y matices de un concepto" in his *Certidumbre de América: estudios de letras, folklore y cultura*, Madrid, Gredos, 1971, 11–26.

A thorough etymological and historical examination of the term.

González Echevarría, Roberto. "Doña Bárbara writes the plain" in his *The Voice of the Masters: Writing and authority in modern Latin American literature*, Austin, University of Texas Press, 1985, 33–63.

Sees the novel as the representation of two mutually exclusive concepts of signification.

Leland, Christopher. "The failure of myth: Ricardo Güiraldes and *Don Segundo Sombra*" in his *The Last Happy Men: The Generation of 1922, fiction and the Argentine reality*, N.Y., Syracuse University Press, 1986, 119–47.

A reading of the novel in light of the literary debates of the 1920s in Argentina.

Marinello, Juan. "Tres novelas ejemplares," in Juan Loveluck (ed.), *La novela hispanoamericana*, Santiago, Editorial Universitaria, 1969, 421–33.

The article that solidified the now standard novelistic triad of *Don Segundo Sombra*, *La vorágine*, and *Doña Bárbara*.

Meléndez, Concha. "Tres novelas de la naturaleza americana: *Don Segundo Sombra*, *La vorágine*, *Doña Bárbara*," *Revista Bimestre Cubana*, 28 (1931), 82–93.

Discusses the representation of Nature in the three works.

Menton, Seymour. "*La vorágine*: circling the triangle," *Hispania*, 59 (1976), 418–34.

Proposes the triangle as the key organizing figure for the novel.

Molloy, Sylvia. "Contagio narrativo y gesticulación retórica en *La vorágine*," *Revista Iberoamericana*, 141 (1987), 745–66.

An excellent study of the text's internal inconsistencies and contradictions.

Osorio, Nelson T. "*Doña Bárbara* y el fantasma de Sarmiento," *Escritura*, 15 (1983), 19–35.

A consideration of Gallegos's novel within the "civilization versus barbarism" rhetorical tradition.

Pope, Randolph D. "*La vorágine*: autobiografía de un intelectual" in Randolph Pope (ed.), *The Analysis of Literary Texts: Current trends in methodology*, Ypsilanti, Mich., The Bilingual Press, 1980, 256–67.

Studies the protagonist's status as a poet–intellectual in confrontation with the jungle.

Rodríguez Luis, Julio. "*La vorágine*: una escritura en busca de la novela," *Diálogos* (El Colegio de México), 130 (1985), 14–21; 131 (1985), 25–31.

Examines the relationship between the development of Rivera's authorial *persona* and the novel's narrator.

Schwartz, Jorge. "*Don Segundo Sombra*: una novela monológica," *Revista Iberoamericana*, 42 (1976), 427–46.

An intelligent ideological reading of Güiraldes's novel.

Chapter 7: The novel of the Mexican Revolution

Primary sources

Azuela, Mariano. *Obras completas*, 3 vols., Mexico, Fondo de Cultura Económica, 1958–1960.

A reliable and fairly complete compilation.

Los de abajo, ed. W. A. R. Richardson, London, Harrap, 1973.

A useful edition with an introduction in English, maps, notes, and glossary.
The Underdogs, tr. Enrique Munguia, New York, Brentanos, 1929.
Castro Leal, Antonio (ed.). *La novela de la Revolución mexicana*, 2 vols., Madrid, Mexico, and Buenos Aires, Aguilar, 1960.
An anthology which includes most of the novels discussed in this chapter.
Guzmán, Martín Luis. *Obras completas*, 2 vols., Mexico, Fondo de Cultura Económica, 1984.
Romero, José Rubén. *Obras completas*, Mexico, Porrúa, 1963.
Vasconcelos, José. *Ulises criollo*, Mexico, Ediciones Botas, 1935.

Secondary sources

Books

Abreu Gómez, Ermilo. *Martín Luis Guzmán*, Mexico, Empresas Editoriales, 1968.
A survey of the life and works.
Brushwood, John S. *Mexico in its Novel: A nation's search for identity*, Austin and London, University of Texas Press, 1968.
Chapters 7–10 discuss the novels of the Revolution.
Dessau, Adalbert. *La novela de la Revolución mexicana*, Mexico, Fondo de Cultura Económica, 1972.
A Marxist approach, more political than literary.
González, Manuel Pedro. *Trayectoria de la novela en México*, Mexico, Botas, 1951.
Contains essays on the novel of the Revolution, Azuela, Guzmán, Romero, López y Fuentes, and Rojas González.
Griffin, Clive. *A Critical Guide to "Los de abajo,"* London, Grant & Cutler, 1990.
By far the best analysis of Azuela's novel, particularly strong on characterization and structure.
Leal, Luis. *Mariano Azuela, vida y obra*, Mexico, Ediciones de Andrea, 1961.
The only general account of Azuela's output.
Robe, Stanley. *Azuela and the Mexican Underdogs*, Los Angeles, University of California Press, 1979.
A detailed study of the genesis of the first version of *Los de abajo*, here reproduced and translated.
Rodríguez Coronel, Rogelio (ed.). *Recopilación de textos sobre la novela de la Revolución mexicana*, Havana, Casa de las Américas, 1976.
A useful but uneven anthology of critical articles.
Ruddinelli, Jorge. *Literatura e ideología: el primer Mariano Azuela (1896–1918)*, Mexico, La Red de Jonás, 1982.
An intelligent Marxist literary analysis.
Rutherford, John. *Mexican Society During the Revolution: A literary approach*, Oxford University Press, 1971.
Social history rather than literary criticism. Chapter 3 is a history of the production of the novels of the Revolution.
An Annotated Bibliography of the Novels of the Mexican Revolution of 1910–1917, in English and Spanish, New York, Whitston, 1972.
All first editions are listed in this bibliography.

La sociedad mexicana durante la Revolución, Mexico, El Caballito, 1978.
> The earlier work above, revised and translated.

Sommers, Joseph. *After the Storm: Landmarks of the modern Mexican novel*, Albuquerque, University of New Mexico Press, 1968.
> A survey of the twentieth-century Mexican novel.

Thomas, D. G. *The Novel of the Spanish Civil War (1936–1975)*, Cambridge University Press, 1990.
> Develops the two waves theory.

Articles

Bradley, D. "Aspects of Realism in Azuela's *Los de abajo*," *Ibero-amerikanisches Archiv*, 4 (1978), 39–55.
"The thematic import of *Los de abajo*: a defence," *Forum for Modern Language Studies*, 15 (1979), 14–25.

Cortínez, Carlos. "Simetría y sutileza en la narrativa de Martín Luis Guzmán," *Revista Canadiense de Estudios Hispánicos*, 12 (1988), 221–34.

Gerdes, Dick. "Point of view in *Los de abajo*," *Hispania*, 64 (1981), 557–63.

Griffin, Clive. "The structure of *Los de abajo*," *Revista Canadiense de Estudios Hispánicos*, 6 (1981), 25–41.

Menton, Seymour. "La estructura épica de *Los de abajo* y un prólogo especulativo," *Hispania*, 50 (1967), 1001–11.

Murad, Timothy. "Animal imagery and structural unity in Mariano Azuela's *Los de abajo*," *Journal of Spanish Studies: Twentieth Century*, 7 (1979), 207–22.
"Foreshadowing, duplication and structural unity in Mariano Azuela's *Los de abajo*," *Hispania*, 64 (1981), 550–6.

Parle, Dennis J. "Narrative style and technique in Nellie Campobello's *Cartucho*," *Kentucky Romance Quarterly*, 32 (1985), 201–11.

Pupo-Walker, Enrique. "El protagonista en la evolución textual de *Los de abajo*" in Andrew P. Debicki and Enrique Pupo-Walker (eds.), *Estudios de literatura hispanoamericana en honor a José J. Arrom*, Chapel Hill, University of North Carolina, 1974, 155–66.

Rama, Angel. "Mariano Azuela: ambición y frustración de las clases medias" in his *Literatura y clase social*, Mexico, Folios Ediciones, 1984, 144–83.

Young, R. "Narrative structure in two novels by Mariano Azuela: *Los caciques* and *Los de abajo*," *Revista Canadiense de Estudios Hispánicos*, 2 (1978), 169–81.

Chapter 8: The Latin American novel from 1950 to 1975

This bibliography includes the first Spanish edition and the translation into English of the novels written in the period 1950–1975 by the authors studied in this chapter. The most important books of criticism on their work are also mentioned. When no commentary follows, I believe the book is informative or otherwise useful. To include a full bibliography of each author would have taken several volumes. Secondary sources listed include general studies of the period and a selection of books containing interviews, as well as works dealing with individual authors.

Primary sources

Aguilera Malta, Demetrio. *Una cruz en la Sierra Maestra*, Buenos Aires, Sophos, 1960.
  La caballeresa del sol: el gran amor de Bolívar, Madrid, Guadarrama, 1964.
  El Quijote de El Dorado: Orellana y el río de las Amazonas, Madrid, Guadarrama, 1964.
  Un nuevo mar para el rey: Balboa, Anayansi y el Océano Pacífico, Madrid, Guadarrama, 1965.
  Siete lunas y siete serpientes, Mexico, Fondo de Cultura Económica, 1970.
  El secuestro del general, Mexico, Mortiz, 1973.
  Manuela, la caballeresa del sol, tr. Willis Knapp Jones, Carbondale, Southern Illinois University Press, 1967.
  Seven Serpents and Seven Moons, tr. Gregory Rabassa, Austin, University of Texas Press, 1979.
Alegría, Fernando. *Caballo de copas*, Santiago, Zig-Zag, 1957.
  El cataclismo, Santiago: Nascimento, 1960.
  Noches del cazador, Santiago, Zig-Zag, 1961.
  Mañana, los guerreros, Santiago, Zig-Zag, 1965.
  Los días contados, Mexico, Siglo Veintiuno Editores, 1968.
  El paso de los gansos, New York, Puelche, 1975.
  My Horse Gonzalez, tr. Carlos Lozano, New York, Las Américas Publishing Co., 1964.
  The Chilean Spring, tr. Stephen Fredman, Pittsburgh, Latin American Literary Review Press, 1980.
      Translates from *El paso de los gansos*.
Alvarez Gardeazábal, Gustavo. *Cóndores no entierran todos los días*, Barcelona, Destino, 1972.
  Dabeiba, Barcelona, Destino, 1972.
  La tara del papa, Buenos Aires, Fabril, 1971.
  El bazar de los idiotas, Bogotá, Editorial Plaza & Janés, 1974.
Angel, Albalucía. *Los girasoles en invierno*, Bogotá, Linotipia Bolívar, 1970.
  Dos veces Alicia, Barcelona, Seix Barral, 1972.
  Estaba la pájara pinta sentada en el verde limón, Bogotá, Colcultura, 1975.
Arenas, Reinaldo. *Celestino antes del alba*, Buenos Aires, Brújula, 1968.
  El mundo alucinante. (Una novela de aventuras.). Mexico, Diógenes, 1969.
  Hallucinations: Being an account of the life and adventures of Friar Servando Teresa de Mier, tr. Gordon Brotherson, New York, Harper & Row, 1971.
Arguedas, José María. *Los ríos profundos*, Buenos Aires, Editorial Losada, 1958.
  El sexto, Lima, Librería Editorial J. Mejía Baca, 1961.
  Todas las sangres, Buenos Aires, Editorial Losada, 1964.
  El zorro de arriba y el zorro de abajo, Buenos Aires, Editorial Losada, 1971.
  Deep Rivers, tr. Frances Horning Barraclough, intro. by John V. Murra, afterword by Mario Vargas Llosa, Austin, University of Texas Press, 1978.
Arreola, Juan José. *La feria*, Mexico, Mortiz, 1963.
  The Fair, tr. John Upton, Austin, University of Texas Press, 1977.
Asturias, Miguel Angel. *Viento fuerte*, Buenos Aires, Editorial Losada, 1950.
  El papa verde, Buenos Aires, Editorial Losada, 1954.

Los ojos de los enterrados, Buenos Aires, Editorial Losada, 1960.

El alhajadito, Buenos Aires, Goyanarte, 1961.

Mulata de tal, Buenos Aires, Editorial Losada, 1963.

Maladrón. Epopeya de los Andes verdes, Buenos Aires, Editorial Losada, 1969.

Viernes de dolores, Buenos Aires, Editorial Losada, 1972.

Mulatta, tr. Gregory Rabassa, New York, Delacorte Press, 1967.

The Cyclon, tr. Darwin Flakoll and Claribel Alegría, London, Peter Owen, 1967.

Strong Wind, tr. Gregory Rabassa, New York, Delacorte Press, 1968.

The Eyes of the Interred, tr. Gregory Rabassa, New York, Delacorte Press, 1973.

The Green Pope, tr. Gregory Rabassa, New York, Delacorte Press, 1973.

Barrios, Eduardo. *Los hombres del hombre*, Santiago, Nascimento, 1950.

Benedetti, Mario. *Quién de nosotros*, Montevideo, Número, 1953.

La tregua, Montevideo, Alfa, 1960.

Gracias por el fuego, Montevideo, Alfa, 1965.

The Truce, tr. Benjamin Graham, New York, Harper & Row, 1969.

Bianco, José. *La pérdida del reino*, Buenos Aires, Siglo Veintiuno Editores, 1972.

Brunet, Marta. *Humo hacia el sur*, Buenos Aires, Editorial Losada, 1946.

La mampara, Buenos Aires, Emecé, 1946.

María Nadie, Santiago de Chile, Zig-Zag, 1957.

Amasijo, Santiago de Chile, Zig-Zag, 1962.

Bryce Echenique, Alfredo. *Un mundo para Julius*, Barcelona, Seix Barral, 1970.

Bullrich, Silvina. *Bodas de cristal*, Buenos Aires, Sudamericana, 1951.

Los burgueses, Buenos Aires, Sudamericana, 1964.

Silvina Bullrich published twelve other novels in this period.

Caballero Calderón, Eduardo. *El Cristo de espaldas*, Bogotá, Organización de los festivales del Libro, 1952.

Cabrera Infante, Guillermo. *Tres tristes tigres*, Barcelona, Seix Barral, 1967.

Three Trapped Tigers, tr. Donald Gardner and Suzanne Jill Levine, New York, Harper & Row, 1971.

Campos, Julieta. *Muerte por agua*, Mexico, Fondo de Cultura Económica, 1965.

Tiene los cabellos rojizos y se llama Sabina, Mexico, Mortiz, 1974.

Carpentier, Alejo. *Los pasos perdidos*, Mexico, Distribución Iberoamericana de Publicaciones, 1953.

The best edition, with an excellent introduction, is the one edited by Roberto González Echevarría, Madrid, Cátedra, 1985.

El acoso, Buenos Aires, Editorial Losada, 1956.

El siglo de las luces, Mexico, Compañía General de Ediciones, 1962.

Concierto barroco, Mexico, Siglo Veintiuno Editores, 1974.

El recurso del método, Mexico, Siglo Veintiuno Editores, 1974.

The Lost Steps, tr. Harriet de Onís, New York, Knopf, 1956.

"Manhunt," *Noonday*, 2 (1959), 109–80.

Explosion in a Cathedral, tr. John Sturrock, Boston, Little, Brown & Co., 1963.

Reasons of State, tr. Frances Partridge, New York, Knopf, 1976.

Concierto Barroco, tr. Asa Zatz, Tulsa, Okla. Council Oak Books, 1988.

Castellanos, Rosario. *Balún canán*, Mexico, Fondo de Cultura Económica, 1957.

Oficio de tinieblas, Mexico, Mortiz, 1962.

Los convidados de agosto, Mexico, Ediciones Era, 1964.

The Nine Guardians, tr. Irene Nicholson, New York, Vanguard Press, 1960.
A translation of *Balún canán*.

Cepeda Samudio, Alvaro. *La casa grande*, Bogotá, Mito, 1962.

Cofiño López, Manuel. *La última mujer y el próximo combate*, Havana, Casa de las Américas, 1971.

Collazos, Oscar. *Crónica de tiempo muerto*, Barcelona, Editorial Planeta, 1975.

Conti, Haroldo. *Sudeste*, Buenos Aires, Fabril, 1962.

Alrededor de la jaula, Xalapa, Mexico, Universidad Veracruzana, 1966.

En vida, Barcelona, Barral Editores, 1971.

Mascaró, el cazador americano, Havana, Casa de las Américas, 1975.

Cortázar, Julio. *Los premios*, Buenos Aires, Sudamericana, 1960.

Rayuela, Buenos Aires, Sudamericana, 1963.

62 Modelo para armar, Buenos Aires, Sudamericana, 1968.

Libro de Manuel, Buenos Aires, Sudamericana, 1973.

The Winners, tr. Elaine Kerrigan, New York, Pantheon, 1965.

Hopscotch, tr. Gregory Rabassa, New York, Random House, 1966.

62: A model kit, tr. Gregory Rabassa, New York, Pantheon, 1972.

A Manual for Manuel, tr. Gregory Rabassa, New York, Pantheon, 1978.

Denevi, Marco. *Rosaura a las diez*, Buenos Aires, G. Kraft, 1955.

Rosa at Ten O'clock, tr. Donald A. Yates, New York, Holt, Rinehart & Winston, 1964.

Desnoes, Edmundo. *No hay problema*, Havana, Ediciones R, 1961.

El cataclismo, Havana, Ediciones R, 1965.

Memorias del subdesarrollo, Havana Unión, 1965.

Inconsolable Memories, tr. Edmundo Desnoes, New York, New American Library, 1967.

Díaz Valcárcel, Emilio. *Figuraciones en el mes de marzo*, Barcelona, Seix Barral, 1972.

El hombre que trabajó lunes, Río Piedras, Ediciones Puerto, 1973.

Schemes in the Month of March, tr. Nancy Sebastiani, New York, Bilingual Review Press, 1979.

Donoso, José. *Coronación*, Santiago, Nascimento, 1957.

El lugar sin límites, Mexico, Mortiz, 1966.

Este domingo, Santiago, Zig-Zag, 1966.

El obsceno pájaro de la noche, Barcelona, Seix Barral, 1970.

Historia personal del "boom", Barcelona, Anagrama, 1972.

Coronation, tr. Jocasta Goodwin, New York, Knopf, 1965.

This Sunday, tr. Lorraine O'Grady Freeman, New York, Knopf, 1967.

Hell Hath No Limits, tr. Suzanne Jill Levine, in *Triple Cross*, New York, E. P. Dutton, 1972.

The Obscene Bird of Night, tr. Leonard Mades and Hardie St. Martin, New York, Knopf, 1973.

The Boom in Spanish American Literature: A personal history, tr. Gregory Kolovskos, New York, Columbia University Press, 1977.

Droguett, Carlos. *Sesenta muertos en la escalera*, Santiago, Nascimento, 1953.

Eloy, Barcelona, Seix Barral, 1960.

100 gotas de sangre y 200 de sudor, Santiago, Zig-Zag, 1961.

Patas de perro, Santiago, Zig-Zag, 1965.

El compadre. Mexico, Mortiz, 1967.
Supay el cristiano, Santiago, Zig-Zag, 1967.
El hombre que había olvidado, Buenos Aires, Sudamericana, 1968.
Todas esas muertes, Madrid, Alfaguara, 1971.
El hombre que trasladaba ciudades, Barcelona, Noguer, 1973.
Edwards, Jorge. *El peso de la noche*, Barcelona, Seix Barral, 1965.
Elizondo, Salvador. *Farabeuf o la crónica de un instante*, Mexico, Mortiz, 1965.
Salvador Elizondo. Nuevos escritores mexicanos del siglo XX presentados por sí mismos, Mexico, Empresas Editoriales, 1966.
El hipogeo secreto, Mexico, Mortiz, 1968.
Fernández, Macedonio. *Museo de la novela de la eterna: (primera novela buena)*, Buenos Aires, Centro Editor de Américan Latina, 1967.
Fuentes, Carlos. *La región más transparente*, Mexico, Fondo de Cultura Económica, 1958.
Las buenas conciencias, Mexico, Fondo de Cultura Económica, 1959.
Aura, Mexico, Era, 1962.
La muerte de Artemio Cruz, Mexico, Fondo de Cultura Económica, 1962.
Cambio de piel, Mexico, Mortiz, 1967.
Zona sagrada, Mexico, Siglo Vientiuno Editores, 1967.
Cumpleaños, Mexico, Mortiz, 1969.
La nueva novela hispanoamericana, Mexico, Mortiz, 1969.
Terra nostra, Mexico, Mortiz, 1975.
Where the Air is Clear, tr. Sam Hileman, New York, Ivan Obolensky, 1960.
The Good Conscience, tr. Sam Hileman, New York, Ivan Obolensky, 1961.
The Death of Artemio Cruz, tr. Sam Hileman, New York, Farrar, Straus, & Girous, 1964.
A Change of Skin, tr. Sam Hileman, New York, Farrar, Straus, & Girous, 1968.
"*Holy place*," tr. Suzanne Jill Levine, in *Triple Cross*, New York, E. P. Dutton, 1972.
Aura, tr. Lysander Kemp, New York, Farrar, Straus, & Girous, 1975.
Terra Nostra, tr. Margaret Sayers Peden, New York, Farrar, Straus, & Giroux, 1976.
Gálvez, Manuel. *Han tocado a degüello*, Buenos Aires, Espasa-Calpe, 1951.
Tiempo de odio y angustia, Buenos Aires, Espasa-Calpe, 1951.
Bajo la garra anglo-francesa, Buenos Aires, Espasa-Calpe, 1953.
Las dos vidas del pobre Napoleón, Buenos Aires, Editorial Losada, 1954.
Y así cayó don Juan Manuel, Buenos Aires, Espasa-Calpe, 1954.
El uno y la multitud, Buenos Aires, Ediciones Alpe, 1955.
Tránsito Guzmán, Buenos Aires, Ediciones Theoría, 1956.
Perdido en su noche, Buenos Aires, Sudamericana, 1958.
Me mataron entre todos, Buenos Aires, Emecé, 1962.
La locura de ser santo, Buenos Aires, Ediciones Puma, 1967.
García Márquez, Gabriel. *La hojarasca*, Bogotá, Ediciones Sipa, 1955.
El coronel no tiene quien le escriba, Medellín, Aguirre Editor, 1961.
La mala hora, Madrid, Talleres de Gráficas Luis Pérez, 1962; corrected edn., Mexico, Ediciones Era, 1966.
Cien años de soledad, Buenos Aires, Sudamericana, 1967.

El otoño del patriarca, Barcelona, Editorial Plaza & Janés, 1975.

No One Writes to the Colonel and Other Stories, tr. J. S. Bernstein, New York, Harper & Row, 1968.

One Hundred Years of Solitude, tr. Gregory Rabassa, New York, Harper & Row, 1970.

The Autumn of the Patriarch, tr. Gregory Rabassa, New York, Harper & Row, 1976.

Leafstorm and Other Stories, tr. Gregory Rabassa, New York, Avon, 1978.

In Evil Hour, tr. Gregory Rabassa, New York, Harper & Row, 1979.

Garmendia, Salvador. *Los pequeños seres*, Caracas, Sardio, 1959.

Los habitantes, Caracas, Dirección de Cultura, 1961.

Díaz de ceniza, Caracas, Monte Avila, 1968.

La mala vida, Montevideo, Arca, 1968.

Los pies de barro, Caracas, Monte Avila, 1973.

Memorias de Altagracia, Barcelona, Barral Editores, 1974.

Garro, Elena. *Recuerdos del porvenir*, Mexico, Mortiz, 1963.

Recollections of Things to Come, tr. Ruth L. C. Simms, Austin, University of Texas Press, 1986.

González León, Adriano. *País portátil*, Barcelona, Seix Barral, 1969.

Guido, Beatriz. *La casa del ángel*, Buenos Aires, Emecé, 1954.

La caída, Buenos Aires, Editorial Losada, 1956.

Fin de fiesta, Buenos Aires, Editorial Losada, 1958.

La mano en la trampa, Buenos Aires, Editorial Losada, 1961.

El incendio y las vísperas, Buenos Aires, Editorial Losada, 1964.

Escándalos y soledades, Buenos Aires, Editorial Losada, 1970.

The House of the Angel, tr. Joan Coyner MacLean, New York, McGraw Hill, 1957.

End of a Day, tr. A. D. Towers, New York, Scribners, 1966.

  Translates *El incendio y las vísperas*.

Lafourcade, Enrique. *Pena de muerte*, Santiago, Zig-Zag, 1953.

Para subir al cielo, Santiago, Zig-Zag, 1958.

La fiesta del rey Acab, Santiago, Editorial del Pacífico, 1959.

El príncipe y las ovejas, Santiago, Zig-Zag, 1962.

Novela de Navidad, Santiago, Zig-Zag, 1965.

Pronombres personales, Santiago, Zig-Zag, 1967.

Frecuencia modulada, Mexico, Mortiz, 1968.

King Ahab's Feast, tr. Renate and Ray Morrison, New York, St. Martin's Press, 1963.

Leñero, Vicente. *La voz adolorida*, Xalapa, Mexico, Universidad Veracruzana, 1961.

Los albañiles, Barcelona, Seix Barral, 1964.

Estudio Q, Mexico, Mortiz, 1965.

A fuerza de palabras, Buenos Aires, Centro Editor de América, 1967.

El garabato, Mexico, Mortiz, 1967.

Redil de ovejas, Mexico, Mortiz, 1973.

Lezama Lima, José. *Paradiso*, Havana, Ediciones Unión, 1966.

Paradiso, tr. Gregory Rabassa, New York, Farrar, Straus, & Giroux, 1974.

Lynch, Marta. *La alfombra roja*, Buenos Aires, Fabril, 1962.

Al vencedor, Buenos Aires, Editorial Losada, 1965.

La señora Ordóñez, Buenos Aires, Alvarez, 1967.

El cruce del río, Buenos Aires, Sudamericana, 1972.

Un árbol lleno de manzanas, Buenos Aires, Sudamericana, 1974.

Mallea, Eduardo. *Los enemigos del alma*, Buenos Aires, Sudamericana, 1950.

La torre, Buenos Aires, Sudamericana, 1951.

Chaves, Buenos Aires, Sudamericana, 1953.

La sala de espera, Buenos Aires, Sudamericana, 1953.

Simbad, Buenos Aires, Sudamericana, 1957.

Posesión, Buenos Aires, Sudamericana, 1958.

La vida blanca, Buenos Aires, Sur, 1960.

El resentimiento, Buenos Aires, Sudamericana, 1966.

La barca de hielo, Buenos Aires, Sudamericana, 1967.

La penúltima puerta, Buenos Aires, Sudamericana, 1969.

Gabriel Andaral, Buenos Aires, Sudamericana, 1971.

Triste piel del universo, Buenos Aires, Sudamericana, 1971.

Marechal, Leopoldo. *El banquete de Severo Arcángelo*, Buenos Aires, Sudamericana, 1965.

Megafón, o la guerra, Buenos Aires, Sudamericana, 1970.

Mejía Vallejo, Manuel. *Al pie de la ciudad*, Buenos Aires, Editorial Losada, 1958.

El día señalado, Barcelona, Destino, 1964.

Aire de tango, Medellín, Bedout, 1973.

Melo, Juan Vicente. *Juan Vicente Melo: nuevos escritores del siglo XX presentados por sí mismos*, Mexico, Empresas Editoriales, 1966.

La obediencia nocturna, Mexico, Era, 1969.

Mujica Lainez, Manuel. *Los ídolos*, Buenos Aires, Sudamericana, 1953.

La casa, Buenos Aires, Sudamericana, 1954.

Los viajeros, Buenos Aires, Sudamericana, 1955.

Invitados en "El Paraíso", Buenos Aires, Sudamericana, 1957.

Bomarzo, Buenos Aires, Sudamericana, 1962.

El unicornio, Buenos Aires, Sudamericana, 1965.

De milagros y de melancolías, Buenos Aires, Sudamericana, 1968.

Cecil, Buenos Aires, Sudamericana, 1972.

El laberinto, Buenos Aires, Sudamericana, 1974.

El viaje de los siete demonios, Buenos Aires, Sudamericana, 1974.

Bomarzo, tr. Gregory Rabassa, New York, Simon & Schuster, 1969.

The Wandering Unicorn, tr. Mary Fitton, New York, Taplinger, 1983.

Murena, Héctor A. *La fatalidad de los cuerpos*, Buenos Aires, Sur, 1955.

Las leyes de la noche, Buenos Aires, Sur, 1958.

Los herederos de la promesa, Buenos Aires, Sur, 1965.

Epitalámica, Buenos Aires, Sudamericana, 1969.

Polispuercón, Buenos Aires, Sudamericana, 1970.

Caína muerte, Buenos Aires, Sudamericana, 1971.

Folisofía, Caracas, Monte Avila, 1976.

The Laws of the Night, tr. Rachel Caffyn, New York, Scribner's, 1970.

Onetti, Juan Carlos. *La vida breve*, Buenos Aires, Sudamericana, 1950.

Los adioses, Buenos Aires, Sur, 1954.

Para una tumba sin nombre, Montevideo, Biblioteca de Marcha, 1959.

Volume 2

La cara de la desgracia, Montevideo, Alfa, 1960.

El astillero, Buenos Aires, Fabril, 1961.

Tan triste como ella, Montevideo, Alfa, 1963.

Juntacadáveres, Montevideo, Alfa, 1964.

La muerte y la niña, Buenos Aires, Corregidor, 1973.

The Shipyard, tr. Rachel Caffyn, New York, Scribner's, 1968.

A Brief Life, tr. Hortense Carpentier, New York, Grossman Publishers, 1976.

Orphée, Elvira. *Dos veranos*, Buenos Aires, Sudamericana, 1956.

Uno, Buenos Aires, Fabril, 1961.

Aire tan dulce, Buenos Aires, Sudamericana, 1966.

En el fondo, Buenos Aires, Galerna, 1969.

Pacheco, José Emilio. *Morirás lejos*, Mexico, Mortiz, 1967.

Paso, Fernando del. *José Trigo*, Mexico, Siglo Veintiuno Editores, 1966.

Peri Rossi, Cristina. *El libro de mis primos*, Montevideo, Biblioteca de Marcha, 1969.

Puig, Manuel. *La traición de Rita Hayworth*, Buenos Aires, Editorial Jorge Alvarez, 1968.

Boquitas pintadas, Buenos Aires, Sudamericana, 1969.

The Buenos Aires Affair, Buenos Aires, Sudamericana, 1973.

Betrayed by Rita Hayworth, tr. Suzanne Jill Levine, New York, E. P. Dutton, 1971.

Heartbreak Tango, tr. Suzanne Jill Levine, New York, E. P. Dutton, 1973.

The Buenos Aires Affair, tr. Suzanne Jill Levine, New York, E. P. Dutton, 1976.

Roa Bastos, Augusto. *Hijo de hombre*, Buenos Aires, Editorial Losada, 1960.

Yo el Supremo, Buenos Aires, Siglo Veintiuno Editores, 1974.

Son of Man, tr. Rachel Caffyn, London, Victor Gollancz, 1965.

I the Supreme, tr. Helen Lane, New York, Knopf, 1986.

Rojas, Manuel. *Hijo de ladrón*, Santiago, Zig-Zag, 1951.

Mejor que el vino, Santiago, Zig-Zag, 1958.

Punta de rieles, Santiago, Zig-Zag, 1960.

Sombras contra el muro, Santiago, Zig-Zag, 1963.

La oscura vida radiante, Buenos Aires, Sudamericana, 1971.

Born Guilty, tr. Frank Gaynor, New York, Library Publishers, 1955.

Rulfo, Juan. *Pedro Páramo*, Mexico, Fondo de Cultura Económica, 1955.

Pedro Páramo, tr. Lysander Kemp, New York, Grove Press, 1959.

Sábato, Ernesto. *Sobre héroes y tumbas*, Buenos Aires, Fabril, 1961.

Abaddón el exterminador, Buenos Aires, Sudamericana, 1974.

On Heroes and Tombs, tr. Helen R. Lane, Boston, Godine, 1981.

Sainz, Gustavo. *Gazapo*. Mexico, Mortiz, 1965.

Obsesivos días circulares, Mexico, Mortiz, 1969.

La princesa del Palacio de Hierro, Mexico, Mortiz, 1974.

Gazapo, tr. Hardie St. Martin, New York, Farrar, Straus, & Giroux, 1968.

The Princess of the Iron Palace, tr. Andrew Hurley, New York, Grove Press, 1987.

Sánchez, Néstor. *Nosotros dos*, Buenos Aires, Sudamericana, 1966.

Siberia Blues, Buenos Aires, Sudamericana, 1967.

El amhor, los orsinis y la muerte, Buenos Aires, Sudamericana, 1969.

Cómico de la lengua, Barcelona, Seix Barral, 1973.

Sarduy, Severo. *Gestos*, Barcelona, Seix Barral, 1963.

De dónde son los cantantes, Mexico, Mortiz, 1967.

Cobra, Buenos Aires, Sudamericana, 1972.

From Cuba with a Song, tr. Suzanne Jill Levine and Hallie D. Taylor, in *Triple Cross*, New York, E. P. Dutton, 1972.

Cobra, tr. Suzanne Jill Levine, New York, E. P. Dutton, 1975.

Scorza, Manuel. *Redoble por Rancas*, Barcelona, Editorial Plaza & Janér, 1970.

Historia de Garabombo, el Invisible, Barcelona, Planeta, 1972.

Skármeta, Antonio. *Soñé que la nieve ardía*, Barcelona, Editorial Planeta, 1975.

I Dreamt the Snow Was Burning, tr. Malcolm Coad, Columbia, La., Readers International, 1985.

Traba, Marta. *Las ceremonias del verano*, Havana, Casa de las Américas, 1966.

Los laberintos insolados, Barcelona, Seix Barral, 1967.

La jugada del sexto día, Santiago, Editorial Universitaria, 1970.

Valenzuela, Luisa. *Hay que sonreír*, Buenos Aires, Américalee, 1966.

El gato eficaz, Mexico, Mortiz, 1972.

Clara: Thirteen short stories and a novel, tr. Hortense Carpentier and J. Jorge Castello, New York, Harcourt Brace Jovanovich, 1976.

Includes *Hay que sonreír*.

Vargas Llosa, Mario. *La ciudad y los perros*, Barcelona, Seix Barral, 1963.

La casa verde, Barcelona, Seix Barral, 1966.

Conversación en La Catedral, Barcelona, Seix Barral, 1969.

Pantaleón y las visitadoras, Barcelona, Seix Barral, 1973.

Time of the Hero, tr. Lysander Kemp, New York, Grove Press, 1966.

The Green House, tr. Gregory Rabassa, New York, Harper & Row, 1968.

Conversation in the Cathedral, tr. Gregory Rabassa, New York, Harper & Row, 1975.

Captain Pantoja and the Special Service, tr. Gregory Kolovakos and Ronald Christ, New York, Harper & Row, 1978.

Viñas, David. *Cayó sobre su rostro*, Buenos Aires, Doble P, 1955.

Los años despiadados, Buenos Aires, Letras Universitarias, 1956.

Un dios cotidiano, Buenos Aires, G. Kraft, 1957.

Los dueños de la tierra, Buenos Aires, Editorial Losada, 1958.

Dar la cara, Buenos Aires, Jamcana, 1962.

Los hombres de a caballo, Buenos Aires, Siglo Veintiuno Editores, 1968.

Cosas concretas, Buenos Aires, Tiempo Contemporáneo, 1969.

Jauría, Buenos Aires, Granica Editor, 1974.

Yáñez, Agustín. *La creación*, Mexico, Fondo de Cultura Económica, 1959.

La tierra pródiga, Mexico, Fondo de Cultura Económica, 1960.

Ojerosa y pintada. La vida en la Ciudad de México, Mexico, Libro Mex Editores, 1960.

Las tierras flacas, Mexico, Mortiz, 1962.

The Lean Lands, tr. Ethel Brinton, Austin, University of Texas Press, 1968.

Secondary sources

Books

Achúgar, Hugo. *Ideología y estructuras narrativas en José Donoso, 1950–1970*,

Caracas, Centro de Estudios Latinoamericanos Rómulo Gallegos, 1979.

Ahern, Maureen. *A Rosario Castellanos Reader: An anthology of her poetry, short fiction, essays, and drama*, Austin, University of Texas Press, 1988.

It does not include selections from Castellanos's novels, but there is a comprehensive introductory essay by M. Ahern, pp. 1–70, and a good bibliography, pp. 70–7.

Aínsa, Fernando. *Las trampas de Onetti*, Montevideo, Alfa, 1970.

Alegría, Fernando. *Nueva historia de la novela hispanoamericana*, Hanover, N.H., Ediciones del Norte, 1986.

Devotes many insightful pages to the period 1950–1975.

Bedoya, Luis Iván, and Augusto Escobar. *El día señalado de Manuel Mejía Vallejo: lectura crítica*, Medellín, Ediciones Hombre Nuevo, 1981.

Detailed analysis.

Bellini, Giuseppe. *La narrativa di Miguel Angel Asturias*, Milan, Istituto Editoriale Cisalpino, 1966.

Benasso, Rodolfo. *El mundo de Haroldo Conti*, Buenos Aires, Editorial Galerna, 1969.

Informative, including a critical study, photographs, interviews, and texts by Conti.

Boldori de Baldussi, Rosa. *Vargas Llosa: un narrador y sus demonios*, Buenos Aires, Fernando García Cambeiro, 1974.

Boldy, Steven. *The Novels of Julio Cortázar*, Cambridge University Press, 1980.

Brody, Robert. *Julio Cortázar, Rayuela*, London, Grant & Cutler, 1976.

A clear and well-informed guide.

Brody, Robert, and Charles Rossman (eds.). *Carlos Fuentes, a Critical View*, Austin, University of Texas Press, 1982.

Brushwood, John S. *The Spanish American Novel: A twentieth-century survey*, Austin, University of Texas Press, 1975.

Very well-informed, with brief analyses of the many authors mentioned.

Callan, Richard. *Miguel Angel Asturias*, New York, Twayne, 1970.

Campos, René Alberto. *Espejos: la textura cinemática en "La traición de Rita Hayworth,"* Madrid, Pliegos, 1985.

Carballo, Emmanuel. *Agustín Yáñez*, Havana, Cuaderno de la Casa de las Américas, 1966.

Castro-Klarén, Sara. *El mundo mágico de José María Arguedas*, Lima, Instituto de Estudios Peruanos, 1973.

Mario Vargas Llosa: análisis introductorio, Lima, Latinoamericana Editores, 1988.

Catania, Carlos. *Genio y figura de Ernesto Sábato*, Buenos Aires, EUDEBA, 1987.

Collazos, Oscar. *Literatura en la revolución y revolución en la literatura*, Mexico, Siglo Veintiuno Editores, 1970.

The texts of an important polemic between Collazos, Cortázar, and Vargas Llosa.

García Márquez: la soledad y la gloria, Bogotá, Editorial Plaza & Janés, 1983.

A lively biography.

Cornejo Polar, Antonio. *Los universos narrativos de José María Arguedas*, Buenos Aires, Editorial Losada, 1973.

Cortázar, Julio, and Ana María Barrenechea. *Cuaderno de bitácora de "Rayuela,"* Buenos Aires, Sudamericana, 1983.

An excellent study and the best edition of Cortázar's manuscript.

Coulson, Gabriela. *Marechal: la pasión metafísica*, Buenos Aires, García Cambeiro, 1974.

A very informative book.

Crovetto, Pier Luigi, and Ernesto Franco (eds.). *Omaggio a Juan Rufo. Studi di letteratura ispanoamericana*, 20 (1988).

Davison, Ned J. *Eduardo Barrios*, New York, Twayne, 1970.

Earle, Peter G. (ed.). *García Márquez*, Madrid, Taurus, 1981.

A selection of nineteen studies and an interview.

Fama, Antonio. *Realismo mágico en la narrativa de Aguilera Malta*, Madrid, Playor, 1977.

Fau, Margaret Eustella. *Gabriel García Márquez: An annotated bibliography, 1947–1979*, Westport, Conn., Greenwood Press, 1980.

Fau, Margaret Estella, and Nelly Sfeir de González. *Bibliographical Guide to Gabriel García Márquez, 1979–1985*, New York, Greenwood Press, 1986.

Flasher, John J. *México contemporáneo en las novelas de Agustín*, Mexico, Porrúa, 1969.

Foster, David William. *Augusto Roa Bastos*, Boston, Twayne, 1978.

Franco, Jean. *An Introduction to Spanish-American Literature*, London, Cambridge University Press, 1969.

García-Gutiérrez, Georgina. *Los disfraces: la obra mestiza de Carlos Fuentes*, Mexico, El Colegio de México, 1981. See also her excellent introduction to her edition of Carlos Fuentes's *La región más transparente*, Madrid Cátedra, 1982, pp. 11–83.

García Pinto, Magdalena. *Historias íntimas: conversaciones con diez escritoras latinoamericanas*, Hanover, N.H., Ediciones del Norte, 1988.

Interviews, among others, Albalucía Angel, Elvira Orphée, Marta Traba, and Luisa Valenzuela.

Garfield, Evelyn Picón. *Julio Cortázar*, New York, Ungar, 1975.

Gazarian Gautier, Marie-Lise. *Interviews with Latin American Writers*, Elmwood Park, Ill., Dalkey Archive Press, 1989.

Interviews, among others, Cabrera Infante, Donoso, Fuentes, Onetti, Puig, Sábato, Sarduy, Valenzuela, and Vargas Llosa.

Gerdes, Dick. *Mario Vargas Llosa*, Boston, Twayne, 1985.

Giacoman, Helmy F. *Homenaje a Augusto Roa Bastos*, New York, Anaya/Las Americas, 1973.

A mixed bag of useful articles.

Giacoman, Helmy F. (ed.). *Homenaje a Fernando Alegría*, New York, Las Américas Publishing Co., 1972.

An uneven collection of articles.

Giacoman, Helmy F., and José Miguel Oviedo. *Homenaje a Mario Vargas Llosa*, New York, Las Américas, 1972.

González Echevarría, Roberto. *Alejo Carpentier: The pilgrim at home*, Ithaca, Cornell University Press, 1977.

The best overall criticism of Carpentier's novels.

La ruta de Severo Sarduy, Hanover, N.H., Ediciones del Norte, 1987.

Provides essential background and lucid interpretations.

González Echevarría, Roberto, and Klaus Müller-Bergh. *Alejo Carpentier: Bibliogra-*

phical guide, Westport, Conn., Greenwood Press, 1983.

Grieben, Carlos F. *Eduardo Mallea*, Buenos Aires, Ediciones Culturales Argentinas, 1961.

Guibert, Rita. *Seven Voices*, New York, Knopf, 1973.
    Interviews with Asturias, Cabrera Infante, Cortázar, García Márquez, among others.

Gullón, Ricardo. *García Márquez o el olvidado arte de contar*, Madrid, Taurus, 1970.

Gutiérrez Mouat, Ricardo. *José Donoso, impostura e impostación: la modelización lúdica y carnavalesca de una producción literaria*, Gaithersburgh, Md., His-pamérica, 1983.

Guzmán, Daniel de. *Carlos Fuentes*, New York, Twayne, 1972.

Faris, Wendy B. *Carlos Fuentes*, New York, Ungar, 1983.

Harss, Luis, and Barbara Dohmann. *Into the Mainstream: Conversations with Latin-American writers*, New York, Harper & Row, 1967.
    Includes interpretations and interviews of Asturias, Borges, Cortázar, Carpen-tier, Fuentes, García Márquez, Onetti, Rulfo, and Vargas Llosa.

Jiménez de Báez, Diana Morán, and Edith Negrín. *La narrativa de José Emilio Pacheco*, El Colegio de México, 1979.
    A very detailed study of *Morirás lejos*.

Kadir, Djelal. *Juan Carlos Onetti*, Boston, Twayne, 1977.
    Questing Fictions: Latin America's family romance, Minneapolis, University of Minnesota Press, 1986 – pp. 107–40 study *Terra Nostra*'s philosophical background.

Kerr, Lucille. *Suspended Fictions: Reading novels by Manuel Puig*, Urbana, University of Illinois Press, 1987.

Lagos, María Inés. *H. A. Murena en sus ensayos y narraciones: de líder revisionista a marginado*, Santiago, Monografías del Maitén, 1989.

Larco, Juan (ed.). *Recopilación de textos sobre José María Arguedas*, Havana: Casa de las Américas, 1976.

Lastra, Pedro (ed.). *Julio Cortázar*, Madrid, Taurus, 1981.
    Twenty-five excellent essays.

Lewald, Ernest H. *Eduardo Mallea*, Boston, Twayne, 1977.

Lichtblau, Myron I. *El arte estilistico de Eduardo Mallea*, Buenos Aires, Goyanarte, 1967.
    Complete and balanced.
    Manuel Gálvez, New York, Twayne, 1972.

Loveluck, Juan (ed.). *Novelistas Hispanoamericanos de Hoy*, Madrid, Taurus, 1976.
    A good selection of articles on Onetti, Arguedas, Yáñez, Carpentier, Rulfo, Donoso, Sábato, Vargas Llosa, Fuentes, Cortázar, and García Márquez.

Luchting, Wolfgang A. *Mario Vargas Llosa: desarticulador de realidades*, Bogotá, Editorial Plaza & Janés, 1978.

Ludmer, Josefina. *Cien años de soledad: una interpretación*, Buenos Aires Tiempo Contemporáneo, 1972.
    A psychoanalytic interpretation; excellent insights.
    Onetti: los procesos de construcción del relato, Buenos Aires, Sudamericana, 1977.

Magnarelli, Sharon. *Reflections/Refractions: Reading Luisa Valenzuela*, New York, Peter Lang, 1988.

Includes an interview.

Marcos, Juan Manuel. *Roa Bastos, precursor del post-boom*, Mexico, Katún, 1983.
While the *Post-Boom* theory is unconvincing, the author knows Roa Bastos very well.

Márquez Rodríguez, Alexis. *Lo barroco y lo real-maravilloso en la obra de Alejo Carpentier*, Mexico, Siglo Veintiuno Editores, 1982.
A complete study of Carpentier's works.

Mcguirk, Bernard, and Richard Cardwell (eds.). *Gabriel García Márquez: New readings*, Cambridge University Press, 1987.
Twelve new essays, uniformly excellent.

McMurray, George. *Gabriel García Márquez*, New York, Ungar, 1977.
José Donoso, New York, Twayne, 1979.

Melón de Díaz, Esther. *La narrativa de Marta Brunet*, Barcelona, UPREX, 1975.
Reviews all Brunet's works, in an encomiastic but uncritical way.

Mena, Lucila Inés. *La función de la historia en "Cien años de soledad,"* Barcelona, Editorial Plaza & Janés, 1979.
Historical background.

Méndez Rodenas, Adriana. *Severo Sarduy: el neobarroco de la transgresión*, Mexico, Universidad Nacional Autónoma de México, 1983.
Well thought-out study.

Menton, Seymour. *Prose Fiction of the Cuban Revolution*, Latin American Monographs, 37, Austin, University of Texas Press, 1975. Also in Spanish, *La narrativa de la revolución cubana*, Colección Nova Scholar, Madrid, Playor.
Very informative.
La novela colombiana: planetas y satélites, Bogotá, Editorial Plaza & Janés, 1978.
Includes a chapter on *El otoño del patriarca*.

Millington, Mark. *Reading Onetti: Language, narrative and the subject*, Liverpool Monographs in Hispanic Studies, 1985.
A revisionist interpretation with merit.

Moore, Richard E. *Asturias: A checklist of works and criticism*, New York, American Institute for Marxist Studies, 1979.

Morsella, Astur. *Eduardo Mallea*, Buenos Aires, Mac-Co, 1957.

Müller-Bergh, Klaus. *Alejo Carpentier: estudio biográfico-crítico*, New York, Las Americas Publishing Co., 1972.
A detailed biography and excellent analysis of the early novels.

Muñoz, Elías Miguel. *El discurso utópico de la sexualidad en Manuel Puig*, Madrid, Pliegos, 1987.

Muñoz, Silverio. *José María Arguedas y el mito de la salvación por la cultura*, Minneapolis, Institute for the Study of Ideologies and Literatures, 1980.

Oberhelman, Harley Dean. *Ernesto Sábato*, New York, Twayne, 1970.

Ocampo, Victoria. *Diálogo con Mallea*, Buenos Aires, Sur, 1969.
Important, significant, and delightful.

Ortega, Julio, *et al. Guillermo Cabrera Infante*, Madrid, Fundamentos, 1974.

Oviedo, José Miguel. *Mario Vargas Llosa: la invención de una realidad*, Barcelona, Seix Barral, 1970. 2nd edn., 1977.
Mario Vargas Llosa: el escritor y la crítica, Madrid, Taurus, 1981.

Pellón, Gustavo. *José Lezama Lima's Joyful Vision: A study of "Paradiso" and other prose works*, Austin, University of Texas Press, 1989.

Picón Garfield, Evelyn. *Women's Voices from Latin America: Interviews with six contemporary authors*, Detroit, Wayne State University Press, 1985.

Excellent introductions to, and interviews with, Julieta Campos, Elvira Orphée, Marta Traba, and Luisa Valenzuela, among others. Good bibliography.

Predmore, James R. *Un estudio crítico de las novelas de Ernesto Sábato*, Madrid, José Porrúa Turanzas, 1981.

Commendably critical and balanced.

Rabassa, Clementine Christos. *Demetrio Aguilera-Malta and Social Justice*, London, Associated University Presses, 1980.

Rama, Angel. *Salvador Garmendia y la narrativa informalista*, Caracas, Universidad Central de Venezuela, 1975.

La novela en América Latina: panoramas 1920–1980, Bogotá, Procultura, 1982.

Important essays, among them one on the *Boom* and another on the novels about Latin American dictators.

Rangel Guerra, Alfonso. *Un mexicano y su obra: Agustín Yáñez*, Mexico, Empresas Editoriales, 1969.

Rivelli, Carmen. *Eduardo Mallea. La continuidad temática de su obra*, New York, Las Américas, 1969.

Rodríguez Monegal, Emir. *El arte de narrar*, Caracas, Monte Avila, 1968.

El boom de la novela latinoamericana, Caracas, Tiempo Nuevo, 1972.

A classic book of essays.

Roffe, Reina (ed.). *Espejo de escritores*, Hanover, N.H. Ediciones del Norte, 1985.

Interviews with Cortázar, Fuentes, Onetti, Puig, Rama, Rulfo, and Vargas Llosa.

Rogmann, Horst. *Narrative Strukturen und "Magischer Realismus" in den Ersten Romanen von Miguel Angel Asturias*, Frankfurt, Lang Verlag, 1978.

Studies the early novels, but from an unusually critical and refreshing point of view.

Rossman, Charles, and Alan Warren Friedman (eds.). *Mario Vargas Llosa: A collection of critical essays*, Austin, University of Texas Press, 1978.

Sáenz, Jimena. *Genio y figura de Miguel Angel Asturias*, Buenos Aires, EUDEBA, 1974.

Shaw, Donald L. *Nueva narrativa hispanoamericana*, Madrid, Cátedra, 1983.

Thorough, the best guide available for the period 1950–1975.

Smith, Verity. *Carpentier: los pasos perdidos*, London, Grant & Cutler, 1983.

A good introduction.

Sommers, Joseph. *After the Storm: landmarks of the modern Mexican novel*, Albuquerque, University of New Mexico Press, 1968.

Yáñez, Rulfo, Fuentes: la novela mexicana moderna, Caracas, Monte Avila, 1970.

Sommers, Joseph (ed.). *La narrativa de Juan Rulfo: interpretaciones críticas*, Mexico, SepSetentas, 1974.

Excellent collection of twelve articles.

Sosnowski, Saúl (ed.). *Augusto Roa Bastos y la producción cultural americana*, Buenos Aires, Ediciones de la Flor, 1986.

An excellent collection of essays.

Souza, Raymond D. *Major Cuban Novelists: Innovation and tradition*, Columbia,

University of Missouri Press, 1976.
 Chapter 2 is "Alejo Carpentier's timeless history," pp. 30–52. Chapter 4, pp. 80–100, is devoted to Cabrera Infante. The introduction places him in the context of Cuban literature.
The Poetic Fiction of José Lezama Lima, Columbia, University of Missouri Press, 1983.
 A very useful book.
Sur, 358–9 (1986), special issue dedicated to Mujica Lainez.

Tovar, Francisco. *Las historias del dictador "Yo el Supremo," de Augusto Roa Bastos*, Barcelona, Edicions del Mall, 1987.
 Useful information, but wordy.

Ulloa, Justo. *Sobre Lezama Lima y sus lectores: guía y compendio bibliográfico*, Boulder, Society of Spanish and Spanish American Studies, 1987.

Vargas Llosa, Mario. *García Márquez: historia de un deicidio*, Barcelona, Barral, 1971.
 Heavy on biographical interpretation and with unconvincing theories about the demons and obsessions of the writer, but still a major work.
José María Arguedas, entre sapos y halcones, Madrid, Ediciones Cultura Hispánica, 1978.

Vázquez, María Esther. *El mundo de Manuel Mujica Lainez*, Buenos Aires, Editorial de Belgrano, 1983.

Verani, Hugo. *Onetti: el ritual de la impostura*, Caracas, Monte Avila, 1981.
José Emilio Pacheco ante la crítica, Mexico, Universidad Autónoma Metropolitana, 1987.

Verani, Hugo (ed.). *Juan Carlos Onetti*, Madrid, Taurus, 1987.
 A selection of nineteen articles by major critics. Includes a good bibliography.

Vidal, Hernán. *José Donoso: surrealismo y rebelión de los instintos*, Gerona, Ediciones Aubí, 1972.
Para llegar a Manuel Cofiño: estudio de una narrativa revolucionaria cubana, Minneapolis, Institute for the Study of Ideologies and Literatures, 1984.

Villordo, Oscar Hermes. *Genio y figura de Eduardo Mallea*, Buenos Aires, EUDEBA, 1973.

Walker, John. *Metaphysics and Aesthetics in the Works of Eduardo Barrios*, London, Tamesis Books, 1983.
 A complete and profound study of Barrios's novels.

Washburn, Yulan M. *Juan José Arreola*, Boston, Twayne, 1983.

Williams, Raymond Leslie. *Una década en la novela colombiana: la experiencia de los setenta*, Bogotá, Editorial Plaza & Janés, 1981.
Gabriel García Márquez, Boston, Twayne, 1984.
Mario Vargas Llosa, New York, Ungar, 1986.
 An excellent study of the narratological aspects.

Williams, Raymond Leslie (ed.). *Aproximaciones a Gustavo Alvarez Gardeazábal*, Bogotá, Colombia, 1977.
 Studies *Dabreiba* and *El bazar de los idiotas*. A good collection of articles on different novels.

World Literature Today, 47 (Summer 1973), focuses on García Márquez; 52 (Winter 1978) focuses on Vargas Llosa; 57 (Autumn 1983), focuses on the work of Carlos Fuentes; 61 (Autumn 1987) is a special issue focusing on Cabrera Infante.

Volume 2

Articles

Urbina, Nicasio. "Bibliografía crítica completa de Ernesto Sábato, con un índice temático," *Revista, de Crítica Literaria Latinoamericana*, 14 (1988), 117–222.

Chapter 9: *The Spanish American novel: recent developments, 1975 to 1990*

Primary sources

Allende, Isabel. *La casa de los espíritus*, Barcelona, Editorial Plaza & Janés, 1982.
  De amor y de sombra, Barcelona, Editorial Plaza & Janés, 1984.
  Eva Luna, Barcelona, Editorial Plaza & Janés, 1987.
  The House of the Spirits, tr. Magda Bogin, New York, Knopf. 1985.
  Of Love and Shadows, tr. Margaret Sayers Peden, New York, Alfred A. Knopf. 1987.
  Eva Luna, tr. Margaret Sayers Peden, New York, Knopf. 1988.
Barnet, Miguel. *Biografía de un cimarrón*, Havana, Academia de Ciencias de Cuba, Instituto de Etnología y Folklore, 1968.
  Canción de Rachel, Havana, Instituto Cubano del Libro, 1969.
  Gallego, Madrid, Alfaguara, 1981.
  La vida real, Madrid, Alfaguara, 1986.
  The Autobiography of a Runaway Slave, tr. Jocasta Innes, New York, Pantheon, 1968.
Benítez Rojo, Antonio. *El mar de las lentejas*, Havana, Editorial Letras Cubanas, 1979.
  Sea of Lentils, tr. James Maraniss, Amherst, University of Massachusetts Press, 1990.
Ferré, Rosario. *Maldito amor*, Mexico, Mortiz, 1986.
Fuentes, Carlos. *Gringo viejo*, Mexico, Fondo de Cultura Económica, 1985.
  The Old Gringo, tr. Margaret Sayers Peden, New York, Farrar, Straus, & Giroux, 1985.
García Márquez, Gabriel. *El general en su laberinto*, Bogotá, Oveja Negra, 1989.
  The General in his Labyrinth, tr. Edith Grossman, New York, Knopf, 1990.
Giardinelli, Mempo. *¿Por qué prohibieron el circo?*, Buenos Aires, Editorial Losada, 1976 (edition destroyed); Mexico, Oasis, 1983.
  La revolución en bicicleta, Barcelona, Editorial Pomaire, 1980.
  El cielo con las manos, Hanover, N.H. Ediciones del Norte, 1981.
  Luna caliente, Mexico, Oasis, 1983.
  Qué solos se quedan los muertos, Buenos Aires, Sudamericana, 1985.
Goldemberg, Isaac. *La vida a plazos de don Jacobo Lerner*, Lima, Libre-1, 1978.
  Tiempo al tiempo, Hanover, N.H., Ediciones del Norte, 1984.
  The Fragmented Life of Don Jacobo Lerner, tr. Roberto Picciotto, New York, Persea Books, 1976.
  Play by Play, tr. Hardie St. Martin, New York, Persea Books, 1985.
Martínez, Tomas Eloy. *La novela de Perón*, Buenos Aires, Editorial Legasa, 1985.
  The Perón Novel, tr. Asa Zatz, New York, Pantheon Books, 1988.
Paso, Fernando del. *José Trigo*, Mexico, Siglo Veintiuno Editores, 1966.
  Palinuro de Mexico, Mexico, Mortiz, 1977.
  Noticias del Imperio, Mexico, Editorial Diana, 1987.

Peri Rossi, Cristina. *La nave de los locos*, Barcelona, Seix Barral, 1984.

    The Ship of Fools, tr. Psiche Hughes, Columbia, L., Readers International, 1989.

Poniatowska, Elena. *Hasta no verte Jesús mío*, Mexico, Ediciones Era, 1969.

    La noche de Tlatelolco, Mexico, Ediciones Era, 1971.

    Querido Diego, te abraza Quiela, Mexico, Ediciones Era, 1978.

    Fuerte es el silencio, Mexico, Ediciones Era, 1980.

    De noche vienes, Mexico, Ediciones Era, 1985.

    Massacre in Mexico, tr. Helen R. Lane, New York, Viking Press, 1975.

    Dear Diego, tr. Katherine Silver, New York, Pantheon Books, 1986.

Puga, María Luisa. *La posibilidades del odio*, Mexico, Siglo Veintiuno Editores, 1978.

Roffé, Reina. *La rompiente*, Buenos Aires, Puntosur Editores, 1987.

Sánchez, Luis Rafael. *La guaracha del Macho Camacho*, Buenos Aires, Ediciones de la Flor, 1976.

    Macho Camacho's Beat, tr. Gregory Rabassa, New York, Avon Books, 1980.

Skarmeta, Antonio. *Soñé que la nieve ardía*, Barcelona, Editorial Planeta, 1975.

    La insurrección, Hanover. N.H., Ediciones del Norte, 1982.

    Ardiente paciencia, Buenos Aires, Sudamericana, 1985.

    Match ball, Buenos Aires, Sudamericana, 1989.

    The Insurrection, tr. Paula Sharp, Hanover, N.H., Ediciones del Norte, 1982.

    I Dreamt the Snow Was Burning, tr. Malcolm Coad. New York, Readers International, 1985.

    Burning Patience, tr. Katherine Silver, New York, Pantheon Books, 1987.

Soriano, Osvaldo. *Triste, solitario y final*, Buenos Aires, Ediciones Corregidor, 1973.

    No habrá más penas ni olvido, Barcelona, Editorial Bruguera, 1980.

    Cuarteles de invierno, Barcelona, Editorial Bruguera, 1982.

    A sus plantas rendido un león, Buenos Aires, Sudamericana, 1986.

    Una sombra ya pronto serás. Madrid, Mondadori, 1990.

    A Funny Dirty Little War, tr. Nick Caistor, New York, Readers International, 1986.

    Winter Quarters: A novel of Argentina, tr. Nick Caistor, Columbia, L., Readers International, 1989.

Szichman, Mario. *Crónica falsa*, Buenos Aires, Editorial Jorge Alvarez, 1969.

    Los judíos del mar dulce, Buenos Aires, Editorial Galerna, 1971.

    La verdadera crónica falsa, Buenos Aires, Centro Editor de American Latina, 1972.

    A las 20:25 la señora entró en la inmortalidad, Hanover, N.H., 1981.

    At 8:25, Evita Became Inmortal, tr. Roberto Picciotto, Hanover, N.H., Ediciones del Norte, 1983.

Valenzuela, Luisa. *Cola de lagartija*, Buenos Aires, Editorial Bruguera, 1983.

    Novela negra con argentinos, Buenos Aires, Editorial Plaza & Janés, 1990.

    Realidad nacional desde la cama, Buenos Aires, Grupo Editor Latinoamericano, 1990.

    The Lizard's Tail, tr. Gregory Rabassa, New York, Farrar, Straus, & Giroux, 1983.

Vargas Llosa, Mario. *La guerra del fin del mundo*, Barcelona, Editorial Plaza & Janés, 1981.

    The War of the End of the World, tr. Helen R. Lane, New York, Farrar, Straus, & Giroux, 1984.

Volume 2

Secondary sources

Books

Hart, Patricia. *Narrative Magic in the Fiction of Isabel Allende*, Cranbury, N.J., Associated University Presses, 1989.

Argues that the relationship between magic and Realism in Allende's novels takes the form of a "magical feminism."

Kohut, Karl (ed.). *Un universo cargado de violencia: presentación, aproximación y documentación de la obra de Mempo Giardinelli*, Frankfurt-am-Main, Vervuert Verlag, 1990.

Includes interview with Giardinelli, essays by Jorge Rufinelli, Ricardo Gutiérrez Mouat, and John L. Marambio, essays by Giardinelli, and a complete bibliography.

Lindstrom, Naomi. *Jewish Issues in Argentine Literature: From Gerchunoff to Szichman*, Columbia, University of Missouri Press, 1989.

Studies the works of Alberto Gerchunoff, César Tiempo, Bernardo Verbitsky, David Viñas, José Rabinovich, José Isaacson, Marcos Ricardo Barnatán, Mario Szichman.

Sosnowski, Saúl. *La orilla inminente: escritores judíos argentinos*, Buenos Aires, Editorial Legasa, 1987.

Chapters on the concept of "Latin American Jewishness," and on Germán Rozenmacher, Gerardo Mario Goloboff, and Mario Szichman.

Articles

González Echevarría, Roberto. "Sarduy, the Boom and the Post-boom," *Latin American Literary Review*, 15:26 (1987), 57–72.

Argues for the *Post-Boom* as a postmodern phenomenon and the importance of Sarduy's work in that respect.

Menton, Seymour. "*Noticias de Imperio* y la nueva novela histórica" in his *Narrativa mexicana (desde "Los de abajo" hasta "Noticias del Imperio."* Tlaxcala and Puebla (joint publication), Universidad Autónoma de Tlaxcala and Centro de Ciencias del Lenguaje de la Universidad Autónoma de Puebla, 1991, 141–50.

Differentiates between the new historical novel and previous forms and makes a very positive evaluation of del Paso's novel.

Poniatowska, Elena. "Hasta no verte Jesús mío," *Vuelta*, 24 (1978), 5–11.

Describes her relationship with her informant and how she wrote the novel.

Shaw, Donald L. "Towards a description of the Post-Boom," *Bulletin of Hispanic Studies*, 66 (1989), 87–94.

Clear outline of the tendencies of the *Post-Boom*. Shaw sees these as "the three P's of the Post-Boom": parody, poetry, and pop.

Swanson, Philip. "Conclusion: after the Boom" in Philip Swanson (ed.), *Landmarks in Modern Latin American Fiction*, London, Routledge, 1990, 222–45.

Differentiates between the *Boom* and the *Post-Boom* stressing the diversity of the latter.

Chapter 10: *Spanish American poetry from 1922 to 1975*

Primary sources

Ballagas, Emilio. *Obra poética*, Havana, Editorial Letras Cubanas, 1984.

Borges, Jorge Luis. *Fervor de Buenos Aires*, Buenos Aires, Imprenta Serantes, 1923.
  Luna de enfrente, Buenos Aires, Ediciones Proa, 1925.
  Cuaderno San Martín, Buenos Aires, Ediciones Proa, 1929.
  Poemas, 1922–1943, Buenos Aires, Editorial Losada, 1943.
  Poemas, 1923–1953, Buenos Aires, Emecé, 1954.
  Poemas 1923–1958, Buenos Aires, Emecé, 1958.
  El hacedor, Buenos Aires, Emecé, 1960.
  Obra poética, 1923–1964, Buenos Aires, Emecé, 1964.
  Para las seis cuerdas, Buenos Aires, Emecé, 1965.
  Obra poética, 1923–1967, Buenos Aires, Emecé, 1967.
  El otro, el mismo, Buenos Aires, Emecé, 1969.
  Obra poética, 1923–1977, Buenos Aires, Emecé, 1977.
  Selected Poems, 1923–1967, ed. and intro. Norman Thomas di Giovanni, New York, Delacorte Press, 1972.
  In Praise of Darkness, tr. Norman Thomas di Giovanni, preface Jorge Luis Borges, New York, E. P. Dutton, 1974.

Brull, Mariano. *Poesía*, ed. Emilio de Armas, Havana, Editorial Letras Cubanas, 1983.

Cardenal, Ernesto. *Hora O*, Mexico, Universidad Nacional Autónoma a de México, 1960.
  Epigramas; poemas, Mexico, Universidad Nacional Autónoma de México, 1961.
  Salmos, Medellín, Universidad de Antioquía, 1964.
  Oración por Marilyn Monroe y otros poemas, Medellín, Ediciones La Tertulia, 1965.
  El estrecho dudoso, Madrid, Ediciones Cultura Hispánica, 1966.
  Homenaje a los indios americanos, Buenos Aires and Mexico, Ediciones Carlos Lohlé, 1971.
  Canto nacional, Mexico, Siglo Veintiuno Editores, 1973.
  Nueva antología poética, Mexico, Siglo Veintiuno Editores, 1978. 2nd. edn. 1979.
  Homage to the American Indians, tr. Monique and Carlos Altschul, Baltimore, Johns Hopkins University Press, 1973.
  Psalms of Struggle and Liberation, tr. Emile G. McAnany, foreword Thomas Merton, New York, Herder & Herder, 1971; rpt. New York, Seabury Press, 1973.

Castellanos, Rosario. *Apuntes para una declaración de fé*, Mexico, Ediciones de América, 1948.
  Trayectoria del polvo, Mexico, Colección El Cristal Fugitivo, 1948.
  De la vigilia estéril, Mexico, Ediciones de América, 1950.
  Dos poemas, Mexico, Icaro, 1950.
  El rescate del mundo, Mexico, Ediciones de América, 1952.
  Poemas (1953–1955), Mexico, Colección metáfora, 1957.
  Al pie de la letra, Xalapa, Mexico, Universidad Veracruzana, 1959.
  Salomé y Judith: poemas dramáticos, Mexico, Editorial Jus, 1959.
  Lívida luz, Mexico, Universidad Nacional Autónoma de México, 1960.

Poesía no eres tú: obra poética 1948–1971, Mexico, Fondo de Cultura Económica, 1972; 2nd. edn. 1975.

Cuadra, Pablo Antonio. *Poemas nicaragüenses, 1930–1933*, Santiago, Nascimento, 1934.

Canto temporal, Granada, Cuadernos del Taller de San Lucas, 1943.

Poemas con un crepúsculo a cuestas, Madrid, Ediciones Cultura Hispánica, 1949.

La tierra prometida, ed. Ernesto Cardenal, Managua, El Hilo Azul, 1952.

El jaguar y la luna, Managua, Editorial Artes Gráficas, 1959.

Zoo, San Salvador, Publicaciones del Ministerio de Educación, 1962.

The Jaguar & the Moon, tr. Thomas Merton, Greensboro, N.C., Unicorn Press, 1963.

Cantos de Cifar, Avila, "Institución Gran Duque de Alba," Diputación Provincial, 1971.

Songs of Cifar and the Sweet Sea, tr. and ed. Grace Schulman and Ann McCarthy de Zavala, New York, Columbia University Press, 1979.

Dalton, Roque. *Poemas*, San Salvador, Editorial Universitaria, 1967.

La taberna y otros lugares, Havana, Casa de las Américas, 1969.

Las historias prohibidas de Pulgarcito, Mexico, Siglo Veintiuno Editores, 1974.

Poemas clandestinos. Historia y poemas de una lucha de clases, Mexico, Universidad Autónoma de Puebla, 1980.

Girondo, Oliverio. *Calcomanías*, Madrid, Espasa-Calpe, Imprenta Sucesores de Rivadeneyra, 1925.

Espantapájaros (al alcance de todos), Buenos Aires, Ediciones Proa, 1932.

Persuasión de los días, Buenos Aires, Editorial Losada, Imprenta López, 1942.

En la masmédula, Buenos Aires, Editorial Losada, 1956.

Obras completas, Buenos Aires, Editorial Losada, 1968.

Homenaje a Girondo, ed. Jorge Schwartz, Buenos Aires, Ediciones Corregidor, 1987.

Gorostiza, José. *Canciones para cantar en las barcas*, Mexico, Cultura, 1925.

Muerte sin fin, Mexico, R. Loera & Chávez, 1939.

Poesía, Mexico, Fondo de Cultura Económica, 1964.

Death Without End, tr. Laura Villaseñor, Austin, University of Texas Press, 1969.

Guillén, Nicolás. *Motivos de son*, Havana, Rambla & Bouza, 1930.

Sóngoro Cosongo. Poemas mulatos, Havana, Imprenta Ucar, García, & Cía., 1931.

West Indies, Ltd., Havana, Imprenta Ucar, García, & Cía, 1934.

Cantos para soldados y sones para turistas, Mexico, Editorial Masa, 1937.

España, poema en cuatro angustias y una esperanza, Valencia, Ediciones Españolas, 1937.

El son entero. Suma poética, 1929–1946, Buenos Aires, Pleamar, 1947.

La paloma de vuelo popular y Elegías, Buenos Aires, Editorial Losada, 1959.

Tengo, Santa Clara, Cuba, Universidad Central de Las Villas, 1964.

El gran zoo, Havana, Empresa Consolidada de Artes Gráficas, 1967.

El diario que a diario, Havana, Unión, 1972.

Summa poética, ed. Luis Iñigo Madrigal, Madrid, Cátedra, 1976.

Obra poética, 2 vols., Havana, Editorial Letras Cubanas, 1980.

Cuba Libre; poems by Nicolás Guillén, tr. Langston Hughes and Ben Frederic Caruthers, Los Angeles, Anderson Ritchie (The Ward Ritchie Press), 1948.

¡Patria o muerte! The Great Zoo and other poems by Nicolas Guillén, tr., and intro., Roberto Márquez, New York and London, Monthly Review Press, 1972.

Tengo, tr. Richard J. Carr., Detroit, Broadside Press, 1974.

The Daily Daily, tr. Vera M. Kutzinski, Berkeley, University of California Press, 1989.

Huidobro, Vicente. *La gruta del silencio*, Santiago, Imprenta Universitaria, n.d. [1913].

Pasando y pasando . . . crónicas y comentarios, Santiago, Imprenta Chile, 1914.

Hallali. Poème de Guerre, Madrid, 1918.

Manifestes, Paris, Editions de la Revue Mondiale, 1925.

Altazor o el viaje en paracaídas, Madrid, Compañía Iberoamericana de Publicaciones, 1931.

Temblor de cielo, Madrid, Editorial Plutarco, n.d. [1931].

Obras completas, prologue Hugo Montes, Santiago, Editorial Andrés Bello, 1976.

Arctic Poems, tr. William Witherup and Serge Echeverría, Austin, Texas, Desert Review Press, 1974.

The Selected Poetry of Vicente Huidobro, ed. David M. Guss, New York, New Directions, 1981.

Altazor, or a voyage in a parachute, tr. Eliot Weinberger, Saint Paul, Minn., Graywolf Press, 1988.

Ibáñez, Sara de. *Canto*, Buenos Aires, Editorial Losada, 1940.

Jamís, Fayad. *Los puentes (poesía, 1956–1957)*, Havana, Ediciones R, 1962.

Cuerpos, Havana, Unión, 1966.

Juárroz, Roberto. *Segunda poesía vertical*, Buenos Aires, Ediciones Equis, 1963.

Tercera poesía vertical, Buenos Aires, Ediciones Equis, 1965.

Poesía vertical, Barcelona, Barral Editores, 1974.

Quinta poesía vertical, Buenos Aires, Ediciones Equis, 1974.

Poesía vertical, antología mayor, Buenos Aires, Ediciones C. Lohlé, 1978.

Séptima poesía vertical, Caracas, Monte Avila, 1982.

Vertical Poetry, tr. W. S. Merwin, San Francisco, North Point Press, 1988.

Lezama Lima, José. *Muerte de Narciso*, Havana, Ucar, García, & Cía., 1937.

Coloquio con Juan Ramón Jiménez, Havana, Secretaría de Educación, Dirección de Cultura, 1938.

Enemigo rumor, Havana, Ucar, García, & Cía., 1941.

Aventuras sigilosas, Havana, Orígenes, 1945.

La fijeza, Havana, Orígenes, 1949.

Dador, Havana, (private edn.), 1960.

Poesías completas, Havana, Instituto del Libro, 1970.

Fragmentos a su imán, Havana, Editorial Arte y Literatura, 1977.

Obras completas de José Lezama Lima, 2 vols., Mexico, Aguilar, 1977.

Poesía completa, Havana, Editorial Letras Cubanas, 1985.

Mistral, Gabriela. *Desolación*, New York, Instituto de las Españas, 1922.

Ternura, Madrid, Calleja, 1924.

Tala, Buenos Aires, Sur, 1938.

Lagar, Santiago, Editorial del Pacífico, 1954.

Poesías completas, ed. Margaret Bates, Madrid, Aguilar, 1958.

Antología poética de Gabriela Mistral, ed. Alfonso Calderón, Santiago, Editorial

Universitaria, 1974.

Moro, César. *Le château de grisou*, Mexico, Editions Tigrondine, 1943.

Lettre d'amour, Mexico, Editions Dyn, 1944.

Trafalgar Square, Lima, Editions Tigrondine, 1954.

Amour à mort, Paris, Le cheval marin, 1957.

La tortuga ecuestre y otros poemas, 1924–1949, Lima, Editorial San Marcos, 1958.

Derniers poèmes. Ultimos poemas (1953–1955), tr. Ricardo Silva-Santisteban, Lima, Ediciones Capulí, 1976.

La tortuga ecuestre y otros textos, ed. Julio Ortega, Caracas, Monte Avila, 1976.

Obra poética, ed. Ricardo Silva-Santisteban, Lima, Instituto Nacional de Cultura, 1980.

The Scandalous Life of César Moro, in his own words, tr. from French and Spanish by Philip Ward, New York and Cambridge, The Oleander Press, 1976.

Neruda, Pablo. *Crepusculario*, Santiago, Editorial Claridad, 1923.

Veinte poemas de amor y una canción desesperada, Santiago, Nascimento, 1924.

Tentativa del hombre infinito, Santiago, Nascimento, 1926.

Residencia en la tierra (1925/1931), Santiago, Nascimento, 1933.

Residencia en la tierra (1925/1935), 2 vols., Madrid, Cruz & Raya, 1935.

Tercera residencia (1935/1945), Buenos Aires, Editorial Losada, 1947.

Alturas de Macchu Picchu, Santiago, Libreria Neira, 1948.

Canto general. Mexico, Ediciones Océano, 1950.

Los versos del capitán, Buenos Aires, Editorial Losada, 1953.

Odas elementales, Buenos Aires, Editorial Losada, 1954.

Nuevas odas elementales, Buenos Aires, Editorial Losada, 1956.

Tercer libro de las odas, Buenos Aires, Editorial Losada, 1957.

Estravagario, Buenos Aires, Editorial Losada, 1958.

Cien sonetos de amor, Buenos Aires, Editorial Losada, 1959.

Canción de gesta, Havana, Imprenta Nacional de Cuba, 1960.

Plenos poderes, Buenos Aires, Editorial Losada, 1962.

Memorial de Isla Negra, Buenos Aires, Editorial Losada, 1964.

Fin del mundo, Santiago de Chile, Sociedad de Arte Contemporáneo, 1969.

La espada encendida, Buenos Aires, Editorial Losada, 1970.

Las piedras del cielo, Buenos Aires, Editorial Losada, 1970.

Geografía infructuosa, Buenos Aires, Editorial Losada, 1972.

El mar y las campanas, Buenos Aires, Editorial Losada, 1973.

Incitación al nixonicidio y alabanza de la revolución chilena, Santiago, Quimantú, 1973.

Obras completas, ed. Margarita Aguirre, Alfonso Escudero, Hernán Loyola, 4th edn., 3 vols., Buenos Aires, Editorial Losada, 1973.

2000, Buenos Aires, Editorial Losada, 1974.

Confieso que he vivido, memorias, Barcelona, Seix Barral, 1974.

El corazón amarillo, Buenos Aires, Editorial Losada, 1974.

Poesía, 2 vols., Bilbao, Editorial Noguer, 1974.

Canto general, ed. Enrico Mario Santí, Madrid, Cátedra, 1990.

The Heights of Macchu Picchu, tr. Nathaniel Tarn, New York, Farrar, Straus, & Giroux, 1967, rpt. New York, Noonday Press, 1967.

A New Decade: Poems 1956–1967, ed. and tr. Ben Belitt and Alastair Reid, New

York, Grove Press, 1969.

Twenty Love Songs and a Song of Despair, tr. W. S. Merwin, London, Cape, 1969, rpt. New York, Grossman, 1971.

Neruda and Vallejo: Selected poems, ed. Robert Bly, tr. Robert Bly, John Knoepfle, James Wright, Boston, Beacon Press, 1971.

Estravagaria, tr. Alistair Reid, London, Jonathan Cape, 1972, rpt. New York, Farrar, Straus, & Giroux, 1974.

Residence on Earth, tr. Donald D. Walsh, New York, New Directions, 1973.

Five Decades, A Selection (Poems 1925–1970), ed. and tr. Ben Belitt, New York, Grove Press, 1974.

Memoirs, tr. Hardie St. Martin, New York, Farrar, Straus, & Giroux, 1977.

Isla Negra, tr. Alastair Reid, New York, Farrar, Straus, & Giroux, 1981.

Canto general, tr. Jack Schmitt, Berkeley, University of California Press, 1990.

Pacheco, José Emilio. *Los elementos de la noche*, Mexico, Universidad Nacional Autónoma de México, 1963.

El reposo del fuego, Mexico, Fondo de Cultura Económica, 1966.

No me preguntes cómo pasa el tiempo, Mexico, Mortiz, 1969; 1977.

Irás y no volverás, Mexico, Fondo de Cultura Económica, 1973.

Islas a la deriva, Mexico, Siglo Veintiuno Editores, 1976.

Desde entonces, Mexico, Ediciones Era, 1980.

Los trabajos del mar, Madrid, Cátedra, 1983.

Miro la tierra, Mexico, Ediciones Era, 1986.

Don't Ask Me How the Time Goes By, tr. Alistair Reid, New York, Columbia University Press, 1969.

Tree Between Two Walls, tr. and ed. Dorn and Gordon Brotherston, Los Angeles, Black Sparrow Press, 1969.

Signals from the Flames, tr. Thomas Hoeksema, Pittsburgh, Latin American Literary Review Press, 1980.

Selected Poems, ed. George McWhirter, New York, New Directions, 1987.

Padilla, Heberto. *El justo tiempo humano*, Havana, UEAC, 1962.

Fuera del juego, Buenos Aires, Aditor, 1969.

El hombre junto al mar, Barcelona, Seix Barral, 1981.

Sent Off the Field; A selection from the poetry of Heberto Padilla, tr. J. M. Cohen, London, Deutsch, 1972.

Subversive Poetry: The Padilla affair, various translators, Washington, Georgetown University Cuban Students Association, n.d. [1972].

Legacies: Selected poems, tr. Alastair Reid and Andrew Hurley, New York, Farrar, Straus, & Giroux, 1982.

Palés Matos, Luis. *Azaleas*, Guayama, Puerto Rico, Casa Editorial Rodríguez y Cía., 1915.

Tuntún de pasa y grifería. Poemas afroantillanos, San Juan, Biblioteca de Autores Puertorriqueños, 1937.

Poesía, 1915–1956, Río Piedras, Puerto Rico, Editorial Universitaria, 1964.

Parra, Nicanor. *Cancionero sin nombre*, Santiago, Nascimento, 1937.

Poemas y antipoemas, Santiago, Nascimento, 1954.

La cueca larga, Santiago, Editorial Universitaria, 1958.

Versos de salón, Santiago, Nascimento, 1962.

La cueca larga y otros poemas, ed. Margarita Aguirre, Buenos Aires, EUDEBA, 1964.
Canciones rusas, Santiago, Editorial Universitaria, 1967.
Obra gruesa, Santiago, Editorial Universitaria, 1969.
Poemas y antipoemas, ed. René de Costa, Madrid, Cátedra, 1988.
Anti-poems, tr. Jorge Elliott, San Francisco, City Lights Books, 1960.
Poems and Antipoems, ed. Miller Williams, New York, New Directions, 1967.
Emergency Poems, tr. Miller Williams, New York, New Directions, 1972.
Antipoems, New and Selected, tr. Lawrence Ferlinguetti, *et al.*, New York, New Directions, 1985.
Paz, Octavio. *Luna silvestre*, Mexico, Fabula, 1933.
Libertad bajo palabra, Mexico, Tenzontle, 1949.
El laberinto de la soledad, Mexico, D. F. Cuadernos Americanos, 1950.
¿Aguila o sol?, Mexico, Tentzontle, 1951.
Semillas para un himno, Mexico, Tenzontle, 1954.
Piedra de sol, Mexico, Tenzontle, 1957.
La estación violenta, Mexico, Fondo de Cultura Económica, 1958.
Libertad bajo palabra: obra poética, 1935–1958, Mexico, Fondo de Cultura Económica, 1960.
Salamandra (1958–1961). Mexico, Mortíz, 1962, 2nd. edn., revised, 1969.
Viento entero, Delhi, 1965.
El arco y la lira, Mexico, Fondo de Cultura Económica, 1967.
Blanco, Mexico, Mortiz, 1967.
Libertad bajo palabra (1935–1957), Mexico, Fondo de Cultura Económica, 1968.
La centena (poemas: 1935–1968), Barcelona, Barral Editores, 1969.
Ladera este (1962–1968), Mexico, Mortiz, 1969.
¿Aguila o sol? – Eagle or Sun? tr. Eliot Weinberger, New York, Center for Inter-American Relations, Inc, October House [1970?].
Topoemas, Mexico, Ediciones Era, 1971.
Renga, Mexico, Mortiz, 1971.
Poemas (1935–1975), Barcelona, Seix Barral, 1979.
Libertad bajo palabra, ed. Enrico Mario Santí, Madrid, Cátedra, 1988.
Selected Poems of Octavio Paz, Bloomington, University of Indiana Press, 1963.
Configurations, (various translators), New York, New Directions, 1971.
The Bow and the Lyre, tr. Ruth L. C. Simons, Austin, University of Texas Press, 1973.
Early Poems. 1935–1955, tr. Murial Rukeyser and others, New York, New Directions, 1974.
The Collected Poems of Octavio Paz. 1957–1987, ed. Eliot Weinberger, New York, New Directions, 1987.
Pizarnik, Alejandra. *Arbol de Diana*, Buenos Aires, Sur, 1962.
Los trabajos y las noches, Buenos Aires, Sudamericana, 1965.
Extracción de la piedra de la locura, Buenos Aires, Sudamericana, 1968.
El infierno musical, Buenos Aires, Siglo Veintiuno Editores, 1971.
El deseo de la palabra, Barcelona, Barral Editores, 1975.
Textos de sombra y últimos poemas, Buenos Aires, Sudamericana, 1982.
Alejandra Pizarnik: a profile, ed, intro. Frank Graziano, tr. Maria Rosa Fort and

Frank Graziano, additional translations by Suzanne Jill Levine, Durango, Colo., Logbridge-Rhodes, 1987.

Vallejo, César. *Los heraldos negros*, Lima, [Imprenta Souza Ferreyra], 1918.

Trilce, Lima, Talleres Tip. de la Penitenciaría, 1922; 2nd. edn. Madrid, Compañía Iberoamericana de Publicaciones, 1930.

España, aparta de mi este cáliz, Spain, Ediciones Literarias del Comisariado del Ejército del Este, 1939.

Poemas humanos (with *España, aparta de mi este cáliz*), Paris, Les Editions des Presses Modernes, 1939.

Obra poética completa, Lima, Francisco Moncloa Editores, 1968.

Obra poética, ed. Américo Ferrari, Madrid, Colección Archivos, 1988.

Poemas humanos. Human Poems, tr. Clayton Eschleman, New York, Grove Press, 1968, rpt. London, Cape, 1969.

César Vallejo. An anthology of his poetry, intro. and notes, James Higgins, Oxford, Pergamon Press, 1970.

Neruda and Vallejo: Selected poems, ed. Robert Bly, tr. Robert Bly, John Knoepfle, and James Wright, Boston, Beacon Press, 1971.

Spain, Take this Cup Away from Me, tr. Clayton Eschleman and José Rubia Barcia, New York, Grove Press, 1974.

Trilce, tr. David Smith, Tokyo, Mushinsha, 1973; rpt. New York, Grossman Publishers, 1974.

César Vallejo. Selected poems, tr. and ed. Dorn and Gordon Brotherston, Harmondsworth, Penguin Books, 1976.

The Complete Posthumous Poetry, tr. Clayton Eshleman and José Rubia Barcia, Berkeley, University of California Press, 1978.

Villaurrutia, Xavier. *Reflejos*, Mexico, Editora Cultura, 1926.

Dos nocturnos, Mexico, Barandal, 1931.

Nocturnos, Mexico, Fábula, 1931.

Nocturno de los ángeles, Mexico, Hipocampo, 1936.

Nocturno mar, Mexico, Hipocampo, 1937.

Nostalgia de la muerte, Buenos Aires, Sur, 1938; 2nd. edn., revised, Mexico, Ediciones Mictlán, 1946.

Décima muerte y otros poemas no coleccionados, Mexico, Nueva Voz, 1941.

Canto a la primavera y otros poemas, Mexico, Editorial Stylo, 1948.

Poesía y teatro completos, Mexico, Fondo de Cultura Económica, 1953.

Vitier, Cintio. *Luz ya sueño*, Havana, Imprenta Ucar, García, & Cía., 1938.

De mi provincia, Havana, Orígenes, 1945.

Extrañeza de estar, Havana, Imprenta Ucar, García, & Cía., 1945.

Vísperas, 1938–1953, Havana, Orígenes, 1953.

Canto llano, 1954–1955, Havana, Orígenes, 1956.

Escrito y cantado, 1954–1959, Havana, Imprenta Ucar, García, & Cía., 1959.

Antología poética, Havana, Editorial Letras Cubanas, 1981.

Westphalen, Emilio Adolfo. *Las insulas extrañas*, Lima, Compañía de Impresiones y Publicidad, 1933.

Abolición de la muerte, Lima, Ediciones Perú Actual, 1935.

Otra imagen deleznable. . ., Mexico, Fondo de Cultura Económica, 1980.

Ruiz del Vizo, Hortensia (ed.). *Black Poetry of the Americas (a bilingual survey)*, Miami, Ediciones Universal, 1972.

Secondary sources

Books

Albornoz, Aurora de, and Julio Rodríguez Luis (eds.). *Sensemayá: la poesía negra en el mundo hispanoahablante*, Madrid, Orígenes, 1980.

Alegría, Fernando. *Walt Whitman en Hispanoamérica*, Mexico, Colección Studium, 1954.

Encyclopedic study of Whitman's influence in Spanish America.

Alonso, Amado. *Poesía y estilo de Pablo Neruda. Interpretación de una poesía hermética*, Buenos Aires, Editorial Losada, 1940.

Pathbreaking book-length study of the early Neruda. A classic by one of the major Spanish stylistic critics.

Angiula, Eduardo, and Volodía Teitelboim, *Antología de poesía chilena nueva*, Santiago, Zig-Zag, 1935.

Ardjis, Homero. *Seis poetas hispanoamericanos de hoy*, New York, Harcourt Brace Jovanovich, 1972.

Baciu, Stefan. *Antología de la poesía surrealista latinoamericana*, Mexico, Mortiz, 1974.

Bajarlía, Juan Jacobo. *La polémica Reverdy-Huidobro: origen del ultraísmo*, Buenos Aires, Devenir, 1964.

Best on a polemic that was important for Huidobro and the Spanish American Avant-Garde.

Balakian, Anna. *Surrealism: The road to the Absolute*, 2nd edn., New York, E. P. Dutton, 1970.

Examines the roots of the movement from the nineteenth century to Breton and after. Lucid, informed, one of the best.

Ballagas, Emilio. *Mapas de la poesía negra americana*, Buenos Aires, Pleamar, 1946.

Bary, David. *Huidobro o la vocación poética*, Universidad de Granada, 1963.

One of the first books dedicated to Huidobro.

Benedetti, Mario. *Los poetas comunicantes*. Interviews with Roque Dalton, Nicanor Parra, Jorge Enrique Adoum, Ernesto Cardenal, Carlos María Gutiérrez, Gonzalo Rojas, Eliseo Diego, Roberto Fernández Retamar, Juan Gelman and Idea Vilariño, Montevideo, Biblioteca de Marcha, 1972.

Interviews portray the cultural atmosphere of the 1960s in Spanish America. Emphasis on socially committed poetry.

Bruns, Gerald L. *Modern Poetry and the Idea of Language*, New Haven, Yale University Press, 1974.

Classic book on the Orphic and hermetic visions of language in poetry.

Bürger, Peter. *Theory of the Avant-Garde*, tr. Michael Shaw, foreword Jochen Schulte-Sasse, Theory and History of Literature, 4, Minneapolis, University of Minnesota Press, 1984.

Rigorous study of the Avant-Garde and its problems. Still unsurpassed for its theoretical framework.

Camurati, Mireya. *Poesía y poética de Vicente Huidobro*, Buenos Aires, Fernando García Cambeiro, 1980.

Good book on Huidobro's poetics.

Caracciolo Trejo, Enrique, (ed.). *The Penguin Book of Latin American Verse*, intro. Henry Gifford, Harmondsworth and Baltimore, Penguin Books, 1971.

Carter, Boyd G. *Las revistas literarias de hispanoamérica. Breve historia y contenido*, Mexico, Ediciones de Andrea, 1959.

Excellent work on Spanish American journals.

Cobo Borda, Juan Jacobo. *Antología de la poesía hispanoamericana*, Mexico, Fondo de Cultura Económica, 1985.

Cohen, John Michael (ed. and tr.). *The Penguin Book of Spanish Verse*, Harmondsworth and Baltimore, Penguin Books, 1956.

Cortínez, Carlos (ed.). *Borges the Poet*, Fayeteville, University of Arkansas Press, 1986.

A collection of excellent articles on Borges's poetry by various authors.

Costa, René de (ed.). *Vicente Huidobro y el creacionismo*, Madrid, Taurus, 1975.

Reprints documents related to Huidobro and the Avant-Garde and the most important essays written at the time.

The Poetry of Pablo Neruda, Cambridge, Mass., Harvard University Press, 1979.

Insightful book-length study of the author.

Vicente Huidobro: The careers of a poet, Oxford, Clarendon Press, 1984.

The most thorough study of Huidobro to date. Includes previously unpublished primary sources.

Debicki, Andrew Peter. *Poetas hispanoamericanos contemporáneos: punto de vista, perspectiva, experiencia*, Madrid, Gredos, 1976.

Well-written essays on Borges, Villaurrutia, Paz, Parra, and others by an excellent critic of Mexican poetry. Examines relations between poetry and narrative.

De Onís, Federico. *Antología de la poesía española e hispanoamericana (1882–1932)*, Madrid, Imprenta de la librería y casa editora Hernández, 1934.

De Torre, Guillermo. *Literaturas europeas de vanguardia*, Madrid, Rafael Caro Raggio, 1925.

A classic that has spawned countless polemics, the best book on the Avant-Garde written by a first-person witness.

Historia de las literaturas de vanguardia, Madrid, Ediciones Guardarrama, 1965.

A very revised version of the above, written with more historical distance and in a much more tempered language.

Durán, Manuel, and Margery Safir. *Earth Tones. The poetry of Pablo Neruda*, Bloomington, Indiana University Press, 1981.

One of the best books on Neruda.

Edwards, Jorge. *Persona non grata*, Barcelona, Seix Barral, 1973.

Includes biographical accounts of Neruda and his relationships with the poets of the Cuban Revolution.

Adios, poeta. . ., Barcelona, Tusquets Editores, 1990.

Interesting memoirs of the writer's friendship with Neruda.

Escalona-Escalona, José Antonio (ed.). *Muestra de poesía hispanoamericana del siglo XX*, 2 vols., Caracas, Biblioteca Ayacucho, 1985.

Fein, John. *Toward Octavio Paz. A reading of his major poems 1957–1976*, Lexington, University of Kentucky Press, 1986.

Some of the best readings of Paz's major works to date.

Felstiner, John. *Translating Neruda, The Way to Macchu Picchu*, Stanford University Press, 1980.

Excellent study of the problems of translating Neruda's major poem.

Fernández, Teodosio. *La poesía hispanoamericana (hasta final del modernismo)*, Madrid, Taurus, 1989.

Good general history of Spanish American poetry.

Fitts, Dudley (ed.). *Anthology of Contemporary Latin American Poetry*, Norfolk, Conn., New Directions, 1942.

Flores, Angel. *Aproximaciones a Octavio Paz*, Mexico, Mortiz, 1974.

Collection of important essays on Octavio Paz written during perhaps the most productive period of Paz's life.

Florit, Eugenio, and José Olivio Jiménez. *La poesía hispanoamericana desde el Modernismo*, New York, Appleton-Century-Crofts, 1968.

Forster, Merlin H. *Tradition and Renewal: Essays on twentieth century Latin American literature and culture*, Urbana, University of Illinois Press, 1975.

One of the best books on the modern tradition in Latin America.

Fire and Ice: The poetry of Xavier Villaurrutia, University of North Carolina at Chapel Hill, 1976.

Good work on Villaurrutia, one of a few.

Franco, Jean. *César Vallejo. The dialectics of poetry and silence*, Cambridge University Press, 1976.

Comprehensive book on the aesthetics of a very complex poet.

Gelpí, Juan. *Enunciación y dependencia en José Gorostiza. Estudio de una máscara poética*, Mexico, Universidad Nacional Autónoma de México, 1984.

A lucid interpretation that examines Gorostiza and his relationships with modern poetry.

Gertal, Zunilda. *Borges y su retorno a la poesía*, New York, The University of Iowa and Las Américas, 1969.

Very good study of Borges's poetry.

Gimferrer, Pere (ed.). *Octavio Paz*, Madrid, Taurus, 1982.

Good selection of essays.

González Echevarría, Roberto. *Alejo Carpentier: The pilgrim at home*, Ithaca, Cornell University Press, 1977.

Of particular interest to students of poetry is the context of Afro-Caribbean cultural politics, aesthetics, and practice in the Cuba of the 1930s. A reading of its unsurpassed examination of Carpentier's polemics with Surrealism is also recommended.

Hidalgo, Alberto, Vicente Huidobro, and Jorge Luis Borges. *Indice de la nueva poesía americana*, Buenos Aires, Sociedad de Publicaciones El Inca, 1926.

Jiménez, José Olivio. *Antología de la poesía hispanoamericana contemporánea: 1914–1970*, Madrid, Alianza Editorial, 1978.

Jiménez, Juan Ramón. *Españoles de tres mundos*, Buenos Aires, Editorial Losada,

1942.

For his acerbic comments on Pablo Neruda.

Kirkpatrick, Gwen. *The Dissonant Legacy of Modernismo: Lugones, Herrera y Reissig, and the voices of modern Spanish American poetry*, Berkeley, University of California Press, 1989.

The best study on late *Modernismo* in its transition to the Avant-Garde.

Kushigian, Julia. *Orientalism in the Hispanic Literary Tradition. In dialogue with Borges, Paz, and Sarduy*, Albuquerque, University of New Mexico Press, 1991.

Establishes the different orientalist readings of three major writers.

Kutzinski, Vera M. *Against the American Grain: Myth and history in William Carlos Williams, Jay Wright, and Nicolás Guillén*, Baltimore, Johns Hopkins University Press, 1987.

One of the few books that deal with a Pan-American framework; some of the best readings of Guillén.

Larrea, Juan. *Del Surrealismo a Macchu Picchu*, Mexico, Mortiz, 1967.

A negative reading of Neruda, an important document for the polemics of the time.

López Adorno-Pedro, J. *Vías teóricas a 'Altazor' de Vicente Huidobro*, American University Studies, Series II, Romance Languages and Literature, 33, New York, Peter Lang, 1987.

Good and original reading of *Altazor*, based on new language theories.

Morejón, Nancy (ed.), *Recopilación de textos sobre Nicolás Guillén*, Havana, Casa de las Américas, 1974.

A canonical and by now dated collection of criticism on Guillén. Still an important publication.

Murray, Frederic W. *The Aesthetics of Contemporary Spanish American Social Protest Poetry*, Lewiston, N.Y., E. Mellen Press, 1990.

Examines Spanish American poetry with an eye for its aesthetics.

Neale-Silva, Eduardo. *César Vallejo en su fase trílcica*, University of Wisconsin Press, 1975.

Still the most comprehensive work on Vallejo's most difficult book, the obligatory point of departure for all later critiques.

Ogden, Estela Busto. *El creacionismo de Vicente Huidobro en sus relaciones con la estética cubista*, Madrid, Playor, 1983.

Very useful and informative account of Huidobro's relationship with his cubist Parisian milieu.

Ortega, Julio. *Antología de la poesía hispanoamericana actual*, Mexico, Siglo Veintiuno Editores, 1987.

Ortega, Julio (ed.). *César Vallejo*, Madrid, Taurus 1974.

Documents, testimonials, and very good essays.

Paz, Octavio. *Las peras del olmo*, Barcelona, Seix Barral, 1971.

Collection of essays on varied figures.

Los hijos del limo: del romanticismo a la vanguardia, Barcelona, Seix Barral, 1974.

A classic book on modernity in Europe and the Americas.

Xavier Villaurrutia en persona y obra, Mexico, Fondo de Cultura Económica, 1978.

Villaurrutia as he is remembered, read, and narrated by Paz. An excellent account of the problems that faced the *Contemporáneos*.

Children of the Mire: Modern poetry from Romanticism to the Avant-Garde, tr. Roches Phillips, Cambridge, Mass., Harvard University Press, 1974.

Paz, Octavio (ed. and intro.). *Anthology of Mexican Poetry*, tr. Samuel Beckett, preface C. M. Bowra, Bloomington, Indiana University Press, 1958; rpt. London, Thames & Hudson, 1959; London, Calder & Boyars, 1970.

Paz, Octavio *et al. Poesía en movimiento, México, 1915–1966*, Mexico, Siglo Veintiuno Editores, 1966.

Reyes, Alfonso. *La experiencia literaria*, Buenos Aires, Editorial Losada, 1952.

Essay on "Las jitanjáforas" is included in this collection of essays on the different genres by one of the master Spanish American intellectuals of the twentieth century.

Rodríguez Monegal, Emir. *El viajero inmóvil*, Buenos Aires, Editorial Losada, 1966.

One of the best books on Neruda. It blends biographical information with Monegal's lucid and sharp readings of the poems.

Jorge Luis Borges: a literary biography, New York, E. P. Dutton, 1978.

Still the only biography on Borges. Part II, in particular, is good on Borges's early poetry.

Rodríguez Monegal, Emir, and Enrico Mario Santí. *Pablo Neruda*, Madrid, Taurus, 1980.

Collection of excellent essays and interesting testimonials.

Roggiano, Alfredo (ed.). *Octavio Paz*, Madrid, Editorial Fundamentos, 1979.

Essays by José Emilio Pacheco, Manuel Durán, and others. It includes a useful bibliography.

Ruiz del Vizo, Hortensia (ed.) *Black Poetry of the Americas (a bilingual survey)*, Miami, Ediciones Universal, 1972.

Santí, Enrico Mario. *Pablo Neruda. The poetics of prophecy*, Ithaca, Cornell University Press, 1982.

Indispensable reading on Neruda, one of the best books on the poet.

Schopf, Federico. *Del vanguardismo a la antipoesía*, Rome, Bulzoni, 1986.

Very useful account of Spanish American poetry.

Schwartz, Jorge (ed.). *Las vanguardias latinoamericanas. Textos programáticos y críticos*, tr. of Portuguese texts by Estela dos Santos, Madrid, Cátedra, 1991.

Sheridan, Guillermo. *Los "Contemporáneos" ayer*, Mexico, Fondo de Cultura Económica, 1985.

The best history and account of the group. Sees *Contemporáneos* as an imaginary place and not strictly as a generation.

Sefamí, Jacobo. *Contemporary Spanish American Poets: A bibliography of primary and secondary sources*, New York, Greenwood Press, 1992.

Most recent and complete bibliography of living poets.

Smart, Ian I. *Nicolás Guillén: Popular poet of the Caribbean*, Columbia and London, University of Missouri Press, 1990.

Good readings on Guillén and on his importance in the wider Caribbean setting.

Strand, Mark (ed.). *New Poetry of Mexico, Selected with Notes by Octavio Paz, Alí Cumacero, José Emilio Pacheco and Homero Aridjis*, intro. Octavio Paz, New York, E. P. Dutton, 1970, rpt. London, Secker & Warburg, 1972.

Sucre, Guillermo. *Borges el poeta*, Caracas, Monte Avila, 1974.

One of the first books dedicated to Borges as poet, written with Sucre's usual sensitivity and intelligent readings.

La máscara, la transparencia: ensayos sobre poesía hispanoamericana, 2nd edn., revised, Mexico, Fondo de Cultura Económica, 1985.

The best book on Spanish American poetry and poetics available to date.

Verani, Hugo. *Octavio Paz: bibliografía*, Universidad Nacional Autónoma de México, 1983.

Indispensable and most up-to-date source for Paz.

Las vanguardias literarias en Hispanoamérica (manifiestos, proclamas y otros escritos), Rome, Bulzoni, 1986.

Videla, Gloria. *El ultraísmo: estudios sobre movimientos de vanguardia en España*, Madrid, Gredos, 1963.

First, and still the best, book on Spanish and Argentinian Ultraism. Reproduces documents of the time.

Videla de Rivero, Gloria. *Direcciones del vanguardismo hispanoamericano*, 2 vols., Mendoza, Argentina, Universidad Nacional de Cuyo, Facultad de Filosofía y Letras, 1990.

Examines various ramifications of the Avant-Garde.

Villaurrutia, Xavier (ed.). *Laurel. Antología de la poesía moderna en lengua española*, Mexico, Editorial Séneca, 1941, rpt. with afterword by Octavio Paz, Mexico, Editorial Trillas, 1986.

Vitier, Cintio. *Lo cubano en la poesía*, Havana, Universidad de Las Villas, 1958.

A classic work by one of Cuba's best poet–critics. A search for the distinctive Cuban elements as defined by a prominent member of the *Orígenes* group.

Weisgerber, Jean (ed.). *Les avant-gardes littéraires au XXème siècle*, 2 vols., Budapest, Akadémiai Kiadó, 1984.

The most encyclopedic to date on the world-wide manifestations of the Avant-Garde.

Wood, Cecil G. *The creacionismo of Vicente Huidobro*, Fredericktown, York Press, 1978.

Early readings on Huidobro, focuses on the Chilean's poetic movement.

Xirau, Ramón. *Poesía hispanoamericana y española*, Mexico, Imprenta Universitaria, 1961.

Essays on Borges, Huidobro, Paz, and others by a major Mexican philosopher.

Poesía y conocimiento: Borges, Lezama Lima, Octavio Paz, Mexico, Mortiz, 1978.

Another indispensable book on three major Spanish American poets. Xirau is concerned with their philosophy and aesthetics.

Yúdice, George. *Vicente Huidobro y la motivación del lenguaje*, Buenos Aires, Galera, 1978.

Good structuralist book-length reading of Huidobro.

Yurkievich, Saul. *Poesía hispanoamericana: 1960–1970: una antología a través de un certamen continental*, Mexico, Siglo Veintiuno Editores, 1972.

Fundadores de la nueva poesía latinoamericana: Vallejo, Huidobro, Borges, Neruda, Paz, Barcelona, Seix Barral, 1971, 2nd. edn., rev., Ariel, 1984.

Important and influential book. The second edition adds Girondo and Lezama Lima.

Volume 2

Articles

Alazraki, Jaime. "Enumerations as evocations: on the use of a device in Borges' latest poetry" in Carlos Cortínez (ed.), *Borges, the Poet*, Fayeteville, University of Arkansas Press, 1986, 149–57.
> Study of the sources of enumerations in Borges's poetry.

Borinsky, Alicia. "'Altazor': entierros y comienzos," *Revista Iberoamericana*, 40 (1974), 125–8.
> Studies literary motifs embedded in the poem.

Camurati, Mireya. "Emerson y el creacionismo" in Alan M. Gordon (ed.). *Actas del Sexto Congreso Internacional de Hispanistas celebrado en Toronto del 22 al 27 de agosto de 1977*, University of Toronto, 1980, 143–6.
> Fundamental essay on the presence of Emerson in Huidobro's early works.

Doudoroff, Michael J. "José Emilio Pacheco: an overview of the poetry, 1963–86," *Hispania*, 72 (1989), 264–76.
> Excellent introduction to the major themes of Pacheco's poetry.

Durán, Manuel. "Irony and sympathy in *Blanco* and *Ladera este*" in Ivar Ivask, (ed.), *The Perpetual Present: The poetry and prose of Octavio Paz*, Norman, University of Oklahoma Press, 1973, 67–74.
> Examines themes of love and culture as underlying tropes of Paz's major books.

"'Contemporáneos': ¿grupo, promoción, generación, conspiración?" *Revista Iberoamericana*, 48 (1982), 37–46.
> Analyzes the critical revisions of the Mexican group.

Echavarría Ferrari, Arturo. "From expression to allusion: towards a theory of poetic language in Borges" in Carlos Cortínez (ed.), *Borges the Poet*, Fayeteville, University of Arkansas Press, 1986.
> Examines Borges's systems of allusion.

Gertel, Zunilda. "La imagen metafísica en la poesía de Borges," *Revista Iberoamericana*, 43 (1977), 433–48.
> Examines Borges's images and his vision of the oxymoron up to 1969.
> Good on Ultraism.

González Echevarría, Roberto. "Guillén as baroque: meaning in *Motivos de son*," *Callalloo*, 10 (1987), 302–17.
> Excellent reading that illuminates the classical tradition that underlies Guillén's *Motivos*.

Gordon, Samuel. "Los poetas ya no cantan, ahora hablan: aproximaciones a la poesía de José Emilio Pacheco," *Revista Iberoamericana*, 56 (1990), 255–66.
> Examines Pacheco's conversational style in relation to the new poetry of Mexico.

Maier, Linda S. "Three 'new' avant-garde poems of Jorge Luis Borges," *MLN*, 102 (1987), 393–98.
> Excellent essay on the early ultraist Borges.

Man, Paul de. "A modern master: Jorge Luis Borges," *New York Review of Books*, 3 (November 19, 1964), 8–10; rpt. in Lindsay Waters (ed.), *Critical Writings, 1953–1978*, Minneapolis, University of Minnesota Press, 1989.

Lucid and concise review of Borges's *Labyrinths and Dreamtigers* by the modern master of literary criticism.

Mandlove, Nancy B. "At the outer limits of language: Mallarmé's 'Un coup de dés' and Huidobro's 'Altazor'," *Studies in Twentieth Century Literature*, 8, (1984), 163–83.
One of the more lucid and suggestive readings of *Altazor*.

Mignolo, Walter D. "La figura del poeta en la lírica de vanguardia," *Revista Iberoamericana*, 48 (1982), 131–48.
Examines the figure of the poet in Huidobro's lyric and in others.

Müller-Bergh, Klaus. "El hombre y la técnica: contribución al conocimiento de corrientes vanguardistas hispanoamericanas," *Revista Iberoamericana*, 48 (1982), 149–76.
Historical survey of the context of the first Avant-Garde. Erudite and well-informed.

Oviedo, José Miguel. "Borges: the poet according to his prologues" in Carlos Cortínez (ed.), *Borges the Poet*, Fayeteville, University of Arkansas Press, 1986, 121–33.
One of the first to read carefully Borges's poetics as they appear in successive introductions to his works.

Paz, Octavio. "Decir sin decir," *Vuelta*, 107 (October, 1985), 12–13.
Concise and brilliant reading of Huidobro's *Altazor*.

Quiroga, José. "El entierro de la poesía: Huidobro, Nietzsche y Altazor," *MLN*, 107, (1992), 342–62.
On the Nietzsche and his presence in Huidobro's work.

"Vicente Huidobro and the poetics of the invisible texts," *Hispania*, 75 (1992), 516–26.
On Huidobro and Emerson.

Ríos-Avila, Rubén. "The origin and the island: Lezama and Mallarmé," *Latin American Literary Review*, 8 (1980), 242–55.
A classic essay on the language and poetics of Lezama.

Santí, Enrico Mario. "The accidental tourist: Walt Whitman in Latin America" in Gustavo Pérez Firmat (ed.), *Do the Americas Have a Common Literature?* Durham, Duke University Press, 1990, 156–76; 364–71.
A fascinating and brilliant account of the translations of Whitman in the work of Neruda and Borges.

Undurraga, Antonio de. "Teoría del creacionismo" in *Vicente Huidobro, poesía y prosa*, Madrid, Aguilar, 1957, 19–186.
Emphasis on Creationism. Distinguishes it from other avant-garde movements and reads Hhuidobro's work according to its various stages.

Chapter 11: The modern essay in Spanish America

Primary sources

(The works of some critics who are studied in this text as authors of essays can also be read as secondary sources for other authors. In such cases, they will be included in the list of secondary sources.)

Arciniegas, Germán. *Páginas escogidas (1932–1973)*, Madrid, Gredos, 1975.

Benedetti, Mario. *El ejercicio del criterio: crítica literaria (1950–1970)*, Mexico, Nueva Imagen, 1981.

Bianco, José. *Ficción y realidad (1946–1976)*, Caracas, Monte Avila, 1977.

Blanco Fombona, Rufino. *Ensayos históricos*, ed. Rafael Ramón Castellanos, prologue Jesús Sanoja Hernández, Caracas, Biblioteca Ayacucho, 1981.

Borges, Jorge Luis. *Discusión*, Buenos Aires, Gleizer, 1932.

Otras inquisiciones, Buenos Aires, Sur, 1952.

Historia de la eternidad, Buenos Aires, Emecé, 1953.

Other Inquisitions, 1937–1952, Ruth L. C. Simms, intro. James E. Irby, Austin, University of Texas Press, 1964.

Cardoza y Aragón, Luis. *Guatemala: las líneas de su mano*, Mexico, Fondo de Cultura Económica, 1955.

Carpentier, Alejo. *Tientos y diferencias*, Mexico, Universidad Nacional Autónoma de México, 1964.

Cortázar, Julio. *La vuelta al día en ochenta mundos*, Mexico, Siglo Veintiuno Editores, 1967.

Ultimo round, Mexico, Siglo Veintiuno Editores, 1969.

Territorios, Mexico, Siglo Veintiuno Editores, 1978.

La vuelta al día en 80 mundos, 2 vols., Madrid, Siglo Veintiuno Editores, 1984.

Fernández, Macedonio. *Papeles de reciénvenido. Continuación de la nada*, Buenos Aires, Editorial Losada [1944].

Fuentes, Carlos. *Cervantes o la crítica de la lectura*, Mexico, Mortiz, 1976.

Myself with Others, New York, Farrar, Straus & Giroux, 1988.

Galeano, Eduardo. *Las venas abiertas de América Latina*, Montevideo, Universidad Nacional de la República, 1971.

García Calderón, Francisco. *Las democracias latinas. La creación de un continente*, prologue Luis Alberto Sánchez, Caracas, Biblioteca Ayacucho, 1979.

Gómez Dávila, Nicolás. *Escolios a un texto implícito*, 2 vols., Bogotá, Instituto Colombiano de Cultura, 1977.

Guevara, Ernesto. *Diario del Che en Bolivia*, Buenos Aires, Siglo Veintiuno Editores, 1973.

Haya de la Torre, Víctor Raúl. *El antimperialismo y el APRA*, Santiago de Chile, Ediciones Ercilla, 1936.

Henríquez Ureña, Pedro. *La utopía de América*, ed. Angel Rama, prologue Rafael Gutiérrez Girardot, Caracas, Biblioteca Ayacucho, 1978.

Lezama Lima, José. *El reino imaginario*, ed. Julio Ortega, Caracas, Biblioteca Ayacucho, 1981.

Lugones, Leopoldo. *El payador y antología de poesía y prosa*, ed. Guillermo Ara, prologue Jorge Luis Borges, Caracas, Biblioteca Ayacucho, 1979.

Mariátegui, José Carlos. *7 ensayos de interpretación de la realidad peruana*, 13th. edn., Lima, Biblioteca Amauta, 1968.

7 ensayos de interpretación de la realidad peruana, prologue Aníbal Quijano, notes and chronology Elizabeth Garrels, Caracas, Biblioteca Ayacucho, 1979.

Seven Interpretative Essays on Peruvian Reality, tr. Marjory Urquidi, intro Jorge Basadre, Austin, University of Texas Press, 1971.

Martínez Estrada, Ezequiel. *Muerte y transfiguración de Martín Fierro*, 2nd. edn., 2 vols., Mexico, Fondo de Cultura Económica, 1958.

Monterroso, Augusto. *La palabra mágica*, Mexico, Ediciones Era, 1983.

Moro, César. *Los anteojos de azufre*, Lima, Editorial San Marcos, 1958.

Neruda, Pablo. *Confieso que he vivido*, Barcelona, Seix Barral, 1974.

Memoirs, tr. Hardie St. Martin, New York, Farrar, Straus & Giroux, 1977.

Paz, Octavio. *El laberinto de la soledad*, 2nd. edn., Mexico, Fondo de Cultura Económica, 1959.

El arco y la lira; el poema; la revelación poética; poesía e historia, 2nd. edn., Mexico, Fondo de Cultura Económica, 1967.

Conjunciones y disyunciones, Mexico, Mortiz, 1969.

El mono gramático. Barcelona, Seix Barral, 1974.

Los hijos del limo: del romanticismo a la vanguardia, Barcelona, Seix Barral, 1974.

Sor Juana Inés de la Cruz o las trampas de la fe, Mexico, Fondo de Cultura Económica, 1982.

The Labyrinth of Solitude, tr. Lysander Kemp, 2nd. edn., London. A. Lane – The Penguin Press, 1967.

The Bow and the Lyre, tr. Ruth L. C. Simms, Austin, University of Texas Press, 1973.

Children of the Mire: modern poetry from Romanticism to the Avant-Garde, tr. Rachel Phillips, Cambridge, Mass. Harvard University Press, 1974.

Conjunctions and Disjunctions, tr. Helen R. Lane, New York, Viking Press, 1974.

Sor Juana or the Traps of Faith, tr. Margaret Sayers Peden, Cambridge, Mass., Harvard University Press, 1988.

Picón Salas, Mariano. *Viejos y nuevos mundos*, ed. Guillermo Sucre, Caracas, Biblioteca Ayacucho, 1983.

Poniatowska, Elena. *La noche de Tlatelolco*, Mexico, Ediciones Era, 1971.

Massacre in Mexico, tr. Helen R. Lane, New York, Viking Press, 1976.

Rama, Angel, *La ciudad letrada*, Hanover, N.H., Ediciones del Norte, 1984.

Ramos, Samuel. *Obras completas*, 3 vols., Mexico, Universidad Nacional Autónoma de México, 1975.

Reyes, Alfonso, *Obras completas*, vol. I, *Cuestiones estéticas. Capítulos de literatura mexicana. Varia*, Mexico, Fondo de Cultura Económica, 1955.

Obras completas, vol. II: *Visión de Anáhuac. Las vísperas de España. Calendario*, Mexico, Fondo de Cultura Económica, 1956.

Obras completas, vol. XIV: *La experiencia literaria. Tres puntos de exegética literaria. Páginas adicionales*, Mexico, Fondo de Cultura Económica, 1962.

Obras completas, vol. XV, *El deslinde*, Mexico, Fondo de Cultura Económica, 1963.

Rodó, José Enrique. *Ariel*, ed. and intro. Gordon Brotherston, Cambridge University Press, 1967.

Obras completas, ed. and notes Emir Rodríguez Monegal, Madrid, Aguilar, 1967.

Ariel. Motivos de Proteo, ed. and chronology Angel Rama, prologue Carlos Real de Azúa, Caracas, Biblioteca Ayacucho, 1976.

Ariel, reader's reference, and annotated bibliography, Margaret Sayers Peden, foreword James W. Symington, prologue Carlos Fuentes, Austin, University of Texas Press, 1988.

Romero, Francisco. *Sobre la filosofía en América*, Buenos Aires, Raigal, 1952.

Sábato, Ernesto. *El escritor y sus fantasmas*, Buenos Aires, Aguilar, 1963.

Salazar Bondy, Sebastián. *Lima la horrible*, Mexico, Ediciones Era, 1964.

Sánchez, Luis Alberto. *Aladino o vida y obra de José Santos Chocano*, Mexico, Libro Mex, 1960.

Sanín Cano, Baldomero. *Ensayos*, Bogotá, Biblioteca Popular de Cultura, 1942.

Escritos, ed. J. G. Cobo Borda, Bogotá, Instituto Colombiano de Cultura Colombiana, 1977.

Sierra, Justo. *Evolución política del pueblo mexicano*, prologue and chronology Abelardo Villegas, Caracas, Biblioteca Ayacucho, 1977.

Tamayo, Franz. *Obra escogida*, ed. Mariano Baptista Gumucio, Caracas, Biblioteca Ayacucho, 1979.

Uslar Pietri, Arturo. *Veinticinco ensayos*, Caracas, Monte Avila, 1969.

Vargas Llosa, Mario. *La orgía perpetua: Flaubert y "Madame Bovary,"* Barcelona, Seix Barral, 1975.

Contra viento y marea, 2nd. edn., 2 vols., Barcelona, Seix Barral, 1986.

The Perpetual Orgy: Flaubert and "Madame Bovary," tr. Helen R. Lane, New York, Farrar, Strauss & Giroux, 1986.

Varona, Enrique José. *Textos escogidos*, ed. Raimundo Lazo, Mexico, Porrúa, 1968.

Vaz Ferreira, Carlos. *Lógica viva. Moral para intelectuales*, ed. Manuel Claps and Sara Vaz Ferreira, Caracas, Biblioteca Ayacucho, 1979.

Vitier, Cintio. *Crítica sucesiva*, Havana, Unión, 1971.

Zea, Leopoldo. *La filosofía americana como filosofía sin más*, Mexico, Siglo Veintiuno Editores, 1969.

Secondary sources

Books

Beer, Gabriella de. *José Vasconcelos and his World*, New York, Las Américas Publishing Co. 1966.

    Wide-ranging study of the work and times of Vasconcelos.

Bloom, Harold (ed.). *Jorge Luis Borges*, New York, Chelsea House, 1986.

    Important collection of essays including texts by Paul de Man, Rodríguez Monegal, and others.

Borges, Jorge Luis. *Leopoldo Lugones*, 2nd. edn., Buenos Aires, Pleamar, 1965. Brief introductory essay to the work of Lugones, whose intellectual ties with Borges are profound.

Cobo Borda, Juan Gustavo. *La tradición de la pobreza*, Bogotá, Carlos Valencia Editores, 1980.

    Essays about twentieth-century Colombian literature, including one each on Sanín Cano and Gómez Dávila.

La otra literatura latinoamericana, Bogotá, Procultura-Colcultura-El Ancora, 1982.

    Notes and brief essays, among which figure texts on Raimundo Lida, Victoria Ocampo, Zaid, Monsiváis, Volkening, and others.

Constábile de Amorim, Helena, and María Rosario Fernández Alonso. *Rodó, pensador y estilista*, Montevideo, Academia Nacional de Letras, 1973.

    Studies Rodó's Americanism, his philosophic foundations, and his aesthetics.

Davis, Harold Eugene. *Latin American Thought*, Baton Rouge, Louisiana State

University Press, 1972.

Traces the great currents in the American history of ideas, beginning with its colonial antecedents.

Díaz Quiñones, Arcadio. *Cintio Vitier: la memoria integradora*, San Juan, Editorial sin Nombre, 1987.

Study on "Cubanness" and on the relations between poetry and history in Vitier's work, followed by dialogues between Vitier and Díaz Quiñones.

Earle, Peter G. *Prophet of the Wilderness. The works of Ezekiel Martínez Estrada*, Austin, University of Texas Press, 1971.

The most complete study on Martínez Estrada.

Earle, Peter G., and Robert G. Mead, Jr. *Historia del ensayo hispanoamericano*, Mexico, Ediciones de Andrea, 1973.

Basic reference text for tracing the history of the essayistic genre from its origins through the twentieth century.

Férnandez Moreno, César (ed.). *América Latina en su literatura*, Mexico, UNESCO Siglo Veintiuno Editores, 1972.

While this critical collection does not specifically concern the essay genre, numerous references are made to it in the context of some fundamental issues of the literary phenomenon.

Foster, David William. *Para una lectura semiótica del ensayo latinoamericano*, Madrid, Porrúa Turanzas, 1986.

Following the methodology highlighted in the title, examines works of Sarmiento, Rodó, Reyes, Vasconcelos, Mariátegui, and others.

Giordano, Jaime (ed.). *La identidad cultural de Hispanoamérica*, Santiago, Ediciones del Maitén, 1986.

Contains a selection of Americanist texts written over the last twenty-five years.

Goic, Cedomil (ed.). *Historia y crítica de la literatura hispanoamericana*, vol. III, Barcelona, Editorial Crítica, 1988.

The final section of the volume is devoted to important figures of the contemporary essay.

González Echevarría, Roberto. *The Voice of the Masters: Writing and authority in modern Latin American literature*, Austin, University of Texas Press, 1985.

Contains various critical essays about literature and ideology; the first chapter is a good study of Rodó's *Ariel*.

Gracia, Jorge J. E., and Iván Jaksic (eds.). *Filosofía e identidad cultural en América Latina*, Caracas, Monte Avila, 1988.

Valuable collection of philosophic and Americanist texts, including those of little-known authors.

Haddox, John H. *Antonio Caso. Philosopher of Mexico*, Austin, University of Texas Press, 1971.

Among the few extensive and detailed studies of Caso's work.

Ivask, Ivar (ed.). *The Perpetual Present. The poetry and prose of Octavio Paz*, Norman, University of Oklahoma, 1973.

Collection of essays and conferences on various works of Paz.

Leander, Birgitta (ed.). *Cultural Identity in Latin America*, special issue of *Culturas*, Paris, 1968.

Repertoire of multidisciplinary works on various aspects of thought, literature, and culture; includes Brazil and the Caribbean.

Lévy, Isaac Jack, and Juan Loveluck (eds.). *Simposio. El ensayo hispánico. Actas, Hispanic Studies* 3, Columbia, University of South Carolina, 1984.

Assembles works in both English and Spanish about theoretical issues and about Spanish and Spanish American authors; contains an extensive annotated bibliography.

Levy, Kurt L., and Keith Ellis (eds.). *El ensayo y la crítica literaria en Iberoamérica*, University of Toronto, 1970.

North American and Latin American critics discuss diverse topics and authors.

Lipp, Solomon. *Three Argentine Thinkers*, New York, Philosophical Library, 1969.

Studies the principal works of Korn, Ingenieros, and Romero.

Marichal, Juan. *Cuatro fases de la historia intelectual latinoamericana*, Madrid, Fundación Juan March, 1978.

The final two chapters (which cover from Rodó to Octavio Paz) are very pertinent and useful to the issues discussed throughout our study.

Martí, Oscar R. (ed.). *The Gabino Barreda Centennial Issue*, special issue of *Aztlán*, 14:2 (1983).

Interpretations of Mexican Positivism, with references to the "Ateneo" group and to Vasconcelos.

Martínez, José Luis (ed.). *El ensayo mexicano moderno*, 2nd. edn., 2 vols., Mexico, Fondo de Cultura Económica, 1984.

The second volume covers the twentieth century through Carlos Monsiváis.

Mejía Sánchez, Ernesto (ed.). *El ensayo actual latinoamericano*, Mexico, Ediciones de Andrea, 1971.

Selects one essayist per country, including Brazil and Haiti.

Meyer, Doris. *Victoria Ocampo. Against the wind and tide*, New York, George Brazilier, 1979.

Comprehensive literary biography of Ocampo, with a selection of her texts.

Monsiváis, Carlos (ed.). *A ustedes les consta*, Mexico, Ediciones Era, 1980.

Collects chronicles and testimony on the history and cultural life of Mexico during the last two centuries.

Morse, Richard M. *El espejo de Próspero*, Mexico, Siglo Veintiuno Editores, 1982.

Original study of contrasts between Latin and North American historical and cultural experiences.

Oberhelman, Harley Dean. *Ernesto Sábato*, New York, Twayne, 1970.

General study of Sábato's works; the third chapter is devoted to his essayistic production.

Revista Iberoamericana, special issue on Octavio Paz, 37:74 (1971).

While the majority of articles concern Paz's poetry, there are references to his essayistic production as well as Rodríguez Monegal's review of *El arco y la lira*.

Ripoll, Carlos (ed.). *Conciencia intelectual de América. Antología del ensayo hispanoamericano (1836–1959)*, 2nd. edn., New York, Las Américas Publishing Co. 1971.

Selection of the works of the most important Americanists and ideologists.

Robb, James Willis. *El estilo de Alfonso Reyes*, Mexico, Fondo de Cultura Económica, 1965.

Extremely detailed, if somewhat conventional, study of Reyes's language.

Rodríguez Monegal, Emir. *Jorge Luis Borges, a literary biography*, New York, E. P. Dutton, 1978.

Borges's most exhaustive biography, with abundant critical references to his works.

Roggiano, Alfredo, A. *Pedro Henríquez Ureña en los Estados Unidos*, Mexico, Editorial Cultura, 1961.

Well-documented work about an important period of Henríquez Ureña's life and work.

Roig, Arturo Andrés. *Teoría y crítica del pensamiento latinoamericano*, Mexico, Fondo de Cultura Económica, 1981.

A somewhat disorderly review of the evolution of ideas in Latin America.

Santí, Enrico Mario. *Escritura y tradición*, Barcelona, Laia, 1987.

Includes important works about Borges, Lezama, Vitier, Ortega y Gasset, Paz, and Sarduy, among others.

Skirius, John (ed.). *El ensayo latinoamericano del siglo XX*, 3rd edn., Mexico, Fondo de Cultura Económica, 1994.

Includes essays from González Prada to Monsiváis and Libertella; good bibliography on the genre.

Stabb, Martin S. *In Quest of Identity: Patterns in the Spanish American essay of ideas, 1890–1960*, Chapel Hill, University of North Carolina Press, 1967.

Extremely useful reference work on the ideological essay in modern times.

Texto Crítico, special issue in homage to Angel Rama, 10:31–2 (1985).

Multiple appreciations of Rama by numerous Spanish American critics.

The Philosophical Forum, special issue on "Latin American Philosophy Today," 20:1–2 (1988–1989).

Various thinkers (among them Zea and Adolfo Sánchez Vázquez) examine Latin American philosophical currents from the beginning of the twentieth century through the present.

Villegas, Abelardo. *Panorama de la filosofía iberoamericana actual*, Buenos Aires, EUDEBA, 1963.

Brief summary of the historical process of Spanish American philosophy, from Positivism onward.

Reformismo y revolución en el pensamiento latinoamericano, 2nd. edn., Mexico, Siglo Veintiuno Editores, 1974.

Review of Latin American political ideologies; Chapter 7 studies Mariátegui and Haya de la Torre.

Vitier, Medardo. *Del ensayo americano*, Mexico, Fondo de Cultura Económica, 1945.

Despite its age, a useful and extremely readable study of the essay as a genre and of various modern essayists.

Wilson, Jason. *Octavio Paz. A study of his poetics*, Cambridge University Press, 1979.

While this study is devoted to Paz's poetry, there are various references to his essays, particularly throughout the fourth chapter which contains an analysis of *El mono gramático*.

Yurkievich, Saúl (ed.). *Identidad cultural de Iberoamérica en su literatura*, Madrid, Editorial Alhambra, 1986.

Some of the works included in the collection are related to the major themes of the Spanish American essay.

Zea, Leopoldo (ed.). *Pensamiento positivista latinoamericano*, 2 vols., Caracas, Biblioteca Ayacucho, 1980.

Important collection of works about nineteenth- and twentieth-century Latin American thinkers, ideologues, and Americanists.

América Latina en sus ideas, Mexico, UNESCO/Siglo Veintiuno Editores, 1986.

Collection of critical works about the history of ideas, the relations between Latin America and Europe, and cultural identity.

Articles

Foster, David William. "Latin American documentary narrative," *PMLA*, 99:1 (1984), 41–55.

Valuable article about new narrative forms that are intricately related with the essay; includes a bibliography.

Rodríguez Monegal, Emir. "Octavio Paz: crítica y poesía," *Mundo Nuevo*, 21 (1968), 55–62.

Key article on the relation between the critical and the poetic in Paz.

Stabb, Martin. "Utopia and anti-utopia: the theme in selected essayistic writing of Spanish America," *Revista de Estudios Hispánicos*, 15:3 (1981), 377–93.

Examines the theme in works of Reyes, Paz, Martínez Estrada, Cortázar, Borges, and others.

Chapter 12: Literary criticism in Spanish America

Primary sources

Alonso, Amado. *Poesía y estilo de Pablo Neruda*. Buenos Aires, Editoria Losada, 1940.

Ensayo sobre la novela história. El modernismo en "La gloria de don Ramiro," Buenos Aires, Instituto de Filología, Imprenta y Casa Editora Coni, 1942.

Bello, Andrés. *Obras completas*, vols. I: Poesías; IV: *Gramática de la lengua castellana destinada al uso de los americanos*; VI: *Estudios filológicos*: 1, *Principios de ortología y métrica de la lengua castellana y otros escritos*; VII: *Estudios filológicos* 2, *Poema del Cid y otros escritos*; IX: *Temas de crítica literaria*, Caracas, Ministerio de Educación, 1951–1969.

"La Araucana, por Don Alonso de Ercilla y Zúñiga" in *Obras completas de Andrés Bello*, vol. IX, *Temas de crítica literaria*, Caracas, La Casa de Bello, 1981.

Anthology of Andrés Bello, compiled by Pedro Grases, foreword Rafael Caldera, tr. Barbara D. Huntley and Pilar Liria, Washington, General Secretariat, Organization of American States, 1981.

Blanco-Fombona, Rufino. *Letras y letrados de Hispanoamérica*, Paris, Sociedad de Ediciones Literarias y Artísticas, 1908.

Grandes escritores de América, Madrid, Renacimiento, 1917.

El modernismo y los poetas modernistas, Madrid, Mundo Latino, 1929.

Borges, Jorge Luis. *Discusión*, Buenos Aires, Emecé, 1957.

Otras inquisiciones, Buenos Aires, Emecé, 1960.

Borges on Writing, ed. Norman Thomas di Giovanni, Daniel Halpern, and Frank MacShane, New York, E. P. Dutton, 1973.

Prólogos, con un prólogo de Prólogos, Buenos Aires, Torres Aguero, 1975.

Textos cautivos. Ensayos y reseñas en "El Hogar" (1936–1939), ed. Enrique Sacerio-Garí and Emir Rodríguez Monegal, Barcelona, Tusquets, 1986.

"Discurso pronunciado en la instalación de la Universidad de Chile el día 17 de septiembre de 1843" in *Obras completas de Andrés Bello*, vol. XVIIIA: *Temas educacionales*, Caracas, La Casa de Bello, 1981.

Other Inquisitions, 1937–1952, tr. Ruth L. C. Simms, intro. James E. Irby, Austin, University of Texas Press, 1964.

Borges, a Reader: A selection from the writings of Jorge Luis Borges, ed. Emir Rodríguez Monegal and Alastair Reid, New York, E. P. Dutton, 1981.

Seven Nights, tr. Eliot Weinberger, intro. Alastair Reid, New York, New Directions, 1984.

Darío, Rubén. *Los raros*, Buenos Aires, Talleres de "La Vasconia," 1896.

El viaje a Nicaragua e Historia de mis libros, Madrid. Biblioteca del Ateneo, 1909.

Obras completas, II, Madrid, Afrodasio Aguado, 1950.

Delmonte, Domingo. *Centón epistolario*, preface and notes by Domingo Figarola-Caneda, 5 vols., Havana, Imprenta "El Siglo XX," 1923.

Escritos, intro. and notes by José A. Fernández de Castro, 2 vols., Havana, Editorial Cultural, 1929.

Fernández Retamar, Roberto. *Calibán. Apuntes sobre la cultura en Nuestra América*, Mexico, Editorial Diógenes, 1971.

Para una teoría de la literatura latinoamericana y otras aproximaciones, Havana, Casa de las Américas, 1975.

García Calderón, Ventura. *Literatura peruana (1535–1914)*, New York and Paris, offprint from *Revue Hispanique*, 31 (1914).

Semblanzas de América, Madrid, La Revista Hispanoamericana "Cervantes," 1920.

Groussac, Paul. *Del Plata al Niágara*, Buenos Aires, n.p., 1897.

El viaje intelectual. Impresiones de naturaleza y arte (primera serie), Madrid, V. Suárez, 1904.

El viaje intelectual. Impresiones de naturaleza y arte (segunda serie), Buenos Aires, J. Menéndez, 1920.

Crítica literaria, Buenos Aires, J. Menéndez & hijo, 1924.

Gutiérrez, Juan María. *Estudios biográficos y críticos sobre algunos poetas sudamericanos anteriores al siglo XIX*, Buenos Aires, Imprenta El Siglo, 1865.

"Estudios histórico-críticos sobre la literatura en Sud-América" in *Críticas y narraciones*, Buenos Aires, Librería El Ateneo, 1928.

Henríquez Ureña, Pedro. *Seis ensayos en busca de nuestra expresión*, Buenos Aires, Babel, 1928.

La cultura y las letras coloniales en Santo Domingo, Buenos Aires, Biblioteca de Dialectología Hispanoamericana, appendix 2, 1936.

Literary Currents in Hispanic America, Cambridge, Mass., Harvard University Press, 1945.

Historia de la cultura en la América Hispánica, Mexico, Fondo de Cultura Económica, 1947.

Las corrientes literarias en la América Hispánica, tr. into Spanish Joaquín Diez-
Canedo, Mexico, Fondo de Cultura Económica, 1949.
Jitrik, Noé. *Las contradicciones del modernismo. Productividad poética y situación
sociológica*, Mexico, El Colegio de México, 1978.
Lezama Lima, José. *La expresión americana*, Havana, Instituto Nacional de Cultura,
Ministerio de Educación, 1957.
Tratados en La Habana, Santa Clara, Cuba, Universidad Central de Las Villas,
1958.
Esferaimagen. Sierpe de don Luis de Góngora, Barcelona, Tusquets, 1970.
La cantidad hechizada, Havana, UNEAC, 1970.
Mariátegui, José Carlos. *7 ensayos de interpretación de la realidad peruana*, Lima,
Amauta, 1928.
Seven Interpretive Essays on Peruvian Reality, tr. Marjory Urquidi, intro. Jorge
Basadre, Austin, University of Texas Press, 1971.
Marinello, Juan. "Americanismo y cubanismo literarios," prologue to Luis Felipe
Rodríguez, *Marcos Antilla, cuentos de cañaveral*, Havana, Editorial Hermes,
1932.
Literatura hispanoamericana: hombres, meditaciones, Mexico, Editorial de la
Universidad Nacional de México, 1937.
Martí, José. *Obras completas*, vols. v (Cuba; Mujeres, Artículos varios, Letras,
educación pintura y música "En Casa"), vi–vii (Nuestra América i, ii, iii), xiii (En
los Estados Unidos; Norteamericanos, Letras, pintura y Artículos varios), xiv
(Europa i; Escenas europeas), xv (Europa ii; Crítica y arte), Havana Editorial
Nacional de Cuba, 1963–1965.
On Art and Literature: Critical writings, tr. Elinor Randall, Luis A. Baralt, Juan
Onís, and Roslin Held Foner, ed. with intro. and notes by Philip S. Foner, New
York, Monthly Review Press, 1982.
Molloy, Sylvia. *Las letras de Borges*, Buenos Aires, Sudamericana, 1979.
Paz, Octavio. *El laberinto de la soledad*, Mexico, Cuadernos Americanos, 1950.
El arco y la lira. El poema; la revelación poética; poesía e historia, Mexico, Fondo de
Cultura Económica, 1956.
Conjunciones y disyunciones, Mexico, Mortiz, 1969.
Los hijos del limo: del romanticismo a la vanguardia, Barcelona, Seix Barral, 1974.
Sor Juana Inés de la Cruz, o las trampas de la fe, Barcelona, Seix Barral, 1983.
The Labyrinth of Solitude, tr. Lysander Kemp, New York, Grove Press, 1962.
The Bow and the Lyre, tr. Ruth L. C. Simms, Austin, University of Texas Press,
1973.
Children of the Mire: modern poetry from Romanticism to the Avant-Garde, tr.
Rachel Phillips, Cambridge, Mass, Harvard University Press, 1974.
Conjunctions and Disjunctions, tr. Helen R. Lane, New York, Viking Press, 1974.
Sor Juana, tr. Margaret Sayers Peden, Cambridge, Mass., Harvard University Press,
1988.
Picón Salas, Mariano. *De la Conquista a la Independencia: tres siglos de historia
cultural hispanoamericana*, Mexico, Fondo de Cultura Económica, 1944.
Europa-América: preguntas a la esfinge de la cultura, Mexico, Cuadernos America-
nos, 1947.
A Cultural History of Spanish America: from Conquest to Independence, tr. with

foreword by Irving Leonard, Berkeley, University of California Press, 1962.

Ponce, Anibal. *Humanismo burgués y humanismo proletario. De Erasmo a Romain Rolland*, Mexico, Editorial América, 1938.

Rama, Angel. *Rubén Darío y el modernismo (Circunstancia socioeconómica de un arte americano)*, Caracas, Ediciones de la Biblioteca de la Universidad Central de Venezuela, 1970.

Transculturación narrativa en América Latina, Mexico, Siglo Veintiuno Editores, 1982.

La ciudad letrada, Hanover, N.H., Ediciones del Norte, 1984.

Las máscaras democráticas del modernismo, Montevideo, Fundación Angel Rama, 1985.

Reyes, Alfonso. *Cuestiones estéticas*, Paris, Ollendorf, 1911.

Visión de Anáhuac, San José, Costa Rica, El Convivio, 1917.

Cuestiones gongorinas, Madrid, Espasa-Calpe, 1927.

Discurso por Virgilio, Mexico, Contemporáneos, 1931.

La experiencia literaria, Buenos Aires, Editorial Losada, 1942.

Ultima Tule, Mexico, Imprenta Universitaria, 1942.

El deslinde. Prolegómenos a la teoría literaria, Mexico, Fondo de Cultura Económica, 1944.

Estudios helénicos, Mexico, El Colegio Nacional, 1957.

Rodó, José Enrique. *Ariel*, Montevideo, Dornaleche & Reyes, 1900.

Motivos de Proteo, Montevideo, J. M. Serrano & Cía., 1909.

El mirador de Próspero, Montevideo, J. M. Serrano & Cía, 1913.

Ultimos Motivos de Proteo, Montevideo, n. p., 1932.

Obras completas, ed., with intro., prologue and notes, by Emir Rodríguez Monegal, Madrid, Aguilar, 1967.

The Motives of Proteus, tr. Angel Flores, intro. Havelock Ellis, London, Allen & Unwin, 1929.

Ariel, tr., reader's reference, and annotated bibliography Margaret Sayers Peden, foreword James W. Symington, prologue Carlos Fuentes, Austin, University of Texas Press, 1988.

Rodríguez Monegal, Emir. *El viajero inmóvil: introducción a Pablo Neruda*, Buenos Aires, Editorial Losada, 1966.

El desterrado. Vida y obra de Horacio Quiroga, Buenos Aires, Editorial Losada, 1968.

El otro Andrés Bello, Caracas, Monte Avila, 1969.

Jorge Luis Borges: a literary biography, New York, E. P. Dutton, 1978.

Sanín Cano, Baldomero, *La civilización manual y otros ensayos*, Buenos Aires, Babel, 1925.

Sarduy, Severo. *Escrito sobre un cuerpo*, Buenos Aires, Sudamericana, 1969.

Barroco, Buenos Aires, Sudamericana, 1974.

La simulación, Caracas, Monte Avila, 1982.

Sarmiento, Domingo Faustino. *Obras de D. F. Sarmiento*, vol. 1, Paris, Belen Hermanos, 1885.

Varona, Enrique José. *Estudios literarios y filosóficos*, Havana, Librería "La Nueva Principal," 1883.

Seis conferencias, Barcelona, Gorgas & Cía, 1887.

Desde mi belvedere, Havana, Imprenta y Papelería de Rambla & Bouza, 1907.
Violetas y ortigas, Madrid, Editorial América, 1917.

Secondary sources

Books

Anderson-Imbert, Enrique. *La crítica literaria contemporánea*, Buenos Aires, Eds. Gure SRL, 1957.

Has useful appendix (up to 1957) on "Estado actual de la crítica literaria hispanoamericana," and "Bibliografía sobre la crítica hispanoamericana."

Aponte, Barbara B. *Alfonso Reyes and Spain. His dialogue with Unamuno, Valle-Inclán, Ortega y Gasset, Jiménez, and Gómez de la Serna*, Austin, University of Texas Press, 1972.

Good overview of Reyes's background, his early years as a writer, and his relationship with Spanish writers.

Blixen, Carina, and Alvaro Barros-Lemez. *Cronología y bibliografía de Angel Rama*, Montevideo, Fundación Angel Rama, 1986.

Thorough and generally reliable chronology and bibliography of Rama and his works.

Bueno, Salvador. *La crítica literaria cubana del siglo XIX*, Havana, Editorial Letras Cubanas, 1979.

An introductory and somewhat fragmentary history of criticism in Cuba in the nineteenth century. Devotes specific chapters to Domingo Deimonte, Enrique Piñeyro, and José Martí.

Fernández Retamar, Roberto. *Idea de la estilística*, Havana, Casa de las Américas, 1976.

Well-informed introduction to the history and methodology of stylistics. Originally published in 1958.

González, Aníbal. *La crónica modernista hispanoamericana*, Madrid, José Porrúa Turanzas, 1983.

Studies the relation between the Modernists' journalistic writings and the works of philologists such as Renan, Taine, and Menéndez y Pelayo.

González Echevarría, Roberto. *The Voice of the Masters: Writing and authority in modern Latin American literature*, Austin, University of Texas Press, 1985.

Chapters 1 and 2 contain extensive and useful comments on the telluric critics and the crisis in contemporary criticism.

La ruta de Severo Sarduy, Hanover, N.H., Ediciones del Norte, 1987.

Studies the interaction between Sarduy's French-influenced criticism and his novels.

Grases, Pedro. *Estudios sobre Andrés Bello*, 2 vols., Caracas/Barcelona/Mexico, Seix Barral, 1981.

A collection of essays on bibliographical, biographical, and literary aspects of Bello's work, by an eminent *bellista*.

Morin, Thomas D. *Mariano Picón Salas*, Boston, Twayne, 1979.

A study of the life and works of Picón Salas, with emphasis on his ideological evolution.

Roggiano, Alfredo. *Pedro Henríquez Ureña en los Estados Unidos*, Mexico, Editorial Cultura, 1961.

A collection of writings by Henríquez Ureña during his various periods in the United States, with introductory comments by Roggiano.

Vitier, Cintio (ed.). *La crítica literaria y estética en el siglo XIX cubano*, 2 vols., prologue by editor, Havana, Biblioteca Nacional "José Martí," 1968–1970.

Anthology of nineteenth-century Cuban critics with substantial prologues by Vitier. Contains selections from Domingo Delmonte, Rafael María Merchán, Enrique José Varona, Manuel Sanguily, and José Martí, among others.

Wellek, René. *A History of Modern Criticism: 1750–1950*, IV, *The Later Nineteenth Century*, New Haven, Yale University Press, 1965.

Wold, Ruth. *Diario de México: primer cotidiano de Nueva España*, Madrid, Gredos, 1970.

Studies the *Diario de México* in the context of the impact of the Enlightenment on New Spain.

Zum Felde, Alberto. *Indice crítico de la literatura hispanoamericana. La ensayística*, Mexico, Editorial Guarania, 1954.

Highly detailed though often rambling and impressionistic history of the essay in Spanish America. Devotes separate sections to literary criticism in each period covered.

Articles

Block de Behar, Lisa. "Emir Rodríguez Monegal: medio siglo de una (di)visión crítica" in *Homenaje a Emir Rodríguez Monegal*, Montevideo, Ministerio de Educación y Cultura, 1987.

Studies Rodríguez Monegal's role in the Uruguayan critical tradition, with emphasis on literary polemics.

Coleman, Alexander. "El otro Emir en *El otro Andrés Bello*" in *Homenaje a Emir Rodríguez Monegal*, Montevideo, Ministerio de Educación y Cultura, 1987.

Remarks on "novelty and anachronism" in the work of Rodríguez Monegal, with emphasis on *El otro Andrés Bello*.

Dwyer, John P. "Emir Rodríguez Monegal: autor/actor y antagonista" in *Homenaje a Emir Rodríguez Monegal*, Montevideo, Ministerio de Educación y Cultura, 1987.

Personal and professional reminiscences of Rodríguez Monegal.

González Echevarría, Roberto. "Nota crítica sobre *The Borzoi Anthology of Latin American Literature*" in *Isla a su vuelo fugitiva. Ensayos críticos sobre literatura hispanoamericana*, Madrid, José Porrúa Turanzas, 1983, 227–34.

Points out Rodríguez Monegal's role in defining the current canon of Latin American literature.

"Emir and the Canon. An obituary note," *Latin American Literary Review*, 4 (July–Dec., 1986), 7–10.

Remarks on Rodríguez Monegal's contribution to the teaching of Latin American literature in the United States.

Hozven, Roberto. "Pedro Henríquez Ureña: el maestro viajero," *Revista Iberoamericana. Número Especial sobre la Literatura Dominicana en el Siglo XX*, 142 (Jan.–Mar., 1988), 291–320.

Well-documented though somewhat confusing attempt to summarize Henríquez Ureña's critical ideas.

Martínez, Tomás Eloy. "Angel Rama o la crítica como gozo," *Revista Iberoamericana*, 135–6 (April–Sept., 1986), 645–64.
    Broad and useful summary of Rama's critical career, interwoven with personal reminiscences.

Martínez Antonini, Agustín. "Problemas de la crítica literaria latinoamericana," *Cuadernos Americanos*, 6 (1987), 92–108.
    Abstract analysis of the history of Spanish American criticism in terms of a theory of "modernization."

Paz, Octavio. "Alrededores de la literatura hispanoamericana, "*Vuelta*, 5 (April 1977), 21–4.
    Contains insightful comments on the relationship between literature and criticism in Spanish America.

Rodríguez Monegal, Emir. "Introducción general" in José Enrique Rodó, *Obras completas*, ed. with intro., prologue, and notes, Emir Rodríguez Monegal, Madrid, Aguilar, 1967.
    Gives a detailed account of Rodó's life and works in his social and literary context.

Roggiano, Alfredo. "Emir Rodríguez Monegal, o el crítico necesario" in *Homenaje a Emir Rodríguez Monegal*, Montevideo, Ministerio de Educación y Cultura, 1987.
    Outlines Rodríguez Monegal's intellectual evolution.

Santí, Enrico Mario. "Borges y Emir" in *Homenaje a Emir Rodríguez Monegal*, Montevideo, Ministerio de Educación y Cultura, 1987.
    Studies the influence of Borges on Rodríguez Monegal's criticism.

Sosnowski, Saúl. "Sobre la crítica de la literatura hispanoamericana: balance y perspectivas," *Cuadernos Hispanoamericanos: Revista Mensual de Cultura Hispánica*, 443 (May 1987), 143–59.
    Wide-ranging and detailed (if somewhat chaotic) overview of Spanish American criticism since the 1960s.

Sucre, Guillermo. "La nueva crítica" in César Fernández Moreno (ed.), *América Latina en su literatura*, with intro. by editor, Mexico, Siglo Veintiuno Editores/ UNESCO, 1976, 259–78.
    Useful, if now dated, overview of the various tendencies in Spanish American criticism since the 1940s.

Uslar Pietri, Arturo. "Prólogo," in Uslar Pietri (ed.), *Obras completas de Andrés Bello*. *Vol. IX. Temas de crítica literaria*, Caracas, La Casa de Bello, 1981.
    Overview of Bello's contribution to Spanish American literary criticism.

Chapter 13: The autobiographical narrative

Primary sources

Alberdi, Juan Bautista. *Autobiografía: mi vida privada*, prologue Jean Jaurès, Buenos Aires, El Ateneo, 1927.

Barnet, Miguel. *Biografía de un cimarrón*, Havana, Academia de Ciencias de Cuba,

Instituto de Etnología y Folklore, 1966.

Autobiography of a Runaway Slave, tr. Jocasta Innes, London, Bodley Head, 1966.

Cané, Miguel. *Juvenilia*, Vienna, 1882; rpt. Buenos Aires, Talleres Gráficos Argentinos, 1927.

Chocano, José Santos. *Memorias. Las mil y una aventuras*, Santiago, Nascimento, 1940.

Cortázar, Julio. *Rayuela*, Buenos Aires, Sudamericana, 1963.

Hopscotch, tr. Gregory Rabassa, New York, Random House, 1966.

Darío, Rubén. *La vida de Rubén Darío escrita por él mismo*, Barcelona, Casa Editorial Maucci, n.d. [1915]; rpt. in *Obras completas*, I, Madrid, Afrodisio Aguado, 1950.

Elizondo, Salvador. *Salvador Elizondo*, Mexico, Empresa Editorial, 1968.

Fernández Moreno, Baldomero. *Vida, memorias de Fernández Moreno*, intro. Fernández Moreno, Buenos Aires, G. Kraft, 1957.

Gómez Carrillo, Enrique. *Obras completas*, vol. X: *Treinta años de mi vida*, Book I, *El despertar de un alma*, Madrid, Mundo Latino, n.d. [1918].

Obras completas, vol. XVI: *Treinta años de mi vida*, Book II, *En plena bohemia*, Madrid, Mundo Latino, n.d. [1919].

Treinta años de mi vida, Book III, *La miseria de Madrid*, Buenos Aires, Casa Vaccaro, 1921.

Gómez de Avellaneda, Gertrudis. *Autobiografía y cartas (hasta ahora inéditas) de la ilustre poetisa Gertrudis Gómez de Avellaneda, con un prólogo y una necrología por Don Lorenzo Cruz de Fuentes*, 2nd. rev. edn., Madrid, Imprenta Helénica, 1914.

González Martínez, Enrique. *El hombre del búho. Misterio de una vocación*, Mexico, Cuadernos Americanos, 1944; rpt. *Obras completas*, Mexico, El Colegio Nacional, 1971.

La apacible locura. Segunda parte del hombre del búho, Mexico, Cuadernos Americanos, 1951; rpt. *Obras Completas*, Mexico, El Colegio Nacional, 1971.

González Vera, José Santos. *Cuando era muchacho*, Santiago, Nascimento, 1951.

Guridi y Alcocer, José Miguel. *Apuntes de la vida de D. José Miguel Guridi y Alcocer*, Mexico, Moderna Librería Religiosa de José L. Vallejo, 1906.

Lange, Norah. *Cuadernos de infancia*, Buenos Aires, Editorial Losada, 1937.

Larreta, Enrique. *Tiempos iluminados*, Buenos Aires/Mexico, Espasa-Calpe Argentina, 1939.

López Albújar, Enrique. *De mi casona. Un poco de historia piurana a través de la biografía del autor*, Lima, Imprenta Lux, 1924.

Memorias, preface Ciro Alegría, Lima, Talleres Gráficos Villanueva, 1963.

Mansilla, Lucio V. *Mis memorias*, Paris, 1904; rpt. intro. Juan Carlos Ghiano, Buenos Aires, Hachette, 1955.

Manzano, Juan Francisco. *Autobiografía*, intro. José L. Franco, Havana, Municipio de La Habana, 1937.

The Life and Poems of a Cuban Slave, intro. Edward J. Mullen, Richard Madden, Hamden, Conn., Archon Book, 1981.

Menchú, Rigoberta. *Me llamo Rigoberta Menchú y así me nació la conciencia*, ed. E. Burgos, Barcelona, Argos Vergara, 1983.

I . . . Rigoberta Menchu. An Indian woman in Guatemala, ed. and intro. by Elizabeth Burgos-Debray, Ann Wright, London and New York, Verso Books,

1984.

Méndez Capote, Renée. *Memorias de una cubanita que nació con el siglo*, Buenos Aires, 1964; rpt. Barcelona, Argos Vergara, 1984.

Neruda, Pablo. *Confieso que he vivido. Memorias*, Buenos Aires, Editorial Losada, 1974.

Memoirs, Hardie St. Martin, New York, Farrar, Straus, & Giroux, 1976.

Ocampo, Victoria. *El archipiélago. Autobiografía*, I, Buenos Aires, Ediciones Revista Sur, 1979.

El imperio insular. Autobiografía, II, Buenos Aires, Ediciones Revista Sur, 1980.

La rama de Salzburgo. Autobiografía, III, Buenos Aires, Ediciones Revista Sur, 1981.

Virajes. Autobiografía, IV. Buenos Aires, Ediciones Revista Sur, 1982.

Figuras simbólicas. Medida de Francia. Autobiografía, V, Buenos Aires, Ediciones Revista Sur, 1983.

Sur y Cia. Autobiografía, VI, Buenos Aires, Ediciones Revista Sur, 1984.

Oliver, María Rosa. *Mundo, mi casa*, Buenos Aires, 1965; rpt. Buenos Aires, Sudamericana, 1970.

La vida cotidiana, Buenos Aires, Sudamericana, 1969.

Mi fe en el hombre, Buenos Aires, Carlos Lohlé, 1981.

Orrego Luco, Luis. *Memorias del tiempo viejo*, intro. Héctor Fuenzalida Villegas, Santiago, Ediciones de la Universidad de Chile, 1984.

Pérez Rosales, Vicente. *Recuerdos del pasado (1814–1860)*, 1882; rpt. Santiago, Biblioteca de Escritores de Chile, 1910.

Picón Salas, Mariano. *Mundo imaginario*, Santiago, Nascimento, 1927.

Viaje al amanecer, Mexico, Ediciones Mensaje, 1943.

Regreso de tres mundos. Un hombre en su generación, Mexico, Fondo de Cultura Económica, 1959.

Pitol, Sergio. *Sergio Pitol*, Mexico, Empresa Editorial, 1967.

Rojas, Manuel. *Imágenes de infancia*, Santiago, Babel, 1955.

Samper, José María. *Historia de una alma. Memorias íntimas y de historia contemporánea*, Bogotá, Imprenta de Zalamea Hermanos, 1881.

Sanín Cano, Baldomero. *De mis vidas y otras vidas*, Bogotá, Editorial ABC, 1949.

Santa Cruz y Montalvo, Mercedes, Countess of Merlin. *Mis doce primeros años e Historia de Sor Inés*, 1831; rpt. Havana, Imprenta "El Siglo XX," 1922.

Santiván, Fernando (Fernando Santibáñez). *Memorias de un tolstoyano*, Santiago, Zig-Zag, 1955; rpt. in *Obras completas*, II, Zig-Zag, 1965.

Confesiones de Santiván, Santiago, Zig-Zag, 1958; rpt. in *Obras completas*, II, Santiago, Zig-Zag, 1965.

Sarmiento, Domingo Faustino. *Mi defensa*, 1843; rpt. in *Obras*, III, Buenos Aires, Imprenta y Litografía Mariano Moreno, 1896.

Recuerdos de provincia. 1850; rpt. in *Obras*, III, Buenos Aires, Imprenta y Litografía Mariano Moreno, 1896.

Subercaseaux, Ramón. *Memorias de cincuenta años*, Santiago, Imprenta y Litografía Barcelona, 1908.

Tapia y Rivera, Alejandro. *Mis memorias, o Puerto Rico como lo encontré y como lo dejo*, New York, De Laisne & Rossboro, 1928; rpt. Río Piedras, Editorial Edil, 1979.

Torres Bodet, Jaime, *Tiempo de arena*, Mexico, Fondo de Cultura Económica, 1965.

Vasconcelos, José. *Ulises criollo. La vida del autor escrita por él mismo*, I: *Ulises criollo*; II; *La tormenta*; III; *El desastre*; IV; *El proconsulado*, Mexico, Botas, 1935–1939; rpt. as *Memorias*, I–II, Mexico, Fondo de Cultura Económica, 1982.

    Ulises criollo. Primera edición expurgada, Mexico, Editorial Jus, 1958.

    A Mexican Ulysses: An autobiography, tr. William Rex Crawford, Westport, Conn., Greenwood Press, 1972.

Vega, Bernardo. *Memorias de Bernardo Vega*, ed. César Andreu Iglesias, 1977; rpt. Río Piedras, Eds. Huracán, 1984.

Vientós Gaston, Nilita. *El mundo de la infancia*, Mexico, Editorial Cultural, 1984.

Secondary sources

Books

L'Autobiographie dans le monde hispanique. Actes du Colloque International de la Baume-lès-Aix, 11–13 Mai 1979, Aix-en-Provence, Université de Provence, 1980.

    Proceedings of conference, with a few papers, mainly monographic, devoted to Latin American autobiography and first-person narrative (Neruda, Gómez de Avellaneda, Macedonio Fernández, Che Guevara, Rulfo).

Azzario, Ester. *La prosa autobiográfica de Mariano Picón Salas*, Caracas, Ediciones de la Universidad Simón Bolívar, 1980.

    A detailed, mainly descriptive study of Picón Salas's autobiographical writings.

Catelli, Nora. *El espacio autobiográfico*, Barcelona, Lumen, 1991.

    Excellent theoretical reflection on the genre, with special attention devoted to the imposture of self-writing, and a subtle analysis of gendered self-figuration in Gertrudis Gómez de Avellaneda.

Díaz Arrieta, Hernán (Alone). *Memorialistas chilenos*, Santiago, Zig-Zag, 1960.

    A collection of journalistic essays, consisting of brief presentations of Chilean autobiographers from the colonial period to the present. Informative, though basically anecdotal and lacking critical depth.

Feal, Rosemary Geisdorfer. *Novel Lives: The fictional autobiographies of Guillermo Cabrera Infante and Mario Vargas Llosa*, Chapel Hill, North Carolina Studies in the Romance Languages and Literatures, 1986.

    An excellent analysis of the rhetorical devices informing the autobiographical novels of the two authors, with a solid theoretical reflection and a good bibliography.

Molloy, Sylvia. *At Face Value: Autobiographical writing in Spanish America*, Cambridge University Press, 1991.

    A study of autobiography with special emphasis on textual strategies, generic attributions, and perceptions of self-informing self-writing from the nineteenth century on. (Sarmiento, Manzano, Picón Salas, Ocampo, Lange, Mansilla, Vasconcelos.)

Prieto, Adolfo. *La literatura autobiográfica argentina*, Rosario, Instituto de Letras, 1966; rpt. Buenos Aires, Centro Editor de América Latina, 1982.

    The first book of its kind in Latin America. A perceptive study of the evolution of the genre in the late nineteenth and early twentieth centuries in Argentina, with particular emphasis on the sociocultural context of autobiographical texts. (Saavedra, Belgrano, Sarmiento, Alberdi, Mitre, Paz, La Madrid, Mansilla, Guido y Spano, Cané, López, Quesada, etc.)

Ramos, Raymundo. *Memorias y autobiografías de escritores mexicanos*, Mexico, Universidad Nacional Autónoma de México, 1967.

A critical anthology, mainly descriptive in its approach.

Articles

Altamirano, Carlos, and Beatriz Sarlo. "Una vida ejemplar: la estrategia de *Recuerdos de provincia*" in *Literatura/Sociedad*, Buenos Aires, Hachette, 1983, 163–208.

Superb study of Sarmiento's tactics in *Recuerdos*, with special emphasis on the modelling function of reading in Sarmiento's construction of self.

Bastos, María Luisa. "Escrituras ajenas, expresión propia: *Sur* y los *Testimonios* de Victoria Ocampo," *Revista Iberoamericana*, 110–11 (1980), 123–37.

Intelligent analysis of Ocampo's oblique self-figuration through the writing of others and through her own review, *Sur*.

Halperín Donghi, Tulio. "Sarmiento: su lugar en la sociedad argentina posrevolucionaria," *Sur*, 341 (1977), 121–35.

A close examination of Sarmiento's shifting ideological allegiances and the manner in which these shifts affect the construction of his self-image.

"Lamartine en Sarmiento: *Les Confidences* y *Recuerdos de provincia*," *Filología*, 20:2 (1985), 177–90.

A perceptive analysis of Sarmiento's use of Lamartine as a precursor text.

"Intelectuales, sociedad y vida pública en Hispanoamérica a través de la literatura autobiográfica" in *El espejo de la historia. Problemas argentinos y perspectivas latinoamericanas*, Buenos Aires, Sudamericana, 1987, 41–64.

An incisive reflection on the ideological function of autobiography as the self-defining gesture of new liberal intellectuals in nineteenth-century Latin America.

Lugo-Ortiz, Agnes. "Memoria infantil y perspectiva histórica en *El archipiélago* de Victoria Ocampo," *Revista Iberoamericana*, 140 (1987), 651–61.

Thoughtful study of the interplay between individual and collective memory in Ocampo's childhood recollections.

Sklodowska, Elzbieta. "Hacia una tipología del testimonio hispanoamericano," *Siglo XX/20th Century* (1990–1991), 103–20.

Intelligent, thorough analysis of the particulars of this form, and of the way it relates both to autobiography and to fiction.

Sommer, Doris. "'Not Just a Personal Story': Women's *Testimonios* and the plural self" in Bella Brodzki and Celeste Schenk (eds.), *Life/Lines: Theorizing women's autobiography*, Ithaca and London, Cornell University Press, 1988, 107–30.

Excellent critical reflection on the status of testimonial literature within autobiographical discourse, with special attention to the way in which gender inflects the genre.

Chapter 14: The twentieth-century short story in Spanish America

Primary sources

Bianco, José. "Sombras suele vestir" (1941) in Bianco, *Ficción y reflexión*, Mexico, Fondo de Cultura Económica, 1988, 19–46.
    Shadow Play and The Rats, tr. Daniel Balderston, Pittsburgh, Latin American Literary Review Press, 1983, 1–33.

Borges, Jorge Luis. "Abenjacán el Bojarí, muerto en su laberinto" (1951) in Borges, *Obras completas*, Buenos Aires, Emecé, 1974, 600–7.
    "Ibn Hakkan al-Bokhari, dead in his labyrinth," tr. Norman Thomas di Giovanni with the author, in *The Aleph and Other Stories (1933–1969)*, New York, E. P. Dutton, 1970, 115–25.
    "La busca de Averroes" (1947) in Borges, *Obras completas*, Buenos Aires, Emecé, 1974, 582–8.
    "Averroes' search," tr. James E. Irby, in Donald A. Yates and James E. Irby, (eds.) *Labyrinths: Selected stories and other writings*, New York, New Directions, 1964, 148–55.
    "El Aleph" (1945) in Borges, *Obras completas*, Buenos Aires, Emecé, 1974, 617–28.
    "The Aleph," tr. Norman Thomas di Giovanni with the author, in *The Aleph and Other Stories (1933–1969)*, New York, E. P. Dutton, 1970, 15–30.
    "El hombre en el umbral" (1952) in Borges, *Obras completas*, Buenos Aires, Emecé, 1974, 612–16.
    "The man on the threshold," tr. Norman Thomas di Giovanni with the author, in *The Aleph and Other Stories (1933–1969)*, New York, E. P. Dutton, 1970, 129–35.
    "La muerte y la brújula" (1942) in Borges, *Obras completas*, Buenos Aires, Emecé, 1974, 499–507.
    "Death and the compass," tr. Donald A. Yates, in Donald A. Yates and James E. Irby (eds.), *Labyrinths: Selected stories and other writings*, New York, New Directions, 1964, 76–87.
    "Pierre Menard, autor del Quijote" (1939) in Borges, *Obras completas*, Buenos Aires, Emecé, 1974, 444–50.
    "Pierre Menard, author of the *Quixote*," tr. James E. Irby, in Donald A. Yates and James E. Irby (eds.), *Labyrinths: Selected stories and other writings*, New York, New Directions, 1964, 36–44.

Carpentier, Alejo. "Viaje a la semilla" in Carpentier, *Guerra del tiempo*, Mexico, Compañía General de Ediciones, 1958, 77–107.
    "Journey to the seed," tr. Jean Franco, in J. M. Cohen (ed.), *Latin American Writing Today*, Harmondsworth, Penguin Books, 1967, 53–66.

Cortázar, Julio. "Apocalipsis en Solentiname" in Cortázar, *Alguien que anda por ahí y otros relatos*, Madrid, Ediciones Alfaguara, 1977. 93–105.
    "Apocalypse at Solentiname" in *We Love Glenda So Much and A Change of Light*, tr. Gregory Rabassa, New York, Vintage Books, 1984, 265–73.
    "Axolotl" in Cortázar, *Final de Juego*, Buenos Aires, Sudamericana, 1964, 161–8.
    "Axolotl" in *Blow-Up and Other Stories*, tr. Paul Blackburn, New York, Collier, 1968, 3–8.

"Las babas del diablo" in Cortázar, *Las armas secretas*, Buenos Aires, Sudamericana, 1964, 77–98.

"Blow-Up" in *Blow-Up and Other Stories*, tr. Paul Blackburn, New York, Collier, 1968, 100–15.

"Continuidad de los parques" in Cortázar, *Final de juego*, Buenos Aires, Sudamericana, 1964, 9–11.

"Continuity of parks" in *Blow-Up and Other Stories*, tr. Paul Blackburn, New York, Collier, 1968, 55–6.

"Final de juego" in Cortázar, *Final de juego*, Buenos Aires, Sudamericana, 1964, 181–96.

"End of the game" in *Blow-Up and Other Stories*, tr. Paul Blackburn, New York, Collier, 1968, 119–31.

Ferré, Rosario. "La muñeca menor" in Ferré *Papeles de Pandora*, Mexico, Mortiz, 1976, 9–15.

"The youngest doll," tr. Rosario Ferré and Diana Vélez, in Pamela Mordecai and Betty Wilson (eds.), *Her True-True Name: An anthology of women's writing from the Caribbean*, Oxford, Heinemann, 1989, 93–8; also in Rosario Ferré, *The Youngest Doll and Other Stories*, Minneapolis, University of Minnesota Press, 1990.

García Márquez, Gabriel. "La increíble y triste historia de la cándida Eréndira y de su abuela desalmada" in García Márquez, *La increíble y triste historia de la cándida Eréndira y de su abuela desalmada: siete cuentos*, Mexico, Editorial Hermes, 1972, 95–163.

"The incredible and sad tale of innocent Eréndira and her heartless grandmother" in *Innocent Eréndira and Other Stories*, tr. Gregory Rabassa, New York, Harper & Row, 1979, 1–59.

Garro, Elena, "La culpa es de los tlaxcaltecas" in Garro, *La semana de colores*, Xalapa, Mexico, Universidad Veracruzana, 1964, 11–29.

"It's the fault of the Tlaxcaltecas," Alberto Manguel, in Alberto Manguel (ed.), *Other Fires: Short fiction by Latin American women*, New York, Clarkson N. Potter, 1986, 159–78; another English translation, "Blame the Tlaxcaltecs" in Celia Correas de Zapata (ed.), *Short Stories by Latin American Women: The magic and the real*, Houston, Arte Público Press, 1990, 74–88.

"La primera vez que me vi" in Garro, *Andamos huyendo Lola*, Mexico, Mortiz, 1980, 33–54.

González, José Luis. "La noche que volvimos a ser gente" in González, *Mambrú se fue a la guerra (y otros relatos)*, Mexico, Mortiz, 1972, 117–34.

"The night we became people again" in Kal Wagenheim (ed. and tr.), *Cuentos: An anthology of short stories from Puerto Rico*, New York, Schocken, 1978, 117–41.

Hernández, Felisberto. "Las Hortensias" (1949) in María Luisa Puga (ed.), *Obras completas*, 3 vols., Mexico, Siglo Veintiuno Editores, 1983, II, 176–233.

"El acomodador" (1946) in María Luisa Puga (ed.), *Obras completas*, Mexico, Siglo Veintiuno Editores, 1983, II, 75–92.

Ocampo, Silvina. "Las fotografías" (1959) in Ocampo, *La furia y otros cuentos*, Madrid, Alianza Editorial, 1982, 89–93.

"The photographs" in *Leopoldina's Dream*, tr. Daniel Balderston, Markham, Ontario, Penguin Books, 1988, 25–9.

"La furia" in Ocampo, *La furia y otros cuentos* [1959], Madrid, Alianza Editorial, 1982, 113–21.

"The fury" in *Leopoldina's Dream*. tr. Daniel Balderston, Markham, Ontario, Penguin Books, 1988, 17–24.

"Icera" in Ocampo, *Las invitadas*, Buenos Aires, Editorial Losada, 1961, 124–7.

"Icera" in *Leopoldina's Dream*, tr. Daniel Balderston, Markham, Ontario, Penguin Books, 1988, 103–7.

"La revelación" in Ocampo, *Las invitadas*, Buenos Aires, Editorial Losada, 1961, 23–5.

"Revelation" in *Leopoldina's Dream*, tr. Daniel Balderston, Markham, Ontario, Penguin Books, 1988, 13–16.

"Tales eran sus rostros" in Ocampo, *Las invitadas*, Buenos Aires, Editorial Losada, 1961, 7–12.

"Thus were their faces" in *Leopoldina's Dream*, Markham, Ontario, Penguin Books, 1988, 1–7.

Onetti, Juan Carlos. "El album" (1953) in Onetti, *Cuentos completos*, intro. Jorge Ruffinelli, Buenos Aires, Corregidor, 1974, 155–72.

"The photograph album" in *Goodbyes and Stories*, tr. Daniel Balderston, Austin, University of Texas Press, 1990, 79–90.

"La cara de la desgracia" (1960) in Onetti, *Cuentos completos*, intro. Jorge Ruffinelli, Buenos Aires, Corregidor, 1974, 221–55.

"The image of misfortune" in *Goodbyes and Stories*, tr. Daniel Balderston, Austin, University of Texas Press, 1990, 104–28.

"El infierno tan temido" (1957) in Onetti, *Cuentos completos*, intro. Jorge Ruffinelli, Buenos Aires, Corregidor, 1974, 203–20.

"Hell most feared" in *Goodbyes and Stories*, tr. Daniel Balderston, Austin, University of Texas Press, 1990, 91–103.

Piglia, Ricardo. "Homenaje a Roberto Arlt" in Piglia, *Nombre falso*, Buenos Aires, Siglo Veintiuno Editores, 1975, 97–172.

Piñera, Virgilio. "El álbum" in Piñera, *Cuentos*, Madrid, Alfaguara, 1983, 65–86.

"The album" in *Cold Tales*, tr. Mark Schafer, Hygiene, Colo., Eridanos Press, 1988, 37–54.

Poniatowska, Elena. "Cine Prado" in Poniatowska, *Los cuentos de Lilus Kikus*, Xalapa, Mexico, Universidad Veracruzana, 1967, 67–75.

"Park Cinema" in Celia Correas de Zapata (ed.), *Short Stories by Latin American Women: The magic and the real*, Houston, Arte Público Press, 1990, 171–5.

"De noche vienes" in Poniatowska, *De noche vienes*, Mexico, Editorial Grijalbo, 1979, 209–31.

"The night visitor," tr. Catherine S. White-House, in Alberto Manguel (ed.), *Other Fires: Short fiction by Latin American women*, New York, Clarkson N. Potter, 1986, 125–45.

Quiroga, Horacio. "El hijo" (1928) in Emir Rodríguez Monegal (ed.), *Cuentos*, Caracas, Biblioteca Ayacucho, 1981, 294–7.

"The son" in *The Decapitated Chicken and Other Stories*, tr. Margaret Sayers Peden, Austin, University of Texas Press, 1976, 189–94.

"El hombre muerto" (1920) in Emir Rodríguez Monegal (ed.), *Cuentos*, Caracas, Biblioteca Ayacucho, 1981, 190–3.

"The dead man" in *The Decapitated Chicken and Other Stories*, tr. Margaret Sayers Peden, Austin, University of Texas Press, 1976, 121–5.

"Las moscas" (1923) in Emir Rodríguez Monegal (ed.), *Cuentos*, Caracas, Biblioteca Ayacucho, 1981, 304–6.

Ribeyro, Julio Ramón. "La juventud en la otra ribera" (1969) in Ribeyro, *La juventud en la otra ribera*, Barcelona, Argos Vergara, 1981, 275–309.

Roa Bastos, Augusto. "Contar un cuento" in Roa Bastos, *Moriencia* [1969], 2nd edn., Barcelona, Editorial Plaza & Janés, 1984, 89–96.

Rulfo, Juan. "Anacleto Morones" in Rulfo, *El llano en llamas*, Mexico, Fondo de Cultura Económica, 1953, 117–33.

"Anacleto Morones," tr. George D. Schade, in *The Burning Plain*, Austin, University of Texas Press, 1967, 157–75.

Wilcock, Juan Rodolfo. "El caos" in Wilcock, *El caos*, Buenos Aires, Sudamericana, 1974, 7–36.

"La engañosa" in Wilcock, *El caos*, Buenos Aires, Sudamericana, 1974, 119–27.

"La fiesta de los enanos" in Wilcock, *El caos*, Buenos Aires, Sudamericana, 1974, 37–63.

Secondary sources

Note: I have excluded all anthologies from the following list, although the introductions to the anthologies have included some of the most widely read statements on the genre. For a full list of anthologies see Balderston, *The Latin American Short Story*, listed below.

Books

Acker, Bertie. *El cuento mexicano contemporáneo: Rulfo, Arreola y Fuentes: temas y cosmovisión*, Colección Nova Scholar, Madrid, Playor, 1984.

Thematic studies of the three authors, focusing on themes such as women, society, art, free will, nostalgia, life, liberty, and the pursuit of happiness.

Aldrich, Earl M., Jr. *The Modern Short Story in Peru*, Madison, University of Wisconsin Press, 1966.

Important study of the development of the genre of the modern short story in Peru, focusing on the questions of national identity, local color, and social protest. Includes useful studies of Arguedas, Ciro Alegría, and others. Unsophisticated literary analysis.

Anderson Imbert, Enrique. *Teoría y técnica del cuento*, Buenos Aires, Marymar, 1979.

An ambitious survey of questions of genre, literary history, narrative structure, etc. Anderson Imbert as Structuralist.

Araujo, Orlando. *Narrativa venezolana contemporánea: ensayo*, Caracas, Editorial Tiempo Nuevo, 1972.

Includes discussion of the short story as well as the novel. Disjointed impressionist survey.

Balderston, Daniel. *The Latin American Short Story: An annotated guide to anthologies and criticism*, Westport, Conn. Greenwood Press, 1992.

A comprehensive survey of anthologies and general criticism of the short story in Spanish America and Brazil.

Baquero Goyanes, Mariano. *¿Qué es el cuento?*, Colección Esquemas, 83, Buenos Aires, Columba, 1967; 2nd edn., 1974.

Focuses on questions of definition. A general study, with few references to examples of the genre in Spanish America.

Barbagelata, Hugo D. (ed. and intro.). *La novela y el cuento en Hispanoamérica*, Montevideo, Enrique Miguez, 1947.

Organized by groupings of countries: (1) Chile, Peru, Bolivia, (2) Argentina, Uruguay, Paraguay, (3) Colombia, Venezuela, Ecuador, (4) Mexico, (5) Cuba, Santo Domingo, Puerto Rico, and (6) Central America. A cursory overview of literary history.

Bullrich, Silvina. *Carta a un joven cuentista*, Buenos Aires, Rueda, 1968.

A mixture of personal experience and earnest advice by the bestselling Argentinian writer, loosely modeled on Rilke's *Letters to a Young Poet*.

Carballo, Emmanuel. *Bibliografía del cuento mexicano del siglo XX*, Serie Textos, 3, Mexico, Universidad Nacional Autónoma de México, 1988.

Introduction (pp. 9–30) consists of critical discussion of Torri, Efrén Hernández, Revueltas, Arreola, Rulfo, and Fuentes. Bibliographies in chronological order (from 1900 to 1987) and in alphabetical order by author.

Carrión, Benjamín. *El nuevo relato ecuatoriano: crítica y antología*, 2 vols., Quito, Casa de la Cultura Ecuatoriana, 1950.

The first volume is the critical study. It is divided into three parts: Part I (pp. 9–101) is a general survey of Ecuadorian and Spanish American literature from Romanticism to 1930; Part II (pp 103–287) deals with the Guayaquil group of 1930; Part III (pp. 291–387) is largely miscellaneous.

Castagnino, Raúl H. *"Cuento-artefacto" y artificios del cuento*, Buenos Aires, Editorial Nova, 1977.

An introductory survey of narratology, with extended discussion of Roa Bastos's "El baldío."

Castellanos, Luis Arturo. *El cuento en la Argentina*, Santa Fe, Colmegna, 1967.

Discussion of social realism, the fantastic, and other tendencies, with focus on younger writers: Heker, Poletti, Constantini, and others.

Englekirk, John E., and Margaret M. Ramos. *La narrativa uruguaya: estudio crítico bibliográfico*, Berkeley, University of California Press, 1967.

Extensive introductory essay on history of the genre in Uruguay since Romanticism, with particular attention to Acevedo Díaz, the Generation of 1900 and the nativist writers of the 1920s; brief discussion of Onetti and Felisberto Hernández at the end of the essay. Extensive annotated bibliography.

Fleak, Kenneth. *The Chilean Short Story: Writers from the Generation of 1950*, New York, Peter Lang, 1989.

A useful study of the Chilean short story, focusing on Lafourcade, Giaconi, Donoso, Edwards, and Guillermo Blanco. Excellent bibliographies.

Flores, Angel (ed.). *El realismo mágico en el cuento hispanoamericano*, La Red de Jonás, Estudios, 18, Tlahuapán, Mexico, Premiá, 1985.

This collection includes Flores's important essay on Magical Realism (1955) as well as essays by Ghiano, Bratosevich, Yurkievich, Jitrik, Ruffinelli, and others. Also includes texts of stories by Lugones, Quiroga, Onetti, and others, considered by Flores to be examples of this current in Spanish American short fiction.

Foster, David William. *Studies in the Contemporary Spanish-American Short Story*, Columbia, University of Missouri Press, 1979.

A study of narrative *écriture*, with chapters on Borges, Rulfo, García Márquez, Cortázar, Benedetti, and Cabrera Infante.

Gotlib, Nádia Batella. *Teoria do conto*, 5th edn., São Paulo, Editora Atica, 1990.

Fine introduction to short-story theory. Includes discussion of Quiroga and Cortázar as well as of Brazilian, and other, authors.

Lancelotti, Mario. *De Poe a Kafka. Para una teoría del cuento*, Buenos Aires, EUDEBA, 1965.

Consists of seven chapters, four on general topics, one on Poe and two on Kafka.

Teoría del cuento, Buenos Aires, Ediciones Culturales Argentinas, 1973.

Much less systematic than the title suggests. The work is actually a collection of thirty-two brief essays on Mallea, Hawthorne, Poe, Maupassant, and other practitioners of the genre, as well as on the difference between story and novel, the reader, narrative time, and other topics.

Leal, Luis. *Breve historia del cuento mexicano*, Manuales Studium, 2, Mexico, Ediciones de Andrea, 1956.

As with Leal's history of the Spanish American short story listed below, consists largely of lists of authors and titles, though the critical judgments are well informed. Broad scope, from pre-Hispanic tales to literary Expressionism.

Bibliografía del cuento mexicano, Colección Studium, 21, Mexico, Ediciones de Andrea, 1958.

Bibliographical volume to complement Leal's anthology and history of the Mexican short story. Lacks annotations.

Historia del cuento hispanoamericano, Mexico, Ediciones de Andrea, 1966.

This book, like others in the Ediciones de Andrea series, consists largely of lists of authors and works, but is the only traditional literary history of the genre with such broad scope.

Mancera Galletti, Angel. *Quiénes narran y cuentan en Venezuela: fichero bibliográfico para una historia de la novela y del cuento venezolanos*, Caracas, Ediciones Caribe, 1958.

Chaotic collection of essays on novel and short story in Venezuela, with discussions of 143 writers.

Mastrángelo, Carlos. *El cuento argentino, contribución al conocimiento de su historia, teoría y práctica*, Buenos Aires, Editorial Nova, 1963.

A poorly written, extraordinarily belligerent study, which won a prize in 1961 from the Sociedad Argentina de Escritores. Disjointed essays on various short-story anthologies, on questions of definition, on short-story theory, and on the avant-garde short story.

Matlowsky, Bernice D. *Antologías del cuento hispanoamericano: guía bibliográfica*, Monografías Bibliográficas, 3, Washington, Unión Panamericana, División de Filosofía, Letras y Ciencias, 1950.

A brief bibliographical guide, now very out of date.

Menton, Seymour. *Prose Fiction of the Cuban Revolution*, Latin American Monographs, 37, Austin, University of Texas Press, 1975; also in Spanish, *La narrativa de la revolución cubana*, Colección Nova Scholar, Madrid, Playor.

Discussion of the prose fiction of the revolutionary period, including works written both for and against the Revolution, and by foreign as well as Cuban authors. Part III and a chapter of Part IV are specifically about the short story.

Minc, Rose S. *The Contemporary Latin American Short Story*, New York, Senda Nueva de Ediciones, 1979.

Proceedings of a conference held in New Jersey in 1978. Includes articles by Luis Harss and many others.

Mora, Gabriela. *En torno al cuento: de la teoría general y de su práctica en Hispanoamérica*, Madrid, José Porrúa Turanzas, 1985.

Important study. The first part includes discussions of definitions of the genre since Poe, a survey of Spanish American theoretical statements on the genre from Spanish America (Quiroga, Cortázar, Mastrángelo, Lancelotti, Castagnino, Serra, and Anderson Imbert), and a summary of current narratological approaches to the genre. The second part consists of analyses of stories by Felisberto Hernández, García Márquez, Brunet, Bombal, and Cortázar.

Navarro, Armando. *Narradores venezolanos de la nueva generación*, Caracas, Monte Avila, 1970.

Discussion of twenty-seven works published between 1959 and 1969. The twelve authors discussed include Salvador Garmendia, González León, and Balza.

Omil, Alba, and Raúl A. Piérola. *El cuento y sus claves*, Buenos Aires, Editorial Nova, 1967.

First three chapters focus on questions of definition of the genre. Next four chapters trace a history of the short story from the fourteenth to the twentieth century. Ninth chapter focuses on the short story in Argentina.

Parodi, Roberto A. *Los límites del cuento y la novela*, Santa Fe, Argentina, Universidad del Litoral, 1968; rpt. Concepción del Uruguay, Argentina, Revista Ser, 1971.

General survey of the literature on definitions of the short story and novel.

Pavón, Alfredo. *El universo del relato literario (el sentido narrativo de "Polvos de arroz")*, Colección Maciel, 3, Tuxtla Gutiérrez, Mexico, Universidad Autónoma de Chiapas, 1984.

A general study of narratology (pp. 13–120) followed by analysis of a volume of stories by the Mexican author Sergio Galindo (pp. 125–212). Theoretical bibliography.

Peden, Margaret Sayers (ed.). *The Latin American Short Story: A critical history*, Twayne's Critical History of the Short Story, Boston, G. K. Hall, 1973.

Includes articles by David William Foster, Naomi Lindstrom, John Brushwood, and George McMurray. Useful survey.

Pupo-Walker, Enrique (ed.). *El cuento hispanoamericano ante la crítica*, Madrid, Editorial Castalia, 1973.

Includes articles by Arrom, Pupo-Walker, Alazraki, Anderson Imbert, Rodríguez Monegal, and numerous others. Widely consulted collection.

Quiles de la Luz, Lillian. *El cuento en la literatura puertorriqueña*, Río Piedras, Editorial Universitaria de Puerto Rico, 1968.

Initial essay begins with general questions of definition and history of the genre, then provides thumbnail sketches of more than fifty authors. The latter half of the book consists of a bibliographical index of the short story in Puerto Rico from 1843 to 1963.

Ramos, Elías A. *El cuento venezolano (1950–1970): estudio temático y estilístico*, Colección Nova Scholar, Madrid, Playor, 1979.

The following aspects of the modern Venezuelan short story are considered: the short story as portrait and critique of society, the representation of violence and existential anguish, short-story technique. Includes extensive final bibliography.

Reyes, Graciela. *Polifonía textual: la citación en el relato literario*, Madrid, Gredos, 1984.

Sophisticated discussion, by the Argentinian critic, of narratological functions of quotation, polyphony, and indirect free style, with most examples from Borges, Cortázar, and García Márquez.

Rivera Rodas, Oscar. *La nueva narrativa boliviana: aproximación a sus aspectos formales*, La Paz, Ediciones Camarlingi, 1972.

A study of both the novel and the short story in Bolivia in the late 1960s and early 1970s, focusing on style, content, and structure.

Rivera Silvestrini, José. *El cuento moderno venezolano*. Río Piedras, Colección Prometeo, 1967.

Broad literary history of short story in Venezuela since *Modernismo*, with brief discussions of fifty-eight writers as well as cursory accounts of major movements and literary magazines.

Sáenz, Dalmiro. *El oficio de escribir cuentos*, Buenos Aires, Emecé, 1968.

Commentary by the Argentinian writer on a number of his own stories, with observations on short-story technique.

Serra, Edelweis. *Tipología del cuento literario: textos hispanoamericanos*, Madrid, Cupsa Editorial, 1978.

Excellent introduction to questions of short-story technique and theory, with examples drawn from Spanish American authors from Arévalo Martínez and Quiroga to the present.

Tijeras, Eduardo. *Relato breve en Argentina*, Madrid, Ediciones Cultura Hispánica, 1973.

A general survey focusing on the period since the 1920s. Well-informed traditional literary history.

Articles

Andrade, Ramiro. "Apuntes sobre la nueva cuentística nacional," *Bolívar*, 13:55–8 (1960), 175–80.

Discussion of Colombian short story, focusing on García Márquez, Cardona Jaramillo, and Truque.

Aponte, Barbara B. "El rito de la iniciación en el cuento hispanoamericano," *Hispanic Review*, 51:2 (1983), 129–46.

A rather thin article on images of children in the genre, following the molds of archetypal criticism. Discussion of stories by Donoso, García, Márquez, and Roa Bastos.

Borges, Jorge Luis. "Los laberintos policiales y Chesterton," *Sur*, 10 (1935), 92–4.
Most important of Borges's discussions of the detective story.

Bosch, Juan. "La forma en el cuento," *Revista Nacional de Cultura*, 144 (1966), 40–8.
The Dominican writer argues that the short story is ruled by two essential laws: that there must be constant action, and that the writer should choose only those words that are indispensable for expressing that action. He does not discuss the role of description in the short story.

Bueno, Salvador. "El cuento actual en la América hispana" in Bueno, *La letra como testigo*, Santa Clara, Cuba, Universidad Central de Las Villas, 1957. 127–43.
A 1953 article in which the Cuban critic and anthologist surveys the *criollista* and the "subjective" or "psychological" tendencies in the Spanish American short story since Quiroga.

Chang-Rodríguez, Raquel. "La experiencia revolucionaria en la cuentística cubana actual: *Los años duros* y *Tute de reyes*," *Cuadernos Americanos*, 222 (1979), 59–75.
Focus on collections of short stories by Antonio Benítez Rojo and Jesús Díaz, with emphasis on intellectuals' engagement in revolutionary struggle.

Cortázar, Julio. "Algunos aspectos del cuento," *Casa de las Américas*, 15–16 (1963), 3–14; also included in Cortázar, *Literatura y arte nuevo en Cuba*, Barcelona, Editorial Estela, 1971.
Famous Cortázar speech, originally presented in Havana in 1962.

"Some aspects of the short story," Tr. Naomi Lindstrom, *Review of Contemporary Fiction*, 3:3 (1983), 24–33; also trans. by Aden Hayes in *Arizona Quarterly*, 38:1 (1982), 5–18.

"Del cuento breve y sus alrededores" in Cortázar, *Ultimo round*, Mexico, Siglo Veintiuno Editores, 1969, 35–45.
Important discussion of short-story technique by the Argentinian writer.

Coulson, Graciela. "El texto ausente: notas a propósito de algunos relatos hispanoamericanos," *Cuadernos Americanos*, 223 (1979), 111–21.
Interesting article on use of ellipsis in genre, with examples from Cortázar, Arreola, Borges, and others.

D'Halmar, Augusto. "Cuento cómo cuento un cuento," *Atenea*, 279–80 (1948), 8–19.
This practical essay by the Chilean writer forms part of a large special issue of *Atenea* dedicated to the short story in Chile.

Durán-Cerda, Julio. "Sobre el concepto de cuento moderno," *Explicación de textos literarios*, 5:2 (1976), 119–32.
Choppy article on questions of definition of short story.

Earle, Peter G. "Dreams of creation: short fiction in Spanish America," *University of Denver Quarterly*, 12 (1977), 67–79.
General survey from "El matadero" to García Márquez, directed to non-specialist audience.

Escobar, Alberto. "El cuento peruano," *Estudios Americanos*, 9:43 (1955), 289–312.
Useful survey of evolution of genre from *costumbrista* sketch and *tradiciones* to modern short stories of Ciro Alegría and José María Arguedas.

Foster, Jerald. "Towards a bibliography of Latin American short story anthologies," *Latin American Research Review*, 12:2 (1977), 103–8.
Annotated list of more than fifty anthologies.

Fraser, Howard M. "The structure of violence in contemporary Spanish-American short fiction" in Frank Northen Magill and Walton Beacham (eds.), *Critical Survey of Short Fiction*, II, Englewood Cliffs, N.J., Salem, 1981, 690–705.

Considers use of violence in climactic moments of stories, from "El matadero" to Quiroga to García Márquez.

Freilich de Segal, Alicia. "El niño en el cuento venezolano," *Revista Nacional de Cultura*, 24:153 (1962), 126–63.

Sentimental exploration of the theme in works of Blanco Fombona, Pocaterra, Díaz Solís, and others.

García, Germán. "El cuento" in García, *La novela argentina. Un itinerario*, Buenos Aires, Sudamericana 1952, 269–94.

A good survey of the short story from Echeverría to Martínez Estrada, organized by theme.

García Ramis, Magali. "Women's tales" in Asela Rodríguez de Laguna (ed.), *Images and Identities: The Puerto Rican in two world contexts*, New Brunswick, N.J., Transaction, 1987, 109–15.

Brief account of writing on Puerto Rican women (by male as well as female authors) by a leading figure in the "Generation of 1970."

Gilgen, Read G. "Absurdist humor in the Spanish American short story," *Perspectives on Contemporary Literature*, 7 (1981), 81–7.

Brief article that uses Bergson, Jarry, and others to talk about the function of laughter and of black humor in such writers as Piñera, Arreola, and Cortázar.

Gómez Lance, Betty R. "¿Existe una 'Promoción del Cuarenta' en el cuento puertorriqueño?" *Revista Iberoamericana*, 30:58 (1964), 283–92.

Useful introduction to Díaz Alfaro, Marqués, González, and others, though question asked in title is not answered in an interesting way.

Hasson, Liliane. "Le Conte cubain de la révolution," *Europe*, 666 (1984), 21–8.

Survey of Cuban writing during the revolutionary period, with mention of such ideologically diverse figures as Lydia Cabrera, Onelio Jorge Cardoso, Piñera, Casey, and Benítez Rojo.

Hozven, Roberto. "Un modelo estructural y tres relatos orales chilenos," *Estudios Filológicos*, 13 (1978), 113–54.

Structuralist study grounded in Lévi-Strauss, Greimas, and others of "Los tres chanchitos," "El cuentos de las adivinanzas," and "El cuento de la adivinanza."

Koch, Dolores M. "El micro-relato en México: Torri, Arreola, Monterroso" in Merlin H. Forster and Julio Ortega (eds.), *De la crónica a la nueva narrativa: coloquio sobre literatura mexicana*, Mexico Oasis, 1986, 161–77.

Consideration of what Anglo-American critics call the "short short story."

Koenenkampf, Guillermo. "Visión del cuento chileno del siglo XX," *Atenea*, 279–80 (1948), 63—81.

Useful survey, from Gana and Lillo to Latorre and d'Halmar.

Lagmanovich, David. "Images of reality: Latin American short stories of today," *Dispositio*, 9:24–6 (1984), 53–63.

Disjointed comments on stories by Quiroga, Borges, García Márquez, Cortázar, and Pacheco, with brief comment at the end on the ways in which these violate readers' expectations with regard to story plots and characters.

Langford, Walter M. "The short story in Mexico," *Kentucky Foreign Language*

Quarterly, 1:2 (1954), 52–9.

Brief survey of evolution of genre in Mexico, from Roa Bárcena to Rafael Muñoz.

Leal, Luis. "La revolución mexicana y el cuento" in Edmundo Valadés and Luis Leal, *La revolución y las letras: 2 estudios sobre la novel y el cuento de la Revolución Mexicana*, Mexico, Instituto Nacional de Bellas Artes, 1960, 97–133.

A useful survey complements the more numerous studies of the novel of the Mexican Revolution.

Lindo, Hugo. "Ambiente, cuentistas y cuentos," *Síntesis* (San Salvador), 1:5 (1954), 109–15.

A brief article by the Salvadoran writer of the development of the genre of El Salvador, especially in the works of Ambrogi and Salarrué.

"Una generación de cuentistas salvadoreños," *Atenea*, 369 (1956), 297–306.

A survey of Salvadoran short-story writers born in the second decade of the twentieth century.

Liscano, Juan. "El cuento hispano-americano," *Revista Nacional de Cultura*, 20 (1958), 7–14.

Comments on the importance of the short story genre in Spanish America and its relative lack of importance in Europe. Overly general comments on numerous Spanish American authors.

Mancisidor, José. "Realidad del cuento mexicano," *Revista de Guatemala*, 2:4 (1946), 87–93.

Interesting discussion of the representation of the Mexican Revolution in the short story; the critic holds that the Mexican short story has tended to be overly realistic or photographic.

Meléndez, Concha. "El cuento en la edad de *Asomante*: 1945–1955," *Asomante*, 11:1 (1955), 39–68.

Useful account of evolution of genre in Puerto Rico, followed by survey of contemporary writers such as Blanco, Belaval, Díaz Alfaro, González, and Marqués.

"La literatura de ficción en Puerto Rico (1955–1963)," *Asomante*, 20:3 (1964), 7–23.

Updated account, supplementing Meléndez's 1955 article, focusing on recent works by Soto, Luis Rafael Sánchez, Díaz Valcárcel, and others.

Miliani, Domingo. "Diez años de narrativa venezolana (1960–70)," *Nueva Narrativa Hispanoamericana*, 2:1 (1972), 131–43.

Important analysis of appearance of new narrative in Venezuela in the 1960s, with emphasis on social context.

Miranda Hevia, Alicia. "El cuento contemporáneo en Costa Rica," *Kañina*, 5:1 (1981), 35–8.

General survey from 1948 to 1977, with mention of such writers as Naranjo, Dobles, and Duncan.

Muñoz, Luis G. "'El verdadero cuento en Chile': hacia la determinación de una generación," *Acta Literaria*, 8 (1983), 53–65.

Discussion of critical debate around the so-called "Generation of 1940" in Chile.

Núñez, Estuardo. "El cuento peruano contemporáneo," *Revista Nacional de Cultura*, 24:154 (1962), 68–90.

Useful survey of evolution of genre from Clemente Palma to Ribeyro, though categories used in classification are questionable.

Orantes, Alfonso. "El cuento en Centroamérica," *Cultura* (San Salvador), 32 (1964), 42–50; 33 (1964), 40–9.

Survey of history of the genre in the Central American republics since nineteenth-century *costumbrismo*. Little space is devoted to discussion of each writer.

Pla y Beltrán, Pascual. "Cinco cuentistas venezolanos," *Cuadernos Americanos*, 18 (1959), 210–19.

Discussion of Guaramato, Márquez Salas, Armas Alfonzo, Dorante, and González León. Pla y Beltrán's solution to the problem of definition of the genre: "For me, paradoxically as it may seem, a story is a story. I don't believe in theories."

Pollman, Leo. "Función del cuento latinoamericano," *Revista Iberoamericana*, 48:118–19 (1982), 207–15.

Confused discussion of questions of definition of genre, of the Latin American identity of Latin American literature, of Palma, Borges, Roa Bastos, and others, of the relation between the novel and the short story.

Polo García, Victorino. "La formalización del cuento hispanoamericano," *Cuadernos para Investigación de la Literatura Hispánica*, 1 (1978), 99–119.

Thin formalist study of stories by Agustín, Arreola, Bombal, and others.

Portuondo, José Antonio. "Lino Novás Calvo y el cuento hispanoamericano," *Cuadernos Americanos*, 6:5 (1947), 245–63. Important article by the Cuban critic, the first half of which is a general consideration of the genre from Quiroga to Borges and Piñera; the discussion of Novás Calvo focuses on questions of technique.

Quiroga, Horacio. "Ante el tribunal" in Emir Rodríguez Monegal (ed.), *Cuentos*, Caracas, Biblioteca Ayacucho, 1981, 316–18.

"Decálogo del perfecto cuentista" in Emir Rodríguez Monegal (ed.), *Cuentos*, Caracas, Biblioteca Ayacucho, 1981, 307–8.

"La retórica del cuento" in Emir Rodríguez Monegal (ed.), *Cuentos*, Caracas, Biblioteca Ayacucho, 1981, 308–10.

Influential writings on the genre by the Uruguayan master.

Rest, Jaime. "El cuento" in Rest, *Novela, cuento, teatro: apogeo y crisis*, Buenos Aires, Centro Editor de América Latina, 1971, 52–107.

A learned consideration of questions of definition of the genre, place of oral narrative, development of the genre from the medieval story to the modern short story. Oddly, almost no mention is made of the Spanish American short story.

Rodríguez, Juan. "El desarrollo del cuento chicano: del folklore al tenebroso mundo del yo" in Francisco Jiménez (ed.), *The Identification and Analysis of Chicano Literature*, New York, Bilingual Press/Editorial Bilingüe, 1979, 58–67.

Useful survey of a new literature, with emphasis on Tomás Rivera. First published in 1973 in *Mester*.

Rodríguez, Rafael. "Apuntes sobre el último decenio de narrativa puertorriqueña: el cuento," *Nueva Narrativa Hispanoamericana*, 2:1 (1972), 179–91.

Focuses on developments subsequent to publication of René Marqués's important 1960 anthology, with emphasis on Edwin Figueroa, Luis Rafael

Sánchez, and Díaz Valcárcel.

Rodríguez Rea, Miguel Angel. "El cuento peruano contemporáneo: indice bibliográfico, I: 1900–1930," *Lexis*, 7:2 (1983), 287–309.

"El cuento peruano contemporáneo: indice bibliográfico, II: 1931–1945," *Lexis*, 8:2 (1984), 249–73.

Bibliographical indexes to volumes of short stories published in the period. Give tables of contents but no annotations.

Rojas, Elena M. "Lenguaje y realidad regional en los cuentos del noroeste argentino," *Estudios Filológicos*, 18 (1983), 85–95.

Consideration of use of regional lexicon and idioms in stories by Juan José Hernández and others.

Rueda, Ana. "El cuento hispanoamericano actual: operaciones de desmantelamiento," *Insula*, 512–13 (1989), 29–30.

Focuses on technical innovations in the genre, with reference made to Bareiro Saguier, Peri Rossi, Valenzuela, and others.

Salinas Paguada, Manuel. "Breve reseña del cuento moderno hondureño," *Cuadernos Hispanoamericanos*, 371 (1981), 385–96.

Good survey of evolution of genre in Honduras since the 1920s, with discussion of seven authors.

Sarfati-Arnaud, Monique, and Gaston Lillo. "El cuento mexicano a través del título: apuntes sobre la ideología de los años 1940 hasta 1958," *Imprévue*, 1 (1983), 7–46.

Fascinating semiotic study of short story titles.

Sarlo, Beatriz. "Panorama del cuento" in Susana Zanetti (ed.), *Historia de la literatura argentina*, 5 vols., Buenos Aires, Centro Editor de América Latina, 1980, I, 25–48.

Excellent overview of the genre in Argentina. The third, fourth, and fifth volumes of the same collection contain more detailed articles by Eduardo Romano, Marta Bustos, and others, on the history of the genre in the twentieth century.

Siles, Juan Ignacio. "El cuento y la difícil coexistencia boliviana," *Ensayistas*, 20–1 (1986), 161–73.

Thematic study of representation of social conflict in the short story, organized around topics: "El indigenismo," "El Oriente," "El cuento minero," "La guerrilla," "La cuentística urbana."

Soto, Luis Emilio. "El cuento" in Rafael Alberto Arrieta (ed.), *Historia de la literatura argentina*, 6 vols., Buenos Aires, Peuser, 1959, IV, 285–450.

Book-length essay on history of genre in Argentina from Fray Mocho to Mujica Lainez and Verbitsky.

Torrico Arroyo, Wilma, and Rubén Vargas Portugal. "Indice bibliográfico de libros de cuentos bolivianos publicados entre 1960–1980" in Javier Sanjinés (ed.), *Tendencias actuales en la literatura boliviana*, Minneapolis, Institute for the Study of Ideologies and Literatures, 1985, 265–73.

Bibliography lists 128 collections of short stories. Not annotated.

Uslar Pietri, Arturo. "El cuento venezolano" in *Letras y hombres de Venezuela*, Mexico, Fondo de Cultura Económica, 1948, 154–63; rpt. in *Obras selectas*, Madrid, Ediciones Edime, 1956, 1065–72.

Brief survey of evolution of genre since 1896 by one of Venezuela's best-known writers.

Wheelock, Carter. "Fantastic symbolism in the Spanish American short story," *Hispanic Review*, 48:4 (1980), 415–34.

 Discussion of what is here termed the "primal fantastic" in short stories of Montalvo, Darío, Quiroga, Murena, and Fuentes. Cortázar and Borges are excluded from consideration.

Yates, Donald A. "The Spanish American detective story," *Modern Language Journal*, 40:5 (1956), 228–32.

 A brief overview of the detective story in Mexico, Chile, Uruguay, and Argentina.

"The Mexican detective story," *Kentucky Foreign Language Quarterly*, 8:1 (1961), 42–7.

 A chatty article on the recent history of the detective story in Mexico, focusing particularly on an anthology of crime fiction edited by María Elvira Bermúdez.

Chapter 15: Spanish American theatre in the twentieth century

Secondary sources

Books

Arcila, Gonzalo. *Nuevo teatro en Colombia: actividad creadora, política cultural*, Bogotá, Ediciones CEIS, 1983.

 Contains valuable study of New Theatre groups since 1957, with separate chapters on Teatro Experimental de Cali (TEC), La Candelaria, and different theatre festivals.

Argudín, Yolanda, with María Luna Argudín. *Historia del teatro en México*, Mexico, Panorama Editorial, 1986.

 Compendium of short but informative essays on the development of theatre from pre-Hispanic times to the dramatists of 1980, including material on directors, actors, and play productions.

Artaud, Antonin. *The Theater and its Double*, trans. Mary Caroline Richards, New York, Grove Press, 1958.

Blanco Amores de Pagella, Angela. *Nuevos temas en el teatro argentino. La influencia europea*, Buenos Aires, Editorial Huemul, 1965.

 Useful study of the manner in which the Argentinian stage accepted influences from the *sainete*, Pirandello, Greek myths, Expressionism, Beckett, Brecht.

Bravo-Elizondo, Pedro. *Teatro hispanoamericano de crítica social*, Madrid, Playor, 1975.

 Uses eight representative plays to show the relationship of Spanish American theatre to its European sources.

 (ed.) *La dramaturgia de Egon Wolff: interpretaciones críticas 1971–1981*, selection, introduction and notes by Pedro Bravo-Elizondo, Santiago, Nascimento, 1985.

 Useful compilation of essays, some published previously, that substantiates Wolff's position as a dramatist of importance.

Castagnino, Raúl H. *Semiótica, ideología y teatro hispanoamericano*, Buenos Aires, Editorial Nova, 1974.

 One of the early applications of a semiotic reading of Spanish American plays chosen from the selection of Carlos Solórzano's anthology. Helpful historical introduction to the theatrical tradition of eight countries.

Castedo-Ellerman, Elena. *El teatro chileno de mediados del siglo XX*, Santiago, Editorial Andrés Bello, 1982.

Perceptive overview of important period of productivity from 1955 to 1970. Divides plays into five types of theatre, from social realist plays, through folkloric, absurdist, Brechtian, and the "taller" or workshop groups.

Castillo, Susana D. *El desarraigo en el teatro venezolano. Marco histórico y manifestaciones modernas*, Caracas, Editorial Ateneo de Caracas, 1980.

Solid study focusing on psychological developments in Venezuelan theatre, with textual analyses of eight important contemporary authors.

Dauster, Frank. *Xavier Villaurrutia*, New York, Twayne, 1971.

Historia del teatro hispanoamericano (Siglos XIX y XX), 2nd. edn., Mexico, Ediciones de Andrea, 1973.

A useful compendium that follows a combination of the periodic and national approaches to summarize the whole panorama of plays, writers, and national movements from the nineteenth to twentieth centuries.

Ensayos sobre teatro hispanoamericano, Mexico, SepSetentas, 1975.

The nine essays give perceptive readings of important playwrights from Cuba (Triana and Arrufat), Puerto Rico (Marqués and Arriví), Mexico (Hernández, Garro, and Carballido), Guatemala–Mexico (Solórzano), and Argentina (Dragún).

Eidelberg, Nora. *Teatro experimental hispanoamericano. 1960–1980*, Minneapolis, Institute for the Study of Ideologies and Literature, 1985.

Divides plays from the period 1960–1980 into three main categories: ludic theatre, didactic theatre, and popular theatre. While the categories are not definitive, the plays analyzed merit critical attention.

Foster, David William. *The Argentine Teatro Independiente 1930–1955*, York, S.C., Spanish Literature Publishing Co., 1986.

Uses a semiotic approach to read plays of the Teatro Independiente period, from Arlt to Dragún. Substantiates the importance of the movement in Argentina during a twenty-five year period.

Giordano, Enrique. *La teatralización de la obra dramática. De Florencio Sánchez a Roberto Arlt*, Mexico, Premia, 1982.

A useful study that attempts to distinguish between "theatricalization" and "theatricality" in the theoretical section and then applies the methodology to study works of River Plate writers Sánchez, Eichelbaum, Nalé Roxlo, Arlt.

González Cajiao, Fernando. *Historia del teatro en Colombia*, Bogotá, Instituto Colombiano de Cultura, 1986.

Considered one of the most important books on Colombian theatre for its comprehensive history, extensive documentation, photographs, thorough index of references to plays, playwrights, critical authors, and theatrical companies.

Herzfeld, Anita and Teresa Cajiao-Salas. *El teatro de hoy en Costa Rica; perspectiva crítica y antología*, San José, Editorial Costa Rica, 1973.

A valuable essay on the development of theatrical activity in Costa Rica precedes an anthology of five plays, with bio-bibliographical information, interviews with authors.

Kaiser-Lenoir, Eva Claudia. *El grotesco criollo: estilo teatral de una época*, Havana, Casa de las Américas, 1977.

> An excellent study of the native form of the Grotesque in Argentina. Carefully researched, giving antecedents, and studying major plays of Discépolo, Ghiano, and others.

(ed.) *Theater Research International*, 14:2 (1989), 111–85.

> Issue focuses on studies of popular theatre in several Latin American countries by D. Frischmann, Kaiser-Lenoir, B. Rizk, J. Weiss, D. George, M. Pianca.

Leal, Rine. *Breve historia del teatro cubano*, Havana, Editorial Letras Cubanas, 1980.

> Well-documented history that deals with works of the theatre from a sociological perspective.

Luzuriaga, Gerardo (ed.). *Popular Theater for Social Change in Latin America: Essays in Spanish and English*, Los Angeles, University of California, Latin American Center, 1978.

> A collection of twenty-six contributions, including pieces by such noted Latin American practitioners of popular theatre as Augusto Boal, Enrique Buenaventura, and Segio Corrieri. Has an extensive bibliography.

Lyday, Leon F., and George W. Woodyard (eds.). *Dramatists in Revolt*, Austin, University of Texas Press, 1976.

> One of the first collections of essays in English on fifteen individual playwrights from Spanish America and Brazil by a number of experts in the field.

Molinaza, José. *Historia crítica del teatro dominicano*, Editora Universidad Autónoma de Santo Domingo, 1984.

> Of importance since it is one of the few studies dedicated to Dominican theatre. Two volumes contain titles, reviews, dates, and texts; some critical material.

Montes Huidobro, Matías. *Persona, vida y máscara en el teatro cubano*, Miami, Ediciones Universal, 1973.

> History of Cuban theatre, including a good discussion of "teatro bufo" and plays of the post-revolutionary period, written from the perspective of a Cuban playwright who left the island after the Revolution. Uses a combination of Freudian psychology and politics to read the plays.

Morfi, Angelina. *Historia crítica de un siglo de teatro puertorriqueño*, San Juan, Instituto de Cultura Puertorriqueña, 1980.

> Well-documented review of theatre in Puerto Rico, with special attention focused on the earlier periods.

Morris, Robert J. *The Contemporary Peruvian Theater*, Lubbock, Texas Tech Press, 1977.

> Insightful review of playwrights and plays that gives the reader a thorough source of information on Peruvian theatre not found elsewhere.

Neglia, Erminio. *Aspectos del teatro moderno hispanoamericano*, Bogotá, Editorial Stella, 1975.

> Useful essays on a variety of trends in the modern theatre, from "grotesco criollo" to committed theatre.

Ordaz, Luis, *et al. Historia del teatro argentino*, Buenos Aires, Centro Editor de América Latina, 1982.

> Valuable study of Argentinian theatre from its origins to Teatro Abierto of 1981. Includes illustrations.

Orenstein, Gloria. *The Theater of the Marvelous*, New York University Press, 1975.
Comparative study of surrealist theatre with selected plays from Latin
America, including Garro, Paz, Díaz, Jodorowsky.

Peden, Margaret Sayers. *Emilio Carballido*, Boston, Twayne, 1980.
An exellent example of coverage of a multifaceted writer, which transcends the
limitations of the Twayne series.

Pianca, Marina (ed.). *Diógenes: anuario critico del teatro Latinoamericano*. vol. I:
(1985), vol. II: *(1986)*, Ottawa, GIROL Books, 1987.
Includes a series of interviews, reports, and essays describing theatrical activity
both in and outside Latin America. Many entries focus on aspects of popular
theatre.

Pignataro, Jorge. *El teatro independiente uruguayo*, Montevideo, Editorial Aiser,
1968.
Excellent history that analyzes four phases of independent theatre movements
from 1937 to 1967.

Rela, Walter. *Teatro uruguayo 1907–1979*, Montevideo, Alianza Cultural Uruguay-
Estados Unidos, 1980.
Useful for its bibliographical and historical information on the period covered.

Rizk, Beatriz J. *El nuevo teatro latinoamericano: una lectura histórica*, Minneapolis,
Institute for the Study of Ideologies and Literature/Prisma Institute, 1987.
Good example of research being done on New Theatre.

Revista/Review Interamericana, 9:1 (1979).
Contains articles on theatre in Puerto Rico and the Caribbean, including essays
by Pilditch, Waldman, Cypess, Woodyard, Martin, and Quackenbush.

Rodríguez Seda de la Laguna, Asela. *Shaw en el mundo hispánico*, San Juan, Puerto
Rico, Editorial Universitaria, 1981.
Designed to be an analysis of Shaw's presence in plays by both Spaniards and
Spanish American playwrights, although concludes that, except by Usigli, Shaw
was not well accepted.

Rojo, Grínor. *Orígenes del teatro hispanoamericano contemporáneo*, Valparaíso,
Ediciones Universitarias, 1972.
Studies the break with costumbrism on the Latin American stage as seen in the
manifestations of theatre of the imagination and psychological theatre. Also
presents a review of the state of critical texts of importance (by Jones, Dauster,
and Solórzano) at the time of its publication.

Muerte y resurrección del teatro chileno, 1973–1983, Madrid, Michay, 1985.
Review of the effects on conditions in the theatre after the coup of September,
1973.

Solórzano, Carlos. *El teatro latinoamericano en el siglo XX*, Mexico, Editorial
Pormaca, 1964.
One of the first serious critical studies of Latin American dramaturgy, it deals
with thematic topics (theatre of universal tendencies, national concerns, etc.) that
then subdivide according to countries, with a focus on individual playwrights of
importance.

The Contemporary Latin American Theater, tr. Rafael Sanchez, Lincoln, Nebr.,
Prairie Schooner Press, 1965–1966.
This translation marks one of the rare examples of drama criticism from

Spanish made available in English.

Soria, Mario T. *Teatro boliviano en el siglo XX*, La Paz, Editorial Casa Municipal de la Cultura, 1980.

Written as an insightful guide to little-known theatrical activity in Bolivia. Includes a bibliography of twentieth-century Bolivian plays and a selective bibliography of articles on Bolivian theatre.

Suárez Radillo, Carlos Miguel. *Lo social en el teatro hispanoamericano contemporáneo*, Caracas, Equinoccio, 1976.

Gives a historical overview of each national theatre, with biographical sketches of authors.

Toro, Fernando de. *Brecht en el teatro hispanoamericano contemporáneo*, Ottawa, GIROL Books, 1984.

Divided into two parts: the first is theoretical, using the semiotic model of Greimas modified by Pavis and Ubersfeld; the second part focuses on individual plays that are examples of Brechtian techniques.

Semiótica del teatro. Del texto a la puesta en escena, Buenos Aires, Editorial Galerna, 1987.

Offers a useful summary of the terminology of semiotics for the theatre as well as presenting an application of the theory to specific plays. Includes an extensive bibliography.

Tschudi, Lilian. *Teatro argentino actual*, Buenos Aires, Fenando García Gambeiro, 1974.

Covers the period from 1960 to 1970. Analyzes three different aspects of plays: the plot, dialogue, and the style of representation, an approach that helps the reader visualize the play as performance.

Unger, Roni. *Poesía en Voz Alta in the Theater of Mexico*, Columbia, University of Missouri Press, 1981.

A careful history of an ensemble of the 1950s in Mexico which included Octavio Paz and Juan José Arreola. Formed as a reaction against the dominant mode of dramatic realism on the Mexican stage, this group had its major impact on the fields of directing and stage design.

Zayas de Lima, Perla. *Diccionario de autores argentinos, 1950–1980*, Buenos Aires, Editorial R. Alonso, 1981.

Provides brief information about numerous authors and plays.

Articles

Benedetti, Mario. "Carlos Maggi y su meridiano de risa," *La Palabra y el Hombre*, 45 (1968), 133–46.

Although focusing on Maggi's work to show his importance, writer Benedetti offers interesting dramatic insights.

Bixler, Jacqueline. "Games and reality on the Latin American stage," *Latin American Literary Review*, 12:24 (1984), 22–35.

Offers insights into the plays of three female dramatists of different countries (M. Romero, S. Torres Molina, and R. Mahhieu) and the way each explores game-playing as an attack on the power structure.

Bravo-Elizondo, Pedro. "La realidad latinoamericana y el teatro documental," *Texto*

Crítico, 14 (1979), 200–10.

Good introduction to definition of documentary theatre that mentions playwrights and plays that fit the category.

Burgess, Ronald D. "Building a basic Spanish American theatre bibliography," *Latin American Research Review*, 23:2 (1988), 226–33.

Useful review of pertinent bibliographic material and includes a list of works to consult.

Carballido, Emilio. "Sobre creación colectiva," *Tramoya*, 20 (1980), 34–6.

Discussion of the practice of collective creation, and what are "false" collective creations from the perspective of an experienced playwright.

Conjunto, Cuba, Casa de las Américas, 1964–.

Established in 1964 in post-revolutionary Cuba, making it the oldest Spanish American theatre review in continuous publication. Although covers all of Latin America, it is not all-inclusive with regard to playwrights and trends, for it is primarily concerned with socialist theatre. Contains essays, interviews, performance reviews, book summaries, photographs. Also, a play script is published in each issue.

Cypess, Sandra Messinger. "The influence of the French theater in the plays of Xavier Villaurrutia," *Latin American Theater Review*, 3:1 (1969), 9–15.

"Overview of an oversight: Latin American women dramatists" in Cypess (ed.), *Studies in Romance Languages and Literature* Lawrence, Kans., Coronado Press, 1979, 36–47.

One of the first feminist reviews of the works of twentieth-century women dramatists.

"La dramaturgia femenina y su contexto socio-cultural," *Latin American Theater Review*, (Summer Supplement 1980), 63–8.

Dauster, Frank. "Towards a definition of tragedy," *Revista Canadiense de Estudios Hispánicos*, 7:1 (1982), 3–17.

Analysis of several plays based on Francis Fergusson's theories of tragedy.

Gambaro, Griselda. "Teatro de vanguardia en la Argentina de hoy," *Revista de la Universidad Nacional del Litoral* (Santa Fe, Argentina), 81 (1970), 301–31.

Gambaro's comments on vanguardist theatre in Argentina draw upon her experience as a dramatist and make this an informative study.

Gestos, Irvine, University of California, Department of Spanish and Portuguese, 1986–.

Begun in 1986 under the editorship of Juan Villegas, the journal focuses on theoretical articles but also includes play scripts and reviews.

Green, Joan Rea. "Character and conflict in contemporary central American theater" in Harvey L. Johnson and Philip B. Taylor (eds.), *Contemporary Latin American Literature*, University of Houston Press, 1973.

Covers a wide variety of dramatists in Central America.

Latin American Theater Review, Lawrence, Kans. Centre for Latin American Studies, 1967–.

Begun in 1967, *LATR* is under the editorship of George Woodyard and is the first journal dedicated to Latin American theatre in the United States. Articles, in Spanish and Portuguese, as well as in English, range from studies of individual authors and plays, to reports of festivals, theatre seasons, and reviews of books pertinent to the field.

Layera, Ramón. "La revista *Conjunto* y el nuevo teatro latinoamericano," *Latin American Research Review*, 18:2 (1983), 35–55.

Offers an informative review of the role of *Conjunto* in revitalizing political theatre practices in Latin America.

Lindo, Hugo. "La literatura dramática en el Salvador," *Revista Interamericana de Bibliografía*, 18:3 (1968), 258–327.

Useful guide to a little-studied area that focuses on recent writers.

Luzuriaga, Gerardo. "La generación del sesenta y el teatro," *Caravelle*, 34 (1980), 157–70.

Important for its historical review of Ecuadorian theatre, with references to groups, dominant figures, and plays.

Peden, Margaret Sayers. "Theory and practice in Artaud and Carballido," *Modern Drama* (1968), 132–42.

Not only an excellent study of Carballido's three-act play, *La hebra de oro*, and the fantastic trilogy, *El lugar y la hora*, but an insightful review of Artaud's Theatre of Cruelty.

Ramos-Perea, Roberto. "De cómo y por qué la Nueva Dramaturgia Puertorriqueña es una revolución," *Intermedio de Puerto Rico*, 1:1 (1985), 11–16.

Important for an understanding of "New Dramaturgy" from the perspective of one of its participants. Journal is dedicated to theatre topics.

Rojo, Grínor. "Muerte y resurrección del teatro chileno. Observaciones preliminares," *Caravelle*, 40 (1983), 67–81.

Important essay for its review of Chilean theatre from 1943 to the 1980s; proposes three phases which are tied to political changes.

San Félix, Alvaro. "Teatro de intención política en el Ecuador," *Cultura Banco Central del Ecuador*, 5:13 (1982), 209–25.

Review of political theatre from colonial times to the present. Useful article for learning about revolutionary tendencies in Ecuadorian theatre.

Serulle, Haffe. "Teatro universitario en la República Dominicana," *Intermedio de Puerto Rico*, 1:1 (1985), 24–5.

Provides useful information about aspects of theatre in the Dominican Republic.

Texto Crítico, Xalapa, Mexico, 10 (1978).

This issue is dedicated to sixteen articles dealing with Spanish American theatre, from general reviews to specific play analyses, using a variety of critical approaches.

Tramoya–Cuaderno de Teatro, Xalapa, Mexico, and Camden, N.J.

Directed by Emilio Carballido since 1975; added "Nueva Epoca" to its title in 1986 when it began to be published jointly with Eladio Cortés from Camden New Jersey. Contains previously unedited play-scripts, reviews, and essays.

Viñas, David. "Prólogo" in Jorge Lafforgue (ed.), *Teatro rioplatense (1886–1930)*, Caracas, Biblioteca Ayacucho, 1977.

In addition to reprinting plays from the period, the book contains a historical overview by Viñas and a chronology of theatrical events for Latin America and the international scene.

Vodanovic, Sergio. "Theater in society in Latin America," *Journal of Inter-American*

Studies and World Affairs, 18:4 (1976), 495–504.

The Chilean dramatist explains his ideas about Latin American theatre as a cultural expression that must be understood from a political perspective.

Wellwarth, George E. "The theatrical theories of Augusto Boal" in Sandra Messinger Cypess (ed.), *Studies in Romance Languages and Literature*, Kans., Coronado Press, 1979, 36–47.

Good review in English of Boal's theories on popular theatre using versions of Boal's texts in Spanish.

Woodyard, George. "The Theater of the Absurd in Spanish America," *Comparative Drama*, 3:3 (1969), 183–92.

One of the first overviews in English of the leading playwrights of absurdist tendencies. Indicates differences between the European and Spanish American playwrights, the latter being more concerned with social issues as a cause for contemporary angst.

"Towards a radical theater in Spanish America" in Harvey L. Johnson and Philip B. Taylor (eds.), *Contemporary Latin American Literature*, University of Houston Press, 1973.

Comparative review of plays called "radical," or those that have a political ideology along with a new approach to dramatic techniques. Covers from the Southern Cone to the Caribbean area.

Chapter 16: Latin American (Hispanic Caribbean) literature written in the United States

Primary sources

Acosta, Iván. *El súper*, Miami, Ediciones Universal, 1982.

Un cubiche en la luna, Houston, Arte Público, 1989.

Algarín, Miguel. *Canción de gesta / A Song of Protest*, New York, William Morrow & Co., 1976.

Mongo Affair, New York, Nuyorican Poets Cafe, 1978.

On Call, Houston, Arte Público, 1980.

Body Bee Calling From the 21st Century, Houston, Arte Público, 1982.

Time's Now, Houston, Arte Público, 1985.

Alonso, Ricardo. *Cimarrón*, Middletown, Conn., Wesleyan University Press, 1979.

Note: In this bibliography, I have decided not to include the primary works, written in their country of origin, by established nineteenth-century writers such as José María Heredia and José Martí, nor secondary works about them. Works by and about them are well known and are available in numerous critical studies. Nevertheless, I have included those primary works written and published in the United States.

Instead, I have concentrated on the works of and about contemporary Hispanic Caribbean writers who were either born or raised and live in the United States. With this in mind, I have included in the secondary bibliography anthologies which in their introduction provide a critical appraisal of the works of the writers featured.

Many of the works written by Hispanic Caribbean writers living in the United States have been published in numerous newspapers, journals, and magazines. I have omitted these from the bibliography preferring to cite those works which have been published in book form.

Volume 2

Alvarez, Julia. *The Housekeeping Book*, Burlington Vt., Alvarez, MacDonald, Schall, 1984.
    Homecoming, New York, Grove Press, 1984.
    How the Garcia Girls Lost Their Accents, N.C., Algonquin Books of Chapel Hill, 1991.
Arenas, Reinaldo. *El central*, Barcelona, Seix Barral, 1981.
    Arturo, la estrella más brillante, Barcelona, Montesinos Editor, 1984.
    Necesidad de libertad: testimonio de un intelectual disidente, Mexico, Kosmos-Editorial, 1986.
    Persecución: cinco piezas de teatro experimental, Miami, Editorial Universal, 1986.
    La loma del Angel, Miami, Mariel Press, 1987.
    El portero, Malaga, Dador, 1989.
    Voluntad de vivir manifestándose, Madrid, Editorial Betania, 1989.
    El asalto, Miami, Universal, 1990.
    Leprosorio: (trilogía poética), Madrid, Editorial Betania, 1990.
    Viaje a La Habana, Miami, Ediciones Universal, 1990.
    Adios a Mamá, Paris, Le Serpent à Plumes, 1993.
    Antes que anochezca, Barcelona, Tusquets, 1992.
    El color del verano, Miami, Universal, 1991.
Armand, Octavio. *Horizonte no es siempre lejanía*, New York, Las Américas, 1970.
    Entre testigos, Madrid, 1974.
    Cómo escribir con erizo, 1976: La página se llenará, no hay mirada, habeas corpus, tal vez el asombro, Mexico, Asociación de Escritores de México, 1979.
    Cosas pasan, Caracas, Monte Avila, 1979.
    20 poemas, tr. and intro. Mark Strand, Caracas, Fundarte, 1979.
    Piel menos mía (1973–1974), Los Angeles, Freedmens Organizations, 1979.
    Biografía para feacios (1977–1979), Valencia, Pre-Textos, 1980.
    Superficies, Caracas, Monte Avila, 1980.
    With Dusk, tr. Carol Maier, Durango, Colo., Logbridge-Rhodes, 1984.
Barreto, Lefty. *Nobody's Hero*, New York, New American Library, 1976.
Benítez Rojo, Antonio, *La isla que se repite*, Hanover, N.H., El Norte, 1989.
Burgos, Julia. *El mar y tú, otros poemas*, San Juan, Puerto Rico Printing Co., 1954.
Cachán, Manuel. *Al son del triple y el güiro*, Miami, Ediciones Universal, 1987.
    Cuentos de aquí y allá, Miami, Ediciones Universal, 1988.
Carrero, Jaime. *Jet neorriqueño-Neo-Rican Jetliner*, San German, P.R., Universidad Interamericana, 1964.
    Raquelo tiene un mensaje, San Juan, n.p., 1970.
    Pipo Subway no sabe leer in *Flag Inside*, Río Piedras, P.R., Ediciones Puerto, 1973, 113–57.
    "The FM Safe," *Revista Chicano-Riqueña*, 7:1 (1979), 110–50.
    El hombre que no sudaba, Houston, Arte Público, 1982.
Casal, Lourdes. *Los fundadores y otros cuentos*, Miami, Ediciones Universal, 1973.
    Palabras juntan revolución, Havana, Casa de las Américas, 1981.
Caulfield, Carlota. *A veces me llamo infancia = Sometimes I Call Myself Childhood*, Miami, Solar, 1985.
    Fanaim: poems, San Francisco, Ediciones El Gato Tuerto, 1985.
    Oscuridad divina, San Francisco, Ediciones El Gato Tuerto, 1985.

El tiempo es una mujer que espera, Madrid, Ediciones Torremozas, 1986.

34th Street and Other Poems (1982–1984), tr. Chris Allen and the author, San Francisco, Ediciones El Gato Tuerto, 1987.

Cintrón, Humberto. *Frankie Cristo*, New York, Taino Publishing Co., 1972.

Clavijo, Uva A. *Eternidad: ensayos*, New York, Plaza Mayor Ediciones, 1971.

Versos del exilio, Miami, n.p., 1975.

Versos de exilio, n.p., 1976.

Ni verdad ni mentira y otros cuentos, Miami, Ediciones Universal, 1977.

Entre semáforos, Miami, Ediciones Universal, 1981.

Secretariado bilingüe ahora, Editorial Cernuda, 1982.

Tus ojos y yo, Miami, Ediciones Universal, 1985.

No puedo más y otros cuentos, Miami, Ediciones Universal, 1989.

Colón, Jesús. *A Puerto Rican in New York and Other Sketches*, New York, Mainstream Publisher, 1961.

Colón, Ramón. *Carlos Tapia: A Puerto Rican hero in New York*, New York, Vantage Press, 1976.

Comas, Ester. *Hello Stranger*, New York, n.p., 1971.

Correa, Miguel. *Peregrino sediento*, n.p., 1982.

Al norte del infierno, Miami, Editorial Sibi, 1983.

Cotto-Thorner, Guillermo. *Trópico en Manhattan*, San Juan, Editorial Cordillera, 1967.

Cruz, Nick. *Run Baby Run*, Plainfield, N.J., Logos Books, 1968.

Díaz Valcárcel, Emilio. *Harlem todos los días*, San Juan, Ediciones Huracán, 1978.

Espada, Martín. *The Immigrant Iceboy's Bolero*, Madison, Wis., Ghost Pony Press, 1982.

Trumpets from the Islands of Their Eviction, Tempe, Ariz., Bilingual Press/ Editorial Bilingüe, 1987.

Rebellion is the Circle of a Lover's Hands, Willimantic, Conn., Curbstone Press, 1990.

Esteves, Sandra María. *Yerba Buena*, Greenfield Center, N.Y., Greenfield Press, 1980.

Tropical Rains: A bilingual downpour. New York, Caribbean Poetry Theatre, 1984.

Bluestown Mockingbird Mambo, Houston, Arte Público, 1990.

Fernández, Damián. "Litany," *Nuestro*, 1:95 (Aug. 1977), 22–3.

Fernández, Pablo Armando. *Nuevos poemas (1953–1955)*, New York, Las Américas, 1956.

Fernández, Roberto. *Cuentos sin rumbos*, Miami, Ediciones Universal, 1975.

"La encadenada," in Leonardo Fernández-Marcané (ed.), *20 cuentistas cubanos*, Miami, Ediciones Universal, 1978, 38–41.

La vida es un special, Miami, Ediciones Universal, 1981.

La montaña rusa, Houston, Arte Público, 1985.

Raining Backwards, Houston, Arte Público, 1991.

Fernández Fragoso, Víctor. *El reino de la espiga*, New York, Colección Nueva Sangre, 1973.

Ser Islas/Being Islands, New York, Editorial El Libro Viaje, 1976.

Figueroa, José-Angel. *East 110th Street*, Detroit, Broadside Press, 1973.

Noo Jork, New York, Plus Ultra Publications, 1978.

Volume 2

Florit, Eugenio. *Conversación a mi padre*, Havana, Yagruima, 1949.
  Asonante final y otros poemas, Mexico, Studium, 1955.
  Siete poemas, Montevideo, Cuadernos Julio Herrera y Reissig, 1960.
  Hábito de esperanza. Poemas (1936–1964), Madrid, Insula, 1965.
  Antología penúltima. Madrid, Editorial Plenitud, 1970.
  De tiempo y agonía (versos del hombre solo), Madrid, Revista de Occidente, 1974.
  Versos pequeños (1938–1975), Miami, El Marco, 1979.
  Obras completas, Lincoln, University of Nebraska, Society of Spanish and Spanish American Studies, 1982.
  Momentos, Miami, private edition, 1985.
Gómez Rosa, Alexis. *Cabeza de alquiler*, Santo Domingo, Dominican Republic, Luna Cabeza Caliente, 1990.
González, Celedonio. *Los primos*, Miami, Ediciones Universal, 1971.
  La soledad es una amiga que vendrá, Miami, Ediciones Universal, 1971.
  Los cuatro embajadores, Miami, Ediciones Universal, 1973.
  El espesor del pellejo de un gato ya cadáver, Miami, Ediciones Universal, 1978.
  Que veinte años no es nada, Miami, Ediciones Universal, 1987.
González, José Luis. *El hombre en la calle*, San Juan, Editorial Borinque, 1948.
  Paisa, San Juan, Fondo de Cultura Popular, 1950.
  En este lado, Mexico, Los Presentes, 1954.
  Mambrú se fue a la guerra, Mexico, Mortiz, 1972.
  En Nueva York y otras desgracias, Mexico, Siglo Veintiuno Editores, 1973.
González-Cruz, Luis Francisco. *Tirando al blanco/Shooting Gallery*, Miami, Ediciones Universal, 1975.
  Disgregaciones, Madrid, Catoblepas, 1986.
Gutiérrez, Franklin. *Hojas de octubre: poemas*, New York, n.p., 1982.
  Inriri, New York, Ediciones Alcance, 1984.
  Helen, Editorial Santo Domingo, 1986.
Heredia, José María. *Poesías*, New York, Librería de Behr y Khal (Imprenta de Gray y Bunce), 1825.
Hernández, Norma Iris. *Precious Moments*, New York, Parnaso, 1981.
Hernández Cruz, Victor. *Papo Got His Gun*, New York, Calle Once Publications, 1966.
  Snaps, New York, Vintage-Random House, 1969.
  Mainland, New York, Random House, 1973.
  Tropicalization, New York, Reed, Cannon & Johnson, 1976.
  By Lingual Wholes, San Francisco, Momo's Press, 1982.
  Rhythm, Content and Flavor, Houston, Arte Público, 1989.
Hijuelos, Oscar. *Our House in the Last World*, New York, Washington Square Press, 1984.
  The Mambo Kings Play Songs of Love, New York, Farrar Straus, & Giroux, 1989.
Iglesias, César Andreu (ed.). *Memorias de Bernardo Vega*, San Juan, Ediciones Huracán, 1977.
Kozer, José. *Padres y otras profesiones*, New York, Editorial Villa Miseria, 1972.
  Este judío de números y letras, Tenerife, Canary Islands, Editorial Católica, Ediciones Nuestro Arte, 1975.
  Así tomaron posesión en las ciudades, Barcelona, Editorial Ambito Literario, 1978.

Jarrón de las abreviaturas, Mexico, Editorial Premiá, 1980.

La rueca de los semblantes, Leon, Spain, Editorial Instituto Gray Bernardino de Sahagún, 1980.

Antología breve, Santo Domingo, Dominican Republic, Editorial Luna Cabeza Caliente, 1981.

Bajo este cien, Mexico, Editorial Fondo de Cultura Económica, 1983.

La garza sin sombras, Barcelona, Ediciones Libres del Mall, 1985.

El carillón de los muertos, Buenos Aires, Ultimo Reino, 1987.

Carece de causa. Buenos Aires: Ultimo Reino, 1988.

Labarthe, Pedro Juan. *The Son of Two Nations: The private life of a Columbia student*, New York, Caranza, 1931.

Laviera, Tato. *La Carreta Made a U-Turn*, Houston, Arte Público, 1979.

Enclave, Houston, Arte Público, 1981.

AmeRican, Houston, Arte Público, 1986.

Mainstream Ethics, Houston, Arte Público, 1988.

Levine, Barry B. *Benjy López*, New York, Basic Books, 1979.

Levins Morales, Aurora, and Rosario Morales. *Getting Home Alive*, Ithaca, N.Y., Firebrand Books, 1986.

Manrique, Manuel. *Una isla en Harlem*, Madrid, Alfaguara, 1965.

Marín, Francisco Gonzalo (Pachín). *Romances*, New York, Modesto A. Tirado, 1892.

Marqués, René. "La carreta," *Asomante*, 4:2 (1951), 67–87.

Martí, José. *Ismaelillo*, New York, Imprenta de Thompson y Moreau, 1882.

Amistad funesta, (under the pseudonym Adelaida Ral) in *El Latino Americano* (1885), Berlin, G. de Quesada, 1911.

Versos sencillos, New York, Louis Weiss & Co., 1891.

Nuestra América, Havana, Imprenta y papelería de Rambla y Bouza, 1909–10.

Ismaelillo; Versos sencillos; Versos libres, Havana, Imprenta de Rambla y Bouza, 1913.

Versos libres, Buenos Aires, Editorial Claridad, ?1920/1929.

"Carta de Nueva York," *Revista Cubana*, 3:8–9 (1935), 286–93.

Medina, Pablo. *Pork Rind and Cuban Songs*, Washington, Nuclassics and Science, 1975.

Exiled Memories: A Cuban childhood, Austin, University of Texas Press, 1990.

Arching into the Afterlife, Tempe, Ariz., Bilingual Press/Editorial Bilingüe, 1991.

Meléndez, Jesús (Papoleto). *Street Poetry and Other Poems*, New York, Barlenmir House, 1972.

Mohr, Nicholasa. *Nilda*, New York, Harper & Row, 1973.

El Bronx Remembered, New York, Harper & Row, 1975.

In Nueva York, New York, Dial Press, 1977.

Felita, New York, Dial Press, 1979.

Ritual of Survival: A woman's portfolio, Houston, Arte Público, 1985.

Going Home, New York, Dial Books, 1986.

In My Own Words: Growing up inside the sanctuary of my imagination, New York, Julian Meissner, 1994.

Montes Huidobro, Matías. *Desterrados al fuego*, Mexico, Fondo de Cultura Económica, 1975.

Ojos para no ver, Miami, Ediciones Universal, 1979.

Segar a los muertos, Miami, Ediciones Universal, 1980.

"Funeral en Teruel," *Verbena*, 4:1 (1982), 2–29.

"La navaja de Olofé," *Prismal cabral* 7/8, (1982), 120–33.

Muñoz, Elías Miguel. *Los viajes de Orlando Cachumbambé*, Miami, Ediciones Universal, 1984.

Crazy Love. Houston, Arte Público, 1989.

En estas tierras, Tempe, Ariz, Bilingual Press Editorial Bilingüe, 1989.

No fue posible el sol, Madrid, Editorial Betania, 1989.

The Greatest Performance, Houston, Arte Público, 1991.

Novás Calvo, Lino. *Maneras de contar*, New York, Las Américas, 1970.

Núñez, Ana Rosa. *Las siete lunas de enero*, Miami, Cuadernos del Hombre Libre, 1967.

Cinco poetisas cubanas, 1935–1969: Mercedes García Tuduri, Pura del Prado, Teresa María Rojas, Rita Geada, Ana Rosa Núñez, Miami, Ediciones Universal, 1970.

Viaje al Casabe, Miami, Ediciones Universal, 1970.

Los oficialeros, Miami, Ediciones Universal, 1973.

Sol de un solo día, Miami, E. Márquez, 1973.

Atlas poético, Miami, Atabex, 1982.

Verde sobre azul: un verano en Puerto Rico, Miami, Editorial Cartel, 1987.

Crisantemos, chrysanthemums, tr. Jay H. Leal, Madrid, Editorial Betania, 1990.

Oliva, Jorge. *La captura y otros cuentos*, Guatemala, Unión, 1966.

Donde una llama nunca se apaga, Madrid, Playor, 1984.

Ortiz Cofer, Judith. *Latin Women Pray*, Fort Lauderdale, Florida Arts Gazette Press, 1980.

Peregrina, New York, Riverstone Press, 1986.

Terms of Survival: Poems, Houston, Arte Público, 1987.

Triple Crown, Tempe, Ariz., Bilingual Press Editorial Bilingüe, 1987.

The Line of the Sun: A novel, Athens, University of Georgia Press, 1989.

Silent Dancing: A partial remembrance of a Puerto Rican childhood, Houston, Arte Público, 1990.

Padilla, Heberto. *La mala memoria*, Barcelona, Editorial Plaza & Janés, 1989.

Pau-Llosa, Ricardo. *Sorting Metaphors*, Tallahassee, Fla., Anhinga Press, 1983.

Perera, Hilda. *El sitio de nadie*, Barcelona, Editorial Planeta, 1972.

Pérez Firmat, Gustavo. "Carolina Cuban" in Roberto Durán, Judith Ortiz Cofer, and Gustavo Pérez Firmat, *Triple Crown: Chicano, Puerto Rican, and Cuban American Poetry*, Tempe, Ariz., Bilingual Press Editorial Bilingüe, 1987, 121–67.

Equivocaciones, Madrid, Editorial Betania, 1989.

Pietri, Pedro. *Puerto Rican Obituary*, New York, Monthly Review Press, 1973.

The Masses Are Asses, Maplewood, N.J., Waterfront Press, 1984.

Piñero, Miguel. *Short Eyes*, New York, Hill & Wang, 1974.

The Sun Always Shines for the Cool, New York, BMC Productions, 1979.

La Bodaga Sold Dreams, Houston, Arte Público, 1980.

Plays, Houston, Arte Público, 1984.

Outrageous One Act Plays, Houston, Arte Público, 1986.

Prida, Dolores. *Treinta y un poemas*, Brooklyn, N.Y., Fancy Press Editors, 1967.

Women of the Hour, New York, Nuevasangre, 1971.

Coser y cantar: A one-act bilingual fantasy for two women, New York, n.p., 1981.

Beautiful Señoritas and Other Plays, Houston, Arte Público, 1991.

Reyes Rivera, Louis. *Poets in Motion*, New York, Shamal Books, 1977.

Who Pays the Cost, New York, Shamal Books, 1977.

Rivera, Héctor. *Biografía del silencio*, n.p., 1985.

Rivero, Isel. *Tundra*, New York, Las Américas, 1963.

Robles, Mireya. *Hagiografía de Narcisa la Bella*, Hanover, N.H., Ediciones del Norte, 1985.

Ruiz, Richard. *The Hungry American*, Bend, Oreg., Maverick Publications, 1978.

Sánchez-Boudy, José. *Homo Sapiens*, Miami, Ediciones Universal, 1971.

Lilayando, Miami, Ediciones Universal, 1971.

Los cruzados de la aurora, Miami, Ediciones Universal, 1972.

Crocante de maní, Miami, Ediciones Universal, 1973.

Orbus terrarum. La ciudad de humanitas, Miami, Ediciones Universal, 1974.

Aché Babalú Ayé, Miami, Ediciones Universal, 1975.

La soledad de la playa larga (mañana mariposa), Miami, Ediciones Universal, 1975.

Pregones, Miami, Ediciones Universal, 1975.

El corredor Kresto, Miami, Ediciones Universal, 1976.

Ekué, Abanakué, Ekué, Miami, Ediciones Universal, 1977.

El picúo, el fisto, el barrio y otras estampas cubanas, Miami, Ediciones Universal, 1977.

Leyendas de azúcar prieta (Cabio Silo), Miami, Ediciones Universal, 1977.

Los sarracenos del ocaso, Miami, Ediciones Universal, 1977.

Lilayando pal tu, Miami, Ediciones Universal, 1978.

Ninquín el cesante, Miami, Ediciones Universal, 1978.

Tiempo congelado, Miami, Ediciones Universal, 1979.

La rebelión de los negros, Miami, Ediciones Universal, 1980.

Cuentos blancos y negros, Miami, Ediciones Universal, 1983.

Cuentos de la niñez, Miami, Ediciones Universal, 1984.

Dile a Catalina que se compre un guayo, Miami, Ediciones Universal, 1991.

Partiendo el "Jon," Miami, Ediciones Universal, 1991.

Sierra Berdecía, Fernando. *Esta noche juega el joker*, San Juan, Biblioteca de Autores Puertorriqueños, 1939.

Soto, Pedro Juan, *Spiks*, Mexico, Los Presentes, 1956.

Ardiente suelo, fría estación, Xalapa, Mexico, Universidad Veracruzana, 1961.

Sutton, Lorraine. *SAYcred LAYdy*, New York, Sunbury, 1975.

Suárez, Virgil. *Latin Jazz*, New York, William Morrow & Co., 1989.

The Cutter, New York, Balentine Books, 1991.

Welcome to the Oasis and Other Stories, Houston, Arte Público, 1992.

Thomas, Piri. *Down These Mean Streets*, New York, New American Library, 1967.

Savior, Savior, Hold My Hand, New York, Doubleday, 1972.

Seven Long Times, New York, Praeger, 1974.

Stories from El Barrio, New York, Knopf, 1978.

Torres, Edwin. *Carlito's Way*, New York, Saturday Review Press, 1975.

After Hours, New York, Dial Press, 1976.

Q and A, New York, Dial Press, 1977.

Torres, Omar. *Conversación primera*. New York, Editorial Niurklen, 1975.

Ecos de un laberinto, New York, n.p., 1976.

Tiempo robado, Hoboken, N.J., Ediciones Contra Viento y Marea, 1978.

Apenas un bolero, Miami, Ediciones Universal, 1981.

De nunca a siempre, Miami Ediciones Universal, 1981.

Al partir, Houston, Arte Público, 1986.

Fallen Angels Sing, Houston, Arte Público Press, 1991.

Umpierre, Luz María. *En el país de las maravillas*, Bloomington, Ind., Third Woman Press, 1972.

Una puertorriqueña en Penna, San Juan, Masters, 1979.

Y otras desgracias and Other Misfortunes, Bloomington, Ind., Third Woman Press, 1985.

The Margarita Poems, Bloomington, Ind., Third Woman Press, 1987.

Valero, Roberto. *Venias*, Madrid, Editorial Betania, 1990.

Valle, Carmen. *Un poco de lo no dicho*, New York, Editorial La Ceiba, 1979.

Glenn Miller y varias vidas después, Mexico, Premia, 1983.

Vázquez, Miguel A. *Mejorar la raza*, Santo Domingo, Dominican Republic, Editora Taller, 1977.

Vega, Ed. *The Comeback*, Houston, Arte Público, 1985.

Mendoza's Dreams, Houston, Arte Público, 1987.

Vicioso, Chiqui. *Un extraño ulular traía el viento*, Santo Domingo, Dominican Republic, Alfa y Omega, 1985.

Villaverde, Cirilo. *General López, the Cuban Patriot* [New York], 1850.

El señor Saco con respecto a la revolución de Cuba, New York, La Verdad, 1852.

La revolución de Cuba vista desde Nueva York, New York, 1869.

Cecilia Valdés, New York, El Espejo, 1882.

Cuentos de mi abuelo El penitente, New York, M. M. Hernández, 1889.

Vivas Maldonado, J. L. *A vellón las esperanzas, o Melania*, New York, Las Américas, 1971.

Zeno Gandía, Manuel. *El negocio: crónica de un mundo enfermo*, New York, Geo. A. Powers Printing Co., 1922.

Secondary sources

Books

Algarín, Miguel, and Miguel Piñero (eds.). *Nuyorican Poetry, An Anthology of Puerto Rican Words and Feelings*, New York, William Morrow & Co., 1975.

Contains a useful introduction by Algarín in which he attempts to define Nuyorican culture.

Aparicio Laurencio, Angel. *Cinco poetisas cubanas*, Miami, Ediciones Universal, 1970.

The poets included are Mercedes García Tuduri, Pura del Prado, Teresa María Rojas, Rita Geada, and Ana Rosa Núñez. The prologue comments on exile poetry as a means of preserving Cuban culture.

Avendaño, Fausto (ed.). *Literatura hispana de los Estados Unidos, Explicación de Textos Literarios*, 15:2 (1986–1987).

This special issue explores themes by Puerto Rican, Cuban, and Chicano

authors and includes panoramic essays on Cuban Americans by Caroline
Hospital and on Puerto Ricans in the United States by Alfredo Matilla.

Babin, María Teresa, and Stan Steiner (eds.). *Borinquen: An anthology of Puerto
Rican literature*, New York, Vintage Books, 1974.

Although this study is dedicated mostly to Puerto Ricans on the island, it also
contains writers from the mainland such as Piri Thomas and Pedro Pietri.

Barradas, Efraín, and Rafael Rodríguez (eds.). *Herejes y mitificadores: muestra de la
poesía puertorriqueña en los Estados Unidos*, Río Piedras P.R., Ediciones
Huracán, 1980.

A bilingual edition of Puerto Rican poetry written in the United States. Not all
poems pertain to Nuyorican culture. Barradas's introduction points to key
historical and literary components of the literature.

Binder, Wolfgang. *Los puertorriqueños en Nueva York*, Germany, Universidad de
Erlangen, 1979.

Situates Puerto Ricans within a hostile environment and underscores their
need to retain their cultural identity.

Cocco de Felippis, Daisy (ed.). *Sin otro profeta que su canto*, Santo Domingo, P.R.,
Editora Taller, 1988.

An anthology of Dominican women poets, arranged chronologically, which
also includes the works of poets Julia Alvarez and Chiqui Vicioso who write
about New York. Cocco de Felippis's introduction provides a literary history of
key women figures and a commentary on Chiqui Vicioso.

Fabre, Genvieve (ed.). *European Perspectives on Hispanic Literature of the United
States*, Houston, Arte Público, 1988.

Selection of papers from the 1986 conference on "Hispanic cultures and
identities in the United States," sponsored by Université Paris VII. Essays pertain
to Chicano and Nuyorican authors and works. Of interest are Wolfgang Binder's
" 'A Midnight Reality': Puerto Rican poetry in New York, a poetry of dreams";
Dieter Herm's "Chicano and Nuyorican literature – elements of a democratic
and socialist culture in the U.S. of A.?"; and Frances R. Aparicio's "La vida es un
spanglish disparatero: Bilingualism in Nuyorican Poetry."

Fernández, José B., and Roberto G. Fernández. *Indice bibliográfico de autores
cubanos: diáspora, 1959–1979/Bibliographical Index of Cuban Authors: Diaspora, 1959–1979*, Miami, Ediciones Universal, 1983.

Gathers literature of writers outside Cuba and some non-Cuban born authors,
independent of ideology. Prepared for both Spanish and English readers.
Contains 971 entries divided into short story, novel, poetry, theatre, folklore,
literary criticism and culture, and linguistics, arranged in alphabetical order.

Fernández Olmos, Margarita. *Sobre la literatura puertorriqueña de aquí y de allá:
aproximaciones feministas*, Santo Domingo, Dominican Republic, Alfa y
Omega, 1989.

A collection of seven uneven essays in which the problematics of exile and
immigrant writers and feminist literature in and outside the island are discussed.

Grupo Areito. *Contra viento y marea*, Havana, Casa de las Américas, 1978.

Testimony of the sons of Cuban exiles who questioned their parents'
conservative position and wanted to rediscover the island they left. This work
documents their experiences in exile.

Gutiérrez de la Solana, Alberto. *Maneras de contar: contraste de Lino Novás Calvo y Alfonso Hernández Catá*, New York, Eliseo Torres & Sons, 1972.

Treats the exile period of these two important writers.

Hernández-Mijares, Julio (ed.). *Narradores cubanos de hoy*, Miami, Ediciones Universal, 1975.

A collection of eleven Cuban exile writers of the most recent generations. The work is intended to promote exile literature.

Horno-Delgado, Asunción, *et al. Breaking Boundaries: Latina writings and critical readings*, Amherst, University of Massachusetts Press, 1989.

An anthology of essays about Hispanic American women authors writing in the United States. This work is divided into four parts: "Chicanas," "Puertorriqueñas," "Cubanas," and "Latinoamericanas from other countries."

Hospital, Carolina (ed.). *Cuban American Writers: Los atrevidos*, Princeton, N.J., Ediciones Ellas/Linden Lane Press, 1988.

A collection of literary works by Cuban Americans who left the island at a young age and write in English. Hospital's introduction is brief and attempts to explain the vision and language of the writers. Includes a brief biography on each writer.

Kanellos, Nicólas. *A History of Hispanic Theatre in the United States: Origins to 1940*, Austin, University of Texas Press, 1990.

Traces the Hispanic Caribbean theatre to the mid nineteenth century. Of particular interest are the chapters on the development of theatre in New York and Tampa.

Lázaro, Felipe. *Poetas cubanos en Nueva York*, Madrid, Editorial Betania, 1988.

The prologue is written by José Olivio Jiménez and in it he underscores the historical presence of exile writers in New York which began with Heredia, Martí, and Florit. The anthology continues with writers such as José Kozer, Reinaldo Arenas, and Jorge Valls.

Le Riverend, Pablo. *Diccionario biográfico de poetas cubanos en el exilio (contemporáneos)*, Newark, N.J., Ediciones Q-21, 1988.

A brief but useful dictionary which contains pertinent information about exile-poets. It reproduces information normally found in a *curriculum vitae*, even current mailing addresses of writers.

Luis, William. *Literary Bondage: Slavery in Cuban narrative*, Austin, University of Texas Press, 1990.

Analyzes the Cuban anti-slavery narrative and contains chapters on Cirilo Villaverde's *Cecilia Valdés* and Reinaldo Arenas's *La loma del Angel*.

Martínez, Julio A. (ed.). *Dictionary of Twentieth-Century Cuban Literature*, Westport, Conn., Greenwood Press, 1990.

This dictionary also contains entries on the most recognized Cuban exile writers.

Matilla, Alfredo, and Iván Silén (eds.). *The Puerto Rican Poets: Los poetas puertorriqueños*, New York, Bantam, 1972.

A bilingual edition in which Matillan and Silen mistakenly believe that there is a similarity between poetry written on the island and on the mainland.

Menton, Seymour. *Prose Fiction of the Cuban Revolution*, Latin American Monographs, 37, Austin, University of Texas Press, 1975; also in Spanish, *La narrativa de la revolución cubana*, Colección Nova Scholar, Madrid, Playor.

Dedicates Part IV of this comprehensive monograph to "Antirevolutionary prose fiction" in which Menton studies short stories and novels written by exile-writers. With some exceptions, these works have not reached the level of maturity seen in the works of authors living on the island.

Mohr, Eugene. *The Nuyorican Experience: Literature of the Puerto Rican minority*, Westport, Conn.; Greenwood Press, 1982.

The only full-length study about Nuyorican narratives written in English. Mohr provides an introduction to many of the published works.

Montes Huidobro, Matías, and Yara González Montes. *Bibliografía crítica de la poesía cubana (exilio: 1959–1971)*, Madrid, Playor, 1973.

A bibliography about the works of Cuban exile-writers. The authors make a distinction between those writers who wrote in Cuba and those who began to write in exile.

Muñoz, Elías Miguel. *Desde esta orilla*, Madrid, Editorial Betania, 1988.

The only book to date on Cuban poetry in exile. Muñoz accepts a Cuban exile consciousness but also argues for a Cuban American ethnic literature.

Núñez, Ana Rosa. *Poesía en éxodo*, Miami, Ediciones Universal, 1970.

A listing of the works of exile-poets up to 1959, in mainstream and marginal publications. The works are viewed as a testament against the Castro government.

Rodríguez Seda de Laguna, Asela (ed.). *Images and Identities: The Puerto Rican in two world contexts*, New Brunswick, N.J., Transaction, Inc., 1987.

A collection of essays which focuses on the life and works of Puerto Ricans. In her introduction, the editor attempts to define Puerto Rican literature but instead provides a list of authors and works. Of particular interest is Part III, which contains essays on Puerto Rican literature written in English and includes Piri Thomas's "A Neorican in Puerto Rico or Coming home," Nicholasa Mohr's "Puerto Ricans in New York: cultural evolution and identity," Miguel Algarín's "Nuyorican aesthetics," Sandra María Esteves's "Ambivalence or activism from the Nuyorican perspective in poetry," and her "The feminist viewpoint in the poetry of Puerto Rican women in the United States."

Rodríguez Sardiñas, Orlando (ed.). *La última poesía cubana (1960–1973)*, New York, Hispanova de Ediciones, 1973.

Includes Cuban poets both in and outside the island. The introduction divides poets into three generational categories.

Sánchez-Boudy, José. *Historia de la literatura cubana (en el exilio)*, Miami, Ediciones Universal, 1975.

Studies the works of anti-revolutionary writers who are not well known outside the exile community. Sánchez-Boudy gives publicity to them and their works.

Silén, Iván (ed.). *Los paraguas amarillos: los poetas latinos en Nueva York*, Hanover, N.H., Ediciones del Norte, 1983.

Anthology of Hispanic poets writing in New York. Of these, Pedro Pietri is the only one writing in English. Silén's introduction addresses the issues confronted by these writers.

Soto, Pedro Juan. *A solas con Pedro Juan Soto*, Río Piedras, P.R., Ediciones Puerta.

In this interview by the author, Soto discusses his experience while teaching at the State University of New York at Buffalo, and the presence of Puerto Ricans in the United States. He also provides useful information about his life and works.

Woman of Her Word: Hispanic women write, Revista Chicano-Riqueña, 11:3–4 (1983).

Rpt. as Evangelina Vigel (ed.), *Woman of Her World: Hispanic Women Write*, Houston, Arte Público Press, 1987. This issue is dedicated to the works of incipient and well-known women writers of this literature. It also contains an introductory essay about works and authors contained therein and an essay by Luz María Umpierre on Sandra María Estevez and Marjorie Agosin (Chile).

Articles

Acosta-Belén, Edna. "The literature of the Puerto Rican minority in the United States," *The Bilingual Review/La Revista Bilingüe*, 5:1–2 (1978), 107–16.

Views the literature as a response to the social conditions of a national minority in the United States, even though she also discusses works by island-dwelling authors who write about the US experience.

"Conversations with Nicholasa Mohr," *Revista Chicano-Riqueña*, 8:2 (1980), 35–41.

Interview regarding Mohr's life and works.

Acosta-Belén, Edna, and Elsa Hidalgo Christensen (eds.). "Ideology and images of women in contemporary Puerto Rican literature" in *The Puerto Rican Woman*, New York, Praeger Publishers, 1979, 85–109.

An ideological study of the treatment of women in the works of some of the writers of the Generation of 1950: José Luis González, René Marqués, Pedro Juan Soto, and Emilio Díaz Valcárcel. According to the author, these writers cast Puerto Ricans in New York.

Algarín, Miguel. "Volume and value of the breath in Poetry," *Revista Chicano-Riqueña*, 6:3 (1978), 52–69.

Algarín looks at poetry within the context of Nuyorican culture.

"Nuyorican aesthetics" in Asela Rodríguez Seda de Laguna (ed.), *Images and Identities: The Puerto Rican in two world contexts*, New Brunswick, N.J., Transaction, Inc., 1987, 161–3; also published in *Meluse*, 8 (1981).

Traces the roots of Puerto Ricans in the United States and divides Nuyorican aesthetics into three categories: (1) oral expression; (2) safeguard the future; (3) promote the expression of art.

Aparicio, Frances R. "La vida es un spanglish disparatero: Bilingualism in Nuyorican Poetry" in Genvieve Fabre (ed.), *European Perspectives on Hispanic Literature of the United States*, Houston, Arte Público, 1988, 147–60.

Considers the use of Spanish and English as a means of defining the writer's political and cultural position regarding his community. Nuyorican writers are documenting and preserving the speech of the Hispanic community.

Ardura, Ernesto. "José Martí: Latin America's U.S. correspondent," *Americas*, 32:11–12 (1980), 38–42.

Traces Martí's writings in the United States for Latin American newspapers.

Barradas, Efraín. "Historia y ficción: las memorias de un emigrante puertorriqueño

[*Memorias (Contribución a la historia de la comunidad puertorriqueña en Nueva York)*, Bernardo Vega]" *The Bilingual Review/La Revista Bilingüe*, 5:3 (1978), 247–9.

A review of this important work, in which Barradas highlights the testimonial rather than the artistic.

"De lejos en sueños verla . . .: visión mítica de Puerto Rico en la poesía neorrican," *Revista Chicano-Riqueña*, 7: 4 (1979), 46–56.

Studies in nostalgic view of Puerto Rico in Nuyorican poetry.

"Puerto Rico acá, Puerto Rico allá," *Revista Chicano-Riqueña*, 8:2 (1980).

Starts from the common notion that Puerto Ricans are a people divided between those living on the island and those on the mainland and shows that both are exploited.

" 'Entre la esencia y la forma': el momento neoyorquino en la poesía de Julia de Burgos," *Explicación de Textos Literarios*, 15:2 (1986–1987), 138–52.

Limits this study to Burgos's poems about New York, dividing them into two categories: those of a political nature and those of a personal one.

Betances, Samuel. "Race and the search for identity" in María Teresa Babin and Stan Steiner (eds.), *Borinquen: An anthology of Puerto Rican literature*, New York, Vintage Books, 1974, 425–38.

Looks at race as a variable for attaining a sense of identity.

Binder, Wolfgang. " 'A Midnight Reality': Puerto Rican poetry in New York, a poetry of dreams" in Genvieve Fabre (ed.), *European Perspectives on Hispanic Literature of the United States*, Houston, Arte Público, 1988, 22–32.

Concentrates on Puerto Rican poetry written in English by various mainland Puerto Rican writers who compose militant, hypertrophied, feminist, apocalyptic, utopian, and creolized poetry.

Burunat, Silvia. "Omar Torres a través de sus textos," *Explicación de Textos Literarios*, 15:2 (1986–1987), 60–76.

The works of this poet, playwright, and novelist capture with precision the lives and expectations of Cuban Americans.

Campa, Román de la. "En torno a la crítica de la literatura cubana en Estados Unidos," *Ideologies and Literature*, 4:16 (1983), 276–89.

Taking into account the few theoretical works which analyze this literature, de la Campa attempts to provide an ideological framework for his study.

"En la utopía redentora del lenguaje: Pedro Pietri y Miguel Algarín," *Explicación de Textos Literarios*, 15:2 (1986–1987), 32–49.

Uses Lotman's ideas to analyze the poems of these two writers.

Casal, Lourdes, and Andrés R. Hernández. "Cubans in the U.S.: a survey of the literature," *Cuban Studies*, 5:2 (1975), 25–52.

An early study regarding the emergence of a Cuban American literature since 1960.

Cocco de Felippis, Daisy, and Emma Jane Robinett (eds.). *Poemas del exilio y de otras inquietudes*, New York, Ediciones Alcance, 1988.

A bilingual edition of Dominican poetry written in the United States which contains a brief but useful introduction by Cocco de Felippis.

Dauster, Frank. "Image of the city: three Puerto Rican generations in New York" in Asela Rodríguez Seda de Laguna (ed.), *Images and Identities: The Puerto Rican in two world contexts*, New Brunswick, N.J., Transaction, Inc., 1987, 60–4.

Studies the importance of New York in three plays: Sierra Berdecía's *Esta noche juega el joker*, Méndez Ballester's *Encrucijada*, and Carrero's *Caja de caudales F M*.

Esteves, Sandra María. "Ambivalence or activism from the Nuyorican perspective in poetry" in Asela Rodríguez Seda de Laguna (ed.), *Images and Identities: The Puerto Rican in two world contexts*, New Brunswick, N.J., Transaction, Inc., 1987, 165–70.

Reviews the works of Algarín, Louis Reyes Rivera, Roberto Márquez, Lucky Cienfuegos, Piñero, Laviera, and other Nuyorican writers.

"The feminist viewpoint in the poetry of Puerto Rican women in the United States" in Asela Rodríguez Seda de Laguna (ed.), *Images and Identities: The Puerto Rican in two world contexts*, New Brunswick, N.J., Transaction, Inc., 1987, 171–7.

Traces the feminist perspective from Julia de Burgos, to Lorraine Sutton, to Luz María Umpierre, and to a younger generation which includes Magdalena Gómez, Amina Muñoz, and Rota Silverstrini.

"Open letter to Eliana (testimonio)" in Asunción Horno-Delgado, Eliana Ortega, Nina M. Scott, and Nancy Sapporta Sternbach (eds.), *Breaking Boundaries: Latina writings and critical readings*, Amherst, University of Massachusetts Press, 1989, 117–21.

An autobiographical letter in which Esteves lists the important moments and people in her life which have made her the poet she is.

Flores, Juan. "Back down these mean streets: introducing Nicholasa Mohr and Louis Reyes Rivera," *Revista Chicano-Riqueña*, 8:2 (1980), 51–6.

An introduction to Mohr's narrative and Reyes's poetry, two Nuyorican writers who write in English.

" 'Que assimilated, brother, yo soy asimilao': the structuring of Puerto Rican identity in the U.S.," *The Journal of Ethnic Studies*, 13:3 (1985), 1–16: also published in *Casa de las Américas*, 26:152 (1985), 54–63.

Influenced by Tato Laviera's poem, Flores studies Nuyorican culture which for him is composed of four moments linked to three transitional phases.

Flores, Juan, John Attenasi, and Pedro Pedraza. "*La Carreta Made a U-Turn*: Puerto Rican language and culture in the United States," *Daedalus*, 110 (1981), 193–217.

An important sociological analysis of Tato Laviera's poems.

González Montes, Yara, and Matías Montes Huidobro. "La novela cubana: el sitio de la palabra," *Caribe*, 1:1 (1976), 129–46.

This work discusses four novels by Hilda Perera, Alvaro de Villa, José Sánchez-Boudy, and Celedonio González. These Cuban exile narratives contain a fragmented structure and the characters undergo change.

Gutiérrez de la Solana, Alberto. "La novela cubana escrita fuera de Cuba," *Anales de Literatura Hispanoamericana*, 2–3 (1973–1974), 767–89.

Examines the works of Cuban exile writers, including those who hold teaching positions in US universities.

Herms, Dieter. "Chicano and Nuyorican literature – Elements of a democratic and socialist culture in the U.S. of A.?" in Genvieve Fabre (ed.), *European Perspectives on Hispanic Literature of the United States*, Houston, Arte Público, 1988, 118–29.

Uses Lenin's theory of the two cultures to understand Nuyorican and Chicano ethnic literatures as containing national and international dimensions. Regarding Puerto Rican literature, Thomas's *Down These Mean Streets* and Pietri's *Puerto Rican Obituary* respond to the question of identity and to Third-World experience and anti-imperialist struggle.

Hernández Cruz, Víctor. "Mountains in the north: Hispanic writing in the U.S.A." *The Americas Review*, 14:3–4 (1986), 110–14.

US Hispanics have maintained their own cultural identity and unlike other groups have not been absorbed by North American culture.

Hernández-Mijares, Julio. "La poesía cubana del exterior: testimonio y recuento," *Norte*, 7:3–4 (1971), 58–68.

Lists groups of Cuban exile writers, where they publish, and secondary sources about their works.

Herrera-Sobek, María. "Identidad cultural e interacción dinámica entre texto y lector destinatario en *Mi mamá me ama*," *Explicación de Textos Literarios*, 15:2 (1986–1987), 123–37.

The work's multiple meanings suggest Hispanic, Puerto Rican, and North American cultural referents.

Horno-Delgado, Asunción. "Señores, don't leibol mi, please!! ya Luz María Umpierre" in Asunción Horno-Delgado, Eliana Ortega, Nina M. Scott, and Nancy Sapporta Sternbach (eds.), *Breaking Boundaries: Latina writings and critical readings*, Amherst, University of Massachusetts Press, 1989, 136–45.

Analyzes Umpierre's *En el país de las maravillas* as a book of identity and the acceptance of marginality.

Hospital, Carolina. "Los hijos del exilio cubano y su literatura," *Explicación de Textos Literarios*, 15:2 (1986–1987), 103–14.

Concentrates on the generation of Cuban American writers born after 1949.

"Los atrevidos," *Linden Lane Magazine*, 6:4 (1987), 22–3.

Supports a unique Cuban American exile experience which is still present in the second and third generations of writers. These authors are trapped in their condition which leads them to think creatively.

Kanellos, Nicolás. "US Hispanic literature in the Anglo-American empire," *The Americas Review*, 14:3–4 (1986), 103–5.

Speech to the PEN Club in which Kanellos describes the difficulty Hispanic writers face when publishing their works.

"Toward a history of Hispanic literature in the United States" in Asela Rodríguez Seda de Laguna (ed.), *Images and Identities: The Puerto Rican in two world contexts*, New Brunswick, N.J., Transaction, Inc., 1987, 236–45.

Traces the origin of Hispanic literature to a period before the American Revolutionary War. It developed from a monolingual to a bilingual discourse.

Lewis, Marvin A. "The Puerto Rican in popular U.S. literature: a culturalist perspective" in Asela Rodríguez Seda de Laguna (ed.), *Images and Identities: The Puerto Rican in two world contexts*, New Brunswick, N.J., Transaction, Inc., 1987, 65–75.

Looks at the presence of Puerto Rican characters in four works which interpret the Puerto Rican experience: *A Welfare Mother*, *Manny: A criminal addict's story*, *Fort Apache*, and *Benjy Lopez*.

Lindstrom, Naomi E. "Cuban American and continental Puerto Rican literature" in

David William Foster (ed.), *Sourcebook of Hispanic Culture in the United States*, Chicago, American Library Association, 1982, 221–45.

An annotated bibliography of Cuban American and continental Puerto Rican literatures divided into periodicals, critical monographs and short studies, bibliography, anthologies, poetry (single-author volumes), short stories, personal writings, drama, and fiction. Also includes a useful but brief introductory essay.

Lipp, Solomon. "The anti-Castro novel," *Hispania*, 58 (1975), 284–96.

Views as simplistic the anti-Castro novels in which authors project their own experiences.

López, Adalberto. "Literature for the Puerto Rican diaspora: Part II," *Caribbean Review*, 6:4 (1974), 41–6.

A review of the literature of, and about, Puerto Ricans in the United States for an English-speaking audience. He includes commentaries on Thomas and Soto.

Luis, William. "From New York to the world: An interview with Tato Laviera," *Callaloo*, 15:4 (1992), 1022–33.

Explores Laviera's life and works and in particular his important poem "Jesús Papote." Luis also discusses the poet's social and political responsibilities and the development of his poetic voice.

"A search for identity in Julia Alvarez's *How the Garcia Girls Lost Their Accent*," *Latinos in the US Review*, (Spring 1994), 52–7.

Studies the regressive unfolding of the narration as a desire by the protagonist to revisit the past of her childhood in order to come to terms with her identity as an adult.

Maffi, Mario. "The Nuyorican experience in the plays of Pedro Pietri and Miguel Piñero" in Mirko Juark (ed.), *Cross-Cultural Studies: American, Canadian and European literatures: 1945–1985)*, Slovenia, Yugoslavia, Ljublajaria, English Dept., Filozofska Fakulteta, 1988, 483–9.

Situates the development of Nuyorican literature during the decade of the 1970s. Maffi studies Pietri's and Piñero's plays as a portrayal of ghetto society.

Matilla, Alfredo. "The broken English dream: Puerto Rican poetry in New York" in Iris M. Zavala and Rafael Rodríguez (eds.), *The Intellectual Roots of Independence: An anthology of Puerto Rican political essays*, New York, Monthly Review Press, 1980.

Divides Puerto Rican poets into two categories: those who write in Spanish and those who write in English.

"Breve panorámica de las letras puertorriqueñas en los Estados Unidos," *Explicación de Textos Literarios*, 15:2 (1986–1987), 19–31.

Overview of the most important Puerto Rican and Nuyorican authors writing about the North American experience.

Miller, John C. "Hispanic theater in New York, 1965–1977," *Revista Chicano-Riqueña*, 6:1 (1978), 40–59.

Studies mainly Puerto Rican, but also Cuban, theatre in New York, and the dramatists' attempt to create a "minority" theatre.

"Cross-currents in Hispanic literature in the United States" in Asela Rodríguez Seda de Laguna (ed.), *Images and Identities: The Puerto Rican in two world contexts*, New Brunswick, N.J., Transaction, Inc., 1987, 246–53.

Provides a historical development of the theatre and concentrates on the decades of the 1960s and 1970s. Regarding Puerto Rican drama, he comments on the works by Jaime Carrero and Miguel Piñero. In addition, he introduces younger Cuban American, Puerto Rican, and Dominican writers.

Mohr, Eugene. "Lives from El Barrio," *Revista Chicano-Riqueña*, 3:4 (1980), 60–8.

Compares five novels by Nuyorican male writers. This is Chapter 4 of his book, *The Nuyorican Experience* (above).

Mohr, Nicholasa. "On being authentic," *The American Review*, 14:3–4 (1986), 106–9.

Comments on her works which cover about thirty years of her past, but has not successfully written about the present.

"Puerto Ricans in New York: cultural evolution and identity" in Asela Rodríguez Seda de Laguna (ed.), *Images and Identities: The Puerto Rican in two world contexts*, New Brunswick, N.J., Transaction, Inc., 1987, 157–60.

Provides a historical understanding of the lives of Puerto Ricans in New York and the difficulties they had to endure. In spite of these difficulties, they are contributing to the culture of New York.

"Puerto Rican writers in the United States, Puerto Rican writers in Puerto Rico: a separation beyond languages," *The Americas Review*, 15:2 (1987), 87–92; reprinted in Asunción Horno-Delgado, Eliana Ortega, Nina M. Scott, and Nancy Sapporta Sternbach (eds.) *Breaking Boundaries: Latina writings and critical readings*. Amherst, University of Massachusetts Press, 1989, 111–16.

Explains why she writes in English, which separates her from the majority of Puerto Rican writers. She also outlines differences between writers living on the island and those living on the mainland.

Ortega, Eliana. "Poetic discourse of the Puerto Rican woman in the U.S.: new voices of Anacaonian liberation" in Asunción Horno-Delgado, Eliana Ortega, Nina M. Scott, and Nancy Sapporta Sternbach (eds.), *Breaking Boundaries: Latina writings and critical readings*, Amherst, University of Massachusetts Press, 1989, 122–35.

Traces the image of Anacaona from Fernández de Oviedo's *Crónicas* to Cheo Feliciano's popular song. For the author, Anacaona is a symbol of present-day women writers.

Pérez Firmat, Gustavo. "Spic chic: Spanglish as equipment for living," *Caribbean Review*, 15 (1987), 20–1, 36–7.

Looks at *salsa* as a necessity of life for those living in a multi-ethnic environment.

"Transcending exile: Cuban-American literature Today" in *Occasional Papers Series. Dialogues*, Miami, Florida International University, Latin American and Caribbean Center, 1987, 1–13.

Groups the literature of Cuban American writers into immigrant, exile, and ethnic literatures. The latter, which is the most recent one, attempts to preserve a Cuban identity without rejecting a North American one.

"Noción de José Kozer," *Revista Iberoamericana*, 152–3 (1990), 1247–56.

A useful essay on this important but difficult-to-classify poet, in which Pérez Firmat explores two related concepts: "capacidad" and "alteración." Pérez Firmat does a close reading of poems contained mainly in *Bajo este cien* and *Jarrón de las abreviaturas* and underscores the grammatical use of multiple languages and parenthesis.

Prida, Dolores. "The show does go on (testimonio)" in Asunción Horno-Delgado, Eliana Ortega, Nina M. Scott, and Nancy Sapporta Sternbach (eds.), *Breaking Boundaries: Latina writings and critical readings*, Amherst, University of Massachusetts Press, 1989, 181–8.

Provides information about her life and works and her role as a Hispanic playwright living and writing in the United States.

Rivero, Eliana S. "Hispanic literature in the United States: self-image and conflict," *Revista Chicano-Riqueña*, 13:3–4 (1985), 173–92.

Draws on similarities between Chicano and Nuyorican literatures and similarities and differences between these and Cuban American writings. Divides Hispanics into the following groups: those born outside and those born or raised inside the United States; and those writing in Spanish and those writing in English.

"From immigrants to ethnics: Cuban women writers in the U.S." in Asunción Horno-Delgado, Eliana Ortega, Nina M. Scott, and Nancy Sapporta Sternbach (eds.), *Breaking Boundaries: Latina writings and critical readings*, Amherst, University of Massachusetts Press, 1989, 189–200.

Views Lourdes Casal as a pioneer among Cuban American women writers. However, ethnic awareness developed in the mid 1980s with the works of writers such as Achy Obejas.

Rodriguez Sardiñas, Orlando. "Cuba: poesía entre revolución y exilio," *Revista/ Review Interamericana*, 4:3 (1974), 359–69.

This study pertains to the works of first and second generations of Cuban exile-writers.

Rojas, Lourdes. "Latinas at the crossroads: an affirmation of life in Rosario Morales and Aurora Levins Morales's *Getting Home Alive*" in Asunción Horno-Delgado, Eliana Ortega, Nina M. Scott, and Nancy Sapporta Sternbach (eds.), *Breaking Boundaries: Latina writings and critical readings*, Amherst, University of Massachusetts Press, 1989, 166–77.

The author views the lives of Morales and Levins Morales, mother and daughter, as being at the crossroads of the coming together of various cultures. The two women are a symbol of all of them.

Ruiz, Ariel. "Raza, sexo y política en *Short Eyes* de Miguel Piñero," *The Americas Review*, 15:2 (1987), 93–102).

As the title suggests, race, sex, and politics are the main themes of this important play.

Saldívar, José David. "The dialectics of our America" in Gustavo Pérez Firmat (ed.), *Do the Americas Have a Common Literature?*, Durham, N.C., Duke University Press, 1990.

Discusses "Nuestra América" to show Martí's cultural critique of the United States and his knowledge of US literature, culture, and politics.

Sandoval, Alberto. "Dolores Prida's *Coser y cantar*: mapping the dialectics of ethnic identity and assimilation" in Asunción Horno-Delgado, Eliana Ortega, Nina M. Scott, and Nancy Sapporta Sternbach (eds.), *Breaking Boundaries: Latina writings and critical readings*, Amherst, University of Massachusetts Press, 1989, 201–20.

Coser y cantar, a play about a bilingual bicultural woman in Manhattan, describes how Ella and She struggle with their identity or lack of identity.

Tatum, Charles A. "Geographic displacement as spiritual desolation in Puertorican and Chicano prose fiction" in Asela Rodríguez Seda de Laguna (ed.), *Images and Identities: The Puerto Rican in two world contexts*, New Brunswick, N.J., Transaction, Inc., 1987, 254–64.

Associates spiritual desolation with geographical displacement as a common link between Puerto Rican and Chicano literatures. To support his ideas he studies the works of Puerto Rican writers José Luis González, Piri Thomas, Lefty Barreto, and Pedro Juan Soto, and Chicano writers José Antonio Villarreal, Richard Vásquez, Ernesto Galarza, John Rechy, Rudolfo Anaya, and Oscar Zeta Acosta.

Thomas, Piri. "A Neorican in Puerto Rico or Coming home" in Asela Seda Rodríguez de Laguna (ed.), *Images and Identities: The Puerto Rican in two world contexts*, New Brunswick, N.J., Transaction, Inc., 1987, 153–6.

Thomas refers to his life and his quest for identity and explains the motivation behind *Down These Mean Streets*, and recounts his troubling experiences in Puerto Rico.

Vargas, Yamila Azize. "A commentary on the works of three Puerto Rican women poets in New York" in Asunción Horno-Delgado, Eliana Ortega, Nina M. Scott, and Nancy Sapporta Sternbach (eds.), *Breaking Boundaries: Latina writings and critical readings*, Amherst, University of Massachusetts Press, 1989, 1146–65.

Studies the works of Carmen Valle, Sandra María Esteves, and Luz María Umpierre. All of them contribute to a feminist ideology.

Velez, Diana L. "'Pollito chicken': split subjectivity, national identity and the articulation of female sexuality in a narrative by Ana Lydia Vega," *The Americas Review*, 14:2 (1986), 68–76.

A social, linguistic, and sexual study of Vega's story.

Vicioso, Sherezada (Chiqui). "An oral history (testimonio)" in Asunción Horno-Delgado, Eliana Ortega, Nina M. Scott, and Nancy Sapporta Sternbach (eds.), *Breaking Boundaries: Latina writings and critical readings*, Amherst, University of Massachusetts Press, 1989, 229–34.

Talks about her life and how she was able to find a true voice in New York.

Watson-Espener, Maida Isabel. "Observaciones sobre el teatro chicano, nuyorriqueño y cubano en los Estados Unidos," *The Bilingual Review/La Revista Bilingüe*, 5:1–2 (1978), 117–25.

Studies similarities and differences between the three theatre groups, noting that both Chicano and Nuyoricans write about the present and Cubans about the past. Gives more space to dramas written by Cuban Americans and includes unpublished works.

Volume 2

Chapter 17: Chicano literature

Secondary sources

Books

Anaya, Rudolfo A., and Francisco Lomelí (eds.). *Aztlán: Essays on the Chicano homeland*, Albuquerque, N.M., El Norte, 1989.
  A compilation of thirteen articles and documents on Aztlán.

Arellano, Anselmo F. *Los pobladores nuevo mexicanos y su poesía, 1889–1959*, Albuquerque, N.M., Pajarito Publications, 1976.
  Poems collected from Spanish-language newspapers published in New Mexico, with brief introductory notes.

Baker, Houston A., Jr. (ed.). *Three American Literatures: Essays in Chicano, Native American, and Asian-American literature for teachers of American literature*, New York, Modern Language Association of America, 1982.
  Contains two essays on Chicano literature, the first by Luis Leal and Pepe Barrón, and the second by Raymund A. Paredes.

Bardeleben, Renate von, *et al.* (eds.). *Missions in Conflict: Essays on U.S. Mexican relations and Chicano culture*, Tübingen, Germany, Gunter Narr Verlag, 1988.
  Twenty-six papers presented at the First International Symposium on Chicano Culture, July 5–7, 1984, at the University of Mainz in Germersheim.

Binder, Wolfgang (ed.). *Partial Autobiographies: Interviews with twenty Chicano poets*, Erlangen, Germany, Verlag Palm & Enke Erlangen, 1985.
  An important collection of interviews with representative poets.

Bruce-Novoa, Juan. *Chicano Authors: Inquiry by interview*, Austin, University of Texas Press, 1980.
  Interviews with fourteen writers.

  Chicano Poetry: A response to chaos, Austin, University of Texas Press, 1982.
  First book-length critical study of Chicano poetry.

Candelaria, Cordelia. *Chicano Poetry: A critical introduction*, Westport, Conn., Greenwood Press, 1986.
  A survey of the genre, outlining major trends and features.

Eger, Ernestina. *A Bibliography of Criticism of Chicano Literature*, Berkeley, Calif., Chicano Studies Library, 1982.
  An exhaustive listing which facilitates the analysis of critical trends.

Gonzales, Rodolfo. *I Am Joaquín/ Yo soy Joaquín: An epic poem*, New York, Bantam Books, 1972.

Gonzales-Berry, Erlinda (ed.). *Pasó por aquí: Critical Essays on the New Mexican Literary Tradition, 1542–1988*, Albuquerque, University of New Mexico Press, 1989.
  Fifteen essays and a bibliography that provide the most comprehensive historical introduction to New Mexican culture available.

González-T., César A. (ed.). *Rudolfo A. Anaya: Focus on criticism*, La Jolla, Calif., Lalo Press, 1990.
  Contains fifteen articles on Anaya's works, as well as several appendixes

739

(bibliography, interviews, round tables). Most materials had not been published before.

Herrera-Sobek, María (ed.). *Beyond Stereotypes: The critical analysis of Chicana literature*, Binghamton, N.Y., Bilingual Press/Editorial Bilingüe, 1985.
   Six essays about Chicana poets and novelists.

Huerta, Jorge A. *Chicano Theatre: Themes and forms*, Ypsilanti, Mich., Bilingual Press/Editorial Bilingüe, 1982.
   The most complete survey of the genre.

Jiménez, Francisco (ed.). *The Identification and Analysis of Chicano Literature*, Binghamton, N.Y., Bilingual Press/Editorial Bilingüe, 1979.
   A collection of twenty-five critical articles with a bibliography.

Kanellos, Nicolás. *Mexican American Theatre: Legacy and reality*, Pittsburgh, Penn., Latin America Literary Review Press, 1987.
   A collection of seven articles.

A History of Hispanic Theatre in the United States: Origins to 1940, Austin, University of Texas Press, 1990.
   A thorough study of the genre, with abundant graphical documentation.

Lattin, Vernon E. (ed.). *Contemporary Chicano Fiction: A critical survey*, Binghamton, N.Y., Bilingual Press/Editorial Bilingüe, 1986.
   A collection of twenty-six critical studies and a bibliography.

Leal, Luis. *Atzlán y México: perfiles literarios e históricos*, Binghamton, N.Y., Bilingual Press/Editorial Bilingüe, 1985.
   A collection of twenty-three articles on literature and culture.

Lewis, Marvin A. *Introduction to the Chicano Novel*, Milwaukee, University of Wisconsin Spanish Speaking Outreach Institute, 1982.
   A study giving emphasis to the regional variations found in the Chicano novel.

Lomelí, Francisco A., and Donaldo W. Urioste. *Chicano Perspectives in Literature: A critical and annotated bibliography*, Albuquerque, N.M., Pajarito Publications, 1976.
   One of the earliest critical bibliographies, still quoted.

Martín-Rodríguez, Manuel M. *Rolando Hinojosa y su "cronicón" chicano: una novela del lector*, Seville, Universidad de Sevilla Press, 1993.

Martínez, Julio A., and Francisco A. Lomelí (eds.). *Chicano Literature: A reference guide*, Westpoint, Conn., Greenwood Press, 1985.
   An important reference work containing numerous entries written by a large group of Chicano critics. Includes useful bibliographies for each author.

Núñez Cabeza de Vaca, Alvar. *Castaways*, ed. Enrique Pupo-Walker, Berkeley, University of California Press, 1993.
   The first account of the Southwest as experienced by a sixteenth-century *conquistador*.

Olivares, Julián (ed.). *International Studies in Honor of Tomás Rivera*, Houston, Arte Público, 1986.
   Essays on Rivera and other aspects of Chicano literature.

Pérez de Villagrá, Gaspar. *Historia de la Nueva México*, Alaclá, Luis Martínez Grande, 1610; rpt. with intro. by Luis González Obregón, 2 vols., vol. II: *Apéndice de documentos y opúsculos*, Mexico, Museo Nacional de México, 1900.

The conquest of New Mexico in 1598 as told in epic form by one of the explorers.

History of New Mexico, tr. Gilberto Espinosa, Los Angeles, Calif., The Quivira Society, 1933.

Prose translation of Pérez de Villagrá's poem.

Rechy, John. *The Fourth Angel*, Viking, 1972.

Bodies and Souls, Carrol & Graf, 1988.

Marilyn's Daughter, Carrol & Graf, 1988.

The Miraculous Day of Amalia Gómez, Little, Brown & Co., 1991.

Rodríguez del Pino, Salvador. *La novela chicana escrita en español: cinco autores comprometidos*, Ypsilanti, Mich., Bilingual Press/Editorial Bilingüe, 1982.

The novels of Tomás Rivera, Aristeo Brito, Miguel Méndez-M, Alejandro Morales and Rolando Hinojosa-Smith are examined in their cultural context.

Saldívar, José David (ed.). *The Rolando Hinojosa Reader: Essays historical and critical*, Houston Arte Público, 1985.

Contains four essays by Hinojosa, nine studies of his works, and an interview.

Saldívar, Ramón. *Chicano Narrative: The dialectics of difference*, Madison, University of Wisconsin Press, 1990.

An analysis of Chicano prose based on race, class, and gender differences.

Sánchez, Marta Ester. *Contemporary Chicana Poetry: A critical approach to an emerging literature*, Berkeley, University of California Press, 1985.

Analyzes the poetry of Alma Villanueva, Lorna Dee Cervantes, Lucha Corpi, and Bernice Zamora.

Shirley, Carl R., and Paula W. Shirley. *Understanding Chicano Literature*, Columbia, University of South Carolina Press, 1988.

A survey of Chicano literature organized by genres, including a chapter on "Literatura chicanesca," that is, literature about Chicanos written by non-Chicanos. Useful list of suggested readings and bibliographies.

Sommers, Joseph, and Tomás Ybarra-Frausto (eds.). *Modern Chicano Writers*, Englewood Cliffs, N.J., Prentice-Hall, 1979.

Critics have rated this collection of essays on Chicano literature as one of the best in the field.

Tatum, Charles M. *Chicano Literature*, Boston, Twayne, 1982.

A general survey of Chicano literature from its early origins to the beginning of the 1980s.

Trujillo, Roberto G., and Andrés Rodríguez. *Literatura chicana: Creative and critical writings through 1984*, Oakland, Calif., Floricanto Press, 1985.

This is the most complete bibliography of Chicano literature available; listing of seventy-eight works, organized by genres.

Vasallo, Paul (ed.). *The Magic of Words: Rudolfo A. Anaya and his writings*, Albuquerque, University of New Mexico Press, 1982.

Critical essays about Anaya, with an annotated bibliography.

Articles

Campa, Arthur L. "*Los Comanches*, a New Mexico folk drama," *The University of New Mexico Bulletin*, 7:1 (April 1942), 1–43.

Other edition published by Espinosa (see below).

Espinosa, Aurelio M. "*Los Comanches*," *Bulletin University of New Mexico*, 45 (1907), 1–46.

Text and study of eighteenth-century secular folk drama. Other edition published by Campa (see above).

Espinosa, Aurelio M., and Manuel Espinosa. "*The Texans*: a New Mexico folk play of the middle ninetenth century," *The New Mexico Quarterly Review*, 13:3 (Autumn 1943), 299–308.

Text and study of play discovered by Professor Espinosa.

Ortego, Philip D. "Chicano poetry: roots and writers" in his *New Voices in Literature*, Edinburgh, Tex., Pan American University, 1971, 1–7.

One of the earliest studies of Chicano poetry, and still useful.

Volume 3: Brazilian Literature

Chapter 1: The literary historiography of Brazil

Primary sources

Amoroso Lima, Alceu. *Quadro sintético da literatura brasileira*, 2nd edn., Rio de Janeiro, Agir, 1959.

"Introdução à literatura brasileira" in Gilberto Mendonça Teles (ed.), *Tristão de Athayde: teoria, crítica e história literária*, Rio de Janeiro, Livros Técnicos e Científicos Ltda, 1980, 459–521.

Andrade, Mário de. "O movimento modernista" (1942) in his *Aspectos da literatura brasileira*, São Paulo, Livraria Martins Editora, 1974, 231–55.

Azevedo, Fernando de. *A cultura brasileira*, 5th. edn., São Paulo, Edições Melhoramentos, 1971.

Brazilian Culture, tr. William Rex Crawford, New York, Macmillan, 1950.

Bandeira, Manuel. *Noções de história das literaturas*, São Paulo, Companhia Editora Nacional, 1942.

Barbosa, João Alexandre. *A tradição do impasse: linguagem da crítica e crítica da linguagem em José Veríssimo*, São Paulo, Editora Atica, 1974.

Broca, Brito. *A vida literária no Brasil: 1900*, Rio de Janeiro, Ministério da Educação e Cultura, 1956.

Caio Prado, Jr. *Evolução política do Brasil*, São Paulo, Editora Brasiliense, 1932.

Campos, Augusto, and Haroldo de. *Re-visão de Sousândrade*, São Paulo, Edições Invenção, 1964.

Campos, Haroldo de. *O sequestro do barroco na formação da literatura brasileira: o caso Gregório de Mattos*, Salvador, Fundação Casa de Jorge Amado, 1989.

Cândido, Antônio. *Formação da literatura brasileira: momentos decisivos*, vol. I: *1750–1836*; vol. II: *1836–1880*, São Paulo, Livraria Martins Editora, 1959.

"Letras e idéias no período colonial" in his *Literatura e sociedade: estudos de teoria e história literária*, São Paulo, Companhia Editora Nacional, 1965.

"Literatura e cultura de 1900 a 1945 – panorama para estrangeiros" in his *Literatura e sociedade: estudos de teoria e história literária*, São Paulo, Companhia Editora Nacional, 1965.

Carvalho, Ronald de. *Estudos brasileiros*, Rio de Janeiro, Edição do Anuário do Brasil, 1924.

Pequena história da literatura brasileira, 7th edn., Rio de Janeiro, F. Briguiet & Cia., Editores, 1944.

743

César, Guilhermino. *Historiadores e críticos do Romantismo*, I, *A contribuição europeia: crítica e história literária*, Editora da Universidade de São Paulo, 1978.

Coutinho, Afrânio. *Introdução à literatura no Brasil*, Rio de Janeiro, São José, 1964.

A tradição afortunada (o espírito de nacionalidade na crítica brasileira), Rio de Janeiro, Livraria José Olympio Editora, 1968.

An Introduction to Literature in Brazil, tr. Gregory Rabassa, New York, Columbia University Press, 1969.

Coutinho, Afrânio (ed.). *A literatura no Brasil*, 3rd edn., 6 vols., Rio de Janeiro, Livraria José Olympio Editora, 1986.

Cruz Costa, João. *Contribuição à história das ideias no Brasil (O desenvolvimento da filosofia no Brasil e a evolução histórica nacional)*, Rio de Janeiro, Livraria José Olympio Editora, 1956.

Cunha, Euclides da. "Nativismo provisório" in Dermal de Camargo Monfrê (ed.) *Contrastes e confrontos*, Porto, Empresa Litterária e Typographica, 1907, 291–9.

Os sertões, critical edn. Walnice Nogueira Galvão, São Paulo, Editora Brasiliense, 1985.

Rebellion in the Backlands, tr. Samuel Putnam, University of Chicago Press, 1944.

Denis, Ferdinand. *Résumé de l'histoire littéraire du Portugal suivi du résumé de l'histoire littéraire du Brésil*, Paris, Lecointe & Durey, 1826: *O resumo da história literária do Brasil*, Porto Alegre, Editora Lima, 1968.

Fernandes Pinheiro, Joaquim Caetano. *Curso elementar de literatura nacional*, Rio de Janeiro, 1862.

Resumo de história literária, 2 vols., Rio de Janeiro, 1872.

González Echevarría, Roberto. *The Voice of the Masters: Writing and authority in modern Latin American literature*, Austin, University of Texas Press, 1985.

Hauser, Arnold. *The Social History of Art*, III, *Rococo, Classicism and Romanticism*, London, Routledge & Kegan Paul, 1962.

Holanda, Sérgio Buarque de. "Prefácio" (to 1939 edn), in Domingos José Gonçalves de Magalhães, *Suspiros poéticos e saudades*, 5th edn., Editora Universidade de Brasília, 1986, 13–32.

Honório Rodrigues, José. *Vida e história*, Rio de Janeiro, Editora Civilização Brasileira, 1966.

A pesquisa histórica no Brasil, 2nd. edn., São Paulo, Companhia Editora Nacional, 1969.

Kermode, Frank. "Canon and period" in his *History and Value*, Oxford, Clarendon Press, 1989, 108–27.

Leite, Dante Moreira. *O caráter nacional brasileiro: história de uma ideologia*, São Paulo, Livraria Pioneira Editora, 1969.

Lisboa, João Francisco. "Apontamentos para a história do Maranhão" in *Obras de João Francisco Lisboa*, vol. II. *Jornal de Timon*, São Luís, 1864–5.

Lobato, Monteiro. *Urupês*, 26th. edn., São Paulo, Editora Brasiliense, 1982.

Lucas, Fábio. "Literatura e história: história da literatura" in *Revista de Letras* (São Paulo), 22 (1982), 83–98.

Magalhães, Domingos José Gonçalves de. "Ensaio sobre a história da literatura do Brasil," *Niterói, Revista Brasiliense* (1986), vol. I, Biblioteca Nacional, 132–59.

Suspiros poéticos e saudades, 5th. edn. Editora da Universidade de Brasília, 1986.

Mattos Monteiro, Hamilton de. "Da independência à vitória da ordem" in Maria

Yedda Linhares *et al.*, *História geral do Brasil*, Rio de Janeiro, Editora Campus, 1990, 111–30.

"Da República Velha ao Estado Novo – Parte A: O aprofundamento do regionalismo e a crise do modelo liberal," in Maria Yedda Linhares *et al.*, *História geral do Brasil*, Rio de Janeiro, Editora Campus, 1990, 211–28.

Mendonça, Sônia Regina de. "As bases do desenvolvimento capitalista dependente: da industrialização restringida à internacionalização" in Maria Yedda Linhares, *et al.*, *História geral do Brasil*, Rio de Janeiro, Editora Campus, 1990, 243–72.

Mendonça Teles, Gilberto. "Introdução a uma filosofia da história literária," *Revista de Letras de Hoje* (Rio Grande do Sul-PUC), 33 (Sept. 1978), 1–31.

Miguel-Pereira, Lúcia. *Tendências e repercussões literárias do Modernismo, Revista Cultura*, Rio de Janeiro, Ministério da Educação e Saúde, 3 (Dec. 1952), 5.

História da literatura brasileira, vol. XII; *Prosa de ficção: de 1870 a 1920* 3rd. edn., Rio de Janeiro, Livraria José Olympio Editora, 1973.

Oliveira, José Osório de. *História breve da literatura brasileira*, São Paulo, Livraria Martins Editora, 1956.

Paim, Antônio. *História das idéias filosóficas no Brasil*, 2nd. edn., São Paulo, Editora da Universidade de São Paulo/Editorial Grijalbo Ltda., 1974.

Romero, Sílvio. *A América Latina*, Porto, Livraria Chardron, 1906.

História da literatura brasileira, 5th. edn., 5 vols., Rio de Janeiro, Livraria José Olympio Editora, 1953.

Quadro sintético da evolução dos gêneros na literatura brasileira. Rio de Janeiro, 1909.

Romero, Sílvio, and João Ribeiro. *Compêndio de história da literatura brasileira*. 2nd. rev. edn. Rio de Janeiro, Livraria Francisco Alves, 1909.

Salgado Guimarães, Manoel Luiz Lima. "Idéias filosóficas e sociais e estruturas de poder no Segundo Reinado" in Arno Wehling (ed.), *Origens do Instituto Histórico e Geográfico Brasileiro*, Rio de Janeiro, Instituto Histórico e Geográfico Brasileiro, 1989, 21–41.

Sevcenko, Nicolau. *Literatura como missão: tensões sociais e criação cultural na Primeira República*, São Paulo, Editora Brasiliense, 1983.

Sodré, Nelson Werneck. *História da literatura brasileira: seus fundamentos econômicos*, 4th. edn., Rio de Janeiro, Civilização Brasileira, 1964.

Sotero dos Reis, Francisco. *Curso de literatura portuguesa e brasileira*, 5 vols., Maranhão: I–IV, Typografia de B. de Mattos, 1866; V, Typografia de Paiz, 1873.

Varnhagen, Francisco Adolfo (Visconde de Porto Seguro). *História geral do Brasil: antes de sua separação e Independência de Portugal*, 3rd. edn., 5 vols., São Paulo, Companhia Melhoramentos, 1926.

"Ensaio histórico sobre as letras no Brasil" in José Aderaldo Castelo, *Textos que interessam à história do Romantismo*, São Paulo, Conselho Estadual de Cultura, Comissão de Literatura, 1960.

Veríssimo, José. *Estudos brazileiros*, 2nd. series (1889–1893), São Paulo, Laemmert & Co. Editores, 1894.

História da literatura brasileira. Rio de Janeiro, Livraria Francisco Alves, 1916.

Wellek, René. *História da crítica moderna*, 3 vols., São Paulo, Editora Herder, 1967–1971.

Wolf, Ferdinand. *O Brasil literário – história da literatura brasileira*. Translation, preface and notes Jamil Almansur Haddad, São Paulo, Companhia Editora Nacional, 1955.

Secondary sources

Books

The panoramas, anthologies, and histories of period and genre included below are recommended for their selection of texts and clarity of information.

Amora, Antônio Soares. *História da literatura brasileira (séculos XVI a XX)*, São Paulo, Edição Saraiva, 1960.
> Defines questions of origin and identity of Brazilian literature, with special attention to romantic historiography.

Bandeira, Manuel. *Apresentação da poesia brasileira*, Rio de Janeiro, Ed. Casa do Estudante do Brasil, 1946.

Bosi, Alfredo. *História concisa da literatura brasileira*, São Paulo, Cultrix, 1970.
> Extremely clear synthesis, uniting aesthetic and sociological points of view.

Brito, Mário da Silva. *História do modernismo brasileiro*, I: *Antecedentes da Semana de Arte Moderna*, Rio de Janeiro, Civilização Brasileira, 1964.

Broca, Brito. *Vida literária e Romantismo brasileiro*, São Paulo, Livraria e Editora Polis Ltda., 1979.

Broca, Brito, and J. Galante de Sousa. *Introdução ao estudo da literatura brasileira*, Rio de Janeiro, Instituto Nacional do Livro, 1963.

Cândido, Antônio, and J. Aderaldo Castello. *Presença da literatura brasileira*, 3 vols., São Paulo, Difusão Européia do Livro, 1968.

Carpeaux, Otto Maria. *Pequena bibliografia crítica da literatura brasileira*, 3rd. edn., Rio de Janeiro, Editora Letras e Artes, 1964.

Holanda, Sérgio Buarque de. *Antologia dos poetas brasileiros da fase colonial*, Rio de Janeiro, INL, 1952.
> *A literatura brasileira*, I: Castello, José Aderaldo. *Manifestações literárias da era colonial* (1965), II: Amora, Antônio Soares. *O romantismo* (1966); III: Pacheco, João. *O realismo* (1963); IV: Moisés, Massaud. *O simbolismo* (1966); V: Bosi, Alfredo. *O pré-modernismo* (1966); VI: Martins, Wilson. *O modernismo* (1967), São Paulo, Editora Cultrix.

Leite, Dante Moreira. *O caráter nacional brasileiro*, 3rd. edn. São Paulo, Livraria Pioneira Editora, 1976.

Martins, Wilson. *História da inteligência brasileira*, 7 vols., São Paulo, Cultrix, 1976–1979.
> *A crítica literária no Brasil*, 2 vols., Rio de Janeiro, Francisco Alves, 1983.

Merquior, José Guilherme. *De Anchieta a Euclides: breve história da literatura brasileira*, I, Rio de Janeiro, Livraria José Olympio Editora, 1977.
> Penetrating essay as an aesthetic re-reading of Brazilian literature up to the impressionist phase.

Moisés, Massaud. *História da literatura brasileira*, I: *Origens, Barroco, Arcadismo;* II: *Romantismo, realismo;* III: *Simbolismo;* IV: *Modernismo (1922-atualidade)*, São Paulo, Cultrix, 1985–1989.
> Up-to-date, with a rich bibliography reaching into Postmodernism.

Moog, Vianna. *Uma interpretação da literatura brasileira, um arquipélago cultural*, Rio de Janeiro, CEB, 1942.
  A study of regionalization in literary history.
Muricy, Andrade. *Panorama do movimento simbolista brasileiro*, 2 vols., Rio de Janeiro, Instituto Nacional do Livro, 1973.
Ortiz, Renato. *Cultura brasileira e identidade nacional*, São Paulo, Editora Brasiliense, 1985.
Picchio, Luciana Stegagno. *La letteratura brasiliana*, Milano, Sansori Academia, 1972.
  Splendid overall view up to 1970, with sections on criticism and historiography.
Putnam, Samuel. *Marvelous Journey: A survey of four centuries of Brazilian literature*, New York, Knopf, 1948.
  A pioneering study in English.
Sodré, Nelson Werneck. *A ideologia do colonialismo (seus reflexos no pensamento brasileiro)*, Rio de Janeiro, Instituto Superior de Estudos Brasileiros, 1961.
Sousa, J. Galante de. *O teatro no Brasil*, 2 vols., Rio de Janeiro, MEC/INL, 1960.

Articles

Barbosa, João Alexandre. "História da literatura e literatura brasileira" in *Anais do Segundo Congresso Brasileiro de Crítica e História Literária*, São Paulo, Faculdade de Filosofia, Ciências e Letras de Assis, 1963, 159–79.
  For a knowledge of historiographical sources, of literary bibliography, of the general movement of ideas, including criticism and historiography.
Cândido, Antônio. "Literatura y subdesarrollo" in *América Latina en su literatura*, intro. César Fernández Moreno, Mexico, Siglo Veintiuno Editores/UNESCO, 1972, 335–44.
  "Una palabra inestable," *Escritura, Teoría y Crítica Literaria* (Caracas) Año 14:27, 1989, 31–9.
Lucas, Fábio. "O Romantismo e a fundação da nacionalidade" in his *Do Barroco ao Moderno*, São Paulo, Editora Atica, 1989.

Chapter 2: Colonial Brazilian literature

Primary sources

Alvarenga Peixoto, Inácio José de. *Obras poéticas*, Rio de Janeiro, Garnier, 1865.
Anchieta, José de. *Arte de gramática da língua mais usada na costa do Brasil*, Coimbra, Antônio de Mariz, 1595.
  De Beata Virgine Dei Matre Maria in Simão de Vasconcelos, *Crônica da companhia de Jesus*, Lisbon, Valente de Oliveira, 1663.
  Cartas, informações, fragmentos históricos e sermões, Rio de Janeiro, Civilização Brasileira, 1933.
  Poesias, São Paulo, Museu Paulista, 1954.
  De gestis Mendi de Saa, Rio de Janeiro, Arquivo Nacional, 1958.
  Teatro, São Paulo, Edições Loyola, 1977.
Botelho de Oliveira, Manuel. *Música do Parnasso*, Lisbon, Miguel Manescal, 1705.

Brandão, Ambrósio Fernandes. *Diálogos das grandezas do Brasil*, Rio de Janeiro, Oficina Industrial Gráfica, 1930.
Dialogues of the Great Things of Brazil, tr. and ed. F. H. Hall, W. F. Harrison, and D. W. Welker, Albuquerque, University of New Mexico Press, 1987.
Caldas Barbosa, Domingos. *Viola de Lereno*, vol. I, Lisbon, Nunesiana, 1798.
Viola de Lereno, vol. II, Lisbon, Lacerdina, 1826.
Viola de Lereno, Rio de Janeiro, Civilização Brasileira, 1980.
Caminha, Pero Vaz de. "Carta do descobrimento do Brasil" in Manuel Aires do Casal, *Corografia brasílica*, Rio de Janeiro, Impressão Régia, 1817, 12–34.
"The discovery of Brazil" in *Portuguese Voyages, 1498–1663*, tr. and ed. C. D. Ley, London, Dent, 1947, 40–59.
Cardim, Fernão. *Tratados da terra e gente do Brasil*, Rio de Janeiro, J. Leite, 1925.
Costa, Cláudio Manuel da. *Orbas (sic)*, Coimbra, Ferreira, 1768.
Durão, José de Santa Rita. *Caramuru*, Lisbon, Régia Oficina Tipográfica, 1779; Rio de Janeiro, Agir, 1961.
Eça, Matias Aires Ramos da Silva de. *Reflexões sobre a vaidade dos homens*, Lisbon, Francisco Ameno, 1752.
Gama, José Basílio da. *O Uraguai*, Lisbon, Régia Oficina Tipográfica, 1769.
The Uruguay, tr. Sir Richard Burton, ed. Frederick C. H. Garcia and Edward F. Stanton, Berkeley, University of California Press, 1982.
Gonzaga, Tomás Antônio. *Marília de Dirceu*, Lisbon, Nunesiana, 1792; São Paulo, Livraria Martins Editora, 1972.
Léry, Jean de. *Histoire d'un voyage fait en la terre du Brésil*, La Rochelle, Antoine Chuppin, 1578.
Madre de Deus, Gaspar da. *Memórias para a história da capitania de São Vicente, hoje província de São Paulo*, Lisbon, Tipografia da Academia, 1797.
Magalhães Gândavo, Pero de. *História da província de Santa Cruz a que vulgarmente chamamos Brasil*, Lisbon, Antônio Gonçalves, 1576.
Tratado da terra do Brasil, Lisbon, Academia Real das Ciências, 1827.
The Histories of Brazil, tr. and ed. John B. Stetson, with facsimile of 1576 edition, New York, The Cortes Society, 1922.
Marques Pereira, Nuno. *Compêndio narrativo do peregrino da América*, part I, Lisbon, Manuel Fernandes da Costa, 1728; the second part was first published in 1939 (Rio de Janeiro, Academia Brasileira de Letras).
Matos, Gregório de. *Obras poéticas*, vol. I, Rio de Janeiro, Tip. Nacional, 1882.
Obras, ed. Afrânio Peixoto, 7 vols., Rio de Janeiro, Academia Brasileira de Letras, 1923–1933.
Obras completas: crônica do viver baiano seiscentista, ed. James Amado, Bahia, Janaína, 1969.
Natividade Saldanha, José da. *Poesias oferecidas aos amantes do Brasil*, Coimbra, Imprensa da Universidade, 1822.
Nóbrega, Manuel da. *Cartas do Brasil*, Rio de Janeiro, Imprensa Nacional, 1886.
Diálogo sobre a conversão do gentio, Lisbon, Comissão do IV Centenário, 1954.
Cartas do Brasil e mais escritos, ed. Serafim Leite, Coimbra, Universidade de Coimbra, 1955.
Orta, Teresa Margarida da Silva e. *Máximas de virtude e formosura* (after this first edition entitled *Aventuras de Diófanes*), Lisbon, Miguel Manescal, 1752.

Volume 3

Otôni, José Elói. *Paráfrase dos Provérbios de Salomão em verso português*, Bahia, Manuel Antônio da Silva Serva, 1815.

Rocha Pita, Sebastião da. *História da América portuguesa*, Lisbon, José Antônio da Silva, 1730.

Salvador, Frei Vicente do. *História do Brasil*, Rio de Janeiro, Leuzinger, 1889.

São Carlos, Francisco de. *A Assunção da Santíssima Virgem*, Rio de Janeiro, Tip. Régia, 1819.

Silva, Antônio José da. *Teatro cômico português*, 2 vols., Lisbon, Oficina Silviana, 1744.

Silva Alvarenga, Manuel Inácio da. *Glaura: poemas eróticos*, Lisbon, Nunesiana, 1799.

Soares de Sousa, Gabriel. *Tratado descritivo do Brasil em 1587*, Rio de Janeiro, Laemmert, 1851.

Sousa Caldas, Antônio Pereira de. *Psalmos de David*, Paris, P. N. Rougeron, 1820.

Staden, Hans. *Warhaftige Historia und beschreibung einer Landtschafft der Wilden, Nacketen, Grimmigen, Menschenfresser Leuthen, in der Newenwelt America gelegen*, Marburg, A. Kolben, 1557.

The True History of his Captivity, tr. and ed. Malcolm Letts, London, George Routledge & Sons, 1928.

Teixeira, Bento. *Prosopopéia*, Lisbon, Antônio Álvares, 1601.

Thévet, André. *Les singularités de la France Antartique autrement nommée Amérique*, Paris, Maurice de la Porte, 1557.

The New Found World, or Antarctike, probably tr. Thomas Hacket, London, Thomas Hacket, 1568.

Vieira, Antônio. *Cartas*, 3 vols., Lisbon, Oficina da Congregação do Oratório, 1735–1746.

Sermões, 16 vols., Lisbon, João da Costa and others, 1679–1748.

Sermões, 15 vols. in 5, Oporto, Lello, 1959.

Secondary sources

Books

Alves, Luiz Roberto. *Confissão, poesia e Inquisição*, São Paulo, Editora Atica, 1983.
  Best study to date of life of Bento Teixeira, using Inquisition documents.

Borba de Moraes, Rubens. *Bibliografia brasileira do período colonial*, São Paulo, Instituto de Estudos Brasileiros, 1969.
  Indispensable and utterly reliable.

Bosi, Alfredo. *História concisa da literatura brasileira*, São Paulo, Cultrix, 1970.
  Excellent summary and analysis, particularly of seventeenth century.

Boxer, Charles Ralph. *A Great Luso-Brazilian Figure: Padre Antônio Vieira*, London, Hispanic and Luso-Brazilian Councils, 1957.
  Good brief summary of life and work, in English; includes some translations.

Cândido, Antônio. *Formação da literatura brasileira*, 5th edn., vol. I, Editora da Universidade de São Paulo, 1975.
  The best and most complete study of the period.

Cantel, Raymond. *Les sermons de Vieira: étude du style*, Paris, Ed. Hispano-

Americanas, 1959.

Prophétisme et messianisme dans l'oeuvre d'Antônio Vieira, Paris, Ed. Hispano-Americanas, 1960.

Both of Cantel's books are solidly researched and critically innovative.

Castello, José Aderaldo. *Manifestações literárias do Brasil colonial*, 3rd. edn., São Paulo, Cultrix, 1972.

An excellent summary, particularly strong on the academic movement.

Cidade, Hernani. *Padre Antônio Vieira*, 4 vols., Lisbon, Agência Geral das Colônias, 1940.

A good modern biographical account, with sound critical assessments.

Cortesão, Jaime. *A Carta de Pêro Vaz de Caminha*, Lisbon, Portugália, 1967.

Contains a facsimile of the manuscript, a diplomatic edition, and a historical study.

Coutinho, Afrânio (ed.). *A literatura no Brasil*, vol. I, part I, Rio de Janeiro, Editorial Sul Americana, 1955.

A collection of generally excellent critical articles, by various scholars, on individual movements and authors.

Driver, David Miller. *The Indian in Brazilian Literature*, New York, The Hispanic Institute, 1942.

A pioneering work in English, now considerably dated.

Franco, Afonso Arinos de Melo. *O índio brasileiro e a revolução francesa*, Rio de Janeiro, INL, 1937.

Early but first-rate study of influence of Thévet and Léry, among others, on eighteenth-century French ideas.

Galante de Sousa, José. *Em tôrno do poeta Bento Teixeira*, São Paulo, Instituto de Estudos Brasileiros, 1972.

Careful study, with emphasis on bibliographical questions.

Gomes, João Carlos Teixeira. *Gregório de Matos, O boca de brasa*, Petrópolis, Vozes, 1985.

Excellent study of poet's life and work.

Holanda, Sérgio Buarque de. *Visão do Paraíso: os motivos edênicos no descobrimento e colonização do Brasil*, Rio de Janeiro, Livraria José Olympio Editora, 1959.

Still an original and provocative study of the Eden theme.

Jucá Filho, Cândido. *Antônio José, O Judeu*, Rio de Janeiro, Editora Civilização Brasileira, 1940.

Early effort to reclaim da Silva as a Brazilian.

Martins, Wilson. *História da inteligência brasileira*, 2nd. edn., vol. I, São Paulo, Cultrix, 1977.

A massive account of the period, with enormously useful details but less critical commentary than Cândido's *Formação*.

Merquior, José Guilherme. *De Anchieta a Euclides*, Rio de Janeiro, Livraria José Olympio Editora, 1977.

Innovative summary and analysis by a leading modern critic.

Oliveira, Almir de. *Gonzaga e a Inconfidência mineira*, 2nd edn., Belo Horizonte, Itatiaia, 1985.

Best historical and biographical study to date.

Oliveira Lima, Manuel de. *Aspectos da literatura colonial brasileira*, Leipzig,

Brockhaus, 1896.

Marred by the author's nineteenth-century "scientific" racism, but still one of the most influential accounts of the period.

Pereira, Carlos de Assis. *Fontes do "Caramuru" de Santa Rita Durão*, Assis, Brazil, Faculdade de Filosofia, Ciências e Letras, 1971.

Useful, comprehensive study of Durão's sources.

Peres, Fernando da Rocha. *Gregório de Matos e Guerra: uma re-visão biográfica*, Salvador, Ed. Macunaíma, 1983.

Painstaking archival research greatly revises our view of the poet's life. Brief but very well-considered discussion of his poetry and its purpose.

Putnam, Samuel. *Marvelous Journey: A survey of four centuries of Brazilian literature*, New York, Knopf, 1948.

Remarkably detailed summary in English, with interesting comparative remarks on North American literature.

Romero, Sílvio. *História da literatura brasileira*, 3rd. edn. 5 vols. Rio de Janeiro, Livraria José Olympio Editora, 1943.

Very useful, with information not found elsewhere, but Romero is consistently tendentious and occasionally very wrong-headed.

Sayers, Raymond S. *The Negro in Brazilian Literature*, New York, The Hispanic Institute, 1956.

Still the best, most thorough study of the topic for the colonial period.

Sousa, Ronald W. *The Rediscoverers*, University Park, Pennsylvania State University Press, 1981.

Excellent study of Vieira, pp. 46–75.

Unali, Anna. *La "Carta do Achamento" di Pero Vaz de Caminha*, Milan, Cisalpino-Goliardica, 1984.

Excellent facsimile, more readable than that found in Cortesão, *A Carta*; solid edition and commentary.

Van den Besselaar, José. *Antônio Vieira: o homem, a obra, as idéias*, Lisbon, Ministério da Educação e Ciência, 1981.

Useful summary of life and work.

Veríssimo, José. *História da literatura brasileira*, 5th. edn., Rio de Janeiro, Livraria José Olympio Editora; (first edition Rio de Janeiro, Livraria Francisco Alves, 1916), 1969.

Less inclusive than Romero's *História*, but more reliable.

Vilanova, José Brasileiro. *A literatura no Brasil colonial*, Recife, Universidade Federal de Pernambuco, 1977.

One of the best relatively brief summations of the period.

Articles

Cândido, Antônio. "A dois séculos d'O Uraguai" in his *Vários escritos*, São Paulo, Duas Cidades, 1970, 161–82.

Excellent analysis of poem and its influence.

Fernández, Oscar. "José de Anchieta and early theatre activity in Brazil," *Luso-Brazilian Review*, 15:1, 1978, 26–43.

Good account in English of the Jesuit plays.

Helena, Lúcia. "Gonzaga, a lira e o poder" in her *Escrita e poder*, Rio de Janeiro, Cátedra, 1985, 15–29.
  Relationship between poetry and political ideas.
Malinoff-Kamide, Jane. "Domingos Caldas Barbosa: Afro-Brazilian poet at the court of D. Maria I" in B. H. Bichakjian (ed.), *From Linguistics to Literature*, Amsterdam, John Benjamins, 1981, 196–203.
  Good brief account in English, with emphasis on African musical influences.
Preto-Rodas, Richard. "Anchieta and Vieira: drama as sermon, sermon as drama," *Luso-Brazilian Review*, 7:2, 1970, 96–103.
  Interesting linkage of these two major figures.
Sousa, Ronald W. "The divided discourse of *As Aventuras de Diófanes* and its socio-historical implications" in Sousa (ed.), *Problems of Enlightenment in Portugal*, Minneapolis, Institute for the Study of Ideologies and Literatures, 1984, 75–88.
  Innovative and fascinating study of Teresa Margarida da Silva e Orta.
Sturm, Fred. G. " 'Estes têm alma como nós?': Manuel de Nóbrega's view of the Brazilian Indians" in Alfred Hower and Richard Preto-Rodas (eds.), *Empire in Transition: The Portuguese world in the time of Camões*, Gainesville, University Presses of Florida, 1985, 72–82.
  Analysis of the *Diálogo sobre a conversão do gentio*.

Chapter 3: Brazilian poetry from the 1830s to the 1880s

Primary sources

Abreu, Casimiro José Marques de. *Primaveras*, Rio de Janeiro, Tip. Paula Brito, 1859.
Alves, Antônio Frederico de Castro. *Espumas flutuantes*, Bahia, Camilo Lellis Masson, 1870.
  Gonzaga ou a revolução de Minas, Rio de Janeiro, Cruz Coutinho, 1875 (posthumous).
  A cachoeira de Paulo Afonso, Bahia, Imprensa Econômica, 1876 (posthumous).
  Vozes d'Africa, Rio de Janeiro, S. I. Alves, 1880 (posthumous).
  Os escravos, Rio de Janeiro, S. I. Alves, 1883 (posthumous).
Azevedo, Manuel Antônio Álvares de. *Poesias (lira dos vinte anos)*, Rio de Janeiro, Tip. Americana, 1853.
  Obras, Rio de Janeiro, Laemmert, 1855 (posthumous).
  Conde Lopo, Rio de Janeiro, Leuzinger, 1886 (posthumous).
Barreto de Meneses, Tobias. *Dias e noites*, Rio de Janeiro, Imprensa Industrial, 1893 (posthumous).
Fagundes Varela, Luís Nicolau. *Noturnas*, São Paulo, Azevedo Marques, 1861.
  O estandarte auriverde, São Paulo, Azevedo Marques, 1863.
  Vozes da América, São Paulo, Azevedo Marques, 1864.
  Cantos e fantasias, São Paulo, Garraux, 1865.
  Cantos do ermo e da cidade, Rio de Janeiro, Garnier, 1869.
  Cantos meridionais, Rio de Janeiro, Laemmert, 1869.
  Anchieta ou o evangelho nas selvas, Rio de Janeiro, Liv. Imperial de E. G. Possolo, 1975.

Gonçalves de Magalhães, Domingos José. *Suspiros poéticos e saudades*, Paris, Mausot, 1836.

A confederação dos tamoios, Rio de Janeiro, Tip. Paula Brito, 1856.

Guimarães, Bernardo Joaquim da Silva. *Cantos da solidão*, São Paulo, Tip. Liberal, 1852.

Poesias, Rio de Janeiro, Garnier, 1865.

Novas poesias, Rio de Janeiro, Garnier, 1876.

Folhas de outono, Rio de Janeiro, Garnier, 1886.

Junqueira Freire, Luís José. *Inspirações do claustro*, Bahia, Camillo Lellis Masson, 1855.

Obras poéticas, Rio de Janeiro, Garnier, 2 vols., n.d.

Lessa, Aureliano José. *Poesias póstumas*, Rio de Janeiro, Tip. A Luz, 1873.

Porto Alegre, Manuel José de Araújo. *Colombo*, Vienna, Rio de Janeiro, Garnier, 1866.

Rabelo, Laurindo José da Silva. *Trovas*, Bahia, 1853.

Sousândrade, Joaquim de; consult Augusto and Haroldo de Campos, *Re-visão de Sousândrade*.

Inéditos, compiled by Frederick G. Williams & Jomar Moraes, São Luís, Departamento de Cultura do Estado, 1970.

Secondary sources

In order to get an all-encompassing perspective of the romantic movement it is important to consult the principle histories of Brazilian literature. The most important ones have therefore been included in the list of secondary sources.

Amora, Antônio Soares. *A literatura brasileira*, 5th. edn., vol. II: *O Romantismo*, São Paulo, Cultrix, 1977.

Synthesis of poetry and prose between 1833 and 1881. Omits poets such as Bernardo Guimarães and Sousândrade.

Andrade, Mário de. *Aspectos da literatura brasileira*, São Paulo, Americ-Edit, 1943.

Revealing essay about Castro Alves.

O Aleijadinho e Alvares de Azevedo, Rio de Janeiro, Ed. Revista Acadêmica, 1946.

Good study of treatment of love and fear by romantic writers.

Bandeira, Manuel. *Apresentação da poesia brasileira*, Rio de Janeiro, Ed. Casa do Estudante do Brasil, 1946.

Anthology accompanied by good synthesis.

Campos, Augusto and Haroldo de, *Re-visão de Sousândrade*, São Paulo, Edições Invenção, 1964.

Carpeaux, Otto Maria. *Pequena bibliografia crítica da literatura brasileira*, Rio de Janeiro, Ministério da Educação e Cultura, 1951.

Pioneer of bibliographic methodology. There are omissions.

Carvalho, Ronald de. *Pequena história da literatura brasileira*, Rio de Janeiro, Briguiet, 1919.

Aesthetician, irregular. Academic prose. Exaggerates indication of physical determinism.

Castello, José Aderaldo. *Textos que interessam à historia do romantismo*, São Paulo, Conselho Estadual de Cultura, 1961.

Documents giving special attention to José Bonifácio de Andrada e Silva, João Salomé Queiroga, Francisco Adolfo de Varnhagen, Manuel Antônio Alvares de Azevedo, Luís Nicolau Fagundes Varela, and Bernardo Joaquim da Silva Guimarães.

Cesár, Guilhermino. *Historiadores e críticos do romantismo*, Editora da Universidade de São Paulo, 1978.

Presents the European contribution to the study of Brazilian Romanticism: Friedrich Bouterwek, Simonde de Sismondi, Ferdinand Denis, Almeida Garrett, C. Schlichthorst, José da Gama e Castro, Alexandre Herculano, and Ferdinand Wolf.

Coutinho, Afrânio (ed.). *A literatura no Brasil*, Rio de Janeiro, Editorial Sul América, vol. I, tome 2, "Romantismo," 1956.

Tried to present the history of Brazilian literature from just one perspective, that of intrinsic analysis. Irregular, but useful.

Cunha, Fausto. *O romantismo no Brasil*, Rio de Janeiro, Paz e Terra, 1971.

Comparative analysis of the poets and the study of influences.

Lopes, Hélio. *A divisão das águas*, São Paulo, Secretaria da Cultura, Ciência e Tecnologia, 1978.

Contributes to the study of romantic journals: *Minerva Brasiliense* (1843–1845) and *Guanabara* (1849–1856).

Moisés, Massaud. *História da literatura brasileira*, vol. II: *Romantismo/Realismo*, São Paulo, Cultrix/EDUSP, 1984.

Lucid and detailed presentation of Romanticism. Didactic, informative.

Ramos, Péricles Eugênio da Silva. *Do barroco ao modernismo*, São Paulo, Secretaria da Cultura do Estado, 1979.

A study of the phonic, morpho-syntactical, and stylistic occurrences in such poets as Gonçalves Dias, Castro Alves, Alvares de Azevedo, Sousândrade, and Fagundes Varela.

Ricardo, Cassiano. *O indianismo de Gonçalves Dias*, São Paulo, Conselho Estadual de Cultura, 1964.

Important analysis of Indianism, written expressly for the centennial commemoration of the death of Gonçalves Dias.

Romero, Sílvio. *História da literatura brasileira*, Rio de Janeiro, Garnier, 1888.

Hasty critical judgments. Full of information. Exaggerated appreciation of Tobias Barreto as a poet.

Veríssimo, José. *História da literatura brasileira*, Rio de Janeiro, Livraria Francisco Alves, 1916.

Balanced judgments, very seldom wrong. Considers Bernardo Guimarães a "minor poet." Omits Sousândrade.

Chapter 4: Brazilian poetry from 1878 to 1902

Primary sources

Bilac, Olavo Brás Martins dos Guimarães. *Poesias* [1884–1887], São Paulo, Teixeira & Irmão, 1888 (contains *Panóplias*, *Via láctea*, *Sarças de fogo*); Rio de Janeiro and Paris, Garnier, 1902 (definitive edn., containing, in addition to the previously

mentioned works, *Alma inquieta, As viagens, O caçador de esmeraldas*); Rio de Janeiro, Francisco Alves, 1921 (containing the two previous books).
Sagres, Rio de Janeiro, Jornal do Comércio, 1898.
Tarde, Rio de Janeiro, Francisco Alves, 1919.
Carvalho, Vicente de. *Ardentias*, Santos, Diário de Santos, 1888.
Rosa, Rosa de amor, Rio de Janeiro, Laemmert & Co., 1902.
Poemas e canções, São Paulo, Cardozo, Filho & Co., 1908.
Versos da mocidade, Oporto, Livraria Chardron, 1912.
    Contains his first two books and *Avulsas*.
A voz do sino, São Paulo, Editora A Cigarra, n.d. [1916].
Correia, Raimundo. *Primeiros sonhos*, São Paulo, Tribuna Liberal, 1879.
Sinfonias, Rio de Janeiro, Livraria Editora de Faro & Lino, 1883.
Versos e versões [1883–1886], Rio de Janeiro, Moreira Maximino & Co., 1887.
Aleluias [1888–1890], Rio de Janeiro, Cia. Editora Fluminense, 1891.
Poesias, Lisbon, Parceria António Maria Pereira, 1898.
Poesia completa e prosa, Rio de Janeiro, Aguilar, 1961.
Cruz e Sousa, João da. *Tropos e fantasias*, in partnership with Virgílio Várzea, Desterro, Regeneração, 1885.
Broquéis, Rio de Janeiro, Magalhães & Co., 1893.
Missal, Rio de Janeiro, Magalhães & Co., 1893.
Faróis, Rio de Janeiro, Instituto Profissional, 1900.
Evocações, Rio de Janeiro, Aldina, 1898.
Ultimos sonetos, Paris, Aillaud & Co., 1905.
Obra completa, Rio de Janeiro, Aguilar, 1961.
Guimaraens, Alphonsus de. *Setenário das dores da Nossa Senhora* and *Câmara ardente*, Rio de Janeiro, Leuzinger, 1899.
Dona mística, Rio de Janeiro, Leuzinger, 1899.
Kyriale, Oporto, Tip. Universal de António Figueirinhas, 1902.
Pauvre lyre, Ouro Preto, Editora Mineira, 1921.
Pastoral aos crentes do amor e da morte, São Paulo, Monteiro Lobato, 1923.
Poesias, Rio de Janeiro, Ministério da Educação, 1938.
    Contains all the previous books.
Obra completa, Rio de Janeiro, Aguilar, 1960.
Oliveira, Alberto de. *Canções românticas* [1877–1878], Rio de Janeiro, Gazeta de Notícias, 1878.
Meridionais, Rio de Janeiro, Gazeta de Notícias, 1884.
Sonetos e poemas, Rio de Janeiro, Moreira Maximino & Co., 1885.
Versos e rimas, Rio de Janeiro, L'Etoile du Sud, 1895.
Poesias completas, Rio de Janeiro, Garnier, 1900.
    Reunites all previous books, except for his first one; also includes *Por amor de uma lágrima* and *Livro de Ema*.
Poesias, 2nd. series, Rio de Janeiro, Garnier, 1905.
    Contains *Alma livre, Terra natal, Alma em flor, Flores da serra*, and *Versos de saudade*.
Poesias [1877–1895], 1st. series, rev. edn., Rio de Janeiro, Garnier, 1912.
    Contains *Canções românticas, Meridionais, Sonetos e poemas, Versos e rimas, Por amor de uma lágrima*.

Poesias, 2nd. series, rev. edn. [1892–1903], Rio de Janeiro, Garnier, 1912.
Contains *Livro de Ema, Alma livre, Terra natal, Alma em flor, Flores da serra, Versos de saudade.*

Poesias, 3rd. series [1904–1911], Rio de Janeiro, Francisco Alves, 1913.
Contains *Sol de verão, Céu noturno, Alma das coisas, Sala de baile, Rimas várias, No seio do cosmos, Natália.*

Ramo de árvore, Rio de Janeiro, Anuário do Brasil, 1922.

Poesias, 4th. series, Rio de Janeiro, Francisco Alves, 1927.
Contains *Ode cívica, Alma e céu, Cheiro de flor, Ruínas que falam, Câmara ardente,* and *Ramo de árvore.*

Póstuma, Rio de Janeiro, Publicações da Academia Brasileira de Letras, 1944.

Secondary sources

Books

Araripe Jr., Tristão de Alencar. *Literatura brasileira. Movimento de 1893. O crepúsculo dos povos*, Rio de Janeiro, Empresa Democrática, 1896.
Classic study dealing with Symbolism, contemporaneous with the movement.

Azevedo, Octávio d'. *Vicente de Carvalho e os Poemas e canções*, Rio de Janeiro, Livraria José Olympio Editora, 1970.
"Impressionistic" study of the principal themes, technique, and language of the poet.

Bandeira, Manuel. *Antologia dos poetas brasileiros da fase parnasiana*, 3rd. edn., Rio de Janeiro, INL, 1951.
Valuable anthology due to the introduction and to the rigorous selection of texts.

Carollo, Cassiana Lacerda (ed.). *Decadismo e simbolismo no Brasil. Crítica e poesia*, 2 vols., Rio de Janeiro and Brasilia, Livros Técnicos e Científicos and INL, 1980–1981.
Broad and useful collection of doctrinal and critical texts, in prose and verse.

Carvalho, Afonso de. *Bilac: o homem, o poeta, o patriota*, Rio de Janeiro, Livraria José Olympio Editora, 1942.
Long, laudatory study, well-documented in terms of poetry and biography, enhanced by the civic campaigns of the author, written by a follower of Parnassianism.

Carvalho, Maria da Conceição Vicente de, and Arnaldo Vicente de Carvalho. *Vicente de Carvalho*, Rio de Janeiro, Publicações da Academia Brasileira de Letras, 1943.
Study of the author's bibliography, little critical awareness.

Coutinho, Afrânio (ed.). *Cruz e Sousa*, Rio de Janeiro, Civilização Brasileira, 1979.
Collection reuniting some of the best essays dealing with the work of Cruz e Sousa.

Góes, Fernando. *Panorama da poesia brasileira*, vol. IV: *O simbolismo*, Rio de Janeiro, Civilização Brasileira, 1959.
Anthology, useful due to bibliographical notes and introductory essay.

Haberly, David T. *Three Sad Races: Racial identity and national consciousness in Brazilian literature*, Cambridge University Press, 1983.

Volume 3

Jorge, Fernando. *Vida e poesia de Olavo Bilac*, 2nd. edn., revised and augmented, São Paulo and Rio de Janeiro, Edições Mundo Musical, 1972.
  Biography reviewed with insight; 1st. edn. (1963) provoked controversy.
Lima, Alceu Amoroso. *Poesia brasileira contemporânea*, Belo Horizonte, Livraria Editora Paulo Bluhm, 1941, 49–78.
  Study of the criticism of Guimaraens.
Lisboa, Henriqueta. *Alphonsus de Guimaraens*, Rio de Janeiro, AGIR, 1945.
  Brief but penetrating study.
Magalhães, Raimundo, Jr. *Poesia e vida de Cruz e Sousa*, São Paulo, Edameris, 1961.
  Study of the life and work of the poet, with original information and commentary.
Muricy, José Cândido de Andrade. *Panorama do movimento simbolista brasileiro*, 2nd. edn., 2 vols., Brasilia, INL, 1973.
  Indispensable source for the study of symbolist poetry.
Pacheco, João. *A literatura brasileira*, vol. III: *O realismo*, 4th. edn., São Paulo, Cultrix, 1971.
  Contains useful monographic studies of Parnassian poets.
Pontes, Elói. *A vida exuberante de Olavo Bilac*, 2 vols., Rio de Janeiro, Livraria José Olympio Editora, 1944.
  The most exhaustive biography of the poet, unfortunately without rigorous critical documentation.
Ramos, Péricles Eugênio da Silva. *Poesia simbolista: antologia*, São Paulo, Edições Melhoramentos, 1967.
  Anthology with the same degree of quality as Ramos's *Poesia parnasiana*.
Resende, Enrique de. *Retrato de Alphonsus de Guimaraens*, Rio de Janeiro, Livraria José Olympio Editora, 1938.
  Critical and biographical study, objective, but also laudatory.
Sequeira, F. M. B. de. *Raimundo Correia*, Rio de Janeiro, Publicações da Academia Brasileira de Letras, 1942.
  Study of the bibliography and life of the author, with insightful criticisms. Transcribes documents pertaining to the author.
Serpa, Phocion. *Alberto de Oliveira*, Rio de Janeiro, Livraria São José, 1957.
  One of the most informed works dealing with the author's life and work.
Torres, Artur de Almeida. *Cruz e Sousa (aspectos estilísticos)*, Rio de Janeiro, Livraria São José, 1975.
  Linguistic study, covering the principal stylistic aspects of Cruz e Sousa.
Val, Waldir Ribeiro do. *Vida e obra de Raimundo Correia*, Rio de Janeiro, INL, 1960.
  Indispensable.
Vieira, Hermes. *Vicente de Carvalho, o sabiá da Ilha do Sol*, 2nd. edn., São Paulo, Revista dos Tribunais, 1943.
  Study of the life and work of the author.
Vítor, Nestor. *Cruz e Sousa*, Rio de Janeiro, n.p. 1899.
  Study made by a contemporary and friend of the poet, still valid and useful.

Articles

Bandeira, Manuel. "Raimundo Correia e o seu sortilégio verbal," preface to

Raimundo Correia, *Poesia completa e prosa*, Rio de Janeiro, Aguilar, 1961, 13–32.
> Study of the poetic trajectory of Raimundo Correia, with the critical acuteness we have come to expect of Manuel Bandeira.

Bastide, Roger. "Quatro estudos sobre Cruz e Sousa" in his *A poesia afro-brasileira*, São Paulo, Livraria Martins Editora, 1943, 87–128.
> Sociological study, high level of understanding and interpretation.

Campos, Geir. "Apresentação" to Alberto de Oliveira, *Poesia*, Nossos Clássicos, 32, Rio de Janeiro, AGIR, 1959, 6–13.
> Brief and objective study.

Cunha, Euclides da. "Prefácio" to Vicente de Carvalho, *Poemas e canções*, São Paulo, Cardozo, Filho & Co., 1908, 1–11.
> Brief but astute study, done by a well-known contemporary.

Cunha, Fausto. "Apresentação" to Vicente de Carvalho, *Poesia*, Nossos Clássicos, 81, Rio de Janeiro, AGIR, 1965, 8–30.
> One of the best studies on the poet, contains controversial observations, softened in the second and revised edition (1977).

Gomes, Eugênio. "Alberto de Oliveira," "Alberto de Oliveira e o simbolismo" in his *Visões e revisões*, Rio de Janeiro, INL, 1958, 87–100.
> Two studies dealing with the sensuality and Symbolism of the author.

"Raimundo Correia e o idealismo horaciano" in his *Visões e revisões*, Rio de Janeiro, INL, 1958, 111–18.
> Brief, but suggestive, study dealing with the Arcadic and Horatian reminiscences in the work of Correia.

"Uma fonte de Bilac," "Ouvir estrelas," "Outras fontes de Bilac" in his *Visões e revisões*, Rio de Janeiro, INL, 1958, 126–48.
> Important studies about the poet's influences.

Grieco, Agripino. "Raimundo Correia" in his *Evolução da poesia brasileira*, 3rd. edn., Rio de Janeiro, Livraria José Olympio Editora, 1947, 55–7.
> Succinct and laudatory study, by a critic not given to easy praise.

Ivo, Ledo. "Apresentação" to Raimundo Correia, *Poesia*, Nossos Clássicos, 20, Rio de Janeiro, AGIR, 1958, 6–13.
> Brief study covering, with balance, the poetic trajectory of Correia.

Leão, Múcio. "Prefácio" to Raimundo Correia, *Poesias completas*, 2 vols., São Paulo, Editora Nacional, 1948, I, 5–33.
> Valuable due to bibliography.

Lima, Alceu Amoroso. "Apresentação" to Olavo Bilac, *Poesia*, Nossos Clássicos, 2, Rio de Janeiro, AGIR, 1957, 6–13.
> Takes into consideration the life, the work, and the civic action of the poet.

Melo, Gladstone Chaves de. "Apresentação" to Alphonsus de Guimaraens, *Poesia*, Nossos Clássicos, 19, Rio de Janeiro, AGIR, 1958, 5–18.
> Critical study dealing with theme and style.

Muricy, José Cândido de Andrade. "Introdução" to Cruz e Sousa, *Obra completa*, Rio de Janeiro, Aguilar, 1961, 17–58.
> Critical synthesis, notable for its rigor, by one of the most praised scholars of Symbolism.

Queiroz, Maria José de. "Verlaine e Alphonsus no mosteiro simbolista," *Kriterion*,

Belo Horizonte, 71 (1978), 165–200.

Comparative study of style and biography.

Sayers, Raymond. "O poeta negro no Brasil: o caso de João da Cruz e Sousa" in his *Onze estudos de literatura brasileira*, Rio de Janeiro and Brasilia, Civilização Brasileira and INL, 1983, 81–114.

Well-rounded study of the poet's existential drama.

Silva, João Pinto da. "Vicente de Carvalho" in his *Vultos do meu caminho*, vol. II, 2nd. edn., revised and amplified, Porto Alegre, Santa Maria and Pelotas, Editora Globo, 1927, 117–43.

Study of the poetry and prose of Carvalho that continues to have merit.

Veríssimo, José. "O parnasianismo no Brasil," "O Sr. Alberto Oliveira" in his *Estudos de literatura brasileira*, 2nd. and 6th. series, Belo Horizonte and São Paulo, Itatiaia and EDUSP, 1977, 153–61; 75–81.

Two important studies, due to their critical rigor, contemporaneous with poet.

Chapter 5: The Brazilian theatre up to 1900

Primary sources

Alencar, José Martiniano de. *Teatro completo*, 2 vols., Rio de Janeiro, Serviço Nacional de Teatro, 1977.

Volume I reproduces the *crônicas* of 1854–1855, and Volume II, the complete plays.

"The Jesuit," tr. Edgardo R. de Britto, *Poet Lore: A Magazine of Letters*, 30 (1919), 475–547.

Anchieta, José de. *Auto representado na Festa de São Lourenço*, ed. Maria de Lourdes de Paula Martins, São Paulo, Museu Paulista, 1948.

The definitive text of one of Anchieta's best works.

Na vila de Vitória e Na visitação de Santa Isabel, ed. Maria de Lourdes de Paula Martins, São Paulo, Museu Paulista, 1950.

Carefully annotated edition of two of the *autos* composed in Spanish and Portuguese.

Poesias: manuscrito do século XVI, em português, castelhano, latim e tupi, ed. Maria de Lourdes de Paula Martins, São Paulo, Museu Paulista, 1954.

This landmark publication by the eminent Anchieta scholar includes a meticulous study of the manuscript compilation of the *autos* (Archives of the Society of Jesus, Rome, Opp. NN. 24).

Assis, Joaquim Maria Machado de. *Obra completa*, vol. XXX: *Crítica teatral*, Rio de Janeiro, W. M. Jackson, 1938.

A selection of Machado's important dramatic theory and criticism written between 1859 and 1879.

Teatro completo, ed. Teresinha Marinho, Rio de Janeiro, Serviço Nacional de Teatro, 1982.

This modern volume is far more carefully edited than those in the 1938 W. M. Jackson series.

Azevedo, Artur Nabantino Gonçalves de. *A capital federal: comédia-opereta de costumes brasileiros em tres actos e doze quadros*, Rio de Janeiro, Casa

Mont'Alverne, 1897.

The first edition of Azevedo's masterpiece and the highlight of the *teatro de revista*.

Teatro a vapor, ed. Gerald M. Moser, São Paulo, Cultrix/INL, 1977.

Carefully edited and annotated texts of the 1906–1908 vignettes. The introductory essay is a Portuguese translation of Moser's 1976 article, "Artur Azevedo's last dramatic writings," listed below.

Teatro de Artur Azevedo, ed. Antônio Martins de Araújo, Rio de Janeiro, Serviço Nacional de Teatro, 1983–.

The two published volumes include some of Azevedo's most important plays. The editorial plan calls for publication of Azevedo's dramatic works in five volumes.

O tribofe: revista fluminense do ano de 1891, ed. Rachel Teixeira Valença, Rio de Janeiro, Nova Fronteira/Fundação Casa de Rui Barbosa, 1986.

Carefully annotated edition of the *revista* that generated *A capital federal*. Includes a helpful introduction and two perceptive articles.

Costa, Cláudio Manuel da. *O Parnazo obsequioso, drama para se recitar em muzica no dia 5 de dezembro de 1768 em que faz annos o Illmo. e Exmo. Snr. D. José Luiz de Menezes, Conde de Valladares, Gor. e Cappm. General da cappitania de Minas Geraes* in Caio de Mello Franco (ed.), *O inconfidente Claudio Manoel da Costa: O parnazo obsequioso e As cartas chilenas*, Rio de Janeiro, Schmidt Editor, 1931, 63–84.

The first printing of Costa's encomiastic drama dedicated to Governor Menezes.

Dias, Antônio Gonçalves. *Leonor de Mendonça: drama original em tres actos e cinco quadros*, Rio de Janeiro, J. Villeneuve & Cia., 1847.

The first edition of Brazilian Romanticism's best serious drama.

Teatro completo, ed. Edwaldo Cafezeiro, Rio de Janeiro, Serviço Nacional de Teatro, 1979.

Careful edition of Dias's four original plays and his translation of Schiller's *Die Braut von Messina*.

França, Joaquim José da, Jr. *Teatro de França Júnior*, ed. Edwaldo Cafezeiro, 2 vols., Rio de Janeiro, Serviço Nacional de Teatro, 1980.

This long-due first edition of França Júnior's theatre includes the fourteen extant plays. The texts of ten other works remain lost.

Leão, José Joaquim de Campos (Qorpo-Santo). *Teatro completo*, ed. Guilhermino César, Rio de Janeiro, Serviço Nacional de Teatro, 1980.

The complete edition of Qorpo-Santo's theatre, published at long last, only three years before the centenary of the playwright's death.

Macedo, Joaquim Manuel de. *Teatro completo*, ed. Antônio Geraldo da Cunha, Rio de Janeiro, Serviço Nacional de Teatro, 1979 .

The definitive edition of Macedo's complete drama. The editorial plan calls for publication of four volumes.

Magalhães, Domingos José Gonçalves de. *Antônio José ou o poeta e a Inquisição*, Rio de Janeiro, Typographia Imparcial de F. de Paula Brito, 1839.

The first edition of the play credited with introducing romantic theatre in Brazil.

Oliveira, Manuel Botelho de. *Música do Parnasso dividida em quatro coros e rimas portuguesas, castelhanas, italianas & latinas com seu descante comico redusido em duas comedias*, Lisbon, Na Oficina de Miguel Manescal, 1705.

Multilingual collection of poetry. Includes *Hay amigo para amigo* and *Amor, engaños y celos*, the first two plays published by a Brazilian playwright. Both plays in Spanish.

Pena, Luís Carlos Martins. *O juiz de paz na roça*, Rio de Janeiro, Typographia Imparcial de F. de Paula Brito, 1843.

Like the now-lost first edition, this second edition of Martins Pena's masterpiece identifies the author simply as "Hum fluminense" ["a native of Rio de Janeiro"].

"A rural Justice of the Peace," tr. Willis Knapp Jones, *Poet Lore: A Quarterly of World Literature*, 54:2 (1948), 99–119.

Teatro de Martins Pena, ed. Darcy Damasceno and Maria Filgueiras, 2 vols., Rio de Janeiro, MEC/INL, 1956.

The definitive edition of Martins Pena's complete theatre. Abundantly annotated and documented. Volume I comprises the comedies and volume II, the dramas. Some of the plays were printed here for the first time.

Porto Alegre, Manuel de Araújo. *Prólogo dramático*, Rio de Janeiro, Typographia Imparcial de F. de Paula Brito, 1837.

The first edition of Porto Alegre's pioneering romantic play.

Secondary sources

Books

Aguiar, Flávio. *Os homens precários: inovação e convenção na dramaturgia de Qorpo-Santo*, Porto Alegre, A Nação/Instituto Estadual do Livro, 1975.

The major critical work on Qorpo-Santo's theatre.

A comédia nacional no teatro de José de Alencar, São Paulo, Editora Atica, 1984.

The best book-length study of Alencar's theatre.

Araripe, Tristão de Alencar, Jr. *Literatura brazileira: José de Alencar*, Rio de Janeiro, Fauchon & Cia., 1894.

Includes early, perceptive criticism of Alencar's theatre.

Arêas, Vilma Sant'Anna. *Na tapera de Santa Cruz: uma leitura de Martins Pena*, São Paulo, Livraria Martins Fontes Editora, 1987.

One of the major critical works on Martins Pena's theatre.

Fraga, Eudinyr. *Qorpo-Santo: surrealismo ou absurdo?*, São Paulo, Editora Perspectiva, 1988.

Argues that Surrealism, rather than the Absurd, is the essential characteristic of Qorpo-Santo's theatre.

Gonçalves, Augusto de Freitas Lopes. *Dicionário histórico e literário do teatro no Brasil*, Rio de Janeiro, Cátedra, 1975–.

The result of a life-time endeavor, this multi-volume work is an essential research tool for students of the Brazilian theatre.

Hessel, Lothar, and Georges Raeders. *O teatro jesuítico no Brasil*, Porto Alegre, Editora da Universidade Federal do Rio Grande do Sul, 1972.

A short introduction to Jesuit theatre in Brazil. Includes close readings of six of Anchieta's more relevant *autos*.

Khéde, Sônia Salomão. *Censores de pincenê e gravata: dois momentos da censura teatral no Brasil*, Rio de Janeiro, Editora Codecri, 1981.

Part I examines the role of the Conservatório Dramático as the Empire's censorship office. Essential reading on the institution of censorship in Brazil.

Magalhães, Raimundo, Jr. *Arthur Azevedo e sua época*, 3rd. edn., Rio de Janeiro, Civilização Brasileira, 1966.

Useful study of the life and works. Places Azevedo in the context of the theatre of his time and evaluates his contribution to it.

Martins, Antônio (Antônio Martins de Araújo). *Arthur Azevedo, a palavra e o riso: uma introdução aos processos lingüísticos de comicidade no teatro e na sátira de Arthur Azevedo*, São Paulo, Editora Perspectiva/Rio de Janeiro, Editora da Universidade Federal do Rio de Janeiro, 1988.

Seminal study of Azevedo's use of popular language in his comedies.

Mendes, Miriam Garcia. *A personagem negra no teatro brasileiro entre 1838 e 1888*, São Paulo, Editora Atica, 1982.

A ground-breaking study offering a substantive analysis of the portrayal of Blacks in a crucial period of Brazilian drama.

Pontes, Joel. *Machado de Assis e o teatro*, São Paulo, Campanha Nacional de Teatro, 1960.

The first and only major book-length study on Machado's theatre.

Teatro de Anchieta, Rio de Janeiro, MEC/Serviço Nacional de Teatro, 1978.

This very provocative study emphasizes performance elements and gives special consideration to Anchieta's indigenous audiences.

Prado, Décio de Almeida. *João Caetano: o ator, o empresário, o repertório*, São Paulo, Editora Perspectiva, 1972.

João Caetano e a arte do ator: estudo de fontes, São Paulo, Editora Ática, 1984.

Two seminal studies by the eminent critic and leading scholar on the most important actor of nineteenth-century Brazil.

Ruiz, Roberto. *O teatro de revista no Brasil: das origens à Primeira Guerra Mundial*, Rio de Janeiro, Instituto Nacional de Artes Cênicas, 1988.

A substantive analysis of the development of the genre. Abundantly documented.

Silva, Lafayette. *João Caetano e sua época: subsídios para a história do teatro brasileiro*, Rio de Janeiro, Imprensa Nacional, 1936.

A very informative work by the respected chronicler of Brazilian theatre; combines biography and theatre history.

Sousa, José Galante de. "A censura teatral. Anexos II, III, IV" in his *O teatro no Brasil*, vol. I, Rio de Janeiro, MEC/INL, 1960, 309–21, 326–7.

Provides essential information on censorship of the theatre in nineteenth-century Brazil.

Sussekind, Flora. *As revistas de ano e a invenção do Rio de Janeiro*, Rio de Janeiro, Nova Fronteira/Fundação Casa de Rui Barbosa, 1986.

Studies the development of the *revista de ano* in connection with the social and political background of the former capital city.

Windmüller, Kathe. *"O Judeu" no teatro romântico brasileiro: uma revisão da tragédia de Gonçalves de Magalhães, "Antônio José ou o poeta e a Inquisição,"* Centro de Estudos Judaicos da Faculdade de Filosofia, Letras e Ciências Humanas da Universidade de São Paulo, 1984.

A major study of Magalhães's play.

Articles

Aiex, Nora K. "Martins Pena: parodist," *Luso-Brazilian Review*, 18:1 (1981), 155–60.

Examines two of Martins Pena's comedies, *O diletante* and *Os ciúmes de um pedestre*, as parodies of Bellini's opera, *Norma*, and Shakespeare's *Othello*, respectively.

Araújo, Antônio Martins de. "A vocação do riso: um panorama da dramaturgia de Artur Azevedo" in Antônio Martins de Araújo (ed.), *Teatro de Artur Azevedo*, vol. I, Rio de Janeiro, Serviço Nacional de Teatro, 1983, [ix–xxii].

"Para uma poética de Artur Azevedo" in Antônio Martins de Araújo (ed.) *Teatro de Artur Azevedo*, vol. II, Rio de Janeiro, Instituto Nacional de Artes Cênicas, 1985, [xv–xxviii].

Two perceptive introductory studies by the editor of Azevedo's theatre.

Bacarelli, Milton João. "Introdução ao Teatro Jesuítico no Brasil" in *Primeiro Concurso Nacional de Monografias*, Brasília, MEC/Serviço Nacional de Teatro, 1977, 43–131.

Emphasizes the Jesuit's use of the theatre as a missionary tool. Provides a detailed analysis of Anchieta's *Na vila de Vitória*.

Barman, Roderick J. "Politics on the stage: the late Brazilian Empire as dramatized by França Júnior," *Luso-Brazilian Review*, 13:2 (1976), 244–60.

A reading of the plays as social documents of great relevance to the historian.

Brower, Keith H. "The theater of Machado de Assis," *Tinta*, 1:4 (1984), 21–5.

An accurate summary of the characteristics of Machado's theatre.

Carvalho, Armando. "A literatura jesuítica" in Afrânio Coutinho (ed.), *A literatura no Brasil*, revised edn., vol. I, Rio de Janeiro, Editorial Sul Americana, 1968, 194–213.

Most of the essay is dedicated to Anchieta's theatre. Also examines the Jesuit theatre in Portugal and the influence of Gil Vicente's *autos* on Anchieta's works.

César, Guilhermino. "O que era e o que não devia ser" and "O criador do Teatro do Absurdo" in Qorpo-Santo, *As relações naturais e outras comédias*, ed. Guilhermino César, Porto Alegre, Edições da Faculdade de Filosofia da Universidade Federal do Rio Grande do Sul, 1969, 9–37, 39–61.

The first major studies of Qorpo-Santo appeared in this pioneering edition by the playwright's most thorough and perceptive critic.

Correia, Marlene de Castro. "O teatro de Gonçalves Dias" in Antônio Gonçalves Dias, *Teatro completo*, ed. Edwaldo Cafezeiro, Rio de Janeiro, Serviço Nacional de Teatro, 1979. [vii–xxiii].

A short but perceptive assessment of Gonçalves Dias's theatre.

Fernández, Oscar. 1978. "José de Anchieta and early theater activity in Brazil," *Luso-Brazilian Review*, 15:1 (1978), 26–43.

Places Anchieta in the Vicentean tradition but also acknowledges the Jesuit's innovations. Provides close readings of several *autos*. A very informative summation of Anchieta's career and importance.

Gomes, Eugênio. "Manuel Botelho de Oliveira" in Afrânio Coutinho (ed.), *A literatura no Brasil*, revised edn., vol. I, Rio de Janeiro, Editorial Sul Americana, 1968, 255–76.

Studies Oliveira's two plays in the broader context of his poetry and in the light of the overwhelming Spanish influence on the literature of his time.

Lyday, Leon F. "Satire in the comedies of Martins Pena," *Luso-Brazilian Review*, 5:2 (1968), 63–70.

Shows the clear satirical intent in some of the comedies. Argues that the most prevalent form of satire in the comedies is farcical.

Magaldi, Sábato. "Criação da comédia brasileira" in his *Panorama do teatro brasileiro*, São Paulo, Difusão Européia do Livro, 1962, 40–58.

A major critical study of Martins Pena's place in Brazilian theatre. Offers detailed discussions of the dramas as well as the comedies.

Michalski, Yan. "Qorpo-Santo: o Teatro do Absurdo nasceu no Brasil?" *Cultura*, 12 (1974), 18–25.

An important discussion of Qorpo-Santo as a precursor of the Theatre of the Absurd.

Moser, Gerald. "Artur Azevedo's last dramatic writings: the 'Teatro a vapor' vignettes (1906–1908)," *Latin American Theater Review*, 10:1 (1976), 23–35.

Provides sensitive and detailed discussion of Azevedo's innovative, sketched comedies.

Pádua, Antônio de. "Aspectos do estilo cômico em França Júnior" in his *Coletânea*, Rio de Janeiro, MEC, 1963, 11–32.

Interesting stylistic study of França Júnior's major plays.

Pierson, Colin M. "Martins Pena: a view of character types," *Latin American Theater Review*, 11:2 (1978), 41–8.

Discusses Martins Pena's use of caricatures and stereotypes in several comedies.

Prado, Décio de Almeida. "*Leonor de Mendonça*, de Gonçalves Dias," *Revista do Instituto de Estudos Brasileiros*, 8 (1970), 91–106.

"*Leonor de Mendonça*: amor e morte em Gonçalves Dias" in *Esboço de figura: homenagem a Antônio Cândido*, São Paulo, Duas Cidades, 1979, 227–64.

Both of these are major studies of Gonçalves Dias's best play, by the playwright's most thorough critic.

"Do *Tribofe* a *Capital federal*" in Artur Azevedo, *O Tribofe: revista fluminense do ano de 1891*, ed. Rachel Teixeira Valença, Rio de Janeiro, Nova Fronteira/ Fundação Casa de Rui Barbosa, 1986, 253–81.

Traces Azevedo's rewriting of parts of the earlier *revista* into his most important work.

Quackenbush, Louis H. "The *auto* tradition in the Brazilian drama," *Latin American Theater Review* 5:2 (1972), 29–43.

Traces the development of the *auto* from early peninsular models to contemporary Brazilian theatre. Particular attention is given to Anchieta.

Sousa, José Galante de. "O teatro dos jesuítas: século XVI"; "Declínio do teatro jesuítico: século XVII"; "O teatro regular: século XVIII" in *O teatro no Brasil*, vol. I, Rio de Janeiro, MEC/INL, 1960, 81–102, 103–7, 108–37.

Part of a seminal two-volume history of the theatre in Brazil, these three chapters provide extremely important information on the theatre of the colonial period.

Valença, Rachel Teixeira. "Arthur Azevedo e a língua falada no teatro" in Artur Azevedo, *O Tribofe: revista fluminense do ano de 1891*, ed. Rachel Teixeira Valença, Rio de Janeiro, Nova Fronteira/Fundação Casa de Rui Barbosa, 1986, 22–47.

An excellent examination of language in Azevedo's plays.

Weinhardt, Marilene. "Os dramas de Martins Pena e o teatro romântico," *Estudos Brasileiros*, 10 (1980), 237–48.

A useful discussion of Martins Pena's five completed serious dramas.

Yunes, Márcio Jabur. "Introdução ao teatro de Joaquim Manuel de Macedo" in Joaquim Manuel de Macedo, *Teatro completo*, ed. Antônio Geraldo da Cunha, vol. I, Rio de Janeiro, Serviço Nacional de Teatro, 1979, [ix–xx].

A thorough summary of the characteristics of Macedo's theatre.

Chapter 6: Brazilian fiction from 1800 to 1855

Primary sources

Almeida, Manuel Antônio de. *Memórias de um sargento de milícias*, Rio de Janeiro Tipografia Brasiliense, 1854.

Memoirs of a Militia Sergeant, tr. L. L. Barrett, Washington, Pan American Union, 1959.

Macedo, Joaquim Manuel de. *A moreninha*, Rio de Janeiro, Tipografia Francesa, 1844.

O moço loiro, Rio de Janeiro n.p., 1945.

Teixeira e Sousa, Antônio Gonçalves. *O filho do pescador*, Rio de Janeiro, n.p., 1843.

Secondary sources

Amora, Antônio Soares. *Classicismo e romantismo no Brasil*, São Paulo, Conselho Estadual de Cultura, 1966.

Contains information on "Brazilian" magazines published in Europe in the early nineteenth century.

A literatura brasileira, vol. II: *O romantismo*, São Paulo, Cultrix, 1967.

Treats literary and cultural relations between Brazil and Europe and the development of a "Brazilian" literary conscience.

Barbosa Lima Sobrinho, Alexandre. *Panorama do conto brasileiro*, vol. I: *Os precursores*, Rio de Janeiro, Civilização Brasileira, 1960.

A succinct, informative general introduction to the subject.

Broca, Brito. *Obras reunidas*, vol. I: *Românticos, pré-românticos, ultra-românticos*, São Paulo, Polis, 1979.

Contains several salient chapters on the early romantic fiction of Brazil.

Câmara, Adauto da. *História de Nísia Floresta*, Rio de Janeiro, Pongetti, 1941.

First of a slowly growing series of research pieces on this writer; my thanks to Prof. Peggy Sharpe-Valadares for providing useful bibliographical suggestions.

Cândido, Antônio. *Formação da literatura brasileira*, 2nd. edn., vol. II, São Paulo, Livraria Martins Editora, 1964.
General presentation which helps set the context for the subject.

Floresta, Nísia (Dionísia Gonçalves). *Opúsculo humano*, ed. Peggy Sharpe-Valadares, São Paulo, Cortez, 1989.

Freitas, José Bezerra de. *Forma e expressão no romance brasileiro*, Rio de Janeiro, Pongetti, 1947.
Contains chapters on European antecedents and the ethnic influence on the development of the New World conscience.

Martins, Wilson. *História da inteligência brasileira*, vol. II, São Paulo, Cultrix, 1977.
Single most complete source of intellectual, political, and socio-economic context of early nineteenth-century fiction and journalism.

Menezes, Raimundo de. *Dicionário literário brasileiro*, 2nd edn., Rio de Janeiro, Livros Técnicos e Científicos, 1978.
Single most complete source of bio-bibliographical information on authors of the period.

Moisés, Massaud. *História da literatura brasileira*, vol. II: *Romantismo, realismo*, São Paulo, Cultrix, 1984.
Good source of solid critical evaluations of authors treated.

Paranhos, Haroldo. *História do romantismo no Brasil*, vol. II, São Paulo, Cultura Brasileira, 1937.
Offers general cultural background of the period in question.

Salles, David (ed.). *Primeiras manifestações da ficção na Bahia*, São Paulo, Cultrix, 1979.
Historical essay preceding anthology selections is best current source of information on incipient fictional development in northeastern Brazil.

Chapter 7: The Brazilian novel from 1850 to 1900

Primary sources

Alencar, José Martiniano de. *Cinco minutos*, Tip. do Diário do Rio de Janeiro, 1857.
O guaraní, Tip. do Diário de Rio do Janeiro, 1857.
Cinco minutos; A viuvinha, Rio de Janeiro, Garnier, 1860.
Lucíola, Rio de Janeiro, Tip. Francesa de F. Arfvedson, 1862.
Diva, Rio de Janeiro, Garnier, 1864.
As minas de prata, 3 vols., Rio de Janeiro, Garnier, 1865–1866.
Iracema, Rio de Janeiro, Tip. de Viana & Filhos, 1865.
A pata da gazela, Rio de Janeiro, Garnier, 1870.
O gaúcho, 2 vols., Rio de Janeiro, Garnier, 1870.
A guerra dos Mascates, 2 vols., Rio de Janeiro, Garnier, 1871–1873.
O tronco do Ipê. Rio de Janeiro, Garnier, 1871.
Sonhos de ouro, 2 vols., Rio de Janeiro, Garnier, 1872.
Til, Rio de Janeiro, Garnier, 1872.
Alfarrábios, 2 vols., Rio de Janeiro, Garnier, 1873.
O sertanejo, 2 vols., Rio de Janeiro, Garnier, 1875.
Senhora, Rio de Janeiro, Garnier, 1875.
Ubirajara. Rio de Janeiro, Garnier, 1875.

Volume 3

Como e por que sou romancista, Rio de Janeiro, Leuzinger, 1893.

Encarnação. Rio de Janeiro, Domingos de Magalhães, 1893.

Obra completa, 4 vols., Rio de Janeiro, Aguilar, 1958–1960.

Iracema, the Honey-Lips: A legend of Brazil, tr. Isabel Burton, London, Bickers & Sons, 1886.

Almeida, Manuel Antônio de. *Memórias de um sargento de milícias*, 2 vols., Rio de Janeiro, Tip. Brasiliense, 1854–1855; São Paulo, Cultrix, 1970.

Memoirs of a Militia Sergeant, tr. L. L. Barrett, Washington, Pan American Union, 1959.

Álvares de Azevedo, Manuel Antônio. *Obras*, Rio de Janeiro, Laemmert, 1855.

Macário, Noite na taverna, e Poemas malditos, Rio de Janeiro, F. Alves, 1983.

Araripe, Tristão de Alencar, Jr. *O reino encantado*, Rio de Janeiro, Gazeta de Notícias, 1878.

Azevedo, Aluísio Tancredo Belo Gonçalves de. *Uma lágrima de mulher*, São Luís do Maranhão, Tip. Frias, 1879.

O mulato, São Luís do Maranhão, Tip. do País, 1881; São Paulo, Livraria Martins Editora, 1970.

Casa de pensão, Rio de Janeiro, Tip. Santos, 1884.

Filomena Borges, Rio de Janeiro, Gazeta de Notícias, 1884.

O homem, Rio de Janeiro, Castro Silva, 1887.

O cortiço, Rio de Janeiro, Garnier, 1890; São Paulo, Livraria Martins Editora, 1973.

O coruja, Rio de Janeiro, Garnier, 1890.

Demônios, São Paulo, Teixeira e Irmão, 1893.

A mortalha de Alzira, Rio de Janeiro, Fauchon, 1894.

Livro de uma sogra, Rio de Janeiro, Domingos de Magalhães, 1895.

Pegadas, Rio de Janeiro, Garnier, 1897.

A Brazilian Tenement (O cortiço), tr. Harry W. Brown, New York, R. M. McBride, 1926; re-issued, New York, H. Fertig, 1976.

Mulatto, tr. Murray Graeme MacNicoll, Rutherford, N.J., Fairleigh Dickinson University Press, 1990.

Caminha, Adolfo Ferreira. *A normalista*, Rio de Janeiro, Domingos de Magalhães, 1892; São Paulo, Editora Atica, 1985.

Bom-Crioulo, Rio de Janeiro, Domingos de Magalhães, 1895; São Paulo, Editora Atica, 1983.

The Black Man and the Cabin Boy (Bom-Crioulo), tr. E. A. Lacey, San Francisco, Gay Sunshine Press, 1982.

Coelho Neto, Henrique Maximiano. *A capital federal*, Rio de Janeiro, O País, 1893.

Miragem, Rio de Janeiro, Domingos de Magalhães, 1895.

Sertão, Rio de Janeiro, Leuzinger, 1896.

Inverno em flor, Rio de Janeiro, Laemmert, 1897.

O morto, Rio de Janeiro, Laemmert, 1898.

A conquista, Rio de Janeiro, Laemmert, 1899; Rio de Janeiro, Civilização Brasileira, 1985.

Obra selecta, 3 vols., Rio de Janeiro, Aguilar, 1958.

Guimarães, Bernardo Joaquim da Silva. *O ermitão de Muquém*, Rio de Janeiro, Garnier, 1869.

Lendas e romances, Rio de Janeiro, Garnier, 1871.

Histórias e tradições, Rio de Janeiro, Garnier, 1872.

O garimpeiro, Rio de Janeiro, Garnier, 1872.

O seminarista, Rio de Janeiro, Garnier, 1872.

O índio Afonso, Rio de Janeiro, Garnier, 1873.

A escrava Isaura, Rio de Janeiro, Garnier, 1875; Rio de Janeiro, Edições de Ouro, 1968.

Maurício ou os paulistas em São João d'El Rei, Rio de Janeiro, Garnier, 1877.

A ilha maldita, Rio de Janeiro, Garnier, 1879.

Rosaura, a enjeitada, Rio de Janeiro, Garnier, 1883.

Inglês de Sousa, Herculano Marcos. *O cacaulista*, Tip. do Diário de Santos, 1876; 2nd. edn., Belém, Universidade Federal do Pará, 1973.

O coronel Sangrado, Tip. do Diário de Santos, 1877; 2nd. edn., Belém, Universidade Federal do Pará, 1968.

O missionário, Tip. do Diário de Santos, 1888; 3rd. edn., Rio de Janeiro, Edições de Ouro, 1967.

Contos amazônicos, Rio de Janeiro, Laemmert, 1892.

Lopes de Almeida, Júlia. *A família Medeiros*, new edn. Rio de Janeiro, Empresa nacional de publicidade, 1919.

A viuva Simões, Lisbon, A.M. Pereira, 1897.

A falência, Rio de Janeiro, A Tribuna, 1901; São Paulo, Hucitec, 1978.

Macedo, Joaquim Manuel de. *A moreninha*, Rio de Janeiro, Tip. Francesa, 1844.

As vítimas algozes, Rio de Janeiro, Tip. Americana (vol. I) and Tip. Perseverança (vol. II), 1869.

Machado de Assis, Joaquim Maria. 1870. *Contos fluminenses*, Rio de Janeiro, Garnier, 1870.

Ressurreição, Rio de Janeiro, Garnier, 1872.

Histórias da meia-noite, Rio de Janeiro, Garnier, 1873.

A mão e a luva, Rio de Janeiro, Gomes de Oliveira, 1874.

Helena, Rio de Janeiro, Garnier, 1876.

Yaiá Garcia, Rio de Janeiro, G. Vianna, 1878.

Memórias póstumas de Braz Cubas, Rio de Janeiro, Tip. Nacional, 1881.

Papéis avulsos, Rio de Janeiro, Lombaerts, 1882.

Histórias sem data, Rio de Janeiro, Garnier, 1884.

Quincas Borba, Rio de Janeiro, Garnier, 1891.

Várias histórias, Rio de Janeiro, Laemmert, 1896.

Páginas recolhidas, Rio de Janeiro, Garnier, 1899.

Dom Casmurro, Rio de Janeiro, Garnier, 1900.

Esaú e Jacó, Rio de Janeiro, Garnier, 1904.

Relíquias de casa velha, Rio de Janeiro, Garnier, 1906.

Memorial de Aires, Rio de Janeiro, Garnier, 1908.

Casa Velha, ed. Lúcia Miguel-Pereira, São Paulo, Livraria Martins Editora, 1944.

Obras completas, 3 vols., Rio de Janeiro, Aguilar, 1959–1962.

Epitaph of a Small Winner (Memórias póstumas de Brás Cubas), tr. W. L. Grossman, New York, Noonday, 1952.

Dom Casmurro, tr. Helen Caldwell, New York, Noonday, 1953.

Philosopher or Dog (Quincas Borba), tr. Clotilde Wilson, Berkeley, University of California Press, 1954; published in England as *The Heritage of Quincas Borba*, London, Allen, 1954.

Volume 3

The Psychiatrist, and Other Stories, tr. W. L. Grossman and Helen Caldwell, Berkeley, University of California Press, 1963.

Esau and Jacob, Helen Caldwell, Berkeley, University of California Press, 1965.

The Hand and the Glove (A mão e a luva), tr. Albert I. Bagby, Lexington, University of Kentucky Press, 1970.

Counselor Ayres' Memorial (Memorial de Aires), tr. Helen Caldwell, Berkeley, University of California Press, 1972.

Yaya Garcia, tr. R. L. Scott-Buccleuch, London, Peter Owen, 1976.

The Devil's Church and Other Stories, tr. Jack Schmitt and Lori Ishimatsu, Austin, University of Texas Press, 1977.

Helena, tr. Helen Caldwell, Berkeley, University of California Press, 1984.

The Wager: Aires' Journal (Memorial de Aires), tr. R. Scott-Buccleuch, London, Owens, 1990.

Olímpio (Domingos Olímpio Braga Cavalcanti), Domingos. *Luzia-Homem*, Rio de Janeiro, Comp. Lito-Tip, 1903, São Paulo, Editora Atica, 1978.

Oliveira Paiva, Manuel de. *Dona Guidinha do Poço*, São Paulo, Saraiva, 1952; São Paulo, Editora Atica, 1981.

Pompéia, Raul d'Avila. *O Ateneu*, Rio de Janeiro, Gazeta de Notícias, 1888.

Obras, Rio de Janeiro, Editora Civilização Brasileira, 1981.

Porto Alegre, Apolinário. *A tapera*, Pelotas, Correio Mercantil, 1875.

Paisagens, Porto Alegre, Biblioteca Riograndense de J. J. da Silva, 1875; Brasília, INL, 1987.

O vaqueano, Porto Alegre, Movimento, 1987.

Ribeiro, Júlio César. *A carne*, São Paulo, Teixeira, 1888; Rio de Janeiro, Edições de Ouro, 1964.

Taunay, Alfredo d'Escragnolle. *Inocência*, Rio de Janeiro, Tip. Nacional, 1872, São Paulo, Editora Atica, 1974.

O encilhamento, Rio de Janeiro, Domingos de Magalhães, 1894.

Innocencia: A story of the prairie regions of Brazil, tr. James W. Wells, London, Chapman & Hall, 1889.

Inocencia, tr. Henriqueta Chamberlain, New York, Macmillan, 1945.

Távora, João Franklin da Silveira. *A casa de palha*, Rio de Janeiro, Tip. Nacional, 1866.

Um casamento no arrabalde, Rio de Janeiro, Tip. Nacional, 1869.

Cartas a Cincinato, 2nd. edn., Recife, J. W. de Medeiros, 1872.

O cabeleira, Rio de Janeiro, Tip. Nacional, 1876; Rio de Janeiro, Edições de Ouro, 1966.

O matuto, Rio de Janeiro, Tip. Perseverança, 1878.

Lourenço, Rio de Janeiro, Tip. Nacional, 1881; Rio de Janeiro, Edições de Ouro, 1966.

Secondary sources

Books

The bibliography on Machado de Assis is immense. The brief selection included below is limited to classic studies published before 1970, plus a few of the most interesting recent books and articles.

Alvim Corrêa, Roberto. *O mito de Prometeu*, Rio de Janeiro, AGIR, 1951.

Contains a useful essay on Taunay, beginning modern critical reappraisals of this author.

Amora, Antônio Soares. *A literatura brasileira*, vol. II: *O romantismo*, São Paulo, Cultrix, 1967.

A useful study of all genres of Brazilian Romanticism.

Andrade, Mário de. *O Aleijadinho e Álvares de Azevedo*, Rio de Janeiro, Revista Acadêmica, 1935.

As always, Mário is perceptive and convincing; like Mário's study of Almeida, this text documents the modernist re-discovery of Brazilian Romanticism.

Aspectos da literatura brasileira, Rio de Janeiro, Americ-Edit, 1943.

A fundamental text in the modernist rediscovery of Almeida. Still one of the best studies of the *Memórias*.

Beiguelman, Paula. *Viagem sentimental a Dona Guidinha do Poço*, São Paulo, Centro Universitário, 1966.

This study, and that of Pinto (below), documents the relatively recent rediscovery of Oliveira Paiva. Both are interesting and useful, but both also make clear just how much remains to be done in understanding this remarkable and still under-rated author.

Bosi, Alfredo. *História concisa da literatura brasileira*, São Paulo, Cultrix, 1970.

Very useful, well-organized survey.

Bosi, Alfredo, *et al.* (eds.) *Machado de Assis*, São Paulo, Editora Ática, 1982.

An anthology of Machado's writings, plus selections from a wide range of critical appreciations; includes an excellent bibliography.

Brayner, Sônia. *A metáfora do corpo no romance naturalista*, Rio de Janeiro, Livraria São José, 1973.

The best study of Azevedo's use of naturalist techniques.

Broca, Brito. *Pontos de referência*, Rio de Janeiro, MEC, 1972.

Contains a first-rate essay on Macedo's social vision and novelistic practice.

Machado de Assis e a política mais outros estudos, São Paulo, Polis, 1983.

The title essay is fundamental, beginning the reevaluation of Machado as a product of his time and place rather than as a detached, universal craftsman.

Caldwell, Helen. *The Brazilian Othello of Machado de Assis: A study of "Dom Casmurro,"* Berkeley, University of California Press, 1960.

A revolutionary reinterpretation of *Dom Casmurro*, the starting point for much of subsequent Anglo-American criticism on Machado.

Machado de Assis, Berkeley, University of California Press, 1970.

A good but intensely personal introduction to Machado's life and writings.

Cândido, Antônio. *Formação da literatura brasileira*, 5th. edn., 2 vols., Belo Horizonte, Itatiaia, 1975.

First published in 1959, this is without a doubt the best account of the development of Brazilian fiction before Machado de Assis.

A educação pela noite, São Paulo, Editora Ática, 1987.

The title essay is the most perceptive critical study to date of Álvares de Azevedo's "Noite na taverna."

Castello, José Aderaldo. *Realidade e ilusão em Machado de Assis*, São Paulo, CEN,

1969.

Probably the best New Criticism study, in Portuguese, of Machado's novels.

Cavalcanti Proença, Manuel. *José de Alencar na literatura brasileira*, 2nd. edn., Rio de Janeiro, Civilização Brasileira, 1972.

This scholarly and perceptive text marks the beginning of twentieth-century reappraisals of Alencar's works and ideology.

Chaves, Flávio Loureiro. *O mundo social de Quincas Borba*, Porto Alegre, Movimento, 1974.

A studied analysis of Machado's novel as a reflection of Brazilian society and contemporary social ideologies.

Coelho Netto, Paulo. *Bibliografia de Coelho Netto*, Brasília, INL, 1972.

The first step toward making some sense of the author's massive opus.

Cordeiro, Francisca de Basto. *Machado de Assis que eu vi*, Rio de Janeiro, Livraria São José, 1961.

Written by a woman who grew up next door to Machado, this simple, unpretentious text is one of the few unposed glimpses we have of Machado the man.

Coutinho, Afrânio (ed.). *A literatura no Brasil*, 2nd. edn., revised, 6 vols., Rio de Janeiro, Editorial Sul Americana, 1968–1971.

A massive collection of articles, by a number of Brazilian scholars, on the whole development of the national literature. Inevitably, there is considerable variation in the quality of individual articles.

Raul Pompéia, Rio de Janeiro, Civilização Brasileira, 1981.

An anthology of original texts and critical appreciations, with an extremely complete and useful bibliography.

Dixon, Paul B. *Retired Dreams: Dom Casmurro, myth and modernity*, West Lafayette, Ind., Purdue University Press, 1989.

An attempt to apply the lastest critical methodologies to Machado's text.

Faoro, Raymundo. *Machado de Assis: a pirâmide e o trapézio*, São Paulo, CEN, 1974.

This influential and massive study remains the most complete account of Machado's social ideas.

Fitz, Earl E. *Machado de Assis*. Boston, Twayne, 1989.

An informative and solid introduction, in English, to Machado's life and works, more objective and up-to-date than Caldwell's biography.

Galante de Sousa, José. *Bibliografia de Machado de Assis*, 2nd. edn., Rio de Janeiro, INL, 1969.

The most complete compilation for the period it covers.

Gledson, John. *The Deceptive Realism of Machado de Assis*, Liverpool, Francis Cairns, 1984.

Focus on *Dom Casmurro* and its links to contemporary social and political events.

Machado de Assis: ficção e história, Rio de Janeiro, Paz e Terra, 1986.

Includes a Portuguese translation of the "*Casa Velha*" article (below), as well as perceptive re-readings of most of the major novels and of some of Machado's *crônicas*.

Guimarães, Reginaldo. *O folclore na ficção brasileira: roteiro das "Memórias de um sargento de milícias,"* Rio de Janeiro, Cátedra, 1977.

Not critically sophisticated, but useful information on the popular culture described by Almedia.

Haberly, David T. *Three Sad Races: Racial identity and national consciousness in Brazilian literature*, Cambridge University Press, 1983.
Includes studies of Alencar and Machado de Assis.

Ivo, Ledo. *O universo poético de Raul Pompéia*, Rio de Janeiro, Livraria São José, 1963.
A critical first step in modern reinterpretation of Pompéia.

Loos, Dorothy S. *The Naturalistic Novel of Brazil*, New York, The Hispanic Institute, 1963.
Now rather dated, but a useful general account of the movement.

López Heredia, José. *Matéria e forma narrativa de "O Ateneu,"* São Paulo, Quíron, 1979.
A narratological approach to the text.

MacAdam, Alfred A. *Modern Latin American Narratives: The dreams of reason*, University of Chicago Press, 1977.
The original and fasincating section on Machado argues that the fictional texts should be read as satires rather than as novels.

Magalhães, Basílio de. *Bernardo Guimarães*, Rio de Janeiro, Anuário do Brasil, 1926.
Dated, but the best book-length biography of the author.

Magalhães, Raimundo, Jr. *Poesia e vida de Álvares de Azevedo*, 2nd. edn., São Paulo, LISA, 1971.
The best biography of the author, although its focus is on the poetry rather than the prose.

José de Alencar e a sua época, 2nd. edn. Rio de Janeiro, Civilização Brasileira, 1977.
The most complete and accurate biography of Alencar; particularly useful for its account of Alencar's political ideas and career.

Magalhães, Raimundo, Jr. *Vida e obra de Machado de Assis*, 4 vols., Rio de Janeiro, Civilização Brasileira, 1981.
The best and most detailed biography – a goldmine of information.

Marco, Valéria de. *O império da cortesã*, São Paulo, M. Fontes, 1986.
Focus on Alencar's use of the prostitution theme in his plays and fiction – particularly in the novel *Lucíola*.

Marotti, Giorgio. *Black Characters in the Brazilian Novel*, tr. Maria O. Marotti and Henry Lawton, Los Angeles, Center for Afro-American Studies of the University of California, 1987.
Important study, by a leading Italian critic. Particularly useful for Araripe Júnior's *O reino encantado* and Azevedo's *O mulato*.

Marques Rebelo (Edi Dias da Cruz) (ed.). *Para conhecer melhor Manuel Antônio de Almeida*, Rio de Janeiro, Bloch, 1973.
An anthology of Almeida's writings, with brief extracts from critical appraisals and a useful bibliography.

Massa, Jean-Michel. *A juventude de Machado de Assis (1839–1870): ensaio de biografia intelectual*, Rio de Janeiro, Civilização Brasileira, 1971.
A ground-breaking study of Machado's family and early life.

Menezes, Raimundo de. *Aluísio Azevedo*, São Paulo, Livraria Martins Editora, 1958.
The first scholarly biography of the author.

Mérian, Jean-Yves. *Aluísio Azevedo, vida e obra*, Rio de Janeiro, Espaço e Tempo, 1988.
> A very traditional study, despite its recent date. Useful, nonetheless, for its detailed account of Azevedo's life and times.

Merquior, José Guilherme. *De Anchieta a Euclides*, Rio de Janeiro, Livraria José Olympio Editora, 1977.
> A perceptive survey of the literature from the colonial period to about 1900.

Miguel-Pereira, Lúcia. *Machado de Assis: estudo crítico e biográfico*, 5th. edn., Rio de Janeiro, Livraria José Olympio Editora, 1955.
> Perceptive comments, but marred by a desire to read the fiction as reflections of specific events in Machado's life.

História da literatura brasileira: prosa de ficção de 1870 a 1920, 3rd. edn., Rio de Janeiro, José Olympio Editora, 1973.
> Still far and away the best account of fiction for the period it covers.

Montello, Josué. *Aluísio Azevedo e a polêmica de "O Mulato,"* Rio de Janeiro, Livraria José Olympio Editora, 1975.
> An informative account of contemporary reactions to Azevedo's best-seller.

Montenegro, Olívio. *O romance brasileiro*, Rio de Janeiro, Livraria José Olympio Editora, 1938.
> Critically dated, but contains much useful information, particularly on writers from the North-East.

Nunes, Maria Luísa. *The Craft of an Absolute Winner*, Westport, Conn., Greenwood Press, 1983.
> A narratological analysis of Machado's major novels.

Octávio Filho, Rodrigo. *Inglês de Sousa*, Rio de Janeiro, Academia Brasileira de Letras, 1955.
> Dated and somewhat superficial, the only book-length study of this underrated novelist.

Pacheco, João. *A Literatura brasileira*, vol. III: *O realismo*, São Paulo, Cultrix, 1963.
> Flawed by the author's efforts to force late nineteenth-century Brazilian literature into the mold of European literary history, but still useful.

Pereira, Astrojildo. *Interpretações*, Rio de Janeiro, Casa do Estudante do Brasil, 1944.
> An excellent essay on Macedo and the first important twentieth-century text on this fundamental author.

Pinto, Rolando Morel. *Experiência e ficção de Oliveira Paiva*, São Paulo, Instituto de Estudos Brasileiros, 1967.
> See note to Beiguelman, above.

Putnam, Samuel. *Marvelous Journey: A survey of four centuries of Brazilian literature*, New York, Knopf, 1948.
> The best general survey of Brazilian literature in English, despite its age.

Ribeiro, João Felipe de Sabóia. *O romancista Adolfo Caminha*, Rio de Janeiro, Pongetti, 1967.
> Not very satisfactory, but nonetheless the best biography of Caminha.

Ribeiro, José Antônio Pereira. *O universo romântico de Joaquim Manoel de Macedo*, São Paulo, R. Kempf, 1987.
> Not as complete as the title suggests, but very useful nonetheless.

Romero, Sílvio. *História da literatura brasileira*, 3rd. edn., 5 vols., Rio de Janeiro,

Livraria José Olympio Editora, 1943.

    Highly personal and often aggravating account of the whole of the nation's literature. First published in 1888, Romero's text is nonetheless one of the fundamental texts in Brazilian literary historiography as well as a goldmine of facts and flawed, but very revealing, interpretations.

Santiago, Silviano. *Uma literatura nos trópicos*, São Paulo, Perspectiva, 1978.

    Contains a very useful article on Machado's *Dom Casmurro* and its relationship with the earlier *Ressurreição*.

Schwarz, Roberto. *A sereia e o desconfiado*, Rio de Janeiro, Civilização Brasileira, 1965.

Ao vencedor as batatas: forma literária e processo social nos inícios do romance brasileiro, São Paulo, Duas Cidades, 1977.

    Roberto Schwarz's two books, it can be said without exaggeration, revolutionized approaches to the nineteenth-century Brazilian novel and its links to contemporary society; he focuses, in these brilliantly conceived and argued works, on Alencar's urban novels and on the early novels of Machado de Assis.

Serpa, Phocion. *Visconde de Taunay: ensaio biobibliográfico*, Rio de Janeiro, Academia Brasileira de Letras, 1952.

    Dated and not always accurate, but the most useful general survey of Taunay's life. Bibliographical information represents a good start at sorting out Taunay's many publications and various pseudonyms, but much work clearly remains to be done.

Sodré, Nelson Werneck. *O naturalismo no Brasil*, Rio de Janeiro, Civilização Brasileira, 1965.

    An early attempt to apply Marxist ideas to criticism; often dogmatic, but also astonishingly perceptive at times.

Veríssimo, José. *História da literatura brasileira*, 5th. edn., Rio de Janeiro, Livraria José Olympio Editora, 1969.

    A useful counter-weight to Sílvio Romero's *História*; Veríssimo's survey is more objective and balanced and closer to modern tastes in literary history.

Wasserman, Renata R. Mautner. *Exotic Nations: Literature and cultural identity in the United States and Brazil, 1839–1930*, Ithaca, N.Y., Cornell University Press, 1994.

Articles

Andrews, Norwood, Jr. "Modern classification of Bernardo Guimarães's prose narratives," *Luso-Brazilian Review*, 3 (1966), 59–82.

    Very useful analysis of Guimarães's sub-genres.

Bagby, Alberto I., Jr. "Eighteen years of Machado de Assis: a critical annotated bibliography for 1956–74," *Hispania*, 58 (1975), 648–83.

    An essential compilation.

Cândido, Antônio. "Dialética da malandragem," *Revista do Instituto de Estudos Brasileiros*, 8 (1970), 67–89.

    The second fundamental reappraisal of the *Memórias* in the last fifty years.

Foster, David William. "Adolfo Caminha's *Bom-Crioulo*: a founding text of Brazilian gay literature," *Chasqui*, 17:2 (1988) 13–23.

    A useful study of the novel.

Garcia, Frederick C. H. "Três versões de um romance de Taunay," *Revista do Instituto de Estudos Brasileiros*, 9 (1970), 83–97.

An excellent piece of scholarship, allowing us to see how Taunay went about creating his novels.

Gledson, John. "*Casa Velha*: a contribution to a better understanding of Machado de Assis," *Bulletin of Hispanic Studies*, 60 (1983), 31–48.

A superlative reevaluation of one of Machado's most important and least-known texts.

Kinnear, J. C. 1976. "Machado de Assis: to believe or not to believe," *Modern Language Review*, 71 (1976), 54–65.

Focus on narrative technique in *Quincas Borba*; an outstanding and innovative interpretation.

Lopez, Maria Angélica. 1989. "Júlia Lopes de Almeida e o trabalho feminino na burguesia," *Luso-Brazilian Review*, 26 (1989), 45–57.

An important first step in the rediscovery of the only major female novelist of the period.

MacAdam, Alfred A. "Rereading *Ressurreição*," *Luso-Brazilian Review*, 9 (1972), 47–57.

An important reevaluation of this early novel by Machado, with very useful contemporary reactions to it.

MacNicoll, Murray Graeme. "*O Mulato* and Maranhão: the socio-historical context," *Luso-Brazilian Review*, 12 (1975), 234–40.

Very useful documentary information of the setting of Azevedo's novel.

Parker, John M. 1971. "The nature of realism in *Memórias de um sargento de milícias*," *Bulletin of Hispanic Studies*, 48 (1971), 128–50.

An important article, focused on what has become a central question in studies of Almeida – can he be viewed as a Realist before his time?

Peixoto, Marta. "Aires as narrator and Aires as character in *Esaú e Jacó*," *Luso-Brazilian Review*, 17 (1980), 79–92.

An excellent study of narrative technique in one of Machado's least-studied later novels.

Santiago, Silviano. "*O Ateneu*: contradições e perquirições," *Luso-Brazilian Review*, 4 (1967), 53–78.

Reprinted in *Uma literatura nos trópicos* (see above, under "Books"). Perhaps the best critical study yet of the novel.

Schwarz, Roberto. "The form of the novel of the periphery of capitalism," *Social Science Information*, 22 (1983), 51–60.

A useful summary, in English, of Schwarz's ideas.

Sontag, Susan. "Afterlives: the case of Machado de Assis," *New Yorker*, 66 (1990), 102–8 (May 7).

An example of what has practically become a sub-genre: the astonished and enthusiastic discovery of Machado by leading Anglo-American intellectuals.

Turner, Doris J. "A clarification of some 'strange' chapters in Machado's *Dom Casmurro*," *Luso-Brazilian Review*, 13 (1976), 55–66.

An extremely useful article – even if it doesn't have all the answers as to what these "strange" chapters mean.

Wasserman, Renata R. Mautner. "The red and the white: the 'Indian' novels of José de

775

Alencar," *PMLA*, 98:5 (1983), 815–27.
"Re-inventing the new world: Cooper and Alencar," *Comparative Literature*, 36: 2 (1984), 130–45.
　　Two excellent articles on Alencar's Indianism and its relationship to similar developments in North American literature.
Wolff, Maria Tai. "*Lucíola*: critical frames," *Bulletin of Hispanic Studies*, 65:1 (1988), 61–72.
"Re-reading José de Alencar: the case of *A pata da gazela*," *Hispania*, 71:4 (1988), 812–19.
　　Interesting and useful reappraisals of Alencar's female characterization.
Zilberman, Regina. "Natureza e mulher: uma visão do Brasil no romance romântico," *Modern Language Studies*, 19:2 (1989), 50–64.
　　A recent and important revisionist look at Alencar and other romantic novelists; also focuses on Taunay's *Inocência*.

Chapter 8: Brazilian fiction from 1900 to 1945

Primary sources

Almeida, José Américo de. *A bagaceira*, Paraíba, Imp. Oficial, 1928.
Amado, Jorge. *Jubiabá*, Rio de Janeiro, Livraria José Olympio Editora, 1935.
　　Mar morto, Rio de Janeiro, Livraria José Olympio Editora, 1936.
　　Capitães da areia, Rio de Janeiro, Livraria José Olympio Editora, 1937.
　　Terras do sem fim, São Paulo, Livraria Martins Editora, 1942.
　　Seara vermelha. São Paulo, Livraria Martins Editora, 1946.
　　Gabriela, cravo e canela, São Paulo, Livraria Martins Editora, 1958.
　　Os velhos marinheiros, São Paulo, Livraria Martins Editora, 1965.
　　Os pastores da noite, São Paulo, Martins, 1964.
　　Dona Flor e seus dois maridos, São Paulo, Martins, 1967.
　　The Violent Land, New York, Knopf, 1945.
　　Gabriela, Clove and Cinnamon, New York, Knopf, 1962.
　　The Two Deaths of Quincas Wateryell, New York, Knopf, 1963.
　　Home Is the Sailor, New York, Knopf, 1964.
　　Shepherds of the Night, New York, Knopf, 1967.
　　Dona Flor and her Two Husbands, New York, Knopf, 1969.
　　Tent of Miracles, New York, Knopf, 1971.
　　Tereza Batista: Home from the wars, tr. Barbara Shelby, New York, Knopf/ Random House, 1975.
　　Tieta the Goat Girl, New York, Knopf, 1979.
　　Jubiabá, New York, Avon, 1984.
　　Sea of Death, New York, Avon, 1984.
　　Pen, Sword, Camisole, Boston, Godine, 1985.
Andrade, J. Oswald de. *Memórias sentimentais de João Miramar*, São Paulo, Independência, 1924.
　　Serafim Ponte Grande, Rio de Janeiro, Ariel, 1933.
　　Seraphim Grosse Pointe, Austin, Texas, New Latin Quarter Editions, 1979.
Andrade, Mário de. *Amor, verbo intransitivo*, São Paulo, A. Tisi, 1927.

Volume 3

Macunaíma, São Paulo, Eugênio Cupolo, 1928.
Fräulein, New York, Macauley, 1933.
Macunaima, New York, Random House, 1984.
Anjos, Ciro dos. *O amanuense Belmiro*, Belo Horizonte, Os amigos do livro, 1937.
Aranha, José Pereira da Graça. *Canaã*, Rio de Janeiro, Garnier, 1902.
Aranha, José Pereira da Graça, *Canaan*, Boston, Four Seas, 1920.
Cardoso, Lúcio. *A luz no subsolo*, Rio de Janeiro, Livraria José Olympio Editora, 1936.
Mãos vazias, Rio de Janeiro, Livraria José Olympio Editora, 1938.
Crônica da casa assassinada, Rio de Janeiro, Livraria José Olympio Editora, 1959.
Coelho Neto, Henrique Maximiano. *A capital federal*, Rio de Janeiro, O País, 1893.
Miragem, Rio de Janeiro, Domingos de Magalhães, 1895.
Sertão, Rio de Janeiro, Leuzinger, 1896.
Inverno em flor, Rio de Janeiro, Laemmert, 1897.
O morto, Rio de Janeiro, Laemmert, 1898.
A conquista, Rio de Janeiro, Laemmert, 1899.
Tormenta, Rio de Janeiro, Laemmert, 1901.
Turbilhão, Rio de Janeiro, Laemmert, 1906.
Banzo, Porto, Lello, 1913.
O rei negro, Porto, Lello, 1914.
Faria, Otávio de. *Tragédia burguesa*, 13 vols., Rio de Janeiro, Livraria José Olympio Editora, 1937–1971.
Fontes, Amando. *Os corumbas*, Rio de Janeiro, Schmidt, 1933.
Rua do Siriri, Rio de Janeiro, Livraria José Olympio Editora, 1937.
Lima Barreto, Afonso Henriques de. *Recordações do escrivão Isaías Caminha*, Lisbon, Teixeira, 1909.
Numa e a ninfa, Rio de Janeiro, A Noite, 1915.
Triste fim de Policarpo Quaresma, Rio de Janeiro, Revista dos Tribunais, 1915.
Vida e morte de M. J. Gonzaga de Sá, São Paulo, Ed. Revista do Brasil, 1919.
The Patriot, London, Collins, 1978.
Lobato, José Bento Monteiro. *Urupês*, São Paulo, Ed. Revista do Brasil, 1918.
Cidades mortas, São Paulo, Ed. Revista do Brasil, 1919.
Negrinha, São Paulo, Monteiro Lobato, 1920.
Machado, Antônio de Alcântara. *Brás, Bexiga e Barra Funda*, São Paulo, Hélios, 1927.
Laranja da China, São Paulo, Empresa Gráfica, 1928.
Machado, Dionélio. *Os ratos*, Porto Alegre, Ed. Globo, 1935.
Pena, Cornélio de Oliveira. *Fronteira*, Rio de Janeiro, Ariel, 1936.
Threshold, Philadelphia, Franklin, 1975.
Queiroz, Raquel de. *O quinze*, Rio de Janeiro, Livraria José Olympio Editora, 1930.
Caminho de pedras, Rio de Janeiro, Livraria José Olympio Editora, 1937.
As três Marias, Rio de Janeiro, Livraria José Olympio Editora, 1939.
The Three Marias, Austin, University of Texas Press, 1963.
Ramos, Graciliano. *Caetés*. Rio de Janeiro, Livraria José Olympio Editora, 1933.
São Bernardo, Rio de Janeiro, Livraria José Olympio Editora, 1934.
Angústia, Rio de Janeiro, Livraria José Olympio Editora, 1936.
Vidas secas, Rio de Janeiro, Livraria José Olympio Editora, 1938.
Anguish, New York, Knopf, 1946.

Barren Lives, Austin, University of Texas Press, 1965.

Rego, José Lins do. *Menino de engenho*, Rio de Janeiro, Livraria José Olympio Editora, 1932.

Doidinho, Rio de Janeiro, Livraria José Olympio Editora, 1933.

Bangüê, Rio de Janeiro, Livraria José Olympio Editora, 1934.

Moleque Ricardo, Rio de Janeiro, Livraria José Olympio Editora, 1935.

Usina, Rio de Janeiro, Livraria José Olympio Editora, 1936.

Pedra Bonita, Rio de Janeiro, Livraria José Olympio Editora, 1938.

Fogo morto, Rio de Janeiro, Livraria José Olympio Editora, 1943.

Pureza, Rio de Janeiro, Livraria José Olympio Editora, 1937.

Cangaceiros, Rio de Janeiro, Livraria José Olympio Editora, 1953.

Pureza, London, Hutchinson, 1947.

Plantation Boy, New York, Knopf, 1966.

Veríssimo, Erico. *Caminhos cruzados*, Porto Alegre, Globo, 1935.

Música ao longe, Porto Alegre, Globo, 1935.

Um lugar ao sol, Porto Alegre, Globo, 1936.

Olhai os lírios do campo, Porto Alegre, Globo, 1938.

O resto é silêncio, Porto Alegre, Globo, 1943.

O tempo e o vento, 3 vols., Porto Alegre, Globo, vol. I: *O continente*, 1949; vol. II: *O retrato*, 1951; vol. III: *O arquipélago*, 1961/1962.

Noite, Porto Alegre, Globo, 1954.

Incidente em Antares, Porto Alegre, Globo, 1971.

Crossroads, New York, Macmillan, 1943.

The Rest is Silence, New York, Macmillan, 1946.

Consider the Lilies of the Field, New York, Macmillan, 1947.

Time and the Wind, New York, Macmillan, 1951.

Night, New York, Macmillan, 1956.

His Excellency, the Ambassador, New York, Macmillan, 1967.

Vieira, José Geraldo. *A mulher que fugiu de Sodoma*, São Paulo, Livraria Martins Editora, 1931.

Território humano, São Paulo, Livraria Martins Editora, 1936.

A quadragésima porta, São Paulo, Livraria Martins Editora, 1943.

A túnica e os dados, São Paulo, Livraria Martins Editora, 1947.

Secondary sources

Books

Almeida, Alfredo W. B. de. *Jorge Amado: política e literatura*, Rio de Janeiro, Campus, 1979.

Aranha, José Pereira da Graça. *O espírito moderno*, São Paulo, Monteiro Lobato, e Cia, 1925.

Araújo, Murillo. *Quadrantes do modernismo brasileiro*, Rio de Janeiro, MEC, 1958.
    Contains a polemic essay on Graça Aranha and his relationship to Modernism.

Bosi, Alfredo. *História concisa da literatura brasileira*, São Paulo, Cultrix, 1970.
    The final portion of this book offers thoughtful insights into the overall flow of Brazilian fiction during the first half of the twentieth century.

Brasil, Assis. *História crítica da literatura brasileira: o modernismo*, Rio de Janeiro, Pallas, 1976.

Offers special focus on fictional works of Mário de Andrade, Oswald de Andrade, Antônio de Alcântara Machado, and Adelino Magalhães.

Brayner, Sônia. *Labirinto do espaço romanesco*, Rio de Janeiro, Civilização Brasileira, 1979.

Work treats the period 1880–1920.

Brito, Mário da Silva. *História do modernismo brasileiro*, 2nd. edn. revised, Rio de Janeiro, Civilização Brasileira, 1964.

Dedicated principally to poetry, this work contains a short but informative section on the fiction of the 1920s.

Buarque de Holanda, Aurélio (ed.). *O romance brasileiro*, Rio de Janeiro, O Cruzeiro, 1952.

Contains balanced, informative essays on Lima Barreto (by Astrojildo Pereira), Graça Aranha (by Orris Soares), and Coelho Neto (by Brito Broca).

Cândido, Antônio. *Literatura e sociedade – estudos de teoria e história literária*, São Paulo, Companhia Editora Nacional, 1965.

Chapter 6 – "Literatura e cultura de 1900 a 1945" – is a well-written, concise essay on the period in question, while remainder of work gives good background.

Carvalho, Castelar de. *Ensaios gracilianos*. Série Universitária 6, Rio de Janeiro, Rio, 1978.

A mixed group of essays.

Chaves, Flávio Loureiro, Hildebrando Dacanal, *et al. Aspectos do modernismo brasileiro*, Porto Alegre, Universidade Federal do Rio Grande do Sul, 1970.

The Chaves essay treats "disintegration" of traditional concepts of protagonist, plot, and language in Oswald de Andrade and Mário de Andrade, while the Dacanal piece suggests the crisis and collapse of the "middle-class synthesis" in European novels of the early twentieth century and the emergence of vigorous new literatures in the New World.

Coutinho, Carlos Nelson, *et al. Realismo e anti-realismo na literatura brasileira*, Rio de Janeiro, Paz e Terra, 1972.

Offers a Marxist interpretation of the novels of Lima Barreto.

Ellison, Fred P. *Brazil's New Novel: Four northeastern masters*, Berkeley and Los Angeles, University of California Press, 1954.

Offers general overview of northeastern regionalistic fiction from mid-centery viewpoint, plus individual essays on José Lins do Rego, Jorge Amado, Graciliano Ramos, and Raquel de Queiroz; good introduction for English speakers.

Fantinati, Carlos Erivany. *O profeta e o escrivão: estudo sobre Lima Barreto*, São Paulo, Hucitec, 1978.

Freyre, Gilberto. *Heróis e vilões no romance brasileiro em torno das projeções de tipos sócio-antropológicos em personagens de romances do século XIX e do atual*, São Paulo, Cultrix, 1979.

Fusco, Rosário. *Política e letras*, Rio de Janeiro, Livraria José Olympio Editora, 1940.

A subjective synthesis of political and stylistic aspects of Brazilian literature of the 1930s from an "insider's" point of view.

Landars, Vasda B. *De Jeca a Macunaíma*, Rio de Janeiro, Editora Civilização Brasileira, 1987.

Presents Monteiro Lobato as a forerunner of Brazilian Modernism.

Lins, Osman. *Lima Barreto e o espaço romanesco*, São Paulo, Editora Ática, 1976.

Martins, Eduardo. *José Lins de Rego: o homem e a obra*, Recife, Secretaria de Educação e Cultura, 1980.

Martins, Wilson. *The Modernist Idea*, tr. Jack E. Tomlins, New York University Press, 1970.

Informative period essays followed by more detailed analysis of eight representative works and nineteen representative authors, the majority fiction writers.

História da inteligência brasileira, vols. V: *(1897–1914)*, VI: *(1915–1933)*, and VII: *(1933–1960)*, São Paulo, Cultrix, 1978–1979.

Offers detailed background information on events, trends, and year-by-year publication of works in all literary genres, politics, philosophy, and the social sciences, for the period in question.

Menezes, Raimundo de. *Dicionário literário brasileiro*, 2nd. edn., Rio de Janeiro, Livros Técnicos e Científicos, 1978.

Offers essential bio-bibliographical data on all authors of relevance, plus a brief valorative commentary on the majority.

Miguel-Pereira, Lúcia. *História da literatura brasileira: prosa de ficção de 1870 a 1920*, Rio de Janeiro, Livraria José Olympio Editora, 1950.

Best in-depth analysis of fictional trends and writers of the first half of the period in question.

Moisés, Massaud, and José Paulo Paes (eds.). *Pequeno dicionário de literatura brasileira*, 2nd. edn., São Paulo, Cultrix, 1980.

Handy reference work for essential bio-bibliographical information on the most salient writers of the period.

Ramos, Clara. *Mestre Graciliano: confirmação de uma obra*, Rio de Janeiro, Editora Civilização Brasileira, 1979.

A family view of the writer.

Rodríguez Suro, Joaquín. *Érico Veríssimo: história e literatura*, Porto Alegre, Luzzatto, 1985.

A sociohistoric study.

Sodré, Nelson Werneck. *História da literatura brasileira: seus fundamentos econômicos*, 4th. edn., Rio de Janeiro, Civilização Brasileira, 1964.

Focuses on various dimensions of the expression of *Regionalismo/sertanismo/geografismo* in Brazilian fiction of the nineteenth and twentieth centuries.

Zilberman, Regina. *São Bernardo e os processos de comunicação*, Porto Alegre, Movimento, 1975.

Articles

Alves, Ieda Maria. "O vocabulário da cana-de-açúcar nas obras de José Lins do Rego," *Alfa*, 25 (1981), 5–14.

Américo, José. "Lúcio Cardoso – o escritor e a lenda: a queda." *Minas Gerais, Suplemento Literário* 958, 20 (Feb. 9, 1985), 3.

Batchelor, C. Malcolm. "João do Rio: o esboço de um retrato e espelhos de ilusão," *Hispania*, 1985; 68:4 (1985), 700–8.

Cerqueira, Nelson. "Hermeneutics and literature: a study of William Faulkner's *As I*

Lay Dying and Graciliano Ramos' *Vidas secas*," *Dissertation Abstracts*, 47:6 (Nov. 1986), 1719A.

A Marxist interpretation.

Chang, Linda. "Social problems in the novel cycle *Tragédia Burguesa* by Octávio de Faria," *Dissertation Abstracts*, 43:11 (May 1983), 3610A–3611A.

Cintra, Ismael Ângelo. "Consciência e crítica da linguagem: Graciliano Ramos," *Revista de Letras*, 20 (1980): 49–57.

A linguistic study applying the theories of Jakobson.

Courteau, Joanna. "The problematic heroines in the novels of Rachel de Queiroz," *Luso-Brazilian Review*, 22:2 (1985), 123–44.

Daniel, Mary L. "El lenguaje figurado en las novelas de Erico Veríssimo," *Revista de Cultura Brasileña*, 4:12 (1965), 22–34.

Frizzi, Adria. "Life and letters of a chameleon: the carnival of memoirs in *Serafim Ponte Grande*," *Luso-Brazilian Review*, 23:2 (1986), 61–9.

A study of narrative technique.

Garcia, Frederick C. H. "Erico Veríssimo e a literatura infantil," *Prismal/Cabral*, 6 (Spring 1981), 87–105.

Helena, Lúcia. "A propósito dos romances experimentais de Oswald de Andrade," *Colóquio*, 82 (1984), 81–5.

Johnson, Lemuel A. "The *Romance Bárbaro* as an agent of disappearance: Henrique Coelho Neto's *Rei Negro* and its conventions" in William Luis (ed.), *Voices From Under: Black narrative in Latin America and the Caribbean*, Westport, Conn., Greenwood Press, 1984, 223–48.

Jordan, Dawn M. "Building a history of women's literature in Brazil," *Plaza*, 56 (1981–1982), 75–96.

Includes biographical and substantive information on Júlia Lopes de Almeida and others writing from 1800 to 1920.

Lee, Cremilda Toledo. "John Steinbeck, Graciliano Ramos, and Jorge Amado: a comparative study," *Dissertation Abstracts*, 41:12 (June 1981), 5091A–5092A.

A structural study of narrative technique.

Lemos, Brunilda Reichmann. "The essence of tragedy: a comparative study between the tragedies by Thomas Hardy and by Octávio de Faria," *Dissertation Abstracts*, 43:3 (Sept. 1982), 809A.

Focuses on bird imagery and treatment of hero figures.

Nunes, Maria Luísa. "Lima Barreto's theory of literature" in *From Linguistics to Literature: Romance studies offered to Francis M. Rogers*, Amsterdam, Benjamins, 1981, 223–34.

Patai, Daphne. "Race and politics in two Brazilian utopias," *Luso-Brazilian Review*, 19:1 (1982), 66–81.

Focuses on Monteiro Lobato's *Presidente negro* and Chico Buarque's *Fazenda modelo*.

Pereira, José Carlos Seabra. "Programas de gêneros e sintagmática narrativa: sobre *A bagaceira* como romance de formação," *Revista Brasileira de Língua e Literatura*, 3:7 (1981), 5–8.

Pestino, Joseph F. "Mário de Andrade and André Breton: strange bedfellows," *Tinta*, 1:4 (1984), 15–20.

A short comparative study of Modernism and Surrealism.

Potter, Norman M. "The construction of narrative space in the modern Brazilian novel (1902–1938)," *Dissertation Abstracts*, 42:1 (July, 1981), 240A.

Santiago, Silviano. "Uma ferroada no peito do pé: dupla leitura de *Triste fim de Policarpo Quaresma*," *Revista Iberoamericana*, 50:126 (1984), 31–46.
A structuralist study of narrative structure.

Standley, Arline. "Here and there: now and then," *Luso-Brazilian Review*, 23:1 (1986), 61–75.
A comparative study of Faulkner's *The Sound and the Fury* and Lins do Rego's *Fogo morto*.

Suárez, José I. "The neglected fiction of Amando Fontes," *Selected Proceedings: 32nd Mountain Interstate Foreign Language Conference*, Winston-Salem, Wake Forest University, 1984, 353–60.

Wasserman, Renata R. Mautner. "*Preguiça* and power: Mário de Andrade's *Macunaíma*," *Luso-Brazilian Review*, 21:1 (1984), 99–116.

Chapter 9: Brazilian prose from 1940 to 1980

Primary sources

Adonias Filho, *Os servos da morte*, Rio de Janeiro, José Olympio, 1946.
Memórias de Lázaro, Rio de Janeiro, O Cruzeiro, 1952.
Corpo vivo, Rio de Janeiro, Civilização Brasileira, 1962.
Memories of Lazarus, Austin and London, University of Texas Press, 1969.

Amado, Jorge. *Terras do sem fim*, São Paulo, Livraria Martins Editora, 1942.
São Jorge dos Ilhéus, São Paulo, Livraria Martins Editora, 1944.
Seara vermelha, São Paulo, Martins, 1946.
Gabriela, cravo e canela, São Paulo, Livraria Martins Editora, 1958.
Dona Flor e seus dois maridos, São Paulo, Livraria Martins Editora, 1966.
Tenda dos milagres, São Paulo, Livraria Martins Editora, 1969.
Tereza Batista: cansada de guerra, São Paulo, Livraria Martins Editora, 1972.
Tieta do agreste, São Paulo, Livraria Martins Editora, 1977.
Gabriela, Clove and Cinnamon, New York, Knopf, 1962; London, Souvenir Press, 1983.
The Violent Land, New York, Knopf, 1965.
Dona Flor and her Two Husbands, New York, Knopf, 1969; London, Weidenfeld & Nicolson, 1970.
Tent of Miracles, New York, Knopf, 1971.
Tereza Batista, Home from the Wars, tr. Barbara Shelby, New York, Knopf, 1974; London, Souvenir Press, 1982.
Tieta, New York, Knopf, 1979.

Ângelo, Ivan. *A festa*, São Paulo, Summus, 1975.
A casa de vidro, São Paulo, Livraria Cultura, 1979.
The Celebration, New York, Avon, 1982.
The Tower of Glass, tr. Ellen Watson, New York, Avon, 1982.

Antônio (Ferreira Filho), João. *Malagueta, Perus e Bacanaço*, Rio de Janeiro, Civilização Brasileira, 1963.

Brandão, Ignácio de Loyola. *Zero*, Rome, Feltrinelli, 1974.

Volume 3

Callado, Antônio. *Quarup*, Rio de Janeiro, Civilização Brasileira, 1967.

    Bar Don Juan, Rio de Janeiro, Civilização Brasileira, 1971.

Cardoso, Lúcio. *Crônica da casa assassinada*, Rio de Janeiro, José Olympio, 1959.

Dourado, Valdomiro Autran. *A barca dos homens*, Rio de Janeiro, Editora do Autor, 1961.

    Opera dos mortos, Rio de Janeiro, Civilização Brasileira, 1967.

    O risco do bordado, Rio de Janeiro, Expressão e Cultura, 1970.

    Os sinos da agonia, Rio de Janeiro, Expressão e Cultura, 1974.

    Novelário de Donga Novais, Rio de Janeiro, Difel, 1976.

    The Voices of the Dead, London, Peter Owen, 1980; New York, Tapingler, 1981.

    Pattern for a Tapestry, London, Peter Owen, 1984.

Faria, Otávio de. *Mundos mortos*, Rio de Janeiro, José Olympio, 1937.

    Os caminhos da vida, Rio de Janeiro, José Olympio, 1939.

    O lodo das ruas, Rio de Janeiro, José Olympio, 1942.

    O anjo de pedra, Rio de Janeiro, José Olympio, 1944.

    Os renegados, Rio de Janeiro, José Olympio, 1947.

    Os loucos, Rio de Janeiro, José Olympio, 1952.

    O senhor do mundo, Rio de Janeiro, José Olympio, 1957.

    O retrato da morte, Rio de Janeiro, José Olympio, 1961.

    Ângela ou as areias do mundo, Rio de Janeiro, José Olympio, 1963.

    A sombra de Deus, Rio de Janeiro, José Olympio, 1966.

    O cavaleiro da Virgem, Rio de Janeiro, José Olympio, 1971.

    O indigno, Rio de Janeiro, José Olympio, 1976.

    O pássaro oculto, Rio de Janeiro, José Olympio, 1979.

Fonseca, Rubem. *A coleira do cão*, Rio de Janeiro, GRD, 1965.

    Feliz ano novo, Rio de Janeiro, Artenova, 1975.

    A grande arte, Rio de Janeiro, Francisco Alves, 1983.

    High Art, New York, Harper & Row, 1986.

Lins, Osman. *O visitante*, Rio de Janeiro, Livraria José Olympio Editora, 1955.

    Os gestos, Rio de Janeiro, Livraria José Olympio Editora, 1957.

    O fiel e a pedra, São Paulo, Summus, 1961.

    Avalovara, São Paulo, Summus, 1973.

    Nove, novena: narrativas, São Paulo, Melhoramentos, 1966.

    Nine, Novena, tr. Adria Frizzi, diss., Austin, University of Texas Press, 1988.

Lispector, Clarice. *Perto do coração selvagem*, Rio de Janeiro, A Noite, 1944.

    O lustre, Rio de Janeiro, Agir, 1946.

    Alguns contos, Rio de Janeiro, Ministério da Educação e Saúde, 1952.

    Laços de família, Rio de Janeiro, Francisco Alves, 1960.

    A maçã no escuro, Rio de Janeiro, Francisco Alves, 1961.

    A Legião Estrangeira, Rio de Janeiro, Editora do Autor, 1964.

    A paixão segundo G. H., Rio de Janeiro, Editora do Autor, 1964.

    Uma aprendizagem ou o livro dos prazeres, Rio de Janeiro, Sabiá, 1971.

    A hora da estrela, Rio de Janeiro, Livraria José Olympio Editora, 1977.

    The Apple in the Dark, New York, Knopf, 1967; London, Virago, 1983.

    Family Ties, tr. Giovanni Pontiero, Austin, University of Texas Press, 1972; Manchester, Carcanet, 1985.

    An Apprenticeship or the Book of Delights, Austin, University of Texas Press, 1986.

The Foreign Legion: Stories and chronicles, tr. Giovanni Pontiero, Manchester, Carcanet, 1986.

The Hour of the Star, tr. and afterword Giovanni Pontiero, Manchester, Carcanet, 1986.

Nassar, Raduan. *Lavoura arcaica*, Rio de Janeiro, Livraria José Olympio Editora, 1975.

Um copo de cólera, São Paulo, Cultura, 1978.

Nava, Pedro. *Baú de ossos*, Rio de Janeiro, Livraria José Olympio Editora, 1972.

Balão cativo, Rio de Janeiro, Livraria José Olympio Editora, 1973.

Chão de ferro, Rio de Janeiro, Livraria José Olympio Editora, 1976.

Beira mar, Rio de Janeiro, Livraria José Olympio Editora, 1978.

Galo-das-trevas, Rio de Janeiro, Nova Fronteira, 1980.

O círio perfeito, Rio de Janeiro, Nova Fronteira, 1983.

Pena, Cornélio. *A menina morta*, Rio de Janeiro, Livraria José Olympio Editora, 1954.

Pompeu, Renato, *Quatro olhos*, São Paulo, Alfa/Omega, 1976.

Resende, Otto Lara. *O braço direito*, Rio de Janeiro, Civilização Brasileira, 1963.

The Inspector of Orphans, London, André Deutsch, 1968.

Ramos, Graciliano. *Memórias do cárcere*, São Paulo, Livraria Martins Editora, 1953.

Ribeiro, Darcy. *Maíra*, Rio de Janeiro, Civilização Brasileira, 1975.

Maíra, tr., New York, Random House, 1984; London, Picador, 1986.

Ribeiro, João Ubaldo. *Sargento Getúlio*, Rio de Janeiro, Nova Fronteira, 1971.

Sergeant Getúlio, Boston, Houghton & Mifflin, 1978; London, Faber & Faber, 1986.

Rosa, João Guimarães. *Sagarana*, Rio de Janeiro, Universal, 1946.

Corpo de baile, Rio de Janeiro, Livraria José Olympio Editora, 1956.

Grande sertão: veredas, Rio de Janeiro, Livraria José Olympio Editora, 1956.

Primeiras estórias, Rio de Janeiro, Livraria José Olympio Editora, 1962.

Tutaméia (terceiras estórias), Rio de Janeiro, Livraria José Olympio Editora, 1967.

The Devil to Pay in the Backlands, tr. James L. Taylor and Harriet de Onís, New York, Knopf, 1963.

Sagarana, tr. Harriet de Onís, New York, Knopf, 1966.

The Third Bank of the River and Other Stories, tr. Barbara Shelby, New York, Knopf, 1968.

Rubião, Murilo. *O ex-mágico*, Rio de Janeiro, Universal, 1947.

Os dragões e outros contos, Belo Horizonte, Movimento/Perspectiva, 1965.

O convidado, São Paulo, Quíron, 1974.

The Ex-Magician and Other Stories, tr. Thomas Colchie, New York, Harper & Row, 1965.

    This volume contains stories from both *Os dragões e outros contos* and *O ex-mágico*.

Sabino, Fernando. *O encontro marcado*, Rio de Janeiro, Civilização Brasileira, 1956.

A Time to Meet, London, Souvenir Press, 1967; Toronto, Ryerson Press, 1967.

Santiago, Silviano. *Em liberdade*, Rio de Janeiro, Paz e Terra, 1981.

Suassuna, Ariano. *A pedra do reino*, Rio de Janeiro, Livraria José Olympio Editora, 1971.

Sussekind, Carlos. *Armadilha para Lamartine*, Rio de Janeiro, Labor do Brasil, 1975.

Telles, Lygia Fagundes. *Ciranda de pedra*, Rio de Janeiro, O Cruzeiro, 1955.

Volume 3

As meninas, São Paulo, Livraria Martins Editora, 1973.
  The Girl in the Photograph, New York, Avon Books, 1982.
Torres, Antônio. *Essa terra*, São Paulo, Editora Ática, 1976.
  The Land, London, Readers International, 1987.
Trevisan, Dalton. *Novelas nada exemplares*, Rio de Janeiro, Livraria José Olympio Editora, 1959.
  Cemitério de elefantes, Rio de Janeiro, Civilização Brasileira, 1964.
  Morte na praça, Rio de Janeiro, Editora do Autor, 1964.
  O vampiro de Curitiba, Rio de Janeiro, Civilização Brasileira, 1965.
  Desastres do amor, Rio de Janeiro, Civilização Brasileira, 1968.
  A guerra conjugal, Rio de Janeiro, Civilização Brasileira, 1969.
  The Vampire of Curitiba and Other Stories, tr. Gregory Rabassa, New York, Knopf, 1972.
    An anthology of Trevisan's stories.
Veiga, José J. *Os cavalinhos de Platiplanto*, Rio de Janeiro, Nítida, 1959.
  A hora dos ruminantes, Rio de Janeiro, Civilização Brasileira, 1966.
  A máquina extraviada, Rio de Janeiro, Prelo, 1968.
  Sombras de reis barbudos, Rio de Janeiro, Civilização Brasileira, 1973.
  The Misplaced Machine and Other Stories, tr. Pamela G. Bird, New York, Knopf, 1970.
  The Three Trials of Manirema, New York, Knopf, 1970; London, Peter Owen, 1979.
Veríssimo, Erico. *O tempo e o vento*, 3 vols., Porto Alegre, Globo, vol. I: *O continente*, 1949; vol. II: *O retrato*, 1951; vol. III: *O arquipélago*, 1961 and 1962 (published in two parts).
  Incidente em Antares, Porto Alegre, Globo, 1971.
  Time and the Wind, New York, Macmillan, 1951.

Secondary sources

N.B.: In this section of the bibliography, I have attempted to give the best general introductions to the subject, written at different stages in the last forty years or so. Where individual authors are concerned, I have tried to select the most useful work on each, in English in the (rare) cases in which this is possible: in some cases, there is no really adequate work of which I am aware. Many of the works themselves contain complete bibliographies.

Books

Andrade, Ana Luiza. *Osman Lins: crítica e criação*, São Paulo, HUCITEC, 1987.
  The fullest discussion of Lins's work.
Arrigucci, Davi, Jr. *Enigma e comentário*, São Paulo, Companhia das Letras, 1987.
    Contains excellent essays on Rubem Braga, the *crônica*, Pedro Nava, Fernando Gabeira, and Murilo Rubião.
Bosi, Alfredo. *História concisa da literatura brasileira*, São Paulo, Cultrix, n.d.
  O conto brasileiro contemporâneo, São Paulo, Cultrix, 1975.
    Both these works are sensible and authoritative.

Chaves, Flávio Loureiro. *Erico Veríssimo: realismo e sociedade*, Porto Alegre, Globo, 1976.
Complete – sees Veríssimo as a consistent Humanist.
Coutinho, Afrânio (ed.). *A literatura no Brasil*, vol. v, Rio de Janeiro, Editora Sul Americana, 1970.
Individual essays on more important writers – general essay on the younger (i.e., in 1970) generation.
Cunha, Fausto. *Situações da ficção brasileira*, Rio de Janeiro, Paz e Terra, 1970.
Important essays, notably "Situação atual do romance brasileiro."
Fitz, Earl E. *Clarice Lispector*, Boston, Twayne, 1985.
Complete, with good bibliography.
Foster, David William, and Roberto Reis. *A Dictionary of Contemporary Brazilian Authors*, Tempe, Arizona State University Center for Latin American Studies, 1981.
Useful, though some important authors missing or undervalued.
Lepecki, Maria Lúcia. *Autran Dourado*, São Paulo, Quíron, 1974.
A study of mythical structures in his work, not a basic introduction, which is still lacking.
Lima, Luiz Costa. *A perversão do trapezista: o romance em Cornélio Pena*, Rio de Janeiro, Imago, 1986.
A complex account of Pena's fiction, the only one which studies it in depth.
Lins, Osman. *Guerra sem testemunhas*, São Paulo, Livraria Martins Editora, 1969.
Part-criticism, part-confession.
Lowe, Elizabeth. *The City in Brazilian Literature*, London and Toronto, Associated University Presses, 1982.
General study, concentrating on recent authors.
Machado, Janete Gaspar. *Os romances brasileiros nos anos 70: fragmentação social e estética*, Florianópolis, Editora da Universidade Federal de Santa Catarina, 1981.
Discusses eleven novels.
Parker, J. M. *Brazilian Fiction, 1950–70*, Glasgow Latin-American Institute Occasional Papers, 9 (1974).
Short, but very useful as a view of the matter before the end of censorship.
Patai, Daphne. *Myth and Ideology in Contemporary Brazilian Fiction*, London and Toronto, Associated University Presses, 1983.
Original and well-argued, critical of some of the authors discussed (e.g., Amado, Adonias Filho, Lispector).
Perez, Renard. *Escritores brasileiros contemporâneos*, 2 vols., Rio de Janeiro, Civilização Brasileira, 1960 and 1964.
Contains a biographical essay and a selection from forty authors, many of fiction.
Rama, Ángel. *La novela en América Latina*, Xalapa, Mexico, Universidad Veracruzana, 1986.
Several sections on Brazilian authors, giving useful comparative perspectives.
Schwartz, Jorge. *Murilo Rubião: a poética do Uroboro*, São Paulo, Editora Atica, 1981.
Excellent dicussion of a relatively ignored author.
Silverman, Malcolm. *Moderna ficção brasileira*, 2 vols., Rio de Janeiro, Civilização

Brasileira, 1978 and 1981.

    Informative discussions of some twenty-five authors.

Steen, Edla Van. *Viver e escrever*, Porto Alegre, L & PM, 1981.

    Lively interviews with eighteen authors, including many discussed here – very useful.

Sussekind, Flora. *Literatura e vida literária*, Rio de Janeiro, Jorge Zahar, 1985.

    One of a series on the dictatorship years – well-argued, with an anti-Realist *parti-pris*.

Tavares, Paulo. *O baiano Jorge Amado e sua obra*, Rio de Janeiro, Record, 1980.

    Uncritical, but contains much useful information.

Vincent, Jon S. *João Guimarães Rosa*, Boston, Twayne, 1978.

    Sensible introduction for English-speaking readers.

Waldman, Berta. *Do vampiro ao cafajeste: uma leitura da obra de Dalton Trevisan*, São Paulo, HUCITEC, 1982.

    Focuses on Trevisan's elliptical style and its implications.

Articles

Arrigucci, Davi, Jr. "Jornal, realismo, alegoria: o romance brasileiro recente," in *Achados e perdidos*, São Paulo, Polis, 1979, 79–115.

    An influential discussion with other critics.

Cândido, Antônio. "A literatura brasileira em 1972," *Revista Iberoamericana*, 98–99 (Jan.–June 1977), 5–16.

"A nova narrativa" in *A educação pela noite e outros ensaios*, São Paulo, Editora Atica, 1987, 199–215.

    A panorama comparing and contrasting Brazilian and Spanish American fiction since about 1930.

Galvão, Walnice Nogueira. "Amado: respeitoso, respeitável" in *Saco de gatos*, São Paulo, Duas Cidades, 1972, 13–22.

    The most perceptive of the attacks on Amado.

Holanda, Heloísa Buarque de, and Marcos Augusto Gonçalves. "Política e literatura: a ficção da realidade brasileira" in Adauto Neves (ed.), *Anos 70: Literatura*, Rio de Janeiro, Europa Empresa Gráfica e Editora, 1979–1980, 7–81.

    A lively and complete essay, interleaved with interviews with writers.

Lima, Luiz Costa. "O cão pop e a alegoria cobradora" in *Dispersa demanda*, Rio de Janeiro, Francisco Alves, 1981, 144–3.

    On Rubem Fonseca.

"Réquiem para a aquarela do Brasil" in *Dispersa demanda*, Rio de Janeiro, Francisco Alves, 1981, 124–43.

    On *Armadilha para Lamartine* and *Quatro olhos*.

Parker, John M. "The novels of Carlos Heitor Cony," *Luso-Brazilian Review*, 10 (1979), 18–29.

Santiago, Silviano, "Vale quanto pesa (A ficção brasileira moderna)" in his *Vale quanto pesa*, Rio de Janeiro, Paz e Terra, 1982, 25–40.

"O teorema de Walnice e sua recíproca" in his *Vale quanto pesa*, Rio de Janeiro, Paz e Terra, 1982, 57–88.

"Repressão e censura no campo das artes na década de 70" in his *Vale quanto pesa*,

Rio de Janeiro, Paz e Terra, 1982, 47–57.

"Poder e alegria: a literatura brasileira pós-64" in *Nas malhas da letra*, São Paulo, Companhia das Letras, 1989, 11–23.

"Prosa literária atual no Brasil," *Revista do Brasil*, 1 (1984), 46–53.

Schwarz, Roberto. "Cultura e política, 1964–69" in his *O pai de família o outros estudos*, Rio de Janeiro, Paz e Terra, 1978, 61–92.

Chapter 10: The Brazilian short story

Primary sources

Abreu, Caio Fernando. *Inventário do irremediável*, Porto Alegre, Movimento, 1970.

O ovo apunhalado, Porto Alegre, Globo, 1975.

Pedras de Calcutá, São Paulo, Alfa y Omega, 1977.

Morangos mofados, São Paulo, Editora Brasiliense, 1982.

Triângulo das águas, Rio de Janeiro, Nova Fronteira, 1983.

Os dragões não conhecem o Paraíso, São Paulo, Companhia das Letras, 1987.

Accioli, Breno. *João Urso*, Rio de Janeiro, Epasa, 1944.

Cogumelos, Rio de Janeiro, A Noite, 1950.

Marina Pudim, Rio de Janeiro, Livraria José Olympio Editora, 1955.

Os cataventos, Rio de Janeiro, Livraria José Olympio Editora, 1962.

Aguiar, Flávio. *Os caninos do vampiro*, São Paulo, Editora Atica, 1979.

Alcântara Machado, Antônio de. *Brás, Bexiga e Barra Funda*, São Paulo, Hélio, 1927.

Laranja da China, São Paulo, Gráfica Editora, 1928.

Mana Maria e vários contos, Rio de Janeiro, Livraria José Olympio Editora, 1936.

Cavaquinho e saxofone, Rio de Janeiro, José Olympio, 1940.

Novelas paulistanas, 4 vols., Rio de Janeiro, José Olympio, 1959.

Alencar, José Martiniano de. *Cinco minutos*, Rio de Janeiro, Typ. do Diário, 1856.

Almeida, Júlia Lopes de. *Traços e illuminuras*, Lisbon, Typ. Castro & Irmão, 1887.

Ansia eterna, Rio de Janeiro, Garnier, 1903.

Elles e ellas, Rio de Janeiro, Francisco Alves, 1910.

Era uma vez, Rio de Janeiro, J. Ribeiro dos Santos, 1917.

Alphonsus, João. *Galinha cega*, Belo Horizonte, Os Amigos do Livro, 1931.

Pesca da baleia, Belo Horizonte, Paulo Bluhm, 1942.

Eis a noite, São Paulo, Livraria Martins Editora, 1943.

Amâncio, Moacir. *Chame o ladrão*, São Paulo, Edições Populares, 1978.

O riso do dragão, São Paulo, Editora Atica, 1981.

Andrade, Carlos Drummond de. *Contos de aprendiz*, Rio de Janeiro, José Olympio Editora, 1951.

Contos plausíveis, Rio de Janeiro, Livraria José Olympio Editora, 1981.

Andrade, Jefferson Ribeiro de. *No carnaval, confetes e serpentinas*, Belo Horizonte, Liberdade, 1973.

Um homem bebe cerveja no bar do Odilon, Rio de Janeiro, Codecri, 1978.

A origem de Deus e de tudo, Rio de Janeiro, Record, 1983.

Um prazer imenso, Rio de Janeiro, Record, 1986.

Andrade, Mário de. *Primeiro andar*, São Paulo, A. Tisi, 1926.

Belazarte, São Paulo, Piratininga, 1934.

Volume 3

Contos novos, São Paulo, Livraria Martins Editoria, 1947.

"The Christmas turkey," *Latin American Literary Review*, 7:14 (1979), 96–102.

Andrade, Rodrigo Melo Franco de. *Velórios*, Belo Horizonte, Os Amigos do Livro, 1935.

Angelo, Ivan. *Duas faces*, Belo Horizonte, Itatiaia, 1961.

A casa de vidro: cinco histórias do Brasil, São Paulo, Livraria Cultura, 1979.

Festa, tr. Thomas Colchie, New York, Avon, 1982.

The Tower of Glass, tr. Ellen Watson, New York, Avon, 1986.

Anísio, Chico. *O batizado da vaca*, Rio de Janeiro, Sabiá, 1972.

O enterro do anão, Rio de Janeiro Livraria José Olympio Editora, 1973.

A curva do Calombo, Rio de Janeiro, Livaria José Olympio Editora, 1974.

Teje preso, Rio de Janeiro, Rocco, 1975.

Feijoada no Copa, Rio de Janeiro, Rocco, 1976.

Antônio (Ferreira Filho), João. *Malagueta, Perus e Bacanaço*, Rio de Janeiro, Editora Civilização Brasileira, 1963.

Leão-de-chácara, Rio de Janeiro, Civilização Brasileira, 1975.

O Copacabana!, Rio de Janeiro, Civilização Brasileira, 1978.

Dedo duro, Rio de Janeiro, Record, 1982.

10 contos escolhidos, Brasília, Horizonte, 1983.

Abraçado ao meu rancor, Rio de Janeiro, Guanabara, 1986.

Araripe, Tristão de Alencar, Jr. *Contos brazileiros*, Recife, Typ. do Correio Pernambucano, 1868.

Arinos, Afonso. *Os jagunços*, Rio de Janeiro, Philobiblion, 1898; 3rd. edn., 1985.

Pelo sertão, Rio de Janeiro, Laemmert, 1898.

Lendas e tradições brasileiras, São Paulo, Typographia Levi, 1917.

O mestre de campo: romance do século dezoito, Rio de Janeiro, Francisco Alves, 1918.

Histórias e paisagens, Rio de Janeiro, Francisco Alves, 1921.

Azambuja, Darci Pereira de. *No galpão*, Porto Alegre, Globo, 1925.

A prodigiosa aventura e outras histórias possíveis, Porto Alegre, Globo, 1939.

Coxilhas, Porto Alegre, Globo, 1956.

Azevedo, Aluísio de. *Demônios*, São Paulo, Teixeira & Irmãos, 1893.

Pegados, Rio de Janeiro, H. Garnier, 1897.

Azevedo, Artur de. *Contos possíveis*, Rio de Janeiro, B. L. Garnier, 1889.

Contos fora da moda, Rio de Janeiro, Garnier, 1893.

Contos efêmeros, Rio de Janeiro/Paris, Garnier, 1900.

Contos em versos, Rio de Janeiro, H. Garnier, 1910.

Azevedo, Manuel Antônio Alvares de. "A noite na taverna" in his *Obras*, vol. II, ed. H. Pires, 8th. edn., São Paulo, Companhia Editora Nacional, 1942, 87–164.

Barreto, Afonso Henriques de Lima. *Histórias e sonhos*, Rio de Janeiro, Schettino, 1920.

Barroso, Juarez. *Mundinha Panchico e o resto do pessoal*, Rio de Janeiro, Livraria José Olympio Editora, 1969.

Bastos, Orlando. *De repente*, São Paulo, Editora Atica, 1984.

Bulhões, Antônio. *Estudos para a mão direita*, Rio de Janeiro, Civilização Brasileira, 1976.

Campos, José Maria Moreira. *Portas fechadas*, Rio de Janeiro, Edicões Cruzeiro,

1957.

As vozes do morto, São Paulo, Francisco Alves, 1963.

O puxador de têrco: contos, Rio de Janeiro, Livraria José Olympio Editora, 1969.

Contos escolhidos, Fortaleza, Imprensa da Universidade Federal do Ceará, 1971.

Os doze parafusos, São Paulo, Cultrix, 1978.

A grande mosca no copo de leite: contos, Rio de Janeiro, Nova Fronteira, 1985.

Dizem que os cães vêem coisas, Fortaleza, Universidade Federal do Ceará, 1988.

Carbonieri, José Fernando de Mafra. *Arma e bagagem*, São Paulo, Livraria Martins Editora, 1973.

Homem esvaziando os bolsos, Rio de Janeiro, Civilização Brasileira, 1977.

Carneiro, Caio Porfírio. 1975. *O casarão*, São Paulo, Editora do Escritor, 1975.

Chuva, São Paulo, HUCITEC, 1977.

10 contos escolhidos, Brasília, Horizonte/INL, 1983.

Carone, Modesto. *Aos pés de Matilde*, São Paulo, Summus, 1980.

Dias melhores, São Paulo, Editora Brasiliense, 1984.

Cavalcante, Joyce. *O discurso da mulher absurda*, São Paulo, Global, 1985.

Cavalcanti, João Ulchoa. *O diabo*, Petrópolis, Vozes, 1968.

Coelho, Nélson. *Depois do nada*, São Paulo, Global, 1983.

Coelho Neto, Henrique. *Sertão*, Rio de Janeiro, Leuzinger, 1896.

Colasanti, Marina. *E por falar em amor e outros contos*, Rio de Janeiro, Salamandra, 1984.

Contos de amor rasgados, Rio de Janeiro, Rocco, 1986.

Condé, José. *Histórias da cidade morta*, Rio de Janeiro, Jornal de Letras, 1951.

Pensão riso da noite, Rio de Janeiro, Civilização Brasileira, 1966.

As chuvas, Rio de Janeiro, Civilização Brasileira, 1972.

Consolin, Aércio. 1974. *O cabide*, Campinas, Nova Teixeira, 1974.

A dança das auras, São Paulo, Moderna, 1980.

Cony, Carlos Heitor. 1973. *Quinze anos*, Rio de Janeiro, Tecnoprint, 1973.

Sobre todas as coisas, Rio de Janeiro, Civilização Brasileira, 1986.

Costa, Flávio Moreira da. *Os espectadores*, São Paulo, Edições Símbolo, 1976.

Malvadeza Durão, Rio de Janeiro, Record, 1981.

Coutinho, Edilberto. *Um negro vai à forra*, São Paulo, Editora Moderna, 1977.

Sangue na praça, Rio de Janeiro, Codecri, 1979.

Maracanã, Adeus, Rio de Janeiro, Civilização Brasileira, 1980.

O jogo terminado, Rio de Janeiro, Livraria José Olympio Editora, 1983.

Coutinho, Sônia. *Do herói inútil*, Salvador, Macunaíma, 1966.

Nascimento de uma mulher, Rio de Janeiro, Editora Civilização Brasileira, 1970.

Uma certa felicidade, Rio de Janeiro, Francisco Alves, 1976.

Os venenos de Lucrécia, São Paulo, Editora Atica, 1978.

O ultimo verão de Copacabana, Rio de Janeiro, Livraria José Olympio Editora, 1985.

Couto, Rui Ribeiro. *A casa do gato cinzento*, São Paulo, Monteiro Lobato, 1922.

O crime do estudante baptista, São Paulo, Monteiro Lobato, 1922.

Baianinha e outras mulheres, Rio de Janeiro, Anuário do Brasil, 1927.

Clube das esposas enganadas, Rio de Janeiro, Schmidt, 1933.

Largo da matriz, Rio de Janeiro, G. Costa, 1940.

Uma noite chuvosa e outros contos, Lisbon, Inquérito, 1944.

Cruls, Gastão. *Ao embalo da rede*, Rio de Janeiro, A. J. de Castilho, 1923.

História puxa história, Rio de Janeiro, Ariel, 1938.

Cunha, Helena Parente. *Os provisórios*, Rio de Janeiro, Antares; Brasília, INL, 1980.

Cem mentiras de verdade, Rio de Janeiro, Livraria José Olympio Editora, 1985.

Daunt Neto, Ricardo. *Juan*, Rio de Janeiro, Livraria José Olympio Editora, 1975.

Homem na prateleira, São Paulo, Editora Atica, 1979.

Denser, Márcia. *Tango fantasma*, São Paulo, Alfay Omega, 1976.

Animal dos motéis, Rio de Janeiro, Civilização Brasileira; São Paulo, Massao Ohno, 1981.

1986. *Diana caçadora*, São Paulo, Global, 1986.

Dourado, Valdomiro Autran. 1955. *Três histórias na praia*, Rio de Janeiro, MEC, 1955.

Nove histórias em grupos de três, Rio de Janeiro, Livraria José Olympio Editora, 1957.

O risco do bordado, Rio de Janeiro, Expressão e Cultura, 1970.

Solidão, solitude, Rio de Janeiro, Civilização Brasileira, 1972.

Armas & corações, Rio de Janeiro, Difel, 1978.

As imaginações pecaminosas, Rio de Janeiro, Record, 1981.

Drummond, Roberto. *A morte de D. J. em Paris*, Rio de Janeiro, Sabiá, 1975.

Quando fui morto em Cuba, São Paulo, Editora Atica, 1982.

Duque Estrada, Luiz Gonzaga. *Horto de mágoas*, Rio de Janeiro, B. de Aquila, 1914.

Elis, Bernardo. *Ermos e gerais*, São Paulo, Revista dos Tribunais, 1944.

Caminhos e descaminhos, Goiânia, IGL/Brasil-Central, 1965.

Veranico de Janeiro, Rio de Janeiro, Livraria José Olympio Editora, 1966.

Caminhos dos gerais, Rio de Janeiro, Civilizaçãs Brasileira, 1975.

André Louco, Rio de Janeiro, Livraria José Olympio Editora, 1978.

Apenas um violão, Rio de Janeiro, Nova Fronteira, 1984.

Emediato, Luiz Fernando. *Não passarás o Jordão*, São Paulo, Alfa y Omega, 1977.

Os lábios húmidos de Marilyn Monroe, São Paulo, Editora Atica, 1978.

Rebelião dos mortos, Rio de Janeiro, Codecri, 1978.

Faillace, Tânia Jamardo. *O 35° ano de Inês*, Porto Alegre, Movimento, 1971.

Contos, Porto Alegre, Lume Editora, 1977.

Tradição, família e outras histórias, São Paulo, Editora Atica, 1978.

Ferraz, Geraldo. *Km 73: 9 contos desiguais*, São Paulo Editora Atica, 1979.

Figueiredo, Guilherme. *Rondinella e outras histórias*, Rio de Janeiro, O Cruzeiro, 1943.

Fiorani, Sílvio. *Os estandartes de Atila*, Rio de Janeiro, Codecri, 1980.

A morte de Natália, Rio de Janeiro, Nova Fronteira, 1981.

Fischer, Almeida. *10 contos escolhidos*, Brasília, Horizonte, 1980.

Fonseca, Rubem. *Os prisioneiros*, Rio de Janeiro, GRD, 1965.

A coleira do cão, Rio de Janeiro, GRD, 1965.

Lúcia McCartney, Rio de Janeiro, Olivé, 1969.

O homem de fevereiro ou março, Rio de Janeiro, Artenova, 1973.

Feliz ano novo, Rio de Janeiro, Artenova, 1975.

O cobrador, Rio de Janeiro, Nova Fronteira, 1979.

Giúdice, Vítor. *Necrológio*, Rio de Janeiro, O Cruzeiro, 1972.

Os banheiros, Rio de Janeiro, Codecri, 1979.

Gomes, Alvaro Cardoso. *Teia de aranha*, São Paulo, Editora Moderna, 1978.

O senhor dos porcos, São Paulo, Editora Moderna, 1979.

Gomes, Duílio. *O nascimento dos leões*, Belo Horizonte, Interlivros, 1975.

Verde suicida, São Paulo, Editora Atica, 1977.

Janeiro digestivo, Belo Horizonte, Comunicação, 1982.

Gomes, José Edson. *Agonia no Natal*, Porto Alegre, Mercado Aberto, 1986.

Gomes, Lindolfo. *Contos populares*, Juiz de Fora, D. Cardoso & Cía., 1918.

Gomes, Paulo Emílio Salles. *Três mulheres de três PPPes*, São Paulo, Perspectiva, 1977.

P's Three Women, tr. Margaret A. Neves, New York, Avon, 1984.

Gomide, Júlio. *Liberdade para os pirilampos*, Rio de Janeiro, Codecri, 1980.

Grossmann, Judith. *O meio da pedra*, Rio de Janeiro, J. Alvaro, 1970.

A noite estrelada, Rio de Janeiro, Francisco Alves, 1977.

Grossman, William L. (tr.). *Modem Brazilian Short Stories*, intro. by translator, Berkeley, University of California Press, 1974.

Guimarães, Bernardo. *Lendas e romances*, Rio de Janeiro, B. L. Garnier, 1871.

Historias e tradicções da provincia de Minas Geraes, Rio de Janeiro, B. L. Garnier, 1872.

Guimarães, Josué. *Os ladrões*, Rio de Janeiro, Forum, 1970.

O gato no escuro, Porto Alegre, L & PM Editores, 1982.

Hilst, Hilda. *Ficções*, São Paulo, Quíron, 1977.

Com meus olhos de cão, São Paulo, Editora Brasiliense, 1986.

Ivo, Ledo. *Use a passagem subterrânea*, São Paulo, DEL, 1961.

O flautim e outras histórias cariocas, Rio de Janeiro, Bloch, 1966.

10 contos escolhidos, Brasília, Horizonte, 1987.

Jardim, Luiz. *Maria perigosa*, Rio de Janeiro, Livraria José Olympio Editora, 1939.

Jardim, Rachel. *Cheiros e ruídos*, Rio de Janeiro, Livraria José Olympio Editora, 1975.

A cristaleira invisível, Rio de Janeiro, Nova Fronteira, 1982.

Jatobá, Roniwalter. *Ciriaco Martins e outras histórias*, São Paulo, Alfa y Omega, 1977.

Jorge, Miguel. *Avarmas*, São Paulo, Editora Atica, 1978.

Urubanda, Rio de Janeiro, Nova Fronteira, 1985.

José, Elias. *A mal amada*, Belo Horizonte, Imprensa Oficial, 1970.

O tempo, Camila, Belo Horizonte, Imprensa Oficial, 1971.

Inquieta viagem no fundo do poço, Belo Horizonte, Imprensa Oficial, 1974.

Um pássaro em pânico, São Paulo, Editora Atica, 1977.

O grito dos torturados, Rio de Janeiro, Nova Fronteira, 1986.

Ladeira, Julieta de Godoy. *Passe as férias em Nassau*, Rio de Janeiro, GRD, 1962.

Dia de matar o patrão, São Paulo, Summus, 1978.

10 contos escolhidos, Brasilia, Horizonte, 1984.

Era sempre feriado nacional, São Paulo, Summus, 1984.

Leão, Múcio. *A promessa inútil e outros contos*, Rio de Janeiro, Leite Ribeiro, 1928.

Lessa, Orígenes. *Omelete em Bombaim: contos*, Rio de Janeiro, O Cruzeiro, 1946.

A desintegração da morte, Rio de Janeiro, O Cruzeiro, 1948.

Nove mulheres, Rio de Janeiro, Record, 1968.

Mulher na calçada, Rio de Janeiro, Nova Fronteira, 1984.

Dez contos escolhidos, Brasilia, Horizonte, 1985.

Volume 3

Lima Campos, César Câmara de. *Confessor supremo*, Rio de Janeiro, Laemmert, 1904.

Lins, Osman. *Os gestos*, Rio de Janeiro, Livraria José Olympio Editora, 1957.
Nove, Novena: narrativas, São Paulo, Livraria Martins Editora, 1966.
Nine, Novena, tr. Adria Frizzi, Los Angeles, Sun & Moon Press, 1995.

Lispector, Clarice. *Alguns contos*, Rio de Janeiro, MEC, 1952.
Laços de família, Rio de Janeiro, Franciso Alves, 1960.
A Legião Estrangeira, Rio de Janeiro, Editora do Autor, 1964.
Felicidade clandestina, Rio de Janeiro, Sabiá, 1971.
A via crucis do corpo, Rio de Janeiro, Artenova, 1974.
Onde estivestes de noite, Rio de Janeiro, Artenova, 1974.
Family Ties, tr. Giovanni Pontiero, Austin, University of Texas Press, 1972.
The Foreign Legion: Stories and chronicles, tr. Giovanni Pontiero, Manchester, Carcanet, 1986.

Lispector, Eliza. *Sangue no sol*, Brasília, EBRSA, 1970.

Lobato, José Bento Monteiro. *Urupês*, São Paulo, Ed. Revista do Brasil, 1918.
Cidades mortas, São Paulo, Ed. Revista do Brasil, 1919.
Negrinha, São Paulo, Revista do Brasil Monteiro Lobato, 1920.
Brazilian Short Stories, n.p., Halderman – Julius Co., 1925.

Lobato, Manoel. *Garrucha 44*, Rio de Janeiro, Elos, 1961.
Contos de agora, Belo Horizonte, Oficina, 1970.
Os outros são diferentes, Rio de Janeiro, Artenova, 1971.
Flecha em repouso, São Paulo, Editora Atica, 1977.
Você precisa de mim?/O antúrio não é uma flor séria, Belo Horizonte, Comunicação, 1980.

Lobo, Luzia. *Vôo livre*, Rio de Janeiro, Cátedra/INL, 1982.

Lopes Neto, João Simões. *Contos gauchescos*, Pelotas, Echenique, 1912.
Lendas do sul, Pelotas, Echenique, 1913.

Louzeiro, José. *Depois da luta*, Rio de Janeiro, Record, 1980.
Judas arrependido, Rio de Janeiro, Record, 1980.

Machado, Aníbal. *Vida feliz*, Rio de Janeiro, Livraria José Olympio Editora, 1944.
Histórias reunidas, Rio de Janeiro, Livraria José Olympio Editora, 1959.

Machado, Dionélio. *Um pobre homem*, Porto Alegre, Globo, 1927.

Machado, Rubem Mauro. *Jacaré ao sol*, São Paulo, Editora Atica, 1976.
Jantar envenenado, São Paulo, Editora Atica, 1979.

Machado de Assis, Joaquim Maria. *Contos fluminenses*, Rio de Janeiro, B. L. Garnier, 1870.
Histórias da meia noite, Rio de Janeiro, B. L. Garnier, 1873.
Papéis avulsos, Rio de Janeiro, Typ. Lombaerts, 1882.
Histórias sem data, Rio de Janeiro, B. L. Garnier, 1884.
Várias histórias, Rio de Janeiro, Laemmert, 1896.
Páginas recolhidas, Rio de Janeiro, H. Garnier, 1899.
Relíquias de casa velha, Rio de Janeiro, H. Garnier, 1906.
The Psychiatrist and Other Stories, tr. William L. Grossman and Helen Caldwell, Berkeley, University of California Press, 1963.
The Devil's Church and Other Stories, tr. Jack Schmitt and Lorie Ishimatsu, Austin, University of Texas Press, 1977.

"The Siamese academies," tr. Lorie Ishimatsu, *Latin American Literary Review*, 14:27 (1986), 35–41.

Magalhães, Adelino. *Casos e impressões*, Rio de Janeiro, Typ. Revista dos Tribunais, 1916.

1926. *A hora veloz*, Rio de Janeiro, Typ. Revista dos Tribunais, 1926.

Maia, Alcides. *Tapera*, Rio de Janeiro, H. Garnier, 1911.

Alma bárbara, Rio de Janeiro, Typ. Pimenta de Melo, 1922.

Maranhão, Haroldo. *A estranha xícara*, Rio de Janeiro, Saga, 1968.

O chapéu de três bicos, Rio de Janeiro, Estrela, 1975.

A morte de Haroldo Maranhão, Brasília, GPM Editora, 1981.

Flauta de bambu, Rio de Janeiro, Edição Mobral, 1982.

As peles frias, Rio de Janeiro, Francisco Alves, 1983.

Jogos infantis, Rio de Janeiro, Francisco Alves, 1986.

Marques, Xavier. *Simples histórias*, Salvador, Typ. Jornal de Notícias, 1886.

A cidade encantada, Bahia, Catilina, 1920.

Terras mortas, Rio de Janeiro, Livraria José Olympio Editora, 1936.

Martins, Ana Maria. *A trilogia do emparedado e outros contos*, São Paulo, Livraria Martins Editora; Brasília, INL, 1973.

Sala de espera, São Paulo, Melhoramentos, 1978.

Katmandu, São Paulo, Global Editora, 1983.

Martins, Ciro. *Campo fora*, Porto Alegre, Globo, 1934.

Martins, Júlio César. *Sabe quem dançou?*, Rio de Janeiro, Codecri, 1978.

Ao oeste de nada, Rio de Janeiro, Civilização Brasileira, 1981.

Muamba, Rio de Janeiro, Anima, 1985.

Medauar, Jorge. *Agua preta*, São Paulo, Editora Brasiliense, 1958.

A procissão e os porcos, São Paulo, P. de Azevedo, 1960.

O incêndio: contos, Rio de Janeiro, Civilização Brasileira, 1963.

Miguel, Salim. *O primeiro gosto*, Porto Alegre, Movimento, 1973.

A morte do tenente e outras mortes, Rio de Janeiro, Antares, 1979.

10 contos escolhidos, Brasília, Horizonte, 1985.

Morais, Eneida de. *Alguns personagens*, Rio de Janeiro, MEC, 1954.

Boa noite, Professor, Rio de Janeiro, Civilização Brasileira, 1965.

Neme, Mário. *Donana sofredora*, Curitiba, Guaira, 1941.

Mulher que sabe latim, São Paulo, Flama, 1944.

Nepomuceno, Eric. *Contradança*, Rio de Janeiro, Folhetim, 1976.

A palavra nunca, Rio de Janeiro, Nova Fronteira, 1985.

Nery, Adalgisa. *Og*, Rio de Janeiro, Livraria José Olympio Editora, 1943.

22 menos 1, Rio de Janeiro, Expressão e Cultura, 1972.

Noll, João Gilberto. *O cego e a dançarina*, Rio de Janeiro, Civilização Brasileira, 1980.

Onofre, Manuel, Jr. *Histórias do meu povo*, Natal, Americana/Instituto Nacional do Livro, 1969.

Paiva, Mário Garcia de. *Festa*, Rio de Janeiro, Artenova, 1970.

Os Planelúpedes, Rio de Janeiro, Ed. Brasília, 1975.

Dois cavalos num fuscazul, Belo Horizonte, Comunicação, 1976.

Os agricultores arrancam paralelepípedos, São Paulo, Editora Atica, 1977.

Peixoto, Afrânio. *Parábolas*, Rio de Janeiro, Francisco Alves, 1920.

Amor sagrado e amor profano, São Paulo, Editora Nacional, 1942.

Volume 3

Pellegrini, Domingos. *Paixões*, São Paulo, Editora Atica, 1984.

Os meninos crescem, Rio de Janeiro, Nova Fronteira, 1986.

Peregrino, João, Jr. *Pussanga*, Rio de Janeiro, Typ. Hispano-americana, 1929.

Matupá, Rio de Janeiro, Ed. Livraria Católica, 1933.

História da Amazônia, Rio de Janeiro, Livraria José Olympio Editora, 1936.

Perez, Renard. *Irmãos da noite*, Rio de Janeiro, Civilização Brasileira, 1979.

10 contos escolhidos, Brasília, Horizonte, 1983.

Trio, São Paulo, LR, 1983.

Picchia, Paulo Menotti del. *O crime daquela noite*, São Paulo, Monteiro Lobato, 1924.

Piñón, Nélida. *Tempo das frutas*, Rio de Janeiro, José Alvaro, 1966.

Sala de armas, Rio de Janeiro, Sabiá, 1973.

O calor das coisas, Rio de Janeiro, Nova Fronteira, 1980.

Piroli, Wander. *A mãe e o filho da mãe*, Belo Horizonte, Imprensa Publicações, 1966.

A máquina de fazer amor, São Paulo, Editora Atica, 1980.

Minha bela putana, Rio de Janeiro, Nova Fronteira, 1984.

Pólvora, Hélio. 1980. *Massacre no Km.13*, Rio de Janeiro, Antares, 1980.

O grito da perdiz, São Paulo, Difel, 1983.

10 contos escolhidos, Brasília, Horizonte, 1984.

Mar de azor, São Paulo, Melhoramentos, 1986.

Pompéia, Raul de Avila. *Canções sem metro*, Rio de Janeiro, Typ. Aldina, 1900.

Porto Alegre, Apolinário. *Paisagens: Contos*, Porto Alegre, Movimento/Brasília, INL, 1987.

Prada, Cecília. *O cão na sala de jantar*, São Paulo, Editora Moderna, 1985.

Prade, Péricles. *Alçapão para gigantes*, São Paulo, Alfa y Omega, 1980.

Queiroz, Dinah Silveira de. *A sereia verde*, Rio de Janeiro, Livraria José Olympio Editora, 1941.

As noites do morro do encanto, Rio de Janeiro, Civilização Brasileira, 1957.

Eles herdarão a terra e outros contos absurdos, Rio de Janeiro, GRD, 1960.

Comba malina, Rio de Janeiro, Laudes, 1969.

Quintela, Ary. *Um certo senhor tranqüilo*, Rio de Janeiro, Bonde, 1971.

Ramos, Graciliano. *Dois dedos*, n.p., R.A., 194–.

Histórias incompletas, Porto Alegre, Globo, 1946.

Insônia, Rio de Janeiro, Livraria José Olympio Editora, 1947.

7 histórias verdadeiras, Rio de Janeiro, Vitória, 1951.

Ramos, Hugo de Carvalho. *Tropas e boiadas*, Rio de Janeiro, Revista dos Tribunais, 1917.

Ramos, Ricardo. *Tempo de espera*, Rio de Janeiro, Livraria José Olympio Editora, 1954.

Terno de reis, Rio de Janeiro, Livraria José Olympio Editora, 1957.

Os desertos, São Paulo, Melhoramentos, 1961.

Rua desfeita, Rio de Janeiro, J. Alvaro, 1963.

Matar um homem, São Paulo, Livraria Martins Editora, 1970.

Circuito fechado, São Paulo, Livraria Martins Editora, 1972.

Toada para surdos, Rio de Janeiro, Record, 1977.

Os inventores estão vivos, Rio de Janeiro, Nova Fronteira, 1980.

10 contos escolhidos, Brasília, Horizonte/INL, 1983.

O sobrevivente, São Paulo, Global Editora, 1984.

Rangel, Alberto. *Inferno verde*, Genoa, Bacigalupi, 1908.
  Sombras n'água, Leipzig, F. A. Brockhaus, 1913.
  Lume e cinza, Fantasmagorias, Rio de Janeiro, Scientífica Brasileira, 1924.
Rawet, Samuel. *Contos do imigrante*, Rio de Janeiro, Livraria José Olympio Editora, 1956.
  Diálogo, Rio de Janeiro, GRD, 1963.
  O terreno de uma polegada quadrada, Rio de Janeiro, Orfeu, 1969.
Rebelo, Marques. *Stela me abriu a porta*, Porto Alegre, Globo, 1924.
  Oscarina, Rio de Janeiro, Schmidt, 1931.
  Três caminhos, Rio de Janeiro, Ariel, 1933.
Resende, Otto Lara. *O lado humano*, Rio de Janeiro, A Noite, 1952.
  Boca do inferno, Rio de Janeiro, Livraria José Olympio Editora, 1957.
  O retrato na gaveta, Rio de Janeiro, Editora do Autor, 1962.
  As pompas do mundo, Rio de Janeiro, Rocco, 1975.
Ribeiro, João. *O folk-lore*, Rio de Janeiro, J. Ribeiro dos Santos, 1919.
Ribeiro, João Ubaldo. *Reunião*, Universidade da Bahia, 1961.
  Vencecavalo e o outro povo, Rio de Janeiro, Artenova, 1974.
  Livro de histórias, Rio de Janeiro, Nova Fronteira, 1981.
Rio, João do. *A alma encantadora das ruas*, Paris, H. Garnier, 1908.
  Dentro da noite, Rio de Janeiro, H. Garnier, 1910.
  Rosário da ilusão, Lisbon, Portugal-Brasil, [1912?].
  A mulher e os espelhos, Lisbon, Portugal-Brasil, 1918.
Romero, Sílvio. *Contos populares do Brazil*, Lisbon Nova Livraria Internacional, 1885.
Rosa, João Guimarães. *Sagarana*, Rio de Janeiro, Universal, 1946.
  Primeiras estórias, Rio de Janeiro, Livraria José Olympio Editora, 1962.
  Tutaméia:Terceiras estórias, Rio de Janeiro, Livraria José Olympio Editora, 1967.
  Estas estórias, Rio de Janeiro, Livraria José Olympio Editora, 1969.
  Sagarana, tr. Harriet de Onís, New York, Knopf, 1966.
  The Third Bank of the River and Other Stories, tr. Barbara Shelby, New York, Knopf, 1968.
Rosa, Vilma Guimarães. *Acontecências*, Rio de Janeiro, Livraria José Olympio Editora, 1967.
  Setestórias, Rio de Janeiro, Livraria José Olympio Editora, 1970.
  Por que não?, Rio de Janeiro, Livraria José Olympio Editora, 1972.
  Serendipity, Rio de Janeiro, Livraria José Olympio Editora, 1974.
Rubião, Murilo. *O ex-mágico*, Rio de Janeiro, Universal, 1947.
  A estrela vermelha, Rio de Janeiro, Hipocampo, 1953.
  Os dragões e outros contos, Belo Horizonte, Movimento/Perspectiva, 1965.
  O convidado, São Paulo, Quíron, 1974.
  O pirotécnico Zacarias, São Paulo, Editora Atica, 1974.
  A casa do girassol vermelho, São Paulo, Editora Atica, 1978.
  The Ex-Magician and Other Stories, tr. Thomas Colchie, New York, Harper & Row, 1979.
Sabino, Fernando. *Os grilos não cantam mais*, Rio de Janeiro, Pongetti, 1941.
  A companheira de viagem, Rio de Janeiro, Editora do Autor, 1965.
  A faca de dois gumes, Rio de Janeiro, Record, 1985.

Volume 3

Sales, Herberto. *Histórias ordinárias*, Rio de Janeiro, O Cruzeiro, 1966.

Sant'Anna (e Silva), Sérgio Andrade. *O sobrevivente*, Belo Horizonte, Estória, 1969.

Notas de Manfredo Rangel, repórter, Rio de Janeiro, Editora Civilização Brasileira, 1973.

O concerto de João Gilberto no Rio de Janeiro, São Paulo, Editora Atica, 1982.

Santiago, Silviano. *O banquete*, Rio de Janeiro, Saga, 1970.

O olhar, Belo Horizonte, Tendência, 1974.

Schmidt, Afonso. *Brutalidade*, Santos, Inst. D.E. Rosa, 1922.

Os impunes, São Paulo, Liv. Santos, 1923.

Curiango, Rio de Janeiro, Livraria José Olympio Editora, 1935.

O tesouro de Cananéia, São Paulo, Anchieta, 1941.

Scliar, Moacyr. *Histórias de médico em formação*, Porto Alegre, Difusão de Cultura, 1962.

O carnaval dos animais, Porto Alegre, Movimento, 1968.

A balada do falso Messias, São Paulo, Editora Atica, 1976.

Histórias de terra trêmula, São Paulo, Vertente, 1977.

O anão no televisor, Porto Alegre, RBS Globo, 1979.

A massagista japonesa, Porto Alegre, L & PM, 1984.

O olho enigmático, Rio de Janeiro, Guanabara, 1986.

Carnival of the Animals, tr. Eloah F. Giacomelli, New York, Available Press, Ballantine Books, 1986.

The Ballad of the False Messiah, tr. Eloah F. Giacomelli, New York, Ballantine, 1987.

Silva, Deonísio da. *Cenas indecorosas*, Rio de Janeiro, Artenova, 1976.

Exposição de motivos, Rio de Janeiro, Artenova, 1977.

A mesa dos inocentes, Rio de Janeiro, Artenova, 1978.

Livrai-me das tentações, Rio de Janeiro, Nova Fronteira, 1984.

Tratado dos homens perdidos, Porto Alegre, Mercado Aberto, 1987.

Silva, Domingos Carvalho da. 1966. *A véspera dos mortos*. São Paulo, Coliseu, 1966.

Silva, Joaquim Norberto de Sousa e. *As duas orphãs*, Rio de Janeiro, Typographia Francesa, 1841.

Silveira, Francisco Maciel. *Esfinges*, São Paulo, Editora Atica, 1978.

Silveira, Helena. *A humilde espera*, Porto Alegre, Globo, 1944.

Mulheres freqüentemente, São Paulo, Livraria Martins Editora, 1953.

Silveira, Valdomiro. *Os caboclos*, São Paulo, R. do Brasil Monteiro Lobato, 1920.

Nas serras e nas furnas, São Paulo, Ed. Nacional, 1931.

Mixuangos, Rio de Janeiro, Livraria José Olympio Editora, 1937.

Histórias contadas por eles mesmos, São Paulo, Livraria Martins Editora, 1945.

Sousa, Herculano Marcos Inglês de. *Contos amazônicos*, Rio de Janeiro, Laemmert, 1893.

Sousa, João da Cruz e. *Missal*, Rio de Janeiro, Magalhães/Typ. G. Leuzinger & Filhos, 1893.

Evocações, Rio de Janeiro, Typ. Aldina, 1898.

Steen, Edla van. *Cio*, São Paulo, Schmidt Editora, 1965.

Antes do amanhecer, São Paulo, Editora Moderna, 1977.

Até sempre, São Paulo, Global Editora, 1985.

"The Misadventures of João," tr. David George, *Latin American Literary Review*,

14:27 (1986), 168–74.

Steen, Edla van (ed.) *O conto da mulher brasileira*, São Paulo, Vertente, 1978. (Anthology.)

    O papel do amor, São Paulo, Livraria Cultura, 1979. (Anthology.)

Sussekind, Carlos. *Armadilha para Lamartine*, Rio de Janeiro, Labor do Brasil, 1976.

Taunay, Alfredo d'Escragnolle. *Histórias brazileiras*, Rio de Janeiro, B. L. Garnier, 1874.

    Ao entardecer, Rio de Janeiro, H. Garnier, 1901.

Tavares, Zulmira Ribeiro. *Termos de comparação*, São Paulo, Perspectiva, 1974.

Telles, Lygia Fagundes. *Praia viva*, São Paulo, Livraria Martins Editora, 1944.

    O cacto vermelho, São Paulo, Mérito, 1949.

    Histórias do desencontro, Rio de Janeiro, Livraria José Olympio Editora, 1958.

    Histórias escolhidas, São Paulo, Livraria Cultura, 1964.

    O jardim selvagem, São Paulo, Livraria Martins Editora, 1965.

    Antes do baile verde, Rio de Janeiro, Bloch, 1970.

    Seminário dos ratos, Rio de Janeiro, Livraria José Olympio Editora, 1977.

    Filhos pródigos, São Paulo, Livraria Cultura, 1978.

    Mistérios, Rio de Janeiro, Nova Fronteira, 1981.

    10 contos escolhidos, Brasília, Horizonte, 1984.

    Tigrela and Other Stories, tr. Margaret A. Neves, New York, Avon, 1986.

Trevisan, Dalton. *Sonata ao luar: novela*, Curitiba, Gráfica Mundial, 1945.

    Sete anos de pastor, Curitiba, Joaquim, 1948.

    Crônicas da província de Curitiba, Curitiba, Ed. Particular, 1954.

    Novelas nada exemplares, Rio de Janeiro, Livraria José Olympio Editora, 1959.

    Minha cidade, Curitiba, Editora do Autor, 1960.

    Lamentações de Curitiba, Curitiba, Joaquim, 1961.

    Cemitério de elefantes, Curitiba, Joaquim, 1962.

    Morte na praça, Rio de Janeiro, Editora do Autor, 1964.

    O vampiro de Curitiba, Curitiba, Requião, 1965.

    Desastres do amor, Rio de Janeiro, Civilização Brasileira, 1968.

    Mistérios de Curitiba, Rio de Janeiro, Record, 1968.

    A guerra conjugal, Rio de Janeiro, Civilização Brasileira, 1969.

    Brinquedo, São Paulo, Editora do Autor, 1972.

    O rei da terra, Rio de Janeiro, Civilização Brasileira, 1972.

    O pássaro de cinco asas, Rio de Janeiro, Civilização Brasileira, 1974.

    A faca no coração, Rio de Janeiro, Civilização Brasileira, 1975.

    Abismo de rosas, Rio de Janeiro, Civilização Brasileira, 1976.

    A trombeta do anjo vingador, Rio de Janeiro, Codecri, 1977.

    Crimes de paixão, Rio de Janeiro, Record, 1978.

    Primeiro livro de contos: antologia pessoal, Rio de Janeiro, Record, 1979.

    Lincha tarado, Rio de Janeiro, Record, 1980.

    Virgem louca, loucos beijos, Rio de Janeiro, Record, 1980.

    Chorinho brejeiro, Rio de Janeiro, Record, 1981.

    Essas malditas mulheres, Rio de Janeiro, Record, 1982.

    Meu querido assassino, Rio de Janeiro, Record, 1983.

    Contos eróticos, Rio de Janeiro, Record, 1984.

    Pão e sangue, Rio de Janeiro, Record, 1988.

Volume 3

The Vampire of Curitiba and Other Stories, tr. Gregory Rabassa, New York, Knopf, 1972.

Veiga, José J. Os cavalinhos de Platiplanto, Rio de Janeiro, Nítida, 1959.

A máquina extraviada, Rio de Janeiro, Prelo, 1968.

The Misplaced Machine and Other Stories, tr. Pamela G. Bird, New York, Knopf, 1970.

Veríssimo, Érico. Fantoches, Porto Alegre, Globo, 1932.

O ataque, Porto Alegre, Globo, 1959.

Veríssimo, José. Scenas da vida amazónica, Lisbon, Tavares Cardoso & Irmão, 1886.

Vilela, Luiz. Tremor de terra, Belo Horizonte, Editora do Autor, 1967.

No bar. Rio de Janeiro, Bloch, 1968.

Tarde da noite, São Paulo, Vertente, 1970.

O fim de tudo, Belo Horizonte, Liberdade, 1973.

Contos escolhidos, Brasília, Horizonte, 1978.

Lindas pernas, São Paulo, Livraria Cultura, 1979.

Vítor, Nestor. Signos, Rio de Janeiro, Typ. Correia Noves, 1897.

Secondary sources

Books

Bosi, Alfredo. História concisa da literatura brasileira, São Paulo, Cultrix, 1970.
    An outstanding interpretive history of Brazilian literature.

Brasil, Assis. O conto, Rio de Janeiro, Americana Brasília/INL, 1975.

Brayner, Sônia. O conto de Machado de Assis, Rio de Janeiro, Civilização Brasileira/INL/MEC, 1980.

Campos, Maria Consuelo Cunha. Sobre o conto brasileiro, Rio de Janeiro, Gradus, 1977.

Carmo, José Animateia Pinto do. Novelas e novelistas brasileiros: indicações bibliográficas, Rio de Janeiro, Organização Simões, 1957.

Cavalheiro, Edgard. Evolução do conto brasileiro, Rio de Janeiro, MEC. 1954.
    A history of the Brazilian short story.

Curso de conto. Conferências. Rio de Janeiro, Academia Brasileira de Letras, 1958.

Gomes, Celuta Moreira. O conto brasileiro e sua crítica: bibliografia (1841–1974), 2 vols., Rio de Janeiro, Biblioteca Nacional, 1977.
    A monumental collection.

Gotlib, Nádia Batella. 1985. Teoria do conto, São Paulo, Editora Atica.
    Basic orientation for studies of the story as a literary genre.

Hohlfeldt, Antônio. Conto brasileiro contemporâneo, Porto Alegre, Mercado Aberto, 1981.

Jolles, André. Einfache Formen, Legende, Sage, Mythe, Prätsel, Spruch, Kasus, Memorabile, Mächen, Witz, Halle, M. Niemeyer, 1930.

Lima, Herman. O conto, Salvador, Progresso/Universidade Federal da Bahia, 1958.
    Variações sobre o conto, Rio de Janeiro, MEC n.d.

Lima Sobrinho, Barbosa. Os precursores do conto no Brasil, Rio de Janeiro, Civilização Brasileira, 1960.

Linhares, Temístocles. 22 diálogos sobre o conto brasileiro atual, Rio de Janeiro,

Livraria José Olympio Editora, 1973.

Literary Review (Summer 1984) ed. Jon M. Tolman, special issue on Brazilian stories, 1956–1977.

Magalhães Junior, Raimundo. *Panorama do conto brasileiro*, 11 vols., Rio de Janeiro, Civilização Brasileira, 1959.

A arte do conto, Rio de Janeiro, Bloch, 1972.

Moisés, Massaud. *História da literatura brasileira*, vol. V, São Paulo, Cultrix/EDUSP, 1989.

Nunes, Benedito. *Clarice Lispector*, São Paulo, Quíron, 1973.

Lucid and penetrating essay on one of Brazil's greatest writers.

Santos, Wendel. *Os três reais da ficção: O conto brasileiro hoje*, Petrópolis, Vozes, 1978.

Schwartz, Jorge. *Murilo Rubião: a poética do Uroboro*, São Paulo, Editora Atica, 1981.

The only book on the father of magical realism in Brazil.

Xavier, Elódia. *O conto brasileiro e sua trajetória; a modalidade urbana dos anos 20 aos anos 70*, Rio de Janeiro, Padrão, 1987.

Detailed analysis of selected modern writers.

Articles

Andrade, Mário de. "Contos e contistas" in his *O empalhador de passarinho*, São Paulo, Livraria Martins Editora, [1943?]. 7–10.

Reflections on the genre by Modernism's critical genius.

Barbosa, Francisco de Assis. "Romance, novela e conto no Brasil (1893–1949)," *Cultura*, 1:3 (1949), 193–242.

Barbosa, João Alexandre. "Nove, novena novidade" in Osman Lins, *Nove, novena*, 2nd edn., São Paulo, Melhoramentos, 1975, vii–4.

An illuminating study of innovative features in Lins's stories.

Bosi, Alfredo. "Situação e formas do conto brasileiro contemporâneo" in Bosi (ed.), *O conto brasileiro contemporâneo*, São Paulo, Cultrix, 1975, 7–22.

A historical and interpretive survey.

Campos, Haroldo de. "A linguagem do Iauaretê" in his *Metalinguagem*, Petrópolis, Vozes, 1967, 47–53.

A revelation of the linguistic inventiveness of Guimarães Rosa.

Cândido, Antônio. "Esquema de Machado de Assis" in his *Vários escritos*, 2nd. edn., São Paulo, Duas Cidades, 1977, 13–32.

A concise presentation of the literary and psychological depths in Machado's stories.

Galvão, Walnice Nogueira. "Cinco teses sobre o conto" in *O livro do seminário*, São Paulo, L. R. Editores Ltda, 1983, 165–72.

Theories of the nature and origins of the Brazilian story.

Lima, Herman. "Evolução do conto" in Afrânio Coutinho (ed.), *A literatura no Brasil*, 2nd. edn., Rio de Janeiro, Sul Americana, 1971, VI, 39–56.

Lima, Luiz Costa. "O conto na modernidade brasileira" in *O livro do seminário*, São Paulo, L. R. Editores Ltda, 1983, 173–218.

Investigation of the nature of the contemporary Brazilian story.

Volume 3

Lins, Osman. "O mundo recusado, o mundo aceito e o mundo enfrentado" in
Graciliano Ramos, *Alexandre e outros heróis*, 13th edn., Rio de Janeiro, Record,
São Paulo, Livraria Martins Editora, 1976, 175–86.
> Analysis of Graciliano by a contemporary northeastern master.

Lucas, Fábio. "O conto no Brasil moderno" in *O livro do seminário*, São Paulo, L. R.
Editores Ltda, 1983, 103–64.
> Fundamental history and characterization of the modern story.

Martins, Marília. "Retrato de um intelectual brasileiro: entrevista com Dr. Benedito
Nunes," *Jornal do Brasil. Suplemento de Livros*, (Nov. 5, 1988), 7–10.

Moisés, Massaud. "O conto" in his *A criação literária*, São Paulo, Melhoramentos,
1967.

"Contistas" in his *História da literatura brasileira*, vol. II: *Romantismo, realismo*,
São Paulo, Cultrix/EDUSP, 1984, 451–7.

"Conto" in his *História da literatura brasileira*, vol. V: *Modernismo (1922–
atualidade)*, São Paulo, Cultrix/EDUSP, 1989, 5, 493–514.

Nunes, Benedito. "Guimarães Rosa" in his *O dorso do tigre*, São Paulo, Perspectiva,
1976.
> Lucid and penetrating essay on one of Brazil's greatest writers.

Teles, Gilberto Mendonça. "Para uma teoria do conto," *Letras de Hoje* (PUC-Porto
Alegre), 16 (1974), 7–9.
> Reflections from a general course on the short story.

Vargas Llosa, Mario. "Thugs who know their Greek," *New York Times Book
Review*, (Sept. 7, 1976), 7.
> An analysis of Rubem Fonseca's literary method.

Chapter 11: Brazilian poetry from 1900 to 1922

Primary sources

Albano, José. *Rimas* (1912), Fortaleza, Imprensa Universitária do Ceará, 1966.

Anjos, Augusto dos. *Eu*, Rio de Janeiro, private editions, 1912; 29th. edn., Rio de
Janeiro, São José, 1963.

Bandeira, Manuel. *Poesia completa e prosa*, Rio de Janeiro, Nova Aguilar, 1983.

Campos, Augusto de. *Revisão de Kilkerry*, 2nd edn., revised, São Paulo, Editora
Brasiliense, 1985.

Gama, Marcelo. *Via-Sacra*, Porto Alegre, 1902.
Noite de insônia, Porto Alegre, 1907.
Via-Sacra e outros poemas, Rio de Janeiro, Sociedade Felipe d'Oliveira, 1944.

Leoni, Raul de. *Luz mediterrânea*, Rio de Janeiro, Jacinto Ribeiro dos Santos, 1922;
11th. edn., São Paulo, Livraria Martins Editora, 1965.

Machado, Gilka. *Cristais partidos*, Rio de Janeiro, Jacinto Ribeiro dos Santos, 1915.
Estados d'alma, Rio de Janeiro, Jacinto Ribeiro dos Santos, 1917.
Mulher nua, Rio de Janeiro, Jacinto Ribeiro dos Santos, 1922.
Poesias completas, Rio de Janeiro, Cátedra, 1978.

Melo Neto, João Cabral de. *Poesias completas*, Rio de Janeiro, José Olympio, 1978.

Secondary sources

Books

Bandeira, Manuel. *Antologia dos poetas brasileiros da fase parnasiana*, 2nd. edn., Rio de Janeiro, Ministério de Educação e Saúde, 1940.

This, and the *Antologia . . . simbolista* below, contain useful introductions by a connoisseur of the periods.

Itinerário de Pasárgada, Rio de Janeiro, Jornal de Letras, 1954.

Apresentação da poesia brasileira, 3rd. edn., Rio de Janeiro, Ed. Casa do Estudante do Brasil, 1957.

Brief but useful survey.

Antologia dos poetas brasileiros da fase simbolista, Rio de Janeiro, Edições de Ouro, 1967.

See note to *Antologia . . . parnasiana*, above.

Bosi, Alfredo. *A literatura brasileira*, vol. v: *O pré-modernismo*, São Paulo, Cultrix, 1966.

Contains a survey of neo-Parnassian poets, 1900–1922.

Broca, Brito. *A vida literária no Brasil: 1900*, 2nd. edn., revised, Rio de Janeiro, Livraria José Olympio Editora, 1960.

Erudite and elegant history of literary life around the turn of the century.

Carpeaux, Otto Maria. *Pequena bibliografia crítica da literatura brasileira*, 3rd. edn., Rio de Janeiro, Editora Letras e Artes, 1964.

Acute comments on writers and periods preceded by bibliographies, now somewhat outdated.

Coelho, Joaquim Francisco. *Manuel Bandeira pré-modernista*, Rio de Janeiro, Livraria José Olympio Editora, 1982.

A detailed analysis of Bandeira's first three books.

Coutinho, Afrânio (ed.). *A literatura no Brasil*, vol. iii: *Simbolismo, modernismo, impressionismo*, Rio de Janeiro, São José, 1959.

Relevant chapters, of uneven quality, by J. Andrade Muricy, Rodrigo Otávio Filho, and Darcy Damasceno.

Góes, Fernando. *Panorama da poesia brasileira*, vol. v: *O Pré-modernismo*, Rio de Janeiro, Civilização Brasileira, 1960.

A useful introductory survey of poetry, 1900–1922, and samples of the work of sixty-four poets.

Gullar, Ferreira, "Augusto dos Anjos ou vida e morte nordestina" in Augusto dos Anjos, *Toda a poesia*, Rio de Janeiro, Paz e Terra, 1976.

Especially interesting with regard to Anjos's intellectual and cultural milieu. Detailed analysis of his language.

Moisés, Massaud. *História da literatura brasileira*, vol. iii: *O simbolismo*, São Paulo, Cultrix, 1985.

This recent history contains discussions of a selection of symbolist and neo-symbolist poets.

Muricy, José Cândido de Andrade. *Panorama do movimento simbolista brasileiro*, 3 vols., Rio de Janeiro, Departamento de Imprensa Nacional, 1952.

The first major work of scholarship on the subject.

Ramos, Péricles Eugênio da Silva. *Panorama da poesia brasileira*, vol. III: *Parnasia-nismo*, Rio de Janeiro, Civilização Brasileira, 1959.

A useful anthology with reliable introductions to the poets.

Poesia simbolista: antologia, Rio de Janeiro, Edições Melhoramentos, 1965.

Poesia parnasiana: antologia, Rio de Janeiro, Edições Melhoramentos, 1967.

Both of the above anthologies are especially useful regarding stylistic and metrical particularities of each period.

Articles

Gotlib, Nádia Batella. "Com Dona Gilka Machado, Eros pede a palavra (poesia erótica feminina brasileira dos inícios do século XX)," *Polêmica*, 4 (1982), 23–47.

A balanced reevaluation from a feminist perspective.

Leite, Sebastião Uchoa. "Marcelo Gama. Farandulagem. Flânerie" in his *Crítica clandestina*, Rio de Janeiro, Taurus, 1986, 99–107.

A recent reading of this neglected poet.

Proença, M. Cavalcanti. "Artesanato em Augusto dos Anjos" (1955) and "Notas para um rimário de Augusto dos Anjos" (1957) in Afrânio Coutinho and Sônia Brayner (eds.), *Augusto dos Anjos: textos críticos*, Brasília, MEC/INL, 1973.

Detailed studies of meter, rhythm, lexicon, and rhyme in Anjos's poetry.

Chapter 12: Brazilian poetry from Modernism to the 1990s

There is a vast corpus of reliable criticism dealing with Brazilian poetry from Modernism to the 1990s. The following list, therefore, should be regarded as selective rather than comprehensive.

Bio-Bibliographies

Carpeaux, Otto Maria. *Pequena bibliografia crítica da literatura brasileira*, 3rd edn., Rio de Janeiro, Editora Letras e Artes, 1964.

Cunha, Dulce Salles. *Autores contemporâneos brasileiros*, São Paulo, Ed. Cúpolo, 1951.

Cunha, Fausto, and Waltensir Dutra. *Biografia crítica das letras mineiras*, Rio de Janeiro, INL, 1956.

Martins, Ari. *Escritores do Rio Grande do Sul*, Porto Alegre, Universidade do Rio Grande do Sul, 1978.

Menezes, Raimundo de. *Dicionário literário brasileiro ilustrado*, 5 vols., São Paulo, Savaiva, 1969; 2nd. edn., revised, Rio de Janeiro, Livros Técnicos e Científicos, 1978.

Paes, José Paulo, and Massaud Moisés. *Pequeno dicionário de literatura brasileira*, 2nd. edn., São Paulo, Cultrix, 1980.

Pontual, Roberto. *Dicionário das artes plásticas no Brasil*, Rio de Janeiro, Civilização Brasileira, 1969.

Placer, Xavier (ed.). *Modernismo brasileiro: bibliografia (1918–1971)*, Rio de Janeiro, Biblioteca Nacional, 1972.

Histories of the genesis and evolution of Modernism in Brazil

Amora, Antônio Soares. *História da literatura brasileira*, São Paulo, Saraiva, 1955.

Azevedo, Fernando de. *A cultura brasileira*, São Paulo, Instituto Brasileiro de Geografia e Estatística, 1944.
Brazilian Culture, tr. William Rex Crawford, New York, Macmillan, 1950.

Bandeira, Manuel. *Brief History of Brazilian Literature*, Washington, Pan American Union, 1958.

Bosi, Alfredo. *História concisa da literatura brasileira*, São Paulo, Cultrix, 1970.

Cândido, Antônio. *Brigada ligeira: ensaios*, São Paulo, Livraria Martins, Editora, 1945.
Formação da literatura brasileira, 2 vols., São Paulo, Livraria Martins Editora, 1959.
Vários escritos, São Paulo, Duas Cidades, 1970.

Cândido, Antônio, and José Aderaldo Castello. *Presença da literatura brasileira*, vol. III, São Paulo, Difusão Européia do Livro, 1964.

Coutinho, Afrânio. *Introdução à literatura no Brasil*, Rio de Janeiro, São José, 1959.
Conceito de literatura brasileira, Rio de Janeiro, Livraria Acadêmica, 1960.
An Introduction to Literature in Brazil, tr. Gregory Rabassa, New York, Columbia University Press, 1969.

Coutinho, Afrânio (ed.). *A literatura no Brasil*, vol. III: *Simbolismo, modernismo, impressionismo*, 1. Rio de Janeiro, Sul Americana, 1959.
Three chapters (9–11) focus on Modernism.

Lima, Alceu Amoroso. *Introdução à literatura brasileira*, Rio de Janeiro, AGIR, 1956.
Quadro sintético da literatura brasileira, Rio de Janeiro, AGIR, 1956.

Miguel-Pereira, Lúcia. *Cinqüenta anos de literatura*, Rio de Janeiro, Ministério de Educação e Saúde, 1952.

Muricy, José Cândido de Andrade. *A nova literatura brasileira*, Porto Alegre, Globo, 1936.

Sodré, Nelson Werneck. *Síntese do desenvolvimento literário no Brasil*, São Paulo, Livaria Martins Editora, 1943.

Essays on Brazilian poetry

Alvim Correia, Roberto. *Anteu e a crítica*, Rio de Janeiro, Livraria José Olympio Editora, 1948.
O mito de Prometeu, Rio de Janeiro, AGIR, 1951.

Andrade, Mário de. "Mestres do passado," *Jornal do Comércio*, São Paulo, Aug.–Sept. 1921.

Bandeira, Manuel. *Obras completas*, Rio de Janeiro, Aguilar, 1958.
See the critical essays in volume II.

Buarque de Holanda, Sérgio. *Cobra de vidro: crítica literária*, São Paulo, Livraria Martins Editora, 1944.

Góes, Fernando. *O espelho infiel*, São Paulo, Conselho Estadual de Cultura, 1966.

Lima, Alceu Amoroso. *Estudos*, Rio de Janeiro, various publishers, 1927–1933.
Estudos literários, Rio de Janeiro, Aguilar, 1966.

Criticism dealing specifically with modernist and postmodernist poetry

Bandeira, Manuel. *Apresentação da poesia brasileira*, Rio de Janeiro, Ed. Casa do Estudante do Brasil, 1954.
De poetas e de poesia, Rio de Janeiro, Edições de Ouro, 1967.

Barata, Manoel Sarmento. *Canto melhor: uma perspectiva da poesia brasileira*, Rio de Janeiro, Paz e Terra, 1969.

Brotherston, Gordon. *Latin American Poetry: Origins and presence*, Cambridge University Press, 1975.
Considers Brazilian poetry alongside developments in Spanish America.

Chaves, Flávio Loureiro (ed.). *Aspectos do modernismo brasileiro*, Porto Alegre, Universidade Federal do Rio Grande do Sul, 1970.
Contains interesting contributions from Chaves, Donaldo Schüler, Bruno Kiefer, Leonor Scliar Cabral, Tânia Franco Carvalhal, and José Hildebrando Daconal.

Cidade, Hernani. *O conceito de poesia como expressão da cultura*, São Paulo, Saraiva, 1946.

Grieco, Agripino. *Evolução da poesia brasileira*, 3rd. edn., Rio de Janeiro, Livraria José Olympio Editora, 1947.

Ivo, Ledo. *Poesia observada*, Rio de Janeiro, Orfeu, 1967.

Leite, Sebastião Uchoa. *Participação da palavra poética: do modernismo à poesia contemporânea*, Petrópolis, Vozes, 1966.

Lima, Alceu Amoroso. *Poesia brasileira contemporânea*, Belo Horizonte, Livraria Editora Paulo Bluhm, 1941.

Lima, Luiz Costa. *Lira e anti-lira*, Rio de Janeiro, Civilização Brasileira, 1968.

Lins, Edison. *História e crítica da poesia brasileira*, Rio de Janeiro, Ariel, 1937.

Merquior, José Guilherme. *A razão do poema*, Rio de Janeiro, Civilização Brasileira, 1965.

Muricy, José Cândido de Andrade. *Panorama do movimento simbolista brasileiro*, 2 vols., Rio de Janeiro, INL, 1952.

Ramos, Péricles Eugênio da Silva. *Do barroco ao modernismo*, São Paulo, Conselho Estadual de Cultura, 1967; 2nd. edn., revised, Rio de Janeiro, Livros Técnicos e Científicos, 1979.

Rio Branco, Miguel de. *Etapas da poesia brasileira*, Lisbon, Livros do Brasil, 1955.

Teles, Gilberto Mendonça. *Estudos de poesia brasileira*, Coimbra, Livraria Almedina, 1985.
Probes new dimensions in Brazilian poetry.

The testimony of participants

The essays of poets and writers who pioneered and promoted the aesthetics and reforms of the Brazilian Avant-Garde are most valuable of all. The following contributions should be regarded as essential reading for any real understanding of modernist aesthetics.

The various testimonies and manifestos of Mário de Andrade are at once colourful and incisive.

Andrade, Mário de. *Paulicéia desvairada*, São Paulo, Mayença, 1922.
   A escrava que não é Isaura, São Paulo, Lealdade, 1925.
   O movimento modernista, Rio de Janeiro, Casa do Estudante do Brasil, 1942.
   Aspectos da literatura brasileira, Rio de Janeiro, Americ-Edit, 1943.
   O baile das quatro artes, São Paulo, Livraria Martins Editora, 1943.
   O empalhador de passarinho, São Paulo, Livraria Martins Editora, 1945.
   Cartas a Manuel Bandeira, Rio de Janeiro, Edições de Ouro, 1966.
   Hallucinated City (Paulicéia Desvairada), tr. Jack E. Tomlins, Nashville, Tenn.,
   Vanderbilt University Press, 1968.
      These letters further clarify Mário's central role in launching the modernist
   program of reform.

Essays on Mário de Andrade's contribution
Cavalcanti Proença, Manuel. *Roteiro de Macunaíma*, São Paulo, Anhembi, 1955.
Câmara Cascudo, Luís da. "Mário de Andrade," *Boletim de Ariel*, 3:9 (June 1934),
   233–5. *A Manhã*, literary supplement, 4:491 (Jan. 1951), 9, 11, and 14.

Testimony of other participants and studies of the initial phase of Modernism.
Andrade, Oswald de. *Ponta de lança*, São Paulo, n.p., 1945.
   "Modernismo," *Anhembi*, 17:49 (1954), 25–32.
      Oswald de Andrade's personal definition of the modernist movement.
Aranha, J. Pereira da Graça. *O espírito moderno*, 2nd. edn., São Paulo, CEN, 1932.
Carvalho, Ronald de. *Toda a América*, Rio de Janeiro, Pimenta de Melo, 1926.
   Estudos brasileiros II, Rio de Janeiro, Briguiet, 1931.
Cavalheiro, Edgar. *Testamento de uma geração*, Porto Alegre, Globo, 1944.
Discursos Acadêmicos (Rio de Janeiro), vol. 3 *(1914–1918)*, 1935. Lecture by Alberto
   de Oliveira.
   Vol. 11 *(1938–1943)*, 1944. Lectures given by Cassiano Ricardo and Menotti del
   Picchia.
Milliet, Sérgio. *Terminus seco e outros coquetéis*, São Paulo, Irmãos Ferraz, 1932.
   Diário crítico, 10 vols., São Paulo, Editora Brasiliense Livraria Martins Editora,
   1944–1957.
Prado, Paulo. *Retrato do Brasil*, São Paulo, Duprat-Mayença, 1928.
Ricardo, Cassiano. "Oswald de Andrade e o neo-indianismo de 22," *Anhembi*, 24:100
   (1959), 97–112, and 24:101, (1959), 327–40.
   22 e a poesia de hoje, Rio de Janeiro, MEC, 1964.
Revista de Arquivo Municipal (São Paulo), 1946. Ano 3, vol. 106.
      Contains important statements by Sérgio Milliet, Antônio Cândido, Fernando
   Góes, and Jamil Almansur Haddad.
Silveira, Tasso da. *Definição do modernismo brasileiro*, Rio de Janeiro, Forta, 1931.
Vítor, Nestor. *Cartas à gente nova*, Rio de Janeiro, Anuário do Brasil, 1924.
   Os de hoje, São Paulo, Cultura Moderna, 1938.

Volume 3

The pre-modernist phase

Bosi, Alfredo. *A literatura brasileira*, vol. v: *O pré-modernismo*, São Paulo, Cultrix, 1966.

Goldstein, Norma. *Do penumbrismo ao modernismo*, São Paulo, Editora Atica, 1983.

Góes, Fernando. *O pré-modernismo*, Rio de Janeiro, Civilização Brasileira, 1960.

Lara, Cecília de. *Nova cruzada: contribuição para o estudo do pré-modernismo*, Universidade de São Paulo, 1971.

Silva Brito, Mário da. *História de modernismo brasileiro*, 4th. edn., Rio de Janeiro, Civilização Brasileira, 1974.

Clear and comprehensive accounts of the movement's growth and subsequent divergences

Bopp, Raul. *Movimentos modernistas no Brasil, 1922–1928*, Rio de Janeiro, São José, 1966.

Bruzzi, Nilo. *O modernismo*, Rio de Janeiro, Aurora, 1960.

Casais Monteiro, Adolfo. *A moderna poesia brasileira*, São Paulo, Clube de Poesia, 1956.

Cavalcanti Proença Manuel. "Tendencias e repercussões literárias do modernismo," *Cultura* (Rio de Janeiro), 5 (1952).

Chiacchio, Carlos. *Modernistas e ultramodernistas*, Salvador, Progresso, 1951.

Martins, Wilson. "Cendrars e o Brasil," *Revista do Livro*, 5:18 (1960), 177–83.

A literatura brasileira, vol. vi: *O modernismo*, São Paulo, Cultrix, 1967.

"A crítica modernista" in Afrânio Coutinho (ed.), *A literatura no Brasil*, vol. v, Rio de Janeiro, Editorial Sul Americana, 1970.

The Modernist Idea, tr. Jack E. Tomlins, New York University Press, 1970.

    Lacks the cohesion and readability of his works in Portuguese.

Nist, John. *The Modernist Movement in Brazil*, Austin, University of Texas Press, 1967.

Peregrino, João, Jr. *O movimiento modernista*, Rio de Janeiro, MEC, 1954.

Três ensaios, Rio de Janeiro, São José, 1969.

Ribeiro, João Felipe de Sabóia. *Os modernos*, Rio de Janeiro, Academia Brasileira de Letras, 1952.

Saldanha Coelho, José (ed.). *Modernismo: estudos críticos*, Rio de Janeiro, Revista Branca, 1954.

Sena, Homero (ed.) *República das letras*, Rio de Janeiro, São José, 1957.

Silva Brito, Mário da. *História do modernismo brasileiro*, 4th. edn., Rio de Janeiro, Civilização Brasileira, 1974.

Modernism and Regionalism

Drummond de Andrade, Carlos. 1944. *Confissões de Minas*, Rio de Janeiro, Americ-Edit, 1944.

Passeios na Ilha, 2nd. edn., revised, Rio de Janeiro, Livraria José Olympio Editora, 1975.

    These two texts are the best illustrations of the inter-related concepts of Modernism and Regionalism.

Modernism in the Northeast

Câmara Cascudo, Luís da. *Dicionário do folclore brasileiro*, Rio de Janeiro, MEC, 1967.
    Gente viva, Recife, Universidade Federal de Pernambuco, 1970.
    These two volumes are indispensable for any understanding of northeastern customs and traditions.
Freyre, Gilberto. *Interpretação do Brasil*, Rio de Janeiro, Livraria José Olympio Editora, 1947.
Inojosa, Joaquim. *O movimento modernista em Pernambuco*, 3 vols., Rio de Janeiro, Tupy, 1968.
Mota, Mauro. *Imagens do nordeste*, Rio de Janeiro, MEC, 1961.
    Terra e gente, Universidade do Recife, 1963.

Modernism in Brazil's southern states

Leite, Lígia Chiappini Moraes. *Modernismo no Rio Grande do Sul*, São Paulo, Instituto de Estudos Brasileiros, 1972.

Other important aspects of Modernism

Britto, Jomard Muniz de. *Do modernismo à bossa nova*, Rio de Janeiro, Civilização Brasileira, 1966.
Carvalho da Silva, Domingos. *Introdução ao estudo do ritmo da poesia*, São Paulo, Revista Brasileira de Poesia, 1950.
    Explores Modernism's influence on rhythm.
Cavalcanti Proença, Manuel. *Estudos literários*, 3rd. edn., Rio de Janeiro, Livraria José Olympio Editora, 1982.
Ivo, Ledo. *Modernismo e modernidade* (Rio de Janeiro, 1972).
Jornal do Brasil (Rio de Janeiro). Ano 2, 13 (January 29, 1972).
    This special issue of the literary supplement marked the fiftieth anniversary of the Modern Art Week.
Lessa, Luíz Carlos. *O modernismo brasileiro e a língua portuguesa*, Rio de Janeiro, Grifo, 1976.
    Opens up the questions of modernist influence over language.
Schwarz, Roberto. *A sereia e o desconfiado*, 2nd. edn., Rio de Janeiro, Paz e Terra, 1981.
Schwarz, Roberto (ed.) *Os pobres na literatura brasileira*, São Paulo, Editora Brasiliense, 1983.

Modern manifestos

The various manifestos of Modernism were more frequently quoted than analyzed until the 1970s.
RASM: Revista Anual do Salão de Maio (São Paulo), (1939).
    Includes testimonies by Anita Malfatti, Cassiano Ricardo, and Tarsila do Amaral.

Revista do Livro (Rio de Janeiro), 1959. "Arquivo: manifestos modernistas," 4:16. A collection of the most significant of these manifestos.

Freyre, Gilberto. *Manifesto regionalista*, 6th. edn., Recife, Instituto Joaquim Nabuco, 1976.

Mendonça Teles, Gilberto. *Vanguarda européia e modernismo brasileiro*, Petrópolis, Vozes, 1976.

Important monographs on modernist periodicals

Caccese, Neusa Pinsard. *"Festa,"* São Paulo, Instituto de Estudos Brasileiros, 1971.

Lara, Cecília de. *"Klaxon" e "Terra Roxa e Outras Terras"; dois periódicos modernistas de São Paulo*, São Paulo, Instituto de Estudos Brasileiros, 1972.

Napoli, Roselis Oliveira de. *"Lanterna Verde" e o modernismo*, São Paulo, Instituto de Estudos Brasileiros, 1970.

Anthologies

The anthologies edited by Perícles Eugênio da Silva Ramos and Mário da Silva Brito stand out among those listed here, both for the range of material selected and for the depth of their critical perceptions. In the anthologies published in the United States, the selections tend to be somewhat arbitrary and narrow, and the Nist anthology is marred by weak criticism and even weaker translations.

Azevedo Filho, Lodegário A. (ed.). *Poetas do modernismo*, 6 vols., Brasilia, INL, 1972.

Bandeira, Manuel (ed.) *Poesia do Brasil*, Porto Alegre, Editora do Autor, 1963.

Bandeira, Manuel, and Walmir Ayala (eds.). *Antologia dos poetas brasileiros*, 2 vols., Rio de Janeiro, Edições de Ouro, 1967.

Bastide, Roger (ed.). *Poetas do Brasil*, Curitiba, Guaíra, 1947.

Bishop, Elizabeth, and Emanuel Brasil (eds.). *An Anthology of Twentieth-Century Brazilian Poetry*, Middletown, Conn., Wesleyan University Press, 1972.

Brasil, Emanuel, and William Jay Smith (eds.). *Brazilian Poetry (1950–1980)*, Middletown, Conn., Wesleyan University Press, 1983.

Burlamáqui Kopke, Carlos (ed.). *Antologia da poesia brasileira moderna*, Clube de Poesia de São Paulo, 1953.

Caracciolo-Trejo, Enrique (ed.). *The Penguin Book of Latin-American Verse*, Harmondsworth, Penguin Books, 1971.

Carvalho da Silva, Domingos (ed.). *Vozes femininas da poesia brasileira*, São Paulo, Conselho Estadual de Cultura, 1959.

Downes, Leonard S. (ed.). *An Introduction to Modern Brazilian Poetry*, São Paulo, Clube de Poesia do Brasil, 1954.

Gonzalez, Mike, and David Treece (eds.). *The Gathering of Voices. The twentieth century poetry of Latin America*, London, Verso, 1992.

Mendonça, Antonio Sérgio. *Poesia de Vanguarda no Brasil*, Rio de Janeiro, Antares, 1983.

Milano, Dante (ed.). *Antologia de poetas modernos*, Rio de Janeiro, Ariel, 1935.

Neistein, José, and Manuel Cardozo (eds.). *Poesia brasileira moderna*, Washington, Brazilian-American Cultural Institute, 1972.

Nejar, Carlos (ed.). *Antologia da poesia brasileira contemporânea*, Lisbon, Imprensa Nacional-Casa da Moeda, 1986.

Nist, John (ed.). *Modern Brazilian Poetry: An anthology*, Bloomington, Indiana University Press, 1962.

Pontiero, Giovanni (ed.). *An Anthology of Brazilian Modernist Poetry*, Oxford, Pergamon Press, 1969.

Ramos, Péricles Eugênio da Silva (ed.). *Poesia moderna*, São Paulo, Edições Melhoramentos, 1967.

Sampaio, Adovaldo Fernandes (ed.). *Voces femininas de la poesía brasileña*, Goiânia, Brazil, Oriente, 1979.

Silva Brito, Mário de (ed.). *Panorama da poesia brasileira: o modernismo*, 2nd. edn., revised, Rio de Janeiro, Civilização Brasileira, 1968.

Anthologies of the postmodernist phase and the so-called Generation of 1945

Campos, Milton de Godoy. *Antologia poética da Geração de 45*, Clube de Poesia de São Paulo, 1966.

Haddad, Jamil Almansur. *Poesia religiosa brasileira*, Rio de Janeiro, Edições de Ouro, 1966.

Houaiss, Antônio. *Seis poetas e um problema*, Rio de Janeiro, Edições de Ouro, 1967.

Loanda, Fernando Ferreira de. *Panorama da nova poesia brasileira*, Rio de Janeiro, Orfeu, 1951.

    Antologia da nova poesia brasileira, Rio de Janeiro, Livros de Portugal, 1965.

    Antologia de moderna poesia brasileira, Rio de Janeiro, Orfeu, 1967.

Martins, Hélcio. *A rima na poesia de Carlos Drummond de Andrade*, Rio de Janeiro, Livraria José Olympio Editora, 1968.

    Illustrates the poetics not only of Drummond, but also those of the poets whom he influenced.

Portella, Eduardo. *Literatura e realidade nacional*, Rio de Janeiro, Tempo Brasileiro, 1963.

The transition from the 1940s to a new phase of experimentation in the 1960s

Ayala, Walmir. *A novíssima poesia brasileira*, Rio de Janeiro, Gráfica Lux, 1962.

Matos, Gramiro de, and Manuel de Seabra. *Antologia da novíssima poesia brasileira*, Lisbon, Horizonte, 1977.

Mendoça Teles, Gilberto. *Vanguarda européia e modernismo*, Petrópolis, Vozes, 1972.

Sant'Anna, Affonso Romano de. *Música popular e moderna poesia brasileira*, Petrópolis, Vozes, 1978.

Concretism and Post-Concretism

Concretism and Post-Concretism have attracted a great deal of critical attention in Brazil and abroad. The debates and polemics provoked by the movements and the various splinter groups are often couched in dense technical jargon which tends to obscure rather than elucidate complex theories. The following anthologies and essays are reliable notwithstanding intermittent lapses into turgid explication.

Azevedo Filho, Lodegário A. (ed.). *Poetas do modernismo*, vol. VI, Brasilia, INL, 1972.

Bann, Stephen. *Concrete Poetry: An international anthology*, London Magazine, 1967.

Campos, Augusto de, Décio Pignatario, and Haroldo de Campos. *Teoria da poesia concreta (Textos críticos e manifestos 1950–1960)*, 2nd edn., São Paulo, Duas Cidades, 1975.

Campos, Augusto de, Décio Pignatari, Haroldo de Campos, José Lino Grunewald, and Ronaldo Azeredo. *Antologia noigandres (do verso à poesia concreta)*, São Paulo, Massao Ohno, 1962.

Campos, Haroldo de. *Metalinguagem*, 2nd. edn., Petrópolis, Vozes, 1970.

"The rule of anthropophagy: Europe under the sign of devoration," tr. Maria Tai Wolff, *Latin American Literary Review*, 14 (1986), 42–60.

Crespo, Ángel, and Pilar Gomes Bedate. "Tendência: poesia e crítica em situação," *Revista de Cultura Brasileira* (Madrid), 15 (1963).

Faustino, Mário. *Cinco ensaios sobre poesia*, Rio de Janeiro, Ed. GRD, 1964:

Grunewald, José Lino. "Poesia concreta," *Revista do Livro*, 10 (1960).

Invenção (São Paulo), 1962–1967.

This influential journal was edited by the *Noigandres* group.

Mendonça, Antônio Sérgio Lima. *Poesia de Vanguarda no Brasil*, Petrópolis, Vozes, 1970.

Pignatari, Décio. *Informação, linguagem, comunicação*, São Paulo, Perspectiva, 1968.

Contracomunicação, São Paulo, Perspectiva, 1971.

Semiótica e literatura, 2nd. edn., São Paulo, Cultrix, 1987.

Three crucial studies.

Poesia Brasileira (São Paulo), special issue on *Concretismo*, 7:5/6 (1965).

Solt, Mary Ellen. *Concrete Poetry: A world view*, Bloomington, Indiana University Press, 1968.

Sarduy, Severo. "Towards concreteness," tr. Amelia Simpson, *Latin American Literary Review*, 14 (1986), 61–9.

Times Literary Supplement (London), August and September, 1964.

Two special issues devoted to "The changing guard," which include critical commentaries and a selection of concrete poems.

Williams, Emmett. *An Anthology of Concrete Poetry*, New York, Something Else Press, 1967.

The *Poesia Praxis* movement

Chamie, Mário. *Intertexto*. São Paulo, Ed. Praxis, 1970.

A transgressão do texto, São Paulo, Ed. Praxis, 1972.

Cirne, Moacy. *Vanguarda: um projecto semiológico*, Petrópolis, Vozes, 1975.

Pino, Wlademir Dias. *Processo: linguagem e comunicação*, Petrópolis, Vozes, 1971.

Ricardo, Cassiano. *Algumas reflexões sobre poética de vanguarda*, Rio de Janeiro, Livraria José Olympio Editora, 1964.

Poesia Praxis e 22, Rio de Janeiro, Livraria José Olympio Editora, 1966.

Sá, Álvaro de. "Poema-Processo: contribuição à vanguarda," *Revista de Cultura Vozes*, 1 (1970).

Xisto, Pedro. *Poesia em situação*, Fortaleza, Imprensa Oficial do Ceará, 1960.

The emerging talents

A nova poesia brasileira, 10 vols., Rio de Janeiro, Shogun Arte, 1983– .
  Sadly, all ten volumes dispense with any bio-bibliographical notes or critical prefaces.

Prado, Adélia. *The Alphabet in the Park*, tr. Ellen Watson, Middletown, Conn., Wesleyan University Press, 1990.

Chapter 13: *The Brazilian theatre in the twentieth century*

Primary sources

Amaral, Maria Adelaide. *De braços abertos*, Rio de Janeiro, Memórias Futuras Edições, 1985.
  The best work by one of the few notable playwrights of the 1980s.

Andrade, Jorge. *Marta, a árvore e o relógio*, São Paulo, Perspectiva, 1970.
  Careful edition of the ten-play São Paulo Cycle. Includes several important critical studies.

Andrade, Oswald de. *Obras completas*, vol. VIII: *Teatro: A morta; O rei da vela; O homem e o cavalo*, Rio de Janeiro, Civilização Brasileira, 1976.
  The first compilation of Oswald's three major plays, all long out of print before this publication.

Assunção, Leilah. *Da fala ao grito*, São Paulo, Edições Símbolo, 1977.
  A collection of the playwright's major works from the 1960s and 1970s, including her best play to date, *Fala baixo senão eu grito*.

Moist Lips, Quiet Passion, in Elzbieta Szoka and Joe W. Bratcher III (eds.), *3 Contemporary Brazilian Plays*, Austin, Host Publications, 1988, 218–92.

Athayde, Roberto. *Apareceu a Margarida*, Editora Brasília, 1973.
  Important allegorical commentary on the nature of repression.

Miss Margarida's Way, New York, Avon, 1979.

Boal, Augusto, and Gianfrancesco Guarnieri. "Arena conta Zumbi," *Revista de Teatro*, 378 (1970), 31–54.
  The first edition of the ground-breaking musical. An explanatory script is appended.

Arena conta Tiradentes, São Paulo, Editora Sagarana, 1967.
  The first edition of the authors' second collaboration in the *Arena conta* series. Includes important prefatory material by Boal.

Buarque, Chico, and Paulo Pontes. *Gota d'água: uma tragédia carioca*, Rio de Janeiro, Civilização Brasileira, 1975.
  Modern rendering of Euripides' *Medea* in the slums of Rio de Janeiro. Playwrights' preface emphasizes importance of verbal language over spectacle in the theatre.

Buarque, Chico, and Ruy Guerra. *Calabar: o elogio da traição*, Rio de Janeiro, Civilização Brasileira, 1974.
  Dramatic examination of the notion of treason in a key episode of colonial history with obvious contemporary parallels.

Callado, Antônio. *Frankel*, tr. anon., Rio de Janeiro, Serviço de Documentação do

Ministério da Educação e Cultura, 1955.

"Pedro the monkey," tr. Hilda Wickerhauser and William L. Grossman, *Odyssey Review*, 1 (1961), 72–99.

Camargo, Joracy. *Teatro de Joracy Camargo*, São Paulo, Livraria Martins Editora, 1961.

    Includes the most reliable edition of *Deus lhe pague*, Camargo's groundbreaking play of 1932.

Castro, Consuelo de. *Walking Papers*, in Elzbieta Szoka and Joe W. Bratcher III (eds.), *3 Contemporary Brazilian Plays*, Austin, Host Publications, 1988, 368–448.

Chaves Neto, João Ribeiro. *Patética*, Rio de Janeiro, Civilização Brasileira, 1977.

    Award-winning protest drama about the torture and murder of a prominent Jewish journalist in São Paulo.

Figueiredo, Guilherme. *A God Slept Here*, tr. Lloyd F. George, Rio de Janeiro, Serviço de Documentação do Ministério da Educação e Cultura, 1957.

Gomes, Alfredo Dias. *O pagador de promessas*, Rio de Janeiro, AGIR, 1961.

    The first edition of the foremost regionalist drama and one of the most popular Brazilian plays of the twentieth century.

Teatro, 2 vols., Rio de Janeiro, Civilização Brasileira, 1972.

    Includes the playwright's most important works and useful studies of his theatre.

"Payment as pledged," tr. Oscar Fernández, in George Woodyard (ed.), *The Modern Stage of Latin America: Six plays*, New York, E. P. Dutton, 1971, 43–117.

"The cradle of the hero," tr. Leon Lyday, *Modern International Drama*, 11:2 (1978), 5–51.

Guarnieri, Gianfrancesco. "Eles não usam black tie," *Boletim da SBAT*, 54 (1959), 1–32.

    The first edition of Guarnieri's celebrated play about the conflict of father and son in the midst of a labor strike.

O melhor teatro de Gianfrancesco Guarnieri, São Paulo, Global Editora, 1986.

    The playwright's four best plays, selected, and with an introduction, by Décio de Almeida Prado.

Machado, Maria Clara. *Teatro infantil*, Rio de Janeiro, AGIR, 1957.

    Includes the first edition of *Pluft, o fantasminha*, *A bruxinha que era boa*, and other plays.

Marcos, Plínio. *Navalha na carne*, São Paulo, Editora Senzala, 1968.

    This first edition boasts an original layout with graphics and photographs; also includes critical essays at the end.

Dois perdidos numa noite suja, São Paulo, Global Editora, 1979.

    The first edition of Marcos's banned masterpiece, which premiered in 1966.

Two Lost in a Filthy Night, in Elzbieta Szoka and Joe W. Bratcher III (eds.), *3 Contemporary Brazilian Plays*, Austin, Host Publications, 14–112.

Melo Neto, João Cabral de. "Morte e vida severina: auto de natal pernambucano" in *Duas águas*, Rio de Janeiro, Livraria José Olympio Editora, 1956, 169–222.

    The first edition of the noted contemporary "Auto de natal."

"From 'The death and life of a Severino,' a Pernambuco Christmas play, 1954–1955," tr. Elizabeth Bishop, in Elizabeth Bishop and Emanuel Brasil (eds.), *An*

Anthology of Twentieth-Century Brazilian Poetry, Middletown, Conn., Wesleyan University Press, 1972, 126–39.

Moreyra, Alvaro. *Adão, Eva e outros membros da família*, Rio de Janeiro, Serviço Nacional de Teatro, 1959.

The most reliable edition of the ground-breaking production by the Teatro de Brinquedo.

Rodrigues, Nelson. *Vestido de noiva* e *A mulher sem pecado*, Rio de Janeiro, Empresa Gráfica O Cruzeiro, 1944.

The first edition of *Vestido de noiva*, the twentieth century's most important Brazilian play. Includes numerous photos of Ziembinsky's innovatory staging.

Teatro completo, ed. Sábato Magaldi, 4 vols., Rio de Janeiro, Nova Fronteira, 1981–1989.

The definitive edition of Rodrigues's drama. Each volume includes a long, scholarly introduction by the distinguished editor.

The Wedding Dress, tr. Fred M. Clark, Chapel Hill, Hispanófila/Valencia, Albatrós, 1980.

Sampaio, José da Silveira. "The need for polygamy," tr. Gail Mirza, *Modern International Drama*, 9:2 (1976), 47–63.

Souza, Naum Alves de. *A aurora da minha vida*, São Paulo, MG Editores Associados, 1982.

The best play in Souza's memorialist cycle of the early 1980s.

Suassuna, Ariano. *Auto da compadecida*, Rio de Janeiro, AGIR, 1957.

The first edition of one of the most important works in all of Brazilian theatre.

The Rogue's Trial, tr. Dillwyn F. Ratcliff, Berkeley and Los Angeles, University of California Press, 1963.

Viana Filho, Oduvaldo. *Rasga coração*, Rio de Janeiro, Serviço Nacional de Teatro, 1980.

The first edition of Vianinha's last work, which is the best Brazilian play of the 1970s.

Teatro, ed. Yan Michalski, Rio de Janeiro, Edições Muro, 1981–.

The editorial plan calls for an eight-volume edition of the playwright's complete works.

Secondary sources

Books

Almeida, Maria Inez Barros de. *Panorama visto do Rio: a Companhia Tônia-Celi-Autran*, Rio de Janeiro, Ministério da Cultura/INACEN, 1987.

Provides important information on one of the leading professional acting companies of the 1950s.

Arrabal, José and Mariângela Alves de Lima. *Teatro: o seu nome é beato*, O Nacional e o Popular na Cultura Brasileira, São Paulo, Editora Brasiliense, 1983.

Provocative study of key moments in the history of Brazilian theatre which highlight national identity and a synthesis of popular and aesthetic elements.

Arte em Revista, special issue *Teatro brasileiro contemporâneo*, 6 (October 1981).

Includes key texts on Arena, Oficina, student theatre, censorship, and other issues of the 1960s and 1970s.

Boal, Augusto. *Teatro do Oprimido e outras poéticas políticas*, Rio de Janeiro, Civilização Brasileira, 1976.

First Brazilian edition of Boal's seminal work, which was first published in Spanish while the author was in exile in Argentina.

Theater of the Oppressed, trs. Charles and Maria Odília McBride, New York, Urizen Books, 1979.

Ténicas latino-americanas de teatro popular: uma revolução copernicana ao contrário, São Paulo, HUCITEC, 1979.

This first Brazilian edition of another key text by Boal includes *Categorias de teatro popular*, which first appeared in 1972 in Argentina.

Brecht no Brasil: experiências e influências, ed. Wolfgang Bader. Rio de Janeiro, Paz e Terra, 1987.

An excellent collection of essays on the Brechtian influence on the Brazilian theatre of the 1950s, 1960s, and 1970s.

Campos, Cláudia de Arruda. *Zumbi, Tiradentes e outras histórias contadas pelo Arena*, São Paulo, Perspectiva, 1988.

An outstanding study of Arena and its two best productions.

Ciclo de palestras sobre o teatro brasileiro, 12 vols., Rio de Janeiro, Ministério da Cultura/INACEN, 1986–1988.

Transcripts of lectures by leading names in contemporary Brazilian theatre.

Clark, Fred M. *Impermanent Structures: Semiotic readings of Nelson Rodrigues' "Vestido de Noiva," "Album de Família," and "Anjo Negro,"* Chapel Hill, North Carolina Studies in the Romance Languages and Literatures, 1991.

Best semiotic reading of Rodrigues' three masterpieces from the 1940s.

Clark, Fred M., and Ana Lúcia Gazolla de García. *Twentieth-Century Brazilian Theatre: Essays*, Chapel Hill and Valencia: Hispanófila/Albatrós, 1978.

A collection of essays of particular importance to the study of the theatre of Oswald de Andrade, Nelson Rodrigues, Dias Gomes, and Plínio Marcos.

Damasceno, Leslie Hawkins. *Espaço cultural e convenções teatrais na obra de Oduvaldo Vianna Filho*, trans. Iná Camargo Costa, Campinas, Editora da Universidade Estadual de Campinas, 1994.

A superlative analysis of Vianinha's plays, theoretical writings, and political activism. Also constitutes indispensable reading on the overall cultural scene of the 1950s, 1960s, and early 1970s in Brazil.

de Vincenzo, Elza Cunha. *Um teatro da mulher: dramaturgia feminina no palco brasileiro contemporâneo*, São Paulo, Editora Perspectiva/Editora da Universidade de São Paulo, 1992.

Excellent study of women Brazilian playwrights since 1969.

Depoimentos, n. ed., 6 vols., Rio de Janeiro, Serviço Nacional de Teatro, 1976–1982.

This collection of interviews includes fundamental information on twentieth-century Brazilian actors, playwrights, directors, groups, and critics.

Dionysos, special issue, *Os comediantes*, ed. Gustavo Dória, 22 (Dec. 1975).

Dionysos, special issue, *Teatro do Estudante do Brasil; Teatro Universitário; Teatro Duse*, ed. José Arrabal, 23 (Sept. 1978).

Dionysos, special issue, *Teatro de Arena de São Paulo*, ed. Carmelinda Guimarães, Mariângela Alves de Lima, and Maria Thereza Vargas, 24 (Oct. 1978).

Dionysos, special issue, *Teatro Brasileiro de Comédia*, ed. Alberto Guzik and Maria Lúcia Pereira, 25 (Sept. 1980).

Dionysos, special issue, *Teatro Oficina*, ed. Fernando Peixoto, 26 (Jan. 1982).

Dionysos, special issue, *O Tablado*, ed. Flora Sussekind, 27 (1986).

Dionysos, special issue, *Teatro Experimental do Negro*, ed. Ricardo G. Müller, 28 (1988).

Dionysos, special issue, *Escola de Arte Dramática*, ed. Ilka Marinho Zanotto, Mariângela Alves de Lima, Maria Thereza Vargas, and Nanci Fernandes, 29 (1989).

Each of the eight special issues includes essays, brief memoirs, a chronology, and abundant documentation on productions.

Dória, Gustavo A. *Moderno teatro brasileiro: crônica de suas raízes*, Rio de Janeiro, Serviço Nacional de Teatro, 1975.

A major source of information on amateur and professional theatre groups from the 1920s to the 1960s.

George, David. *Teatro e antropofagia*, tr. Eduardo Brandão, São Paulo, Global Editora, 1985.

A provocative consideration of the theatrical applications of a central tenet of Brazilian Modernism.

Grupo Macunaíma: carnavalização e mito, São Paulo, Perspectiva/EDUSP, 1990.

First book-length study of the most important theatre group of the 1980s.

The Modern Brazilian Stage, Austin, University of Texas Press, 1992.

By far the most important book in English on contemporary Brazilian theatre.

Guimarães, Carmelinda. *Um ato de resistência: o teatro de Oduvaldo Vianna Filho*, São Paulo, MG Editores Associados, 1984.

Introduction to Vianinha's life and works. Good thematic study of the major plays. A lengthy bibliography and a useful chronology are appended.

Guzik, Alberto. *TBC: crônica de um sonho. O Teatro Brasileiro de Comédia, 1948–1964*, São Paulo, Perspectiva, 1986.

Carefully researched history of the important professional company.

Khéde, Sônia Salomão. *Censores de pincenê e gravata: dois momentos da censura teatral no Brasil*, Rio de Janeiro, Editora Codecri, 1981.

Highly informative account of the trials and tribulations the Brazilian theatre has had to endure because of the institution of censorship.

Kühner, Maria Helena. *Teatro popular: uma experiência*, Rio de Janeiro, Francisco Alves, 1975.

Reflections on the theory and practice of popular theatre by a leading student of the mode.

Leite, Luiza Barreto. *A mulher no teatro brasileiro*, Rio de Janeiro, Edições Espetáculo, 1965.

This study by the actress, critic and drama professor provides invaluable information on some of the most important figures of the Brazilian theatre through the mid 1960s.

Lins, Ronaldo Lima. *O teatro de Nelson Rodrigues: uma realidade em agonia*, Rio de Janeiro, Francisco Alves, 1979.

Interesting study of the psychological dimension of Rodrigues's theatre.

Magaldi, Sábato. *Panorama do teatro brasileiro*, São Paulo, Difusão Européia do

Livro, 1962.

Essential reading on the theatre through 1960.

Um palco brasileiro: o Arena de São Paulo, São Paulo, Editora Brasiliense, 1984.

Short but very useful history of the seminal group.

Nelson Rodrigues: dramaturgia e encenações, São Paulo, Perspectiva/EDUSP, 1987.

The only book-length study of the stagings of Rodrigues's plays. Includes numerous photographs.

Martuscello, Carmine. *O teatro de Nelson Rodrigues: uma leitura psicanalítica*, São Paulo, Editora Siciliano, 1993.

Best book-length psychanalytic study of Rodrigues's seventeen plays.

Mendes, Miriam Garcia. *O negro e o teatro brasileiro entre 1889 e 1982*, São Paulo, Rio de Janeiro, and Brasília, HUCITEC/Instituto Brasileiro de Arte e Cultura/ Fundação Cultural Palmares, 1993.

Essential reading on the African presence in the theatre of Brazil. Complements author's 1982 book (see ch. 5's bibliography).

Michalski, Yan. *O palco amordaçado: 15 anos de censura teatral no Brasil*, Rio de Janeiro, Avenir Editores, 1979.

O teatro sob pressão: uma frente de resistência, Rio de Janeiro, Jorge Zahar, 1985.

Two short but extremely important records of the hardships the theatre faced during the dark years of the military regime.

Mostaço, Edelcio. *Teatro e política: Arena, Oficina e Opinião*, São Paulo, Proposta Editorial, 1982.

Places the contributions of the three groups in the context of the politics of the left before and after the coup of 1964.

O espetáculo autoritário: pontos, riscos, fragmentos críticos, São Paulo, Proposta Editorial, 1983.

Collection of provocative essays by a noted critic.

Nunes, Mário. *Quarenta anos de teatro*, 4 vols., Rio de Janeiro, Serviço Nacional de Teatro, 1956.

Indispensable reading on the first four decades of the twentieth century.

Peixoto, Fernando. *Teatro em pedaços, 1959–1977*, São Paulo, HUCITEC, 1980.

Collection of essays and reviews – several of which had been previously censored – by the influential actor, director, and critic.

Teatro Oficina, 1958–1982: trajetória de uma rebeldia cultural, São Paulo, Editora Brasiliense, 1982.

Short but insightful account of the group's history, by one of its leaders.

Teatro em movimento, 1959–1984, São Paulo, HUCITEC, 1986.

Further essays and reviews by the author of *Teatro em pedaços*.

Prado, Décio de Almeida. *Apresentação do teatro brasileiro moderno: crítica teatral 1947–1955*, São Paulo, Livraria Martins Editora, 1956.

A selection of the reviews written for the newspaper *O Estado de São Paulo*, during the heyday of the Teatro Brasileiro de Comédia.

Teatro em progresso: crítica teatral, 1955–1964, São Paulo, Livraria Martins Editora, 1964.

Continuation of the highly perceptive *O Estado de São Paulo* reviews by the doyen of Brazilian theatre critics of the twentieth century.

Exercício Findo: crítica teatral, 1964–1968, São Paulo, Perspectiva, 1987.
This last installment of Prado's collected critical reviews covers the first years of the military dictatorship.

O teatro brasileiro moderno, 1930–1980, São Paulo, Perspectiva/DUSP, 1988.
Short but indispensable reading on the most important half-century in the history of the Brazilian theatre.

Praia do Flamengo, 132, ed. Yan Michalski, Rio de Janeiro, Edições Muro, 1980.
Examines the pivotal role of the National Student Union and its theatrical arm, the CPC, in the cultural and political scene prior to the 1964 coup. Includes interviews with some of the founding members of the CPC.

Revista Civilização Brasileira, caderno especial # 2, *Teatro e realidade brasileira*, (July 1968).
Collection of essays of great importance for an understanding of the Brazilian theatre at a critical juncture in its history.

Rosenfeld, Anatol. *O mito e o herói no moderno teatro brasileiro*, São Paulo, Perspectiva, 1982.
An enlightening investigation of the tragic hero in modern Brazilian theatre, with strong emphasis on the works of Dias Gomes, Jorge Andrade, and Boal and Guarnieri.

Silva, Armando Sérgio da. *Oficina: do teatro ao te-ato*, São Paulo, Perspectiva, 1981.
A thorough study of the leading group of the late 1960s and early 1970s.

Uma oficina de atores: a Escola de Arte Dramática de Alfredo Mesquita, São Paulo, EDUSP, 1988.
A superlative study of the influential school, and its acting company. Highly informative and abundantly documented.

Silveira, Miroel. *A contribuição italiana ao teatro brasileiro, 1895–1964*, São Paulo and Brasília, Quíron/INL, 1976.
Interesting study of the Italian influence on the twentieth-century Brazilian comedy of manners.

A outra crítica, São Paulo, Edições Símbolo, 1976.
A collection of reviews written for daily newspapers by the critic and participant of such groups as Os Comediantes and Teatro Popular de Arte.

Teatro Experimental do Negro: Testemunhos, n. ed., Rio de Janeiro, Edições GRD, 1966.
Collection of essays about the important group by Paschoal C. Magno, Roger Bastide, Florestan Fernandes, Décio de A. Prado, A. Boal, and many others.

Teatro Ruth Escobar: 20 anos de resistência, ed. Rofran Fernandes, São Paulo, Global Editora, 1985.
Detailed chronicle of the efforts of the distinguished producer, director, and actress.

Uma atriz: Cacilda Becker, ed. Nanci Fernandes and Maria Thereza Vargas, São Paulo, Perspectiva, 1984.
Provides useful information and abundant documentation on the career and times of the distinguished actress.

Vianinha: teatro, televisão, política, ed. Fernando Peixoto, São Paulo, Editora Brasiliense, 1983.
Major source of information on Arena, CPC, and Opinião, as well as on

Vianinha's career. Editor's comments are extremely informative.

Viver e escrever, ed. Edla van Steen, 2 vols., Porto Alegre, L & PM, 1981–1982.
Includes important interviews with Nelson Rodrigues, Jorge Andrade, Dias Gomes, and Plínio Marcos.

Woodyard, George W., and Leon F. Lyday (eds.). *Dramatists in Revolt: The new Latin American theatre*, Austin, University of Texas Press, 1976.

Articles

Aslan, Odette, and Marlyse Meyer. "*Mort et Vie Séverine* de João Cabral de Melo Neto" in *Les voies de la création théâtrale*, 2, 297–339.
Thorough study of Cabral's *auto de natal*, with emphasis on the staging by the Teatro da Universidade Católica de São Paulo. Includes numerous photos and diagrams.

Bailey, Dale S. "*Pagador de Promessas*: A Brazilian morality," *Latin American Theatre Review*, 6:1 (1972), 35–9.
Persuasive reading of Dias Gomes's work as a modern morality play.

Bissett, Judith Ishamel. "Brecht e cordel: distanciamento e protesto em *Se correr o bicho pega*," *Latin American Theater Review*, 11:1 (1977), 59–64.
Analysis of use of Brechtian techniques and adaptation of *cordel* conventions in Vianinha and Gullar's Opinião play.

Brandão, Tânia. "Oficina: o trabalho da crise" in *Monografias 1979*, Rio de Janeiro, Instituto Nacional de Artes Cênicas, 1983, 7–62.
Useful study of the first ten years of the company's troubled history.

Brownell, Virginia A. "Martyrs, victims and gods: a view of religion in contemporary Brazilian drama," *Luso-Brazilian Review*, 15 (Summer supplement, 1978), 129–50.
Examines one play by Jorge Andrade and three works by Dias Gomes as attempts to define the role of the Catholic church in Brazilian life.

Brownell-Levine, Virginia. "Religious syncretism in contemporary Brazilian theatre," *Latin American Theater Review*, 13:2 (Summer supplement, 1980), 111–17.
A study of several plays in which the blending of Catholic and Afro-Brazilian creeds plays a major role.

Burgess, Ronald D. "Birth. Life. *A Morta*. de Andrade," *Luso-Brazilian Review*, 22:2 (1985), 103–10.
A sound examination of Oswald's play as an attempt to subvert literary conventions.

Butler, Ross E., Jr. "Social themes in selected contemporary Brazilian dramas," *Romance Notes*, 15:1 (1973), 52–60.
A useful survey of the most important protest plays of the 1950s and 1960s.

Chamie, Mário. "A vela do pan-sexualismo" in Oswald de Andrade, *O rei da vela*, São Paulo, Difusão Européia do Livro, 1967, 17–27.
Freudian analysis of Oswald's seminal play.

Clark, Fred M. "Tragedy and the tragic: Andrade's *Pedreira das almas*," *Latin American Theatre Review*, 15:1 (1981), 21–30.
Departs from previous studies of Andrade's tragedy by detecting the highly positive values in conflict within the character of Mariana.

"Oswald and Mayakovsky: *O homem e o cavalo* and *Mystery-Bouffe*," *Revista de Estudios Hispánicos*, 16 (1982), 241–56.

Provocative comparative essay by a leading authority on the theatre of Oswald de Andrade.

Correa, José Celso Martínez. "*O rei da vela*: manifesto do Oficina" in O. de Andrade, *O rei da vela*, São Paulo, Difusão Européia do Livro, 1967, 45–52.

Important document on the salient group of the late 1960s and early 1970s.

Dória, Gustavo. "Semana de 22: Teatro," *Cultura*, 5 (1972), 51–63.

Useful account of the modernist movement's interest in the theatre.

Driskell, Charles. "The Teatro de Arena of São Paulo: an innovative professional theater for the people" in Gerardo Luzuriaga (ed.), *Popular Theater for Social Change in Latin America: Essays in Spanish and English*, Los Angeles, UCLA Latin American Center Publications, 1978, 270–80.

Good study of the importance of Arena; includes a synopsis of the different phases, and of the careers of the group's major playwrights.

Dutra, Francis A. "The theatre of Dias Gomes: Brazil's social conscience," *Cithara*, 4:2 (1965), 3–13.

An early, perceptive analysis of *O pagador de promessas*, *A invasão*, and *A revolução dos beatos*.

Faria, João Roberto Gomes de. "Graça Aranha e o teatro," *Estudos Brasileiros*, 10 (1980), 225–36.

Informative account of a neglected facet of the early Modernist's career.

Fernández, Oscar. "Black theatre in Brazil," *Educational Theater Journal*, 29:1 (1977), 5–17.

Surveys the few successes of black theatre in Brazil and examines the factors that have impeded its development.

George, David. "The staging of *Macunaíma* and the search for national theatre," *Latin American Theatre Review*, 17:1 (1983), 47–58.

Excellent study of the stage adaptation of the cornerstone text of Brazilian Modernism.

"Os Comediantes e *Bridal gown*," *Latin American Theatre Review*, 21:1 (1987), 29–41.

Jungian analysis of *Vestido de noiva*; also examines the play's first staging, a ground-breaking production by the group Os Comediantes.

"Nelson 2 Rodrigues," *Latin American Theatre Review*, 21:2 (1988), 79–93.

Discussion of the 1984 staging by Grupo Macunaíma of Nelson Rodrigues's *Album de família* and *Toda nudez será castigada*.

Guimarães, Maria Ignez de Oliveira. "A *Gota d'água* de Chico Buarque e Paulo Pontes: palavra poética como ação dramática e denúncia," *Estudos Brasileiros*, 13 (1982), 40–82.

Excellent study of verbal language in one of the best plays of the 1970s.

Kühner, Gilberto, and Maria Helena de Oliveira Kühner. "Os centros populares de cultura: momento ou modelo" in *Monografias 1980*, Rio de Janeiro, INACEN, 1983, 141–213.

Good study of the history, goals, and key role of the CPC in the Brazilian theatre of the early 1960s.

Lopes, Angela Leite. "Nelson Rodrigues e o fato do palco" in *Monografias 1980*, Rio de Janeiro, INACEN, 1983, 105–40.

Reevaluation of Rodrigues's theatre in the light of productions of his plays.

Lyday, Leon F. "The *Barcas* and the *Compadecida*: autos past and present," *Luso-Brazilian Review*, 11:1 (1974), 84–8.

Argues persuasively that certain features and passages of Suassuna's play are traceable to Gil Vicente's trilogy.

"The theater of Alfredo Dias Gomes" in Woodyard and Lyday, *Dramatists in Revolt*, 221–42.

Outstanding study of Dias Gomes's theatre, with detailed analysis of the major plays through the early 1970s.

Magaldi, Sábato. "Teatro: marco zero" in Oswald de Andrade, *O rei da vela*, São Paulo, Difusão Européia do Livro, 1967, 7–16.

Perceptive analysis of *O rei da vela*, by one of Brazil's leading theatre critics.

Mazzara, Richard A. "Alfredo Dias Gomes, social commentator and artist," *Latin American Theatre Review*, 2:2 (1969), 41–59.

This useful survey of Dias Gomes's theatre purports to show that the two roles of social commentator and artist are inextricably bound together in the playwright.

"Regionalism and modern Brazilian theater," *Revista de Estudios Hispánicos*, 9:1 (1975), 11–32.

Studies the theatre of the late 1950s and 1960s from a regionalist perspective, with particular attention to Suassuna, Borba Filho, Dias Gomes, and Jorge Andrade.

"The theater of Jorge Andrade" in Woodyard and Lyday, *Dramatists in Revolt*, 205–20.

Traces the playwright's career up to and including the publication of *Marta, a árvore e o relógio*. Includes detailed analysis of each play.

Milleret, Margo. "Entrapment and flights of fantasy in three plays by Leilah Assunção," *Luso-Brazilian Review*, 21:1 (1984), 49–56.

Excellent introductory study of the theatre of Brazil's best woman playwright.

"Acting into action: Teatro Arena's *Zumbi*," *Latin American Theatre Review*, 21:1 (1987), 19–27.

This outstanding essay situates the Arena and its production of *Zumbi* in the political context of the 1960s.

Moser, Gerald M. "Jorge Andrade's São Paulo Cycle," *Latin American Theatre Review*, 5:1 (1971), 17–24.

Excellent study of the devices used to bind the ten diverse plays into one cohesive whole.

Nascimento, Abdias do. "The negro theater in Brazil," *African Forum*, 2:4 (1967), 35–53.

A short introduction by the founder of TEN. Also outlines the dismal situation for Blacks on the Brazilian stage before Nascimento came to the fore.

Peixoto, Fernando. "Uma dramaturgia lúcida e radical" in Oswald de Andrade, *O rei da vela*, São Paulo, Difusão Européia do Livro, 1967, 28–44.

Good introduction to Oswald's theatre by the noted critic, director, and Oficina actor who was directly involved in the first production of *O rei da vela*.

"Como transmitir sinais de dentro das chamas," *Latin American Theatre Review*,

7:1 (1973), 91–8.

Important account of the deleterious consequences of repression for the Brazilian stage.

Pelegrino, Hélio. "A obra e O beijo no asfalto" in Nelson Rodrigues, Teatro quase completo, vol. IV, Rio de Janeiro, Tempo Brasileiro, 1966, 9–25.

Excellent study of Rodrigues's work in general and of Beijo in particular.

Perrone, Charles A. "Dissonance and dissent: the musical dramatics of Chico Buarque," Latin American Theatre Review, 22:2 (1989), 81–94.

Best introduction in English to the theatre of Chico Buarque.

Pinto, Paul A. "Jorge Andrade's three enigmas," Hispania, 67:3 (1984), 364–76.

Good study of the symbolism that informs Marta, a árvore e o relógio.

Pontes, Joel. "Plínio Marcos, dramaturgo da violência," Latin American Theatre Review, 3:1 (1969), 17–27.

A good study of verbal and non-verbal violence in Marcos's early theatre.

Prado, Décio de Almeida. "A evolução da literatura dramática" in Afrânio Coutinho (ed.) A literatura no Brasil, 2nd. edn., vol. VI, Rio de Janeiro, Sul Americana, 1971, 7–37.

The pages covering the twentieth century present a good, if somewhat succinct, summation of the period.

"O teatro" in Affonso Avila (ed.), O modernismo, São Paulo, Perspectiva, 1975, 139–51.

Indispensable reading on the theatrical concerns of several participants of the movement.

"O teatro, 1930–1980: ensaio de interpretação" in Boris Fausto (ed.), O Brasil republicano, vol. VI, São Paulo, DIFEL, 1984, 525–89.

Earlier, shorter version of Prado's O teatro brasileiro moderno.

Quackenbush, Louis H. "The auto tradition in Brazilian drama," Latin American Theatre Review, 5:2 (1972), 29–43.

An excellent study of the auto form in Brazilian theatre from Anchieta to Suassuna and Cabral de Melo.

Rosenfeld, Anatol. "Visão do Ciclo" in Jorge Andrade, Marta, a árvore e o relógio, São Paulo, Perspectiva, 1970, 599–617.

Sheds some valuable light on each of the ten plays and on the cycle as a whole.

Santiago, Silviano. "A moratória em processo," PMLA, 83:2 (1968), 332–9.

Good thematic study of Andrade's play. Argues that the play reflects the passage from a patriarchal society to a matriarchal one and faults the playwright for being too soft on the older generation.

Schoenbach, Peter J. "Plínio Marcos: reporter of bad times" in Woodyard and Lyday, Dramatists in Revolt, 243–57.

An excellent introduction to the theatre of Plínio Marcos, with detailed examinations of the major plays through 1970.

"Themes and directions of the Brazilian theatre, 1973–1978," Latin American Theatre Review, 13:2 (Summer supplement 1980), 43–50.

Good overview of the theatre in the 1970s. Gives special attention to Gota d'água, Ponto de partida, Patética, and Rasga coração.

Schwarz, Roberto. "Cultura, 1964–1969 (o teatro)" in his O pai de família e outros estudos, Rio de Janeiro, Paz e Terra, 1978, 78–89.

Argues persuasively that the musicals of the period functioned as an ample forum for political debate.

Soares, Lúcia Maria MacDowell. "O teatro político do Arena e de Guarnieri" in *Monografias 1980*, Rio de Janeiro, MEC/INACEN, 1983, 7–103.

Studies the development of Guarnieri's theatre in the light of Teatro de Arena's political orientation.

Sussekind, Flora Maria. "Nelson Rodrigues e o fundo falso" in *Primeiro Concurso Nacional de Monografias*, Brasília, Departamento de Documentação e Divulgação do Ministério da Educação e Cultura, 1977, 5–42.

One of the few studies that deliberately disregards previous moralist preconceptions regarding Nelson's theatre.

Teixeira, Selma Suely. "Análise da dramaturgia de Chico Buarque de Hollanda," *Estudos Brasileiros*, 12 (1981), 37–68.

Excellent survey of the theatre of one of the most important playwrights of the 1970s.

Tolman, Jon M. "An allegorical interpretation of João Cabral de Melo Neto's *Morte e vida severina*," *Hispania*, 61:1 (1978), 57–68.

Emphasizes the role of allegory and ambiguity in Cabral's *auto de natal*. An interview with the poet is appended.

Turner, Doris J. "Black theater in a 'racial democracy': the case of the Brazilian Black Experimental Theater," *College Language Association Journal*, 30:1 (1986), 30–45.

Informative historical account of the group's contributions to Brazilian theatre, culture, and political debate.

Unruh, Vicky. "Andrade's *Milagre na cela*: theatrical space and body movement," *Latin American Theatre Review*, 15:1 (1981), 45–51.

Excellent analysis of the breakdown in Andrade's play of traditional dichotomies through dialogue and use of theatrical space and movement.

"Language and power in *Miss Margarida's way* and *The lesson*," *Latin American Literary Review*, 14:27 (1986), 126–35.

Outstanding examination of language manipulation by two classroom autocrats.

"Eluding the censor: from script to improvisation in *Patética*," *Modern Drama*, 32:3 (1989), 345–55.

Provocative reading of Chaves Neto's play with special attention to the use of metatheatrical metaphors to promote improvisation as a form of resistance.

Woodyard, George W. "A metaphor for repression: two Portuguese Inquisition plays," *Luso-Brazilian Review*, 10:1 (1973), 68–75.

Posits that, in *O santo inquérito* and *O judeu*, Dias Gomes and Bernardo Santareno use the Inquisition as a metaphor for political and military repression in Brazil and Portugal in the 1960s.

"The dynamics of tragedy in *Gota d'água*," *Luso-Brazilian Review*, 15 (Summer supplement 1978), 151–60.

Compares the play by Buarque and Pontes with Euripides' *Medea*. Emphasizes departures from the Greek classic, especially the strong note of social protest in the modern adaptation.

Chapter 14: *Brazilian popular literature (the* literatura de cordel)

Primary sources

Amado, Jorge. *Tereza Batista cansada de guerra*, São Paulo, Livraria Martins Editora, 1972.

Tereza Batista, Home from the wars, tr. Barbara Shelby, New York, Knopf, 1975.

Andrade, Mário de. "O romanceiro de Lampeão" in *O baile das quatro artes*, 3rd. edn., São Paulo, Martins/INL/MEC, 1975, 85–119.

Ataíde, João Martins de. *A vida de uma meretriz*, Juazeiro do Norte, Tipografia São Bernardo, n.d.

Uma noite de amor, Recife, n.d.

Bandeira, Manuel. "Itinerário de Pasárgada" in *Estrela da vida inteira*, Rio de Janeiro, Livraria José Olympio Editora, 1966.

"Pasárgada" in *This Earth, That Sky: Poems by Manuel Bandeira, trans., notes and intro. by Candace Slater*, Berkeley and Los Angeles, University of California Press, 1989, 105–7.

Barros, Leandro Gomes de. *O dinheiro*, Recife, n.d.

Callado, Antônio. *Forró no Engenho Cananéia*, Rio de Janeiro, Civilização Brasileira, 1964.

Lins, Osman. *Lisbela e o prisioneiro*, Coleção Teatro, Rio de Janeiro, Editora Letras e Artes, 1964.

Guerra do "Cansa Cavalo," Petrópolis, Vozes, 1967.

Nove, novena: narrativas, 2nd. edn., São Paulo, Edições Melhoramentos, 1975.

Nine, Novena, tr. Adria Frizzi, Austin, University of Texas Press, 1988.

Lispector, Clarice. *A hora da estrela*, Rio de Janeiro, Nova Fronteira, 1977.

The Hour of the Star, tr. and afterword, Giovanni Pontiero, Manchester Carcanet, 1986.

Melo Neto, João Cabral de. *Morte e vida severina, e outros poemas em voz alta*, 20th. edn., Rio de Janeiro, LJOE, 1984.

"From 'The death and life of a Severino,' a Pernambuco Christmas play, 1954–1955," tr. Elizabeth Bishop, in Elizabeth Bishop and Emanuel Brasil (eds.), *An Anthology of Twentieth-Century Brazilian Poetry*, Middletown, Conn., Wesleyan University Press, 126–39.

O castigo da soberba, (anon.) n.p., n.d.

Olímpio, Domingos. *Luzia-Homem*, Memória Literária 6th edn., Edições Melhoramentos, 1977.

Rosa, João Guimarães. *Grande sertão: veredas*, Rio de Janeiro, Livraria José Olympio Editora, 1956.

The Devil to Pay in the Backlands, tr. James L. Taylor and Harriet de Onís, New York, Knopf, 1963.

Suassuna, Ariano. *Auto da compadecida*, Rio de Janeiro, Livraria José Olympio Editora, 1957.

The Rogues' Trial, tr. Dillwyn F. Ratcliff, Berkeley and Los Angeles, University of California Press, 1963.

Távora, João Franklin da Silveira. *O Cabeleira, biografia, introdução e notas de M. Cavalcanti Proença*, Rio de Janeiro, Edições de Ouro, 1966.

Volume 3

Secondary sources

In line with its importance, there is a vast and steadily growing critical bibliography on the *literatura de cordel*. I have attempted here to give the reader a sense of its dimensions, as well as to indicate some of the best analyses of the *cordel*.

Books

Batista, Francisco das Chagas. *Cantadores e poetas populares*, João Pessoa, Editora F.C. Batista Irmão, 1929.
> Of considerable historical interest.

Calasans, José. *Ciclo folclórico do Bom Jesus Conselheiro*, Salvador, Tip. Beneditina, 1950.
> A study of popular poetry relating to the messianic community of Canudos, crushed by republican forces in the last decade of the nineteenth century.

Cantel, Raymond. *Temas de atualidade na literatura de cordel*, tr. Alice Mitika Koshiyama *et al.*, Universidade de São Paulo, Escola de Comunicações e Artes, 1972.
> Study of topical themes by a French scholar largely responsible for introducing *cordel* studies into the Sorbonne.

Cascudo, Luís da Câmara. *Cinco livros do povo*, Rio de Janeiro, Livraria José Olympio Editora, 1953.
> A study of Portuguese classics, such as *A Donzela Teodora* and *A Princesa Magalona*, which became an integral part of the Brazilian *cordel*.

Dicionário do folclore brasileiro, 4th. edn., revised, São Paulo, Edições Melhoramentos, 1979.
> A indispensable reference work containing entries on the *cordel* and a wide variety of Brazilian oral traditions.

Curran, Mark. *Literatura de cordel*, Recife, Universidade Federal de Pernambuco, 1973.
> Includes a useful discussion of the *folheto* sources of Ariano Suassuna's *Auto da compadecida*.

A presença de Rodolfo Coelho Cavalcante na moderna literatura de cordel, Rio de Janeiro, Nova Fronteira/Fundação Casa de Rui Barbosa, 1987.
> A study of one of the better-known *cordel* poets and organizers, Rodolfo Coelho Cavalcante (1919–1987).

Daus, Ronald. *O ciclo épico dos cangaceiros na poesia popular do nordeste*, tr. Rachel Teixeira Valença, Literatura Popular em Verso, Estudos – n.s. 1, Rio de Janeiro, Fundação Casa de Rui Barbosa, 1982.
> Portuguese translation of a study first published in German in 1969. A study of *cordel* presentations of the northeastern outlaws known as *cangaceiros*.

Ferreira, Jerusa Pires. *Cavalaria em cordel: o passo das águas mortas*, São Paulo, HUCITEC, 1979.
> An excellent discussion of Carolingian themes in the *cordel*.

Lessa, Orígenes. *A voz dos poetas*, Literatura Popular em Verso, Estudos, n.s. 6, Rio de Janeiro, Fundação Casa de Rui Barbosa, 1984.
> Engaging interviews with a series of contemporary *cordel* poets.

Literatura popular em verso: antologia, vol. 1, Rio de Janeiro, Fundação Casa de Rui

Barbosa/MEC, 1964.

Reproductions of some of the most important *folheto* texts. The publication of this and a companion catalogue volume marked a growing interest within Brazil in popular culture and initiated a new era in *cordel* scholarship.

Literatura popular em verso: antologia, vol. II, Rio de Janeiro, Fundação Casa de Rui Barbosa/Fundação Universidade Regional do Nordeste, 1976.

A collection of stories by the first great *folheto* writer, Leandro Gomes de Barros.

Literatura popular em verso: antologia, vol. III, Rio de Janeiro and João Pessoa, MEC/Fundação Casa de Rui Barbosa/Universidade Federal da Paraíba, 1977.

More *folhetos* by Leandro. The volume contains an introduction by Ariano Suassuna and a Proppian analysis by Idelette Muzart Fonseca dos Santos.

Literatura popular em verso: antologia, vol. IV, Rio de Janeiro, MEC/Fundação Casa de Rui Barbosa, 1977.

A collection of *folhetos* by Francisco das Chagas Batista (1882–1930) with an introduction by his son, *cordel* researcher Sebastião Nunes Batista.

Literatura popular em verso: catálogo, Rio de Janeiro, Fundação Casa de Rui Barbosa/MEC, 1962.

A catalogue of the Rui Barbosa collection, the most important public *cordel* library in Brazil.

Literatura popular em verso: estudos, Rio de Janeiro, Fundação Casa de Rui Barbosa/MEC, 1973.

A number of useful studies by diverse authors. The introduction by Manuel Cavalcanti Proença is particularly good.

Luyten, Joseph Maria. *A literatura de cordel em São Paulo: saudosismo e agressividade*, Série Comunicação, 23, São Paulo, Edições Loyola, 1981.

A study of the *cordel* in São Paulo. Although the analysis leaves much unsaid, the theme is extremely important.

Mota, Leonardo. *Cantadores: poesia e linguagem do sertão cearense*, 3rd. edn., Fortaleza, Imprensa Universitária do Ceará, 1961.

One of three volumes by Mota of great historical interest.

Nascimento, Bráulio do. *Bibliografia do folclore brasileiro*, Rio de Janeiro, Biblioteca Nacional/MEC, 1971.

A comprehensive guide to research on the *cordel* as well as a variety of other folk and popular traditions. An update is sorely needed.

O cordel e os desmantelos do mundo, Antologia, n.s. 1, Rio de Janeiro, Fundação Casa de Rui Barbosa, 1983.

A series of *folhetos* on the theme of "o tempora, o mores."

Salles, Vicente. *Repente e cordel: literatura popular em versos na Amazônia*, Rio de Janeiro, FUNARTE/Instituto Nacional do Folclore, 1985.

An examination of present-day descendants of the chap-book tradition brought to the Amazon by northeastern immigrants during the Rubber Boom.

Slater, Candace. *Stories on a String; The Brazilian "Literatura de cordel,"* reissued with new preface by author, Berkeley and Los Angeles, University of California Press, 1989.

To date the only English-language comprehensive overview of the *cordel*. Followed by an extensive bibliography, the study discusses *cordel* poets and their public(s) as well as various texts. The paperback edition cited here contains an update to the 1982 original.

Souza, Liêdo Maranhão de. *Classificação popular da literatura de cordel*, Coleção Cultura Popular, 1, Petrópolis, Vozes, 1976.

> Although it is doubtful that all *cordel* poets would agree on the categories proposed here, they are nonetheless worthy of attention.

Suassuna, Ariano. "Notas sobre o romanceiro popular do nordeste" in Silviano Santiago (ed.), *Ariano Suassuna: seleta em prosa e verso*, pp. 162–90, Rio de Janeiro, Livraria José Olympio Editora/INL/MEC, 1974.

> Suassuna's comments on the *cordel* are particularly interesting in the light of his work's heavy dependence on *folheto* themes.

Terra, Ruth Brito Lemos. *Memória de lutas: literatura de folhetos do nordeste, 1893–1930*, Teses, 13, São Paulo, Global Editora, 1983.

> An interesting discussion of the social conflicts apparent in early *folhetos*.

Articles

Amado, Jorge. "Biblioteca do povo e coleção moderna" in Gilberto Freyre *et al.*, *Novos estudos afro-brasileiros*, vol. II, Rio de Janeiro, Civilização Brasileira, 1937, 262–324.

> An indication of Amado's very early interest in *cordel* poetry and other folk and popular traditions.

Baden, Nancy T. "Popular poetry in the novels of Jorge Amado," *Journal of Latin American Lore*, 2 (1976), 3–22.

> A discussion of the role of the *cordel* in several of Amado's novels.

Bandeira, Manuel. "Saudação aos cantadores do nordeste," *Jornal do Brasil* (Rio de Janeiro), (Sept. 12, 1959).

> An occasional poem in honor of poet–improvisers. Testifies to Bandeira's awareness of popular poetry and emphasizes the longstanding give-and-take between educated and popular writers in Brazil.

Lewin, Linda. "Oral tradition and elite myth: the legend of the 'Good' Thief Antônio Silvino in Brazilian popular culture," *Journal of Latin American Lore*, 5 (1980), 157–204.

> The author, a historian, seriously downplays the weight of literary tradition in the depiction of historical figures, but her discussion of *folhetos* about Antônio Silvino is interesting and perceptive.

Slater, Candace. "Joe Bumpkin in the wilds of Rio de Janeiro," *Journal of Latin American Lore*, 6 (1980), 5–53.

> An examination of changes in the traditional hillbilly theme as a key to larger differences between the northeastern and southern *cordel*.

"Why One Evil King Could Not Be Brazilian: A comparative study of the Portuguese and Brazilian *literatura de cordel*," *Luso-Brazilian Review*, 18 (1981), 279–94.

> A brief comparison of Portuguese and Brazilian *cordel* stories.

Suassuna, Ariano. "Coletânea da poesia popular nordestina: romances do heróico," *Revista do DECA* (Recife), 6 (1964), 7–117.

> A discussion of *folhetos* about backlands heroes and bandits. Once again

particularly interesting because of the author's close reliance on the *cordel* in his novels and plays.

Terra, Ruth Brito Lemos, and Mauro W. B. de Almeida. "A análise morfológica da literatura popular em verso: uma hipótese de trabalho," *Revista do Instituto de Estudos Brasileiros*, 16 (1975), 1–28.

A Proppian analysis of the *literatura de cordel*.

Chapter 15: Literary criticism in Brazil

Primary sources

Amaral, Aracy. *Artes plásticas na Semana de 22*, São Paulo, Perspectiva, 1970.

Treats the relationship between literature and the arts in early Modernism.

Amora, Antônio Soares. *A literatura brasileira*, vol. II: *O romantismo*, São Paulo, Cultrix, 1966.

A history of Romanticism in Brazil.

Andrade, Mário de. *A escrava que não é Isaura*, São Paulo, Lealdade, 1925.

A creative treatise on the origins and principles of modernist aesthetics.

Aspectos da literatura brasileira, Rio de Janeiro, Améric-Edit, 1943.

Collected essays on literary themes by a leader of Modernism.

Andrade, Oswald de. *Ponta de lança*, São Paulo, Livraria Martins Editora, 1945.

Polemical social and literary criticism by a major modernist author.

"Cannibal Manifesto," tr. Leslie Bary, *Latin American Literary Review*, 19 (1991), 35–47.

Aranha, José Pereira da Graça. *A estética da vida*, Rio de Janeiro, Garnier, 1921.

An essay on decadentist aesthetics by an aristocrat tied to early Modernism.

O espírito moderno, São Paulo, Monteiro Lobato, 1925.

An essay describing and defending a sense of modernity.

Araripe, Tristão de Alencar Jr. *Cartas sobre a literatura brasileira*, Rio de Janeiro, Tipografia de J. A. dos Santos Cardoso, 1869.

An early work of a northeastern naturalist critic.

Azevedo, Fernando de. *A cultura brasileira*, Rio de Janeiro, Instituto Brasileiro de Geografia e Estatística, 1943.

Panoramic and thematic compendium of national folklore and culture.

Brazilian Culture, tr. William Rex Crawford, New York, Macmillan, 1950.

Bosi, Alfredo. *A literatura brasileira*, vol. V: *O Pré-modernismo*, São Paulo, Cultrix, 1966.

História concisa da literatura brasileira, São Paulo, Cultrix, 1970.

A thorough one-volume history of Brazilian literature covering authors, periods, genres, and selected criticism.

Brito, Mário da Silva. *História do modernismo brasileiro*, vol. I. *Antecedentes da Semana de Arte Moderna*, Rio de Janeiro, Civilização Brasileira, 1964.

The first volume of a never-completed history of the modernist movement.

Campos, Augusto de. *Poesia, antipoesia, antropofagia*, São Paulo, Cortez & Moraes, 1978.

Essays on experimentation in Brazilian literature, from Oswald de Andrade to Guimarães Rosa and concrete poetry.

O anticrítico, São Paulo, ed. Schwarcz, 1986.
   Creative translation of poetry as anti-literary criticism.
À margem da margem, São Paulo, Companhia das Letras, 1989.
   Essays on contemporary poetics, translation, and literary theory.
Campos, Haroldo de. *A arte no horizonte do provável*, São Paulo, Perspectiva, 1969.
   Essays on critical theory and praxis by a leader of the concrete poetry movement.
Metalinguagem, 2nd. edn., Petrópolis, Vozes, 1970.
   Literary studies involving innovation in language or theory.
A operação do texto, São Paulo, Perspectiva, 1977.
   Theory of textual functions.
Ruptura dos gêneros na literatura latino-americana, São Paulo, Perspectiva, 1977.
   A chronology of innovation in literary forms in Latin American literature.
"Da razão antropofágica: a Europa sob o signo da devoração," *Colóquio-Letras*, 62 (July 1981).
O sequestro do barroco na formação da literatura brasileira: o caso Gregório de Mattos, Salvador, Fundação Casa de Jorge Amado, 1989.
   A reappraisal of the baroque aesthetic in Brazilian literature.
Cândido, Antônio. *Brigada Ligeira*, São Paulo, Livraria Martins Editora, 1945.
   Literary essays.
O método crítico de Sílvio Romero, São Paulo, Revista dos Tribunais, 1945.
   A study of Romero's critical background in the naturalist school.
Ficção e confissão, Rio de Janeiro, Livraria José Olympio Editora, 1956.
   A study of the works of Graciliano Ramos.
Formação da literatura brasileira, 2 vols., São Paulo, Livraria Martins Editora, 1959.
   A groundbreaking history of the development of national literature from eighteenth-century beginnings.
O observador literário, São Paulo, CEC, 1959.
   Literary essays.
Tese e antítese, São Paulo, Companhia Editora Nacional, 1964.
   The literary method of Graciliano Ramos.
Literatura e sociedade: estudos de teoria e história literária, São Paulo, Companhia Editora Nacional, 1965.
   The relationship of literature to society and social background.
Vários escritos, São Paulo, Duas Cidades, 1970.
   Literary essays.
Na sala de aula, São Paulo, Editora Atica, 1985.
   Practical criticism of selected texts.
A educação pela noite, São Paulo, Editora Atica, 1987.
   Essays on problems of history and literature.
(ed.) *Sílvio Romero: teoria crítica e história literária*, Rio de Janeiro, Livros Técnicos e Científicos Editora, 1978.
Carpeaux, Otto Maria. *História da literatura ocidental*, Rio de Janeiro, O Cruzeiro, 1959–1966.
   A multi-volume history of Western literature.
Carvalho, Ronald de. *Pequena história da literatura brasileira*, Rio de Janeiro, F.

Briguiet & Cia., 1919.

A short history of Brazilian literature by a modernist writer.

Castello, José Aderaldo. *Manifestações literárias da era colonial*, São Paulo, Cultrix, 1966.

A history of colonial Brazilian literature.

Cavalheiro, Edgard. *Testamento de uma geração*, Porto Alegre, Globo, 1944.

Written interviews and questionnaires completed by authors and critics on social and literary perspectives.

Coutinho, Afrânio (ed.). *A literatura no Brasil*, 5 vols., Rio de Janeiro, Sul Americana, 1956–1959.

A massive project of national literary history, divided into volumes on different periods.

A tradição afortunada, Rio de Janeiro, Livraria José Olympio Editora, 1968.

An interpretation of the nature and character of Brazilian literature.

Conceito de literatura brasileira, Rio de Janeiro, Pallas, 1976.

Denis, Ferdinand. *Résumé de l'histoire littéraire du Portugal, suivi du résumé de l'histoire littéraire du Brésil*, Paris, Lecointe & Durey, 1826.

One of the earliest anthologies to include Brazilian literature along with the Portuguese.

Faustino, Mário (ed.). "Poesia-Experiência," *Jornal do Brasil* (1956–1958).

Collected newspaper supplements on poetry and criticism.

Freyre, Gilberto. *Casa grande e senzala*, Rio de Janeiro, Maia & Schmidt, 1933.

Galvão, Patrícia. "Antologia da literatura estrangeira," *Diário de São Paulo* (1946–1950).

An introduction and translated anthology of approximately ninety world literary figures.

Galvão, Walnice Nogueira. *Formas do falso*, São Paulo, Perspectiva, 1972.

A study of ambiguity and opposites in João Guimarães Rosa.

Saco de gatos, São Paulo, Duas Cidades, 1976.

Literary essays.

Mitológica rosiana, São Paulo, Editora Atica, 1978.

Mythology in the works of João Guimarães Rosa.

Gatos de outro saco, São Paulo, Editora Brasiliense, 1981.

Literary essays.

Gotlib, Nádia Batella (ed.). *A mulher na literatura*, Belo Horizonte, UFMG, 1988.

Assorted essays on women authors in Brazilian literature.

Grieco, Agripino. *Evolução da poesia brasileira*, Rio de Janeiro, Ariel, 1932.

Interpretive history of Brazilian poetry.

Evolução da prosa brasileira, Rio de Janeiro, Ariel, 1933.

Interpretive history of Brazilian prose.

Holanda, Sérgio Buarque de. *Raízes do Brasil*, Rio de Janeiro, Livraria José Olympio Editora, 1936.

Lima, Alceu Amoroso. *Estudos*, 5 vols., Rio de Janeiro, Terra de Sol/Editora Civilização Brasileira, 1927–1935.

Collected criticism of a professional modernist critic.

Estudos literários, Rio de Janeiro, Aguilar, 1966.

A new phase of cultural, literary, and philosophical essays.

Volume 3

Lima, José Inácio de Abreu e. *Bosquejo histórico, político e literário do Brasil*, Niterói, 1835.
  A romantic essay linking national literature to history and politics.
Lima, Luiz Costa. *Lira e antilira*, Rio de Janeiro, Civilização Brasileira, 1968.
  A study of modernist poetics in Carlos Drummond de Andrade.
Estruturalismo e teoria da literatura, Petrópolis, Vozes, 1973.
  A presentation of structuralist theory and analysis.
Teoria da literatura em suas fontes, Rio de Janeiro, Francisco Alves, 1975.
  A survey of sources of modern currents in literary theory.
O controle do imaginário, São Paulo, Editora Brasiliense, 1984.
  Sets forth the author's concept of inherent limits on imaginative constructs in the development of Western thought.
A aguarrás do tempo, Rio de Janeiro, Rocco, 1989.
  Literary essays.
Lins, Alvaro. *Jornal de Crítica*, 7 vols., Rio de Janeiro, Livraria José Olympio Editora, 1941–1963.
  Collected criticism of a major critical voice of Modernism.
López, Telê Porto Ancona. *Mário de Andrade, ramais e caminho*, São Paulo, Duas Cidades, 1968.
  Interpretive study of Mário de Andrade as a modernist thinker and author.
Machado de Assis, Joaquim Maria de. "O instinto da nacionalidade," *A literatura brasileira e a crítica moderna*, Rio de Janeiro, Impresa Industrial de João Ferreira Dias, 1880.
Crítica, Rio de Janeiro, Garnier, 1910.
  Literary criticism by Brazil's most celebrated author.
"O ideal do crítico" in *Obra completa*, vol. III, ed. Afrânio Coutinho, Rio de Janeiro, Aguilar, 1962, 789–801.
Martins, Wilson. *A literatura brasileira*, vol. VI: *O Modernismo*, São Paulo, Cultrix, 1965.
  A history and criticism of the modernist movement.
História da inteligência brasileira, 7 vols., São Paulo, Cultrix, 1976–1979.
  A massive compendium of authors and titles by year, tracing the published intellectual history of Brazil by periods.
Merquior, José Guilherme. *A astúcia da mimese*, Rio de Janeiro, Livraria José Olympio Editora, 1972.
  A theoretical study of literary mimesis.
Formalismo e tradição moderna, Rio de Janeiro, Forense-Universitária, 1974.
  A critique of Formalism in literary studies.
Verso universo em Drummond, Rio de Janeiro, Livraria José Olympio Editora, 1975.
  A comprehensive reading of the poetic works of Carlos Drummond de Andrade.
O fantasma romântico, Petrópolis, Vozes, 1980.
  Literary essays.
Miguel-Pereira, Lúcia. *História da literatura brasileira, Prosa de ficção: 1880–1920*, Rio de Janeiro, Livraria José Olympio Editora, 1950.
  A study of prose fiction from Realism to Modernism.

Milliet, Sérgio. *Diário crítico*, 10 vols., São Paulo, Livraria Martins Editors/Editora Brasiliense, 1944–1959.
   Collected literary criticism of a distinguished modernist author and intellectual.
Moisés, Massaud. *A literatura brasileira*, vol. IV: *O Simbolismo*, São Paulo, Cultrix, 1966.
   História da literatura brasileira, 5 vols., São Paulo, Cultrix/Editora da Universidade de São Paulo, 1983–1989.
   A normative history of Brazilian literature by authors and periods.
Neme, Mário. *Plataforma da nova geração*, Porto Alegre, Globo, 1945.
   Statements on culture and aesthetics by young writers at the time.
Nunes, Benedito. *O dorso do tigre*, São Paulo, Perspectiva, 1976.
   Literary essays on Pessoa, Lispector, and Guimarães Rosa.
   Oswald, canibal. São Paulo, Perspectiva, 1979.
   An exposition and defense of Oswald de Andrade's "cannibal" movement.
   Passagem para o poético: filosofia e poesia em Heidegger, São Paulo, Editora Atica, 1986.
   A study of poetry and philosophy in Heidegger.
   O tempo na narrativa, São Paulo, Editora Atica, 1988.
   A study of time in literary narration.
   O drama da linguagem, São Paulo, Editora Atica, 1989.
   Interpretive essays on Clarice Lispector.
Pacheco, João. *A literatura brasileira*, vol. III: *O Realismo*, São Paulo, Cultrix, 1963.
Perrone-Moisés, Leyla. *Texto, crítica, escritura*, São Paulo, Editora Atica, 1978.
   A critical review of principal currents in literary criticism.
   Flores da escrivaninha, São Paulo, Companhia das Letras, 1990.
   Literary essays.
Prado, Paulo. *Retrato do Brasil*, São Paulo, Mayença, 1928.
   A classic modernist work interpreting national character and values.
I^{ro} *encontro de crítica textual: o manuscrito moderno e as edições*, Faculdade de Filosofia, Letras e Ciências Humanas da Universidade de São Paulo, 1986.
   From a symposium on textual criticism and editions.
Ribeiro, João Felipe de Saboía. *Crítica*, 6 vols., Rio de Janeiro, Academia Brasileira de Letras, 1952.
   Collected works of a distinguished symbolist critic.
Romero, Sílvio. *História da literatura brasileira*, 2 vols., Rio de Janeiro, Garnier, 1888.
   A celebrated naturalistic history of Brazilian literature.
Sant'Anna, Affonso Romano de. *O canibalismo amoroso: o desejo e a interdição em nossa cultura através de poesia*, São Paulo, Brasiliense, 1984.
Santiago, Silviano. *Uma literatura nos trópicos*, São Paulo, Perspectiva, 1978.
   Literary essays.
   Vale quanto pesa, Rio de Janeiro, Paz e Terra, 1982.
   Literary essays.
   Nas malhas da letra, São Paulo, Companhia das Letras, 1989.
   Literary essays.
Schwarz, Roberto. *A sereia e o desconfiado*, Rio de Janeiro, Civilização Brasileira, 1965.

Literary essays.

Ao vencedor as batatas: forma literária e processo social nos inícios do romance brasileiro, São Paulo, Duas Cidades, 1977.

A classic study of fiction by Machado de Assis.

O pai de família o outros estudos, Rio de Janeiro, Paz e Terra, 1978.

Literary essays.

Que horas são? ensaios, São Paulo, Companhia das Letras, 1987.

Literary essays.

Um mestre na periferia do capitalismo: Machado de Assis, São Paulo, Duas Cidades, 1990.

A continuation of the study of fiction by Machado de Assis.

"Brazilian Culture: Nationalism by elimination," in John Gledson (ed.), *Misplaced Ideas*, New York and London, Verso, 1992, 1–18.

Translation of "Nacional por subtração," *Que horas são?*

Sodré, Nelson Werneck. *História da literatura brasileira; seus fundamentos econômicos*, 2nd. edn., Rio de Janeiro, José Olympio, 1940.

A history of national literature from socio-economic viewpoints.

Formação da sociedade brasileira, Rio de Janeiro, Livraria José Olympio Editora, 1944.

Essay on the development of Brazilian society.

Sussekind, Flora. *Tal Brasil, qual romance?*, Rio de Janeiro, Achiamé, 1984.

Interpretations of the nineteenth-century Brazilian novel.

Literatura e vida literária, Rio de Janeiro, Jorge Zahar, 1985.

Essays on censorship and poetry of the self.

Veríssimo, José. *História da literatura brasileira*, Rio de Janeiro, Francisco Alves, 1916.

Secondary sources

Carpeaux, Otto Maria. *Pequena bibliografia crítica da literatura brasileira*, Rio de Janeiro, Edições de Ouro, 1980.

A classic list, updated and revised, of authors, works, and selected criticism.

Forster, Merlin H., and K. David Jackson. *Vanguardism in Latin American Literature: An annotated bibliographical guide, 1920–1935*, New York, Greenwood Press, 1990.

The guide covers primary and secondary works and recent critical studies of Latin American avant-garde movements.

Martins, Wilson. *A crítica literária no Brasil*, 2nd. edn., 2 vols., Rio de Janeiro, Francisco Alves, 1983.

The second volume contains a research bibliography on the subject.

Placer, Xavier. *Modernismo brasileiro: bibliografia, 1918–1971*, Rio de Janeiro, Biblioteca Nacional, 1972.

Placer's is the only comprehensive bibliography of Brazilian literary Modernism.

Stern, Irwin (ed.). *Dictionary of Brazilian Literature*, New York, Greenwood Press, 1988.

A dictionary of concise essays on authors and currents in Brazilian literature.

Chapter 16: The essay: architects of Brazilian national identity

Primary sources

Cunha, Euclides da. *Os sertões, edição crítica* by Walnice Nogueira Galvão, São Paulo, Editora Brasiliense, 1985; 1st. edn., Laemmert, São Paulo, 1902.
The 1985 edition is a meticulous compilation of all variations in the successive editions.
Rebellion in the Backlands, tr. Samuel Putnam, University of Chicago Press, 1944.
With highly useful translator's notes.
Da Matta, Roberto. *Carnavais, malandros e heróis: para uma sociologia do dilema brasileiro*, Rio de Janeiro, Jorge Zahar, 1978.
Relativizando: uma introdução à antropologia social, Petrópolis, Vozes, 1981.
O que faz o brasil, Brasil?, Rio de Janeiro, Rocco, 1986.
Carnivals, Rogues and Heroes: An interpretation of the Brazilian dilemma, tr. John Drury, University of Notre Dame Press, 1991.
Freyre, Gilberto. *Casa grande e senzala*, Rio de Janeiro, Maia & Schmidt, 1933.
Ordem e progresso, 2 vols., Rio de Janeiro, Livraria José Olympio Editora, 1959.
Vida social no Brasil nos meados do século XIX, 3rd. edn., Recife, Editora Massangana, 1985; first published *Hispanic American Historical Review*, 5 (1922), 597–630.
The Masters and the Slaves, tr. Samuel Putnam, 2nd. edn., New York, Knopf, 1956.
Includes Freyre's lengthy prefaces to the two English-language editions, along with Putnam's valuable notes.
The Mansions and the Shanties, tr. Harriet de Onís, New York, Knopf, 1963.
Order and Progress, tr. Rod W. Horton, New York, Knopf, 1970.
Holanda, Heloísa Buarque de. "Os estudos sobre mulher e literatura no Brasil: uma primeira avaliação" in Albertina de Oliveira Costa and Cristina Bruschini (eds.), *Uma questão de gênero*, Rio de Janeiro, Rosa dos Tempos, 1992.
Holanda, Sérgio Buarque de. *Raízes do Brasil*, 3rd. edn., Rio de Janeiro, Livraria José Olympio Editora, 1956; 1st. edn., Rio de Janeiro, Livraria José Olympio Editora, 1936.
Moog, Vianna. *Bandeirantes e pioneiros*, Porto Alegre, Globo, 1961; 1st. edn., Globo, Porto Alegre, 1955.
Bandeirantes and Pioneers, tr. L. L. Barrett, New York, George Braziller, 1964.
Prado, Paulo. *Retrato do Brasil: ensaio sobre a tristeza brasileira*, 6th edn., Rio de Janeiro, Livraria José Olympio Editora, 1962; 1st edn., São Paulo, 1928.
Ribeiro, Darcy. *As Américas e a civilização*, Petrópolis, Vozes, 1988; 1st. Brazilian edn., Rio de Janeiro, Editora Civilização Brasileira, 1970.
Os brasileiros, Petrópolis, Vozes, 1991; 1st. Brazilian edn., Rio de Janeiro, Paz e Terra, 1972.
Romero, Sílvio. *Machado de Assis*, Rio de Janeiro, Laemmert, 1897.
História da literatura brasileira, 2nd. edn., 2 vols., Rio de Janeiro, H. Garnier, 1902; 1st. edn., Rio de Janeiro, Garnier, 1888.
Vianna, Oliveira. *Populações meridionais do Brasil*, 5th. edn., 2 vols., Rio de Janeiro, Livraria José Olympio Editora, 1952; 1st edn., São Paulo, Monteiro Lobato, 1922.

Secondary sources

Books

Andrews, George Reid. *Blacks and Whites in São Paulo, 1888–1988*, Madison, University of Wisconsin Press, 1991.
   The first comprehensive and historically documented look at the evolution of race relations in a key Brazilian state during the century after Abolition.
Broca, Brito. *A vida literária no Brasil: 1900*, 3rd. edn., Rio de Janeiro, Livraria José Olympio Editora, 1975.
   The most stimulating single work on Rio de Janeiro's turn-of-the-century bohemian literary world.
Cândido, Antônio. *Literatura e sociedade: estudos de teoria e história literária*, 7th. edn., São Paulo, Editora Nacional, 1985.
   First published in 1965, it has remained one of the most incisive studies of pre-1945 culture.
Corrêa, Mariza. *História da antropologia no Brasil: 1930–1960*, São Paulo, Vertice, 1987.
   Includes extensive interviews with Emílio Willems and Donald Pierson, two foreign anthropologists who played key roles in the development of the discipline in Brazil.
Fontaine, Pierre-Michel (ed.). *Race, Class and Power in Brazil*, University of California, Los Angeles, Center for Afro-American Studies, 1985.
   A collection of papers documenting racial inequality and the rise of Afro-Brazilian political consciousness in the 1970s.
Freyre, Gilberto. *Perfil de Euclides e outros perfis*, Rio de Janeiro, Record, 1987.
   Important both as an interpretation of Euclides and as an expression of Freyre's thought.
Hallewell, L. *Books in Brazil: A history of the publishing trade*, Metuchen, N. J., Scarecrow, 1982.
   A fascinating exploration of the personalities and institutions that made cultural life possible.
Leite, Dante Moreira, *O caráter nacional brasileiro-história de uma ideologia*, 4th. edn., São Paulo, Livraria Pioneira Editora, 1983.
   Study by a social psychologist, analyzing all the pre-1960 authors treated in this chapter. The first edition was published in 1959.
Lovell, Peggy A. (ed.). *Desigualdade racial no Brasil contemporâneo*, Belo Horizonte, UFMG/CEDEPLAR, 1991.
   Documents the pervasive racial inequalities in Brazil as revealed in the official data.
Martins, Wilson, *História da inteligência brasileira*, 7 vols., São Paulo, Cultrix, 1976–1979.
   The last four volumes offer a highly eclectic interpretation of the period, covered by this chapter, concentrating on literature.
Miceli, Sérgio. *Intelectuais e classe dirigente no Brasil: 1920–1945*, São Paulo, DIFEL, 1979.
   Excellent analysis of the social background and institutional context of

writers.

Mota, Carlos Guilherme. *Ideologia da cultura brasileira: 1933–1974*, 4th. edn. São Paulo, Editora Atica, 1978.

Stressing class analysis, Mota critically scrutinizes the "nationalist" bent of traditionalist figures such as Gilberto Freyre.

Needell, Jeffrey D. *A Tropical Belle Epoque: Elite culture and society in turn-of-the-century Rio de Janeiro*, Cambridge University Press, 1987.

A wealth of detail on the Europeanized elite atmosphere of the 1898–1914 period.

Oliveira, Lúcia Lippi. *A questão nacional na Primeira República*, São Paulo, Editora Brasiliense, 1990.

Analyzes the concept of Brazilian nationality as expressed by the principal intellectuals of the 1889–1930 period.

Os sertões: juízos críticos, Rio de Janeiro, Laemmert, 1904.

A collection of the initial reviews.

Rodrigues, José Honório. *História da história do Brasil*, vol. II, part 2: *A metafísica do latifúndio: o ultrareacionário Oliveira Vianna*, São Paulo, Editora Nacional, 1988.

An unrelenting screed against Oliveira Vianna.

Schwarz, Roberto. *Ao vencedor as batatas: forma literária e processo social nos inícios do romance brasileiro*, São Paulo, Duas Cidades, 1977.

Includes the classic essay, "As ideias fora do lugar," which analyzes the distortion European ideas suffered when transplanted to a slave-holding colony.

Que horas são? ensaios, São Paulo, Companhia das Letras, 1987.

The chapter on "Nacional por subtração" examines the anomalies of an imitative culture.

Sevcenko, Nicolau. *Literatura como missão: tensões sociais e criação cultural na Primeira República*, São Paulo, Editora Brasiliense, 1983.

Includes detailed analysis of the milieu in which Euclides da Cunha worked and wrote.

Skidmore, Thomas E. *Black Into White: Race and nationality in Brazilian thought*, New York, Oxford University Press, 1974.

An attempt to analyze, for the period 1870–1930, the *corpus* of major writers who discussed the related themes of race and nationality. Includes extensive discussion of the secondary literature on Sílvio Romero, Euclides da Cunha, Oliveira Vianna, Paulo Prado, and other intellectuals of the 1870–1930 era.

Sodré, Nelson Werneck. *A ideologia do colonialismo (seus reflexos no pensamento brasileiro)*, Rio de Janeiro, Instituto Superior de Estudos Brasileiros, 1961.

A pioneering Marxist interpretation which includes chapters on Sílvio Romero, Euclides da Cunha, and Oliveira Vianna.

Ventura, Roberto. *Estilo tropical: história cultural e polêmicas literárias no Brasil, 1870–1914*, São Paulo, Companhia das Letras, 1991.

A study of racial ideologies and the unique role played by Sílvio Romero in the intellectual life of his era.

Articles

Skidmore, Thomas E. "Fato e mito: descobrindo um problema racial no Brasil," *Cadernos da Pesquisa*, 79 (1991), 5–16.

Summarizes the extensive data on racial inequality in Brazil and discusses the failure of the intellectual elite to come to terms with its implications for their country's enduring myth of "racial democracy."

Chapter 17: *The Brazilian and the Spanish American literary traditions: a contrastive view*

Bibliographical note

Detailed bibliographical information for the Spanish American and Brazilian authors discussed in this essay may be found in the relevant chapters of this *History*.

There are very few book-length studies which draw explicit parallels between Spanish American and Brazilian writers. Two which should be mentioned are: Gordon Brotherston, *Latin American Poetry: Origins and presence* (Cambridge University Press, 1975) on Vallejo, Neruda, Paz, Parra, Drummond, and Cabral; and Jorge Schwartz's monograph, *Vanguarda e cosmopolitismo* (Universidade de São Paulo, 1983), a sustained comparison of Oliverio Girondo and Oswald de Andrade. See also César Fernández Moreno (ed.), *América latina en su literatura* (Mexico, Siglo Veintiuno Editores XXI, 1972), in which critics Rubén Bareiro Saguier, Antônio Houaiss, José Luís Martínez, Guillermo Sucre, Antônio Cândido, and the present author discuss both Spanish America and Brazil.

Brazilian critics with a keen interest in Spanish American writers have included José Veríssimo, Oliveira Lima, Manoel Bonfim, Alexandre Eulálio, Eduardo Portella, Luiz Costa Lima, and Davi Arrigucci, Jr. Conversely, the Spanish Americans Ramón Xirau, Antonio Alatorre, Francisco Cervantes, Santiago Kovadlof, and Carlos Montemayor, and the Spanish poet and critic Ángel Crespo, have written illuminating pages on Brazilian literature.

For panoramas with a sense of Western literary trends (and their transformation in the Brazilian context), see: Antônio Cândido, *Formação da literatura brasileira* (São Paulo, Livraria Martins Editora, 1959), on Neo-classicism and Romanticism; Luciana Stegagno Picchio, *La Letteratura Brasiliana* (Florence, Sansoni, 1972; an abridged version in French was published in Paris, by Presses Universitaires de France, in 1981); J. G. Merquior, *De Anchieta a Euclides: breve história de literatura brasileira* (Rio de Janeiro, Livraria José Olympio Editora, 1977). Also useful is the reader edited by Mechtild Strausfeld, *Brasilianische Literatur* (Frankfurt, Suhrkamp, 1984); the chapter on Mário de Andrade, Bandeira, and Jorge de Lima is also available in Portuguese in J. G. Merquior's *O elixir do Apocalipse* (Rio de Janeiro, Nova Fronteira, 1983), and Mario Carelli's chapter on the post-1964 novel can also be read in French as an article in *Les Langues Néo-latines*, 249 (Paris, 1984).

For an interesting comparison of Brazilian and Spanish American authors – as well as literary movements – see: Bella Josef *A máscara e o enigma* (Rio de Janeiro), Francisco Alves, 1986).

Also see:

Cândido, Antônio. *Introducción a la literatura del Brasil*, Caracas, Monte Avila, 1968.

Echeverría, Esteban. *Fondo y forma de las obras de imaginación*, in *Obras completas*, ed. J. Maria Gutiérrez, Buenos Aires, Ediciones Antonio Zamora, 1972, I, pp. 341–5.

Friedrich, Hugo. *The Structure of Modern Poetry: from the mid nineteenth century to the mid twentieth century*, tr. Joachim Neugroschel, Evanston, Ill., Northwestern University Press, 1974.

Index

Index

Index

Index

Index

Index